# *Veterinary*
# Bacteriology and Virology

# *Veterinary*
# BACTERIOLOGY

# *and* VIROLOGY

Seventh Edition

**I. A. Merchant,** D.V.M., Ph.D., M.P.H.

*Dean Emeritus, College of Veterinary Medicine,*
*and Professor of Veterinary Microbiology and Preventive Medicine*
*Iowa State University*

**R. A. Packer,** B.S., D.V.M., Ph.D.

*Professor and Head,*
*Department of Veterinary Microbiology and Preventive Medicine*
*College of Veterinary Medicine*
*Iowa State University*

**CBS Publishers & Distributors** Pvt. Ltd.

New Delhi • Bengaluru • Chennai • Kochi • Kolkata • Mumbai
Hyderabad • Nagpur • Patna • Pune • Vijayawada

## ABOUT THE AUTHORS

IVAL A. MERCHANT, Dean Emeritus, College of Veterinary Medicine, and professor of Veterinary Microbiology and Preventive Medicine at Iowa State University, holds the D.V.M. degree from Colorado State University, the M.S. and Ph.D. degrees from Iowa State University, and the M.P.H. degree from Yale University. In 1958 he received the Iowa State University Faculty Citation, in 1961 Iowa State University Alumni Merit Award, and in 1964 the Colorado State University Honor Alumnus Award. Dr. Merchant is a Fellow in the American College of Public Health Veterinarians and the American College of Microbiologists; a member of the Iowa State Veterinary Medical Association, the American Veterinary Medical Association, Phi Zeta, Gamma Sigma Delta, Phi Kappa Phi, Sigma Xi, Delta Omega, and the Osborn Research Club. Besides this book, he is the author of *Outline of Infectious Diseases of Domestic Animals*, *Characteristics of the Pasteurellae*, *Differentiation of Corynebacteria of Animals*, and is coauthor of the *Laboratory Guide for Veterinary Microbiology*.

R. ALLEN PACKER, professor and head of the Department of Veterinary Microbiology and Preventive Medicine at Iowa State University, holds the B.S., D.V.M., M.S., and Ph.D. degrees from Iowa State University, and in 1966 received the Iowa State University Faculty Citation. He is a member of the Iowa State Veterinary Medical Association, the American Veterinary Medical Association, the American Society for Microbiology, the American College of Veterinary Microbiologists, Sigma Xi, Phi Zeta, Phi Kappa Phi, and Gamma Sigma Delta. Besides this book, Dr. Packer has coauthored the *Laboratory Guide for Veterinary Microbiology*, and has published articles in numerous journals, including the *American Journal of Veterinary Research*, the *Journal of Veterinary Medicine*, the *North American Veterinarian*, and the *Journal of Bacteriology*.

ISBN: 81-239-0844-X

First Indian Edition: 1983
Reprint: 1999, 2002, 2005

This edition has been reprinted in India by arrangement with
The Iowa State University Press, USA



Published by **Satish Kumar Jain** and produced by **Varun Jain** for
**CBS Publishers & Distributors Pvt. Ltd.**,
4819/XI Prahlad Street, 24 Ansari Road, Daryaganj, New Delhi - 110002
delhi@cbspd.com, cbspubs@airtelmail.in • www.cbspd.com
• Ph.: 23289259, 23266861, 23266867 • Fax: 011-23243014

*Corporate Office:* 204 FIE, Industrial Area, Patparganj, Delhi - 110 092
Ph: 49344934 • Fax: 011-49344935 • E-mail: publishing@cbspd.com • publicity@cbspd.com

*Branches:*
- ***Bengaluru:*** 2975, 17th Cross, K.R. Road, Bansankari 2nd Stage, Bengaluru - 70 • Ph: +91-80-26771678/79 • Fax: +91-80-26771680 • E-mail: cbsbng@gmail.com, bangalore@cbspd.com
- ***Chennai:*** No. 7, Subbaraya Street, Shenoy Nagar, Chennai - 600030 Ph: +91-44-26681266, 26680620 • Fax: +91-44-42032115 • E-mail: chennai@cbspd.com
- ***Kochi:*** Ashana House, 39/1904, A.M. Thomas Road, Valanjambalam, Ernakulum, Kochi • Ph: +91-484-4059061-65 • Fax: +91-484-4059065 • E-mail: cochin@cbspd.com
- ***Kolkata:*** 6-B, Ground Floor, Rameshwar Shaw Road, Kolkata - 700014 Ph: +91-33-22891126/7/8 • E-mail: kolkata@cbspd.com
- ***Mumbai:*** 83-C, Dr. E. Moses Road, Worli, Mumbai - 400018 Ph: +91-9833017933, 022-24902340/41 • E-mail: mumbai@cbspd.com

*Representatives:*
- Hyderabad: 0-9885175004
- Pune: 0-9623451994
- Nagpur: 0-9021734563
- Vijayawada: 0-9000660880
- Patna: 0-9334159340

*Printed at:* Neekunj Print Process, Delhi (India)

# Preface

THIS TEXTBOOK IS CONCERNED PRIMARILY WITH THOSE SPECIES OF bacteria, mycoplasma, rickettsia, yeasts, molds, and viruses that are pathogenic to animals. The general morphological, physiological, and pathogenic characteristics of these microorganisms are emphasized. An introduction to the fundamental techniques of bacteriology and the principles of immunology are included to establish a working basis for the study of pathogenic forms.

Although this book is primarily intended for students in veterinary medicine, it is believed that the information given will be of value to veterinarians in the many fields of the profession—research workers, livestock disease control officials, public health epidemiologists, and those who are engaged in the field of private practice. An attempt has been made to include all significant data concerning the various microorganisms, but some of the details which would be of interest to those in advanced research have not been included.

It is imperative that the veterinarian acquaint himself with bacteria which are pathogenic only to animals, with those which are pathogenic to both man and animals, and with certain of those which are pathogenic only to man. The intimate relationship of man with animals and the consumption of animal products emphasize the fact that all students of Medical Microbiology must be familiar with the infectious agents found in man and animals if they are to understand the diseases produced.

A great deal of information relative to Veterinary Bacteriology and Virology has been published since the last edition. An attempt has been made to include this information in this edition, but it is apparent that much detailed data could not be given due to limitations of space.

Many of the chapters have been completely rewritten and many extensively revised. Friends and colleagues have kindly consented to revise certain chapters, and their intimate knowledge of the various subjects adds great value to the book. The names of these contributing authors are given in the Table of Contents.

The book has been completely reset into a two-column format which will make it more readable.

The authors wish to express their gratitude to the staff of the Iowa State University Press, especially to Merritt E. Bailey, Jr., and to Mrs. Gertrude C. Burrell.

IVAL A. MERCHANT

R. ALLEN PACKER

January, 1967

# Contents

## PART 1
## *General Biology of Microorganisms*



## PART 2
## *Infection, Resistance, and Immunity*

PART 3

## *Classification and Characteristics of Pathogenic Microorganisms*

## PART 4
## *The Viruses*

# 1

# The Scope and History of Bacteriology

THE 1960'S WILL GO DOWN IN HISTORY AS THE "nuclear energy—space exploration era." One hundred years ago the bacteriological era was beginning to unfold. It is apparent that bacteria, nuclear energy, and space have been a part of the universe for a long time, but slowly and surely man has become more adept at breaking through the veil of the unknown.

The importance of bacteria in the lives of people and the environment about them was not immediately recognized, but in 1893 Theobald Smith wrote, "In the study of the microscopic forms known as bacteria we have what might be fitly called the focal point of the various branches of biological science." The development of bacteriology during the years since that statement was made has revealed the truth of it. This has been true particularly of the relationship of bacteria to disease, for the entire conception of infectious disease, its prevention, and its treatment has been developed during the past 90 years. Bacteriology, as a science, has had a phenomenal growth, yet, the knowledge which is included in all the branches of the subject is so commonplace today, one wonders why its development was delayed so long. Even today, however, in scrutinizing the volumes written about bacteria it is observed that these microscopic forms have been known more for *what they do* than for *what they are.* This is understandable in light of the important changes that bacteria produce in materials in which they live. During recent years the trend of investigation has been toward the determination of the nature of bacteria, their chemical composition, and their variations in morphology and physiology. With this added knowledge we shall understand more clearly *why* bacteria bring about the changes by which they have been recognized for years.

Bacteriology is the branch of biology which deals with four different types of minute living organisms: the *bacteria,* the *filterable viruses,* the *yeasts,* and the *molds.*

Bacteriology, as a science, has numerous divisions, all of which have a common technical foundation, but each division is distinctive because different types of bacteria are found in various habitats. There are definite lines marking some of the divisions while others merge into one another. Any classification of the entire subject would be an arbitrary one, but the one given here is considered appropriate. Bacteriology may be divided into the following: *General Bacteriology, Systematic Bacteriology, Industrial Bacteriology, Agricultural Bacteriology, Dairy Bacteriology, Sanitary Bacteriology,* and *Medical Bacteriology.*

*General Bacteriology* is the study of the general characteristics of all bacteria. It is of academic importance and probably does not deserve the distinction of a separate division; yet, it is an important part of the science because students of this subject become acquainted with the entire field of bacteriology. Research in general bacteriology is of value because it is usually directed toward the nature of bacteria regardless of their origin.

*Systematic Bacteriology* embraces the classification and nomenclature of bacteria.

It also is of academic value and gives order and organization to the entire field. There has been an unfortunate tendency on the part of workers in all branches of bacteriology to disregard the sincere attempts which have been made by systematic bacteriologists to classify bacteria. It is freely admitted that methods which are used in classification may be faulty and at times confusing, but it is hoped that as the nature of bacteria becomes fully known, a satisfactory classification may be accomplished and adopted by all.

*Industrial Bacteriology* includes all the procedures which involve the action of bacteria in the various industries. In the utilization of agricultural by-products bacteria are playing an important rôle. The function of yeasts in the manufacture of alcohols and gases used in beverages is common knowledge. Bacterial action is fundamental in the manufacture of many organic acids, of which vinegar is a good example. The use of bacteria in the fermentation of corn to prepare alcohols of value as motor fuel is a promising industrial venture. The curing of tobacco, the retting of hemp, and the tanning of leather all depend on bacteria in various stages of the process. The discovery of penicillin initiated the development of a tremendous industry, the manufacture of antibiotics, which is included in this category.

*Agricultural Bacteriology* is the study o any of the forms of bacteria relating to agri culture and may be divided very appropriately into *soil bacteriology* and *plant bacteriology;* the former embraces the study of those bacteria which are found in the soil and which are of value in maintaining fertility; the latter is the study of bacteria found in plants and is an important part of the subject *Plant Pathology*.

*Food Bacteriology* includes the various processes which are used in the preparation of foods in the canning industry. This usually is confined to the control of those procedures which prevent spoilage of food and the elimination of conditions of bacterial origin which may impart undesirable flavors to foods.

*Dairy Bacteriology* embraces the study of all the bacteria, yeasts, and molds which are found in the manufacture of dairy products. This subject includes all bacteria which are harmful as well as those which are useful. In the sanitary control of milk and milk products this field overlaps those of sanitary and medical bacteriology.

*Sanitary Bacteriology* is so closely allied with Medical Bacteriology that there has been constant hesitation in placing it in a separate division; yet, certain bacteriologic techniques sufficiently definite to be placed in a separate category have been developed which aid man in the control of his environment. The bacteriology of water, foods, and sewage makes up the most important part of this subject. It is the study of all bacteria significant to health, which are found in the environment of man and animals.

*Medical Bacteriology* embraces the study of those bacteria, viruses, yeasts, and molds which are detrimental to the health of man and animals, primarily by their ability to produce disease. This division may be subdivided into *Human Bacteriology* and *Animal Bacteriology,* the latter commonly called *Veterinary Bacteriology*. Accumulated research reveals, however, that the division of these two subjects is becoming increasingly indistinct. Many bacteria are capable of producing disease in both man and animals, and although we are more familiar with the ones transmissible from animals to man, evidence points to the fact that the reverse occurs in some instances. No doubt much overcrossing of infection would be present if man and animals lived in close contact with one another. *Human Bacteriology* may be defined as that portion of Medical Bacteriology which concerns those microorganisms (bacteria, yeasts, molds, and filterable viruses) which affect the health of man only, and those which are transmitted from animals to man, or from man to animals, either directly or in food products. *Veterinary Bacteriology* includes that portion of Medical Bacteriology which concerns those microorganisms (bacteria, yeasts, molds, and viruses) which affect the health of animals only, and those which are transmitted from animals to man, either directly or in food products. Both branches of Medical Bacteriology have as their very able ally, *Immunology*, which considers the resistance of the body to disease and the means which may be used to increase such resistance.

During recent years the study of the filterable viruses which affect man and animals has progressed so much that the study of such agents is embraced under the general term *Virology*.

## THE HISTORY OF MEDICAL BACTERIOLOGY

The development of bacteriology has been due to the true scientific curiosity and energy of great men, aided in many instances by their fortitude in standing for what they knew to be true in the face of apparent disproof and the disdain of their associates. The history of Medical Bacteriology is a story of the evolution of knowledge concerning the causes of disease. It is a most fascinating story, particularly as revealed by Bullock in "The History of Bacteriology," which every student is urged to read. Space allotted to the discussion of this subject in this book permits only a brief review of the significant discoveries of the foremost contributors to the subject.

### Early Theories of the Cause of Disease

The life of early man was governed by superstition. It is not surprising that such an affliction as disease, often followed by death, was attributed to the wrath of divine spirits for the punishment of individual sins. This is known as the *Theurgical Theory of Disease*. The Bible gives several interesting accounts of contagious disease. One of the most significant is the discussion of the treatment of lepers as given in Leviticus, Chapters XIII and XIV. The fact that the Jews required leprous people to be segregated indicates that they were aware that the disease was spread by contact, but the cause always was considered to be supernatural. That the infected were required to shield their faces with their hands and to cry "unclean" also indicated a knowledge of transmission. Sometimes an enraged Deity was credited with transmitting evil spirits on poisoned darts as was described in the great classic, "The Iliad," when Apollo apparently became angry and supposedly inflicted the army before Troy with epidemic sickness by means of darts. The Theurgical Theory of Disease persisted through many centuries. The belief in supernatural inflictions of disease is still observed among uncivilized peoples, and occasionally vestiges of it are evident among races considered civilized.

This belief was replaced by the *Miasmatic Theory of Disease* which taught that all disease was due to the emanations from the earth, the influence of the stars, the moon, the winds, the waters, and the seasons. This explanation of the cause of disease was enhanced by the teachings of Hippocrates (460–370 B.C.) who is commonly given the credit of being the originator of the theory. In his treatise, "On Airs, Waters and Places," Hippocrates stressed the relationship of disease to different waters, to the direction of the wind, and to the slope of the land. He also postulated that the four elements—fire, air, water, and earth, and the four qualities—heat, cold, moisture, and dryness, corresponded to the four fluids, or humors, of the body—blood, phlegm, yellow bile, and black bile. All were closely related according to Hippocrates, and the different types of disease were caused by the changes in temperature and moisture during the various seasons of the year. Hippocrates did not think of disease as being caused by transmissible agents; consequently, he did not advance knowledge a great deal from the early ancient beliefs. He did free medicine from superstition, however, and his clear method of analysis of cases of disease and his descriptions of them certainly make him worthy of the great honor accorded him in his title, "The Father of Medicine."

The teachings of Hippocrates were the starting point for theorizing on disease by all medical-minded individuals. This resulted in discarding the Miasmatic explanation for a period. The *Pore Theory* came into vogue and was supported by Asclepiades (124 B.C.), Themison (143–23 B.C.), and Thessalus (A.D. 60). Although each of these men based his conception on the function of pores, their resulting theories varied somewhat. The first two investigators believed that a symmetry of proportion of the pores resulted in health and a disproportion of pores caused disease. Thessalus, on the other hand, believed that the pores should be changed in afflicted parts to assure recovery from disease. So positive was he of his theory that he vigorously denounced Hippocrates' Miasmatic Theory.

The close relationship of disease to nature was too apparent for the Miasmatic Theory to be discarded for long. Galen (A.D. 120–200) revived all the medical teachings of the master, Hippocrates, and embellished them with his own observations and imagination. He recognized the four elements, qualities, and humors as postulated by Hippocrates and taught that an excess or deficiency of these humors resulted in disease. Based upon his observation of the individual humoral capacity of each person, Galen classified the temperaments of people as (1) sanguine, (2) phlegmatic, (3) bilious, or (4) melancholic. In order to equalize humors, Galen often found it necessary to draw what he considered excess blood. He advocated bloodletting as one of the cures of disease. No advance in the knowledge of contagion was made during this period. The Miasmatic Theory was accepted wholeheartedly.

The teachings of Hippocrates and Galen were accepted during the Medieval period (1096–1438); however, most scientific investigations and teachings were dominated by the rise of Christianity and its power in the State. Great powers of healing were attributed to the Saints, and fortunate indeed was he who had in his possession, as a charm for healing, a bone or any other article reputed to have come from a Saint. During this period pandemics of plague, epidemic chorea (St. Vitus' dance), and other epidemics swept the civilized world. Ample material was available for the observation of the contagiousness of disease. If such observations were made at that time, very few of them found their way into the medical literature of the period; however, some interesting observations were made by laymen such as Boccaccio (1313–75) who tells an interesting story concerning the transmission of plague in his "Decameron" (1358). He wrote:[1]

> A marvellous thing to hear is that which I have to tell and one which, had it not been seen of many men's eyes and of mine own, I had scarce dared credit, much less set down in writing, though I had heard it from one worthy of belief. I say, then, that of such efficience was the nature of the pestilence in question in communicating itself from one to another, that, not only did it pass from man to man, but this, which is much more, it many times visibly did; to wit, a thing which pertained to a man sick or dead of the aforesaid sickness, being touched by an animal foreign to the human species, not only infected this latter with the plague, but in a very brief space of time killed it. Of this mine own eyes (as hath a little before been said) had one day, among others, experience on this wise; to wit, that the rags of a poor man, who had died of the plague, being cast out into the public way, two hogs came up to them and having first, after their wont, rooted amain among them with their snouts, took them in their mouths and tossed them about their jaws; then, in a little while, after turning round and round, they both, as if they had taken poison, fell down dead upon the rags with which they had in an ill hour intermeddled.

Science rose with the Renaissance, and during the period (1400–1600) made tremendous advances. The conception of the causes of disease, however, was still retarded by beliefs in divine powers and miasms. Paracelsus (1493–1541) speculated that diseases arose from five main causes: (1) the effect of the stars, (2) the poisons in foods, (3) natural phenomena controlled by the stars and moon, (4) spirits and demons, and (5) effects of the acts of God.

The speculations of Fracastorius (1478–1553) represent the earliest doctrine of infection that came close to the truth. He based his observations on epidemics of plague, syphilis, and typhus of man and of foot-and-mouth disease of cattle which were known to be prevalent in Italy at the time. Contagion was attributed to three possible sources: (1) contagion by contact, (2) contagion by fomites (clothes, wooden

[1] Giovanni Boccaccio. *The Decameron,* 1358. Trans. John Payne, The Modern Library, New York, p. 9.

things, etc.), and (3) contagion at a distance. He wrote of *seminaria,* or seeds, of disease, showing that he did believe that some seed or living agent was involved. This represented the greatest advance toward solving the actual cause of infection until the most important barrier to the real discovery, the minuteness of bacteria, had been overcome.

### The Influence of the Microscope

Although the early Greek physicians had conjectured that invisible living plants existed, the discovery of them awaited the development of the microscope.

Sir E. Ray Lankester has written most appropriately, "The microscope is the means by which our modern understanding of the structure and nature of living things has been gained, as contrasted with the baseless fancies and blank ignorance of three centuries ago."

Among the early believers in the existence of invisible forms was Athanasius Kircher (1602–80). He is given the credit of using a microscope of about 32-power magnification with which he saw "worms" in the blood of plague patients. His descriptions were so embellished by imagination that most of his observations are discounted. The first compound microscope is believed to have been made in Holland by Cornelius Drebbel and by Hans and Zaccharias Janssen at about 1590–1610. Galileo, in 1609, is also credited with being one of the first to place a series of lenses in a tube to produce higher magnifications. Toward the end of the seventeenth century two Englishmen, Robert Hooke and Nehemiah Grew, used a microscope in the study of natural objects and the structure of plants. An Italian, Marcello Malpighi (1628–94), who is known as the founder of histology, obviously used a microscope in order to see the detailed cellular structures of the lungs which he described in 1661. The description of the erythrocytes by Jan Swammerdam in 1658 was made possible by the use of a microscope.

The manufacture and use of a microscope of a higher magnifying power than any formerly used is credited to Antony van Leeuwenhoek of Delft, Holland, who lived during the period 1632–1723. The story of the life of this true scientist and of his discoveries has been perpetuated by Dobell. Every student of science dealing with microscopy should read this fascinating account. There is little doubt that Leeuwenhoek should be credited as being the Father of Bacteriology. His letters to the Royal Society of London and the illustrations (Fig. 1.1) which accompanied them

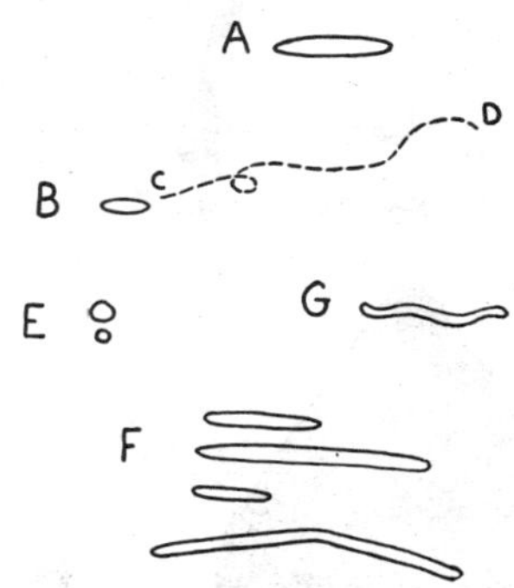


FIG. 1.1—Leeuwenhoek's figures of bacteria: **A** and **B**, probably bacilli; **C–D**, path of motile form; **E**, cocci; **F**, Leptothrix; **G**, spirochete.

prove conclusively that he had seen bacteria of various shapes and sizes in a variety of substances. His microscopes revealed that he was a craftsman of ability, although his interest in his instruments was based upon what they allowed him to see, rather than his ability in manufacturing them. The microscopes of Leeuwenhoek were rough and unfinished although they were mechanically efficient (Fig. 1.2). He made 247 microscopes, very few of which have been handed down to posterity. The highest magnification which he was able to obtain was about 200 diameters. He guarded his instruments jealously, and very few persons were privileged to see them.

The microscope passed through a gradual series of developments until it has become the splendid instrument of the present day (Fig. 1.3). In 1739, J. N. Lieberkühn perfected the solar microscope

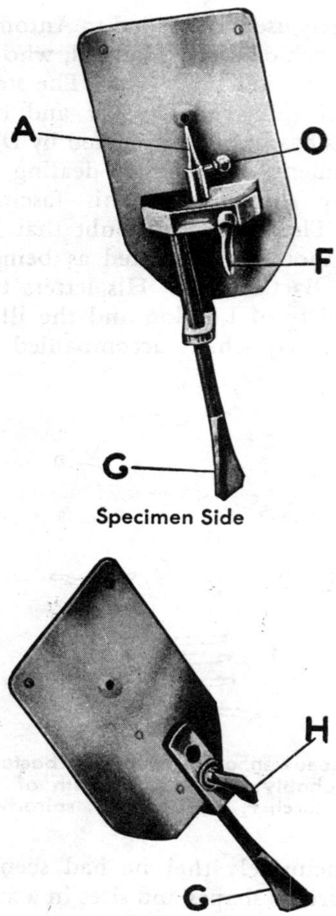


**FIG. 1.2—Replica of Leeuwenhoek's microscope. A, needle on which to mount specimen; F, screw for focusing specimen; G, screw for raising and lowering specimen; H, clamp screw; O, handle for rotating specimen. (Courtesy Bausch and Lomb.)**

of Leeuwenhoek. The light transmitted through the glass lenses of the early microscope was broken into its component colors. Chester Moor Hall and John Dollond (1733) are given the credit for independently preparing achromatic lenses which corrected this dispersion. The use of a combination of lenses is attributed to Chevalier of Paris in 1824. Joseph Jackson Lister developed important detailed principles of the modern microscope in 1830. From that date the microscope has been improved by many mechanical innovations. An advance in the knowledge of microorganisms has followed each improvement in the microscope. The compensating ocular, the Abbe condenser and the oil immersion objective enables us to see objects magnified 1,500 diameters; however, there does appear to be a limit to the visibility of highly magnified objects. Physicists agree that the resolving power of the microscope is limited by the length of the waves of light used for illumination.

The development of the electron microscope during recent years has opened an entirely new invisible world for man to observe. With this instrument, objects which are magnified 25,000 times are photographed and made available for study.

### Spontaneous Generation

The spontaneous origin of life (heterogenesis or abiogenesis) among all living things, other than animals manifestly the result of the act of creation, was the firm conviction of early scientists. The origin of maggots from decaying flesh, and rats from filthy clothing are examples of early beliefs. It is obvious that microscopic living things were believed to arise spontaneously. The proof that such was not the case removed one of the serious barriers to the development of knowledge of the nature of bacteria. Francisco Redi (1626–97) was one of the first to show that maggots did not develop in meat when the meat was covered with fine gauze. Louis Joblot (1647–1723) demonstrated in 1711 that heated infusions were not able to produce animalcules, whereas cold infusions soon teemed with living things. The belief in the theory of spontaneous generation persisted, however, largely due to the efforts of such men as Needham who was an ardent believer in this theory. The experimental work of Spallanzani in 1756 and 1776, which disproved the theory conclusively, served to fan the flame of controversy over the subject. The experiments of Theodore Schwann (1810–82), published during the first part of the nineteenth century, definitely established that fermen-

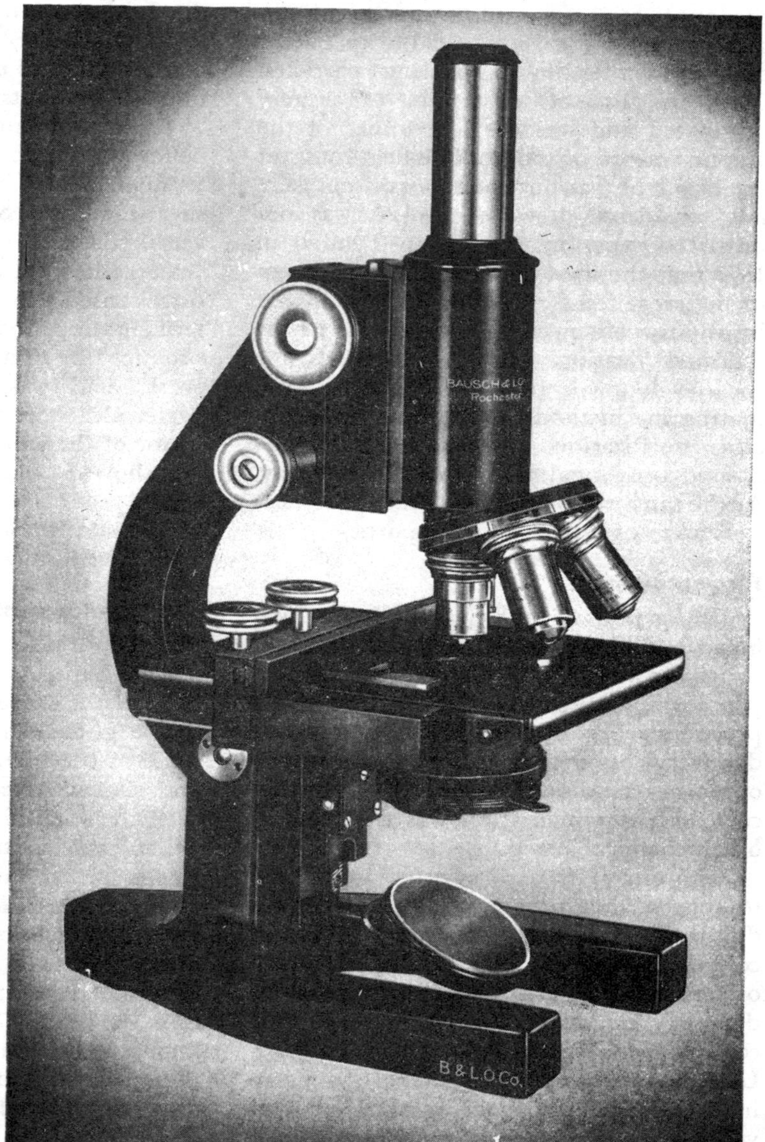


FIG. 1.3—A modern student microscope. (Courtesy Bausch and Lomb.)

tation and decay were results of microorganisms rather than the creation of them. Schröeder and Dusch in 1854 demonstrated that cotton wool satisfactorily protected a freshly boiled infusion from fermentation, thereby establishing the use of the cotton plug in laboratory procedures. A staggering blow to the theory of spontaneous generation was dealt by Louis Pasteur in a series of experiments the results of which were published in 1860. In these experiments he demonstrated that the dust in the air was laden with microbes, and when it was prevented from entering flasks containing infusions, the infusions remained sterile.

The results of these experiments were of great practical value. Joseph Lister (1827–1912), a Scottish surgeon, found that infection following surgery was prevented by the application of a dressing containing some material (carbolic acid) capable of destroying the life of floating particles. Thus the use of antiseptics in surgery originated and was the forerunner of the aseptic surgery of today. The heat-resistant stages of the various microorganisms were not considered, however, and it was not until the experiments of John Tyndall in 1877 that the final decisive blow was given to heterogenesis. He demonstrated that infusions were made absolutely sterile by repeated heating, allowing intervals for the development of spores, thereby originating the method of fractional (intermittent) sterilization (Tyndallization) which is used occasionally in laboratories today. At the same time he demonstrated the heat resistance of bacterial endospores.

### Fermentation

The action of the leaven in making bread and the fermentation and decay of fruits and vegetables were magic to ancient people. The discovery of the nature of the processes really laid the foundation to the discovery of the relationship of microorganisms to disease. Early chemists conceived that fermentation was the same as other chemical reactions.

Fabbroni (1787) apparently was the first to suggest that fermentation of wine was due to the action of a glutinous substance contained in grapes. The biological nature of fermentation was made obvious by the discovery of yeast cells. This important contribution was shared by Cagniard-Latour (1836), Schwann (1837), and Kutzing (1837). Of these Schwann is credited with being the one to explain alcoholic fermentation and is known as the Father of Fermentation.

The role of microorganisms in fermentation was definitely shown by Louis Pasteur (1822–95). His exactness in experimentation and his enthusiastic support of his results epitomize the character of Pasteur. These characteristics explain why his results were accepted when the results of others were not. As a chemist, it was natural that he should become involved in the subject of fermentation. During the period 1854–80 he demonstrated and explained most of the processes of fermentation. His results were opposed, however, by the German chemist, Liebig, who believed that fermentation was due to a ferment formed by the action of air on the sugar molecule. Spurred on by this controversy, Pasteur conclusively proved that yeast cells produced a ferment which in turn caused the reactions characteristic of fermentation, that lactic acid in milk was produced by ferments of bacteria, and that acetic acid was formed as a result of bacterial ferments. He was hailed as the savior of the wine industry of France when he showed that undesirable organisms caused sour wine. He showed that the proper sterilization of vats eliminated these undesirable organisms.

### The Development of the Germ Theory of Disease

In the discussion of the ancient conceptions of the cause of disease it was observed that a glimmering of the truth existed in some of the literature during the fifteenth and sixteenth centuries. In general, however, the scientific world did not accept the belief that contagion was due to living things which grow and multiply in the body of the infected. This hesitance of scientific workers is substantiated by the fact that a very significant book on the nature of consumptions, written by Benjamin Martin in 1720, was comparatively unknown to his contemporaries. He theorized that consumption was caused by some species of animalcules which were inimical to the nature of man; that they were able to exist in the juices and vessels of the body and be carried to the lungs where they localized and wounded or gnawed the tender vessels, thereby producing the disease. It was the adherence to accepted dogma, no doubt, that explained why the discovery of small animalcules by Leeuwenhoek was of so little significance in the understanding of the cause of disease. It is surprising that the keen mind of Bretonneau (1778–1862), who is known as the first to believe in the specificity of disease, did not grasp the significance of animalcules as an aid in explaining specificity of disease.

An Italian layman, Agostino Bassi, discovered in 1835 that a disease of silkworms, known by the Italians as "calcino" and by the French as "muscardine," was caused by a fungus. He demonstrated that the organism could be transmitted from diseased to healthy silkworms by contact and by infected food.

The real basis for the foundation of the *Germ Theory of Disease* was laid by Jacob Henle in 1840 when he speculated "On Miasmata and Contagia." George Rosen has translated this treatise into English which makes it more available to students of this continent. Henle based his theories upon Bassi's discovery of the cause of silkworm disease and the discovery of the relationship of yeast cells to fermentation by Cagniard-Latour and by Schwann. These definite findings, in addition to his own observations, led Henle to give the following reasons which to him proved the individual life of the contagions:[2]

1. The ability to multiply by assimilating foreign materials is known to us only in living organic beings.
2. The action of contagia was also compared with fermentation in that the quantity of the effect is in no relation to the quantity of ferment used. A needle dipped into diluted chicken-pox material having been mixed with a half dram of water is still capable of infecting. This action depends on the ability of the agent to multiply, as has been demonstrated in fermentation and putrefaction; consequently, this is a further proof of the animate nature of the contagia.
3. The precise, typical course of the miasmatic-contagious diseases, and the relations in the course of the corresponding epidemics themselves seem to speak for an independent, temporal development of the disease cause, which occurs only among organic beings.

Although Henle recognized that his theory needed experimental substantiation, he realized that in order for the experiments to develop they needed the light of reasonable theory. The experiments did develop, and it was one of his pupils, Robert Koch, who later expanded the theory into fact which proved the relationship of germs to disease.

The discovery of the fungus of silkworms by Bassi opened the way for the discovery of numerous fungus diseases of man and animals. Some of the discoveries were based on fact, but most of them were without value.

In 1849 John Snow observed epidemic cholera was water-borne; this added proof to the germ theory. The classic, "Typhoid Fever," by William Budd, illustrated his conception of the relationship of living, growing germs to that disease.

The discovery of small filiform bodies in the blood of anthrax-infected sheep and the subsequent proof of the relationship of these bodies to the disease was conclusive evidence that germs could cause disease. The discovery of the bacilli was made, independently, by P. F. O. Rayer and his associate, C. J. Davaine, in 1850 and by F. A. A. Pollender in 1885. F. A. Brauell established the transmissibility of the disease in 1857 by infecting sheep and horses with anthrax blood. During the period 1863–68, Davaine established the definite relationship of the "bacteria," as he called them, to the disease by observing that they were present in blood of animals having the disease and, also, by observing that when they were not present anthrax did not occur. He demonstrated that the disease could be produced by the injection of one-millionth of a drop of anthrax blood.

Pasteur added materially to the formulation of the Germ Theory of Disease by his discovery in 1870 that pebrine, a disease of the silkworm, was caused by a protozoan parasite. The crystallization of the Germ Theory of Disease during the 1860's came as a result of a converging of numerous approaches to the nature of microorganisms which may be summarized as follows: first, fermentation had been shown to be due to the action of yeasts; second, spontaneous generation had been exploded; third, wound infection following surgical operations had been prevented by the use of antiseptics; fourth, epidemiological obser-

[2] Jacob Henle. *On Miasmata and Contagia*, 1840. Trans. George Rosen, Johns Hopkins Press, Baltimore, 1938, p. 19.

vations by Henle, Snow, Budd, and a host of others substantiated the particulate and living nature of contagion; fifth, the injection of putrid blood from a case of septicemia reproduced the disease; sixth, the following specific causes of disease were discovered: fungi were present in the disease of silkworms, fungi were found in skin infection of man, and bacteria were always present in cases of anthrax.

The absolute proof of the Germ Theory came as a result of the classical work of Robert Koch (1843–1910) on anthrax in 1876. Working with crude equipment Koch succeeded in tracing the development of the anthrax bacillus through the spore-forming stage to the germination of the spore and the formation of the bacterial cell. He demonstrated the capacity of the organism to kill mice and to produce the same type of lesions repeatedly. He found that other similar types of bacteria did not produce disease, thereby establishing the specific nature of infectious disease and forming the basis of his postulates or laws for which he has become famous. Koch's discovery was lauded and abetted by Ferdinand Cohn, a botanist, to whom great credit is given for classifying the species of bacteria known at that time and forming a basis of classification and nomenclature on which subsequent systems have been built.

Pasteur had deserted the field of fermentation when he investigated the cause of silkworm disease. Koch's definite discovery of the anthrax organism stimulated Pasteur to delve into the causes of animal and human diseases. He confirmed Koch's work on anthrax, and in 1877 clarified the relationship of another organism to an acute and fatal disease. He established the cause of malignant edema as being due to an anaerobic organism which he termed *Vibrion septique.* Pasteur then turned his attention to the nature of disease and to immunity. His classical studies on anthrax immunity laid the foundation of prophylactic treatment of infectious diseases. Koch turned his attention to the perfection of laboratory procedures during the course of which he made monumental discoveries of bacteria, the most important of which was the tubercle bacillus which he demonstrated in 1882. So it was due largely to the efforts of Koch and Pasteur that the Germ Theory of Disease became a fact, the science of medical bacteriology became established, and the field of medicine became revolutionized.

### The Development of Laboratory Methods

The perfection of the microscope, the discovery that cotton plugs protect culture media from air-dust contamination, and the conclusion that intermittent boiling kills bacterial spores are three very important contributions to laboratory techniques previously discussed. Progress in bacteriology was delayed, however, by the lack of proper methods of staining bacteria and of separating one type of microorganism from another in a pure culture.

Dyes, such as carmine, had been used for the staining of tissues until aniline and the coal-tar dyes were prepared in 1856. Herman Hoffman is given first credit for using carmine and fuchsin in staining bacteria in 1869. The practical use of dyes in bacteriology dates from 1875 when Carl Weigert used methyl violet to stain cocci in tissues. Koch turned his attention to the use of stains which he perfected in 1877 enabling him to stain the flagella of bacteria. He used heat to fix the bacterial film to the slide in 1881. On March 24, 1882, Koch read his first paper on the cause of tuberculosis, a discovery brought about by staining the films of tuberculosis matter with alkaline methylene blue and subsequent treatment with vesuvin and Bismarck brown. Paul Ehrlich, a cousin of Weigert, contributed to the chemical knowledge of stains, introduced the technique of staining blood-films in 1881, and in 1882 improved on the technique of Koch for staining tubercle bacilli. Christian Gram of Denmark introduced the technique now known as the "Gram stain" in 1884; by this method all bacteria are separated into two groups, gram-negative and gram-positive.

Numerous methods were employed by

the early bacteriologists to separate different species of bacteria and obtain pure cultures. The most popular and successful method was by multiple dilution. Raw potato, however, was commonly used as a solid medium. To Robert Koch goes the credit of first using solid media in 1881. He added gelatin to meat infusion and poured the liquid medium on a glass plate to harden; the medium was protected from dust contamination by placing a bell jar over it. The medium was inoculated by streaking the surface with a platinum wire charged with the material containing bacteria. The use of agar-agar in culture media was introduced by Frau Hesse, the wife of Walther Hesse, one of Koch's early coworkers. Koch used coagulated blood serum for a culture medium in 1882. The value of solid media which enabled bacteriologists to obtain pure cultures cannot be overestimated. It was one of the most valuable contributions to the development of the science. It enabled Koch to fulfill his postulates by isolating organisms in pure culture; accordingly, most of the discoveries of the causes of the various infections were made possible by the use of solid media. It served to stimulate all bacteriological research, for it enabled workers to study the action of pure cultures.

New advances in laboratory technique have aided in the discovery of new organisms and of additional knowledge concerning old ones. The technique of filtration, first employed as a method of purifying media and to test the toxicity of bacteria-free filtrates, led to the discovery of the large group of disease agents known as filterable viruses. Constant improvements in methods of sterilization were to reduce the hazards of contamination. Various tests for the metabolic products of bacterial growth were devised to aid in differentiating and classifying bacteria. Methods of culturing bacteria in the absence of free air revealed a large group of anaerobic bacteria and increased knowledge concerning bacterial respiration. Out of all the laboratory procedures, however, three stand out as being the most significant in the development of the science of bacteriology. Those three are: *use of the microscope, sterilization,* and *use of solid media.*

### The Development of Theories of Immunity

A resistance to a second attack of the same disease after recovery from the first was an observation by early physicians. This was thought to be the result of magic as was disease itself. The development of immunology as a science closely followed that of bacteriology and cannot be separated from it.

Methods of immunizing against disease were practiced long before the Germ Theory of Disease was formulated. In 1798 Edward Jenner described his method of immunizing against smallpox by using attenuated virus. His method was an outgrowth of the commonly known fact that milkmaids became immune to smallpox because of their contact with cows suffering with cowpox. Almost 100 years later (1877–80) Pasteur accidentally found that cultures of the fowl cholera organism lost their ability to produce disease after they had been grown on artificial media in contact with air. These cultures did have the property, however, of producing an immunity in chickens which rendered them resistant to virulent cultures of the same organism. The triumphant entry of artificial immunization into the field of medicine resulted from Pasteur's classical work on anthrax at Pouilly-le-Fort in 1881. In those experiments he demonstrated that cultures of the anthrax bacillus, attenuated by growing at 42°C., were able to cause the development of a marked immunity in sheep against highly virulent anthrax organisms. His subsequent work on swine erysipelas and rabies was almost as noteworthy, for it substantiated his earlier work and opened the way for other applications of his methods. In the United States, Theobald Smith and D. E. Salmon demonstrated the use of heat-killed cultures of an organism then thought to be the cause of hog cholera. Although the use of the heat-killed cultures of *Salmonella choleraesuis* was of no value in hog cholera immunization, it was of great value in initiating the technique of bacterin therapy which has been widely practiced since that time.

About 1881 Elie Metchnikoff, a Russian zoologist, observed that motile cells in the body of the water flea were able to engulf invading microorganisms. This led to further observations of the phenomenon in man and animals and the formulation of the *Phagocytic,* or *Cellular Theory of Immunity.*

A few years later (1888), G. H. F. Nuttall demonstrated that blood of various animals possessed a bactericidal action for anthrax bacilli. This fact was confirmed and explained further by Hans Buchner in 1889. In 1890 E. Fraenkel and E. Behring produced an immunity against diphtheria by injecting old broth cultures. In the same year Behring and Kitasato revealed that the immunity in rabbits against the tetanus organism was due to a material in the blood stream capable of neutralizing the toxin formed by the bacillus. This fact was demonstrated also for the diphtheria bacillus. From these discoveries arose the *Humoral Theory of Immunity* which contends that immunity is due to the action of specific substances in the blood and not due to the action of phagocytic cells entirely.

In attempts to explain the methods by which the pathogenic organisms and their toxins were neutralized by blood serum, other discoveries were made which, for the most part, were results of test-tube experimentation. In 1895 Jules Bordet contended that neutralization was due to a physical sensitization process and a subsequent lytic process. Paul Ehrlich, in 1897, insisted that the neutralization process was chemical in nature and upon this premise he formulated his *Side-Chain Theory of Immunity.* He visualized that the body cell produced receptors which were superabundant in immune serum and which caused a chemical neutralization of the invading organism or its toxins when they came in contact. Although Ehrlich's side-chain theory has been relegated to the "historic background" of the subject of immunity, it has served a useful purpose. It has stimulated research out of which have grown more plausible explanations of the phenomenon and has been useful in explaining to the beginning student the intricacies of the various reactions. Ehrlich's terminology is still used to a great extent, and some of his fundamental theories linger with a vestige of truth in them.

In 1896 Herbert Durham and Max Gruber demonstrated that a suspension of organisms was agglutinated by a specific immune serum. The practical application of the phenomenon in the diagnosis of typhoid fever was made by F. Widal in 1896. This test, known as the "Widal Microscopic Test," has been modified during the years until the "Macroscopic Tube Test" is now one of the most common diagnostic methods for certain diseases. R. Kraus demonstrated in 1897 that immune serum also had a specific reaction for a bacterial filtrate which caused it to precipitate. This gave origin to the precipitation test which is used for the diagnosis of disease and for the study of immune reactions.

Simon Flexner demonstrated in 1894 that "animals that had withstood one dose of dog serum would succumb to a second dose given after the lapse of some days or weeks, even when this dose was sublethal for a control animal." Thus he clearly demonstrated that a hypersensitive condition, the exact opposite of immunity, was produced. This reaction was observed also by C. Richet and J. Hericourt in 1898 when eel serum was injected into dogs after allowing a lapse of approximately two weeks from the time the first injection was given. In 1903 M. Arthus observed a skin necrosis in rabbits which followed successive injections of horse serum. In 1904 Theobald Smith found that guinea pigs became hypersensitive to subsequent injections of horse serum during the course of diphtheria antitoxin standardization. From these original observations a mass of data was accumulated about the subject of anaphylaxis and allergy, a study which today is still in its formative stage.

### The Development of Antibiotic Agents

The bacteria are no exception to the the general rule that all life is beset by antagonism. This appears to be a matter of competition for food. This function in the microscopic world was detected by Pasteur when he observed that anthrax bacilli were inhibited in growth by airborne contaminants. Bouchard, in 1888, recorded the inhibitory effect of the products of *Pseudomonas aeruginosa* on many species of bacteria. Sir Alexander Fleming reported that the growth of staphylococci was inhibited by the growth of a penicillium mold. Dubos, in 1939, found that a substance produced by *Bacillus brevis* inhibited the growth of streptococci and pneumococci.

All of these early observations were really crystallized by the work of Florey and Chain in 1940 and by Waksman in 1942, who showed beyond doubt that antibiotics could play a tremendous role in curing infectious diseases. Governments and industry immediately recognized the potential of these agents and, provided with "wartime money," they ushered in the antibiotic era.

## REFERENCES


Adams, F. The Genuine Works of Hippocrates. Williams & Wilkins Co., Baltimore, 1939.

Ainsworth, G. C. A Century of Medical and Veterinary Mycology in Great Britain. Trans. Brit. Mycol. Soc. 34:1, 1951.

Brock, T. D. Milestones in Microbiology. Prentice-Hall, Inc., Inglewood Cliffs, N. J., 1961.

Bulloch, W. The History of Bacteriology. Oxford University Press, New York, 1938. (Reprinted 1960.)

Clendening, Logan. Source Book of Medical History. Paul B. Hoeber, New York, 1942.

Dobell, C. Anton van Leeuwenhoek and His "Little Animals." John Bale, Sons & Danielsson, London, 1932.

Dubos, R. J. Louis Pasteur: Free Lance of Science. Little, Brown and Co., Boston, 1950.

Duclaux, E. Pasteur, A History of a Mind. Eng. Transl. E. F. Smith and Florence Hedges. W. B. Saunders Co., Philadelphia, 1920.

Ford, W. W. The Life and Work of Robert Koch. Bull. Johns Hopkins Hosp. 22:415–24, 1911.

Frobisher, M. Fundamentals of Microbiology. 7th Ed. W. B. Saunders Co., Philadelphia, 1962.

Grainger, T. H. A Guide to the History of Bacteriology. Ronald Press Co., New York, 1958.

Holmes, W. H. Bacillary and Rickettsial Infections: Black Death to White Plague. Macmillan Co., New York, 1940.

Kendall, A. I. Civilization and the Microbe. Houghton Mifflin Co., Boston and New York, 1923.

Kluyver, A. J., and Van Niel, C. B. The Microbe's Contribution to Biology. Harvard Univ. Press, Cambridge, 1956.

Knight, B. C. J. G. The Growth of Microbiology. Jour. Gen. Microbiol. 27:357–72, 1962.

Metchnikoff, Olga. Life of Elie Metchnikoff. Houghton Mifflin Co., Boston, 1921.

Oliver, Wade W. Stalkers of Pestilence. Paul B. Hoeber, New York, 1930.

Rosen, George. Jacob Henle: On Miasmata and Contagia. Transl. Johns Hopkins Press, Baltimore, 1938.

Stephenson, M. Bacterial Metabolism. Longmans, Green and Co., London, 1930.

Waksman, S. A. Microbial Antagonisms and Antibiotic Substances. 2nd Ed. Commomwealth Fund, New York, 1947.

Williams, G. Virus Hunters. Alfred A. Knopf, Inc., New York, 1959.

# 2

# Morphology and Colony Characteristics of Bacteria, Yeasts, and Molds

THE CLASSIFICATION OF PLANTS AND ANIMALS in their respective kingdoms is not difficult when their parts can be seen with the naked eye. Even with the low powers of a microscope, anatomical areas may be used as a basis for classification. The characteristics by which plants and animals are differentiated become less significant among the microscopic forms of life; therefore, it is necessary to understand the factors that are considered in assigning a particular microorganism to the animal or plant kingdom. Difficulty arises particularly in the differentiation of the bacteria and the protozoa. All bacteria probably have a cell membrane which, in function, is closely related to that of plants, and in some species cellulose and chitin may be found. The cell membrane of protozoa is not so well defined and may be described more aptly as a limiting membrane. In shape, habit of growth, and reproduction, the bacteria resemble the blue-green algae and molds much more than they do the protozoa. Motility is of no value in placing the bacteria in either kingdom inasmuch as flagellated forms are found in both the plant and animal kingdoms. Although there is no particular reason why bacteria might not represent a position intermediate to the plants and animals, the evidence, on the whole, is in favor of the classification of true bacteria with plants.

## THE PLANT KINGDOM

The position of the bacteria and fungi in relation to other plants should be understood. The plant kingdom traditionally contains five divisions (formerly considered as phyla) according to the following classification:

| DIVISION | |
|---|---|
| **Scientific Names** | **Common Names** |
| **SPERMATOPHYTA** | |
| Gymnospermae | Conifers and related plants |
| Angiospermae | Flowering plants |
| **PTERIDOPHYTA** | |
| Lycopodineae | Club mosses |
| Equisetineae | Horse-tails |
| Filicineae | Ferns |
| **BRYOPHYTA** | |
| Hepaticae | Liver-worts |
| Musci | Mosses |
| **THALLOPHYTA** | |
| *Algae* | |
| Chlorophyceae | Green algae |
| Phaeophyceae | Brown algae |
| Rhodophyceae | Red algae |
| Diatomeae | Diatoms |
| *Fungi* | |
| Myxomycetes | Slime fungi |
| Phycomycetes | Algal fungi |
| Ascomycetes | Sac fungi |
| Basidiomycetes | Club fungi |
| Deuteromycetes *(Fungi Imperfecti)* | Imperfect fungi |
| **PROTOPHYTA** | |
| Schizophyceae | Blue-green algae |
| Schizomycetes | Bacteria and Actinomycetes |

The Thallophyta are those plants devoid of leaves, stems, or true roots, but otherwise have very little in common. Several of the fungal thallophytes have developed a parasitic capacity for plants, animals, and man.

The Protophyta are those organisms devoid of a nuclear envelope or membrane which is considered to be a more primitive feature than that found in the Thallophyta. Many of the bacterial protophytes have developed a parasitic capacity for plants, animals, and man. A discussion of the general morphology of these two different divisions follows.

## MORPHOLOGY OF BACTERIA

### Shape

The bacteria are grouped according to shape into spherical forms, straight rods, curved or spiral rods, and filamentous forms (Fig. 2.1).

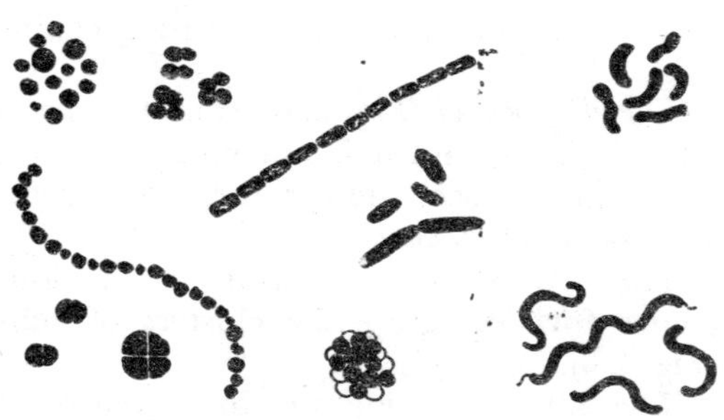

FIG. 2.1—Types of bacteria: cocci, bacilli, and spirilla.

The spherical bacteria are called *cocci* (sing. *coccus*). (See Fig. 2.2.)

The straight rods are called *bacilli* (sing. *bacillus*). (See Fig. 2.3.)

The curved or spiral rods are represented by cells which may vary from a comma shape to a tightly twisted, corkscrew-like cell. The more loosely curved cells are known as *spirilla* (sing. *spirillum*), and the more tightly coiled forms are called *spirochetes* (sing. *spirochete*).

Many of the bacteria resemble the molds in morphology. These forms are elongated and threadlike, and some of them are branched. They are known as the *filamentous bacteria* and are sometimes called *trichobacteria*.

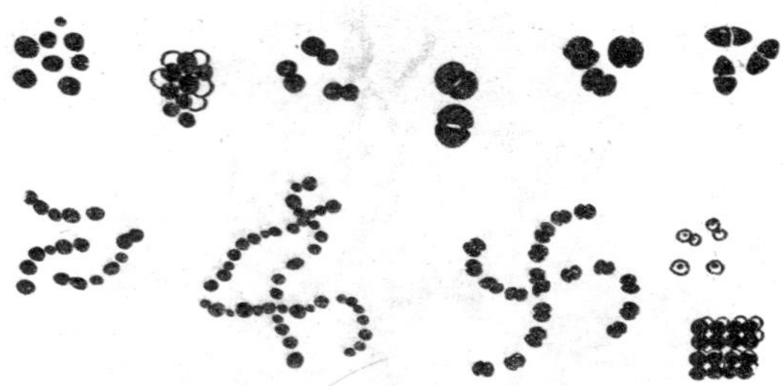

FIG. 2.2—Various groups of cocci.

The different morphologic groups of bacteria are well defined, and on that basis may be classified into various subgroups. As a result of certain stimuli or when grown under unfavorable conditions, however, many bacteria assume unusual and abnormal shapes. Cells of this type have been called involution forms or pleomorphic types, and more recently, variant and dissociative forms. For many years little significance was attached to such changes, and they were thought to be due, in many cases, to contamination. Eventually, however, the changes were recognized, and at the present time are considered to represent normal characteristics of bacteria. Most of the variations which occur are of a temporary nature, and are due to a change in the environment of the organism; nevertheless, changes occur where the resulting type is permanent. The student must not be too alarmed when extremely long rods are found in a culture which is supposed to be composed of short, plump rods; nor should he be surprised to find coccoid forms in the same culture. Some investigators explain that this variation is due to a cyclic development of the organism. In some species of bacteria such cyclic changes may occur, but bacteriologists in general are not ready to accept such explanations for all the organisms, nor for

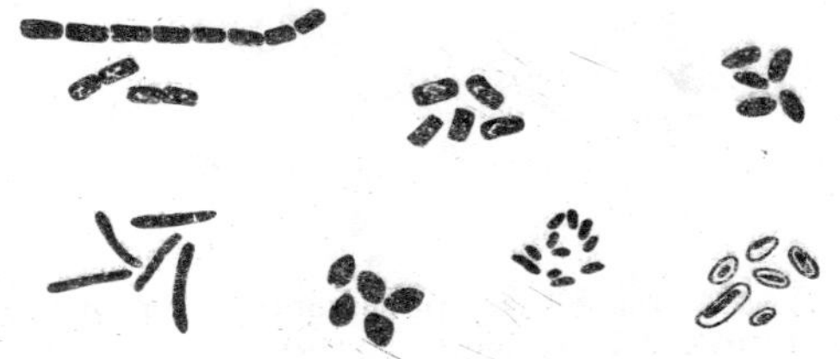

FIG. 2.3—Types of bacilli.

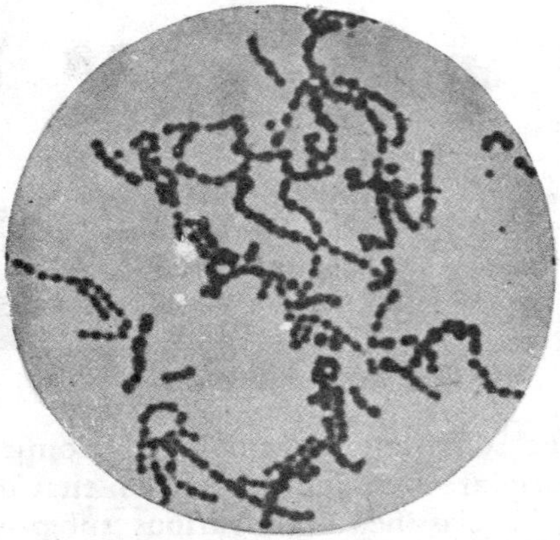

FIG. 2.4—**Streptococcus pyogenes** bouillon culture, ×2,500. (From Nowak: Documenta Microbiologica, courtesy Gustav Fischer.)

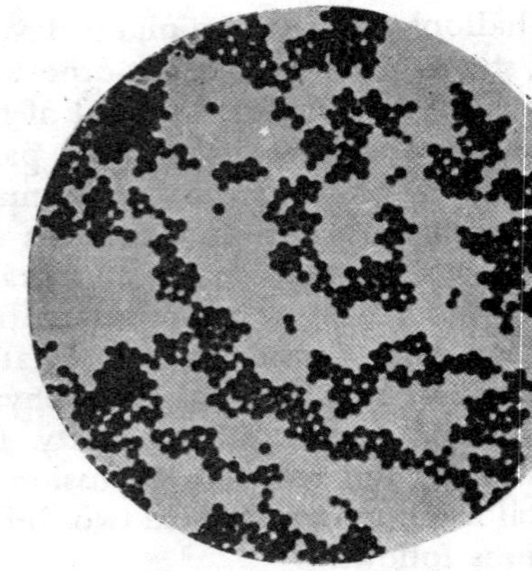

FIG. 2.6—**Staphylococcus aureus** agar culture, ×2,000. (From Nowak: Documenta Microbiologica, courtesy Gustav Fischer.)

all the morphologic dissociative changes which have been described.

### Cell Grouping

Bacterial cells divide by simple fission, and after division some remain attached to one another while others quickly break apart. Those that remain in groups or chains are held together by *plasmodesma,* a protoplasmic bridge between cells. The cell grouping is so constant that it, also, is used to differentiate various genera from each other, and in some cases, the species.

Bacteria divide normally at right angles to the longest axis of the cells. This permits little variation in the cell arrangement of the bacilli, spirilla, and filamentous forms, but the cocci have no longest axis; hence they may divide in various planes. On this basis the cocci are divided into the following groups.

The *streptococci* (chain cocci) divide in a constantly parallel plane, forming chains (Fig. 2.4).

The *diplococci* (Fig. 2.5) remain in pairs after division, and it is not unusual to see such paired cocci among the streptococci and the staphylococci.

The *staphylococci* divide at various angles forming grapelike clusters of cells (Fig. 2.6).

The *sarcina* divide in three planes at right angles to each other, resulting in the formation of cubes or packets.

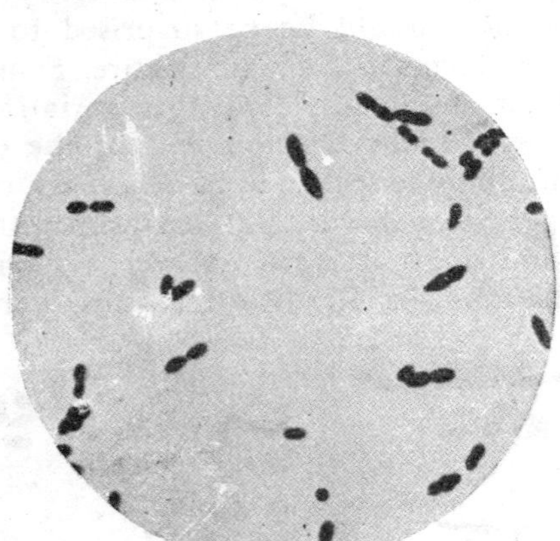

FIG. 2.5—**Diplococcus pneumoniae** from an agar culture, ×2,000. (From Nowak: Documenta Microbiologica, courtesy Gustav Fischer.)

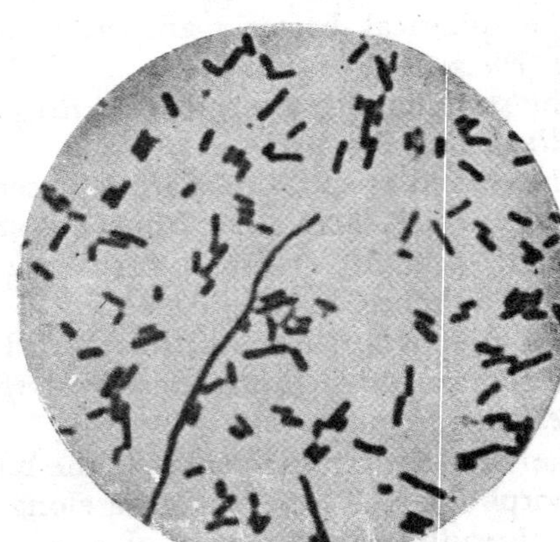

FIG. 2.7—**Escherichia coli** 24-hour agar culture, ×2,000 (From Nowak: Documenta Microbiologica, courtesy Gustav Fischer.)

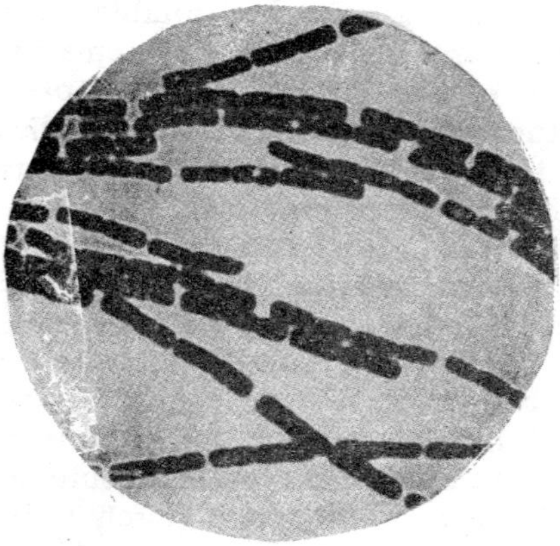

FIG. 2.8—**Bacillus anthracis** impression smear from a 48-hour-old agar plate colony, ×2,000. (From Nowak: Documenta Microbiologica, courtesy Gustav Fischer.)

Bacilli grow either singly or in chains (Figs. 2.7 and 2.8).

The spirilla form short chains of two or three cells, but usually occur singly (Figs. 2.9 and 2.10).

The filamentous types of bacteria occur singly and in tangled masses or in clumps, and occasionally in palisade arrangement (Figs. 2.11 and 2.12).

### Size of Bacteria

The size of bacteria is altogether dependent upon the type of morphology. The cocci range from 0.8$\mu$ to 1.2$\mu$ in size, although some as small as 0.5$\mu$ may be found. (The micron, designated by the

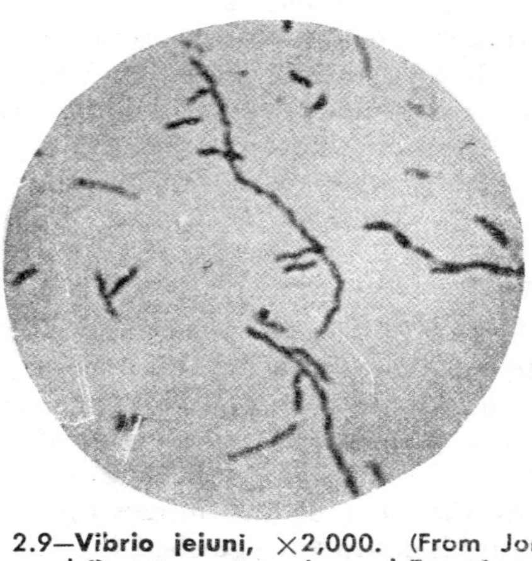

FIG. 2.9—**Vibrio jejuni**, ×2,000. (From Jones, Little, and Orcutt, courtesy Journal Experimental Medicine.)

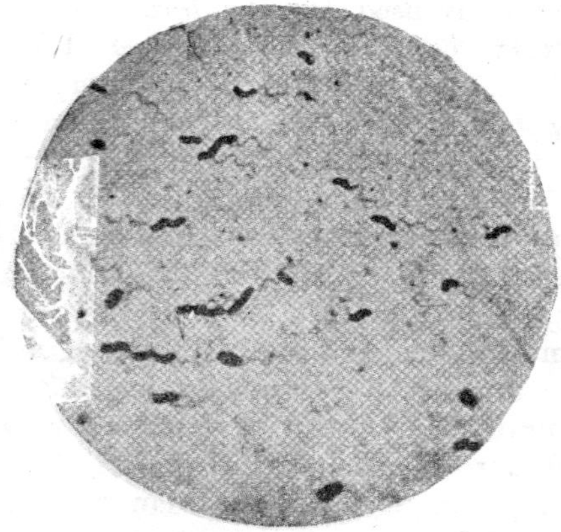

FIG. 2.10—**Vibrio fetus** showing normal, curved, flagellated cells, ×1,000. (From Smith, courtesy Journal Experimental Medicine.)

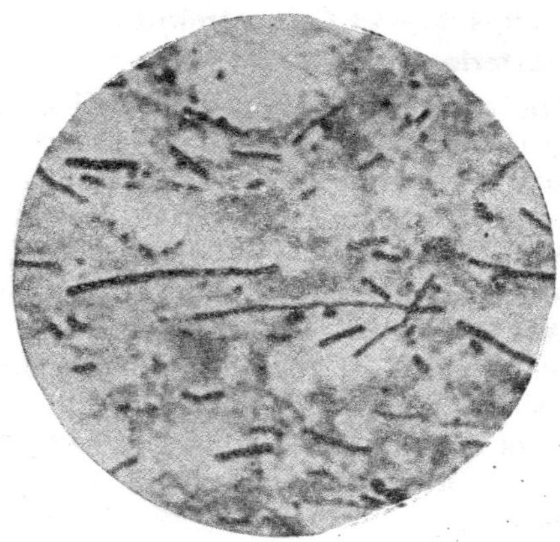

FIG. 2.11—**Spherophorus necrophorus** in smear of infected tissue, ×2,000. (From Nowak: Documenta Microbiologica, courtesy Gustav Fischer.)

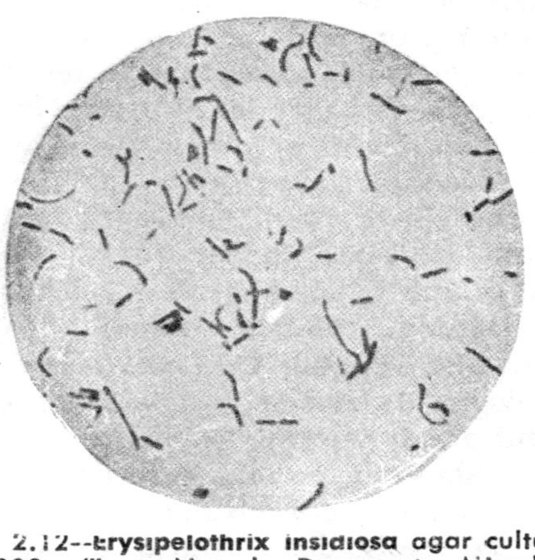

FIG. 2.12—**Erysipelothrix insidiosa** agar culture, ×2,000. (From Nowak: Documenta Microbiologica, courtesy Gustav Fischer.)

letter $\mu$, is used for the measurement of bacteria; $1\mu = 1/1{,}000$ mm. $= 1/25{,}000$ inch.) The rod-shaped microorganisms vary in size. The smallest representative is the influenza organism which is about $0.2\mu$ x $0.5\mu$. The typhoid bacillus, $0.5\mu$ x $2\mu$ to $3\mu$, represents the medium-sized bacilli. The tetanus bacillus is slender, $0.3\mu$, but rather long, $3\mu$ to $5\mu$. The spirilla vary in size from $3\mu$ to $50\mu$, and some of the longest bacteria are found in this group. The filamentous bacteria can be described only according to the diameter of the cell which is usually $0.5\mu$ to $1\mu$. Measurements for all types of bacteria must be based upon the average of normal cells because variation in size always exists.

### The Capsule and Cell Membrane of Bacteria

The cell membrane or cell wall of bacteria is similar in many respects to that of plants, serving as an envelope to give the organism form and to permit the permeation of nutrient substances and waste products. There is little doubt that such a membrane exists because bacterial cells have been shown to undergo *plasmolysis,* the shrinking of the protoplasm and subsequent pulling away from the cell membrane. The composition of this membrane in bacteria is not cellulose or chitin as in higher plants or fungi. Polysaccharide substances are present in the cell membrane, and the membrane is composed of combinations of carbohydrate-protein substances, depending on the species of organism. Electron microphotographs of bacterial cell walls reveal that they are surprisingly rigid, and when devoid of protoplasm they appear much like a grape skin after the contents have been eaten. Obviously, they are a great, great deal smaller.

A capsule composed of a mucoid or mucilagenous substance covers the cell membrane of some bacteria. Many bacteriologists believe it is present to some extent on all bacteria, but in the majority the substance is too thin to be detected by the usual staining procedures. The capsule may be easily demonstrated on certain species of bacteria by suitable staining methods and is recognized on some by the nature of the growth, for example, the "mother of vinegar" and slimy milk and bread. Capsular substance is an extension of the cell membrane and probably produced by it. It is chemically different for the various bacteria. In some it is composed of mucin, a slimy material made up of a protein-like substance united with a carbohydrate, resembling the mucus secreted by the cells of the mucous membrane. In others the capsule is composed of pure carbohydrates and is closely allied to certain of the vegetable gums, such as gum arabic. In still others the material is lipoid in nature, forming a compact, waxy coating over the organism. The complex polysaccharide capsular materials found in some of the bacteria have been used extensively in determining the antigenic relationships of closely related strains of bacteria. These substances seem to be responsible for the specific reactions which are obtained in the serologic study of bacteria.

A relationship apparently exists between capsular substance and virulence, largely due to the resistance of the capsulated organism to phagocytosis; furthermore, the capsulated organism is not as virulent when devoid of its capsule. Many of the capsulated bacteria lose the capsule when grown on artificial media. The anthrax bacillus, for example, is always found to be capsulated when smears of blood from an anthrax-infected animal are examined (Fig. 2.13), but organisms grown on laboratory media are without capsules. This is not a permanent loss, however, for the capsules are formed when such organisms are injected into a susceptible animal.

### Flagella

Fine threads of protoplasm, called *flagella,* extend from the cell membrane of certain of the bacteria. Such organisms are actively motile and, when viewed in a hanging drop, will be seen to pass quickly across the field of the microscope. This motility is easily distinguished from *Brown-*

FIG. 2.13—**Bacillus anthracis** in smear from spleen, showing capsules, ×2,000. (From Nowak: Documenta Microbiologica, courtesy Gustav Fischer.)

*ian movement* which is thought to be due to molecular bombardment on the surface of the particle and produces a vibrating or oscillating motion. Flagellated bacteria in large numbers are inhibited in their movement, however, and may give a picture similar to Brownian movement; hence, it is necessary to examine motility in dilute suspensions.

The presence of flagella is almost entirely limited to the spirilla and bacilli. Motility has been observed among the cocci, *Sarcina agilis,* but that group of organisms may be generally considered as nonmotile. Filamentous bacteria are nonflagellated.

Motility may be seen by viewing an organism in a suspended drop, but the flagella cannot be seen in such a preparation. Special fixing and staining techniques are required to make the flagella visible. The arrangement of flagella (Fig. 2.14) on the surface of the bacterial cell varies among the different types and is used as a basis of classifying them in the following groups:

1. *Atrichous* bacteria possess no flagella.
2. *Monotrichous* bacteria have a single flagellum on one end.
3. *Lophotrichous* bacteria have a group of flagella at one pole.
4. *Amphitrichous* bacteria have flagella at both poles.
5. *Peritrichous* bacteria are completely surrounded by flagella.

Flagella are usually present on young cells grown in fluid media. Older cells are devoid of flagella, and an organism grown on artificial media for some time may lose its ability to form flagella. This is one type of bacterial variation which must be remembered in forming a complete description of the organism. The flagella also enter into the antigenic composition of the organism as will be observed in a later chapter.

Electron microscope photographs of flagellated bacteria show the presence of minute appendages called *fimbriae* extending from the cell wall.

### Cell Protoplasm

The small size of bacterial cells makes it difficult to determine the composition of the cell substance or endoplasm. The complex chemical reactions initiated by bacteria make it obvious that they contain protoplasm similar to other cells. Food material diffuses through the cell membrane, is converted into simpler substances which may be utilized by the bacterium for energy, and the end products are eliminated from the cell into the surrounding medium.

The type of nucleus which is possessed by the bacterial cell has been a subject of much controversy and it cannot be said that the problem is settled even today. Three different theories of the nature of chromatin, or nuclear material, have been advanced. *First,* the reaction of bacteria with basic dyes has been suggested as proof

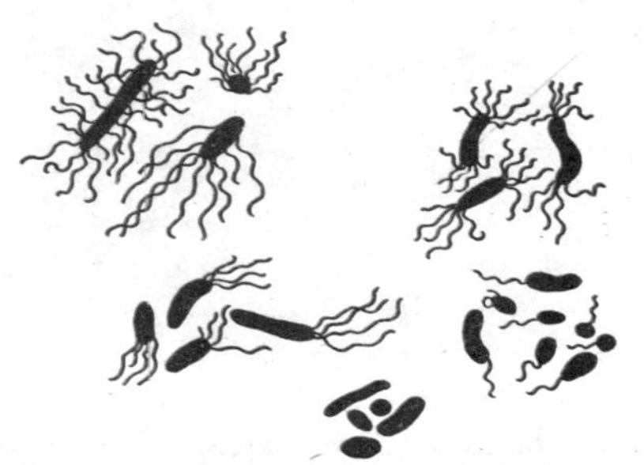

FIG. 2.14—Arrangement of flagella on bacteria.

that the cell is composed of one large nucleus surrounded by very little cytoplasm. *Second,* some of the larger types of bacteria have been shown to have a small nucleus surrounded by cytoplasm; therefore, it has been assumed that all bacteria possess nuclei, even though they are too small to be visible by maximum magnification. Barnard has shown that microphotographs of bacteria taken with dark-field illumination and ultraviolet light show structures highly suggestive of nuclei. Furthermore, the electron microscope has made it possible to learn more about the internal structure of cells. Nuclei are clearly seen in electron micrographs of bacteria. *Third,* a reticular network is present in the bacterial cytoplasm, and chromatin granules lie in the spaces of this network. It has been suggested that in sporeforming bacteria this granular material is concentrated into the spore which functions as the resistant state of the organism and which germinates under favorable conditions to form the bacterial cell. The refractibility of bacteria makes it extremely difficult to study their internal structure in the usual unstained preparation. So far no satisfactory differential staining techniques have been perfected to demonstrate the different structures in bacterial cells. The fractionation of the various nucleoproteins of bacterial cells has indicated that true nuclear material does exist. It is not wise to generalize concerning all the various types of cells which are included under the term, bacteria; it may be possible that some bacteria are composed of one large nucleus, that some of the larger and more highly developed types of bacteria have one small nucleus similar to those found in plant and animal cells, and that still others may have a primitive, diffuse nuclear material.

In some species of bacteria, notably those belonging to the diphtheria group or *Corynebacteria,* small granules are found to be stained more intensely than the surrounding protoplasm by the basic aniline dyes. Because of the resemblance of these granules to chromatin they are called *metachromatic granules,* otherwise known as *Babes-Ernst granules* (Fig. 2.15). The nature and function of these granules are not known. They are not associated with the nuclear apparatus; they do not represent the resting stage of the organism; they are not associated with the virulence of the organism. It has been assumed that they represent a reserve food supply for the organism.

Many of the different species of bacteria present a granular, irregular appearance when stained with the basic aniline dyes. The *Pasteurella* organisms commonly associated with hemorrhagic septicemia of ani-

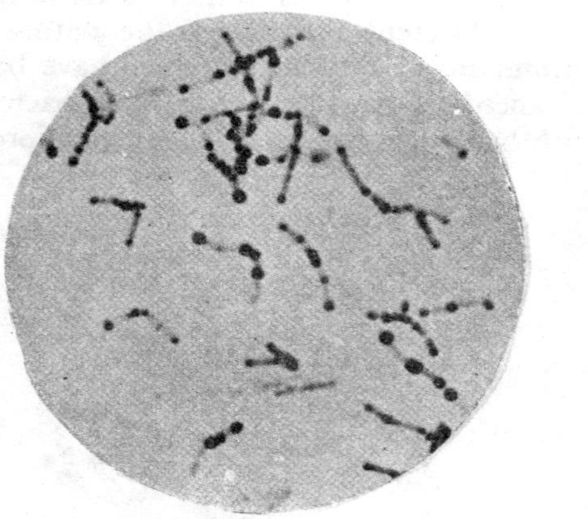

FIG. 2.15—Metachromatic granules in diphtheria bacilli. (From Nowak: Documenta Microbiologica, courtesy Gustav Fischer.)

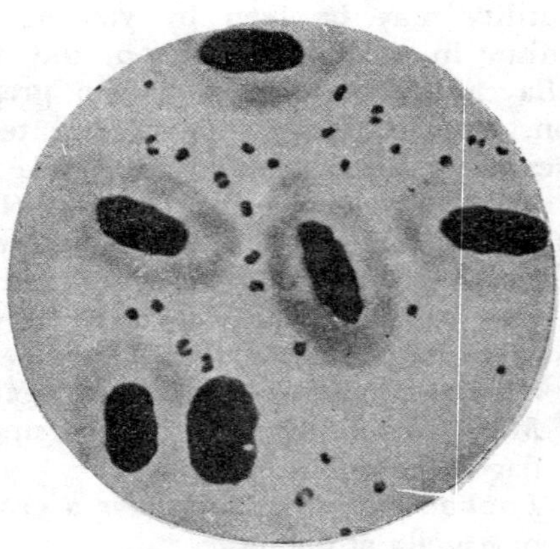

FIG. 2.16—**Pasteurella multocida** blood smear, fowl cholera, ×2,000. (From Nowak: Documenta Microbiologica, courtesy Gustav Fischer.)

mals present a *bipolar* appearance (Fig. 2.16). The protoplasm appears to be concentrated at both poles of the organism, leaving a vacuole-like, unstained space in the center. The various members of the *Clostridium* group, especially the blackleg bacillus, are stained unevenly, showing that the protoplasm accumulates in various parts of the cell.

Among the species of bacteria that live in water are found some that contain sulfur granules in the protoplasm. Fat globules and glycogen granules are found in some bacteria.

### Reproduction of Bacteria

Under standard conditions normal multiplication of all bacteria is a simple process. The cell elongates or enlarges, a cell wall develops across the middle, and the two cells either separate completely or remain attached, forming the different arrangements described previously. This process is known as *binary fission*. It may occur with considerable rapidity; some organisms in a favorable medium may grow to their full size and divide to form two individuals in as short a time as twenty minutes. If the organism multiplies at this rate for a short time, the number of resultant organisms is extremely high. For example, if a bacterium divides every half hour, at the end of two days the progeny is represented by $2^{96}$, a number having twenty-eight figures. Such rapid multiplication is never long continued, for food supply is not favorable over a long period of time, and waste products of the bacterial growth tend to accumulate and diminish the rate. The rapidity of bacterial multiplication accounts, in a large measure, for the many changes produced in a short time, such as in the souring of milk and the invasion of the body, causing disease.

While the most common mode of reproduction among bacteria is binary fission, other methods have been observed. Buds have been seen in some of the true bacteria —members of the typhoid-dysentery group. Branching has also been noted, although it is difficult to differentiate from budding. After the branches are formed, they segment, giving rise to new cells. This process has been observed among many of the more filamentous types of bacteria as well as in the organism causing typhoid fever.

The filamentous bacteria, or trichobacteria, produce arthrospores *(conidia)* by the disintegration of some of the filaments into short rods or spheres which are capable of reproducing the parent type. In many cases the threads which break up into the arthospores are somewhat differentiated from the normal cells of the plant and are serial, resembling closely some of the molds.

It has been suggested by numerous workers that gonidia, which function as part of the reproduction process in higher living things, are formed by certain bacteria. *Gonidia* are formed within the cell —two, four, or more in each cell—and they escape through the cell wall or are liberated upon the disintegration of the cell. Development of mature bacterial cells from these minute granules has been described by numerous workers, many of whom have suggested that the gonidia are filterable; so it is possible that the filterable stages of bacteria may be represented by these forms.

Sexual reproduction has been described by some investigators but doubted by others. By demonstrating conjugation and showing that gonidia result from actual contact, a very interesting life cycle for bacteria may be constructed, but conclusive evidence to show that such a procedure exists is still lacking. However, a type of sexual reproduction does exist among bacteria and the subject of bacterial genetics is of great research interest. This will be discussed in Chapter 14.

Many bacteria produce spores. Although spores, strictly speaking, cannot be considered a part of reproduction, they do play a part in the continuity of the life of the organism, and it is well to discuss spore development in connection with reproduction.

*Endospores,* commonly referred to as

*spores,* are produced definitely by bacilli and possibly by some spirilla. The cocci and filamentous forms do not produce spores. The factors which are responsible for the formation of spores are not thoroughly understood. The process appears to be a natural one for those species in which it occurs, but when the period of spore formation in the life of the organism is reached, environmental conditions appear to hasten spore development. These environmental factors are: accumulation of waste products, change in the reaction of the medium, and a decrease for some species or increase for others in oxygen tension. The spore is essentially a portion of the protoplasm of the cell, almost devoid of water, and shrunken in size until it occupies only a portion of the space within the cell; it is surrounded by a heavy wall, probably chitinous in nature. In practically all cases there is but one spore in a cell. The spore may be equatorial or polar in position, and may be of smaller or greater diameter than the cell which produces it. The position and size of the spore are used in the classification of sporeforming bacilli. The term *Clostridium* is used to indicate a sporebearing rod in which the spore is equatorial and greater in diameter than the cell, resulting in a spindle-shaped cell. Tennis racket or drumstick-shaped cells are produced by spores that are polar and are greater in diameter than the cell (Fig. 2.17).

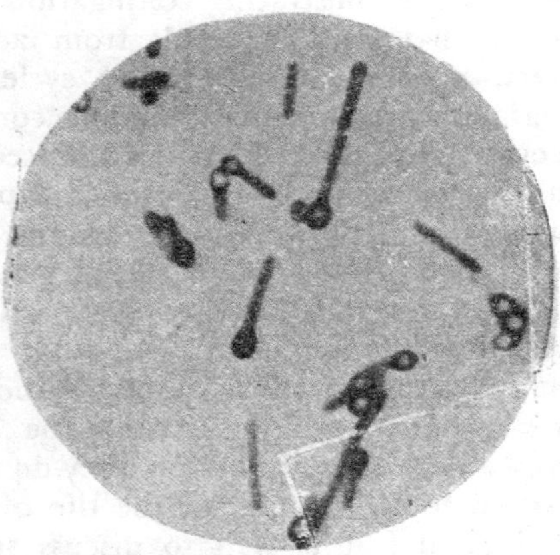

FIG. 2.17--**Clostridium tetani** showing polar spores, ×2,000. (From Nowak: Documenta Microbiologica, courtesy Gustav Fischer.)

Endospores contain only about 20 per cent water as compared with 80 to 90 per cent in the cells which produce them. An organism without a spore is usually differentiated by the term *vegetative rod* or *vegetative cell.* Spores are much more resistant to desiccation, heat, light, and chemicals than the vegetative cells. They are of use in carrying the organism over unfavorable conditions, but it must not be assumed that this is their main function. Sporebearing bacteria are abundant in the soil where they are exposed to great ranges of moisture, temperature, and light. When a spore again comes under favorable conditions for growth, it germinates and produces a cell typical of its species. Germination is accomplished by an elongation of the spore with a resulting stretching and bursting of the spore wall. Spores may germinate equatorially in the same manner.

## COLONY CHARACTERISTICS OF BACTERIA

When a single bacterial cell is allowed to grow upon the surface of nutrient agar or nutrient gelatin, the newly formed cells accumulate and form the bacterial colony. The different forms of bacteria produce various types of colonies. The streptococci grow in minute, dewdrop-like colonies. The staphylococci produce larger, more opaque, smooth, glistening colonies. The sporeforming bacilli form irregular, grayish, lusterless colonies. The nonsporeforming rods are found in colonies that are whitish-gray, smooth, and glistening. Filamentous bacteria form a thin, transparent, spreading growth on the surface of the medium (Figs. 2.18, 2.19, 2.20, 2.21 and 2.22).

The colonies of closely related species of bacteria may differ in some characteristics, yet many of the colonies of closely related species, and even genera, may be practically alike.

External conditions, such as moisture, temperature, oxygen, and pressure, exert an effect upon the appearance of the

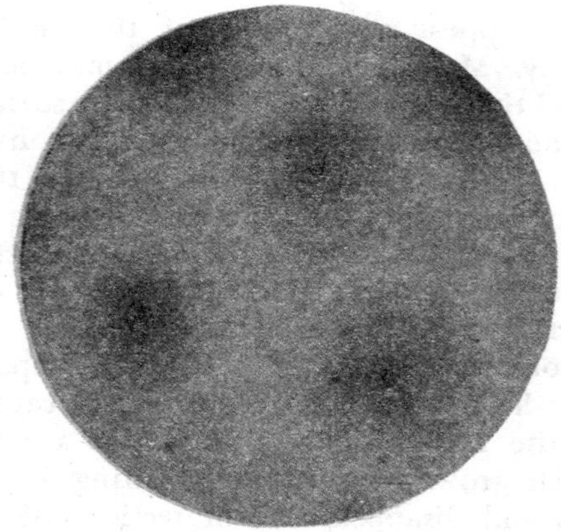

FIG. 2.18—Colonies of streptococci. (From Nowak: Documenta Microbiologica, courtesy Gustav Fischer.)

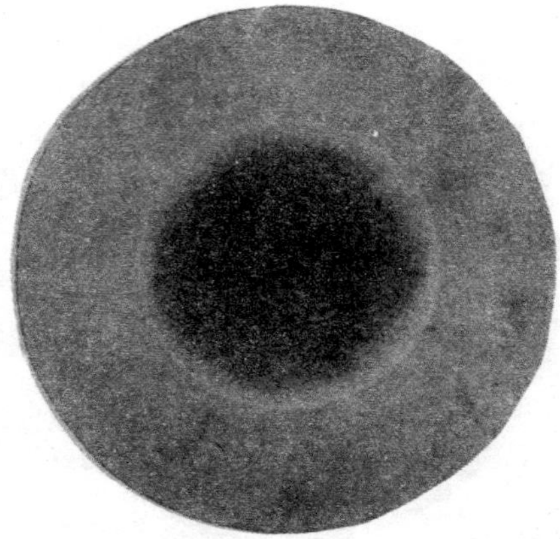

FIG. 2.21—Colony of bacteria. (From Nowak: Documenta Microbiologica, courtesy Gustav Fischer.)

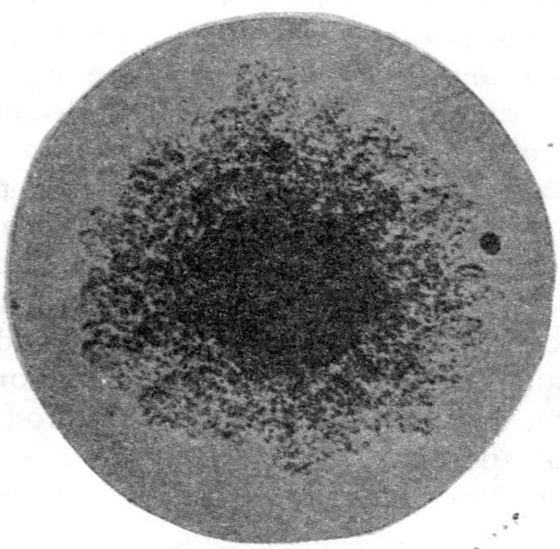

FIG. 2.19—Colony of bacilli. (From Nowak: Documenta Microbiologica, courtesy Gustav Fischer.)

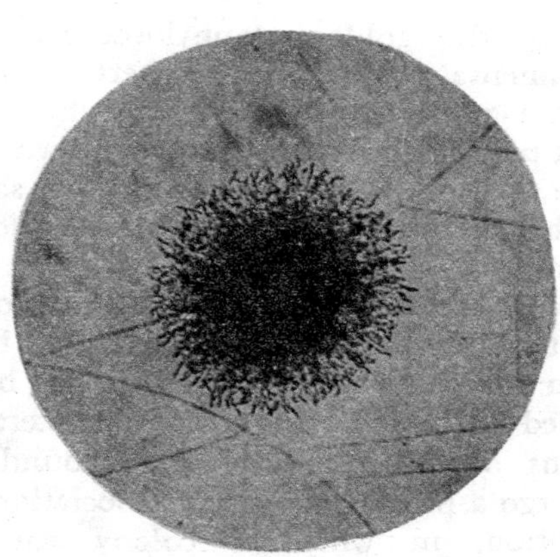

FIG. 2.22—Colony of filamentous bacteria. (From Nowak: Documenta Microbiologica, courtesy Gustav Fischer.)

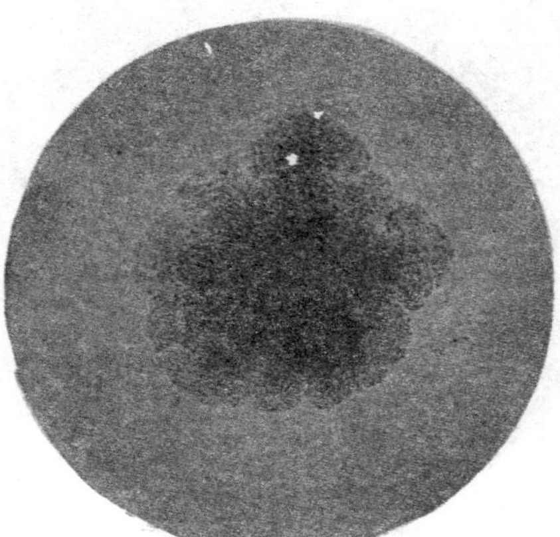

FIG. 2.20—Colony of bacilli. (From Nowak: Documenta Microbiologica, courtesy Gustav Fischer.)

colonies of bacteria; hence, standard conditions for growth must be maintained.

Pigmentation of the colony, also, is often used as a distinguishing feature. Bacterial pigments are water soluble or water insoluble. The water-soluble pigments are of no value in colony differentiation. The water-insoluble pigments, however, impart definite colors to colonies. Some of the colors found in bacterial colonies are white, cream, gold, yellow, orange, brown, violet, and red. Varying shades of each color are present in different species. The color of the colony has been used often in naming bacteria, for example: *Staphylococcus albus,* the white staphylococcus; *Staphylococcus*

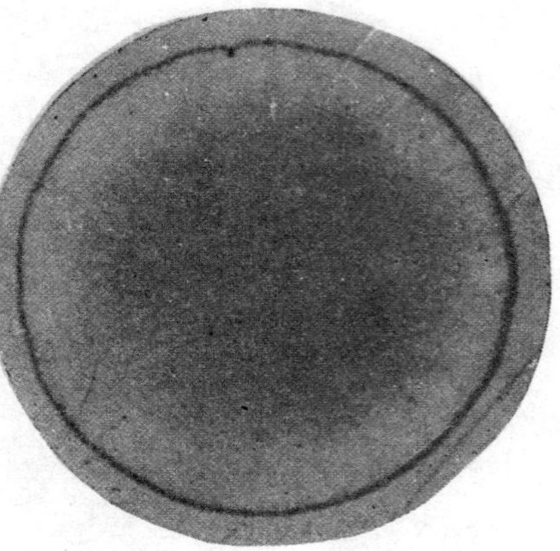

FIG. 2.23—**Salmonella pullorum** normal smooth S colony, ×125. (Courtesy Van Roekel.)

*aureus,* the golden staphylococcus. Environmental conditions also exert an effect upon pigment production, and when pigment-producing organisms are grown for some time under artificial conditions, some of the bacteria lose the power to form color.

Early bacteriologists believed that only one type of colony could be produced by a given species of organism. This has been proved to be true in general, but certain strains of bacteria have been found to undergo a process known as dissociation or variation, in which a colony entirely different from the original one may be produced. The most common type of dissociation is that from a round, convex, smooth, finely granular, and entire type of colony, commonly designated S (Fig. 2.23), to an irregular, flat, rough, coarsely granular, undulate, and dull type of colony, commonly designated R (Fig. 2.24). The organism in the S colony shows many characteristics of physiology and virulence which may be absent in organisms in the R colony. This dissociation may be caused by some environmental effect, such as lack of nutrition, which may be temporary, or it may be caused by factors not understood, which cause a permanent variation. The newly formed dissociative types of colonies may be observed growing as small daughter colonies in the original mother colony or many appear as a sector of the mother colony. Mucoid variants, which may be so viscid that the growth flows over the surface of the agar when the plate is tilted, have been described also. The discovery that dissociation is a normal characteristic of some strains of bacteria has necessitated the inclusion of the dissociative types in the description of organisms.

Colonies having a moth-eaten appearance have been described. This is caused by the action of bacteriophage, a virus which grows in bacteria, resulting in the lysis and disappearance of sections of the colony.

## MORPHOLOGY OF YEASTS

The yeasts are generally characterized by their morphology and their reproduction by budding. They represent a type of plant more complete than bacteria, although some of the various types resemble some of the bacteria. Yeasts are divided into two groups: the true yeasts and the false yeasts. The former are recognized by the formation of sexual spores which develop in a spore case commonly called an *ascus,* and as a result these organisms are called *Ascomycetes.* The false yeasts do not produce sexual spores.

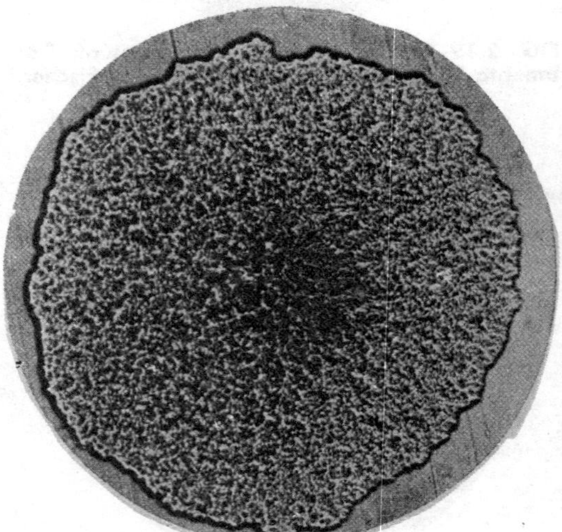

FIG. 2.24—**Salmonella pullorum** variant rough R colony, ×125. (Courtesy Van Roekel.)

### Shape, Size, and Grouping

True yeasts are unicellular organisms which may be spherical, elliptical, or cylindrical in shape. The size of yeasts varies with the different types of morphology. In general, they are larger than bacteria, although some of the larger bacteria and the average yeast cells may be the same size—4μ to 5μ in diameter. Most of the true yeasts occur as individual cells; however, the newly formed daughter cell having developed by the budding process may cling to the mother cell for some time. Some species of false yeasts form into long threads giving rise to a mycelium. These yeasts are much like the molds in this respect. Yeasts grow in a variety of types of colonies.

### Structure of the Yeast Cell

The usual structures found in plant and animal cells are found in the yeast cells, as can be seen in Figure 2.25. The limiting membrane of the cell protoplasm forms first, and from it the cell wall develops. In old cells it is quite distinct. The cell wall is composed of a carbohydrate-nitrogenous substance to which the name *yeastcellulose* has been given. Capsules are found covering some species of yeast. Yeasts are non-flagellated.

The nucleus of the yeast cell is rather large, and together with the nuclear vacuole takes up considerable space in the cell. The nucleus undergoes division during the budding process, and part of it goes with the newly developed bud or cell.

Vacuoles are frequent in yeasts and may be recognized as highly refractive bodies. They increase in size and number as the food supply of the cell diminishes. Glycogen granules are found in the cytoplasm and have been observed in the vacuoles. Fat droplets are commonly seen in certain yeast cells; in fact, such cells are known to be able to convert simple substances into fat. Glycogen and fat represent the reserve food material of yeasts.

### Reproduction of Yeasts

The majority of the yeasts multiply by budding. In this process, a small bud de-

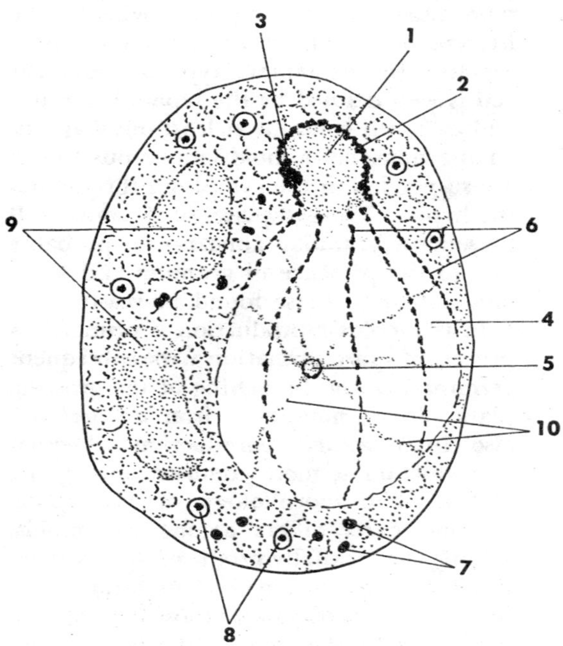


FIG. 2.25—Detailed structure of the yeast cell. (After Wager.) **1**, nucleolus; **2**, peripheral layer of chromatin; **3**, chromatin on side of nucleolus; **4**, nuclear vacuole; **5**, central volutin granule in the vacuole; **6**, chromatin network; **7**, granules of fatty substance; **8**, volutin granules; **9**, glycogen vacuoles; **10**, suspending threads for the central volutin granule.

velops from the cell wall of the mother cell and contains all the essential structures of the mother cell. It gradually increases in size, develops a cell wall, and is constricted off as a distinct individual. Mature yeast cells may produce numerous buds when the environment and food supply are favorable.

The production of ascospores by true yeasts is different from the production of endospores by bacteria in that it is a sexual process. A typical yeast cell produces eight ascospores while only one spore develops in the individual bacterial cell. The formation of the ascospores in yeasts does not appear to be influenced by the factors operative in stimulating spore development in bacteria; therefore, it would appear to represent a reproductive process more than a resting stage in the life of the cell. Ascospores are formed only when water is present, when the cell is well nourished, and when the temperature is around 25°C. The ascus results from the fusion of two mature yeast cells which act as gametes; the contents of one cell pass into the other through a minute tube or copulation canal. The nucleus of the newly formed cell divides into the required number of parts to form ascospores, each of which, together with its surrounding protoplasm, becomes surrounded by a membrane (Fig. 2.26).

## MORPHOLOGY OF THE MOLDS

All of the fungi that grow in a colony composed of loose cottony threads are classed under the general term of molds. Some of these forms are related to the algae and are placed with the *Phycomycetes;* others are grouped with the *Ascomycetes;*

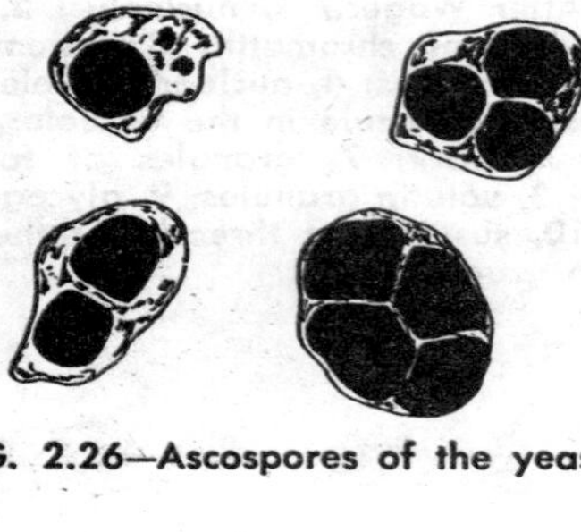

FIG. 2.26—Ascospores of the yeast cell.

others such as the smuts, rusts, and toadstools are *Basidiomycetes.* Those which apparently lack a sexual means of reproduction are the *Deuteromycetes (Fungi Imperfecti).*

Molds are multicellular organisms and, consequently, are easily distinguished from the bacteria and yeasts. The mold plant is made up of a tangled mass of threads called a *mycelium* (Fig. 2.27). Each thread of the mycelium is called a mycelial thread or *hypha* (plural, *hyphae).* The hyphae are designed for two purposes: the vegetative hyphae are for the purpose of supplying nutrition to the mold plant, and the fertile hyphae are differentiated for the purpose of reproduction in the process of spore formation. The hyphae of most of the common molds have numerous cross walls, known as *septa,* dividing one cell from another. Certain species of molds, however are nonseptated. All molds may be classified upon the basis of this characteristic into *septated* and *nonseptated* molds.

The cells of the mold are much like the higher plants. The cell wall is composed of cellulose or chitinous material. The protoplasm of the cell contains one or more nuclei, depending upon whether the hyphae of the mold are septate or nonseptate. In the septate type of mold the cell is well defined by the separating walls, and each cell contains at least one nucleus. In the nonseptate molds numerous nuclei are suspended in the cytoplasm throughout the hypha. The cytoplasm of the mold cell presents a granular appearance, probably due to the presence of granules and vacuoles similar to those found in yeasts.

In the molds reproduction is primarily a process of spore formation with subsequent germination and branching of the growing plant. Spores may result from *asexual* and also from *sexual* reproduction. Asexual reproduction is more common among the molds. The morphology of the spore-forming parts differs among the molds. Among the asexually produced spores there are three different types: those formed in a spore case or *sporangium;* those not incased, *conidia;* those that result from breaking-up

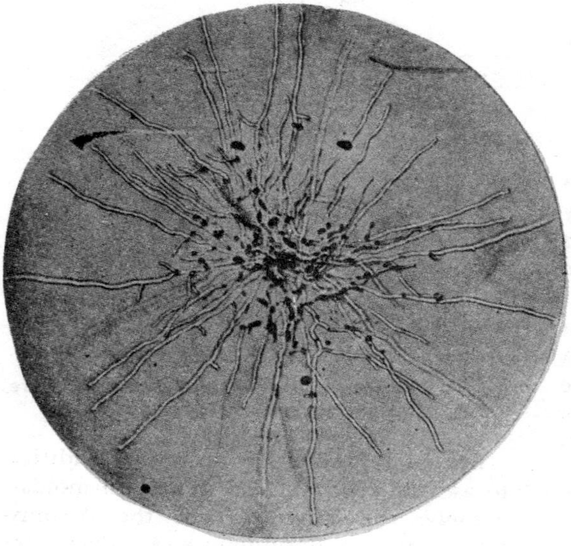

FIG. 2.27—Developing mycelium of **Aspergillus fumigatus.** (From Nowak: Documenta Microbiologica, courtesy Gustav Fischer.)

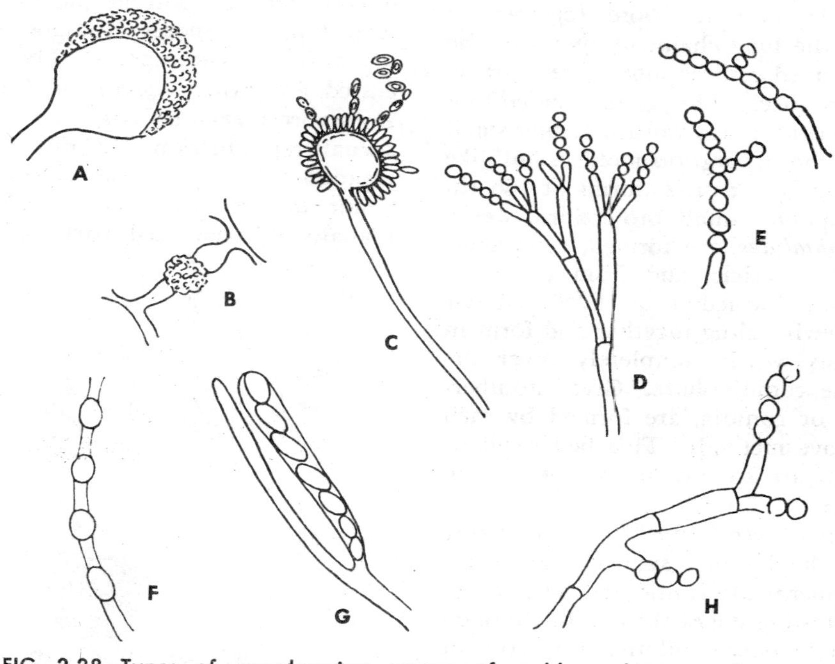


FIG. 2.28—Types of sporebearing organs of molds and types of spores. **A,** sporangium of Mucor; **B,** zygospore of Mucor; **C,** conidiophore of Aspergillus; **D,** conidiophore of Penicillium; **E,** oidium type of spore formation; **F,** chlamydospores in the hypha of Chlamydomucor; **G,** ascospore of Peziza; **H,** differentiation of hypha into spores.

of the hypha into segments, *arthrospores* and *chlamydospores* (Fig. 2.28).

The *sporangium* is formed on the tip of a branch, *sporangiophore,* from a specialized hyphal thread designated for reproductive purposes. The tip gradually increases in size, forming the columella, and the spores are formed and are held in the spore case until maturity. When fully ripened, the sporangium breaks open, as does a pea or bean pod, liberating the spores.

In the formation of *conidia,* the hypha designated for reproduction is called a *conidiophore.* The conidia, or spores, are formed at the tip of the conidiophore. Two morphologic types of conidiophores are observed in the common molds (Fig. 2.28). In the *Penicillium* molds, the conidiophore branches at the end, and from the tip of each branch the conidia develop, forming long chains. The branches of this conidiophore are close together so these and the long chains of spores of the fully developed conidiophore give a brushlike appearance. The term *Penicillium* comes from the Latin word meaning small brush. In the *Aspergillus* molds a bulblike enlargement, the *vesicle,* forms at the tip of conidiophore; small projections, *sterigmata* or *phialides,* are formed, completely covering the vesicle, and from these the conidia are formed (Fig. 2.29). These spores, likewise, cling together and form in long chains which completely cover the end of the conidiophore. Great numbers of spores, or conidia, are formed by each of the above methods. This fact explains why molds are so prolific and are found everywhere.

*Arthrospores* are formed by the breaking up of the hypha into sporelike segments. These segments are considered by some to represent resting stages of the cell, although they seem to possess all the properties of spores. Some of the fungi, particularly the fungus of grain smut, form thick-wall spores known as *chlamydospores.* They are formed at irregular points along the hyphae and do not appear to be the result of a segmentation process.

FIG. 2.29—**Aspergillus fumigatus** conidiophore, sterigmata, and conidia, ×250.

Sexual reproduction occurs in addition to asexual reproduction in certain molds—namely, the Phycomycetes, the Ascomycetes, and the Basidiomycetes. There are several different methods of sexual reproduction which result in the formation of such types of spores as zygospores, ascospores, and basidiospores. These are discussed in greater detail in Chapter 39. Zygospore formation is a good example of sexual reproduction. In this method of reproduction, sexual spores form as the result of the fusion of two hyphae or sexually differentiated parts of the mold

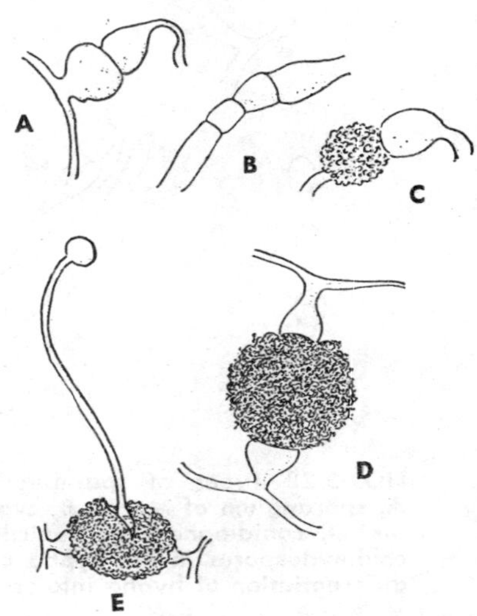


FIG. 2.30—Diagram of sexual fertilization of **Mucor mucedo.** (After Brefeld.)

plant (A in Fig. 2.30). After this fusion occurs, articulation into two gametes and two suspensors takes place (B). The cell wall then begins to develop and thicken, forming the zygospore (C and D) still held in place by the suspending parts of the mold plant. The zygospore ripens, may become free of the parent cell, and may function as any mold spore. If it is in a favorable medium, the zygospore may germinate, forming a sporangium stem (E).

The colonies of the various types of molds are different. Some grow in loose cottony masses which will quickly cover any object upon which the mold is growing. Others grow in moderately cottony colonies. Some form low, flat, velvety colonies and a few chalky colonies. All of the mold colonies have color which is imparted to them by the color of the spores; some of the colors found are black, blue, green, and brown. Color is used as a differentiating criterion in classification and is used in some cases in naming the mold, for example, *Aspergillus niger*.

Molds are capable of producing a variety of diseases in animals through infection or intoxication. With the exception of the dermatophytes which cause ringworm, fungal infections are not contagious but are usually contracted sporadically from environmental foci.

## REFERENCES


Alexopoulas, C. J. Introductory Mycology. 2nd Ed. John Wiley & Sons, Inc., New York, 1962.

Black, S. H., and Gerhardt, P. Permeability of Bacterial Spores. Jour. Bact. 82:743–49, 750–60, 1961. Jour. Bact. 83:301–8, 1962.

Buchanan, R. E., and Buchanan, Estelle D. Bacteriology. 5th Ed. Macmillan Co., New York, 1951.

Burrows, William. Textbook of Microbiology. 16th Ed. W. B. Saunders Co., Philadelphia, 1954.

Clements, F. E., and Shear, C. H. The Genera of Fungi. H. W. Wilson Co., New York, 1931.

Conn, H. W., and Conn, H. J. Bacteriology. 4th Ed. Williams & Wilkins Co., Baltimore, 1929.

Dubos, R. J. The Bacterial Cell. Harvard Univ. Press, Cambridge, 1945.

Frobisher, M. Fundamentals of Bacteriology. 7th Ed. W. B. Saunders Co., Philadelphia, 1962.

Koch, A. L., and Schaechter, M. A Model for Statistics of the Cell Division Process. Jour. Gen. Microbiol. 29:435–54, 1962.

Lamanna, Carl, and Malette, M. Frank. Basic Bacteriology. Williams & Wilkins Co., Baltimore, 1959.

Leifson, Einer. Atlas of Bacterial Flagellation. Academic Press, Inc., New York and London, 1960.

Robinow, C. F. Problems of Nuclear Behavior in Bacteria and Fungi. Univ. of Maryland, Dept. of Microbiol., College Park. Lecture, March 26, 1963.

Salle, A. J. Fundamental Principles of Bacteriology. 5th Ed. McGraw-Hill Book Co., Inc., New York, 1961.

Salton, M. R. J. Cell-wall Structure and Biosynthesis. Jour. Gen. Microbiol. 29:15–23, 1962.

Schaecter, M., *et al.* Growth, Cell and Nuclear Divisions in Some Bacteria. Jour. Gen. Microbiol. 29:421–34, 1962.

Smith, D. T., *et al.* (eds.). Zinsser Microbiology. 13th Ed. Appleton-Century-Crofts, Inc., New York, 1962

# 3

# The Physiology of Microorganisms

**MILO N. MICKELSON, *Ph.D.***
*National Animal Disease Laboratory*
*Ames, Iowa*

ALL LIVING ORGANISMS ARE COMPOSED OF water and inorganic and organic constituents. From these materials, which are found in its environment, the bacterial cell must obtain its energy and structural units. These nutrient materials are assembled through a complex series of chemical reactions into the material substance of which the cell is composed. The nutrient requirements, special structural units, and energy needs for the synthesis of new microbial substance varies with each different microorganism. The chemical changes carried out by the organism upon the nutrients found in its environment are called *metabolism*.

The varied chemical activities of microorganisms are at times useful, and at other times harmful, to man. Microorganisms are used industrially to produce chemicals such as ethyl alcohol, lactic acid, citric acid, and others which result from the partial degradation of carbohydrates; and from their synthetic activities result products such as the numerous antibiotics, a variety of enzymes, and several of the B vitamins. The synthesis of toxins of various kinds is also an expression of the biochemical activities of microorganisms which cause diseases in man, animals, and various forms of plant life. The specific biochemical activities of bacteria along with their morphology are valuable aids in their recognition and identification.

## CHEMICAL COMPOSITION OF MICROORGANISMS

The chemical composition of microbial cells is not qualitatively different from that of cells of other forms of life. The percentage of the various components present in a particular microorganism varies somewhat with the composition of the medium in which it is grown.

### Elemental Composition

The water content of bacteria is in the range of 75 to 95 per cent.

The dry matter is made up of carbon, hydrogen, oxygen, nitrogen, and ash (6–12 per cent) which is composed of all of the inorganic elements found in other forms of plant life. For some of the mineral elements, the amount contained is very small and it is difficult to construct a medium sufficiently free of impurities to establish absolute requirements. Magnesium, manganese, zinc, iron, and cobalt are all known to be indispensable for some microorganisms, but in only trace amounts for activation of enzymes or as an integral part of some molecule such as iron in cytochrome or cobalt in vitamin $B_{12}$.

Phosphorus is at the center of energy metabolism and sulfur is a component of several amino acids, so the requirements for these two inorganic elements are greater than for the others.

The manner in which substances required for growth are used in the construction of the molecular units of the living microbial cell is the key to understanding how bacteria differ from other living forms and how various bacteria differ from each other. In many cases, the organic components of the bacterial cell are of real importance in their identification, in their immunological characteristics, and in their pathogenicity.

## Organic Components of Microbial Cells

**Carbohydrates and Related Substances.** Bacterial cells contain 45 to 55 per cent of their dry weight as carbon. Some bacteria store carbon as reserve materials in the cytoplasm in the form of starch and glycogen-like polymers of glucose. Other organisms store polymers of poly-beta-hydroxybutyric acid. As polymers of the simple units, glucose and $\beta$-hydroxybutyric acid, these substances are relatively insoluble. Storage forms of carbon may make up a large part of the dry weight when the organism is grown in a medium with an abundant carbon but limited nitrogen source, which prevents it from synthesizing protein and nucleic acid. Many bacteria secrete polymers of sugar of limited solubility which tend to accumulate in layers just outside the cell wall. These structures are referred to as *capsules* or *slime layers*. Among the bacteria there are many different capsular substances. *Acetobacter* deposits a polysaccharide with the structure of cellulose that tends to bind the cells into a tough film. Certain streptococci *(Leuconostoc* sp.) convert sucrose into a viscous slime known as dextran which is used as a blood plasma substitute. In some instances, differences in the composition of the capsular material is the basis for the typing of the microorganism, i.e., pneumococci. In other instances, the polysaccharide occurs in the cell wall and has been useful in the immunological typing of the streptococci into the various Lancefield groups. The polysaccharide capsule of a bacterium may also protect it against the defensive phagocytic mechanism of the host.

**Proteins, Nucleic Acids and Other Nitrogen-Containing Substances.** Proteins are polymers of amino acids. Since there are about 20 different amino acids and each protein molecule contains about 200 amino-acid units, the number of possible different proteins is very great. About 50 per cent of the organic matter in bacterial cells is protein. The protein molecule is built by formation of peptide linkages between the —COOH of one amino acid with the $—NH_2$ group of another into long polypeptide chains of molecular weights ranging from 10,000 to one million.

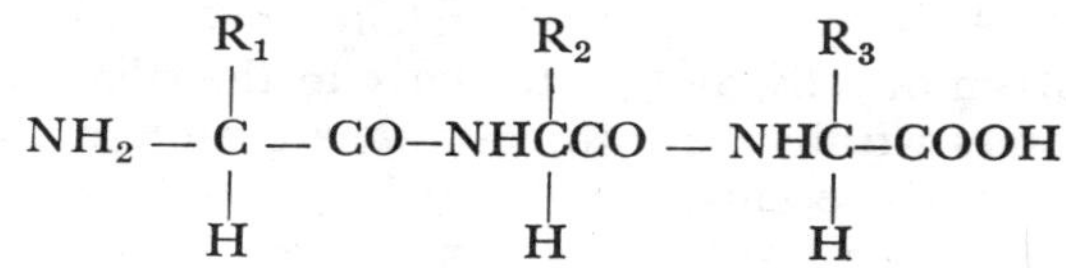

The almost infinite number of different kinds of protein molecules which are possible make them ideal for catalytic functions. Enzymes are proteins and it is estimated that most of the proteins in the cell have catalytic properties. The high substrate specificity results from the surface architecture of the enzyme protein. Anything which alters the surface configuration of the molecule will destroy enzyme activity. They are labile to heat, and their activity is greatly affected by changes in hydrogen-ion concentration.

Nucleic acids are complex polymers of great size, made up of repeating nonidentical units, and reaching molecular weights of several million. Bound to proteins, they form the nucleoprotein of the cell nucleus and cytoplasm. From 2 to 5 per cent of bacterial dry substance is nucleoprotein. The repeating nonidentical units of the nucleic-acid polymers are known as nucleotides. Each nucleotide is composed of a nitrogenous base (purine or pyrimidine), a five-carbon sugar (ribose or deoxyribose), and phosphoric acid. Each nucleotide is joined to the other through their sugar and phosphate groups.

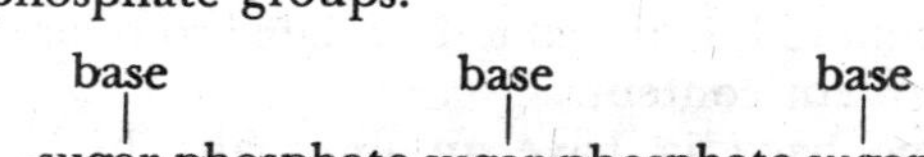

There are two types of nucleic acids which differ in the base and sugar components they contain. Ribonucleic acids (RNA) contain the sugar, ribose, and the bases, adenine, guanine, cytosine, and uracil. Deoxyribonucleic acids (DNA) contain the sugar, deoxyribose, and the bases, adenine, guanine, cytosine, and thymine instead of uracil. Deoxyribonucleic acids are found in the nuclei of cells and are thought to be the genetic substance of the cell. It is believed that the hereditary information needed to direct growth and reproduction is in the DNA molecule and is passed from generation to generation in this form. RNA is found in the nucleus and cytoplasm of cells, and particularly in the ribosomes within the cytoplasm where protein synthesis occurs. It is believed that a specialized form of RNA (messenger RNA) transmits the information from the DNA to the sites of protein synthesis in the cell. These RNA molecules move from the nucleus, where they are formed on the DNA template, to the cytoplasm, where the specific sequence of amino acids is directed for the new protein molecules. The sequence of amino acids in the enzyme protein determines its configuration and specificity. The biochemistry of genetics is presently a very active field of investigation.

**Lipoproteins and Other Lipid Materials.** Lipoproteins are another group of nitrogenous substances found in living cells. They are conjugates of proteins with lipids and are main constituents of cell membranes. The lipid portions of lipoproteins are often not simple fatty acids, but phospholipids of the following general composition:

```
fatty acid
     |
fatty acid-glycerol-phosphate-ethanolamine
```

The insolubility of lipids in water confers on the lipoprotein certain functional properties. The selective permeability of cell membranes is believed to be related to their lipoprotein content.

Some bacteria have an unusually high content of ether-soluble material. The tubercle bacillus is noted for a high content of waxy material which is nonsaponifiable. This accounts for its acid-fast properties and difficulty in staining. The glanders bacillus also contains lipid in higher than usual concentrations. Certain yeasts are known to synthesize large amounts of fat and have been exploited commercially for this property.

**Other Components Found in Bacterial Cells.** Many microoganisms are pigmented. Some of the pigments are water soluble, some are soluble only in lipid solvents. Often the water-insoluble pigments are carotenoids, either of the carotene or xanthophyll type such as found in the mycobacteria, staphylococci, and neisseria.

Recent investigations into the composition of bacterial cells have revealed a new class of polymers. They are composed of nonidentical subunits and form the structure of the cell wall which comprises 20 to 35 per cent of the dry weight of bacterial cells. A component that is common to all bacterial cell walls examined is the *mucocomplex substance* which is primarily responsible for maintaining structural rigidity. This substance is formed from amino sugars (N-acetylglucosamine (Ag) and muramic acid (AMC)) and amino acids. (See formulas at top of next page.) The amino acids that have been found in the mucocomplex are glutamic acid, alanine, glycine, and either lysine or diaminopimelic acid, a compound not found in naturally occurring proteins. Alanine and glutamic acid are often the unnatural D-forms, also not found in naturally occurring proteins. The general structure of the mucocomplex polymers is as follows with

```
- AG - AMA - AG - AMA - AG - AMA
        |           |
     peptide     peptide
     or amino    or amino
      acid        acid
```

the peptide or amino acid linked as an amide to the free carboxyl of muramic acid.

There are major differences in the composition of the cell walls of gram-positive

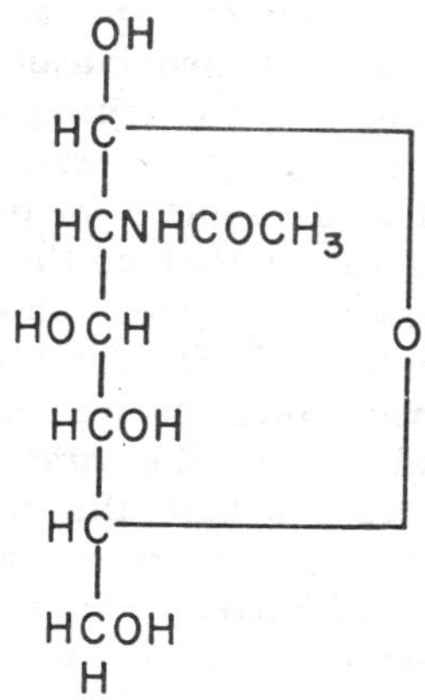

N-ACETYLGLUCOSAMINE

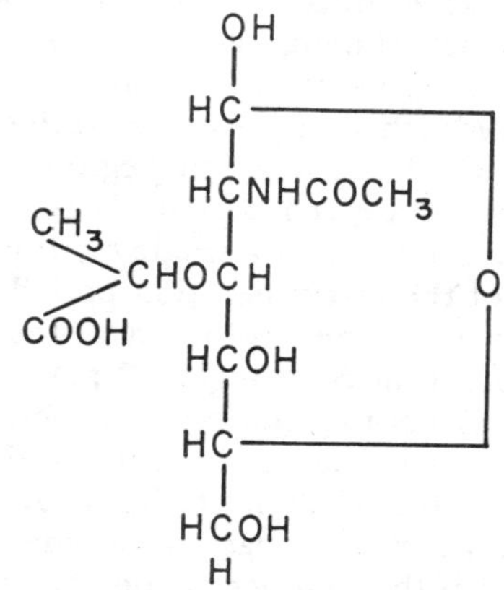

MURAMIC ACID

and gram-negative bacteria. In some gram-positive bacteria, the mucocomplex polymer is the only substance of the cell wall. In other cases, in addition are found simple polysaccharides and another class of heteropolymers known as teichoic acids. Upon hydrolysis, the teichoic acids yield glucose, phosphoric acid, a sugar alcohol, ribitol or glycerol, glucosamine, and a single amino acid, alanine. In the walls of gram-negative bacteria, in addition to the mucocomplex, are found large amounts of protein, lipid, and polysaccharide, but no teichoic acid as yet.

Lysozyme solubilizes the mucocomplex polymer and those gram-positive bacteria in which this is the only constituent are lysed by this enzyme. Gram-negative bacteria are not lysed because their cell walls are not composed solely of the mucocomplex polymer.

An unusual compound has been found to make up 5 to 10 per cent of the dry weight of bacterial spores and is not found in vegetative cells.

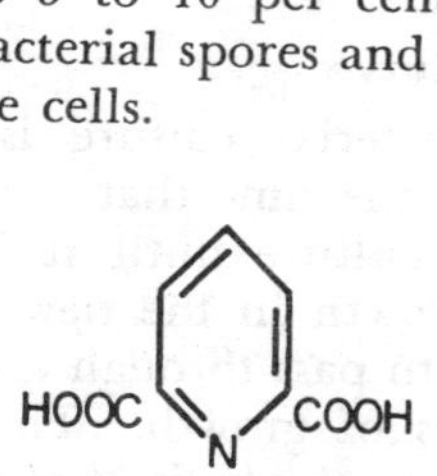

DIPICOLINIC ACID

The synthesis of dipicolinic acid is regarded as essential for spore formation. It is believed to be of importance during the dehydration of the vegetative cell during spore formation.

## GROWTH RATES AND DEATH RATES OF MICROORGANISMS

The various physical and chemical agents manifest their action upon microorganisms by their effect upon the rate of growth and death. Before these agents can be discussed adequately, certain general considerations concerning rates of growth and death must be presented.

### Rates of Growth

When bacteria or other organisms are planted in a suitable culture medium and optimum conditions for growth are maintained, the bacteria soon reach a maximum rate of gro[illegible] This can be measured best by determining the average length of time required for an organism to grow to its full size, divide, and form two individuals. This has been termed the *generation time.* It is the average time elapsing between cell divisions. It may be most conveniently determined in any given case, not by watching the bacteria under the microscope, but by counting the number of living cells present in a given amount of culture after varying lengths of time. It is evident that the shorter the generation time, the more rapid is the rate of multiplication. Any factor, therefore, which tends to shorten the generation time increases the rate of growth.

The actual length of the generation time

may be determined if the bacteria are definitely multiplying at a uniform rate, that is, that the cultures are not too young or too old; this may be determined by counting the bacteria at the beginning and at the end of a given period. It is evident that if one starts with a single organism, at the end of the first generation period there will be two; at the end of the next, four ($2^2$); at the end of the next, eight ($2^3$); and so on. If n represents the number of generations, then there will be at the end of the $n^{th}$ generation period $2^n$ bacteria. If B represents the number of bacteria at the beginning, and b the number at the end, then

$$b = B2^n$$

If b and B are known, their values may be substituted into the equation, and the value of n may be determined by solving the equation.

Careful studies of bacteria growing in culture media show that the length of the generation time does not remain a constant throughout the time of cultivation. When bacteria are first planted in a culture, particularly if they have been taken from an old culture, they frequently grow slowly at first. As they become accustomed to their environment, they multiply more rapidly. After a time the maximum rate of growth occurs. Still later the bacteria become crowded and the rate of growth diminishes, and finally the bacteria cease to grow and begin to die.

### Rates of Death

It is equally important to know something of the laws which govern the rates at which bacteria die under unfavorable conditions. In most of the cases which have been carefully studied, the bacteria die in accordance with a definite law which may be stated as follows: With a given kind of organism under uniform unfavorable conditions, the number of bacteria present in a culture will always be reduced one-half in equal periods of time; that is, regardless of how many bacteria there are at the beginning of a definite period of time, one-half that number will always be alive at the end of the proper interval. For example, suppose that two cultures of the same organism, one containing a million bacteria and the other a thousand bacteria, are subjected to the same unfavorable conditions. It is found that at the end of a definite period of time, possibly ten minutes, the bacteria in the less concentrated suspension number five hundred. It will be found that in the same period of time there are one-half the number of bacteria in the other culture also; that is, there are 500,000 bacteria. Obviously, *during each equal interval of time a definite percentage of those bacteria living at the beginning of the period will be killed.* The effect of unfavorable conditions upon the death of microorganisms is compared to the length of time required to reduce the numbers of bacteria by a definite percentage. If at one temperature, for example, half of the bacteria are killed in ten minutes, and at another temperature one-half are killed in five minutes, it is evident that the second temperature is far more destructive than the first. It will be noted that the time required to kill half the bacteria is mathematically converse to the generation time.

In summary, all effects of environment upon microorganisms are manifest in growing cultures by changes in the length of the generation time, changes in morphology, and in the physiological and cultural reactions. Likewise, the effect of environment will be noted upon the death rate by observing the length of time necessary to kill a definite percentage of the microorganisms present.

### The Growth Curve

When a bacterial culture is observed carefully from the time that it is removed from a stock culture until it has passed through its growth in the new culture, it will be found to pass through a number of definite phases of growth. These *growth phases* have been the basis of much investigation, for knowledge of them aids in the study of the morphology and physiology of the organism. Various interpretations have

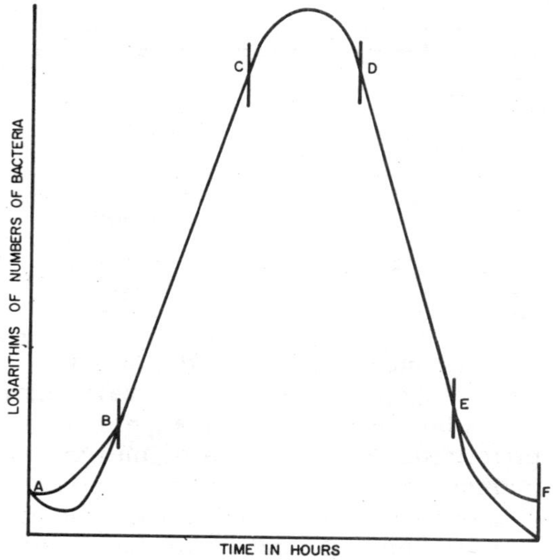


**FIG. 3.1—Growth curve of a bacterial culture. A–B, phase of adjustment; B–C, phase of increase; C–D, phase of crisis; D–E, phase of decrease; E–F, phase of readjustment.**

been given concerning the different phases of growth in a bacterial culture. The curve presented in Figure 3.1, representing the phases of growth, is considered typical by most authorities.

## FACTORS INFLUENCING THE GROWTH OF MICROORGANISMS

### Moisture

Since a high percentage of the bacterial protoplasm is composed of water, it is apparent that moisture is one of the most important substances for the optimum growth of bacteria. The optimum condition for growth in most cases is saturation; however, bacteria vary in their response to moisture. The streptococci grow only when the medium is moist, while tubercle bacilli grow abundantly on a medium which is quite dry.

The morphology of some microorganisms and the arrangement of the cells may be different in fluid media and on solid media. Streptococci grow in long chains in fluid media, while the chains are short on agar surfaces; and some types of bacteria are elongated rods in fluids and more coccoid on solid surfaces.

The amount of moisture in solid media is important in the study of the colonies of bacteria. When the medium is very moist, the colony has a tendency to spread, but it remains quite compact when the medium is dry.

### Temperature

The *optimum* growth temperature is that which most favors the development of the microorganism; that is, that temperature which gives the shortest generation time. The optimum varies with the species. A few organisms found in the ocean, in cold waters, and in alpine regions prefer a low temperature from 0° to 15° C. These are called *psychrophilic*. Those which prefer a somewhat higher temperature are called *mesophilic;* these may be again subdivided into those that prefer a "room" temperature of 18° to 25°C., and those that prefer body temperature (man, 37.5°C.) for the most parasitic forms. Temperatures such as are found in hot springs, interior of compost heaps, and in milk pasteurizers, ranging from 50° to 70°C., favor the development of *thermophilic* bacteria. Fischer has summarized the relationships of bacteria to temperature as given in Table 3.1.

The lowest temperature at which an organism will continue growth is said to be its *minimum*. This temperature varies for different species. Some organisms multiply in brine held at temperatures lower than the freezing point of water.

The highest temperature at which an organism will multiply is called its maximum and varies for the three general classes of organisms previously defined. Obviously, the maximum temperature of a psychrophilic organism may be the minimum temperature of a mesophile, while the maximum temperature of the thermophile may be high enough to cause the death of the other two.

The differences between the minimum and maximum growth temperatures vary within rather wide limits. Those organisms which exhibit considerable adaptability and are able to grow through a wide range of temperature are called *eurythermic*. Most

TABLE 3.1
TEMPERATURE RELATIONSHIPS OF BACTERIA

| Groups | Temperature Changes in Degrees Centigrade | | | Types |
|---|---|---|---|---|
| | Minimum | Optimum | Maximum | |
| Psychrophilic | 0 | 15–20 | 30 | many water bacteria cold storage growth |
| Mesophilic | 15–20 | 37 | 43 | most pathogens |
| Thermophilic | 25–45 | 50–55 | 85 | bacteria from soils, water, thermal springs |

of the saprophytic organisms belong in this class. The parasitic types which have minimum and maximum varying but little from the optimum are *stenothermic*.

Harmful effects of temperature will be discussed in the chapter on disinfection and disinfectants.

### Nutrition

The nutrient substances required by bacteria can be generally classified into four groups of substances: a carbon source, nitrogen, minerals, and often growth accessory substances such as B vitamins, and purine and pyrimidine bases. The complexity of materials required in each of these groups varies over a wide spectrum, depending on the synthetic capabilities of the microorganism. One bacterium may grow in a simple medium composed of only carbon dioxide, ammonia, mineral salts, and elemental sulfur. Another may require glucose, twenty or more amino acids, purine and pyrimidine bases, and all the known B vitamins and mineral salts. In fact, there are some organisms which have not yet been cultured in a medium in which all components are known. Sometimes a purified protein is necessary, or blood or other tissue fluid of unknown composition is needed for maximum growth.

Organisms which grow in a medium composed of a few simple chemicals have greater synthetic capabilities since all the complex structures of bacterial protoplasm such as carbohydrate, protein, and lipid are synthesized from a few simple nutrients. Organisms which require media of complex composition can be considered to have less synthetic capabilities and must have many of the building blocks of their protoplasm preformed. All gradations of nutrient requirements exist between the extremes. Organisms which can use carbon dioxide as a sole source of carbon are called *autotrophic;* those which require an organic source of carbon are called *heterotrophic*. Organisms which exist in nature only in a living host are called *parasites,* while those which exist in nature on nonliving matter are called *saprophytes*. The true parasite does not possess the complete biochemical equipment necessary for propagation and depends on the living host cell to supply the missing components. There are few bacteria in this category, and in our present state of knowledge the viruses are the best known *obligate parasites*. One marked expression of the parasitic nature of organisms is disease production. Those which cause disease, recognized by a change which they produce in living tissue, are known as *pathogenic* organisms. The pathogenic microorganisms are all heterotrophic.

The organisms which cause disease are of special interest to students of veterinary medicine. However, a false impression of the scope of microbiology is obtained if only disease-producing microorganisms are recognized. Microorganisms are widely distributed in soil, air, and water. Fortunately, most of them are beneficial rather than harmful to man and animals. They are necessary in the nutritional economy of all living forms on earth. Dead plant and animal tissues are decomposed by microorganisms returning the carbon to carbon dioxide, organic nitrogen compounds to ammonia and atmospheric nitrogen, and the minerals back to a state where they can be used as food for new life. Some bacteria live in symbiosis with leguminous plants and aid in their transformation of free nitrogen of the atmosphere into plant protein, while some live in the digestive tract of animals and assist in the nutrition of the animal by synthesizing vitamins which the animal uses. Especially important in this respect is the microflora of the rumen which enables the ruminant to convert forage crops and simple nitrogen compounds into high-grade animal protein such as meat and milk. Others are important in the production and preservation of foods for human use such as cheese, fermented milk products, sauerkraut, and vinegar. The chemical changes brought about by bacteria are considered so important that both plant and animal life would cease to exist if all bacteria should perish.

A study of the nutritional requirements of microorganisms has resulted in sensitive, accurate, and specific laboratory methods for the quantitative assay of the B vitamins and amino acids.

## Carbon Compounds as Nutrients

*Organic Carbon.* Microorganisms vary from those which can use carbon dioxide as a sole carbon source to those which are obligate parasites and require the complex organic compounds synthesized by the host in which they grow. Many bacteria have their carbon requirements satisfied with a simple sugar such as glucose, or even simpler organic carbon molecules like ethanol or acetic acid. One species of Pseudomonas has been reported to be able to use over one hundred different organic compounds as a sole carbon source. These carbon sources may vary from a simple two-carbon compound to almost any type of complex structure, including paraffinic hydrocarbons.

*Carbon Dioxide.* It is well known that those organisms which carry out photosynthesis and those which obtain their energy from the oxidation of inorganic compounds can use carbon dioxide as a sole or principal source of carbon. What is less well known is the utilization of carbon dioxide by many organisms which use organic compounds as their principal carbon source. Most of these organisms normally form large amounts of carbon dioxide from the organic compounds which they metabolize, so a net uptake of carbon dioxide is difficult to establish. If, however, labeled carbon dioxide is added to growing cultures, it becomes mixed with that formed metabolically. Some of it will be reassimilated and the label will be found in cellular material and various other compounds formed during growth. Carbon dioxide serves as a unit necessary for the biosynthesis of purines, pyrimidines, and dicarboxylic acids. Some organisms grow better if the atmosphere in which they are incubated is enriched with carbon dioxide. Growth of the tubercle bacillus, gonococcus, and meningococcus is stimulated by carbon dioxide in the atmosphere, and *Brucella abortus* requires carbon dioxide for primary isolation.

**Nitrogen Compounds.** The nitrogen compounds needed by bacteria vary from simple inorganic forms as ammonia and nitrate, or a single simple amino acid to a complete mixture of amino acids, purines, and pyrimidines. Organisms such as Azotobacter can obtain their nitrogen as elemental nitrogen from the atmosphere when they are grown in a sugar-mineral salts medium. Bacteria of the genus Rhizobium growing in the nodules on roots of leguminous plants *(symbiosis)* fix atmospheric nitrogen to the benefit of the plant. A few other bacteria have been found to assimilate atmospheric nitrogen to a limited extent. The process is called *nitrogen fixation.*

**Growth Factors.** In addition to the principal nutrients such as a source of carbon and nitrogen, some organisms of limited synthetic capabilities must be supplied with some of the B vitamins. The amount required is much less than that of the principal nutrients and is for the purpose of supplying to the organism preformed molecular structures which it is unable to synthesize. For some bacteria only a part of a vitamin molecule is needed in order for the organism to make the complete vitamin, for others only one or several of the complete factors, and for others a complete mixture of B vitamins is required. The B vitamins are known to function as prosthetic groups of enzymes.

**Mineral Elements.** In addition to an energy source, carbon, and nitrogen, microorganisms need for growth a variety of mineral elements—some in amounts so small that the requirement is difficult to establish. Phosphorous compounds function in the generation and utilization of energy, and sulfur for the synthesis of several of the amino acids. Other minerals such as iron, copper, zinc, magnesium, manganese, cobalt, calcium, sodium, and potassium are perhaps needed, but in lower concentration, because of physiological functions in which these elements participate.

**Relationship to Oxygen.** Some bacteria rely solely on respiration as their ultimate source of energy. They cannot grow or even survive without molecular oxygen and are *obligate aerobes*. At the other extreme are bacteria which depend for their source of energy on reactions not involving molecular oxygen. They are inhibited in their growth or killed by the presence of atmospheric oxygen and are *obligate anaerobes*. Some obligate anaerobes are very sensitive to oxygen, and its complete exclusion is necessary for growth. An adequate explanation for their sensitivity to oxygen is not available. One likely explanation is that their enzyme systems for supplying energy for growth must be maintained in a reduced state in order to function. Certain sulfhydryl enzymes are very sensitive to oxidative conditions. The obligate anaerobes contain none or very little of the iron-porphyrin respiratory enzymes, i.e., catalase, peroxidase, and the cytochrome-cytochrome oxidase system. They do possess flavoprotein enzymes which catalyze substrate dehydrogenations which are coupled directly to oxygen and lead to hydrogen peroxide formation. The lack of classical catalase and peroxidase in obligate anaerobes has led to the theory of peroxide toxicity as the reason for being unable to grow in air. Organisms which can grow in either the presence or absence of oxygen are called *facultative anaerobes*. Many bacteria are facultative anaerobes and can carry out fermentation and respiration simultaneously. They are able to shift their metabolism, depending on the presence or absence of oxygen.

Many of the bacteria that cause disease in animals are aerobic, some are facultative, and a few are anaerobic. Obligate anaerobes cause diseases such as blackleg, tetanus, malignant edema, and botulism.

**Hydrogen-Ion Concentration.** Hydrogen-ion concentration is an important factor in the growth of microorganisms. The pH range for most bacteria is from a minimum of 4.5–5.0 to a maximum of 8.0–8.5. Nearly all pathogenic bacteria grow best at or near neutrality from pH 6.8 to 7.5. An extreme example of acid tolerance is *Thiobacillus thiooxidans* which grows well at pH 0 to 1.0. Some of the lactobacilli grow well at the minimum range of 4.5 to 5.0. Many yeasts and molds also grow well at reactions below neutrality. From the metabolism of components of the medium, both acidic and basic substances may arise, so it is advisable to add to culture media a hydrogen-ion buffer such as mono- or dipotassium phosphate, or their combination, to keep the reaction of the medium within the optimum growth range.

**Chemicals Other Than Nutrients and Their Effect on Growth.** The effect of chemicals, other than nutrients, on growth is considered in Chapter 5.

## MICROBIAL METABOLISM

Bacteria and other living cells are able to carry out an exceedingly large variety of complex chemical reactions associated with growth, reproduction, and maintenance. Most of the reactions would be difficult or impossible to carry out by the procedures available to the laboratory chemist, yet in the living cell they occur in a controlled manner at normal temperatures and pressures. Furthermore, molecules which are considered to be very stable even to high temperatures in the presence of strong acid are often easily degraded by bacterial cells. The living cell is able to accomplish these reactions with specific catalysts called *enzymes.*

### Enzymes: Kinds and Activity

Enzymes are organic catalysts, produced only in living cells, which exhibit a high degree of specificity in the substrates they activate. A more modern definition is: a protein with catalytic properties due to its power of specific activation. Enzymes increase the rate at which the equilibrium state of a chemical reaction is attained without themselves appearing as a product of the reaction. Nearly one hundred enzymes have been obtained in a purified crystalline state, and all have proved to be proteins. Of the several hundred that have been studied, whether purified or not, all possess the properties of proteins. It is believed that most of the protein in the cell is enzyme protein. As proteins, enzymes are nondialyzable, thermolabile, and their activity is affected by pH, temperature, etc. The substance acted upon by the enzyme is called a *substrate.* In some cases an additional component besides the enzyme and substrate are required before the reaction will proceed. These substances are called *cofactors.* Usually they are relatively small organic molecules which are dialyzable and thermostable, in which case they are called *coenzymes.* The B vitamins, i.e., thiamine, riboflavin, nicotinic acid, pantothenic acid, biotin, pyridoxal, etc., function as coenzymes (Table 3.2.) A single coenzyme, for instance the nicotinamide nucleotides, may function with several different enzyme proteins such as lactic acid dehydrogenase and ethyl alcohol dehydrogenase in performing hydrogen transfer functions. In other cases, the cofactor may be an inorganic ion, such as $Mg^{++}$, $Mn^{++}$, or $Zn^{++}$, and is referred to as an activator. In either case the enzyme,

TABLE 3.2

RELATION OF SOME WATER–SOLUBLE VITAMINS TO COENZYMES

| Vitamin | Coenzyme | Enzymatic Reaction in Which Coenzyme Functions |
|---|---|---|
| Thiamin (vitamin $B_1$) | thiaminpyrophosphate (cocarboxylase) | decarboxylation |
| Riboflavin (vitamin $B_2$) | flavin monophosphate (FMN)<br>flavin adenine dinucleotide (FAD) | dehydrogenation<br>electron transport |
| Nicotinic acid (niacin) | pyridine nucleotides (NAD, NADP) | dehydrogenations |
| Pyridoxine (vitamin $B_6$) | pyridoxal phosphate | amino acid decarboxylation deamination transamination |
| Pantothenic acid | coenzyme A | keto acid oxidation<br>fatty acid synthesis |
| Biotin | prosthetic group of biotin coenzymes | transcarboxylations<br>$CO_2$ fixation |
| Folic acid (vitamin $B_2$) | tetrahydrofolic acid | transfer of 1-carbon units HCHO, $CH_3$- |
| Cobamide (vitamin $B_{12}$) | cobamide coenzymes | carbon chain rearrangement |

substrate, and cofactor are all necessary for catalysis to occur.

Enzymes may be *extracellular* or *intracellular*. Certain bacteria are able to use as nutrients insoluble substances such as starch, cellulose, insoluble proteins, and lipids. The bacterial cell produces and excretes into the medium extracellular enzymes which degrade the carbohydrate polymers to glucose, proteins to amino acids, and lipids to fatty acids and alcohols. The substrate is thus solubilized so it can enter the cell and undergo biochemical transformations by the intracellular enzymes. The extracellular enzymes of bacteria are sometimes called digestive enzymes, and several are prepared commercially on a large scale for use in industry. The intracellular enzymes are held within the cell and can be released only on rupture of the cell membrane. The enzymes concerned with energy transformations of the cell are intracellular. Many of the studies of oxidative reactions of the cell have been done with enzymes extracted from the cell, some of which have been purified and crystallized.

Enzymes are commonly named after the specific substrate they attack by adding the ending "ase" to the name of the substrate. Thus, we have carbohydrases (amylase, cellulase, pectinase); lipases, sometimes called esterases, which hydrolyze the ester linkage of fats; proteinases which hydrolyze the amide linkage in proteins; decarboxylases which split carbon dioxide from carboxyl groups; and deaminases which remove amino groups from amino acids. In some cases the substrate can undergo a variety of reactions such as decarboxylation, oxidation, and reduction. In such cases one adds the name of the reaction to the substrate and adds the ending "ase" to the reaction, i.e., pyruvic decarboxylase or pyruvic dehydrogenase.

Because of the complexity of the reactions which go on in living cells, we should expect a large number of enzymes. Over 650 have been described, and perhaps many are yet unknown (Dixon and Webb, 1958). Of this large group of enzymes, about three-fourths of them catalyze only seven reaction types. In addition to classification of enzymes as extra- or intracellular, they may be grouped according to the type of reaction they carry out under the following headings as proposed by Baldwin (1960).

**Hydrolases.** These are enzymes which catalyze hydrolytic cleavage of their substrates by addition of water. The best known in this group are the extracellular digestive hydrolases which convert large, complex carbohydrate, protein, and fat molecules into simple units. There are, however, intracellular hydrolases concerned with processes other than digestion.

*Peptidases.* These proteolytic enzymes are concerned with the splitting of large molecules of food proteins to amino acids. Usually a mixture of more than one enzyme is involved. Examples are: pepsin, trypsin, and rennin from the animal world; and papain, ficin, and bromelin from plants. Many bacteria can completely digest proteins, and they are a good source of proteolytic enzymes. *Endopeptidases* are those which convert large protein molecules to smaller fragments with several amino acid molecules, while *exopeptidases* liberate free terminal amino acids until only dipeptides remain, and the latter are finally split by *dipeptidases* to the amino acids.

*Carbohydrases.* These are enzymes concerned with the digestion of carbohydrate polymers such as cellulose, starch, and glycogen to simpler units such as tri- and di- and monosaccharides. They are very widely distributed and occur in digestive secretions of animals and in cells of plants and microorganisms of all kinds. Usually, at least two enzymes are involved in the complete digestion of a large substrate molecule to glucose—a *polysaccharidase*

EXAMPLE 3.1

1. Citric acid $\xleftrightarrow[\text{aconitase}]{\pm H_2O}$ cis-aconitic acid $\xleftrightarrow{\pm H_2O}$ isocitric acid

2. l-malic acid $\xleftrightarrow[\text{fumarase}]{\pm H_2O}$ fumaric acid

3. Glyceric acid 2-phosphate $\xleftrightarrow[\text{enolase}]{\pm H_2O}$ enol pyruvic acid phosphate

which attacks the large unit, and *glycosidases* which digest the smaller subunits to a simple monosaccharide. Examples of enzymes and their substrates are: amylases (starch, glycogen); cellulases (cellulose); pectinase (pectin); maltase (maltose); saccharase (sucrose); and lactase (lactose).

*Lipases and Esterases.* These enzymes catalyze the hydrolysis of esters of alcohols with organic acids and the esters of alcohols with inorganic acids such as phosphoric and sulfuric acid. The most common food substance digested by these enzymes is fat. Lipases occur in the digestive juices of vertebrates, in plant seeds, and in many bacteria. Specificity of lipases and esterases is not as high as is true for most other enzymes. Examples are: gastric lipase, pancreatic lipase, castor bean lipase, and lecithinase. The enzymes of *Clostridium welchii* include a lecithinase which acts on lecithin to produce a toxin. The phosphoric acid esters of organic compounds are important in cellular metabolism. The esterases in general hydrolyze smaller molecules than lipases and hydrolyze esters of low molecular weight such as those formed from inorganic acids and alcohols.

*Other Hydrolytic Enzymes.* A very important group of hydrolytic enzymes is that which hydrolyzes mono-, di-, and polyphosphate esters; an example of the latter being adenosinetriphosphatase. Urease, which is produced by many bacteria, is an enzyme which converts urea to carbon dioxide and ammonia. It has a high substrate specificity and was the first enzyme to be crystallized and shown to be a protein.

**Adding Enzymes.** There are certain enzymes which perform very important biological functions by interconversion of substrates by adding or removing water. (See Example 3.1.)

Others perform an important biological function by addition or removal of carbon dioxide. (See Example 3.2.)

**Transferring Enzymes.** There exist many enzymes that are fundamentally important in energy transfer and biological synthesis. These enzymes catalyze the transfer of a

EXAMPLE 3.2

1. Pyruvic acid $\xrightarrow[\text{decarboxylase}]{}$ acetaldehyde + $CO_2$

2. $RCHNH_2COOH \xrightarrow[\text{amino acid decarboxylase}]{} RCHNH_2 + CO_2$

3. Oxalacetic acid $\xleftrightarrow[\text{oxalacetic decarboxylase}]{}$ pyruvic acid + $CO_2$

group or radical, such as pairs of hydrogen atoms, methyl, amino, phosphate and glycosyl groups, from one organic molecule to another. The reaction may be represented as: AG + B = A + BG where A stands for the donor of the radical G, and B its acceptor.

*Dehydrogenases.* In this category there is the large and important group of enzymes concerned with tissue respiration. Respiration is defined as a reaction in which the substrate (electron donor) transfers electrons to gaseous oxygen (electron acceptor) under the influence of specific enzymes. The substrate is oxidized through loss of hydrogen and electrons, and the oxygen is reduced to water by gain of hydrogen and electrons. Biological oxidations are for the most part hydrogen transfers, and the term dehydrogenation is used to describe the reaction. The enzymes concerned are called *dehydrogenases.* It must be remembered that when a substance is oxidized and another reduced, electrons are also transferred from the hydrogen donor to the hydrogen acceptor. The following model is used to illustrate biological hydrogen transfer:

$$AH_2 + B \longrightarrow A + BH_2$$

in which *A* is the substrate being oxidized (hydrogen donor) and *B* the substance being reduced (hydrogen acceptor).

If the hydrogen acceptor is oxygen, it is defined as respiration and it is an aerobic process.

$$AH_2 + 1/2O_2 \xrightarrow[\text{(respiration)}]{} A + H_2O$$

The formation of water in respiration is the result of a combination of hydrogen and oxygen ions.

$$2H^+ + O^- \longrightarrow H_2O$$

The dehydrogenation of the substrate produces hydrogen ions and electrons rather than neutral hydrogen.

$$AH_2 \longrightarrow A + 2H^+ + 2e$$

The role of the oxidases is to transfer the electrons to oxygen.

$$H^+ + 1/2O_2 + 2e \longrightarrow HO^-$$

$$H^+ + HO^- \longrightarrow H_2O$$

The hydrogen acceptor may be a substance other than oxygen, such as pyruvic acid, in which case lactic acid is formed instead of water. When hydrogen transfer is accomplished without oxygen, the process is referred to as fermentation. (See Example 3.3.)

Anaerobic organisms carry out their energy-yielding reactions without oxygen. However, the basic mechanism of aerobic and anaerobic metabolism is the same, only the final hydrogen acceptor is different. The process of hydrogen transfer has been studied a great deal and many specific hydrogen-transferring enzymes are known.

*Transphosphatases.* These enzymes, sometimes called phosphokinases, accomplish the transfer of phosphate radicals from one of a pair of molecules to the other in which adenosine di- and triphosphates are usually the carrier system. Certain phosphorylated compounds occupy a unique position in the energy transfer reactions in the living cell: (1) those reactions which proceed with a release of energy, and (2) those which require energy in order to proceed. In order that both types may proceed in an orderly fashion, there are intermediate compounds

EXAMPLE 3.3

$$AH_2 + \underset{\text{pyruvic acid}}{CH_3\,CO\,COOH} \longrightarrow A + \underset{\text{lactic acid}}{CH_3CHOH\,COOH}\ \text{(fermentation)}$$

EXAMPLE 3.4

glucose + adenosine triphosphate $\underset{\text{hexokinase}}{\rightleftharpoons}$ glucose-6-phosphate + adenosine diphosphate

of phosphorus which are common to both. Phosphate compounds, of which adenosine triphosphate (ATP) is the most common example, serve as carriers of energy and the transferring enzymes are called kinases. Most of the substances which undergo enzyme-catalyzed transformations do so as phosphorylated compounds. For phosphorylation of glucose, see Example 3.4.

This is an example of transphosphorylation in an energy-requiring reaction. Adenosine triphosphate was previously synthesized in an energy-releasing reaction, usually an oxidative reaction, and the energy of the reaction was stored in the phosphate bond to be used in the phosphorylation of glucose. The phosphate transferred from the ATP is known as an energy-rich phosphate bond and the resulting ester linkage in glucose-6-phosphate as a bond with a low level of stored energy.

*Other Transferring Enzymes.* Transaminases are enzymes involved in transfer of amino groups such as in glutamic-alanine transaminase. (See Example 3.5.)

Transaminases are widely distributed among bacteria and supply the cell with the capability of synthesizing the amino acids necessary for protein formation. The corresponding alpha keto acids are products of carbohydrate or fatty acid metabolism.

Transglycosylases are of importance in polysaccharide synthesis from nucleoside diphosphate sugars.

Transmethylases transfer methyl groups and transacetylases acetyl groups. Other group- or radical-transferring enzymes are known, and they are all implicated in specific reactions concerned with synthesis of molecules necessary as structural units for cell protoplasm.

**Oxidases**

*Aerobic Oxidases.* Oxidases are dehydrogenating enzymes which are characterized by their ability to use oxygen directly as a hydrogen acceptor. The *aerobic oxidases* are confined to the use of oxygen as a hydrogen acceptor. The phenol oxidases of plant tissues responsible for the rapid darkening of the surfaces of freshly cut fruits and vegetables are examples of aerobic oxidases. In the phenol oxidases and ascorbic acid oxidase, copper is part of the prosthetic group. As yet, there has been no role assigned to the aerobic oxidases in microbial metabolism except for those organisms known to respire through the cytochrome-

EXAMPLE 3.5

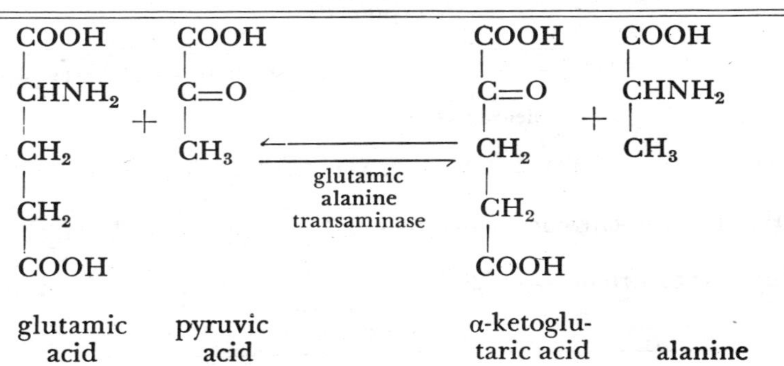

EXAMPLE 3.6

$$\text{(a) lactic acid} + \text{FP} \xrightarrow[\text{dehydrogenase}]{\text{lactic}} \text{pyruvic acid} + \text{FPH}_2$$

$$\text{(b) FPH}_2 + \text{O}_2 \xrightarrow[\text{oxidase}]{\text{FP}} \text{FP} + \text{H}_2\text{O}_2$$

cytochrome oxidase system. Cytochrome oxidase is an iron and copper containing aerobic oxidase, widely distributed in plant and animal tissues and in aerobic bacteria, which oxidizes reduced cytochrome with molecular oxygen, forming water as the final reaction product.

*Aerobic Dehydrogenases.* The *aerobic dehydrogenases* are metal protein complexes containing flavin adenine dinucleotide that can use methylene blue or other reducible dyes as well as oxygen as a hydrogen acceptor. When oxygen is the hydrogen acceptor, the final reaction product is hydrogen peroxide. These enzymes have been shown to function in the respiration of the lactobacilli and in other facultative anaerobes which do not possess cytochrome pigments. Evidently, the flavoprotein (FP) in these organisms constitutes the final link to oxygen. As a rule, the respiration is too slow to be a major source of energy, and it is not inhibited by cyanide or carbon monoxide. These organisms rely primarily on fermentation for their energy. (See Example 3.6.)

The only aerobic system which is known to function rapidly enough to be a major oxidative source of energy for microorganisms is the cytochrome-cytochrome oxidase pathway. The cytochromes are iron porphyrin protein pigments which are present in most all plant and animal cells and in all aerobic bacteria. They have been found in azotobacter, acetobacter, pseudomonads, staphylococci, coliforms, members of the genus Bacillus, and others. Many dehydrogenases are able to reduce the nicotinamide coenzymes (NAD). The reduced coenzyme is oxidized by special flavoprotein enzymes (FP) which are able to reduce the cytochrome pigments. The flavoproteins which reduce cytochromes are called cytochrome reductases. They contain a firmly bound yellow prosthetic group, flavin-adenine-dinucleotide (FAD), which can be reversibly oxidized and reduced. The reduced cytochrome is oxidized by cytochrome oxidases and molecular oxygen. (See Example 3.7.)

The iron atom in cytochrome can be re-

EXAMPLE 3.7

$$\text{(a) lactic acid} + \text{NAD}^+ \xrightarrow[\text{dehydrogenase}]{\text{lactic acid}} \text{pyruvic acid} + \text{NADH} + \text{H}^+$$

$$\text{(b) NADH} + \text{H}^+ + \text{FAD} \longrightarrow \text{NAD}^+ + \text{FADH}_2$$

$$\text{(c) FADH}_2 + \text{2-cytochrome} \longrightarrow \text{FAD} + 2 \text{ reduced cytochrome}$$

$$\text{(d) 2 reduced cytochrome} + 1/2\text{O}_2 \xrightarrow[\text{oxidase}]{\text{cytochrome}} \text{oxidized cytochrome} + \text{H}_2\text{O}$$

EXAMPLE 3.8

$$FADH_2 + 2\ Fe^{+++} \longrightarrow 2\ FAD + 2\ H^+ + 2\ Fe^{++}$$

versibly oxidized and reduced by donating or accepting one electron:

$$Fe^{+++} \underset{+e}{\overset{-e}{\rightleftharpoons}} Fe^{++}$$

When cytochrome accepts an electron from reduced flavoprotein, there is released a hydrogen ion for each electron transferred to the cytochrome. (See Example 3.8.)

If there is more than one cytochrome component in the system, the last one in the chain transfers the electrons to molecular oxygen by means of a special iron-containing enzyme, cytochrome oxidase. When the iron in the reduced form in cytochrome oxidase is reoxidized, molecular oxygen is reduced.

$$4\ Fe^{++} + O_2 \longrightarrow 4\ Fe^{+++} + 2\ O^{--}$$

The reduced oxygen atom reacts with hydrogen ions from the oxidation of reduced flavoprotein to form water.

$$2\ H^+ + O^{--} \longrightarrow H_2O$$

This electron transport system has been shown to account for the major portion of the respiration in those bacteria which contain the cytochromes. Several different cytochromes have been found in bacteria other than the cytochrome C of mammalian tissues and yeast. Some have been found which pass electrons to acceptors other than molecular oxygen, such as nitrate and sulfate, and function in anaerobic electron transport (Gunsalus and Stanier, 1961).

Respiratory poisons such as cyanide and carbon monoxide react with the iron and copper in cytochrome oxidase and function as inhibitors of aerobic metabolism.

### Anaerobic Carbohydrate Metabolism

Pyruvic acid is one of the important intermediates used as a starting point for many biosynthetic reactions in the living bacterial cell. It is formed in the degradation of carbohydrates, amino acids, fats, and other organic molecules. In the metabolism of a simple sugar, it is formed as a result of oxidation. Several different pathways may be used by different microorganisms in the conversion of sugars to pyruvic acid. The most widely distributed and most studied of the pathways of sugar metabolism is the *glycolytic pathway* (Figure 3.2). It is a sequence of reactions elucidated from studies of yeast and muscle metabolism which, in the absence of oxygen, leads from glucose to ethanol and carbon dioxide, or lactic acid, in the cases of yeast and muscle tissue, respectively. In an examination of the successive steps of the glycolytic cycle, the function of phosphate compounds, B vitamins, purine nucleotides, and various inorganic ions in the various enzyme reactions becomes apparent. Adenosine triphosphate, nicotinamide dinucleotides, and thiamine pyrophosphate, $Mg^{++}$ and $Zn^{++}$, all have important roles in glycolysis. The transformation of glucose during operation of the glycolytic cycle may be summarized as:

(1) A phosphorylation of the glucose to form the fructose 1,6 diphosphate ester in which 2 moles of ATP are converted to ADP. (Note that two energy-rich phosphate bonds are used to esterify each mole of hexose, Steps 1 through 4.)

(2) Cleavage of the sugar diphosphate ester into two moles of triosephosphate, glyceraldehyde phosphate and dihydroxyacetone phosphate. All three of these compounds are in equilibrium (Step 5).

(3) An oxidation of glyceraldehyde-3-phosphate to 3-phosphoglyceric acid by a sequence of reactions in which a mole of NAD is reduced and a mole of ATP is

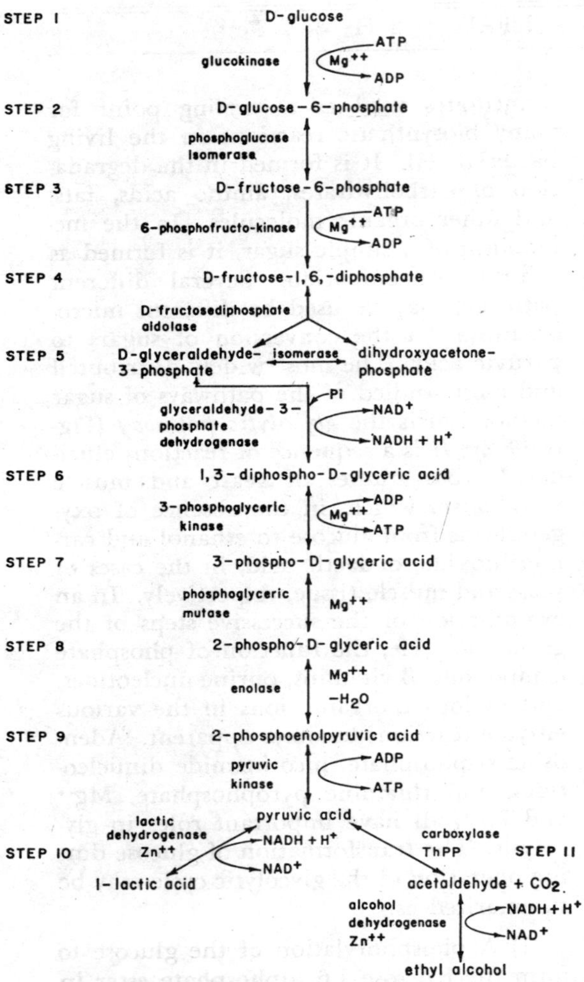


ATP = adenosine triphosphate
NAD+ = nicotinamide dinucleotide (oxidized form) (also called cozymase, Coenzyme I, DPN, diphosphopyridine nucleotide)
NADH + H+ = reduced form
ThPP = thiamine pyrophosphate (cocarboxylase)
Pi = inorganic phosphate

FIG. 3.2—Glycolytic pathway (Embden-Meyer-hof-Parnas).

generated. From each hexose unit, therefore, two moles of ATP are generated, two moles of NAD are reduced, and two moles of phosphoglyceric acid are formed (Steps 6 and 7).

(4) Transformation of the 2-phosphoglyceric acid to pyruvic acid through a loss of water and a transfer of the phosphate to ADP forming ATP. The rearrangement of the molecule in going to pyruvic acid results in a distribution of bond energy so a mole of ATP can be generated for each mole of pyruvate formed from phosphoglyceric acid. In the conversion of one mole of hexose to two moles of pyruvic acid, two moles of ATP are used up in phosphorylation of the sugar but four moles of ATP are formed—a net yield of two energy-rich phosphate bonds for each mole of hexose fermented (Steps 6 to 9).

(5) In muscle extracts which contain lactic dehydrogenase and reduced NAD (Step 5) the pyruvic acid is reduced to l-lactic acid, and NADH + $H^+$ is oxidized (Step 10) to function as a coenzyme again in Step 5 with glyceraldehyde-3-phosphate dehydrogenase.

(6) In yeast extracts which contain carboxylase, cocarboxylase, and alcohol dehydrogenase, the pyruvic acid is decarboxylated to acetaldehyde and carbon dioxide. Reduced NAD from Step 5 donates its electrons to acetaldehyde to form ethanol and oxidized NAD (Step 11). The oxidized NAD returns to Step 5 to function with glyceraldehyde-3-phosphate dehydrogenase in the oxidation of more glyceraldehyde-3-phosphate to 1,3-diphosphoglyceric acid.

This cycle is typical of the reactions in the lactic acid bacteria and yeast when they grow in the absence of oxygen.

The lactic and alcoholic fermentations are widespread among microorganisms. There are other types of microbial fermentations of hexose sugars which are different in the amount and kinds of end products formed. Several kinds of bacterial fermentations and the products formed are listed in Table 3.3. Wood has discussed types of bacterial fermentations extensively (Gunsalus and Stanier, 1961).

## TABLE 3.3

Fermentation Products From Glucose (millimoles per 100 millimoles fermented glucose)

| Fermentation Type | Alcoholic | Homolactic | | Hetero-lactic | Enterobacteria | | | Pro-pionic | Butyric | Butyl | Iso-propyl |
|---|---|---|---|---|---|---|---|---|---|---|---|
| Organism | *Sac. cerevisiae* | *Lac. delbruckii* | *Str. pyogenes* | *Leuc. dextranicum* | *Es. coli* | *Aero. aerogenes* | *Sal. typhosa* | *Prop. arabinosum* | *Cl. perfringens* | *Cl. acetobutylicum* | *Cl. butylicum* |
| Gases | | | | | | | | | | | |
| $CO_2$ | 177.0 | ... | ... | 86.5 | 56.5 | 177.2 | ... | 63.6 | 176.0 | 220.0 | 197.0 |
| $H_2$ | ... | ... | ... | ... | 53.7 | 56.8 | ... | ... | 214.0 | 165.9 | 72.7 |
| Acids | | | | | | | | | | | |
| formic | .82 | ... | ... | ... | 5.82 | 1.25 | 39.5 | ... | ... | ... | ... |
| acetic | 4.03 | ... | ... | ... | 30.10 | 1.02 | 25.6 | 17.0 | 60.0 | 24.8 | 21.2 |
| propionic | ... | ... | ... | 10.8 | ... | ... | ... | 139.0 | ... | ... | ... |
| butyric | .36 | ... | ... | ... | ... | ... | ... | ... | 34.0 | 7.1 | 6.1 |
| lactic | 1.63 | 192.0 | 196.0 | 83.5 | 119.0 | 6.30 | 121.7 | ... | 33.0 | ... | ... |
| succinic | .49 | ... | ... | ... | 4.88 | ... | 10.8 | 13.6 | ... | ... | ... |
| Alcohols | | | | | | | | | | | |
| ethyl | 160.5 | ... | ... | 81.2 | 37.0 | 52.40 | 25.4 | ... | 26.0 | 4.9 | ... |
| isopropyl | ... | ... | ... | ... | ... | ... | ... | ... | ... | ... | 15.1 |
| butyl | ... | ... | ... | ... | ... | ... | ... | ... | ... | 47.4 | 66.6 |
| glycerol | 16.2 | ... | ... | 24.0 | ... | 2.60 | ... | ... | ... | ... | ... |
| acetylmethylcarbinol | ... | ... | ... | ... | ... | 64.30 | ... | ... | ... | 5.7 | ... |
| butanediol–2,3 | .53 | ... | ... | ... | ... | ... | ... | ... | ... | ... | ... |
| Ketones | | | | | | | | | | | |
| acetone | ... | ... | ... | ... | ... | ... | ... | ... | ... | 22.3 | ... |
| Carbon recovery % | 96.4 | 97.0 | 98.0 | 98.9 | 95.4 | 94.5 | 93.0 | 97.6 | 97.1 | 98.0 | 95.0 |
| O/R balance | 1.05 | 1.0 | 1.0 | 0.95 | 0.95 | 0.99 | 0.99 | 1.01 | 1.05 | 1.01 | 1.02 |

## Aerobic Metabolism of Carbohydrates

The oxidation of carbohydrates with oxygen as an electron acceptor is more complicated and is in most cases a continuation of the initial anaerobic changes. In the presence of oxygen, pyruvic acid, instead of being converted to ethanol and carbon dioxide or lactic acid, enters a cycle of reactions known as the *citric acid cycle* or *tricarboxylic acid cycle*. The citric acid cycle is one of the several cyclic mechanisms used in respiration wherein dehydrogenations are coupled with reduction of oxygen through mediation of the nicotinamide nucleotides, flavoprotein, and finally the cytochrome-cytochrome oxidase system.

We have seen how nicotinamide nucleotide functions as a hydrogen transfer coenzyme of dehydrogenases in the glycolytic pathway. The flavoprotein enzymes are able to accept electrons from the reduced nicotinamide nucleotide; the reduced flavoprotein becomes reoxidized by transfer of its electrons to one of the cytochromes from which the electrons are passed to gaseous oxygen by means of the cytochromes and cytochrome oxidase. The flavoprotein enzymes and nicotinamide coenzymes illustrate biochemical functions of the B vitamins, riboflavin, and nicotinic acid, respectively. The series of enzymic reactions that function between the substrate and oxygen is called the *electron transport system*. This stepwise manner of oxidation allows for a smooth flow of energy and permits the conversion of part of it into a storage form of phosphate bond energy (ATP) which can be used for the synthesis of the molecules essential for growth and maintenance of the living cell by reactions which require energy.

**Tricarboxylic Acid Cycle.** This metabolic pathway, sometimes called the citric acid cycle, is important to the organism because it can provide intermediates for biosynthesis of amino acids and fatty acids, and also provides energy from the synthesis of ATP through phosphorylations associated with electron transport. It is an aerobic cycle and accounts for the oxidation (to carbon

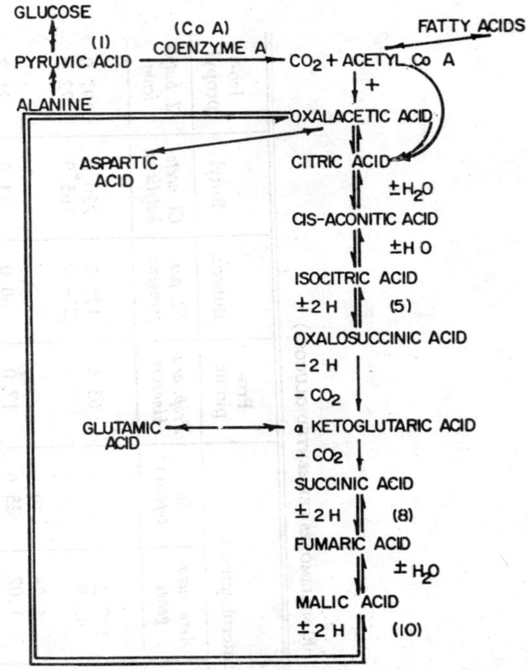


FIG. 3.3—Tricarboxylic acid cycle (Kreb's cycle).

dioxide and water) of two-carbon units in the form of acetyl Co A[1] units "active acetate" which arise from the metabolism of carbohydrate, fatty acids, and amino acids. Active two-carbon fragments (acetyl Co A) resulting from oxidative decarboxylation of pyruvic acid

$$\text{CoA} + \text{pyruvic acid} \longrightarrow \text{acetyl CoA} + CO_2$$

condense with oxaloacetic acid to form citric acid. The compounds involved and their transformation during operation of the citric acid cycle are shown in Figure 3.3.

Each step of the cycle has been established through the work of many investigators since the outline of the scheme was first proposed in 1937. The reactions of the cycle may be reviewed briefly:

(1) Pyruvic acid arising from glucose, fatty acid, or amino acid metabolism is oxidatively decarboxylated yielding acetyl Co A which condenses with the enol form of oxalacetic acid to form citric acid.

[1] Pantothenic acid coenzyme (3′-phospho-ADP-pantoyl-β-alanyl-cystiamine).

(2) Citric acid is interconverted to isocitric acid by means of the enzyme aconitase and the intermediate cis-aconitic acid. Removal of a water molecule from citric acid to yield cis-aconitic acid and replacement in a different manner yields the isomer isocitric acid.

(3) Isocitric acid is dehydrogenated by its specific dehydrogenase to yield oxalosuccinic acid. This is an energy-yielding reaction estimated to give three energy-rich phosphate bonds as ATP.

(4) Oxalosuccinic acid is decarboxylated by oxalosuccinic decarboxylase to give alpha ketoglutaric acid and carbon dioxide. Alpha ketoglutaric acid can be used as the substrate for synthesis of glutamic acid by the transamination reaction.

(5) Alpha ketoglutaric acid is oxidatively decarboxylated to yield succinic acid and carbon dioxide. This oxidation is estimated to give four energy-rich phosphate bonds as ATP. (At this stage in the cycle, two molecules of carbon dioxide have been formed, the equivalent of the oxidation of one acetyl group. Starting with pyruvic acid, there was also one molecule of carbon dioxide lost in its oxidative decarboxylation to acetyl Co A. This is also an energy-yielding reaction estimated to give three energy-rich phosphate bonds. Thus, a molecule of pyruvic acid is oxidized to carbon dioxide and water with each turn of the cycle.)

(6) Succinic acid is dehydrogenated to fumaric acid, estimated to yield three energy-rich phosphate bonds.

(7) Fumaric acid is hydrated to give malic acid.

(8) Malic acid is dehydrogenated to oxalacetic acid, estimated to yield three energy-rich phosphate bonds. The oxalacetic acid enolizes and reenters the cycle.

Each time a pyruvic acid molecule traverses the cycle, it is completely oxidized and a molecule of oxalacetic acid is generated to begin the cycle again. Five pairs of hydrogen atoms are removed with each turn of the cycle which may be passed through appropriate hydrogen acceptors on through the cytochrome system to unite with oxygen and form water. About 15 energy-rich phosphate bonds are generated for each mole of pyruvate oxidized through the cycle. It is therefore an important energy pathway for biosynthesis. The reactions of the citric acid cycle are found in many microorganisms. The cycle accounts for the complete oxidation of any substances which are in the cycle and any substances which can be converted to one of the compounds in the cycle. Another important feature of the cycle is that at various steps intermediates can be withdrawn for synthesis of amino acids, fatty acids, and other cellular constituents, and the cycle provides for replacement of the cycle components.

**Hexosemonophosphate Shunt Pathway.** An alternative pathway for the oxidation of phosphorylated glucose to carbon dioxide and water not involving the glycolytic pathway and the citric acid cycle has been found in microorganisms. It is referred to as the *hexosemonophosphate shunt* or the *oxidative pentose phosphate cycle.* For the preliminary steps of the cycle, see Example 3.9.

EXAMPLE 3.9

$$\text{glucose-6-phosphate} \xrightarrow{-2H} \text{6-phosphogluconic acid}$$

$$\text{6-phosphogluconic acid} \xrightarrow[-CO_2]{-2H} \text{ribulose-5-phosphate}$$

$$\text{ribulose-5-phosphate} \underset{\text{isomerase}}{\rightleftharpoons} \text{xylulose-5-phosphate} \rightleftharpoons \text{ribose-5-phosphate}$$

EXAMPLE 3.10

$$6 \text{ glucose-6-phosphate} \longrightarrow 6\ CO_2 + 5 \text{ glucose-6-phosphate}$$

The five-carbon sugars from the oxidative decarboxylation of 6-phosphogluconic acid enter into a series of reactions wherein for each six moles of glucose-6-phosphate, one is oxidized to carbon dioxide and water and five mole. of glucose-6-phosphate are regenerated. $NADP^+$ is the coenzyme for these reactions and two moles of NADPH + $H^+$ are formed for each mole of glucose-6-phosphate which is oxidized to ribulose-5-phosphate. For the overall reaction, see Example 3.10.

By the use of isotopically labeled sugars, the relative amounts of respiration that proceed through the hexosemonophosphate shunt pathway and the glycolysis-citric acid cycle pathway has been determined for many bacteria and several microorganisms other than bacteria (Cheldelin *et al.*, 1962).

For *Acetobacter suboxydans* which does not ferment, but oxidizes glucose, the hexosemonophosphate shunt has been found to account for 100 per cent of the carbon dioxide evolved. For many other organisms, the respiration by this pathway ranges from 10 to 30 per cent with the rest going through the glycolytic pathway and the citric acid cycle. It is a major pathway of respiration and is of significance in supplying five-carbon sugars for nucleotide synthesis and in formation of NADPH + $H^+$ for fatty acid biosynthesis.[2]

Many bacteria use more than one pathway in the aerobic degradation of carbohydrate. A detailed discussion of aerobic pathways of sugar degradation by microorganisms is given by Cheldelin (Cheldelin *et al.*, 1962). The amount of energy available to the organism from aerobic (respiratory) and anaerobic (fermentative) metabolism is different. In the ethanol or lactic acid fermentation of glucose, the potential energy available is about 50,000 and 57,000 calories per mole of glucose. (See Example 3.11.) There is a net synthesis of two molecules of ATP (energy-rich phosphate) for each hexose unit fermented, each representing about 11,500 calories or a total of about 46 per cent of the total energy becoming available to the cell in the alcoholic fermentation. In the complete oxidation of glucose, the potential energy available is about 688,000 calories. (See Example 3.12.) Of this amount, about 64 per cent is available to the cell in the form of phosphate bond energy, 30 moles of ATP from each two moles of pyruvate oxidized via the citric acid cycle, and 8 moles of ATP from the aerobic conversion of glucose to two moles of pyruvate. Some of the energy not captured as phosphate bond energy is degraded in the form of heat during fermentation and respiration. While certain assumptions are made in the calculations, experiments with muscle tissue have shown from 1 to 3 moles of ATP are formed for each atom of oxygen consumed in biological oxidation.

For a more thorough discussion of microbial metabolism, the student is urged to read the material relating to this subject in Stanier *et al.* (1963), Thimann (1963), Baldwin (1960), Oginsky and Umbreit (1959), and Gunsalus and Stanier (1961).

## USEFULNESS OF BIOCHEMICAL INFORMATION IN IDENTIFICATION AND CLASSIFICATION OF MICROOGANISMS

The extreme diversity among the bacteria is expressed more strongly in their physiology and biochemistry than in their

[2] $NADP^+$ = triphosphopyridine nucleotide (oxidized form), also called coenzyme II, TPN. NADPH + $H^+$ = reduced form.

EXAMPLE 3.11

$$\text{(a)}\quad C_6H_{12}O_6 \longrightarrow 2\ CO_2 + 2C_2H_5OH + 50{,}000 \text{ calories}$$

$$\text{(b)}\quad C_6H_{12}O_6 \longrightarrow 2\ CH_3CHOHCOOH + 57{,}000 \text{ calories}$$

TABLE 3.4

TESTS FOR SPECIFIC ENZYME ACTIVITY

| Enzyme | Substrate | Products of Reaction | Observed Result |
|---|---|---|---|
| Catalase | $H_2O_2$ | $H_2O + O_2$ | evolution of oxygen |
| Cytochrome oxidase | p-phenylenediamine | oxidized dye | leuco. to colored dye |
| Urease | urea | $CO_2 + NH_3$ | test for alkaline reaction |
| Phosphatase | phenolphthaleinphosphate | phenolphthalein + inorganic phosphate | test for phenolphthalein |
| Amino acid decarboxylase | amino acid | corresponding amine + $CO_2$ | increase in alkalinity |
| Arginine dihydrolase | arginine | ornithine + $CO_2$ + $NH_3$ | increase in alkalinity |
| Substrate dehydrogenase | specific substrate + reducible dye | oxidized substrate + reduced dye | colorless dye |
| Proteolytic Enzymes | | | |
| gelatinase | gelatin | peptides and amino acids | liquified gelatin |
| casein digestion | casein | peptides and amino acids | liquified casein |
| rennin | milk | coagulated casein | curdled milk |
| coagulase | blood plasma | clotting of plasma | plasma clot |
| Carbohydrases | | | |
| amylase | starch agar | dextrin, maltose, glucose | solubilized starch, clear zone adjacent to colonies |
| Lipase | tributyrin or fat agar | fatty acids + glycerol | clear zone adjacent to colonies |

Tests for Fermentation Products

| Test | Substrate | Product(s) Formed | Observed Result |
|---|---|---|---|
| Indol | media containing tryptophane | indol | color test for indol |
| Voges–Proskauer | glucose broth | acetylmethylcarbinol | color test for AMC |
| Methyl red | glucose broth | formic, acetic, lactic, succinic acids | acid to methyl red |
| Hydrogen sulfide from proteins | proteose peptone Fe citrate agar | $H_2S$ | black Fe S |
| Sulfate reduction | sulfate containing broth + Fe citrate | $H_2S$ | black Fe S |
| Nitrate reduction | nitrate containing broth | $NaNO_2$ | color test for nitrite or test for absence of nitrate |

Fermentation of Various Organic Compounds

| | | | |
|---|---|---|---|
| Fermentability of various organic carbon sources—sugars, alcohols, organic acids | nutrient broth containing a specific carbon source | acid formation and sometimes gaseous $CO_2$ and $H_2$ | change in indicator from neutral to acid color or, in some cases, growth or its absence |

EXAMPLE 3.12

$$C_6H_{12}O_6 + 6O_2 \longrightarrow 6\ CO_2 + 6H_2O + 688{,}000 \text{ calories}$$

morphology. A limited number of morphological characters are available with which to identify and classify the bacteria. Therefore, it is necessary to exploit for this purpose properties concerned with the activity of microorganisms. An adequate definition of bacteria requires an understanding of what they do in addition to how they look. Biochemical characteristics, physiological characteristics, and serological characteristics (the latter based on chemistry of the structural components of the bacterial cell) are of extreme usefulness in describing microorganisms. A microscopic examination permits the placing of microorganisms into several groups based on shape alone; however, each group will have an extreme diversity of types based on characteristics such as biochemical activity, serology, and pathogenicity. The latter two characteristics will be considered in succeeding chapters.

In tabular form (Table 3.4) are listed some of the biochemical tests which are routinely used in describing and helping to identify bacteria.

## REFERENCES

BALDWIN, E. Dynamic Aspects of Biochemistry. 3rd Ed. Cambridge Univ. Press, London, 1960.

BURROWS, W. Textbook of Microbiology. 18th Ed. W. B. Saunders Co., Philadelphia, 1963.

CHELDELIN, V. H., *et al.* Comparative Biochemistry, Vol. III, pp. 429–92, M. Florkin and H. S. Mason (eds.) Academic Press, Inc., New York, 1962.

DIXON, M., and WEBB, E. C. Enzymes. Academic Press, Inc., New York, 1958.

GUNSALUS, I. C., and STANIER, R. Y. The Bacteria; A Treatise on Structure and Function, Vol. II, Metabolism. Academic Press, Inc., New York, 1961.

OGINSKY, E., and UMBREIT, W. W. An Introduction to Bacterial Physiology. 2nd Ed. W. H. Freeman and Co., San Francisco, 1959.

STANIER, R. Y., *et al.* The Microbial World. 2nd Ed. Prentice-Hall, Inc., Englewood Cliffs, N. J., 1963.

THIMANN, K. V. The Life of Bacteria; Their Growth, Metabolism and Relationships. 2nd Ed. Macmillan Co., New York, 1966.

# 4

# Bacteriological Techniques and Methods

The details of technical procedures which are used in the study of microorganisms are found in books entirely devoted to the subject, but a brief discussion of some of the techniques is desirable in this text also. This discussion is based upon the reasons for and the results of the various laboratory procedures, as well as upon the techniques themselves. A chapter such as this one is found in the back pages of many textbooks, but is here deliberately so the student may realize the importance of this subject to his success in learning bacteriology.

The most fundamental technique in the study of bacteria is the procedure whereby a pure culture is obtained. Since bacteria, yeasts, molds, and filterable viruses are able to produce such varied changes in the food on which they live, it is evident that each species must play a part in the process. All knowledge of bacterial metabolism as represented by chemical changes in inanimate material and by disease in living plants and animals is built upon the *specificity* of microorganisms for the particular kind of food from which they obtain the essentials for life. It is obvious, therefore, that the study of any metabolic process involving microorganisms or their products must be based upon the *pure culture.*

The morphology of bacteria is used as a basis for recognition and differentiation. It also reveals something of the nature of the various types of cells which aids in the understanding of metabolic processes. The microscope is an essential instrument in microbiology, and a knowledge of the manipulation of the instrument facilitates the work of the student and assures his success in learning. Living microorganisms suspended in a fluid medium are so refractive for light rays that their structure is not easily seen when examined under the microscope; in fact, their exact shape and size are difficult to obtain in an unstained preparation. Methods of staining the various cells have added definitely to the knowledge concerning them. Bacteria react differently to the various staining processes. Their varied reactions are of value in classifying them into groups.

Most of the knowledge concerning microorganisms is based upon a study of them under artificial conditions, that is, in captivity. The effect of large numbers of them upon a particular medium is different from the effect of just a few, as might be expected. The effect of large numbers in an environment of optimum conditions for growth is different from the effect of small numbers in a natural environment surrounded by all the hazards of normal life. The study of the natural life of bacteria is difficult because of their small size and their association with different bacterial species. Our knowledge, therefore, out of necessity, is based upon the results obtained from the study of bacteria in an artificial environment.

The methods used for bacteriological analyses are varied. An assortment of special equipment, tubes, dishes, flasks, etc., is peculiar to bacteriology. Many different foods are concocted for microorganisms. These foods are changed by the action of

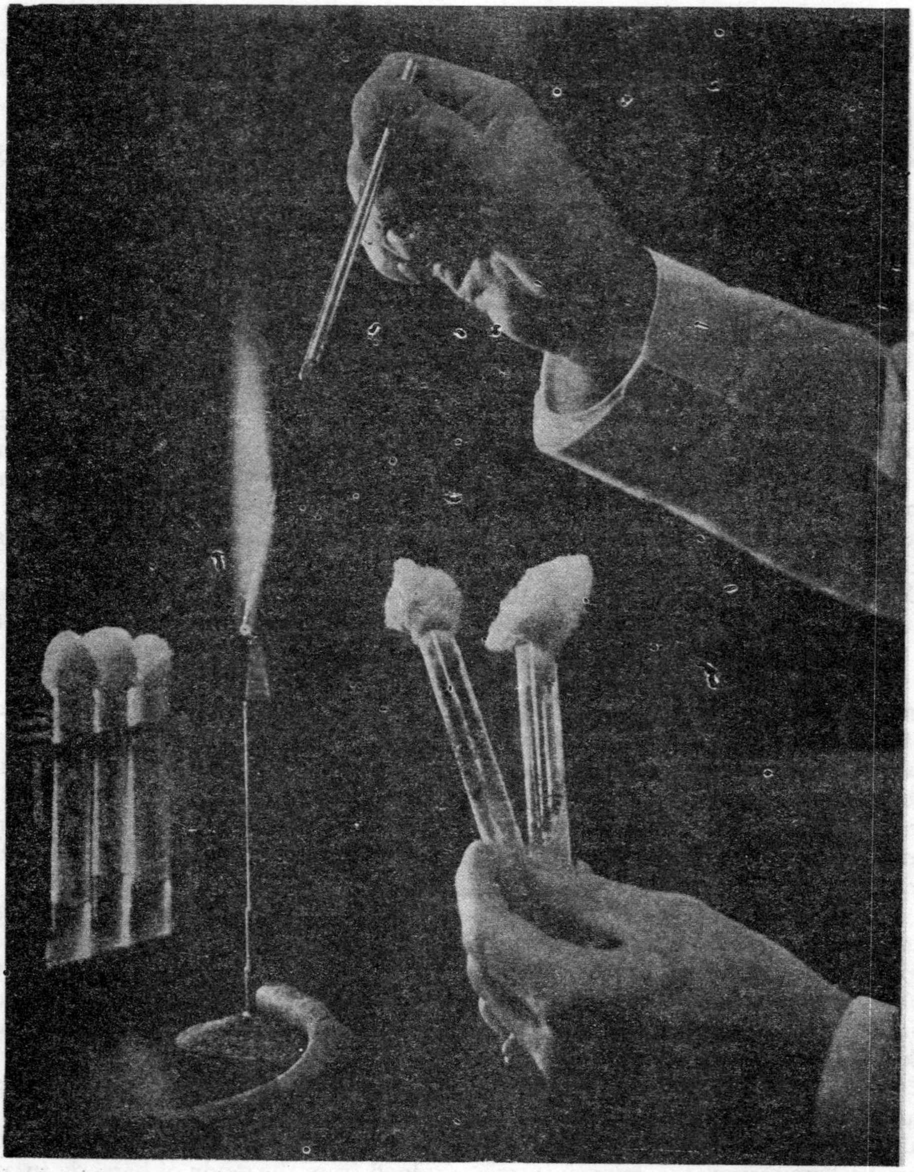

FIG. 4.1—Technique of media inoculation. (Photo by John Barry, courtesy The Iowa State University Veterinarian.)

bacteria so that numerous tests are necessary to detect the resulting products.

The discussion of bacteriological techniques and methods is divided into the following parts: *Isolation and Cultivation Techniques, Microscopic Examination, Stains and Staining Methods,* and *Culture Media and Tests.*

## ISOLATION AND CULTIVATION TECHNIQUES

Cultures of bacteria and materials suspected of containing pathogenic bacteria are transferred to culture media by means of a platinum wire or other wire which is not easily disintegrated by the flame (Fig. 4.1). In cases where a large amount of inoculum is transferred, a sterile glass pipette is used. In the collection of material for bacteriological examination, care must be used to eliminate contamination. Fluids must be collected in sterile glass tubes; tissue surfaces must be seared with a hot spatula before a specimen is taken. Even when all precautions are used, material such as water, urine, milk, tissues, and tissue exudates may contain more than one species of bacteria. In some cases the organism may be present in pure culture, but this cannot be depended upon as being a general rule.

### Methods of Securing Pure Cultures

Prior to the use of solid media by Koch, pure cultures of bacteria were obtained by the dilution method. This method is rarely, if ever, used today for that purpose, although it is commonly employed to decrease the number of bacteria in material previous to the use of other techniques, whereby the organism is obtained in pure culture.

The method most commonly used for isolating bacteria in pure culture is known as the *plating method;* "plating" because Koch used a glass plate in his original technique. The *Petri dish* or *Petri plate* (Fig. 4.2) is now used for that purpose. The Petri dish is composed of two circular glass plates, one slightly smaller than the other so that it fits into the outer one loosely

FIG. 4.2—The Petri culture dish.

enough to permit the passage of air and sufficiently tight to prevent the passage of dust particles. After the dishes are once sterilized they remain so when they are given reasonable care, but they should be stored in metal or cardboard containers to assure sterility. Two methods are used in the plating technique—the streak plate and the pour plate. The objective of both methods is to obtain the growth of the desired organism in pure culture in well-isolated colonies. In the streak plate the material from which the organism is to be isolated is streaked across the surface of solid medium in parallel lines; the organisms grow in separated colonies along the ends of the last few streaks. In making a pour plate, a solid medium contained in a test tube is melted, cooled to 45°C., and inoculated with the organism. The medium and organism are mixed by rapidly rotating the tube between the palms of the hands. The lid of a sterile Petri dish is elevated just enough to permit the insertion of the open end of the test tube from which the medium is poured into the dish. The medium in the dish is allowed to cool. The organisms grow throughout the medium in well-isolated colonies from which the desired organism is "fished" and transferred to a tube of medium in a pure culture. In case the material to be examined is heavily seeded with bacteria, preliminary dilution in sterile water or bouillon is necessary in order to diminish the number of organisms. It is obvious that if bacteria are too numerous, one colony grows over another, and isolation of a pure culture is impossible.

Barber has devised a capillary pipette method whereby it is possible to pick up a single bacterial cell from a drop of suspended medium and transfer it into another drop of medium. This method has been found useful in the study of bacterial dissociation and essential in the study of bacterial cyclogeny. Modifications of the Barber method have been made by many investigators.

A sporeforming organism may be isolated from a nonsporeproducing one by heating the medium in which both are contained to 80°C. for 15 minutes. The spores will resist that temperature while all other cells are killed.

Some chemicals such as crystal violet inhibit the growth of certain bacteria but permit the growth of others. When these chemicals, in correct proportions, are added to media, the isolation of organisms in pure cultures is obtained. Crystal violet inhibits the growth of gram-positive bacteria but permits the growth of gram-negative forms. Antiformin permits the growth of tubercle bacilli but inhibits the growth of other species. The various inhibiting agents will be discussed more fully in chapters devoted to specific organisms.

A pure culture of a pathogenic microorganism can be obtained in many cases by the injection of the suspected mixture of bacteria into a susceptible experimental animal. Tissues from a suspected case of blackleg may be contaminated with putrefactive bacteria before they are submitted to the laboratory for diagnosis. Since many putrefactive bacteria, as well as the blackleg organism, are anaerobic the isolation of the latter is at times difficult. It may be accomplished by plating the material and incubating the plates anaerobically. Fluid from the suspected material, however, is often injected into a guinea pig. The putrefactive contaminating bacteria do not multiply in the tissues of the guinea pig, whereas *Clostridium chauvoei* grows freely and causes the death of the animal. A pure culture of the organism can be obtained from the infected tissues.

The filterable viruses can be isolated in pure culture by the process of passing the fluid containing the virus through a sterile filter and collecting it in a sterile test tube or flask. An illustration of an apparatus

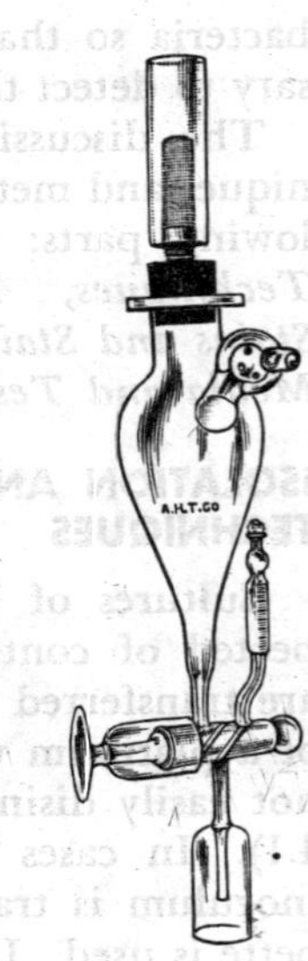

FIG. 4.3—Filtering apparatus for small amounts of fluid.

suitable for filtering small amounts of fluids is given in Figure 4.3.

In a previous chapter, the factors such as temperature and oxygen, which influence the growth of microorganisms, were discussed. A brief description of the techniques for obtaining those conditions follows.

### Incubation of Cultures

Cultures of various kinds of microorganisms are grown in an incubator which is well insulated, assuring a constant temperature. Incubators vary in size and in the material with which they are constructed. Usually heat is supplied from two sources, the gas flame and the electric element. Temperature is controlled by means of a thermostat.

The usual temperature at which pathogenic bacteria are grown is 37.5°C. Gelatin cultures, however, are liquefied at this temperature; consequently, they are usually kept in an incubator regulated to 20°C. Many of the nonpathogenic organisms grow more abundantly at temperatures ranging from 25°–30°C. Since various microorganisms have an optimum temperature for growth, the thermostat of the incubator must be adjusted to the desired temperature. In laboratories where different varieties of organisms are studied, it is obvious that an incubator for each desired temperature must be available.

### Anaerobic Methods

In the cultivation of anaerobic bacteria two general principles are involved: the reduction of oxygen tension, and the maintenance of the reduced tension. Hall has outlined the anaerobic methods under those two principles as follows:

I. Reduction of oxygen tension
  A. Biological reduction
    Aerobic-anaerobic symbiosis
      Symbiont in the medium
      Symbiont in the air chamber
    Use of animal and plant tissues
  B. Physical reduction
    Boiling
    Evacuation
    Use of inert gases
  C. Chemical reduction
    Agent in air chamber
      Catalytic ignition of hydrogen and residual oxygen
      Reduction by phosphorus
      Reduction by iron compounds
      Reduction by alkaline pyrogallol
    Agent in the medium
II. Maintenance of reduced oxygen tension
  A. Portion of medium sealed off
    Deep medium seals
    Insoluble liquid seals
    Mechanical seals
  B. Air chamber sealed
    Fusion of glass outlet
    Mechanical seals

The biological reduction of oxygen tension is nature's way of producing optimum conditions for the growth of anaerobic bacteria inasmuch as they grow in the presence of aerobic forms or in tissues which absorb oxygen. In the laboratory two common methods are patterned after this process. Aerobic bacilli, such as *Bacillus subtilis,* are grown symbiotically in the same tube with an anaerobe, such as *Clost. tetani.* The growth and toxin production of the latter can be demonstrated in the filtrate of the medium. If the two organisms are grown in separate tubes or flasks, these results are not obtained. One of the most common media used in laboratories is minced meat. Liver, spleen, brain, or any other tissue may be finely divided and added to nutrient broth. Fresh, sterile tissues are more suitable than the ground, cooked tissues, but the latter are satisfactory for general use. When the medium is sterilized, all air is driven from it. Upon cooling, air permeates the upper few centimeters of the medium, but anaerobic conditions exist below that area because the particles of meat block its passage. Bits of steel wool or iron filings will accomplish the same results.

Fluid media of any kind can be used for the cultivation of anaerobes if a layer of oil is placed upon the medium prior to sterilization. Obviously the heavy oil does not permit oxygen to enter the medium.

A common method used in most bacteriology laboratories is to exhaust air from an anaerobic apparatus (Fig. 4.4) and then add $CO_2$ and/or nitrogen. A pressure cooker fitted with two valves also provides a suitable container. Any medium may be inoculated with an anaerobic organism and placed in the container.

Special anaerobic media are available which are routinely used for the growth of anaerobic bacteria. Alkaline sulfides and sulfhydryl compounds such as thioglycollate, glutathione, cystine, and sodium formaldehyde sulfoxylate may be incorporated into any appropriate medium. The above compounds reduce the oxygen potential to

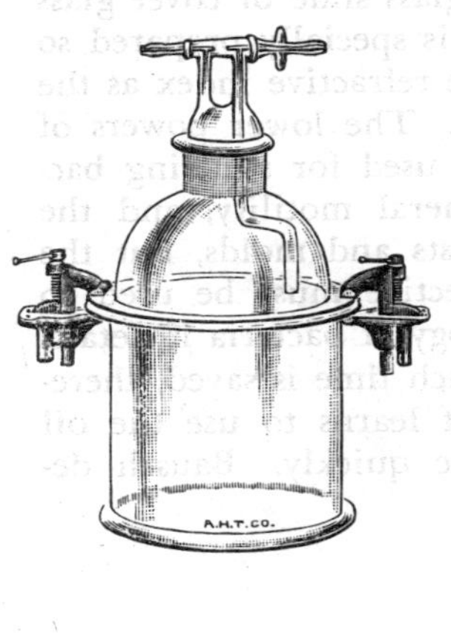

FIG. 4.4 — Novy anaerobic apparatus.

provide suitable anaerobic conditions. A small amount of agar added to the medium will also provide anaerobic conditions.

## MICROSCOPIC TECHNIQUE

The use of the microscope is indispensable in the study of bacteria. The student must understand the mechanism of magnification and the essentials of correct illumination if he is to study cultures of bacteria with success. The student in veterinary medicine has had previous courses in which he has become familiar with the manipulation of the microscope and with the general technique of microscopy, and for this reason it is not necessary to repeat these procedures; however, a few minimum essentials of technique which are used in the study of microorganisms are outlined.

### Oil Immersion Objectives

The small size of bacteria requires the use of the highest powers of magnification possible. The total magnification of a microscope is obtained by multiplying the magnification due to the objective by the magnification due to the eyepiece. The magnification of the usual student microscope is the total of a 97 × objective and a 10 × eyepiece or 970. The higher the power of the objective, the smaller is the opening through which the light may reach the eye. It is necessary, therefore, that all possible light shall enter the lens in order to assure a well-illuminated field. This means that light must not be lost by refraction as it passes through the glass slide. For this reason, immersion contact is made between the objective and glass slide or cover glass with oil. This oil is specially prepared so as to have the same refractive index as the oil immersion lens. The lower powers of the microscope are used for studying bacterial colonies, general motility, and the morphology of yeasts and molds, but the oil immersion objective must be used to study the morphology of bacteria if details are to be seen. Much time is saved, therefore, if the student learns to use the oil immersion objective quickly. Bausch describes this technique as follows:[1]

> **Apply a small quantity of oil to the front lens of the objective or to the cover glass, using for this purpose the rod in the oil bottle. Lower the objective very carefully with the coarse adjustment until contact is made. This can best be determined by watching the space between objective and slide with the eye well down to the level of the stage. At the instant contact is made, a flash of light will illuminate the oil. When this flash is seen, the objective will be near enough to focus by means of the fine adjustment.**

The presence of dust or air bubbles in the immersion oil may destroy the definition of the best objective; therefore, it is very essential to keep the oil bottle stoppered at all times. If bubbles are trapped between objective and slide, it may be necessary to apply fresh oil and to refocus in order to get rid of them.

Special care must be observed if a low power objective is used after an oil immersion. The oil must invariably be removed from the top of the cover glass by wiping with lens paper. The front of the objective should always be cleaned in the same manner immediately after it has been used. If oil does dry, it may be removed by using lens paper moistened with a *minute* amount of *xylol.*

### Illumination

The regulation of the light which illuminates the object is of great importance in microscopic work of all kinds and is of utmost importance in the study of bacteria.

Natural and artificial light are used. Natural light from a north window is an excellent source but has the disadvantage of variability due to cloudy weather. Direct sunlight is too bright for microscopic use. The electric light is the most common source of illumination. A variety of lamps is available for this purpose. Blue and white, frosted and nonfrosted bulbs are used. When the white bulb is used the light is most satisfactory when filtered through a blue glass in the form of a shade or a disc placed in the microscope substage

[1] E. Bausch. *The Use and Care of the Microscope.* Bausch and Lomb Optical Co., Rochester, 1948, p. 9.

condenser. The light is adjusted after the object has been brought into focus by manipulation of the mirror and the condenser.

The mirror on the microscope is double, plane on one side and concave on the other. When skylight is used as a light source, either side may be used, but the plane side gives a more even light. The plane mirror is always used with the substage condenser (Fig. 4.5).

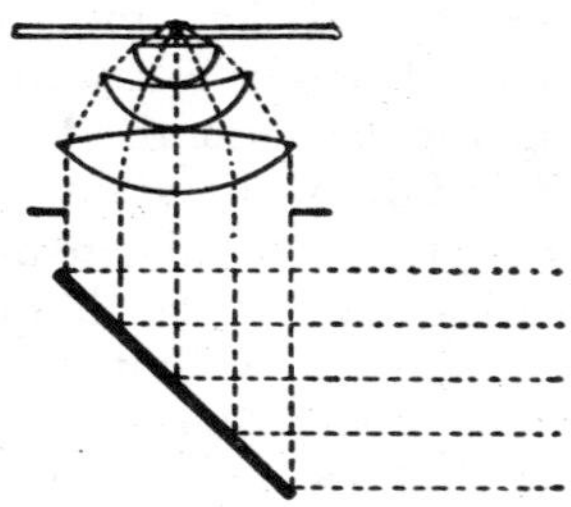

**FIG. 4.5—The path of light reflected from the mirror through the substage condenser. (Courtesy Bausch and Lomb.)**

The substage condenser, frequently called the Abbe condenser, is used to concentrate light rays on the object. It is a system of lenses so arranged that the light is refracted, and the rays converge a short distance above the top lens (Fig. 4.5). The intensity of light is governed by lowering or elevating the condenser. For oil immersion magnification the condenser is raised near the level of the stage in order to assure a maximum amount of light.

The substage iris diaphragm is also used to adjust illumination. It should not be used to control the density of illumination but to bring out details in the object which is being studied.

### Dark-Field Illumination

Some types of microorganisms, such as the spirochetes, are not stained by the usual methods but are made visible by the dark-field method. Details of the structure of some of the large bacteria, as well as yeasts and molds, are demonstrated by this technique. Various methods are available to demonstrate dark-field illumination. All of them depend on the blocking of the central rays of light but allowing the passage of a ring of rays around the outer edge of the condenser. These light rays do not enter the microscope unless they are reflected from the object which appears brightly illuminated against a dark background. The three common condensers which are used for this method of illumination are illustrated in Figure 4.6. The dark ground stop is a metal disc which is inserted into the slot in the lower part of

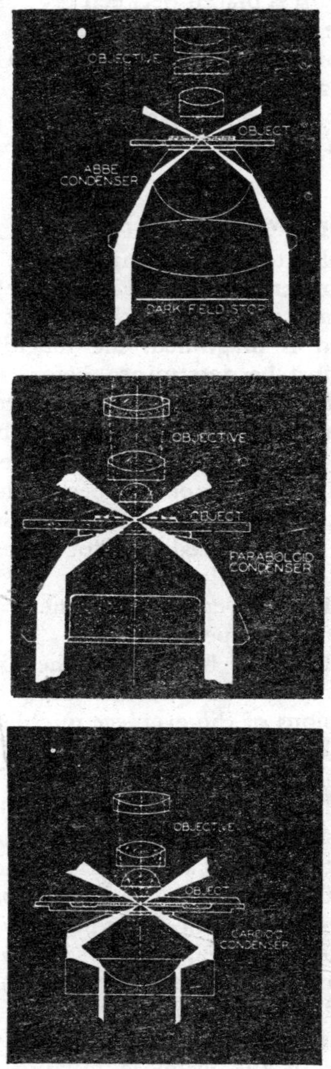


FIG. 4.6—Condensers used for dark-field illumination. (Courtesy Bausch and Lomb.)

the Abbe condenser. It is used satisfactorily to demonstrate the principle of dark-field illumination with the lower powers of magnification. In the paraboloid condenser the central light rays are blocked out by means of an enamel disc on the lens of the condenser. There is no disc in the cardioid condenser since the rays are reflected as they enter the object from the side.

In dark-field illumination, water or immersion oil is placed between the condenser and the object slide. When the higher power of magnification is used, a funnel stop, or a special objective, must be inserted in the oil immersion objective to prevent direct rays from entering the margin of the lens.

### Measuring Microorganisms

In order to measure microscopic objects a micrometer scale is used in the eyepiece of the microscope. Since the object to be measured is magnified, the magnification factor must be determined before the size of the object is known. A stage micrometer is used to determine the distance between the lines of the eyepiece micrometer scale. When the microscope has been calibrated, the eyepiece may be used to measure objects. The procedure for measuring bacteria is as follows:

1. Insert eyepiece micrometer in the microscope.
2. Examine bacteria on the slide and record their size in terms of divisions of the eyepiece micrometer.
3. Remove the slide of bacteria and insert the stage micrometer.
4. Determine the relation of the division of the eyepiece micrometer to that of the stage micrometer.

5. Compute the size of the bacteria. The divisions on the stage micrometer are usually 0.01 mm. The unit of measurement of bacteria is the micron (0.001 mm); therefore, the divisions are $10\mu$ in size. If the calibration of the eyepiece shows that two divisions of the eyepiece micrometer are equal to one division of the stage micrometer, then each eyepiece division represents $5\mu$. The size of the bacteria which have been measured are computed on that basis.

### The Hanging Drop

The motility of bacteria is observed best by examining a hanging drop in which the organisms are able to move about freely. A special glass slide with a hollow depression in the center is used for this purpose. The technique is as follows:

Place a thin layer of petrolatum or vaseline around the rim of the hollow-ground slide. Transfer a loopful of broth containing the bacteria to the center of a cover slip. Lower the slide onto the cover slip and press it firmly in place in the rim of petrolatum. Invert it quickly and handle carefully so as not to disturb the drop which is hanging from the cover slip into the hollow of the slide. Examine the preparation with the lower power objective in order to locate the edge of the drop. The organisms may be studied for detail with the higher powers of magnification. The glass slide and cover slip must be absolutely free of dust and fingerprints to assure clear vision.

## STAINING METHODS

Bacteria are generally so transparent when they are examined in the living condition that the details of their morphology are difficult to discern. It is customary to stain these organisms with various aniline dyes which render them distinctly visible. Some progress has been made in differential staining of the various parts of bacterial cells. Bacteria react differentially to some strains. This is an aid in classifying them.

The stains used in biologic work for the most part are known as "coal-tar" dyes because most of them are derivatives of the hydrocarbon, benzene ($C_6H_6$). "Coal-tar" dyes are nonacid salts of color bases or alkali salts of color bases. "Acidic" and "basic" as applied to dyes refer to the affinity of the chromogenic radicle for acidic and basic groups. The dye is acidic or basic according to the character of its auxochromes. Acidic or basic as applied to dyes has no reference to the hydrogen-hydroxyl-ion reaction and is not to be interpreted in the true chemical sense. Both acidic and basic dyes are more potent in alkaline media. Basic dyes are sold as salts of a colorless acid such as hydrochloric, sulfuric, oxalic, or acetic. Acid dyes are sold as sodium, potassium, calcium, or ammonium salts.

The present-day conception of dyes is based on molecular structure. The basis of the structure is the benzene ring of Kekule. If derivatives, with this structure, contain groups of elements known as "chromophores," they impart the property of color. Chromogenes, although colored, are not dyes. They may coat the cells superficially, but the color can be easily removed by the mechanical process of washing. To become a dye the chromogen derivative must contain, in addition to the chromophore, other groups known as "auxochromes." These auxochromes impart to the compound the property of electrolytic dissociation, furnishing it with salt-forming properties, and thus converting it into a dye.

Dyes probably fulfill their function by both chemical and physical processes. The chemical process of staining is thought to be enhanced by the number of auxochromic groups in the dye as well as the number and adequacy of the chromophilic groups in the cells to be stained. The physical process depends on surface attraction, osmosis, diffusion, and adsorption. Factors which no doubt promote these processes are the size of the dye molecule and adequate pore-volume of the material to be stained.

The abundance of nucleoprotein in bacteria appears to explain their affinity, at least for basic "coal-tar" dyes. In their staining reactions bacteria behave as if they are composed largely of protein. The amount of dye taken up by bacteria and the firmness with which it is held doubtless depend, in a large part, on the hydrogen-ion concentration of the bacterial protein. The general rule is that the larger the number of hydrogen atoms that have been replaced by methyl, ethyl, or phenyl groups, the deeper the color. A dye retains its color only as long as its affinities for hydrogen are not completely satisfied. Since the pH of bacterial protein changes with age, this may account for the variations in staining between young and old cultures of the same organism.

### Mordants and Decolorizing Agents

When bacteria are present in tissues or exudates, they may not be observed because of their small size unless correct staining methods are used. Various methods are available whereby the organisms are stained more deeply than the tissue cells, or the stain in the tissue cells is removed by decolorizing agents, leaving the bacteria as previously colored. Chemical agents which fix the stain, or cause it to penetrate more deeply into the organism, are called *mordants*. Aniline oil, phenol, potassium iodide, tannic acid, and various metallic salts are all used as mordants for different organisms and in various staining procedures. Prolongation of the period of staining and heating increases the intensity with which bacteria and their spores are stained. After the organism has been stained deeply and the stain has been fixed by the action of a mordant, the dye is not removed easily; however, bacteria vary in this respect. Tissue cells also vary, which makes differential staining possible. The stain is removed from certain bacteria and tissue cells by decolorizing agents such as dilute alcohols, acetone, ether, dilute mineral and organic acids, and hot water. The decolorized cells are counterstained with a dye of a contrasting color.

### Method of Preparing a Bacterial Film for Staining

A glass slide is cleaned until it is perfectly free from grease. If a drop of water does not spread evenly over the slide, it is not suitable for use. Hot water and alkaline washing powder usually clean the slide satisfactorily. It is necessary to place some slides in dilute acid or alcohol in order to remove the film which prevents the even spread of a drop of water. When the slide is clean, place a drop of bouillon containing the culture on the slide with the loop of the inoculating needle and smear it over a surface about the size of the small fingernail. When it has dried, fix the smear to the slide by passing it through the Bunsen flame a few times.

In making smears from cultures which have grown on solid media, an inoculating loop full of water is placed on the slide. Into this is mixed a small amount of the culture which has been removed from the growth with the tip of the straight inoculating needle. Too much of the culture must not be transferred or the smear will be too thick to be studied satisfactorily. Films of blood, pus, lymph, milk, and urine are prepared in the same manner. Tissue cells must be spread thinly, however, or the cells will obscure the bacteria which may be present, even when a differential stain is used.

The smears are allowed to dry in the air and are then passed through the Bunsen flame which fixes the film to the slide. Fixation by chemicals, such as methyl alcohol, saturated aqueous mercuric chloride, or formalin, is often used for tissue smears.

The preparation is then stained with the method which is most applicable to the particular organism.

The excess stain is removed by washing the slide with water which is removed by placing the slide between two layers of blotting paper. To assure the removal of all water the slide is passed through the flame.

Immersion oil may be placed directly on the stained film, or a glass cover slip mounted in oil may be placed upon the film.

In summary, the technique of preparing a bacterial film for examination consists of the following steps: (1) preparing the film; (2) drying in air; (3) fixing; (4) staining; (5) washing with water; (6) blotting; (7) drying; and (8) mounting.

## STAINS

### The Gram Stain

Christian Gram, a Dane, devised a method of staining bacteria in 1884. This method, universally called the Gram stain, has become the most common staining technique used in bacteriology. It consists of staining a prepared bacterial smear with gentian violet or crystal violet, mordanting with Lugol's iodine solution, washing with alcohol or acetone until all of the violet stain is removed, and counterstaining with a contrasting dye such as basic fuchsin or safranin. Those bacteria which retain the violet stain are called gram-positive, and those which are decolorized and stained red by the counterstain are gram-negative.

The detailed technique for the staining process is as follows:

1. Stain the film 2 minutes with Hucker's gentian violet prepared as follows:
   1 ml. saturated alcoholic solution of gentian violet or crystal violet (4 grams dye in 20 ml. of 95% ethyl alcohol).
   10 ml. of 1% ammonuim oxalate.
2. Wash with water and apply Gram's iodine 1 minute. Gram's iodine is prepared as follows:

| | |
|---|---|
| Iodine | 1 gm. |
| Potassium iodide | 2 gms. |
| Distilled water | 300 ml. |

3. Pour off excess fluid and wash with acetone (30 parts) and 95% alcohol (70 parts) until the smear ceases to lose color.
4. Wash with water.
5. Counterstain with 2% aqueous solution of safranin.
6. Wash with water, blot, dry, and examine.

Various theories have been advanced to explain the Gram-staining reaction. Benians contends that the iodine forms a large alcohol-soluble molecule with the gentian violet which is removed from the gram-negative bacteria but retained by those which stain gram-positive; the difference is due to the permeability of the cell walls of the two types. Churchman believes that gram-positive cells possess an outer cortex which is responsible for the retention of the gentian violet stain. Stearns and Stearns have shown that the proteins of gram-positive bacteria have an isoelectric point more toward the acid side than the gram-negative bacteria, which explains why gram-positive bacteria show a greater affinity for basic dyes. Deuszen has explained that Gram staining is due to a chemical reaction resulting from the compound-forming properties of the nucleoprotein of the bacterial cells.

The theory of Churchman has been upheld by Henry and Stacey, who have been able to "strip" gram-positive bacteria of an essential part of their gram-positive material, leaving gram-negative cytoskeletons and a gram-negative extract. These investigators were able to obtain this result by extracting washed bacterial cells at 60°C. with a 2 per cent aqueous solution of a bile salt in the presence of oxygen. The material in the extract can be precipitated by alcohol and consists of magnesium ribonucleate, inert polysaccharides, and traces of protein. It was possible to reconstitute the gram-positive cell by "plating" the extract back on the cytoskeleton. Those bacteria which are fundamentally gram-negative do not respond to such technique.

As further proof, Henry and Stacey were able to produce gram-negative bacteria from known gram-positive species, such as *Streptococcus salivarus,* by growing in a medium completely devoid of magnesium.

The most plausible explanation of the Gram process is that the gram-positive material is a high-molecular complex formed by the combination of a reduced basic protein substrate with magnesium ribonucleate.

### Alkaline Methylene Blue Stain

In some cases it is desirable to stain a bacterial smear without the use of a differential technique. Methylene blue has been one of the old "standby" stains for this purpose in bacteriology. It is also of value as a counterstain in many methods.

SOLUTION A

| | |
|---|---|
| Methylene blue (90% dye content) | 0.3 gm. |
| Ethyl alcohol (95%) | 30.0 ml. |

SOLUTION B

| | |
|---|---|
| KOH (0.01% by weight) | 100 ml. |

Solutions A and B are mixed, and the mixture is allowed to stain the smear 3–5 minutes. The preparation is then thoroughly washed with water.

### Carbol Fuchsin

This stain is often used in differential staining methods but is effective when used alone.

| | |
|---|---|
| Basic fuchsin | 1 ml. |
| Ethyl alcohol (absolute) | 10 ml. |
| 5% aqueous carbolic acid | 90 ml. |

The stain is allowed to act 1 to 2 minutes.

### Spore Stains

The compact nature of the bacterial spore prevents stains from penetrating to a depth which imparts color. The penetrability of the stain is usually increased by heat or prolonged contact. When once stained, the spore is not decolorized easily.

HANSEN'S METHOD

1. Prepare the film containing the sporeforming bacteria as usual.
2. Stain with steaming carbol fuchsin 5 minutes.
3. Decolorize with 5% acetic acid until the film is a light pink and then wash with water.
4. Counterstain 3 minutes with methylene blue.

The spores will be stained a bright red, and the vegetative part of the cell will be blue.

SCHAEFFER AND FULTON'S METHOD

1. Flood the slide with malachite green (5% aqueous solution allowed to stand ½ hour and filtered) and heat to steaming three or four times within ½ a minute.
2. Wash off excess stain and continue washing ½ minute.
3. Apply 0.5% aqueous safranin for ½ minute.

The spores will retain the green stain, and the vegetative cells will stain red.

### Flagella Stains

The flagella of bacteria are not visible in ordinary stained mounts and can be demonstrated only by a special technique. Young 12- to 18-hour cultures of bacteria should be used to demonstrate flagella. A tube containing 5 ml. of bouillon is inoculated with sufficient quantity of the growth removed from the agar surface to produce a slight turbidity. Incubate for an hour at 37°C. Drop two or three drops without mixing or spreading on a slide which is absolutely clean. It is essential that the slide be free of any acid, therefore such cleaning solutions must not be used. In passing the slide through the flame, one must always use the blue portion so as to eliminate carbon particles which may be deposited from the upper flame. The smear is allowed to dry in the air and *must not* be fixed by passing through the flame as is the usual practice. When completely dry the preparation is ready for staining.

Numerous staining methods are available, but the one proposed by Leifson gives satisfactory results.

### LEIFSON'S METHOD

Prepare basic fuchsin which has been certified for flagellar staining by making a 1.2% solution in 95% ethyl alcohol. Make a 3.0% solution of tannic acid in distilled water and a 1.5% solution of sodium chloride. The latter two compounds must be free of impurities of any kind.

A stock solution is made by mixing equal quantities of the three ingredients. In order to prevent change during storage the stain is kept in the refrigerator.

In the staining process 1 ml. of stain is applied to the smear and allowed to remain 5 to 15 minutes depending on the age of the stain and the temperature of the air in the laboratory. Upon standing, a precipitate forms on the slide due to the evaporation of alcohol. When the precipitate has changed to a rust color, the stain may be washed from the slide. After washing, the slide may be blotted lightly and allowed to dry in the air.

The smear must be examined under the oil-immersion lens. The flagella are pink or red, depending on the depth of the stain, and the bacterial body may not be stained or be faintly pink.

In order to have a contrasting stain the smear may be counterstained with methylene blue by allowing the stain to flow across the slide.

The staining of flagella is not an easy process, so numerous trials must be made in order to secure a satisfactory preparation.

## Capsule Stains

The capsules of bacteria are fragile and cannot be stained by the usual methods.

### HISS'S METHOD

1. Prepare film, dry, and fix.
2. Stain with aniline oil gentian violet, or carbol fuchsin for 5 seconds, or until steam rises.
3. Wash off the stain with 20% aqueous copper sulfate solution.
4. Blot and dry in air. Do not wash.

### JOHNE'S METHOD

This is particularly suited for the demonstration of the capsules of the anthrax bacillus in smears from blood or tissues.

1. Dry the smear in air, and fix.
2. Stain with 2% aqueous gentian violet, heating slightly for ¼ to ½ minute.
3. Wash quickly in water.
4. Wash in 1% to 2% acetic acid 6 to 10 seconds.
5. Wash in water; mount in water under a cover slip to examine.

### INDIA INK METHOD

India ink may be used to demonstrate the presence of capsules. The organisms to be examined are mixed into a drop of ink placed on a glass slide. The mixture is pulled into a thin smear by the use of the end of another slide, in the same manner as blood smears are made. The preparation is allowed to dry and then examined under the high-dry objective. The capsulated bacteria will appear as clear zones surrounding the organism. The ink has been held back by the capsular material. Those bacteria which are noncapsulated appear as minute bright specks.

Instead of allowing the ink to dry, a cover slip may be placed on the drop and examined under the high-dry objective. Encapsulated bacteria will be seen floating in the ink.

Although these methods are not staining

processes they are simple and convenient techniques to use in the student laboratory.

### Stains for Metachromatic Granules

#### NEISSER'S STAIN

1. The smear of the organism is prepared in the usual way.
2. Flood the smear 10 to 30 seconds with Solution 1 prepared as follows:

| | |
|---|---|
| Methylene blue | 0.1 gm. |
| Absolute alcohol | 20 ml. |
| Glacial acetic acid | 5 ml. |
| Distilled water | 100 ml. |

3. Wash in water.
4. Counterstain with Bismarck brown or dilute safranin (preferably the latter) for a few seconds.
5. Blot, dry, and examine.

The granules will be a blackish-blue, and the body of the cells will be brown or pink, depending upon the counterstain.

#### ALBERT'S STAIN

1. Prepare the smear as usual.
2. Stain for 1 minute with Solution 1 which is prepared as follows:

| | |
|---|---|
| Toluidin blue | 0.15 gm. |
| Methyl green | 0.20 gm. |
| Acetic acid (glacial) | 1 ml. |
| Alcohol (95%) | 2 ml. |
| Distilled water | 100 ml. |

After standing for one day the solution is filtered and is ready for use.

3. Stain for 1 minute with Solution 2 prepared as follows:

| | |
|---|---|
| Iodine | 2 gms. |
| Potassium iodide | 3 gms. |
| Distilled water | 300 ml. |

4. Wash with water, blot, dry, and examine.

The granules stain black, the cross striations blue, and the intermediate portions a light green.

### Stains for Acid-fast Organisms

Bacteria of a certain group, of which the tubercle bacillus is the most important member, are spoken of as being acid-fast. It is difficult to stain them, but when they are once stained, the color is retained after a treatment with dilute acid. The cause of this acid-fast property is supposedly due to the lipoids which are present on the surface of the organism and also within the cell.

#### ZIEHL-NEELSEN'S METHOD

1. Smears are fixed with heat as usual.
2. Flood with carbol fuchsin and heat gently to steaming for 3 minutes.
3. Decolorize with acid alcohol composed as follows:

| | |
|---|---|
| Hydrochloric acid | 2 ml. |
| Alcohol (95%) | 98 ml. |

The smear is decolorized until the thinner parts are decolorized, and the heavier portions remain pink.

4. Counterstain with methylene blue for 1 minute.
5. Wash in water, blot, and dry.

The acid-fast bacteria are stained red, and the tissue cells and other bacteria are blue.

#### GABBETT'S METHOD

1. Prepare a film and stain as above with carbol fuchsin.
2. Stain for 1 minute with Gabbett's methylene blue prepared as follows:

| | |
|---|---|
| Methylene blue (dry) | 2 gms. |
| Sulfuric acid (sp. gr. 1.84) | 25 ml. |
| Distilled water | 75 ml. |

3. Wash in water and examine.

The acid-fast organisms will be red in a blue field.

### Stains for Blood Cells

Many special stains have been devised for demonstrating blood cells, some of which are used in bacteriologic and immunologic studies. A reliable blood stain is necessary in the study of phagocytosis and in studying bacteria which cause septicemic conditions. The stains most commonly used are the Romanowsky and Giemsa, each with numerous modifications. These stains may be purchased in tablet or powder form from a reliable dealer and are ready for use when mixed with the proper diluent.

#### WRIGHT'S STAIN

One of the most satisfactory blood stains for routine work is that of Wright. This stain can be purchased in liquid form ready for use, or in powder form from which a saturated solution is made as a stock solution. The stain is prepared for use by adding to 20 ml. of the filtered stock solution 5 ml. of methyl alcohol. This is applied to a blood smear and allowed to stand 1 minute. Distilled water is then added drop by drop until a metallic luster appears on the surface. The stain is allowed to act for 5 minutes; then it is washed off with distilled water, dried, and examined with or without oil immersion.

*Care must be taken in washing to float off the metallic sheen, for it forms a precipitate on the smear if allowed to settle there.*

### GIEMSA'S STAIN

1. Apply the following fixing agent to moist films for 12 hours:
   95% ethyl alcohol .................. 1 part
   Saturated aqueous $HgCl_2$ ........... 2 parts
2. Wash in water for a few seconds.
3. Apply Lugol's solution for 5 minutes.
4. Wash in water, then in 0.5% sodium thiosulfate.
5. Stain with Giemsa stain 8 to 10 hours.
6. Wash and mount.

A modification of this method consists of mixing 1 drop of concentrated Giesma in 20 drops of distilled water. After fixing the smear for 5 minutes in methyl alcohol, it is immersed in dilute stain and placed in a 37.5° incubator for 10 to 12 hours. It is then washed off with distilled water until the film has a slightly pink tinge. This method is recommended for staining brain tissue for Negri bodies.

## CULTURE MEDIA AND TESTS FOR METABOLIC PRODUCTS

Many different types of foods must be available for bacteria which are to be cultivated artificially; however, culture media are used for purposes other than supplying bacteria with the food essential for life. Microscopic examination alone is insufficient to differentiate closely related species of bacteria. For example, it is microscopically impossible to detect the difference between an organism which causes a specific intestinal infection such as typhoid fever and one which is a normal inhabitant of the intestinal tract such as *E. coli*. It is essential, therefore, to use different media in the differentiation of morphologically closely related types of bacteria.

Many different kinds of media which demonstrate the metabolism of the various species of microorganisms can be prepared, as was explained in the discussion of physiology in Chapter 2.

It must be emphasized that the listing of many media and differential tests is beyond the scope of this text. Many periodicals are devoted to this service and many laboratories manufacture dehydrated culture media which can be easily and quickly prepared. Those formulas which are given here are used in our laboratory for undergraduate and graduate courses and in research. Laboratories in parts of the world reached by this book may find them useful.

Some of the tests for metabolic products and the formulas for preparing common media are as follows:

### Meat Infusion Broth

This is a medium commonly used in the laboratory, and serves as a basis for the preparation of many others.

Fresh lean meat, beef or horse, is finely ground. Place 500 gms. in 1 liter of distilled water. Place in refrigerator overnight. Boil vigorously for ½ hour, maintaining the volume throughout by adding water. Filter through gauze and then paper to remove all meat particles. To each 1,000 ml. of infusion add 10 gms. peptone and 5 gms. of sodium chloride, then heat to dissolve. Adjust to pH 7.4–7.6. Boil for ½ hour and allow to cool. Filter through paper. Dispense in test tubes or flasks and sterilize 15 minutes at 15 pounds pressure.

Meat infusion broth is usually used to determine the type of growth produced in a fluid medium. Growth characteristics noted are (1) abundance and pellicle formation, (2) growth throughout the medium, and (3) the mucoid or granular character of the sediment.

### Beef Extract Broth

In much of the routine work, particularly in student laboratories, beef extract is substituted for meat infusion broth.

| Formula: | | |
|---|---|---|
| | beef extract | 5 gms. |
| | peptone | 10 gms. |
| | sodium chloride | 5 gms. |
| | distilled water | 1,000 ml. |

The ingredients are mixed together and heated until dissolved. The medium is then filtered, tubed, and sterilized.

### Sugar-free Broth

In all meat infusion and meat extract media, there is always a small percentage of sugar. Such media cannot be used for exact fermentation studies unless the sugar has been removed. In order to render a medium sugar-free, the meat infusion is inoculated with a culture of *E. coli* and incubated at 37°C. for 18 hours. The infusion is then sterilized and filtered, and is ready for use.

### Carbohydrate Broth

Any desired carbohydrate is added to sugar-free broth in preparing a medium for testing the fermenting ability of an organism. A 1% solution of the carbohydrate is usually used although a 0.5% solution is sufficient in some cases. A suitable indicator is commonly added to such a medium to detect acid formation. Sugar media are sterilized at lower temperatures or for shorter periods than most media because heat is apt to cause the decomposition of some of the carbohydrates. Sterilization with flowing steam for 30 minutes on three consecutive days is the usual procedure. The carbohydrates may be sterilized by filtration through a porcelain filter and then added to the basic medium. In addition to heat sterilization, the medium with the carbohydrate may be sterilized by filtration.

Two products of carbohydrate disintegration which are useful in the differentiation of bacteria are *acid* and *gas*.

The formation of acid is usually detected by the use of an indicator in the medium. If the total acidity or the final pH of the medium is desired, it is necessary to titrate the medium or to use a suitable indicator or potentiometer. The kind of acid which is formed is rarely determined in the study of the pathogenic species of bacteria.

In order to detect the formation of gas in carbohydrate fermentation, special tubes are used in which the gas collects. Two types of tubes commonly used are the Smith tube and the Durham tube. In the Smith tube the gas collects in the closed arm of the tube. In the Durham tube the gas collects in the small inverted vial. A considerable amount of gas escapes from both tubes since both have portions open to the air. The type of gas which is formed by fermentation is of use in the study of some bacteria. Two of the gases commonly produced are *carbon dioxide* and *hydrogen.*

**Voges-Proskauer Test.** Acetyl methyl carbinol is a product of dextrose cleavage which is formed by some bacteria in the presence of peptone. It is recognized by the addition of 1 ml. of a 10% solution of sodium hydroxide to approximately 5 ml. of the medium, then adding three or four drops of a 2% solution of ferric chloride. An eosin pink or red color develops near the surface of the medium when it is allowed to stand a few hours.

### Serum Broth

Many of the pathogenic bacteria grow more abundantly when the medium is enriched with blood serum. Blood serum is poured or aspirated from blood which has been taken under aseptic conditions and allowed to coagulate in flasks. The sterile serum is added to the basic meat infusion medium by means of a special filler pipette which has been sterilized. Serum may be poured directly into culture tubes if due caution is observed. Serum is added to the ratio of 1 ml. to 10 ml. of medium.

### Hiss Serum Water

Horse or cow serum is dialized to remove the salts and sugars which are normally present, diluted with three times its volume of distilled water, tubed, and sterilized at 100°C. for 20 minutes on three consecutive days. A 1% peptone water or sugar and salt-free nutrient broth may be used instead of distilled water. For fermentation tests an indicator and 1% of the desired carbohydrate is added. Acid formation is indicated by a change in reaction and a resulting coagulation of the serum. Gas production is apparent by bubbles of gas in the coagulated mass.

### Dunham's Solution

Peptone water is prepared by mixing 10 gms. of peptone and 5 gms. of sodium chloride in 1,000 ml. of distilled water. The medium is boiled for 5 minutes, adjusted to pH 7.6–7.8, cooled, and filtered through paper.

This medium is used as a basic medium to which carbohydrates may be added for fermentation studies and for indol production.

### Tryptophane Broth

This medium is prepared by using tryptone instead of peptone in the method described above. It is used almost exclusively to detect the formation of indol by bacteria.

**The Indol Test.** The medium is inoculated and incubated for two days. Various reagents may be used to detect the presence of indol but Kovac's reagent is considered very reliable.

KOVAC'S REAGENT

| | |
|---|---|
| Amyl alcohol | 75 ml. |
| Hydrochloric acid, conc. | 25 ml. |
| p-dimethyl-aminobenzaldehyde | 5 gms. |

The test is conducted by overlaying the medium with 2 ml. chloroform followed by 2 ml. Kovac's reagent. The medium and test reagents are not agitated. A positive test is apparent by the formation of a pink to deep red color in the alcohol layer.

Strips of filter paper may be soaked with saturated oxalic acid solution and suspended in the test tube above the medium. Indol formation is noted by the formation of a pink color in the paper strip during incubation.

### Milk

Most bacteria grow in milk, so it is used alone, or as an enriching substance for other media. Litmus milk is prepared by adding aqueous litmus solution to fresh skimmed milk until a deep purple color is obtained. Bromcresol purple milk is rapidly replacing litmus milk in many laboratories. It is prepared by adding 10 ml. of a 1.6% alcoholic solution of bromcresol purple to 1,000 ml. of milk.

The changes which bacteria are able to cause in milk are quite varied; this makes it an important differential medium. Milk is coagulated by a rennet-like enzyme or by the formation of acid produced by the fermentation of lactose. The coagulum may be soft or hard. Lactose may be fermented to gas which can be observed in the curd. Milk casein is peptonized by some bacteria but not by others. Casein may be digested but not coagulated. Many species of bacteria grow in milk without causing any physical change in the medium.

### Nutrient Gelatin

A good grade of granulated gelatin is added to meat broth or beef extract broth. Twelve to 15% is usually added; it is advisable to use 15% during hot weather whereas 12% is satisfactory during cold weather. To dissolve the gelatin, the medium is heated over an asbestos pad or in a double boiler. The medium is then adjusted to pH 7.4–7.6. After the medium has cooled, the white of egg which is added for clearing is thoroughly stirred into the medium. It is again heated to the boiling point and then filtered through a cotton pad. The medium is tubed and then sterilized in flowing steam for 20 minutes on three consecutive days. It is cooled at once upon removal from the sterilizer.

In addition to being a medium which produces a solid surface, gelatin is of value because it is liquefied (hydrolyzed) by some types of bacteria. Since the medium becomes liquid at about 25°C., it is necessary to incubate it at a lower temperature; 20°C. is usually used. The gelatin-liquefying bacteria produce different types of liquefaction when stab cultures are made (Fig. 4.7).

### Nutrient Agar

Agar is a carbohydrate-like material which comes from seaweed found in Japanese and Chinese seas. It is used in the granulated form in the laboratory; 1.5% is the usual amount added to a fluid medium. The mixture must be boiled vigorously 10–15 minutes to melt the agar. Egg white is then added for clearing, and the medium is filtered through a cotton pad, after which it is tubed and sterilized in the autoclave at 15 pounds for 15 minutes.

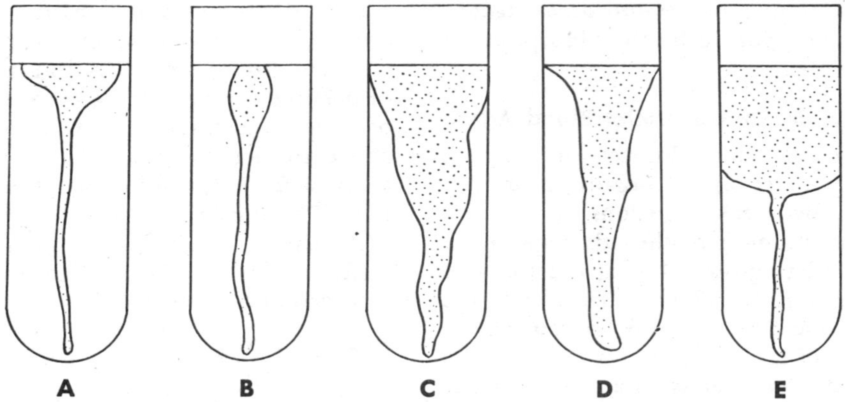


FIG. 4.7—Types of liquefaction of gelatin. **A**, crateriform; **B**, napiform; **C**, infundibuliform; **D**, saccate; **E**, stratiform.

Agar is not utilized by bacteria as food and is not liquefied by any of the usual temperatures of incubation; consequently, it is an ideal solidifying agent for many different types of media.

### Blood-Serum Agar

Sterile blood serum (10%) is mixed with sterile melted nutrient agar which has been cooled to 45°C. The medium is then solidified and is ready for use. Ascites fluid may be substituted for serum.

### Blood Agar

Whole blood is often used in the cultivation of pathogenic bacteria. It not only serves as an excellent nutritive medium but also as a diagnostic one, for some bacteria are able to hemolize red blood cells.

Under *strictly aseptic* conditions blood is removed from the jugular vein of one of the larger animals (horse, cow, sheep) and collected in a sterile flask. Sodium citrate or sodium oxalate solution may be placed in the flask prior to sterilization in order to prevent coagulation of the blood. After collection, the whole blood is distributed in 10 ml. amounts in sterile tubes. These may be kept in the refrigerator for three weeks without deterioration. Add 5% of the blood to any suitable carbohydrate-free agar base which has been melted and cooled to 45°C. After the addition of the blood, the tubes are rotated carefully to prevent the formation of bubbles. The medium contained in the test tubes is then slanted for hardening. Petri dishes may be poured after the blood has been added to the medium. To insure a perfectly smooth surface and medium free of bubbles, the lid of the dish is raised and the surface of the medium is heated momentarily with the Bunsen flame. It is best to incubate blood agar for 24 hours to determine sterility before it is used.

### Edwards' Medium

The examination of milk samples to detect the presence of streptococci is facilitated by the use of special media. Edwards has suggested the following media which are helpful in the diagnosis of bovine mastitis.

| *Liquid medium.* | |
|---|---|
| Meat infusion broth pH 7.4 | 950 ml. |
| Sterile ox or horse serum | 50 ml. |
| Dextrose | 10 gms. |
| Crystal violet q.s. | 1:200,000 concentration |
| *Solid medium.* | |
| Meat extract agar pH 7.4 | 1,000 ml. |
| Defibrinated ox blood | 50 ml. |
| Esculin | 1 gm. |
| Crystal violet (0.1%) | 2 ml. |

Put esculin in solution by boiling in a small amount of water and then add last three ingredients to melted agar at 50°C.

The crystal violet inhibits the staphylococci; colonies of *E. coli* and related species are black, due to the reaction with esculin. Colonies of *Streptococcus agalactiae* are made purple by the absorption of gentian violet.

### Sodium Azide, Crystal Violet Blood Agar

Streptococci, staphylococci, micrococci, and the swine erysipelas organisms are not inhibited by weak dilutions of sodium azide, whereas most of the other species of bacteria fail to grow. During the study of udder streptococci, Packer has found the following medium valuable in routine examination of milk samples for the presence of *Str. agalactiae* and as an aid in the isolation of streptococci from various sources.

| | | |
|---|---|---|
| Meat infusion | 500 | ml. |
| Tryptose | 15 | gms. |
| Sodium chloride | 5 | gms. |
| Agar-agar | 18 | gms. |
| Sodium azide | 0.5 | gms. |
| Crystal violet (dye cont. 94%) 0.1% aqueous solution | 2 | ml. |
| Dist. $H_2O$ q.s. | 1,000 | ml. |

Adjust to pH 7.0
Sterilize by autoclaving 20 min. at 15 lbs. pressure.
Cool to 50° C.
Add 50 cc. sterile citrated or defibrinated blood.
Pour into Petri dishes or test tubes for slants as desired.

The final concentration of sodium azide in the above formula is 1:2,000 and of crystal violet 1:500,000.

Some species of streptococci, especially *Str. agalactiae,* absorb the crystal violet from the medium producing violet-colored colonies. Hemolysis is more distinct and the zones of hemolysis around the colonies of streptococci are wider when the above medium is used as compared to those on ordinary blood agar. Certain species classified as nonhemolytic upon ordinary blood agar are distinctly beta hemolytic when grown upon this medium.

A selective medium on which only *Erysipelothrix insidiosa* may be grown can be obtained by increasing the concentration of sodium azide to 1:1,000 and of crystal violet to 1:100,000.

### PPLO Enrichment Broth

| | | |
|---|---|---|
| Beef heart, infusion from | 50 | gms. |
| Bacto-peptone | 10 | gms. |
| Sodium chloride | 5 | gms. |
| Bacto-crystal violet | 0.01 | gm. |
| Distilled water | 1,000 | ml. |

The above medium is used for primary growth of pleuropneumonia-like organisms (PPLO). In order to inhibit the growth of possible contaminating bacteria, 2.85 ml. of Bacto-Chapman tellurite solution is added to each 1,000 ml. of medium, giving a 1:35,000 concentration of potassium tellurite. The final pH should be 7.8.

Potassium tellurite is added to other media which may be used to isolate streptococci and corynebacteria.

### Chocolate Agar

To a suitable nutrient agar heated to about 90°C., 5 to 10% sterile defibrinated blood is added. The tubes, or flasks, are shaken gently to mix the blood thoroughly with the agar, and then they are cooled. The medium will have a decided chocolate color. It is not suitable for the isolation of bacteria but serves as a stock medium for species which require blood as a source of food.

### Liver Infusion Agar

Boil 500 gms. of finely chopped beef liver in 1,000 ml. of water for 2 hours and then filter through glass wool. Add 20 gms. of peptone and 1 gm. of dipotassium phosphate. Adjust reaction to pH 6.8. To this add 15 gms. agar and heat until thoroughly melted. The medium is again filtered and is then tubed and sterilized at 15 pounds pressure for 15 minutes.

### Potato-Glycerin Agar

Grind 500 gms. of potato and place in an open vessel. Two liters of distilled water are added and the vessel is placed in a water bath and heated at 60°C. for 12 to 16 hours. The mixture is then filtered through cheesecloth and again made up to 2 liters by the addition of distilled water. By this method the finely ground potato is removed, leaving the clear extract. To the extract are added 50 gms. of shredded or powdered agar, 10 gms. of beef extract, 20 gms. of dextrose, and 40 ml. of glycerin. The mixture is then subjected to 15 pounds of pressure for 30 minutes to dissolve the agar. Following this the pH is adjusted to

6.8 and the medium is placed in tubes or stored in flasks which are sterilized for 15 minutes at 15 pounds pressure in the autoclave.

### Brilliant Green-Bile Medium

| | | |
|---|---|---|
| Bacto-peptone | 10 | gms. |
| Bacto-lactose | 10 | gms. |
| Bacto-oxgall | 20 | gms. |
| Bacto-brilliant green | 0.0133 | gm. |
| Distilled water | 1,000 | ml. |

This medium is used in milk and water analysis as a presumptive test for the presence of *E. coli.* The presence of bile and brilliant green in the medium inhibits the growth of many contaminating types of bacteria. After the above ingredients have been dissolved in the distilled water, the medium is placed in fermentation tubes and sterilized for 15 min. at 15 pounds pressure. The final pH should be 7.2.

### Brilliant Green Agar

| | | |
|---|---|---|
| Bacto-yeast extract | 3 | gms. |
| Proteose peptone no. 3, Difco | 10 | gms. |
| Sodium chloride | 5 | gms. |
| Bacto-lactose | 10 | gms. |
| Saccharose, Difco | 10 | gms. |
| Bacto-phenol red | 0.08 | gm. |
| Bacto-brilliant green | 0.0125 | gm. |
| Bacto-agar | 20 | gms. |
| Distilled water | 1,000 | ml. |

This medium is used for the isolation of members of the genus Salmonella. These organisms appear as slightly pink-white opaque colonies surrounded by a brilliant red medium.

### E.M.B. Agar

| | | |
|---|---|---|
| Bacto-peptone | 10 | gms. |
| Bacto-lactose | 5 | gms. |
| Saccharose, Difco | 5 | gms. |
| Dipotassium phosphate | 2 | gms. |
| Bacto-agar | 13.5 | gms. |
| Bacto-eosin Y | 0.4 | gm. |
| Bacto-methylene blue | 0.065 | gm. |
| Distilled water | 1,000 | ml. |

In some formulations of E.M.B. agar, saccharose may be omitted and in others any desired carbohydrate may be added. This medium is universally used for the detection of *E. coli.* This organism grows in colonies which have a dark center giving a distinct indelible-ink, greenish-black, metallic sheen to the bacterial growth.

The above ingredients or Difco dehydrated medium are completely dissolved by heating and then by putting into the autoclave for 15 minutes at 15 pounds pressure. Following sterilization the medium is distributed into Petri plates or into test tubes with a long slant.

### Formate Ricinoleate Broth

| | |
|---|---|
| Bacto-peptone | 5 gms. |
| Bacto-lactose | 5 gms. |
| Sodium formate | 5 gms. |
| Sodium ricinoleate | 1 gm. |
| Distilled water | 1,000 ml. |

This medium is used in milk and water analysis as a selective medium for the colon group. The sodium formate increases acid and gas formation by *E. coli,* while sodium ricinoleate inhibits the growth of gram-positive types of bacteria.

The medium is prepared by dissolving the ingredients in boiling distilled water, distributing in fermentation tubes, and autoclaving 15 minutes at 15 pounds pressure.

### Desoxycholate Agar

| | | |
|---|---|---|
| Proteose peptone | 10 | gms. |
| Bacto-lactose | 10 | gms. |
| Sodium desoxycholate | 1 | gm. |
| Sodium chloride | 5 | gms. |
| Dipotassium phosphate | 2 | gms. |
| Ferric ammonium citrate | 2 | gms. |
| Bacto-agar | 15 | gms. |
| Bacto-neutral red | 0.03 | gm. |
| Distilled water | 1,000 | ml. |

This medium is used for the isolation and direct enumeration of coliform bacteria in milk and water. It is of value also in the isolation of Salmonella and Shigella species. In this medium Salmonella colonies are colorless and Shigella are colorless but somewhat opaque.

After the ingredients are dissolved in boiling water the medium is cooled to 45°–50°C. to be added to the Petri plate used for counting. When the medium in this inoculated plate has solidified, the surface is covered with a thin layer of the medium. The final pH of the medium is 7.3. It must not be autoclaved during preparation.

### Tetrathionate Broth Base

| | |
|---|---|
| Proteose peptone | 5 gms. |
| Bacto-bile salts | 1 gm. |

| | |
|---|---|
| Calcium carbonate | 10 gms. |
| Sodium thiosulfate | 30 gms. |
| Distilled water | 1,000 ml. |

The medium is prepared by dissolving the ingredients in the hot distilled water. It is then dispensed in 100-ml. flasks and sterilized in the autoclave 15 minutes at 15 pounds pressure. The day the medium is used, 2.0 ml. of iodine solution is added to each 100 ml. of medium. The iodine solution is prepared by dissolving 6 gms. iodine crystals and 5 gms. potassium iodide in 20 ml. of water. The medium is thoroughly shaken and distributed in test tubes for inoculation.

Tetrathionate broth is used as a selective enrichment medium for the isolation of Salmonella from feces or intestinal contents. After inoculation the medium is incubated 24 hours and then streaked out on differential plates for positive selection and identification.

### Simmons Citrate Agar

| | | |
|---|---|---|
| Magnesium sulfate | 0.2 | gm. |
| Monoammonium phosphate | 1 | gm. |
| Dipotassium phosphate | 1 | gm. |
| Sodium citrate | 2 | gms. |
| Sodium chloride | 5 | gms. |
| Bacto-agar | 15 | gms. |
| Bacto-bromthymol blue | 0.08 | gm. |
| Distilled water | 1,000 | ml. |

Adjust to pH 6.8.

This medium is used for the differentiation of fecal *E. coli* strains from the aerogenes group which grow abundantly on this medium because of the utilization of citrate. Members of the Salmonella group, especially *Sal. typhimurium,* utilize citrate, so this medium may be used to differentiate this organism from *Sal. typhosa* and *Sal. paratyphi*. It also serves as a medium for isolating certain mold species.

### Selenite Broth

| | |
|---|---|
| Bacto-tryptone | 4 gms. |
| Bacto-lactose | 4 gms. |
| Disodium phosphate | 10 gms. |
| Sodium acid selenite | 5 gms. |
| Distilled water | 1,000 ml. |

The medium is prepared by dissolving the above ingredients in the boiling water. It is then dispensed in sterile culture tubes. Excessive heating must be avoided and the medium must not be autoclaved.

Selenite broth is used as a preliminary enrichment medium for the isolation of Salmonella. It inhibits coliform bacteria and enterococci. After 24 hours incubation of the inoculated tubes, plates of SS agar are streaked in order to isolate the Salmonella.

### Endo's Agar (Modified)

A basic medium is prepared by adding 5 gms. of beef extract, 10 gms. of peptone, and 30 gms. of agar to 1,000 ml. of distilled water. The mixture is heated and adjusted to a pH of 7.8–8.2, is then filtered and placed in 100-ml. lots in small flasks to which are added 10 gms. of lactose. The medium is then sterilized 15 minutes at 10 pounds. Just before the medium is to be used, add aseptically 10 ml. of a 2.5% solution of sodium sulfite and 0.5 ml. of an alcoholic solution of basic fuchsin which is decolorized to a light straw by the sodium sulfite. The medium is then poured into Petri dishes and incubated overnight to test sterility.

This medium is used as a confirming medium for the presence of *Escherichia coli* and related microorganisms. The colonies of colon bacilli are vermilion in color, and color the surrounding medium. Colonies of the typhoid-dysentery group are grayish; streptococci are deep red. The reactions are due to the fermentation of lactose and the formation of acetaldehyde which is fixed by sodium sulfite; this reaction in turn restores the color to basic fuchsin.

### SS (Salmonella Shigella) Agar

| | | |
|---|---|---|
| Bacto-beef extract | 5 | gms. |
| Proteose peptone | 5 | gms. |
| Bacto-lactose | 10 | gms. |
| Bacto-bile salts no. 3 | 8.5 | gms. |
| Sodium citrate | 8.5 | gms. |
| Sodium thiosulfate | 8.5 | gms. |
| Ferric citrate | 1 | gm. |
| Bacto-agar | 13.5 | gms. |
| Bacto-brilliant green | 0.00033 | gm. |
| Bacto-neutral red | 0.025 | gm. |
| Distilled water | 1,000 | ml. |

This medium is employed to differentiate those bacteria which ferment lactose from those which do not. It likewise is designed to inhibit the coliform bacteria yet allow the growth of the more delicate types.

On this medium the Salmonella and Shigella, as well as other bacteria not fermenting lactose, grow in transparent or translucent uncolored colonies. The lactose-fermenting bacteria which may grow in the medium form red colonies.

The medium is prepared by placing the ingredients in cold distilled water and then boiling to completely dissolve. It must not be sterilized in the autoclave. Petri dishes are poured with the medium which is allowed to harden and stand for 2 hours with the lids partly removed. This allows the surface of the medium to dry, which is important for maximum results. The final pH of the medium is 7.0.

### Urea Agar Base

| | | |
|---|---|---|
| Bacto-peptone | 1 | gm. |
| Dextrose | 1 | gm. |
| Sodium chloride | 5 | gms. |
| Monopotassium phosphate | 2 | gms. |
| Urea-Difco | 20 | gms. |
| Phenol red | 0.012 | gm. |

The medium is prepared by dissolving all the above ingredients, 29 grams, in 100 ml. distilled water, and *filter sterilizing.* In 900 ml. distilled water dissolve 15 grams agar and sterilize in the autoclave for 15 minutes at 15 pounds. This medium is then cooled and the concentrated urea base medium is added under aseptic conditions. The completed medium is then dispensed in test tubes and allowed to solidify in the slanted position. Inasmuch as this medium cannot be reheated it is essential that slants are made at the time of preparation. For this reason smaller batches are desirable. This can be done by adding 10 ml. of urea base to 90 ml. agar.

Urea base agar is used for the detection of Proteus and to differentiate these organisms from other enteric species. It may be used for any species of bacteria able to hydrolize urea. Proteus cultures are able to hydrolize urea rapidly, producing a marked alkaline reaction within 4 hours after inoculation. While aerobacter and paracolon types do hydrolize this medium, they do so more slowly, requiring 3–5 days to completely alkalinize the medium. Salmonella and Shigella are not able to produce alkalinity in this medium.

### Decarboxylase Medium Base

| | | |
|---|---|---|
| Bacto-peptone | 5 | gms. |
| Bacto-yeast extract | 3 | gms. |
| Bacto-dextrose | 1 | gm. |
| Bacto-bromcresol purple | 0.02 | gm. |
| Distilled water | 1,000 | ml. |

Many different types of bacteria, especially those of the enteric group, can be differentiated by their ability to decarboxylate certain of the amino acids. The amino acids most commonly used for differential purposes are lysine, arginine, and ornithine. To the base medium, 5 grams of the desired amino acid are added to each 1,000 ml. of medium. The pH should be 6.5. The medium is dispensed in screw cap culture tubes and sterilized 15 minutes at 15 pounds pressure. After the medium has been inoculated, the screw cap must be tightened as much as possible. Other culture tubes may be used if the medium is overlayered with oil, to reduce aeration.

Positive reactions, decarboxylation, are noted by alkaline production which increases the purple color of the bromcresol purple. Negative reactions are indicated by a yellow color due to acid production.

### Phenylalanine Agar

| | |
|---|---|
| Bacto-yeast extract | 3 gms. |
| Diphenylalanine | 2 gms. |
| Disodium phosphate | 1 gm. |
| Sodium chloride | 5 gms. |
| Bacto-agar | 12 gms. |
| Distilled water | 1,000 ml. |

This medium is used to differentiate members of the Proteus and Arizona groups from other gram-negative enteric bacteria. After the medium has been prepared it is distributed in culture tubes and autoclaved 15 minutes at 15 pounds pressure. The pH will be 7.3. The tubes are slanted, and the organisms to be differentiated are inoculated thereon. After incubation the production of phenyl pyruvic acid is determined by flowing 5 drops of an acidified ammonium sulfate-ferric ammonium sulfate solution across the culture. A positive test is the formation of a green color indicative of Proteus or closely related species. Other Enterobacteriaceae are negative.

### Nitrate Agar

| | |
|---|---|
| Beef extract | 3 gms. |
| Peptone | 5 gms. |
| Potassium nitrate | 1 gm. |
| Agar | 12 gms. |
| Distilled water | 1,000 ml. |

The above ingredients are heated thoroughly to melt the agar, and the pH adjusted to about 6.8. The medium is tubed and sterilized in the autoclave at 15 pounds for 15 minutes, and the tubes are then slanted. Inoculation with the test organism is made by streaking the slant and stabbing into the butt of the medium. The cultures are incubated 24 to 48 hours.

The above medium is used to detect the reduction of nitrate to nitrite. It is tested for the presence of nitrite by the following reagents:

SOLUTION A

| | |
|---|---|
| 5/N Acetic acid | 1,000 ml. |
| Sulfanilic acid | 8 gms. |

SOLUTION B

| | |
|---|---|
| 5/N Acetic acid | 1,000 ml. |
| Alpha-amidonaphthylene | 5 gms. |

Add 2 ml. of each solution (A and B) to the tube to be tested. A red rose color will indicate the presence of nitrite. A control in check tubes of uninoculated agar should always be tested at the same time.

### Lead Acetate Agar

| | |
|---|---|
| Agar | 15 gms. |
| Bacto-tryptone | 20 gms. |
| Dextrose | 1 gm. |
| Lead acetate | 0.2 gm. |
| Distilled water | 1,000 ml. |

The ingredients are boiled until the agar is melted and the pH is then adjusted to 6.8. The medium is tubed and sterilized at 15 pounds pressure for 15 minutes. The tubes are slanted leaving generous butts. Inoculation is made by streaking the slant and a stab into the butt.

The ability of some species of bacteria to form hydrogen sulfide is used as a differential criterion. In the above medium those species which form $H_2S$ cause a blackening of the medium adjacent to the culture, both on the surface of the slant and along the needle track of the stab inoculation.

The formation of hydrogen sulfide by bacteria may also be detected by placing strips of paper soaked in lead acetate solution in the test tube with a medium which does not contain lead acetate. Some authorities contend that even a trace of lead is inhibitory to some bacteria; therefore, the incorporation of the chemical in the medium may explain why growth is not obtained in some instances. The amount of lead acetate in a medium should be below 0.02% which is considered nontoxic.

### Kligler Iron Agar

| | |
|---|---|
| Bacto-beef extract | 3 gms. |
| Bacto-yeast extract | 3 gms. |
| Bacto-peptone | 15 gms. |
| Proteose peptone | 5 gms. |
| Lactose | 10 gms. |
| Dextrose | 1 gm. |
| Ferrous sulfate | 0.2 gm. |
| Sodium chloride | 5 gms. |
| Sodium thiosulfate | 0.3 gm. |
| Agar | 12 gms. |
| Phenol red | 0.024 gm. |
| Distilled water | 1,000 ml. |

The medium is prepared by dissolving the ingredients in boiling distilled water, dispensing in tubes or flasks as desired, and sterilizing in the autoclave 15 minutes at 15 pounds pressure (120°C.).

Kligler iron agar is used in the study of the gram-negative enterobacteria. It differentiates the lactose-fermenting species from those which do not ferment lactose. It detects those which ferment dextrose. The fermentation reactions on this medium are noted by the change of phenol red to yellow in case of lactose fermentation; gas is apparent by bubbles which form in the medium. In dextrose fermentation the butt of the slant is changed to yellow but the slant remains red. Hydrogen sulfide production is noted by the blackening of the medium.

### SIM Medium

| | | |
|---|---|---|
| Bacto-beef extract | 3 | gms. |
| Peptone | 30 | gms. |
| Peptonized iron, Difco | 0.2 | gm. |
| Sodium thiosulfate | 0.025 | gm. |
| Bacto-agar | 3 | gms. |
| Distilled water | 1,000 | ml. |

This medium is prepared by dissolving the above ingredients in the boiling distilled water. It is then dispensed in tubes at a depth of 1½ inches. After sterilization for 15 minutes at 15 pounds pressure the medium is allowed to solidify by placing the tubes in a vertical position.

SIM medium serves the triple function of detecting hydrogen sulfide, indol, and motility. The medium is inoculated by the stab method. A small amount of blackening along the needle tract is considered positive for hydrogen sulfide production due to the small amount of sodium thiosulfate in the medium. Motility is noted by the formation of a test tube brush type of growth around the central needle tract. Nonmotile bacteria do not penetrate into the semisolid agar in this manner. Indol production can be detected by placing paper strips soaked with saturated oxalic acid into the tubes hanging below the cotton plug about one inch. Kovac's reagent may also be used, following the same procedure as is used in Dunham's peptone or tryptophane broth.

### Hibler's Brain Medium

Boil either sheep or beef brain in equal amounts of water. Decant the fluid and press the brain through a potato ricer. Add to the decanted water 2% peptone and 0.1% dextrose. Mix the brain and fluid together and adjust to pH 7.2. Tube in large tubes, filling them one-half full. Sterilize in the Arnold for 30 minutes on three consecutive days.

### Dorset's Egg Medium

Wash eggs with 5% phenol solution, allow to dry partially, pierce the ends, and blow into sterile flasks. Add 10% water by volume to the weight of the eggs. Mix gently, filter through cheesecloth, tube, and slant in an inspissator. Coagulate by heating to 70°C. 2 to 2½ hours on three consecutive days. Incubate 4 days to determine sterility.

### Loeffler's Blood Serum Medium

| | |
|---|---|
| Fresh ox serum | 3 parts |
| 1% dextrose broth | 1 part |

Tube and sterilize either by inspissating as above or by sterilizing in the autoclave. To prevent the formation of bubbles the following procedure must be followed: The steam is turned on suddenly with *all* outlets tightly closed until the pressure records 15 pounds. The mixture of air and high pressure prevents boiling. After the medium has been heated in this manner for 15 minutes, the steam is turned on slowly until the safety valve is slightly open. Heating is continued under this condition for 20 minutes. All outlets must remain closed tightly until pressure has been entirely reduced and medium has had an opportunity to cool. Under the above conditions an entirely smooth and absolutely sterile medium is produced.

### Glycerin Agar-Egg Medium

To a basic meat infusion agar add 3% glycerin. Add one egg yolk to each 150 ml. of this medium. A sterile egg yolk is obtained as follows: Place the eggs in 80% ethyl alcohol for 30 minutes, remove one end with a flamed forceps, and pour out the egg white. The yolk is then placed directly into the medium which has been melted and cooled to 45°–50°C. Shake until the egg yolk and medium are completely mixed. Under aseptic conditions the medium is tubed, slanted, and then incubated for sterility. Incubation is essential because the yolks of some eggs are known to be infected.

The medium is used for the cultivation of tubercle bacilli, but is an excellent medium for the cultivation of most of the pathogenic bacteria. The addition of 10% blood serum to the medium increases its nutritive qualities.

### Lowenstein-Jensen Medium

| | |
|---|---|
| Bacto-asparagine | 3.6 gms. |
| Monopotassium phospate | 2.4 gms. |
| Magnesium sulfate | 2.4 gms. |
| Magnesium citrate | 0.6 gm. |
| Potato flour | 30 gms. |
| Glycerol | 12 ml. |
| Malachite green | 0.4 gm. |
| Whole egg | 1,000 ml. |
| Distilled water | 600 ml. |

The above medium is also used for the primary culture of tubercle bacilli. In its preparation, care must be observed in sterilization following distribution into culture tubes. The tubes are placed in a slanted position in a steam sterilizer and heated slowly until the egg has coagulated. If heated too suddenly, air bubbles will form in the medium giving it a "blown-out" appearance. After the egg has solidified, use time and pressure which ordinarily assure sterility.

### Dorset's Synthetic Medium

Dorset devised the following medium for the preparation of tuberculin which is free of meat protein.

| | |
|---|---|
| l-asparagin | 14 gms. |
| Dipotassium phosphate C.P. | 1.80 gms. |
| Sodium citrate C.P. | 0.90 gm. |
| Magnesium sulfate U.S.P. | 1.50 gms. |
| Ferric citrate U.S.P. scales | 0.30 gm. |
| Dextrose (cerelose) | 10 gms. |
| Gycerol C.P. | 100 ml. |
| Distilled water to | 1,000 ml. |

The medium is adjusted to pH 7.0 and sterilized in the autoclave at 15 pounds for 15 minutes. It is usually placed in large flasks.

### Blood Glucose Cystine Agar (Francis)

*Pasteurella tularensis* is most easily grown on a medium in which cystine has been incorporated. For the cultivation of the organism, Francis devised the following medium: To a meat infusion agar add 0.1% cystine and 1% glucose. This is placed in the Arnold and heated long enough to melt the agar and sterilize the cystine and glucose. The medium is cooled to 60°C., and 5% to 8% of defibrinated or whole rabbit blood is added. The medium is then sterilized in a water bath for 2 hours at 60°C.

### Staphylococcus Medium No. 110

| | |
|---|---|
| Bacto-yeast extract | 2.5 gms. |
| Bacto-tryptone | 10 gms. |
| Bacto-gelatin | 30 gms. |
| Bacto-lactose | 2 gms. |
| d-mannitol | 10 gms. |
| Sodium chloride | 75 gms. |
| Dipotassium phosphate | 5 gms. |
| Bacto-agar | 15 gms. |
| Distilled water | 1,000 ml. |

The ingredients are heated in boiling water until completely dissolved and then sterilized in the autoclave 15 minutes at 15 pounds pressure. Plates are poured while the medium is still hot, at which time the flask is agitated to resuspend the precipitate which usually forms upon sterilization.

The above medium is used for the selective isolation of pathogenic staphylococci, but it also may be used to detect those strains which produce gelatinase. In order to detect the latter characteristic, the inoculated plate is flooded with 5 ml. saturated solution of ammonium sulfate and let stand in the incubator 10 minutes. Those organisms which are gelatinase-producing are surrounded by a clear zone while the rest of the medium is opaque due to the precipitation of the nonliquefied gelatin by the ammonium sulfate

Other media, such as mannitol salt agar and Chapman Stone medium, may be used for the isolation of staphylocci.

### Bacto-Middlebrook 7H10 Agar

| | |
|---|---|
| Ammonium sulfate | 0.5 gm. |
| l glutamic acid | 0.5 gm. |
| Sodium citrate | 0.4 gm. |
| Disodium phosphate | 1.5 gms. |
| Monopotassium phosphate | 1.5 gms. |
| Ferric ammonium citrate | 0.04 gm. |
| Magnesium sulfate | 0.05 gm. |
| Pyridoxine | 0.001 gm. |
| Biotin | 0.0005 gm. |
| Bacto-malachite green | 0.001 gm. |
| Bacto-agar | 15 gms. |

The above ingredients may be obtained from Digestive Ferments Company. To rehydrate the medium, 20 grams are suspended in 1,000 ml. cold distilled water containing 0.5 per cent glycerol. Heat to boiling to completely dissolve. Distribute in 180 ml. amounts in flasks, and autoclave at 15 pounds for 15 minutes. To each 180 ml. sterile medium add 20 ml. Bacto-Middlebrook OADC Enrichment under aseptic conditions. Dispense the medium in tubes and allow it to solidify in a slanted position.

This medium is used for primary isolation of tubercle bacilli and for antibiotic sensitivity tests.

### Bacto-Middlebrook OADC Enrichment

| | | |
|---|---|---|
| Oleic acid | 0.5 | gm. |
| Albumin fraction V, bovine | 50 | gms. |
| Dextrose | 20 | gms. |
| Catalase (beef) | 0.04 | gm. |
| Sodium chloride | 8.5 | gms. |
| Distilled water | 1,000 | ml. |

The above ingredients are dissolved in the distilled water, dispensed in 20 ml. amounts in test tubes, and autoclaved at 15 pounds pressure for 15 minutes.

### Bacto-Dubos Oleic Agar Base

| | | |
|---|---|---|
| Bacto-casitone | 0.5 | gm. |
| Bacto-asparagine | 1 | gm. |
| Disodium phosphate | 2.5 | gms. |
| Monopotassium phosphate | 1 | gm. |
| Ferric ammonium citrate | 50 | mg. |
| Magnesium sulfate | 10 | mg. |
| Calcium chloride | 0.5 | mg. |
| Zinc sulfate | 0.1 | mg. |
| Copper sulfate | 0.1 | mg. |
| Bacto-agar | 15 | gms. |
| Distilled water | 1,000 | ml. |

Difco dehydrated medium is used in most laboratories, so in preparing the above medium 4.0 grams are suspended in 180 ml. cold distilled water and heated until completely dissolved. Each flask is then autoclaved at 15 pounds for 15 minutes. To each 180-ml. flask, cooled to 50°–55°C., 20 ml. of Bacto-Dubos Oleic Albumin Complex are added along with 5,000 to 10,000 units of penicillin, under aseptic conditions. Mix thoroughly, distribute in test tubes and allow to solidify in a slanted position.

### Staphylococcus Toxin Medium

The following medium has been found very satisfactory for the cultivation of *Staph. aureus* for toxin formation:

| | | |
|---|---|---|
| Sugar-free veal infusion broth | 1,000 | ml. |
| Proteose peptone | 40 | gms. |
| Sodium chloride | 4 | gms. |
| $KH_2PO_4$ | 2 | gms. |
| $MgSO_4$ | 0.3 | gm. |
| Glycerol | 100 | ml. |
| Agar | 6 | gms. |

The above ingredients are heated in the Arnold for 30 minutes, filtered, and the pH is adjusted to 7.6. It is then distributed into flat-bottomed flasks or medicine bottles to a depth of 5 mm., and then autoclaved. The medium is inoculated with a pipette, allowing the inoculum to flow entirely over the surface. The cultures are placed in a suitable jar or other container and the air volume is adjusted to 20% $CO_2$. The organism is incubated at 37°C. for six to eight days. To each 10 ml. of medium is added 1 ml. of 0.8% NaCl solution and medium is thoroughly broken by shaking. The liquid is then squeezed through cheesecloth and passed through a porcelain filter. The filtrate contains the toxin.

### Thioglycollate Medium

| | | |
|---|---|---|
| Bacto-yeast extract | 5 | gms. |
| Bacto-casitone | 15 | gms. |
| Dextrose | 1 | gm. |
| Sodium chloride | 2.5 | gms |
| l-cystine, Difco | 0.05 | gm. |
| Thioglycollic acid | 0.3 | ml. |
| Agar | 0.75 | gm. |
| Distilled water | 1,000 | ml. |

The medium is prepared by dissolving the ingredients in boiling distilled water. It is then dispensed in tubes or flasks as desired, and sterilized in the autoclave 15 minutes at 15 pounds pressure.

Thioglycollate medium is used for the growth of facultative anaerobic and anaerobic bacteria without placing the medium under anaerobic conditions. It is used also for testing biologics and antibiotics for sterility.

### Potato

Cylinders are cut from potatoes by means of an apple corer or special potato borer. They are then divided by a diagonal longitudinal cut so that each half has one long, sloping surface. It is well to soak the pieces in running water for a few hours to prevent their turning dark when sterilized. They are placed with the sloping surface up in test tubes with a bit of saturated absorbent cotton or any solid object (glass tubing) in the bottom, or in special potato tubes. The space below the potato is filled with water to prevent undue desiccation of the potato.

The tubes are sterilized in the autoclave for 15 minutes at 15 pounds pressure.

The appearance of bacterial growth on the potato is manifest by abundance, pigmentation, and the changes produced in the medium, such as blackening.

### Other Vegetable Media

Carrots and other vegetables may be prepared in the same manner as potatoes. Tomato juice is often used in the same proportions as meat infusion and has been found to be a satisfactory medium for certain of the organisms used in the manufacture of milk products.

## REFERENCES

BALTIMORE BIOLOGICAL LABORATORY. Products for the Microbiological Laboratory. Baltimore, 1965.

CONN, H. J. Biological Stains. 2nd Ed. Biological Stain Commission, Geneva and New York, 1929.

DIGESTIVE FERMENTS CO. Manual of Dehydrated Culture Media and Reagents. Detroit, 1953. (Reprinted 1965.)

———. Supplementary Literature to Difco Manual. Detroit, 1962.

EDWARDS, P. R., and EWING, W. H. Identification of Enterobacteriaceae. Burgess Publ. Co., Minneapolis, 1962.

FISHER SCIENTIFIC CO. Fisher Bacteriological Culture Media. Chicago, 1963.

FROBISHER, M. Fundamentals of Microbiology. 7th Ed. W. B. Saunders Co., Philadelphia, 1962.

GAGE, S. H. The Microscope. Comstock Publ. Co., Ithaca, 1941.

HENRY, H., and STACY, M. Histochemistry of the Gram-staining Reaction for Microorganisms. Nature, London 151:671, 1943.

LEIFSON, EINAR. Atlas of Bacterial Flagellation. Academic Press, Inc., New York and London, 1960.

LEVINE, MAX, and SCHOENLEIN, H. W. A Compilation of Culture Media. Williams & Wilkins Co., Baltimore, 1930.

PACKER, R. A. The Use of Sodium Azide ($NaN_3$) and Crystal Violet in a Selective Medium for Streptococci and *Erysipelothrix rhusiopathiae.* Jour. Bact. 46:343–49, 1943.

SALLE, A. J. Fundamental Principles of Bacteriology. 5th Ed. McGraw-Hill Book Co., New York, 1961.

SOCIETY OF AMERICAN BACTERIOLOGISTS. Manual of Microbiological Methods. H. J. Conn and M. W. Jennison (eds.). McGraw-Hill Book Co., New York, 1957.

# 5

# Sterilization and Disinfection

BACTERIA ARE PRESENT UPON THE SURFACE of all laboratory apparatus, in the dust, and upon the hands; they are everywhere. Hence, sterilization is a necessity. The use of sterile instruments and dressings in surgical operations emphasizes the need of various procedures for killing bacteria. The preparation of operative fields, the treatment of wounds, the sterilization of milking equipment, and the disinfection of poultry houses, cattle barns, swine rearing and breeding establishments, trucks, railroad cars, ships, and airplanes are examples of the use and need of methods to destroy bacteria.

The destruction of microorganisms may be accomplished by physical and chemical means. The former method is often called *sterilization* while the latter is termed *disinfection;* this is not a set rule, however, for the ultimate action which kills the organism may be the same when either a physical or a chemical method is employed. Boiling coagulates bacterial protoplasm, and so does a salt of a heavy metal. Natural desiccation removes water from the bacterial cell, so does a dehydrating chemical. It cannot be said that sterilization refers to the destruction of nonpathogenic bacteria, and disinfection refers to the pathogenic bacteria. Sterilization is always aimed at both types, while disinfection, in its true sense, applies only to the pathogenic varieties.

Many general terms, such as *bactericide,* are used to designate methods of destroying bacteria. Anything that kills germs is a *germicide;* that which kills algae is known as an *algacide;* that which kills fungi is called a *fungicide;* that which kills a virus is a *virucide.* The term *antiseptic* is commonly applied when chemicals are used to inhibit the growth of bacteria. This inhibition of growth is often referred to as *bacteriostasis* or *microbiostasis.* The chemical does not need to be the type nor the concentration to actually kill organisms which are present. The term antiseptic is used in the true meaning of the word, *anti* = against and *sepis* = decay. When no pathogenic bacteria are present the term *aseptic* is often used. Asepsis may be brought about by physical or chemical methods. Certain disinfectants and antiseptics are added to *sera* and bacterial suspensions in small quantities which act as *preservatives;* organisms which accidentally may be present are inhibited in growth and in time actually perish. A *deodorant* is anything, usually a chemical, which removes or masks odors. It is not to be inferred that a deodorant is always a disinfectant; frequently it is not. People have associated disinfectants with odor, however, and they often judge the killing power of a chemical mixture by its odor. It is an unfortunate circumstance in the practice of medicine when a disinfectant with a disagreeable odor is used. Undesirable professional odors should be avoided; especially since many disinfectants with pleasant odors and high efficiency are available.

For convenience of presentation the

physical agencies which cause the destruction of bacteria will precede the discussion of the chemical compounds.

## PHYSICAL DISINFECTION

### Light

It was noted in Chapter 3 that most bacteria require an environment of darkness for optimum growth. Light is probably the most effective germicide in the universe. In judging the effect of sunlight and other radiations on bacteria, a number of factors must be considered: (1) the wave length and intensity of the radiation, (2) the kind of organism, (3) the medium in which the organism is contained, and (4) the time of exposure.

Early in the study of the action of sunlight on bacteria it was found that various portions of the spectrum were more germicidal than others. A review of a portion of the spectrum (Fig. 5.1) will emphasize that it is divided into various portions based upon the wave length of the radiation. Wave length is expressed in Ångstrom units, Å (1Å = 1 x $10^{-7}$ mm. or 1/10,000,000 mm.).

The most germicidal rays are those ranging from 2,540 Å to 2,800 Å, but those from 2,100 Å to approximately 3,200 Å possess high bactericidal properties. It is seen that these rays are found in the ultraviolet section of the spectrum. The other rays, however, are not without effect in inhibiting bacterial life. Light from which the ultraviolet rays have been filtered is inhibitory to the multiplication of bacteria. Infrared heat radiation is a valuable adjunct to the action of ultraviolet rays, for it has been shown in tropical countries that the increased action of ultraviolet light is partially due to increased heat.

The Cooper-Hewitt and other mercury vapor arc lights and carbon arc lamps are used to produce ultraviolet light. The glass usually used in lamps does not permit the passage of ultraviolet rays; so it is replaced by quartz. Artificial ultraviolet radiation may be used for a variety of purposes, chief among which in bacteriology is the sterilization of water and the study of the germicidal effect of the intensity and length of such rays.

Bacteria vary in their resistance to the action of light. Obviously, the sporeforming types are the most resistant due to the compact nature of spore protoplasm. The vegetative cells of the different types of pathogenic microorganisms do not differ a great deal in the length of time they are destroyed by direct sunlight; this is within 5 minutes for the majority. It has been observed, however, that fluorescent bacteria are not as easily destroyed as the nonfluorescent. This is explained by the supposition that the short germicidal waves may be converted by fluorescent pigments into longer ones which are without so much effect.

The medium in which the organism is suspended is an important factor in judging the effect of light. A turbid, opalescent, or opaque medium does not permit the penetration of light. In nature, bacteria are protected from sunlight by many materials in which they live. It has been shown, however, by numerous scientists that an uninoculated medium which has been exposed to ultraviolet light becomes definitely inhibitory to the growth of bacteria. Just what change occurs in the me-

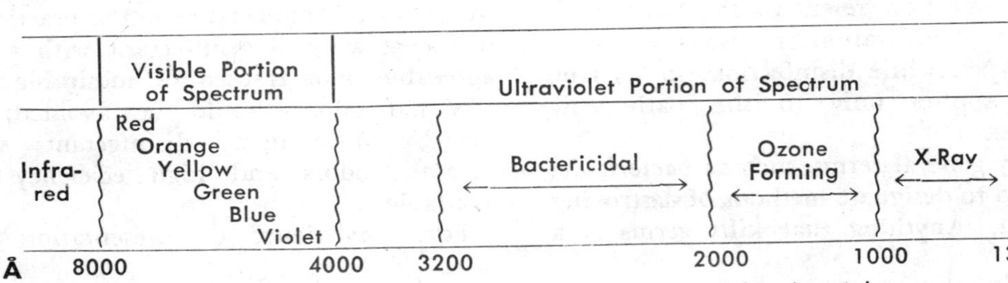


FIG. 5.1 — A portion of the spectrum showing the position of the ultraviolet rays.

dium has not been conclusively explained. Some claim hydrogen peroxide is increased by radiation while others believe that the effect is due to oxidation. It is of little practical significance because most media are contained in glass which does not permit the passage of ultraviolet radiation and, moreover, they are commonly stored in the dark.

Light apparently produces the death of microorganisms in a variety of ways. The accumulation of inhibitory substances in the medium, as suggested above, may be one factor. The most common explanation, however, is that the surface colloids of bacterial cells are coagulated, thereby rendering the cell wall more permeable, which enhances the action of surrounding ions and may also bring about the dissolution of the organism. A more recent explanation is that of Buckholz and Jeney who claim that the energy produced by waves 2,530 to 2,650 Å displace sufficient electrons from the bacterial protoplasm to produce irreversible photochemical changes and subsequent death of the cell.

### Electricity

Currents of both low-frequency and high-frequency electricity have been used in order to detect their effect on bacteria. The effect of such currents is difficult to evaluate, however, since many varied conditions are used in the experiments. Most investigators report that bacteria are rendered nonmotile in some cases, and in other instances they are killed. Death is due to the action of chemicals liberated by electrolysis, such as chlorine from sodium chloride, or to the heat generated by the electric current. No practical use has been made of the destructive action of electricity upon microorganisms because the method is difficult to apply and, as yet, is considered quite inefficient.

### Other Rays and Waves

The action of roentgen ray (X rays) upon bacteria has been subjected to much study, but the reports which have been made are too contradictory to conclude that such rays are extremely detrimental to bacteria. The same is true of cathode rays, radium, sonic, and supersonic waves. However, the ionizing action of any type of energy must have an effect on rapidly dividing bacteria, so it may be presumed that a certain amount of lethal action may occur in all irradiations.

### Heat

Another effective physical agency which is commonly used to destroy bacteria is heat. It was noted in Chapter 4 that temperature is an important factor in the growth of bacteria and that different types of microorganisms react differently to temperature variations. This must be stressed again here, for it is obvious that the maximum growth temperature of a thermophilic organism may be the thermal death point of a mesophilic organism. The *thermal death point* of an organism may be defined as that temperature which, under given conditions, will certainly destroy all the cells. The accurate determination of the exact temperature that is necessary to destroy various species of bacteria is frequently of great economic importance. Efficient sterilization and pasteurization can be accomplished only when facts are known. Many methods have been suggested. In the laboratory the determination is frequently made by subjecting freshly inoculated tubes of broth to different temperatures in a water bath for ten minutes each. For reliable results, more accurate methods are needed. One of the most common and best is the use of a long, slender, glass vial. A definite amount of culture is introduced into the vial, and the open end is sealed in the flame. The vial is completely immersed in a water bath and suspended by wires or by some other method, so that it does not come in contact with the walls or bottom of the bath as it is heated. A number of vials are prepared. One is heated five minutes, another 10 minutes, at 50°C. The temperature is raised two degrees and two more vials are exposed. This procedure of heating two vials with each increase of two degrees is continued up to 70°C. for the sporeless bacteria. The vials are cooled quickly, and after exposure, their contents are mixed with agar in a Petri dish, or are added to a tube of other suitable medium. This is then incubated several days. The minimum temperature required to destroy the bacteria can readily be determined by a comparison of the tubes. Bacteria do not die instantaneously even under the action of heat. The following factors must be taken into consideration in determining the thermal death point of bacteria and the rate of death:

1. *The Specific Character of the Organism.* The intrinsic variations in the character of protoplasm of different species make it necessary to determine the thermal death point for each species. Young cultures of bacteria are more quickly killed than old ones.

2. *The Absence or Presence of Spores.* Spores are much more resistant to high temperatures than are the vegetative cells. Forms having spores, therefore, have two rates of death, one for the vegetative cell and the other for the spores.

3. *Presence or Absence of Moisture.* Bacteria are more resistant to dry than to moist heat. The thermal death point is probably the temperature at which *incipient coagulation of the albuminous protoplasm* occurs, resulting in an inability to function. Water is necessary for this coagulation. The following table from Frost and McCampbell illustrates this point:[1]

Egg albumen plus 50 per cent water coagulates at 56°C.
Egg albumen plus 25 per cent water coagulates at 74°–80°C.
Egg albumen plus 18 per cent water coagulates at 80°–90°C.
Egg albumen plus 6 per cent water coagulates at 145°C.
Egg albumen plus no water coagulates at 160°–170°C.

The action of water is emphasized by the laboratory methods of sterilization discussed below. The autoclave, with live steam at a temperature of 120°C., will destroy in ten minutes the most resistant spores, while in the hot-air oven a temperature of 150° to 170°C. for an hour is necessary.

4. *Reaction and Composition of Medium.* The reaction and composition of the medium have been found to exert a marked influence on the thermal death point; the hydrogen-ion concentration of the medium, that is, the actual acidity, should be noted particularly. It is a well-known fact, for example, that acid fruits are more easily sterilized than are the more nearly neutral vegetables. This is due to the increased dissociation of acids as the temperature increases. The composition of the medium may also alter the rate at which heat diffuses through it and comes in contact with the bacteria.

5. *Time of Exposure.* In general, the higher the temperature the shorter is the period required to destroy life in the cells. Ten minutes exposure is the usual standard. When the thermal death point of an organism is mentioned, it is without meaning unless the time is given.

### Sterilization by the Flame

The destruction of microorganisms by the use of the flame is highly effective when the material to be sterilized is either indestructible or is to be destroyed. The platinum wire used in the laboratory in the transfer of bacteria is sterilized by heating to a red heat in the flame of the Bunsen burner. The open flame is also used to kill bacteria smeared on slides preparatory to staining. The destruction of infected clothing, bedding, buildings, etc., by flame during an epidemic of disease is effective. The burning of carcasses of animals having died with infectious diseases is practiced. The flame also has been used as a means of disinfecting concrete floors and the surfaces of ground.

### Sterilization by Hot Air

Glassware is commonly sterilized by subjecting it to a temperature of 150° to 170°C. in a hot-air oven for an hour. All bacteria will be destroyed at this tempera-

[1] William D. Frost and Eugene F. McCampbell. *A Textbook of General Bacteriology.* The Macmillan Co., New York, 1910, p. 140.

ture providing the material to be sterilized is of such nature that heat can penetrate readily to all parts. This method cannot be used, however, in the sterilization of liquids or of any organic material which might be decomposed at such a temperature.

### Sterilization at Temperatures Lower Than the Boiling Point

It is sometimes necessary to sterilize a medium, particularly blood serum, at a temperature lower than the boiling point of water. This is accomplished by placing the material to be sterilized in an apparatus where it may be heated to the desired temperature, usually 70° to 80°C., for 1 to 2 hours on each of five or more consecutive days. When it is known that only vegetative cells are present, this method of sterilization is effective, but if large numbers of spores of certain organisms, such as *Bacillus subtilis,* are present, it is almost impossible to sterilize efficiently by this method. The inspissation of certain culture media, especially egg and blood serum media, should be done at temperatures lower than boiling in order to obtain a uniformly smooth-surfaced product.

### Pasteurization

A practical use of lower-than-boiling temperatures for the killing of bacteria is in the process generally known as *pasteurization.* In the pasteurization of milk two methods are employed. The holding method requires the heating of milk to 142° to 145°F. for a period of 30 minutes. The flash method requires the milk to be held for 15 seconds at 160°F. Both temperatures are high enough to kill the vegetative cells of pathogenic bacteria, but not high enough to kill spores or heat resistant forms. It is a process intended to make milk safer for human consumption and to prolong its keeping period, but is not intended as a substitute for sanitation in the production and handling of milk. Pasteurization is also used in the treatment of antisera used for the immunization of animals, for the canning of fruits and vegetables, and for the preparation of wines and other beverages.

FIG. 5.2—The Arnold sterilizer.

### Sterilization by Steam

It is well known that live steam is an efficient sterilizing medium. Steam is used in the surgery for sterilizing instruments, in the milk plant and dairy for sterilizing equipment, in canning procedures, and for many other purposes. Steam under atmospheric pressure at sea level has a temperature of about 100°C. Some type of apparatus should be used so that the live steam comes in direct contact with the material to be sterilized. One type of apparatus used in the laboratory is called the Arnold steam sterilizer (Fig. 5.2).

A single exposure to live steam for 15 minutes is sufficient to kill all vegetative bacteria, but spores are not thus destroyed. It is customary, therefore, to heat for 30 minutes on one day, keep the medium for 24 hours at a temperature suitable for the germination and development of any spores present, then heat again for 30 minutes in the same manner. Those spores which have germinated will be destroyed by this second heating. A third heating, 24 hours later, will certainly destroy all the bacteria which may have been present. This process is called *intermittent sterilization,* or *fractional sterilization,* or *tyndallization.* It finds its principal application in the sterilization of materials which may be changed or broken down by heating at a higher temperature. Among such materials are media containing sugars which undergo incipient caramelization when heated for too long a time or at too high a temperature.

### Sterilization by Steam Under Pressure

In order to have complete and rapid destruction of bacterial spores, it is necessary to have temperatures higher than boiling point. This is accomplished in the autoclave (Fig. 5.3), which consists of a chamber into which steam may be introduced and maintained under pressure.

Live steam under pressure unmixed with air has a constant temperature; therefore, if the pressure of the live steam is known, one can determine easily the temperature as well. A technical difficulty often presents itself in the use of the autoclave. It is necessary that all the air in the chamber first be eliminated. This is usually accomplished by allowing the stopcock, which is always present upon the steam chamber of the autoclave, to remain open until all the air has escaped and the steam issues in a constant stream. It is much more satisfactory, however, to use an autoclave equipped with a temperature control device on the steam discharge outlet. This means that sterilization is controlled by temperature rather than by pressure. When the required temperature is reached, the steam pressure is adjusted to maintain the temper-

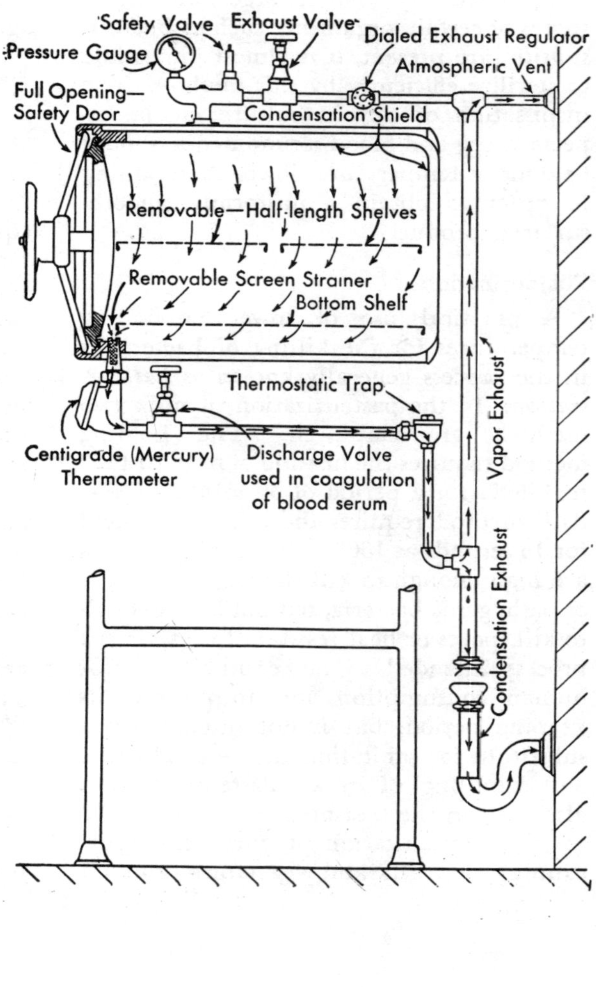


FIG. 5.3—Cross section of autoclave sterilizer showing path of steam. (Courtesy American Sterilizer Company.)

ature for the required length of time. Material to be sterilized should be allowed to remain 15 minutes in most cases. If large bulks such as flasks of media and packages of dressing are to be sterilized, a longer period must be allowed for the heat to penetrate into the center of the objects. Material wrapped in cloth or paper should be placed on edge, instead of flat, so steam will circulate through the packages more easily. When properly carried out, sterilization by this method will certainly destroy all the bacteria present. Its principal disadvantage is that certain organic substances may be decomposed at such high temperatures.

### Freezing

Freezing cannot be depended upon as an effective method to destroy microorganisms. Alternate freezing and thawing cause a marked decrease in a bacterial population. Death probably occurs with the solidification of the bacterial protoplasm and, no doubt, is mechanical in nature. Bacteria kept frozen in ice, however, remain alive for considerable periods of time.

### Desiccation

Since water is so essential to the life of microorganisms, it is apparent that the removal of it would be detrimental. Drying is one of nature's most effective means of controlling the growth of all bacterial life. We see it active in the preservation of fruits and meat and in the prevention of the decay of trees and other vegetation.

A number of factors must be considered in evaluating the effects of desiccation on bacteria. The various species of microorganisms differ in their ability to survive drying. The cocci and actinomyces, in general, are more resistant than the rod-shaped bacteria. Whether the organism produces an endospore is of great significance in the maintenance of life. It will be recalled that spores are compact, dehydrated bodies of bacterial protoplasm and for this reason are able to resist desiccation for indefinite periods. A young, actively growing culture of an organism is more readily killed by drying than one which has passed through the different growth phases and survived into a resistant state. The conditions under which the water is removed from bacteria play an important role. This is particularly true of temperature, rapidity of drying, and the gases present. Generally, the higher the temperature the more rapid is the death of bacteria. It has been shown that bacteria dehydrated at nearly freezing temperatures and kept at that temperature will remain viable for some time. This process, known as *lyophilization,* is a technical process whereby water is extracted from the bacterial cell by vacuum; the moisture being condensed by drawing it into a chamber kept frigid by a dry ice-alcohol mixture. The small tubes containing the bacteria are then completely sealed and stored at cold temperatures. This method may be used for the preservation of various immunizing substances such as vaccines, bacterins, and immune sera. Organisms dried rapidly are not as apt to be killed as quickly as those dried slowly.

The death of microorganisms by desiccation is probably due to any or all of the following factors: concentration of salts producing plasmolysis, denaturation of proteins, destruction of intracellular enzymes, and the germicidal effect produced by oxidation.

### Filtration

Bacteria may be removed from a liquid by passing the liquid through a filter with pores so fine that the organism cannot enter. Such filters are made up in a great variety of shapes and densities. They are extensively used in the isolation of *filterable viruses* in pure culture; therefore, a more complete discussion of filters and filtration will be found in a later chapter. A laboratory "setup" of a filter apparatus is given in Figure 5.4. This method of sterilization is often used in the sterilization of media which may be altered by heat sterilization.

Filtration is also used for the removal of bacteria from culture media when it is necessary to study their soluble metabolic

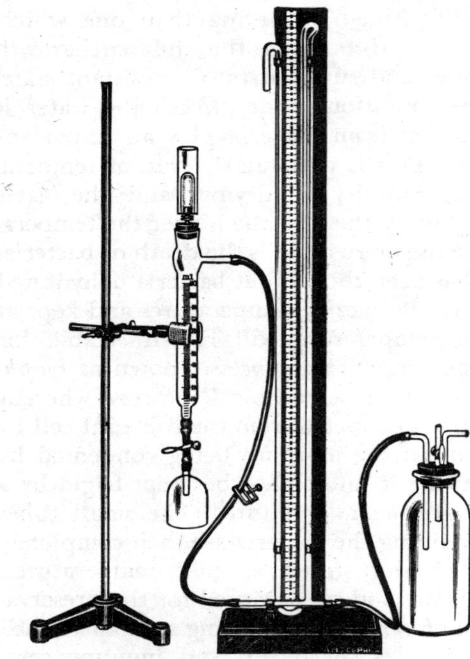

FIG. 5.4—Laboratory filter apparatus for removing bacteria from fluids.

products as well as in the removal of bacteria from sera which contain antitoxins and other antibodies. Filters of this character have been used for the filtration of a limited supply of drinking water. When first installed they are quite efficient, but it has been observed that the organisms rapidly penetrate through the filter walls, and in the course of time are found in the filtrate; consequently, such filters must be sterilized at intervals if they are to remain efficient.

Although it cannot be considered a method of sterilization, it should be noted here that nature purifies water by filtration. The seeping of water through the ground and the various rock strata underlying it serves as a most effective way of removing bacteria. This process is used extensively by man in an artificial way, by passing water through sand filters in order to remove bacteria and organic materials. It is true that biological action occurs in the surface of the earth and in the top layer of sand which, also, aids in the destruction of bacteria, but filtration is the most important step of the process.

## CHEMICAL DISINFECTION

The destruction of bacteria by chemicals is most important to anyone wishing to control the growth of bacteria, and is of special interest to students of medicine. The process of disinfection by the use of chemicals in a practical way dates from the time of Lister. Since that time volumes of literature have accumulated about the subject. Only a brief discussion of some of the common chemicals and a summary of some of the factors pertaining to the process of chemical disinfection, the mode of action, and the methods of evaluating the relative efficiency of disinfectants can be given here.

### Factors Affecting Chemical Disinfection

The factors which influence the process of chemical disinfection are extremely varied. Zinsser and Bayne-Jones have summarized them under three separate heads as follows:[2]

A. Factors relating to the chemical disinfectant.
   1. Chemical nature of the substance, inorganic, organic, structure.
   2. Ionization constant.
   3. Concentration.
   4. Solubility in the menstruum and in bacterial cellular constituents.
   5. Affinities for bacterial cell protoplasm or constituents.
   6. Mode of action, oxidation, precipitation, etc.

B. Factors relating to the bacteria.
   1. Species of organism.
   2. Chemical composition of the organism.
   3. Growth phase, especially in relation to differences in susceptibility of young cells as compared with old cells or differences between cells of same age. Young cells are often more susceptible than older ones.
   4. Special structures, spores, capsules.
   5. Previous history of the culture. Resistant forms can be selected or produced by gradually increased exposure to toxic agents.
   6. Dissociation in relation to differences in susceptibility.
   7. Number of bacteria in test mixture.

---

[2] H. Zinsser and S. Bayne-Jones, *A Textbook of Bacteriology,* D. Appleton-Century Co., New York, 1949.

C. General factors affecting both components and the process as a whole.
   1. Temperature. The temperature coefficient of disinfection is high, $Q_{10} = 2$ to 5.
   2. Surface phenomena, especially adsorption and surface tension, and the relationship of these to changes in concentration of substances in interfacial films, changes in permeability and diffusion.
   3. Hydrogen-ion concentration.
   4. Presence of other electrolytes, which influence both ionization of the chemical and the properties of the cells. This is especially true of sodium chloride as shown by numerous investigators.
   5. Presence of organic substances, especially proteins, which may react with the substance or form protective films on the organisms, usually reducing the action of the disinfectant.
   6. Pressure. Important in some cases, especially in reference to gaseous substances.
   7. Time.

It is obvious that since so many factors influence the process of killing bacteria by chemicals, it is rather difficult to choose the best disinfectant or set of conditions for disinfection. It must be remembered, also, that these factors apply to the use of chemicals in vitro, and that many more must be considered when chemicals are applied to live tissues.

### Characteristics of an Ideal Disinfectant

Certain characteristics may be listed as belonging to an ideal disinfectant. If a particular disinfectant measures up to the characteristics of the ideal, it is valuable for general use. The most important of these characteristics are as follows:

1. *Germicidal power*. The ideal disinfectant should possess high germicidal power; that is, it should kill bacteria in dilute solution. The ability of a disinfectant to kill microorganisms is usually compared with that of phenol. In making such comparisons it is customary to use *Salmonella typhosa,* the cause of typhoid fever, as the test organism. Most commercial disinfectants, particularly the coal-tar products, are sold upon the basis of their phenol coefficient.

2. *Stability*. A disinfectant to be most valuable should be relatively stable in the presence of organic matter. Some of the most powerful of the disinfectants combine with organic matter, forming insoluble compounds, and pass out of solution quite completely. The strength of the disinfectant thereby may be rapidly decreased to a point where it no longer destroys microorganisms.

3. *Homogeneity*. Disinfectants should be homogeneous in composition. Substances which may be bought in pure condition or in crystalline form, such as mercuric chloride, are ideal from this point of view. Many of the commercial disinfectants, particularly those prepared from coal tar, may vary considerably in their composition from time to time, and consequently in their germicidal value.

4. *Solubility*. The ideal disinfectant is one which will dissolve in all proportions in water. Alcohol is a typical example.

5. *Nontoxic to higher life*. An ideal disinfectant is nonpoisonous to man and to the higher animals. Obviously, disinfectants which will kill one kind of cell and not injure another are not very common. Most of the valuable disinfectants are somewhat injurious to tissues. Certain disinfectants, however, may be injected into the blood stream exerting a more harmful influence upon microorganisms than upon tissues of the body, destroying the former without seriously injuring the latter. A true example of this type is the arsphenamine used in the treatment of infections.

6. *Noncorrosive*. Inasmuch as disinfectants must frequently be used in contact with metals, fabrics, and other materials, it is highly desirable that they should not attack metal, injure fabrics, leave stains, or bleach color.

7. *Penetration*. Disinfectants differ decidedly in their power to penetrate materials to be sterilized. An ideal disinfectant is one which penetrates rapidly and efficiently.

8. *Economy*. The ideal disinfectant should be low in cost. Cost must not be judged by volume but by killing power. One disinfectant may cost more per gallon than another, yet it may have twice the killing power. Since certain effective chem-

icals are very expensive, they can be used only in limited quantities and for special purposes. The high cost of salts of silver, for example, practically limits silver to medicinal uses. If the entire water supply of a city is to be sterilized, a disinfectant must be chosen which is relatively inexpensive. This also applies to the disinfection of public stock yards.

9. *Power to remove dirt and grease.* A film of oil or grease over the surface of certain materials may wholly prevent the action of many disinfectants. Those which have power to dissolve or remove grease and all kinds of dirt are naturally more efficient.

10. *Deodorizing power.* A disinfectant which can combine with and destroy malodorous substances is preferable to one which does not, provided, of course, it does not have a disagreeable odor.

### The Action of Chemical Disinfectants

Chemicals destroy microorganisms in a variety of ways. A few of the chemicals have only one type of action, while others bring about death by a number of different types of chemical action.

Probably the most varied of any of the chemicals are the inorganic salts. It has been observed previously that salts of various kinds in low concentrations are stimulating to the growth of bacteria and are of importance as buffers in media. In high concentrations, however, most salts are definitely toxic and hasten death. Salts vary in toxicity; sodium chloride is toxic only in high concentrations while mercury bichloride is toxic in low concentrations. It has been shown, however, that the toxic action of many salts and other types of disinfectants may be increased by the addition of sodium chloride. This is due to the increased dissociation and dispersion of the disinfectant, and as a result, there is an increased effect upon the bacterial cells. This is not true of other salts. The addition of NaCl to $HgCl_2$ definitely lowers the toxicity of the latter. Salts do not produce bacterial death by osmotic effects. Bacteria are quite resistant to changes in osmotic pressure, living in distilled water as well as in rather high salt concentrations. Salts do, however, exert a dehydrating action upon the media in which bacteria grow, and thereby cause inhibition of growth and eventual death. Due to the dissociation of salts, most of the germicidal action is caused by the effect of ions (ion effect) upon the bacterial cell. This effect may be the result of the influence upon cell permeability, the lyotropic action upon cell protoplasm altering cell metabolism, and the inactivation of enzymes on which the cell depends for the synthesis of food substances.

Oxidation is one of the most common methods by which chemicals cause death. Many of the salts, for example, potassium permanganate and sodium perborate, are active oxidizing agents. The halogen compounds also are noted for this kind of chemical action.

Some chemicals which are used in sterilization are active reducing compounds. These, it is true, are not as commonly used as the oxidizing agents. The ferrous salts, sulfites, and thiosulfites are good examples of this type of chemical.

Many of the most effective chemicals form irreversible compounds with bacterial protoplasm by the coagulation of the protein. The salts of the heavy metals, i.e., silver, mercury, zinc, copper, and bismuth, are active in this manner. The derivatives of benzene, the coal-tar products, chief among which are phenol and cresol, are used widely as the basis of many commercial disinfectants. These chemicals in their pure state, saponified or altered by the replacement of an H atom by another chemical, cause the death of bacteria by the coagulation of bacterial protein.

It must be emphasized that all chemical disinfectants are more effective in their aqueous state and that germicidal activity is increased with an increase of temperature. Relative humidity alone has been shown to be detrimental to gram-negative bacteria. McDade and Hall have reported that die-away of surface-exposed gram-negative bacteria is accelerated and progressive at 25°C. and 53 to 85 per cent relative humidity.

**Bacteriostatic Compounds**

The bacteriostatic or microbiostatic effect of dyes, and other chemicals not classed as dyes, is commonly employed to control the growth of bacteria. Since many of the dyes are specific for certain species of bacteria, this method of control has three definite uses. *First,* it is possible to incorporate dyes in media to inhibit the growth of undesirable species; for example, the addition of crystal violet to media inhibits the growth of gram-positive bacteria but permits the growth of gram-negative types. *Second,* the bacteriostatic action of dyes is used to differentiate closely related species of bacteria, which is best illustrated by the use of basic fuchsin, thionin, and pyronin in differentiating the members of the brucella group. *Third,* dyes are used in the treatment of disease. Skin infections caused by gram-positive cocci may be controlled by the use of crystal violet. The acridine dyes, acriflavine and proflavine, are used internally as general antiseptics. Chemicals not classed as dyes may be used in the same manner as has been demonstrated by sodium cacodylate which has been used for years as a pulmonary and general antiseptic. It has always been the hope of those interested in chemotherapy that chemicals which would inhibit the growth of bacteria in vivo would be discovered. Ehrlich's discovery of salvarsan resulted from such investigations. The subsequent use of arsenicals and compounds of bismuth and antimony in treating spirochaetal infections has stimulated the search for other agents which would be effective against bacteria.

The discovery by Domagk in 1932 that prontosil was an effective chemotherapeutic agent against experimental streptococcal infection in mice opened the pathway for the subsequent development of the sulfonamide compounds. The most significant contribution to this development was the discovery by Tréfouëls and his associates that the active part of the prontosil was para-aminobenzene-sulfonamide, commonly known as *sulfanilamide;* subsequently, other compounds have been prepared by attaching other radicals to the nitrogen of the sulfonamide group. These compounds possess different solubilities, toxicities, and specific chemotherapeutic effects. The period between 1935 and 1942 may be called the "sulfonamide era" in chemotherapeutic research.

It is quite likely that this era has not entirely ended, for new compounds are being created, each claiming lesser toxicity for animal tissues and greater specificity for the various types of pathogenic bacteria.

The sulfonamide compounds which have been developed and found to be therapeutically useful are as follows: sulfanilamide, sulfathiazole, sulfapyridine, sulfadiazine, sulfasuxidine (succinylsulfathiazole), sulfaguanidine, sulfathaladine, sulfamethazine, sulfamerazine, and promin. To this list also must be added the parent compounds prontosil and neoprontosil. The sulfonamides are incorporated in many different types of vehicles for therapeutic purposes. They are prepared as water-soluble jellies, fatty ointments, oil-in-water emulsions, pastes, powders, and solutions. These drugs are frequently used in combination with other drugs for specific purposes. The discussions of the specificity of each of the above compounds for certain species of bacteria and the toxicity of each is beyond the scope of this brief summary.

The method by which the sulfonamides produce bacteriostasis is a subject of interest. It must be emphasized that this action is not a sterilization of fluids and tissues which are infected. These compounds inhibit the reproduction of bacteria; hence the living ones either perish because of their inability to convert food to energy or they become phagocytized by body cells. Numerous theories have been proposed to explain the mechanism by which these compounds act, but the most accepted one at present is known as the *Woods-Fildes theory of competitive inhibition.* In 1940 Woods reported that the action of sulfanilamide is neutralized by *p*-aminobenzoic acid. This compound is required by most

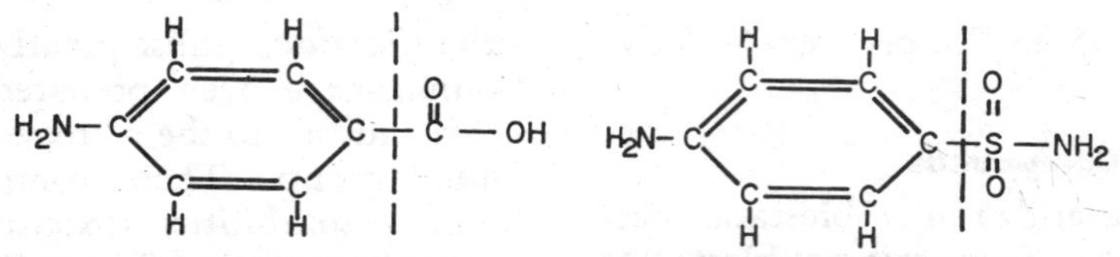

PARA-AMINOBENZOIC ACID SULFONAMIDE

FIG. 5.5—Structural resemblance of molecules of para-aminobenzoic acid and sulfonamide.

bacteria as an essential growth accessory substance *(metabolite)*, many being able to synthesize it. The structural formula of *p*-aminobenzoic acid (PABA) is similar to sulfanilamide (Fig. 5.5), and it has been postulated by Woods and Fildes that sulfanilamide replaces *p*-aminobenzoic acid in cellular metabolism. None of the sulfonamides have the ability to carry on PABA function, thus serving as *antimetabolites.* Folic acid, composed of three molecular groups—pterin, PABA, and glutamic acid, is an essential bacterial metabolite. If a sulfonamide is placed in a culture of bacteria which depends upon folic acid for growth, it competes with PABA, thus inhibiting growth. This occurs in the treatment of infectious diseases. Unfortunately some bacterial populations may have mutations in their midst which are unaffected by a sulfonamide. These are drug resistant and would be able to grow after a short period of inhibition, causing the appearance of symptoms of disease. Obviously another drug should be chosen for which the mutant is susceptible.

"Furacin" is another type of bacteriostatic agent. In 1944 Dodd and Stillman observed that several investigators had recorded the bacteriostatic action of furan compounds. Following the study of 42 different furan compounds, they found that the nitro group was essential in activating the furans to produce greater bacteriostasis. Later Cramer and Dodd found that the most effective agent was nitrofurazone N.N.R.: *5-nitro-2 furaldehyde semicarbazone,* known now by the trademark, Furacin.[3] Numerous reports have been made showing that this compound is quite effective against skin infections in man, particularly those caused by *Staphylococcus aureus.* Reports of the value of Furacin in animal infections are not numerous. Kaplan has shown that external infections in dogs and cats responded quickly to the drug, and Knowles, Knowles, and Knowles reported it of definite value in treating cases of otitis externa of dogs and cats. In addition to its bacteriostatic qualities Furacin may be used in wounds and incisions without fear of interference with healing.

Other nitrofuran compounds, such as furaltadone, are available for the treatment of both human and animal infections. Some of these may be combined with one or more of the antibiotics in order to be specific for a variety of bacteria. Furaltadone, for example, has been found effective against staphylococcic infections.

During very recent years the value of all bacteriostatic agents has been overshadowed by the antibiotics. The latter substances are discussed in the next chapter.

## THE EVALUATION OF DISINFECTANTS

The many chemicals which have germicidal power have made desirable the adoption of methods which determine the effectiveness of such chemical substances. In order to make wise selections of disinfectants, the user must have some value to which he may refer; furthermore, the testing of antiseptics and disinfectants is required by the federal government because all chemicals offered for interstate shipment or for import into or export from the United States are subject to the provisions of the Federal Insecticide Act and the Federal Food and Drugs Act, or both.

Various methods of testing the germicidal value of chemicals have been devised. In

[3] Eaton Laboratories, Inc., Norwich, Conn.

1881 Koch saturated silk threads with cultures of bacteria, treated them with the disinfectant, and then transferred them into tubes of sterile broth in order to detect the growth of surviving cells. Krönig and Paul (1897) introduced the use of garnets which were submerged in the test culture, then transferred to the disinfectant, and then washed in sterile water. The wash water was cultured to determine the effect of the treatment. Rideal and Walker (1903) were the first to use phenol as a standard with which the action of other disinfectants was compared under standard conditions. Chick and Martin (1908) believed that the addition of 3 per cent dried human feces to the test solution would give a more natural condition for the test because most disinfectants were commonly used in the presence of organic matter. Subsequent tests which have been developed to measure disinfectants have been based largely upon the technique outlined by Rideal and Walker. The comparison of all chemicals to phenol has been criticized justly, however, and for that reason other methods which give a truer picture of the value of nonphenol compounds have been advocated. The real test of the ability of a chemical to kill bacteria, and its value as a disinfectant for use on skin and other tissues is not obtained by its action on bacteria suspended in distilled water in a test tube; therefore, toxicity tests have been devised which measure the effect of the disinfectant or antiseptic on live tissue along with its ability to kill bacteria.

It is not desirable in this book to outline in detail the various tests used in the testing of disinfectants and antiseptics. The student is referred to more complete treatises for further information, a list of which is given at the end of this chapter. Only a brief description of each method will be given here.

### The Phenol Coefficient

The *phenol coefficient* of a disinfectant may be defined as the ratio of the killing power of the disinfectant to the killing power of pure phenol when determined under standard conditions. It is obvious, therefore, that the most important factors in such a determination are the conditions under which the test is made. The conditions under which phenol coefficients and other germicide tests are determined are given in Circular No. 198 by Ruehle and Brewer of the United States Department of Agriculture, and form the basis for the following discussion.

1. Choice of microorganism: *Salmonella typhosa* (Hopkins strain) and *Staphylococcus aureus*.
2. Composition of medium: 5 gms. of Liebig's beef extract, 5 gms. of chemically pure sodium chloride, and 10 gms. of Armour's peptone (for disinfectant testing) in 1,000 ml. of distilled water.
3. Acidity of medium: pH 6.8.
4. Amount of culture medium in tube: 10 ml.
5. Phenol: Must meet the requirements of the United States Pharmacopoeia, and in addition, the congealing point must not be below 40°C. A 5% stock solution is required.
6. Amount of culture added to diluted disinfectants: 0.5 ml. to 5.0 ml.
7. Resistance of test culture to phenol (dilutions killing in 10 minutes, but not in 5 minutes): 1–90.
8. Condition of tube in test: plugged with cotton.
9. Temperature of test: 20°C.
10. Time intervals of the test: 5, 10, and 15 minutes.
11. Amount of medication mixture transferred (size of loop): 4 mm. loop (of No. 23 B. and S. gage wire).
12. Calculation of phenol coefficient: highest dilution not killing in 5 minutes but killing in 10 minutes divided by same for phenol.

It is apparent that the highest dilution of disinfectant (X) not killing in 5 minutes, but killing in 10 minutes, is 1:350; likewise the dilution for phenol is 1:90.

The phenol coefficient is $350/90 = 3.89$.

In order to avoid an impression of assumed accuracy, the phenol coefficient is calculated to the nearest 0.1, unless the coefficient is less than 1.0, which in the above case would be 3.90.

The calculation of the phenol coefficient will be clarified by the following example:

| | 5 Minutes | 10 Minutes | 15 Minutes |
|---|---|---|---|
| Disinfectant (X) | | | |
| 1-300 .......... | 0 | 0 | 0 |
| 1-325 .......... | + | 0 | 0 |
| 1-350 .......... | + | 0 | 0 |
| 1-370 .......... | + | + | 0 |
| 1-400 .......... | + | + | + |
| Phenol: | | | |
| 1- 90 .......... | + | 0 | 0 |
| 1-100 .......... | + | + | + |

### The Wet Filter-Paper Method

The wet filter-paper method is a germicidal test rather than a test of inhibitory properties. It is used when the substance to be tested is not soluble or completely miscible with water, or for substances that are to be used in high concentration, such as soaps, toothpastes, suppositories, dyes, dusting powders, salves, and ointments. If the substance is to be used in the body cavities the test is carried out at 37°C.; if not, the test is carried out at 20°C. or at room temperature.

No. 2 Whatman filter paper is cut into pieces about 0.5 cm. square, and sterilized in a plugged test tube at temperatures below 170°C. to prevent charring. A suitable number of the paper squares are then impregnated with *Staph. aureus,* or other test organisms, by immersion in a 24-hour broth culture of the organism. The culture must have the standard resistance required for phenol coefficient testing. The wet inoculated squares are then placed in the liquid or solid substance to be tested, arranged in intimate contact, and completely covered. At the end of 5 minutes, 10 minutes, 15 minutes, 1 hour, or any other desired length of time, the wet papers are removed with a sterilized, stiff, platinum wire bent at a sharp angle to form a hook and placed in 10 ml. of sterile broth. After all possible disinfectant has been removed (in the case of sticky substances the needle must be used to aid in freeing the squares of adherent germicide) the squares are retransferred to a fresh tube of sterile broth (10 ml.), and the tubes are incubated at 37°C. for 48 hours; they are then observed for evidence of growth.

Resubcultures are always required in this test because the first tube of broth to which the filter-paper squares have been added frequently contains sufficient antiseptic to exhibit inhibition of growth. Both tubes of broth are usually incubated.

### The Dry Filter-Paper Method

The dry filter-paper method is used in tests of fumigants and of oils that are to be used where moisture is absent. It is similar to the wet filter-paper test, using squares of paper that have been impregnated as described under the test above, with the exception that squares are dried for two days in a sterile Petri dish in the 37°C. incubator. This test can be used successfully only with organisms capable of resisting the drying. *Sal. typhosa* will not withstand the drying. *Staph. aureus* is the usual test organism. The inoculated, dried-paper squares may be used at any time up to 30 days after the drying period, but the resistance of the organism at no time should fall so low that it is incapable of withstanding a 1–80 dilution of phenol for 5 minutes at 20°C. It should be emphasized that control tests with nonmedicated squares should always be carried out to test the viability of the test organism. As is true in the wet filter-paper method, resubcultures are always necessary.

### The Agar-Plate Method

The agar-plate method is a test for inhibitory properties and is used for substances remaining in contact with the body in the absence of serous body fluids. Examples of substances which may be tested by this method are salves, dusting powders, creams, plasters, pads, adhesive tape, catgut, and suppositories. The test organism ordinarily used is *Staph. aureus,* but for special purposes the test may be used with any organism capable of growing on agar. The agar is of the same composition as that previously described for carrying stock cultures of the test organism.

Fifteen to 20 ml. of agar are melted and cooled to 42°–45°C. To this is added 0.1 ml. of a 24-hour broth culture of the test organism. The inoculated agar is then poured into a sterile Petri plate and allowed to harden. As soon as the agar has hardened, the test substance is placed in intimate contact with the surface of the agar. If it is a salve, it is first warmed sufficiently to soften and thus secure a complete peripheral contact. As a control, warmed sterile petrolatum may be placed on another portion of the plate. The plates are incubated 24 to 48 hours under unglazed porcelain tops at 37°C. and are then examined for evidence of inhibition. If the preparation is antiseptic or inhibitory, a zone of clear agar will be observed around the portion where the substance has been in contact with the agar, and the width of the zone will indicate the diffusibility of the inhibitory (antiseptic) agent. If there is no inhibition, growth of the test organism will be observed adjacent to and even under the test substance.

### The Serum Agar-Plate Method

Preparations recommended for use on open wounds, cuts, and abrasions are effective only if they exhibit activity in the presence of serous fluids. In testing such preparations the agar-plate method is modified by the addition of 10 per cent sterile horse serum to the agar.

### The Agar Cup-Plate Method

The agar cup-plate method is merely a variation of the agar-plate method. It is used on products liquid at the temperature of the test. The agar, or serum agar, is inoculated as in the agar-plate method. Before the agar cools, a depression or cup is made in the medium by standing a sterile flat-bottomed glass tube, 1.5 cm. in diameter, in the liquefied agar; after hardening, the glass tube is removed by slightly twisting and pulling at the same time. Insertion of a sterile wire down the side of the tube for the introduction of air will eliminate much of the cracking of the agar. Another method of preparing the agar cup plate is to allow the medium to harden and then cut out a disk in the agar, by means of a cork borer, 1.5 cm. in diameter. Several drops of melted agar are placed in the cup to seal cracks or crevices. After the agar cup plate is prepared, 6 drops of the test liquid are placed in the cup, and the plate is incubated under an unglazed porcelain top for 24 to 48 hours. If there is a clear zone about the cup, the substance under test has inhibitory properties. Here, as well as in the agar-plate test, the agar in the clear zone may be tested for growth by subculture in broth to indicate whether the action is germicidal or merely inhibitory.

### Tests in the Presence of Organic Matter

In general, the tests outlined above will take care of most of the preparations; however, special tests may be required to determine the value of products recommended for certain purposes. For example, recommendations on the label may make advisable the use of various additions of organic matter, such as increased amounts of peptone or the addition of gelatin, blood, ascitic fluid, saliva, urine, or feces, depending upon the information desired.

### The Toxicity Index

The use of various chemicals to disinfect skin and other tissues prior to surgical operations and for the treatment of infections has prompted the development of methods which measure the toxicity of such antiseptics for tissues. An ideal antiseptic, obviously, would be one which would kill bacteria but would not injure tissue cells. Numerous investigators have devised methods which may be used to measure the *toxicity index* of a disinfectant, that is, *the highest dilution of disinfectant required to prevent the growth of embryonic tissue divided by the highest dilution to kill the test organism.*

A technique introduced to determine the *toxicity index* of antiseptics is that of Salle

TABLE 5.1

TOXICITY INDEX OF VARIOUS GERMICIDES

| Germicide | Highest Dilution Showing No Tissue Growth = A | Highest Dilution Showing No Growth of *Staph. aureus* = B | Toxicity Index = A/B | *Staph. aureus* Phenol Coefficient |
|---|---|---|---|---|
| Iodine | 1– 1,800 | 1–20,000 | 0.09 | 308 |
| Iodine trichloride | 1– 2,400 | 1– 6,000 | 0.4 | 92 |
| Mercuric chloride | 1– 45,000 | 1–16,000 | 2.8 | 246 |
| Hexylresorcinol | 1– 21,000 | 1– 7,000 | 3.0 | 108 |
| Metaphen | 1– 76,000 | 1– 6,000 | 12.7 | 92 |
| Phenol | 1– 840 | 1– 65 | 12.9 | ... |
| Potassium mercuric iodide | 1– 12,000 | 1– 900 | 13.3 | 13.8 |
| Merthiolate | 1–176,400 | 1– 4,000 | 35 | 71 |
| Mercurochrome | 1– 10,500 | 1– 40 | 262 | 0.6 |

and associates. Fundamental to the test is the determination of the *Staph. aureus* phenol coefficients for various antiseptics by using the technique which has been described previously. Heart tissue fragments from 9-day-old chick embryos embedded in guinea pig plasma diluted with three parts of Tyrode's solution and one part of embryonic fluid are used as the test-tissue cultures. Various dilutions of the disinfectants are made in chick embryonic fluid, added to the flasks containing the tissue cultures, and examined for evidence of growth after 48 hours incubation. The toxicity index for the antiseptics is determined by dividing the highest dilution showing no tissue growth by the highest dilution showing no growth of *Staph. aureus.* The most efficient antiseptic is the one having the lowest toxicity index. Table 5.1 shows results of the testing of several germicides obtained by Salle and Lazarus. Note that iodine appears to be the most ideal antiseptic as measured by the tissue culture technique as well as by the phenol coefficient methods.

## DISINFECTANTS AND ANTISEPTICS IN COMMON USE

Space does not permit the listing of all chemicals which are available as disinfectants and antiseptics, nor is it the function of this book to discuss the chemical structure and the application of chemicals in the field or laboratory. Chemicals used as antiseptics and disinfectants may be classed in definite groups, such as acids and alkalies. Various combinations of one group of chemicals with another (mercuric iodide) may be utilized in preparing more ideal disinfectants. Certain chemicals may be treated in specific ways—saponification of the cresols, for example, to make a more ideal compound. It is obvious that these combinations are almost limitless; hence it is easily understood why so many preparations are available to the user with each individual compound making its claim to being the most suitable for all types of disinfection. It is doubtful if there is a universal "ideal disinfectant," nor is it essential that there should be such a substance. Different chemicals should be chosen for different types of disinfection. One may excel in one situation where another is entirely inapplicable.

### Acids

The addition of acid to any solution containing bacteria, with the consequent increase in hydrogen-ion concentration, increases the rate of death. Some bacteria, termed the *acidophiles,* will grow well in relatively high hydrogen-ion concentrations. The ability of these organisms to grow in the presence of high concentrations of acid is sometimes utilized in their isolation. Some types of bacteria are able to survive the hydrogen-ion concentration of gastric juice, which makes them of greater consequence in intestinal infections.

Acids are most commonly used as preservatives. The most important are the acetic (usually in the form of vinegar) and the lactic acids, the latter being the preservative agent in sour milk, sauerkraut, and silage. Benzoic acid, salicylic acid, sulfurous acid, formic acid, pyroligneous acid, carbonic acid, and citric acid have been used, and some continue to be used as preservatives for fruits and meats. They are not active germicides but do prohibit the growth of microorganisms.

Boric acid is used extensively as an antiseptic wash for mucous membranes, particularly of the conjunctiva. It is a poor germicide but does have antiseptic qualities. It is toxic and must be used in high dilutions.

### Alkalies

High alkalinity, that is, high concentration of hydroxyl ions, likewise exerts a destructive action upon microorganisms. Sodium hydroxide is one of the most widely used chemicals of this group. In a 0.5 per cent concentration it is valuable as a germicide for mechanical milking equipment. In stronger solutions it is used in the disinfection of stanchion floors, maternity stalls, and farrowing pens. It has been shown to be almost a specific virucide, especially for the viruses of foot-and-mouth disease and hog cholera.

Unslaked lime (quick lime) added to water is converted into calcium hydroxide, and when used in strong solutions, as in whitewash, it has a marked disinfecting action.

Various detergents, chief among which is trisodium phosphate, are used in the dairy industry in washing milk equipment, in the washing of dishes, and in washing bottles for beverages. While they are not as active as the hydroxides, such compounds are definitely germicidal when used in hot solutions.

### Salts of Heavy Metals

The salts of silver, mercury, arsenic, copper, and zinc are all used in a variety of combinations as disinfectants and antiseptics.

Silver nitrate is one of the most commonly used compounds containing silver. It is objectionable, however, because of its corrosive and irritating action on tissue. Silver proteinates such as argyrol, silvol, and neosilvol are not as irritating to live tissue and are frequently used to disinfect surfaces of mucous membranes.

The mercury compounds are well known for their germicidal value. Mercuric chloride is the most widely used of these chemicals. The biniodide of mercury is also quite popular. Because of the toxic and corrosive action of simple mercury compounds, various complex mixtures have been prepared. Mercurochrome has had periods of popularity. Metaphen and Merthiolate are two comparatively new mercury compounds which appear to be satisfactory germicides.

Arsenic compounds are not used to a great extent as germicides because they are toxic to human and animal life; however, the value of the complex salts of arsenic in the treatment of spirochetal infections is well known.

The salts of copper cannot be depended upon for their germicidal action. As an algacide, however, copper sulfate has no equal and is used extensively in the control of algae in water supplies.

Zinc salts are practically devoid of germicidal activity, but zinc oxide is widely used in the treatment of many conditions where infection may exist. The beneficial results are due to an astringent action which promotes healing.

### Phenols and Related Compounds

Phenol, or carbolic acid, $C_6H_5OH$, either pure or in mixtures with alcohol, glycerin, or various oils, ranks among the most efficient of the disinfectants. Weak dilutions, 0.5 per cent, are used in the preservation of antigens, viruses, and antisera used in immunizing procedures. The methyl phenols or cresols, $C_6H_4CH_3OH$, either pure or in trade mixtures—tricresol, creolin and liquor cresolis—are also effective germicides. They are most frequently used in 1 to 5 per cent solutions and will destroy bacteria even in the presence of quantities of organic matter. For this reason they are universally used for the disinfection of barns, pens, railway cars, trucks, and many other places where infected animals have been kept.

Orthophenylphenol is an odorless disinfectant which has rather wide use as a barn disinfectant. It is effective against *Mycobacterium tuberculosis,* hence is useful as a disinfectant for barns after tuberculin reactors have been removed. This disinfectant is much more satisfactory for dairy barn use because it does not impart odors to milk as is the case when the phenolic compounds are used.

### The Halogens

The halogens and the variety of compounds which are prepared by mixing them with other chemicals have the distinction of being the most widely used of any of the disinfectants. Halogens are not effective in the presence of organic matter, and for that reason their use is limited.

Chlorine is used more than any other chemical of the group. Chlorine gas, or the various mixtures, such as hypochlorite prepared by the action of chlorine on lime, all exert a germicidal action on bacteria by oxidation resulting from the union of chlorine with hydrogen in water. Chlorine is used in the sterilization of water supplies, in the treatment of sewage water, for the sterilization of all dairy equipment used in the transfer of milk from the farm to the consumer, and for sterilizing dishes, glassware, and many other articles. Some of the more stable chlorine compounds are used in the treatment of wounds and other disease processes; among these are chloramine-T, dichloramine-T, Javelle water, Dakin's solution, and azochloramide.

Iodine is one of the most efficient disinfectants for use on skin surfaces. Usually it is used in alcoholic solutions with potassium iodide, and for that reason is irritating to tissue. The value of low concentrations, such as 1 per cent of iodine, as antiseptics has been proved during recent years. Reference was made to this fact in the preceding discussion of the toxicity index, which the student should review at this point. Colloidal iodine is used as an intestinal antiseptic and a parasiticide. Iodine is commonly used in combination with other chemicals—biniodide of mercury, for example, forming stable and effective disinfectants. Iodoform is one of the iodine compounds which is used in wounds and other septic processes; it is valuable for this purpose, but to some the odor of the compound is disagreeable, and for that reason the use of it in medicine is objectionable.

Fluorine is too reactive and toxic to be of great use as a disinfectant. Sodium fluoride is a valuable insecticide and may be added in small quantities, 10 mg. per ml. of blood, for the preservation of blood intended for laboratory examination. Bromine is too reactive to be of any use as a disinfectant or antiseptic.

### Miscellaneous Compounds

Alcohol, especially ethyl alcohol, is considered by many to be a most effective antiseptic, and is credited by some as a disinfectant. The efficacy of this alcohol is dependent upon the concentration. Investigation and experience have shown that 70 per cent alcohol is most efficient. Concentrations above and below that concentration are ineffective. Alcohols in general are more bactericidal in the higher molecular weight. This fact is shown clearly by the *Sal. typhosa* phenol coefficients of various alcohols tested by Tilley and Schaffer given in Table 5.2.

Isopropyl alcohol has been shown to be a more effective germicide than the more commonly used ethyl alcohol. It is used in the 98–99 per cent pure state and is noncorrosive to instruments. The pungent odor of this alcohol is objectionable, and for that reason it has not come into wide use.

Chloroform is used as an attenuating agent for vaccines. It may be added as a preservative to blood serum which is to be used in the preparation of Loeffler's

TABLE 5.2

PHENOL COEFFICIENTS OF VARIOUS ALCOHOLS

| | Phenol Co-efficients |
|---|---|
| Primary Normal Alcohols | |
| Methyl | 0.026 |
| Ethyl | 0.040 |
| Propyl | 0.102 |
| Butyl | 0.237 |
| Amyl | 0.78 |
| Hexyl | 2.30 |
| Heptyl | 6.80 |
| Octyl | 21.00 |
| Secondary Alcohols | |
| Propyl | 0.064 |
| Butyl | 0.152 |
| Amyl | 0.38 |
| Hexyl | 1.00 |
| Tertiary Alcohols | |
| Butyl | 0.081 |
| Amyl | 0.182 |
| Hexyl | 0.45 |

Source: Tilley and Schaffer, Jour. Bact. 12:303, 1926.

medium or to enrich other media; likewise, ether is used for the above purposes.

Formaldehyde gained great popularity as a disinfectant when it was popular to fumigate contaminated dwellings. Its value as a disinfectant in that procedure was due to its solubility in water; on account of this characteristic it is usually sold commercially as Formalin, an aqueous alcoholic solution containing approximately 40 per cent formaldehyde. Formalin is an effective germicide and is used not only in the killing of animal and human pathogenic bacteria, but also for treating seeds and potato tubers in order to kill fungi with which they may be contaminated. This chemical is used as an attenuating agent for bacteria, toxins, and viruses which are to be used as immunizing agents. Formaldehyde forms hexamethylenamine with ammonia, a compound which is used extensively as a urinary antiseptic.

Potassium permanganate is used extensively in veterinary medicine as an antiseptic in drinking water for poultry for which it seems to have definite value. It is used as a wound dressing also. The stains produced by the chemical have been factors preventing its general use as an antiseptic. Hydrogen peroxide is not employed extensively as a disinfectant due to the ease with which it combines with organic matter; however, it does have some virtue as a cleansing agent for deep wounds, but its effervescing action belies its real value, and it should not be depended upon to any great extent. Metallic peroxides, $CaO_2$, $MgO_2$, $ZnO_2$, and $NaO_2$, are claimed to be less reactive than $H_2O_2$. They are usually found in ointments and toothpastes. Their antiseptic values are not great.

One of the most important factors influencing all disinfection is freedom from oily compounds and organic matter. The virtues of soap as a cleansing agent, serving to remove many bacteria from surfaces of the skin, are common knowledge. Numerous investigators have shown that most soaps also have a certain amount of antiseptic value. In general it has been found that the activity of soaps depends upon the fatty acid radicals present, the state of saturation of the fatty acids, the concentration of the soapy solutions, the temperature, and the amount of foreign material present. Various compounds of known disinfecting value have been added to soap with the assumption that a more effective process of sterilization could be accomplished. Critical evaluation of such compounds has failed to reveal a greater effectiveness than with the disinfectant alone. In some instances the presence of soap interfered rather than enhanced the action of the disinfectant.

Investigations of the synthetic soaps or detergents have revealed that they have germicidal activity. Such compounds are classified as either *cationic* or *anionic* detergents. The cationic detergents have been found to have greater germicidal activity than the anionic compounds. Cationic detergents are more active in the alkaline range and anionic in the acid range. The great popularity of these compounds as detergents, wetting agents, and emulsifiers has resulted in the synthesis of over 1,000 different ones since Domagk showed the value of roccal in 1935. Most of these compounds are nontoxic to living tissues and are safe to use as skin disinfectants. Some have been given internally to experimental animals without showing toxic effects. Zephiran, an alkyl-dimethyl-benzyl-ammonium chloride similar to roccal, has been shown to be an active germicide. In a dilution of 1:80,000 it may be used as a preservative for biological products, such as antiserums. Triethanolamine lauryl sulfate, commonly known as Drene, is an anionic compound effective against gram-positive bacteria. McCulloch demonstrated that this compound was effective against *Streptococcus agalactiae* and *Erysipelothrix insidiosa*.

The quaternary ammonium salts, cationic surface-active agents, are the most recent additions to the long list of germicidal agents. Numerous compounds known by various trade names are widely used in disinfection. As a group these agents are satisfactory against nonsporeforming bacteria. They have the distinct value of being active in the presence of organic matter. Acetyl-beta-methylcholine chloride (mecholyl), a compound belonging to this group, ionizes to a high degree in solution and resembles the alkali metals in stability.

## REFERENCES


BARBER, EDDA, and FLYNN, PATRICIA. Effects of Sterilizing Agents on Microorganisms. (Abst.) Jet Propulsion Laboratory, Calif. Inst. Tech., Pasadena, 1961.

CHICK, H., and BROWNING, C. H. The Theory of Disinfection. A System of Bacteriology in Relation to Medicine, Privy Council, Med. Res. Council. His Majesty's Stationery Office, London, Vol. I, Chap. 5, 1930.

DAILY, L. E. The Nitrofurans—A New Group of Chemotherapeutic Agents. Printed by the Eaton Laboratories, Norwich, N. Y., 1947.

FILDES, PAUL. A Rational Approach to Research in Chemotherapy. Lancet 1(238):955–57, 1940.

FROBISHER, M. Fundamentals of Microbiology. W. B. Saunders Co., Philadelphia, 1962.

JONES, L. M. Veterinary Pharmacology and Therapeutics. 3rd Ed. Iowa State Univ. Press Ames, 1965.

KAPLAN, A. D. Vet. Med. 43, 1948.

KLATZ, I. M., and MELLODY, M. Jour. Bact. 57:477, 1949.

KNOWLES, A. T., *et al.* No. Amer. Vet. 29:495–96, 1948.

LAWRENCE, C. A. Surface-active Quaternary Ammonium Germicides. Academic Press, Inc., New York, 1950.

LUCHIESCH, MATTHEW. Applications of Germicidal, Erythermal and Infrared Energy. D. Van Nostrand Co., Inc., New York, 1946.

MAXCY, K. F. Rosenau Preventive Medicine and Public Health. 8th Ed. Appleton-Century-Crofts, Inc., New York, 1956.

MCCABE, W. R., *et al.* Furaltadone. New Eng. Jour. Med. 263:927–34, 1960.

MCCULLOCH, E. C. Disinfection and Sterilization. 2nd Ed. Lea & Febiger, Philadelphia, 1945.

MCDADE, J. J., and HALL, L. B. Survival of Gram-negative Bacteria in the Environment. Amer. Jour. Hyg. 80:192–204, 1964.

PERKINS, J. J. Principles and Methods of Sterilization. Charles C Thomas, Springfield, Ill., 1956.

REDDISH, G. F. Antiseptics, Disinfectants, Fungicides and Chemical and Physical Sterilization. 2nd Ed. Lea & Febiger, Philadelphia, 1957.

SALLE, A. J., and Lazarus, A. S. Proc. Soc. Exp. Biol. Med. 32:665, 1935.

———, *et al.* Jour. Bact 34:267, 1937.

———, *et al.* Proc. Soc. Exp. Biol. Med. 37:694, 1938.

———, *et al.* Jour. Bact. 37:639, 1939.

SHECHMEISTER, I. L., and SALLE, A. J. Proc. Soc. Exp. Biol. Med. 38:295, 1938.

WILSON, G. S., and MILES, A. A. Topley's Principles of Bacteriology and Immunity. 5th Ed. Williams & Wilkins Co., Baltimore, 1964.

WOODS, D. D. Brit. Jour. Exp. Path. 21:74–90, 1940.

WOOLEY, D. W. Science 100:579, 1944.

# 6

# Antibiotic Agents

THE DISCOVERY AND THERAPEUTIC USE OF penicillin will be recorded as one of the most significant contributions to medicine. This discovery is of significance to the entire field of bacteriology as well as to medicine. It has increased the scope of bacteriology, opening a broad new avenue for scientific endeavor. In principle, the antibiotic or antagonistic association of bacteria, yeasts, and molds is not new. It has been an interesting phase in the study of bacteria since the early contributions of Pasteur. Generally, the association of microscopic forms with each other has been lost from view because of the stress placed upon the study of pure cultures. For that reason every bacteriologist has disregarded contaminants on a Petri plate culture which show inhibition of the organism under study. Plates of milk, water, and soil samples have shown the presence of colonies which inhibit the growth of neighboring colonies.

Numerous well-known examples of antagonistic or antibiotic action may be cited. It is evident that a strict aerobic organism cannot live in the presence of an anaerobe. The pH of the medium produced by the acid-producing organism becames too high for many types of bacteria to continue growth. Likewise marked alkalinity of a medium due to the hydrolysis of proteins inhibits the growth of still other types. These are examples of antagonisms commonly used to explain inhibition of growth. It is understandable, then, that the advent of specific antibiotic agents has increased tremendously the significance of antagonistic association.

## HISTORICAL DEVELOPMENT

Although the search for antibiotic agents was stimulated by the discovery and use of penicillin, this substance was not the first one to be recognized. In 1877 Pasteur observed that the growth of the anthrax bacillus was inhibited by air-borne contaminants. Bouchard noted in 1888 that *Pseudomonas aeruginosa* was antagonistic to *Bacillus anthracis* and at one time filtrates of that organism were advocated in the treatment of anthrax. The early work of Bouchard was substantiated by other workers who showed that the products of *Ps. aeruginosa* were inhibitory to many different species of bacteria; futhermore, Emmerich and Löw were able to prepare an extract from the filtrate of cultures of this organism. This material was called *pyocyanase* and was found to have a destructive bacteriolytic effect upon numerous species of bacteria. This lytic substance was thought to be a proteolytic enzyme by early workers; however, recently Shoental has found three antibacterial substances in chloroform extracts of *Ps. aeruginosa* filtrates: pyocyanin, α-oxyphenazine, and a colorless substance. The antibacterial action of pyocyanin and other extracts has been shown by many, but the toxicity of the material has prevented its therapeutic use.

Antibiotic substances similar in action to pyocyanin have been found to be produced by numerous species of bacteria. In his comprehensive survey of this subject, Waksman lists 16 different strains of sporeforming bacteria and approximately the same number of nonsporeforming strains which show antibiotic activity against different bacteria.

Antibiotic action was not observed in bacteria alone. In 1922 Alexander Fleming, in England, observed that egg white contained a material which dissolved bacteria. He called it lysozyme. Although this material attracted considerable attention at the time, it did not gain chemotherapeutic popularity; nevertheless this discovery did bear fruit, for it enabled Fleming to recognize the antibiotic effect of a contaminating mold in a culture of staphylocci in 1929. Fleming recorded this observation as follows:[1]

> While working with staphylococcus variants a number of culture-plates were set aside on the laboratory bench and examined from time to time. In the examinations these plates were necessarily exposed to the air and they became contaminated with various micro-organisms. It was noticed that around a large colony of a contaminating mould the staphylococcus colonies became transparent and were obviously undergoing lysis. Subcultures of this mould were made and experiments conducted with a view to ascertaining something of the properties of the bacteriolytic substance which had evidently been formed in the mould culture and which had diffused into the surrounding medium. It was found that the broth in which the mould had been grown at room temperature for one or two weeks had acquired marked inhibiting, bactericidal and bacteriolytic properties to many of the more common pathogenic bacteria.

Nutrient broth in which the mold was grown contained the inhibiting agent which Fleming called "penicillin" because the mold was a species of Penicillium. The species later was identified as *Penicillium notatum.* He suggested at the time that this agent had chemotherapeutic potentialities but, like so many discoveries of this type, the time was not right for acceptance. Fleming did find use for the agent in the isolation of influenza bacilli from cocci, for the former organisms were not sensitive to penicillin whereas the latter were inhibited.

The application of antibiotic agents in the treatment of disease was really crystallized by the discovery of gramicidin by Dubos in 1939. This substance, produced by the sporeforming organism *Bacillus brevis,* was found to inhibit the growth of streptococci and pneumococci.

Penicillin was not to be forgotten. Bacteriologists and chemists, particularly Florey and Chain at Oxford University, England, had continued research on this important antibiotic and in 1940 had purified enough penicillin to prove that it was highly effective against infections caused by streptococci, staphylococci, and gas-gangrene bacilli. By 1943 the value of penicillin was proved beyond any doubt and, due to the insistency by the army that it be made available for use, the therapeutical manufacturing industry in the United States centered upon the manufacture of it.

Penicillin has one shortcoming. It is not particularly active against the gram-negative rods. In 1942 Waksman and Woodruff described an antibiotic agent *streptothricin,* which was produced by a soil organism *Actinomyces lavendulae.* This agent inhibited the growth of gram-negative bacteria. In 1944 Schatz, Bugie, and Waksman discovered that *Actinomyces griseus* produced an antibiotic agent which was more active against gram-negative organisms than was streptothricin. This new substance was named *streptomycin.*

During the 1940 decade practically every microbiologist kept his eyes open for organisms with antibiotic properties. Bacteria as well as molds were studied. In 1945 Johnson, Anker, and Meleney isolated an organism *Bacillus licheniformis,* a species closely related to *Bacillus subtilis,* which produced an antibiotic agent which they called *bacitracin.*

During the process of examining soils from various parts of the world for fungi which have antibiotic properties, Burkholder isolated an actinomycete, which he called *Streptomyces venezuelae,* from soil from Venezuela. It has been revealed that this organism is present in American soils also. The antibiotic agent produced by this organism was first reported in 1947 by Ehrlich, Bartz, Smith, Joslyn, and Burk-

[1] A. Fleming. On the Antibacterial Action of Cultures of a Penicillium With Special Reference to Their Use in the Isolation of *B. influenzae.* Brit. Jour. Exp. Path. 10:226, 1929.

holder. It was originally called chloromycetin but is now known as *chloramphenicol.* Chemical studies of this antibiotic have shown that it is a derivative of dichloroacetic acid and has the following chemical structure:

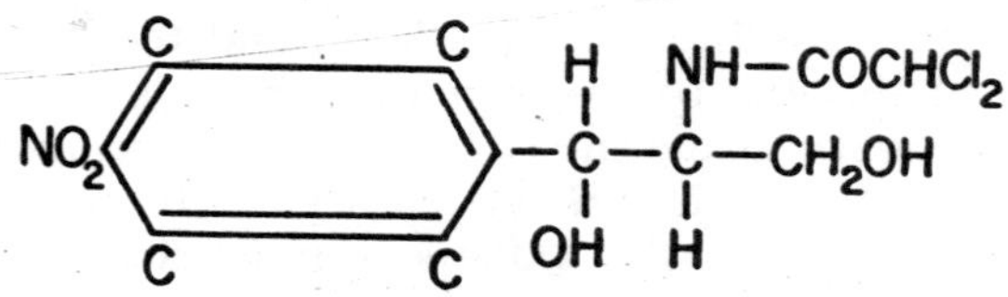

Chloramphenicol has the distinction of being the first of the important antibiotics to be synthetically produced in large quantities. It has been shown to be active against a large number of bacteria, thus gaining the distinction of being a "broad spectrum" antibiotic. Although it has not been shown to inhibit the growth of viruses, it is effective against the rickettsiae and other infectious agents of similar characteristics.

The discovery of chlortetracycline by Duggar in 1948 revealed another antibiotic with a "broad spectrum" inasmuch as it is effective against a large variety of both gram-positive and gram-negative bacteria, as well as other infectious agents. Chlortetracycline (produced under the trademark name of Aureomycin by the Lederle Laboratories) is produced by a soil actinomyces, *Streptomyces aureofaciens.* It is manufactured in large quantities and is widely used as a therapeutic agent. In addition to this important use, this antibiotic has been shown to increase the growth rate of swine and chickens when fed in small amounts. The exact manner by which this effect is produced is not known. It is theorized that bacteria of low toxicity which are present in the intestinal tract are inhibited in growth, or that the antibiotic may enter into the metabolism of cells as an additional nutrient substance, or that it produces an increased activity of enzymes essential for cell metabolism.

In 1950 Finlay and associates of the Charles Pfizer Company announced the discovery of an agent they called Terramycin. This name is now used as a trademark name for the antibiotic by the Pfizer Company, but the scientific name is *oxytetracycline.* The antibiotic is produced by the soil actinomycete, *Streptomyces rimosus.* It, also, has a wide spectrum of activity and it has been shown to promote more rapid growth in young animals.

The close similarity of chlortetracycline and oxytetracycline led to the detailed chemical study of both compounds. In 1952 Stephens and associates announced the discovery of tetracycline, an antibiotic agent common to, but different from, the two parent substances. This agent is produced by both *Strep. aureofaciens* and *Strep. rimosus.* In addition to the production of this antibiotic by fermentation, it can be produced by the catalytic hydrogenation of chlortetracycline. This latter discovery has opened the door to the probable development of various agents with slightly different chemical structures and with very specific activities against specific organisms.

The similarity of the three tetracyclines is shown by the structural formula of each, given on the following page. It is apparent that tetracycline differs from oxytetracycline by an OH group at carbon 5 and from chlortetracycline by a chlorine atom at carbon 7.

The above historical sketch mentions only those antibiotics which are of practical importance as pharmaceutical agents. The search for microorganisms which produce antibiotic substances continues. Literally hundreds have been discovered; in fact, many are known which have not been thoroughly tested. There is a natural tendency to conclude that the antibiotic agents produced commercially today are the superior ones. While this may be true at present, one should always expect to learn of new superior agents which will be produced from time to time.

So the search for antibiotic agents active against specific types of bacteria, and especially for filterable viruses, still goes on.

In this search it is well to keep the desirable properties of an antibiotic for medical use constantly in mind. Florey, who contributed so much to the early clinical application of penicillin, lists these desirable properties as follows:

1. It must have a powerful action against some bacteria. It is improbable that any of the weaker antibiotics, of which there are many, will find a place as chemotherapeutic agents.

2. It must have specificity of action. From a study of bacteria affected has emerged the fact that the antibiotics possess in many instances remarkable specificity of action. They may have no action whatever against certain species, and yet be powerfully active against others. At one time we had the idea that any substance which would act against both gram-positive and gram-negative organisms—that is, a substance without any great specificity of action as between one bacterial species and another—would in all probability be toxic to animal cells. This we now know is not a completely valid generalization. Nevertheless, all the antibiotics so far investigated which have any prospect of being used in medicine have specific action.

3. A substance must possess little toxicity to the intact animal body, and the less of this the better. Not only must it lack toxicity to the intact body but also to individual cells such as leucocytes. It must not damage the kidneys if it is excreted and possibly concentrated by them, and its toxicity must not only be low following a single dose but it must not cause any changes in the body when given in frequent doses for a considerable length of time.

4. A substance must be active in the presence of body fluids such as serum, pus, and cerebrospinal fluid; substances very

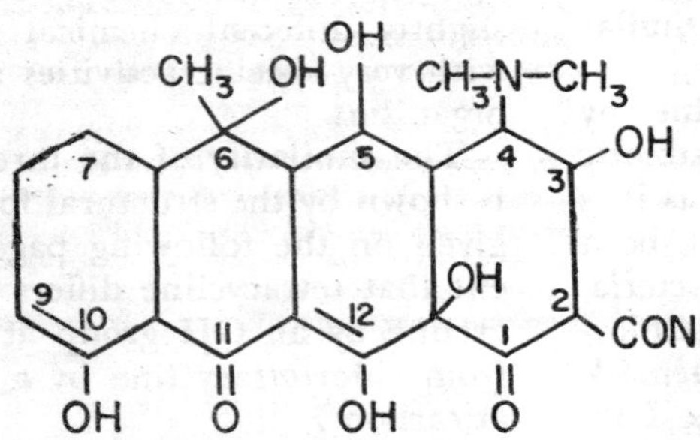

OXYTETRACYCLINE

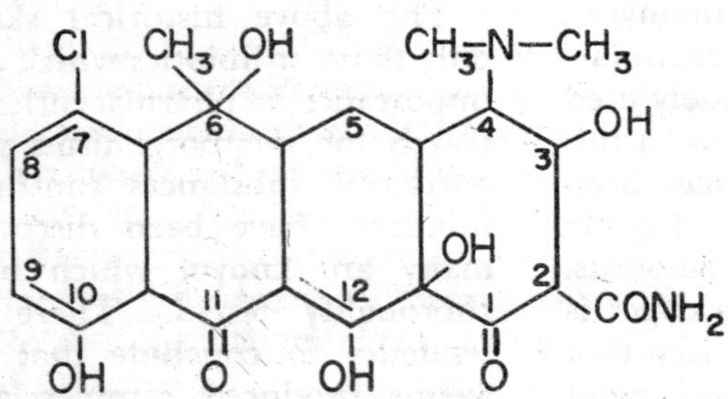

CHLORTETRACYCLINE

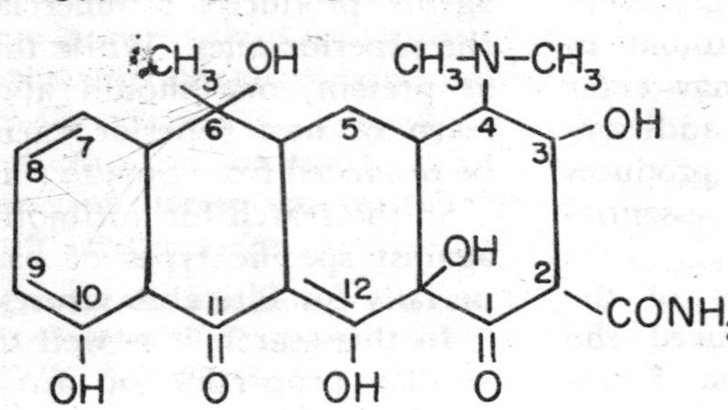

TETRACYCLINE

active in the test tube may be completely inactive in the body because of the inhibitory effect of body fluids.

5. The chemotherapeutic agent must not be destroyed by tissue enzymes. An indication of likely behavior in this respect is obtained by the reaction to trypsin. It is improbable that any substance which is destroyed by tissue enzymes or by trypsin will survive for long after injection into the blood stream; it will probably be destroyed rapidly and with it any possibility of its exerting antibacterial action. Though it is not essential, it is highly desirable that the drug should be absorbed from the gastrointestinal tract, so that it can be taken by mouth.

6. It should be stable. Penicillin has caused a great deal of trouble through its instability. Many of the difficulties in the early days of penicillin would have been avoided but for its particular liability to destruction.

7. It is also desirable that it should not be too rapidly excreted by the kidneys. Penicillin has this great disadvantage. Because it is excreted by the tubules, it leaves the body with great rapidity.

8. Another property which we have come to recognize as being serious is the capacity to produce in infecting bacteria a resistance to the chemotherapeutic drug itself. This was first noted with the sulfonamide compounds, for bacteria can become resistant to the sulfonamide drugs both in vitro and in vivo. It was also shown that bacteria became resistant to penicillin in vitro, and this is especially true of the staphylococci. Fortunately it appears to be much more difficult to acquire resistance to penicillin in vivo than in vitro, but the induction of resistance, even in vivo, is a marked property of streptomycin and this does interfere with its therapeutic use.

Complete books have been written about the antibiotics, so the student is referred to the list at the end of the chapter for more extensive study. Most of the significant antibiotics in veterinary medicine will be listed and discussed below very briefly.

## ANTIBIOTIC AGENTS FROM BACTERIA

Previous mention has been made of the antibiotic action of the substances pyocyanase, pyocyanin, and hemipyocyanin produced by *Ps. aeruginosa.* Likewise, gramicidin produced by *B. brevis* has been noted; in addition to this agent, inhibitory substances are known to be produced by other bacteria.

*Bacillus subtilis* (Jansen and Hirschman, 1944) has been found to produce an agent called *subtilin,* which is inhibitory to gram-positive bacteria.

*Bacitracin* (Johnson, Anker, and Meleney, 1945) is another agent produced by *B. licheniformis,* a species closely related to *B. subtilis.* This antibiotic received its name because the culture was isolated from the dirt débrided from the fractured leg of a child named Tracy. Bacitracin is produced commercially, and has been found to be effective against the gram-positive cocci and not affected by bacteria which do produce penicillinase. It has value in the topical treatment of cellulitis, wounds, ulcers, and superficial abscesses. Initial investigations demonstrated that the nephrotoxic property of the drug decreased its usefulness; however, that undesirable characteristic can be overcome by regulated dosage. Bacitracin may be given by the oral route, and is retained in the intestine and not readily absorbed. It is lethal to *Entamoeba histolytica,* and is one of the first of the antibiotic agents shown to affect protozoa. It has been used in the treatment of bovine mastitis with some success. Further investigation will reveal the value of this agent in the treatment of the various animal diseases.

In 1946 Foster and Woodruff recovered an agent they called *bacillin* from a culture of *B. subtilis.* This material was a water-soluble, thermostable substance but was somewhat toxic. Johnson and Burdon (1946) reported the extraction from cultures of *B. subtilis* a hemolytic agent called *eumycin* which was too toxic for internal use.

The *polymyxins* (Stansly, Shepherd, and

White, 1947) are related antibiotics which are derived from *Bacillus polymyxa,* a sporeforming organism isolated from the soil. These substances are simple, basic polypeptides which form water-soluble salts with mineral acids. Five distinct antibiotic agents, designated polymyxin A, B, C, D, and E, have been isolated. The polymyxins are particularly active against gram-negative bacteria and almost totally inactive against gram-positive species. One gram-negative genus, Proteus, is peculiarly resistant to the action of these antibiotics but most of the other genera, including Aerobacter, Brucella, Eberthella, Escherichia, Hemophilus, Klebsiella, Pasteurella, Pseudomonas, Salmonella, Shigella, and Vibrio, are sensitive. Among the above genera an occasional resistant species is observed, but the development of resistance by sensitive strains has not been observed.

According to Newton, the polymyxins produce their effect on bacteria by a disorganization of the cell membrane which controls the osmotic equilibrium of the cell. The antibiotic combines with ionized phosphate groups of phospholipid components. Those bacteria, the gram-positive species and some of the gram-negative, which are not affected by polymyxin, possess cell walls which do not permit the penetration of the antibiotic to the underlying membrane controlling osmosis.

The use of polymyxin has been limited because of toxicity. It has been found that polymyxin B is less nephrotoxic than the others; consequently, it is produced commercially. This antibiotic has especial value in being active against several species of bacteria, particularly *Ps. aeruginosa,* which are resistant to many other antibiotics. Various preparations of the drug are available, the topical and oral types being the most desirable inasmuch as no toxic effects have been noted following those methods of administration.

Bacteriolytic and bactericidal properties have been observed in filtrates of *Bacillus mesentericus.* Another one of the sporeforming aerobic species, *Bacillus mycoides,* produces a thermostable substance which inhibits the growth of many different species of bacteria, including *Mycobacterium tuberculosis.*

Among the nonsporeproducing bacteria, *Pseudomonas fluorescens* has been shown to produce a thermostable filterable agent which is antagonistic to *B. anthracis* and *Corynebacterium diphtheriae.* In the red pigment produced by *Serratia marcescens,* an alcohol-soluble substance has been shown to inhibit the growth of various gram-positive bacteria. Other species of bacteria have been shown to be antagonistic to different pathogenic species grown in contact with them.

Up to the present time the bacteria-produced antibiotic agent gaining most prominence as a chemotherapeutic substance has been tyrothricin. Tyrothricin is a polypeptide, insoluble in water but soluble in alcohol. When treated with acetone-ether, tyrothricin yields two substances: soluble fraction *gramicidin* and the insoluble substance *tyrocidine hydrochloride,* commonly referred to as *tyrocidine.* Tyrothricin is active mainly against gram-positive bacteria and because of its hemolytic property is limited to topical applications. It has been used in the treatment of bovine mastitis, being administered by infusion into the mammary gland through the teat canal. Although minor inflammation is produced in the mucosa by this treatment, the agent has been proved effective in treating streptococcal mastitis. Gramicidin is active against gram-positive bacteria, particularly the streptococci. It, too, is toxic, which limits its use in the treatment of generalized infections. Tyrocidine is active against both gram-positive and gram-negative bacteria and no doubt would have gained greater popularity as a therapeutic agent had it not been for the discovery of more effective agents.

In addition to those discussed above, other bacteria have been shown to produce antibiotic substances. *Streptococcus lactis* strains have produced two substances: *nisin* and *diplococcin.* The former are high molecular weight polypeptids and have been designated as A, B, C, and D, differing in the number and type of amino acids they contain. In general, *nisin* is active against gram-positive bacteria including *Streptococcus agalactiae,* the Clostridia, and Mycobacteria. *Iodinin* has been produced by *Chromobacterium iodinum; phthicol* by *Mycobacterium tuberculosis; micrococcin* by *Micrococcus varians; prodigiosin* by *Serratia marcescens* (*Chromobacterium prodigio sum*); *simplexin* by *Bacillus simplex; mycobacillin* by a strain of *Bacillus subtilis,* and active against *Candida albicans.*

The antibiotics produced by bacteria have had limited therapeutic use because of their toxicity. However, the fact that such a wide variety of bacteria do produce antibiotic substances makes it worthwhile to proceed with further investigation of them with the hope of finding the right one or the correct modification of molecular structure. Furthermore, it is difficult to know how much naturally produced antibiotics maintain "balance in nature." Man must not deceive himself by believing that antibiotics came into being with his discovery of them.

## ANTIBIOTIC AGENTS FROM ACTINOMYCES

Since the research of Waksman and coworkers, a number of different species of actinomyces have been found to produce antibiotic substances. The first organism in this group was *Actinomyces antibioticus,* which produced inhibiting agents designated as *actinomycin* A and *actinomycin* B. The first of these agents has been studied in greater detail than the second. It is soluble in alcohol and ether but not in water. A large group of different bacteria are sensitive to it but it has not been useful as a therapeutic agent because of its marked toxicity for animal tissue. This toxicity, however, has some promise as an antitumor agent according to Pugle, Katz, and Waksman.

*Streptothrycin* is produced by *Actinomyces lavendulae.* This material is a thermostable organic base. It is soluble in water and in acid alcohol, but not in ether. The growth of various gram-negative bacteria is inhibited by it and it has specific action against a few of the gram-positive forms. It is not toxic to animal tissues.

The antibiotic agent which parallels penicillin as an effective chemotherapeutic agent is *streptomycin.* It has been previously noted that this agent was found to be produced by *Actinomyces griseus* by Schatz, Bugie, and Waksman in 1944. Since then this agent has been subjected to considerable investigation and is now being prepared in large quantities.

Streptomycin is produced by growing the culture of *A. griseus* in a meat extract medium to which glucose is added. After five to twelve days incubation the medium is filtered and the active agent is extracted with acid and further purified by alcohol extraction. It is an organic base, soluble in dilute acids and in water, but insoluble in chloroform and ether. It is a thermostable compound so does not deteriorate as quickly as penicillin. Streptomycin produces in some patients dizziness and deafness, due to the action of the agent on the auditory nerve. Some nephrotoxic effects have been noted also. These toxic characteristics have been largely removed by the addition of two hydrogen atoms to streptomycin creating *dihydrostreptomycin.*

In order to regulate the dosage of streptomycin, it is evident that a standard potency must be available. Since this agent is effective against gram-negative bacteria, a standard strain of *E. coli* was chosen as the organism for the development of a standard.

The unit of streptomycin was originally defined as that quantity of dry material which would inhibit the growth of *Escherichia coli* in 1 ml. of nutrient broth. This was found to approximate one microgram. Consequently, when amounts of streptomycin are specified in dosage or assay, they are expressed in micrograms or grams.

As prepared and dispensed commercially, streptomycin is a white powder contained in sterile vials in 1-gram quantities. A suitable diluent is placed in the vial and from this known dilution, dosages containing the desired amount per cubic centimeter may be obtained.

The early investigations of Waksman and coworkers revealed that streptomycin was active against *Mycobacterium tuberculosis,* in addition to such gram-negative bacteria as *Brucella abortus, Proteus vulgaris, Pseudomonas aeruginosa,* and *Salmonella schottmulleri.* This discovery is acknowledged to be the motivating force behind the rapid development of this agent. In 1944 Feldman and Hinshaw demonstrated that streptomycin suppressed the effect of experimentally induced tuberculosis in guinea pigs and now much of the streptomycin produced is used in the treatment of tuberculosis. Stubbs has found streptomycin effective in preventing the death of guinea pigs used for experimental brucellosis. The sensitivity of the Pasteurella to streptomycin has been revealed by Heilman by in vitro studies with *Pasteurella tularensis* as well as with experimental tularemia in mice. Coles tested the sensitivity of a number of species of bacteria pathogenic for animals, finding that the gram-negative species were most sensitive while the gram-positive cocci were least so. *Pasteurella multocida* and *Brucella abortus* are two important species which are quite sensitive to streptomycin. Hinshaw and McNeil demonstrated the value of this agent in the treatment of fowl cholera in turkeys.

Mention has been made previously to chloramphenicol, chlortetracycline, oxytetracycline, and tetracycline, so they will not be discussed here.

In addition to the above-mentioned antibiotics produced by actinomyces, two others deserve discussion. *Neomycin* is produced by *Streptomyces fradiae,* and was first reported by Waksman and Lechevalier in 1949. Upon more complete study, this antibiotic has been shown to consist of at least three closely related chemical substances which are designated neomycin A, B, and C. This antibiotic is active against a wide range of bacteria, but unfortunately it contains a nephrotoxic substance which limits its use as a pharmaceutical agent.

*Viomycin* is produced by *Streptomyces puniceus* and was reported by Bartz and associates in 1950. However, research workers of Pfizer Laboratories had previously reported this antibiotic and they are given credit for its discovery. Likewise it became apparent that an antibiotic agent called *Vinactin,* which was reported by Mayer *et al.* in 1951, was identical to viomycin. It is now recognized that vinactin is composed of three active substances A, B, and C. Viomycin is considered to be Vinactin A, which is the trademark name used by Ciba Pharmaceutical Products, Inc. Viomycin is active against the gram-negative types of bacteria and has shown promise in the treatment of tuberculosis in man.

In 1952 McGuire and associates reported an antibiotic agent, *Erythromycin,* produced by *Streptomyces erythreus.* This antibiotic is active against the gram-positive bacteria, being similar to penicillin in that respect. It has the added advantage of being effective against those strains of bacteria which have developed resistance to penicillin. While the trademark name of Erythromycin is used by Upjohn Company, the name Ilotycin is used by the Eli Lilly Company, and Erythrocin by Abbott Laboratories.

*Carbomycin* was first reported by Tanner *et al.* in 1952. It is produced by *Streptomyces halstedii.* The Chas. Pfizer Company, manufacturers of this new drug, use the trademark name, Magnamycin. Carbomycin is a mixture of two antibiotics designated A and B, and differing in that B is more readily absorbed from the intestinal tract with resulting higher blood levels. Both are active against the gram-positive types of bacteria.

*Tylosin* of the Eli Lilly Company is produced by a strain of *Actinomyces fradiae.* Experimentally it shows promise in the treatment of PPLO infections as well as those caused by spirochetes and certain of the large viruses. This antibiotic, along with erythromycin, picromycin, and others, belongs to the group of antibiotics known as *macrolide antibiotics.* This class of antibiotics is characterized by a large lactone ring, a ketone function, and an amino-sugar attached by a glycosidic linkage.

## ANTIBIOTIC AGENTS FROM MOLDS

Penicillin is the best known agent produced by molds. Probably no subject has accumulated such extensive literature in so short a period of time as has penicillin. In addition to the thousands of periodical articles and annual symposiums, several books have been written on the subject—one by Waksman; others by Herrell, Kolmer, and Goldberg.

Numerous strains of *Penicillium notatum* have been found, many of them producing a more potent penicillin than the original strain studied by Fleming. Furthermore, other species of Penicillium, notably *Penicillium chrysogenum,* have been found to produce different forms of *penicillin.*

In the production of penicillin three general methods may be used. The mold may be grown as a surface culture on fluid medium; it may be grown as a submerged culture in a fluid medium which is aerated and agitated; or it may be grown in a moist bran medium. The composition of the fluid media used in the growth of the mold varies to some extent, but it has been found that corn-steep liquor and zinc are two ingredients which are definitely of value in producing a greater yield of penicillin. The maximum yield of penicillin is obtained after approximately seven days of incubation between 22°C. and 25°C. The mold growth is removed from the medium by filtration, leaving a clear, yellowish-brown filtrate. Penicillin exists in the filtrate as an organic acid and can be extracted with numerous solvents such as ether, amyl acetate, and n-butyl alcohol. While in solution, penicillin may be combined with various salts, of which sodium, procaine, potassium, and calcium have been the most widely investigated.

During recent years research has centered upon the chemistry of penicillin with the hope that a synthetic compound may be prepared. This has been accomplished but is not considered commercially applicable in replacing methods now in use for penicillin production. Nevertheless, from chemical research has come a number of penicillins which have been developed by modifications of the side-chain molecule. The great variety of penicillins and the types of bacteria sensitive to them may be noted by studying Table 6.1.

The potency of penicillin is determined by the inhibition of growth of selected strains of staphylococci. A variety of techniques such as serial dilution, turbidimetric, and agar-cup methods have been developed to demonstrate the inhibition which is expressed in units per cubic centimeter. The original unit of potency determined by the Oxford group was based upon the comparison of any sample of penicillin with a standard. This group devised the method known as the Oxford-cup method. This consists of inoculating an agar plate with a standard strain of *Staphylococcus aureus.* Upon the surface of the medium, small cylinders of a standard diameter (9 mm.) are placed. One cylinder is filled with a standard penicillin containing 1 unit of penicillin per cubic centimeter. The other dilutions of the unknown are placed in other cylinders. After incubating the plate, the extent of the clear zones around the cylinders is determined and compared with that of the standard. A unit of penicillin is that amount which, when dissolved in 1 ml. of water, gives the same area of inhibition as the standard. In order to have a more exact method of measurement, an International Unit for penicillin has been established. It is 0.6 microgram of the sodium salt of penicillin G, which is approximately equivalent to the Oxford unit.

It has been noted that penicillin is more active against gram-positive than against gram-negative bacteria. Many of the gram-positive forms are more susceptible to penicillin than others. Occasionally a strain of a sensitive organism such as *Staph. aureus* is found, which is very resistant to the drug. This appears to be an inherent characteristic of the organism in many instances;

however, it has been shown that sensitive organisms may develop drug fastness upon prolonged contact with penicillin. The mechanism by which such strains become resistant is not clear. It was discovered in the early period of research on this agent that the gram-negative bacteria were resistant because of their ability to secrete an enzyme, called penicillinase, which was able to destroy penicillin. Naturally resistant strains of staphylococci have been shown to produce a penicillinase-like substance. Geronimus and Cohen have found that staphylococci do develop penicillinase activity when injected into mice simultaneously with penicillin.

The mechanism by which penicillin inhibits the growth of bacteria has not been thoroughly explained. It is generally conceded that the action is bacteriostatic, but numerous investigators have shown that under certain conditions penicillin is bactericidal. The action of penicillin is not instantaneous as is the case of a chemical disinfectant. For this reason it has been postulated that this agent interferes with cell metabolism during the active growth phase of bacteria, probably by "neutralizing" the action of enzyme systems essential for the formation of the cell wall. The amount of penicillin in a medium is not decreased by its action on living bacteria; therefore, it does not enter into chemical reactions whereby its chemical nature may be altered.

Some of the gram-negative species of bacteria which are known to be resistant to penicillin do show that penicillin affects them when grown in a medium of increased osmotic pressure and nonlethal amounts of penicillin. These organisms do not develop a cell wall, but *L forms* (also called *protoplasts* or *spheroplasts)* are produced. Under ordinary osmotic pressure these forms are so fragile they burst.

## ANTIBIOTIC RESISTANCE

Not long after penicillin and streptomycin came into general use it was obvious that not all individual bacterial cells perished during a course of antibiotic therapy. The significance of this fact becomes more and more apparent, so it is necessary to determine the susceptibility of individual isolates to a group of antibiotics in order to determine the proper one for therapy.

The staphylococci have become the greatest offenders in developing strains resistant to penicillin. Fortunately these strains are susceptible to other antibiotics so that the treatment of an infection can proceed, although at times the delay is longer than should be the case.

The exact process by which drug resistance is developed by bacteria is not known. It seems plausible to assume that some rapidly multiplying cells may become mutants which do not possess the particular molecule to which the antibiotic may react or become attached. These resistant cells are allowed to multiply without inhibition even in the presence of a known toxic amount of the drug. McDermott has advanced an interesting explanation of the phenomenon which he calls "microbial persistence." Survival of living things in the face of adversity is an essential factor in all life. Microbes have a "high degree of adaptive plasticity" to the environment in which they may be living. Reflection on the evolution of living things makes apparent the fact that adaptive plasticity is the underlying mechanism for survival and that microbes, since their origin, have been adjusting themselves to all sorts of antibiotic agents which man isolates and produces artificially.

## ANTIBIOTIC ALLERGY

The development of an allergic reaction to an antibiotic is one of the unfortunate results of therapeutic use. The antibiotics produced by molds appear to be the most capable of producing sensitivity. Usually a reaction follows upon receiving an antibiotic, such as penicillin, some time after the first injection. Allergic reactions may be a mild urticaria, hives, anaphylactoid symptoms, or, in some cases, sudden death.

In some cases persons are hypersensitive although they never have been injected with the antibiotic. This probably has

COMPARATIVE ACTIVITY OF THE PENICILLINS IN VITRO

| Type of Bacteria | Penicillins Compared | Relative Sensitivity and Activity |
|---|---|---|
| A. Group A beta hemolytic streptococci<br>pneumococci<br>alpha hemolytic streptococci<br>nonhemolytic steptococci | (1) penicillin G<br>phenoxymethyl penicillin<br>potassium phenethicillin<br>ampicillin | (1) All streptococci, pneumococci, and staphylococci are extremely sensitive. Some strains of alpha of nonhemolytic streptococci from bacterial endocarditis are relatively less sensitive. |
| *Staphylococcus aureus* (nonpenicillinase-producing) | (2) sodium methicillin<br>sodium oxacillin | (2) Oxacillin 5 to 8 times more active than methicillin, but both considerably less active on weight basis than (1) above. Order of sensitivity about the same as (1). |
| B. *Staphylococcus aureus* (penicillinase-producing) | (1) penicillin G<br>phenoxymethyl penicillin<br>potassium phenethicillin<br>ampicillin | (1) Moderately to extremely resistant. Two-thirds of strains more sensitive to phenethisillin than to penicillin G or V. |
| | (2) sodium methicillin<br>sodium oxacillin | (2) Strains tested almost uniformly sensitive. Three strains not sensitive. |
| C. Gonococci (all strains) | all penicillins | All sensitive; penicillin G most active. |
| D. Enterococci (all strains) | (1) penicillin G<br>phenoxymethyl penicillin<br>potassium phenethicillin<br>ampicillin | (1) All strains sensitive; penicillin G and ampicillin most active; however, bactericidal only if penicillin combined with streptomycin or kanamycin. |
| | (2) sodium methicillin<br>sodium oxacillin | (2) Resistant to concentrations attainable in vivo. |
| E. *Hemophilus influenzae* | penicillin G<br>ampicillin | Highly sensitive (1 μg/ml). |
| *Proteus mirabilis* | penicillin G<br>ampicillin | Moderately sensitive (most strains inhibited by 15 μg/ml). |
| *Proteus vulgaris;* other Proteus species | all | Generally resistant. |
| Other gram-negative bacilli<br>Salmonella (most strains)<br>Shigella (most strains)<br>*Escherichia coli* (many strains)<br>*Alcaligenes faecalis* (some strains) | (1) all penicillins except ampicillin<br>(2) ampicillin | (1) Relatively or highly resistant.<br>(2) Quite active. |
| *Klebsiella pneumoniae*<br>*Aerobacter aerogenes*<br>*Pseudomonas aeruginosa* | ampicillin | Inactive |
| F. Anaerobic bacteria (Clostridia, anaerobic streptococci, Bacteroides) | (1) penicillin G<br>ampicillin<br>(2) sodium oxacillin<br>(3) sodium methicillin | (1) Approximately equal sensitivity.<br>(2) Less sensitive.<br>(3) Resistant. |
| *Bacteroides fragilis* (most frequent species isolated) | penicillin G<br>ampicillin | Resistant. |

Source: Hewitt, W. L. The Penicillins. A Review of Strategy and Tactics. Jour. Amer. Med. Assn. 185:264–72, 1963.

been due to having consumed milk which contains the drug as a result of mastitis treatment. Also, antibiotics are used to preserve meat, such as chickens, and the antibiotic could have been obtained in this way.

Because of antibiotic allergy, the antibiotics are not used as freely by physicians as they were a few years ago. These drugs should be considered valuable in the treatment of infectious diseases and reserved for serious cases.

## ANTIBIOTIC SENSITIVITY

It has been emphasized that certain bacteria are sensitive to a certain antibiotic. Obviously this fact should be basic in the decision to use a certain antibiotic for the treatment of an infection. In order to determine this, it is essential that a culture of the infecting organism be obtained from the patient. After this is accomplished, a number of paper discs, each impregnated with a different antibiotic, are placed upon the culture plate containing the organism. After incubation, the zone of inhibition is easily seen around the disc containing the antibiotic for which the organism is sensitive. This technique has become routine in human and veterinary medicine, and anyone who would not avail himself of such information is indeed negligent.

## REFERENCES


ALLISON, J. L., *et al.* Mode of Action of Chloramphenicol. Jour. Bact. 83:609–15, 1962.

ARNSTEIN, H. R. V., and GRANT, T. P. The Metabolism of the Penicillia in Relation to Penicillin Biosynthesis. Bact. Rev. 20:133, 1956.

AYLIFFE, G. A. J. Amphicillin Inactivation and Sensitivity of Coliform Bacilli. Jour. Gen. Microbiol. 30:339–48, 1963.

BANERJEE, N., and BOSE, S. K. Mode of Action of Mycobacillin, A New Antifungal Antibiotic. Jour. Bact. 86:387–91, 1963.

BLISS, E. A., and ALTER, B. M. Bacterial Resistance to Antibiotics in Vivo. II. Population Patterns Among Staphylococci. Jour. Bact. 84:125–29, 1962.

BROCK, T. D. Chloramphenicol. Bact. Rev. 25:32–48, 1961.

CHAIN, E., *et al.* Brit. Jour. Exp. Path. 23:202, 1942.

COLLIER, H. O. J. Chemotherapy of Infections. John Wiley & Sons, Inc., New York, 1954.

DINEEN, P. Further Studies on the Period of Microbial Susceptibility. Jour. Inf. Dis. 111:169–74, 1962.

DUBOS, R. J. Proc. Soc. Exp. Biol. Med. 40:311, 1939. Jour. Exp. Med. 70:1, 11, 1939.

DUGGAR, B. M., *et al.* Aureomycin—A New Antibiotic. Ann. New York Acad. Med. 51:175–342, 1948.

FLEMING, A. Proc. Roy. Soc. London 93:306, 1922.

———. Brit. Jour. Exp. Path. 10:226, 1929.

FOSTER, J. W., and WOODRUFF, H. B. Jour. Bact. 51:363, 1946.

GARDNER, A. D., and CHAIN, E. Brit. Jour. Exp. Path. 23:123, 1942.

GERONIMUS, L. H., and COHEN, S. Increased Staphylococcal Penicillinase Activity Accompanying Penicillin Treatment of Experimentally Infected Mice. Jour. Bact. 74:507, 1957.

GOLDBERG, H. S. (ed.). Antibiotics, Their Chemistry and Non-Medical Uses. D. Van Nostrand Co., Inc., Princeton, N. J., 1959.

GOSIO, B., 1896, in Florey, H. W. Brit. Med. Jour. 2:635, 1945.

GROVE, D. C., and RANDALL, W. A. Assay Methods of Antibiotics. Medical Encyclopedia, Inc., New York, 1956.

HEWITT, W. L. The Penicillins—A Review of Strategy and Tactics. Jour. Amer. Med. Assn. 185:264–72, 1963.

JAWETZ, E., and GUNNISON, J. B. Antibiotic Synergism and Antagonism: An Assessment of the Problem. Pharmacol. Rev. 5:175–92, 1953.

KAREL, L., and ROACH, E. S. A Dictionary of Antibiosis. Columbia Univ. Press, 1951.

LEDERBERG, J. Mechanism of the Action of Penicillin. Jour. Bact. 73:144, 1953.

MARTIN, G. J. Biological Antagonism. Blakiston Co., New York, 1953.

MAYER, R. L., *et al.* Proc. XII Intl. Cong., Pure and Applied Chemistry, New York, 1951.

MCDERMOTT, W. Microbial Persistence. Yale Jour. Biol. Med. 30:257–91, 1958.

MCGUIRE, J. M., *et al.* Ilotycin, a New Antibiotic. Antibiotics and Chemotherapy 2:281, 1952.

NEWTON, B. A. The Properties and Mode of Action of the Polymyxins. Bact. Rev. 20:14, 1956.

Pratt, R., and Younker, H. W., Jr. Pharmacognosy: The Study of Natural Drug Substances and Certain Allied Products. 2nd Ed. J. B. Lippincott Co., Philadelphia, 1956.

Pugh, L. H., *et al.* Antibiotic and Cytostatic Properties of the Actinomycins. Jour. Bact. 72:660, 1956.

Routien, J. B. Distribution of Streptomycetes That Produce Antibiotics. Jour. Bact. 81:218–25, 1961.

Schatz, A., *et al.* Proc. Soc. Exp. Biol. Med. 55:66, 1944.

Smith, J. L., and Weinberg, E. D. Mechanisms of Antibacterial Action of Bacitracin. Jour. Gen. Microbiol. 28:559–69, 1962.

Sokoloff, B. The Miracle Drugs. Ziff-Davis Co., Chicago, 1949.

Tanner, F. W., Jr., *et al.* Some Properties of Magnamycin, a New Antibiotic. Antibiotics and Chemotherapy 2:441, 1952.

Thompsett, R. Protection of Pathogenic Staphylococci by Phagocytes. Trans. Assn. Amer. Physiol. 69:84–92, 1956.

Townley, R. W., *et al.* Proc. XII Intl. Cong., Pure and Applied Chemistry, New York, 1951.

Trans. Ninth Streptomycin Conference, St. Louis, 1950.

Waksman, S. A. Microbial Antagonisms and Antibiotic Substances, 2nd Ed. Commonwealth Fund, New York 1947.

———, and Lechevalier, H. A. Science 109:305, 1949.

———, and Woodruff, H. B. Jour. Bact. 44:373, 1942.

———, *et al.* Science 96:202, 1942.

Weinberg, E. D. The Mutual Effects of Antimicrobial Compounds and Metallic Cations. Bact. Rev. 21:46, 1957.

———. Known and Suspected Role of Metal Coordination in Action of Antimicrobial Drugs. Fed. Proc. 20: 132–35, 1961.

Welch, Henry, *et al.* Antibiotic Therapy. Blakiston Co., New York, 1954.

Wiley, P. F. Macrolide Antibiotics. Research Today. Eli Lilly Co., 1960.

Wilson, G. S., and Miles, A. A. Topley's Principles of Bacteriology and Immunity. Vol. I. Williams & Wilkins Co., Baltimore, 1964.

PART 2

# Infection, Resistance, and Immunity

# 7

# The Mechanism of Infection

DISEASES ARE GENERALLY RECOGNIZED BY A definite chain of symptoms, and when they are sufficiently severe they represent an alteration of body fluids and cells. The agents of disease produce different effects; consequently, the various diseases are recognized by the differences in symptoms and the differences in the changes produced in body fluids and cells.

*Diseases* are divided into two general types, infectious and noninfectious. An *infectious* disease is one which is caused by a microorganism. The mere presence of microorganisms in the body, however, does not constitute *infection.* General infection is not regarded as occurring unless the organisms multiply in the body and produce symptoms of disease and pathological changes in tissues. A *noninfectious* disease is one which is caused by injury, vegetable or mineral poison, heat or cold, faulty nutrition, abnormal physiology, or abnormal tissue growth. A *contagious* disease is one which is caused by an organism that is readily transferred from one individual to another by direct or indirect contact. The terms *infectious* and *contagious* are sometimes used interchangeably. It is best, however, to limit the terms. *Infectious defines the cause of a disease, and contagious defines the ease and method of transmission.* Contagious diseases are all infectious, but all infectious diseases are not contagious; for example, tetanus and botulism in man and animals cannot be regarded as contagious because they result from contact with infected soil and foods which never may have been in contact with infected animals. Every gradation between highly contagious and noncontagious disease is known; hence, it is customary to indicate the degree of contagiousness by the use of modifiers, such as highly contagious and slightly contagious. There has been a tendency to refer to the infectious diseases as communicable diseases and to eliminate using "contagious."

Among the infectious, or communicable, diseases of animals are the following: abscesses and similar pyogenic infections, strangles, pneumonia, meningitis, brucellosis, tuberculosis, paratuberculosis, pseudotuberculosis, swine erysipelas, glanders, dysentery, hemorrhagic septicemia, swine plague, fowl cholera, anthrax, blackleg, malignant edema, actinomycosis, aspergillosis, ringworm, pleuropneumonia, foot-and-mouth disease, rinderpest, hog cholera, equine encephalomyelitis, fowl plague, rabies, and the poxes, such as fowl pox.

Examples of noninfectious, or noncommunicable, diseases are: diabetes, azoturia, vitamin deficiency diseases such as rickets, mineral deficiencies, sweet clover disease, and plant poisoning.

## KINDS OF BACTERIA IN RELATIONSHIP TO DISEASE

Reference has been made previously to the relationship of bacteria to their food supply. It is desirable at this point to discuss them in relationship to their ability to produce disease as a result of their presence on or in a living animal. Bacteria may be classified as saprophytic and parasitic.

*Saprophytic* bacteria are those which live on dead matter. Since pathogenic bacteriology is almost completely concerned with the effect of bacteria on the living animal, the saprophytes do not appear to be of great significance. While this is true generally, there are some instances where the growth of bacteria on dead tissue may be harmful. For example, the putrefaction of retained placental tissues by bacteria may result in the absorption of the end products. This may cause a condition commonly referred to as toxemia, which in this instance may be more specifically called *sapremia.*

*Parasitic* bacteria are those which live at the expense of the host to which they may produce severe injury. The ideal parasite is one which does not injure the host sufficiently to cause great debility or death. Unfortunately many parasites do not possess the power to control the desirable characteristics of parasitism for their own good. During the evolution of their parasitic existence they have acquired properties which injure the host. These bacteria are called *pathogenic* bacteria. The injury produced by the pathogenic microorganism to the host varies from minor tissue damage to death. The variables operating in infectious disease are those contributed by the infecting agent and those possessed by the host. The student can understand, therefore, the complexity of disease when he realizes the interrelationships of numerous species of bacteria, numerous types of body tissues and fluids, and numerous species of animals.

## VIRULENCE

The characteristics which make one organism a harmless saprophyte and another a deadly pathogen are not thoroughly understood. Infectious disease is primarily a result of the action of certain chemical components of the organism along with the reaction to this chemical on the part of the tissues of the host. Whether disease is a result of the potency of the organism or the weakness of the host is difficult to determine. There is a tendency to refer to the causal microorganism as the inciter of disease and to the host merely as a susceptible recipient. Bacteria vary in their ability to cause disease. This ability is usually summed up in the use of the terms *virulence* or *pathogenicity;* hence an organism is referred to as avirulent, slightly virulent, very virulent, or extremely virulent. The use of such modifying terms for various species of bacteria is based upon factors emphasized in the following discussion.

Some species of bacteria are able to produce toxins which are more lethal than those of other bacteria. This is true also in some strains of the same species. A good example of a toxin-producing organism is the bacillus responsible for tetanus in man and animals. This organism may be classified as a saprophyte, but the effects of its deadly toxin make it apparent that it should be called a pathogen. Washed spores of this organism may be given orally to animals without producing injury; in fact, they may be introduced into healthy tissue without causing symptoms of the disease. However, if such spores are introduced into tissues along with necrotic tissue or with chemicals which may kill tissue cells, they germinate and produce a toxin which is disseminated throughout the body causing the muscle contraction characteristic of the disease. If the organism is grown artificially, so that toxin is produced, minute amounts of it, entirely free of the bacilli, will cause the same typical symptoms. An example of an entirely different type of organism is *Bacillus anthracis,* the cause of anthrax. This is a sporeforming bacillus. When washed spores are placed in healthy tissues, they germinate, and the resulting organisms multiply rapidly and spread throughout the body of the animal, quickly producing death. When this organism is grown in artificial media, the cell-free filtrate will not produce symptoms of the disease. These two examples represent the two extremes of pathogenic activity, with many species of bacteria being both toxic and invasive.

In addition to toxin, mentioned above, there are other substances produced by bacteria which endow them with virulence. Some of these substances are toxins, while others are extracellular enzymes.

The production of hemolysin by bacteria has long been associated with virulence. While this may be true of some species it is not true of others, because entirely nonpathogenic species produce hemolysin. Studies on hemolysin (Bernheimer, 1947) indicate that this material is enzymatic. The substrates in which these enzymes reside are not known. Quite likely the substrates act as antigens, explaining why hemolysins have been classified as toxins. A single bacterial species may produce more than one hemolysin. The Group A hemolytic streptococci, for example, produce two hemolysins which differ in their chemical properties and the method by which they cause hemolysis of erythrocytes. These hemolysins have been designated streptolysin O and streptolysin S. Streptolysin O is a rather labile protein containing sulfur and is oxidized by atmospheric oxygen. It can be reactivated by such a reducing agent as sodium hydrosulfite. This type of hemolysin is produced by many different species of bacteria. It is neutralized by specific immune serum and by cholesterol. The antisera from an animal immunized by one of the O hemolysins will neutralize the others, hence, it appears that they are not specific.

Streptolysin S is a lipoprotein and is not neutralized by cholesterol and is not reversely oxidizable. Antiserum for this hemolysin is prepared with difficulty, and it does not neutralize streptolysin O. It is extractable from the streptococcal cells by means of serum—the S means serum extractable. It is very unstable, being preserved only by lyophilization. This hemolysin produces degenerative effects on heart muscle and other parenchymatous organs as well as hemolysis. There is little doubt that it is associated with virulence. Hemolysis noted on the blood agar plate is considered due to streptolysin S. However, this does not mean that O has not been produced. It may have been oxidized. Blood of horses has been shown to possess antistreptolysin O which prevents the elaboration of this substance. The blood of all animals has not been assayed for the presence of antihemolysin, but rabbit blood is known to be comparatively free of it, and consequently is most suitable for the preparation of blood agar.

Many different species, particularly the staphylococci, produce *leucocidin* which is able to cause the destruction of leucocytes. It appears likely that this material is identical to hemolysin O, inasmuch as it is oxidized in the same reverse manner. The accumulation of leucocytes in suppurative processes, and the destruction of those leucocytes which have phagocytized masses of bacteria, make it evident that the substance leucocidin is a protective mechanism which enables bacteria to multiply more abundantly in infected tissue.

The description of "fibrinolysin" by Tillett and Garner in 1933 contributed another substance by which certain of the streptococci and staphylococci may be enhanced in virulence. This substance, now called *streptokinase,* causes the dissolution of fibrin clots in a few minutes. It is known to be a kinase which activates a proteolytic enzyme normally present in plasma in an inactive form. The absence of fibrin is one of the characteristics of certain acute types of streptococcal infections, so it is presumed that this is due to streptokinase. This is supported by the fact that when the specific antibody, antistreptokinase, appears in the blood stream, fibrin appears in the infected tissues.

Pathogenic strains of *Staphylococcus aureus* produce an enzyme-like substance called *coagulase,* which is able to cause the coagulation of blood plasma from rabbits and human beings. The role this substance plays in virulence is not known. However, since most staphylococcic infections are localized, it may be presumed that the formation of coagulated masses of plasma about colonies of the organism in tissue prevents the penetration of leucocytes and lytic agents of the body defense mechanism.

*Clostridium perfringens,* as well as other

members of the gangrene group of Clostridia, produces toxins which have a marked effect upon the blood-vascular system. It has been shown that this toxin is a *lecithinase* which brings about the hydrolysis of lecithin when acted upon by calcium ions. Lecithinase causes marked hemolysis and necrosis of other cells, so it is apparent that it has a direct influence on disease produced by these organisms.

Culture filtrates of *Clost. perfringens* also contain another proteolytic enzyme which has been called *collagenase*. This substance causes the disintegration of muscle tissue of laboratory animals by decomposing the reticular scaffolding. It has been suggested by MacFarlane and MacLennon, 1945, that collagenase may be responsible for the pulpy condition of muscle found in cases of gas gangrene. Both lecithinase and collagenase are neutralized by the action of commercial antitoxin.

Hyaluronic acid is a viscous, polysaccharide acid of high molecular weight, present in the intercellular ground substance of many different tissues. Numerous bacteria produce the enzyme *hyaluronidase* which hydrolyzes hyaluronic acid. Duran-Reynals, 1942, found that the injection of this enzyme into tissues increased permeability and allowed the rapid spread of injected solutions, India ink, and bacteria. He referred to the substance as a spreading factor. Previous to 1945 this investigator had observed the presence of this material in aqueous extracts of rabbit, guinea pig, and rat testes. It has since been shown that numerous bacteria, staphylococci, streptococci, pneumococci, corynebacteria, and clostridia produce hyaluronidase. The invasive qualities of these bacteria are enhanced, no doubt, by this substance which enables the bacteria to penetrate through the barrier of endothelial and epithelial cells.

It must be kept in mind, when considering the relationship of the toxins and enzymes to virulence, that all of these substances are not produced by all bacteria. One substance may be of aid to one species and another substance to another species. In general the bacteria producing disease in animals have not been sufficiently investigated to know the virulence pattern of all of them. The specific significance of each substance will be discussed along with the particular organism in subsequent chapters.

Bacteria in general may lose their virulence when subjected to certain environmental conditions such as growth on ordinary artificial media, high temperatures, and contact with chemicals. This decrease in virulence is known as *attenuation*. The anthrax bacillus maintains its virulence when grown on ordinary media but loses it when grown at 42°C. The virulence of bacteria can be increased also. The less virulent strains of hemorrhagic septicemia bacteria can be increased by successive passages through mice and egg embryos. Certain avirulent strains of bacteria can be made fully virulent when grown on media containing blood or blood serum. The loss, as well as the acquisition, of virulence appears to be involved in the phenomenon of dissociation. Bacteria in the S stage are more fully virulent than those in the R. Capsulated bacteria are more virulent when the capsule is present than in the dissociative noncapsulated state. Organisms are more virulent when they contain as a part of their chemical structure a specific polysaccharide, a substance which also has an important role in immunity. The gram-negative bacteria possess an endotoxic substance known as O, or somatic, antigen, which is composed of carbohydrate, protein, and phospholipid. This component is located at or near the cell surface and is liberated upon the lysis of the cell. It is known to be highly toxic, but not in the manner of the various toxins and enzymes produced by gram-positive cocci and bacilli. Injections of small amounts of purified endotoxin will produce a sharp rise in temperature, increase in blood sugar, and decrease in organic blood phosphorus in experimental animals. The pyrogenic substances present in water are believed to be endotoxic material resulting from the autol-

TABLE 7.1

Effect of Various Numbers of Anthrax Bacilli on Mice

| Number Mice | Number Bacilli | Number Died | Percentage Died | Duration of Life |
|---|---|---|---|---|
| 10 | 20 | 10 | 100 | 2.6 da. |
| 11 | 10 | 8 | 73 | 4.3 |
| 20 | 5 | 13 | 65 | 4.0 |
| 20 | 2 | 10 | 50 | 5.2 |
| 50 | 1 | 14 | 28 | 5.6 |

ysis of gram-negative bacteria present in the water. For this reason solutions used for intravenous injections should be made of freshly distilled water.

The number of bacteria present in the initial invasion of a host undoubtedly is a factor in virulence. The apparent increase in the virulence of a microorganism causing an infection in a herd is partially due to the increase in the number of bacteria to which the susceptible animals have access. It is obvious that two infected animals would liberate more bacteria than one, four more than two, etc. The relationship of the number of bacteria to virulence is illustrated in Table 7.1, by Martos, which shows the effect of various numbers of anthrax bacilli on mice.

The specificity of one species of bacteria for certain tissue has a marked bearing upon the determination of the virulence of that species; that is, the degree of virulence can be determined somewhat by the type of tissue affected. It is obvious that a microorganism which produces a rapid and fatal pneumonia is more virulent than one which attacks intestinal tissue. One organ, in this instance, is more vital than the other, and its destruction causes the death of the host more quickly. The extent to which bacteria are able to multiply in tissue also has some bearing upon its virulence and is governed greatly by the response of the defense mechanism of the tissues of the host. Some types of bacteria have the ability to repel this defense and multiply rapidly; others are easily destroyed by it.

Lastly, the host itself plays an important role in determining the virulence of a microorganism. Cuts, abrasions, and other effects of traumatism upon skin and mucous membranes may permit the entrance and establishment of bacteria which otherwise would not occur. The age of the host has an important bearing upon the establishment of bacteria and production of disease. As a rule young animals are more susceptible to infection than old ones. This is illustrated best by numerous diseases to which adults are resistant and children highly susceptible. Baby chicks are especially susceptible to *Salmonella pullorum* which produces a fatal septicemia and enteritis, while in the mature hen the organism localizes in the ovary where it causes a chronic type of infection. The reverse is true in avian tuberculosis which is found most commonly in old birds. Malnutrition has a bearing upon the susceptibility of the host to infection. Vitamin D deficiency produces an increased susceptibility of respiratory mucous membranes to infection. Experimentally it has been possible to infect pigeons, which are resistant otherwise, with anthrax subsequent to a period of starvation. Sudden and extreme exposure to cold has a bearing upon host resistance. Influenza appears in swine herds following sudden drops of temperature and exposure to cold, sleet, and rain. Hens which are naturally resistant to the anthrax bacillus may be infected with that organism when submerged in cold water which lowers their normal temperature. The reverse effect of cold is noted in cold-blooded animals: frogs die quickly with "red leg" when kept in warm water, but deaths cease when the water is decreased in temperature by a block of ice. The effect of fatigue on susceptibility is illustrated by the classical experiment of placing white rats, which are normally resistant to anthrax, upon a tread mill, and then injecting them with anthrax bacilli. After they have become fatigued, they will succumb to the disease. The genetic constitution of the host is a factor in resistance. Strains of chickens which are resistant to *Sal. pullorum* infection have been produced by inbreeding; likewise, strains of mice which are resistant to mouse typhoid have been produced.

In summary, virulence depends upon (1) the toxins and enzymes produced, (2) the number of invaders, (3) the specificity of bacterial products for certain types of tissue, (4) the inherent resistance of the host, and (5) the factors which alter that resistance.

## TRANSMISSION OF INFECTIOUS AGENTS

Pathogenic microorganisms are transmitted from infected to susceptible animals in a variety of ways. Many species of bacteria are not capable of existing for long periods of time away from the body of the live animal. Other species are able to exist for long periods when protected from the action of sunlight and putrefaction. Certain species, especially the sporeforming types, remain viable after indefinite periods away from the host.

The majority of infections are transmitted by direct or indirect contact with animals harboring the infection. The habit of licking, characteristic of some animals, is a ready means of transmission. This is illustrated by the spread of diarrhea among calves and brucellosis among cattle. Rabies is spread among animals and to man by the bite of animals infected with the virus of that disease. The spread of mastitis among dairy cattle is due to the transmission of the microorganisms on the hands of the milker and by contaminated mechanical milking equipment. The streptococci of scarlet fever and septic sore throat are occasionally transmitted from infected milkers to the udder of the cow and then to man through the raw milk supply. Animals do not need to show symptoms of disease to eliminate pathogenic organisms. Many harbor the infection for some time after apparent recovery. Such is the case in *Sal. pullorum* infection: an infected chick may recover and grow to be a normal hen, but the organism will be localized in the ovary, and be transmitted from there. As a result of infection, animals may become immune to further effects of the organism, and yet they may harbor and eliminate organisms in great numbers. Typhoid fever in man is a typical example. Some people who recover from typhoid fever remain immune carriers. Bacteria are eliminated in the feces, which may contaminate water and milk supplies. Beyond any doubt, such conditions prevail among animals, and the persistence of infection of various kinds in herds is explained by the presence of the immune carrier. Animals may harbor pathogenic bacteria without revealing svmptoms of disease. Cows may harbor and transmit *Brucella abortus,* the organism of brucellosis, yet they may never have aborted nor shown any other marked evidence of infection. The role of the goat in the transmission of brucellosis to man by the milk supply is another example. Animals of one species may harbor infectious agents but may not be visibly affected, yet when these agents are transmitted to animals of another species serious infection results. This is commonly referred to as *inapparent infection.* Pseudorabies is a good example. This virus disease is most severe in cattle, yet is not easily transmitted from animal to animal of that species. Swine do harbor the virus, yet are not severely affected; in fact, in many outbreaks they are not visibly abnormal. Such animals do transmit the virus to the skin of cattle by biting or rubbing the skin with the snout.

Ticks, fleas, lice, and mosquitoes are often involved in the transmission of infection. In some of the protozoan infections such as malaria, the passage of the parasites through the mosquito is an essential step in the life cycle. Bacteria are passively transferred by the bloodsucking parts of various arthropods, with no evidence of the presence of a bacterial life cycle which is completed by passage through an intermediate host. Bacteria, classed as Rickettsia, live in the cells lining the intestine of certain lice and ticks, from which they are transmitted to man causing such diseases as typhus and Rocky Mountain spotted fever. The length of time which pathogenic bacteria may survive in the transmitting insect is not known; in some instances, they apparently remain viable for a considerable period of time. The following diseases are known to be transmitted in this matter: bubonic plague in man and rodents by the rat flea, tularemia in man and rodents by ticks and bloodsucking flies, typhus and trench fever in man by lice, Rocky Mountain spotted fever in man by ticks, yellow fever in man by the mosquito, equine encephalomyelitis by mosquitoes and probably other bloodsucking insects, and anthrax in animals by bloodsucking flies.

The house fly is of importance in the transfer of pathogenic bacteria. This is especially true of typhoid fever because flies feed upon human feces which may contain typhoid bacteria and then feed upon or light upon dairy equipment, or directly upon food intended for human consumption.

Bacteria are transported from place to place by the dust of the air. Pullorum disease among chicks is spread by the soft down from chicks and by dust in the brooder house. Spores of bacteria and some of the more resistant actinomyces are spread for considerable distances by dust; this contaminates soil to which animals have access.

The living habits of animals make possible the spread of disease by the medium of the soil. Such diseases are generally due to sporeforming bacteria which enter the deeper tissues of the body through wounds. Tetanus is an excellent example of this method of transmission. The foods of animals are easily contaminated by bacteria of all types—the intestinal bacteria, those that are sporeforming, and even those of the respiratory tract; in fact, most of the secretions and excretions of animals have ample opportunities for reaching the food and water which animals consume. The watering tank on the farm is often a source of infection to the whole herd. Flowing streams have been known to carry the spores of anthrax bacilli for considerable distances. Experiments have revealed that tuberculosis is sometimes spread by streams.

The transmission of disease among animals by coition is not of common occurrence; however, suppurative infections involving the genital organs of the cow and horse are spread in this manner. Gonorrhea and syphilis are excellent examples of diseases of man which are commonly spread by sexual contact.

## ATRIA OF INFECTION

The avenue through which an organism gains entrance to the body is called its *portal of entry* or its infection atrium. An infection arising from contact with infective external objects is termed *exogenous;* one caused by organisms constantly or normally present in the body or on it is termed *endogenous*. Infection frequently occurs through a break in the continuity of the skin or mucous membranes caused by wounds, the bites of animals, and bloodsucking parasites. Ordinarily, the intact skin is an efficient barrier against infection, but microorganisms occasionally enter through the glands or hair follicles. Some bacteria, such as the diphtheria bacillus, injure the unbroken mucous surface. Some disease organisms are known to have passed unharmed through the intestinal walls and to have entered the lymph vessels and the thoracic duct.

The lungs constitute the infection atrium in some types of pneumonia, probably in many cases of tuberculosis and aspergillosis. Many other infectious agents, especially the viruses, may enter into the general circulation through this channel.

The genital tract is the common infection atrium in syphilis and gonorrhea of man. *Brucella abortus* infection in cows frequently involves the cotyledons arriving there via the blood stream. The entrance of this organism through the external genitalia rarely occurs.

*Cryptogenic infections* are those in which it is impossible to determine the infection atrium. In some cases of tetanus, for example, careful search fails to reveal the channel through which the organism reaches the deeper tissues where toxin is liberated.

The path by which the organism enters the body of the host usually determines the type of infection which results. As a general rule, microorganisms show a marked specificity, or affinity, for certain types of tissue; for example, the typhoid bacillus infects intestinal tissue and the pneumococcus infects pulmonary tissue. These organisms, therefore, cause the typical disease when they gain access directly to the susceptible tissue; neither is dangerous when entrance is made through scratches in the skin. The reverse is true of tetanus which most frequently results from the penetration of the skin by sharp objects which introduce the spores of the organism; however, the organism can be isolated from the intestines and feces of normal animals. A few species of bacteria produce disease when entering by any or all of the infection atria; for example, the tularemia organism causes infection when it enters scratches in the skin, wounds caused by insect bites, the conjunctiva of the eye, the lungs, on dust particles or hair, and when taken into the intestinal tract in infected food. Some bacteria produce no lesions at the site of entry but localize at distant points. *Br. abortus* enters through the digestive tract but most frequently involves lymphoid, uterine, and mammary tissues.

## THE NORMAL PROTECTIVE MECHANISM OF THE ANIMAL BODY

A discussion of the relationship of microorganisms to disease would not be complete without a brief description of the normal mechanism by which all animals are protected against infection. That this mechanism is an efficient one is apparent when one considers all of the possibilities of infection which animals encounter in their daily life; in fact, it is only when this natural protection fails to function that infection results. The type of tissue, the nature of secretions and their drainage, acidity, and alkalinity all function in normal protection against the infection.

### The Skin

The hair coat of mammals and the feathers of birds serve to protect the skin. The layer of epithelial cells of the normal skin constitutes an effective barrier against bacterial invasion. The skin of animals is constantly covered with bacteria which are potentially disease-producing when they invade the subcutaneous tissues. Many bacteria do penetrate into the crypts of sweat glands and into hair follicles from which they enter into deeper tissues. Even under such conditions they encounter an additional protective mechanism, the tissue phagocytes.

### The Mucous Membranes

The epithelial covering of the mucous membranes also constitutes an effective barrier against bacteria. This tissue is constantly bathed in mucus which prevents bacteria from becoming established in crypts and folds. The mucous membranes of the eyes are continually washed by lacrimal secretion and those of the external genitalia and the urinary tract are periodically flushed with urine which prevents the lodgement of bacteria.

### The Lungs

The mucous membranes, the mucus, and the tortuous characteristic of the nasal cavity protect the upper air passages against infection and also prevent the passage of dust particles into the lower part of the pulmonary system. The trachea is lined with mucous membrane, and in the bronchi ciliated epithelium tends to sweep foreign particles outward; however, when bacteria surmount these barriers and reach the bronchioles and alveoli, infection results if they are in sufficient numbers to overcome the humoral and cellular defense of those tissues. The act of coughing makes it possible for bacteria to be carried outward in the mucus in which they have been entrapped.

### The Intestinal Tract

The epithelial and mucous cells are most valuable barriers against infection throughout the digestive canal. Various secretions, however, have a protective function in addition to being primarily concerned with the digestion of food. Saliva has a feeble germicidal power and, in addition, keeps the mouth and esophagus bathed. Gastric juice is definitely inhibitory to many kinds of bacteria and their toxins because of the high hydrogen-ion concentration. Arnold has shown that the pH of the upper part of the intestinal tract governs the bacterial flora found there and that alteration of the pH toward alkalinity causes the anterior movement of lower intestinal types of bacteria. The peristaltic movement of the intestinal tract prevents the lodgement of bacteria, and accumulated masses of bacteria are dispersed by the constant mixing of the intestinal contents.

### The Genito-urinary Tract

Previous mention has been made of the protective value of epithelium, mucous secretion, and urine lavage to the urinary tract and external genitalia. These factors prevent the establishment of infection in such tissues unless there has been massive contamination. The function of the urinary bladder as a collecting reservoir for urine prevents, except in rare instances, the ascent of bacteria into the ureters. The vital reproductive glands, testes and ovaries, are protected from external contamination by tortuous tubes which connect them with external parts. In the female the ciliated epithelium of the Fallopian tubes serves as a noteworthy obstacle to bacteria. In the pregnant animal the cervix is sealed with a tenacious substance which is a most effective protection for the developing embryo.

### The Eyes and Ears

The eyelashes and eyelids protect the eyes against foreign objects which may be contaminated with bacteria. The voluntary response of lacrimal glands when foreign particles do reach the eye aids in diluting the invading substance, and if it is not too heavy or does not become lodged, it will wash it away. The delicate mechanism of hearing is protected by the shell of the ear, the ear hairs, and ear wax. The invasion of the ear by bacteria from the exterior is rare.

## THE PROOF OF THE RELATIONSHIP OF A MICROORGANISM TO A DISEASE—KOCH'S RULES

In order to prove the relationship of an organism to a disease, Koch proposed rules which must be fulfilled. The finding of an organism in diseased tissue is not enough proof that the organism is the cause. Koch found that:

1. The organism must be found in each case of disease.
2. The organism must be isolated and grown in pure culture.
3. The organism must reproduce the disease in the susceptible animal or in suitable experimental animals.
4. The organism must be isolated from the tissues of the experimental animal in pure culture.

These rules or postulates have been of great value in the study of infectious diseases since the time of Koch, and the observance of them has formed a firm basis for medical bacteriology. These rules have been fulfilled in practically all of the infectious diseases. In some cases it has been found difficult to satisfy each of the requirements, and exceptions based on the following reasons have been acknowledged:

(a) Organisms which have grown on artificial media for some time may dissociate to such an extent that virulence is lost. They are no longer able to reproduce the disease. Some strains of bacteria may be isolated directly from the infected animal and not be able to reproduce the disease until they have been increased in virulence by serial passage through experimental animals.

(b) One organism may be most effective in the presence of another one. This synergistic action has been proved in the relationship of the virus of swine influenza and the organism *Hemophilus suis*.

(c) In some cases the filterable viruses

cannot be grown on artificial medi.., but when living tissues are used in which viruses will multiply, even this rule can be fulfilled.

The relationship of an organism to the disease also is obtained by the use of serological tests such as agglutination, precipitation, and protein sensitization.

## INOCULATION OF ANIMALS

In addition to the proving of the relationship of a microorganism to a disease, animals are inoculated for the following purposes:

1. To maintain microorganisms that do not grow on artificial media.
   (a) Viruses.
   (b) Rickettsia.
   (c) Spirochetes.
2. To obtain a pure culture of an organism.
   (a) When mixed with other bacteria.
   (b) When present in small numbers.
   (c) When the organism grows poorly on artificial media.
3. To determine virulence or toxicity.
4. To produce vaccines for immunizing purposes, e.g.:
   (a) Rabies vaccine.
   (b) Canine distemper vaccine.
5. To produce antisera which are used for therapeutic or diagnostic purposes.
6. To standardize toxins and antitoxins.
7. To increase the virulence of bacteria which have been grown on artificial media for some time.

Animals may be inoculated by numerous parenteral methods. *Parenteral* methods are those in which material is inoculated into body tissues by any route except the intestinal tract. The method which is used in the inoculation of animals is governed by the type of organism, the type of material which is to be injected, and the purpose of the inoculation. Any of the following methods may be used:

1. *Cutaneous.* The material is placed upon or rubbed into the skin.
2. *Intracutaneous, intradermal.* The material is injected into the skin. Proteins, such as tuberculin, are usually injected in this manner to determine hypersensitivity.
3. *Subcutaneous.* Inoculation just beneath the skin is the most common method used in the study of bacteria.
4. *Intramuscular.* The inoculum is injected into the body of large muscles, such as those in the neck and the gluteal region.
5. *Intravenous.* The material is injected directly into a vein. The vein which is chosen varies with the different animals. In the rabbit the posterior auricular vein is used. In the horse, cow, and sheep the jugular vein is used. If rapid action is desired, this method is most frequently employed.
6. *Intracardial.* In small animals such as the rabbit and guinea pig, the material is injected directly into the heart.
7. *Intrathoracic.* Injections into the thorax are not made commonly.
8. *Intraperitoneal.* In guinea pigs this method is used for the injection of pathogenic bacteria in the process of diagnosis.
9. *Intraneural.* This method is not used except in the study of certain neurotropic viruses.
10. *Intracranial.* Injections are made directly into the cranium usually through a trephine opening or by means of a sharp, heavy needle at thin parts of the skull. The material is injected into the brain substance, or subdurally.
11. *Intraocular.* Substances which affect the eye are placed beneath the eyelids, injected into the cornea, or into the anterior chamber.
12. *Intraspinal.* In some cases it is necessary to inject material directly into the spinal canal.

13. *Inhalation.* Material in the form of vapor or dust is inhaled into the deeper air passages.
14. *Intrapulmonary.* Substances are injected into the lungs.
15. *Intratracheal.* Fluids are injected into the trachea.
16. *Oral.* Material is fed or injected through a stomach tube.
17. *Rectal.* Fluids are injected into the rectum by an enema.
18. *Intramammary.* Drugs are commonly injected into the mammary gland of the cow for the treatment of mastitis.

## GENERAL TYPES OF INFECTIOUS DISEASES

After the animal body has been invaded. the type of organism, its specificity for tissue, the resistance of the individual, and the infection atrium will determine the localization or distribution of the organism and the type of disease produced.

Most bacterial infections are due to one species of an organism, and are termed *primary infections.* Many infections, however, are due to the presence of more than one species of organism. Since it is difficult to determine which organism is responsible for the condition, the disease is called a *mixed infection.* If a primary infection is followed by the invasion of another species of organism, the condition is termed a *secondary infection.* Organisms causing secondary infections are capable of producing primary infections. In some cases, the way must be prepared for the infection of a secondary organism. This is the case in swine influenza, in which the primary invading agent is a filterable virus which produces an inflammation in the respiratory mucous membrane which is then conducive to invasion by the bacterium *hemophilus suis.* The occurrence of mixed and secondary infections complicates the diagnosis of disease.

After invading the body, many organisms remain localized, producing *focal infections.* The localized lesions may remain quiescent until healed, or the organism may gain access to the lymph or blood stream and be carried to other parts of the body. If the organism is carried to other parts of the body where it again localizes and produces abscesses, the condition is called *pyemia.*

*Bacteriemia* is a general term which denotes the presence of bacteria in the blood-vascular system. If these bacteria are of a certain type such as the hemolytic streptococci, acute disease may result. *Septicemia* is the term given to such an infectious disease which is accompanied by fever, rapid pulse rate, and marked prostration. Pathologically, such a condition is characterized by petechial hemorrhages, hyperemia, and edema; also degenerative changes in parenchymatous tissues.

Certain species of bacteria, notably the diphtheria and tetanus bacilli, produce potent toxins which cause tissue changes by which the diseases are recognized. In tetanus the organism gains entrance through skin wounds. It localizes in subcutaneous tissues where it produces the toxin which finds its way to the central nervous system by way of the motor nerves and the lymph and blood streams.

A disease produced by toxin liberated by an organism and being disseminated throughout the body by the blood stream is called a *toxemia.* The term toxemia is used quite generally in clinical medicine to mean a condition in which toxic materials of any kind are considered the cause of the symptoms. In a later chapter the criteria for the term toxin will be discussed in detail.

A condition which results from the absorption of the end-products of tissue disintegration is called *sapremia.* The absorption of the products of the decomposition of dead fetuses and retained placental membranes causes such a condition.

The diseases which are characterized by skin eruptions are known as *exanthematous* diseases. Scarlet fever, measles, cow pox, and swine erysipelas are typical examples.

## REFERENCES

BANG, F. B. Mucociliary Function as Protective Mechanism in Upper Respiratory Tract. Bact. Rev. 25:228–36 1961.

BARBER, M. A. Jour. Exp. Med. 6:634, 1909.

BERNHEIMER, A. W., and CANTONI, G. L. Jour. Exp. Med. 81:295–306, 1945.

BURNETT, F. M Biological Aspects of Infectious Disease. Cambridge Univ. Press, Cambridge, 1940.

CANTONI, G. L., and BERNHEIMER, A. W. Jour. Exp. Med. 81:307–13, 1945.

CHRISTENSEN, L. R. Jour. Gen. Physiol. 28:363–83, 1945.

———, and MACLEOD, C. M. Jour. Gen. Physiol. 28:559–83, 1945.

CLAPPER, W. E., and MEADE, G. H. Normal Flora of the Nose, Throat, and Lower Intestine of Dogs. Jour. Bact. 85:643–48, 1963.

DINEEN, P. The Effect of Alterations in Intestinal Flora on Host Resistance to Systemic Bacterial Infection. Jour. Inf. Dis. 109:280–86, 1961.

DUBOS, R. J. The Bacterial Cell. Harvard Univ. Press, Cambridge, 1945.

———, and SCHAEDLER, R. W. The Effect of Diet on the Fecal Bacterial Flora of Mice and on Their Resistance to Infection. Jour. Exp. Med. 115:1161–72, 1962.

DURAN-REYNALS, F. Jour. Exp. Med. 58:161–81, 1933.

———. Bact. Rev. 6:197–252, 1942.

EHRLICH, R., and MIESZKUC, B. J. Effects of Space Cabin Environment on Resistance to Infection. Jour. Inf. Dis. 110:278–81, 1962.

EICHENWALD, H. F., *et al.* Some Effects of Viral Infection on Aerial Dissemination of Staphylococci and on Susceptibility to Bacterial Colonization Bact. Rev. 25:274–81, 1961.

GAY, F. P., *et al.* Agents of Disease and Host Resistance. Chaps. 2, 3, 4, 5, 14. Charles C Thomas, Baltimore, 1935.

GLADSTONE, G. P. Brit. Jour. Exp. Path. 27:394–418, 1946.

GOODLOW, R. J., and LEONARD, F. A. Viability and Infectivity of Microorganisms in Experimental Airborne Infection. Bact. Rev. 25:182–87, 1961.

HALE, J. H., and SMITH, W. Brit. Jour. Exp. Path. 26:209–16, 1945.

LANCEFIELD, R. C. The Harvey Lectures. Pp. 251–90, 1940–41.

LONGLEY, M. Y., and BERRY, C. M. Pulmonary Deposition of Aerosols. Archives of Environmental Health 2:535–43, 1961.

MACFARLANE, M. G., and KNIGHT, B. C. J. G. Biochem. Jour. 35:884–902, 1941.

MACLEOD, C. M. Bacterial and Mycotic Infections of Man. 3rd Ed. Chap. 4. J. B. Lippincott Co., Philadelphia, 1958.

PASTEUR, L. Compt. rend. Acad. Sci. 92:209–11, 1881.

PAYNE, J. M., and DERBYSHIRE, J. B. Portals of Entry for Bacterial Infection in Calves and Piglets With Particular Reference to the Tonsil. Jour. Path. Bact. 85:171–78, 1963.

PREVITE, J. J., and BERRY, L. J. The Effect of Environmental Temperature on the Host-Parasite Relationship in Mice. Jour. Inf. Dis. 110:201–9, 1962.

SCHAEDLER, R. W., and DUBOS, R. J. The Fecal Flora of Various Strains of Mice. Its Bearing on Their Susceptibility to Endotoxin. Jour. Exp. Med. 115:1149–60, 1962.

SMITH, D. T., and CONANT, N. F. (eds.). Zinsser Microbiology. 13th Ed. Appleton-Century-Crofts, Inc., New York, 1964.

SMITH, THEOBALD. Parasitism and Disease. Princeton Univ. Press, Princeton, 1934.

SULKIN, S. E. Laboratory-Acquired Infections. Bact. Rev. 25:203–9, 1961.

TAYLOR, C. E. Synergism and Antagonism Between Simultaneously Occurring Diseases—A General Review of the Ways in Which Diseases Modify Each Other. Clinical Conf. Chicago Med. Soc., 1958.

WATSON, D. W., *et al.* Jour. Inf. Dis. 80:28–40, 1947.

WEDUM, A. G. Control of Laboratory Airborne Infection. Bact. Rev. 25:210–16, 1961.

WILSON, G. S., and MILES, A. A. Topley's Principles of Bacteriology and Immunity. 5th Ed. Williams & Wilkins Co., Baltimore, 1964.

WRIGHT, G. W. Structure and Function of Respiratory Tract in Relation to Infection. Bact. Rev. 25:219–27, 1961.

# 8

# The Principles of Immunity

THE WORD IMMUNITY AS APPLIED TO DISEASE refers to a lack of susceptibility on the part of a host. Although the terms immunity and resistance are used interchangeably, the word resistance is often applied to situations in which the host is naturally resistant to a disease. In certain instances protection against a given disease-producing organism appears to be absolute, while in others it is only relative. In the latter case, the number of invading organisms, their relative virulence, and the condition of the host all play a part in the degree of immunity or resistance displayed.

Since the animal body may respond to the injection of many substances other than agents of disease, the principles of immunology and immunological terms are also applicable to nondisease situations.

## NATURAL RESISTANCE

There are many examples of complete resistance to a given disease. Animals are resistant to plant viruses and vice versa. Human beings are resistant to hog cholera virus and horses do not contract foot-and-mouth disease. Such resistance is sometimes referred to as *species resistance.* In other instances only partial resistance is exhibited. Whereas cattle are highly susceptible to anthrax, swine are somewhat resistant as shown by the rapidly fatal and generalized infection observed in cattle as compared to a tendency toward localization of the infection in the pharyngeal region of swine. Specific antibodies are not the basis for natural resistance to disease. The mechanisms involved cannot be fully explained. No doubt the inability of certain organisms to gain entrance and multiply within a given host's tissues concerns biochemical and physiological functions of both the organism and the host.

Some individuals of a species of animal may exhibit a significantly greater resistance to exposure to a given disease than the majority. This has been termed *individual resistance.* Factors which may influence an individual's resistance may be nutrition, fatigue, age, environmental temperatures, or genetic constitution. There are good examples of *genetic resistance* among animals and man. Most strains of laboratory mice are highly susceptible to mouse typhoid, but highly resistant strains have been developed by selection and breeding. Significant differences are noted in the incidence of diseases such as tuberculosis among the various races of human beings.

## ACQUIRED RESISTANCE OR IMMUNITY

Immunity which is acquired may be active or it may be passive.

*Active acquired immunity* is that which the animal produces in his own body as a result of disease followed by recovery or by vaccination. In general, this type of immunity is long lasting; the cells of the immunized animal continue to produce the protective materials several months or years after this process is once started. Immunity acquired in childhood to measles, mumps, or chicken pox usually remains for a lifetime. On the other hand, there are a few diseases in which active immunity is of short duration.

Active immunity requires a period of time for development after vaccination or the onset of a disease. Although it is possible to detect the immune response in an animal within three days after vaccination, it is more often a week or two before definite protection is acquired.

*Passive acquired immunity* is transferred to one animal from another which has previously recovered from a disease or has been vaccinated. This type of immunity is of short duration—20 to 30 days. However, the immune state is almost immediate following the transfer from the immune animal to the nonimmune. The transfer of immunity may be accomplished in several ways: (1) transfusion of whole blood, plasma, or serum, (2) gamma globulin fractions from the blood of an immune animal injected into a nonimmune, (3) the ingestion of colostrum, (4) through the egg from the adult female bird to the newly hatched bird, or (5) through the placenta from mother to offspring.

## ANTIGENS AND ANTIBODIES

The entire field of immunology is based on knowledge of antigens and the behavior of their corresponding antibodies. An *antigen* is the substance introduced, and an *antibody* is produced by the animal in response to the introduction.

An *antigen* is a substance which, if introduced into the animal body, will stimulate the formation of a specific antibody. Antigenic substances are usually protein or protein-linked. Some large polysaccharides can function as antigens without being linked to protein. Larger molecules are usually better antigens. A molecular weight of 10,000 is considered an approximate minimum, with some of the best antigens having molecular weights of several million. Some relatively nonantigenic substances can be made more antigenic if adsorbed onto particulate matter such as kaolin.

Certain lipids and polysaccharides of bacterial or animal origin are able to combine with antibodies, but when injected alone do not stimulate antibody formation. Such substances are called *haptens,* and it is necessary to combine them with protein in order to make them antigenic.

An antigen must be foreign to the individual into which it is introduced. The greater the chemical differences between the antigen and the animal in which it is introduced, the better is the antibody response. For example, it would be expected that a greater response would be obtained by the injection of bovine serum into a chicken than its injection into a sheep. It should be noted that there are exceptions to the general rule that an animal does not produce antibodies to its own tissue components. There are reports of the production of auto-antibodies under certain conditions. Antibodies to one's own lens protein, thyroid tissue, erthyrocytes, or nervous tissue have been reported.

The same antigenic substance may be found in somewhat diverse sources. The term *heterophile antigen* has been applied to these. For example, it has been observed that the injection of guinea pig tissue suspensions into a rabbit gives rise to antibodies which will react with sheep erythrocytes. Undoubtedly the same substance is common to these two tissues of different origin. There are many other examples of the sharing of the same antigens among different animals, between animals and plants, or between animal cells and bacteria.

Some of the more common antigens include animal serum proteins, cellular proteins, and protein-lipid or protein-polysaccharide complexes of animals, plants, protozoa, helminths, and bacteria. Venoms of animals and insects and bacterial toxins are quite antigenic. It must be borne in mind that intact cells of bacteria, plants, or animals contain many different substances, each of which functions as a separate antigen. They are in a sense "packages" of antigens.

Various bacterial and viral antigens are prepared commercially for the purpose of active immunization against disease by vaccination. These may be listed under the following headings:

1. Vaccines—composed of live virulent virus
   —composed of live virus of reduced virulence
   —composed of live bacteria of reduced virulence
   —composed of live bacterial spores
   —composed of killed virus
2. Bacterins—composed of killed bacterial cells
3. Toxoids—detoxified bacterial toxins
4. Aggressins and lysates—cell-free filtrates of infected tissue or cultures of bacteria.

Combinations of antigens are often made in which several strains of the same species of organism are combined to make a bivalent, trivalent, or polyvalent immunizing product. Mixed bacterins composed of two or more species of bacteria are widely used. Bacterin-toxoids are also produced and used.

The introduction of a mixture of antigens into an animal usually results in the production of antibodies specific for each one. However, there are combinations of antigens in which one antigen interferes with another so that the antibody response to one antigen is reduced or absent while the response to the other may be normal.

It is possible and sometimes necessary to increase the antigenicity of a substance by the addition of an *adjuvant*. Examples of materials used as adjuvants are alum, aluminum hydroxide, lanolin, oil-in-water emulsions, killed mycobacteria or extracts of them, and bacterial toxins. Such materials are mildly irritant to the tissues, and the antigen is retained in the resulting area of inflammation for a longer period of time than antigen without adjuvant. The prolonged stimulation due to the slow release of antigen results in the production of a greater quantity of antibodies.

An *antibody* is a molecule of serum globulin which has been modified in such a way that it reacts specifically with its corresponding antigen. The origin of antibodies, mechanisms of their formation, and their actions have been the subjects of a great deal of research. Although much information has accumulated, there are many fundamental aspects of these subjects still to be elucidated.

### Origin of Antibodies

Antibodies are the product of those cells of the animal body which synthesize globulins. Early work pointed to the cells of the reticuloendothelial system (RES) as the producers of antibodies. Experiments were conducted using animals whose RES cells were "blocked" with colloidal carbon. Such animals showed little or no antibody formation. Other work has directed attention to the lymphoid elements. By the injection of an antigen into a hind footpad of a rabbit, it has been observed that antibodies can be detected first in the efferent lymph from the popliteal node. When the cellular elements of the lymph and the lymph plasma are compared, the antibody content of the cells is several times higher than the plasma during the early stages of formation. Later on they are more nearly equal in antibody content. This would indicate that certain lymph cells either synthesize or carry antibodies or may have both functions. It has also been shown that adrenalectomized rabbits with hypertrophy of lymphoid tissues produce much more antibody than normal rabbits. Still further evidence of lymphoid participation is found in experiments in which lymph cells taken from animals undergoing immunization are transferred to donor animals or grown as cell cultures in test tubes. In both instances continued antibody formation can be demonstrated. Considerable published evidence indicates that the *plasma cell* is especially active in the synthesis of antibodies. The introduction of an antigen is followed by an increase in the number of plasma cells in the spleen and lymph nodes. Fluorescent antibody studies definitely show that antibody globulin is contained in plasma cells. Furthermore, it is indicated that these cells may be the only producers of normal, as well as immune, globulins. It is observed that human beings with the anomaly known as agammaglobulinemia produce little or no gamma globulin and have no detectable plasma cells.

## Formation of Antibodies

The mechanisms involved in the formation of antibodies are incompletely understood. It is known that a molecule of immune gamma globulin is chemically the same as a molecule of normal gamma globulin taken from the same species of animal. It can also be shown that antibodies to the same antigen produced in different species of animals react with the antigen in the same way but are chemically different. For example, antibodies to tetanus toxin produced in a horse react by neutralizing the toxin as do antibodies to tetanus toxin produced in a cow, but both antibodies are chemically identical to normal globulins of their respective species.

How does an antigen cause the modification of the molecules of globulin so as to form antibodies? And what is the nature of such modification? Answers to these questions are still in the area of the theoretical. Various theories have been advanced but none are able to explain all of the aspects of antibody formation. The first theory of antibody formation to gain general acceptance was the *side-chain theory* of Ehrlich formulated in the years 1890–1900. The side-chain theory proposed that body cells possessed "receptors" for various antigenic substances such as toxins. The union of the antigen and the receptor resulted in injury to the cell, causing the receptor to become detached. In the regeneration process there was a tendency of the injured cell to overproduce new receptors with the result that large numbers were liberated into the blood and thus became circulating antibodies. Such a theory must assume that there are preexisting receptors in each animal for every antigen to which it could respond. This has been considered as unlikely.

Various investigators, Breinl and Haurowitz, also Mudd, and later Pauling, have proposed the *template theory* of antibody formation. This theory asserts that the presence of an antigen in a globulin-synthesizing cell brings about changes in the configuration of the globulin molecule and its polar forces that mirror those of the antigen. Thus, the antigen must enter the globulin-synthesizing cell and function as the mold from which the newly formed molecules of globulin are made. The complementary shape and arrangement of polar forces give the antibody its specificity and its tendency to combine with its antigen when the two are mixed together.

The template theory does not account for the continued antibody production which occurs after the animal has apparently eliminated that antigen. It is well known that in certain diseases of man, antibodies can be detected throughout a lifetime following infection and recovery during childhood. However, some investigators interpret this observation as evidence that the antigen remains in the tissue cells as long as the specific antibody continues to be produced.

Burnet has proposed the *adaptive enzyme theory,* which explains antibody formation on the basis that the presence of an antigen results in a change in the enzymes of those cells synthesizing globulins. The antigen acts as an indirect template by affecting the enzymes which in turn modify the globulin molecules. Since the enzymes are self-replicating, continued presence of antigen is not required for prolonged antibody formation.

In 1955 Jerne advanced a *natural-selection theory* which was further modified by Burnet in 1957 as the *clonal-selection theory*. These concepts of antibody formation have several features in common with Ehrlich's views. They suggest that the antibody-synthesizing cells of the animal normally produce a large variety of patterns of globulin, each in very minute amount. Among the large population of antibody-producing cells in a given animal there will be some which are producing globulin corresponding to all or practically all of the antigens which exist in biological material except those of the particular animal itself. It is Burnet's suggestion that upon entering the blood or tissue fluids an antigen becomes attached to the lymph or plasma cell which carries reactive sites corresponding to that antigen. This attachment is followed by proliferation of that cell, and the clone of cells which results produces a large amount of the specific antibody. Evidence that each animal has preexisting cells for the production of an antibody for every possible antigen has not been presented. It is well established, however, that many natural antibodies are produced without direct antigen stimulation, such as the antibodies against foreign erythrocytes which are found in many animals. Swine possess natural antibodies for the erythrocytes of sheep, rabbits, rats, horses, and man. Chicken serum has antibodies for rabbits, rats, swine, cats, and dogs. Antibodies to many bacteria can be found in the serum of various animals which obviously have never contacted the particular organism. Just how far the list of naturally occurring antibodies can be extended for each animal remains to be determined.

None of the theories mentioned above disputes the idea that an antibody molecule possesses a configuration complementary to its antigen. They differ in their attempts to explain how an antigen influences the process of globulin synthesis. The template theory is the easiest to visualize but fails to explain the continued production of antibody after the template has apparently been removed, nor does it explain how the antibody is separated from its template. Because of the affinity of antigen and antibody for each other, it might be expected that the first molecule of antibody formed would remain in the "antigen mold." However, it is known that thousands of antibody molecules are produced for each molecule of antigen that is introduced into an animal.

The selection theories offer better explanations for the prolonged antibody response, for immune tolerance, the origin of isohemagglutinins, and several immunopathological conditions such as auto-antibody formation and agammaglobulinemia. On the other hand, it is difficult to conceive of each animal possessing the large number of different cells necessary to initiate the production of antibodies to all of the possible antigens to which that animal could respond. It would seem unlikely that animal cells could anticipate the chemically synthesized antigens which do not occur in nature. More complete explanations of the mechanism of antibody formation must await further experimentation and new approaches to the problem.

A summary of the observable events concerning antibody formation are as follows:

1. Introduction of the antigen.
2. If the antigen is not in a "soluble" form, it is acted upon by phagocytes and possibly by other physiological processes and is reduced to smaller units.
3. The antigen is distributed to antibody-producing cells in various locations, especially the lymphoid tissues, by way of the blood and lymph systems.
4. Plasma cells are observed to proliferate in the lymphoid tissues.
5. The appearance of antibodies is accompanied by the disappearance of the antigen from the tissues.
6. The first contact of an animal with an antigen may produce a good response, or in some instances little or no antibody can be detected. This is referred to as a *primary response*.
7. The reintroduction of the same antigen into an animal results in a more rapid response, and the concentration of antibodies in the serum is higher and persists longer than after the primary response. This is called a *secondary response*.
8. Repeated injections of large amounts of an antigen will produce the maximum antibody response and is called *hyperimmunization*.
9. Upon reaching a peak in two or three weeks after the primary or

secondary responses, the antibody concentration usually declines gradually over the next few weeks or months to a point which remains low or nondetectable.

10. After antibodies decline to very low or nondetectable levels the reinjection of the same antigen results in a secondary type of response. This is termed an *anamnestic* or "recalling" reaction. A reappearance of circulating antibodies in measurable levels may also occur upon the injection of an unrelated antigen.

### Properties of Antibodies

As previously stated, antibodies are modified globulin molecules behaving chemically like molecules of normal globulin taken from the same species of animal. Most antibodies are found in the gamma fraction of the globulin. However, in certain animals antibodies will also occur in the beta fraction. The molecular weight of antibodies is usually around 160,000. In the horse, antibody globulin having a molecular weight of 1,000,000 has been identified. It is also observed in the horse, as well as in other animals, that different antigens stimulate antibodies of different size. Antibodies to pneumococcus polysaccharide occur in the globulin of large size while those to tetanus toxin are relatively small. It was once thought that all antibodies to a given antigen were probably identical. More recent evidence indicates that a great deal of heterogeneity exists among the molecules of antibody which are produced in response to an antigen. While they all have the essential combining sites for reaction with antigen, the antibody molecules may not be exact duplicates in all respects. Perhaps there is some heterogeneity among molecules of the same antigen as well. Evidence of some variation in the specific properties of antibodies is suggested by the terms incomplete antibodies, blocking antibodies, nonprecipitation antibodies, also valence and avidity of antibodies which are to be discussed later.

Biochemical and biophysical studies indicate that antibody molecules have a shape which is cylindrical and elongated like a cigar. Antibodies usually carry a negative electrical charge.

The most important property of an antibody is its selective union with its corresponding antigen. This ability to unite is generally quite specific; that is, the antibody is able to differentiate between antigens which may differ only in the position of a single chemical radical. However, some weak cross reactions may be observed with related antigens.

The rate of combination of antigen and antibody is generally quite rapid. Most of the reaction takes place in seconds and is complete in 10 to 15 minutes. In only a few instances has the reaction continued over a period of hours. The antigen-antibody combination is a relatively stable one. However, they can be dissociated by various chemical means such as dilution with water, varying the salt concentration, or changes in pH. The ratio of antigen and antibody molecules following their combination is variable. It is possible for one molecule of antibody to have more than one combining site and therefore react with more than one molecule of antigen, thus exhibiting differences in *valence*. Antibodies may be monovalent, bivalent, or polyvalent. It is also possible for a molecule of antigen to react with more than one molecule of antibody. The observation that antigen and antibody could react in varying proportions has been termed the *Danysz phenomenon*. Danysz found that if equivalent amounts of toxin and antitoxin were mixed at once, the mixture was nontoxic when injected into susceptible animals, but if the toxin was slowly added to the antitoxin, the mixture was toxic. In the first instance a combining ratio of toxin to antitoxin of approximately one to one was achieved, while in the second, the first toxin molecules added probably united with more than one antibody. Consequently, some of the toxin added last was not combined and remained toxic.

Another property of antibodies is their differences in *avidity* or "aggressiveness." It has been observed that the antibodies in certain sera react more quickly and with greater efficiency than others. Antibodies produced early in the process of immunization have been compared with a similar quantity of antibodies obtained at the peak of the immune response. Those antibodies in late immunization show the greater avidity. It has been theorized that the antibodies produced during the early stages of the immunization do not as completely mirror the configuration of the antigen as those produced later.

The pioneer immunologists such as Ehrlich believed that a different kind of antibody functioned in each different immunological reaction. However, in 1930 it was shown that if the antibody which functioned in precipitation was removed from an immune serum, the agglutinating antibodies were also removed. This led Zinsser to propose his *unitarian theory,* which states that for each antigen there is only one kind of antibody produced, and that this antibody reacts with its antigen. Whether agglutination, precipitation, or any other visible reaction takes place depends upon the physical state of the antigen and the accessory factors that are present.

According to more recent views, although the same antibody may function in various reactions, evidence clearly indicates that more than one kind of antibody may be produced in response to a single antigen or at least to different portions of the antigen. For example, antibodies capable of neutralizing the infectivity of Newcastle disease virus can be distinguished from those which inhibit hemagglutination by this virus, and antibodies which function in anaphylaxis may or may not precipitate the protein used as antigen.

### Action of Antibody

As previously stated, the primary action of an antibody is to combine with its antigen. The union of antigen and antibody results in certain changes in their properties, but they are invisible ones. In order to determine that antigen and antibody have united, various secondary reactions must be observed. These secondary, visible reactions will be discussed in more detail in succeeding chapters. The more common visible reactions will be:

1. Loss of toxicity of a toxin when it is mixed with its antitoxin.
2. Precipitation of molecules of proteins when mixed with their antibodies and an electrolyte.
3. Agglutination or clumping of cells in the presence of their antibody and an electrolyte.
4. Lysis of cells by the addition of antibodies to cell antigens plus complement.
5. Anaphylactic shock will occur when a large amount of an antigen is injected into a hypersensitive animal.
6. Allergic reactions appear when an antigen is introduced into the tissues of a hypersensitive animal.
7. Infectivity of a virus is neutralized by mixing it with antibody to the virus.
8. Hemagglutination by viruses is inhibited by the addition of antibody to the virus.
9. Phagocytosis of disease-producing bacteria in many cases requires that they be first acted on by specific antibodies to the bacteria.

### Distribution of Antibodies

Most work with antibodies and our general concepts of them are based on studies involving circulating or *humoral antibodies.* It should be pointed out that antibodies are also contained in various body cells. Lymphoid cells are known to contain a high concentration of antibodies, especially those originating from a node which has been recently stimulated to activity by an antigen. Smooth muscle cells which contract in the production of anaphylaxis are believed to contain *sessile* or cellular antibody which combines with the injected antigen.

Persistence of acquired immunity after serum antibody can no longer be detected has been explained on the basis of a more rapid decline in antibody content in the blood serum than in the various cells.

During the early stages of immunization there is a greater concentration of antibodies in the efferent lymph coming from lymph nodes which drain the area of antigen deposition. Later on there is a more uniform distribution of the antibody in blood and lymph. Antibodies occur in the milk of lactating animals and usually reflect the same antibodies and the relative concentrations found in the blood. If the antigen is introduced directly into the mammary gland, the antibody response is detectable first in the milk and later in the blood serum, with a tendency to equalize after a period of time. If infection of the mammary gland occurs, the antibody content of the milk remains high as long as the infectious agent persists in the gland.

Colostrum is very high in antibody content and contains antibodies to the various antigens to which the parturient animal is immune. The passive transfer of immunity from the mother to the newborn is of great importance in the prevention of disease. The intestinal mucosa of the newborn animal is able to absorb antibody globulin rapidly during the first few hours of life. With each succeeding hour after birth, the ability to absorb globulins declines until about the 48th hour, when it practically ceases. Whether significant amounts of antibody can be absorbed after the first 2 or 3 days is controversial. Antibodies are also transferred from the hen to the newly hatched chick through the egg yolk Chicks hatched from eggs laid by immune hens resist specific infections during the first 2 or 3 weeks.

Antibodies can also be demonstrated in the urine and feces of animals and are referred to as *urinary* and *coproantibodies,* respectively.

## APPLIED IMMUNOLOGY

The ability of all animals to respond to foreign antigens with the production of specific antibodies is essential to their existence. Throughout the lifetime of each animal, antibody production is constantly in progress and constantly changing. Antibody production does not occur in embryonic life, and it is often several weeks after birth before appreciable amounts of antibody globulin are produced by the newborn animal. During this period maternal antibodies are provided to the young through colostrum, absorption from egg yolk, or placental transfer. It is quite difficult for animals to survive without the benefit of maternal antibody. From the time an animal is able to synthesize its own globulins until its death, the total antibody picture of an animal is probably never exactly the same on two different days. The level of certain antibodies will be increasing while others will be decreasing. Some will be quite high, others low, in concentration. Depending on the environment, diseases contracted, and vaccinations, new antigens are constantly being encountered. It would be impossible to determine accurately the complete immunological history of any animal. Man is able to control through artificial immunization procedures only some of the amounts and kinds of antibodies an animal may produce. There are several practical considerations to be taken into account in successful artificial immunization.

### The Antigen

The careful selection, preparation, and handling of antigens are of great importance in artificial immunization. In the case of bacteria, it is found that certain isolates or strains are more immunogenic than others. Factors which may influence the immunogenicity of an organism and must be given consideration are: dissociation phase, virulence, toxin production, encapsulation, type of medium used for its growth, age of culture, and the method employed for its inactivation. When dealing with viruses it is important that attention be given to careful selection of strains, their antigenic structure, degree of modification if used alive, or the method of inactivation if used as a killed product. Other considerations include the type of diluent used, the addition of adjuvants, preservatives, standardization as to concentration, processes of desiccation, the conditions of storage, and the maintenance of potency during storage. The commercial production of antigens is under government license and regulation. Certain standards of potency, safety, and purity must be met by each immunizing product.

## The Animal

The individuality, species, age, health, and nutritional state of the animal are concerned in the immune response. There are differences between individual animals as well as species in the antibody response to a given antigen. For this reason it is best to use several animals of various species if a maximum response is to be obtained for experimental work. The very young or the very old are less efficient producers and should be avoided. For commercial production of antiserum the horse has often been used because it usually responds well to many antigens, and large quantities of serum can be withdrawn at one time. Since animals may become hypersensitive to horse serum protein, the immune serum is often produced in the same species in which it is to be used.

Animals in a general state of health are more responsive to antigen injections. Sometimes death losses will occur if live attenuated vaccines are administered to sick animals, whereas the healthy ones show little or no reaction.

Malnutrition may impair antibody formation, but some animals will respond normally to antigens even though they are nutritionally deficient.

## Route of Administration of the Antigen

The route of administration is significant with certain antigens but less so with others. It has also been shown that the route of injection may influence the kinds of antibodies that are produced.

Antigens which are readily soluble, such as native proteins, are usually injected intravenously, and those of a particulate nature are injected intramuscularly or subcutaneously. However, the intravenous route is preferred for antibody production to erythrocytes and to the polysaccharides of pneumococci and streptococci. Subcutaneous injections of streptococci result in protein antibodies being formed almost exclusively, whereas antibodies to the polysaccharide are produced following intravenous injection. The intradermal route is specified for anthrax spore vaccines, equine encephalomyelitis vaccine and the intramuscular route for avianized rabies vaccine for dogs. With many live avirulent vaccines the route of injection is less critical since the virus grows and multiplies after it is first distributed to the tissues.

Methods of inoculation employed for birds include intranasal, oral, wing-web puncture, defeathered follicles, and skin scarification.

Oral vaccination has proved successful in certain instances where live attenuated organisms are used. Killed vaccines administered orally have not resulted in satisfactory antibody levels.

## Amount of Antigen Introduced

There is a relationship between the amount of antigen injected and the degree of antibody response obtained. Detectable antibody may result from the injection of extremely small amounts of a highly antigenic substance, but in actual practice fairly large amounts are usually employed. Larger doses are usually given when nonliving products are used than when live organisms are administered. The dose of a bacterin usually consists of several billion killed bacteria. Live immunizing products depend upon some growth of the organism within the vaccinated animal in order to achieve the maximum antigenic stimulation.

The optimum dose of each immunizing agent is established by experimentation, taking into consideration the size of animal, the route of administration, and the character of the immunizing agent. To inject more than this amount may produce no better immunity and in some instances is not well tolerated. The injection of too large a volume of antigen at one site may result in "sterile abscesses" because the limits of tissue absorption of the material have been exceeded.

#### Frequency of Injection

The most efficient immunity is obtained from live vaccines which give a long period of antigenic stimulation. Nonliving antigens must be injected repeatedly for maximum response. With some antigens a single dose is satisfactory and more economical, while in other instances two or more injections spaced from 3 to 7 days apart are necessary. Some weakly antigenic substances require both the addition of adjuvants and multiple injections before a satisfactory antibody response can be achieved.

Periodic booster injections of immunizing materials serve to maintain the level of antibody. Such injections spaced several months or years apart result in a secondary response, with the concentration of antibody increasing more rapidly and reaching higher levels than after the initial stimulation.

#### Effect of Bleeding During Immunization

In the experimental production of antibodies with poorly antigenic materials it is sometimes necessary to bleed on animal severely after the first injections are given. The removal of a quantity of the blood stimulates all blood forming cells to greater activity. Globulin-synthesizing cells thus stimulated appear to be more responsive to additional injections of antigen.

Any benefits of "therapeutic bleedings" by ancient medical men in their efforts to equalize the "body humors" unknowingly might have been based on the above principle.

#### Uses of Antibody

There are many uses of the knowledge of the behavior of antibodies. A list of the more important uses will serve to acquaint the student with the scope of antibody activities.

1. Prevention of infectious diseases.
2. Therapy of infectious diseases.
3. Diagnosis of infectious diseases.
4. Blood typing.
5. Identification of bacteria and viruses.
6. Classification of bacteria, viruses, plants, and animals.
7. Standardization of products used for artificial immunization.
8. Forensic medicine, identification of stains, blood types, etc.
9. Study of certain organic compounds, especially proteins.
10. Basic studies of the immune mechanisms.

## OTHER IMMUNOLOGIC PHENOMENA

#### Acquired Immune Tolerance and Tissue Grafting

Immunological mechanisms are vitally concerned with skin and other tissue transplants in animals and man. With the exception of bone, cartilage, and cornea it seldom has been possible to transfer tissue from one individual to another except between identical twins. This is because the cells of each animal are antigenically unique. Two individuals are never completely identical in composition unless they have originated from a single ovum. A tissue graft from one animal to another is usually rejected within a few days because of an immune response of the receiving animal to foreign antigens in the tissue of the donor. It has been discovered that a recipient animal may be made tolerant of a tissue graft if it has received injections of tissue from the donor during embryonic life or shortly after birth. For some reason not understood, the introduction of foreign antigens before the antibody-producing cells begin to function results in tolerance of that foreign antigen in later life. In other words, animals which are made tolerant in this manner fail to recognize the foreign character of the particular antigen and treat it as their own and do not produce antibodies against it. Such acquired tolerance is specific and does not impair the ability of the animals to respond to other antigens. The term *active acquired tolerance* for this phenomena was suggested by Billingham, Brent, and Medawar in 1953. The terms *acquired immune tolerance* and *immunologic unresponsiveness* have also been used.

Observations leading to the recognition of acquired tolerance were contributed by several workers who noted that the embryo and the very young animal fail to respond to antigenic stimuli. Burnet and Fenner called special attention to these observations in their publication *The Production of Antibodies* and predicted the existence of immune tolerance. In addition to tolerance of tissue grafts, animals have been made tolerant in early life to many different kinds of antigens including erythrocytes, bacterial cells, viruses, toxoids, toxins, and purified proteins.

There are examples of naturally acquired tolerance which are of interest. Owen, in 1945, observed that fraternal cattle twins may possess two antigenically different kinds of erythrocytes. This is an example of a *chimera*. During embryonic development anastomosis of placental blood vessels of the twin embryos results in an exchange of blood. Such animals may continue to tolerate each other's erythrocytes permanently, and an exchange of skin grafts is also possible. The blood chimera of the above type is also observed in other animals, including man. Chicks from double-yolked eggs may show blood chimerism. Immunological "paralysis," which is also a form of acquired tolerance, is sometimes observed in adult animals that have received large doses of an antigen over a period of time. Horses hyperimmunized for commercial production of antiserum may become "exhausted" and fail to respond to further injections of the antigen.

### Immunology and Cancer

A great deal of research on the cancer problem has been directed toward the possible role of antigens and antibodies in the production as well as the control of the disease. It can be demonstrated that there are antigenic differences between cancer cells and normal cells of the individual from which the tumor is taken. Cancer cells obtained during the metastatic stages of the disease can be transplanted to many different animals, whereas cells taken early in the development of the tumor or normal cells from the animal with the cancer are not transplantable. Experimentally, it is possible to immunize animals with suspensions of tumor cells so that they become refractory to transplantation of the tumor. Furthermore, serum from immunized animals will produce specific cytotoxic effects on tumor cells. Whether immune serum will be of value therapeutically in cancer is questionable.

Another immunological approach to the control of neoplastic disease is aimed toward the viral agents known to be the cause of certain kinds of cancer. Whether immunity can be produced to these viruses or if such immunity would be an effective control is problematical.

### Immunology and Parasitism

Like other foreign organic materials, those from various helminths and protozoa are antigenic to the host animal. Antibodies to parasites can be demonstrated by various serological techniques such as complement-fixation, precipitation, and allergic tests.

It is established that immune reactions play a significant role in acquired resistance of mature animals to the effects of parasitism. Vaccination of young animals with X-irradiated larvae is effective in the prevention of infection by certain nematodes and gives promise as a means of control. Losses of fowl and animals from coccidiosis can be reduced by immunization procedures.

## REFERENCES


ALTLAND, P. D., *et al.* Immune Response in Rabbits Exposed to High Altitude. Jour. Inf. Dis. 113:228–32, 1963.

ANSON, M. L. *In* Advances in Protein Chemistry. Academic Press, New York, 1947.

ATTARDI, G., *et al.* Symposium on the Biology of Cells Modified by Viruses or Antigens. II. On the Analysis of Antibody Synthesis at the Cellular Level. Bact. Rev. 23:213, 1959.

BILLINGHAM, R. E., *et al.* Actively Acquired Tolerance of Foreign Cells. Nature 172:603, 1953.

BORDET, JULES, and GAY, F. P. Studies in Immunity. John Wiley & Sons, London, 1909.

BOYD, W. C. Fundamentals of Immunology. 3rd Ed. Interscience Publishers Inc., New York, 1956.

BREINL, F., and HAUROWITZ, F. Zeit. f. Phys. Chem. 192:45, 1930.

BURNET, F. M. A Modification of Jerne's Theory of Antibody Production Using the Concept of Clonal Selection Austral. Jour. Sci. 20:67, 1957.

———. The Clonal Selection Theory of Acquired Immunity. Vanderbilt Univ. Press, Nashville, 1959.

———. Theories of Antibody Production. *In* Immunity and Virus Infection. V. A. Najjar (ed.). John Wiley & Sons, New York, 1959.

———, and FENNER, F. The Production of Antibodies. Melbourne Macmillan Co., Ltd., 1949.

CAMERON, H. S. Amer. Jour. Vet. Res. 8:153–56, 1947.

CHACE, J. H., *et al.* Jour. Immunol. 52:267–78, 1946.

COCHRANE, C. G. Studies on the Localization of Circulating Antigen-Antibody Complexes and Other Macromolecules in Vessels. I. Structural Studies. Jour. Exp. Med. 118:489–502, 1963. II. Pathogenetic and Pharmacodynamic Studies. Jour. Exp. Med. 118:503–13, 1963.

CUSHING, JOHN E., and CAMPBELL, DAN H. Principles of Immunology. McGraw-Hill Co., New York, 1957.

DUBOS, R. J. The Bacterial Cell. Harvard Univ. Press, Cambridge, 1945.

EHRLICH, PAUL. Studies in Immunity. John Wiley & Sons, New York, 1910

FELIX, A. A System of Bacteriology. Med. Res. Council. 7:412. His Majesty's Stationery Office, London, 1930.

GAY, F. P., *et al.* Agents of Disease and Host Resistance. Chap. 18. Charles C Thomas, Baltimore, 1935.

HARRIS, T. N., and EHRICH, W. E. Science 101:28, 1945.

———, and ———. Jour. Exp. Med. 84:157–65, 1946.

———, and HARRIS, S. The Genesis of Antibodies. Amer. Jour. Med. 20:114, 1956.

———, *et al.* Immunologic Response of Neonatal and Older Rabbits to Antigens of Rabbit Leucocytes. Jour. Exp. Med. 116:575–88, 1962.

HAUROWITZ, F. Lancet 252:149–51, 1947.

JERNE, N. K. The Natural Selection Theory of Antibody Formation. Proc. Natl. Acad. Sci. 41:849, 1955.

KABAT, E. A., and MAYER, M. M. Experimental Immunochemistry. Charles C Thomas, Springfield, Ill., 1948.

KAHN, R. L. Effect of Irradiation on Some Aspects of Tissue Immunity. Bol. Inst. Bact. de Chile 11:58–59, 1959.

KAPLAN, M. H., *et al.* Jour. Exp. Med. 91:15–30, 1950.

KOLMER, J. A. Infection, Immunity and Biological Therapy. W. B. Saunders Co., Philadelphia, 1925.

KRAFT, S. C., *et al.* Criteria for Evaluating Autoïmmune Phenomena in Ulcerative Colitis. Gastroenterology 43:330–36, 1962.

KUHNS, W. J. Types and Distribution of Antibodies Amer. Jour. Med. 20:251, 1956.

LANDY, M., *et al.* Bactericidal Method for the Measurement in Normal Serum of Antibody to Gram-Negative Bacteria. Jour. Bact. 83:631–40, 1962.

MCMASTER, P. D. Sites of Antibody Formation. *In* The Nature and Significance of Antibody Response. A. M. Pappenheimer (ed.). New York Acad. Med., 1953.

MARRACK, J. R. Chemistry of Antigens and Antibodies. Special Report Series No. 230. Med. Res. Council. His Majesty's Stationery Office, London, 1938.

MICHAEL, J. G., *et al.* Studies on Natural Antibodies to Gram-Negative Bacteria. Jour. Exp. Med. 115:131–46, 1962.

MUDD, STEWART. Jour. Immunol. 23:423, 1932.

MURPHY, J. B., and STURM, E. Proc. Soc. Exp. Biol. Med. 66:303–7, 1947.

NORRIS, J. R. Bacterial Spore Antigens: A Review. Jour. Gen. Microbiol. 28:393–408, 1961.

NOSSAL, G. J. V. Antibody Production by Single Cells. III. Histology of Antibody Production. Brit. Jour. Exp. Path. 40:301, 1959.

OWEN, R. D. Immunological Tolerance. Fed. Proc. 16:581, 1957.

PAPPENHEIMER, A. M., JR. Antiegg Albumin Antibody in the Horse. Jour. Exp. Med. 71:263, 1940.

PARK, W. H., and WILLIAMS, A. W. Pathogenic Microorganisms. 11th Ed. Lea & Febiger, Philadelphia, 1939.

PATTERSON, R., *et al.* Antibody Production and Transfer to Egg Yolk in Chickens. Jour. Immunol. 89:272–78, 1962.

PAULING, L. A Theory of the Structure and Process of Formation of Antibodies. Jour. Amer. Chem. Soc. 62: 2643, 1940.

QUILLIGAN, J. J., JR. Immunity and Immunization. Med. Arts and Sci. 14:85–91, 1960.

RAFFEL, SIDNEY. Immunity, Hypersensitivity, and Serology. Appleton-Century-Crofts, Inc., New York, 1961.

SHEPEL, M., and KLUGERMAN, M. R. Effect of Adjuvants on Antibody Response of Rabbits Inoculated With Venezuelan Equine Encephalomyelitis Virus. Jour. Bact. 85:1150–55, 1963.

SMITH, D. T., and CONANT, N. F. (eds.). Zinsser Microbiology. 13th Ed. Appleton-Century-Crofts, Inc., New York, 1964.

SOULSBY, E. J. L. Immune Mechanisms in Helminth Infections. Vet. Rec. 73:1053–58, 1961.

TALMADGE, D. W. Allergy and Immunology. Ann. Rev. Med. 8:239, 1957.

TITUS, J. L., and SHORTER, R. G. Second-Set Rejection. Proc. Mayo Clinic 38:249–60, 1963.

WILSON, G. S., and MILES, A. A. Topley's Principles of Bacteriology and Immunity. 5th Ed. Williams & Wilkins Co., Baltimore, 1964.

WISSLER, R. W., *et al.* Jour. Immunol. 52:267–78, 1946.

ZINSSER, HANS. Resistance to Infectious Diseases. 4th Ed. Macmillan Co., New York, 1931.

# 9

# Toxin and Antitoxin

## TOXIN

THE WORD TOXIN IS OFTEN USED TO COVER A wide variety of substances, but generally is used to denote a bacterial substance which is capable of producing disease in a susceptible animal. Bacteriologically speaking, toxins are divided into two types: *exotoxins* and *endotoxins*. Each type has certain characteristics by which it may be recognized.

EXOTOXINS

1. Excreted by bacteria in the medium in which they are grown.
2. Highly specific for certain tissues and cells such as nerve, muscle, erythrocytes, producing typical symptoms of disease of which tetanus is a good example.
3. Very toxic. Amounts small as 0.001 ml. of some toxins lethal to guinea pigs.
4. Unstable, quickly losing toxicity when exposed to 60°C., when exposed to various chemicals, and when stored at room temperature.
5. Highly antigenic, stimulating the formation of specific neutralizing antitoxins in animals which have been injected.
6. Converted into toxoids by treatment with formalin and other chemicals. Retain specific antigenicity but lose toxicity.

ENDOTOXINS

1. Intracellular substances liberated by bacterial disintegration into the medium in which the bacteria are grown.
2. Not specific for tissue, but do produce general effects such as fever. Do not produce specific symptoms of disease.
3. Weakly toxic in general, but certain gram-negative bacteria produce endotoxin lethal in 0.5 ml. amounts in mice.
4. Stable, remaining toxic after exposure to 60°C., unchanged by chemicals, and by storage at room temperature.
5. Not highly antigenic, not stimulating the formation of specific neutralizing antitoxins, but do stimulate formation of antibodies which can be demonstrated by agglutination, precipitation, and complement fixation.
6. Not converted into toxoids by action of chemicals; antigenicity remains unaltered.

Ordinarily the term *toxin* is used to mean *exotoxin* and will be used in this manner in the following discussion.

### Sources of Toxins

Toxins are produced by a number of bacteria, plants, and animals. The bacteria which produce toxins are relatively few, but the list is being increased as the poisonous products of more of the bacteria are discovered. The toxins vary in ability to cause disease; this makes it difficult to form a definite list of toxin-producing bacteria. The best criterion of toxicity is the ability of the toxin to stimulate the formation of an antitoxin which possesses definite neutralizing properties.

Some of the plants are able to produce powerful toxins. *Ricin* from the castor-oil bean and *abrin* from the jequirity bean are typical examples. *Robin* is a toxin from the bark of the locust. Certain of the mushrooms or "toadstools" produce potent toxins.

The poisons of certain snakes, scorpions, and spiders are the oldest toxins known.

### The Nature of Toxins

Although each of the above toxins has characteristics peculiar to itself, there are characteristics common to all. Most toxins are protein in nature. The best known toxins, diptheria, botulinus, and tetanus, are pure proteins and the last two mentioned have been crystallized. Many toxins are relatively easily destroyed by heat,

| EFFECTS OF TOXINS | SOURCES | NAMES OF TOXINS |
|---|---|---|
| Hemolysis | *Strep. pyogenes*<br>*Staph. aureus*<br><br>*Clost. perfringens*<br><br>*Clost. novyi*<br><br>*Clost. septicum*<br>snake venoms | streptolysin O and S<br>alpha, beta, gamma, delta hemotoxins<br>alpha toxin (lecithinase) delta, theta<br>gamma, delta, and epsilon toxins<br>alpha, beta toxins |
| Produce skin rash | *Strep. pyogenes* | erythrogenic toxin |
| Lethal to laboratory animals | *Coryn. diphtheriae*<br>*Clost. septicum*<br>*Clost. novyi*<br>*Clost. chauvoei*<br>*Clost. perfringens*<br>*Staph. aureus* | lethal toxin |
| Produce necrosis of tissues | *Staph. aureus*<br>*Clost. perfringens*<br>*Coryn. diphtheriae* | necrotizing toxin |
| Produce definite neurological symptoms | *Clost. botulinum*<br>*Clost. tetani*<br>*Shigella dysenteriae*<br>snake venoms | neurotoxin<br>tetanospasmin<br>neurotoxin<br>neurotoxin |
| Kill leucocytes | *Staph. aureus* | leucocidin |
| Digest collagen | *Clost. perfringens* | collagenase |

chemicals, and digestive enzymes. However, tetanus and botulinus toxins differ in these respects. Tetanus toxin is easily destroyed by acids and digestive enzymes, while botulinus toxin is resistant. Botulinus toxin has been found to agglutinate the erythrocytes of chickens and sheep, and this reaction is specifically inhibited by antitoxin. The molecular weight of botulinus toxin is approximately 900,000. Toxins are precipitated with albumose and peptone fractions of proteins by the action of ammonium sulfate, aluminum sulfate, zinc chloride, alcohol, or nucleic acid. A temperature of 60°C. is destructive to toxins, and at least 95 per cent of the toxin molecules are destroyed by 56°C.; however, an exception is the streptococcus toxins which are not totally destroyed by boiling for 20 minutes. Light and oxygen are detrimental to toxins. Although many toxins are destroyed by digestive enzymes, the epsilon toxin of *Clost. perfringens* is excreted from the organism in an inactive form and is activated by trypsin.

The action of toxins upon tissues can be studied only by their injection into susceptible animals; in fact, the presence of toxin in a bacterial filtrate usually can be detected only by such a procedure. There are no chemical tests which reveal the presence of toxin. The potency of many of the toxins is an important characteristic. Tetanus toxin is so powerful that 1 ml. of culture filtrate will cause the death of 50,000 to 75,000 guinea pigs. Botulism toxin is considered to be the most powerful poison known. Purified type A botulinus toxin has been assayed as having 31 billion mouse lethal doses per gram. Toxins exert their action, however, only after a "period of incubation," or a sufficient lapse of time following injection to allow the toxin to become fixed to the susceptible tissue.

A very small dose of toxin will stimulate body cells to produce specific antibodies or antitoxins, which will neutralize the toxins in definite proportions. Antitoxic sera are used for the protection of individuals who are immunized by a simultaneous injection of toxin and in the treatment of individuals who are suffering with an infection caused by a toxin-producing organism. In tetanus, for example, the life of the animal is saved by the prompt injection of tetanus antitoxin. After the toxin has become fixed to nerve tissue, however, the neutralizing ability of tetanus antitoxin is considerably reduced.

Animals are immunized against infections caused by toxin-producing bacteria, by the injection of toxin in nonlethal doses, or by the injection of attenuated toxin. Ehrlich demonstrated that the toxin molecule is composed of two parts which he termed *toxophore* and *haptophore*. The action of a toxin in producing disease is due to the toxophore part of the molecule. This is the thermolabile and chemolabile fraction of the molecule. Toxin is combined or united with tissue by the haptophore fraction, and it is this part which functions as the antigen. Ehrlich observed that the toxophore fraction was destroyed upon standing, but that the haptophore fraction was not altered. This same decrease in toxicity is produced by the action of a chemical such as formalin or iodine. Ehrlich called the haptophore portion *toxoid*. These fundamental discoveries of Ehrlich have been of great value in developing methods of producing immunity against toxins. They have facilitated the production of antitoxin without undue losses of producing animals. In the production of tetanus antitoxin, horses are given injections of tetanus toxoid in order to form a basal immunity against subsequent injections of toxin. Toxoids are used without the simultaneous use of antitoxin in producing an immunity against many diseases. Diphtheria and tetanus toxoids are universally used in medicine.

### Tissue Specificity of Toxins

One of the most important characteristics of a toxin is its specificity for a certain tissue. The toxin liberated by *Clostridium tetani* is specific for two types of tissue—nerve tissue and erythrocytes. Toxin which combines with nerve tissue is called *neurotoxin* and in the case of tetanus, *tetanospasmin*. Toxin which acts on erythrocytes is called *hemotoxin* or *hemolysin* because it causes a lysis of the red blood cell with liberation of hemoglobin.

The toxins of *Streptococcus pyogenes* are able to cause hemolysis of erythrocytes and the formation of an erythema. Diphtheria toxin affects the nerve centers of the vascular system and produces degenerative changes in heart muscles, kidneys, and liver. The toxin of botulism causes a paralysis of the muscles supplied by the cranial nerves.

### Determination of the Potency of Toxins

With the more powerful toxins, the death of a susceptible experimental animal is used as a criterion of potency. In order to compare a toxin produced by one strain of an organism with that produced by another, standard doses, methods of injection, time of action, size and species of animal are considered. The smallest dose of a certain toxin which will kill an animal in a definite time is called the *minimum lethal dose*, designated M.L.D. The exact definition of an M.L.D. varies with the toxin. An M.L.D. of tetanus toxin is defined as the least amount that will kill a *350-gram* guinea pig in 96 hours. An M.L.D. of diphtheria toxin is the least amount that will kill a *250-gram* guinea pig in 96 hours.

Toxins which cause the hemolysis of red blood cells also are tested for potency; for example, the minimum hemolytic dose, M.H.D., of staphylococcus toxin is the amount which will hemolyze 1.0 ml. of a 2 per cent suspension of rabbit erythrocytes in one hour at 37°C.

A toxin of the scarlet fever streptococcus produces an erythema. Susceptible children are used in order to test the potency of this toxin. The toxin is injected into the skin of the arm and the unit of measurement is called the skin test dose, S.T.D. The smallest amount which gives a reaction 1.5 cm. in size in 24 hours is designated the S.T.D. of scarlet fever toxin.

Endotoxins are produced by members of various genera of gram-negative bacteria. These include Neisseria, Escherichia, Salmonella, Brucella, Vibrio, Shigella, Pasteurella, and Pseudomonas. Injection of endotoxins into animals results in fever and depression, and in large amounts they may be lethal. The disintegration of organisms in the tissues or circulation of infected animals is one of the mechanisms of disease production.

Other toxic materials which enhance virulence of organisms or produce definite effects but which do not come under the definition of either exotoxin or endotoxin are:

1. Coagulase—produces clotting of plasma.
2. Streptokinase—lyses fibrin (fibrinolysin).
3. Enterotoxin—produces food poisoning.
4. Hyaluronidase—aids in spread of infection in tissues.

## ANTITOXIN

Antitoxin is the name commonly used for antibodies to a toxin.

An antitoxin is produced by body cells in response to a stimulus by a toxin and is specific for the toxin which has stimulated its production. Antitoxins combine with toxins in the body of the immune animal and in test tubes in the laboratory. The toxin is neutralized in proportion to the amount of antitoxin which is adsorbed by it. Ramon has demonstrated that toxin is precipitated by antitoxin and that the reaction is so definite that it may be used as a standardization procedure. This indicates that the union of toxin-antitoxin is similar to any precipitation reaction involving antigen and antibody and the action of an electrolyte.

Antitoxins are relatively stable but are destroyed by a temperature of 62°C. Refrigeration at 3° to 5°C. maintains antitoxin satisfactorily, and when dried *in vacuo* there is little deterioration over long periods of time. The addition of 0.5 per cent chloroform preserves antitoxin.

### Production of Antitoxin

The production of antitoxins for the immunization of animals and man against the various toxins follows the same general procedure. The toxin is prepared and standardized; a suitable animal, usually the horse, is injected to produce antitoxin; the serum is collected, filtered, and concentrated; the antitoxin is standardized or tested for potency. Tetanus antitoxin is used more than any other antitoxin in veterinary medicine; therefore, a brief description of its manufacture will be given to illustrate the general procedure of antitoxin production.

### Tetanus Toxin

A culture of *Clostridium tetani* which produces a highly potent toxin is chosen for toxin production. The organism is grown in veal-infusion broth containing 0.5 per cent sodium chloride and 7 per cent peptone. Dextrose can be added to the medium to enhance the growth of the organism, but apparently it does not increase the potency of the toxin. The medium is covered with a layer of petrolatum and is then sterilized to drive out oxygen previous to inoculation. The medium is incubated at 34° to 35°C. for 10 to 14 days for maximum toxin production. The potency of the toxin decreases after 14 days. The soluble toxin is separated from the living bacteria by passing through a Berkefeld N filter. The filtrate can be preserved by the addition of 0.5 per cent phenol, or the toxin may be precipitated with ammonium sulfate and preserved in the dry state. The toxin in the dry state is easily dissolved in sterile salt solution and may be placed in various dilutions for the purpose of standardization.

The toxin is then tested for potency. This is done by making a series of dilutions of 1:1,000, 1:5,000, 1:10,000, 1:15,000, 1:20,000, 1:25,000, and injecting 1 ml. of each dilution into a series of 350-gram guinea pigs. The highest dilution which causes the death of the guinea pig in 96 hours is chosen as the M.L.D.

### Tetanus Antitoxin

The horse used for production of antitoxin must be in good condition and absolutely free from disease of any kind. The animal is given a foundation immunity by the injection of tetanus toxoid or by the injection of toxin and antitoxin. The animals are then given 10–20 guinea pig M.L.D.'s at three-day intervals; the doses are gradually increased until the animal receives as much as 1,000 ml. of culture filtrate. Toward the end of the fifth or sixth month after immunization is started, samples of serum are taken and tested for the potency of the antitoxin. When the antitoxin has reached a satisfactory potency, the animal is bled (Fig. 9.1), and the clear serum, antitoxin, is removed after the blood has clotted. It is preserved as whole serum by the addition of 0.5 per cent phenol or 0.4 per cent tricresol. The whole serum may be used therapeutically or it may be concentrated.

The concentration of antitoxin is based upon the fact that blood serum is a mixture of various proteins, pigments, and inorganic salts and that antitoxin is in the globulin fraction. Concentration is desirable for two reasons; first, to eliminate those serum fractions which may cause anaphylactic reactions, and second, because there is little reason for injecting inert substances. All of the methods which have been devised for the concentration of antitoxin are based upon the differences in solubility or coagulability of the various serum constituents. The original methods of Gibson and Banzhaf have formed the basis for most of the methods which are in use at present.

Many methods are used throughout the world for standardizing tetanus antitoxin. The method used in the United States follows the one originally described by Rosenau and Anderson in 1908. The standard of measurement of antitoxin is called the immunity unit. The *immunity unit* for tetanus antitoxin is *ten times the least amount of serum necessary to save the life of a 350-gram guinea pig for 96 hours against the official test dose of standard toxin.* The official test dose of toxin consists of a precipitated toxin preserved under

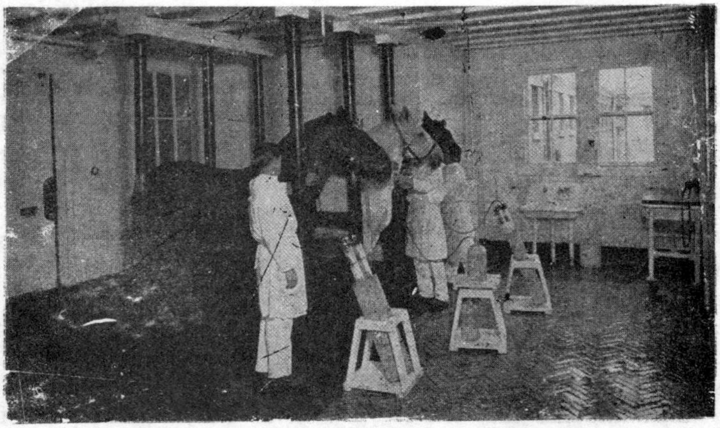

FIG. 9.1—Bleeding horses in antiserum production.

special conditions at the laboratories of the National Institutes of Health in Bethesda, Maryland. This toxin is sent to laboratories to be used in standardizing antitoxin. In order to find the immunity unit (I.U.), various dilutions are made of the antitoxin which are then mixed with a standard dose of toxin. After the toxin and antitoxin are placed together, the mixtures are kept at room temperature and then injected subcutaneously into a series of guinea pigs weighing approximately 350 grams.

After the potency of the antitoxin in terms of immunity units is determined, the antitoxin is placed in vials containing varying amounts and is ready for use. It is common practice to place 1,500 American Units (3000 International Units) of tetanus antitoxin in a vial.

### Other Methods of Standardizing Antitoxins

Ramon demonstrated as early as 1922 that a precipitate results when toxin and antitoxin are mixed in definite proportions. This method has been developed during recent years and is a valuable adjunct to the biological method of standardization. The unit of toxin which is used in the standardization of antitoxin is called the Lf dose. An Lf unit is the volume of toxin flocculating with one unit of antitoxin and is determined by flocculation tests with antitoxin of known potency. The results which are obtained with this method agree with the guinea-pig method although it has not replaced the older technique. Since the toxoids react in the same general proportions with antitoxin as does toxin, the test is of greater value in the standardization of toxoids.

A method of tetanus antitoxin standardization using hemagglutination techniques has been described by Fulthorpe. Tetanus toxin is first adsorbed onto erythrocytes, then with the addition of antitoxin the toxin-coated erythrocytes are agglutinated.

Römer and his coworkers demonstrated that the injection of small amounts of diphtheria toxin into the skin of guinea pigs produces small areas of necrosis at the point of injection. Mixtures of toxin-antitoxin do not result in necrosis unless a small amount of unneutralized toxin is present in the mixture. These investigators were able to determine the amount necessary to produce necrosis; hence they arrived at a method of testing the potency of antitoxin. The rabbit has been substituted for the guinea pig in the test by some investigators. It has been observed that the rabbit skin is more sensitive to the toxin than is that of the guinea pig, and a larger number of tests can be made on one animal. The method has not come into use in the standardization of diphtheria antitoxin in commercial establishments, but it has been found to be of value in detecting the presence of minute amounts of antitoxin in blood serum.

The Schick test in man is a practical application of the principle of the test for determining susceptibility to diphtheria. In this test a minute amount of toxin is given intradermally into the arm. If swelling and redness occur the patient is considered to be susceptible to diphtheria. If no reaction is observed the patient is considered immune.

## REFERENCES

ARRHENIUS, S. Immuno-chemistry. Macmillan Co., New York, 1907.

BANZHAF, E. J. The Preparation and Purification of Toxins, Toxoids and Antitoxins. The Newer Knowledge of Bacteriology and Immunology. Pp. 745–58. Univ. of Chicago Press, Chicago, 1928.

BAYNE-JONES, STANHOPE. The Titration of Toxins and Antitoxins by the Flocculation Method. The Newer Knowledge of Bacteriology and Immunology. Pp. 759–71. Univ. of Chicago Press, Chicago, 1928.

BERRY, L. J., and SMYTHE, D. S. The Role of Tryptophan Pyrrolase in Response of Mice to Endotoxin. Jour. Exp. Med. 118:587–603, 1963.

BORDET, JULES. On the Mode of Action of Antitoxins on Toxins. Studies in Immunity. Transl. F. P. Gay. Pp. 259–79. John Wiley & Sons, London, 1909.

BOYD, W. C. Fundamentals of Immunology. 3rd Ed. Interscience Publishers, New York. 1956.

CONDIE, R. M., *et al.* Comparison of the Properties of Snake Venom and Endotoxin. Jour. Exp. Med. 115: 563–78, 1962.

DUBOS, R. J., and SCHAEDLER, R. W. The Effect of Bacterial Endotoxins on the Water Intake and Body Weight of Mice. Jour. Exp. Med. 113:921–34, 1961.

EHRLICH, PAUL. Collected Studies on Immunity. Transl. C. Bolduan. Pp. 481–560. John Wiley & Sons, London, 1906.

FULTHORPE, A. J. Titration of Antitoxin by Hemagglutination at Low Level of Test. Jour. Hyg. 56:183, 1958.

GAY, F. P., *et al.* Agents of Disease and Host Resistance. Charles C Thomas, Baltimore, 1935.

GLENNY, A. T. Active Immunization With Toxin. A System of Bacteriology. Pp. 107–93. Med. Res. Council. His Majesty's Stationery Office, London, 1931.

GREISMAN, S. E., *et al.* Relationship Between Tolerance and Reticuloendothelial System Phagocytic Activity in the Rabbit. Jour. Exp. Med. 117:663–74, 1963.

———, *et al.* Relationship Between Endotoxin Tolerance and Reticuloendothelial System Phagocytic Activity in Man. Jour. Exp. Med. 119:241–64, 1964.

KAHN, R. L., *et al.* Irradiation and Toxin Neutralization by Antitoxin. Jour. Inf. Dis. 107:325–31, 1960.

KOLMER, J. A. Infection, Immunity and Biologic Therapy. Pp. 203–26. W. B. Saunders Co., Philadelphia, 1923.

KRASNER, R. I., and JANNACH, J. R. Its Effect on the Development of Local Streptococcal Infections in Rabbit Skin. Jour. Inf. Dis. 112:134–42, 1963.

MILNER, K. C., *et al.* Structure and Biological Properties of Surface Antigens From Gram-Negative Bacteria. Bacteriol. Rev. 27:352–68, 1963.

RIBI, E., *et al.* Relationship of Chemical Composition to Biological Activity. Bacteriol. Rev. 25:427–36, 1961.

STAAB, E. V., *et al.* Enhancement of Susceptibility to Snake Venom by Endotoxin. Jour. Exp. Med. 115:579–96, 1962.

STETSON, C. A., JR. Immunological Aspects of the Host Reaction to Endotoxins. Bacteriol. Rev. 25:457–58, 1961.

UHR, J. W. The Effect of Bacterial Endotoxin on the Newborn Guinea Pig. Jour. Exp. Med. 115:685–94, 1962.

VAN HEYNINGEN, W. E. Bacterial Toxins. Blackwell Scientific Publ., Oxford, 1950.

WATSON, D. W., and KIM, Y. B. Specificity of Pyrogenic Tolerance and the Role of Hypersensitivity in Pyrogenicity, Lethality, and Skin Reactivity. Jour. Exp. Med. 118:425–46, 1963.

WHITBY, J. L., *et al.* Possible Mechanisms Whereby Endotoxins Evoke Increased Nonspecific Resistance to Infection. Bacteriol. Rev. 25:437–46, 1961.

WOODS, M. W., *et al.* Metabolic Effects of Endotoxins on Mammalian Cells. Bacteriol. Rev. 25:447–56, 1961.

# 10

# Agglutination and Precipitation

WHEN BACTERIA ARE WASHED FROM THE surface of an agar slant with a salt solution, and if the mixture is diluted until faintly cloudy, the bacteria will remain in suspension for a considerable period of time. If a small amount of homologous immune serum is added to a small volume of the bacterial suspension in a test tube and the mixture is placed in a warm water-bath, it will be observed that aggregates of bacteria are formed. When allowed to stand overnight the clumps may become so large they will settle to the bottom of the test tube. This is called *agglutination.* When a small amount of serum from a rabbit which has received a series of injections of egg white is added to a solution of egg white in a test tube and placed in a warm water-bath, a faintly cloudy layer will form at the junction of the two ingredients. This is called *precipitation.*

The distinction between agglutination and precipitation is as follows: Agglutination occurs when the antigen is in suspension in the form of individual cells or finely divided particles. Precipitation occurs when the antigen is composed of protein molecules in solution. Otherwise the two reactions are fundamentally the same.

## AGGLUTINATION

The clumping of bacterial cells in the presence of an immune serum was observed by Charrin and Roger in 1889, Metchnikoff in 1892, Isaeff and Ivanhoff in 1894, Bordet in 1895, and Washburn in 1896. Of these, Bordet attached much significance to the reaction and sought to explain the mechanism which caused it. Gruber and Durham, in 1896, called attention to the specificity of the reaction and to the possibilities of group agglutination. It was these investigators who first used the term *agglutinin* for the antibody responsible for the reaction. In 1896, when Widal and Grünbaum independently found that the blood serum of typhoid fever patients would agglutinate typhoid bacilli, the true value of the reaction as a means of diagnosing disease was established. Since then, numerous diseases of man and animals have been diagnosed by the agglutination test. The value of the reaction has not been limited to the diagnosis of disease, for it is also of use in the differentiation of closely related types of bacteria. Erythrocytes are also agglutinated; this reaction is universally used in the typing of blood.

### The Antigen

The term *antigen,* as used in connection with agglutination reactions, refers not only to the organisms or other cells responsible for antibody production but more often refers to the suspension of cells used as a reagent in the agglutination test. Bacterial antigens are usually suspensions of killed bacteria in 0.9 per cent NaCl solution. It is necessary to use live organisms in some instances, but this is hazardous to the laboratory worker and special handling precautions must be employed. The strain of organism used must be carefully selected and maintained in pure culture. The conditions of growth and the dissociation phase of the organism must be controlled. The bacteria to be used for agglutination antigens are usually grown in quantity on the surface of agar in large bottles or flasks. When maximum growth has occurred the organisms are removed by washing the surface with saline solution. They are then killed by heat or chemicals such as phenol or formalin and diluted to a predetermined standard density. The density will vary depending on the organism used and the technique of testing to be employed.

A suspension of erythrocytes in 0.9 per cent NaCl is used as the antigen in blood typing of man and animals. For blood typing, a dilution of whole blood in saline may be used. Many techniques require that the plasma be removed and the density of the erythrocyte suspension be carefully standardized. This is done by centrifugation followed by replacement of the plasma with saline. Resuspension, centrifugation, and discard of the saline is repeated three to five times. These "washed cells" are essentially free of plasma constituents.

It has been found that many soluble antigens can be adsorbed onto the surface of erythrocytes or other particles of similar size such as resins, collodion, and rice starch. Particles so treated then can be agglutinated by antibodies to the adsorbed substance. Boyden reported that the treatment of erythrocytes with dilute tannic acid increases their ability to adsorb proteins onto their surface. Tanned erythrocytes have been used to advantage in demonstrating certain antigen-antibody reactions.

### The Antibody

The antibodies which produce agglutination are referred to as *agglutinins.* Blood serum is ordinarily used in agglutination tests although plasma can be employed. Antibodies in milk may be detected in milk serum or whey. The serum is obtained by centrifuging a sample of clotted blood or rennet-coagulated milk obtained from the animal to be tested for the presence of antibodies. Usually it is unnecessary to treat the serum prior to testing, but certain special procedures may require that it be heated to 56°C. for 30 minutes or that it be treated with kaolin to remove interfering substances. In order to quantitate the antibody content of a serum, various dilutions in saline solution are made. The reciprocal of the highest dilution of the serum which produces a definite agglutination reaction is called the *titer.*

### Mechanism of Agglutination

Bacteria or other cells suitable as antigens for the agglutination reaction must be capable of remaining in uniform suspension for a period of time with little or no tendency to settle out. Cells in suspension are kept apart because of their identical repelling electrical charges. When antibodies to the cellular antigens are mixed with the cells in suspension, they unite with these antigens at the cell surface. If adjacent cells come in contact with each other, they stick together. As more and more cells contact each other, large clumps of cells are formed. Agitation or centrifugation of the mixture of cells and antibodies will increase the rate of contact between cells and will hasten agglutination reactions.

Explanations of the mechanisms of agglutination have in the past involved changes in electrical charge and cohesiveness of the cells brought about by the presence of antibody globulin on their surfaces. The effect of electrolyte (saline) is to reduce surface charges on the cell while the combination of antigen and antibody increases their stickiness. The result of the reduction of repelling charges and increased stickiness is agglutination. More recent observations indicate that bridging between cells by bivalent antibodies is important in the formation of aggregates of cells (Fig. 10.1). Further support for the bridging theory will be found in the discussion of prozones and blocking antibodies later in this chapter.

### Factors Influencing Agglutination

Alteration of conditions of the test may influence the results obtained. Salt con-

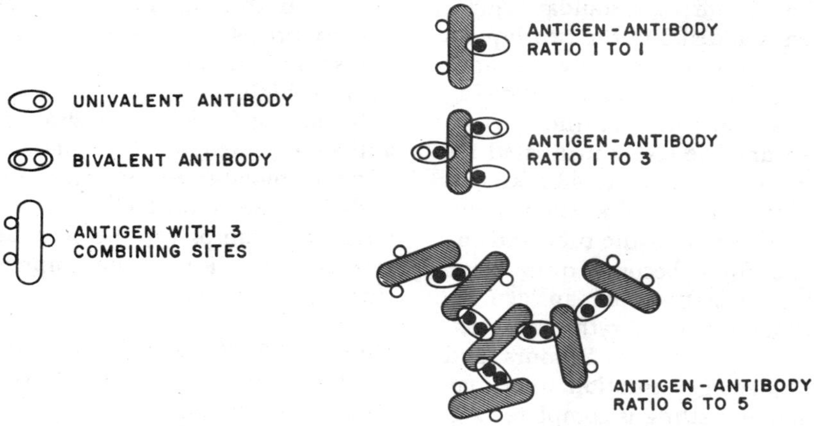


FIG. 10.1—Diagrammatic representation of different ratios of antigen to antibody and the bridging of bivalent antibodies between antigens to produce visible aggregates.

centration is usually 0.9 per cent NaCl or, if buffers are used as diluents, an ionic strength of 0.15 M. Sensitivity of the antigen may be altered if substantial deviation in salt concentration occurs. The pH of the diluent is ordinarily adjusted to 7.0 to 7.2, but agglutination is not affected by a pH range of 5.0 to 8.5. *Acid agglutination* may occur at very low pH values. The temperature of incubation of agglutination reactions is variable, ranging from 5° to 56°C. Many techniques of agglutination, such as those used in blood typing, are carried on at room temperature, while others are traditionally incubated at 37°C. Specialized procedures for brucellosis testing use temperatures of 56°C. Certain agglutinins in the blood serum of man are active only at refrigerator temperatures. These are called *cold agglutinins.*

The addition of small amounts of gelatin to antigens will increase their sensitivity.

## Agglutination Techniques

Agglutination reactions may be demonstrated by a variety of techniques. These include the microscopic, tube, and plate tests. The details of the various techniques as applied to each different organism or cell are too variable to be described in detail but the general procedures are given below.

**The Microscopic Agglutination Test** is conducted by placing a drop of the diluted antigen on a coverslip, and a drop of serum or serum dilution is added. The two drops are mixed and then covered with a hanging drop slide. The preparation is incubated at room temperature and examined every 5 to 10 minutes under low and high power of a microscope for evidence of clumping. Careful rotation of the slide will hasten the reaction. A saline-antigen control should be made and used for comparison.

**The Tube Agglutination Test.** Bacterial antigens usually vary in density with different species of organisms. An amount of the antigen is suspended in saline so that a standard density is obtained. For example, Brucella antigen is standardized at 0.04 per cent by volume. Phenol 0.5 per cent or formalin 0.2 per cent is usually incorporated into the diluent for the antigen to prevent growth of contaminating organisms during incubation of the test. Erythrocyte suspensions are adjusted to a standard density on a basis of the volume of packed cells in relation to diluent. Turbidemetric methods are also in common use for adjusting the density of antigens.

To perform the test, undiluted serum is either pipetted in measured quantities directly into a test tube or dilutions are made in saline or buffer. A standard quantity of antigen is added and the two liquids mixed. Some techniques employ the antigen as diluent for the serum. Following the mixture of antigen and the various dilutions of serum, the test is incubated for a definite period of time, 24 to 48 hours, at 37°C. If agglutination occurs, clumps will gravitate to the bottom of the tube and the top part of the liquid becomes quite clear. If the result is negative, the antigen remains uniformly turbid. Erythrocytes settle out of suspension in 1 to 2 hours, and the results of hemagglutination tests may be read as soon as settling is complete. Agglutinated erythrocytes are easily observed on the bottom of the tube. Brief centrifugation of the test tubes following a period of incubation will hasten the agglutination of cells.

A variation of the technique of tube agglutination is the *capillary tube test.* The same antigen preparation and serum dilutions may be drawn successively into a capillary tube so that one liquid overlays the other. Clumps of antigen will form on the walls of the tube if agglutination occurs.

**The Plate Agglutination Test.** A technique which will give the most rapid agglutination reactions is the plate test. Concentrated antigen suspensions are used. In the case of Brucella antigen, a 12 per cent suspension is employed rather than the 0.04 per cent used in the tube test. Stained antigens are often utilized to aid in the reading. Crystal-violet, methyl violet, or malachite green are used for this purpose.

Varying amounts of undiluted serum are measured onto a glass plate or slide and a standard amount of the concentrated antigen is added. A toothpick is used to mix the serum and antigen. After being left at room temperature for a designated time—2 to 8 minutes depending on the particular test—the plate is rotated and readings made. Agglutinated cells will form large, easily distinguished clumps. Rapid hemagglutination tests can be conducted in this manner. Agglutination of the erythrocytes may be evident within a few seconds if the concentration of agglutinins is high.

In the test for pullorum disease a drop of antigen is placed on a glass plate and a drop of whole blood from the wing vein is mixed with it. The stained bacteria will agglutinate and clumps can be seen among the erythrocytes. It must be emphasized that this is not hemagglutination.

### Application of Agglutination Reactions

The more common applications of agglutination include:

1. Diagnosis of infectious disease of man and animals, such as brucellosis, typhoid and paratyphoid fever, tularemia, pullorum disease, glanders, vibriosis.
2. Blood typing prior to transfusion, for parenthood determination, genetic studies, erythroblastosis of the newborn.
3. Identification and classification of bacteria—Streptococci, Salmonella, Shigella.
4. Detection of the presence of certain viruses.
5. Detection of the presence of antibodies by indirect hemagglutination and hemagglutination-inhibition tests.

### Interpretation of Agglutination Reactions

Agglutination tests are extremely valuable when properly conducted and interpreted, but they have limitations. For diagnosis of bacterial infections certain titers of antibody have been established as significant while reactions in low dilutions are disregarded. For example, reactions to Brucella antigen in dilutions below 1 to 50 are held to be of no significance, while those at that dilution and above indicate the presence of infection. The higher the agglutinin titer the greater is the specificity of the reaction. Agglutination tests detect presence of antibodies to the infectious agent, and presence of the organism then must be assumed. Therefore, agglutination tests are most applicable in diagnosis of those diseases in which immune carriers are frequently found. On a large scale, this approach is more accurate and economical than to attempt to culture the causative organism from the internal tissues of each animal examined. Two further limitations are that animals in the early stages of infection show no antibody response and that if artificial immunizing products are in common use for prevention of the disease in question, the agglutinins may have resulted from vaccination rather than natural infection.

The practice of testing paired sera, one serum sample collected during the acute phase of the disease and a second collected during convalescence, is helpful in interpretation. A fourfold increase in agglutination titer in the convalescent serum over that of the acute serum is good evidence of recent infection.

*Cross reactions* between different species of organisms may be confusing. There are many examples of shared antigens among bacteria. The causative agents of tularemia and brucellosis share antigens and will cross agglutinate. Therefore, serum of animals infected with brucellosis will agglutinate suspensions of tularemia organisms although in somewhat lower dilutions than Brucella antigen.

### Prozones

In many serological reactions, including agglutination, it occasionally is observed that no reaction occurs in low dilutions, 1 to 5 or 1 to 50, while marked reactions occur in higher dilutions. The zone of lower dilutions in which no reaction occurs is called a prozone. This phenomenon is more often observed with high-titered serum and serum which has been stored or heated. It is possible to obtain false negative serological results if the serum being tested is not diluted beyond the prozone.

There are several explanations for prozones which may occur in various serological tests. Different mechanisms may operate in various situations. One explanation of prozones presumes the presence of monovalent antibody in the serum. Since a monovalent molecule of antibody has only one combining site, it cannot "bridge" between antigens in order to build aggregates or clumps. Thus, the monovalent antibody combines with the antigen and "blocks" the bivalent to the extent that no visible reaction can be noted in the test (Fig. 10.2).

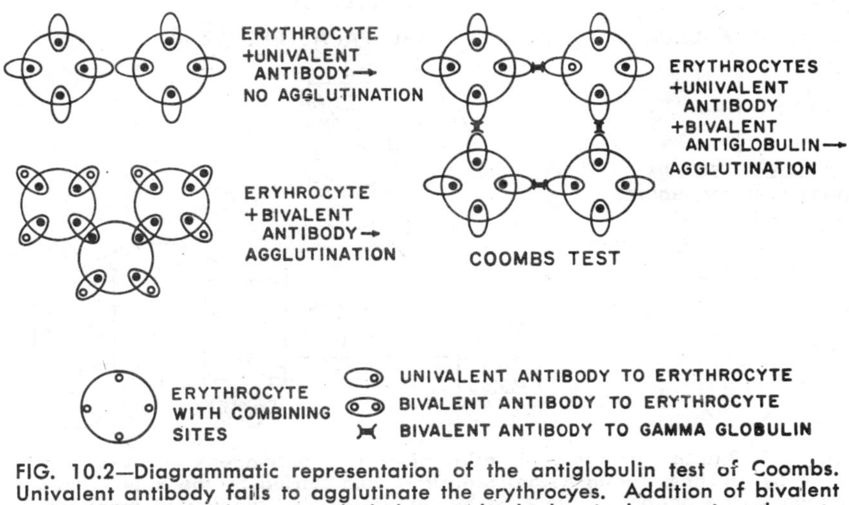


FIG. 10.2—Diagrammatic representation of the antiglobulin test of Coombs. Univalent antibody fails to agglutinate the erythrocyes. Addition of bivalent antiglobulin to erythrocytes which have adsorbed univalent anti-erythrocyte antibody results in agglutination.

Ordinarily the monovalent antibody concentration is less than the bivalent so that as higher dilutions of antiserum are made the monovalent antibody is diluted beyond effect.

Another explanation is that bivalent antibody quickly and completely saturates all antigen-combining sites with only one of the two reacting portions of the antibody being involved. This leaves no room on the antigen for other uncommitted sites to form a bridge between antigens.

Another type of interference with antibody action may occur with bacteria such as *E. coli* and *Sal. typhosa*. Certain antigens appear to be located physically so close to each other in the cell wall that union of antibody to one of the antigens may physically interfere with union of the other antibody with its antigens. Sometimes blocking effects are sufficient to give completely negative tests even though antibodies are present in serum. Coombs has devised a test which is widely used to detect agglutinating antibodies under such circumstances (Fig. 10.2).

The *Coombs test* employs antibodies to the normal globulin of the species of animal from which the serum under test has been obtained. The test is conducted by first setting up the conventional tube agglutination test, mixing antigen and various dilutions of the serum to be tested. Following a period of incubation, the tests are centrifuged and the cells (bacterial or erythrocytes) are washed free of any uncombined antibody. Antiglobulin serum is then added and a second period of incubation is followed by reading for agglutination. If no agglutination occurred in the conventional test but was observed after addition of the antiglobulin serum, it is concluded that specific univalent antibodies for the antigen were present and entered into combination but did not result in agglutination. The bivalent antiglobulin antibodies bridge between cells coated with monovalent antibodies, resulting in the agglutination of the cells in the second phase of the test.

The Coombs antiglobulin test is used in blood typing, especially with Rh factors, and also as a special technique in bacterial agglutination tests.

### Agglutinin Adsorption

The technique of agglutinin adsorption has important applications in identification

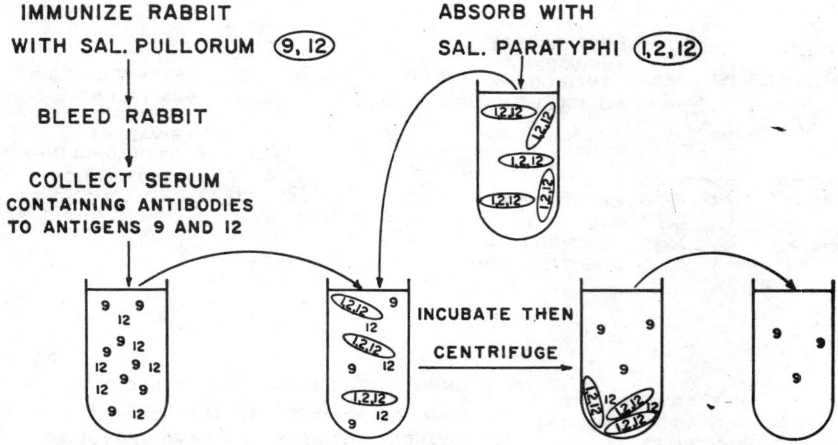


FIG. 10.3—Principle of agglutinin adsorption. One antibody is removed from serum by reacting it with its antigen. It is then carried by the agglutinated antigen to the bottom of the tube by centrifugation. The uncombined antibody is decanted to another tube as "pure" antibody.

and classification of bacteria and in blood typing. Members of the genus Salmonella are to a great extent identified on the basis of their antigenic structure. In order to determine presence or absence of different antigens in various isolates of Salmonella, monospecific sera must be obtained. Such sera are produced by injection of organisms of known antigenic character into an animal. The resulting antibodies could be totally adsorbed from the serum by addition of the same organism that was used for the immunization. If a closely related organism, one which differs by only one antigenic component, is added to the serum, then all but one antibody is combined, and when the mixture of serum and organisms is centrifuged the uncombined antibody remains in the supernatant liquid. In this manner a "pure antibody" for a single antigen is obtained by adsorbing all other antibodies by the closely related organism (Fig. 10.3).

The principle of agglutinin adsorption is used in studying the antigenic structure of other bacteria, and there are many situations in which it is used in connection with antigenic analysis of erythrocytes.

Many technical procedures connected with the three tests described above have been omitted in this discussion. The student should consult manuals of laboratory technique for the details of each test.

## HEMAGGLUTINATION—ISOANTIBODIES

Certain bacteria and toxic substances from some plants and from a few species of animals contain substances which agglutinate red blood cells. Such agglutinins are termed *hemagglutinins*. The extract from the navy bean is used in the agglutination of red blood cells in the clarification of anti-hog cholera serum. The red blood cells are agglutinated by the extract, and when the blood is centrifuged, the cells form in a compact mass in the bottom of the centrifuge cup. Hemagglutinin, like any antibody, is formed by the injection of the red blood cells of one species into another unrelated species.

### Erythrocyte Antigens and Blood Typing

Before 1900 attempts to transfuse blood from animals to man were tried but were unsuccessful. About 50 per cent of the transfusions from person to person were followed by reactions and some were fatal.

The discovery that erythrocyte composition differs from one person to another was made by Landsteiner in 1900. This discovery stimulated a large amount of research which has yielded much that has been applied in the fields of genetics and medicine. It has furnished a basis for safe transfusions of blood from one person to another, explained the mechanism of hemolytic disease of the newborn, made it possible to determine parentage, has become a most important tool for genetic studies, and has enabled the anthropologist and the crime investigator to determine the blood type of human remains even after long periods of time.

Much research has also been done on erythrocyte antigens of animals, especially cattle. Other animals, including horses, swine, sheep, dogs, rabbits, cats, mice, and chickens, have been studied to some extent. Interest in animal blood typing has been pioneered by the geneticist but has also interested the veterinarian from the standpoint of transfusion compatibility between animals and hemolytic disease of the newborn. Most procedures for the typing of blood involve agglutination tests run on glass plates, slides, or ceramic tile surfaces. A typical typing procedure is as follows: Blood from the individual to be typed is drawn into sodium citrate solution or other anticoagulant. The erythrocytes are washed twice in 20 volumes of saline. The packed cells are measured in the bottom of the graduated centrifuge tube after the final centrifugation. The desired concentration, usually 3 to 5 per cent by volume, is prepared ready for use. Equal volumes (approximately 0.03 ml.) of erythrocyte suspension and typing serum are placed on the slide or plate and mixed. The test is read macroscopically after 6 minutes of incubation at room temperature. The slide or plate should be gently rotated several times during the incubation period.

There are many variations of the technique described above which apply to different systems. Some workers prefer to use different concentrations of erythrocytes, different amounts of reagents, microscopic readings, or tests conducted in test tubes followed by centrifugation. It is necessary to use the antiglobulin test of Coombs to detect the presence of certain antigens. In blood typing of cattle and sheep, hemolytic tests employing complement are used.

The preparation of the antiserum for use in blood typing usually requires much planning. The choice of individuals from which erythrocytes are taken, the animal to be immunized, and the elimination of unwanted antibodies by agglutinin adsorption must be carefully considered in order to obtain antiserum of known composition.

**Blood Groups of Man.** The ABO groups discovered by Landsteiner are the most important as far as compatibility of blood transfusions is concerned. Table 10.1 shows the relationship of erythrocyte antigens of the ABO group to the presence or absence of their corresponding antibodies in the serum of the four major blood types.

Reactions resulting from transfusion of blood from one person to another are due to the action of antibodies in the serum of the recipient on the erythrocytes of the donor. Such antibodies which occur in the serum of one individual for antigens in the cells of another of the same species are *isoantibodies*. These antibodies are an example of normal antibodies which appear in the blood without specific antigen stimulation. A type O person has been referred to as a "universal donor" since his erythrocytes contain neither A nor B antigens and an AB person a "universal recipient" because he has no antibodies to these antigens. In practice, however, transfusions are made with blood of the same type as the recipient.

TABLE 10.1

ANTIGENS AND ANTIBODIES OF ABO BLOOD GROUPS OF MAN

| Blood Type | Erythrocyte Antigens | Antibodies in Serum |
|---|---|---|
| O | none | anti-A and anti-B |
| A | A | anti-B |
| B | B | anti-A |
| AB | AB | none |

Occasionally transfusion reactions have occurred as a result of antigens and antibodies other than those of the ABO group.

In the years 1939–41 observations by Levine and Stetson and by Landsteiner and Wiener led to the discovery of the Rh antigens and their significance in man. It was found that antibodies produced in rabbits by the injection of erythrocytes of rhesus monkeys would agglutinate the erythrocytes of about 85 per cent of the human population. It was also observed that the Rh (rhesus) antigens and antibodies were responsible for the clinical condition known as erythroblastosis fetalis.

Six different antigens of the Rh system have been reported. Antigen D is the most important, being responsible for a majority of cases of hemolytic anemia (erythroblastosis). Persons possessing the D antigen in their erythrocytes are Rh positive and those in which the antigen is absent are designated as Rh negative. Rh negative individuals may produce antibodies to the Rh antigen D if they receive erythrocytes from an Rh positive donor. Before 1940 transfusions were made only on the basis of the ABO types and some individuals were immunized to Rh antigens in this way. Immunization to Rh antigens may also occur as a result of the transplacental passage or absorption of Rh antigens from a fetus into the blood of an Rh negative mother. The antibodies are transferred back to the fetus, resulting in the destruction of its erythrocytes and causing hemolytic anemia. It is under these circumstances that nearly all immunizations to Rh antigens occur. Rh antigens which occur in the fetus of an Rh negative mother are inherited from the father.

Other erythrocyte antigens listed in Table 10.2 are occasionally involved in transfusion reactions and erythroblastosis but are more important in genetic studies and are of use in determining the complete antigenic formula of an individual in order to establish identity or parentage. With the antisera available it is possible to identify over 300,000 different kinds of erythrocytes. As more antigens are discovered, the number of kinds may be in the millions. Except for identical twins, each person is probably antigenically unique.

**Animal Blood Typing.** More of the research on animal blood antigens has been oriented toward genetic application. In several species, hemolytic disease of the newborn has been described and transfusion reactions occur. In a few instances, linkage between erythrocyte antigens and economic factors such as butter fat production, growth rates, and egg production have been reported.

Blood typing of cattle is used in genetic studies, parentage determination, and the eligibility of calves for registry, as well as fertility predictions of heifers born twin to a bull. Transfusions can usually be made from one cow to another without reactions. Hemolytic anemia of the newborn has not been reported in cattle.

In the horse the first blood transfusion is usually tolerated but subsequent transfusions may result in mild to severe reactions. Hemolytic anemia and icterus of newborn foals have been reported by several investigators. The mechanism is similar to that of the Rh system of man, the chief difference being that antibodies from the immunized mother reach the circulation of the foal only by way of the colostrum rather than transplacentally. The manner by which the erythrocytes of the fetus (which are like those of the sire) reach the antibody-forming cells of the mare is not clear. Transfusion of the affected foal with compatible blood or restriction of colostrum during the first 24 hours after birth have usually controlled the condition if it can be anticipated by blood typing prior to parturition.

Iso-immunization of sows by erythrocyte antigens of their fetuses of a different blood type has been reported by Bruner and others. An entire litter may be lost from hemolytic anemia within the first 48 hours after birth as a result of the ingestion of colostrum from an iso-immune sow. The occurrence of this condition in swine has been associated with injection of hog cholera vaccines produced from swine blood and tissues.

Transfusions between dogs may result in reactions. Those animals having "A-negative" blood are universal donors, and their blood can be used for transfusion if a negative cross-matching test is obtained using the donor's cells and recipient serum. Hemolytic anemia of newborn pups has been reported by several workers.

Only a limited amount of work has been done on blood typing of cats, rabbits, rats, and mice. Hemolytic anemia has been reported to occur in all four of these species.

The study of erythrocyte antigens of chickens has been directed toward genetic applications and possible association with economically important characteristics. Blood types of turkeys, ducks, doves, and pigeons have been studied to a limited extent.

## PRECIPITATION

Kraus was the first one to observe precipitation in 1897. While working with broth filtrates of *Pasteurella pestis* and the cholera vibrio, he found that upon mixing the clear filtrates with their respective immune sera, a cloudy precipitate was formed. He named the antibodies responsible for the reaction *precipitins.* He, furthermore, found that the reaction was specific, for the immune sera of each of the two organisms which he studied did not produce precipitation in the filtrate of the opposite organism, nor would they precipitate the filtrates of other types of bacteria. These observations of Kraus opened the path for numerous applications of the precipitin reaction, and today it is used in the study of any protein, as well as linkages of protein to other materials.

As was previously stated, the precipitation reaction is similar to agglutination, the only difference being the size of the antigen. The antigen which induces the development of precipitin, doubtlessly, is the protein molecule itself. The precipitins are quite specific but *group precipitation* takes place when related proteins are treated with a serum homologous to one of them. The blood sera of various ruminants, for example, exhibit group precipitation. An

TABLE 10.2

SUMMARY OF THE MORE IMPORTANT SYMBOLS AND DESIGNATIONS USED IN BLOOD TYPING

| | Blood Types or Systems | Erythrocyte Antigens | Occurrence of Hemolytic Disease of Newborn |
|---|---|---|---|
| Man | ABO | $A_1$, $A_2$, B | occasionally |
| | Rh | C* or Rh†<br>D rh′<br>E rh″<br>c $Hr_0$<br>d hr′<br>e hr″ | occasionally<br>+ and most important<br>occasionally<br>occasionally |
| | MNSs | M,N,S,s | rare |
| | P | P | ? |
| | Kell | K | + |
| | Duffy | $Fy^a$, $FY^b$ | rare |
| | Kidd | $Jk^a$, $Jk^b$ | rare |
| | Lewis | $Le^a$, $Le^b$ | ? |
| | Lutheran | $Lu^a$, $Lu^b$ | ? |
| Cattle | | >60 factors<br>A to Z<br>A′ to H′, etc. | |
| Swine | A,B,E,F,G,H,<br>I,J,K,L, | A,O,$B_a$,$E_a$,$E_b$,$E_d$,<br>$E_e$,$E_f$,$E_g$,$F_a$,$G_a$,$G_b$,$H_a$,<br>$H_b$,$I_a$,$J_a$,$K_a$,$K_b$,$K_d$,<br>$L_a$,$L_b$,$L_c$ | + |
| Dogs | | A,B,C,D,E | + |
| Sheep | R,r,i | R,r | |
| Cats | EF,O,F | E,F | + |
| Rabbits | | $G^a$,$G^b$,$G^c$ | + |
| Rats and mice | | | + |
| Chickens | A,B,C,D,E,L | >20 factors<br>$A_1$–$A_8$<br>$B_1$–$B_5$, etc. | |

* Fisher-Race system.
† Wiener.
Although letters of the alphabet are used to designate erythrocyte antigens in various species, this does not imply that they are the same substances. However, "J" antigen of cattle, "A" of swine, and "R" of sheep are related. A and B blood group antigens are found in horses and swine.

antiserum homologous to human serum will precipitate the serum of anthropoid apes. The work of Nuttall has shown quite definitely the limits of group precipitation. He tested 900 kinds of blood, using in all 30 antisera, and made a total of 16,000 combinations. He showed that, on the whole, the closer the relationship the greater was the amount of common or group precipitation. For example, he determined that the blood of apes of the old world yields a heavier precipitate with human antiserum than does that of apes of the new world. Another exception to specificity has been found in the protein of the crystalline lens; an antiserum for lens protein of man or the ox will produce a precipitate in solutions containing the lens protein from other animals that are not at all closely related. It has been suggested that cataract of the eye may be due to the formation of an autoprecipitin for the protein of the lens and its consequent precipitation *in situ*.

There are several techniques used in conducting precipitation tests. The simplest is to mix equal amounts of the antigen dilutions with antiserum in a small test tube. After incubation at 37°C. for 1 hour, the tubes are examined for cloudiness due to the formation of a precipitate. A second reading is often made after the tests have been in a refrigerator overnight. A more sensitive test is the interfacial ring test which is performed by carefully layering the antigen over the antiserum. A ring of precipitate forms at the junction of the two liquids. Ring tests may be performed in the conventional serological test tubes or in capillary tubes, the latter having some advantages in conserving reagents and equipment. It is common practice to dilute the antigen and to use undiluted antiserum in precipitation tests. However, in certain applications such as toxin-antitoxin precipitation, both antigen and antibody are diluted and each dilution of antigen is tried with each different dilution of antibody. In this manner the optimum dilution of each may be determined. The greatest amount of precipitate does not necessarily occur in those tubes containing the most concentrated reagents. Ratios of antigen to antibody which favor 1 to 1 combinations may result in soluble complexes which are invisible in contrast to the larger visible aggregates which are due to lattice formation (Fig. 10.1).

Precipitation tests conducted in gels, usually agar, have been used extensively since 1946. Two techniques, the Oudin and Ouchterlony, are in use although the principle was not originally described by either of these investigators. In the Oudin precipitation technique the antiserum is mixed with melted agar, pipetted into a test tube and allowed to harden. A solution of the antigen is placed above the serum agar column and the tubes are allowed to stand for several days either in the incubator or at room temperature. As the antigen diffuses into the serum agar, zones or lines of precipitate will form. If the antigen is a pure substance, only one line will form. If the antigen solution is composed of more than one antigenic component, a line of precipitate corresponding to each different substance will form because of the differences in their rates of diffusion.

A similar technique has been described by Ouchterlony in which the tests are conducted in Petri dishes instead of test tubes. Melted agar is poured into Petri dishes and allowed to harden. Wells are punched in the agar with a cork borer or some other device, or troughs are cut out of the layer of agar with a knife. The antigen and antiserum are placed in separate wells or troughs and allowed to migrate into the agar between them. Lines of precipitate will form in the agar and the number of lines will correspond to the number of different antigen-antibody systems present (Fig. 10.4).

## Uses Made of the Precipitation Phenomenon

Several practical applications have been made of precipitation in the differentiation of proteins. These are: (1) the recognition of blood stains and stains of other body fluids such as semen, and the differentiation of meats from different species of animals, such as horse from beef, and venison from

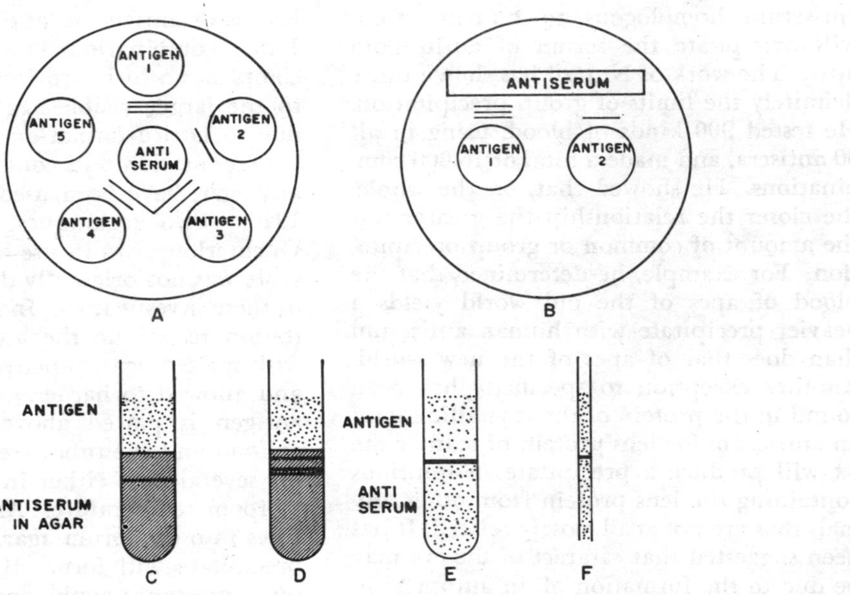


FIG. 10.4—Agar-diffusion precipitation tests. A, Ouchterlony technique. Antigen 1 has three different reacting components; antigen 2, one component. Antigens 3 and 4 appear identical. Antigen 5 is unrelated to any antibody in the antiserum. B, partial duplication of A except serum reservoir is of a different shape. C and D show zones of precipitation in serum agar. Oudin technique. E, ring or interfacial test. F, same as E but conducted in capillary tube.

calf; (2) the classification of bacterial strains as is done with the streptococci; (3) the diagnosis of bacterial infections such as anthrax (Ascoli test) and syphilis (Kahn test); (4) the diagnosis of viral diseases; (5) the standardization of toxins and antitoxins such as diphtheria and tetanus discussed in the last chapter; (6) the diagnosis of parasitic infestations, for example, trichinosis; (7) the identification of closely related plants. Some of these reactions, particularly the differentiation of bacteria and diagnosis of disease, will be discussed in the chapters devoted to those organisms.

## Recognition of Blood Stains

It is sometimes necessary in criminal investigation to determine with certainty the origin of a blood stain. The fact that the stain has been produced by blood may be easily demonstrated by a chemist, but he has no ready means of telling with certainty whether the blood is of animal or human origin. Uhlenhuth was the first to call attention to the value of the precipitation test in legal medicine. The test, when properly carried out, enables the determination to be made with a high degree of certainty. An antiserum specific for human blood first must be secured by injections of human serum into a rabbit, at intervals of a few days, for a period of two weeks. A piece of the material with the blood stain on it is placed in a watch-glass, and 5 ml. of sterile physiological salt solution is added. This is allowed to stand until the blood proteins have been dissolved. If any dirt or sediment appears in the solution, it is removed by filtration. An effort is made to secure a dilution of the suspected blood serum of about 1:1,000. The diluted serum is placed in a series of test tubes and the specific antiserum is added. If the blood stain is human blood, a precipitate will be apparent in the course of a few minutes. The reliability of the test has been recognized by many courts, and the results have been accepted as evidence. By varying the procedure, the same method may be used in differentiating animal blood proteins.

### Differentiation of Meats

Meat inspection, particularly in certain European countries, includes the differentiation of meats. In some localities large quantities of horse flesh are used for food, but the law forbids the sale of horse flesh as beef. There are certain chemical differences between the two, differences in the composition of the fat and in the abundance of glycogen, but these differences require chemical analysis and examination for their recognition. The precipitation test furnishes an easier and more reliable method for differentiation; furthermore, the testing may be extended to an examination of mixed meats, such as sausages, and the various kinds of meat present are determined. Specific antisera are prepared for each type of meat which is to be recognized by mincing the meat and soaking it in physiological salt solution. This extract is then used in the immunization of a rabbit by repeated injections during several weeks. The flesh to be tested is likewise extracted with physiological salt solution; the solution is filtered and tested with the various specific antisera. A prominent precipitate is given with its homologous antiserum, and the differentiation is made.

In many cases the meat which is suspected of adulteration is cooked or smoked; these processes change the nature of the precipitinogen. In such cases it is necessary to use as the antigen, which is injected to produce immune serum, serum or other tissue extracts which have been heated to about 70°C. The precipitins which result from the injections of such antigens are called *cocto-precipitins.*

## REFERENCES


ANDRESEN, E. Investigation on Blood Groups of the Pig. Nord. Vet. Med. 9:274, 1957.

ARRHENIUS, S. Immuno-chemistry. Chap. 9, The Precipitins and Their Antibodies. Macmillan Co., New York, 1907.

BALAKRISHNAN, C. S., and YERAVDEKAR, S. N. Blood Groups in Horses. Indian Vet. Jour. 26:86, 1949.

BELLANTI, J. A., *et al.* The Development of the Immune Response. Studies on the Agglutinin Response to Salmonella Flagellar Antigens in the Newborn Rabbit. Jour. Exp. Med. 117:479–96, 1963.

BORDET, JULES. The Mechanism of Agglutination. Studies in Immunity. Transl. F. P. Gay. John Wiley & Sons, London, 1909.

BOYDEN, S. U. The Absorption of Proteins on Erythrocytes Treated With Tannic Acid and Subsequent Hemagglutination by Antiprotein Sera. Jour. Exp. Med. 93:107, 1951.

BRILES, W. E., *et al.* Multiple Alleles Effecting Cellular Antigens in Chickens. Genetics 35:633, 1950.

BRUNER, D. W. Cornell Vet. 40:11–16, 1950.

———, *et al.* The Relation of Blood Factors to Icterus in Foals. Amer. Jour. Vet. Res. 9:237–42, 1948.

———, *et al.* Icteric Foals. Jour. Amer. Vet. Med. Assn. 112:440–41, 1948.

———, *et al.* Blood Factors and Baby Pig Anemia. Jour. Amer. Vet. Med. Assn. 115:94–96, 1949.

———, *et al.* Further Studies on Hemolytic Icterus in Foals. Amer. Jour. Vet. Res. 11:22, 1950.

BUXTON, J. C., and BROOKSBAND, N. H. Haemolytic Disease of New-Born Pigs by Iso-Immunization of Pregnancy. Vet. Rec. 65:287, 1953.

CAVELTI, P. A. The Technic of Collodion Particle Agglutination. Jour. Immunol. 57:141–54, 1947.

COOMBS, R. R. A., *et al.* A New Test for the Detection of Weak and "Incomplete" Rh Agglutinins. Brit. Jour. Exp. Path. 26:255, 1945.

DEAN, H. R. The Precipitation Reaction. A System of Bacteriology. Pp. 424–51. Med. Res. Council. His Majesty's Stationery Office, London, 1931.

DOLL, E. R. Observations on the Clinical Features and Pathology of Hemolytic Icterus of Newborn Foals Amer. Jour. Vet. Res. 13:504, 1952.

———. Evidence of the Production of an Anti-isoantibody by Foals Affected With Hemolytic Icterus. Cornell Vet. 43:44, 1953.

———, *et al.* The Influence of an Equine Fetal Tissue Vaccine Upon Hemagglutination Activity of Mare Serums: Its Relation to Hemolytic Icterus of Newborn Foals. Cornell Vet. 42:496, 1952.

FERGUSON, L. C., *et al.* On Additional Antigens in the Erythrocytes of Cattle. Jour. Immunol. 44:1471, 1942.

GAY, F. P., *et al.* Agents of Disease and Host Resistance. Chap. 20, The Phenomenon of Agglutination; Chap. 21, The Precipitin Phenomenon. Charles C Thomas, Baltimore, 1935.

GILMAN, M. A., *et al.* Immunohematologic Studies of the Thoroughbred Horse. Amer. Jour. Vet. Res. 21:393, 1960.

HOLMES, R. The Occurrence of Blood Groups of Cats. Jour. Exp. Biol. 30:350, 1953.

HUBERT, E. G., *et al.* Preservation of Antigen-Coated Sheep Erythrocytes by Freezing for Use in Indirect Hemagglutination Procedure. Jour. Bact. 86:569–72, 1963.

JOYSEY, V. A Study of the Blood Groups of the Rabbit With Reference to the Inheritance of Three Antigens, and the Agglutinability of the Red Cells Carrying Them. Jour. Exp. Biol. 32:440, 1955.

KOLMER, J. A. Infection, Immunity and Biologic Therapy. Pp. 254–335. W. B. Saunders Co., Philadelphia, 1923.

LANDSTEINER, K. The Specificity of Serological Reactions. Charles C Thomas, Baltimore, 1936.

———, and WIENER, A. S. An Agglutinable Factor in Human Blood Recognized by Immune Sera for Rhesus Blood. Proc. Soc. Exp. Biol. N.Y. 43:223, 1940.

LEVINE, P., and STETSON, R. E. An Unusual Case of Intragroup Agglutination. Jour. Amer. Med. Assn. 113: 126, 1939.

———, *et al.* The Role of Isoimmunization in the Pathogenesis of Erythroblastosis Fetalis. Amer. Jour. Obst. Gynec. 42:925, 1941.

MITCHESON, N. A. The Effect on the Offspring of Maternal Immunization in Mice. Jour. Genet. 51:406, 1953.

NORTHROP, J. H. The Mechanism of Agglutination. The Newer Knowledge of Bacteriology and Immunology. Pp. 782–801. Univ. of Chicago Press, Chicago, 1928.

OUCHTERLONY, Ö. Antigen-Antibody Reactions in Gels. Acta Path. Microbiol. Scand. 26:507, 1949.

OUDIN, J. Méthode d'analyse immunochemique par précipitation spécifique in mililieu gélifié. Comp. rend. Acad. Sci. 222:115, 1946.

———. *In* Methods in Medical Research, A. C. Corcoran (ed.). 5:335. Yearbook Publishers, Chicago, 1952.

PATTERSON, R. Use of $I^{131}$-Labeled Antigens in Gel Diffusion Precipitate Reactions. Jour. Lab. Clin. Med. 57: 657–60, 1961.

RACE, R. R., and SANGER, R. Blood Groups in Man. 3rd Ed. Charles C Thomas, Springfield, Ill., 1959.

RAFFEL, SIDNEY. Immunity, Hypersensitivity, and Serology. Appleton-Century-Crofts, Inc., New York, 1961.

RENDEL, J., *et al.* Evidence for Epistatic Action for Antigenic Substances in Sheep. Genetics 39:396, 1954.

SHIEH, T. M., *et al.* Studies on Middlebrook-Dubos, Hemagglutination Test for Tuberculosis in Cattle (1). Jour. Taiwan Assn. An. Husb. Vet. Med., Taiwan, China. 3:39–44, 1959.

STORMONT, C., and CUMLEY, R. W. Cellular Antigens in Cattle Blood. Jour. Hered. 34:35, 1943.

STRATTON, F., and RENTON, P. H. Practical Blood Grouping. Charles C Thomas, Springfield, Ill., 1958.

WILSON, G. S., and MILES, A. A. Topley's Principles of Bacteriology and Immunity. 5th Ed. Williams & Wilkins Co., Baltimore, 1964.

YOUNG, L. E., *et al.* Blood Groups in Dogs. Amer. Jour. Vet. Res. 13:207, 1952.

# 11

# Cytolysis and Complement Fixation

THE FUNCTIONS OF ANTIBODIES PRESENT IN immune serum were discussed in the two preceding chapters. That antitoxin has the ability to neutralize toxin and that antibodies, called agglutinins and precipitins, are able to sensitize particles in suspension, causing flocculation when an electrolyte is present, have been observed. Another important property of sensitizing antibody is the sensitization of bacteria and erythrocytes so that they are acted upon by a normal substance in blood plasma which produces lysis, or cytolysis. As a result of this action, the protoplasm of the cells diffuses into the surrounding medium; this, in the case of erythrocytes, is apparent by the liberation of hemoglobin.

Bacteria which invade the deep tissues of the body and into the blood and lymph streams are destroyed by the lytic action of normal blood plasma. As early as 1792, John Hunter demonstrated that blood did not putrefy readily. Nearly a century later Lister, 1881, von Fodor, 1887, Nuttall, 1888, and Buchner, 1889, revealed the destructive action of normal blood for pathogenic bacteria. Nuttall demonstrated the lytic power of the blood of various species of animals for anthrax bacilli, but he found that this power was lost when the blood stood for a few days or was heated to 60°C. Buchner found that the plasma from clotted blood was able to lyse bacteria and confirmed the action of 60°C. He conceived that the lytic property was due to a ferment, or enzyme, to which he gave the name *alexins,* from a Greek word meaning *to ward off* or *protect.* In 1891 Daremburg discovered that the erythrocytes of one species of animals are lysed by the serum of another species and that this lytic property is also destroyed by 55°C.

## THE PFEIFFER PHENOMENON

In an attempt to find a suitable immunizing material to check an extensive epidemic of cholera caused by the cholera vibrio, Pfeiffer and his coworker, Isaeff, made other fundamental discoveries. They found that normal guinea pigs died when they received injections of the cholera vibrio and that large numbers of the organisms were present in the body. The injection of the organism into the peritoneal cavity of a pig which had survived an experimental injection resulted in the rapid destruction of the bacteria. This protective function was transferred from an immune guinea pig to a normal one, and the vibrios were destroyed when mixed with immune serum and injected into the peritoneal cavity of a normal guinea pig. The reaction was specific, and Pfeiffer used it as a method of identifying the true cholera vibrio.

Metchnikoff demonstrated that the reaction would take place in a test tube when a small quantity of peritoneal exudate was added to the immune serum and suspension of the organism; in this way he proved that the peritoneal endothelium was not essential in the reaction as Pfeiffer believed.

### Bordet's Contributions to the Phenomenon

Bordet found that the addition of fresh

immune serum produced the lysis of the cholera vibrio, but the aging of the serum or heating to 55°C. for one-half hour destroyed the lytic property. The addition of *normal* serum to heated immune serum, however, restored the lytic property. Accordingly, Bordet concluded that the action of the immune serum was due to two substances:

1. A thermostable substance, *sensitizer,* which sensitized the cholera vibrio to the action of the second substance, was present in immune serum but not in normal serum.
2. A thermolabile material, *alexin,* which was able to cause the lysis of cells previously sensitized by the immune serum, was present in normal serum as well as in fresh immune serum.

Subsequently, Bordet demonstrated that the lysis of red blood cells was brought about by the same essential phenomenon. The injection of erythrocytes of one species into another species produced immune bodies, *sensitizers,* for the erythrocytes which were injected. The serum of the immunized animal, therefore, was capable of causing the sensitization of erythrocytes in the presence of the *alexin* in normal serum.

Both phenomena, bacteriolysis and hemolysis, Bordet explained, were due to the modification of the bacterial cells and the erythrocytes by the sensitizer and the subsequent adsorption of the *alexin;* he further demonstrated that the action of the sensitizer was similar to the action of fixing agents or mordants on tissues, which increased the adsorption of dyes that otherwise would not be adsorbed.

## Ehrlich's Explanation of the Phenomenon

The fundamental principles of the phenomenon of the lysis of bacteria and erythrocytes, as shown by Bordet, were accepted by Ehrlich and his pupils. The explanation of the phenomenon, however, was not. In conformity with the receptor conception of antibodies in general, Ehrlich explained that lysis was due to an antibody equipped with two haptophore or combining groups. He called this antibody *amboceptor.* This antibody had the property of combining on the one hand with the antigen, bacteria, or erythrocytes, and on the other with the normal lytic substance which he named *complement.* The term *complement fixation* orginated with Ehrlich. He believed that the complement was united to the antigen by the amboceptor, thereby he differed considerably with Bordet who thought the union was due to the action of amboceptor, or sensitizer, upon the antigen. In light of present-day knowledge the explanation of Bordet is more acceptable.

## Definition of Terms

In the foregoing discussion numerous terms have been used for the antibody and for the lytic substance which are fundamental for this phenomenon. Although the terms used by Bordet and by Ehrlich are still found in current literature, it is well to confine the forthcoming discussion to those terms which are most commonly used, some of which are different from those previously mentioned.

The antibody which is developed as the result of infection or by the injection of bacterial antigens fundamentally acts on antigens as a sensitizing substance. In the description of the reaction which is to follow, the antibody which unites with the infectious agent or with products of the infectious agent will be called *sensitizer.* The antibody operating in the reaction which causes the lysis of erythrocytes, called sensitizer by Bordet and amboceptor by Ehrlich, is now commonly called *hemolysin.* It must be constantly kept in mind that this is likewise a sensitizing antibody, and that a different term is used for the purpose of clarity. There must not be any confusion of the term hemolysin used as an antibody with the term hemolysin used as a toxin. These substances are entirely different although the end result of their action is the liberation of hemoglobin from the erythrocyte.

The lytic substance which is present in normal plasma, called alexin by Bordet and complement by Ehrlich is now called *complement.* This latter term has become well fixed in our contemporary literature. The reaction, as inferred by the chapter heading, which will be explained in the forthcoming discussion is called *complement fixation,* abbreviated CF.

### The Antigens in Complement Fixation

All of the original conceptions of lysis were based upon the effect which was produced upon the intact cell; for example, cholera vibrios were observed to undergo disintegration, and red blood cells were known to lose their hemoglobin. It was assumed, then, that intact cells must be used as the antigen which is to be injected to stimulate the formation of the antibody. In general this theory is still accepted, although the knowledge of complete and partial antigens does reveal that proteins of cells may serve as antigens. In this respect, an antigen which is injected to stimulate antibody formation must be differentiated from the antigen which is used in a complement-fixation test for the diagnosis of disease. In such diseases as brucellosis and glanders the fixation test may be used for the diagnosis. One might presume that since whole organisms are present in the body producing the disease, that whole organisms must be used as the antigen in the test. This is not true, for complement is just as readily fixed when extracts of the organism are used as when whole organisms are used for the test antigen. It has been observed, furthermore, that complement is fixed in the precipitation test. This is of great importance in the complement-fixation test, for in the preparation of an hemolytic antigen, the red blood cells may not be completely washed free of blood serum. A subsequent test, then, may remove complement by virtue of the precipitation of the serum by the specific antibody.

Nonspecific antigens may be used in complement fixation. In the Wassermann test for syphilis, lipid extracts of normal organs, such as beef heart, are used. To such lipid substances cholesterol is added, which makes the antigen more suitable. This antigen, obviously, has nothing in common with the spirochete which is the cause of syphilis, yet the serum of a person affected with that disease causes the fixation of complement to the antigen. This nonspecific reaction is thought to be due to a serological similarity between certain normal tissue lipids and the antigens of the spirochete.

In the fixation of complement by erythrocytes, with the subsequent liberation of hemoglobin, the entire cell must be used. The stroma of the cell appears to function as an antigen in the production of hemolysin as well as serving as the antigen in the fixation of complement. It is obvious that, when the hemolysis of erythrocytes is used as the indicator of complement fixation, entire normal cells must be used. The blood of each species is distinctive in composition and serves as a specific antigen.

Certain antigens are unsuitable for use in complement fixation because of their anticomplementary action. It is apparent that hemolytic toxin cannot be used because of the specific hemolytic action of this substance.

Antigens prepared from tissues of animals affected by various viruses are used as antigens in complement fixation. These will be discussed in greater detail in the section devoted to virology.

The production of lytic antibodies for various types of cells has been investigated; for example, the destruction of cancer cells of rats and mice by the action of a specific lytic antiserum has been shown by Lumsden. The function of blood platelets in controlling hemorrhage has been demonstrated by Ledingham and Bedson by the production of experimental hemorrhagic purpura by the injection of a blood platelet antiserum.

### Antibody in Complement Fixation

The complement-fixation test which may be used for the diagnosis of a disease requires two antibodies. One of these antibodies may be called the bacterial antibody, if the disease to be diagnosed is a bacterial disease. It could be termed the "diagnostic" antibody. It is the antibody sought for in the test, and its presence would determine the cause of the disease in question.

The other antibody used in complement fixation is hemolysin. This is produced artificially by the injection of the erythrocytes of one animal, sheep, into another animal, rabbit. After a series of injections, hemolytic antibody, hemolysin, for sheep erythrocytes is present in the serum of the rabbit.

That both antibodies are sensitizing antibodies can be shown by the fact that the bacterial antibody will agglutinate its homologous antigen, if it is particulate, or will cause precipitation, if it is a protein. The hemolytic antibody will agglutinate a suspension of sheep erythrocytes. The union of antibody with antigen in complement fixation is the same as in other antigen-antibody reactions. Both the bacterial antibody and hemolytic antibody show the properties ascribed to antibody in general, but in complement fixation, complement is fixed by the antigen-antibody complex. One characteristic of antibody which functions in complement fixation is its thermostable nature. It is not destroyed by 56°C. Furthermore, it is not injured by contact with a preservative, such as 0.5 per cent phenol, nor is it altered by standing in the refrigerator for a period of time.

### Nature and Action of Complement

The perishable nature of complement has prevented, until recent years, significant contributions concerning its chemical composition. Since the original conception of its enzyme nature by Büchner, complement has been considered to be a lipase, a protease, a peptidase, an intracellular catalyst, a simple chemical like oleic acid, and a combination of lipids, soaps, and proteins. By some, complement has been considered to be only a colloidal attribute of fresh serum; its action dependent on the physicochemical state of serum.

Certain physical properties and chemical agents which affect complement are recognized as being significant. Complement is inactivated by exposure to 56°C. for 30 minutes, although most serum proteins are not injured by this temperature. Complement is most stable within the pH ranges of 6.0 to 6.5; consequently, strong concentrations of acids and alkalies are detrimental to it. Other agents such as chloroform, ether, alcohols, soaps, and certain alkaloids are destructive. Complement is inactivated in a few hours if allowed to stand at room temperature, and will disappear in three or four days when kept at refrigeration temperatures. Filtration of serum through a Berkefeld filter removes complement. Other materials such as kaolin, shellac, cholesterol, and casein adsorb complement.

Reviews of complement by Pillemer and by Heidelberger reveal that complement is an integral chemical part of serum and that it has numerous functions. Complement is now known to consist of four components. Dialysis of fresh serum against distilled water or treatment with carbon dioxide water or dilute hydrochloric acid will separate complement into two thermolabile fractions. The water-insoluble, carbon-dioxide-insoluble, acid-insoluble component, commonly called "mid-piece," is now called C′1. The water-soluble, carbon-dioxide-soluble component, commonly called "endpiece," is referred to as C′2. Following the above discoveries, subsequent studies of complement revealed that it could be inactivated by treatment with washed yeast cells, hence a third component labeled C′3 was discovered. It was then shown that the exposure of complement to ammonia rendered it inactive, so the fourth component C′4 was revealed. The heating of complement to 56°C. destroys C′1 and C′2 but does not alter the heat-stable components C′3 and C′4. Other detailed chemical properties of these components have been discovered which may be found in the reviews mentioned above.

The origin of complement in the body has been a subject of considerable investigation. Early workers, such as Büchner, believed that it was produced by leucocytes. Metchnikoff was of the opinion that complement was present in blood serum only after leucocyte injury. Extracts of leucocytes, however, have never yielded complement, so it is now believed that the substance does not originate in those cells. Since complement is a mixture of globulins and a mucoprotein, it is presumed that it arises from the same source as globulin. This is conceded to be the cells of the reticuloendothelial system and the lymphocytes.

It is significant that the various components of complement are not all found in the serums of all animals. Normal guinea pig serum contains a greater concentration of all components than other serums. This accounts for the universal choice of guinea pig serum as a source of complement. Cow, horse, sheep, and squirrel serums do not hemolyze sheep erythrocytes because of the absence of C′2 component. These serums consist almost entirely of C′1 component.

The outstanding property of complement is its ability to cause the lysis of sensitized bacterial cells, particularly the gram-negative types. The ability of complement to cause the hemolysis of erythrocytes is fundamental in the complement-fixation test. It combines with numerous antigen-antibody complexes to which it becomes fixed. This substance stimulates the activity of the leucocytes thereby aiding the animal in the destruction of invading bacteria. It aids immune serum in the destruction of certain viruses. It apparently has a role in tissue sensitization. It is considered to play a part in the neutralization of toxin in vivo subsequent to toxin-antitoxin union. Complement appears to influence the sedimentation rate of erythrocytes.

## The Fixation of Complement

The fixation of complement to antigen-antibody has not been satisfactorily explained. It cannot be attached until antigen unites with antibody. The conception of Ehrlich that antibody acted as a "between-body" for antigen and complement has been discarded. Likewise, the explanations of Bordet are not tenable in light of present knowledge about complement.

Heidelberger has studied the combining action of the various components of complement on red blood cells and hemolysin. When the hemolysin combines with the red blood cell, the surface patterns of the antiserum molecules or the antiserum, red-blood-cell aggregate changes and different groups are in contact with the complement components. C′4 combines first or simultaneously with C′1 to the red-blood-cell aggregates. The fixation of C′4 is accompanied by the fixation of C′2. The absorption of these components in this order renders the red blood cell susceptible to the action of unattached C′3, and hemolysis results. C′3 is not taken up by the fixed complex and is not used up in the process of hemolysis, indicating that it has enzymatic properties. It has been rather clearly demonstrated that erythrocytes are not entirely coated with hemolysin and then with complement. The union of hemolysin with erythrocyte apparently occurs in certain places on the cell and it is on such sensitized areas that complement becomes fixed, producing the effect which is recognized as hemolysis.

The fact that the components of complement are variable in different animal species has been mentioned. This has a bearing on the application of the complement-fixation test in the diagnosis of disease. Other factors influence the value of the complement-fixation test as a diagnostic agent. All antigen-antibody complexes do not fix even guinea pig complement. For example, horse antiserum for the type-specific pneumococcus polysaccharides do not. Anticomplementary factors have been found to be of significance in the reaction. The bacterial antigen or tissue extracts or suspensions used as antigens may have an anticomplementary effect, thus reducing the amount of complement in a test, thus preventing a satisfactory result. The size of the antigen-antibody aggregate apparently has an effect on complement fixation. The maximal power of fixation is possessed by particles large enough to cause opalescence but not visible to the eye. Complement is fixed to antigen-antibody mixtures rapidly at first but becomes slower as the particles become larger. Most complete fixation occurs when antigen-antibody and complement are mixed simultaneously.

Early investigators found that definite proportions of antigen-antibody and complement combined. This discovery was, and still is, a fundamental factor in complement fixation. The amount of each reacting substance is not necessarily equal. It has been shown that complement and hemolysin can supplement each other in hemolysis. Within certain limits, hemolysis will result if hemolysin is decreased and complement increased, or if complement is decreased and hemolysin increased. In general, the amount of hemolysin and complement are carefully determined by titration previous to their use in any diagnostic procedure. The reason for this will be made apparent in the discussion which follows.

### Applications of Complement Fixation

Complement fixation has been used to the greatest extent for the diagnosis of disease. At one time this reaction was the only test used for the diagnosis of brucellosis. It was replaced by the agglutination test which is now used. The diagnosis of glanders was considered at one time to be most reliably made by complement fixation, but it has been largely replaced by the mallein test, an allergic skin test. At present the complement-fixation test is not used as a routine diagnostic procedure for any of the animal diseases.

The complement-fixation reaction is used as a research tool in immunology. Many antigen-antibody combinations can be proved only by complement fixation. The reaction has had increased use for this purpose in recent years.

A great deal of the understanding of complement fixation has been made possible by the value of the Wassermann test in the diagnosis of syphilis. This test is still used in public health laboratories for the diagnosis of this disease.

### Description of the Complement-Fixation Test

The understanding of complement fixation will be more complete if the fundamentals of a diagnostic test are given. Brucellosis is chosen as the disease to be diagnosed because almost everyone is familiar with it, and experimentally all of the essential ingredients needed for the test are available in most laboratories.

A. Reacting Agents Required.

1. Dilute suspension of *Brucella abortus,* the bacterial antigen.
2. The serum of the cow suspected of being infected with brucellosis. The normal complement in this serum is inactivated by exposure to 56°C. for one-half hour. The bacterial antibody may or may not be present in this serum. The objective of the test is to detect its presence.
3. Pooled serum from a number of normal guinea pigs. This is the complement. The potency of complement is determined by preliminary titration.
4. A 2 per cent suspension of sheep erythrocytes. These cells have been washed in physiological saline so as to be free of normal complement. This is the hemolytic antigen.
5. Serum from a rabbit which has been given a series of injections of sheep erythrocytes. This is the hemolytic antibody, hemolysin. The potency of hemolysin is determined by preliminary titration.
6. Physiological, 0.85 per cent, sodium chloride solution containing 75 mg. $MgCl_2$ per liter.

B. Titration of Hemolysin.

The potency of hemolysin varies with the individual and with the number of injections of sheep erythrocytes which the rabbit has received. A satisfactory hemolysin is produced by five injections of 5 ml. of a 10 per cent suspension of sheep cells, four days apart. The rabbit is then bled, and the serum collected and preserved by adding an equal part of neutral glycerin.

TABLE 11.1

| | | | |
|---|---|---|---|
| No. 1 | 0.5 ml. hemolysin (1:100 ) | + 4.5 ml. saline solution | = 1:1,000 |
| No. 2 | 0.5 ml. hemolysin (1:1,000) | + 0.5 ml. saline solution | = 1:2,000 |
| No. 3 | 0.5 ml. hemolysin (1:1,000) | + 1.0 ml. saline solution | = 1:3,000 |
| No. 4 | 0.5 ml. hemolysin (1:1,000) | + 1.5 ml. saline solution | = 1:4,000 |
| No. 5 | 0.5 ml. hemolysin (1:1,000) | + 2.0 ml. saline solution | = 1:5,000 |
| No. 6 | 0.5 ml. hemolysin (1:3,000) | + 0.5 ml. saline solution | = 1:6,000 |
| No. 7 | 0.5 ml. hemolysin (1:4,000) | + 0.5 ml. saline solution | = 1:8,000 |
| No. 8 | 0.5 ml. hemolysin (1:5,000) | + 0.5 ml. saline solution | = 1:10,000 |
| No. 9 | 0.5 ml. hemolysin (1:6,000) | + 0.5 ml. saline solution | = 1:12,000 |
| No. 10 | 0.5 ml. hemolysin (1:8,000) | + 0.5 ml. saline solution | = 1:16,000 |

A 1:100 stock dilution is prepared as follows:

Saline solution..........94.0 ml.
Glycerinized hemolysin
(50 per cent).......... 2.0 ml.
Phenol (5 per cent
in phy-saline) ........ 4.0 ml.

For titration, a series of 10 higher dilutions are then prepared. (See Table 11.1.) The titer of hemolysin is obtained by using each of the above dilutions with complement and sheep red blood cells. The amounts of each of these ingredients are given in Table 11.2.

The contents of each tube are thoroughly mixed, and the tubes are placed in a water-bath at 37°C. for one hour. The tubes are then examined to determine the titer of the hemolysin. *The unit of hemolysin is the highest dilution that shows complete hemolysis.*

C. Titration of Complement.

In the titration of complement, varying amounts of the 1:30 dilution are set up in a series of test tubes. Two units of the previously titrated hemolysin are used. Inasmuch as this amount varies, the volume of fluid in each tube is regulated by adding the amount of saline which brings the volume to 3 ml. The various amounts are given in Table 11.3.

*The complement unit is the highest dilution which shows complete hemolysis.*

D. The Complement-Fixation Test.

The titration of hemolysin and complement has emphasized that when definite amounts of these substances are mixed with a suspension of sheep erythrocytes, hemolysis will result. Hemolysis will not result if complement is not present. It is clear, therefore, that a controlled and standardized hemolytic system can be used as an indicator of complement fixation. This is its function in a complement-fixation test for the diagnosis of disease.

It has been stated repeatedly that complement is fixed by most antigen-antibody combinations. In the example, brucellosis, complement would be fixed if the serum of the cow suspected of having brucellosis is

TABLE 11.2
TITRATION OF HEMOLYSIN

| Tube Number | Hemolysin 0.5 ml. | Complement ml. (1:30 dil.) | Sheep R.B.C. ml. (2% susp.) | Saline Solution ml. |
|---|---|---|---|---|
| 1 | 1:1,000 | 0.3 | 0.5 | 1.7 |
| 2 | 1:2,000 | 0.3 | 0.5 | 1.7 |
| 3 | 1:3,000 | 0.3 | 0.5 | 1.7 |
| 4 | 1:4,000 | 0.3 | 0.5 | 1.7 |
| 5 | 1:5,000 | 0.3 | 0.5 | 1.7 |
| 6 | 1:6,000 | 0.3 | 0.5 | 1.7 |
| 7 | 1:8,000 | 0.3 | 0.5 | 1.7 |
| 8 | 1:10,000 | 0.3 | 0.5 | 1.7 |
| 9 | 1:12,000 | 0.3 | 0.5 | 1.7 |
| 10 | 1:16,000 | 0.3 | 0.5 | 1.7 |

TABLE 11.3

TITRATION OF COMPLEMENT

| Tube Number | Complement ml. (1:30 dil.) | Hemolysin 2 units | Sheep R.B.C. ml. (2% susp.) | Saline Solution q.s. 3 ml. |
|---|---|---|---|---|
| | | *(units)* | | |
| 1 | 0.1 | 2 | 0.5 | ... |
| 2 | 0.15 | 2 | 0.5 | ... |
| 3 | 0.2 | 2 | 0.5 | ... |
| 4 | 0.25 | 2 | 0.5 | ... |
| 5 | 0.3 | 2 | 0.5 | ... |
| 6 | 0.35 | 2 | 0.5 | ... |
| 7 | 0.4 | 2 | 0.5 | ... |
| 8 | 0.45 | 2 | 0.5 | ... |
| 9 | 0.5 | none | 0.5 | ... |
| 10 | none | 2 | 0.5 | ... |

TABLE 11.4

THE COMPLEMENT-FIXATION TEST

| Tube Number | *Br. abortus* Antigen | Suspect's Serum | Complement 1:30 | Sheep R.B.C. | Hemolysin | Saline Sol. | Results |
|---|---|---|---|---|---|---|---|
| | *(ml.)* | *(ml.)* | *(units)* | *(ml.)* | *(units)* | | |
| 1 | 0.2 | 0.1 | 2 | 0.5 | 2 | q.s. 3 ml. | no hemolysis if animal infected |
| 2 | ... | 0.1 | 2 | 0.5 | 2 | q.s. 3 ml. | hemolysis, serum control |
| 3 | 0.4 | 0.2 | 2 | 0.5 | 2 | q.s. 3 ml. | no hemolysis if animal infected |
| 4 | ... | 0.2 | 2 | 0.5 | 2 | q.s. 3 ml. | hemolysis, serum control |
| 5 | 0.2 | ... | 2 | 0.5 | 2 | q.s. 3 ml. | hemolysis, antigen control |
| 6 | 0.4 | ... | 2 | 0.5 | 2 | q.s. 3 ml. | hemolysis, antigen control |
| 7 | ... | ... | 2 | 0.5 | 2 | q.s. 3 ml. | hemolysis, hemolytic system control |
| 8 | ... | ... | 2 | 0.5 | ... | q.s. 3 ml. | no hemolysis, complement control |
| 9 | ... | ... | ... | 0.5 | 2 | q.s. 3 ml. | no hemolysis, hemolysin control |
| 10 | ... | ... | ... | 0.5 | ... | q.s. 3 ml. | no hemolysis, saline sol. control |

mixed with a suspension of the causal organism, *Brucella abortus,* in the presence of complement. It is equally obvious that if the suspect serum is from a noninfected animal, there will be no antibody for *Brucella abortus* present; hence, fixation of complement will not result.

The complement-fixation test is a combination of two systems with complement the deviating substance between them. By studying Table 11.4, it is noted that the bacterial antigen, suspect serum, and complement are mixed. This is followed by a period of one hour incubation, which allows the fixation of complement *if antibody for* Br. abortus *is present in the suspect serum.* This is followed by the addition of the hemolytic system, sheep R.B.C., and hemolysin. After a period of incubation the test is read. If the complement has been fixed by the bacterial system—in other words, if the test is positive—the erythrocytes will not be hemolyzed. If the complement has not been fixed in the bacterial system, the erythrocytes will be hemolyzed in all the tubes where the hemolytic agents are present. It is now apparent why it is essential to titrate the sheep-cell hemolysin and the complement. In conducting routine diagnostic complement-fixation tests it is not necessary to use as many controls as given in Table 11.4; they are inserted in this example to emphasize the need for controlling a mechanism as sensitive as the hemolysis of such delicate cells. Figure 11.1 illustrates the reaction in a diagrammatic way.

### Applications of Complement-Fixation Tests

The greatest application of the CF test is for the detection of antibodies as an aid to diagnosis of bacterial, virus, protozoan, and other parasitic infections. It is also useful in the identification of unknown antigens by using serum of known antibody content. CF tests are particularly useful in virology. Since it is difficult to produce pure virus antigens, a test which can employ crude preparations such as brain tissue or chicken embryo tissues as a source of virus antigen has distinct advantages.

Although many antigen-antibody systems can be detected by CF tests, some variations in technique may be necessary in order to arrive at a successful one for any given system. Serum from chickens, turkeys, and mules cannot be tested with the conventional CF system which uses guinea pig complement because of their anticomplementary effects. Swine serum is difficult to test because it exhibits procomplementary activities. An indirect complement-fixation test applicable to avian sera has been described by Rice. A modified direct method of complement fixation for avian sera devised by Brumfield and Pomeroy has been used for the diagnosis of rickettsial diseases.

Complement fixation is also used in blood-typing procedures and also in the study of fundamental mechanisms of immune reactions.

### The Properdin System

While investigating some properties of complement, Pillimer *et al.* discovered a new substance in human serum which they named *properdin.* It has been found that properdin aided by complement and magnesium ions can lyse certain bacteria and is lethal to some animal and bacterial viruses.

Properdin is found in the serum of most warm-blooded animals although in different quantities in different species. It is a globulin but not an antibody. It has a molecular weight of approximately one million and can function as an antigen.

The assay of properdin is usually based on its ability to complex with various polysaccharides, especially zymosan, plus magnesium ions, C′1 and C′4 at 15°C. This properdin-zymosan complex plus additional magnesium at 30° to 37°C. inactivates C′3. There is a quantitative relationship between the amount of C′3 inactivated and the properdin present.

All four components of complement are necessary for the bactericidal and virus-inactivating effects. Most of the susceptible bacteria are gram-negative rods. Viruses killed by the properdin system include

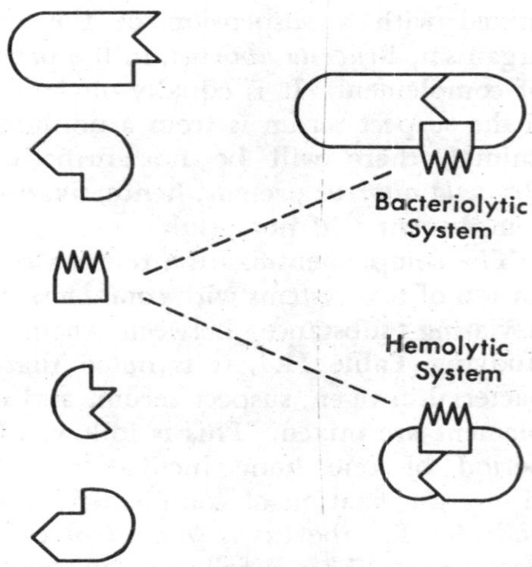


FIG. 11.1 — Diagrammatic scheme of the complement-fixation reaction.

Newcastle, influenza, and herpes simplex. It is believed that the properdin system undoubtedly plays a part in natural resistance of animals. However, it is probably only one of the bactericidal substances in the serum of animals.

### The Phenomenon of Conglutination

Ehrlich and Sachs observed that the addition of fresh, unheated horse serum to a suspension of red blood cells of the guinea pig produced slight hemolysis. They further observed that the addition of heated cow serum to a suspension of the red corpuscles caused no hemolysis. The addition of both heated cow serum and fresh horse serum produced an active hemolysis.

Many other workers have studied the phenomenon. These include Bordet and Gay, Streng, Hole and Coombs, and Ingram. They have found that conglutination occurs not only with the system observed by Ehrlich and Sachs but also with others. Sheep erythrocytes can be substituted for those of the guinea pig, and agglutination is observed instead of hemolysis. Streng found that bacterial cells could be used instead of erythrocytes. It has also been observed that cat and pig serums can be used instead of fresh horse serum as a source of conglutinating complement. Human and dog serums have been used but are less active. Conglutinin is a heat-stable factor found in the serum of normal ruminants, the cow being the most commonly used source.

Many different sources of components might be chosen to demonstrate conglutination. However, the ones most often used are the horse as a source of complement, the cow as a source of conglutinin, and the sheep as a source of erythrocytes. The mechanism of conglutination is as follows: (1) Washed sheep cells are first acted upon by a naturally occurring antibody in normal bovine serum; (2) complement from the fresh unheated horse serum is absorbed by the erythrocyte-antibody complex; (3) then the conglutinin, also from the bovine serum, causes the sheep erythrocytes to agglutinate.

The fact that complement is absorbed in the above reaction enables the use of the phenomenon in serological tests for antibody. The horse complement and the conglutinin must be titrated in much the same way as is done in the conventional CF test. The technique of the test is nearly parallel to the hemolytic CF test except that agglutination is the indicator reaction instead of hemolysis (Fig. 11.2).

The conglutination test is applicable in asses and mules which possess anticomplementary substances in their blood serum; furthermore, the ingredients of the test are more easily obtained than are those for complement fixation. The test is con-

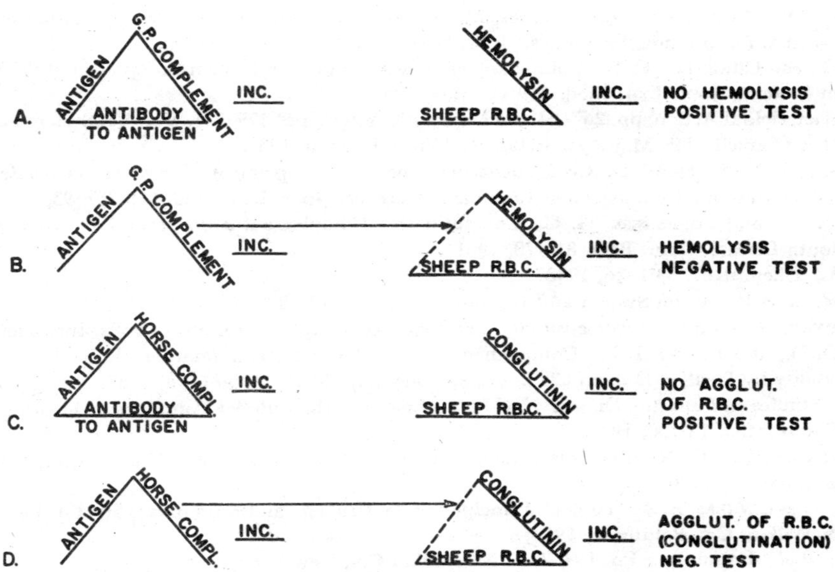


FIG. 11.2—Comparison of the conventional complement-fixation test and the conglutination test. **A** and **B** represent positive and negative tests, respectively, by complement fixation, **C** and **D** conglutination tests.

sidered even more delicate than the complement-fixation test and requires more careful titration of the reagents. Pfeiler believed that it has a greater degree of accuracy, and cited cases in which it was positive where both agglutination and complement fixation were negative; subsequent postmortem examination verified the accuracy of the test.

## REFERENCES


Bordet, Jules. Ann. de l'Inst. Past. 12:668–95, 1898.

———. Studies on Immunity. Pp. 186–258, 280–311, 333–38. Transl. F. P. Gay. John Wiley & Sons, London, 1909.

Boulanger, P., and Bannister, G. L. A Modified Direct Complement-Fixation Test for the Detection of Antibodies in the Serum of Cattle Previously Infected With Vesicular Stomatitis Virus. Jour. Immunol. 85: 368, 1960.

Boyd, W. C. Fundamentals of Immunology. 3rd Ed. Interscience Publishers, New York, 1956.

Brumfield, H. P., and Pomeroy, B. S. Test Based on Normal Component Implementing Fixation of Complement by Turkey Antiserum. Proc. Soc. Exp. Biol. Med. 102:278, 1959.

Dubos, R. J. Bacterial and Mycotic Infections of Man. 3rd Ed. J. B. Lippincott Co., Philadelphia, 1958.

Ehrlich, Paul. Collected Studies on Immunity. Pp. 1–35, 56–142, 181–282, 390–403, 561–76. Transl. Charles Bolduan. John Wiley & Sons, London, 1906.

Gay, F. P., *et al.* Agents of Disease and Host Resistance. Pp. 370–89. Charles C Thomas, Baltimore, 1935.

Heidelberger, M. Amer. Sci. 34:597–610, 1946.

Hole, N. H., and Coombs, R. R. A. The Conglutination Phenomenon. I. An Introduction to the Conglutination Phenomenon and an Account of the Observations and Views of Previous Investigators. Jour. Hyg. 45: 480, 1947.

———, and ———. The Conglutination Phenomenon. II. The Technique of the Conglutinating Complement-Absorption Test Compared With the Hemolytic Complement-Fixation Test. Jour. Hyg. 45:490, 1947.

Ingram, D. G. The Conglutination Phenomenon. XIV. The Resistance-Enhancing Effect of Conglutinin and Immuno-Conglutinin in Experimental Bacterial Infection. Immunol. 2:334, 1959.

Kabat, E. A., and Mayer, M. M. Experimental Immunochemistry. Charles C Thomas, Springfield, Ill., 1948.

LINSCOTT, W. D., and NISHIOKA, K. Components of Guinea Pig Complement. II. Separation of Serum Fractions Essential for Immune Hemolysis. Jour. Exp. Med. 118:795–815, 1963.

MORSE, J. H., and CHRISTIAN, C. L. Immunological Studies of the 11S Protein Component of the Human Complement System. Jour. Exp. Med. 119:195–209, 1964.

MUIR, R. Bactericidal Action, pp. 267–94 and Hemolytic Action, pp. 295–331, Vol. VI, System of Bacteriology. Med. Res. Council. His Majesty's Stationery Office, London, 1931.

NISHIOKA, K., and LINSCOTT, W. D. Components of Guinea Pig Complement. I. Separation of a Serum Fraction Essential for Immune Hemolysis and Immune Adherence. Jour. Exp. Med. 118:767–93, 1963.

NORCROSS, N. L., and POPPENSISK, G. C. Conglutinating Complement-Adsorption Test As Applied to Foot-and-Mouth Disease. Jour. Bact. 81:478, 1961.

PILLEMER, L. Chem. Rev. 33:1–26, 1943.

———, *et al.* The Properdin System and Immunity. Science 120:279, 1954.

RAFFEL, SIDNEY. Immunity, Hypersensitivity, and Serology. Appleton-Century-Crofts, Inc., New York, 1961.

RATNOFF, O. D., and LEPOW, I. H. Complement as a Mediator of Inflammation. Enhancement of Vascular Permeability by Purified Human C'l Esterase. Jour. Exp. Med. 118:681–98, 1963.

RICE, C. E. Studies on Pullorum Disease. XXII. Technique of the Indirect Complement-Fixation Test. Canad. Jour. Comp. Med. 12:130, 1948.

———, and CROWSON, C. N. The Interchangability of the Complement of Different Animal Species. Jour. Immunol. 65:201, 1950.

WILSON, G. S., and MILES, A. A. Topley's Principles of Bacteriology and Immunity. 5th Ed. Pp. 158–66. Williams & Wilkins Co., Baltimore, 1964.

ZINSSER, H., *et al.* Immunity. Pp. 194–232. Macmillan Co., New York, 1939.

# 12

# Phagocytosis

PHAGOCYTOSIS IS THE PROCESS BY WHICH foreign particles, including bacteria, are ingested by leucocytes and by certain endothelial cells of the body. In many respects the phenomenon is similar to the ingestion of food particles by single-celled animals, such as the amoeba. Phagocytosis is a normal function of body cells, but is definitely stimulated by the invasion of pathogenic bacteria.

The discovery of phagocytosis is credited to Eli Metchnikoff. In his study of the origin of the intestine and the process of intracellular digestion, Metchnikoff observed that mobile cells of the mesoderm accumulated about grains of carmine introduced into the body of the jellyfish. He then demonstrated that when sharp thorns were introduced under the skin of starfish larvae, mobile cells clustered about the thorns. From these facts, Metchnikoff concluded that inflammation is a reaction of mesodermic cells against an invading agent, and the function of leucocytes is a protective and curative one. The term *phagocytes,* meaning devouring cells, was coined for these cells. The real function of phagocytes in the disease process was shown by Metchnikoff by his work with small, transparent crustaceans, the *daphniae,* which he found to be infected with a fungus, producing sharp, needle-like spores. These spores penetrated the intestinal wall and were attacked by the mobile phagocytes which digested them. Carrying his researches into the field of the diseases of larger animals, he demonstrated that virulent anthrax bacilli were not phagocytized, but attenuated anthrax bacilli were readily engulfed, and further, that active phagocytosis was apparent in immune animals. Metchnikoff believed that immunity was due entirely to phagocytosis and that the ability of phagocytes to engulf invading microorganisms was caused by the stimulation, or training, of the phagocytes during the immunizing process. He published his first work on the theory in 1884.

Metchnikoff divided the phagocytic cells into two groups: the wandering cells, and the fixed cells. He called the polymorphonuclear leucocytes *microphages,* and the mononuclear leucocytes, *macrophages;* all of which were classed as wandering cells. These cells were the most active phagocytes, and Metchnikoff assigned different functions in disease to them. The fixed phagocytes, he concluded, were prevalent in the lymph nodes and spleen and are the cells which are recognized as part of the reticulo-endothelial system.

The rise of the alexin, or humoral, theory of Buchner and its subsequent development by Pfeiffer, Bordet, Ehrlich, and others caused Metchnikoff a great deal of concern. He fitted the phagocytic theory into the humoral theory, however, by showing, to his satisfaction, that alexin was liberated only after the leucocytes were damaged by the inflammatory process. He called the liberated material *cytase.* His conception of the relationship of the two phenomena has been proved erroneous, but his theory of phagocytosis was not severely shaken and at present is accepted as the most fundamental process in immunity.

### The Antibody in Phagocytosis, Opsonin

The phagocytosis of virulent bacteria is due to the action of specific antibody, which sensitizes the bacteria so that they are approached and engulfed by phagocytic cells. Denys and Leclef, in 1895, were the first to show that the antibodies in immune serum affected the microorganism and made it more easily phagocytized. This was contrary to the belief of Metchnikoff and his pupils who had believed that immune serum stimulated the leucocytes to greater activity.

Wright and Douglas, in 1904, showed that a substance in immune serum increased the number of bacteria which were phagocytized by leucocytes. They also demonstrated that this substance acted upon the microorganisms and not upon the phagocytes. Because this action prepared bacteria as food for the phagocytes, they named the antibody *opsonin,* meaning *to prepare food.*

The role of antibody in the phagocytic process is demonstrated by the following procedure: The blood from a suitable animal is drawn into physiological salt solution, defibrinated, and centrifuged. The cells are thrown to the bottom, and the leucocytes form in a layer between the red cells and the plasma. The leucocytes are removed, washed, and are again centrifuged until free of blood serum and erythrocytes. The leucocytes are mixed with a dilute suspension of bacteria, and the mixture is incubated for 15 minutes. A smear is made of the mixture and is stained by a suitable dye. When the smear is viewed under the microscope, it is observed that the bacteria are not engulfed by the leucocytes. A similar preparation is made with the addition of an homologous immune serum. In this smear a large number of bacteria are found within the leucocytes.

Phagocytosis, as has been stated, is a normal function in the body and is a process by which most of the saprophytic and relatively avirulent bacteria are destroyed. In fact, the virulence of microorganisms is due, in part at least, to their ability to repel phagocytes. Normal serum stimulates the phagocytic process; consequently, there has been considerable speculation concerning the difference between the function of normal serum, as represented presumably by normal opsonin, and immune opsonin. Whether the normal and the immune opsonins are identical has been a controversial subject for many years. Normal opsonin is similar to components C′1 or C′2 of the serum complement for it is thermolabile; that is, 58° to 60°C. destroys it. The immune or specific opsonin, on the other hand, is relatively thermostable. It is generally admitted that normal opsonin is not identical with complement; however, it is known that the presence of complement, or a thermolabile substance similar to complement, does augment the action of immune opsonin. This substance also has been shown to increase the action of immune opsonin in sensitizing cells for phagocytosis. The substance apparently cannot sensitize cells alone, and its action has been described as that of a catalyst which hastens the union of antibody with bacteria, thereby promoting phagocytosis. The specificity and action of opsonin seems to be an extension of the properties of normal serum, not differing from other types of antibody relationships.

### The Opsonic Index

*The opsonic index* is the ratio of the sensitizing power of the serum of an infected animal as compared with that of a healthy individual. The ratio between the two sera is determined by the relative effect they have on phagocytic action. Although it is not always necessary, it is customary to use leucocytes of the species of animal under investigation. The technique is as follows:

*Preparation of Leucocytes.* Leucocytes are secured by collecting blood in physiological salt solution, and defibrinating and centrifuging it. (The use of sodium citrate is contraindicated in this work because of the depressing effect of the citrate ion on phagocytosis.) The cells are washed repeatedly in salt solution until all the serum is removed. The upper layer of corpuscles, rich in leucocytes, is carefully pipetted and placed in a small test tube. Leucocytes can be collected in large quantities from small experimental animals within a few hours after an intraperitoneal injection of peptone or aleurone, which causes the concentration of leucocytes in the peritoneal cavity.

*Preparation of Bacterial Emulsion.* The organisms are prepared in a perfectly homogenous suspension. A 24-hour slant agar culture is used; the growth is washed off with sterile physiological salt solution, and is then shaken and diluted to a faint opalescence. Filtration may be necessary in order to remove unbroken clumps.

*Preparation of Serum.* Normal serum and serum from the animal to be tested are secured by bleeding, allowing the blood to clot, centrifuging and taking off the serum with a pipette, and transferring it to a small test tube. Before they are ready for use, both of the sera are diluted 1:10.

*Technique of the Test.* A capillary pipette is prepared from glass tubing, and a mark is made about 2 cm. from the end. The suspension of leucocytes is then drawn up to the mark, an air bubble is similarly drawn, and then the serum to be tested is drawn to the same mark, followed by a second air bubble, and finally an equal amount of the bacterial suspension. The contents are blown out on a watch glass and thoroughly mixed by drawing up and down in the pipette a few times. The mixture is then drawn into the capillary pipette, the end of which is sealed in the flame. It is then placed in an incubator at 37°C. for 15 minutes, where it is rotated frequently to assure thorough mixing during the incubating period. The procedure is repeated with the use of the normal serum. At the completion of incubation, the end of the pipette is broken, and smears are made of the contents which are stained with Wright's stain.

*Computation of the Opsonic Index.* The total number of bacteria ingested by 100 heterophile leucocytes is tabulated and the average number per leucocyte calculated. This is termed the *phagocytic index.* This number is determined for normal serum and the serum to be tested. The *opsonic index* is now more exactly defined as the *ratio* between the phagocytic index of the test serum and the phagocytic index of the normal serum.

### Phagocytic Cells

The division of phagocytic cells into two groups, motile and fixed, which was made by Metchnikoff, has been found to be entirely valid as has his division of the wandering leucocytes into microphages and macrophages. The cellular elements of the blood have been extensively investigated since the original work of Metchnikoff, and the origin of the cells has been a subject of great interest. While the origin of the majority of them, their relationships with one another, and their function in the animal body have been generally agreed upon, there still are some phases of the subject open to investigation.

The microphages of Metchnikoff embrace the heterophile leucocytes or neutrophiles, the eosinophiles, and basophiles. These cells have their origin from the myeloblasts in bone marrow. The neutrophiles comprise 72 to 75 per cent of the white blood cells and to them has been ascribed the most important task of phagocytosis. The eosinophiles do not appear to have a great deal of phagocytic value although they have been shown to have some ability to engulf bacteria. These cells become more numerous in certain bacterial infections, in animal parasite infestations, and in foreign body invasion; however, their exact function in such disturbances is not well known. The basophiles apparently are not phagocytic, in the true sense of the term, although bacteria have been observed in their cytoplasm.

The macrophages of Metchnikoff, which include the mononuclear leucocytes, the fixed tissue cells, and the wandering tissue cells, have been of increasing interest in immunity. Reference has been made to these cells in the discussion of the origin of antibody in Chapter 7, where it was emphasized that they have an important role in the production of antibody. Their dual purpose makes them even more interesting. These cells have been termed by Aschoff, "The Reticulo-endothelial System." They include: *the reticular cells* of the splenic pulp and of cortical nodules, and the pulp cords in the lymph nodes; the *endothelial cells* of the sinuses of the lymph nodes, the blood sinuses of the spleen, the liver sinusoids, the capillaries of the bone marrow, adrenals, and hypophysis; the *histiocytes,* or the clasmatocytes, of Ranvier; the *splenic pulp cells;* and the *septal cells* of the lung.

## THE PHAGOCYTIC PROCESS

The act of phagocytosis is divided into three distinct parts: the approach of the phagocyte to the particle, or cell, to be phagocytized; the ingestion of the particle, or cell; and the disintegration, or digestion, within the phagocyte.

### The Approach

Phagocytes are drawn to foreign particles, including bacteria which are present in the body tissues, by the force known as *positive chemotaxis.* In this particular phenomenon this force is thought to be a result of surface tension effects. The surface tension on the side of the phagocyte nearest the bacteria is lowered, and as a consequence, the phagocyte migrates toward the particle and engulfs it. That the attraction of leucocytes to bacteria and other particles is positive chemotaxis has been repeatedly demonstrated. It is, in all practical respects, the same phenomenon as that of ingestion of food particles by amoeba and other protozoa. The phagocytosis of foreign particles, dead tissue, and nonpathogenic bacteria is doubtless a function of normal phagocytosis; that is, there is no need for the intervention of an additional amount of the antibody material, opsonin.

One of the important characteristics of pathogenic bacteria is their ability to resist phagocytosis; in fact, they exert such a marked negative chemotaxis that the phagocytes are actually repelled. This property is noted in the action of anthrax bacilli which is due to the capsular substance of the organism. The neutralization of this material is considered the function of opsonin, thereby permitting the phagocytosis of the anthrax bacilli during the process of immunization. This material, which is present within the capsules of capsulated bacteria and is no doubt a part of the ectoplasm of noncapsulated bacteria, has been termed *"aggressin"* by Bail. Its function as an antigen which is used in the stimulation of antibody, or antiaggressin, was discussed in the chapter relating to antigens and antibodies. The neutralization of the negative chemotactic force of pathogenic bacteria by opsonin is referred to as a sensitization process. There is no reason why this procedure should be considered different from the sensitization of bacteria to the action of an electrolyte or complement, and if the unitarian view of antibody is accepted, one realizes that the procedure is the same; that is, the denaturization, or "coating over," of bacterial protoplasm by globulin.

The approach of phagocytes toward bacteria is usually characterized, at least in the case of less pathogenic species, by a mass movement of phagocytes toward the invader. Because of their great number and definite mobility, the heterophile leucocytes predominate in this movement. They possess a greater amount of cytoplasm than other leucocytes and may pass between (diapedesis) the endothelial cells of capillaries and lymph vessels toward the positive chemotactic influence. This influence can become generalized throughout the body in a relatively short time and may cause a condition called *leucocytosis,* which is characterized by a marked increase in the number of leucocytes in the blood stream. This phenomenon is observed in many pyogenic infections as well as other inflammatory reactions and is used as a factor in the diagnosis of disease, an example of which is appendicitis in man.

### The Ingestion

The second phase of the act of phagocytosis, the *ingestion* of the bacteria, is the continuation of the first phase. As the phagocyte comes in contact with the bacteria, it flows around them and incorporates them within its cytoplasm. This process is a simple one for the mobile phagocytes. The fixed phagocytes, however, are held in place by their contact with adjacent cells. In this instance the bacteria must be brought to them; this is done by the blood and lymph streams, and considerable phagocytosis occurs at points where the flow of these streams is slow and in tissues where it becomes static. The act of ingestion does not mean destruction. In many instances the ingested material is not destroyed by the phagocyte. The best example of this is in tuberculosis. Tubercle bacilli are readily engulfed by leucocytes as they wander about in glandular crypts of the mucous membrane and in lymph vessels. In many cases this "accidental phagocytosis" of tubercle bacilli is harmful to the animal. The heterophile leucocytes do not appear to have the ability to digest tubercle bacilli; hence, they carry such organisms to the deeper tissues, the regional lymph nodes, or in many cases into the blood stream, and on to the lungs. This forms a focus of the infection because the tubercle bacilli are able to multiply within the leucocyte and ultimately destroy it; consequently, in tuberculosis, it is necessary for other cells, such as the mononuclear leucocytes, to intervene and to defend the body against the assisted invasion. The act of ingestion is responsible for the concentration of bacteria in certain tissues where body defenses, such as the action of various types of phagocytes, encapsulation of the process, and in many cases calcification, rid the body of the invading organisms.

The ingestion of bacteria by leucocytes results in the death of many of the leucocytes. A substance known as *leucocidin* is produced by many species of bacteria, notably the staphylococci and streptococci. It is by virtue of this substance, in addition to the action of aggressin noted previously, that these bacteria are considered to be virulent. Leucocidin is usually a toxin-like substance produced by bacteria. It is produced in broth cultures, and its effect upon leucocytes is demonstrated by the action of the filtrate. It is able to resist 56°C., and has been shown to be an antigen, in that its injection produces antileucocidin.

### The Digestion

Metchnikoff assumed that the destruction of bacteria was brought about by phagocytes and was due to two substances formed by them. The microphages produced *microcytase* which he considered identical with complement, or alexin, and which was active in the normal destruction of bacteria. The macrophages produced *macrocytase* which was active in the destruction of dead tissue and other debris. In the assumption that phagocytes are able to produce a substance which has a disintegrating action upon bacteria, Metchnikoff was right. His division of the function of the phagocytes was wrong as, also, was his contention that the substance was similar to complement. One of the most substantial proofs for the distinction between "cytase" and complement is the fact that the latter is thermolabile (56°C.) and the former is heat resistant.

The nature of the bactericidal substance present in phagocytes is not entirely known. It does not seem to be identical with various enzymes produced by leucocytes such as leucoprotease which can be purified by precipitation and still show proteolytic activity without bactericidal property. The proteolytic enzymes of the polymorphonuclear cells act in a weakly alkaline medium while those of the mononuclear cells are more effective in a weakly acid medium. Lipase is produced by cells of the macrophage group. This is clearly demonstrated in tuberculosis and leprosy, where it has been shown that the lipoid constituents of the bacilli are removed by mononuclear cells, whereas this is not true of polymorphonuclear leucocytes.

The name *leukin* has been used for the antibacterial factor produced by leucocytes. Skarnes and Watson report that amino acid analysis of a potent antibacterial substance obtained from rabbit leucocytes yielded arginine (17 per cent) and other amino acids. They considered it to be a protamine or protamine derivative. It had marked action against gram-positive bacteria but not against gram-negative species.

Unfortunately, certain types of bacteria may not be destroyed by the phagocyte after they have been ingested. This is apparent in tuberculosis, as noted above, where the tubercle bacilli are ingested by polymorphonuclear leucocytes and transported to regional lymph nodes where the primary lesion of tuberculosis, the tubercle, develops. In other diseases, such as brucellosis, the causal bacteria are ingested, but apparently not quickly digested. Their presence in the phagocyte protects them against antibody and the lytic process. This is thought to explain the chronic nature of that disease as well as the recurring acute attacks of the infection.

## THE SIGNIFICANCE OF PHAGOCYTOSIS IN IMMUNITY

The role of phagocytosis in immunity has been acknowledged as an important phenomenon since its description by Metchnikoff. That it is the only means by which the animal body is protected against pathogenic bacteria, as contended by Metchnikoff, has been doubted by many. The demonstration of the bactericidal action of blood plasma, followed by the advent of the humoral theory of immunity, made it evident that lysis, too, had a part to play in the destruction of microorganisms. The neutralization of toxin by antitoxin has demonstrated that a direct neutralizing process is active in destroying certain toxins of bacteria. The division of immunity into the three parts—neutralization, humoral, and cellular—is logical, but how much of immunity may be ascribed to each is rather difficult to ascertain. We may dispose of the part toxin-antitoxin plays by admitting that this is a function which is operative in all diseases produced by toxins of any marked potency. The division of the resulting immunity into humoral and cellular is a more difficult task. That the lysis of bacteria takes place when the necessary reacting substances are placed in a test tube is well established. It may be assumed that the same thing occurs in the animal body. Furthermore, it has been proved that when leucocytes, bacteria, and antibody are placed together in a test tube, the bacteria are destroyed. This occurs within the body as has been demonstrated. The division of immunity into *temporary* and *permanent* is helpful in showing a difference between the humoral and cellular effects.

It is assumed that humoral immunity is active when antibody is noted in the blood plasma. Antibody is detected by the agglutination, precipitation, or complement-fixation tests. As long as this substance is present in great amounts, high titers, it is supposed that humoral immunity is still an effective means of destroying bacteria. In those conditions where antibody is demonstrated and yet the animal is in the acute stage of the disease, the mere presence of antibody does not assure the animal protection against death, nor does it mean that the animal will be protected against chronic infection. In most cases, however, the presence of antibody is conducive to recovery. During this recovery process, lysis and phagocytosis are no doubt the active forces in bacterial destruction. Ultimately, however, in many conditions it is not possible to demonstrate the presence of antibody in blood plasma, and yet the animal is entirely immune. By what means is the animal protected? Lysis and phagocytosis both are enhanced by the action of antibody, and it seems logical to assume that the absence of antibody affects each equally.

Metchnikoff was of the opinion in his

very early work on phagocytosis that the phenomenon was due to the stimulation of the phagocyte. The discovery of opsonin negated that assumption. Wassermann and Citron, in 1905, were of the opinion that cells could be conditioned to the effects of foreign substances without the action of antibody. This first suggestion of the existence of a "local immunity" has been considerably advanced by the work of Besredka, Gay and his coworkers, and by many others. Definite evidence has accumulated which appears to demonstrate that phagocytic cells can be trained to be effective against a specific type of antigenic substance. This training appears to be an inheritable phenomenon which is possessed by the cells for long periods of time. In a sense, then, the original conception of Metchnikoff, that phagocytosis is due to the stimulation of the phagocyte, seems to be partly true. The action of the antibody, opsonin, speeds up the union of phagocyte and the invading microorganism. The presence of a marked immunity in the absence of demonstrable antibody is explained by the presence of a property in phagocytes which is passed on to the newly formed cells. It is assumed, then, that cellular immunity is more durable than humoral and plays an exceedingly important role in temporary infections. It is generally conceded, also, that natural immunity is due largely to the action of phagocytes.

## PHAGOCYTOSIS IN DISEASE DIAGNOSIS

At one time the determination of the opsonic index of a patient was considered a practical method of diagnosing disease. Experimental error and the availability of more adequate diagnostic tests discouraged its use. A modification of the opsonic index determination under the name of the *opsonocytophagic test* has been suggested as an aid in the diagnosis of brucellosis of man.

## REFERENCES


BESREDKA, A. Local Immunization. Williams & Wilkins Co., Baltimore, 1927.

CARPENTER, P. L. Immunology and Serology. W. B. Saunders Co., Philadelphia, 1956.

DUBOS, R. J. (ed.). Bacterial and Mycotic Infections of Man. 3rd Ed. J. B. Lippincott Co., Philadelphia, 1958.

FENN, W. O. The Mechanism of Phagocytosis. The Newer Knowledge of Bacteriology and Immunology. Pp. 861–69. Univ. of Chicago Press, Chicago, 1928.

GAY, F. P., *et al.* Agents of Disease and Host Resistance. Pp. 296–309, 444–54. Charles C Thomas, Baltimore, 1935.

GOULD, S. E., and HUDDLESON, I. F. Diagnostic Methods in Undulant Fever (Brucellosis). Jour. Amer. Med. Assn. 109:1971–74, 1937.

HALE, A. J., and WILSON, S. J. The Deoxyribonucleic Acid Content of the Leucocytes in Human Blood, Bone-Marrow and Lymph-Glands. Jour. Path. Bact. 82:483–501, 1961.

KOLMER, J. A. Infection, Immunity and Biologic Therapy. Pp. 171–202. W. B. Saunders Co., Philadelphia, 1923.

METCHNIKOFF, ELIE. Immunity in Infective Diseases. English transl. F. G. Binnie. Cambridge Univ. Press, Cambridge, 1907.

METCHNIKOFF, OLGA. The Life of Elie Metchnikoff. Houghton Mifflin Co., Boston, 1921.

MUDD, S., *et al.* Pha gocytosis. Physiological Reviews. 14:210–370, 1934.

PATTERSON, R., *et al.* In Vitro Uptake of Antigen-Antibody Complexes by Phagocytic Cells. Jour. Immunol. 89:471–82, 1962.

RAFFEL, SIDNEY. Immunity. 2nd Ed. Appleton-Century-Crofts, Inc., New York, 1961.

SBARRA, A. J., and SHIRLEY, W. Phagocytosis Inhibition and Reversal. I. Effect of Glycolytic Intermediates and Nucleotides on Particle Uptake. Jour. Bact. 86:259–65, 1963.

WOOD, W. B. Studies on the Cellular Immunology of Bacterial Infections. Harvey Lectures 47:72, 1951–52.

ZINSSER, H., *et al.* Immunity. Pp. 284–339. Macmillan Co., New York, 1939.

# 13

# Allergy

**MERLIN L. KAEBERLE, *D.V.M., Ph.D.***
*Department of Veterinary Microbiology
and Preventive Medicine
Iowa State University
Ames, Iowa*

A PARADOXICAL SITUATION MAY EXIST in that the same immunologic response that renders an animal resistant to disease may lead to pathologic processes. This role of the immunologic mechanism in disease processes will be considered under the general heading of *allergy*. Von Pirquet proposed the term *allergy* in 1906 to describe the altered reactivity of individuals following infectious disease, vaccination, or injection with a foreign protein. As defined by von Pirquet, *allergy* implied both increased and decreased sensitivity to foreign substances which he termed *allergens*. In recent years, usage of the term *allergy* has restricted its application to an altered reactivity that is increased above normal. This concept was stated by Chase[1]: "The allergic state, or the state of hypersensitivity, may be considered as an altered type of reactivity to some substance, transcending the response of those individuals who are undergoing a parallel experience *de novo* with that substance. The altered type of reactivity takes the form of an allergic inflammation of tissues variable in type and site; it witnesses some sort of preparative experience of the individual that sets him apart from his fellows." *Hypersensitivity*, in the immunologic sense, refers to a specifically induced hyper-reactivity and is used synonymously with allergy.

The relationship between *immunity* and *hypersensitivity* is not clear, and there is probably no basis for distinctly separating one from the other. According to von Pirquet[2]: "The term immunity must be restricted to those processes in which the introduction of the foreign substance into the organism causes no clinically evident reaction, where, therefore, complete insensitivity exists." Yet the immunologic response to the antigen may be the same as in the hypersensitive state. Entry of microorganisms into the body or injection of antigenic materials stimulates body cells to produce antibodies. These antibodies react with the antigen to bring about neutralization, opsonization, lysis, or other processes which render the foreign material harmless. A state of immunity has resulted and the condition may be termed *prophylaxis,* meaning "with protection." In contrast to that situation, injection of foreign materials may lead to a hypersensitive state. When a protein substance is injected into an animal parenterally, that is, subcutaneously or intravenously, and is followed in two weeks by another injection,

[1] Chase, M. W. *Mechanisms of Hypersensitivity*. J. H. Shaffer, G. A. Lo Grippo, and M. W. Chase (eds.). Little, Brown and Co., Boston, 1959, pp. 673–78.

[2] von Pirquet, C. Münch. med. Wochenschr. 30:1457, 1906. English translation by Carl Prausnitz, *Clinical Aspects of Immunology*. P. G. H. Gell and R. R. A. Coombs (eds.). F. A. Davis Co., Philadelphia, 1963, Appendix A:805.

a reaction varying from a minor respiratory disturbance to death may be observed. This reaction is termed *anaphylaxis,* meaning "without protection," and is a specific example of a hypersensitive state. Therefore, both immunity and anaphylaxis may be induced by protein substances, both are specific in action, both involve body cells, and both result from the union between antigen and antibody. While the mechanisms are very similar, the effects upon the animal body are quite different. Essentially then, *immunity* and *hypersensitivity* are descriptive clinical terms used to describe the response of an animal to foreign substances. Only elucidation of the basic mechanisms involved in immunologic processes gives promise of differentiating physiologic from pathologic responses.

Allergic reactions have been observed for many years, but clarification of the basic mechanisms underlying many of these reactions has been slow. Jenner was probably the first to observe hypersensitiveness, for in 1798 he reported that patients previously infected with smallpox or cowpox developed an accelerated response when immunized. Some time later, in 1839, Magendie observed that the injection of egg albumen into rabbits produced a hypersensitive state, and subsequent injections of the same substance resulted in death. In 1865 Blackley related hay fever to pollen sensitivity. Robert Koch, who discovered the cause of tuberculosis, observed the delayed allergic reaction to tubercle bacilli and tuberculin in 1890. His name became appended to the reaction that occurred when a suspension of tubercle bacilli was injected into the skin of a tuberculous guinea pig—the *Koch phenomenon.* Koch did not, however, recognize the allergic nature of this reaction.

One of the most significant early contributions to the subject was made by Richet and his coworkers, Herricourt and Portier, in 1898. They first observed that the injection of eel serum into dogs produced a sensitivity to a second injection of the serum. Later, the same workers observed that the same type of reaction, sometimes terminating in death, could be produced in dogs with derivatives of sea anemones and mussels. The term anaphylaxis was applied to this acute shocklike reaction. In 1904 Theobald Smith observed hypersensitiveness in guinea pigs used for diphtheria toxin-antitoxin standardization. Guinea pigs given a second injection of toxin-antitoxin mixture 10 days following an initial injection, frequently developed a violent reaction. Such symptoms as extreme restlessness, dyspnea, itching of the skin, and convulsive seizures were observed, with death occurring in more than 50 per cent of the animals within half an hour. Smith communicated these observations through Ehrlich to Otto in Germany, who studied the reaction further and published in 1906 "the Theobald Smith phenomenon of serum hypersensitiveness." Almost simultaneously with Otto, Rosenau and Anderson in the United States studied the reaction, developed important fundamental criteria, and determined that the response was due to the horse serum protein alone. This phenomenon in the guinea pig is so striking that it has been used by many investigators in the study of the anaphylaxis reaction.

In 1903 Arthus described an unusual phenomenon which has since been named for him—the *Arthus reaction.* He injected rabbits subcutaneously with horse serum at six-day intervals. The first three injections were readily absorbed by the tissues and the fourth was followed by some edema at the site of injection. After the sixth or seventh injection, the skin at the site of injection became gangrenous, and a deep abscess scar was finally formed. The same animal that developed this localized lesion from an Arthus reaction was also subject to anaphylactic shock. If the sensitized animal was injected intravenously with the serum, it appeared restless, lay on its abdomen, and respiration frequently increased; it defecated frequently, finally fell on its side, and usually died, all within the span of 2 or 3 minutes.

In 1903 several observers noted that a reaction in man often followed the injection of diphtheria antitoxin. In some instances, the reaction was so severe that it caused death. Von Pirquet independently, and later with Schick, explained the reaction as one due to an *allergy* caused by horse serum. They named the disease *serum sickness.* In a monograph published in 1951, von Pirquet and Schick quoted numerous workers who had reported serum sickness occurring spontaneously in animals, particularly in calves, after a primary injection of antianthrax horse serum.

Our knowledge of hypersensitivity has increased tremendously in the past half-century and has been extended to include a number of new clinical syndromes. Some of the basic mechanisms have been clarified, but all relationships are far from clear.

## CLASSIFICATION

A variety of clinical syndromes and experimental observations are included under the general heading of allergy. The various reactions must be grouped on some basis into a classification scheme to facilitate discussion of the nature of the reactions. Formerly, hypersensitivities were usually grouped according to the nature of the clinical response. In this scheme the reactions are divided into two classes on the basis of the time of peak reaction following administration of the response-eliciting dose of antigen. Those responses that occur shortly after injection of antigen are grouped with the *immediate hypersensitivities,* are mediated by circulating antibody, and primarily affect blood vessels, smooth muscle, and collagen. Those reactions that reach a peak response several hours after exposure to antigen are termed *delayed hypersensitivities.* A role for circulating antibodies has not been demonstrated in delayed hypersensitivity, and the reaction apparently stems from specifically sensitized cells. The major characteristics of the two types of hypersensitivity are listed in Table 13.1.

More recently, allergists and immunologists have based the classification on the circumstances of the initial reaction between allergen and antibody or specifically sensitized cells. Secondary phenomena such as the site of the reaction, manifestations of the reaction, and the physiopathologic responses of the animal are used to subgroup reactions within the major types. The following classification was proposed by Coombs and Gell:[3]

I. Type I Reaction or Response (Anaphylactic). This reaction is initiated by the allergen or antigen reacting with antibody associated with tissue cells and leading to the release of pharmacologically active substances. Characteristic of this type of reaction are: (1) General anaphylaxis and (2) Local anaphylaxis.

II. Type II Reaction or Response (Cytolytic or Cytotoxic). This type of reaction is initiated by antibody reacting with either (1) an antigenic component of a tissue cell or (2) an antigen or hapten which has become intimately associated with tissue cells. Complement is often involved in production of the cellular damage.

III. Type III Reaction or Response (Arthus Reaction and Toxic-Complex Syndrome). This type of reaction is initiated by the combination of antigen with potentially precipitating antibody either (1) in tissue spaces with the resulting microprecipitates accumulating around the small vessels causing damage to cells secondarily or (2) in the blood stream to form soluble circulating complexes that are subsequently deposited in blood vessel walls where they cause local inflammation. Subgroups of this type of reaction are: (1) the Arthus Reaction and (2) the Serum Sickness Syndrome.

IV. Type IV Reaction or Response (Delayed or Tuberculin-Type Sensitivity). This type of response is initiated by the reaction between an allergen deposited at a local site and specifically sensitized mononuclear cells. Whether the reaction is between the allergen and the cell or a substance associated with the cells is open to question, since the mechanism is still uncertain.

### Type I Reaction

The anaphylactic reaction is mediated by certain pharmacologically active agents that are released following combination of antigen *(anaphylactogen)* with cell-associated antibody *(anaphylactin).* The basic mechanism of the reaction is the same in both generalized and local anaphylaxis, with the characteristic difference being the site and extent of the reaction.

[3] Coombs, R. R. A., and Gell, P. G. H. The Classification of Allergic Reactions Underlying Disease. In *Clinical Aspects of Immunology.* P. G. H. Gell and R. R. A. Coombs (eds.). F. A. Davis Co., Philadelphia, 1963, pp. 317–37.

TABLE 13.1
MAJOR CHARACTERISTICS OF IMMEDIATE AND DELAYED HYPERSENSITIVITIES CONTRASTED*

| Characteristics | Immediate Hypersensitivity | Delayed Hypersensitivity |
|---|---|---|
| Induction | injection of antigen in aqueous solution by any route | usually requires intradermal injection of soluble antigens and use of water-in-oil emulsion |
| Reaction time | appears and recedes rapidly | appears slowly; may last for days |
| Skin reaction | edema, erythema, sometimes petechiae | induration, erythema, necrosis |
| Systemic reaction | shock organs involved | no shock organs |
| Histopathology | edema, hyperemia; in more severe reactions blood stasis, thrombosis, extravasation, infiltration of polymorphonucleocytes | histiocyte infiltration and congregation around blood vessels forming "perivascular islands"; in more severe reactions, necrosis and secondary infiltration by polymorphonucleocytes |
| Passive transfer | by serum or plasma only | by lymphoid cells only |
| Drug susceptibility | antihistamines, antiserotonins, corticosteroids | corticosteroids |
| Irradiation susceptibility | existing allergy unaffected | existing allergy depressed |
| Desensitization | readily and rapidly accomplished, but short-lived | difficult and slow; somewhat longer lasting |

Source: Crowle, Alfred J., Delayed Hypersensitivity in Health and Disease. Publ. 508, American Lecture Series, 1962. (Courtesy Charles C Thomas, Springfield, Ill.)

*Contrasts in this table apply primarily to tuberculin allergy and to anaphylactic hypersensitivity. Limited space does not permit qualification or extension of some points listed as may be necessary for other forms of immediate and delayed hypersensitivities, and which are discussed in the text.

**Generalized Anaphylaxis.** The anaphylactic reaction that occurs in the guinea pig is usually used as a model for experimentation and study. The marked sensitivity of this animal to anaphylaxis has led to extensive study of the mechanisms and characteristics of the response. Anaphylaxis may be induced by either active or passive sensitization of the animal. Active sensitization may be established by the parenteral injection of a small quantity of foreign protein *(sensitizing dose)* and waiting 14 days for the guinea pig to produce antibodies *(incubation* or *sensitizing period)*. Passive sensitization is accomplished by the intravenous injection of serum containing specific antibodies and allowing 12 to 24 hours for the antibodies to associate with body cells. The injection of antigen *(shocking dose)* into a previously sensitized animal elicits the shock syndrome known as anaphylaxis.

***Mechanism of the Reaction.*** Soluble protein antigens combining with their corresponding antibodies are most effective in eliciting the anaphylactic response. While the ability of a serum to confer passive sensitization was shown by Doerr and Russ to be directly proportional to the precipitin titer of the serum, this association may be circumstantial. Recent evidence presented by Ovary and associates indicated that the antibodies responsible for anaphylaxis in the guinea pig are primarily IgA globulins that have limited precipitating activity. Anaphylaxis-mediating antibodies apparently have the property of becoming intimately associated with or passively absorbed to tissue cells. The type of cells that become sensitized has not been specifically identified, but mesenchymal cells have been implicated. The nature of this sensitization is the same whether the antibodies are passively administered or

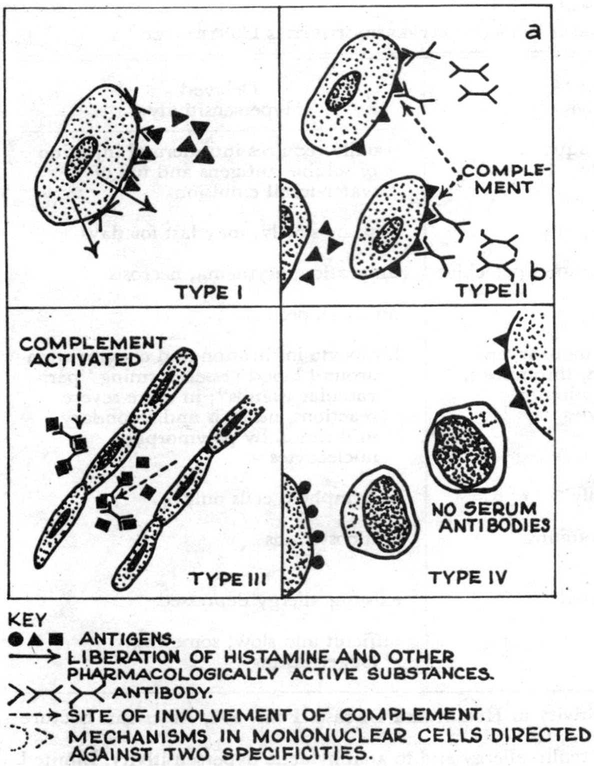


FIG. 13.1—Diagrammatic representation of the four basic mechanisms of allergic reactions. (From Coombs and Gell: The Classification of Allergic Reactions Underlying Disease. In Clinical Aspects of Immunology. P. G. H. Gell and R. R. A. Coombs (eds.). F. A. Davis Co., Philadelphia, 1963, pp. 317–37. (Courtesy authors and Blackwell Scientific Publications, Oxford, England.)

actively produced in the animal by antibody synthesizing cells and released into the circulation.

Antigen reacts with the antibody on the surface of the tissue cells leading to injury to the cells. The mechanism of cell damage is unknown, but available evidence indicates that it is enzymatic in nature. The damaged cells release histamine and other pharmacologically active agents into the circulation. These substances produce the clinical syndrome by their action on tissues that are responsive to their pharmacologic activity.

***Mediators of the Reaction.*** Several distinct pharmacologically active agents are known to be released by the interaction of antigen and antibody and may be involved in the production of anaphylaxis. *Histamine* is probably the most important of these substances for it is definitely associated with anaphylaxis in the guinea pig. However, *serotonin* (5-hydroxytryptamine), *slow reacting substance* (SRS), *acetylcholine, heparin,* and *bradykinin* have also been implicated, at least in some species of animals. The action of a combination of these agents is probably responsible for producing the syndrome, with one or another of the substances being of greater significance in any one species.

Histamine is the base derived by the decarboxylation of histidine and acts to stimulate contraction of certain smooth muscles, to cause vasodilatation, and to increase vascular permeability. These physiopathologic responses occur during the generalized anaphylactic reaction and contribute to the syndrome. Vasodilatation and increased vascular permeability are associated with local anaphylaxis. Histamine was first implicated in the anaphylactic reaction by the experiments of Dale and Laidlaw between 1910 and 1914 in which they demonstrated that a syndrome very similar to anaphylaxis could be induced in the guinea pig by injection of histamine. The evidence was extended by Schultz and Dale who demonstrated the relationship between the antigen-antibody reaction, histamine, and the contraction of smooth muscle. When they suspended the uterus of a previously sensitized guinea pig in a maintenance medium and added a small amount of antigen, the smooth muscle contracted and a release of histamine was detected. A further addition of antigen failed to elicit a response, and unrelated antigens had no effect. This in vitro anaphylactic response has come to be known as the *Schultz-Dale reaction* and can be produced by using a strip of smooth muscle from the uterus or ileum of an unsensitized animal and soaking it in immune serum. The smooth muscle apparently takes up antibody from the serum and the subsequent addition of antigen leads to histamine release and contraction of the muscle tissue. Further evidence for the role of histamine in anaphylaxis was provided by Dragstedt who demonstrated a histamine-like substance in the efferent blood from the liver of dogs during anaphylactic shock. Although rather sensitive methods are required, histamine-like substances have been demonstrated in increased amounts in the blood of other animals during anaphylaxis.

Histamine is released from body cells by an unknown mechanism as a result of the antigen-antibody reaction. While platelets, leucocytes, and perhaps other cell types may liberate histamine, the richest source is the tissue mast cell. Histamine occurs as a constituent of the cytoplasmic granules in association with heparin. The antigen-antibody reaction results in disruption of mast cells, degranulation, and the release of heparin and histamine. However, appreciable quantities of histamine may be detected in tissues such as the lung of the guinea pig during anaphylaxis and there are relatively few mast cells present in these tissues. The reasons for such a finding may be the release of histamine from other cell types or a selective localization of histamine in these tissues following its release into the circulation at another site.

There is evidence to indicate that other substances than histamine mediate anaphylaxis. In the Schultz-Dale reaction, addition of antigen will cause muscle contraction even after the sensitized guinea pig muscle has been fatigued by serial additions of histamine. Blood histamine levels in horses, calves, and rabbits are depressed below normal during anaphylactic shock. Rats and mice are susceptible to anaphylaxis but are very tolerant of histamine. In sensitized rats, for example, cutaneous anaphylaxis may be induced by the injection of antigen even after the administration of histamine-releasing substances.

Serotonin (5-hydroxytryptamine) is a decarboxylated derivative of the amino acid tryptophan that is widely distributed in body tissues. This agent causes rapid contraction of certain smooth muscles, increases capillary permeability, and may have certain other physiological activities. Platelets are rich in serotonin, and mast cells of rodents also contain significant quantities. The role of serotonin in anaphylaxis is still unclear, although there is evidence that it may be involved to some degree. Serotonin may be released from platelets by an antigen-antibody reaction. In the rabbit, large numbers of serotonin-rich platelets accumulate in the lungs during anaphylaxis and may contribute to the reaction. Some workers believe serotonin released from mast cells of the mouse plays a role in anaphylaxis in this species. Guinea pigs exposed to an aerosol of serotonin undergo a systemic reaction that mimics anaphylaxis. While the possibility of serotonin mediating the asthmatic syndrome in man has been suggested, recent evidence indicates that it is not involved in mediating asthma in man or dogs.

Other possible mediators of immediate hypersensitivity include slow reacting substance, bradykinin, and acetylcholine. Slow reacting substance causes a contraction of certain smooth muscles that is slow in onset and quite prolonged. This substance is liberated from sensitized tissues during anaphylaxis, and there is some evidence to indicate that it may be responsible for the bronchial constriction in human asthma that is not antagonized by antihistaminic drugs. Bradykinin is also a slow reacting material that is capable of causing contraction of certain smooth muscles, inducing vasodilatation, and increasing capillary permeability. While it probably has important physiologic activities in the body, bradykinin's role in anaphylaxis has not been demonstrated. The major evidence for implicating acetylcholine in hypersensitivity is the increase of this substance in the circulation during anaphylaxis, but this may only be coincidental.

***Characteristics of the Response.*** The nature of the response differs with the species of animal, and to a lesser degree, with the route of injection of antigen, amount of antigen injected, and time between doses of antigen. The reaction may be extremely acute, with death occurring in 2 to 5 minutes after intravenous injection of the shocking dose. In other instances the response may be prolonged, with death resulting several hours later, or the reaction may be less severe with complete recovery.

Acute anaphylaxis with subsequent death is the usual type in the guinea pig. The animal becomes restless and scratches its nose with the front feet within a few seconds after injection of the shocking dose of antigen. The animal commonly voids urine and feces. Breathing becomes rapid, followed by labored respiration *(dyspnea)* due to intense constriction of the bronchi and bronchioles. The animal rolls onto its side, respiration stops, convulsions ensue, and the animal dies from asphyxia even though the heart may continue to function for a period of time after breathing ceases. In less acute cases, the initial signs of the reaction occur but the animal gradually returns to normal. However, some guinea pigs so affected may die several hours later.

Anaphylaxis may occur in the rabbit, although this animal is not so susceptible to the reaction even though it is a more able producer of antibodies. This observation serves to confirm reports that occurrence of shock is not regularly predictable from determinations of level of circulating antibody. Anaphylactic shock in the rabbit resembles in general the reaction in the guinea pig. However, there are indications that the tissue focus of the reaction is different. The generally accepted cause of death in the rabbit is heart failure resulting from contraction of the pulmonary arterioles and leading to cardiac dilatation. There is some disagreement however, for other workers have proposed that cardiac failure is due to spasms of the coronary vessels. Other experimental evidence indicates that death is the direct result of respiratory failure as in the guinea pig.

The dog is also subject to anaphylactic shock but is not so readily sensitized as the guinea pig. The clinical syndrome in the dog is quite different from that in other species of animals. The initial reaction is acute and characterized by restlessness, weakness, decrease in blood pressure, vomiting, urination, and defecation. The early reaction subsides to some degree, and later there develops increasing weakness, circulatory failure, and death 8 to 10 hours after administration of the shocking dose. The shock organ in the dog appears to be the liver, with this organ of prime importance in the release of histamine. Histamine released by the liver may account for the early signs of shock and acute death in those animals that apparently succumb to respiratory failure. However, in most cases of anaphylactic death in dogs, necropsy reveals a marked congestion of the liver and gastrointestinal tract. These lesions are thought to result from interference with portal circulation, although a general circulatory collapse may be responsible.

Cattle are susceptible to anaphylactic shock, with histamine probably the most significant mediator of the reaction. The anaphylactic reaction in cattle is characterized by respiratory embarrassment, including coughing, choking and difficult breathing, excessive lacrimation, excessive salivation, sweating, and edematous swelling of the vulva, udder, and around the eyes. Death is not an unusual occurrence and probably results from respiratory failure. A syndrome that closely mimics the anaphylactic reaction may be produced in the bovine animal by the intravenous injection of histamine.

Pigs are readily sensitized for anaphylaxis

but seem to be quite resistant to the reaction. The initial sign of anaphylaxis in the pig is a gasping for breath which develops within 15 to 20 seconds following intravenous injection of a shocking dose of antigen. Within 1 minute respiration ceases and the pig falls on its side in a convulsive seizure. Within 30 seconds respiration begins once again and hyperemia of the skin of the ears, eyelids, snout, and abdominal region becomes very evident. Respiration gradually returns to normal and apparent recovery ensues. Some animals may die from respiratory failure during the early acute stage of the reaction, and rather protracted reactions with resultant death have been reported.

***Desensitization.*** The anaphylactic reaction in a sensitized animal may be prevented by a number of different treatments. This process by which an animal becomes nonreactive is termed *desensitization*. Several theories have been proposed to explain the mechanism of desensitization since no procedure is always successful.

A state of relative refractoriness usually exists for a period of time following a nonlethal anaphylactic reaction in an animal. Sensitization may be reduced by repeated small injections of antigen into the sensitized animal. This type of desensitization is usually explained on the basis of antigen neutralization of available antibody. However, this theory is open to question since, in an animal sensitized to two different antigens, desensitization with one antigen also may reduce the sensitivity to the second unrelated antigen.

Desensitization may be accomplished in some instances in sensitized guinea pigs by the parenteral injection of antiserum. This phenomenon has been termed antianaphylaxis and probably results from the increased level of circulating antibody. However, the character of the antibody that is predominant may be of greater importance. Antianaphylaxis is not easily demonstrated and, consequently, the mechanism of the reaction has not been adequately explained.

Another theory that has been proposed would have the state of desensitization resulting from exhaustion of pharmacologic mediators of anaphylaxis. Following an anaphylactic reaction, the source of histamine, for example, might be reduced to such an extent that inadequate quantities would be available to mediate a second reaction. Further, replacement of histamine precursors would be relatively slow and account for a period of refractoriness.

In those species of animals where histamine is the primary mediator of anaphylaxis, antihistaminic agents may act to prevent or reduce the severity of the anaphylactic reaction. A similar effect may result from the administration of such substances as adrenalin, salicylates, aminopyrine, or normal serum. The action of these agents is nonspecific in nature, but they may be used beneficially in the treatment of anaphylactic shock.

***Significance of the Reaction.*** The generalized anaphylactic reaction is of considerable importance in the practice of veterinary medicine. The reaction has been observed quite commonly in cattle during immunization. Taylor and Casserly reported the occurrence of anaphylaxis in cattle following a second administration of anthrax antiserum. Schlotthauer observed anaphylaxis in calves during immunization with paratyphoid bacterin. Numerous cases of anaphylaxis have resulted in cattle immunized with *Leptospira pomona* bacterin in which there was residual rabbit serum. Even though only a small amount of rabbit serum was present and a year elapsed between injections of the bacterin, severe anaphylactic reactions and occasional deaths ensued. Anaphylaxis has also been observed in cattle following attempted manual removal of the cattle grub larvae (*Hypoderma*) from the back of the animal. Crushing of the larvae in the process apparently leads to release and absorption of antigenic substances that induce the reaction. In swine, injections of anti-hog cholera serum have resulted in an anaphylaxis-like reaction. The nature of this reaction is not fully understood because the antiserum is of porcine origin. However, pasteurization of the serum results in aggregation of globulins; the aggregated globulin may fix complement; and a formation of *anaphylatoxin* may mediate the reaction. The obvious significance of the anaphylactic reaction in the practice of veterinary medicine requires that caution be used in giving injections of foreign proteins to animals without obtaining a history of previous treatment.

**Local Anaphylaxis.** The anaphylactic reaction may occur in a limited area or be restricted to certain tissues and is then termed *local anaphylaxis*. Except in situations where sensitization is established at a local site by passive means, the sensitization is general in nature. However, the manifestations are localized due to a limited distribution of a quantity of antigen or allergen which, if it was distributed throughout the body in adequate quantity, could produce generalized anaphylaxis.

If a small quantity of antigen is injected into the skin of man or some species of animals that have previously been sensitized, an *evanescent cutaneous reaction* results. The reaction is identical to the "wheal and flare" response that can be elicited by the local injection of histamine. Therefore, it is assumed that the response results from the release of histamine by an antigen-antibody reaction. The response becomes visible within a few minutes and lasts 3 to 4 hours. The congestion and swelling at the site of the reaction result from dilatation of small venules and capillaries, with accompanying endothelial damage and an escape of circulatory fluids into extravascular spaces.

Immediate hypersensitivity of the local cutaneous type possesses practical usefulness for serologic and diagnostic procedures. One diagnostic procedure of this type is the *Prausnitz-Küstner* (P-K) reaction which will be discussed later along with atopic hypersensitivity. A second type is *passive cutaneous anaphylaxis* (PCA) in which sensitization is established by the injection of antibody into a local area of skin and the reaction developed by intravenous injection of antigen. A dye such as Evans blue is usually injected with the antigen; extravasation of the dye permits better visualization of the reaction. The reaction has been studied extensively due to its great sensitivity in detecting antibodies, its ability to detect hypersensitivity-mediating antibodies, and its potential for elucidation of characteristics of antigens. Antibodies that mediate the reaction must be capable of fixing to the tissues and be able to fix complement. For this reason when the reaction is conducted in the guinea pig, high molecular weight (19S) antibodies of human and rabbit origin are not effective because they do not fix to the tissues. Antibodies produced by the horse and goat are not effective due to their inability to fix guinea pig complement. A modification of the reaction, which is called *reversed passive cutaneous anaphylaxis,* can be produced if the antigen is a gamma globulin capable of fixing to the tissues. The response is identical to PCA even though in this case the antigen is injected locally in the skin and the antibody-dye preparation is administered intravenously.

**Atopic Hypersensitivity.** Atopy was defined by Coca in 1922 as a "type of hypersensitiveness peculiar to man, subject to hereditary influence, presenting the characteristic immediate whealing type reaction, having circulating antibody reagin, and manifesting peculiar clinical syndromes such as asthma and hay fever." The reaction is essentially a local anaphylaxis but possesses certain characteristics that are different. Furthermore, atopic hypersensitivity includes a group of clinical entities which may differ somewhat in basic mechanism as well as manifestations of the response. While Coca's definition is still accepted, newer and, as yet, incomplete knowledge of atopy indicates that the state is much more complex than indicated by the original work of Coca and associates.

Atopic hypersensitivity results from spontaneous sensitization of man or animals by environmental contact with such substances as pollens, dust, animal dandruff, and certain drugs. The antibodies which develop in the sensitized individual are termed *reagins* and, although subjected to extensive study, their physicobiologic characteristics are still not completely understood. These reagins have been termed *nonclassical antibodies* by some workers because they possess characteristics that differentiate them from the better known precipitins and agglutinins. The reaginic antibodies possess the property of fixing to skin and other tissues and react with the corresponding allergen to bring about histamine release but, in contrast to classical 7S antibodies, are not transferred across the human placenta to the fetus. Other workers have described a selective organ fixation of reaginic antibodies corresponding to the shock organ for the particular clinical disease. Such a conclusion might be questioned since the shock organ might be determined by the nature of the antigenic exposure or by limited antigen distribution. Demonstration of antibodies usually requires a skin-test procedure, although in recent years the passive hemagglutination test has proved to be a satisfactory serologic method. While the reagins possess certain characteristics of high molecular weight antibodies, molecular weight and electrophoretic determinations indicate that many of them do not belong in the macroglobulin class. Study of reaginic antibodies and their biologic activities has proved to be rather frustrating in many instances, and additional knowledge of their nature and activities is needed.

A genetic basis for the occurrence of atopic hypersensitivities in man was proposed nearly 50 years ago, but proof has not been forthcoming. Circumstantial evidence indicates that asthma tends to involve family lines, but other factors than a heritable mechanism may be responsible. Available evidence does indicate that certain individuals possess an increased susceptibility to atopic hypersensitivity and may become sensitized to a variety of allergens to which other individuals are completely refractory. The problem is best summarized by the statement of Frankland[4]: "It seems, however, that as the clinicians cannot even agree on a definition of asthma, and as all that wheezes is not asthma and all that wheezes is not allergy, it would appear to be impossible to state whether a disease which cannot be easily defined, can be proved to be inherited."

Contrary to original beliefs, atopy is not peculiar to man but does occur in other animals. Its occurrence in animals has been presumed to be rare, but this may be due to our failure to recognize the conditions. Wittich described hay fever in dogs caused by pollen. The dogs reacted with urticaria, sneezing, and wheezing on exposure to pollen and had positive skin tests on injection of pollen. Patterson *et al.* described a case of spontaneous ragweed sensitivity in a dog. Urticaria is not uncommon in cattle and, although the basis for the reaction is unknown, may be a manifestation of atopic hypersensitivity. Certain types of dermatitis observed in domestic animals possess characteristics of allergic dermatitis or eczema in man. Eczema is rather common in dogs, and many of these cases may be a manifestation of an allergy to food. For example, Pomeroy demonstrated that substances in canned salmon were the cause of an allergic dermatitis in a dog. Other workers, Andrews and Benjamini *et al.*, have presented evidence that the dermatitis resulting from flea bites has an allergic basis. Bradford and Bradford described an allergic dermatitis in a cow. Allergic stomatitis and dermatitis in cattle has been associated with the ingestion of certain forages, including different types of clover and alfalfa.

Diagnostic test procedures for atopic hypersensitivity are usually based on a skin-test procedure. Injection of small doses of the allergen into the skin of a sensitized individual results in the typical "wheal and flare" response. A modification of this procedure is the *Prausnitz-Küstner* reaction in

[4] Frankland, A. W. The Pathogenesis of Asthma, Hay Fever and Atopic Diseases. In *Clinical Aspects of Immunology*. P. G. H. Gell and R. R. A. Coombs (eds.). F. A. Davis Co., Philadelphia, 1963, pp. 338–59.

which a small quantity of serum from the sensitive individual is injected into the skin of a normal person. Several hours later the test allergen is injected into the same site in the skin. A positive test is characterized by the "wheal and flare" response resulting from the release of histamine by tissue-fixed reaginic antibodies combining with the allergen.

Desensitization is commonly practiced in the treatment of atopic hypersensitivity in man even though it cannot be accomplished as readily as in anaphylactic sensitivity. Of the atopic hypersensitivities, hay fever is probably the most amenable to desensitization. In those instances where the sensitivity is due to a specific allergen, ragweed pollen for example, desensitization is accomplished in a high percentage of patients by a series of subcutaneous injections of an extract of the pollen. The proposed mechanism for this desensitization is a conversion in the type of antibody produced by the body from a sensitizing type to a type that is capable of neutralizing the antigen. This neutralizing antibody has been termed "blocking" antibody and possesses characteristics that distinguish it from reaginic antibody. Asthma and atopic dermatitis may also be treated by a similar method of desensitization, but successful results are achieved somewhat less regularly than in hay fever patients.

### Type II Reaction

In the Type II reaction, antibody reacts with an antigenic component of a cell or with an antigen associated with a cell to bring about the cytolytic or cytotoxic destruction of that cell. Whether the destruction is by cytolytic or cytotoxic means is determined by the nature of the antibody and the kind of cell, with complement often involved in the reaction. In those instances where complement is involved, it probably mediates cell destruction by enzymic activity.

**Isoimmunologic Reaction.** The isoimmunologic reaction involves cell destruction as a result of antibodies *(isoantibodies)* of one individual of a species reacting with cell- or tissue-associated antigens *(isoantigens)* from another member of the same species. *Isoantigens* are those antigens associated with certain individuals but not all members of a species. *Isoantibodies* are the corresponding antibodies and are found naturally or develop from artificial stimulation in those members of a species not possessing the respective antigen. The isoantigens are broadly distributed in body cells and tissues, but those of erythrocytes, leucocytes, and platelets have received the most study. Isoantibodies may occur naturally as do the isoagglutinins in the ABO red cell system of man (see Chapter 10), be naturally stimulated as in the case of Rh immunization in primates, or be artificially induced. If a situation arises where cells possessing the isoantigen come in contact with the corresponding isoantibody in the presence of complement, cell destruction may follow.

***Transfusion Reaction.*** In man, the transfusion of blood from a donor into an incompatible recipient leads to destruction of the transfused erythrocytes. For example, if the donor is an A type individual with A antigen associated with the erythrocytes and these cells are transferred to a B type individual that possesses anti-A isoagglutinins, a transfusion reaction is the usual result. Since leucocytes and platelets also possess isoantigens, the interaction between these cells and the corresponding antibodies may lead to certain transfusion reactions not explainable on the basis of an erythrocyte system.

Transfusion reactions are not common in domestic animals because isoantibodies are either absent or present in extremely low titers. For this reason, transfusion reactions with an immunologic basis result only after repeated transfusions of blood from the same donor or a donor with the same isoantigens that are foreign to the recipient.

***Hemolytic Disease of the Newborn.*** This reaction occurs in man and many species of animals as a result of transfer of antibodies to red cell antigens of the fetus from the dam to her offspring. Genetic heterogeneity of the male and female may lead to a fetus possessing red cell antigens not possessed by the mother. When these red cells gain access to the maternal circulation, the mother produces antibodies. Subsequent transfer of these antibodies to the newborn animal may result in destruction of erythrocytes and hemolytic disease. The condition known as erythroblastosis fetalis in man that results from incompatabilities in the Rh blood type system is a good example. In those instances where the mother is Rh negative and the father is Rh positive, the fetus may be Rh positive. The mother may develop anti-Rh antibodies which are transferred to the fetus and cause lysis of the red cells of the fetus.

Hemolytic disease of the newborn occurs in horses and swine with essentially the same mechanism involved. In contrast to man where there is transplacental transfer of antibodies, the transfer takes place after birth in domestic animals by intestinal absorption of antibodies from the colostrum. A hemolytic anemia develops and may cause the death of the newborn animal. The disease is of adequate significance in horses to warrant a compatibility test of the foal's red cells and the mare's serum prior to allowing the foal to nurse.

***Isoallergic Neonatal Thrombocytopenia.*** In man, it has been reported that the mother may produce antibodies against platelet antigens of the fetus. Subsequent transfer of the antibodies to the fetus leads to platelet destruction and thrombocytopenia. The condition has also been reported in pigs in Norway. Clinically, the disease was observed to develop in pigs 5 days old and was characterized by unthriftiness, multiple petechial and ecchymotic hemorrhages, markedly reduced platelet count, reduced blood hemoglobin and death.

***Homograft Rejection.*** A piece of tissue or an organ transferred from one individual to another is called a homograft and, unless the individuals are genetically identical, is usually sloughed 10 to 14 days later. A skin homograft, for example, appears to be taking like an autograft for the first few days. Starting 7 to 10 days after placement of the graft, lymphocytes and plasma cells begin to invade the graft, circulation to the graft is disrupted, and the foreign tissue is sloughed or replaced by tissues of the recipient. A second skin homograft from the same donor is usually rejected even more rapidly *(second set phenomenon)* at a rate dependent on the nature of the first graft and its location on the recipient. However, a skin homograft from a different donor might be rejected by either a first or second set type of rejection. The rejection mechanism can be suppressed to some degree by agents such as irradiation, corticosteroids, and pyridoxine which inhibit immunologic responses. Further evidence that graft rejection has an immunologic basis resides in the findings that immunologic tolerance to homografts can be induced in fetal animals, antibodies are formed to tissue antigens and, while the rejection state cannot be transferred with immune serum, it can be with lymphoid cells from a sensitized individual.

The immunologic mechanism by which homografts are rejected is still open to question. Antibodies of various reactivities are formed to tissue antigens but their role in rejection of homografts has not been demonstrated. With certain exceptions, serum containing antibodies fails to bring about graft rejection and seems to argue against their involvement. However, lymphoid cells and leucocyte extracts are capable of transferring resistance to homografts and a typical delayed hypersensitivity reaction develops when a recipient animal that has rejected a homograft is injected intradermally with an extract of the homograft tissue. For these reasons, rejection of homografts may be due to a Type IV reaction or delayed hypersensitivity. The relative role of immediate and delayed hypersensitivity in homograft rejection is still subject to further experimentation.

**Anti-Tissue Reaction.** Certain species of animals possess naturally occurring Forssman antibody in their serum. Injection of this serum into an animal such as the guinea pig which has Forssman antigen as a constituent of its tissue cells results in a severe reaction characterized by vascular damage and hemorrhages. The reaction is produced by the cytotoxic action of the antibody and complement on tissue cells.

Under certain circumstances, an animal may become autosensitized, that is, be immunized against its own tissue or cellular antigens. This autosensitization may be of a cellular type (Type IV reaction) or it may be a result of antibody formation. Antibodies formed against autologous antigens are known as *autoantibodies* and may be responsible for autoimmune disease.

### Type III Reaction

The formation in vivo of complexes of antigen and antibody in moderate antigen excess may be locally toxic to tissues. Complement also probably participates in this reaction that brings about tissue damage by hormonal, vascular, and cytotoxic mechanisms. Complexes of antigen and antibody in proper proportions can bring about the release of histamine, cause aggregation of blood leucocytes, and alter local vascular endothelium to promote adherence of leucocytes, platelets, and fibrin. The clinical syndrome that results is determined by the nature of the complex, amount of complex, site of formation of the complex, and the histologic site of the reaction. Depending on the amount of complex formed and the site of reaction, the lesion may vary from transient polymorphonuclear infiltration and edema to extensive vascular thrombosis and local necrosis. Two clinical entities, the "Arthus reaction" and "serum sickness," result from a toxicity of this type and other clinical conditions may have a similar basis.

**Arthus Type Reactions.** The Arthus phenomenon results from the local injection of a soluble antigen into an animal that possesses the corresponding antibody in the circulation and tissues. The reaction is named after Maurice Arthus who first observed the response following subcutaneous injection of horse serum into immunized rabbits. Development of the reaction is dependent upon an adequate level of classical, precipitating antibody, an adequate quantity of antigen, and vascularity of the reaction site. One or two hours following injection of antigen into the skin of an immunized rabbit, swelling and hyperemia develop at the site. Subcutaneous edema and erythema increase during the next several hours, and petechial hemorrhages may appear. The reaction may proceed to necrosis in some situations but usually begins to subside after several hours. The extent of the reaction appears to be influenced by the quantity of antigen and antibody.

Extensive study utilizing special techniques has permitted microscopic visualization of the Arthus reaction during the various stages. Shortly after the injection of antigen, histologic sections observed with the fluorescent antibody procedure show antigen which is free or complexed with antibody in the tissue spaces. A few minutes later antigen-antibody complexes may be observed in the subendothelial layer between the endothelial cells and the basement membrane. The concentration of complexes in this location increases apparently as antibody from the circulation meets antigen diffusing from tissue spaces. Associated with the complexing of antigen and antibody are physiopathologic changes in the tissues. Approximately 15 minutes following the addition of antigen the flow of blood through the capillaries appears to slow, and clumps of platelets and polymorphonuclear cells appear within the venules. These clumps of cells then begin to adhere to the capillary and venule endothelium. Circulation through the small vessels may be obstructed as they become plugged with platelet-leucocyte thrombi. Vessel walls may rupture, permitting red cells and other blood components to escape into the extravascular spaces. Polymorphonuclear cells emigrate through the vessel walls and fluorescent antibody techniques indicate that they phagocytose the antigen-antibody complexes. Even though the polymorphonuclear cells digest the complexes quite rapidly, some cells are destroyed in the process. Consequently, macrophages are found to invade the lesion and phagocytose the cellular debris.

The mechanism of tissue damage is not completely understood, although the actual damage is done by the polymorphonuclear leucocytes. If neutrophils are removed temporarily from the circulation, the reaction is delayed until neutrophils again appear. The deposition of the antigen-antibody complexes in vascular walls establishes the environment for toxic activity mediated by the polymorphonuclear cells. While antigen-antibody complexes formed in vitro and injected may have some toxic activity, it is much reduced from that resulting from the formation of complexes in the tissues.

**Serum Sickness.** Serum sickness, as originally described, results from the therapeutic injection into man of an antiserum of heterologous origin. Seven to ten days following the injection of a foreign serum such as equine origin tetanus antitoxin, a reaction begins that occasionally results in death. Clinical manifestations of the reaction include fever, urticaria, edema of the eyelids, leucopenia, swollen and painful joints, reduction in serum complement levels, albuminuria, and occasionally hematuria. The reaction has an immunologic basis and results from the combination between the foreign serum protein and antibodies synthesized by the individual in response to the protein. Although antiserums used therapeutically in man are now enzyme-treated to reduce their antigenicity, approximately 5 per cent of individuals undergoing serotherapy develop serum sickness.

The clinical syndrome most commonly observed is probably a combination of Type I and Type III reactions. The fever, urticaria, edema, and asthmatic symptoms probably result in part from a Type I reaction. Superimposed on that reaction is a Type III response that involves tissue responses to the deposit of antigen-antibody complexes.

The mechanism of the reaction has been clarified by the enlightening work of Dixon and associates who used purified protein antigens in experimental animals. Bovine serum albumin, injected intravenously into rabbits, was removed from the circulation at approximately the same rate as autologous albumin until about the 8th day postinjection. Thereafter, the rate of removal was much more rapid until none could be detected by the 12th day. At this time, antibovine serum albumin antibodies began to appear in the circulation. Antibodies probably began to be secreted into the circulation at about the 7th or 8th day postinjection and complexed with the circulating antigen. Histologic observation of tissues during the period from the 8th to the 14th day showed a generalized arteritis affecting especially the renal glomeruli and endocardium. The condition produced in the rabbit has been termed "experimental glomerulonephritis." Antigen-antibody complexes formed in vitro and injected into rabbits may produce reactions, but they differ somewhat from the serum-sickness type of response. However, injection of in vitro-formed complexes into mice has produced experimental serum sickness.

Certain drugs such as penicillin are capable of producing serum-sickness-like syndromes in man. The reaction invariably develops a few days after penicillin treatment has been discontinued and is characterized by fever, joint pains, and urticaria. Apparently breakdown products of penicillin may bind to certain proteins to form a hapten-protein conjugate against which antibody may be formed. A chronic arteritic inflammation that may be an extension of acute serum sickness has been reported to result from sulfonamide therapy.

### Type IV Reaction

The Type IV reactions include those responses classed as delayed-type hypersensitivity. This reaction is characteristically different from immediate-type hypersensitivity in a number of respects. Induction of the response is commonly associated with an infectious process or application of certain chemical agents to the skin. However, a transient type of delayed hypersensitivity can be established to many purified protein antigens and a more lasting sensitivity to bacterial protein can be produced by using entire bacterial organisms. Passive sensitization can be accomplished only by the transfer of cells from peritoneal exudates, lymph nodes, spleen or blood leucocytes, or of extracts of such cells. The nature of the reactivity also differs from immediate hypersensitivity in that the response is delayed some hours after the individual is exposed to the antigen, reaches its peak after 24 to 72 hours, and may persist for several days. No specific shock organs are involved, but certain cells are responsive and accumulate at the site of antigenic localization to bring about the reaction. Type IV reactions include infection allergy, contact dermatitis, and Jones-Mote hypersensitivity.

**Infection Allergy.** Infection allergy is associated with certain of the fungal, viral, and chronic bacterial diseases. The classical example of this type of response is the tuberculin reaction. Intravenous or intramuscular injection of a small quantity of a protein extract of *Mycobacterium tuberculosis,* called *tuberculin,* into a normal animal fails to elicit a significant response. However, in a tuberculous individual a generalized reaction develops, characterized by changes in body temperature ranging from a moderate hyperthermia in mild reactions to a marked hypothermia in severe reactions. In addition, the animal becomes lethargic, "hunches up," shows respiratory disturbances, develops a marked leucopenia, and commonly dies. Necropsy discloses hemorrhages and congestion in the liver, spleen, lungs, adrenal glands, intestine, and around tubercular foci.

Injection of tuberculin into the skin of a tuberculous animal results in hyperemia and swelling developing at the injection site several hours later and progressing to an indurated lump in 24 to 72 hours. Histologically, the reaction is characterized by mononuclear cell invasion, with the cells congregating around blood vessels to form "perivascular islands." The early lesion is indicative of a vascular reaction with vasodilatation, thrombosis of some vessels, and diapedesis of leucocytes. However, macrophage and lymphocyte infiltration soon predominates. Only in severe reactions do appreciable numbers of polymorphonuclear cells accumulate, and this type of reaction is usually accompanied by necrosis. This severe reaction may be difficult to differentiate histologically from an Arthus reaction, although plasma cells accumulate in the Arthus lesion but are rare in the tuberculin reaction.

The immunologic response to *tuberculosis* contrasts with that to the majority of infectious agents in that delayed hypersensitivity predominates and circulating antibodies are extremely difficult to demonstrate. The reason for this happening is not understood, although the chemical composition of the organism or the intracellular nature of mycobacterial infections may be responsible. Neither is it known whether or not delayed-type hypersensitivity plays a role in immunity to tuberculosis, or even whether there is immunity to that disease. Recent evidence indicates that a cellular type of immunity can be induced in certain laboratory animals by the injection of an attenuated strain of *M. tuberculosis.* This immunity is characterized by enhanced phagocytic activity in engulfing and destroying virulent organisms. However, there is doubt that this activity relates to delayed hypersensitivity which is essentially an inflammatory type of reaction. This inflammatory response may be beneficial to the extent of localizing the invading microorganisms, but necrosis of tissue could lead to extensive dissemination and thereby contribute to the disease process.

Tuberculin hypersensitivity may be responsible for some of the lesions associated with tuberculosis. The tubercle bacillus would probably not be pathogenic if the organism were not so allergenic. The pathogenicity of the bacillus seems to be more related to its ability to survive and multiply in vivo rather than the elaboration of toxins. Aside from hypersensitivity, the organism possesses little power of producing tissue necrosis. This has been demonstrated in guinea pigs where injection of a culture of the bacillus or tuberculoprotein into a nonsensitized animal results in practically no tissue damage. However, injection of pathogenic or nonpathogenic tubercle bacilli into a sensitized animal precipitates a reaction that mimics lesions of tuberculosis. The same reaction can be produced in the lung of the sensitized guinea pig with tuberculoprotein incorporated in a vehicle that will hold the allergen at the site of reaction. The specificity of the reaction and the results of controlled experiments indicate that hypersensitivity may play a very important role in the pathogenesis of tuberculosis.

The tissue reactivity and damage resulting from delayed hypersensitivity of the tuberculin type probably results from an interaction between specifically sensitized cells and the allergen. There is no evidence to indicate that humoral antibody nor any pharmacological agent is involved in the reaction. While it was formerly thought that many cell types could be sensitized by the tubercle antigen, present knowledge indicates that the sensitivity is restricted to macrophages and lymphocytes.

Infection allergy is certainly not restricted to tuberculosis, for the state exists as a result of infection with a variety of bacteria. Delayed-type hypersensitivity may result from brucellosis, Johne's disease, tularemia, and glanders. While there is a tendency to associate the reaction with chronic infections, the allergic state can be demonstrated following more acute infections with such organisms as streptococci, staphylococci, and pneumococci. In every instance of bacterial allergy studied, the hypersensitivity exists to a protein fraction of the organism.

A state of hypersensitivity commonly results from infection of man and animals with fungal organisms. Allergy is most often observed with the systemic mycotic infections such as histoplasmosis, coccidioidomycosis, blastomycosis, and aspergillosis, but has also been reported to occur with superficial cutaneous infections. Available evidence indicates that the antigen associated with delayed-type hypersensitivity to fungi is polysaccharide in nature.

Delayed-type hypersensitivity has been reported to result from viral infections in man. The reaction is commonly seen following revaccination for smallpox and may be observed following infection with influenza, mumps, measles, and herpes viruses. It may be assumed that a similar reactivity occurs in domestic animals, although there is a lack of experimental evidence.

Infection allergy is of considerable importance in veterinary medicine, for the reaction provides the basis for diagnostic tests. The tuberculin test is the key to our bovine tuberculosis eradication program by providing a means for detecting infected animals. Similar tests are used for the diagnosis of Johne's disease in cattle, glanders in horses, and histoplasmosis, blastomycosis, and coccidioidomycosis in dogs.

**Contact Dermatitis.** A delayed-type hypersensitivity that involves primarily the skin may result from contact with a variety of plants, drugs, and chemicals. Contact of a sensitized individual with the inciting agent results in a rather prolonged inflammatory reaction. The first indication of the reaction is the appearance of erythema and papular lesions about 24 hours after exposure. The papules progress to vesicles and then to desquamation of the skin with oozing, crusted lesions. This reaction may continue for a week or longer before healing, with a degree of hyperkeratotic thickening, terminates the response.

A wide variety of substances has been incriminated as the causative agents of hypersensitive dermatitis. Plants, such as poison ivy and poison oak, and cotton seeds contain chemical substances that act as allergens. Penicillin, formalin, sulfonamides, quinine, nickel, and mercury have been reported to cause contact dermatitis. Induction of sensitivity usually takes place by entry of the agent through the skin or mucous membranes. Since many of the inciting agents are not antigenic per se, it is thought that they may complex with tissue proteins to form an antigenic material. Absorption through the skin is believed to be necessary for complexing to take place since injection of the substance does not usually lead to sensitization. Even though the allergen enters at only one site, sensitization is not restricted to that site but is general over the body. However, some skin areas of a sensitized individual are considerably more reactive than others.

The occurrence of contact dermatitis is quite interesting since certain individuals have a predisposition to sensitization while others are quite resistant. This predisposition seems to vary with the allergen in question, however, since some agents are capable of sensitizing a higher proportion of a population than are other substances.

**Jones-Mote Hypersensitivity.** A type of reactivity very similar to delayed-type hypersensitivity has been observed in man and animals following small injections of soluble protein antigens. Injections of antigen into the skin of sensitized individuals evoke a delayed reaction that resembles the tuberculin response grossly and histologically. The sensitization develops before circulating antibodies can be detected and seems to wane with the appearance of serum antibodies. Other characteristics of this so-called "Jones-Mote" hypersensitivity resemble infection allergy, but certain aspects of the two reactions cannot be equated. The reactions differ in the evanescence of the reaction, in their susceptibility to desensitization, and in the response that follows parenteral injection of antigen. Further experimentation should determine whether the reaction is a true Type IV hypersensitivity or belongs in another category.

**Desensitization.** Desensitization of the state of delayed hypersensitivity may be accomplished in some instances, but not nearly so readily as with hypersensitivity of the immediate type. In fact, when the two types of hypersensitivity coexist in an animal, they can often be dissociated by the desensitization process. Immediate hypersensitivity usually yields long before delayed hypersensitivity, which may not be overcome at all. However, persistent treatment of certain types has been successful in some cases of delayed hypersensitivity in man, particularly the contact hypersensitivities. Desensitization of infection allergy is probably very difficult to accomplish, although there are indications that this occurs naturally. In cattle, for example, the animal in the early stages of tuberculosis is usually highly sensitive, but it is not unusual for the advanced case to have lost the sensitivity. Whether this is due to a specific desensitization from tuberculin release in the animal or nonspecific as a result of general debilitation is still open to question. Hypersensitivity of the "Jones-Mote" type also seems to spontaneously disappear.

## Hypersensitive-like Reactions

Man and animals are subject to other hypersensitivities in which the exact mechanisms are unknown. An immunologic basis has been suggested for the reactions to be discussed, although no clear-cut evidence is available. Among the various reactions, physical allergy, the Shwartzman phenomenon, and anaphylactoid reactions appear to have significance in veterinary medicine.

**Physical Allergy.** Physical agents such as cold, heat, and sunlight may elicit such local responses as urticaria and angioedema or generalized responses such as fever, headache, tachycardia, and collapse in certain individuals. The reactions probably result from histamine release but the mechanism for the release of histamine is not clear. The possibility exists that physical agents may act directly on cells to bring about the release of histamine. A second possibility involves some type of immunologic mechanism to mediate the release of histamine. The hypothetical basis for an immunological mechanism would have the physical agent either: (1) influencing an antigen-antibody reaction, (2) altering tissues to bring about the formation of anti-tissue antibodies, or (3) enhancement of an already existing hypersensitive state.

A role for light in physical allergy is particularly interesting since "photosensitivity" reactions involving sunlight are not uncommon in animals. Animals feeding on certain plants or grains such as buckwheat or being treated with drugs such as sulfanilamide may react on exposure to sunlight. While certain of these reactions are due to the localization of photoreactive substances in the tissues and are not immunologic in nature, other responses are probably related to immunologic mechanisms.

**Shwartzman Phenomenon.** A local tissue reactivity following two appropriately spaced injections of bacterial endotoxin was described by Shwartzman in 1928. An initial or preparatory dose of *B. typhosus* culture filtrate was injected intradermally into rabbits and followed by an intravenous-provoking dose of the same filtrate 24 hours later. Four hours after the intravenous injection, severe hemorrhagic necrosis appeared at the prepared site. Grossly it was dark blue, swollen, with an angry red periphery, and histologically it showed disruption of the venules, extensive hemorrhage, thrombosis, and necrobiosis of all the cells. The reaction extended from the superficial layers of the skin through the entire thickness of the abdominal wall to the peritoneum. Subsequently, Shwartzman demonstrated that other tissues and organs could be prepared and provoked in a similar manner. Further, he discovered that unrelated endotoxins could act as the provoking agent. Other workers have since demonstrated that such unrelated agents as antigen-antibody complexes, glycogen, starch, and kaolin may have the same effect.

In 1935 Apitz first described the generalized Shwartzman reaction. In this reaction both injections of endotoxin are given intravenously, and the most striking and most constant lesions produced in rabbits consist of bilateral renal cortical necrosis and hemorrhage. Although unrelated endotoxins can serve as provoking agents in this reaction, other unrelated compounds are less successful in producing the reaction.

Current information indicates that the basic mechanisms operating in the local and the generalized Shwartzman reaction are identical and that many factors may be involved in the production of the lesions. One factor commonly involved in production of the lesions is an altered local tissue metabolism produced by the preparatory dose of endotoxin. Following the provoking dose of endotoxin, it appears that damage to the endothelium, vasoconstriction, the formation of leucocyte and platelet thrombi, the intravascular precipitation of fibrinoid material, and depression of the function of the reticuloendothelial system are all involved in causing thrombosis in the vessels of the prepared tissue. This thrombosis and the subsequent anoxia result in the characteristic hemorrhagic and necrotic changes which are typical of the local and generalized Shwartzman reaction.

**Anaphylactoid Reactions.** A variety of substances are capable of eliciting a shock syndrome resembling anaphylaxis following parenteral injection. The reaction is apparently mediated by histamine, but the mechanism of release is not known. In addition, the lesions that are observed at necropsy differ in some ways from those of generalized anaphylaxis. Such substances as snake venom, bee venom, India ink, colloidal iron, sodium citrate, tragacanth, and aggregated globulins have been observed to elicit such a reaction, although the lesions may vary somewhat with different substances. The anaphylaxis-like reaction observed in pigs following injection of anti-hog cholera serum probably belongs in this category. Pasteurization of the serum aggregates gamma globulins, and complement may be fixed by the aggregates. Recent evidence indicates that the first component of complement is converted to an esterase when fixed and that the esterase is capable of causing the formation of a substance called *anaphylatoxin*. Anaphylatoxin is responsible for mediating the anaphylactoid reaction.

## REFERENCES


ANDREWS, J. M. Parasitism and Allergy. Jour. Parasitol. 48:3, 1962.

APITZ, K. J. A Study of the Generalized Shwartzman Phenomenon. Jour. Immunol. 29:255, 1935.

ARTHUS, M. Injections Répetées de Serum de Cheval Chez Le Lapin. Comp. rend. Soc. Biol. (Paris). 55:817, 1903.

BALYEAT, R. M. Allergic Diseases: Their Diagnosis and Treatment. 4th Ed. F. A. Davis Co., Philadelphia, 1936.

BENJAMINI, E., *et al.* Skin Reactivity in Guinea Pigs Sensitized to Flea Bite: The Sequence of Reactions. Proc. Soc. Exp. Biol. Med. 108:700, 1961.

BRADFORD, F. J., and BRADFORD, V. M. Allergic Dermatosis in the Cow. No. Amer. Vet. 32:396, 1951.

BROWNLEE, A. Allergy in the Domestic Animals. Jour. Comp. Path. Therap. 53:55–74, 1940.

BURNS, P. W. Allergic Reactions in Dogs. Jour. Amer. Vet. Med. Assn. 83:627–37, 1933.

COOKE, R. A. Allergy in Theory and Practice. W. B. Saunders Co., Philadelphia, 1947.

CROWLE, A. J. Delayed Hypersensitivity in Health and Disease. Charles C Thomas, Springfield, Ill., 1962.

DALE, H. H. The Pharmacology of Histamine With a Brief Survey of Evidence for Its Occurrence, Liberation and Participation in Natural Reactions. Ann. N.Y. Acad. Sci. 40:1017, 1950.

DAVIES, G. O. Hypersensitiveness in Animals. Vet. Rec. 58:285–87, 1946.

DOERR, R., and RUSS, V. K. Analyse des Präzipitationsphanomens mit Hilfe der anaphylaktischen Reaktion. Ztsch. f. Immunitätsf. Exper. Therap. 5:125, 1910.

DRAGSTEDT, C. A. Anaphylaxis. Physiol. Rev. 21:563, 1941.

GELL, P. G. H., and COOMBS, R. R. A. (eds.). Clinical Aspects of Immunology. F. A. Davis Co., Philadelphia, 1963.

HUMPHREY, J. H., and WHITE, R. G. Immunology for Students of Medicine. F. A. Davis Co., Philadelphia, 1963.

JOSHUA, J. O. Some Allergic Conditions in the Dog and Cat. Vet. Rec. 68:682–85, 1956.

LAWRENCE, H. S. (ed.). Cellular and Humoral Aspects of the Hypersensitive States. Paul Hoeber, Inc., New York, 1959.

NAJJR, V. A., and ROBINSON, J. P. A Unified Concept of Immunologic Reactions and Allergic States. *In* Immunity and Virus Infections. V. Najjar (ed.). John Wiley & Sons, Inc., New York, 1959.

OVARY, Z., *et al.* Properties of Guinea Pig 7s Antibodies. Jour. Exp. Med. 117:951, 1963.

PATTERSON, R., *et al.* Spontaneous Canine Hypersensitivity to Ragweed. Characterization of the Serum Factor Transferring Skin, Bronchial and Anaphylactic Sensitivity. Jour. Immunol. 90:35, 1963.

POMEROY, B. S. Allergy and Allergic Skin Reactions in the Dog. Cornell Vet. 24:335, 1934.

RAFFEL, S. Immunity. 2nd Ed. Appleton-Century-Crofts, Inc., New York, 1961.

ROSENAU, M. J., and ANDERSON, J. F. No. 29—A Study of the Cause of Sudden Death Following the Injection of Horse Serum. No. 45—Further Studies Upon Anaphylaxis. Bull. U.S. Hyg. Lab. No. 29, 1906 and No. 45, 1908.

SAMPTER, M., and ALEXANDER, H. L. (eds.). Immunological Diseases. Little, Brown and Co., Boston, 1966.

SCHLOTTHAUER, C. F. Anaphylaxis Associated With Treatment of an Enzootic Disease of Calves. No. Amer. Vet. 14:24–27, 1933.

SCHNELLE, G. B. Eczema in Dogs—an Allergy. No. Amer. Vet. 14:37–44, 1933.

SCHROEDER, C. R Classification of the Phenomena of Specific Sensitivity in Lower Animals. Jour. Amer. Vet. Med. Assn. 106:351–54, 1945.

SHAFFER, J. H., *et al.* (eds.). Mechanisms of Hypersensitivity. Little, Brown and Co., Boston, 1959.

SHWARTZMAN, G. Phenomenon of Local Skin Reactivity to Culture Filtrates of Various Microorganisms. Proc. Soc. Exp. Biol. Med. 26:207, 1928.

———. Phenomenon of Local Tissue Reactivity. Paul Hoeber, Inc., New York, 1937.

STORMORKEN, H., *et al.* Thrombocytopenic Bleedings in Young Pigs Due to Maternal Isoimmunization. Nature 198:1116–17, 1963.

TUFT, L. Clinical Allergy. W. B. Saunders Co., Philadelphia, 1938.

VAUGHAN, W. T , and BLACK, J. H. Practice of Allergy. 2nd Ed. C. V. Mosby Co., St. Louis, 1948.

VON PIRQUET, C. Allergie. Münch. mëd. Wschr. 53:1457, 1906.

WEIL, A. J., and REDDIN, L. Supersensitivity in Cattle. Jour. Immunol. 46:345–52, 1943.

WITTICH, F. A. Spontaneous Allergy (Atopy) in the Lower Animal. Jour. Allergy 12:247, 1941.

ZEISSIG, A Hypersensitivity in Domestic Animals. Jour. Amer. Vet. Med. Assn. 88:139–53, 1936.

# PART 3

# Classification and Characteristics of Pathogenic Microorganisms

# 14

# The Classification and Nomenclature of Bacteria

One of the cardinal characteristics of nature is the orderliness of living things. All animals and plants are divided into distinct species. These species of animals and plants are able to reproduce only with their kind. Since this is a genetic truth, similar individuals are reproduced, and the orderliness of all nature is continued. Such simple forms as bacteria follow the same genetic rules as animals and plants. The bacteria, therefore, are classified and named in the same manner as animals and plants, and, as a result, definite information concerning the various groups is available. Furthermore, it is possible to learn the names and to correlate the activities and characteristics of one group with those of another.

Since the bacteria are classified as plants, the system of botanical nomenclature proposed by the Swedish biologist, Carl von Linné (Linnaeus), during the years 1750 and 1760, is taken as the starting point for bacterial nomenclature. In 1773–74 the Danish naturalist, Otto Frederich Müller, arranged the bacteria then known into a system which was subsequently enlarged in 1786. C. G. Ehrenberg extended this classification in 1838 and added the descriptions of numerous types of protozoa and bacteria. During the period between 1872–76, the most fundamental early contributions to the subject of classification were made by Ferdinand Cohn who differentiated between the bacteria and protozoa; his classification has been used as the basis of those which have followed.

The rapid discovery of all the various species of bacteria, as well as characteristics so significant to health and comfort of man, has made the subject of the classification of bacteria a most complex one. The systems of classification now in use have developed about the work of Buchanan, of the various committees on classification and nomenclature of the Society of American Bacteriologists, of the International Society of Microbiologists, and of the National Botanical Congress, as well as of the various contributors throughout numerous editions of *Bergey's Manual of Determinative Bacteriology*. It is obvious that there should be an international system of classification and nomenclature, and as knowledge of the bacteria increases, changes in existing systems will be made. This is an inevitable mark of progress. It must be recognized that bacteriology, as a science, is still quite young and that it takes time to reach the period of organization so characteristic of middle and old age. The student, therefore, must expect to replace new names for old from time to time and to look for a well-known organism in a group different from the one of which he has learned that it is a member.

## RULES OF BACTERIOLOGICAL NOMENCLATURE

Since the time of Linnaeus, botanists and

zoologists have followed the binominal system of nomenclature. Numerous other rules have been adopted from time to time until the lists of rules of Zoological Nomenclature and of Botanical Nomenclature are quite extensive. In 1958 an International Code of Nomenclature of Bacteria and Viruses was published by the Judicial Commission, International Committee on Bacteriological Nomenclature of the International Association of Microbiological Societies. This code culminated the work of a committee of which Buchanan was chairman, and is the guide to which all bacteriologists should adhere.

It is not within the scope and purpose of this text to list all of the rules for naming bacteria. It is desirable, however, that students become familiar with a few of the general principles which are followed.

1. The scientific name of a microorganism is composed of two words, both Latin.

2. The name does not need to be a descriptive one; in fact, descriptive names are apt to be misleading. The name *Staphylococcus aureus* is descriptive of the golden staphylococcus; however, it is now recognized that this organism may become nonpigmented, or white; yet it retains all of its other characteristics. Descriptive names given to bacteria years ago often lose their significance in light of new discoveries. When descriptive names are used, there is a marked tendency to use more than the one species name; this leads to such absurd names as *Bacillus saccharobutyricus fluorescens liquefaciens.*

3. The first name of the organism is a proper noun and always begins with a capital letter. It is the *genus* name of the group to which the organism belongs. The name *Staphylococcus* is a generic name.

4. The second name begins with a small letter and designates the species of the organism. If it is an adjective it must agree grammatically with the generic name *Streptococcus pyogenes* and if it is a noun modifying the generic name, it must be in the possessive case, *Streptococcus equi.*

5. Bacteria are classified into the various taxonomic groups as are animals and plants, hence:

every individual belongs to a species,
every species belongs to a genus,
every genus belongs to a family,
every family belongs to an order,
every order belongs to a class,
every class belongs to a phylum,
and every phylum belongs to a kingdom.

The names of the different groups take different endings. These are illustrated by listing the various taxonomic groups of *Staphylococcus aureus.*

Species—aureus
Genus—Staphylococcus
Family—Micrococcaceae—ending *aceae*
Order—Eubacteriales—ending *ales*
Class—Schizomycetes—ending *cetes*
Phylum—Thallophyta—ending *a*
Kingdom—Plant

If a greater number of intermediate categories are required for lucid classification, subclasses, suborders, subfamilies, tribes and subtribes, subgenera and subspecies, or varieties may be designated.

## BASES FOR BACTERIOLOGICAL CLASSIFICATION

Bacteria are classified by using any of the characteristics which fall under the following general heads:

1. *Morphology.* Morphology is used for differentiation whenever practical. For example, the bacteria are placed in the plant kingdom, the class schizomycetes, into the various orders, and into families largely on this basis.

2. *Physiology.* When considering the more closely related groups, such as the genera, physiological characteristics must be used. For example, the sporeforming, rod-shaped bacteria are placed into the family *Bacillaceae* on the basis of morphology. The two genera *Bacillus* and *Clostridium* are formed, however, on the basis of physiological function, oxygen relationship.

3. *Antigenicity.* Within the genus and in some cases the formation of subspecies, the antigenic structure of bacteria forms

the basis for differentiation. The antigenic relationships of bacteria are detected by the use of serological tests, such as agglutination and precipitation. The value of the use of antigenic structure is noted in the differentiation of the pneumococci into different strains. The species of the genus Salmonella are classified largely upon the basis of antigenic differences.

4. *Pathology*. Bacteria are not grouped into species or genera on the basis of the different types of diseases which are produced; yet the specific pathology of disease is acknowledged as one of the important characteristics of pathogenic bacteria and, from the point of view of medical bacteriology, is not given the prominence it deserves. The type of infection which the organism causes enters into the coining of names such as *Streptococcus pyogenes* and *Salmonella choleraesuis*.

All of the different characteristics considered pertinent to the complete description of bacteria are included in a chart which has been compiled by the Committee on Bacteriological Technic of the Society of American Bacteriologists.

## THE RELATIONSHIP OF BACTERIAL VARIATION TO CLASSIFICATION

Early workers in bacteriology described cultures which are recognized today as being composed of a number of different species of bacteria. For example, Hallier described as pure cultures what were actually numerous types of bacteria; he pictured them as varying in morphology from short rods to forms as complex as molds. Obviously such cultures were not pure, but were contaminated with Aspergillus and Penicillium molds. As methods of obtaining pure cultures of bacteria became available, it was concluded that a pure culture was composed of only one definite type of an organism and that the daughter cell always produced a type of cell, a type of colony, and a type of physiology exactly like that of the mother cell. This conception, aptly called monomorphism, held sway for many years.

As the study of bacteria progressed, it became increasingly apparent that bacteria do vary from the accepted normal forms under certain conditions. This variation, transformation, or dissociation may be morphological or physiological. Some variations appear spontaneously in a culture while others develop slowly, usually augmented by the environment of the culture.

Numerous examples of morphological dissociation may be cited. Changes in the shape of the individual cells of a culture are often observed. A particular organism may be ovoid on solid media but an elongated bacillus in a fluid medium. *E. coli* is normally a flagellated organism when grown in fluid media, yet may not develop flagella when grown for some time on solid media. *Bacillus anthracis,* when grown on a common nutrient medium, is noncapsulated; yet when it is grown on a medium containing a carbohydrate and serum, it will produce a capsule. This same bacillus normally produces spores, but one of the classical experiments performed by Pasteur was to develop a nonsporeproducing culture by cultivation at 42°C.

Greatest emphasis has been given to the different types of colony variations which appear in cultures. These variations often explain the differences in virulence of a bacterial culture. The cocci and gram-negative bacteria normally grow in a type of colony which is smooth (S). However, colonies of this type of microorganism are often encountered which are mucoid (M), and sometimes, when grown on a less nutritive medium, may form rough (R) colonies. In some instances these variations are reversible, but many of the variants are permanent. The R form appears to represent the last stage in reproductive maturity. An organism in its S form has an antigenic structure more complete than in the R form. An organism in the M form is often more virulent when in the S form; however, the S form is more virulent than the R form. Under conditions of artificial cultivation the variation is from S to R, presumably because the individual cells of the R colony are more able to subsist on the food available in artificial media. When such a culture is injected into a susceptible animal and disease results, the S form of the organism is usually isolated. In this instance, the fluids and cells of the animal body apparently provide the nutrient substances essential for the growth of S type organisms. Since they are more virulent than R, they resist body defenses, such as phagocytosis, reproduce at a greater rate, and consequently predominate in the culture.

In certain types of bacteria the R type of colony represents the normal virulent phase. For example, *Bacillus anthracis* is normally R, and when variant S type colonies appear they are less virulent. Colonies of virulent *Myco. tuberculosis* are of the R type.

The change from S to R may occur suddenly or slowly. In the latter instance intermediate variants are observed. These colonies are designated as SR, Sr, or sR depending upon which type the new colony most nearly resembles. These intermediate types are not as stable as the S and R types, showing a tendency to revert to either permanent S or R types of colonies.

Numerous examples of physiological variation could be cited. Some of these are examples of a rather specific mutation, while others appear to be merely adaptive processes of the organism. As long ago as 1907 Massini observed that a nonlactose-fermenting strain of *E. coli* would develop the ability to ferment lactose when grown in the presence of that carbohydrate. This property was reflected in the type of colony which developed in the mother nonlactose-fermenting colony. The loss or acquisition of the ability to ferment a certain carbohydrate appears to be a variant property of many bacteria. Upon this criterion, strains of a given species of a bacterium are recognized. *Sal. pullorum,* for example, is not recognized usually as a maltose-fermenting organism. However, well-defined strains of this bacterium are isolated which do produce acid from maltose. These are referred to as maltose-fermenting strains. Other examples of other physiological reactions of bacteria could be cited, such as variation in $H_2S$ production and nitrate reduction. Many of these variations are due apparently to the adaptive nature of the enzyme systems of bacteria. The enzymes are formed under the influence of the presence of the substrate, calling into action, as it were, certain enzymes which have become dormant but which awaken and become active when a certain type of food is present. This same adaptable property of bacteria is observed when a culture grows not at all or at least poorly upon primary isolation from animal tissue, but grows abundantly after it has been cultivated on artificial medium for some time. This fact often explains the different results obtained in the study of one species of an organism by different investigators. One has studied recently isolated strains while the other has studied old laboratory strains. Their results may agree, in the main, but differences in detailed reactions are common.

Previous mention has been made of the loss of virulence when an organism dissociates from an S colony to an R. Variations in virulence are encountered when there are no visible changes in the type of colony. Loss of virulence, commonly called attenuation, often occurs when cultures are grown artificially for some time. When the various factors which make up the composite picture of virulence are reviewed, it is obvious that certain properties would be lost under artificial conditions, and promptly regained when under natural conditions. The loss of toxin production may mean a great deal in terms of disease, but may mean very little in the life of a microorganism. There is a tendency on the part of many investigators to overemphasize the significance of many physiological processes. There are instances when variable reactions should be considered the rule rather than the exception.

Since the advent of antibiotic agents, another variable characteristic, drug fastness of bacteria, has been introduced. Among the staphylococci, for example, it is not unusual to find strains which are extremely resistant to penicillin. The same is true of many other species which normally are considered to be sensitive to a certain antibiotic agent. In some instances this resistance is an inheritable characteristic of the strain, and in other instances drug fastness is developed as a result of contact of the organism with the drug. This becomes a serious matter when it becomes apparent that a penicillin-resistant strain of organism is developed and may become widespread throughout a herd. In the treatment of tuberculosis of man with streptomycin, it is found that certain cases of that disease are caused by streptomycin-resistant strains of tubercle bacilli. Such instances are quite unfortunate, and other means of treatment must be provided. The explanation of the acquisition of drug fastness by bacteria will not be available until the reason for drug sensitivity becomes known.

## BACTERIAL GENETICS

The relationships of bacterial variation or transformation to bacterial genetics present an interesting phase of bacteriology. Upon first thought, the viruses may be considered to represent the most primitive forms of life, because of their size. However, when the specific cell-parasite nature of viruses is recognized, it is apparent that these forms probably represent the very advanced forms of living agents. The autotrophic bacteria, those which derive their energy from the oxidation of simple inorganic compounds, more nearly represent the most primitive type of life—probably the beginning of life on our planet. It is apparent that as the tremendous numbers of different types of bacteria have developed a parasitic existence on man, plants, and animals, a process of bacterial genetics was in operation. It is entirely conceivable and probable that this process continues, and such examples given in the foregoing discussion are only expressions of evolution.

As research progresses it is becoming more certain that bacteria possess a genetic mechanism. True, it is not the same as in higher plants and in animals. Nevertheless, the changes discussed above—changes from S to R colonies, loss of capsules, fermentation changes, and antibiotic resistance—may be expressions of genetic mechanisms.

Bacteria have not been considered to possess a particulate nucleus, but the nuclear material is well distributed throughout the cell. It has been assumed that bacteria divide by simple fission, each daughter cell being exactly the same as the mother cell. In other words, the nuclear material of the mother cell has been divided equally with the two daughter cells. In higher organisms, plants, and animals, sexual reproduction takes place. Individual characteristics are contained in the genes which are distributed on the chromosomes of the male and female. When fertilization occurs, the chromosomes become "intertwined," with the resulting new individual possessing characteristics of both parents. Genes are essentially nucleic acids which are the fundamental bases on which the science of genetics is based. Nucleic acids combine with proteins to form nucleoproteins, which in various forms are in all living cells. Nucleic acid can be separated from proteins by hydrolysis, yielding phosphoric acid and nucleotide. The nucleotide may be called ribonucleic acid, RNA, if 5-carbon sugar (pentose) is ribose. However, if the pentose is deoxyribose, the nucleic acid is called deoxyribonucleic acid, DNA. In addition, two purine bases, adenine and guanine, and two pyrimidine bases, cytosine and thymine, are present. The double-stranded helix of DNA is composed of phosphate and deoxyribose sugar. The adenine of one strand is attached to the guanine of the other, and the cytosine of one strand is attached to the thymine of the other. Inasmuch as the arrangement of these molecules is practically limitless, the genetic "messages" they transmit are multitudinous. Disarrangements or rearrangements of DNA are considered to be the cause of mutations.

Bacterial geneticists believe that transfer of nuclear (DNA) material from one bacterium to another may take place under certain conditions. This process, called *transformation,* may explain some of the variation changes previously discussed.

Bacteriophage (phage) or bacterial virus is known to play an important role in bacterial genetics. The genetic substance of phage is ribonucleic acid (RNA). Bacterial viruses invade the bacterial cells, live upon the cytoplasm of these cells, and multiply therein. They cause the disruption of the cell, liberating the virus particles. These invade other cells and the process is repeated. During this procedure RNA becomes involved with DNA of the bacterial cell, and the resulting combination is carried to the newly invaded bacterial cells which may be changed in various ways. This process is called *transduction*. Phage may also cause *conversion,* a process whereby the bacterial cell is converted into some function it did not originally possess.

Bacteria have been shown to undergo a process similar to that of higher animals and plants, that is, sexual reproduction. However, among bacteria, it is known as *recombination*. In this process parent strains of bacteria recombine to form offspring which have different characteristics than either parent. Evidently DNA of one parent becomes absorbed by the other, resulting in a different offspring.

The subject of bacterial genetics is becoming quite complex and the foregoing discussion is an oversimplification of the subject. The student is urged to study some of the references given at the end of the chapter for further information.

It must be emphasized that in the majority of cases bacteria multiply by direct fission and the resulting cultures are like the parent ones. Nevertheless, over the period of millions of years the bacteria, like the plants and animals, have been undergoing the relentless process of evolution. We study them as we find them today.

## THE SYSTEMATIC ARRANGEMENT OF BACTERIA

Reference to the position of the bacteria in the plant kingdom was made in Chapter 2; consequently, it is not necessary to repeat that classification here. The phylum Thallophyta is divided into different classes among which is the class Schizomycetes. This class is divided into eight different orders on the basis of morphology. These are listed as follows: I. Eubacteriales, II. Actinomycetales, III. Spirochaetales, IV. Rickettsiales, V. Thiobacteriales, VI. Chlamydobacteriales, VII. Caulobacteriales, and VIII. Myxobacteriales. Of these, the first four contain species of bacteria which produce diseases in animals and man. The orders are divided into numerous families which in turn are divided into tribes; the tribes are divided into genera, and the genera into species.

In most of the systematic bacterial classifications which have been published, the organisms are arranged in what is known as a key. There are a number of types of keys, but the dichotomous key is the type used most often, and it is most satisfactory. In a dichotomous key the organisms are divided into two groups on the basis of a differentiating characteristic; these two groups are in turn divided into two others, and so on until only one group remains; for example:

a. Cells spherical
  b. Cells gram-positive
    c. cells aerobic
    cc. cells anaerobic
  bb. Cells gram-negative
aa. Cells not spherical

Any of the different characteristics of bacteria may be used in forming a key. The orders, families, tribes, genera, and species are usually divided by means of a key. Such a key is found in *Bergey's Manual of Determinative Bacteriology*. The student will become familiar with the use of these keys in his laboratory work.

A list of the orders, families, and genera which contain species of bacteria producing diseases in man and animals is given below. The species which make up each generic group will be discussed in detail in chapters devoted entirely to them.

| *Order* | *Family* | *Genus* |
|---|---|---|
| Eubacteriales | Pseudomonadaceae | Pseudomonas |
| | | Vibrio |
| | Micrococcaceae | Staphylococcus |
| | Neisseriaceae | Neisseria |
| | Lactobacteriaceae | Diplococcus |
| | | Streptococcus |
| | Corynebacteriaceae | Corynebacterium |
| | | Listeria |
| | | Erysipelothrix |
| | Achromobacteriaceae | Alcaligenes |
| | | Aeromonas |
| | Enterobacteriaceae | Escherichia |
| | | Aerobacter |
| | | Klebsiella |
| | | Proteus |
| | | Salmonella |
| | | Shigella |
| | Brucellaceae | Pasteurella |
| | | Bordetella |
| | | Malleomyces |
| | | Actinobacillus |
| | | Brucella |
| | | Bacterioides |
| | | Spherophorus |
| | | Hemophilus |
| | | Moraxella |
| | Bacillaceae | Bacillus |
| | | Clostridium |
| Actinomycetales | Mycobacteriaceae | Mycobacterium |
| | Actinomycetaceae | Nocardia |
| | | Actinomyces |
| Spirochaetales | Spirochaetaceae | Spirochaeta |
| | Treponemataceae | Borrelia |
| | | Treponema |
| | | Leptospira |
| Rickettsiales | Rickettsiaceae | Rickettsia |
| | | Ehrlichia |
| | | Coxiella |
| | | Cowdria |
| | | Neorickettsia |
| | | Wolbachia |
| | | Symbiotes |
| | | Rickettsiella |
| | Chlamydiaceae | Chlamydia |
| | | Ricolesia |
| | | Coletsia |
| | Bartonellaceae | Bartonella |
| | | Grahamella |
| | | Haemobartonella |
| | | Eperythrozoon |
| | Anaplasmataceae | Anaplasma |
| Mycoplasmatales | Mycoplasmataceae | Mycoplasma |

## REFERENCES

ADELBERG, E. A., *et al.* Papers on Bacterial Genetics. Little, Brown and Co., Boston, 1960.

BREED, R. S., *et al.* Bergey's Manual of Determinative Bacteriology. 7th Ed. Williams & Wilkins Co., Baltimore, 1957.

BUCHANAN, R. E. General Systematic Bacteriology. Williams & Wilkins Co., Baltimore, 1925.

———, and BUCHANAN, ESTELLE D. Bacteriology. 5th Ed. Macmillan Co., New York, 1951.

———, *et al.* International Bacteriological Code of Nomenclature. Jour. Bact. 55:287–306, 1948.

BURROWS, WILLIAM. Textbook of Microbiology. 16th Ed. W. B. Saunders Co., Philadelphia, 1954.

DUBOS, R. J. The Bacterial Cell. Harvard Univ. Press, Cambridge, 1945.

HAYES, W. The Genetics of Bacteria and Their Viruses. John Wiley & Sons. Inc., New York, 1964.

INTERNATIONAL CODE OF NOMENCLATURE OF BACTERIA and VIRUSES. Iowa State Univ. Press, Ames, 1958.

Jacob, F., and Wollman, E. L. Sexuality and the Genetics of Bacteria. Academic Press, New York, 1961.
Luria, S. E. Recent Advances in Bacterial Genetics. Bact. Rev. 11:1–40, 1947.
Skerman, V. B. D. A Guide to the Identification of the Genera of Bacteria. Williams & Wilkins Co., Baltimore, 1959.
Smith, D. T., and Conant, N. F. (eds.). Zinsser Microbiology. 13th Ed. Appleton-Century-Crofts, Inc., New York, 1964.
Timakov, V. D. Microbial Variation. Pergamon Press, New York, 1959.

# 15

# The Genus Streptococcus

THE STREPTOCOCCUS GROUP INCLUDES ALL OF those bacteria which are spherical and usually occur in chains of variable lengths. All of the species described are gram-positive. Spores are never produced. The various species show differences in their ability to produce acid from carbohydrates. In general, they produce scant, dewdrop-like growth on the surface of culture media, preferring enriched media and microaerophilic conditions. They are widely distributed, but are most common upon the skin, mucous membranes, and in the intestines of man and animals, as well as in milk. They are not common as saprophytes in nature apart from animals or their excretions.

## CLASSIFICATION

In the early observations of micrococci by Pasteur, Koch, and other investigators, no attempt was made to separate them according to cell arrangement. Rivolta described chain-forming cocci in pus from cases of strangles in the horse in 1873. Ogston (1881) was apparently the first to show that the micrococci were associated with various types of infections in man and that they could be separated into two groups, those growing in chains and those in grape-like clusters. In 1883 Fehleisen described a chain-forming coccus as the cause of erysipelas in man. The following year Rosenbach isolated from an abscess in man a coccus to which he gave the name *Streptococcus pyogenes,* thus establishing the genus name *Streptococcus.* The relationship of a streptococcus to scarlet fever was first demonstrated by Klein in 1886 when he isolated *Micrococcus scarlatinae* from the throats of scarlet fever patients and traced the source of the infection to milk. Nocard and Mollereau, in 1887, isolated a streptococcus from a cow, with which they produced experimental mastitis in a cow and in a goat. As a result of the isolation of streptococci from specific diseases there was a tendency to consider each a separate species and to give it a name similar to the disease produced.

Lingelsheim, in 1891, suggested that two types, to be known as *Streptococcus longus* and *Streptococcus brevis,* be recognized; he believed the more virulent forms produce long chains, usually of more than six cells, and the less virulent forms short chains with fewer than six cells. A strict adoption of this classification proved impractical because variations occurred in different media and under different environments.

Schottmüller's classification in 1903 proposed the use of blood agar in differentiation. The more virulent types he termed *Str. longus* or *Str. erysipelatos.* These formed long chains and hemolyzed blood cells. His *Str. mitis* or *Str. viridans* were found to be less virulent, to produce shorter chains, and to be devoid of the power of hemolysis. His *Str. mucosus* proved to be an encapsulated form and more closely related to the pneumococci.

The classification proposed by Andrewes and Horder in 1906, and adopted by Winslow and Winslow in 1908, was the first to use a combination of pathogenicity and fermentation as a basis of differentiation.

This classification considered only one pathogenic species, *Str. pyogenes;* the remaining five were saprophytic.

Smith and Brown, in 1915, separated pathogenic streptococci which were obtained from milk-borne tonsillitis patients into two groups on the basis of hemolysis. One group, *alpha* hemolytic, produced a greenish discoloration and partial hemolysis of the blood corpuscles surrounding the colony; the other, *beta* group, produced a zone of complete hemolysis around the colony on blood agar.

In 1916 Holman published a classification of the streptococci in which he divided them into two groups on the basis of hemolysis, and subsequently divided each subgroup by means of carbohydrate fermentation. This classification has served as the basis of most of the systematic treatises on the streptococci since that time.

Brown set forth in 1919, in a most comprehensive report, the criteria for studying the hemolytic streptococci and strengthened the position of the different types which he and Smith had described previously. He recognized and described four types which could be distinguished by their action or lack of action on blood agar: alpha type; beta type; $\alpha'$ type, a type intermediate to $\alpha$ and $\beta$; and gamma type, a type which did not alter blood corpuscles, i.e., nonhemolytic.

In a series of reports beginning in 1928, Rebecca Lancefield reported that the hemolytic streptococci may be divided into groups on the basis of the precipitation reaction using specific carbohydrate substance, designated as "C substance," as the antigen. By using the Lancefield typing techniques, the streptococci have been studied by various investigators with the formation of the following groups: Group A, composed of the more virulent human strains typified by *Str. pyogenes;* Group B, includes the bovine mastitis streptococci typified by *Str. agalactiae;* Group C, made up of hemolytic animal and human strains which are now called *Str. equisimilis,* certain strains *Str. canis* from the dog, and a distinct species, *Str. equi;* Group D, in which is placed the enterococci and strains isolated from dairy products; Group E, includes strains isolated from milk and abscesses in swine; Group F, a minute colony type isolated from the respiratory tract of man; Group G, comprised of both a minute colony type and a large colony type, the former of which has been isolated from the respiratory tract of man and the latter from dogs; Group H, isolated from the respiratory tract of man but of doubtful virulence; Group K, comprised of strains isolated from the respiratory tract of man, likewise of doubtful virulence; Group L, includes strains isolated from the genital tract of the dog; Group M, strains which have been isolated from respiratory tissues of the dog; Group N, includes streptococci found in milk, typified by *Str. lactis* and *Str. cremoris.*

Several of the above groups may be divided into serologic types. The antigen which may be used for type differentiation varies with the group. In Group A the various serologic types are determined by protein antigens, in Group B by polysaccharides, in Group C by proteins, and it is believed that the antigens are polysaccharide in nature in Groups D, E, F, and G.

Additional tests for differentiating bacteria in general have been used for the streptococci. It is not feasible to discuss them in detail here, but the following deserve mentioning: optimum growth temperature, survival temperature, optimum hydrogen-ion range, maximum hydrogen-ion production in glucose broth, growth in presence of 6.5 per cent NaCl, growth in and reduction of methylene blue milk, growth in 40 per cent bile-blood agar, reaction to bacteriophage, and fibrinolytic activity. With this formidable array of differential methods it would seem that the streptococci should be adequately classified.

In 1937 Sherman compiled the information then available concerning the streptococci. This review has been of great value to those studying and working with this group of microorganisms. It lists all of the important species of streptococci causing infection in man and animals and the significant nonpathogenic species which frequently are found in fluids and tissues.

The differentiation of the strains of streptococci occurring in man from those found in animals has been one of the problems of bacteriologists. Present-day methods have aided in accomplishing this problem. It has been conceded for many years that two animal species, *Streptococcus agalactiae (mastitidis* of Sherman) and *Streptococcus equi* are distinct species and may be recognized by their cultural and physiological characteristics. Furthermore these species occur in the cow and horse respectively, neither being transmitted to man.

It was demonstrated by Davis in 1912, and since then by other investigators, that *Str. pyogenes* may be transmitted from infected human tissues by the milker to the bovine udder where it may localize and may produce a typical mastitis. The growth of organisms in such tissue serves as a potential hazard to human health in the form of milk-borne epidemics of scarlet fever and septic sore throat. Acute bovine mastitis also may be caused by a hemolytic streptococcus of animal origin. This organism was named *Str. zooepidemicus* by Frost and Engelbrecht in 1936. In the process of detecting the infected cow in milk-borne epidemics, it is obvious that methods should be available for the differentiation of *Str. pyogenes* and *Str. zooepi-*

TABLE 15.1
Differential Characteristics of Streptococci Affecting Animals

| Name | Hemolysis | Salicin | Mannite | Inulin | Lactose | Raffinose | Trehalose | Sorbitol | Sodium hippurate | Litmus milk | | | Lancefield Group |
|---|---|---|---|---|---|---|---|---|---|---|---|---|---|
| | | | | | | | | | | Acid | Coagulation | Reduction | |
| *Str. pyogenes* | beta | +* | ± | − | + | − | + | − | − | + | − | ± | A |
| *Str. zooepidemicus* | beta | + | − | − | + | − | − | + | − | + | − | − | C |
| *Str. equi* | beta | + | − | − | − | − | − | − | − | − | − | − | C |
| *Str. equisimilis* | beta | +* | − | − | ± | − | + | − | − | + | − | ± | C |
| *Str. agalactiae* | gamma, alpha, or narrow beta | +* | − | − | + | − | + | − | + | + | + | ± | B |
| *Str. dysgalactiae* | gamma, alpha, or narrow beta | − | − | − | + | − | + | − | − | + | + | + | C |
| *Str. uberis* | gamma, alpha, or narrow beta | + | + | + | + | − | + | + | + | + | ± | ++ | ? |
| *Str. canis* | beta | + | − | − | + | − | − | − | − | + | − | + | C |
| Group L | beta | − | − | − | ± | − | − | − | − | ± | ± | ± | L |
| Group E | beta | + | + | − | − | − | + | ± | − | − | − | − | E |

*Occasional strains are negative

*demicus.* These differences are clearly established by Lancefield's grouping and by the use of sorbitol (see Table 15.1).

When the technique of serological typing by Lancefield became widely used, it became evident that numerous unrelated strains, in fact species, of streptococci were placed in Group C. The recognition of *Str. equi* as a definite species was accepted but the classification of other strains presented more of a problem. In the absence of better terminology these strains were referred to as "*human* C" or "*animal* C," depending on their source. In their 1940 review of the streptococci, Frost and Engelbrecht described and used the name *Streptococcus equisimilis* for strains of streptococci fitting the characteristics of "*animal* C" strains. The studies of the hemolytic streptococci by Evans in 1944 reveal that *Str. equisimilis* may be found in a wide variety of human and animal tissues where they produce infection. While these studies do not differentiate the strains isolated from man from those isolated from animals, it has been demonstrated by Hansen that they may be distinguished by the fibrinolysis test of Tillett and Garner. Hansen found that twenty-nine of the animal strains failed to cause the lysis of human fibrin, whereas the strains isolated from man were able to do so.

The species of the genus *Streptococcus* which will be discussed in detail are *Streptococcus pyogenes, Streptococcus zooepidemicus, Streptococcus agalactiae, Streptococcus uberis, Streptococcus dysgalactiae, Streptococcus equi, Streptococcus equisimilis,* and *Streptococcus canis.*

### *Streptococcus pyogenes*

**Synonyms.** *Str. erysipelatos, Str. puerperalis, Str. septicus, Str. articulorum, Str. anginosus, Str. scarlatinae, Str. epidemicus, Str. hemolyticus.*

**Distribution and Transmission.** The organism is found universally where human populations have intermingled. It is present on skin and mucous membranes, apparently waiting an opportunity to invade into deeper tissues. Immune carriers, subinfected cases, or severely infected cases serve to spread the organism.

**Morphology and Staining.** *Streptococcus pyogenes* is a coccus 0.5μ to 1μ in size arranged in chains of various lengths (Fig. 15.1). The length and character of the chains are variable in different media and under varying conditions of growth, and likewise in strains isolated from different sources; for example, chains are apt to be shorter in artificial than in natural media. The length of the chain is also increased by the presence of specific antibody and decreased by the absence of antibody. Sometimes there is a tendency toward diplococcus formation, and the chains may be made up of many such diplococci. The organism is nonmotile and does not produce spores. It is gram-positive, although in older cultures a few decolorized cells may be observed. Capsules are not produced by the majority of strains when grown under ordinary conditions. Certain variant strains have been described which do produce capsules. These strains have been known under the name of *Str. epidemicus.* Other strains produce capsules early in the growth period upon enriched media.

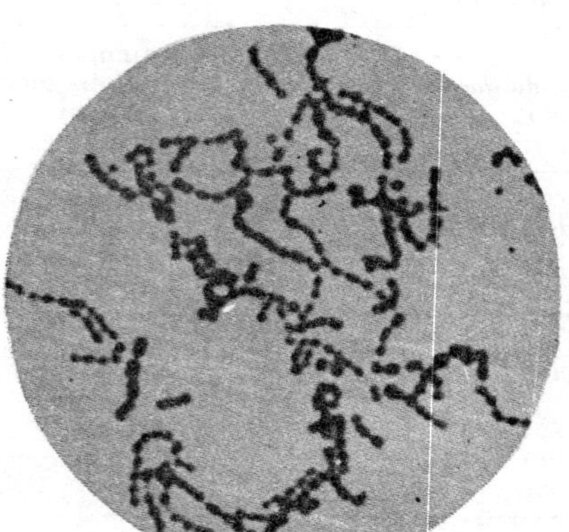

FIG. 15.1—**Streptococcus pyogenes** bouillon culture, X2,500. (From Nowak: Documenta Microbiologica, courtesy Gustav Fischer.)

**Growth Requirements and Characteristics.** The organism may be isolated upon common media from infected tissue, although media to which blood, serum, or ascitic fluid is added obtains and maintains more satisfactory growth. It is aerobic and microaerophilic and has an optimum growth temperature of 37°C.

On solid media the colonies are small, smooth, glistening, dewdrop-like, finely granular, and with age become opaque with a raised central portion. See Figure 15.2. No pigment is produced. On blood agar, beta type of hemolysis is distinct after 24 hours incubation. Bouillon is uniformly clouded in early stages of growth, forming a finely granular sediment as the culture ages, which settles on the sides and bottom of the culture tube. No pellicle is formed.

**Resistance.** A temperature of 60°C. for 30 minutes kills the organism, and boiling is effective immediately. The commonly used disinfectants at standard concentrations are effective. The organism perishes rather quickly on laboratory media, and for that reason must be subcultured at least once each month. Cultures may be maintained longer in blood bouillon, sealed tightly or in a semisolid agar.

This streptococcus, in common with all of the pathogenic species of streptococci, is sensitive to sulfanilamide, penicillin, tetracycline, and chloromycetin.

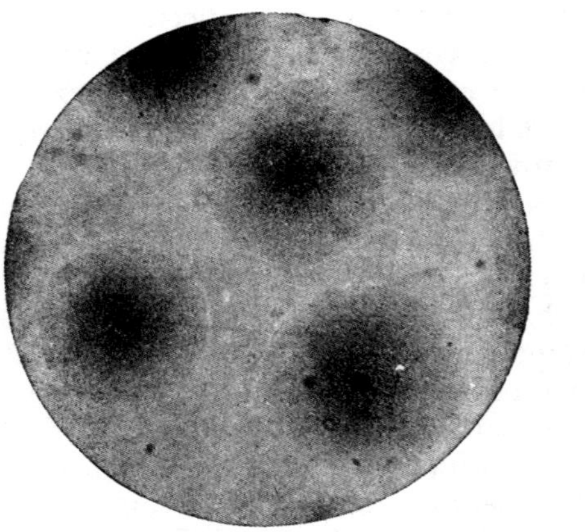

FIG. 15.2—**Streptococcus pyogenes** colonies on agar, ×50. (From Nowak: Documenta Microbiologica, courtesy Gustav Fischer.)

**Biochemical Properties.** *Str. pyogenes* produces acid but no gas from glucose, lactose, salicin, sucrose, trehalose, and some strains from mannitol, and does not ferment sorbitol, inulin, arabinose, or raffinose. It produces a final pH of 6.0–4.8 in glucose broth. Gelatin is not liquefied. Milk is acidified but rarely coagulated. Indol is not formed. Nitrates are not reduced. Sodium hippurate or starch is not hydrolyzed. Esculin is split by some strains. The organism is not soluble in bile but will not grow on 40 per cent bile-blood agar.

On the basis of group-specific carbohydrate substance C, *Str. pyogenes* belongs in Group A. At least 40 serologic types in the Group A streptococci have been determined by the use of two antigenc protein substances. These antigens are called type-specific protein M and T substance. They have been rather thoroughly studied but space does not permit their description here. The reader is referred to the work of Lancefield and Dole for a detailed discussion.

Griffith has found 27 serological types on the basis of agglutination. By using Griffith's agglutination technique Evans studied 444 strains of Group A streptococci obtained from various parts of the world. She concluded that agglutinative types shift from place to place and that certain types are associated with definite diseases. For example, Types 3, 8, and 10 were found to be scarlatinal types, with more or less limited ability to produce other diseases. Type 19 is a predominant scarlatinal type which commonly causes all kinds of streptococcal ailments. Types 5, 13, 14, and 18 do not commonly produce rash, but they have a tendency to produce suppurative and miscellaneous diseases. Type 6, which also has a tendency to produce suppurative diseases, may be found more commonly than the others in scarlet fever.

*Str. pyogenes* produces two soluble hemolysins which cause the hemolysis of erythrocytes. Study of these substances has revealed that one is oxygen labile, and for that reason is called *streptolysin* O. Under ordinary aerobic conditions of growth the production of this hemolysin by a streptococcus culture is not detected. This substance is not lethal to mice in large doses. It is neutralized by streptolysin O antiserum, and the serum of patients suffering with a *Str. pyogenes* infection contains a specific neutralizing antibody. The other type of hemolysin produced by *Str. pyogenes* is called *streptolysin* S because it is extracted from the streptococcal cells by serum. This substance is not oxygen labile; consequently it is the hemolysin responsible for the hemolysis of erythrocytes observed on the blood agar plate. Antibodies against this hemolysin can be induced only by the injection of intact streptococcal cells. This substance is quite toxic to animal tissues, producing degenerative changes in parenchymatous cells and hemolysis of erythrocytes. The animal usually dies within 24 to 48 hours.

*Str. pyogenes* produces a leucocyte-destroying substance known as *leucocidin*. It has been shown that this substance is similar, if not identical, to streptolysin O.

Numerous strains of this streptococcus produce *erythrogenic* toxin responsible for the characteristic skin lesions of scarlet fever. Persons who have had a typical case of scarlet fever develop immunity to this toxin. In order to detect susceptibility to scarlet fever, diluted toxin (Dick test) may be injected intradermally into the arm. Those susceptible to the disease will have a reaction characterized by swelling and erythema surrounding the point of inoculation. No reaction results if the person has had scarlet fever and has become skin immune to the toxin.

The production of a fibrinolysin by streptococci was first shown by Tillett and Garner in 1933. The detection of this substance in filtrates of streptococcal cultures constitutes a test for the differentiation of certain strains of streptococci. It is assumed that fibrinolysin is functional in the infectious process by preventing the formation of fibrin clots which ordinarily control hemorrhage. Christensen has demonstrated that the lysis of fibrin depends on the action of two substances. One is a proenzyme called *plasminogen* which is an inactive proteolytic factor in all human sera. The other substance called *streptokinase* is liberated by the streptococcal cell. The streptokinase acts with the plasminogen to form the active proteolytic enzyme called *plasmin*, which digests fibrin and other proteins. This digestive process may be inhibited by one of the following factors: (a) the presence of the antibody antistreptokinase induced by a natural streptococcal infection; (b) the presence of antiprotease in the blood; (c) a deficiency of the proenzyme, plasminogen, in the blood.

Certain strains of *Str. pyogenes* have been found to produce another proteolytic enzyme called *proteinase*. This substance is distinct from streptokinase; in fact, its presence in a streptococcus culture prevents the formation of streptokinase or destroys it as it is formed. When active, this enzyme digests milk, gelatin, casein, and human and rabbit fibrin. Its role in the infectious process is not known.

Those strains of Group A streptococci which form capsules are known to produce *hyaluronic acid*. This substance is the main component in the capsule of *Str. pyogenes* as well as other species of streptococci of Group C. It is found also as a natural component of many tissues of the animal body where it appears to serve as a "continuity substance" between cells and tissue spaces. It is not antigenic and its role in the infectious process is unknown unless it acts as a phagocytosis-inhibiting material. It has been shown that when capsulated streptococci are treated with hyaluronidase, they become susceptible to phagocytosis.

Certain other strains of streptococci produce *hyaluronidase* that is recognized as the important enzyme in the substance referred to as "spreading factor." The most significant property of this material is its ability to attack hyaluronic acid thereby permitting the spread of streptococci *and* their products. For this reason hyaluronidase is considered a factor in bacterial virulence, although critical experiments to prove this relationship have not been too successful.

**Pathogenicity.** *Streptococcus pyogenes* causes a number of diseases in man. It is associated with scarlet fever, septic sore throat, tonsillitis, various suppurative inflammatory conditions, septicemia, focal infections, ulcerative endocarditis, rheumatic fever, puerperal sepsis, and erysipelas. It may be a secondary invader in such diseases as diphtheria, measles, smallpox, tuberculosis, pleurisy, and pneumonia. The organism invades the bovine mammary gland, producing mastitis. In such instances it is transmitted from an infected person during the milking process. When such occasions occur, a milk-borne epidemic of scarlet fever or septic sore throat may result. Evans studied in some detail the data concerning 29 milk-borne outbreaks of streptococcal infection in man in order to determine the agglutinative type of the organism. The ability of certain strains of *Str. pyogenes* to produce scarlet fever and for other strains to produce only sore throat is emphasized in her report. It has been noted by other investigators that it is difficult to distinguish between septic sore throat and the sore throat present in scarlet fever. The characterization of a milk-borne outbreak as septic sore throat or as scarlet fever often depends on whether the population involved has experienced a recent natural epidemic of scarlet fever. If such is the case, they have become skin immune to erythrogenic toxin but not throat immune to the streptococcus. Alford, Gunter, and Edwards reported the isolation of Group A streptococci from the genital tract of 12 cows in a dairy herd.

Some strains of *Str. pyogenes* are highly virulent for the mouse and rabbit. The guinea pig is more resistant.

**Immunity.** Immunity is not produced by one's having had an infection. The toxin of the scarlet fever streptococcus will produce a skin immunity in persons having that disease. The resistance of throat tissues, however, which are the usual seat of the infection, does not appear to be increased; in fact, recovered patients may remain carriers of the organism for considerable periods of time. Bacterin and vaccine therapy in *Streptococcus pyogenes* infection have been found to be of value in some cases. Immune serum, especially scarlet fever antitoxin, has been shown to be of great value in treating cases of scarlet fever.

**Diagnosis of *Str. pyogenes* Infections.** Direct smears of the exudate from the lesions of the disease usually reveal long-chained streptococci which may be considered sufficient for the usual diagnosis. Hemolysis may be detected only by the use of blood media. To satisfactorily place the organism in its correct group, the Lancefield technique must be used in conjunction with other biochemical tests.

### *Streptococcus zooepidemicus*

**Synonyms and History.** *Str. pyogenes*, "animal pyogenes," *Str. genitalium*.

The organism has been isolated from numerous types of tissue and from a variety of species of animals. In most cases it has been considered similar to *Str. pyogenes*. In 1929 Ogura demonstrated the distinction between the human and animal strains, and in 1933 Edwards definitely revealed that two distinct species exist. The antigenic classification of Lancefield shows that the strains of streptococci usually affecting man belong to Group A, whereas the strains found in animals are placed in Group C.

**Distribution and Transmission.** *Str. zooepidemicus* is universally found where domesticated animals are kept. The organism commonly produces sporadic infection in animals; however, some cases of bovine mastitis have been reported.

In Kentucky the organism has been encountered as a cause of genital infection in mares and is, no doubt, transmitted by coitus. Whether the presence of the organism in the genital tract of normal mares indicates an immune carrier state, or whether the organism is normally present and infection indicates a decrease in resistance is not known. In a study of the hemolytic streptococci isolated from swine, Collier reported two strains of the organism from suppurative arthritis, one strain from a cervical abscess, and one strain from vegetative carditis.

The presence of the organism in so many species of animals suggests that cross infection among animal species may occur; for example, it is possible for this streptococcus to be transmitted from the genital tract of a mare to the udder of a cow if both animals are kept in the same barn lot, or to both or either cows and horses from an infected pig, or to pigs from an infected horse or cow. Whether this organism occurs in chickens has arisen from time to time. It may be confused with *Str. gallinarum;* indeed, some consider the latter organism to be a type of *Str. zooepidemicus.* Soto and Ushijima, in Japan, described an outbreak of infection in chickens shown to be caused by *Str. zooepidemicus.*

**Morphology and Staining.** *Str. zooepidemicus* is not significantly different from *Str. pyogenes* to warrant repetition; however, the fact may be emphasized that recently isolated strains of the organism produce capsules, especially when grown upon blood or serum media. It is gram-positive, although some strains are easily decolorized, and in most stained preparations an occasional gram-negative cell may be found.

**Growth Requirements and Characteristics.** This streptococcus is grown readily on meat infusion agar upon first isolation from infected tissues, but needs serum or blood in the medium in successive subcultures. The addition of tryptose to the medium definitely increases growth. The organism is aerobic and microaerophilic. Optimum growth temperature is 37°C.

A flocculent growth is formed on the bottom of tubes of bouillon with a clear supernatant liquid. Some strains are found to produce a faint cloudiness in bouillon. On serum agar, colonies of this organism are larger and more moist than other species of streptococci. The colonies show a tendency to become dry and slightly wrinkled as they age.

*Str. zooepidemicus* is decidedly beta hemolytic. Wide zones of hemolysis are present around colonies. On pour plates of blood agar the organism forms relatively large spreading colonies between the medium and the bottom of the Petri dish. In the medium itself colonies are flatly lenticular.

**Resistance.** The organism is not resistant to desiccation or sunlight. Laboratory cultures perish unless they are transferred regularly once a month. The thermal death point is 68°C. in 10 minutes. It is easily killed by the ordinary chemicals used in disinfection.

**Biochemical Properties.** *Streptococcus zooepidemicus* forms acid in lactose, salicin, sorbitol, glucose, and sucrose. Some strains produce acid in maltose. Arabinose, trehalose, raffinose, inulin, adonitol, populin, glycerol, rhamnose, dulcitol, sorbose, erythritol, and inositol are not fermented. Sodium hippurate is not hydrolyzed; starch is hydrolyzed; esculin is not split; gelatin is not liquefied. Milk is rendered slightly acid but is not curdled. It produces a final pH of 5.0–4.6 in glucose broth. Indol is not formed. Nitrates are not reduced.

**Antigenic Structure and Toxins.** *Str. zooepidemicus* belongs to Group C of Lancefield. Beta hemolysin is formed as is evident by the marked hemolysis of blood agar. The organism differs from *Str. pyogenes* since it does not produce fibrinolysin as was demonstrated by Tillett and Garner.

**Pathogenicity.** This streptococcus may be called the beta hemolytic streptococcus of animals and bears a pathogenic relationship to those species as does *Str. pyogenes* to man. The organism produces severe infection, often ending in septicemia and death.

Among the animal hosts the horse appears to be the most susceptible. In the mare the organism has been isolated from cases of cervicitis and metritis, and it has been considered to be the cause of abortion and sterility. It is the principal infecting agent in navel infection, joint infection, peritonitis, and septicemia in very young foals. The organism has been recovered from the semen of infected stallions. Infection in the horse is not confined to the genitalia, for cultures have been obtained from the respiratory tract following influenza as well as from subcutaneous wounds in various parts of the body.

In cattle this streptococcus may cause cervicitis and metritis. It is often associated with mastitis in the cow, and some investigators consider it the cause of acute septicemic conditions which follow some cases of mastitis. Fortunately it is not as frequently involved in bovine mastitis as are other udder streptococci. Because of the presence of this organism in the udder of cattle and its resemblance on blood agar to *Str. pyogenes,* it was once thought to be pathogenic to man. At the present time it is not considered capable of producing infection in man, although Frost and Engelbrecht report the isolation of cultures from the throats of dairy employees not in contact with infected cows. It must be remembered that *Str. pyogenes* can cause infection in the bovine udder; hence, it may be transmitted to man through the milk supply. Since this is true, it is imperative that marked beta hemolytic strains of udder streptococci be subjected to further laboratory diagnosis.

This streptococcus has been isolated from cases of arthritis, adenitis, abortion, wound infection, and septicemia in swine.

Cultures of the organism have been recovered from foxes which have died of pneumonia, as well as from the lymph node of a sheep. The organism is capable of killing rabbits by intraperitoneal injection, but guinea pigs and rats are resistant. Mice are susceptible and succumb quickly.

**Immunity.** An animal is not rendered immune by an infection produced by this organism. An increased phagocytic activity probably exists during and following an infection, but it does not persist. It is commonly incorporated in mixed bacterins which are used for domestic animals.

**Diagnosis.** It is apparent that an infection produced by *Str. zooepidemicus* can be diagnosed correctly only by the isolation and identification of the culture. This organism is beta hemolytic, ferments sorbitol, but does not ferment trehalose nor hydrolyze sodium hippurate. These criteria, in addition to the identification of it as belonging to Group C by the Lancefield technique, are sufficient for diagnosis.

### *Streptococcus agalactiae*
### *Streptococcus dysgalactiae*
### *Streptococcus uberis*

These three species of streptococci are biochemically and serologically different; however, they are associated with bovine mastitis and are usually referred to as the "mastitis streptococci." Since these species of streptococci are similar and are encountered in the same tissue, it is deemed advisable to discuss them as a group.

**Synonyms and History.** *Str. agalactiae* was first isolated from cases of mastitis in cows and described by Nocard and Mollereau in 1884 and in subsequent publications in 1885 and 1887. Although numerous udder streptococci were described by various investigators during the following years, the next most significant description was by Kitt in 1893. Lehmann and Neumann used the name *Streptococcus agalactiae* in 1890, and Migula *Str. mastitidis* in 1900. The former name has been generally adopted for the organism.

Up to 1929 nearly all cases of streptococcic mastitis were thought to be caused by *Str. agalactiae.* Minett, Stableforth, and Edwards in that year pointed out that some cases of mastitis were caused by streptococci with characteristics different from those of *Str. agalactiae*. These organisms were designated by them as "non-hemolytic group II." Further work by Edwards revealed a third type of streptococcus which he designated as "nonhemolytic group III." In 1930 Diernhofer described streptococci from mastitis cases which were the same as those of groups II and III of Minett, Stableforth, and Edwards. Later, in 1932, Diernhofer suggested the names *Str. dysgalactiae* and *Str. uberis* for the streptococci which corresponded to groups II and III, respectively. These species names have now been adopted for these two organisms.

**Distribution and Transmission.** These three species of streptococci are widely distributed and are found wherever dairy cows are kept. Incidence of streptococcus mastitis is often high. As high as 80 per cent infection is reported in large dairy herds. Few herds are entirely free from the disease. There are a number of factors concerning transmission of mastitis which are not clearly understood at present; however, it is generally agreed that the most common manner of spreading it is by the hands of the milker or the teat cups of the milking machine. It has been proved that flies are capable of transmitting the disease.

Ingalls and Johnson recovered *Str. agalactiae* from the external surface of the teats of infected quarters nine times in 28 attempts. In all cases a minimum of eight hours had elapsed from the time of milking, and the organisms were recovered as late as the fifth day following the last milking.

**Morphology and Staining.** The morphology and staining of *Str. agalactiae* and *Str. dysgalactiae* are not significantly different from *Str. pyogenes*. *Str. uberis* shows less tendency to form long chains, usually occurring in pairs or short chains.

**Growth Requirements and Characteristics.** These organisms may be isolated directly from milk taken from an infected udder. The incubation of the milk sample for 12 to 24 hours insures greater success. They may be readily grown upon nutrient media to which serum or blood has been added. The use of sodium azide crystal violet blood agar facilitates the isolation of these organisms from milk samples which may have become contaminated with other bacteria. It is aerobic and microaerophilic and grows best at 37°C. There are no significant differences in colony characteristics among these three organisms. They appear upon solid media as discrete, transparent, dewdrop-like colonies which are characteristic of the streptococci. Growth in liquid media is somewhat variable. *Str. agalactiae* and *Str. dysgalactiae* usually produce a flocculent growth in the bottom of the tube with a clear supernatant liquid above, while *Str. uberis* produces a uniform turbidity in broth medium. *Str. agalactiae* produces a narrow zone of beta or alpha hemolysis or no hemolysis at all upon blood agar. Hemolysis never extends as far from the colony as with *Str. pyogenes*. Brown has described characteristic "double-zone" hemolysis by beta hemolytic strains of *Str. agalactiae* if the blood agar cultures are refrigerated after 24 hours incubation at 37°C.

*Str. dysgalactiae* and *Str. uberis* are described as nonhemolytic; however, some strains produce beta hemolysis when they are grown on sodium azide blood agar.

**Resistance.** Resistance of these species in general is similar to that of *Str. pyogenes;* however, *Str. agalactiae* has been found in pasteurized milk. This would suggest that this organism is able to resist pasteurization temperatures occasionally, while *Str. pyogenes* has never been shown to survive proper pasteurization.

Watts has shown that *Str. agalactiae* remained viable for three years after a milk culture had been thoroughly desiccated over pure sulfuric acid. In a relative humidity greater than 60 per cent the organism perished in eleven weeks, but in a relative humidity of 10–25 per cent it remained viable for three years.

Spencer, McCarter, and Beach concluded that *Str. agalactiae* died out rapidly in barn bedding; most of the organisms were dead after 24 hours but a few lived as long as six to nine days. These investigators found the organism on the hands of dairy attendants who hand-milked infected cows.

**Biochemical Properties.** The biochemical properties of these three organisms are alike in that they do not produce indol, liquefy gelatin, or reduce nitrates. Table 15.1 shows the reactions on the various test media which may be used in differentiating these streptococci.

**Antigenic Structure and Toxins.** *Str. agalactiae* is placed in Lancefield's Group B and appears to be the only definite species in this group. Four subgroups, namely Ia, Ib, II, and III, have been described under Group B. *Str. dysgalactiae* has been placed in Lancefield's Group C. The antigenic structure of *Str. uberis* is very heterogeneous. Most strains show no serological relationship to established Lancefield groups or to each other, although they appear to be identical biochemically. Norcross has shown that three antigenically pure antigens of different composition may be produced by *Str. agalactiae*. One of these antigens is proteinaceous and the other two gave positive tests for carbohydrates. The blood serum and colostrum of cows having a history of numerous *Str. agalactiae* infections were titrated by the use of these antigens.

The production of hemolysin by this group of streptococci is not marked. Some strains of *Str. agalactiae* produce a soluble hemolysin, while the other two species do not. An erythrogenic toxin is not formed. Fibrinolysin has not been demonstrated.

**Pathogenicity.** It is generally conceded that a large per cent of the cases of mastitis in badly infected herds is caused by *Str. agalactiae*. It causes a parenchymatous mastitis which is characterized by acute onset followed by a progressively chronic condition resulting in fibrosis of the infected gland. Infection is usually permanent, carrying over from one lactation to another, and with occasional "acute attacks" of the disease. Murphy has shown that if the soft keratin lining of the teat canal is removed by soft plastic cannulas, infection always could be produced.

Hypersensitivity of the mammary gland produced by previous infection has been considered conducive to subsequent infection. Spencer and Simon infused mammary glands with streptococcal polysaccharide, producing a more severe inflammation to subsequent exposure to living *Str. agalactiae* cultures. They also found that polysaccharide was an inflammatory irritant to normal as well as to hypersensitive cows.

Mastitis caused by *Str. dysgalactiae* is less frequent; usually less than 10 per cent of the cases of streptococcic mastitis are due to this organism. The disease is usually more acute with less tendency toward chronic, permanent infection than in the case of *Str. agalactiae*. *Str. uberis* may be associated with an acute mastitis which later becomes chronic. Its course is more transient with less tendency to permanent infection. This organism also has been found in the udder of cows not showing any obvious evidence of infection. Less than 10 per cent of the cases of streptococcic mastitis are found to be caused by this organism.

The character of the milk in mastitis is quite variable depending largely upon the severity and stage of infection. In acute stages it may appear as a curdled mass composed of purulent exudate, dead tissue cells, coagulated milk proteins, and bacteria. In chronic cases it may appear normal macroscopically, but there usually is a slight increase in the number of leucocytes and a large number of streptococci.

These organisms are not pathogenic for farm animals other than the cow and goat nor have they been found to be pathogenic for any other organ except the mammary gland. Although *Str. agalactiae* has been isolated from various tissues of man, it is considered to have only an opportunist role in human disease processes.

Experimental animals have been considered resistant to *Str. agalactiae*. Kaplan *et al.* have shown, however, that when a strain of the organism is passed through a series of four mice, increase of virulence results.

**Immunity.** Immunity is not produced by an attack of mastitis due to *Str. agalactiae*. Cows may be continuously infected for years. Bacterins have been used in treatment with little success. Autogenous bacterins have been used also and have appeared to be of more value. Spontaneous recoveries of cases of mastitis due to *Str. dysgalactiae* suggest a possible immunity; however, little work has been done on this subject.

**Diagnosis.** The cultivation of streptococci from the milk is indicative of mastitis. This may be done by incubating a sample of milk from an infected udder using the milk as the culture medium, or the organism may be grown on any other suitable medium. Blood agar is preferred as it not only grows the organism, but also shows its action upon blood. Sodium azide crystal violet blood agar is a more valuable medium for the routine isolation of streptococci since it inhibits the growth of contaminants which may be confusing. The demonstration of streptococci in milk should be followed by identification of the organism for accurate diagnosis. Inoculation of the organism into the test media shown in Table 15.1 will accurately diagnose the disease and differentiate the organism from the saprophytic streptococci which are occasionally present.

Hotis and Miller have devised a test for the detection of *Str. agalactiae* infection, but it is much less accurate in detecting other streptococci such as *Str. dysgalactiae*. The test is performed by adding 0.5 ml. of sterile 0.5 per cent aqueous solution bromcresol purple to 9.5 ml. of milk. The milk is incubated 24 hours at 37°C., and the test is read. The appearance of canary-yellow colonies of bacterial growth along the walls and in the bottom of the test tube is diagnostic of *Str. agalactiae* infection. The yellow color formed around the colonies is due to the fermentation of lactose to acid which changes the bromcresol purple to the yellow range of the indicator. Although *Str. dysgalactiae* and *Str. uberis* are capable of fermenting lactose, they never grow in clumps as does *Str. agalactiae*. The growth of *Str. agalactiae* in clumps in this test appears to be associated with agglutination.

In 1944 Christie, Atkins, and Munch-Peterson reported a reaction which since has become known as the CAMP Test. They observed that around colonies of staphylococci cultured on bovine blood agar a double zone of hemolysis occurred. In this type of hemolysis, called alpha-beta hemolysis, a clear zone of beta hemolysis is surrounded by a darker zone of incompletely hemolyzed erythrocytes. When milk containing mastitis streptococci was cultured on bovine blood agar plates containing colonies of alpha-beta staphylococci, the colonies of streptococci growing in the beta zone were surrounded by a wider zone of beta hemolysis than was observed in colonies growing elsewhere on the plate. Murphy, Stuart, and Reed, in 1952, observed that 96.6 per cent of the cultures of *Str. agalactiae* were positive to the CAMP Test, 14.9 per cent of the cultures of *Str. uberis* were positive, and none of the cultures of *Str. dysgalactiae* were positive. They have considered the test of value in typing the mastitis streptococci.

Various indirect methods have been devised for the diagnosis of mastitis, but do not identify the causal agent. These tests include the chloride, catalase, strip cup, bromthymol blue, and the California tests.

### *Streptococcus equi*

**Synonyms and History.** The disease, strangles, in horses has a long recorded history. It was described by Solleysel in 1664, and its contagious nature was determined by Lafosse in 1790. Apparently a streptococcus was first considered to be responsible for the disease by Rivolta in 1873 when he described cocci found in exudate from typical cases of strangles. In 1886 Perroncito observed the same type of cells in exudate and considered them to be the cause of the disease. Baruchello is credited with being the first to isolate the organism in 1886 and to reproduce the disease. Sand and Jensen described the organism in 1887 and are credited with being the first to use the name *Streptococcus equi* in 1888. Schütz isolated and distinguished it from other streptococci in 1888. In his classification of 1901, Chester used the name *Streptococcus capelletti.* Matzuschita referred to it as *Streptococcus contagiosae equorum* in 1902. In 1913 Bongert used the name *Streptococcus Schütz.*

**Distribution and Transmission.** *Str. equi* appears wherever there are horses. Epizootics of strangles constantly occur in horse populations. The organism is spread by close contact and by contaminated water and feeds. There is evidence that infected horses remain resistant carriers of the organism and are sources of the infection for considerable periods of time.

**Morphology and Staining.** In its general appearance *Str. equi* does not differ from the other species of the group. Long chains of cocci are usually found in fluids and in pus from infected animals; however, short chains have been observed, and it is believed that they are even more virulent. Capsules may be demonstrated on many of the cocci in smears made from lesions of the disease and from media containing serum. The organism is gram-positive, but it may be decolorized more easily than other members of the group. It is easily stained by the aniline dyes.

**Growth Requirements and Characteristics.** In most cases, the organism is isolated in pure culture from the deeper portion of the characteristic abscesses. More abundant growth is obtained upon primary isolation by the use of slightly alkaline, serumized media under microaerophilic conditions. The organism is the most difficult to cultivate of any of the streptococci. Colonies are small, convex, and transparent. In water of the agar slant it produces a whitish, flocculent precipitate. In agar stabs nodular outgrowths from the line of puncture develop. In broth the majority of strains form a flocculent deposit with a clear supernatant fluid. Some strains produce uniform turbidity. Colonies on blood agar are moist, mucoid-like, even though they are small. A wide zone of beta hemolysis is produced on blood agar.

**Resistance.** *Str. equi* is more resistant to heat than some of the other species although it is not as resistant as some previous investigators believed. It is killed promptly by boiling for 10 minutes at 65°C. to 70°C., and for 50 minutes at 60°C. The cresol compounds destroy the organism readily. Gentian violet also exerts a marked action. Mercury salts appear to be less effective. It is more resistant to disinfectants and to desiccation when it is present in purulent exudate.

**Biochemical Properties.** Acid is formed from glucose, salicin, sucrose, mannose, galactose, and maltose. It fails to ferment lactose and sorbitol, which serves to differentiate it from *Str. pyogenes* and *Str. zooepidemicus.* It also fails to ferment mannitol, trehalose, arabinose, raffinose, inulin, and glycerol. Litmus milk is not changed. Sodium hippurate is not hydrolyzed. Nitrates are not reduced. It does not grow in 40 per cent bile-blood agar. It is not bile-soluble. Gelatin is not liquefied.

**Antigenic Structure and Toxins.** The organism belongs to Group C of Lancefield's classification. Antigenic subtypes have not been reported. Bazeley studied 32 strains of the organism collected from 26 distinct outbreaks of strangles in Australia. By cross-protection tests in mice he found definite cross protection by the univalent serum against all strains. It forms hemolysin and leucocidin, but does not produce erythrogenic toxin. Some strains are reported to lyse human fibrin, although the majority fail to do so.

**Pathogenicity.** *Streptococcus equi* is considered one of the main causes of strangles, which is most prevalent in young horses. It is often a secondary invader in respiratory diseases such as influenza and contagious pleuropneumonia of horses. It may be found in the genital tract of the mare. Strangles is first characterized by a catarrhal discharge, with inflammation of the nasal mucous membranes, followed quickly by a swelling of the pharyngeal lymph nodes in which abscesses generally develop. The infection spreads through the lymph channels, but usually remains localized in the tissues adjacent to the original point of infection. Metastatic infections may occur in any organ of the body; and in the chronic types of the disease, great variations in localization are found. Fatal termination is rare, but sometimes occurs, due to septicemia, pyemia, or pneumonia.

Subcutaneous inoculation of the organism into the horse will usually provoke abscess formation at the point of injection. The introduction of pure cultures into the nasal cavity of young, susceptible horses gives rise to the characteristic purulent catarrh with secondary abscess formation in the lymph nodes. It is obvious that, in addition to age, other predisposing factors, such as exposure to cold and fatigue, lower the resistance of animals to the disease. Variations in the virulence of the organism may account for the epizootic character of the disease. Bazeley has shown that cultures of *Str. equi* four and one-half hours old are much more virulent than cultures twenty-four hours of age. He attributes this to the high surface electric charge of the young cultures as compared to the old. He believes that this explains why young, actively multiplying streptococci are not readily phagocytized.

Pus from abscesses in strangles kills white mice, with evidence of acute septicemia in two to four days, or after a longer period as a result of pyemia. An abscess generally develops at the point of inoculation. Rabbits and guinea pigs succumb to the injection of large quantities of the organism, but are not readily infected. Cattle, sheep, swine, dogs, and birds are very resistant. Man is not susceptible to the organism.

**Immunity.** Immunity is conferred by an attack of *Str. equi* infection. Some animals appear to suffer second attacks of the disease, but this is often due to mistaken diagnosis of the first attack. Animals five years old are usually resistant to the disease. These facts have led to the assumption that artificial immunization is of value.

Immunization with bacterins and vaccines has not given completely satisfactory results. The use of a herd-autogenous bacterin is more successful than the use of polyvalent bacterins. Allen has reported favorable results following the use of a pyovaccine which he prepared by placing the contents of an abscess in contact with ether for 12 hours, followed by subsequent dilution with sterile salt solution. Richters has recommended the use of a polyvalent immune serum simultaneously with a methylene blue treated vaccine.

Bazeley in Australia has produced an effective vaccine by exposing very young cultures of *Str. equi* to moderate heat for a short time. The use of this vaccine reduced the incidence of strangles in horses to a significant degree.

Immune serum used at once after the appearance of symptoms is of value in reducing the severity of the disease and preventing sequelae. Convalescent serum has been used with evident success.

**Diagnosis.** Presumptive bacteriologic diagnosis may be made by identification of a gram-positive streptococcus from the lesions characteristic of the disease. Since *Str. zooepidemicus* and *Str. equisimilis* also may be found in upper-respiratory diseases of horses, it is necessary to distinguish between them and *Str. equi* by the use of appropriate media. Serological reactions have not been used in the diagnosis of the disease.

### *Streptococcus equisimilis*

**Synonyms and History.** This streptococcus has been described under various names, such as *Str. equi,* "animal pyogenes," *Str. pyogenes.* However, most workers have called attention to the characteristics which have indicated that a separate species really exists.

The name *Str. equisimilis* was proposed by Frost and Engelbrecht in 1936 to designate strains of streptococci which belonged in Lancefield Group C but which were biochemically different from *Str. zooepidemicus* and *Str. equi.*

In her detailed studies of the hemolytic streptococci in 1944, Alice Evans has described this species more thoroughly and has called attention to the different species of animals from which it may be isolated as well as from man.

**Distribution and Transmission.** This organism, apparently, is one of the species of streptococci which may be found among people and various species of animals throughout the world. In common with other members of the genus it is transmitted directly from animal to animal by close contact and by water and feed to which animals have common access.

Inasmuch as *Str. equisimilis* is found in both animals and man, there is every reason to assume that animals may serve as a source of human infection. Instances have been reported where infection caused by the organism in man has followed contact with exudate from a case of strangles in the horse, which likewise was caused by this streptococcus. No doubt there is freer exchange of it between animals and man than is generally recognized.

**Morphology and Staining.** There is nothing peculiar nor different about *Str. equisimilis* which can be used to differentiate it from other streptococci. It does not produce capsules.

**Growth Requirements and Characteristics.** *Str. equisimilis* is not as fastidious as *Str. pyogenes* or *Str. equi* in its growth requirements. It will grow rather abundantly on meat infusion agar. Blood agar, which should be used routinely for the primary isolation of all streptococci, is the most suitable medium. On this medium the organism grows abundantly and produces marked beta hemolysis. The zones of hemolysis average 4.0 mm. The colonies are discrete and opaque.

In fluid media this streptococcus forms a fairly heavy sediment in the bottom of the tube. Some strains show initial clouding of the medium which clears as the culture ages.

**Resistance.** The action of chemicals and antibiotics on *Str. equisimilis* is similar to other members of the genus.

**Biochemical Properties.** *Str. equisimilis* produces acid in glucose, maltose, sucrose, trehalose, and glycerol. Animal strains uniformly produce acid in salicin but some strains isolated from man may fail to ferment that carbohydrate. Most strains from either animal or human sources do not ferment lactose, but occasional strains may be isolated which will produce acid. No acid is produced from sorbitol, mannitol, arabinose, inulin, or raffinose. Slight acid may be produced in milk by certain strains, otherwise no change is observed in that medium. It does not hydrolyze starch and esculin. Ammonia is produced in peptone media. Gelatin is not liquefied.

**Antigenic Structure and Toxins.** It has been noted previously that *Str. equisimilis* belongs in Lancefield Group C. On the basis of agglutination, Evans has found that the strains she studied fell into at least three different types.

Antigenic relationships, on the basis of cross-protection tests, between *Str. equisimilis* and *Str. pyogenes* have been recorded. Likewise, on the basis of cross-protection tests antigenic relationships have been observed between *Str. equisimilis* and *Str. equi.*

Although the hemolysins of this streptococcus have not been studied, the marked beta hemolysis produced by it indicates that these toxins probably are similar to those produced by *Str. pyogenes.* It is probable that other toxins are likewise similar.

Evans noted that the animal and human strains of *Str. equisimilis* were not distinguishable by biochemical reactions. Hansen found that human strains of this organism were able to lyse human fibrin whereas the animal strains were unable to do so. Evans has reported the same results.

**Pathogenicity.** *Str. equisimilis* has been isolated from various conditions in many animal species and man.

In her studies Evans reported cultures from strangles and metritis of the horse. In our laboratory Packer has isolated this streptococcus from strangles, cervicitis, and wound infection in the horse.

This microorganism has been encountered by many workers in exudates and tissues from cattle. Hadley and Frost demonstrated artificial infection of the udder and isolated it from milk samples from ten cows. Evans reported it in bovine metritis and mastitis. Packer has isolated it from mastitis in the cow and Ruebke from the prepuce of the bull. It is not considered to be a common streptococcus in cattle, comparing with *Str. zooepidemicus* in this respect.

The distribution of the various species of streptococci in swine has not received detailed study. In his study of the streptococci in this animal, Collier has isolated *Str. equisimilis* from suppurative adenitis, suppurative arthritis, vegetative endocarditis, suppurative periostitis, suppurative dermatitis, pneumonia, septicemia, and an aborted fetus. Of 67 strains isolated from swine, 39 were identified as *Str. equisimilis.*

The presence of this streptococcus in pyometria, purulent rhinitis, and purulent conjunctivitis in the dog has also been observed by Packer. In this regard, attention must be called to another streptococcus, *Str. canis,* of the dog. By referring to Table 15.1 it will be noted that *Str. equisimilis* ferments trehalose but *Str. canis* does not, thus permitting the differentiation of these two streptococci.

Evans has reported avian strains of *Str. equisimilis* which were isolated from bronchitis. In the discussion of *Str. gallinarum* which follows, it will be noted that numerous reports of streptococcal infections in chickens have been made. It is quite difficult to determine the species of organism studied in many of the early reports because many of the important differential carbohydrates were not used. Those investigators who study avian diseases should take particular care in the identification of the streptococci. From such reports it will be possible to distinguish the most important streptococcus in the avian family.

The presence of strains which have been designated as "human C" in various diseases of man has been known for many years. In her study Evans has reported cultures from scarlet fever, pneumonia, hemorrhagic smallpox, erysipelas, lymphadenitis, nasal discharge, abscessation, septicemia, puerperal fever, and empyema. It is apparent that the organism is widely distributed.

**Immunity.** No information is available concerning the immunity produced by an infection with *Str. equisimilis,* but it would be rather safe to presume that there is no deviation from the general rule in all streptococcal infection.

**Diagnosis.** The incrimination of *Str. equisimilis* as the infectious agent in animal and human disease is possible only after the isolation and definite identification of the organism.

### *Streptococcus gallinarum*

**Synonyms and History.** Norgaard and Mohler isolated and described a streptococcus in 1902 which produced a highly fatal septicemia in chickens. Dammann and Mangold described an encapsulated streptococcus in 1905 to which they gave the name, *Streptococcus capsulatus gallinarum.* The organism was associated with an epizootic of "sleeping sickness" in chickens. Moore and Mack, in 1905, described the organism and the disease. In 1908 Grave described a capsulated streptococcus of the chicken. Magnusson, in 1910, investigated a highly acute septicemia of fowls caused by a streptococcus. Kernkamp, in 1927, isolated a streptococcus from chickens which had died with an idiopathic peritonitis. Hudson found a streptococcus associated with fowl septicemia in 1933.

Lack of complete descriptive data does not permit the conclusion that all the above-mentioned streptococci are of the same species, but until more definite results have been established, they will be classified as *Str. gallinarum*. Many of the descriptions suggest that some of the strains should be classified as *Str. zooepidemicus*. The failure to ferment sorbitol has been mentioned in some reports. This suggests that these cultures may have been *Str. equisimilis*.

**Distribution and Transmission.** The organism has been found in the United States, Germany, and Sweden. The method of transmission among birds in the flock is not known, but the nature of the severe type of septicemia indicates that it is spread through water or contaminated feed.

**Morphology and Staining.** Short chains of six to eight cells predominate. Long chains are found in fluid media. Cells are diplococcoid on solid media. Uneven sizes are common. Some strains are capsulated. The organism is gram-positive.

**Growth Requirements and Characteristics.** *Str. gallinarum* can be isolated from the blood and tissues of infected birds. If blood is added to the surface of agar, growth is stimulated. Young colonies on agar are white and gelantinous, and as they become older, brownish centers and bluish borders are evident. A maximum size is reached in 72 hours. A flocculent sediment is formed in bouillon. Beta hemolysis is formed on blood agar.

**Resistance.** Resistance is typical of the group.

**Biochemical Properties.** The organism ferments glucose, fructose, lactose, maltose, sucrose, dextrin, starch, galactose, and salicin; does not ferment arabinose, adonitol, dulcitol, erythritol, inositol, mannitol, and sorbitol; does not ferment lactose in milk sufficiently to produce coagulation.

**Antigenic Structure and Toxins.** Hemolysin and leucocidin are produced. Nothing is known about antigenic types.

**Pathogenicity.** The organism is most pathogenic for chickens in which it produces a typical acute septicemia. It produces a peritonitis which accompanies the septicemia. Rabbits, pigeons, ducks, and white mice succumb to injection of the organism. Guinea pigs are resistant.

**Immunity.** Little is known of the immunity produced naturally by the infection in surviving birds. It has been observed that active immunity can be conferred by the injection of bouillon culture filtrates and by vaccination with killed cultures, and that passive immunity can be established by the injection of the blood serum of an immunized animal. The latter is of doubtful value due to the apoplectiform nature of the disease.

**Diagnosis.** The organism is identified as a gram-positive streptococcus in smears from the blood and internal organs as well as by culture.

### *Streptococcus canis*

A study of the streptococcic infections of dogs by Stafseth, Thompson, and Neu in 1937 revealed a new species, *Streptococcus canis*. This organism and the conditions which it produces in the dog were again discussed by Stafseth in 1940. This organism was the one most commonly found in infected dogs although two other types were isolated.

*Str. canis* is 0.9μ to 1μ in size, occurs singly and in pairs, but often in chains of varying lengths. The shape and size of the individual cells in a single chain vary from well-rounded forms to elliptical or rod-shaped elements. It is gram-positive. It is definitely beta hemolytic, forming a zone on blood agar up to 5 mm. in diameter. Colonies of the organism vary from 0.5 to 1 mm. in size and are convex, smooth, glistening, faintly yellowish white, opaque with entire margins. This streptococcus grows best on blood agar, but it will grow on neopeptone chicken muscle infusion agar. It forms a fine to coarse granular sediment with a clear supernatant fluid when grown on neopeptone chicken infusion broth. *Str. canis* produces acid but no gas in glucose, lactose, maltose, salicin, and sucrose. It does not ferment mannite, sorbitol, or trehalose. It belongs to Group C of Lancefield.

The female genital tract appears to be the natural habitat of this streptococcus, and Stafseth, Thompson, and Neu were able to isolate it from the prepuce of a male dog four days after mating to an infected female. The organism has been isolated from abscesses which have followed antirabies inoculation, emphasizing the fact that care must be taken in cleaning and disinfecting the skin of dogs prior to biological therapy. *Str. canis* has been isolated from the umbilicus, intestines, heart, lungs, kidneys, vagina, blood, peritoneal cavity, and femorotibial articulation of pups; hence, it is thought to be of considerable significance to very young dogs. It is considered to be the cause of "acid milk" in puppies and is thought to be the chief etiological agent in canine tonsillitis.

The female may be a carrier of the organism; consequently, it is doubtful that immunity follows an active infection. Stafseth, Thompson, and Neu treated two cases of articular and muscular rheumatism successfully with an autogenous vaccine.

Since other species of streptococci, not as yet sufficiently studied to warrant description here, are found in the dog, accurate diagnosis of the presence of *Str. canis* can be obtained only by the isolation and identification of the organism.

### Miscellaneous Streptococci

In 1922 Bayne-Jones described a hemolytic streptococcus which causes a respiratory infection and septicemia of cats, to which the name *Streptococcus feline* was given. The organism was culturally and biochemically identical with *Str. pyogenes* but serologically distinct. It is possible that this organism belongs to the *"animal pyogenes"* group.

The presence of beta hemolytic streptococci in the lymph nodes of the cervical region of swine was reported by Newsom in Colorado in 1937 and by Stafseth and Clinton in Michigan in 1941. The organisms described by these investigators did not appear to be identical. Stafseth and Clinton reported that their streptococcus belonged in Lancefield's Group E, which was the first time such a source of this organism had been reported. In his study of streptococci isolated from swine, Collier found 13 out of 67 strains studied were classified as Group L and 5 strains were Group E.

The presence of alpha hemolytic varieties of streptococci in animal disease is not well established. This type is found in animals with mastitis and in some cases of wound infection. Thorp has found viridans type of streptococci associated with pneumonia in the pig. It is probable that these organisms may be of some importance in chronic infections in animals as well as in man. Organisms of this type are found in the mouth and intestinal tract of both man and animals. *Str. equinus* appears to be a rather well-defined species of the viridans type which is found as a saprophyte in the intestine of the horse.

An unusual motile streptococcus has been reported by Bruner, Edwards, Doll, and Moran. This organism was isolated from an aborted equine fetus and was believed to have produced the abortion. It grew readily on meat infusion agar; was gram-positive; individual cells were oblong rather than spherical and arranged in short chains or small groups. The organism was found to be monotrichous and cultures grown in semisolid agar showed slight growth from the needle track, indicating slight motility. This streptococcus produced acid but not gas in glucose, lactose, sucrose, mannitol, sorbitol, trehalose, and salicin. It hydrolyzed sodium hippurate; reduced methylene blue milk; grew on 40 per cent bile blood agar. Narrow zones of beta hemolysis were observed around deep colonies in blood agar. It was found to belong to Group D.

In a study of the distribution of Group D streptococci in cattle and sheep, Medrek and Barnes found *Str. bovis* was the predominant species in cattle and sheep. *Str. faecalis, Str. faecium,* and *Str. durans* were rare in cattle but were quite common in sheep.

Nonhemolytic streptococci are often found in animal tissues. Most gamma types are considered saprophytic, and for that reason have not been completely studied except from the point of view of systematic relationships. Many species are of use in dairy manufacturing. They grow well in milk and in milk products, and for that reason are of significance in milk sanitation. *Str. lactis* is one of the most common organisms of this type; however, it is not a normal inhabitant of the bovine udder; in fact, it is rarely found there. It gains access to milk from contaminated utensils. Recent work indicates that its normal habitat is plants; this explains its prevalence in raw milk. For the detailed description of this and other streptococci of significance in milk processing, the student is advised to consult Hammer's text, *Dairy Bacteriology.*

## REFERENCES


Alford, J. A., *et al.* Cornell Vet. 45:357, 1955.

Bazeley, P. L. Austral. Vet. Jour. 18:189–94, 1940.

———. Austral. Vet. Jour. 19:62–85, 1941.

———. Studies With Equine Streptococci. III. Vaccination Against Strangles. Austral. Vet. Jour. 18:141–55, 1942.

Bergey, D. H., *et al.* Manual of Determinative Bacteriology. 7th Ed. Williams & Wilkins Co., Baltimore, 1957.

Brocq-Rousseu, Forgeot, and Urbain. Le Streptocoque Gourmeux. Five parts. Revue de Pathologie Comparée et d'Hygiène Générale 25, 1925.

Brown, J. H. The Use of Blood Agar for the Study of Streptococci. Rockefeller Inst. Med. Res., Monograph No. 9, 1919

Bruner, D. W., *et al.* Cornell Vet. 38:313–14, 1948.

Christensen, L. R. Jour. Gen. Physiol. 28:363–83, 1945.

Christie, R., *et al.* Austral. Jour. Exp. Biol. Med. Sci. 22:197, 1944.

Collier, J. R. Streptococci Lymphadenitis of the Pharyngeal Region of Swine. Jour. Amer. Vet. Med. Assn. 129:543, 1956.

———. Proc. 88th Ann. Conv. Amer. Vet. Med. Assn. P. 169, 1951.

Czarnetzky, E. J., *et al.* Jour. Exp. Med. 67:643–57, 1938.

Dick, G. F., and Dick, G. H. Jour. Amer. Med. Assn. 82:301–2, 1924.

Dimock, W. W., and Edwards, P. R. Ky. Agr. Exp. Sta. Bull. 338, 1933.

———, and Snyder, Ethel. Jour. Amer. Vet. Med. Assn. 64:288–99, 1923.

Edwards, P. R. Jour. Bact. 23:259–66, 1932.

———. Jour. Bact. 35:527–36, 1933.

———. Jour. Bact. 27:527–34, 1934.

——— Ky. Agr. Exp. Sta. Bull. 536, 1935.

Edwards, S. J. Jour. Comp. Path. Therap. 45:43–57, 1932.

Evans, Alice C. Streptococcus Bacteriophage: A Study of Four Serological Types. Pub. Health Rept., Wash. 49:1386–1401, 1934.

———. Studies on Hemolytic Streptococci. Four parts. Jour. Bact. 31, 32, 1936; 34, 1937.

———. Studies on Hemolytic Streptococci. VIII. *Streptococcus equisimilis.* Jour. Bact. 48:267–84, 1944.

———. Jour. Inf. Dis. 78:1–17, 18–24, 1946.

Garner, R. L., and Tillett, W. S. Jour. Exp. Med. 60:239–67. 1934

GRIFFITH, F. The Serological Classification of *Streptococcus pyogenes*. Jour. Hyg. 34:542–84, 1934.
HAHN, J. J., and COLE, R. M. Studies on the Mechanism of the Long Chain Phenomenon of Group A Streptococci. Jour. Exp. Med. 117:583, 1963.
HAMMER, B. W. Dairy Bacteriology. 3rd Ed. John Wiley & Sons, Inc., New York, 1948.
HANSEN, P. A. A Bibliography on Mastitis. N.Y. (Geneva) Agr. Exp. Sta. Mimeo. Bull. 1, 1934.
———. Mastitis. III. The Identity of *Streptococcus agalactiae*. N.Y. (Geneva) Agr. Exp. Sta. Tech. Bull. 232, 1935.
HANSEN, P. L. Skand. Vet-Tidskr. 33:257–80, 1943.
HOTIS, R. P., and MILLER, W. T. A Simple Method for Detecting Mastitis Streptococci in Milk. USDA, Circ. No. 400, 1936.
HUCKER, G. J. Mastitis. V. The Presence of Mastitis Streptococci in Bovine Mammary Tissue. N.Y. (Geneva) Agr. Exp. Sta. Tech. Bull. 241, 1937.
INGALLS, W. L., and JOHNSON, E. P. Amer. Jour. Vet. Res. 8:321–24, 1947.
LANCEFIELD, REBECCA C. The Antigenic Complex of *Streptococcus haemolyticus*. Five parts. Jour. Exp. Med. 47, 1928.
———. A Serological Differentiation of Human and Other Groups of Hemolytic Streptococci. Jour. Exp. Med. 57:571–95, 1933.
———. Two Serological Types of Group B Hemolytic Streptococci With Related, but Not Identical, Type-specific Substances. Jour. Exp. Med. 67:25–40, 1938.
———. Jour. Exp. Med. 78:465–76, 1943.
———, and DOLE, V. P. Jour. Exp. Med. 84:449–71, 1946.
———, and STEWART, W. A. Jour. Exp. Med. 79:79–88, 1944.
MCCARTY, M. The Hemolytic Streptococci. Chap. 10. *In* Dubos, Bacterial and Mycotic Infections of Man. 3rd Ed. J. B. Lippincott Co., Philadelphia, 1958.
MEDREK, T. F., and BARNES, E. M. The Distribution of Group D Streptococci in Cattle and Sheep. Jour. Appl. Bact. 25:159, 1962.
MICHAEL, J. G., and MASSELL, B. F. Factors Involved in the Induction of Non-specific Resistance to Streptococcal Infection in Mice by Endotoxin. Jour. Exp. Med. 116:101, 1962.
MINETT, F. C. Jour. Path. Bact. 40:357–64, 1935.
———, and STABLEFORTH, A. W. Jour. Dairy Res. 5:223–32, 1934.
MURPHY, J. M. The Effect of Certain Mild Stresses to the Bovine Teat Canal on Infection With *Streptococcus agalactiae*. Cornell Vet. 49:411, 1959.
———, *et al.* Cornell Vet. 42:133, 1952.
NEWSOM, I. E. Vet. Med. 37:137–38, 1937.
NORCROSS, N. L. Antigenic Substances Purified From *Streptococcus agalactiae*. I. Antibody Response in Infected Cattle. Cornell Vet. 53:301–8, 1963.
PERRY, D., and SLADE, H. D. Optimal Conditions for the Transformation of Streptococci. Jour. Bact. 85:636, 1963.
PLASTRIDGE, W. N., and HARTSELL, S. E. Jour. Inf. Dis. 61:110–21, 1937.
SATO, G., and USHIJIMA, J. An Outbreak of Hemolytic-Streptococcal Infection Among Chickens of a Flock. Jap. Jour. Vet. Res. 8:285, 1960.
SHERMAN, JAMES, M. The Streptococci. Bact. Rev. 1:1–97, 1937.
SPENCER, G. R. The Effect of Hypersensitivity on Experimental Streptococcal Mastitis. Res. Studies, State College of Washington 24:247, 1956.
———, *et al.* Amer. Jour. Vet. Res. 7:32–36, 1946.
STABLEFORTH, A. W. Jour. Path. Bact. 45:263–77, 1937.
STAFSETH, H. J. Jour. Amer. Vet. Med. Assn. 96:230–35, 1940
———, and CLINTON, I. Jour. Amer. Vet. Med. Assn. 99:468–70, 1941.
———, *et al.* Jour. Amer. Vet. Med. Assn. 90:769–81, 1937.
STEWART, W. A., *et al.* Jour. Exp. Med. 79:99–114, 1944.
THOMSON, D., and THOMSON, R. The Pathogenic Streptococci. Annals Pickett-Thomson Research Lab. 4, 1928.
WATSON, R. F., and LANCEFIELD, REBECCA C. Jour. Exp. Med. 79:89–98, 1944.
WILSON, G. S., and MILES, A. A. Topley's Principles of Bacteriology and Immunity. 5th Ed. Williams & Wilkins Co., Baltimore, 1964.

# 16

# The Genera Diplococcus and Neisseria

THE ORGANISMS IN THE GROUP OF DIPLOCOCCI are spherical or oval in shape, and the cells are usually in pairs. All the organisms are nonmotile and are nonsporeproducing. One genus, Diplococcus, produces capsules. Species of both genera grow sparsely on solid media in drewdrop-like colonies and ferment carbohydrates with acid formation only. They are strictly parasitic for man and cause specific diseases.

The species of this group are placed in two genera, Diplococcus and Neisseria; the separation is made upon the basis of the reaction to the Gram stain and on morphology. *Diplococcus pneumoniae* is gram-positive; the cells are elongated, pointed, and capsulated. *Neisseria meningitidis* and *Neisseria gonorrhoeae* are gram-negative; the cells are spherical and noncapsulated.

None of the above species produces disease in animals, but all are sufficiently important to the student in animal bacteriology to warrant brief discussion. Additional references are given at the end of the chapter for the convenience of the student.

## THE GENUS DIPLOCOCCUS

### *Diplococcus pneumoniae*

**Synonyms and History.** *Pneumococcus, Streptococcus pneumoniae, Diplococcus lanceolatus,* Fränkel's pneumococcus.

The presence of cocci in the exudate from cases of pneumonia was noted by Klebs (1875), Ebert (1881), Koch (1881), Leyden (1882), and Friedländer (1882). Pasteur, Chamberland, and Roux (1881), and Sternberg (1881) isolated an organism from the blood of rabbits which had died of a septicemia following the injection of human sputum. In cases of pneumonia, Telamon (1883) observed lancet-shaped organisms with which he infected rabbits. Fränkel (1884) is accredited with being the first to isolate the organism and to give a clear description of it and its relationship to pneumonia. Weichselbaum (1886) found it to be the most common organism in pneumonia. In 1900 Neufeld concluded that the organism is bile-soluble. Neufeld and Haendel (1910 observed that the pneumococci are of more than one serological type. This finding was confirmed by Avery, Chickering, Cole, and Dochez in 1917. Since that time Avery and his pupils and many others have contributed to the subject. At present, thirty-two serological types of pneumococci are known.

**Distribution and Transmission.** The pneumococci are found all over the civilized world exempting no class of people from infection. Some of the types of the organism seem to be normal inhabitants of the human mouth. It is believed, however, that immune carriers are responsible for pneumonia which is caused by the more virulent strains. The disease appears as a sporadic one. Epidemics are rarely observed, and for this reason predisposing factors, such as fatigue, exposure, faulty nutrition, and alcoholism, are considered important. The organism is transmitted by hand-to-mouth contact.

**Morphology and Staining.** The organism is $0.5\mu$ to $1.25\mu$ in size. It usually occurs in pairs with occasional chains of four or six cells. It is ovoid or lanceolate with adjacent cells bluntly rounded at the point of contact (Fig. 16.1). Capsules are present in tissue or exudates but absent on artificial media, unless serum is present. The organism is nonmotile, does not form spores, and is gram-positive.

**Growth Requirements and Characteristics.** The organism may be isolated in pure cultures from the blood in some cases. The preliminary injection of sputum into white mice aids in the isolation of pure cultures. It grows best at 37°C., but some strains grow at 25°C. in the presence of carbon dioxide. It is a faculative anaerobe.

On serum agar the colonies are flat, moist, discrete, and transparent, with a slight elevation of the edges. Some strains form mucoid colonies. Dissociation has been found to occur under certain conditions. Typical S (smooth) colonies produce R (rough colonies). The R types are usually noncapsulated and avirulent. Since the R type is often found in convalescent cases, it is thought that recovery may be aided by the dissociation of virulent S to avirulent R types due to the action of immune serum.

Alpha hemolysis with the typical green zone around the colony is formed in blood agar. Broth is clouded initially with subsequent settling of the cells as the culture ages.

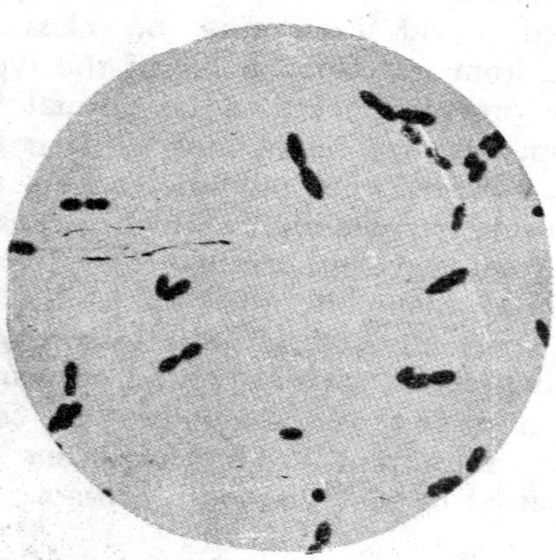

FIG. 16.1—Diplococcus pneumoniae from an agar culture, ×2,000. (From Nowak: Documenta Microbiologica, courtesy Gustav Fischer.)

**Resistance.** The thermal death point for *Dip. pneumoniae* is 60°C. for 30 minutes. It readily perishes in cultures but has been known to live for considerable periods of time in pulmonary exudate. It is readily killed by the common disinfectants. The R forms are more resistant than the S. Penicillin is commonly used in the treatment of pneumonia caused by this diplococcus.

**Biochemical Properties.** *Dip. pneumoniae* produces acid from lactose, sucrose, inulin, usually from raffinose, frequently from salicin; does not ferment mannitol; does not liquefy gelatin; does not reduce nitrates; does not form indol. The organism is soluble in bile (1:10), which is an important distinguishing characteristic. Milk serves as a good medium and is acidified and coagulated, although slowly by some strains.

**Antigenic Structure and Toxins.** The antigenic structure of the pneumococci is better known than that of any other group of micrococci. The basic antigen is composed of nucleoprotein which is contained in the body of the cell. Covering this is a protein-lipoid substance which determines the species. The capsular material is composed of complex polysaccharides by which the different types are recognized.

The agglutination of organisms, the precipitation of extracts, or the swelling of the capsule, "Quellung reaction" of Neufeld, by type-specific antisera may be used as the basis of type determinations. For rapid typing the capsule-swelling reaction is used most often.

Four original types of pneumococci, designated I, II, III, IV, have been considered of greatest importance. At the present time eighty different types have been found. Types I and II appear to be most prevalent in the United States.

The organism produces a soluble hemolysin and leucocidin. It does not produce fibrinolysin for human fibrin, but does produce a substance which prevents the clotting of rabbit serum.

**Pathogenicity.** *Dip. pneumoniae* is the cause of lobar pneumonia in man. It may cause other types of infection, such as sinusitis, otitis media and meningitis, pleurisy, peritonitis, endocarditis, and arthritis. Mice are highly susceptible, and virulent strains kill rabbits. Guinea pigs are resistant, although organisms resembling the pneumococci have been observed in spontaneous outbreaks of pneumonia in that animal. Lobar pneumonia has been produced experimentally in the monkey. Spontaneous pneumonia due to the organism has been reported in monkeys held in captivity. Horses, swine, sheep, dogs, cats, fowls, and pigeons are resistant.

**Immunity.** Type-specific immune serum gives favorable results in both preventive and curative treatment. The determination of the type of pneumococcus causing the disease is imperative for successful treatment. Vaccines and baterins are not widely used in immunization, although numerous investigators report that such materials are of value in decreasing the incidence of the disease in susceptible populations.

One attack of the disease does not confer an immunity. When recovery takes place, increased activity of phagocytes is considered responsible.

**Diagnosis.** The laboratory diagnosis of pneumonia is concerned chiefly with the determination of the type to which the invading pneumococcus belongs.

## THE GENUS NEISSERIA

### *Neisseria meningitidis*

**Synonyms and History.** *Diplococcus intracellularis meningitidis, Diplococcus meningitidis, Micrococcus weichselbaumii, Streptococcus meningitidis, Neisseria intracellularis.*

Marchiofava and Celli were the first to observe the organism in meningeal exudate from man in 1884. It was first cultured and identified as a separate species by Weichselbaum in 1887. The causal relationship of the organism to epidemic cerebrospinal meningitis has been demonstrated since that time by numerous investigators.

**Distribution and Transmission.** The disease caused by this diplococcus occurs in epidemic form in most heavily populated areas. It is a disease of some concern in army life. Serious epidemics were reported in 1965. Numerous epidemics of the disease have occurred in the eastern part of the United States and on the Pacific coast. The resistant carrier seems to constitute the chief source of the infection. The organism is spread by nasal and oral discharges. It gains entrance to the nasopharynx where it may cause slight inflammatory disturbances. Whether the organism enters the meninges by way of the lymph vessels or the blood stream is not known, but the large percentage of blood cultures which are positive favor the latter route.

**Morphology and Staining.** The organism is spherical, and when in diplococcic form the adjacent sides of the cells are flattened. It varies in size from $0.6\mu$ to $1\mu$. It is nonmotile, nonsporeforming, and noncapsulated. Granules of a metachromatic nature are shown by the Neisser stain. It is gram-negative. Masses of cells are found in heterophile leucocytes from spinal fluid (Fig. 16.2).

**Growth Requirements and Characteristics.** The meningococcus is isolated in pure culture from material obtained from the spinal canal by lumbar puncture. It grows best on media to which serum or blood has been added and the pH has been adjusted to 7.4–7.6. The colonies on serum agar are transparent, circular, and hemispherical with a bluish-gray tinge. The colonies are larger than those of the streptococci but not as large and opaque as the staphylococci. No hemolysis is produced in blood

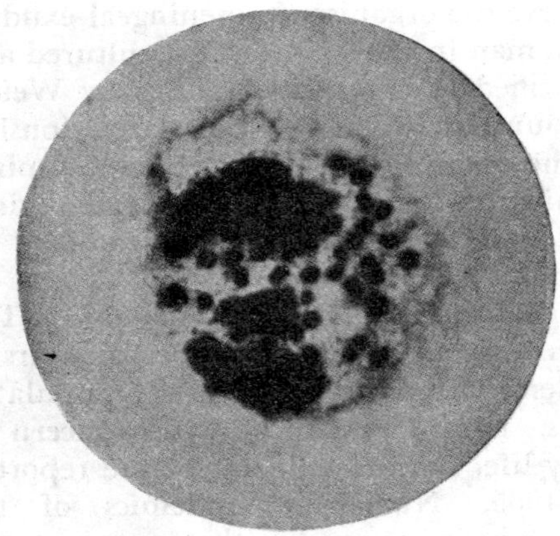

FIG. 16.2—**Neisseria meningitidis** in polymorphonuclear leucocyte of cerebrospinal fluid, ×2,000. (From Nowak: Documenta Microbiologica, courtesy Gustav Fischer.)

agar. Growth in broth occurs near the surface and produces a faint clouding; a granular sediment forms on the bottom of the tube. The optimum temperature for growth is 37°C. Oxygen is essential for maximum growth.

**Resistance.** The organism is easily killed by 55°C. in a few minutes. Desiccation kills cultures quickly, and they must be transplanted often or must be kept tightly sealed in order to maintain them. Ordinary disinfectants destroy the organisms quickly. It is sensitive to penicillin and the broad spectrum antibiotics.

**Biochemical Properties.** *N. meningitidis* forms acid from glucose and maltose; does not ferment fructose, sucrose, and mannitol; does not change litmus milk; reduces methylene blue; does not form indol or $H_2S$.

**Antigenic Structure and Toxins.** The meningococci are not composed of one homogenous antigenic group. According to Gordon, four different groups are recognized by agglutinin-absorption tests. Some investigators maintain that there is considerable overlapping in several of the groups, and it is practical to recognize only two types.

The organism produces a powerful toxin by which typical symptoms and lesions are produced experimentally in rabbits. Whether this toxin is an endotoxin or exotoxin is not known, but evidence points strongly toward the latter. A weak hemolysin and leucocidin are produced.

**Pathogenicity.** *N. meningitidis* infection is observed most commonly in children and young adults. The disease is an acute inflammation of the meninges, accompanied by a purulent exudate. The mortality in the disease is usually high, but not 100 per cent as is often the case in meningitis caused by other bacteria. Death is thought by many to be due to a toxemia.

Injection of pure cultures of the organism into the spinal canal of the goat has been found to produce meningitis, and inoculation into the monkey has resulted in a duplication of the disease as it occurs in man. Rabbits, guinea pigs, and mice are susceptible to intravenous and intraperitoneal injections but are killed more quickly by subdural inoculations.

**Immunity.** It is probable that an attack of the disease results in immunity, although data to this effect are not conclusive. Polyvalent immune serum is used in treating cases of the disease. The serum must be injected directly into the spinal canal in order to be effective. This necessitates the removal of fluid to keep the pressure on the cord equalized. Vaccines have been used on a large scale in armies, but the results are not available. The value of vaccine prophylaxis is still doubtful.

**Diagnosis.** Lumbar puncture, with the demonstration in smears of a gram-negative diplococcus, occurring principally within the leucocytes, constitutes a satisfactory diagnosis. The agglutination test may be applied but is not used in practice. Some investigators believe that the test is of value in detecting resistant carriers of the organism.

### *Neisseria gonorrhoeae*

**Synonyms and History.** *Micrococcus gonorrhoeae, Diplococcus gonorrhoeae,* diplococcus of Neisser, gonococcus.

Neisser, in 1879, noted the occurrence of a characteristic coccus in gonorrheal pus. Bumm, in 1885, obtained the organism in pure cultures and determined the causal relationship of the organism to the disease by inoculations into human subjects.

**Distribution and Transmission.** Gonorrhea is found throughout the civilized world. No class or race is exempt from infection. Transmission occurs in the greatest percentage of cases by direct sexual contact. Infection of the conjuctiva may result from the use of recently infected towels or from infected hands. Infection from toilet seats and toilet accessories is possible, but occurs rarely; this is equally true of bed linen and clothing.

**Morphology and Staining.** *N. gonorrhoeae* is a typical diplococcus. The cells are spherical with adjacent edges flattened and slightly indented, giving the appearance of a kidney bean. It is nonmotile, nonsporeforming, and noncapsulated. It stains gram-negative, which is important, as this renders possible differential diagnosis between the common staphylococci and the gonococcus. Microorganisms are abundant in the purulent secretion of a typical infection; many are present in leucocytes (Fig. 16.3). Methylene blue and Wright's stain are especially suited for the direct staining of such smears.

**Growth Requirements and Characteristics.** Growth is best obtained on media to which serum or ascitic fluid has been added. It is a strict aerobe, and the optimum temperature for growth is 36°C. Surface colonies on serum agar are thin, grayish, opalescent, amorphous, and glistening, with entire edges, and with a slimy consistency. In fluid media, growth is more abundant toward the surface, and a fine, granular sediment forms as the culture ages. Old cultures kept on chocolate agar tend to lose virulence. Walsh and associates have found that virulence can be maintained; in fact, old cultures can be restored in virulence by growing them upon the chick embryo.

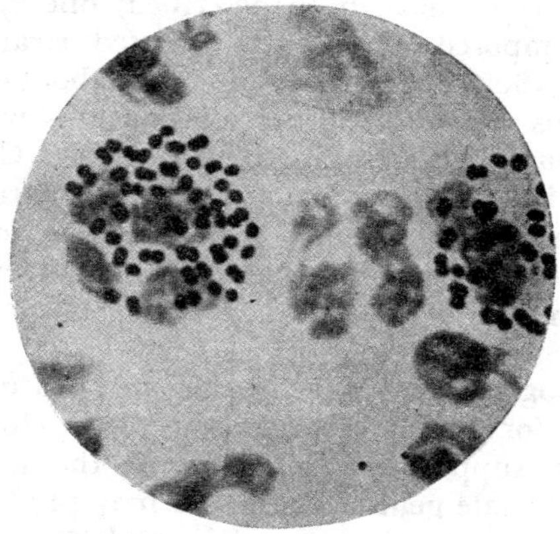

FIG. 16.3—**Neisseria gonorrhoeae** undergoing phagocytosis, ×2,000. (From Nowak: Documenta Microbiologica, courtesy Gustav Fischer.)

**Resistance.** *N. gonorrhoeae* is easily killed by 55°C. in 5 minutes. Drying kills it in a few minutes, although cells may remain viable in undried pus for 18 to 20 hours. The organism quickly succumbs to ordinary surface disinfectants and is especially sensitive to silver nitrate and other silver salts. It is killed by diathermy, 41.5° to 43°C. in 2 to 7 hours. Penicillin is used in treatment which has caused a false assumption that the disease is not serious or frequent. Obviously, the wide use of antibiotic therapy has not decreased the incidence of the disease.

**Biochemical Properties.** The saccharolytic powers of the organisms are negligible; dextrose is fermented with acid formation. Litmus milk is unaltered. Methylene blue reduction is negative. Indol and $H_2S$ formation are negative.

**Antigenic Structure and Toxins.** The group is not antigenically homogenous.

Two types have been described; one type is composed of recently isolated strains, and the other type of old laboratory strains. Some antigenic relationships with *N. intracellularis* apparently exist. Culture filtrates are toxic, but the exact nature of the toxic substance is not known; however, it is probable that it is not an exotoxin.

**Pathogenicity.** Man is the only natural host for the microorganism. It produces acute suppurative infection in the male and female genital tracts and may produce cystitis, proctitis, stomatitis, and conjunctivitis. Sterility in the male and female is a common sequela of the infection. Prior to the discovery of the sulfa drugs and antibiotics it was considered to be the cause of 60 to 75 per cent of the surgical operations on female genitalia, 60 per cent of the blindness in the newborn, and 10 per cent of all blindness. Duration of the infection is indefinite in some cases. Mice, rabbits, and guinea pigs are killed by subcutaneous, intraperitoneal, and intravenous injections. The genital tracts of all animals are resistant to the infection.

**Immunity.** One infection does not confer an immunity. The individual may harbor the infection for years even though the acute stage does not reappear. Agglutinating, precipitating, and complement-fixing antibodies are demonstrated during infections. Vaccines are used, but are of doubtful value. Immune serum has been used, but beneficial results have not been proved.

**Diagnosis.** The demonstration of gram-negative diplococci in pus from typical cases is sufficient for the diagnosis of gonorrhea. Internal infection is diagnosed by agglutination, precipitation, or, in some cases by complement-fixation.

## REFERENCES


AVERY, C. T., *et al.* Acute Lobar Pneumonia. Prevention and Serum Treatment. The Rockefeller Inst. Med. Res., Monograph No. 7, 1917.

Branham, S. E. The Meningococcus (*Neisseria intracellularis*). Bact. Rev. 4:59–96, 1940.

———. Milestones in the History of the Meningococcus. Canad. Jour. Microbiol. 2:175–88, 1956.

BURROWS, W. Textbook of Microbiology. 16th Ed. W. B. Saunders Co., Philadelphia, 1954.

CHEEVER, F. S. The Meningococci. *In* Bacterial and Mycotic Infections of Man, R. J. Dubos (ed.), Chap. 24. J. B. Lippincott Co., Philadelphia, 1958.

GARSON, W., and THAYER, J. D. The Gonococcus. *In* Bacterial and Mycotic Infections of Man, R. J. Dubos (ed.), Chap. 25. J. B. Lippincott Co., Philadelphia, 1958.

McLEOD, J. W., *et al.* The Pneumococcus. A System of Bacteriology in Relation to Medicine. Vol. II, p. 164. His Majesty's Stationery Office, London, 1929.

MURRAY, E. G. D. The Meningococcus. A System of Bacteriology. Vol. II, pp. 291–325, His Majesty's Stationery Office, London, 1929.

PELOUZE, P. S. Gonorrhea in the Male and Female. 2nd Ed. W. B. Saunders Co., Philadelphia, 1931.

TULLOCH, W. J. The Gonococcus. A System of Bacteriology. Vol. II, p. 239. His Majesty's Stationery Office, London, 1929.

WALSH, M. J., *et al.* Use of the Chick Embryo in Maintaining and Restoring Virulence of *Neisseria gonorrhoeae.* Jour. Bact. 86:478, 1963.

WHITE, B. The Biology of the Pneumococcus. The Commonwealth Fund, New York, 1938.

WILSON, G. S., and MILES, A. A. Topley's Principles of Bacteriology and Immunity. 5th Ed. Williams & Wilkins Co., Baltimore, 1964.

# 17

# The Genus Staphylococcus

The staphylococci are spherical or ovoid cells usually arranged in grapelike clusters, although pairs and short chains are seen frequently in fluid media. They are nonsporeforming, nonmotile, noncapsuleproducing, and gram-positive. White, yellow, or orange, water-insoluble pigments are formed. They are aerobic and facultative, liquefy gelatin, and ferment a number of carbohydrates to acid. The organisms are found in suppurative processes in man and animals and produce a variety of toxic substances.

Micrococci were discovered in pus by Ogston in 1881, and in 1883 he divided them into two groups, *Staphylococci* and *Streptococci.* In 1884 Rosenbach cultivated them upon artificial media and differentiated between two species which he named *Staphylococcus pyogenes aureus* and *Staphylococcus pyogenes albus.* Passet, in 1885, isolated a third species, *Staphylococcus pyogenes citreus.* The investigations of Garre in 1885, Bumm in 1885, and Bockhart in 1887, in which they subjected themselves to inoculations, proved the relationship of these cocci to human infections.

Migula, in 1895, assigned the genus name *Micrococcus* to the group. In 1900 in his System der Bacterien, he referred to the species as *Micrococcus aureus, Micrococcus albus,* and *Micrococcus citreus.* Andrewes and Gordon, in 1905–6, reported a study of 300 cultures of staphylococci and concluded that "*Staphylococcus pyogenes albus* is merely a nonpigmented variety of the golden form, and that *Staphylococcus pyogenes citreus* is an intermediate variety. The chromogenesis is a physiological function which is readily lost. Our experiments have not yielded any instance of the gain of a chromogenic function in a primitively white variety. The species may conveniently be termed *Staphylococcus pyogenes,* the suffixes 'aureus,' 'albus,' and 'citreus' being employed when desired. Its cardinal reactions are the formation of acid in mannite media, and the rapid liquefaction of gelatin, usually manifested in 48 hours. This is clearly the most important and virulent of the pathogenic staphylococci as well as the commonest." Andrewes and Gordon also recognized four different types of staphylococci in man—*Staphylococcus pyogenes, Staphylococcus epidermidis albus, Staphyloccus salivarius,* and the scurf staphylococcus. In 1909 Winslow and Rogers formed the genus names *Aurococcus* and *Albococcus* for the golden- and white-pigmented strains. Buchanan, in 1911, used the genus name *Micrococcus* for the group. In 1917 Buchanan placed these cocci in the genus *Staphylococcus.* This genus name has been used in most systematic treatises since that time and seems to be definitely established.

The difficulty in classifying this group of bacteria has been demonstrated by classifications in Bergey's Manual. In the 1948 edition they were called Micrococci, then in the 1957 edition they were called Staphylococci. Although one well-defined species has emerged, it has become more and more evident that numerous strains exist which do not fall into well-defined species.

Classifications by Shaw, Stitt, and Cowan (1951) and by Baird-Parker (1963) have attempted to clarify the problem. The latter recognizes two groups; Group I, Staphyloccus; and Group II, Micrococcus. In Group I he places six subgroups, headed by *Staph aureus.* In Group II he places seven subgroups but does not assign any species names to them.

It can be concluded that there exists one definitely pathogenic species, *Staph. aureus,* and that numerous ill-defined strains may be isolated from man and animals, which can simply be referred to as Micrococci.

The importance of *Staph. aureus* as a pathogenic microorganism to man and animals has been augmented by the variety of toxic substances which it produces. This organism is also fascinating because it has been shown that all strains do not produce all toxic materials, but may have the capacity to gain or lose this ability.

Inasmuch as the virulence of *Staph. aureus* is dependent on its toxins, these substances will be discussed in some detail.

## STAPHYLOCOCCUS TOXINS

The pathogenesis of staphylococcal infection is a type of chain reaction dependent upon the toxin produced and the reaction of the tissues of the host. Staphyloccus toxins may be listed in the order in which they produce their effect upon body tissues as follows: coagulase, fibrinolysin, leucocidin, hyaluronidase, dermonecrotoxin, lethaltoxin, hemolysin, and enterotoxin.

### Coagulase

This substance appears to be the first line of defense of invading pathogenic staphylococci. It is reasoned that the coagulation of plasma about a colony of organisms permits them to multiply and protects them from immediate phagocytosis. It has become an important criterion for determining whether a staphylococcus isolated from a disease process in man or animals is pathogenic.

In 1903 Loeb demonstrated the coagulation of goose plasma by broth cultures of *Staph. aureus.* Since that time, the substance has been studied by many investigators who have shown a close relationship between it and pathogenicity. Rabbit and human plasma are most readily clotted, although dog plasma has been coagulated by some strains. In the routine detection of coagulase-producing strains of staphylococci, an equal volume of broth culture or a loopful of agar plate culture is added to fresh, citrated rabbit plasma, diluted 1:5 in broth. The ingredients are thoroughly mixed and placed in the 37°C. incubator or in a water-bath held at that temperature. The tube is examined for clotting at intervals over a period of three hours. Practically all of the pathogenic strains will show clotting within one hour. Some strains are slow, however, so incubation is usually continued overnight. The clot which is formed is usually quite solid and compact, but occasional strains are observed which produce a "thready" accumulation of fibrin. No one has shown a relationship between the type of clot and pathogenicity.

Coagulase is resistant to heat; some strains produce a more heat-resistant substance than others. Variations of 50° to 100°C. for 30 minutes have been reported. Its antigenicity is doubtful. Staphylococcus antihemotoxin has no effect upon it. The active principle in coagulase is precipitated by alcohol, acetic acid, or half-saturation with ammonium sulfate. The active principle may be dialyzed through cellophane after precipitation with alcohol but not before.

In a study of 32 coagulase-positive strains of staphylococci, Spink and Vivino observed that all but one of these strains were able to resist the bactericidal action of blood. Eleven coagulase-negative strains were all killed by normal defibrinated blood. Four coagulase-positive strains which had been cultured artificially for four years lost the ability to coagulate plasma and also their resistance to the killing action of normal blood. These results substantiate the correlation between the property to coagulate plasma and pathogenicity.

In 1945 Hale and Smith demonstrated that phagocytosis of coagulase-positive staphylococci was reduced by the presence of coagulable plasmas. They suggested that this inhibitory mechanism is due to the production of a fibrin film on the surface of the organisms. As further proof of the relationship of coagulase to pathogenicity, W. Smith, Hale, and M. M. Smith demonstrated that the presence of a coagulable plasma increased the virulence of staphylococci to mice and guinea pigs.

### Fibrinolysin

Like many other types of bacteria, particularly the streptococci, the staphylococci produce a substance which is able to liquefy fibrin. Although Tillett and Garner found that only a few strains of staphylococci possess the property of fibrinolysis, other workers, Fisher, Aci, Madison and Madison, and Dart have found that many strains are so endowed. The power of lysing fibrin appears to be confined to human strains which are isolated from internal lesions. Madison and Dart found that 80 per cent of all strains isolated from human internal processes are capable of liquefying fibrin. They observed that 90 per cent of all strains isolated from superficial human infections were unable to liquefy fibrin and that none of the 24 strains isolated from animals was lytic, except two horse strains which were able to lyse horse fibrin only.

In the pathogenic process, fibrinolysin appears to lyse fibrin which may accumulate about the lesion in an attempt to wall-off the initial invasion and thus prevent its spread.

Fibrinolysin is not known to be antigenic, although it has been precipitated from culture filtrates by alcohol and acetone. It is possible that this property is an expression of the proteolytic ability of certain strains of staphylococci. Christie and Wilson studied the fibrinolytic properties of human and animal strains of staphylococci and concluded that the factor responsible for this property is associated with coagulase and $\alpha$-hemolysin. Fibrinolysis is inhibited or masked by $\beta$-hemolysin; hence, clearing of fibrinogen agar is a good indication of pathogenicity of human strains which do not produce $\beta$-hemolysin under usual conditions of artificial growth. This medium would not be applicable for the identification of animal strains which do produce $\beta$-hemolysin.

### Leucocidin

This toxin principle was described by Van de Velde in 1874 and has the distinction of being the first bacterial leucocidin to be observed. The importance of leucocidin in staphylococcal infections has been recognized for some time, but it has not been studied experimentally to any great extent. As the name implies, this toxin has the ability to kill leucocytes. By doing so, the organism may spread more easily. In fact, it has been shown that some actually may be phagocytized but not killed by the action of the leucocyte. Therefore, they may be carried to other parts of the body where they develop secondary lesions.

In 1901 Neisser and Wechsberg devised a method by which the effect of leucocidin could be determined by noting that live leucocytes consume oxygen whereas dead ones fail to do so. The utilization of oxygen is detected by the use of methylene blue. Valentine, in 1936, outlined a method of studying leucocidin by demonstrating the effect it produces on leucocytes in a series of smears stained with the Leishman stain. He demonstrated that leucocidin is distinct from $\alpha$-hemotoxin by showing that it destroys rabbit and human leucocytes but has little or no effect upon the erythrocytes of either species. The rabbit leucocyte, however, is susceptible to $\alpha$-hemotoxin toward which the human leucocyte is relatively resistant.

Leucocidin is antigenic, and numerous workers have demonstrated the production and neutralizing qualities of antileucocidin. Although some methods have been suggested for measuring this antibody, no standard unit has been formulated.

### Hyaluronidase

The production of "spreading factor" or hyaluronidase by the staphylococci has been shown by numerous investigators. The properties and action of this substance, as produced by staphylococci, is not different from hyaluronidase produced by other bacteria.

The exact role of this substance in staphylococcus infection is not known. The enzyme has been shown to be produced by pathogenic strains. Inasmuch as inhibitors of hyaluronidase are found in normal sera, it is assumed that the substance is most active during early stages of the staphylococcus infection.

### Dermonecrotoxin

As the name implies, this toxin causes a necrosis of skin. It has been demonstrated experimentally in the rabbit and occurs in natural infections in the pustular dermatitis of the dog.

### Lethal Toxin

The injection of a potent staphylococcal toxin into a susceptible rabbit is followed in 5 to 15 minutes, or in some cases longer (2 to 24 hours), by a fatal reaction. The animal becomes unsteady, and paralysis of the hind legs develops; the respiration becomes irregular and gasping; incoordination of movements occurs; pupils of the eyes are contracted, followed by wide dilatation; violent convulsions are often followed by death. On autopsy, serosanguinous exudates are found in the body cavities; hyperemia and hemorrhage with intravascular hemolysis are noted. Tissue destruction ranges from cloudy swelling to intense necrosis. Dolman has reported that the guinea pig, horse, cat, and mouse are also susceptible to this lethal effect.

### Hemotoxin

The staphylococci have been noted for their ability to produce hemolysis on the blood agar plate or in a test tube containing erythrocytes in suspension. This characteristic is one of the definite properties of the pathogenic staphylococci.

Three antigenically distinct hemolysins have been described. These have been designated α-hemolysin, β-hemolysin, and γ-hemolysin. The α- and β-hemolysins may be produced by the same strain of staphylococcus forming a double-zone effect on the agar plate. The α-hemolysin produces the clear zone immediately surrounding the colony while the presence of β-hemolysin is noted by a wider, less hemolytic zone. This hemolysin is augmented by incubation of cultures at 10°–20°C. after sufficient incubation at 37°C. to produce satisfactory growth; consequently, the term "hot-cold" hemolysis may be used. It is not essential to resort to hot-cold incubation to develop the double-zone. The α-hemolysin is particularly active against rabbit erythrocytes, but not active against sheep or human erythrocytes. Both α- and β-hemolysins may be detected by the use of bovine or sheep blood agar. The production of β-hemolysin is a significant characteristic of the animal strains of staphylococci. Minett found that only five out of ninety-seven animal strains failed to produce β-hemolysin. The γ-hemolysin is active on rabbit erythrocytes but is antigenically distinct from α-hemolysin.

Christie and North have observed that β-hemolysin is able to denature globulin and to some extent albumen of human serum, and suggest that this function may be a means of detecting β-toxin-producing strains. These authors suggest that the effect produced upon globulin and albumen may limit the spread of the staphylococcal lesion.

Williams and Harper have observed that strains of staphylococci grown on 2 per cent sheep blood agar and incubated in a chamber containing 30 per cent carbon dioxide would produce both α- and β-hemolysin. It was not possible to distinguish, on the plates, those strains that produced β-hemolysin alone from those which produced both α-and β-hemolysins. These authors observed another hemolysin distinct from $\alpha$ and $\beta$ which was active on a variety of mammalian erythrocytes, including human. They suggest that this hemolysin should be called $\delta$-hemolysin.

**Enterotoxin**

It was reported by Barber in 1914 that an acute gastroenteritis in man was produced by milk that contained large numbers of white staphylococci. The organism was isolated in almost pure culture from the udder of a cow. The ability of certain strains of staphylococci to produce an enterotoxin has been shown by numerous investigators. The most common type of food involved has been bakery products, particularly those filled with custards. Raw milk, cream, and ice cream have been incriminated in some instances. Other foods which have been found to cause staphylococcic food poisoning have been meat, gravy, cheese, oysters, and fish cakes. The natural conditions under which enterotoxin is produced are not well understood; however, a protein medium, warm temperatures, and microaerophilic conditions seem to suffice. The toxin produces nausea accompanied by dizziness and prostration, severe abdominal pain, and diarrhea, usually within 4 hours after the food has been eaten.

This period of "incubation" is significant because it differentiates this type of food poisoning from Salmonella infection which usually appears 24 to 48 hours after consuming the contaminated food. Fatal cases of staphylococcal food poisoning have not been reported.

Surgalla has demonstrated that enterotoxin may be produced in a medium containing from 2 to 16 amino acids as a source of nitrogen. Growth did not occur in a medium containing only three amino acids unless glucose was also present. The amount of enterotoxin formed was reduced in the simple synthetic media as compared to the medium customarily used.

Enterotoxin is not destroyed by 100°C. for 30 minutes. By virtue of this characteristic it is shown to be clearly distinct from the other toxic products of staphylococci. It has been reported that N/100 NaOH and N/100 HCl destroy enterotoxin, and that ethyl ether or chloroform removes it from acid aqueous solution. The material is nonvolatile and nondialyzable; it is less readily adsorbed on filters than hemotoxin. The antigenic properties of enterotoxin have been questioned by many. Reoccurring attacks of food poisoning presumably due to enterotoxin have not indicated substantial resistance. However, Surgalla, Bergdoll, and Dack have demonstrated, by the use of the gel-diffusion precipitation test, the presence of antitoxin in the serum of rabbits immunized with enterotoxin.

The incidence of enterotoxin-producing strains of staphylococci in man and the various species of animals is not known. Outbreaks of food poisoning caused by this toxin have followed the preparation of such food by people later proved to be carriers of the organism. Likewise, outbreaks have followed the use of animal foods, particularly milk, ham, and chicken. The presence of staphylococci on the skin and mucous membranes of cattle, swine, and chickens has been repeatedly demonstrated.

The detection of enterotoxin-producing strains of staphylococci presents a most difficult problem. One certain proof is the vomit reaction produced in the human being, but the use of the "human volunteer" method is not practical for large-scale studies, for obvious reasons. Monkeys are susceptible to enterotoxin, but they become resistant after a period of use; furthermore they are expensive. The "kitten test" has been useful in experimental studies of this substance, but young kittens are not always available, due to seasonal breeding characteristics of that animal. Suckling pigs have been used, but this animal is seasonal, although somewhat elastic in respect to the time of breeding. Fowler has found that dogs are also susceptible and are entirely satisfactory test animals.

All enterotoxin-producing strains of staphylococci are hemolytic and coagulase-positive; however, it must be emphasized that all hemolytic and coagulase-positive strains are not capable of producing enterotoxin.

In a critical assay of the kitten test, Fulton found that three of the four strains of staphylococci isolated from a food poisoning epidemic did not produce reaction in kittens. These three strains produced α-hemolysin whereas the kitten-positive strain produced β-hemolysin. Purified α- and β-lysins produced vomiting in kittens, but α-lysin was nontoxic to human volunteers.

The study of enterotoxin was considerably advanced by the report of Dolman and Wilson that a specific antibody for enterotoxin could be produced. Casman and Bennett contributed more significant information by finding that enterotoxin was antigenic, and that antiserum produced in rabbits would confer a passive immunity when injected into cats. Two serological types (A and B) of enterotoxin have been found. Most of the food-poisoning epidemics due to staphylococci have been found to be Type A. The above authors have developed an extraction-filtration procedure which recovers small amounts of enterotoxin. The tube double-diffusion precipitation of Oakley and Fulthorpe may then be used for the identification of the type of enterotoxin, and to detect its presence in food.

## ANTIGENIC RELATIONSHIP OF THE STAPHYLOCOCCI

Numerous attempts have been made to classify the staphylococci on the basis of antigenic relationship. Most of the work has been directed toward the differentiation of pathogenic from nonpathogenic strains. Agglutination and agglutinin absorption have been used. A correlation between antigenicity and pathogenicity has been reported. Julianelle and Wieghard designated the pathogenic strains of staphylococci Group A on the basis of the precipitation of polysaccharide antigens. They placed the nonpathogenic types in Group B. They noted that Group A is composed largely of orange-pigmented, hemolytic, mannitol-fermenting, and gelatin-liquefying strains of staphylococci.

Cowan, in 1938, classified the staphylococci on the basis of biological and serological characteristics. He included pigmentation, mannitol fermentation, hemolysis plasma coagulation, the Voges-Proskauer reaction, and gelatin liquefaction in his biological tests. On the basis of these tests he divided the staphylococci according to the following scheme:

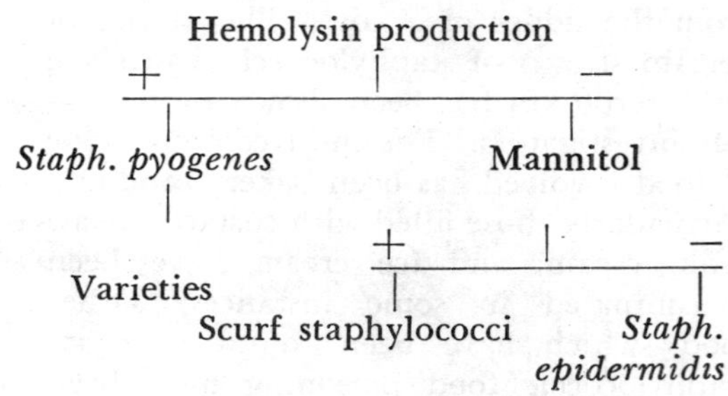


Cowan revived the name *Staph. pyogenes* of Andrewes and Gordon for the hemolytic group. The varieties are represented by strains which produce a hemotoxin, those which produce both α- and β-hemotoxin, and those which produce only β-hemotoxin. The precipitation reactions show that the majority of α and αβ strains belong in one serological group. He found an absolute correlation between hemolysin and coagulase production, and suggested it as the most valuable criterion for pathogenicity. In a series of reports on antigenic properties of *Staph. aureus,* Oeding has shown that this organism can be differentiated into antigenic strains, but he also has concluded that considerable work needs to be done on the subject before a complete antigenic classification is available.

## BACTERIOPHAGE TYPING OF STAPHYLOCOCCI

Staphylococci, as well as many other species of bacteria, may become "infected" by a virus. Inasmuch as this virus causes the lysis of the bacterial cell, the term bacteriophage, or phage, is used for it. In

Chapter 53, bacteriophage is discussed in some detail and the student is urged to read it for greater understanding.

Susceptibility of cultures of staphylococci to various strains of bacteriophage is used as an aid in identifying strains of the organism. When an organism becomes infected with a strain of bacteriophage it retains it throughout successive transplants. In fact, it is retained when the organism is transmitted from host to host. For this reason the identity of the phage type found in a recently isolated organism or the phage type for which the organism may be susceptible is of epidemiologic significance. For example, it has become evident that a strain of *Staph. aureus,* known as 80/81 phage type, has become generally spread throughout the world. So the source and spread of epidemic disease may be traced by determining the strain of bacteriophage for which the organism is susceptible.

Bacteriophage also acts as a genetic transfer agent among bacteria, a process called *transduction.* Strains of *Staph. aureus,* for example, may be changed in their ability to ferment mannitol, produce coagulase, or become resistant to penicillin by the action of phage.

*Staph. aureus* appears to be as prevalent in some species of animals, particularly cattle and dogs, as in man. Consequently, it is important to determine if cross infection may occur. The discovery that 80/81 phage type is found in cattle and in dogs, as well as in man, indicates that this organism is spread from man to animals and from animals to man.

## THE SPECIES OF STAPHYLOCOCCI

As stated previously, *Staph. aureus* appears to be the only species which is pathogenic for man and animals; consequently, it is the only species to be described.

### *Staphylococcus aureus*

**Synonyms and History.** *Staphylococcus pyogenes aureus, Staphylococcus aureus, Staphylococcus pyogenes, Micrococcus pyogenes* var. *aureus, Micrococcus pyogenes* var. *albus.* The organism was first described as present in pus by Ogston, in 1881, and cultivated by Rosenbach in 1884.

**Distribution and Transmission.** This staphylococcus is distributed widely throughout the world and makes up the normal bacterial flora of the skin and mucous membranes of man and animals. It occurs chiefly in the upper respiratory tract of man. It is present in many animal products, such as eggs, milk, and meat. When it is found in those foods its origin may be from infected persons who have prepared or handled the food, or from an infected animal. The organism has been called, very appropriately, an "opportunist type" because it is commonly present on tissues and waits for suitable conditions for invasion.

**Morphology and Staining.** The organism is spherical, and sometimes slightly flattened where two cells are appressed. In pus and blood it is usually found in grapelike clusters, justifying the name staphylococcus. In culture media the cells are grouped irregularly, and pairs and short chains are not uncommon (Figure 17.1). The diameter of the cells varies from $0.8\mu$ to $1\mu$. The organism does not produce spores, cap-

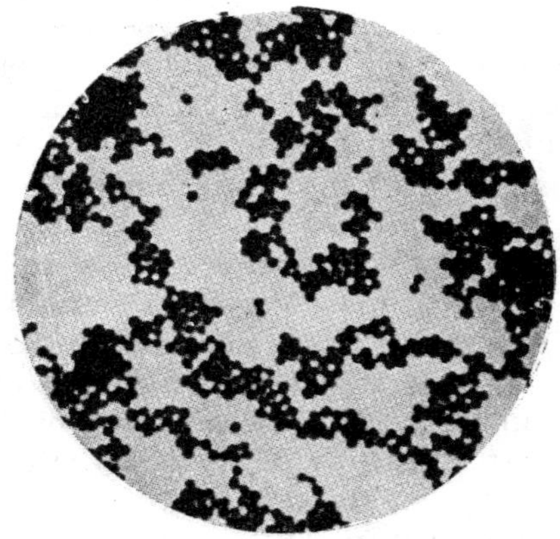

FIG. 17.1—**Staphylococcus aureus** agar culture, ×2,000. (From Nowak: Documenta Microbiologica, courtesy Gustav Fischer.)

sules, or flagella. It stains well with ordinary aniline dyes and is gram-positive.

**Growth Requirements and Characteristics.** *Staph. aureus* is secured frequently in pure culture by making inoculations directly from a suppurating process, first cleaning the outer portion and securing material on a sterile needle. In general, it is best to plate out the drop of pus obtained in this way. The organism grows well in all common laboratory media, and abundant growth is produced on blood or serum media. Selective media are of value in the isolation of staphylococci. This is particularly true of those media containing a high concentration of sodium chloride, such as mannitol salt agar and staphylococcus medium No. 110. In these media the growth of other bacteria is inhibited and colonies of staphylococci which ferment mannitol and produce golden pigment are easily detected. It is an aerobe and a facultative anaerobe. The optimum temperature for growth is 37°C. It has a wide pH range for growth, but the optimum is 7.2.

Agar-plate colonies are round, smooth, glistening, opaque, low, convex, amorphous, edge entire, and of a golden yellow or white color. The growth is butyrous in consistency. In broth a uniform turbidity is present with a powdery sediment. A faint ring forms on the test tube at the surface of the medium. Gelatin liquefaction is infundibuliform or saccate in type. Growth is luxuriant upon potato, and the orange pigment is produced in great abundance. The aureus pigmentation is lost by continued growth upon artificial media.

**Resistance.** Staphylococci are the most resistant of the cocci. Varying reports are given concerning its resistance to heat which, no doubt, is due to the different conditions under which the tests are made. Usually a temperature of 60°C. for half an hour destroys all the cells, but some individual cells require 80°C. for the same length of time. Staphylococci are more resistant to chemicals than many of the nonsporeforming organisms. Death is accomplished in: 1 per cent phenol in 35 minutes; 2 per cent phenol in 15 minutes; 0.5 per cent $HgCl_2$ in 1 hour; 10 per cent formaldehyde in 10 minutes. The organism is surprisingly resistant to drying, remaining alive in dried pus for months. Gentian violet kills the organism in 5 to 10 minutes in dilutions as high as 1:25,000. This dye in 2 per cent aqueous solution is used often in treating staphylococcus skin infections in man and animals.

Staphylococci are sensitive to many antibiotics, including penicillin, streptomycin, chlortetracycline, oxytetracycline, tetracycline, chloramphenicol, erythromycin, bacitracin, neomycin, cathomycin, streptonivicin, spiramycin, and vancomycin.

Penicillin has been the standard antibiotic used in treatment of staphylococcus infections. Although this drug has great value for this purpose, a significant percentage of penicillin-resistant strains of the organism are encountered. Consequently, it is always advisable to determine the antibiotic most applicable to a newly isolated culture by conducting sensitivity tests with a battery of different antibiotics.

**Biochemical Properties.** *Staph. aureus* produces acid from glucose, maltose, mannitol, lactose, sucrose, and glycerol but not from salicin, raffinose, or inulin; acidifies and coagulates litmus milk which is slowly peptonized by some strains; produces hemolysis on blood agar. The organism is indol negative, $NH_3$ positive, methyl red positive, and Voges-Proskauer positive; reduces methylene blue; reduces nitrates to nitrites; forms slight $H_2S$; hydrolyzes gelatin and coagulated serum.

**Antigenic Structure.** Methods used for the antigenic study of many bacteria have failed when applied to staphylococci. For example, capsular substance as used for pneumococci is not applicable. Staphylococci do possess carbohydrate substance which has been used to show antigenic differences by using the precipitation test.

Agglutination tests and also agglutinin-adsorption tests have been used to distinguish strains.

In order to type strains of *Staph. aureus,* antigenic components of the cell wall appear to be the most promising. Although antitoxin can be demonstrated in the serum of infected individuals against hemolysin and lethal toxin, this substance cannot be depended upon for typing various strains which may be isolated. Morse has isolated a surface antigen from the Smith strain of *Staph. aureus* which he has termed Smith Surface Antigen (SSA). This purified compound was capable of absorbing agglutinating antibody from antiserum prepared against the homologous strain and one other strain of *Staph. aureus.*

The above type of research is needed for successful typing of this organism. That there is much more work needed is admirably summarized by Per Oeding, which the student should read.

**Pathogenicity.** *Staph. aureus* is associated with most of the cases of suppurative wound infection in man and animals. It may localize in any tissue of the body; consequently, it is the most common cause of pyemia. The organism is found in man and is considered one of the etiologic agents in the following: osteomyelitis, sinusitis, tonsillitis, boils, mastoiditis, endocarditis, and ulcerative keratitis. It is found as a secondary invader in smallpox, diphtheria, septic sore throat, scarlet fever, tuberculosis, and pneumonia. In animals the organism has been found associated with the following diseases: mastitis in the cow and ewe, pustular dermatitis in the dog, abscess formation in all species, including fowls. The presence of the organism in arthritis in geese was noted by Rowlands and Smith. The prevalence of this organism in bovine mastitis is becoming increasingly apparent. Packer found it in 76 per cent of 2,296 bacteria-positive samples of milk examined for the presence of bacteria causing mastitis. MacDonald found staphylococci in more than half of 280 samples of milk examined in Norfolk, England. This author observed that bovine strains were affected by one type of bacteriophage, which he suggested as a useful clue to the source of certain staphylococcal infections in man. Schalm and Woods reported that variation from test to test is common in dairy herds infected by this organism. However, the average incidence may be over 50 per cent of the cows. Older cows are more prone to be infected although some show the development of resistance.

In a series of studies McDiarmid reported that staphylococci produced pyemia in lambs following infection of tick-bite wounds. It is associated with other bacteria in numerous diseases. Osebold and Gray reported an outbreak of infection in wild jack rabbits *(Lepus californicus)* due to an antibiotic-resistant strain of *Staph. aureus* and having a bacteriophage pattern similar to strains of the organism isolated from the bovine mammary gland.

The severity of the infections in man and animals is probably influenced by the toxins which are produced; for example, wound infections and boils are produced by dermonecrotoxin and leucocidin. Aranow and Wood have reported a case which showed all the cutaneous reactions characteristic of scarlet fever and from which an erythrogenic toxin-producing strain of *Staph. aureus* was isolated from the blood stream. Toxin produced by this organism was neutralized by commercial scarlet fever antitoxin. Gastroenteritis in man, and possibly in dogs, is caused by enterotoxin.

Rabbits and mice are the most susceptible of the laboratory animals and are chosen universally for experimental animals in staphylococcus research. Julianelle observed that staphylococci are not highly infective to the rabbit or mouse in the absence of traumatism or lowered resistance. Johnson and coworkers have demonstrated that hypersensitization and inflammatory reactions increased the severity of staphylococcus infections in experimental rabbits. Generalized infection is obtained in the chick embryo. Rats and pigeons are susceptible. Mice and guinea pigs are comparatively resistant. Kittens, dogs, and monkeys, are sensitive to enterotoxin.

**Immunity.** An infection with *Staph. aureus* does not produce a noticeable immunity to subsequent attacks. Probably there is a temporary rise in the phagocytic power due to opsonin, but this is soon lost. This organism is incorporated in many of the mixed bacterins which are used for animal immunization.

In view of the toxin-producing ability of the organism, it appears that the most satisfactory immunity would be produced by toxoids and antitoxins for the various toxic substances. It has been found that the use of formolized toxin, toxoid, is of value in chronic skin infections in man and produces favorable results in pustular dermatitis of dogs. A beneficial effect of antitoxin upon conditions produced experimentally in animals has been demonstrated, and the use of this immunizing material in natural infections is beginning to show promise. It may be used with success in cases of septicemia and pyemia caused by the organism. Antitoxin may be found in the blood of apparently normal animals. Miller and Heishman found antitoxin in the blood of 57 of 220 cows and heifers. Furthermore, they observed that there was four to six times more antitoxin in the colostrum than in the blood. Richou and Holstein and also Slanetz *et al.* found that the treatment of staphylococcal mastitis of the cow with toxoid reduced the incidence of infection in the herd to a significant extent.

The prevalence of staphylococcal bovine mastitis emphasizes that a dependable vaccine would find ready acceptance. Adjuvant-cell-toxoid vaccine as discussed by Cameron, has shown more promise than other vaccines. However, it is imperative that the strain causing infection in the herd must be similar to those used in making the vaccine. Furthermore, numerous injections of the vaccine must be made, and even then the duration of immunity is only a few months. Unfortunately, the use of vaccines indicates to the animal owner that the need of sanitation and other disease-prevention processes are no longer essential. The false sense of security thus invoked may do more harm than the vaccine does good.

There does not appear to be a better control for bovine mastitis than strict sanitation.

**Diagnosis.** Demonstration of a staphylococcus on direct smears from a lesion is diagnostic if it is present in great numbers and is the only organism to be found. The identification of *Staph. aureus* is accomplished by the use of specific media and tests. The production of toxins, particularly enterotoxin, is essential in the diagnosis of cases of food poisoning. Pathogenic strains of the organism are identified by the production of hemolysis and coagulase.

Schalm, in 1948, observed that toxicogenic coagulase-positive staphylococci produced typical reactions in the Hotis test of milk samples. These organisms produced adherent green, greenish-brown, brown, or russet-colored colonies with white centers after the milk sample had been incubated 16 to 20 hours. Upon further incubation, 40 hours, digestion of the milk was produced. However, Schalm and Woods, in 1953, concluded that the presence of beta hemolysis surrounding colonies of the organism cultured from milk samples was ample for the identification of the organism.

## Miscellaneous Cocci

It must be emphasized again that there are numerous strains of staphylococci and micrococci which can be isolated from man and animals. The pathogenic role of these species is quite questionable; at least no serious infection is attributable to any of them. Their chief importance is the confusion they may cause in the isolation of pathogenic staphylococci. The routine use of blood agar, however, eliminates the confusion caused by the nonpathogenic species of cocci, for none of them is hemolytic.

The genera Gaffkya and Sarcina likewise contain species which may be found on the skin and mucous membranes of man and animals. None of them is pathogenic to any marked extent, although some have been considered to be the causes of the lesions from which they were isolated.

## REFERENCES

ANDREWES, F. W., and GORDON, M. Biological Characters of Staphylococci Pathogenic to Man. Suppl. to 35th Ann. Rept. Loc. Govt. Board, Rept. Med. Officer. App. B., No. 7, 543, 1907.

ARANOW, H., and WOOD, W. B. Jour. Amer. Med. Assn. 119:1491–95, 1942.

BAIRD-PARKER, A. C. A Classification of Micrococci and Staphylococci Based on Physiological and Biochemical Tests. Jour. Gen. Microbiol. 30:409–27, 1963.

———. An Improved Diagnostic and Selective Medium for Isolating Coagulase-Positive Staphylococci. Jour. Appl. Bact. 25:12–19, 1962.

BARBER, M. A. Philippine Jour. Sci. Sect. B. 9:515–19, 1914.

BERGEY, D. H., *et al.* Manual of Determinative Bacteriology. 7th Ed. Williams & Wilkins Co., Baltimore, 1957.

BERNHEIMER, A. W., and SCHWARTZ, L. Isolation and Composition of Staphylococcal Alpha Toxin. Jour. Gen. Microbiol. 30:455–68, 1963.

BLAIR, J. E. The Pathogenic Staphylococci. Bact. Rev. 3:97–146, 1939.

———. The Staphylococci. *In* Bacterial and Mycotic Infections of Man, R. J. Dubos (ed.), Chap. 12. J. B. Lippincott Co., Philadelphia, 1958.

———. What Is a Staphylococcus? Bact. Rev. 26:375–81, 1962.

BLOBEL, H., and BERMAN, D. T. Vaccination of Dairy Cattle Against Staphylococcic Mastitis. Amer. Jour. Vet. Res. 23:7–14, 1962.

BORCHARDT, K. A., and PIERCE, W. A., JR. In Vitro Phagocytosis of *Staphylococcus aureus* With Special Reference to a Possible Antiphagocytic Function of Coagulase. Jour. Bact. 87:311–15, 1964.

BROWN, R. W. Staphylococcic Antitoxins in Dairy Cattle. II. Their Occurrence in the Blood of Cows With Chronic Staphylococcic Udder Infections. Amer. Jour. Vet. Res. 23:251–56, 1962.

———. Staphylococcic Antitoxins in Dairy Cattle. III. Their Occurrence in the Blood of Cows With Acute Staphylococcic Mastitis. Amer. Jour. Vet. Res. 23:257–61, 1962.

———, and SCHERER, R. K. A Study of the Necrotizing Action of Staphylococcic *Alpha Toxin.* Amer. Jour. Vet. Res. 19:354, 1958.

CAMERON, C. M. Immunity to *Staphylococcus aureus* (Rosenbach 1884). Jour. S. Afr. Vet. Med. Assn. 34:363–80, 1963.

———. The Immunization of Cows and Ewes Against Adjuvant Cell Toxoid. A Review. Jour. S. Afr. Vet. Med. Assn. 35:57–63, 1964.

CASMAN, E. P., and BENNETT, R. W. Detection of Staphylococcal Enterotoxin in Food. Appl. Microbiol. 13: 181–89, 1965.

CHRISTIE, R., and NORTH, E. A. Austral. Jour. Exp. Biol. Med. Sci. 19:323–27, 1941.

———, and WILSON, H. Austral. Jour. Exp. Biol. Med. Sci. 19:329–32, 1941.

COLES, E. H., and EISENSTARK, A. Staphylococci Phages. Amer. Jour. Vet. Res. 20:832–40, 1959.

COLLINS, A. M., and MCDONALD, S. Transduction of Tetracycline Resistance in Staphylococci. Jour. Path. Bact. 83:399–404, 1962.

CONTI, C. R, *et al.* Studies on the Pathogenesis of Staphylococcal Infection. Jour. Exp. Med. 113:845–60, 1961.

COWAN, S. T. An Introduction to Chaos, or the Classification of Micrococci and Staphylococci. Jour. Appl. Bact. 25:324–40, 1962.

CRISLEY, F. D., *et al.* Comparative Evaluation of Five Selective and Differential Media for the Detection and Enumeration of Coagulase-Positive Staphylococci in Foods. Appl. Microbiol. 13:140–56, 1965.

DACK, G. M. Staphylococcal Enterotoxin. *In* Chemical and Biological Hazards in Food, J. C. Ayres, *et al.* (eds.), Chap. 18. Iowa State Univ. Press, Ames, 1962.

DOERY, H. M., and NORTH, E. A. The Interaction of Staphylococcal Toxin and Gangliocide. I. Inactivation of the Lethal Effect of Staphylococcal Toxin in Mice. Austral. Jour. Exp. Biol. 39:333–44, 1961.

DOLMAN, C. E., and WILSON, R. J. Experiments With Staphylococcal Enterotoxin. Jour. Immunol. 35:13–30, 1938.

DOLMAN, C. W. Canad. Pub. Health Jour. 23:125–32, 1932.

———. Canad. Med. Assn. Jour. 30:601–10, 1934.

DRURY, A. R., and SAN CLEMENTE, C. L. Response of the Bovine Udder to Artificial Introduction of *Staphylococcus aureus*, Phage Type 80/81, and Subsequent Treatment With Various Drugs. Amer. Jour. Vet. Res. 23:262–66, 1962.

DUDGEON, L. S., and SIMPSON, J. W. H. Jour. Hyg. 27:160–73, 1928.

EKSTEDT, R. D. Studies on Immunity to Staphylococcal Infection in Mice. Jour. Inf. Dis. 112:143–51, 152–57; 113:105–9, 1963.

ELEK, S. D. *Staphylococcus pyogenes*. E. & S. Livingstone, Ltd., Edinburgh and London, 1959.

FLEMING, L. W. Studies on Bovine Staphylococcal Mastitis. III. Inactivation and Antigenicity of Toxins. Cornell Vet. 52:350–62, 1962.

———, and PATON, I. M. Studies on Bovine Staphylococcic Mastitis. II. Characterization of Isolates. Amer. Jour. Vet. Res. 22:970–74, 1961.

FOWLER, J. L. Use of the Dog as a Test Animal for Detecting Staphylococcal Enterotoxin. M.S. Thesis. Iowa State Univ. Library, 1961.

FULTON, F. Brit. Jour. Exp. Path. 24:65–72, 1943.

GALE, E. R. The Development of a Good Round Character. A Speculation on the Origins of the Staphylococcus. Jour. Appl. Bact. 25:309–23, 1962.

HABERMANN, R. T., and WILLIAMS, F. P. Metastatic Micrococcic Infection (Botryomycosis) in a Cat. Jour. Amer. Vet. Med. Assn. 129:30, 1956.

HALE, J. H., and SMITH, W. Brit. Jour. Exp. Path. 26:209–16, 1945.

HAMDY, M. K., and BARTON, N. D. Fate of *Staphylococcus aureus* in Bruised Tissue. Appl. Microbiol. 13:15–21, 1965.

HOUSER, E. D., and BERRY, L. J. The Pathogenesis of Staphylococcus Infections. I. The Use of Diffusion-Chambers in Establishing the Role of Staphylococcus Toxins. Jour. Inf. Dis. 109:24–30, 1961.

JAY, J. M. The Relative Efficacy of Six Selective Media in Isolating Coagulase-Positive Staphylococci From Meats. Jour. Appl. Bact. 26:69–74, 1963.

JOHNSON, J. E., *et al.* Studies on the Pathogenesis of Staphylococcal Infection. Jour. Exp. Med. 113:235, 249, 259, 1961.

JULIANELLE, L. A. Proc. Soc. Exp. Biol. Med. 36:117–19, 1937.

———. Jour. Immunol. 48:155–61, 1944.

———, and WIEGHARD, C. W. Proc. Soc. Exp. Biol. Med. 31:947–49, 1933–34.

———, and ———. Jour. Exp. Med. 62:11, 1935.

KARAS, E. M., and KAPRAL, F. A. Virulence and Coagulases of *Staphylococcus aureus*. III. Survival of Certain Coagulase-Negative Mutants in the Organs of Intravenously Infected Mice. Jour. Inf. Dis. 111:209–14, 1962.

KOENIG, M. G., *et al.* Factors Relating to the Virulence of Staphylococci. II. Observations on Four Mouse-Pathogenic Strains. Jour. Exp. Med. 116:589–99, 1962.

———. Factors Relating to the Virulence of Staphylococci. III. Antibacterial Versus Antitoxic Immunity. Jour. Exp. Med. 116:601–10, 1962.

KORMAN, R. Z. Coagulase-Negative Mutants of *Staphylococcus aureus*: Genetic Studies. Jour. Bact. 86:363–69, 1963.

———, and BERMAN, D. T. Genetic Transduction With Staphylophage. Jour. Bact. 84:228–36, 1962.

KUMAR, S., and LINDORFER, R. K. The Characterization of Staphylococcal Toxins. I. The Electrophoretic Migration of the Alpha Hemolytic, Dermonecrotic, Lethal, and Leucocidal Activities of Crude Toxin. Jour. Exp. Med. 115:1095–1106, 1962.

———, *et al.* The Characterization of Staphylococcal Toxins. II. The Isolation and Characterization of a Homogeneous Staphylococcal Protein Possessing Alpha Hemolytic, Dermonecrotic, Lethal, and Leucocidal Activities. Jour. Exp. Med. 115:1107–15, 1962.

LAM, G. T., *et al.* Abscess-Forming Factor (S) Produced by *Staphylococcus aureus*. I. Collodion Bag Implantation Technique. Jour. Bact. 86:611–15, 1963.

LASMANIS, J., and SPENCER, G. R. The Action of Hypochlorite and Other Disinfectants on Micrococci With and Without Milk. Amer. Jour. Vet. Res. 14:514–16, 1953.

———, and ———. Antibodies for Hemolysins of *Micrococcus pyogenes* in Whey and Serum of Dairy Cattle. Amer. Jour. Vet. Res. 15:517–19, 1954.

LEITNER, F., and COHEN, S. Effect of pH and Inorganic Salts on Penicillinase Formation in *Staphylococcus aureus*. Jour. Bact. 83:314–23, 1962.

LERNAU, H., and SOMPOLINSKY, D. The Laboratory for Milk Hygiene and Mastitis Control of the Veterinary Institute, Rishon le Zion, and the Staphylococcus Reference Laboratory, Serifin, Israel. Cornell Vet. 52: 445–51, 1962.

LI, I. W., and KAPRAL, F. A. Virulence and Coagulases of *Staphylococcus aureus*. II. Survival of Certain Coagulase-Negative Mutants in the Organs of Intravenously Infected Rabbits. Jour. Inf. Dis. 111:204–8, 1962.

LIVE, I., and NICHOLS, A. C. The Animal Hospital as a Source of Antibiotic-Resistant Staphylococci. Jour. Inf. Dis. 108:195–204, 1961.

MACDONALD, A. Mon. Bull. Min. Hlth. Emerg. Pub. Hlth. 5:230–23, 1946.

MARUCCI, A. A. Mechanism of Action of Staphylococcal Alpha-Hemolysin. I. Some Factors Influencing the Measurement of Alpha-Hemolysin. Jour. Bact. 86:1182–88, 1963.

———. Mechanism of Action of Staphylococcal Alpha-Hemolysin. II. Analysis of the Kinetic Curve and Inhibition of Specific Antibody. Jour. Bact. 86:1189–95, 1963.

MCDADE, J. J., and HALL, L. B. Survival of *Staphylococcus aureus* in the Environment. I. Exposure on Surfaces. Amer. Jour. Hyg. 78:330–37, 1963.

———, and ———. Survival of *Staphylococcus aureus* in the Environment. II. Effect of Elevated Temperature on Surface-Exposed Staphylococci. Amer. Jour. Hyg. 80:184–91, 1964.

MCDIARMID, A. Vet. Rec. 58:103–5; 243–44, 1946.

MESSINGER, H. B., *et al.* The Transmission of Hospital Staphylococci by Patients to Household Members. Amer. Jour. Hyg. 78:310–24, 1963.

MILLER, W. T., and HEISHMAN, J. O. Amer. Jour. Vet. Res. 4:265–69, 1943.

MINETT, F. C. Jour. Path. Bact. 42:247–63, 1936.

MOELLER, R. W., *et al.* Transfer of Hospital Staphylococci From Man to Farm Animals. Jour. Amer. Med. Assn., 1963.

MORSE, S. I. Isolation and Properties of a Surface Antigen of *Staphylococcus aureus*. Jour. Exp. Med. 115:295–311, 1962.

———. Isolation and Properties of a Group Antigen of *Staphylococcus albus*. Jour. Exp. Med. 117:19–26, 1963.

NAHMIAS, A., *et al.* The Staphylococcus "80/81 Complex": Epidemiological and Laboratory Observations. Jour. Inf. Dis. 109:211–22, 1961.

NOVICK, R. P. Analysis by Transduction of Mutations Affecting Penicillinase Formation in *Staphylococcus aureus*. Jour. Gen. Microbiol. 33:121–36, 1963.

OAKLEY, C. L., and FULTHORPE, A. J. Antigenic Analysis by Diffusion. Amer. Jour. Pub. Health 31:1191–98, 1953.

OEDING, PER. Antigenic Properties of *S. aureus*. Bact. Rev. 24:374, 1960.

OSEBOLD, J. W., and GRAY, D. M. Disseminated Staphylococcal Infections in Wild Jack Rabbits (*Lepus californicus*). Jour. Inf. Dis. 106:91, 1960.

PACKER, R. A. No. Amer. Vet. 28:591–92, 1947.

PARGAONKER, V. N., *et al.* Phage-Typing of *Staphylococcus aureus* Associated With Cases of Bovine Mastitis. Amer. Jour. Vet. Res. 23:1205–12, 1962.

PARISI, J. T., and BALDWIN, J. N. The Incidence and Persistence of Certain Strains of *Staphylococcus aureus* in Dairy Herds. Amer. Jour. Vet. Res. 24:551–56, 1963.

PARKER, M. T. Phage-Typing and the Epidemiology of *Staphylococcus aureus* Infection. Jour. Appl. Bact. 25: 389–402, 1962.

POUNDEN, W. D., and KRAUSS, W. E. Jour. Amer. Vet. Med. Assn. 111:35–36, 1947.

———, *et al.* Jour. Amer. Vet. Med. Assn. 111:376–77, 1947.

PROCEEDINGS OF THE NATIONAL CONFERENCE ON HOSPITAL-ACQUIRED STAPHYLOCOCCAL DISEASE. Recommended Procedures for Laboratory Investigation of Hospital-Acquired Staphylococcal Disease. U.S. Dept. of Health, Education, and Welfare, Atlanta, Ga., 1958.

REID, W. B., and Wilson, J. B. A Study of Staphylococci Associated With the Bovine Udder. Amer. Jour. Vet. Res. 20:825, 1959.

SATO, G., *et al.* Characters of Staphylococci Isolated From Dead Chick Embryos and From Pathological Conditions in Chickens. Jap. Jour. Vet. Res. 9:1–13, 1961.

SCHALM, O. W. Amer. Jour. Vet. Res. 9:11–19, 1948.

———, and WOODS, G. M. *Micrococcus pyogenes* in Bovine Milk. Amer. Jour. Vet. Res. 14:530, 1953.

———, and ———. Amer. Jour. Vet. Res. 14:534, 1953.

SETO, J. T., and WILSON, J. B. Bacteriophage Typing of Micrococci of Bovine Origin. Amer. Jour. Vet. Res. 19:241, 1958.

SHAYEGANI, M. G., and KAPRAL, F. A. The Immediate Fate of Staphylococci After Phagocytosis. Jour. Gen. Microbiol. 29:625–36, 1962.

———, and ———. The Eventual Intracellular Destruction of Staphylococci by Mononuclear Cells. Jour. Gen. Microbiol. 29:637–44, 1962.

SLANETZ, L. W., and BARTLEY, C. H. Bacteriophage and Serological Typing of Staphylococci From Bovine Mastitis. Jour. Inf. Dis. 110:238–45, 1962.

———, *et al.* The Immunization of Dairy Cattle Against Staphylococcal Mastitis. Jour. Amer. Vet. Med. Assn. 134:155, 1959.

SPENCER, G. R. Effect of Antibodies and Vaccination on Staphylococcic Infection in Veterinary Students. Amer. Jour. Vet. Res. 25:1550–55, 1964.

———, and LASMANIS, J. Reservoirs of Infection of *Micrococcus pyogenes* in Bovine Mastitis. Amer. Jour. Vet. Res. 13:500–503, 1952.

———, *et al.* Preliminary Report on Immunization of Animals Against *Micrococcus pyogenes*. Amer. Jour. Vet. Res. 17:594–98, 1956.

———, *et al.* The Use of a Growth-Agglutination Test for the Detection of Antibodies to *Staphylococcus aureu* in Cattle. Amer. Jour. Vet. Res. 24:83–87, 1963.

SPINK, W. W., and VIVINO, J. J. Jour. Clin. Invest. 21:353–56, 1942.

ST. GEORGE, C., *et al.* Characteristics of Staphylococci From Bovine Milk. Jour. Inf. Dis. 110:75–79, 1962.

SUGANUMA, A. Some Observations on the Fine Structure of *Staphylococcus aureus*. Jour. Inf. Dis. 111:8–16, 1962.

SUGIYAMA, H., *et al.* Early Development of a Temporary Resistance to the Emetic Action of Staphyloeoccal Enterotoxin. Jour. Inf. Dis. 111:233–38, 1962.

SURGALLA, M. J. Jour. Inf. Dis. 81:97–111, 1947.

———, *et al.* Jour. Immunol. 72:398, 1954.

THATCHER, F. S., and ROBINSON, J. Food Poisoning: An Analysis of Staphylococcal Toxins. Jour. Appl. Bact. 25:378–88, 1962.

VALENTINE, F. C. O. Lancet 1:526–31, 1936.

WENTWORTH, B. B. Bacteriophage Typing of the Staphylococci. Bact. Rev. 27:253–72, 1963.

WEST, B., and KELLY, F. C. Relationship of Sodium Chloride Tolerance and Serological Group of Staphylococcal Phages. Jour. Gen. Microbiol. 28:367–73, 1962.

———, *et al.* Effect of Sodium Chloride on Staphylococcus-Phage Relationships. Jour. Bact. 86:773–80, 1963.

WILLIAMS, R. E. O., and HARPER, G. J. Jour. Path. Bact. 59:69–78, 1947.

YOTES, W. W. Effect of the Antibacterial Serum Factor on Staphylococcal Infections. Jour. Bact. 83:137–43, 1962.

ZOLLI, Z., JR., and SAN CLEMENTE, C. L. Purification and Characterization of Staphylocoagulase. Jour. Bact. 86:527–35, 1963.

# 18

# The Genera Pseudomonas, Aeromonas, and Alcaligenes

## THE GENUS PSEUDOMONAS

BACTERIA WHICH BELONG TO THE GENUS Pseudomonas are widely distributed in nature, being found in both fresh and salt water and in the soil. Some are found on plants. Most species produce a water-soluble, green, blue, or yellowish-green pigment which diffuses through the culture medium on which they are grown. The majority of the members of the group are motile, but some either are not or have lost their flagella. All are gram-negative. The taxonomic relationships among the pseudomonads are not clear inasmuch as species which have been classified as vibrios apparently belong to this group. In his classification Hysenko lists 19 strains, but antigenic and biochemical differentiation will, no doubt, identify many more.

For all general purposes only one species, *Pseudomonas aeruginosa,* is associated with infection in man and animals.

### *Pseudomonas aeruginosa*

**Synonyms and History.** *Bacterium aeruginosum, Bacillus pyocyaneus, Pseudomonas pyocyaneus, Pseudomonas pyocyanea, Bacterium pyocyaneum.*

Years ago a blue-green exudate on surgical dressings was common, and in 1850 Sedillot, a French surgeon, showed that the discoloration was transferable. In 1860 Fordas isolated a crystalline substance which he called *pyocyanine* from stained linen removed from suppurating wounds. These results were confirmed in 1862 by Lücke, who showed that the condition was infective and was always associated with the presence of small vibrios. Much of our early knowledge concerning these organisms is due to the work of Gessard who isolated the organism in 1882 and continued his studies until 1925.

**Distribution and Transmission.** *Ps. aeruginosa* is worldwide in distribution and is found in water and soil. Judging from the ease with which it causes skin infection, it is logically concluded that the organism is a common contaminant of the skin of man and animals. It is inserted into deeper tissues by punctures and lacerations. Sinuses are infected often by contaminated water which contains the organism.

**Morphology and Staining.** This organism is a slender rod, 0.5$\mu$ by 1$\mu$ to 3$\mu$ with rounded ends. It is motile by means of one to three polar flagella (Fig. 18.1). It does not produce capsules or spores. The organism is gram-negative and is easily stained by the usual aniline dyes.

**Growth Requirements and Characteristics.** The organism is cultured readily on the ordinary nutrient media of the laboratory under aerobic conditions; however, it can be grown anaerobically. The colonies produced on agar are large, irregular, trans-

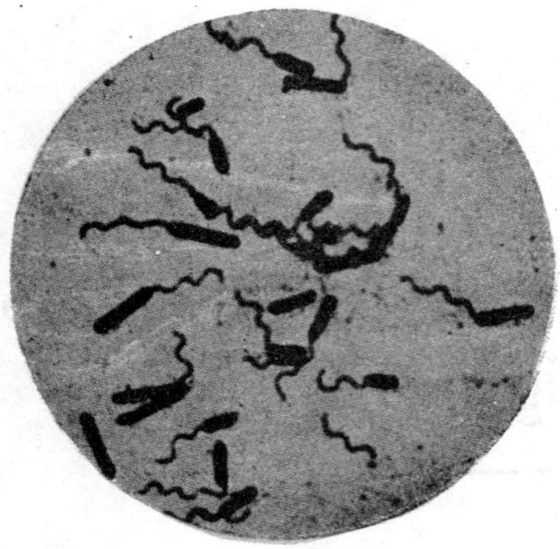

**FIG. 18.1—Pseudomonas aeruginosa** showing polar flagellum, ×2,000. (From Nowak: Documenta Microbiologica, courtesy Gustav Fischer.)

lucent, spreading, and grayish with a dark center and an entire or undulate edge (Fig. 18.2).

An unusual spontaneous lysis has been described for certain strains of *Ps. aeruginosa.* Berk has referred to this as the "autoplaque" phenomenon and has found that maximum plaque formation occurs on a medium with a tryptone concentration of 2.0 to 2.5 per cent. However, lysis was induced by the addition of L-asparagine and L-arginine to 0.5 per cent tryptone medium. A bluish-green, water-soluble pigment diffuses throughout the medium, although all strains of the organism do not produce

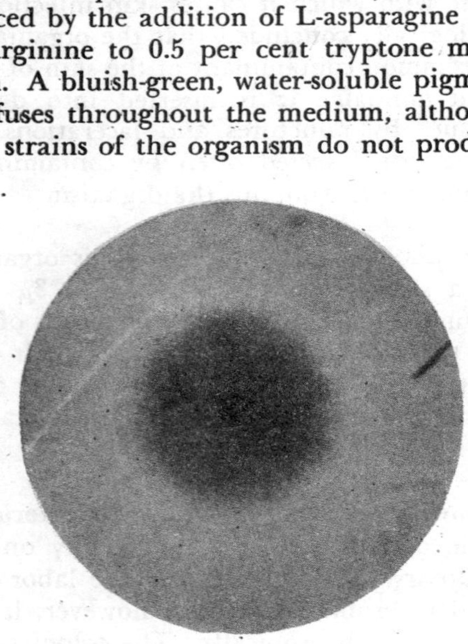

**FIG. 18.2—Pseudomonas aeruginosa** colony on agar plate, ×40. (From Nowak: Documenta Microbiologica, courtesy Gustav Fischer.)

pigment. An abundant growth occurs in broth with the formation of a thick pellicle, dense turbidity, and a heavy sediment. The medium usually becomes green, which changes to brown as the culture ages.

**Resistance.** The ordinary disinfectants easily kill *Ps. aeruginosa.* Heat at 55°C. is destructive in 1 hour. This organism is resistant to practically all of the commonly used antibiotics. However, it is sensitive to sulfonamide compounds, especially sulfadiazine, sulfamerazine, and sulfamethazine, and they are the drugs of choice in the treatment of infections.

**Biochemical Properties.** The carbohydrate-fermenting ability of *Ps. aeruginosa* is variable. This is due to the composition of the medium in which the carbohydrate is tested. Various investigators have reported that glucose is the only carbohydrate which is fermented by this organism; however, others have demonstrated that when the source of nitrogen in the medium is decreased, the detection of acid formation in many different carbohydrates is possible. The organism is able to produce ammonia from peptone, thereby producing an alkalinity which neutralizes acids which are formed when the usual amounts of beef extract and peptone are used. By the use of a medium containing final concentrations of 0.3 per cent beef extract, 0.5 per cent peptone, and 1.0 per cent carbohydrate, Cone detected decided or slight acid reactions in arabinose, xylose, glucose, fructose, galactose, glycerol, and mannitol. Acid was not produced in media containing sucrose, maltose, lactose, raffinose, inulin, dextrin, and dulcitol. In a study of a variety of Pseudomonas species Bender found that the fermenting ability of this group was clearly revealed when a synthetic medium composed of ammonium chloride 0.2 per cent, magnesium sulfate 0.05 per cent, potassium hypophosphate 0.08 per cent, and carbohydrate 0.3 per cent was used.

Kopper has described a strain of the organism which was cultivated in a phosphate-buffered solution containing creatinine as the only source of carbon and nitrogen. This strain produced the enzyme creatinase by which it was able to utilize creatinine.

*Ps. aeruginosa* varies in its ability to form indol; however, the majority of strains fail to do so. Nitrates are reduced to nitrites; $H_2S$ is produced by some strains; catalase is produced. The organism is negative to the methyl red and Voges-Proskauer tests. It hydrolyzes gelatin, with the formation of a slow crateriform liquefaction. The organism coagulates milk by a rennet-like enzyme, and increases the alkalinity of the medium as the culture ages. It slowly hydrolyzes casein and coagulated blood serum.

The production of water-soluble pigments is one of the most outstanding characteristics of most strains of *Ps. aeruginosa.* Cultures which have been isolated recently from the animal body are able to produce two pigments: One is a green pigment called *pyocyanin,* soluble in water and in chloroform; the other is a yellowish-green pigment called *fluorescin,* soluble in water but not in chloroform. Both phosphate and sulfate are required in the medium for the production of fluorescin, but neither is required for pyocyanin. Both pigments are oxidation products of colorless substances and are not produced when the organism is grown under anaerobic conditions. Some cultures lose their ability to produce pigments and never regain this characteristic. Young has demonstrated that *Ps. aeruginosa* does not produce pigment or antibiotic substances if sufficient glucose is present in the medium to be fermented and produce an acid reaction.

Various tests have been used to differentiate the pyocyanogenic strains from the apyocyanogenic ones. Bühlmann, Visher, and Bruhin have reported that growth at 0° and 42°C., testing the ability to decompose acetamide, and determining the virulence for Swiss mice are three methods which are satisfactory.

In addition to the active proteolytic enzymes produced by this organism, an enzyme-like substance, called *pyocyanase* by Emmerich and Low, is produced. This substance is able to hemolyze red blood cells and to cause the inhibition of growth of anthrax bacilli. For that reason it has been advocated as a therapeutic agent for anthrax and other diseases. Fukuhara showed in 1909 that pyocyanase is lipoidal in nature. In 1934 Hettche demonstrated that the bacteriolytic and hemolytic properties of the alcohol and acetone extracts of the organism are due to fatty acids. In the same year Kramer found the chloroform- and ether-soluble pyocyanase to be active against a number of organisms, including the anthrax bacillus, diphtheria bacillus, *Bact. coli, Bact. typhi,* hemolytic streptococci, and *Staphylococcus albus.*

In 1941 Shoental noted that *Ps. aeruginosa* may produce three compounds that are antibacterial in action: pyocyanin, α-hydroxy-phenazine, and an oil that forms an insoluble salt with calcium, barium, and the heavy metals.

In a study of the bactericidal activities of the α-oxyphenazine and the lipoidal substance produced by *Ps. aeruginosa,* Zweig tested these substances against a number of different species of bacteria pathogenic to animals. The concentrations necessary to kill the organisms varied with the organism and time of exposure and ranged from 1:1,000 to 1:1,000,000 for α-oxyphenazine. The lipoidal product was about one-half as active.

**Antigenic Structure and Toxins.** The antigenic classification of this organism was facilitated when Verder and Evans recognized 29 serological types on the basis of O and H antigens. By using the agglutination test they were able to divide 326 strains into ten O groups and thirteen O types. Ten H factors were found to occur in eight distinct combinations. Woktatsch was also able to place animal strains into definite O groups.

A thermostable exotoxin is produced by the organism which, if given in 40- to 60-ml. doses, is able to cause the death of rabbits. An antitoxin which will neutralize the toxin can be produced.

The production of hemolysin by this organism was mentioned above. Berk has shown that the substance is not an enzyme and that cellophane washings of blood agar cultures show stability to heat, acid, and alkali.

**Pathogenicity.** *Ps. aeruginosa* is found in wound infections in a number of the domestic animals, particularly the pig. The pigment produced by the organism imparts a blue-green color to purulent exudate. The organism has been recovered from septicemia in chickens and turkeys. Many infections in man have been attributed to this organism. These include: inner ear infection, pericarditis, meningitis, septicemia, bronchopneumonia, infant diarrhea, and wound infection.

This organism has been isolated from clinical cases of bovine mastitis and although it is not a common cause of this infection, it must be listed with other bacteria as one of the etiological agents. A severe outbreak of mastitis may be caused by the organism, as illustrated by Cone and by Tucker. A case of acute generalized infection in cattle, characterized by fibrinous pleuritis and pericarditis accompanied by extensive renal lesions, was described by Gardiner and Craig.

The presence of *Ps. aeruginosa* in a disease of horses had not been reported until 1949 when Doll, Bruner, and Kinkaid isolated it from an aborted equine fetus. The organism is frequently encountered in the genital tract of both equine and bovine species. As a consequence, it may be found with regularity in bull semen used for artificial insemination. Its marked proteolytic propensities indicate that caution should be used to eliminate it from semen intended for artificial insemination. The above report of the organism in the horse emphasizes that in this animal caution likewise should be used in protecting semen intended for use in artificial insemination.

The organism produces death in guinea pigs, pigeons, rats, and rabbits within 24 to 36 hours following intraperitoneal or subcutaneous injection. Extensive edema and suppuration are caused by the subcutaneous injection of the organism or of exudates containing the organism. A serofibrinous and purulent peritonitis is produced by intraperitoneal inoculation. In a study of the various fractions of the organism, I pyocyanin, II hemolysin, III extracellular enzymes, IV slime, and V bacterial cells, Liu *et al.* found that slime appeared to be the most important pathogenic agent. Furthermore, the susceptibility of animals to infection depends on their content of specific antibodies to each serological type of the slime layer or surface antigens.

**Immunity.** The infections caused by this organism are not frequent enough in animals to warrant immunizing procedures. Experimentally, antitoxins and bacterins have been proved of immunizing value, and the use of small doses of the organism produces localized abscesses, with resulting immunity. The organism is often incorporated into mixed bacterins, particularly for swine.

**Diagnosis.** The organism is recognized by isolation in pure culture. It is often a secondary invader with streptococci and staphylococci and for that reason it is essential to plate the material which is to be examined. Deubler and Cole claim that milk serum titers are high enough to warrant the use of the agglutination test in the diagnosis of mastitis caused by *Ps. aeruginosa.*

## THE GENUS AEROMONAS

Cultures of bacteria which are commonly found in water and soil are sometimes found to be pathogenic for man and animals. Such an organism is *Aeromonas hydrophila* formerly called *Proteus hydrophilus.*

*A. hydrophila* is a short, plump, aerobic rod 0.6$\mu$ by 1.3$\mu$ in size and is motile by means of polar flagella, although peritrichous flagella have been observed by some workers. It is gram-negative. Grayish-white, stippled, translucent, moist colonies are formed on an agar plate and a heavy turbidity and thick pellicle develop in broth. Optimum temperature for growth is 30°C. At that temperature acid and gas are produced in glucose, maltose, sucrose, mannitol, trehalose, arabinose, sorbitol, and salicin. Lactose is not quickly fermented but some strains will produce acid in a few days. Nitrates are reduced to nitrites; indol is formed; gelatin is liquefied; milk is coagulated and peptonized; catalase and oxidase are produced; aesculin is hydrolyzed; $H_2S$ is produced in cysteine broth; most strains are Voges-Proskauer positive; ammonia is produced from arginine.

In animals *A. hydrophila* is found in frogs where it produces a condition known as "redleg" due to the hemorrhagic erosion found in the skin and between toes and limb attachments. The condition is also found in salamanders and fish which may be kept in tanks in laboratories or sales rooms without the circulation of cool, running water. It has been isolated from stored eggs where it causes a condition characterized by the term "black rot." It has been isolated from man, guinea pigs, mice, and rabbits. Pure cultures of the organism produce a tetanic condition in frogs. An alcohol-precipitated toxin causes effects similar to those produced on muscles by caffein, digitalis, and veratrin. Some strains produce $\beta$ hemolysin.

At least two definite serological types of *A. hydrophila* have been described, and when used as bacterins, each type produces immunity in experimental animals against both types; however, passive immunization can be demonstrated only against the homologous type.

## THE GENUS ALCALIGENES

Bacteria which cannot readily be classified are frequently isolated from the intestinal tract of animals and man. As early as 1896 Petruschky isolated a gram-negative bacillus from feces. It was actively motile with peritrichate flagella, and because it produced an alkaline reaction in litmus milk he named it *Bacillus faecalis alcaligenes*. Since that time this organism has been described by many workers but has not been considered to be of pathogenic significance.

In addition to the peritrichate flagella and alkalinization of litmus milk, this organism does not ferment carbohydrates; is aerobic; reduces nitrates; produces $H_2S$; does not liquefy gelatin; has oxidase and catalase reactions which are positive; is indol negative.

The pathogenic possibilities of *A. faecalis* have been reported by Bruner and Hughes as a result of isolating it from an aborted 5-month-old bovine fetus. The organism was found in the stomach fluid and tissues of the fetus and was judged to be the cause of the abortion.

## REFERENCES


BERK, RICHARD S. Production and Characterization of *Pseudomonas aeruginosa*. Jour. Bact. 84:1041, 1962.

———. Intracellular Hemolysis of *Pseudomonas aeruginosa*. Jour. Bact. 85:522, 1963.

———. Nutritional Studies on the "Auto-plaque" Phenomenon in *Pseudomonas aeruginosa*. Jour .Bact .86:728 1963.

BRUNER, D. W., and HUGHES, D. E. *Alcaligenes faecalis* Isolated From a 5-Month-Old Bovine Fetus. Cornell Vet. 45:271–72, 1955.

BUHLMANN, X., *et al.* Identification of Apyocyanogenic Strains of *Pseudomonas aeruginosa*. Jour. Bact. 82:787, 1961.

CAMPBELL, J. J. R., *et al.* Enzyme Distribution in *Pseudomonas aeruginosa*. Jour. Bact. 83:1155, 1962.

CASELITZ, F. H., and GÜNTHER, R. Weitere Beiträge zum Genus Aeromonas. Zentralbl. f. Bakt. 178:15–24, 1960.

COLWELL, R. R., and LISTON, J. Taxonomic Relationships Among the Pseudomonads. Jour. Bact. 82:1, 1961.

DEUBLER, M. J., and COLE, E. J. Preliminary Studies on *Pseudomonas mastitis*. Amer. Jour. Vet. Res. 16:511, 1955.

GABY, W. L., and FREE, E. Differential Diagnosis of Pseudomonas-like Microorganisms in the Clinical Laboratory. Jour. Bact. 76:442, 1958.

GARDINER, M. R., and CRAIG, J. Generalized Pseudomonas Infection in a Cow. Vet. Rec. 73:372, 1961.

GUTHRIE, R., and HITCHNER, E. R. Studies of Microorganisms Classified as *Proteus hydrophilus*. Bergey. Jour. Bact. 45:52, 1943.

HAYNES, W. C., and RHODES, L. J. Comparative Taxonomy of Crystallogenic Strains of *Pseudomonas aeruginosa* and *Pseudomonas chlororaphis*. Jour. Bact. 84:1080, 1962.

HETTCHE, H. O. Untersuchungen über die Natur der bakteriziden und hamölyteschen Bestandteile der Pyozyanenslipoide. Ztsch. f. Immunitätsf. 83:499, 1934.

HOLLOWAY, B. W., and COOPER, G. N. Lysogenic Conversion in *Pseudomonas aeruginosa*. Jour. Bact. 84:1321, 1962.

KOPPER, P. H. An Atypical Strain of *Pseudomonas aeruginosa*. Jour. Bact. 54:359, 1947.

KRAMER, HANS. Neue Untersuchungen über die Antagonistische Wirkung des *Bacillus pyocyansus*. Ztsch. f. Immunitätsf. 84:505, 1935.

KULP, W. L., and BORDEN, D. G. Further Studies on *Proteus hydrophilus*, an Etiological Agent in "Red Leg" Disease of frogs. Jour. Bact. 44:673, 1942.

LIU, P. V., and MERCER, C. B. Growth, Toxigenicity and Virulence of *Pseudomonas aeruginosa*. Jour. Hyg. 61: 485, 1963.

LYSENKO, O. Pseudomonas—An Attempt at a General Classification. Jour. Gen. Microbiol. 25:379, 1961.

MILES, A. A., and HALMAN, E. T. A New Species of Microorganism *Proteus melanovogenes* Causing Black-rot in Eggs. Jour. Hyg. (Cambridge) 37:79, 1937.

MILES, E. M., and MILES, A. A. The Identity of *Proteus hydrophilus*, Bergey *et al.*, and *Proteus melanovogenes*, Miles and Halman, and Their Relation to the Genus *Aeromonas*, Kluyver and vanNiel. Jour. Gen. Microbiol. 5:298–306, 1951.

PETRUSCHKY, J. *Bacillus faecalis alcaligenes*. Zentralbl. f. Bakt. 19:187, 1896.

RUSSELL, F. H. An Epidemic Septicemic Disease Among Frogs Due to *Bacillus hydrophilus fuscus*. Jour. Amer. Med. Assn. 30:442, 1898.

SHOENTAL, R. The Nature of the Antibacterial Agents Present in *Pseudomonas aeruginosa* Cultures. Brit. Jour. Exp. Path. 22:137, 1941.

VERDER, E., and EVANS, J. A Proposed Antigenic Schema for the Identification of Strains of *Pseudomonas aeruginosa*. Jour. Inf. Dis. 109:183, 1961.

WILSON, G. S., and MILES, A. A. Topley's Principles of Bacteriology and Immunity. 5th Ed. Williams & Wilkins Co., Baltimore, 1964.

WOKTATSCH, R. Serologische Untersuchungen an *Pseudomonas aeruginosa* (*Bact. pyocyaneum*) aus verschiedenan Tierarten. Zentralbl. f. Bakt. 192:468, 1964.

YOUNG, G. Pigment Production and Antibiotic Activity in Cultures of *Pseudomonas aeruginosa*. Jour. Bact. 54: 109, 1947.

# 19

# The Genus Vibrio

THE MEMBERS OF THE GENUS VIBRIO ARE short, bent rods occurring singly or in short chains, and are usually motile by means of single or, occasionally, two or three polar flagella. Many species liquefy gelatin and are active ammonifiers; they are aerobic and facultatively anaerobic; no endospores are formed; they are usually gram-negative. Many different types of bacteria from many sources fit into the above description. It is quite likely, as Davis and Park emphasize, that many bacteria now classified as Vibrios in Bergey's Manual may not belong in this genus.

The pathogenic species include: *Vibrio comma,* which produces Asiatic cholera in man; *Vibrio metchnikovii,* the cause of an acute enteritis in chickens; *Vibrio fetus,* the etiologic agent in vibrionic abortion of ewes and cows; and *Vibrio jejuni,* the cause of an acute enteritis in mature cattle and calves. In addition to the specific diseases which they cause, these species differ in other respects. *Vibrio comma* does not coagulate milk, whereas *Vibrio metchnikovii* does; both of these species liquefy gelatin, which is not true of *Vibrio fetus* and *Vibrio jejuni.* Jones, Orcutt, and Little have shown that *Vibrio fetus* and *Vibrio jejuni* can be differentiated by the agglutination test.

### Vibrio comma

**Synonyms and History.** *Spirillum cholerae asiaticae, Pacinia cholerae asiaticae, Microspira comma, Vibrio cholerae, Vibrio cholerae asiaticae.*

The organism was discovered in 1883 by Koch while he was working as head of a commission to study the disease in Alexandria during an Egyptian epidemic. The toxicity of cultures of the organism was noted by Pfeiffer in 1891. The early development of knowledge concerning the natural lysis of bacteria was done with *Vibrio comma;* Gruber and Durham used the organism in much of their early work on agglutination.

**Distribution and Transmission.** The organism has caused numerous widespread epidemics of cholera, some of which have extended to America. The organism has its true home in the dells of the Ganges from which most epidemics have originated. At present the organism causes endemic cholera in various parts of Asia but is not prevalent in any other continent.

Three types of individuals—the infected case, the convalescent case, and the healthy carrier—serve as centers from which the organism is spread. The organism is eliminated in fecal matter and gains access to susceptible individuals by contact, by fomites, and by water and food. Flies are also a means by which the organism is spread.

**Morphology and Staining.** *V. comma* is a short, curved rod, 0.4$\mu$ by 1.5$\mu$ in size. It is commonly called the "comma bacillus" because of its comma shape. Spiral filaments develop in old cultures but are rarely seen in intestinal discharges. In old cultures, thickened and irregularly clubbed and granular shapes are frequent (Fig. 19.1).

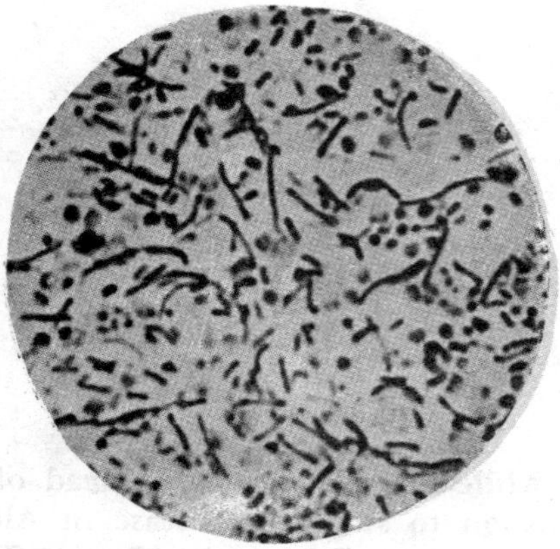

FIG. 19.1—Vibrio comma from an old culture showing numerous coccoid forms, ×2,000. (From Nowak: Documenta Microbiologica, courtesy Gustav Fischer.)

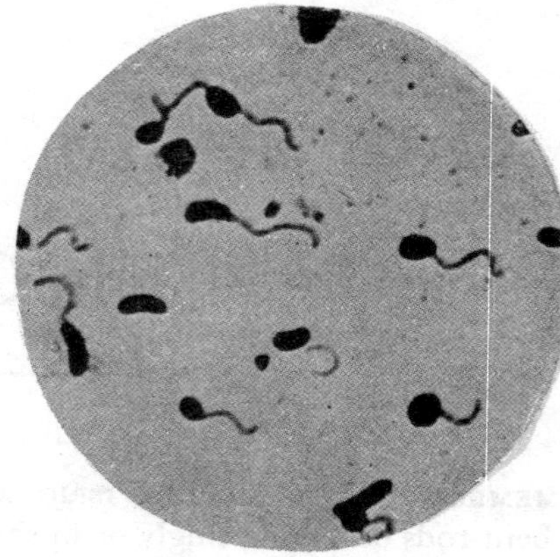

FIG. 19.2—Vibrio comma showing young flagellated cells, Van Erssenghem stain, ×2,000. (From Nowak: Documenta Microbiologica, courtesy Gustav Fischer.)

The organism is actively motile by means of one polar flagellum (Fig. 19.2). It is noncapsulated and nonsporeforming.

The organism is not stained as readily as many other bacteria. It is gram-negative.

**Growth Requirements and Characteristics.** This species of Vibrio is aerobic and is easily isolated from the stools of cholera patients. It grows at room temperature but more abundantly at 37°C. It grows best in an alkaline medium.

Gelatin plate colonies of the organism are round, small, opaque, with smooth or slightly granular surface, and are yellowish-white. A thin transparent extension grows from the central heavier colony (Fig. 19.3). The growth is similar on agar. An abundant growth occurs in broth, producing moderate turbidity, and a powdery sediment and a thick pellicle are formed.

**Resistance.** The cholera vibrio is destroyed by 56°C. in half an hour. It is easily destroyed by desiccation, sunlight, and the common disinfectants.

**Biochemical Properties.** *V. comma* produces acid but no gas from dextrose, maltose, mannitol, galactose, sucrose, and levulose; does not ferment lactose, inulin, or dulcitol; forms hydrogen sulfide; reduces nitrates; liquefies coagulated serum and gelatin; forms indol; produces ammonia and catalase. It causes an increased alkalinity in litmus milk, which is generally not coagulated or peptonized in 14 days.

**Antigenic Structure and Toxins.** An O antigen is common to all strains of the organism, but three subtypes have been described. Bacteriolytic serum causes the liberation of toxic substances which produce death in guinea pigs. Such substances are not classed as true toxins, inasmuch as antitoxins are not produced. Hemolysins are produced by some strains.

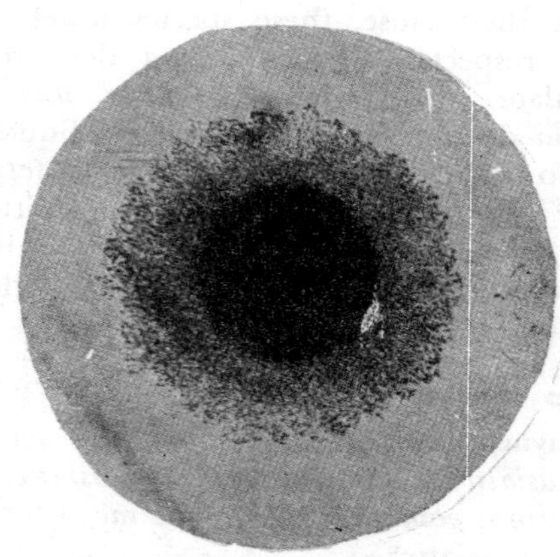

FIG. 19.3—Vibrio comma on gelatin plate, ×45. (From Nowak: Documenta Microbiologica, courtesy Gustav Fischer.)

**Pathogenicity.** The cholera vibrio is not pathogenic for domestic animals. The guinea pig may be infected by the alkalinization of the intestinal tract prior to the feeding of virulent cultures. Intraperitoneal inoculation with a young culture kills the guinea pig within 48 hours. Man is variable in resistance; predisposing factors, such as gastric disorders produced by overeating and drinking, are significant.

The organism produces such a severe diarrhea in man that the intestinal epithelium is desquamated, giving rise to "rice water" stools. Most of the conditions associated with the disease in man are attributed to dehydration during the initial stage of purgation.

**Immunity.** Recovered cases are definitely immune to the disease. Bacterins and vaccines are used in prophylactic treatment but without marked success. Antiserum is not of value. Sensitizing antibodies which are active in agglutination and complement fixation are observed in the serum of recovered patients. The natural disease is too acute, however, for these tests to be of value in diagnosis.

**Diagnosis.** The isolation of the organism is the only sure method of diagnosis.

### *Vibrio metchnikovii*

**Synonyms and History.** *Vibrio nordhafen, Microspora metchnikovii, Spirillum metchnikovii.*

In Odessa, Russia, Gamaléia isolated *Vibrio metchnikovii* in 1888 from chickens which had died of an acute intestinal infection. He observed the similarity of the diseases produced by this organism and the vibrio of human cholera and noted the differences between the disease this vibrio produced and the septicemic cholera of chickens. Metchnikoff, in 1891, described an immunity produced in the guinea pig by the injection of *V. metchnikovii.*

**Distribution and Transmission.** The original work of Gamaléia appears to be the only record made of the isolation of the organisms from the natural disease. The distribution and transmission of the organism, therefore, are not known.

In 1946 Kaschula and Canham observed outbreaks of disease in chickens in Natal, South Africa, from which this organism was isolated. This is the first report of the organism in South Africa. Much of the data on the morphology and physiology of the organism are based upon studies made of strains in culture collections.

**Morphology and Staining.** *V. metchnikovii* is a curved rod, 0.5$\mu$ by 2$\mu$ in size, with round ends. Variable shapes, such as coccoid and spiral, have been observed in old cultures. It is motile by means of a single polar flagellum. It does not produce spores or capsules.

The organism is stained readily by the common dyes and is gram-negative.

**Growth Requirements and Characteristics.** This vibrio is aerobic and grows at room temperature. It is cultivated easily upon most of the common media, such as nutrient agar, upon which it produces small, yellowish, round, glistening colonies. It clouds bouillon and produces a delicate white pellicle.

**Resistance.** A temperature of 50°C. kills the organisms in 5 minutes.

**Biochemical Properties.** *V. metchnikovii* produces acid but no gas from dextrose and lactose; produces indol; reduces nitrates to nitrites; liquefies gelatin and solidifies egg medium; coagulates milk with the formation of acid.

**Antigenic Structure and Toxins.** The organism does not produce true toxins. It is antigenically distinct from *V. comma.*

**Pathogenicity.** The organism produces an acute, fatal gastroenteritis in chickens and is especially pathogenic for young ones. It produces a marked inflammation of the intestinal mucous membrane, causing the formation of a sanguinous, yellowish-gray fluid. It does not affect other tissues; this is noteworthy in regard to the heart, since it differentiates this disease from septicemia.

The temperature of the animal does not increase.

The pigeon and guinea pig are susceptible to the organism; this fact provides a method used to differentiate it from *V. comma*. Large doses cause death in rabbits and mice.

**Diagnosis.** Isolation and identification of the organism are the only positive methods of diagnosis.

### *Vibrio fetus*

**Synonyms and History.** *Spirillum fetus.* In 1913 McFadyean and Stockman isolated a vibrio from cases of abortion in ewes and cows in England. Theobald Smith, in the United States, described an organism in 1918 which he isolated from cows with abortion. He considered it identical with the organism of McFadyean and Stockman, and the following year, 1919, Smith and Taylor named it *Vibrio fetus*. Florent, in 1959, coined the names *V. fetus* var. *intestinalis* and *V. fetus* var. *venerealis* considering that two distinct varieties are found in sheep and cattle. The former is found in the intestinal tract of sheep, cattle, and pigs and is transmitted by ingestion. The latter is never found in the intestinal tract and is transmitted by coitus. Florent has also shown that *V. fetus* var. *venerealis* does not produce $H_2S$ in a medium containing additional cysteine and does not grow in a medium containing 1 per cent glycine, whereas *V. fetus* var. *intestinalis* does. Smibert has added other biochemical data which characterize *V. fetus* var. *intestinalis*. This discussion will be found under Biochemical Properties.

It is becoming apparent that at least two species of Vibrio are being classified as *V. fetus*. Rules of Bacteriological Nomenclature discourage the use of variety names. If two organisms differ enough to be distinguished morphologically, biochemically, or antigenically, each one is entitled to a species name. The present confusion could be solved in two ways. A new species, *Vibrio intestinalis* (Florent), could be recognized, separating it from *V. fetus* which would include all *venerealis* strains, or the name *V. fetus* could be dropped and the name *Vibrio venerealis* (Florent) could be recognized. The next issue of Bergey's Manual should solve this problem.

**Distribution and Transmission.** In addition to the original discovery of the organism in England and in New Jersey, the isolation of the organism from sheep and cattle has been reported from Colorado, Connecticut, Wyoming, New York, Iowa, Illinois, Montana, California, and Virginia. It is quite likely that the organism is well distributed throughout the United States.

Cases of abortion in ewes and cows which are known not to be caused by *Brucella abortus* should be investigated with respect to *V. fetus*.

The organism is eliminated from the infected sheep before and after abortion. Grass pastures and other feeds are thereby contaminated and transmit the organism to susceptible animals. Frank *et al.* observed that eleven of thirteen ewes inoculated orally with infected tissues during the last half of the third month of pregnancy aborted, and the twelfth was nonpregnant. Marsh and associates have shown that infection is not carried over by infected ewes from one breeding season to the next. Miner has observed that the cohabitation of susceptible with infected sheep was more likely to spread infection than were the contaminated boots of the caretaker or the presence of an aborted fetus in the pen. Waldhalm *et al.* report that magpies *(Pica pica)* may carry *V. fetus* for as long as 39 days after artificial infection, and because of their carnivorous habits may spread the organism from place to place.

The persistence of the organism in the intestines of clinically normal sheep, as shown by Smibert, indicates that these animals as well as pigs, in which the organism has been found, may serve as reservoirs of infection and hazards to both preg-

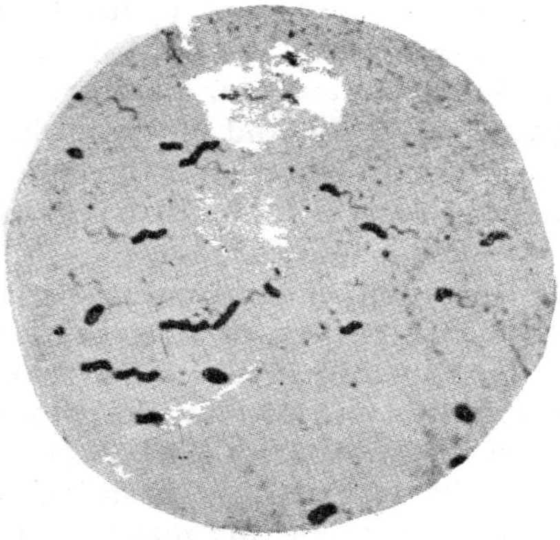

FIG. 19.4—**Vibrio fetus** showing normal, curved, flagellated cells, ×1,000. (From Smith, courtesy Journal Experimental Medicine.)

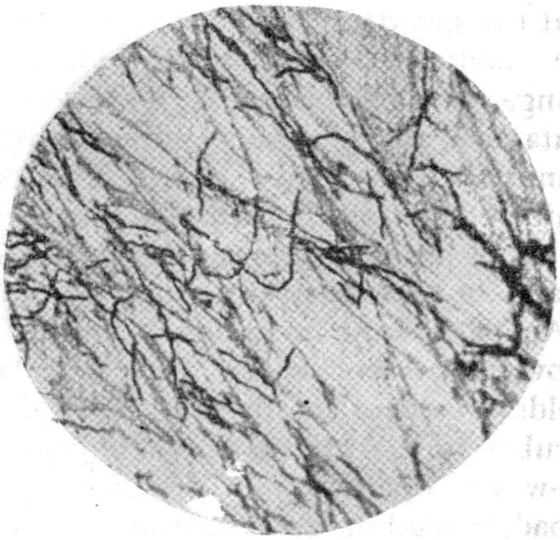

FIG. 19.5—**Vibrio fetus** showing long spirals in old cultures, ×1,000. (From Smith, courtesy Journal Experimental Medicine.)

nant ewes and cows. The ram is not considered to transmit infection from ewe to ewe by coitis. In cattle the bull and bull semen are believed to be the only methods of transmission.

**Morphology and Staining.** In young cultures *V. fetus* is comma-shaped and S-shaped, measuring 0.2$\mu$ to 0.5$\mu$ in breadth by 1.5$\mu$ to 5$\mu$ in length (Fig. 19.4). In old cultures a number of the short cells cling together, forming long spirals which may extend entirely across the field of the oil-immersion objective. Granules, which are stained by 1 per cent toluidin blue and by Wright's or Giemsa's stain, are observed in both young and old cultures, and are often located in one end of a cell. Stockman reports that these granules are filterable, but no growth is obtained from the filtrate. Ogg has found that a coccoid form of the organism could be produced after 72 to 96 hours incubation on thiol, blood, and Albimi Brucella agar. The organism is motile by means of a single polar flagellum. Rhoades has observed by electron microscopy that the comma-shaped organism usually has a polar flagellum, whereas many of the S-forms have bipolar flagella. It is not capsulated and does not form spores. Ryff and Lee have described "ribbon" forms of the organism, which they suggest may be resistant dissociative phases that serve to perpetuate the infection. Smith has described extremely long spiral filaments in old cultures (Fig. 19.5).

*V. fetus* is stained densely by alkaline methylene blue, crystal violet, and carbol fuchsin. It is gram-negative.

**Growth Requirements and Characteristics.** The organism is obtained from the placenta of an aborting animal and from the stomach, liver, lungs, and kidneys of the aborted fetus. It grows best in microaerophilic conditions and in an atmosphere of 10 per cent carbon dioxide, but is not strictly anaerobic. Reich and associates were able to obtain more abundant growth in broth when aerating with a gas mixture of 5 per cent $CO_2$, 35 per cent air, 10 per cent $H_2$, and 50 per cent He. The optimum temperature for growth is 37.5°C.

A medium containing blood serum, whole blood, bits of fresh tissue, or stomach contents is best suited for primary isolation. Huddleson has found that a semisolid agar medium known as "thiol" is superior to other media for the cultivation of *V. fetus*. In this medium the organism grows profusely at or within 0.5 mm. of the surface of the medium, reaching maximum growth in 4 days. He observed that the vibrios will remain alive for at least 150 days without intervening transfer in tubes of this medium. Zemjanis and Hoyt have found that the growth of *V. fetus* is enhanced by the addition of cysteine, magnesium, manganese, iron, lactate, α-ketoglutarate, glutamate and glutamine, uracil, thymine, *p*-aminobenzoic acid, and 17-β-estradiol. Smibert reported that a medium containing 18 amino acids supported the growth of 87 strains of the organism which he studied.

An agar slant, enriched by any of the above tissues and sealed after inoculation, yields growth after three or four days of incubation. It appears as two narrow, grayish-white, opaque lines, less than 1 mm. broad, extending upward from beneath the surface of the condensation water where the agar slant comes in contact with the glass. The growth extends around and between the agar butt and the test tube, producing a thin, veil-like layer. The condensation water is slightly clouded by the organisms in it.

On blood agar, the organism forms fine, pin-point, bluish areas from 1 to 3 mm. in diameter, visibly raised above the surface of the medium.

The organism produces a faint clouding in fluid media after it has become adapted to growth under artificial conditions. As is the case with many species of bacteria, *V. fetus* may grow in smooth, rough (R), and mucoid (M) colonies. The smooth colonies are composed of more virulent cells and the R dissociates are relatively avirulent; in fact, they are referred to as representing the saprophytic strains of *V. fetus.*

**Resistance.** *V. fetus* is killed in 5 minutes at 58°C. and is readily killed by drying, direct sunlight, and chemical disinfectants. Laboratory cultures must be transferred weekly in order to maintain them, and they must be stored in a dark chamber because they are sensitive to light. Cultures of the organism survive in room temperatures longer than at refrigerator temperatures of 5°–6°C.

Ward and Lee found that vibrio cultures covered with heavy mineral oil were viable at the end of 33 days.

Lindenstruth and Ward studied the survival of three strains of this vibrio mixed in hay, soil, and manure. These materials were kept at 6°C., 20°C., and 37°C. and examined for viability of the organism at 10, 20, and 30 days. Survival was noted in all materials at the end of 10 days, survival at 6°C. in 20 days, and no survival at the end of 30 days.

Plastridge and Easterbrooks have found that 500 micrograms of streptomycin per milliliter of diluted bull semen will prevent infection of cows by the process of artificial insemination. The organism is not sensitive to bacitracin, gramicidin, tyrothricin, polymixin, and novobiocin.

**Biochemical Properties.** *V. fetus* does not ferment arabinose, dextrose, dextrin, dulcitol, galactose, inulin, lactose, levulose, maltose, mannitol, raffinose, salicin, sucrose, sorbitol, and trehalose. It does not form indol, but is nitrate-positive. Most investigators report no change in litmus milk, but Price, Poelma, and Faber reported some reduction. The organism does not alter gelatin.

The production of catalase is considered by Bryner and Frank to be a method of differentiating *V. fetus* from nonpathogenic strains of vibrio which are also found in the genital tract of the cow and which do not produce catalase. The latter strains produce $H_2S$ while *V. fetus* does not. Kayser has separated *V. fetus* into three groups which are differentiated by the various reactions given in Table 19.1.

Group I was composed of virulent organisms isolated from aborted fetuses or from cows or bulls and was considered to be typical *V. fetus.* Group II were facultative pathogens, probably variant strains of *V. fetus.* Group III was considered to be *Vibrio bubulus,* a nonpathogenic strain of vibrio which was first described by Florent and which had been observed by many other investigators.

Fletcher and Plastridge reported that microaerophilic vibrios from cattle, chickens, man, and sheep could be placed in four groups on the basis of catalase and $H_2S$ production and glycine tolerance (Table 19.2).

TABLE 19.1

DIFFERENTIATION OF VIBRIO STRAINS

| | Group I | Group II | Group III |
|---|---|---|---|
| Morphology | Short and long cells | Short and long cells | Almost always short, fine cells |
| Growth on blood agar | Bluish-white or metallic sheen | Bluish-white or metallic sheen | Grayish-yellow, greenish, or ocher color |
| Micro-aerophilic growth | + | + | + |
| Aerobic growth | − | + | − |
| Deep growth in Bacto-thiol medium | − | − | + |
| Growth in Bacto-thiol medium with 3.5% NaCl | − | + | + |
| Catalase | + | + | − |
| $H_2S$ | − | − | + |
| Nitrate reduction | + | + | + |
| Urease | − | − | − |
| Gelatin liquefaction | − | − | − |
| Hemolysis | − | − | − |
| Agglutination with *V. fetus* positive vaginal mucus | + | − | − |

All strains in each group required oxygen and carbon dioxide for growth. On yeast-extract agar the optimal oxygen for growth was 2.5 per cent for Group I, and 5 per cent for the other groups, while the optimum $CO_2$ level was 10 per cent for all groups. These authors conclude that Group I strains from cattle differ from Group II strains from cattle, sheep, man, and chickens.

Bryner and associates have summarized some of the biochemical reactions of the vibrios which they consider reliable for classification as shown in Table 19.3.

TABLE 19.2

| | Catalase | $H_2S$ | Glycine Tolerance |
|---|---|---|---|
| Group I | + | − | − |
| Group II | + | − | + |
| Group III | + | + | + |
| Group IV | − | + | + |

It is quite evident that strains classified as *V. fetus* may not be identical biochemically, and that further criteria must be used for the identification of definite species. Smibert has presented an array of characteristics for *V. fetus* var. *intestinalis* as shown in Table 19.4.

**Antigenic Structure and Toxins.** Both H and O antigens have been observed for *V. fetus*. Various strains of the organism studied with the agglutination test have appeared to be antigenically homogeneous, although certain strains have been found to be more agglutinable than others.

Variable results obtained with the agglutination test in the diagnosis of vibriosis in cattle and sheep indicate that there are a number of different antigenic strains of the organism. Marsh and Firehammer found that the majority of ovine strains they

TABLE 19.3

BIOCHEMICAL REACTIONS OF VIBRIOS

| | *Vibrio fetus* | | | *Vibrio bubulus* |
|---|---|---|---|---|
| | Type 1 | Sub-type 1 | Type 2 | |
| Catalase | + | + | + | − |
| $H_2S$ at 24 hr. | − | − | − | ++++ |
| $H_2S$ at 5 days | − | +++ | +++ | ++++ |
| 3.5% NaCl tolerance | − | − | − | + |
| Bile tolerance | + | + | + | − |
| Glycine tolerance | − | − | + | + |

studied were of one type but that there were three other types. The bovine strains were of a fifth type. There was some relationship between the bovine type and two of the less common ovine types.

Price, Poelma, and Faber have shown that cross-agglutination and reciprocal absorption tests, using heat-treated cell suspensions, indicate that the somatic antigens of the bovine strains were of four different types which were designated as Types I, II, III, and IV. An ovine strain, not antigenically related to the bovine strains, was designated Type V.

A heat-stable, water-soluble substance, termed "HS," was isolated by Ristic and Brandly from *V. fetus* cells in the smooth phase. This polysaccharide substance yielded only pentoses on hydrolysis, and seven amino acids were identified. Erythrocytes of sheep can be sensitized with this antigen and are agglutinated and also lysed by serums from artificially infected rabbits and from infected bulls. DePunga also has shown that sensitized sheep erythrocytes are more sensitive indicators of *V. fetus* antibody than bacterial agglutination tests.

Nageswarrao and Blobel studied an acid-precipitable material (APM) which appeared different from the heat-stable polysaccharide antigen of Ristic and Brandly. The cellular components liberated by lysis were distinguished from APM by the double-diffusion precipitation technique.

Winter and Dunne reported that soluble extracts of the organism could not be used to differentiate between strains of the organism.

In addition to the agglutination, agglutinin absorption, and precipitation tests, complement fixation and fluorescent antibody techniques have been used in attempts to differentiate the various strains of *V. fetus*. In general, results have shown that there are two or three strains of the organism, agreeing with biochemical tests. The organism called *Vibrio bubulus,* which is nonpathogenic, is antigenically distinct from *V. fetus*.

It has been shown that antigenic components are shared by *V. fetus* and *Brucella abortus,* thus leading to confusion in the diagnosis of abortion in cattle. For example, Kiggins and associates demonstrated, by using agglutinin absorption tests, that brucella antigen removed both *V. fetus* and brucella agglutinins from *Br. abortus* antiserum, whereas the vibrio antigens absorbed all of the *V. fetus* antibodies from *Br. abortus* antiserum but did not reduce the titer for *Br. abortus* appreciably. They concluded that *V. fetus* infection does not interfere with the agglutination test for brucellosis, but that *Br. abortus* infection may interfere with the aggutination test for vibriosis if the *V. fetus* antigen is made from strains which possess antigenic components similar to those of *Br. abortus*.

Tissue-specific exotoxin has not been demonstrated for *V. fetus*. However, endotoxin is considered to be the bacterial substance which does cause an inflammatory reaction, resulting in abortion. Osborne and Smibert have shown that this is an allergic reaction and may be produced in cattle, goats, swine, sheep, and rabbits by the injection of *V. fetus* cell-free filtrate. Furthermore, a fatal Sanarelli-Schwartzman reaction followed the intravenous injection of *V. fetus* toxin in the pregnant rabbit.

**Pathogenicity.** *V. fetus* causes abortion in the pregnant guinea pig, producing lesions

TABLE 19.4

Some Cultural, Biochemical, and Morphologic Characteristics of Representative Strains of *Vibro fetus* var. *intestinalis* Isolated From the Fecal and Intestinal Contents of Sheep

| Strains | Coccoid Forms | Catalase | Oxidase | TSI, $H_2S$ | Cysteine, $H_2S$ | Reduce $NO_3$ | Reduce Selenite | Ferment Sugars | Alkaline Reaction | Litmus Milk | Growth: 1% Bile | 1% Glycine | 3.5% NaCl | 25 C. | 42 C. | 45 C. | MacConkey's | Defined mediums A | B | C | D | E | Hydrolysis: Phosphatase* | Aryl-sulfatase | Hippurate | Aesculin | Casein | Gelatin | pH (2 wk.) | Serotype |
|---|---|---|---|---|---|---|---|---|---|---|---|---|---|---|---|---|---|---|---|---|---|---|---|---|---|---|---|---|---|---|
| L-1 | + | + | ± | – | + | + | + | – | + | A1.R. | + | + | – | – | + | + | ± | ± | + | + | + | + | – | – | – | – | + | – | 8.5 | – |
| L3 | + | + | ± | – | + | + | + | – | + | A1.R. | + | + | – | – | + | + | ± | ± | + | + | + | + | – | – | – | – | + | – | 8.7 | – |
| L27 | + | + | ± | – | + | + | + | – | + | A1.R. | + | + | – | – | + | + | ± | ± | ± | + | + | + | – | – | – | – | + | – | 8.4 | – |
| 274 PSI | + | + | ± | – | + | + | + | – | + | A1.R. | + | + | – | – | + | + | ± | ± | ± | ± | + | + | – | – | – | – | + | – | 8.7 | – |
| 274 c | + | + | ± | – | + | + | + | – | + | A1.R. | + | + | – | – | + | + | ± | ± | ± | ± | + | + | – | – | – | – | + | – | 8.6 | – |
| L263 | + | + | ± | – | + | + | + | – | + | A1.R. | + | + | – | – | + | + | ± | ± | + | + | + | ± | – | – | – | – | + | – | 8.6 | 1 |
| M6 | + | + | ± | – | + | + | + | – | + | A1.R. | + | + | – | – | + | ± | ± | ± | + | + | + | + | – | – | – | – | + | – | 8.4 | – |
| L278 | + | + | ± | – | + | + | + | – | + | A1.R. | + | + | – | – | + | + | ± | ± | ± | ± | + | + | – | – | – | – | + | – | 8.6 | – |
| L276 | + | + | ± | – | + | + | + | – | + | A1.R. | + | + | – | – | + | + | ± | ± | ± | ± | + | + | – | – | – | – | + | – | 8.5 | – |
| L277 | + | + | ± | – | + | + | + | – | + | A1.R. | + | + | – | – | + | + | ± | – | – | ± | + | + | – | – | – | – | + | – | 8.5 | 3 |
| E861 | + | + | ± | – | + | + | + | – | + | A1.R. | + | + | – | – | + | + | ± | ± | + | + | + | + | – | – | – | – | + | – | 8.3 | – |
| L290 | + | + | ± | – | + | + | + | – | + | A1.R. | + | + | – | – | + | + | ± | ± | ± | ± | + | + | – | – | – | – | + | – | 8.3 | – |
| M4-2 | + | + | ± | – | + | + | + | – | + | A1.R. | + | + | – | – | + | + | ± | ± | + | + | + | + | – | – | – | – | + | – | 8.6 | 1 |
| M4-1 | + | + | ± | – | + | + | + | – | + | A1.R. | + | + | – | – | + | + | ± | ± | + | + | + | + | – | – | – | – | – | – | 8.5 | 1 |
| M2 | + | + | ± | – | + | + | + | – | + | A1.R. | + | + | – | – | + | + | ± | – | – | ± | + | + | – | – | – | – | – | – | 8.5 | – |
| M3 | + | + | ± | – | + | + | + | – | + | A1.R. | + | + | – | – | + | + | ± | ± | ± | ± | + | + | – | – | – | – | – | – | 8.6 | – |
| M31 | + | + | ± | – | + | + | + | – | + | A1.R. | + | + | – | – | + | + | ± | ± | ± | + | + | + | – | – | – | – | – | – | 8.3 | 1 |

Source: Smibert, R. M. Amer. Jour. Vet. Res. 26:324, 1965.

+ = Positive test or growth; ± = weakly positive test or minimal growth; – = negative test or no growth; A1 = alkaline; R = reduction; PSI = posterior small intestine; and c = cecum.

*Negative after 2 days of incubation.

characterized by epithelial sloughing, hyperemia, hemorrhage, myometrial and subendometrial edema, and cystic uterine glands, according to Ristic and associates. The above investigators have also shown that abortion is caused in pregnant hamsters and that the infection may be transmitted by coitus from the infected male to the female.

The organism has not been shown to be pathogenic to swine, rats, and mice.

Plastridge and Williams have observed that the chick embryo is killed within five days by *V. fetus* and that the organism grows in the allantoic fluid. According to Webster and Thorp, the organism grows in the chorioallantoic membranes of infected embryos and, in addition, lesions are found in cutaneous tissues, liver, kidney, spleen, gizzard, and brain.

It localizes in the uterine mucous membrane producing premature parturition in the ewe and cow. Ryff and Lee have found that ewes were not uniformly susceptible to experimental infection and that various strains of the organism were not uniform in pathogenicity. Lee and Scrivner evaluated various methods of producing abortion in pregnant ewes. Some were given a drench containing the fetal fluids, vaginal fluids, and cultures of the organism; some were injected intravenously with the culture; some were given combinations of the above. In general those animals in which the cultures were injected intravenously aborted while those receiving the organisms in a drench did not. The organism may be present in the uterine discharge days before abortion occurs. Specific lesions are not found in organs other than the uterus. Some animals may carry the organism long after abortions have occurred.

Rhoades and Hardenbrook, in 1947, reported *V. fetus* as the cause of abortion in dairy cows in Illinois. This was the first report from that state of the disease in the cow. They did not produce abortion in pregnant cows by injecting cultures of the organism intranvenously. The presence of vibrionic abortion in cattle herds of Connecticut was reported by Plastridge, Williams, and Petrie in 1947 and by Plastridge and Williams in 1948. They were able to demonstrate the presence of the infection in cows by the use of the agglutination test. The above investigators observed that the infection is most prevalent during the first year after its introduction into the herd and that animals over two years of age are all susceptible if they have never been previously exposed. In addition to abortion in the cow, the organism is considered to produce a low-grade infection in the uterus which causes infertility.

Frank and associates and also Dozsa *et al.* found that the bovine pregnant uterus infected with *V. fetus* showed a neutrophilic and lymphocytic infiltration of the endometrium.

In Sweden, Olson observed that abortion in cattle was a sporadic disease even in a herd where the disease was present. Over a period of 20 years, 1924–43, 2,105 cases of vibrionic abortion occurred, being 10 per cent of the total number of aborted placentas examined during that time. Trueblood and Post considered the organism to be a factor in the low conception rate in a herd of antelope *(antilocapra americana).*

The ability of *V. fetus* to produce infection in man was not reported until 1947 when Verge in France described abortion in a woman at the sixth month of pregnancy after an acute illness. During the course of her illness a mixed infection with a staphylococcus was revealed on culture of the peripheral blood. The vibrio which was isolated was identified as *V. fetus,* and Verge claimed that this was the first time it had been isolated in France from either animals or man. Infection is believed to have originated from a cow which had recently aborted. Ward, in 1948, isolated *V. fetus* from a skin wound of a laboratory worker who had handled cultures of the organism. Although a larger gram-positive rod was also present in the lesion, it is considered significant that the vibrio was able to multiply in the human body. King has summarized 19 cases of infection in man caused by *V. fetus,* making it apparent that the organism may be involved in obscure fevers, pulmonary and hepatic conditions, nausea, abdominal discomfort, and abortion.

**Immunity.** An active infection caused by *V. fetus* in either cattle or sheep appears to produce some resistance to subsequent infections. Unfortunately some animals remain carriers, thereby becoming hazards in the herd. This is especially true if the carrier animal is a bull to be used for supplying semen for artificial insemination.

Miller and Jensen in 1963 found that formalin-killed *V. fetus* suspended in mineral oil with aluminum potassium sulfate adjuvants was effective in producing immunity in ewes. Subsequently Hoerlein, in 1964, reported that the same type of vaccine induced immunity in heifers. Firehammer, in Montana, has shown that vaccines are valuable in preventing infection in cattle.

**Diagnosis.** The diagnosis of vibriosis in cattle and sheep is essential to determine the cause of abortion and the cause of infertility. The latter problem is considered to be the most important.

It is essential to isolate *V. fetus* from an aborted fetus in order to differentiate the abortion caused by it from that produced by *Brucella abortus* or any other cause.

In detecting carrier bulls, prepucial swabs are smeared over blood agar plates containing bacitracin, polymixin, and novobiocin which are added to control contaminants but permit *V. fetus* to grow. Prepucial smears may also be mixed with immune serum and then examined by fluorescent antibody technique.

The agglutination test is a method of detecting infected animals which may be spreading the infection. Blood serum and vaginal mucus are used in the agglutination test. Antigens used for the test must be so prepared that H antigen is preserved; hence, the use of hot formolized saline as the diluent. A positive reaction in 1:200 is considered suspicious and 1:400 is positive evidence of infection. Blood serum is usually positive before the vaginal mucus in an infected cow, although the reaction persists in the mucus longer than in blood serum. The tampon method is a valuable technical aid in collecting vaginal mucus for the test.

The sensitization of sheep erythrocytes by placing them in contact with extracts of *V. fetus* cells produces an antigen which may be used for diagnosis. This test, referred to as an indirect hemagglutination test, is more sensitive than the direct agglutination test according to DePunga.

### *Vibrio jejuni*

**Synonyms and History.** In 1927 Smith and Orcutt isolated a vibrio from the spleen of a calf suffering with a severe diarrhea. This vibrio was similar to *V. fetus* in morphology and physiology, but was different antigenically. In a series of papers published in 1931, Jones and Little, and Jones, Orcutt, and Little described an organism which proved to be the etiologic agent of a condition referred to as "winter dysentery" in cows and calves. The morphology and physiology of the organism plus the fact that it was commonly isolated from the jejunum of infected animals led them to name it *Vibrio jejuni*.

**Distribution and Transmission.** The natural cases of the disease from which the organism was isolated were found in cattle herds in New Jersey. The experimental production of the disease by oral inoculation of infective fecal matter and of pure cultures suggests that the organism is naturally transmitted by the medium of contaminated water and feed.

**Morphology and Staining.** *V. jejuni* is notably pleomorphic, presenting three different forms in the same preparation; the first is active, short, and slightly convoluted with a flagellum at one or both poles; the second is less active, with two or more complete coils; the third is comparatively nonmotile and is long and convoluted (Fig. 19.6). As the cultures of the organism age, the cells form into clumps and then disintegrate into fragments and granules.

The organism is stained well by the

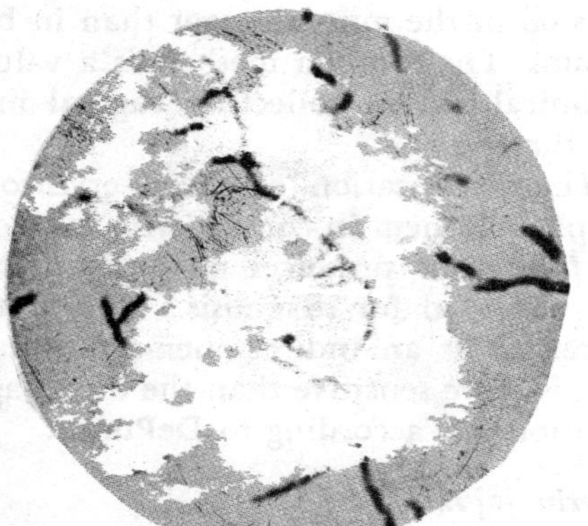

FIG. 19.6—Vibrio jejuni, ×2,000. (From Jones, Little, and Orcutt, courtesy Journal Experimental Medicine.)

ordinary dyes after prolonged exposure. It is gram-negative.

**Growth Requirements and Characteristics.** This organism can be isolated from the material in the lumen of the intestine, but it is more successfully isolated when bits of intestinal mucosa are washed, then ground, and inoculated into the condensation fluid of blood agar. Contamination with colon types of bacteria is prevented by the preliminary washing and by the inoculation of secondary cultures from the primary ones. The organism is microaerophilic; hence, all cultures are sealed.

The optimum pH for growth is 7.6; the organisms fail to grow in slightly acid or in definitely alkaline media. The optimum temperature for growth is 37.5°C.

The growth of the organism is maintained in the laboratory by adding pieces of fresh kidney to veal-infusion agar.

On blood agar the condensation fluid becomes cloudy in four or five days, and later delicate lines become visible at the border of the agar. After several transfers these border lines become well defined, and a delicate film spreads over the lower part of the slant. Many strains grow well on the surface of blood agar after they have been cultured for some time.

In bouillon, old laboratory strains produce a slimy tenacious mass in the bottom of the tube.

**Resistance.** This organism is killed within 5 minutes by a temperature of 55°C. It remains alive for six days when inoculated into moist, autoclaved cow feces but perishes when the feces become thoroughly dry. It survives for 24 hours in distilled water. It is not soluble in bile.

**Biochemical Properties.** *V. jejuni* does not ferment carbohydrate media and does not liquefy gelatin or blood serum.

**Antigenic Structure and Toxins.** The strains of the organism studied by Jones, Orcutt, and Little fall into two groups on the basis of agglutination. One group is composed of two strains isolated from diarrhea in cows, and the other is composed of all the strains isolated from the intestinal tracts and livers of calves. The calf group, in turn, is divided by agglutinin absorption into a group which possesses a complete antigen, and another which has a partial antigen.

No one of the vibrios classified as *V. jejuni* is antigenically similar to *V. fetus.*

Toxin production has not been reported.

**Pathogenicity.** The organism is not pathogenic to laboratory animals under usual conditions. Guinea pigs and white rats resist intraperitoneal injections. Some recently isolated strains produce an increase in temperature and diarrhea in rabbits. The administration of 0.5 gm. of sodium bicarbonate to the rabbit increases the pathogenicity of the organism, resembling *Vibrio cholerae* in this respect. When it is injected intraperitoneally, the organism produces necrotic foci in the liver of white mice.

Jones and Little found that the disease could be produced experimentally in calves, was less severe, but was of the same type of enteritis observed in naturally infected cases. Pure cultures isolated from the infected intestinal tract of such cases were able to reproduce the disease in other susceptible calves. It was observed that the feeding of sodium bicarbonate to calves was not necessary in order to produce infection as was observed in the experimental infection of rabbits by oral administration.

In the cow, the organism causes a severe diarrhea characterized by dark brown or black feces, often containing mucus and blood. The principle lesions are catarrhal inflammation of the jejunum and upper ileum and degenerative changes in the liver. The disease is rarely fatal.

In 1946 Levy described the isolation of an organism which resembled *V. jejuni* by blood culture and from the feces of people suffering from severe gastroenteritis. Milk was suspected as being the vehicle for the organism. Attempts to trace the source of the suspected milk supply failed.

**Immunity.** Agglutinating antibodies are produced by the injection of living cultures into rabbits. Facts are not available concerning the immunity or antibodies produced in the cow during and following an attack of the disease.

**Diagnosis.** The organism is identified by isolation and differentiated from other vibrios, such as *V. fetus,* by the agglutination test.

### *Vibrio coli*

In 1944 Doyle described a vibrio which he isolated in pure culture from the mucosa of the colon of swine which had died of dysentery. In 1948 he published more information about the organism and suggested the name *Vibrio coli.* Roberts, in 1956, isolated a vibrio from cases of swine dysentery in Australia which is considered to be the same organism.

*V. coli* is similar in size and shape to *V. fetus.* It is comma-shaped, although long chainlike cells are found in old cultures. It is actively motile with polar flagella. It is gram-negative. It is grown on blood agar containing tryptose in a chamber containing 15 per cent carbon dioxide. Colonies are round and dewdrop-like, growing sparsely along the needle track. Little change is produced in any of the culture media. Gelatin is not liquefied; nitrate is not reduced; indol is not formed; litmus milk is not altered. Acid is not produced from dextrose, lactose, saccharose, maltose, and mannite. In a study of vibrios of swine origin Davis reported catalase production, nitrate reduction, but only one of eighteen of his cultures was pathogenic for swine.

When the organism is inoculated with mucin into susceptible pigs, typical swine dysentery is produced. No lesions or symptoms of disease are produced in rabbits, white rats, mice, guinea pigs, chickens, and calves.

### A Vibrio From Avian Hepatitis

In 1956 McGehee isolated a vibrio from diseased livers of adult chickens, and Hofstad was able to reproduce a mild disease in chickens with the organism. Peckham reported a similar vibrio which he isolated from cases of avian hepatitis and transmitted to experimental chickens.

## REFERENCES


BARGER, E. H. Report of a Case of Abortion Induced by *Vibrio fetus.* Jour. Amer. Vet. Med. Assn. 72:468–74, 1928.

BLOBEL, H., *et al.* Observations on Experimental Bovine *Vibrio fetus* Infection. Amer. Jour. Vet. Res. 18:579, 1957.

BOND, J. M. Characteristics of Colonial Forms of *Vibrio fetus.* Amer. Jour. Vet. Res. 18:449, 1957.

BRYNER, J. H., and FRANK, A. H. Amer. Jour. Vet. Res. 16:76, 1955.

———, *et al.* Amer. Jour. Vet. Res. 23:32–41, 1962.

DAVIS, G. H. G., and PARK, R. W. A. Jour. Gen. Microbiol. 27:101–19, 1962.

DAVIS, J. W. Studies on Swine Dysentery. Jour. Amer. Vet. Med. Assn. 138:471, 1961.

DEPUNGA, W. A. New Zealand Vet. Jour. 6:157, 161, 1958.

DOYLE, L. P. A Vibrio Associated With Swine Dysentery. Amer. Jour. Vet. Res. 5:3–5, 1944.
———. The Etiology of Swine Dysentery. Amer. Jour. Vet. Res. 9:50, 1948.
DOZZA, L. Jour. Amer. Vet. Med. Assn. 147:620–25, 1965.
———, *et al.* Amer. Jour. Vet. Res. 23:769–76, 1962.
DUNN, H. O., *et al.* Cornell Vet. 55:220–29, 1965.
EASTERBROOKS, H. L., and PLASTRIDGE, W. N. Jour. Amer. Vet. Med. Assn. 120:199, 1952.
EIDE, G. W., and HELLE, O. The Persistence of a Genital Vibrio Infection in a Herd of Sheep After an Outbreak of Vibrionic Abortion. Amer. Jour. Vet. Res. 19:887, 1958.
FIREHAMMER, B. D., and LOVELACE, S. A. The Isolation of *Vibrio bubulus* (Florent) From Sheep. Amer. Jour. Vet. Res. 22:449–61, 1961.
———, and MARSH, H. Amer. Jour. Vet. Res. 14:392, 1953.
FLORENT, A. Isolement d'un Vibriou Saprophyte du Sperme du Taureau et du Vagin de le Vache (*Vibrio bubulis*). C. R. Soc. Biol. 147:2066, 1953.
———. Les Deux Vibrioses Génitales de la Bête Bovine: La Vibriose Vénérienne, due à *V. foetus venerealis*, et la Vibriose d'Origine Intestinale due à *V. foetus intestinale*. Proc. 16th Intl. Vet. Cong., Madrid 2:953–57, 1959.
FRANK, A. H., *et al.* A Comparison of the Effect of Catalase-Positive and Catalase-Negative Vibrio on the Fertility of Cattle. Amer. Jour. Vet. Res. 19:108, 1958.
———, *et al.* Amer. Jour. Vet. Res. 23:1213–16, 1962.
FRANK, F. W., *et al.* Experimental Oral Transmission of Vibrionic Abortion of Sheep. Jour. Amer. Vet. Med. Assn. 131:472, 1957.
GAMALÉIA, M. N. *Vibrio metchnikovi* (n. sp.). Ann. de l'Inst. Past. 2:482–88 and 552–57, 1888.
GRAHAM, R., and THORP, F., JR. Vibrionic Abortion in Sheep. Jour. Amer. Vet. Med. Assn. 76:568–73, 1930.
HOERLEIN, A. B. Amer. Jour. Vet. Res. 25:371–73, 1964.
———, and KRAMER, T. Amer. Jour. Vet. Res. 24:951–55, 1963.
HOFSTAD, M. S. Hepatitis in Chickens. A Report of Progress in Veterinary Medical Research. P. 15. Iowa State Univ., Ames, 1956.
JENSEN, RUE, *et al.* Vibrionic Abortion in Sheep. Amer. Jour. Vet. Res. 18:326, 1957.
JONES, F. S., *et al.* Vibrios (*Vibrio jejuni*, n. sp.) Associated With Intestinal Disorders of Cows and Calves. Jour. Exp. Med. 53:853, 1931.
KASCHULA, V. R., and CANHAM, A. S. Jour. S. Afr. Vet. Med. Assn. 17:150–57, 1946.
KAYSER, J. Beitag zur Bakteriologischen Diagnostik der Genitalen Vibrionen—infektion beim Reind. Inaug. dis. Ludwig—Maximilians—Universität München, Germany, 1959.
KIGGINS, E. M., *et al.* Amer. Jour. Vet. Res. 16:291, 1955.
KING, E. O. Human Infections With *Vibrio fetus* and a Closely Related Vibrio. Jour. Inf. Dis. 101:119, 1957.
KUZDAS, C. D., and MORSE, E. V. Physiological Characteristics Differentiating *Vibrio fetus* and Other Vibrios. Amer. Jour. Vet. Res. 17:331, 1956.
LEE, A. M., and SCRIVNER, L. H. Amer. Jour. Vet. Res. 11:50–54, 1941.
LEVY, A. J. Yale Jour. Biol. Med. 18:243–58, 1946.
LINDENSTRUTH, R. W., and WARD, B. Q. Jour. Amer. Vet. Med. Assn. 113:163, 1948.
MCBRIDE, J. K., and ROBERTSTAD, G. W. Amer. Jour. Vet. Res. 25:1763–68, 1964.
MCENTEE, K., *et al.* Cornell Vet. 44:376, 1954.
MCFADYEAN, SIR JOHN, and STOCKMAN, SIR S. Abortion in Sheep. III. Dept. Comm. Rept. for Board of Agr. and Fisheries of Great Britain Into Epizootic Abortion, 1913.
MARSH, H., and FIREHAMMER, B. D. Amer. Jour. Vet. Res. 14:396, 1953.
———, and TUNNICLIFF, E. A. Jour. Amer. Vet. Med. Assn. 126:100, 1955.
———, *et al.* Amer. Jour. Vet. Res. 15:352, 1954.
MELLICK, P. W., *et al.* Cornell Vet. 55:280–94, 1965.
MILLER, V. A., and JENSEN, R. Experimental Immunization Against Ovine Vibriosis. Amer. Jour. Vet. Res. 22:43, 1961.
———, and ———. Amer. Jour. Vet. Res. 24:65–68, 1963.
———, *et al.* Bacteremia in Pregnant Sheep Following Oral Administration of *Vibrio fetus*. Amer. Jour. Vet. Res. 20:677, 1959.
MINER, M. L. Amer. Jour. Vet. Res. 25:474–77, 1964.
MORSE, E. V., and RISTIC, M. Amer. Jour. Vet. Res. 15:599, 1954.
NAGESWARARAO, G., and BLOBEL, H. Amer. Jour. Vet. Res. 24:1313–20, 1963.
O'BERRY, P. A. Amer. Jour. Vet. Res. 25:1669–72, 1964.

Ogg, J. E. Amer. Jour. Vet. Res. 23:354–58, 1962.
Olson, A. Skand. Vet. Tidskr. 36:1–36, 1946.
Osborne, J. C. Amer. Jour. Vet. Res. 26:1056–67, 1965.
———, and Smibert, R. M. Cornell Vet. 55:561–72, 1964.
Peckham, M. C. Avian Vibrionic Hepatitis. Avian Dis. 2:348, 1958.
Plastridge, W. N. Amer. Jour. Vet. Res. 25:710–13, 1964.
———, and Easterbrooks, H. L. Amer. Jour. Vet. Res. 13:145, 1952.
———, and Williams, L. F. Cornell Vet. 38:165–80, 1948.
———, *et al.* Amer. Jour. Vet. Res. 8:178–83, 1947.
———, *et al.* Jour. Amer. Vet. Med. Assn. 118:367, 1951.
———, *et al.* Vibriosis in Cattle. Storrs Agr. Exp. Sta. Bull. 281. Univ. of Conn., Storrs, 1951.
———, *et al.* Jour. Amer. Vet. Med. Assn. 123:516, 1953.
———, *et al.* Amer. Jour. Vet. Res. 16:493, 1955.
———, *et al.* Incidence and Significance of Vibriosis. Agr. Exp. Sta. Bull. 677. Penn. State Univ., University Park, 1961.
———, *et al.* Amer. Jour. Vet. Res. 23:558–61, 1962.
Price, K. E., *et al.* Amer. Jour. Vet. Res. 16:164, 1955.
Reich, C. V., *et al.* Technique for Rapid Growth of *Vibrio fetus* in Broth. Jour. Bact. 74:246, 1957.
Rhoades, H. E. Amer. Jour. Vet. Res. 15:630, 1954.
———, and Hardenbrook, H., Jr. Cornell Vet. 37:8–13, 1947.
Ristic, M., and Brandly, C. A. Characterization of *Vibrio fetus* Antigens. Amer. Jour. Vet. Res. 20:148, 154, 1959.
———, and Morse, E. V. Amer. Jour. Vet. Res. 14:399, 1953.
———, *et al.* Amer. Jour. Vet. Res. 15:309, 1954.
———, *et al.* Amer. Jour. Vet. Res. 15:137, 1954.
———, *et al.* Amer. Jour. Vet. Res. 16:246, 1955.
———, *et al.* Colonial and Antigenic Variations of *Vibrio fetus*. Amer. Jour. Vet. Res. 17:803, 1956.
———, *et al.* The Characteristics of Agglutinating Antigens of *Vibrio fetus* Variants. Amer. Jour. Vet. Res, 18:764, 1957.
———, *et al.* Morphological and Serological Characteristics of Fresh Isolates of *Vibrio fetus* and Other Vibrios Inhabiting the Bovine and Ovine Genital Tracts. Amer. Jour. Vet. Res. 19:99, 1958.
Roberts, D. S. The Isolation of a Vibrio From an Outbreak in New South Wales. Austral. Vet. Jour. 32:114. 1956.
Ryff, J. F., and Lee, A. H. *Vibrio fetus* in Sheep. Amer. Jour. Vet. Res. 6:149–58, 1945.
Saxegaard, F. A Study of Vibrios Isolated From Cattle and Sheep. Thesis. Iowa State Univ. Library, 1965.
Shepler, V. M. Amer. Jour. Vet. Res. 24:749–55, 1963.
Smibert, R. M. Jour. Bact. 85:394, 1963.
———. *Vibrio fetus* var. *intestinalis*, Isolated From Fecal and Intestinal Contents of Clinically Normal Sheep. Amer. Jour. Vet. Res. 26:315–27, 1965.
Smith, Theobald. Spirilla Associated With Disease of the Fetal Membranes in Cattle (infectious abortion). Jour. Exp. Med. 28:701–20, 1918.
———. Further Studies on the Etiological Significance of *Vibrio fetus*. Jour. Exp. Med. 37:341, 1923.
———, and Orcutt, M. L. Vibrios From Calves and Their Serological Relation to *Vibrio fetus*. Jour. Exp. Med. 45:391–98, 1927.
———, and Taylor, M. S. Some Morphological and Biological Characters of the Spirilla (*Vibrio fetus* n. sp.) Associated With Disease of the Fetal Membranes of Cattle. Jour. Exp. Med. 30:299–312, 1919.
Stockman, Sir S. Vibrionic Abortion. Jour. Amer. Vet. Assn. 60:499–504, 1919.
Trueblood, M. S., and Post, G. Vibriosis as a Factor in the Reproduction of Antelope (*A. americana*). Jour. Amer. Vet. Med. Assn. 134:562, 1959.
Verge, J. Rev. Path. Comp. 47:309–12, 1947.
Wagner, W. C., *et al.* Cornell Vet. 55:209–20, 1965.
Waldhalm, D. G., *et al.* Jour. Amer. Vet. Med. Assn. 144:497–500, 1964.
Ward, B. Q. Jour. Bact. 55:113–14, 1948.
———, and Lee, A. M. Jour. Amer. Vet. Med. Assn. 112:227–28, 1948.
Webster, H. D., and Thorp, F., Jr. Amer. Jour. Vet. Res. 14:118, 1953.
Welch, Howard, and Marsh, H. Vibrionic Abortion in Sheep. Jour. Amer. Vet. Med. Assn. 65:203–11, 1924.

WERNER, H. J., *et al.* Amer. Jour. Vet. Res. 22:1121–23, 1961.
WHITE, F. H., *et al.* Infectivity of Colonial Variants of *Vibrio fetus* Strains for the Chicken Embryo. Amer. Jour. Vet. Res. 19:205, 1958.
WINTER, A. J. Amer. Jour. Vet. Res. 24:193–98, 1963.
———, and DUNNE, H. W. Amer. Jour. Vet. Res. 23:150–58, 1962.
ZEMJANIS, R., and HOYT, H. H. The Effect of Growth Factors on the Growth of *Vibrio fetus*. Amer. Jour. Vet. Res. 21:1109, 1960.

# 20

# The Genera Escherichia, Aerobacter, Klebsiella, Paracolobactrum, and Proteus

## THE ENTEROBACTERIA

INTESTINAL INFECTIONS WHICH OCCUR IN animals and in man are commonly caused by gram-negative rods which do not form spores. These organisms are known under the collective name enterobacteria and are classified in the family Enterobacteriaceae.

This family is characterized as follows: Many are parasitic upon animals and some upon plants; they are gram-negative rods widely distributed in nature; they grow well on artificial media; all species attack carbohydrates, forming acid, or acid and visible gas; all produce nitrites from nitrates; the flagella are peritrichous when present.

The family is divided into tribes which in turn are divided into numerous genera and species. There are seven genera—Escherichia, Citrobacter, Aerobacter, Klebsiella, Proteus, Salmonella, and Shigella—which contain species of special interest to students in veterinary bacteriology. Reactions produced in various media by representative strains of these genera are given in Table 20.1.

TABLE 20.1

DIFFERENTIATION OF ENTEROBACTERIA

| | Escherichia | Klebsiella | Aerobacter | Proteus | Salmonella | Arizona Group | Citrobacter | Shigella |
|---|---|---|---|---|---|---|---|---|
| Glucose | ag | ag | ag | ag | ag | ag | ag | a |
| Lactose | ag | ag | ags | — | — | ag | ag | — |
| Sucrose | v | ag | ag | v | — | — | v | — |
| Dulcitol | v | — | — | — | ag | — | v | v |
| Salicin | v | ag | ags | + | — | — | v | — |
| Adonital | — | ag | v | — | — | — | — | — |
| Inositol | — | ag | v | — | v | — | — | — |
| Indol | + | — | — | + | — | — | — | v |
| Methyl red | + | — | — | + | + | + | + | + |
| Voges-Proskauer | — | + | + | — | — | — | — | — |
| Hydrogen sulfide | — | — | — | + | + | + | + | — |
| Urease | — | + | v | + | — | — | — | — |
| Gelatin liquid | — | — | + | + | — | (+) | — | — |
| Growth KCN | — | + | + | + | — | — | + | — |
| Sod. malonate | — | + | + | — | — | + | — | — |
| Simmons citrate | — | + | + | + | + | + | + | — |
| Nitrate reduction | + | + | + | + | + | + | + | — |
| Motility | + | — | + | + | + | + | + | — |

+ = positive; — = negative; a = acid; (+) = positive slow; v = variable; ag = acid gas; ags = acid gas slow.

## THE GENUS ESCHERICHIA

Organisms which are placed in the genus Escherichia are widely distributed in nature and are commonly found in normal intestinal tracts of man and animals. Due to the widespread nature of the group, a large number of species have been isolated, described, and named.

The 1957 edition of Bergey's Manual recognizes four species of Escherichia which are differentiated by the following key:

I. Citric acid and salts of citric acid are not utilized as sole sources of carbon. Hydrogen not produced.
   A. Usually not pigmented, although a yellow pigment is sometimes produced.
      1. *Escherichia coli*
   B. Golden brown to red pigment produced.
      2. *Escherichia aurescens*

II. Citric acid and salts of citric acid utilized as sole sources of carbon.
   A. Hydrogen sulfide produced.
      3. *Escherichia (Citrobacter) freundii*
   B. Hydrogen sulfide not produced.
      4. *Escherichia (Citrobacter) intermedium*

The name *Escherichia coli* embraces a number of strains of bacteria which have been isolated from the intestinal tract of man and animals where it is frequently associated with disease.

*Escherichia aurescens* is very similar to *E. coli* in morphology, but golden-brown colonies are produced. It has been isolated from human feces and from water supplies. It is not associated with any animal disease.

*Escherichia (Citrobacter) freundii* is an organism most commonly found in soil and water and to some extent in the intestinal tract of man and animals. It is not considered to be pathogenic so will not be described. Its importance in veterinary bacteriology is confined to the confusion it may create in the identification of cultures belonging to the genus Escherichia originating in animals or man.

*Escherichia (Citrobacter) intermedium,* likewise, is found in soil and water and infrequently in the intestinal tract of man and animals. It will not be described. The reader is referred to Bergey's Manual for a complete description of the two organisms mentioned above.

## *Escherichia coli*

**Synonyms and History.** *Bacillus coli, Bacterium coli,* the colon bacillus—these and a host of other synonyms are given in Bergey's Manual, but it is not essential to list them here.

*Escherichia coli* was first isolated by Escherich in 1885 from the feces of infants but was more completely described in 1886. Since that time the organism has been found in the intestinal tract of practically all vertebrates.

**Distribution and Transmission.** The organism is worldwide in distribution. It is transmitted by water, flies, and feed which are contaminated with fecal matter.

**Morphology and Staining.** *E. coli* is a short rod, 0.5μ by 1.0μ to 3.0μ, varying from coccoid bipolar shapes to long filamentous forms (Fig. 20.1). It usually occurs singly but short chains are not uncommon. It does not produce spores. It is usually motile with peritrichous flagella, but some strains do not possess flagella.

The organism is readily stained and is gram-negative.

**Growth Requirements and Characteristics.** The organism is aerobic and facultatively anaerobic in the presence of a fermentable carbohydrate. The optimum temperature for growth is 37.5°C., but growth occurs over a range of 15° to 45°C. It grows best at a pH of 7 but grows within a wide pH

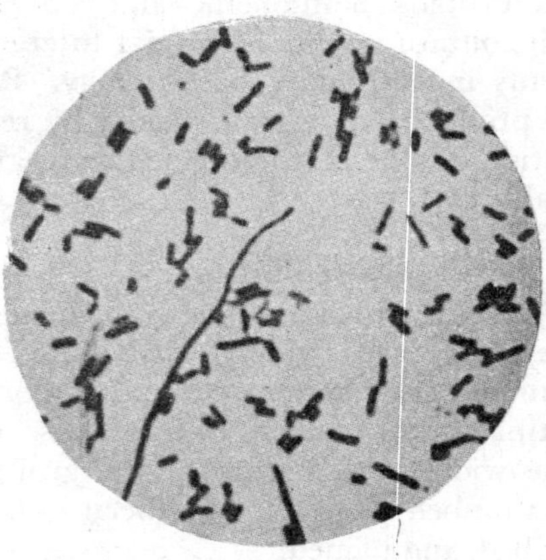

FIG. 20.1—**Escherichia coli** 24-hour agar culture, ×2,000. (From Nowak: Documenta Microbiologica, courtesy Gustav Fischer.)

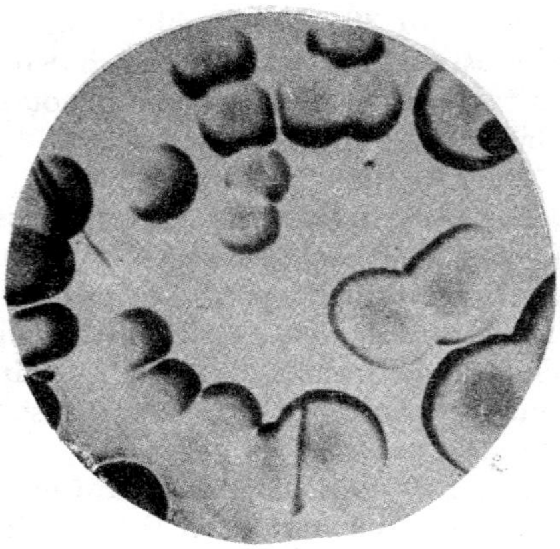

FIG. 20.2—**Escherichia coli** colonies on agar plate, ×10. (From Nowak: Documenta Microbiologica, courtesy Gustav Fischer.)

range. It grows readily upon common laboratory media.

On the agar plate the colonies formed are white to yellowish-white, turning to brown or golden-brown with age; they are moist, glistening, opaque, and circular with an entire edge (Fig. 20.2). Young colonies are finely granular; as they grow older, they become coarsely granular.

In broth the organism produces a diffuse cloudiness and a heavy sediment but no pellicle.

The characteristic appearance of the colonies of *E. coli* on eosin-methylene blue agar is of value for identification. On this medium the colonies formed have blackish centers and a metallic sheen very much like that of indelible ink. On litmus-lactose agar the colonies are red in color and produce a red zone in the medium around the colonies.

**Resistance.** The organism is usually destroyed by 60°C. in 30 minutes, but heat-resistant strains may survive. Some individual cells are able to survive freezing in ice for six months; 95 per cent of the cells are destroyed in 2 hours by freezing in liquid air. Death is readily accomplished by drying and by the action of the common disinfectants.

Glantz studied the antibiotic sensitivity of *E. coli* which had been isolated from animal and poultry diseases. He found that colistin, chloramphoricol, furazolidone, HCO, thiofuradene, and polymixin were the most effective. Dihydrostreptomycin, chlortetracycline, tetracycline, and oxytetracycline were of intermediate activity. Penicillin, oleandomycin, furaltadone, and nicroxyzone were the least effective.

**Biochemical Properties.** *E. coli* produces acid and gas from glucose, lactose, fructose, galactose, maltose, arabinose, xylose, rhamnose, and mannitol; may or may not ferment sucrose, raffinose, salicin, esculin, dulcitol, and glycerol; is variable in the fermentation of sucrose and salicin; rarely ferments pectin and adonitol; never ferments dextrin, starch, glycogen, and inositol. It is methyl red positive and Voges-Proskauer negative; produces catalase; does not liquefy gelatin; forms indol; reduces nitrates; coagulates and acidifies milk with no peptonization; oxidizes potato to a dark brown color; does not produce $H_2S$.

**Antigenic Structure and Toxins.** Following the technique which was used for the antigenic typing of the salmonellae, Kauffmann of Denmark, in 1942–43, published his first results on the typing of *E. coli.* He revealed that certain strains of *E. coli* which were believed to be inagglutinable were bearers of an antigen, L antigen, which prevented O agglutination. Knipschildt, in 1945, showed that these bacteria possessed two other antigens A and B in addition to the L antigen. All three antigens A, B, and L were located in the capsule of the organism, and all inhibited O agglutination. After recognizing the presence of such antigens, it became possible to recognize antigenic strains, and upon this basis Kauffmann demonstrated 55 different antigenic strains and Knipschildt increased the number to 110. Later in 1945 Vahlne showed that the A, B, and L antigens were really only a quantitative relationship rather than qualitative antigens, so the term K antigen was adopted for the capsular antigens. The presence of flagella upon *E. coli* indicated that H antigen should be in the antigenic picture. The maintenance of flagella was solved by Vahlne by the passage of *E. coli* organisms through semisolid agar in a U-tube. Consequently, he was able to add 19 different H antigens to the three discovered by Kauffmann.

The Kauffmann-Knipschildt-Vahlne *E. coli* antigenic scheme is based upon the three antigens O, K, and H. The source of the cultures typed by the above-mentioned investigators was man, and for that reason may have limited application in veterinary bacteriology, although strains common to animals and man have been revealed. For example, Charter found an antigenic strain (0.114) in cultures isolated from calf scours and from human sources.

In a most comprehensive treatise Wramby of Sweden, in 1948, classified the antigenic strains isolated from calves and a few from chickens by using the scheme mentioned above. Many calf strains could be placed with the homo strains but it was clear that a considerable number were confined to calves. In their publication, *Identification of Enterobacteriaceae,* to which the student is referred for details, Edwards and Ewing summarized the antigenic structure of various strains of this organism.

Some of the pathogenic strains of *E. coli* which are isolated from man and animals are shown to be hemolytic. However, until the report of Lovell and Rees, a hemolytic agent was not separated from bacterial cells. Smith has described alpha hemolysin which could be separated from bacterial cells and beta hemolysin which could not. Preparations containing high concentrations of a hemolysin produced intravenous hemolysis when given intravenously into mice, rabbits, and guinea pigs, but not when given by stomach tube or injected into the rectum or duodenum. Some preparations of a hemolysin caused dermonecrosis, but none contained leucocidin.

Further evidence of a toxic substance produced by hemolytic *E. coli* has been presented by Davis, Allen, and Smibert by finding that a sonic extract killed pigs weighing 60 to 80 pounds when injected intravenously. This extract was shown to contain at least seven antigenic components by agar-gel diffusion tests.

**Pathogenicity.** Strains of the organism which have been isolated recently from a disease process will produce death in guinea pigs, mice, rats, and rabbits within 48 hours. The animals die with a fibrinopurulent peritonitis and in some cases a septicemia.

In the larger animals the organism has been isolated from numerous tissues affected with disease. In some cases it appears to be the only organism present, but in many it occurs as a secondary invader. The ease with which the organism grows on culture media is thought to explain its frequent isolation from a wide variety of sources.

Most of the cases of calf dysentery, "white scours," or colibacillosis, are produced by *E. coli;* in fact, all young animals appear to be more susceptible to the organism than old ones.

Lecce and Reep reported that colostrum-free neonatal pigs raised in isolation were particularly susceptible to special strains of *E. coli.* Similarly, Smith and Gay, McKay, and Barnum have described acute disease in colostrum-deprived calves. It is also associated with pyelonephritis, navel infection, joint infection, cervicitis, cystitis, mastitis, and metritis of the cow.

*E. coli* is recognized as an inciter of suppurative exudates and has been isolated from wound infections and abscesses of various animals. It invades the blood stream during the agonal stages of many diseases and for that reason septicemia is commonly attributed to it. In some cases, however, septicemia is caused by particularly virulent strains.

Edema disease of swine which is characterized by massive edema involving the stomach and intestines is considered to be caused by hemolytic strains of *E. coli.* The sonic extract produced by Davis, Allen, and Smibert was able to produce lesions similar to those of edema disease.

Hjärre and Wramby (1945), in Sweden, described a specific granuloma-like condition which was found along the intestinal tract of chickens. The lesion was considered to be an atypical form of avian tuberculosis, but a capsulated culture of *E. coli* was the only organism isolated. These investigators subsequently have found that such an organism is the etiological agent. The disease in chickens is referred to as Hjärre's disease, although the original discoverers prefer the term coligranuloma. Biely and March have reported that this disease was diagnosed in three successive generations of the same strain of white leghorn chickens, while the disease did not appear in other strains on the same premises.

In man the organism produces fatal intestinal infection in infants, and in mature people is associated with peritonitis following intestinal perforations, gallbladder infections, inflammation of the pancreas, infections involving the uro-genital tract, pneumonia, and meningitis. It is found in the majority of the abscesses and fistulae involving the perineal region of man.

An extensive epidemic of diarrhea in the winter of 1960–61 in the metropolitan Chicago-northwestern Indiana region was found to be due to an enteropathogenic strain of *E. coli.*

**Immunity.** Natural infection results in the formation of antibodies, but little is known concerning the immunity which is produced.

Bacterins prepared from the organism have been found of value in chronic cases. The organism is commonly incorporated in the mixed bacterins which are to be used in the various species of animals to protect against intestinal infections. Mixed bacterins containing numerous strains of the organism which have been isolated from cases of calf diarrhea are used for immunization against the disease. The calf is immunized the first day of life. Autogenous bacterins prepared from a single strain of the organism isolated from a herd have been found valuable in the herd.

Gay and associates showed a formalin-killed oil adjuvant vaccine used for vaccination of the dam to be effective in controlling colibacillosis of calves.

It is apparent that the use of strains of *E. coli* in mixed bacterins as prophylactic agents for animal diseases should be based upon antigenic types, but, as yet, no one has typed the strains of *E. coli* found in the United States.

Immune serum has been proved effective in treating calves which are infected with *E. coli.*

**Diagnosis.** This organism is identified by isolation in pure culture and growth on various differential media. In the diagnosis of disease, media which are used for preliminary isolation must be sufficiently nutrient to support the growth of other organisms suspected. If this is not done, one is able to isolate *E. coli* from numerous tissues because it grows on almost any type of medium.

## THE KLEBSIELLA-AEROBACTER GROUP

It has become apparent that the microorganisms which are methyl red negative, Voges-Proskauer positive, and citrate positive, belong in one group. They have been divided into two genera: Klebsiella, which are nonmotile; and Aerobacter, which may be both motile or nonmotile. The nonmotile forms are indistinguishable from Klebsiella, but in the past these have been classified as *Aerobacter aerogenes.* Edwards and Ewing state that these should be classified as Klebsiella and that the motile forms can be classified as *Aerobacter cloacae;* therefore, *Aerobacter aerogenes* should be discarded as a species. No doubt, a future edition of Bergey's Manual will contain the above changes, but until that occurs, it is best to adhere to the nomenclature which is official. For that reason the name *Aerobacter aerogenes* will be used.

*Aerobacter aerogenes* is found frequently in the same environment as *E. coli.* Its natural habitat is considered to be water and soil; this explains its frequency in water as well as its presence in the intestinal tract of man and animals. It is rarely pathogenic but has been isolated from cases of cystitis in man and in the dog. This organism is encountered in bovine mastitis, where it persists and causes clinically apparent cases of the disease.

**The Coli-Aerogenes Test in Water Analysis.** In the bacteriological examination of water supplies, the presence of *Escherichia coli* and *Aerobacter aerogenes* is used as an indication of fecal contamination, and thus indicates that the typhoid fever organism, also, may be present in the water. Routine methods which are designed to detect coli-aerogenes organisms are followed in public health laboratories. A general outline of the test follows.

The test is based upon the assumption that the coli-aerogenes group includes all gram-negative, nonsporeforming bacteria which ferment lactose with the formation of acid and gas and grow aerobically on standard solid media.

The test is divided into three parts: the Presumptive, the Partially Confirmed, and the Completed.

1. The Presumptive test is positive for the coli-aerogenes group if 10 per cent or more gas forms in a standard lactose broth fermentation tube within 24 hours at 37°C.
2. The appearance of aerobic, lactose-splitting colonies on Endo agar or on eosin-methylene blue plates made from a positive lactose fermentation tube constitutes the Partially Confirmed test for the presence of coli-aerogenes organisms.
3. The Completed test requires the inoculation of lactose broth from a typical colony of nonsporeforming, gram-negative bacteria taken from a plate in the Partially Confirmed test. The lactose must be fermented to acid and gas for a positive test.

In the genus Klebsiella one species, *Klebsiella genitalium,* is pathogenic for animals. Bruner considers this organism as a variety of *Klebsiella pneumoniae,* but it would seem that host specificity would be adequate to classify it as a separate species.

Two species, *Klebsiella genitalium* and *Klebsiella pneumoniae,* will be discussed below.

### *Klebsiella genitalium*

**Synonyms and History.** The name *Encapsulatus genitalium* was given to an organism which was isolated from the genital tract of mares. It was discussed in the annual report of the director of the Agricultural Experiment Station of Kentucky in 1924. Dimock and Edwards of Kentucky described more completely in 1926 the organism and the disease it produces.

**Distribution and Transmission.** *Kleb. genitalium* has been found in mares in Kentucky and Virginia, but little is known of its general distribution.

It is readily transmitted through breeding, generally by the infected stallion. Lack of asepsis in artificial insemination and in the examination of a number of mares for genital abnormalities is a factor in the spread of the infection.

**Morphology and Staining.** The organism is a nonmotile, encapsulated rod which varies in morphology from coccoid shapes to long forms. It varies from $0.9\mu$ to $1.7\mu$ in breadth by $1.8\mu$ to $3.7\mu$ in length. The coccoid form is most prevalent in old cultures.

It is stained readily with the ordinary aniline dyes and is gram-negative. The capsule surrounding the organism is easily demonstrated by any of the capsule stains.

**Growth Requirements and Characteristics.** *Kleb. genitalium* is aerobic and facultatively anaerobic, and grows abundantly on the common media incubated at 37°C. The optimum pH for growth is 6.8 to 7.2.

Colonies of the organism on the agar plate are large, raised, and round with an entire edge. On the agar slant, the growth is yellowish in color, moist, glistening, and so viscid that the culture flows to the bottom of the test tube. The organism produces a marked turbidity and a heavy, ropy sediment in broth. A typical nail-head type growth occurs on gelatin.

**Resistance.** The bacterium is easily killed by a temperature of 60°C. for 20 minutes and by the common disinfectants.

**Biochemical Properties.** *Kleb. genitalium* produces acid and gas from glucose, lactose, sucrose, raffinose, xylose, salicin, glycerol, and adonitol; does not ferment inulin; does not form indol; is methyl red negative and Voges-Proskauer positive; reduces nitrates to nitrites; does not liquefy gelatin. It is able to utilize citrate as a source of carbon. It grows abundantly in milk, producing an initial slimy ropiness followed by acidification, coagulation, and gas formation.

**Antigenic Structure and Toxins.** The equine strains of the organism belong to the same antigenic group according to agglutination and precipitation reactions. Cross agglutination has been noted with strains of *Kleb. pneumoniae.*

The organism does not produce exotoxin.

**Pathogenicity.** *Kleb. genitalium* produces septicemia in guinea pigs and rabbits, causing death in 12 to 24 hours. Rabbits injected intravenously with large doses of the organism may die within 24 hours.

Intrauterine injection of saline suspensions of living cultures of the organism into a mare reproduces a marked cervicitis and metritis accompanied by a copious, slimy, purulent exudate in a few days. The organism can be isolated from the cervix, uterus, fallopian tubes, and inguinal lymph glands of mares suffering with a natural infection. Interference with the oestrus cycle and the production of permanent sterility are common sequelae of the infection.

**Immunity.** Data are not available concerning the immunity produced by the organism.

**Diagnosis.** *Kleb. genitalium* infection is diagnosed by the isolation and identification of the organism. Agglutinins are formed, no doubt, during the disease, but the agglutination test is not routinely used in diagnosis.

### *Klebsiella pneumoniae*

In 1882 Friedländer described a "micrococcus" which he had isolated from a case of lobar pneumonia in man. Subsequent investigations of the organism by Fränkel and by Weichselbaum in 1886 revealed that the organism was a short rod which occasionally presented coccoid forms.

*Kleb. pneumoniae* is the type species of the genus Klebsiella, and strains of the organism are commonly used in studying organisms of the same group which have been isolated from other sources. Edwards included strains of the organism and related encapsulated bacteria in his studies of *Kleb. genitalium.*

The organism is normally a short, plump rod with rounded ends. It is extremely pleomorphic, varying in length from 1.5$\mu$ to 5$\mu$. It is surrounded by a heavy capsule two or three times as large as the organism itself (Fig. 20.3). The organism is easily cultured on ordinary agar media on the surface of which it forms white, mucus-like colonies which are slimy and semifluid in consistency. It ferments a number of carbo-

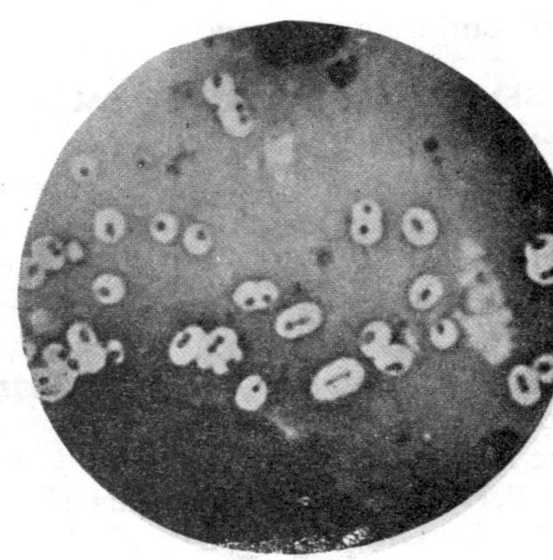

FIG. 20.3—**Klebsiella pneumoniae** in mouse blood showing thick capsules, ×2,000. (From Nowak: Documenta Microbiologica, courtesy Gustav Fischer.)

hydrates, forming both acid and gas, and gives the reactions common to the group on other types of media.

*Kleb. pneumoniae* is composed of a number of different strains which are not agglutinated by the same antisera. Julianelle has shown that the antigenic structure of the organism is changed by dissociation. The S forms are mucoid, encapsulated, virulent, and possess a group-specific antigen in the cell bodies and type-specific polysaccharide partial antigens in the capsules. The noncapsulated, avirulent R forms contain only the group antigen of the cell bodies. Julianelle divided the strains of the Friedländer group into four types, called A, B, C, and X, by using anti-S serum in the agglutination and precipitation tests.

In his comparison of the strains of *Kleb. genitalium* with *Kleb. pneumoniae* and other similar encapsulated bacteria, Edwards recognized only two antigenic types, I and II, by precipitin reactions. The strains of *Kleb. genitalium* were placed in Type I.

*Kleb. pneumoniae* is considered to be one of the causes of pneumonia in man. The isolation of an organism, indistinguishable from it antigenically, has been reported by Barnes from cases of bovine mastitis; also by Easterbrooks and Plastridge. Ludford and Stevens have reported the isolation of the organism from an acute case of canine pneumonia.

## THE GENUS PARACOLOBACTRUM (ARIZONA GROUP)

The isolation and study of the enterobacteria have revealed the existence of a group of bacteria similar to *E. coli* in many respects but differing sufficiently to warrant discussion. These bacteria are commonly called the paracolon group or the Arizona group.

The fermentation of lactose has been the basis of classifying the enteric bacteria since the early days of bacteriology, so it is understandable that an organism should be placed in a separate category if it did not ferment lactose as rapidly as a typical Escherichia. In this instance, however, it is not a question of whether lactose is fermented or not, but how slowly lactose is fermented. Consequently, there have appeared in the literature numerous descriptions of organisms of this group which are characterized by the slow fermentation of lactose.

In classifying these bacteria, Borman, Wheeler, and Stuart, in 1944, formed the genus Paracolobactrum. Bergey's Manual (1957) recognizes four species: *P. aerogenoides, P. intermedium, P. Arizonae,* and *P. coliforme.*

In the course of routine serological typing of the Salmonella cultures which were submitted to them, Edwards and his associates encountered cultures which could not be classified as Salmonella and which resembled the Escherichia. Although this group was, as a rule, somewhat slow in fermenting lactose, this characteristic could not be used entirely as a basis of group selection. Inasmuch as the description of a culture by Caldwell and Ryerson, in 1939, isolated from a horned lizard in Arizona, indicated the existence of a separate group, the name Arizona group was coined. Subsequent descriptions of this group by numerous workers were summarized by Edwards, West, and Bruner in 1947. In this summary the above authors describe the Arizona group of paracolon bacteria as motile coliform bacteria which produce abundant $H_2S$, but fail to form indol; are methyl red positive and Voges-Proskauer negative; produce acid and gas from glucose; do not utilize *d*-tartrate or ferment sucrose, dulcitol or salicin; ferment lactose with varying avidity and liquefy gelatin. In this study of 373 cultures it was found they could be divided into 19 groups and 55 types by antigenic analysis. All of the types were serologically related to Salmonella and the various types were found to be related to infections in animals. The cultures which were studied were isolated from reptiles, fowls, rodents, swine, man, and egg powder.

The close relationship of the Arizona group with the Salmonellae was emphasized by Edwards, Fife, and Ramsey in a

TABLE 20.2

MAJOR BIOCHEMICAL PROPERTIES OF THE GENUS SALMONELLA AND THE ARIZONA GROUP

| Property | Salmonella | Arizona |
|---|---|---|
| Indol production | − | − |
| Methyl red test | + | + |
| Voges-Proskauer test | − | − |
| Growth in Simmons' citrate | + | + |
| $H_2S$ production | + | + |
| Urease production | − | − |
| Growth in KCN medium | − | − |
| Motility | + | − |
| Gelatin liquefaction | − | + |
| Lysine decarboxylation | + | + |
| Phenylalanine deamination | − | (+) |
| Gas from glucose | + | + |
| Fermentation of: lactose | − | (+) |
| sucrose | − | − |
| mannitol | + | + or × |
| dulcitol | + | − |
| salicin | − | − |
| adonitol | − | − |
| inositol | d | − |

\+ = prompt, positive, 1 to 2 days; (+) = delayed positive; × = late and irregularly positive; d = different biochemical types; − = negative.

comprehensive article published in 1955. They set forth criteria which may be used to distinguish the two groups (Table 20.2) but refrain from suggesting a genus name.

In their study of the paracolon bacteria, Hinshaw and McNeil revealed their presence in gopher snakes, lizards, turkey poults, and rattlesnakes. The significance of these bacteria in reptiles was emphasized, and the incrimination of such animals as sources of infection to avian species as well as domestic animals and man was a most worthwhile contribution.

Most of the cultures of the Arizona group have been isolated from animals; however, Edwards, McWhorter, and Fife reported in 1956 that isolations of the organism from man showed a marked increase, which is probably due to the increased presence of it in poultry flocks.

Upon continued study of the characteristics of paracolon bacteria of human origin, Edwards, West, and Bruner described cultures which they designated the Bethesda group, because most of the cultures originated from Bethesda, Maryland. They describe this group as follows: slow lactose-fermenting cultures that are methyl red positive, Voges-Proskauer negative, indol negative, $H_2S$ positive, *d*-tartrate positive, and Simmons' citrate positive. Urea utilization is negative when tested by the method of Rustigian and Stuart (1941), but most cultures give positive tests by the method of Christensen (1946). Dulcitol usually is fermented promptly, although dulcitol negative strains occur. Sucrose generally is not fermented, although occasional cultures may ferment sucrose.

A third group of paracolon bacteria called the Ballerup group was described by Bruner, Edwards, and Hopson in 1949. This group is so named because the original culture which was considered to be the type species of the group was named *Salmonella ballerup*. This group is characterized as follows: motile or nonmotile coliform bacteria which produce abundant $H_2S$ but fail to form indol; usually are methyl red positive and Voges-Proskauer negative; promptly produce acid and gas from glucose, arabinose, maltose, rhamnose, xylose, trehalose, mannitol, and sorbitol; attack lactose, sucrose, dulcitol, and salicin with varying avidity, but fail to ferment inositol; utilize *d*-tartrate, usually utilize sodium citrate, and rarely liquefy gelatin. Practically all of the 45 cultures which were originally placed in this group by the above investigators originated from cases of gastroenteritis in man, but cultures from a hog, a hen, a duck, oysters, and sewage were included.

The latter two groups are now classified

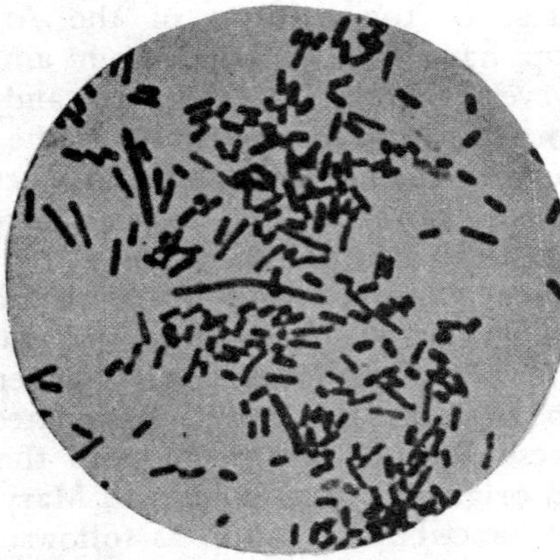

FIG. 20.4—**Proteus vulgaris** from agar culture, ×2,000. (From Nowak: Documenta Microbiologica, courtesy Gustav Fischer.)

together under the term Bethesda-Ballerup group.

## THE GENUS PROTEUS

The bacteria in the genus Proteus are gram-negative, pleomorphic rods (Fig. 20.4) which are actively motile by means of peritrichous flagella. They ferment dextrose and sucrose, forming both acid and gas, but do not ferment lactose. They liquefy gelatin and do not give a positive reaction to the Voges-Proskauer test. On moist media the motile types produce typical ameboid colonies which rapidly spread across the surface of the plate (Fig. 20.5); nonmotile forms produce dense, nonspreading colonies.

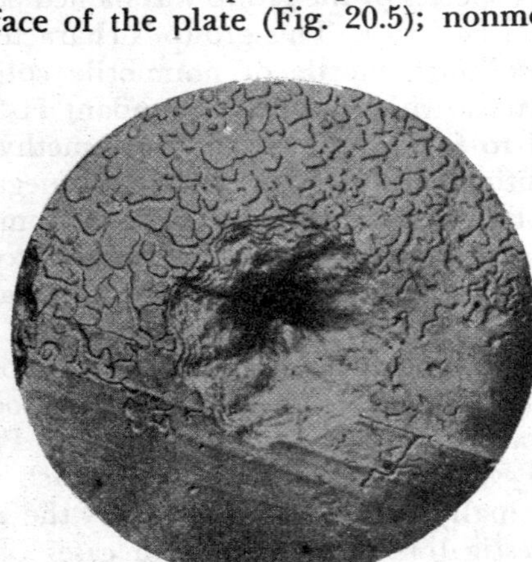

FIG. 20.5—**Proteus vulgaris** colony on agar plate showing thin, filmy growth around the main colony, ×70. (From Nowak: Documenta Microbiologica, courtesy Gustav Fischer.)

Strains of one of the species, *Proteus vulgaris,* have been extensively investigated because of their diagnostic importance in typhus fever of man. Weil and Felix, in 1917, demonstrated that certain strains, which they designated X2 and X19, were agglutinated by the sera of typhus fever patients. In the course of this investigation, Weil and Felix introduced the term H (Hauch = film) for the motile forms and the term O (ohne Hauch = without film) for the nonmotile forms of the organism. Immune sera of rabbits prepared by injecting H and O cultures revealed that two types of agglutinin developed. The O agglutinin caused the agglutination of O organisms, forming fine clumps, and the H agglutinin agglutinated H organisms, forming coarse clumps. The O immune serum contained only O agglutinins, but the H serum contained both H and O agglutinins. Since then, the terms O and H have been adopted as the designations of types of agglutination; that is, O pertains to fine clumps and H to coarse clumps.

*Proteus vulgaris* is not significant as a pathogenic organism. It is not the cause of typhus fever or any other of the Rickettsia diseases. The real explanation of the positive agglutination tests with X2 and X19 strains of the organism is not known. The organism has been associated as a secondary invader with other organisms in wound infections and diseases of mucous membranes. It has been isolated from cases of cystitis and pyelitis in man following the obstruction of the urinary tract by calculi.

### *Proteus ammoniae*

*Proteus ammoniae* and *Proteus mirabilis* are very closely related and considered by some authors to be identical.

**Synonyms and History.** In 1925 Hager and Magath described an organism which they found to be associated with incrusted cystitis in man. They called this organism *Salmonella ammoniae.* In a subsequent study in 1928 Magath gave a detailed description of the organism and suggested that it belonged to the genus Proteus, although some minor characteristics did not conform to a typical Proteus organism. In a study of 32 strains of the organism, isolated from various sources, Fulton and Harrison emphasized that the organism was sufficiently characteristic to be considered a member of the Proteus group.

The relationship of *P. ammoniae* to animal infections has been emphasized during recent years by Packer by the isolation of the organism from a variety of animals.

**Distribution and Transmission.** The distribution of *P. ammoniae* is not known. The presence of the organism in so many different animal species and different tissues indicates that it is rather ubiquitous, and infections caused by it are sporadic due to predisposing factors.

**Morphology and Staining.** *P. ammoniae* is a plump rod 0.5$\mu$ by 1.4$\mu$ in size; is motile with peritrichous flagella; is nonsporeforming and noncapsulated. The organism is easily stained by the commonly used bacteriological stains, and is gram-negative.

**Growth Requirements and Characteristics.** Colonies formed by the organism on solid media are thin and transparent, typical of the veil-like growth characteristics of the genus Proteus.

In fluid media *P. ammoniae* produces a marked turbidity due to abundant growth.

**Resistance.** This organism is not resistant to the common disinfectants. It is not susceptible to penicillin, but its growth is inhibited by streptomycin.

**Biochemical Properties.** *P. ammoniae* produces acid and gas from glucose, galactose, glycerol, trehalose, and xylose. The ability of the organism to ferment sucrose has been of concern to numerous investigators. This led Hager and Magath to question the inclusion of the organism in the genus Proteus. Fulton and Harrison have shown that the organism produces acid and gas in 5 per cent but not in 0.5 per cent sucrose. The rapid growth of actively proteolytic bacteria often causes such a marked alkalinity that acids produced from carbohydrates are neutralized. This has been proved true of *Pseudomonas aeruginosa*. The use of a protein-free medium in which the carbohydrate is placed reveals fermentation which has been considered negative. By using this medium, the composition of which is given in Chapter 18, Packer has demonstrated that *P. ammoniae* produces acid and gas in 0.3 per cent sucrose and salicin in 10 days. The organism does not ferment lactose, mannite, maltose, dulcitol, arabinose, inositol, inulin, raffinose, rhamnose, sorbitol, adonitol, dextrin, fructose, and soluble starch. It liquefies gelatin, and reduces and peptonizes litmus milk. The decomposition of urea is an outstanding characteristic of this organism. Colonies of the organism on S-S medium have black centers and the sulfurous odor characteristic of $H_2S$ production.

**Antigenic Structure and Toxins.** Various species of this organism have not been subjected to detailed antigenic study. On the basis of limited agglutination tests the species is serologically heterogenous. Specific toxins have not been described.

**Pathogenicity.** Previous mention has been made of the relationship of this organism to incrusted cystitis in man. Fulton and Harrison studied cultures isolated from stool specimens and from a mastoidectomy in man. Packer has isolated the organism from nine cases of hematuria and cystitis in the dog, two cases of urinary tract infection in cows, two cases of omphalophlebitis in the turkey; one case of each of the following: prostatitis in the dog, endocarditis in the pig, bacteriemia in the turkey, pneumonia in the dog, skin wound in the dog, and skin wound in the cow.

Craige isolated Proteus organisms from 101 dogs showing a variety of symptoms including peritonitis and omphalitis in newborn puppies, acute bloody diarrhea, chronic dysentery, and nervous disorders.

Autogenous bacterins used in 49 cases gave rather satisfactory results.

White mice usually are killed within 24 hours by intraperitoneal injections of *P. ammoniae*. Some strains are pathogenic for the guinea pig whereas others are not able to produce death. In their study of the organism Hager and Magath were able to produce the lesion of incrusted cystitis in guinea pigs and in rabbits when a primary inflammation was produced in the bladder mucosa by the injection of 0.5 to 1 cc. of a 0.1 per cent alcoholic solution of salicylic acid.

**Immunity.** No information is available concerning the immunitv produced by the organism.

**Diagnosis.** The close similarity of this organism with *E. coli* makes it imperative that urine cultures be subjected to close examination. The usual presence of the swarming, ameboid colony of the organism is sufficient to identify it as a Proteus. Carbohydrate fermentation must be used for definite identification.

## REFERENCES


Barnes, L. E. Jour. Amer. Vet. Med. Assn. 125:50, 1954.

Biely, J., and March, B. B. Avian Dis. 7:1–5, 1963.

Carroll, E. J. Amer. Jour. Vet. Res. 25:720–26, 1964.

Charter, R. E. *Escherichia coli* Type 0.114 Isolated From Infantile Diarrhea and Calf Scours. Jour. Path. Bact. 72:33, 1956.

Craige, J. E. Jour. Amer. Vet. Med. Assn. 113:154, 1948.

Davis, J. W., and Smibert, R. M. Amer. Jour. Vet. Res. 24:324–28, 1963.

———, *et al.* Amer. Jour. Vet. Res. 22:736–40, 1961.

Deibel, R. H., and Silliker, J. H. Jour. Bact. 85:827–32, 1963.

Dimock, W. W., and Edwards, P. R. Jour. Amer. Vet. Med. Assn. 70:469–80, 1927.

Easterbrooks, H. L., and Plastridge, W. N. Acute Klebsiella (Capsulated Coliform) Mastitis. Jour. Amer. Vet. Med. Assn. 128:502, 1956.

Edwards, P. R. Relationships of the Encapsulated Bacilli With Special Reference to *Bact. aerogenes*. Jour. Bact. 17:339–53, 1929.

———. The Relationship of Encapsulated Bacilli Found in Metritis in Mares to Encapsulated Bacilli From Other Sources. Jour. Bact. 15:245–66, 1928.

———, and Ewing, W. H. Identification of Enterobacteriaceae. Burgess Publishing Co., Minneapolis, 1962.

———, and Fife, M. A. Studies on the Klebsiella-Aerobacter Group of Bacteria. Jour. Bact. 70:382, 1955.

———, *et al.* Arizona Group of Paracolon Bacteria. Ky. Agr. Exp. Sta. Bull. 499, Univ. Ky., Lexington, 1947.

———, *et al.* Antigenic Studies of a Group of Paracolon Bacteria (Bethesda Group). Jour. Bact. 55:711, 1948.

———, *et al.* Bull. World Health Org. 14:511–28, 1956.

———, *et al.* The Occurrence of Bacteria of the Arizona Group in Man. Canad. Jour. Microbiol. 2:281–87, 1956.

———, *et al.* Studies on the Arizona Group of Enterobacteriaceae. Bact. Rev. 23:155, 1959.

Erlandson, A. L., and Gagliardi, L. A. Jour. Inf. Dis. 108:181–88, 1961.

———, *et al.* Jour. Inf. Dis. 108:189–94, 1961.

Ewing, W. H. Ann. N.Y. Acad. Sci. 66:61–70, 1956.

———, *et al.* Bull. Pub. Health Lab. 14:106–11, 1956.

Fulton, M., and Harrison, P. E. Jour. Bact. 46:365–67, 1943.

Gay, C. C., *et al.* Canad. Vet. Jour. I. 5:248–61, 1964; II. 5:297–308, 1964; III. 5:314–25, 1964

Glantz, P. J. 64th Ann. Proc. U.S. Livestock Sanit. Assn., 1960.

———, and Rothenbacher, H. Amer. Jour. Vet. Res. 26:258–61, 1965.

———, *et al.* Penn. State Univ., Agr. Exp. Sta. Bull. 645, 1959.

Gregory, D. W. Edema Disease in Swine. Jour. Amer. Vet. Med. Assn. 135:321, 1959.

Hager, B. H., and Magath, T. B. Jour. Amer. Med. Assn. 85:1352, 1925.

Hall, H. E., and Humphries, J. C. The Relationship Between Insusceptibility to Phagocytosis and Virulence of Certain *Klebsiella pneumonia* Strains. Jour. Inf. Dis. 103:157, 1958.

Hinshaw, W. R., and McNeil, E. Jour. Bact. 53:715, 1947.

Hjärre, A., and Wramby, G. Skandinavisk Veterinärtidskrift. 35:449, 1945.

INGRAM, P. L., *et al.* *Bacterium coli* Antibodies in Colostrum and Their Relation to Calf Survival. Jour. Path. Bact. 72:561, 1956.

JULIANELLE, L. A. Jour. Exp. Med. 44:683–96, 735–51, 1926.

KAUFFMANN, F. Jour. Immunol. 57:71, 1947.

KESSNER, D. M. Amer. Jour. Hyg. 76:27–43, 1962.

KNIPSCHILDT, H. E. Undersgelser over Coligruppens Serologi med Saerligt Henblik poa Kapsedformerne. Diss. Copenhagen, 1945.

LECCE, J. G., and REEP, B. R. Jour. Exp. Med. 115:491–501, 1962.

LUDFORD, C. G., and STEVENS, M. S. The Isolation of *Klebsiella pneumonia* From a Case of Canine Pneumonia. Austral. Vet. Jour. 34:253, 1958.

MAGATH, T. B. *Proteus ammoniae*. Jour. Inf. Dis. 43:181–83, 1928.

McCABE, W. R., and JACKSON, G. G. Biology of Pyelonephritis, International Symposium. Little, Brown and Co., Boston, 1960.

PACKER, R. A. *Proteus ammoniae* in Animals. Personal communication.

SANFORD, J. P., *et al.* Jour. Exp. Med. 116:285–94, 1962.

SHAUGHNESSY, H. J., *et al.* Amer. Jour. Hyg. 76:44–51, 1962.

SMIBERT, R. M., *et al.* Amer. Jour. Vet. Res. 23:460–64, 1962.

SMITH, H. W. Jour. Path. Bact. 84:147–68, 1962.

———. Jour. Path. Bact. 85:197–211, 1963.

VAHLNE, G. Serological Typing of the Colon Bacteria, With Special Reference to Occurrence of *B. coli* in Man Under Normal and Pathological Conditions Particularly in Appendicitis. Diss. Lund, 1945. Acta Path. et Microbiol. Scandinav. Suppl. 62, 1945.

WEST, M. G., and Edwards, P. R. The Bethesda-Ballerup Group of Paracolon Bacteria. Pub. Health Serv. Publ. No. 362. U.S. Govt. Print. Off., Washington, D.C., 1954.

WILSON, G. S., and MILES, A. A. Topley's Principles of Bacteriology and Immunity. 5th Ed. Williams & Wilkins Co., Baltimore, 1964.

WILSON, W. J. The Colon Group and Similar Bacteria. A System of Bacteriology. Vol. IV, Chap. 4. Med. Res Council. His Majesty's Stationery Office, London, 1929.

WRAMBY, G. Investigations Into the Antigenic Structure of *Bact. coli* Isolated From Calves. Appelbergs Boktryckeriaktiebolag, Uppsala, 1948.

# 21

# The Genus Salmonella

SALMONELLAE ARE NONSPOREFORMING, GRAM-negative rods closely related morphologically and physiologically to the other genera of the family Enterobacteriaceae. They are usually motile, although nonmotile forms occur; produce acid and gas from glucose, maltose, mannitol, and sorbitol; do not ferment lactose, sucrose, or salicin; do not form indol, coagulate milk, or liquefy gelatin. They are parasitic upon man and animals and usually produce inflammatory reactions in the intestinal tract.

The first organism representative of the group was isolated in 1885 by Smith and Salmon from pigs which had died of hog cholera. They believed the organism to be the cause of the disease; consequently, the name *Bacillus cholerae suis* was given to it. This organism was considered to be the cause of hog cholera until 1904 when de Schweinitz and Dorset discovered that the real cause was a filterable virus. Subsequently this organism has been found to be a secondary invader to the virus disease and to be one of the causes of infectious enteritis in the pig. The second organism of the group was isolated by Gärtner in 1888 from a fatal case of gastroenteritis in a young man who had eaten raw meat taken from a diseased cow. The organism was named *Bacillus enteritidis*. The name Salmonella was proposed for the genus by Lignières in 1900 in honor of D. E. Salmon, the first Chief of the United States Bureau of Animal Industry, now called the Agricultural Research Service.

During the intervening years numerous species of bacteria fulfilling the description for this genus have been described. Four of the group, *Salmonella paratyphi, Salmonella schottmuelleri, Salmonella herschfeldii,* and *Salmonella typhosa* are well known as species which are pathogenic for man. These species are not known to produce infection in animals, and their occasional isolation from animals is considered

TABLE 21.1

TOTAL OUTBREAKS OF SALMONELLOSIS AND NUMBER OF SALMONELLA TYPES ENCOUNTERED IN ANIMALS (FOWLS AND MAN NOT INCLUDED)

| Source | Types | Outbreaks |
|---|---|---|
| Horses | 3 | 42 |
| Cattle | 11 | 60 |
| Sheep | 6 | 33 |
| Other ruminants | 2 | 2 |
| Swine | 38 | 958 |
| Dogs | 4 | 18 |
| Foxes | 7 | 74 |
| Other carnivora | 5 | 6 |
| Rats | 5 | 18 |
| Mice | 4 | 23 |
| Guinea pigs | 4 | 29 |
| Other rodents | 2 | 13 |
| Reptiles | 10 | 8 |
| Lower primates | 5 | 5 |

Source: Edwards, P. R., and Bruner, D. W. Proc. 50th Ann. Meet. U.S. Livestock Sanit. Assn., 1946.

Total animal species, 23; total Salmonella types, 46; total outbreaks, 1,289.

to be as a result of contamination. The rest of the species in the genus which are to be discussed are pathogenic for a wide variety of animals in which they produce enteric infection. The only exceptions are *Sal. abortivoequina* and *Sal. abortusovis*, which cause abortion in the equine and ovine species, respectively.

The selection of the most common species of Salmonella, which infect animals, from the large number of antigenic types for discussion in this textbook has been difficult. The prevalence of various types of Salmonella in domestic animals has also been tabulated (Table 21.1) by Bruner and Edwards. This emphasizes the widespread incidence of organisms of this group and the large number of different species of animals involved.

In 1961 Moran summarized the occurrence and distribution of Salmonella serotypes in animals in the United States. Only 15 species which were the most frequently isolated are included in Table 21.2. A more complete list is given in the article by Moran. It is significant to note that these organisms are exceedingly widespread among various animal hosts, and in many cases animals other than the primary hosts are involved. The prevalence of *Sal. typhimurium* must be emphasized. It appears difficult to select a primary host for this organism.

Food products of animal origin which are used by either man or animals are often the sources of Salmonella which may cause extensive outbreaks of enteric infection. For example, Bayer, Bruner, and Brown reported an outbreak in experimental turkey poults which was produced by feeding a commercial starter mash. They were able to isolate nine serotypes of Salmonella from turkey feed and meat scraps. Pomeroy and Grady found that 175 out of 980

TABLE 21.2

OCCURRENCE AND DISTRIBUTION OF SALMONELLA SEROTYPES IN THE UNITED STATES, JANUARY 1957–JULY 1961

| | Turkeys | Chickens | Other Birds | Swine | Sheep and Goats | Cattle | Horses | Mice and Rats | Other Animals | Total |
|---|---|---|---|---|---|---|---|---|---|---|
| *Sal. typhimurium* | 612 | 282 | 120 | 45 | 11 | 185 | 49 | 40 | 41 | 1385 |
| *Sal. pullorum* | 14 | 987 | 4 | | | 2 | | | 3 | 1010 |
| *Sal. choleraesuis* | | 12 | 1 | 353 | | 4 | | | 8 | 378 |
| *Sal. heidelberg* | 159 | 127 | 2 | 2 | | 2 | | | 2 | 294 |
| *Sal. anatum* | 176 | 59 | 13 | 8 | | 26 | 3 | | 6 | 291 |
| *Sal. enteritidis* | 63 | 25 | 1 | | | 50 | 99 | 10 | 9 | 257 |
| *Sal. newport* | 165 | 6 | 3 | 3 | 3 | 57 | 3 | | 15 | 255 |
| *Sal. san diego* | 215 | 10 | | | | 4 | | | | 229 |
| *Sal. gallinarum* | 22 | 184 | | | | | | | | 206 |
| *Sal. infantis* | 78 | 94 | | 2 | 1 | 1 | 3 | 3 | 4 | 186 |
| *Sal. chester* | 106 | 52 | 3 | | | | | 2 | 1 | 164 |
| *Sal. saintpaul* | 114 | 18 | | | | | 2 | | 2 | 136 |
| *Sal. muenchen* | 95 | 16 | 1 | 1 | | 1 | | | | 114 |
| *Sal. derby* | 52 | 17 | 7 | 27 | 2 | 1 | | | 7 | 113 |
| *Sal. blockley* | 16 | 82 | 1 | 4 | | | | | | 103 |

Source: Moran, Alice, Proc. 65th Ann. Meet. U.S. Livestock Sanit. Assn., 1961.

samples of animal by-products from 22 states which were to be used for animal food were contaminated with 43 different serotypes of Salmonella.

## CLASSIFICATION

The classification of the Salmonella has undergone significant changes during the time such organisms have been recognized as significant agents of disease. In common with other groups of bacteria, carbohydrate fermentation has been recognized as a fundamental basis for classification. The fermentation of the carbohydrates, xylose, arabinose, inositol, maltose, and trehalose, as well as the production of hydrogen sulfide are used in differentiating the group selected for discussion (Table 21.3).

According to Table 21.3, the common species of the Salmonella associated with animal diseases can be differentiated. One exception must be noted; that is, the reactions of *Sal. schottmuelleri* and *Sal. typhimurium*. The similarity in the reactions between these two species appears to indicate that they should be placed in one species. It must be emphasized, however, that physiological reactions are only one set of criteria by which bacteria are classified. In this instance, these two species can be separated on the basis of differences in antigenic structure (Table 21.4). Moreover, they are different in respect to pathogenicity. *Sal. schottmuelleri* is pathogenic for man, whereas *Sal. typhimurium* is primarily associated with animal diseases.

In addition to the carbohydrate fermentations and other tests which are commonly employed in the laboratory for the differentiation of bacteria, a few other specific tests have been designed for the Salmonella group. Stern described a fuchsin-sulfite-glycerol meat-extract medium in which "Stern positive" organisms formed a deep lilac color due to the formation of an aldehyde by the fermentation of the carbohydrate. A second test, known as the Bitter test, specifies a medium containing 0.5 per cent rhamnose in milk; incubation

TABLE 21.3

DIFFERENTIAL METABOLIC CHARACTERISTICS OF REPRESENTATIVE SALMONELLA

| Species | Xylose | Arabinose | Trehalose | Inositol | Maltose | $H_2S$ Produced |
|---|---|---|---|---|---|---|
| *Sal. paratyphi* | — | AG | AG | — | AG | — |
| *Sal. schottmuelleri* | AG | AG | AG | AG | AG | + |
| *Sal. hirschfeldii* | AG | AG | AG | — | AG | + |
| *Sal. typhosa* | V | V | A | — | A | + |
| *Sal. typhimurium* | AG | AG | AG | AG | AG | + |
| *Sal. abortivoequina* | AG | AG | | — | AG | V |
| *Sal. abortusovis* | AG | AG | — | — | AG | + |
| *Sal. choleraesius* | AG | — | — | — | AG | V |
| *Sal. typhisuis* | AG | AG | AG | — | AG | — |
| *Sal. enteritidis* | AG | AG | AG | — | AG | + |
| *Sal. pullorum* | AG | AG | AG | — | V | + |
| *Sal. gallinarum* | A | A | A | — | A | V |
| *Sal. anatis* | AG | AG | AG | — | AG | + |

A = acid; G = gas; — = negative; + = positive; V = variable.

TABLE 21.4

ANTIGENIC STRUCTURE OF REPRESENTATIVE SALMONELLA

| Type | Species | Somatic O-Antigen | Flagellar H-Antigen | |
|---|---|---|---|---|
| | | | Phase 1 | Phase 2 |
| A | *Sal. paratyphi* | 1,2,12 | a | ... |
| B | *Sal. schottmuelleri* | 1,4,5,12 | b | 1,2 |
| | *Sal. typhimurium* | 1,4,5,12 | i | 1,2 |
| | *Sal. abortivoequina* | 4,12 | ... | e,n,x |
| | *Sal. abortusovis* | 4,12 | c | 1,6 |
| | *Sal. bredeny* | 1,4,12,27 | l,v | 1,7 |
| $C_1$ | *Sal. choleraesuis* | 6,7 | c | 1,5 |
| | *Sal. typhisuis* | 6,7 | c | 1,5 |
| D | *Sal. typhosa* | 9,12,Vi | d | ... |
| | *Sal. enteritidis* | 1,9,12 | g,m | ... |
| | *Sal. dublin* | 1,9,12 | g,p | ... |
| | *Sal. gallinarum* | 1,9,12 | ... | ... |
| | *Sal. pullorum* | 9,12 | ... | ... |
| $E_1$ | *Sal. anatum* | 3,10 | e,h | 1,6 |
| | *Sal. meleagridis* | 3,10 | e,h | l,w |
| F | *Sal. rubislaw* | 11 | r | e,n,x |
| G | *Sal. worthington* | 1,13,23 | l,w | z |
| H | *Sal. horsham* | 1,6,14,25 | l,v | e,n,x |
| | *Sal. brazil* | 16 | a | 1,5 |
| | *Sal. hull* | 16 | b | 1,2 |

is required for 15 hours and then methyl red is added to determine acid formation. The medium used in the test has been modified by the use of various salts, 0.5 per cent peptone, and a fermentable carbohydrate such as rhamnose, xylose, and maltose. A third reaction depends on the ability of the organisms to ferment *d*-tartrate which is added to a nutrient medium.

## SEROLOGICAL CLASSIFICATION OF THE SALMONELLA

The classification of bacteria by the use of serological reactions, such as agglutinin absorption, has been used for the Salmonella more than for any other group of bacteria.

This was due to the initial contribution of White and of Kauffmann. In the United States the typing of Salmonella cultures was centered at the Agricultural Experiment Station, University of Kentucky at Lexington, under the guidance of P. R. Edwards, and at the Beth Israel Hospital in New York City under the supervision of F. Schiff. Inasmuch as Edwards studied, mainly, the Salmonella isolated from animals, his reports are of most significance to veterinary bacteriology. In 1949 Edwards moved to the laboratories of the Communicable Disease Center of the United States Public Health Service at Atlanta, Georgia, where he, in association with Ewing, continued his study of the Salmonella and related microorganisms.

It is not considered necessary to list the 151 antigenic types of Salmonella given in Bergey's Manual, but the antigenic formula of the important species will be given.

The serological classification is based upon the antigenic structure of the various species of organisms. The terminology used by Weil and Felix for the Proteus strains has been adopted for the Salmonella; accordingly, the antigens of the organisms are divided into two groups, O antigen and H antigen.

The O antigen, or somatic antigen, is composed of the bacterial cell body and is prepared by heating the bacterial suspension for an hour at 80°–100°C. or by extraction with hot alcohol. These procedures remove the H flagellar antigens. The various O antigens are designated by numerals, 2, 3, 4, etc.; and upon the basis of close relationships the species of the Salmonella are placed into groups designated Types A, B, C, etc. (see Table 21.4). A single species may have more than one O antigen; that is, it has a group antigen which may be common to many of the members of its group.

The H antigen, or flagellar antigen, is composed of cell flagella and is prepared by subjecting the bacterial suspension to formalin which, supposedly, fixes the flagella over the surface of the bacterium, thereby covering the O antigens of the cell body. This antigen is heat labile. The H antigens of the Salmonella are *diphasic;* that is, they are of more than one type. The two phases are designated *specific phase* and *nonspecific phase.* The specific phase is composed of only those antigenic components which are specific for the species, or strain, of the organism. These antigens are designated a, b, c, etc. The nonspecific phase is represented by the antigens shared by other species, in other group types. These antigens are designated 1, 2, 3, 4, etc. The antigenic formulae of all the Salmonella species which are to be discussed in this chapter are listed in Table 21.4, along with other representative antigenic types.

The antisera which are used for typing the Salmonella must be prepared from known strains of organisms in known stages of biology. The production of flagella antiserum presupposes that the organism which is injected possesses flagella. *Sal. pullorum* is nonflagellated; therefore, it does not have H antigen. An S→R dissociation results in the loss of certain components of the cell essential for complete O antigen. Since various environmental conditions produce dissociative changes in the Salmonella, the phase of the organism, S or R, must be known in the recognition of species. It must be emphasized that the recognition of a number of strains of Salmonella requires the use of numerous antisera and scores of agglutinin-adsorption tests.

## THE ISOLATION OF SALMONELLA

The presence of practically all of the species of Salmonella in the intestinal tract of man and animals presents a more complex problem of isolation than is found in those bacteria which may infect lung, liver, kidney, or muscle. The various kinds of bacteria, yeasts, molds, and protozoa in the intestinal tract assure that a culture medium inoculated with a loopful of intestinal fluid would be a very mixed culture. For this reason special media have been devised to assure that a Salmonella can be isolated if it is present.

### Preliminary Enrichment

If intestinal infection is severe and is caused by a Salmonella, it is not essential that a specimen be inoculated into a preliminary enrichment medium. However, there are times, such as surveys of Salmonella incidence, that the number of bacteria may be low, and when increased in a medium favoring growth, isolation will be easier. Media used for this purpose are selenite broth and tetrathionate broth. If these are not available, meat-infusion broth can be used. The student has become familiar with the genus Proteus and the swarming type of growth found on an agar plate. Fundamentally, this is the problem in obtaining pure cultures of any organism from fecal matter. The addition of 0.215 mg. of sodium sulfathiazole to 100 ml. of tetrathionate broth has been found effective in suppressing the growth of Proteus. Lauryl sulfate and bismuth sulfate are also used for this purpose when added to tetrathionate broth.

### Selective Plating Media

EMB agar and Endo's agar are used to

detect the lactose-fermenting bacteria and to inhibit gram-positive bacteria. These media were used in the study of the Escherichia and in plating water samples. Proteus is also inhibited by the use of desoxycholate agar and MacConkey's agar.

The media which are recognized as being selective for Salmonella are: (1) SS agar, (2) bismuth sulfite agar, (3) desoxycholate citrate agar, (4) MacConkey brilliant green agar, and (5) brilliant green-phenol red agar. Of these, the latter is preferred by those working with the Salmonella group.

When colonies which are typical Salmonellae are observed on the selective medium, tryptose broth is inoculated, and when sufficient growth is obtained, carbohydrate and other media are inoculated. This will identify the most common of the Salmonella. If the antigenic type or serotype is to be identified, a culture must be sent to one of the laboratories where antisera for the various types are used.

### *Salmonella paratyphi*

**Synonyms and History.** *Bacterium paratyphi* Type A, *Bacillus paratyphosus* Type A, *Salmonella paratyphi* A.

This organism was first isolated by Gwyn in 1898 from a case which was clinically like typhoid fever, but the serum of the patient did not agglutinate the typhoid organism. In 1900 Schottmüller isolated two different organisms from cases similar to typhoid fever. He termed these organisms paratyphoid A and paratyphoid B: this terminology has become firmly established in medical literature. Extensive study of various strains of these organisms has revealed that they are separate species; consequently, the A and B designations have been dropped, and the names *Salmonella paratyphi* for the type A, and *Salmonella schottmuelleri* for the type B are used.

**Distribution and Transmission.** *Sal. paratyphi* is widely distributed throughout the world. It is transmitted through the agencies of meat, milk, and water which have been contaminated with fecal matter from infected people.

**Morphology and Staining.** The organism is a short, plump rod, 0.6$\mu$ by 3.0$\mu$ to 4.0$\mu$ in size; is motile with peritrichous flagella; is noncapsulated; is nonsporeforming; is stained readily by the common laboratory staining methods; and is gram-negative.

**Growth Requirements and Characteristics.** *Sal. paratyphi* is easily grown on laboratory media enriched with meat extracts. It is aerobic and facultatively anaerobic. It grows best at a pH of 7.2.

On agar surfaces colonies of the organism are grayish, homogeneous, smooth, glistening, with an entire or slightly undulate edge.

In broth the organism produces a light, uniform turbidity and forms a light, powdery sediment.

The growth on potato is not abundant, being limited to a grayish-white streak.

**Resistance.** This organism, in common with all of the gram-negative, nonsporeforming, rod-shaped bacteria, is easily killed by 60°C. in 20 minutes and is quickly destroyed by the common chemical disinfectants. All such organisms, however, survive in fecal material where they are protected from the action of sunlight and desiccation. They survive freezing and, consequently, live through winter periods.

**Biochemical Properties.** *Sal paratyphi* produces acid and gas from glucose, fructose, galactose, mannose, arabinose, maltose, trehalose, dextrin, glycerol, mannitol, dulcitol, isodulcitol, and sorbitol; does not ferment lactose, sucrose, raffinose, xylose, salicin, inulin, adonitol, or inositol; reduces nitrates to nitrites; does not produce indol; does not form $H_2S$; acidifies litmus milk slightly; is negative to the Bitter test; is Stern negative; does not ferment *d*-tartrate; does not liquefy gelatin.

**Antigenic Structure and Toxins.** The antigenic structure of the organism is given in Table 21.4. No exotoxins are produced.

**Pathogenicity.** The organism is pathogenic

for man, producing paratyphoid fever. It is not of significance in the lower animals, although the isolation of the organism from the pig has been reported.

This organism is typical of all of the species of Salmonella which are pathogenic to mice, guinea pigs, and rabbits when suitable doses are inoculated intravenously and intraperitoneally. Variability in pathogenicity of the different strains is observed when cultures are given orally or are injected subcutaneously.

**Immunity.** Recovery from the disease produces an immunity. This organism is commonly incorporated with *Sal. schottmuelleri* and *Sal. typhosa,* forming the triple vaccine usually employed in routine immunization. Antibodies are produced during an infection.

**Diagnosis.** The organism is identified by culture reactions. The agglutination test is valuable as a diagnostic method.

### *Salmonella schottmuelleri*

**Synonyms and History.** *Bacillus paratyphi alcaligenes, Bacterium paratyphi* Type B, *Bacillus schottmuelleri, Salmonella paratyphi* B, *Bacterium schottmuelleri.*

This organism was described first by Schottmüller in 1900 in relationship to an intestinal infection in man.

**Distribution and Transmission.** The organism is widely distributed, and cases of the disease produced by it are more numerous than those produced by *Sal. paratyphi.* Infections often occur as epidemics resulting from the contamination of food and water with human fecal material from an infected case or an immune carrier.

**Morphology and Staining.** This organism is typical of the group.

**Resistance.** *Sal. schottmuelleri* is typical of the group.

**Biochemical Properties.** The organism produces acid and gas from glucose, fructose, galactose, mannose, arabinose, xylose, maltose, dextrin, trehalose, glycerol, mannitol, dulcitol, sorbitol, isodulcitol, and inositol; does not ferment lactose, sucrose, inulin, salicin, adonitol, or usually raffinose; produces $H_2S$; does not reduce nitrates; does not form indol; does not liquefy gelatin; produces an increased alkalinity in litmus milk; is variable in its reaction to the Bitter test and the Stern test. The fermentation of *d*-tartrate is negative in strains isolated in the United States.

**Antigenic Structure and Toxins.** (See Table 21.4.) Exotoxins are not produced.

**Pathogenicity.** *Sal. schottmuelleri* causes paratyphoid fever in man similar to that produced by *Sal. paratyphi.* Its role in acute gastroenteritis of the food-poisoning type is controversial; although it is not a frequent cause of this type of disease, it has been isolated from typical cases. It is not considered a natural pathogen of animals, but strains of the organism have been isolated from enteritis in chickens and other birds and from bovine milk. The close relationship between this organism and *Sal. typhimurium* emphasizes the need of careful identification of it when it is suspected as the cause of animal infections.

**Immunity.** Recovery from an infection produced by the organism results in immunity. This organism is also incorporated into the triple vaccine used for enteric fevers. Agglutinating antibodies are produced by an infection.

**Diagnosis.** The organism is identified by cultural methods. The disease is diagnosed by the use of a specific antigen of the organism in the agglutination test.

### *Salmonella typhosa*

**Synonyms and History.** *Bacillus typhosus, Bacillus typhi abdominalis, Bacterium typhi, Eberthella typhi, Salmonella typhosus, Bacterium typhosum, Eberthella typhosa.*

Typhoid fever is one of the diseases

which led to the belief that living agents were the cause of certain types of disease and that such agents could be transmitted from one person to another. Budd believed this to be true of typhoid fever as early as 1856. The organism was first observed in infected human tissues by Eberth in 1880, but it was isolated and described by Gaffky in 1884.

**Distribution and Transmission.** *Sal. typhosa* is distributed quite generally over the entire world, but is most prevalent in those countries and areas where little is done to prevent the contamination of water and food supplies.

The organism is transmitted from an infected person to a susceptible one by means of any medium which can be contaminated with fecal matter. At one time the infected case was the usual source of the infective material, but the resistant carrier has now become of greater significance. Petruschky reported in 1898 that typhoid organisms remain in urine of typhoid convalescents for months. Subsequently it was shown that the organisms are also present in feces, and that 2 to 3 per cent of infected persons remain typhoid carriers for the rest of their lives. The story of Mary Malone, commonly known as "Typhoid Mary," is one of the classical illustrations of the damage which may result from an immune carrier.

The organism can be transmitted to food by means of contaminated water which comes in contact with the food directly or with utensils which are used in handling food. The fingers of a carrier may transmit the organism to food or to utensils. Flies may carry the organism from fecal matter to food or to utensils. Although water is the most common vehicle in the transmission of the organism, milk is one of the important foods which can be contaminated. A number of milk-borne epidemics of typhoid fever occur in the United States each year. Practically all of them are caused by the consumption of raw milk which has been contaminated by immune carriers or by contaminated water used in washing milk utensils. Whether the typhoid bacillus may invade the bovine mammary gland, become established there, and produce infection has been a question in the minds of many. Scott and Minett, in 1947, contributed to the solution of the problem by their unsuccessful attempt to produce infection in the cow with *Sal. typhosa.* It is obvious that a great many of the methods which are used in milk sanitation should be directed toward the prevention of the spread of this organism.

**Morphology and Staining.** *Salmonella typhosa* is a plump, short rod, 0.5$\mu$ to 0.8$\mu$ in diameter by 1$\mu$ to 3$\mu$ in length (Fig. 21.1). Some individual cells and some cultures are long and threadlike. It is actively motile by means of peritrichous flagella. It is noncapsulated and nonsporeforming.

The organism is stained readily by the usual staining methods and is gram-negative.

**Growth Requirements and Characteristics.** This organism is aerobic and facultatively anaerobic, grows well on meat infusion media at a pH of 7.2, and grows best at 37.5°C.

On the agar surface the organism forms small, grayish, transparent colonies which become opaque as the culture ages.

In broth, the typhoid organism produces a uniform turbidity, rarely a pellicle.

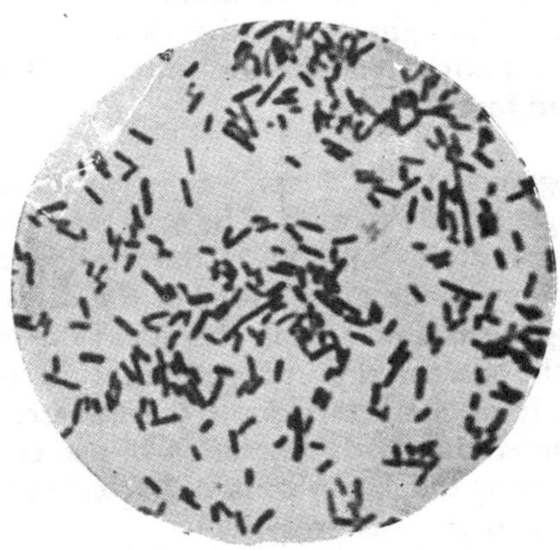

FIG. 21.1—**Salmonella typhosa** from 24-hour agar culture, ×2,000. (From Nowak: Documenta Microbiologica, courtesy Gustav Fischer.)

The growth on potato is thin and glistening and is limited to a narrow streak.

**Resistance.** The organism is easily destroyed by ordinary surface disinfectants such as chlorine 200 p.p.m. Heating at 143°F. for 30 minutes or 160°F. for 15 seconds kills the organism; consequently, the temperatures used in milk pasteurization are important safeguards to health.

**Biochemical Properties.** *Sal. typhosa* produces acid but not gas from glucose, levulose, galactose, xylose, maltose, raffinose, dextrin, glycerol, mannitol, and sorbitol; does not ferment lactose, sucrose, inulin, rhamnose, inositol, salicin, or usually arabinose or dulcitol. It produces $H_2S$; reduces nitrates to nitrites; does not form indol; does not liquefy gelatin; produces a slight initial acidity in litmus milk and an increased alkalinity as the culture ages.

**Antigenic Structure and Toxins.** The organism is closely related antigenically with other salmonellae, and on the basis of antigenic structure is placed in Group D with *Sal. enteritidis, Sal. pullorum,* and *Sal. gallinarum.* An antigen, Vi, which is related to virulence has been described for the organism. The typhoid bacillus does not produce a true toxin; however, a heat-resistant substance, presumably endotoxin, is liberated by the organism. This substance is thought to be the cause of the marked toxicity in persons suffering from typhoid fever.

**Pathogenicity.** *Sal. typhosa* is primarily pathogenic only to man. The organism produces symptoms in 7 to 14 days following infection. In the early stages of the disease the organism is present in the blood stream, and the destruction of intestinal tissue, which is so characteristic of the disease, is considered due to the excretion of bacterial products or the localization of bacteria subsequent to the bacteremia.

Septicemia may be produced in guinea pigs and rabbits by the intravenous injection of large doses of the organism which is found in the gallbladder of some of the surviving animals.

A disease typical of typhoid fever in man can be produced in chimpanzees by feeding cultures of the organism. These animals are commonly used in testing the efficacy of the various immunizing products used for typhoid fever.

**Immunity.** Persons who recover from an attack of typhoid fever are immune to the general effects of the organism; however, the persistence of the organism in the gallbladder of some individuals belies a total immunity. Antibody is formed by the infection, thereby producing a certain degree of humoral immunity.

Typhoid fever vaccines are widely used in prophylactic treatment. While it is difficult to evaluate such treatment exactly, it is believed by most authorities that the incidence of cases is reduced. Vaccines which have been prepared in such a manner as to preserve the heat-labile Vi factor are considered to be of greater value than those which have not been so treated.

### *Salmonella typhimurium*

**Synonyms and History.** *Bacillus typhimurium, Bacterium aertrycke, Salmonella pestis caviae, Salmonella psittacosis.*

In 1892 Loeffler isolated from a natural outbreak of a typhoid-like disease in mice an organism which he called *Bacillus typhimurium.* This animal has been the only one with which the name has been associated until recent years. Biochemical and serological reactions reveal that it is identical with many other heretofore recognized species of Salmonella; consequently, on the basis of priority, it has been chosen as the species name which embraces many others.

*Sal. aertrycke* of de Nobele, 1898, is one of the species of the genus which had become well established in animal bacteriology, but it now becomes a synonym of *Sal. typhimurium.* This constitutes an important change which the student must remember in the study of past literature.

*Sal. pestis caviae,* which was isolated

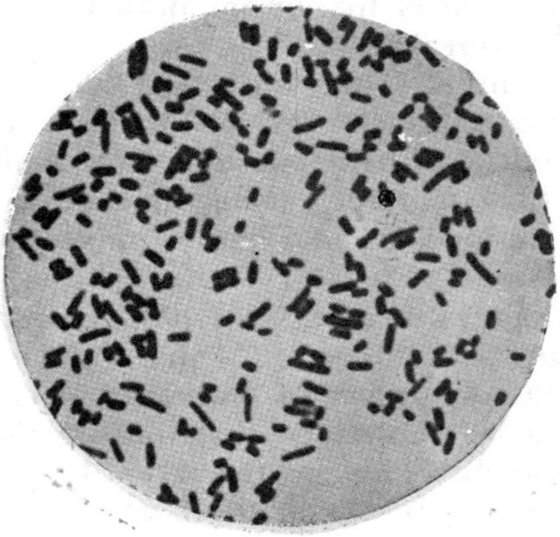

FIG. 21.2—**Salmonella typhimurium** from an agar culture, ×2,000. (From Nowak: Documenta Microbiologica, courtesy Gustav Fischer.)

from an intestinal infection in guinea pigs by Wherry in 1908, is now a synonym of *Sal. typhimurium.*

*Sal. psittacosis,* isolated from parrots by Nocard in 1893 and considered to be the cause of psittacosis until the revelation of a filterable virus as the etiologic agent, is now placed under *Sal. typhimurium.*

**Distribution and Transmission.** The organism is widely distributed geographically, and among numerous species of animals and birds; in fact, it occurs in all warm-blooded vertebrates. (See Table 21.2.) It produces a typical paratyphoid, intestinal inflammation; consequently, it is transmitted by the medium of food and water contaminated by fecal matter. Normal animals are known to harbor the organism. In birds this organism, in common with many of the other salmonellae, is transmitted through the ovary of the mature bird to the embryo.

In a study of the Salmonella isolated from snakes in California, Hinshaw and McNeil found that 11 out of 41 (26.8 per cent) snakes yielded cultures of Salmonella. Five different types were isolated, *Sal. meleagridis, Sal. typhimurium, Sal. newport, Sal. rubislaw,* and *Sal. panama.* The isolation of these cultures from snakes is considered significant since infection in turkey poults yielded the same types of Salmonella in many instances. It is apparent that such reptiles may serve as reservoirs of infection.

Feed and animal by-products such as eggs and poultry meat often have been incriminated as vehicles of infection. Smyser *et al.* have shown that the organism will remain viable for considerable periods of time in feedstuffs kept at 21°–29°C. and longer when stored at 4°C. The *Sal. typhimurium* epidemic in Riverside, California, in 1965 emphasized that a water supply may become contaminated with the organism and transmit it to people.

Flies have been shown by Greenberg *et al.* to be capable of transmitting this organism to man. This is especially true if flies have come from a slaughterhouse where they have had ready access to contamination.

**Morphology and Staining.** This bacterium is typical of the group. See Figures 21.2 and 21.3.

**Resistance.** It is typical of the group.

**Growth Requirements and Characteristics.** It is typical of the group.

**Biochemical Properties.** *Sal. typhimurium* produces acid and gas from glucose, fructose, galactose, arabinose, maltose, xylose,

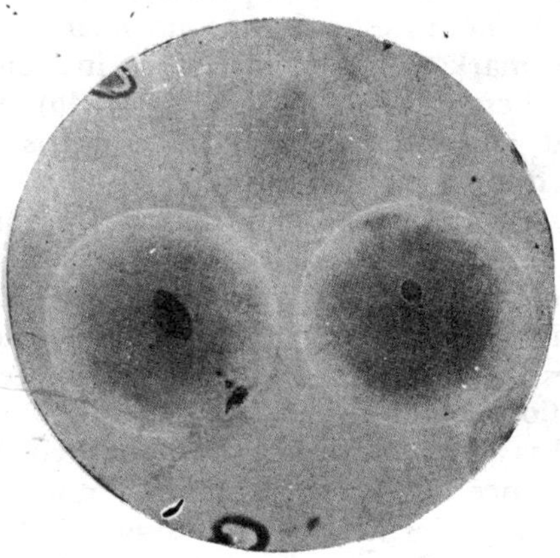

FIG. 21.3—**Salmonella typhimurium** colony on agar plate, ×45. (From Nowak: Documenta Microbiologica, courtesy Gustav Fischer.)

dextrin, mannitol, sorbitol, trehalose, and inositol; does not ferment lactose, sucrose, raffinose, inulin, salicin, or adonitol. It produces $H_2S$; does not form indol; reduces nitrates; produces an increasingly alkaline reaction in litmus milk; does not liquefy gelatin. Strains of the organism vary in reaction to the Bitter test, the Stern test, and in the fermentation of *d*-tartrate. Edwards has shown that the Bitter test, employing maltose and xylose as the fermentable carbohydrate, can be used to determine the epizootic relationships of strains of *Sal. typhimurium*.

**Antigenic Structure.** The antigenic structure of the organism is given in Table 21.4. Edwards has found that the pigeon strains have somatic antigen 4 and are classified as 4 variants, but they do not possess antigen 5 with regularity.

Although old-culture filtrates produce symptoms similar to anaphylactic shock in experimental animals, the organism does not produce specific exotoxins.

**Pathogenicity.** *Sal. typhimurium* is the cause of acute and fatal intestinal infections of mice, rats, guinea pigs, sheep, calves, horses, chickens, white Pekin ducks, turkeys, parrots, and pigeons. The symptoms of the disease are characterized by increased temperature, severe diarrhea, and marked weakness. Upon postmortem examination the intestinal mucous membrane shows marked hyperemia, and in acute cases, hemorrhage. Schofield (1946) recorded an outbreak of fatal enteritis in cattle due to this organism.

*Sal. typhimurium* may depart from its usual role as an enteric pathogen according to Vickers *et al.* They have reported the isolation of the organism from aborted fetuses following an outbreak of dysentery in a flock of ewes.

Lukas and Bradford have emphasized the importance of the organism as a cause of paratyphoid in turkeys by finding that 32.7 per cent of Salmonella cultures were of this species and that it was responsible for 46.5 per cent of the uncomplicated paratyphoid outbreaks.

Chinchillas *(Chinchilla laniger)* have been found susceptible to *Sal. typhimurium*, and in instances of herd infection show a high mortality. Chronic, acute, and peracute cases are observed in a herd of mixed ages and sexes.

The prevalence of *Sal. typhimurium* in so many animal species (Table 21.2) forecasts the occurrence of outbreaks in man. It must be emphasized that this organism was responsible, during the period 1934–47, for more outbreaks in the human family than any other Salmonella species. During May, June, and July, 1965, a water-borne epidemic of enteric disease involved an estimated 18,000 people in Riverside, California. The method by which the water supply became contaminated with *Sal. typhimurium* was not detected, and this epidemic probably will be recorded as one in which the exact source will never be known, according to Stone.

Story and Hanbury report that this organism may produce a wide variety of conditions in man, although the lymphoid cells of the intestines, the mesenteric lymph nodes, and the spleen are more commonly involved. Other organs affected are the lungs, kidneys, heart, liver, and gallbladder. In addition to these, the organism has been isolated from cases of osteomyelitis, meningitis, appendicitis, salpingitis, and furunculosis. Lesions of focal necrosis of the intestinal mucosa are not found as is the case with typhoid fever.

**Immunity.** Artificial immunity has been practiced for mice which have been used for experimentation purposes for *Sal. typhimurium*. The majority of reports reveal that solid immunity is not obtainable without incurring high death losses during treatment.

Infections produced by the organism are so sporadic in nature that widespread immunization of susceptible birds and flocks is not practical. Strains of the organism are commonly incorporated in mixed bacterins which are used for intestinal infections in the various domesticated animals.

Coburn, Armstrong, and Psyche observed that it is advantageous to immunize chinchillas with an autogenous bacterin, and it is especially desirable to immunize the dam early in the period of pregnancy, for it enhances the production of living litters and the survival of the young.

**Diagnosis.** The extensive distribution of *Sal. typhimurium* among animals necessitates the use of specific antisera for correct identification, although the organism is identified in a general way by biochemical reactions. Agglutinins are formed during the progress of the natural disease and may be used for diagnosis.

### *Salmonella abortivoequina*

**Synonyms and History.** *Bacillus abortivus equinus, Bacillus abortus equi, Bacterium abortum-equi, Salmonella abortus-equi.*

In 1893 Smith and Kilborne isolated a gram-negative rod from mares which had aborted. Lignières, in 1905, reported finding a bacillus belonging to this group in aborting mares and in cows in France and Argentina. In 1912 Good, in Kentucky, described an organism which was associated with equine abortion; subsequently, in 1913 he proposed the name *Bacillus abortivus equinus*. Good and Smith, in 1916, published a complete literature summary and a description of the disease and of the organism.

**Distribution and Transmission.** This organism was introduced, apparently, into the United States in 1886, and first made its appearance in states of the Mississippi Valley from which it has spread to numerous other states. Abortion in mares, caused by this organism, is not considered to be prevalent, although sporadic cases do appear. Unfortunately, many of the cases are not studied bacteriologically; consequently, the exact distribution of the organism is not known.

The organism is thought by some to be transmitted by an infected stallion; however, the short incubation period of the disease, and experimental infection of pregnant mares by feeding cultures of the organism have emphasized the fact that the organism is obtained by the ingestion of infected feed, such as grass, from contaminated pastures.

**Morphology and Staining.** It is typical of the group.

**Growth Requirements and Characteristics.** The organism is aerobic and facultatively anaerobic and grows abundantly on common laboratory media.

Colonies of the organism on an agar plate are small, round, slightly elevated, glistening colonies which become finely granular in structure as they age. Older colonies are dry and membranous, and entire colonies can be pushed along the surface of the agar or lifted from it with the inoculating needle. These colonies are irregular and appear like rosettes with a wrinkled surface.

On the agar slant, growth is dull and parchment-like, developing thin wrinkles close to the water in the bottom of the tube as well as a thin pellicle on the water.

In broth a uniform turbidity develops in 24 hours. Cultures which have dissociated to the R develop a heavy pellicle which sinks en masse to the bottom of the tube. Smooth strains do not form a pellicle.

**Resistance.** The organism does not differ from other members of the group in resistance to surface disinfectants. The need of an antiseptic douche for infected mares led Good and Smith to test various chemicals which may be used for that purpose. They found that a one-tenth per cent solution of potassium permanganate kills the organism in 1 minute, 1 per cent carbolic acid in 1 minute, 1:1,000 methylene blue in 5 minutes, and a saturated solution of boric acid in 3 hours.

**Biochemical Properties.** *Sal. abortivoe-*

*quina* produces acid and gas from xylose, raffinose, arabinose, dulcitol, glucose, mannitol, maltose, dextrin, and trehalose; does not ferment lactose, adonitol, and inositol; varies in the fermentation of sorbitol and rhamnose. It does not liquefy gelatin; does not produce indol; varies in the production of $H_2S$; varies in reaction to the Bitter rhamnose test; is negative to Stern glycerol; varies in the fermentation of *d*-tartrate; produced an increased alkalinity in litmus milk.

**Antigenic Structure and Toxins.** The organism belongs to Group B on the basis of somatic antigen. H antigen is shared with other strains of Salmonella not related to equine abortion.

It does not produce an exotoxin, but a comparatively potent endotoxin is released by the organism. Large doses of killed suspensions of the organism injected subcutaneously into horses produce symptoms characterized by inappetence, chills, fever, and stiffness.

**Pathogenicity.** *Sal. abortivoequina* causes abortion in mares and jennets following natural infection. Parenteral injection of the organism produces abortion in guinea pigs, rabbits, sows, ewes, mares, and jennets. Schebitz and Hansen, in Sweden, reported that the organism could be the cause of epididymitis in donkeys. The recovery of the organism from aborted bovine fetuses has been reported. It is not pathogenic for man.

**Immunity.** In 1916 Good and Smith demonstrated that pregnant mares were protected from the infection by the injection of a number of doses of bacterin. Since that time, bacterins have been reported to give highly satisfactory results in preventing abortion. Kelser (1921) reported that bacterins injected during the fourth and ninth months of pregnancy were used widely in United States Army Remount Depots with highly satisfactory results.

**Diagnosis.** Infectious abortion in mares is diagnosed by the isolation and identification of the organism from the aborted fetus and vaginal exudate from the mare. The agglutination test is also of value in detecting infected mares.

### *Salmonella abortusovis*

In 1921 Schermer and Ehrlich isolated an organism from ewes which had aborted. They found the organism belonged to the paratyphoid group; consequently, they named it *Bacillus paratyphi abortus ovis*. In 1925 Bosworth and Glover discovered the organism was the cause of abortion in ewes in England. The organism has not been reported in the United States.

*Salmonella abortusovis* is similar to the other members of the group in morphology and culture characteristics. It produces acid and gas from glucose, maltose, mannitol, xylose, and sorbitol; does not ferment lactose, sucrose, salicin, inositol, or rhamnose; is variable in fermenting arabinose, dulcitol, and dextrin. It produces $H_2S$ slowly and does not change litmus milk.

Lovell found the English and German strains to be antigenically identical. The organism shares somatic antigen with other members of Group B. Apparently it is pathogenic only for sheep, for it has not been reported from other animals or from man.

### *Salmonella choleraesuis*

**Synonyms and History.** *Bacillus cholerae suis, Bacterium cholerae suis, Bacillus suipestifer, Salmonella choleraesuis, Salmonella suipestifer.*

This organism was first isolated and described in 1885 by Salmon and Smith, and was named *Bacillus cholerae suis*. It was considered to be the cause of hog cholera until the real cause, a filterable virus, was discovered in hog cholera, and it was found to be one of the infecting agents in infectious enteritis in Iowa pigs by Murray, Biester, Purwin, and McNutt in 1927 and 1928.

**Distribution and Transmission.** The organism is widely distributed throughout

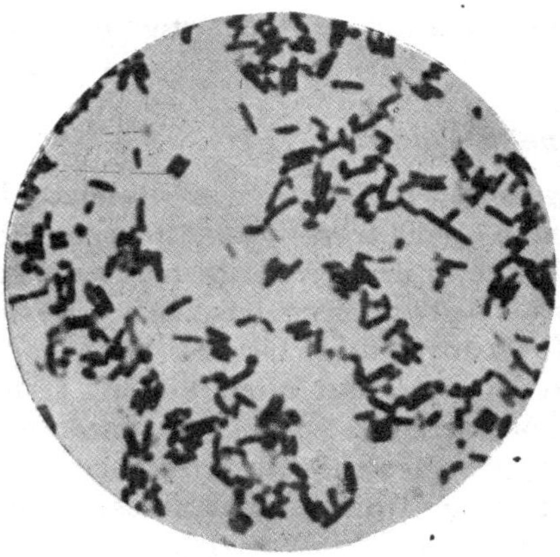

FIG. 21.4—**Salmonella choleraesuis** smear from agar culture, ×2,000. (From Nowak: Documenta Microbiologica, courtesy Gustav Fischer.)

the world where large numbers of pigs are raised. It is transmitted by the ingestion of feed and water contaminated by feces from infected animals. The repetition of the infection on certain farms year after year indicates that the organism lives through the winter season in fecal material or is present in animals which have become immune carriers.

**Morphology and Staining.** It is typical of the group. See Figures 21.4 and 21.5.

**Resistance.** The organism is typical of the group.

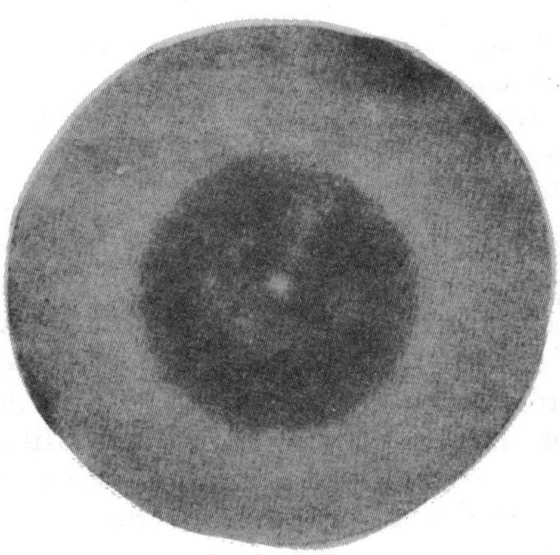

FIG. 21.5—**Salmonella choleraesuis** colony on agar plate, ×30. (From Nowak: Documenta Microbiologica, courtesy Gustav Fischer.)

**Growth Requirements and Characteristics.** It is typical of the group.

**Biochemical Properties.** *Sal. choleraesuis* produces acid and gas from glucose, fructose, galactose, mannose, xylose, maltose, glycerol, mannitol, dulcitol, isodulcitol, sorbitol, and dextrin; does not ferment arabinose, inositol, lactose, sucrose, salicin, inulin, raffinose, and trehalose. It reduces nitrates; does not form indol; does not liquefy gelatin; produces a slight initial acidity in milk, followed by alkalinity and clearing of the medium; ferments *d*-tartrate. It is negative to the Bitter rhamnose test and to the Stern test. *Sal. choleraesuis* does not produce $H_2S$; however, it must be emphasized that *Sal. choleraesuis* var. *kunzendorf* does produce $H_2S$ and the two species may be identified on that basis.

**Antigenic Structure and Toxins.** See Table 21.4. The antigens of this organism are similar to *Sal. paratyphosum* C, an organism producing a certain type of enteric fever in man. It is also closely related in antigenic structure to *Sal. choleraesuis* var. *kunzendorf* which lacks a type specific H antigen.

**Pathogenicity.** *Sal. choleraesuis* is the cause of acute infectious enteritis found in pigs of all ages throughout the United States. Freshly isolated cultures of the organism reproduce the typical disease when they are fed or injected parenterally. The organism has also been recovered from cattle, dogs, and fowls and occurs more frequently than any other Salmonella in foxes.

Mice are more susceptible than any of the other laboratory animals; they die of a septicemia within a few days after inoculation. Guinea pigs are susceptible when cultures are fed or injected. The rabbit is especially susceptible to this organism, succumbing to very small doses given parenterally.

The organism has been recovered from cases of food poisoning in man. The Kunzendorf variety has been isolated most frequently from such cases. Henderson isolated the organism from a urinary tract infection in a farmer 49 years of age.

Three cases of pneumonia in man caused by *Sal. choleraesuis* were reported by Levine and Plattner in 1944. These authors suggest that blood cultures and the agglutination test with *Sal. choleraesuis* antigen should be used in cases of atypical pneumonia in man.

In a study of 318 cultures of *Sal. choleraesuis,* Saphra and Wasserman noted that patients from whom the organisms were isolated rarely showed enteric pathology, fecal excretion of the organism, or a carrier state. However, there were frequent septicemias, focal lesions, and a high mortality rate.

**Immunity.** Mature animals which recover from an attack of this organism are presumably immune. It was the first organism to be used in the preparation of a bacterin for immunizing purposes by Salmon and Smith; bacterin-therapy was used for hog cholera until the discovery of the virus and virus antiserum. The function of bacterins in producing immunity in pigs is of doubtful value due to the massive doses of the organism which enter the susceptible intestinal tract of pigs on contaminated feeds. Infectious enteritis due to this organism can be prevented best by observing well-established rules of swine sanitation and nutrition.

The close association of hog cholera with *Sal. choleraesuis* infection has led to the assumption that there exists a synergistic relationship between the two agents. It has been believed that *Sal. choleraesuis* infection interfered with the production of immunity by hog chólera virus immunization products. Rodabaugh, Wright, and Elder have shown that this does not happen, at least when *Sal. choleraesuis* infection is induced at the time of vaccination with hog cholera vaccine of rabbit origin.

**Diagnosis.** Infection due to *Sal. choleraesuis* is detected by the isolation and identification of the organism. This includes the determination of the antigenic structure.

### Salmonella typhisuis

*Salmonella typhisuis* was isolated by Glässer in 1909 from young pigs with a typhoid-like infection known as ferkeltyphus. This organism has been reported from Germany, but as far as is known it is not present in the United States. It has been considered a strain of *Salmonella choleraesuis* since the two are antigenically alike. It varies from *Sal. choleraesuis,* however, since it produces acid and gas from arabinose and trehalose but does not form hydrogen sulfide. The organism forms a more delicate growth on solid media and produces gas more slowly in fermentable media than *Sal. choleraesuis.*

It is pathogenic only for young pigs and has not been involved in human infection.

### Salmonella enteritidis

**Synonyms and History.** *Bacillus enteritidis, Bacterium enteritidis.* This organism was first isolated by Gärtner in 1888 from a fatal case of meat poisoning in man and from beef that had produced the disease. Since then, the organism and its different varieties have been isolated from numerous animals and from man.

Antigenic classification and other special tests have revealed that there are a number of varieties of *Salmonella enteritidis.*

All of the strains are similar in morphology, colony characteristics, and resistance to the other members of the Salmonella group.

**Biochemical Properties.** *Salmonella enteritidis* produces acid and gas from glucose, fructose, galactose, mannose, arabinose, xylose, maltose, trehalose, dextrin, glycerol, mannitol, dulcitol, and sorbitol; does not ferment lactose, sucrose, inulin, salicin, raffinose, adonitol, and inositol. The organism does not form indol; forms $H_2S$; reduces nitrates to nitrites; does not liquefy gelatin.

**Pathogenicity.** *Sal. enteritidis* produces enteritis in rodents and in man. It has been isolated from cattle but is not of any consequence as the cause of disease in that animal in this country.

*Salmonella enteritidis* var. *danysz* was originally isolated from an epidemic of enteritis in field mice, but is now thought to be more pathogenic for rats.

*Salmonella enteritidis* var. *essen* has been isolated from ducks' eggs and from ducks. It also has been known to produce gastroenteritis in man.

*Salmonella enteritidis* var. *dublin* is considered one of the primary causes of calf diarrhea. It has been found also in pigs and foals. This strain is one of the important causes of food poisoning in man.

*Salmonella enteritidis* var. *rostock* has been isolated from cattle but has not been known to produce disease in man.

Higgens, Christiansen, and Schroeder report an infection in a flock of 900 turkeys caused by *Sal. enteritidis.* The disease involved 100 birds and was characterized by purulent exudate in the tendon sheaths of the hock joint.

The different varieties of *Sal. enteritidis* are able to produce a severe gastroenteritis in mice and guinea pigs. The inflammatory reaction is produced by a potent endotoxin which is liberated by the organism. The endotoxin is resistant to heat and is not antigenic, resembling the enterotoxin of the staphylococci.

**Immunity.** Infections which are caused by *Sal. enteritidis* and its different varieties are so sporadic that little is known about the immunity which may result following the active disease. It is presumed that these infections, in common with those which are produced by other salmonellae, produce an immunity. Calf enteritis produced by the organism seems to support this presumption, for this animal is resistant to infection as it grows to maturity.

*Sal. enteritidis* is commonly incorporated in mixed bacterins which are used to immunize calves. The antiserum which is used in the treatment of cases of calf enteritis should be polyvalent; that is, it should include antibodies against this organism along with those of other organisms which are known to be the cause of the disease.

**Diagnosis.** The presence of this organism is detected by isolating and identifying it by the use of biochemical reactions.

### *Salmonella pullorum*

**Synonyms and History.** *Bacterium pullorum, Bacillus pullorum.*

*Salmonella pullorum* was first isolated from chicks suffering from severe diarrhea and was described by Rettger in 1899, and more completely described by Rettger and Stoneburn in 1909. At that time considerable confusion existed concerning this organism and the one responsible for typhoid in chickens, now called *Salmonella gallinarum.* Smith and Ten Broeck, in 1915, were the first to show the differences between the two organisms. Because the antigenic structure of the two organisms is identical, there has been an inclination by some authors to place them in the same species. They are clearly distinguishable by biochemical tests as shown by Trabulsi and Edwards. Their results are summarized in Table 21.5.

TABLE 21.5

BIOCHEMICAL REACTIONS OF *Sal. pullorum* AND *Sal. gallinarum*

| | *Sal. pullorum* | *Sal. gallinarum* |
|---|---|---|
| Glucose (gas) | + | − |
| Maltose | − | + |
| Dulcitol | − | + |
| D-tartrate | − | + |
| Cysteine gelatin | − | + |
| Ornithine | − | + |
| Mucate | − | + |

Source: Trabulsi, L. R., and Edwards, P. R. Cornell Vet. 52:563–69, 1962.

**Distribution and Transmission.** The organism is widely distributed over the world where chickens are present in large numbers.

The transmission of *Sal. pullorum* from an infected chick to a susceptible one is commonly through feed and water. An unusual mode of transmission exists in this disease. Many of the infected chicks which survive an infection remain carriers of the organism. The organism shows a definite affinity for the developing ovary of the pullet in which it localizes and produces a condition typified by shrunken, distorted, and undeveloped ova; however, many ova do develop into eggs. These eggs contain the organism, and when they are incubated and hatched, an infected chick results. This chick will then infect others; hence, the cycle of the infection is continued.

*Sal. pullorum* may be transmitted from an infected adult member of a flock to other adults. Gwatkin has shown that adult turkeys also may be infected by contact with infected adult chickens. Although turkeys do not maintain the infection as do adult hens during the period of infection, they lay eggs which contain the organism.

The role of the infected rooster in the transmission of *Sal. pullorum* has been investigated by many. In general it is believed that this manner of transmission is not too frequent but may happen. The hazard is great enough to warrant the removal of infected males of all species of domestic fowl from the flock.

**Morphology and Staining.** The organism is similar to the other gram-negative rods in size and shape. It does not possess flagella, which is an important characteristic in respect to antigenic structure. The normal shape of the organism is short and plump, but Van Roekel has described variants which are extremely long and filamentous (Fig. 21.6).

**Growth Requirements and Characteristics.** The organism is isolated in pure culture

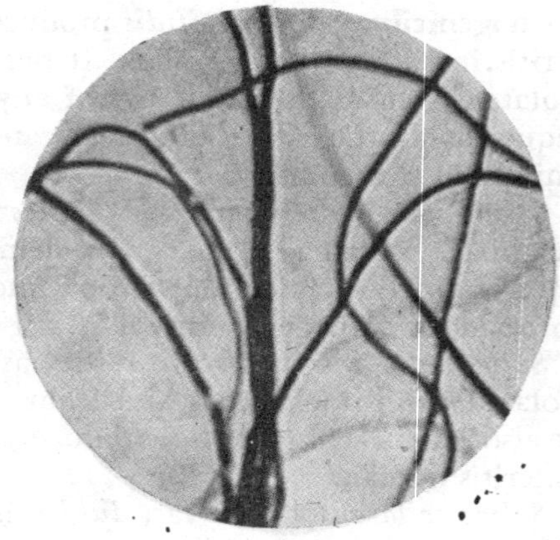

FIG. 21.6—**Salmonella pullorum** showing long filamentous variant types, ×1,200. (Courtesy Van Roekel.)

by opening the infected chick with aseptic precautions and streaking blood or liver and spleen pulp upon the surface of meat infusion agar. The organism is aerobic and facultatively anaerobic; grows best at 37°C. and a pH of 7.2.

The normal organism produces smooth, glistening, opalescent, entire colonies on nutrient agar (Fig. 21.7). Van Roekel has described variants which form rough, dry, and opaque colonies with markedly irregular edges (Fig. 21.8). Mucoid colonies also have been described. Variation is induced more easily by growing the organism on liver infusion agar.

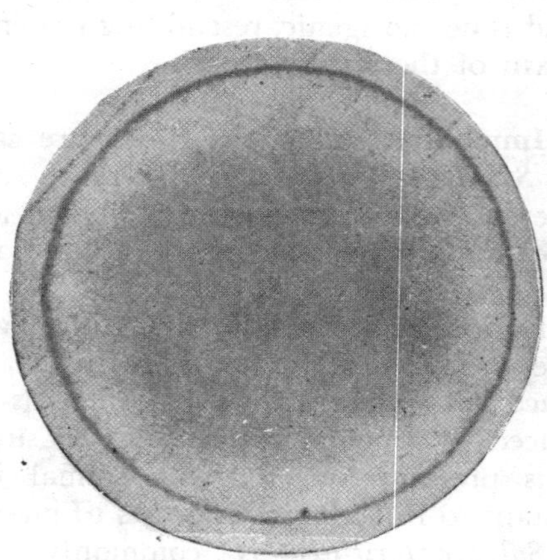

FIG. 21.7—**Salmonella pullorum** normal smooth S colony, ×125. (Courtesy Van Roekel.)

**Resistance.** It is typical of the group.

**Biochemical Properties.** *Sal. pullorum* produces acid and gas from glucose, fructose, galactose, mannose, arabinose, xylose, mannitol, and isodulcitol; does not attack lactose, sucrose, dextrin, salicin, raffinose, sorbitol, adonitol, dulcitol, or inositol. The organism has been considered unable to ferment maltose. Hinshaw reports the finding of an occasional strain which produces acid from this carbohydrate. In a study of 300 strains of the organism, Hinshaw, Browne, and Taylor found 40 strains which did not ferment maltose, 27 anaerobic strains which did ferment maltose, and 260 aerobic strains which were able to produce acid in this carbohydrate. They were able to isolate nonmaltose-fermenting strains as variants from stock cultures of maltose-fermenting strains. It produces $H_2S$; reduces nitrates to nitrites; does not form indol; does not liquefy gelatin; produces initial slight acidity in milk with increasing alkalinity; is negative to the Bitter rhamnose test and the Stern glycerol test; does not ferment *d*-tartrate.

**Antigenic Structure and Toxins.** *Sal. pullorum* possesses only somatic antigen since it is nonmotile. The complete antigenic formula of the organism is considered to be 9, 12. However, antigenic variants $12_1$, $12_2$, and $12_3$ have been observed. Strains of the organism are classified as standard, variant, or intermediate types. Williams has found that the three antigenic types may be differentiated by a macroscopic ammonium sulfate sedimentation test. The significance of antigenic variability of *Sal. pullorum* is emphasized in agglutination testing of adult hens for the detection of reactors (Wright). It is apparent that a testing antigen should contain both regular and variant forms if the variant is known to exist in the territory to be tested.

**Pathogenicity.** *Sal. pullorum* produces an acute disease in chicks during their first few days of life and is characterized by a severe enteritis and bacteremia. The organism multiplies rapidly in the chicken embryo. Jeffries and Holtman have found that the minimum lethal dose for embryonating eggs was as little as one organism, following intra-allantoic inoculation. The fecal material is white in color and pasty in consistency. This color led to the name bacillary white diarrhea, but one of the terms salmonellosis, paratyphoid, or pullorum disease is considered more appropriate. In mature hens the organism produces a chronic infection characterized by a shrunken and misshaped ovary. Acute septicemia has been reported in mature chickens.

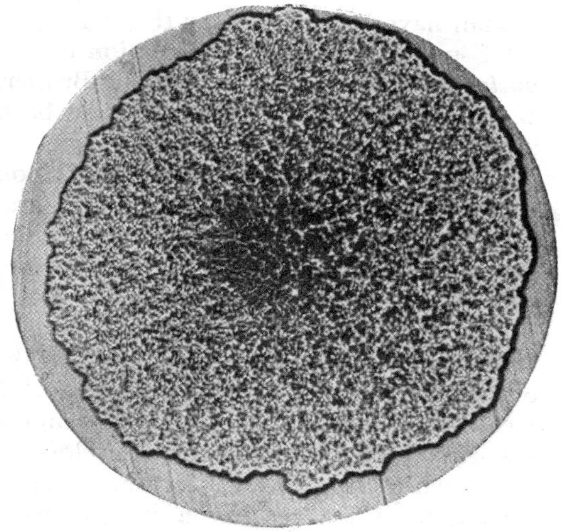

FIG. 21.8—**Salmonella pullorum** variant rough R colony, ×125. (Courtesy Van Roekel.)

In an outbreak of *Sal. pullorum* infection in canaries in which 50 birds of a flock of 75 died, Edwards was able to isolate the organism from 13 of the birds autopsied.

This organism infects turkeys in the same manner as chickens, but as previously noted it does not appear to be as chronic a disease in the turkey hen as in the chicken.

*Sal. pullorum* has been isolated from other species of animals including the cow, pig, and fox. The importance of it as an agent of disease in mammals is not considered very great. It is significant to observe that no serious outbreaks of infection in man have been caused by this organism.

Of special interest is the isolation of *Sal. pullorum* from a dog by Brown, Bruner, and Moran in 1948. The animal had been in poor condition and received a diet of raw eggs before it was destroyed. Upon necropsy an intense icterus was found along with an enlarged liver and petechial hemorrhages in the lungs. The organism was isolated from many different tissues.

**Immunity.** An absolute immunity to the organism does not appear to develop. A local tissue immunity, particularly in the intestinal tract, appears to develop in chicks which survive an infection. The localization of *Sal. pullorum* in the ovary makes it evident that a generalized immune condition does not exist. Agglutinins are present in the blood stream of the hen which harbors the organism in the ovary.

**Diagnosis.** The presence of the organism in the chick is determined by the isolation and identification of it.

The agglutination test is used to diagnose the condition in mature hens. Two types of tests are commonly used, the macroscopic tube test and the macroscopic plate test, or rapid test. The rapid plate test can be done in the field, employing whole blood instead of the clear serum which is used in the laboratory. The dissociation or variation of the organism from the normal S to the abnormal R necessitates care in the selection of strains of the organism for the production of suitable bacterial suspensions for the agglutination test. It is also essential to include all antigenic types in the antigen.

Rice has described an indirect complement-fixation test which has been found to be of value as a supplementary serologic method in experimental studies where the agglutination reaction may give indeterminate results.

### *Salmonella anatum*

In 1919 Rettger reported a disease which he observed in ducklings from which he isolated an organism typical of the Salmonella group. The following year Rettger and Scoville described the organism in detail and named it *Bacterium anatis.*

The disease is extremely acute and fatal. Rettger and Scoville describe the symptoms as follows:[1]

> The affected individuals appeared weak and sluggish, and remained close to the heating pipes. They were not easily aroused, and did not go in search of food, as did the others. They ate at times, however, and their crops were distended. One of the marked symptoms was intense thirst. After drinking, some of the ducklings drew themselves to full height, staggered a few seconds, keeled over and after one or two gasps died—hence the name "keel" for the disease. Few of the ducklings died after they were from three to four weeks of age; the greatest mortality occurring within the first week or ten days. Examination of the dead ducklings revealed no lesions of any pathologic condition except, perhaps, paleness of the tissues as a whole and light body weight.

The organism is obtained from ovarian and abdominal cysts of breeding ducks which appear to be carriers of the infection; consequently, it resembles the infection cycle of the disease in chickens caused by *Sal. pullorum. Sal. anatum* has been considered the only organism responsible for the disease described above. However, Price *et al.* have shown that *Sal. anatum* is the most important infectious agent, but a number of other Salmonella have been isolated from cases of the disease. These are *Sal. enteritidis, Sal. bredeny, Sal. panama, Sal. give, Sal. senftenberg, Sal. newport, Sal. oregon, Sal. saintpaul, Sal. manhattan,* and *Sal. manchester.*

In an epidemic among chukar partridges caused by *Sal. anatum* and *Sal. derby,* Francis and associates found that it was due to a gradual buildup of bacteria because the brooder pen floors were not disinfected as frequently as they should have been.

Craige isolated *Sal. anatum* from the feces of a dog showing symptoms of diarrhea and encephalitis.

The prevalence of *Sal. anatum* in many different species of animals has become evident since the antigenic typing of the

[1] L. F. Rettger, and M. M. Scoville, Jour. Inf. Dis. 26:215, 1920.

Salmonella became the customary method of identification. Reference to Table 21.2 emphasizes that the organism has been recovered from many different animal species including the turkey, chicken, pig, cow, and horse. The presence of *Sal. anatum* in dogs is emphasized by the report of Galton, McElrath, Stucker, and Hardy in 1950, in which 297 cultures of this organism were identified out of 937 of all salmonellae. Likewise, the presence of the organism in swine was noted in 547 of 1,476 total fecal isolations of salmonellae by Galton and associates.

*Sal. anatum* is similar to *Sal. pullorum* in morphology, but cultures of the organism on solid media are heavier than *Sal. pullorum.*

The organism produces acid and gas from glucose, fructose, galactose, maltose, dextrin, arabinose, xylose, mannitol, dulcitol, trehalose, and rhamnose; does not ferment lactose, sucrose, inulin, raffinose, salicin, or inositol. It is positive to the Bitter rhamnose test and the Stern glycerol test; ferments *d*-tartrate; produces an alkaline reaction in litmus milk; does not liquefy gelatin; reduces nitrates to nitrites; does not form indol. It produces $H_2S$.

The antigenic structure of *Sal. anatum* is sufficiently different from the other species in the genus to place it in Group $E_1$. See Table 21.4.

Agglutinating antibody is produced in breeding ducks which are infected with the organism; consequently, it is possible to detect such cases by the agglutination reaction.

### *Salmonella gallinarum*

**Synonyms and History.** *Shigella gallinarum.* This organism was first isolated in 1889 by Klein in England from chickens suffering with a disease referred to as fowl typhoid. He named the organism *Bacillus gallinarum.* In 1895 Moore, in the United States, isolated an organism which he called *Bacterium sanguinarum* from cases of "infectious leukemia" in fowls.

The isolation of a similar organism, *Salmonella pullorum,* from chicks in 1900 by Rettger opened the way for extensive investigation of the two organisms, and various conclusions have been reached by different individuals. In Germany it has been concluded that the two organisms are identical or that *Salmonella pullorum* is just a variety of *Salmonella gallinarum.* This opinion has not been accepted by all. The Salmonella subcommittee places the organism in the genus Salmonella because its O antigen is identical with *Salmonella pullorum.*

An organism isolated by Hadley, Elkins, and Caldwell in 1918, and named *Bacterium jeffersonii,* has been found to be antigenically identical with *Salmonella gallinarium;* consequently, it is now considered to be a synonym of the organism under discussion.

**Morphology and Staining.** *Sal. gallinarum* is a short, plump rod, 0.4μ to 0.6μ by 0.8μ to 1.6μ in size. It usually occurs singly, but short chains are sometimes observed in blood smears. It is nonflagellated, nonsporeforming, and noncapsulated.

The organism is stained with the common dyes and is gram-negative. If blood smears are stained with methylene blue or dilute carbol fuchsin, the organism appears distinctly bipolar, not unlike the typical *Pasteurella avicida* of fowl cholera.

**Growth Requirements and Characteristics.** The organism is easily isolated from the blood and liver of typical cases of fowl typhoid. It grows well on meat infusion media adjusted to pH 7.2. It is aerobic, facultatively anaerobic, and grows best at 37°C.

On the agar plate the colony of the organism is small, blue-gray, moist, circular, and entire.

The organism produces a uniform turbidity in broth and the formation of a granular sediment. A thin, filmy pellicle is observed in some strains.

**Resistance.** The organism is easily killed by any of the disinfectants. Its thermal death point is 60°C. in 10 minutes. It is not resistant to desiccation but does live for some time in fecal material from infected chickens.

**Biochemical Properties.** *Sal. gallinarum* produces acid but no gas from glucose, fructose, galactose, mannose, xylose, arabinose, maltose, dextrin, mannitol, dulcitol, and isodulcitol; does not ferment lactose, sucrose, glycerol, salicin, or sorbitol. It reduces nitrates in the presence of Difco peptone; does not liquefy gelatin; does not form indol. The organism does not acidify or coagulate litmus milk. Some strains produce hydrogen sulfide.

**Antigenic Structure and Toxins.** *Sal. gallinarum* possesses the O antigen 1, 9, and 12, which is similar to *Sal. pullorum* and many other species in Group D of the Salmonella antigenic classification. Numerous reports are found which emphasize the close antigenic relationship of *Sal. pullorum* and *Sal. gallinarum.* For the most part, these reports have resulted from studies of the problems related to the testing of flocks of laying hens in order to detect fowls infected with *Sal. pullorum.* The blood from a chicken infected with either organism will cause the agglutination of a suspension of either organism.

*Sal. gallinarum* does not produce a true toxin, although endotoxin has been demonstrated.

**Pathogenicity.** *Sal. gallinarum* is the cause of an acute intestinal and generalized infection of fowls, usually past the first few weeks of life. Artificial infection of young chicks produces a disease typical of the infection caused by *Sal. pullorum.* Leucocytic infiltration of the liver and other parenchymatous tissue is characteristic of fowl typhoid; however, this disease differs from the leucosis which is caused by a filterable virus. Boney, in 1947, reported the isolation of this organism from turkeys.

When fed or injected parenterally, the organism is capable of producing disease in rabbits and all poultry as well as in wild birds and canaries.

**Immunity.** Fowl typhoid bacterins have been used in flocks which are periodically affected with the disease, but are not considered a substantial method of controlling the disease; furthermore, Runnells and Thorp have demonstrated that the sera of such birds give a positive agglutination test with *Sal. pullorum* antigen.

**Diagnosis.** Fowl typhoid is diagnosed by the isolation and identification of *Sal. gallinarum.* Since *Sal. pullorum, Sal. typhimurium, Past. avicida,* and other species of closely related organisms also may produce a disease in the fowls and birds similar to fowl typhoid, suitable culture media must be chosen for differentiation. Hinshaw has found that a gelatin medium containing 0.15 per cent cysteine hydrochloride is valuable for identification. *Sal. gallinarum* produces a characteristic yellowish-white or grayish turbidity in this medium when incubated at 37°C. for 72 hours, whereas *Sal. pullorum* does not produce turbidity.

The cross reaction of this organism with *Sal. pullorum* limits the value of the agglutination test as a method of diagnosing fowl typhoid. However, Moore has shown that polyvalent *Sal. gallinarum* antigen is more sensitive than standard *Sal. pullorum* antigen.

### *Salmonella dublin*

This serotype has been isolated from cases of enteritis of cattle in many areas of the world. In the United States it is confined to the western states. Rokey and Erling have found that the organism was present in other species of animals including the horse, dog, chicken, dove, rabbit, and mouse. In one dairy herd in Arizona 85 per cent calf mortality due to the organism was observed.

### *Salmonella derby*

The increasing prevalence of this organism in human infections is indicated by the report of Sanders and associates in their study of hospital infections. *Sal. derby* is found most often in poultry and in eggs, but has been isolated from ducks, game birds, cattle, and swine.

## REFERENCES

BAYER, C. I., *et al.* Salmonella Organisms Isolated From Turkey Feed. Avian Dis. 2:396, 1958.

BERGEY, D. H., *et al.* Manual of Determinative Bacteriology. 7th Ed. Williams & Wilkins Co., Baltimore, 1957.

BOHNHOFF, M., and MILLER, C. P. Enhanced Susceptibility to Salmonella Infection in Streptomycin-Treated Mice. Jour. Inf. Dis. 111:117–27, 1962.

BONEY, W. A. Amer. Jour. Vet. Res. 8:133, 1947.

BOSWORTH, T. J., and GLOVER, R. E. Contagious Abortion in Ewes. Vet. Jour. 81:319–34, 1925.

BROWN, R. G., *et al.* Jour. Amer. Vet. Med. Assn. 114:29, 1949.

BRUNER, D. W., and EDWARDS, P. R. Biochemical and Serological Studies of Microorganisms of the *Salmonella cholerae-suis* Group. Ky. Agr. Exp. Sta. Bull. 404, Lexington, 1940.

———, and MORAN, A. B. Cornell Vet. 39:53, 1949.

BRYANS, J. T., *et al.* Equine Salmonellosis. Cornell Vet. 51:468–77, 1961.

COBURN, D. R., *et al.* Amer. Jour. Vet. Res. 3:96–99, 1942.

CRAIGE, J. E. Jour. Amer. Vet. Med. Assn. 105:33, 1944.

DAY, W. H., *et al.* Salmonellosis in the Dog. Amer. Jour. Vet. Res. 24:156–58, 1963.

DIMOCK, W. W., and GOOD, E. S. Jour. Amer. Vet. Med. Assn. 71:25–31, 1927.

DOUGHERTY, E. The Pathology of Paratyphoid Infection in the White Pekin Duck, Particularly the Lesions in the Central Nervous System. Avian Dis. 5:415–20, 1961.

EDWARDS, P. R. Standard Strains of Salmonella. Ky. Agr. Exp. Sta. Circ. 50, 1939.

———. Jour. Amer. Vet. Med. Assn. 107:545, 1945.

———, and BRUNER, D. W. The Significance of Biological Types of *Salmonella typhimurium*. Ky. Agr. Exp. Sta. Bull. 400, Lexington, 1940.

———, and ———. Cornell Vet. 36:318, 1946.

———, and EWING, W. H. Identification of Enterobacteriaceae. Burgess Publ. Co., Minneapolis, 1962.

———, and HULL, F. E. Bacillary White Diarrhea and Related Diseases of Chickens. Ky. Agr. Exp. Sta. Res. Bull. 296, 1929.

———, *et al.* The Genus Salmonella: Its Occurrence and Distribution in the United States. Ky. Agr. Exp. Sta. Bull. 525, Univ. of Ky., Lexington, 1948.

———, *et al.* Further Studies on the Occurrence and Distribution of Salmonella Types in the United States. Jour. Inf. Dis. 83:220, 1948.

EWING, W. H. Enterobacteriaceae. Biochemical Methods for Group Differentiation. Pub. Health Serv. Publ. 734, U.S. Govt. Print. Off., Washington, D.C., 1960.

FRANCIS, D. W., *et al.* A Study of a Salmonella Infection in a Flock of Chukar Partridges. Avian Dis. 6:501–6, 1963.

GALTON, M. M. Laboratory Procedures for the Isolation of Salmonella From Human and Animal Food Products. Proc. 65th Ann. Meet. U.S. Livestock Sanit. Assn., p. 434, 1961.

———, *et al.* Proc. 87th Ann. Conv. Amer. Vet. Med. Assn., 1950.

———, *et al.* Jour. Inf. Dis. 95:232, 1954.

———, *et al.* Jour. Inf. Dis. 95:236, 1954.

GAUGER, H. C., *et al.* Paratyphoid of Pigeons. No. Carolina State Agr. Exp. Sta. Tech. Bull. 62, Raleigh, 1940.

GERSHMAN, M., *et al.* The Laboratory Application of Anhydrous *Salmonella pullorum* Antigen. Avian Dis. 6:107–11, 1962.

GOOD, E. S., and SMITH, W. V. Further Investigations of the Etiology and Control of Infectious Abortion in Mares. Ky. Agr. Exp. Sta. Bull. 204, 1916.

GREENBERG, B. Experimental Transmission of *Salmonella typhimurium* by Houseflies to Man. Amer. Jour. Hyg. 80:149–56, 1964.

———, and BORNSTEIN, A. A. Fly Dispersion From a Rural Mexican Slaughterhouse. Amer. Jour. Trop. Med. Hyg. 13:881–86, 1964.

———, and MIGGIANO, V. Host-Contaminant Biology of Muscoid Flies. Jour. Inf. Dis. 112:37–46, 1963.

———, *et al.* Salmonellae From Flies in a Mexican Slaughterhouse. Amer. Jour. Hyg. 77:177–83, 1963.

GWATKIN, R. Efficiency of Homologous and Heterologous Antigens in Detecting Reacting Birds in a Variant-Infected Flock. Canad. Jour. Comp. Med. 9:183, 1945.

———. Serological Reactions of Regular and Variant Types of *Salmonella pullorum*. Canad. Jour. Comp. Med. 10:254, 1946.

———. Antigenic Differences in Strains of *Salmonella pullorum*. Amer. Jour. Vet. Res. 8:204, 1947.

GWATKIN, R. Response to Oral Infection With *Salmonella pullorum* in Comparable Groups of Turkeys and Chickens. Canad. Jour. Comp. Med. 12:47, 1948.

———. Infection of Adult Turkeys by Mouth and by Contact With Infected Hens. Canad. Jour. Comp. Med. 13:103, 1949.

———, and BOND, E. W. Examination of Colonies From Regular and Variant Form Subcultures of *Salmonella pullorum*. Canad. Jour. Comp. Med. 11:289, 1947.

HIGGENS, W. A., *et al.* Poult. Sci. 23:340–41, 1944.

HINSHAW, W. R. Cysteine and Related Compounds for Differentiating Members of the Genus Salmonella. Hilgardia 13:583–621, 1941.

———. Salmonellosis of Turkeys. Vet. Med. 42:179, 1947.

———, and MCNEIL, E. The Use of the Agglutination Test in Detecting *Salmonella typhimurium* Carriers in Turkey Flocks. Proc. 47th Ann. Meet. U.S. Livestock Sanit. Assn., p. 106, 1943.

———, and ———. Avian Salmonellosis. Its Economic and Public Health Significance. Off. Rept. 8th World's Poultry Cong., 1948.

———, *et al.* Jour. Inf. Dis. 72:197–201, 1943.

JEFFRIES, C. D., and HOLTMAN, D. F. Growth Response of *Sal. pullorum* in the Chicken Embryo. Amer. Jour. Vet. Res. 19:736, 1957.

LEVINE, M. G., and PLATTNER, E. B. Amer. Jour. Clin. Path. 14:342–43, 1944.

LUKAS, G. N., and BRADFORD, D. R. Jour. Amer. Vet. Med. Assn. 125:215, 1954.

MCCOY, J. H. The Isolation of Salmonellae. Jour. Appl. Bact. 25:213–24, 1962.

MALLMANN, W. L. *Bacterium pullorum* Studies. Mich. Agr. Exp. Sta. Tech. Bull. 68, 1925.

MILLER, C. P., and BOHNHOFF, M. A Study of Experimental Salmonella Infection in the Mouse. Jour. Inf. Dis. 111:107–16, 1962.

MIRAGLIA, G. J., and BERRY, L. J. Enhancement of Salmonellosis and Emergence of Secondary Infection in Mice Exposed to Cold. Jour. Bact. 84:1173–80, 1962.

MOORE, E. N. Cornell Vet. 37:21, 1947.

MORAN, A. Occurrence and Distribution of Salmonella in Animals in the United States. Proc. 65th Ann. Meet. U.S. Livestock Sanit. Assn., p. 441, 1961.

MURRAY, CHARLES, *et al.* Studies in Infectious Enteritis of Swine. Jour. Amer. Vet. Med. Assn. 72; first paper, pp. 34–90, 1927; second paper, pp. 1003–22, 1928.

POMEROY, B. S., and GRADY, M. K. Salmonella Organisms Isolated From Feed Ingredients. Proc. 65th Ann. Meet. U.S. Livestock Sanit. Assn., p. 449, 1961.

PRICE, J. I., *et al.* Salmonella Infections in White Pekin Duck. Avian Dis. 6:145–47, 1962.

RETTGER, L. F., and SCOVILLE, M. M. *Bacterium anatum* (n. sp.). Jour. Inf. Dis. 26:215–29, 1920.

RODABAUGH, D. E., *et al.* The Effect of *Salmonella choleraesuis* Infection on Immunity to Hog Cholera. Jour. Amer. Vet. Med. Assn. 145:252–57, 1964.

ROKEY, N. W., and ERLING, H. G. *Salmonella dublin* Infection in Calves. Jour. Amer. Vet. Med. Assn. 135:117, 1959.

———, and ———. Natural Occurrences of *Salmonella dublin* in Arizona. Jour. Amer. Vet. Med. Assn. 1:36 381, 1960.

RUDE, T. A. *Salmonella typhimurium* Infections in Cattle. Jour. Amer. Vet. Med. Assn. 142:751–53, 1963.

SANDERS, E., *et al.* An Outbreak of Hospital-Associated Infections Due to *Salmonella derby*. Jour. Amer. Med. Assn. 186:984–86, 1963.

SAPHRA, I., and WASSERMANN, M. *Salmonella cholerae suis*. A Clinical and Epidemiological Evaluation of 329 Infections Identified Between 1940 and 1954 in the New York Salmonella Center. Amer. Jour. Med. Sci. 228:525–33, 1954.

SCHEBITZ, VON H., and HANSEN, H. J. Uber eine durch *Salmonella abortus equi* verursachte epididymitis infectiosa beim Esebhengst. Deut. tierärztl. Woch. 66:212, 1959.

SCHOFIELD, F. W. Canad. Jour. Comp. Med. 10:271, 1946.

SCOTT, W. M., and MINETT, F. C. Jour. Hyg., Cambridge, 45:159, 1947.

SHANDS, J. W. Growth Rate and Toxicity of *Salmonella typhimurium*. Jour. Bact. 89:799–802, 1965.

SMYSER, C. F., *et al.* Detection of *Salmonella typhimurium* From Artificially Contaminated Poultry Feed and Animal By-Products. Avian Dis. 7:423–34, 1963.

STOKES, J. L., and BAYNE, H. G. Growth Rates of Salmonella Colonies. Jour. Bact. 74:200, 1957.

———, and ———. Growth-Factor-Dependent Strains of Salmonellae. Jour. Bact. 76:417, 1958.

STONE, E. Personal communication.

STORY, P., and HANBURY, W. J. Morphological Changes in *Salmonella typhimurium* Infections. Jour. Path. Bact. 73:443, 1957.

TRABULSI, L. R., and EDWARDS, P. R. The Differentiation of *Salmonella pullorum* and *Salmonella gallinarum* by Biochemical Methods. Cornell Vet. 52:563–69, 1962.

TULLY, J. G., *et al.* Studies on Infection and Immunity in Experimental Typhoid Fever. IV. Role of H Antigen in Protection. Jour. Inf. Dis. 112:118–24, 1963. V. Respiratory Challenge of Chimpanzees With *Salmonella typhosa*. Jour. Inf. Dis. 113:131–38, 1964.

VAN ROEKEL, H. A Study of Variation of *Salmonella pullorum*. Mass. Agr. Exp. Sta. Bull. 319, 1935.

WHITE, P. B. The Salmonella Group. A System of Bacteriology. Vol. IV, pp. 86–158. Med. Res. Council. His Majesty's Stationery Office, London, 1929.

WILLIAMS, J. E. Amer. Jour. Vet. Res. 14:465, 1953.

YAMAMOTO, R., *et al.* A Study of *Salmonella typhimurium* Infection in Market-Age Turkeys. Amer. Jour. Vet. Res. 22:382, 1961.

# 22

# The Genus Shigella

THE SHIGELLA GROUP OF BACTERIA SHOW characteristics similar to the Escherichia group including methyl red positive, but are Voges-Proskauer, citrate, $H_2S$, urease, KCN, and phenylalanine negative. They also may be differentiated by many other tests (see Table 20.1). They are nonmotile and are not reactive in a number of carbohydrate media. They are associated with enteric disease in man and animals, and for that reason are commonly called the "dysentery group."

They are composed of a number of varieties which have many characteristics in common, especially pathogenicity; yet they vary in carbohydrate fermentation much more than some of the other types of bacteria which are placed in separate species on that basis. The first and most typical organism of the group was isolated by Shiga in Japan in 1898. A second type was isolated by Flexner in the Philippines in 1900, although at that time he considered it to be the same organism discovered by Shiga. Kruse demonstrated that the two types were serologically distinct. In 1902 Martini and Lentz showed that the Shiga and Flexner strains were easily distinguishable by fermentation reactions.

In 1904 Duval described a lactose-fermenting organism in cases of typical dysentery. This type was included with the dysentery bacilli and was commonly designated the Sonne type. A fourth organism, first described by Schmitz in 1917 as the cause of an epidemic dysentery in a Rumanian war prison camp, was included in the dysentery group. This organism was known as the Schmitz dysentery bacillus.

Numerous contributions were made to the literature of this group after World War I when dysentery was so prevalent. The history of the group is completely discussed by Bensted (1956) to which the student is referred. In this publication Bensted places the Shigella in four subgroups.

Subgroup A. *Shigella dysenteriae* (all nonlactose, mannite fermenters).

Subgroup B. *Shigella flexneri* (nonlactose, nonmannite fermenters, but with different antigenic structure than A).

Subgroup C. *Shigella boydii* (nonlactose, mannite fermenters possessing distinct type antigen, but no characteristic group complex).

Subgroup D. *Shigella sonnei* (slow lactose and mannite fermenters).

In addition to the four species given above, one species, *Shigella equirulis,* is associated with purulent nephritis, septicemia, and joint infection in foals. Two species, *Shigella pfaffi* and *Shigella rettgeri,* have been isolated from chickens which had shown symptoms of severe intestinal infection. The classification of the latter organism as a Shigella may be doubtful because its description fits the genus Proteus.

**Distribution and Transmission.** The dysentery organisms are widely distributed throughout the world and are frequently associated with epidemic disease where a large number of persons congregate together and live under insanitary conditions.

The organism is commonly transmitted

by water and food which have been contaminated by human excreta. Hand contamination of food and cooking utensils is not as common as in typhoid fever. Flies are considered to be a more significant transmitting factor in dysentery than in typhoid. The immune carrier is known to exist in dysentery but is not as great a factor as in typhoid.

**Morphology and Staining.** *Shig. dysenteriae* is a short, plump rod, 0.4$\mu$ to 0.6$\mu$ by 1.0$\mu$ to 3.0$\mu$. It occurs singly. It is nonmotile.

The organism is gram-negative. All other species are similar.

**Growth Requirements and Characteristics.** This group of organisms is typical of the other gram-negative rods of the genus Salmonella. Smooth S to rough R colony dissociation is frequently observed among the Shigella organisms.

**Biochemical Properties.** The strains or types of dysentery bacilli differ in respect to many of the biochemical reactions.

TABLE 22.1

BIOCHEMICAL REACTIONS OF SHIGELLA

| | *Shig. dysenteriae* | *Shig. flexneri* | *Shig. boydii* | *Shig. sonnei* |
|---|---|---|---|---|
| Mannitol | − | + | + | + |
| Dulcitol | − | − | v | − |
| Arabinose | + | + | + | + |
| Sorbitol | v | + | + | − |
| Xylose | − | − | + | − |
| Rhamnose | − | − | − | + |
| Raffinose | − | − | − | v |
| Glycerol | + | − | + | v |
| Indol | v | + | v | − |
| Ornithine decarboxylase | − | − | − | + |

Source: Edwards, P. R., and Ewing, W. H. Identification of Enterobacteriaceae, p. 31. Burgess Publ. Co., Minneapolis, 1962.

The biochemical reactions of the four species of dysentery bacteria are given in Table 22.1.

**Antigenic Structure and Toxins.** The different strains of dysentery bacilli appear to be antigenically homogenous for each type with the exception of the Flexner type which is composed of a number of heterogenous strains. The group lacks the flagellar specific antigen which is so significant in the Salmonella group.

The four subgroups are composed of numerous antigenic types. Newly isolated species are typed much like the Salmonellae and placed in their appropriate antigenic group.

The Shiga type is characterized by the soluble exotoxin which it produces. This toxin is fatal to the rabbit, producing diarrhea and paralysis of the limbs; but is less active in guinea pigs, producing diarrhea with no paralysis. The other types do not produce true toxin although the endotoxins of all are fatal to rabbits when given in large doses intravenously.

Formal and associates, working with *Shig. flexneri,* found that when the intestinal tract of the guinea pig is immobilized with opiates, a more severe infection results. They believe this emphasizes the fact that intestinal mobility is a defense mechanism of the intestine against infection and, also, that opium addiction may predispose to intestinal infection.

**Pathogenicity.** The dysentery bacilli are pathogenic to man and resemble the typhoid bacillus in this respect. They produce a type of intestinal infection in man which is distinguished from typhoid fever by a shorter incubation period (two to three days), by a more persistent diarrhea, by a lower temperature, and by the localization of the infection in the colon instead of in the small intestine. The condition is prone to become chronic, producing a persistent diarrhea over a period of several weeks. The Shiga variety produces the most severe type of case and is more fatal than the others.

When cultures of dysentery bacilli are injected intravenously or intraperitoneally into rabbits and guinea pigs, they produce lesions in the intestines which are similar to those produced by the natural disease in man. The same type of infection is not produced by feeding virulent cultures or toxins. These results suggest that the seat of the infection is in the submucous cells due to the elimination of the organism or its toxins.

**Immunity.** Vaccines have been proved to be of value in prophylactic procedures; however, they must be of a polyvalent nature to be effective. Antiserum has been used in the treatment of cases of the disease, and in the case of Shiga antiserum, the results have been satisfactory.

**Diagnosis.** The blood serum of a dysentery patient agglutinates dysentery bacilli. The various types must be identified by culture reactions.

### *Shigella equirulis*

**Synonyms and History.** This organism was first observed in 1908 by Theiler in South Africa in cases of purulent nephritis of horses. In a report covering the years 1908–9, Meyer in South Africa called the organisms *Bacillus nephritidis equi.* Van Straaten referred to the organism as *Bacillus equuli* in 1916–17. Magnusson called the organism *Bacterium viscosum equi* in 1917. In the United States it was first isolated and described by Snyder in 1925. She used the name *Eberthella viscosa.*

The 1957 edition of Bergey's Manual classifies this organism as *Actinobacillus equuli.*

Much of the information concerning this organism and the disease it produces has been contributed by Dimock and Edwards of Kentucky. In 1931 Edwards published a detailed study of the organism in which he advanced reasons for using the name *Shigella equirulis.*

**Distribution and Transmission.** The reports of the organism from various parts of the world indicate that it is widely distributed. In the United States it has been reported from Kentucky, New York, and Indiana. Britton has observed this organism as the cause of the death of foals in California.

The methods by which foals are infected with the organism are not known. Dimock, Edwards, and Bullard reported the average age at death as 2.9 days; the appearance of the disease so soon after birth indicates that infection occurs *in utero.* The organism has been isolated from verminous aneurysms in old horses, and it has been claimed that the organism is carried by the larvae of intestinal nematode parasites.

**Morphology and Staining.** *Shig. equirulis* is a small, nonmotile rod, 0.3$\mu$ to 0.4$\mu$ by 0.4$\mu$ to 0.8$\mu$ in size. It is notably pleomorphic, and single cells, streptococcus-like chains, and long filaments occur in the same smear. The organism is considered noncapsuleproducing, although some investigators report the presence of capsular material.

Young cultures of the organism are stained easily by the usual stains and are gram-negative.

**Growth Requirements and Characteristics.** The organism is an aerobe and a facultative anaerobe, and grows readily in media containing fresh meat infusion.

When the organism is isolated from infected tissue and grown on the surface of agar media, it forms a characteristically rough, irregular mucoid colony. Well-isolated colonies frequently attain 3 to 5 mm. in size. The colonies are raised, are sometimes hemispherical, and are opaque. The surface is definitely lobulated, which makes the colony appear radially striated in transmitted light. As the culture ages, a clear, smooth border develops from the edge of the colony.

Many of the cultures dissociate from the normal rough type to a smooth nonmucoid colony. Edwards found that incubation above 37°C. combined with an acid reaction in the medium tends to accelerate the change from rough to smooth. Some cultures show dwarf colonies.

In broth the growth of the rough form of the organism is first apparent as a collection of small masses of bacteria along the side of the tube and floating in the medium near the surface. A thin pellicle then develops, and the sides of the tube become covered with bacteria. A thick viscid sediment forms as the culture ages, and the medium becomes decidedly turbid. The smooth form of the organism produces a uniform turbidity in broth and does not form a pellicle or much sediment.

**Resistance.** The organism is readily destroyed by chemical disinfectants and by 60°C. in 15 minutes. It does not remain viable on laboratory media unless it is subcultured every week.

**Biochemical Properties.** *Shig. equirulis* produces acid from glucose, fructose, xylose, lactose, galactose, maltose, sucrose, mannitol, dextrin, raffinose, and glycerol; does not ferment rhamnose, dulcitol, isodulcitol, sorbitol, or inositol; varies in fermenting salicin, inulin, starch, adonitol, and arabinose. It does not produce indol; reduces nitrates to nitrites; is negative to the Voges-Proskauer test; does not liquefy gelatin; acidifies, and some strains coagulate litmus milk; is negative to the methyl red test.

**Antigenic Structure and Toxins.** The organism is composed of a number of heterogenous strains which give positive agglutination and precipitation reactions only with their homologous antisera.

Toxin production has not been reported for the organism.

**Pathogenicity.** *Shig. equirulis* has been isolated from horses only. In foals it produces arthritis which usually involves the back, hip, and knee joints; glomerulonephritis followed by suppuration and necrosis; and septicemia. The condition is frequently called pyosepticemia and "joint ill." The organism produces the same typical lesions when it is injected subcutaneously into a young foal. Older colts and adult horses are more resistant although abscesses develop at the point of inoculation.

In an examination of 2,025 specimens, of which 1,150 were aborted fetuses and 875 were dead foals, Dimock, Edwards, and Bruner (1947) reported that *Shig. equirulis* was responsible for the death of a larger number of foals than any other microorganism.

It is generally conceded that the organism is not pathogenic for rabbits, guinea pigs, and rats, although enormous doses do produce death within 24 hours.

**Immunity.** The sudden and acute nature of the disease in the newborn foal eliminates the opportunity for any very definite immunizing treatment. The dam's blood has been used, but the value of it in accurately diagnosed cases of the disease is doubtful.

**Diagnosis.** *Shig. equirulis* infection in foals is diagnosed by the isolation and identification of the organism.

### *Shigella pfaffii*

In 1905 Franz Pfaff reported the isolation of an organism from canary birds which had died of an acute infectious disease characterized by a severe enteritis and necrotic foci in the liver and spleen. In 1918 in the course of the study of the colon-typhoid organisms in birds, Hadley, Elkins, and Caldwell reported the characteristics of the Pfaff culture which they obtained from the Kral collection. These investigators assigned the name *Bacterium pfaffi* to the organism.

*Shigella pfaffii,* as it is now known, is a short, gram-negative, nonmotile rod averaging 1.4$\mu$ in length. It is stained readily by ordinary dyes, but peripheral or bipolar staining characteristics are not prominent. There are no colony characteristics formed by the organism by which it is distinguished from *Salmonella gallinarum.* The organism does not alter litmus milk, produce indol, form $H_2S$, or reduce nitrates. It produces acid but no gas from dextrose, levulose, xylose, arabinose, maltose, dextrin, mannite, and salicin; does not ferment sucrose, raffinose, lactose, inulin, adonitol, or dulcitol. Its distribution and pathogenicity for birds other than the canary are not known. It does not produce infection in the rabbit.

No antigenic relationship exists with any known member of the paratyphoid-enteritidis group.

### *Shigella rettgeri (Proteus rettgeri)*

This organism was first isolated in Connecticut by Rettger in 1909 from chickens which were infected with a disease resembling fowl cholera. This original culture was studied by Hadley, Elkins, and Caldwell in 1918 and designated *Bacterium rettgeri*. *Shigella rettgeri* is a short, gram-negative, nonmotile rod, 0.5μ to 0.8μ in length. It is stained readily with ordinary dyes, but the bipolar characteristics are not apparent. The growth of the organism on the surfaces of solid media is similar to other members of the group. It grows luxuriantly on potato. It changes litmus milk to an alkaline reaction in eight days but does not alter its consistency. The organism produces acid but not gas from dextrose, levulose, galactose, mannose, xylose, adonitol, mannite, and salicin; does not ferment arabinose, raffinose, sucrose, lactose, maltose, dextrin, inulin, dulcitol, and erythritol. It does not form indol or $H_2S$, nor reduce nitrates. It is urease-positive.

The organism does not exhibit an antigenic relationship with any other member of the paratyphoid-enteritidis group. Its distribution and pathogenicity for other fowls are not known.

## REFERENCES


Bensted, H. J. Dysentery Bacilla—Shigella. A Brief Historical Review. Canad. Jour. Microbiol. 2:163–74, 1956.

Britton, J. W. Cornell Vet. 35:375, 1945.

Cheever, F. S. The Shigella and Bacillary Dysentery. Chap. 17. *In* Dubos, Bacterial and Mycotic Diseases of Man. 3rd Ed. J. B. Lippincott Co., Philadelphia, 1958.

Dimock, W. W., *et al.* *Bacterium viscosum equi.* A Factor in Joint-ill and Septicemia in Young Foals. Jour. Amer. Vet. Med. Assn. 73:163, 1928.

———, *et al.* Cornell Vet. 37:89, 1947.

Edwards, P. R. Studies on *Shigella equirulis* (*Bact. viscosum equi*). Ky. Agr. Exp. Sta. Bull. 320, 1931.

———, and Ewing, W. H. Identification of Enterobacteriaceae. Burgess Publ. Co., Minneapolis, 1962.

Formal, S. B., *et al.* Experimental Shigella Infections. VI. Role of the Small Intestine in an Experimental Infection in Guinea Pigs. Jour. Bact. 85:119–25, 1963.

Gardner, A. D., and O'Brien, R. A. The Dysentery Group of Bacilli. A System of Bacteriology. 4:161–253. Med. Res. Council. His Majesty's Stationery Office, London, 1929.

Hadley, P., *et al.* The Colon-Typhoid Intermediates as Causative Agents of Disease in Birds. R.I. Agr. Exp. Sta. Bull. 174, May, 1918.

Pfaff, F. Eine infektiöse Erkrankung der Kanarienvögel. Zentralbl. f. Bakt. Abt. I. Orig. 38:281, 1905.

Smith, D. T., and Conant, N. F. Zinsser Bacteriology. 12th Ed. Appleton-Century-Crofts, New York, 1960.

# 23

# The Genera Brucella and Bordetella

THE MICROORGANISMS OF THE GENUS Brucella are minute, nonmotile, nonspore-forming, coccoid rods which are gram-negative. On initial culture, one of the group, *Brucella abortus,* requires an atmosphere containing an increased amount of carbon dioxide, but when adjusted to aerobic conditions it grows readily. The organisms produce an increased alkalinity in milk, but are almost inactive in the fermentation of carbohydrates, except for limited utilization of some of the simple sugars such as glucose. There were four species in the genus, *Brucella melitensis, Brucella abortus, Brucella suis,* and *Brucella bronchiseptica.*

The position of *Brucella melitensis, Brucella abortus,* and *Brucella suis* in the genus Brucella has never been questioned to any extent, although at one time they were classified in the genus Alcaligenes. *Brucella bronchiseptica* is the only motile species and its classification in the genus has been seriously questioned by many. The only basis for placing this organism along with the other three species is the increased alkalinity it produces in protein media, especially milk. It was on this basis that the Brucella were once classified as Alcaligenes. In 1936 Topley and Wilson called the canine distemper organism *Brucella bronchiseptica.* This classification was followed in the 1939 and 1948 editions of Bergey's Manual. In the 1957 edition the name was changed to *Bordetella bronchiseptica.*

## THE GENUS BRUCELLA

Inasmuch as the three closely related species of Brucella are usually discussed as a group and the disease which they produce is known as brucellosis, they will be discussed here as a group.

### *Brucella melitensis*
### *Brucella abortus*
### *Brucella suis*

**Synonyms and History.** In 1887 Bruce described the first member of the genus Brucella from cases of Malta fever on the Island of Malta. He later named it *Micrococcus melitensis.* In 1905 it was shown that goats were usually infected and that people contracted the disease mainly from infective goat milk. In 1897 Bang, in Denmark, discovered *Br. abortus* in cases of abortion in cows and showed that it was the cause of the disease now known as Bang's disease, or brucellosis, an infectious abortion of cattle. In 1914 Traum found *Br. suis* in cases of abortion in swine. It was not until the work of Evans in 1918 that the close relationship of *Br. melitensis* and *Br. abortus* was established. She found them to be closely related morphologically, physiologically, and serologically, but showed by agglutinin absorption tests that they could be distinguished.

It has been proved that even though agglutination tests and agglutinin absorption tests are very useful, differentiation by this means alone often is impossible. For example, it is difficult to classify rough types by this means because they elicit a different type of agglutinin than when they were smooth. Smooth strains will not absorb the agglutinin produced by the rough type and rough strains will not absorb the agglutinin produced by the smooth. Absorption furnishes valuable additional information where other tests prove inconclusive.

Meyer, in 1920, suggested the name Brucella for the genus. Evans concluded that the organisms were so much alike that they might produce similar disease conditions in different species of animals. In general, this has been proved to be true. The first recognized case of undulant fever caused by *Br. abortus* in man is credited to Keefer in 1924. These findings stimulated research and resulted in the discovery of many cases, not only in this country, but in many parts of the world. It was found that all three species affect man. In this country the early cases of undulant fever were found in the east and southwest. Woodward recognized the first case in Iowa; this led to the extensive and meritorious work of Hardy and his associates. It has been generally concluded that *Br. melitensis* is most pathogenic for man, *Br. abortus* the least so, and *Br. suis* intermediate. In their study of cases of undulant fever in Iowa, Borts and Jordan found that *Br. suis* produced the most severe type of the disease, and that *Br. melitensis* was intermediate. Each species has its natural host.

The goat is the natural or true host for *Br. melitensis,* cattle for *Br. abortus,* and swine for *Br. suis.* Each species spreads readily among members of its natural host, tending to persist indefinitely in large groups. Other species of animals, including man, are accidentally infected and are considered foreign hosts; thus, cattle may be infected with *Br. suis* but are quite resistant. Epidemics of milk-borne brucellosis due to *Br. suis* have been reported. In a study of the pathogenicity of *Br. suis* for cattle, Washko, Hutchings, and Donham found that the organism became established in the bovine udder following inoculation into the open teat orifice. *Br. abortus* is of no importance as a disease-producing agent in swine. Subcutaneous injection of *Br. abortus* into hogs produces a low agglutination titer for Brucella in such animals and it is possible that natural exposure occasionally might result in a like reaction, but no significant disease is produced, and evidence that hogs act as spreaders of *Br. abortus* has not been obtained. Artificial exposure of hogs to *Br. melitensis* results in a disease much like that caused by *Br. suis.* An epidemiological study of *Br. melitensis* infection in man has led to the discovery of herds of Iowa hogs naturally infected with *Br. melitensis.* This study also indicates that infection with *Br. melitensis* may persist for long periods of time in herds of hogs and that the organism spreads from hog to hog. Damon and Scruggs have reported the isolation of this organism from hogs in Indiana. The isolation of *Br. melitensis* from human patients whose only known source of infection has been cow's milk has indicated that the cow may harbor that species of organism. As support of this probability, Damon and Fagan (1947) reported the isolation of *Br. melitensis* from a guinea pig which had been injected with milk from cows that had aborted.

**Distribution and Transmission.** Brucella infections are worldwide. Infection by *Br. melitensis* is largely confined to those regions where goats are raised, especially Europe and North Africa. *Br. suis* is confined to hog-raising regions. Cattle are raised in most parts of the world, and the disease is nearly universal. In the United States, *Br. melitensis* is confined largely to the southwest, and perhaps to the hog-growing areas; *Br. suis* is especially prevalent where there are large hog populations, and *Br. abortus* is found among cattle everywhere. The incidence of infection, especially in cattle, is proportional to the amount of traffic; in certain parts of the southern states and range country, there has been little traffic in cattle, and the incidence of infection is low. This is also true of hogs. It is interesting to note that there are no reports of infection in sheep in this country although it is common in Europe. This indicates that sheep are resistant to American strains of *Br. abortus* and *Br. suis* and possibly more susceptible to *Br. melitensis.*

Wild ruminant animals may become infected with any of the three species of Brucella and constitute a hazard to domesticated animals of the area. Carnivorous animals, also, may become carriers of the organism. In some, infection is produced, while in others the organism may be deposited in fecal matter, thereby contaminating feed materials.

Brucellosis is most commonly contracted through ingestion of infective material. The organisms can pass through any mucous membrane. A few drops of a suspension of *Br. abortus* placed in the conjunctival sac of a cow quickly results in infection. The organisms are known to pass through the broken skin, and it is also thought that they can pass the unbroken skin. Tovar has shown that ticks, bed bugs, and fleas can be infected with all three species of Brucella. Only ticks are able to infect by biting, and they are able to transmit the bacteria to the eggs and larvae. The Brucella are obligate parasites but can live for a considerable time outside the animal body. For this reason infected animals are the main source of danger in transmission. Food and water contaminated by diseased animals are always dangerous. It is apparent that direct or indirect association of clean animals with infected animals, or the eating of infective materials, will lead to infection. For man, the handling of diseased animals and their products, eating of infective meat, and drinking of infective milk are especially dangerous. Laboratory workers who handle Brucella organisms often become infected.

**Morphology and Staining.** *Br. abortus, Br. suis,* and *Br. melitensis* are almost identical in size and shape. As has been mentioned, *Br. melitensis* was considered to be a micrococcus for many years. All species are distinctly coccoid in shape (Fig. 23.1). They are best described as coccobacillary organisms about $0.5\mu$ in diameter by $0.5\mu$ to $2\mu$ in length. They are nonmotile and do not form endospores.

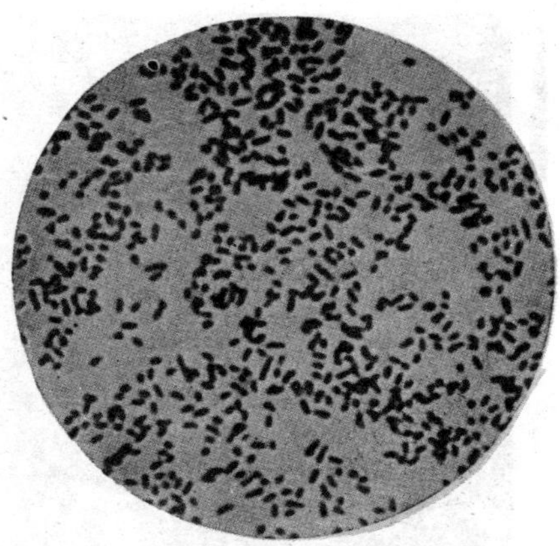

FIG. 23.1—**Brucella abortus,** ×2,000. (From Nowak: Documenta Microbiologica, courtesy Gustav Fischer.)

The cell wall of the Brucellae, as is also true of all gram-negative bacteria, is more complex than it was thought to be before the advent of the electron microscope. It is now known to be composed of three layers which are quite rigid, and when disrupted appear as thin collapsed membranes (Fig. 23.2). The importance of the cell wall in the pathogenic process, and as antigenic material will be discussed later. Although thin capsules have been demonstrated by a special staining technique, these bacteria are not considered capsulated as is *Bacillus anthracis*.

Brucella are readily stained, are not acid-fast, and are gram-negative.

**Growth Requirements and Characteristics.** Brucella grow on most ordinary laboratory media but thrive especially well if the pH is 6.6 to 6.8; however, when very few are transplanted, initial growth is delayed. They grow best in the presence of many of their kind. For this reason, in primary isolation many of the usual contaminating organisms outgrow them; hence, if many contaminators are present, it is best to attempt isolation by guinea pig inoculation. This is also true when only a few Brucella are present in relatively large amounts of material such as milk. Where contamination with other organisms is scant or absent, inoculations are made on solid or in liquid medium. Serum dextrose

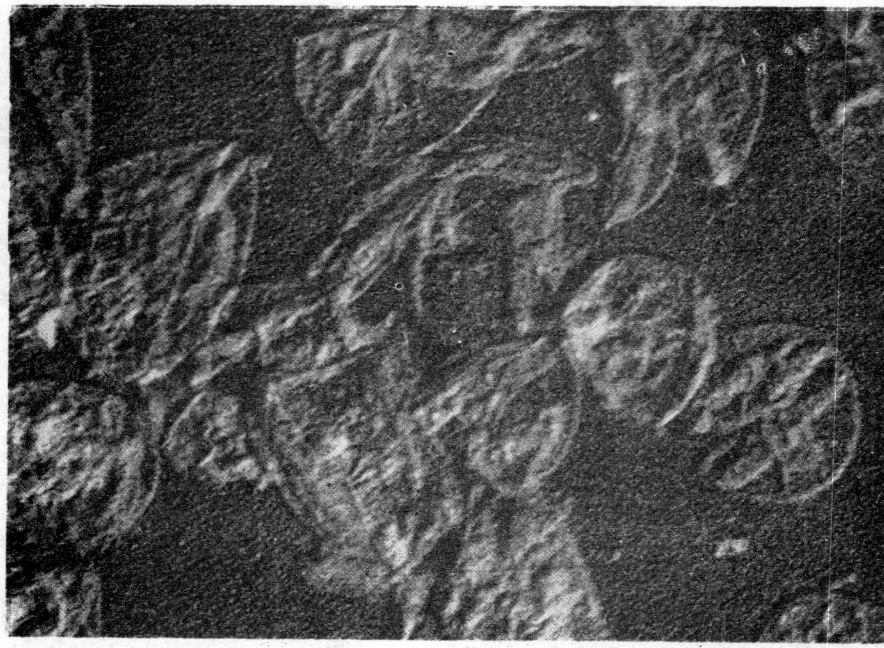

FIG. 23.2—Electron photomicrograph showing **Brucella abortus** cell walls, ×70,000. (Courtesy J. W. Foster and E. Ribi.)

agar, serum potato infusion agar, trypticase soy agar, tryptose thiamine agar, and blood agar are all used for both primary isolation and the growth of stock cultures. When a Brucella culture becomes adapted to growing in vitro it does very well on any of the basic media. On prolonged incubation the surface of a solid medium is apt to become too dry. This can be corrected if the cultures are placed in tight containers.

In common with most other bacteria the Brucella have rather specific nutritional requirements. In a study of *Br. suis,* McCullough *et al.* found that thiamine, niacin, cystine, histidine, tyrosine, phenylalanine, tryptophane, and magnesium salts were essential for growth, whereas glycine, lysine, arginine, methionine, glutamic acid, isoleucine, aspartic acid, serine, biotin, calcium pantothenate, manganese, and iron salts were stimulating, and 1 per cent glucose also essential, for maximum growth. Gerhardt and Wilson have found that a nitrogen source such as asparagine, glutamic acid, or histidine was essential for maximum growth.

The organisms are aerobic and facultatively anaerobic. In a semisolid agar medium, colonies form at varying distances from the surface (Fig. 23.3).

All Brucella require carbon dioxide for growth; although *Br. suis* and *Br. melitensis* need no more than is naturally found in the air, it is often desirable to place initial cultures of Brucella in containers that can be sealed and to which may be added 5–10 per cent $CO_2$. It is absolutely necessary to do this with initial cultures of *Br. abortus* or to increase the $CO_2$ tension by some other method. It has been shown that *Br. abortus* obtained directly from infected animals will not grow in the air. Bang first isolated the organism in deep solid medium. Later it was grown in sealed containers in which a part of the oxygen had been exhausted by the reaction of hydroxides on pyrogallic acid. Smith grew *Br. abortus* in test tubes sealed with sealing

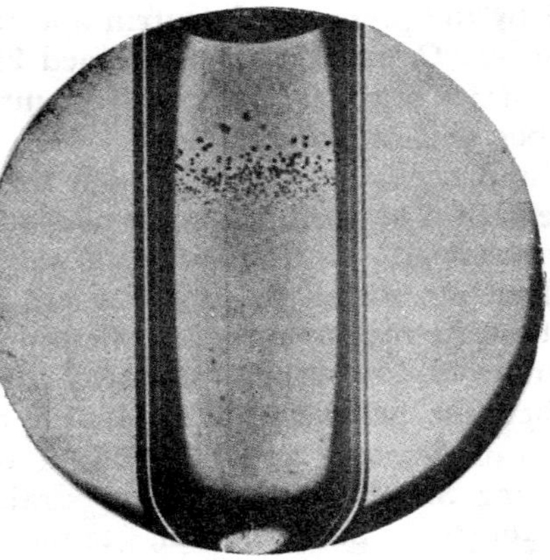

FIG. 23.3—**Brucella abortus** deep colonies in agar shake culture, natural size. (From Nowak: Documenta Microbiologica, courtesy Gustav Fischer.)

wax. Later, Huddleson used 10 per cent $CO_2$ in closed containers. The last method is most satisfactory. Visible colonies should develop in 72 hours, but are often delayed; consequently, it is best to allow negative cultures to incubate 15–20 days or even longer, especially if the $CO_2$ requirements are not optimum. Borts found some cultures that required more than 30 days incubation for growth in initial isolations.

On serum dextrose agar the colonies appear small and delicate, but in one or two days reach a diameter of 1–2 mm., and after continued incubation may be 8–9 mm. (Fig. 23.4). At first the colonies are semi-transparent with a light bluish tinge by transmitted light, and in older colonies this coloring is retained about the margins. This character is in no way distinctive since it is a common characteristic with many of the enterobacteria; however, most of the tissues cultured for Brucella are not contaminated with other organisms that have this characteristic. Colonies, especially old ones, are in the shape of a very low cone. They are distinctly pointed in the centers with a smooth circular margin and a smooth, shining, glistening surface; thus it is easy to differentiate them from other colonies which are flat, have irregular margins and dry or granular surfaces. Brucella colonies are not opaque as are those of many organisms, but are translucent and semitransparent. Old colonies show a distinct, small, dark area in their centers when viewed by transmitted light. Pigmentation on liver agar is not marked. Growth appears light brown or yellowish-brown. Pigmentation is most apparent on potato; here the colors are dull yellows, browns, or even bordering on slate. Color may vary with the same strain at different times.

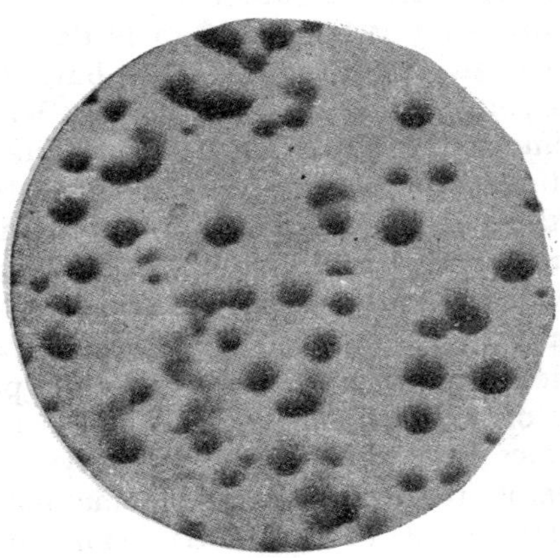

FIG. 23.4—**Brucella abortus** colonies on agar plate, ×25. (From Nowak: Documenta Microbiologica, courtesy Gustav Fischer.)

Huddleson and associates have shown that all three species of Brucella undergo colony dissociation and they have described the dissociation pattern for each species. Assuming that the normal colony is smooth (S), other types may be described as smooth intermediate (SI), sector smooth intermediate (Sec.SI), mucoid (M), sector smooth mucoid (Sec.SM), sector mucoid (Sec.M), rough (R), and pseudosmooth (PS). By using the above terminology and by designating subtypes as $R_1$, $R_2$, etc., eighteen dissociation types have been described for *Br. abortus,* thirty-four for *Br. suis,* and nineteen for *Br. melitensis.* The student is referred to Memoir 6, 1952, by Huddleson *et al.* for the detailed description of each of the dissociation types.

Tetrazolium salts have been shown by Huddleson to be of value in differentiating the three species of Brucella and also the different colony dissociation types.

Huddleson recommends gentian violet 1:200,000 in liver agar for isolation on solid medium. This concentration does not inhibit any of the Brucella but does delay or prevent growth of many gram-positive organisms. Brucella colonies on this medium have the same general characteristics as those on liver agar, but are stained bluish-violet.

Blood cultures are commonly employed for isolation in cases of undulant fever. For one satisfactory method, 60 ml. of blood are withdrawn from the patient during the height of the fever; 10 cc. of this are placed in a small flask containing 40–50 ml. of liver infusion broth or other suitable liquid medium, and the remainder of the blood is placed in a second flask containing the same amount of broth. Incubation is continued for about 14 days or longer if growth is not obtained before. If contamination is found, injections of the blood-broth culture are made into guinea pigs from time to time during the incubating period.

**Resistance.** The three species exhibit no differences in their ability to resist adverse conditions. All are killed in the pasteurization of milk in 10–15 minutes. In salt solution and broth cultures they are killed more quickly and at a lower temperature. Dry heat at 70°C. for one hour does not kill. In agar cultures they may live a year or more; on the other hand, they may die in six to eight weeks. The determining factor seems to be the amount and concentration of end products in such cultures. Masses of organisms dried at 55°–60°C., stoppered, and kept in a refrigerator may live a year or more. They have been found to survive for about seventy days in soil and for about thirty-five days in water. They are readily killed by the common disinfectants. In this respect they are similar to most members of the colon-typhoid group.

According to Elberg and Glassman, aerated broth cultures of *Br. suis,* stabilized by the presence of dextrin and ascorbic acid, retain their original, viable cell count after storage for two months at 20°–25°C. An aerated broth culture of *Br. suis* stabilized by the presence of dextrin and stored at 20°–25°C. for 175 days retained 25 per cent of its original viable cell count and 100 per cent of its virulence.

The Brucella are not sufficiently sensitive to penicillin to warrant the use of that drug in treatment. Kraft has observed that virulent strains of *Br. abortus* are more resistant to the action of penicillin than is Strain 19 (see under Immunity, below). In fact, she believes that penicillin resistance can be used as a method of differentiating Strain 19 from other strains of *Br. abortus.* Streptomycin, tetracycline, chloramphenicol, and para-aminobenzoic acid, however, do inhibit the growth of these organisms, and these drugs have been found to be of value in treating cases of brucellosis in man. The use of these drugs in animals has been limited to experimental procedures.

**Biochemical Properties.** The Brucella organisms do not produce indol; do not liquefy gelatin; are Voges-Proskauer and methyl red negative; reduce nitrates to nitrites. Urease and catalase are produced, but Sanders and Warner have shown that *Br. melitensis* varies according to geographic area in the number of strains which are urease and catalase positive. Biochemical differences are found, however, that help to divide the group. *Br. suis* always produces hydrogen sulfide in considerable quantities for as long as 10 to 14 days. *Br. abortus* usually produces $H_2S$ but, ordinarily, not to the extent or for the length of time found for *Br. suis. Br. melitensis* produces little or no $H_2S$. The growth of the three species on a medium containing thionin and basic fuchsin, as originally shown by Huddleson, has become a routine laboratory procedure. The oxidative rates of these organisms when grown in the presence of various amino acids and carbohydrates have been shown by Meyer and Cameron to be a dependable method of differentiation (Table 23.1). The utilization of glucose, as well as other carbohydrates, by the Brucella also has been used for differentiation.

TABLE 23.1

DIFFERENTIATION OF BRUCELLA SPECIES

| | *Br. abortus* | *Br. melitensis* | *Br. suis* | *Br. ovis* |
|---|---|---|---|---|
| Requires $CO_2$ | + | – | – | + |
| Produces $H_2S$ | + (4 days) | – | ++ (5 days) | – |
| Growth on thionin | – | + | + | + |
| Growth on basic fuchsin | + | + | – | + |
| Oxidizes<br>L-alanine | + | + | + | + |
| D-alanine | + | + | + | + |
| L-asparagine | + | + | – | + |
| L-glutamic acid | + | + | + | + |
| L-arabinose | + | – | + | – |
| D-galactose | + | – | + | – |
| D-ribose | + | – | + | – |
| Does not oxidize<br>D-xylose | – | – | + | – |
| L-arginine | – | – | + | – |
| DL-citrulline | – | – | + | – |
| DL-ornithine | – | – | + | – |
| L-lysine | – | – | + | – |
| Agglutination in monospecific sera<br>*Br. abortus* | + | – | + | – |
| *Br. melitensis* | – | + | – | – |
| Bacteriophage (Tb) susceptibility | + | – | – | – |

The typing of bacteria by the use of bacteriophage has proved reliable for certain species. A phage specific for *Br. abortus,* identified as Tb, has been used for classification. Only smooth colonies of *Br. abortus* are susceptible to this phage. *Br. melitensis* are resistant.

**Antigenic Structure and Toxins.** All of the species of Brucella have major antigens in common, but agglutinin absorption tests reveal minor antigenic differences. Dissociation or variation from smooth to rough affects the antigenic structure. Exotoxins have not been demonstrated. The bacteria are capable of producing an allergic condition in infected individuals which may persist indefinitely. Ottosen and Plum have prepared a purified extract of *Br. abortus* which did not elicit the formation of agglutinin or complement-fixing antibodies in rabbits but did produce marked allergic sensitivity in guinea pigs.

The relationship of capsular material to virulence has been shown by Gonzalez, who was able to increase virulence of *Br. melitensis* and *Br. abortus* for mice by serial passage and the injection of starch or mucin along with the bacteria. The highly virulent cultures produced in this manner were capsulated. The sera of animals which had been immunized with capsulated strains produced agglutination for capsulated strains. The agglutinins appear to be different from those produced by smooth, noncapsulated strains. The serum of patients suffering from *Br. melitensis* infection agglutinated the capsulated strains. It was shown in 1950 by Olitski and Oren that the virulence of *Br. abortus* for mice can be enhanced by injecting 0.5 cc. of a 10 per cent suspension of mucin along with 0.5 cc. of a 4-fold concentration of a 48-hour culture.

The ability of gram-negative bacteria to evoke an inflammatory reaction in tissues of the host animals is usually considered due to endotoxin. The revelation that the cell walls of bacteria may be or may contain the substance called endotoxin changes the long-time concept of that substance. Apparently the cytoplasm of all bacteria does not contain endotoxin. The work of Rogers and Ribi, for example, shows that the cell walls of *Br. abortus* contain substances which are lethal to mice and responsible for primary inflammation of rabbit skin. Furthermore, antigens capable of protecting mice against *Br. abortus* infection and reacting with immune serum prepared by injection of whole cells were present in the cell wall.

**Pathogenicity.** The Brucella produce infection which is most acute in laboratory animals, less so in man, and still less in cattle. In hogs the disease resembles that of both man and cattle in varying from symptoms which are pronounced, general, and local to those which are difficult to detect. Brucellosis in sows can result in abortion as it can in cows. The symptom of abortion has been greatly overemphasized, not only in hogs, but in cattle also. It has been proved that inoculation of pregnant sows may cause infection, but abortion does not always result; that is, abortion is not the disease but rather a symptom that is sometimes observed. This is also true for cattle, but to a lesser degree. In certain herds, free of brucellosis, it has been observed that about 3 per cent of all pregnant cows abort. Consideration of these facts shows that total numbers of abortions are enormous, even where brucellosis is not a factor. Abortions are encountered in diseased goats; they are rare in mares and in human beings. In cases of abortion, a placentitis is produced; with brucellosis, this is a serious matter, not only because it endangers the life of the fetus, but also because it results in injury to the uterus that may affect future pregnancies. Such inflammation results in a lowered tone of the uterus and renders it susceptible to secondary infections following abortion or parturition. After secondary invaders are once established, they often do more damage than Brucella. The retention of the placenta is also considered a symptom of brucellosis, but retained membranes may be, and often are, as common in brucellosis-free herds as they are in infected herds. The only difference lies in the ease with which the retained membranes may be removed. In brucellosis such membranes are removed with difficulty; those retained from other causes are more easily removed. *Br. abortus* is not found in the nongravid uterus of cows and disappears from that organ soon after parturition or abortion. Its most favored site is the udder, where it causes an interstitial mastitis; it is also considered a predisposing factor to other infections of the udder. The Brucella have a predilection for the male sex glands. Manthei, DeTray, and Goode have demonstrated the organism in the semen of a naturally infected bull on 80 consecutive collections. It is evident that bulls used for natural service or for artificial breeding should be free of infection. The organisms are easily isolated from the internal organs of infected hogs, especially the lymph nodes, spleen, liver, uterus, and kidneys, as well as from the blood stream. Isolation from cattle is usually difficult when the organism is not present in the udder, pregnant uterus, or associated lymph nodes. The Brucella are often found in lesions in and about articulations of many animals, and are sometimes associated with pneumonia and enteritis of newborn calves.

It is emphasized again that cattle are the true hosts for *Br. abortus,* swine for *Br. suis,* and goats for *Br. melitensis,* but each natural host may be infected with the other two species. It has been shown by Hoerlein, for example, that *Br. melitensis* is as pathogenic as *Br. suis* for swine. With the possible exception of man and some laboratory animals, other animals are quite resistant to the Brucella. The guinea pig, rabbit, mouse, rat, sheep, horse, and dog can be infected. The guinea pig is easily infected, while the dog, although having much chance of exposure, rarely shows symptoms and is thought to be relatively resistant. Abortion in the dog, due to brucellosis, has been observed, and Morse and coworkers have isolated the organisms from aborted fetuses as well as from surviving puppies. The infection is usually associated with fistula of the poll and withers in the horse. The sheep appears to be most susceptible to *Br. melitensis.* White rats inoculated with small amounts of any of the Brucella are thereafter immune, but if they are injected with initial large amounts, they die in a day or so. In pregnant rats the organism produces hyperemia and hemorrhage in the placental membranes followed by leucocyte invasion. The fetus may become edematous and die. Chickens are considered to be naturally resistant to Brucella, although experimental infections may be produced. For example, Felsenfeld and associates produced bacteremia in chickens by intramuscular and intraperitoneal injection and by feeding live cultures. They considered *Br. melitensis* more pathogenic to chickens than the other two species.

The Brucella have a very wide host range and are considered capable of infecting any mammal. Most of the infection of mammals originates in the three natural hosts. However, infection of hippopotami, rodents, and herbivora in Africa is thought to be independent of cattle, goats, and swine. In most areas wild deer constitute a reservoir of infection, and in some areas wild boars. It is apparent that "reservoirs of infection" constitute a real challenge to absolute eradication of the disease.

**Immunity.** Although the act of abortion would appear to be the result of an acute disease, brucellosis is really a chronic disease. Inasmuch as lymph tissue usually is predominantly infected, one may argue that most animals show natural resistance to the disease. *Br. abortus* is known to persist for long periods of time after initial infection. Lambert and coworkers have shown that the organism persisted for as long as four years after exposure; the organism was isolated from 132 of the 169 animals exposed; the organism was isolated from the udder and supramammary lymph glands of 123 of the 132; the tissues most frequently involved were (1) supramammary lymph glands, (2) udder, (3) iliac lymph glands, and (4) retropharyngeal lymph glands.

There is also an age resistance that can be easily demonstrated; in general, the usual infectious disease attacks the young more often and more severely than the older animals. In brucellosis the order is reversed in man and cattle. Young calves can be infected but "throw off" the disease readily. The sexually mature cattle are as easily infected, if not more so, and the infection is more lasting. In calves there is more antagonism between the host and the parasite; therefore, soon after infective feed is eliminated, the calf rids itself of Brucella, unless, as is true in some rare instances, the infection becomes dormant, and the agglutination test becomes negative. Such rare dormant infections become active when the animal reaches sexual maturity.

Some infected cattle remain diseased throughout their lives; others recover in a few months. Between these extremes all the other possibilities occur. It is generally believed that many recovered animals are highly resistant to subsequent reinfection; it is further believed that some animals that recover can be reinfected. Again, between these two extremes, many possibilities exist. It is thought that the character of the particular strain with which the animal is infected has much to do with the duration of disease and the amount of immunity acquired.

The use of an avirulent strain of *Br. abortus* by Buck in 1930 for the vaccination during calfhood indicated a superior method of immunization. This strain, known as Strain 19, was used on an extensive experimental scale by the Federal Bureau of Animal Industry, and in 1940 permission was given for its use as an aid in controlling brucellosis in the various states. This strain of *Br. abortus* is quite stable, not varying in virulence or antigenicity. Cameron and Meyer have shown that the consecutive passage of it through 26 swine did not alter its characteristics.

Strain 19 vaccine is a living culture which must be prepared according to procedures outlined by the U.S. Department of Agriculture. The relative avirulence of this strain has been mentioned, but because it is a living culture, the inoculation of it into calves produces a positive agglutination reaction. This reaction is lost in the majority of vaccinates by the time they reach breeding maturity. Unfortunately, a small per cent do not become negative and this is one objection to its use.

Calves are vaccinated with Strain 19 vaccine when 4 to 8 months old with 5 ml. subcutaneously. It has been shown by Rabstein and Cotton that 0.2 ml. of vaccine given intradermally produces just as high an agglutinin titer as 5 ml. given subcutaneously and that the titer tends to disappear sooner. McDiarmid in England found that the immunity produced in guinea pigs by 0.04 ml. of Strain 19 vaccine given intradermally compared favorably with 1 ml. given subcutaneously. Campbell and Rodwell in Australia introduced the intracaudal (tip of the tail) method of vaccination for brucellosis, giving a 0.2 ml. dose. Neither the intradermal nor the intracaudal method of vaccination is practiced much in the United States. Berman, Beach, and Irwin could find no significant difference in the immunity produced by vaccinating sexually mature cattle with 5 ml. of Strain 19 subcutaneously or 0.25 ml. intracaudally.

Unfortunately, *Br. abortus* Strain 19 may persist in body tissues of the animal vaccinated. When this does occur a continued agglutination reaction will result. Obviously, this presents a problem in eradication of the disease by the "test and slaughter method" because it is difficult to tell whether the positive agglutination reaction is due to Strain 19 vaccination or a virulent field strain of the organism. Lambert, Deyoe, and Painter have described the postvaccinal persistence of Strain 19 in two bulls. The organism had localized in the genital tissue of both animals.

In 1946 Verwey and Scheidy found that desiccation of *Br. abortus* Strain 19 vaccine by lyophilization affords a satisfactory method of preserving and maintaining the culture in a viable state. This method reduces the hazard of having a nonviable vaccine for use in the field and allows a longer use-date after its manufacture. Most of the vaccine used is prepared by this procedure.

Brucellosis in hogs may be self-limiting. In small droves of swine the disease can run through the entire lot and recovery may take place in a few months. In larger herds the infection is apt to persist. The amount of immunity afforded by one attack of Brucella infection in swine is not known. The use of Strain 19 for producing immunity in swine has been of little value.

In general, it is believed that, in most animals, recovery from one attack of brucellosis affords sufficient immunity to protect against subsequent exposures to natural infection. This is especially true of infection in man, but is difficult to determine because an initial infection may become dormant only to resume activity at a later date. When symptoms again develop in a supposedly recovered individual, the question arises as to whether or not a new infection is present.

Anti-Brucella serum contains agglutinins and complement-binding antibodies. Im-

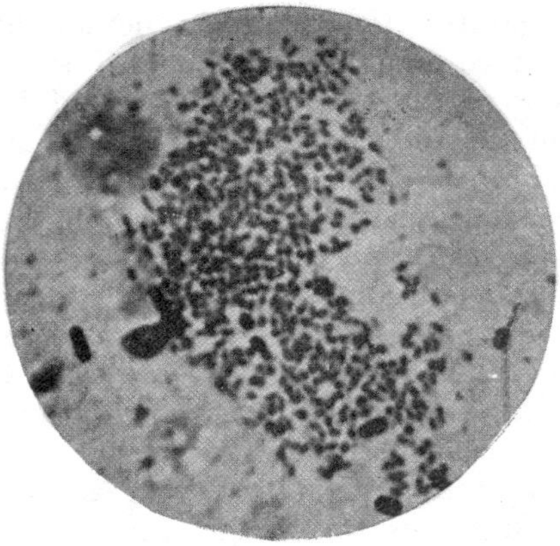

FIG. 23.5—**Brucella abortus** smear of uterine exudate, ×2,000. (From Nowak: Documenta Microbiologica, courtesy Gustav Fischer.)

mune serum, so far produced, has little or no influence on the course of the disease.

**Diagnosis.** The organism is found in large numbers on stained smears made of uterine exudate which has been obtained from a cow that has recently aborted (Fig. 23.5). The isolation of Brucella from the tissues or excretions of the animal body also establishes a diagnosis; however, a diagnosis is usually made by serological methods that have proved reliable. A combination guinea pig inoculation and the agglutination test of its blood at a later date is also reliable. In this case it is not absolutely necessary to isolate the organism. Many guinea pigs will recover from inoculations with Brucella, and it is obviously impossible to obtain cultures from them, but even these animals, if bled at the proper time, will show agglutinins in their blood; hence, the agglutination test of the guinea pig's blood should be employed in conjunction with an attempt to isolate the organism from the animal's tissues. The blood of normal guinea pigs does not contain agglutinins for Brucella. Some laboratories allow the inoculated guinea pigs to go 36 days before they are bled and examined. Others allow only 24 days. A period of approximately 24 days has some advantages because it allows ample time for agglutinins to develop and for the infection to develop, and at the same time is sufficiently short to test many guinea pigs before they recover. Lesions which will heal in 36 days are often present at the end of the 24-day period.

Complement fixation is a reliable diagnostic test. It is believed that complement-fixing antibody is formed in the blood of infected animals a short time before agglutinins appear; otherwise it holds no advantage over the agglutinin test; in fact, the latter has supplanted it because it can be conducted more easily, more quickly, and with less chance of error on the part of the operator. Selection of proper strains of the Brucella is one of the important factors in the agglutination test. Rough or variant strains must be avoided. The smooth type is disease-producing, stays in uniform suspension exceedingly well, and in all ways is an ideal type for the test. Different variants often show different characters; for instance, some are auto- or thermoagglutinating; some are only slightly so; others agglutinate in any serum; still others do not. It appears that there are different types of variants, all of which should be avoided.

*Br. melitensis* is most apt to become variant in culture media and for this reason is little used. *Br. suis* strains are satisfactory, but they, too, are apt to become rough. *Br. abortus* strains are the best, and although some become rough, others have been kept for years on laboratory media without producing variants. Such strains are nearly fixed in type if kept on a solid medium. All laboratories employ only strains that have not shown variants. If it should become necessary to rid a strain of its variants, this can be done by guinea pig inoculation. In about 14 days after inoculation the variants will disappear in the animal's body, leaving only the smooth type. This is not true of at least some of the mucoid variants mentioned above which may persist in the body of the guinea pig for more than 50 days. Isolation of desirable agglutinating types can be obtained from mixed cultures by plating and examination of likely colonies. It is necessary to test the growth from several colonies because with the usual variant on the common laboratory medium, there is little or no difference between the colonies of variants and those of smooth types.

In routine diagnosis two kinds of agglutination tests are employed. One is usually referred to as the tube test and the other the plate or rapid test. Both have their advantages, and both give about the same final results; in fact, the plate test is standardized to conform to the tube test. If one prepares the materials and conducts the test himself, the tube test is simpler. It is necessary to understand the tube test in order to prepare sera and standardize plate-test antigen. For the tube test, the suspension of the organism is made in physiological salt solution containing 0.5 of 1 per cent phenol. The density of the suspension is made to compare with tube No. 1 of the McFarland nephelometer. Donham and Fitch estimate that this should be 0.04 per cent suspension of bacteria. The serum from the suspect is added to the bacterial suspension making dilutions 1:25, 1:50, 1:100, 1:200, and higher if desired. Readings are made after 48 hours incubation at about 37°C.

In brucellosis of cattle a reaction of 1:25 is without significance; a reaction of 1:50 is considered suspicious; and one of 1:100 is generally regarded as indicating infection. An exception is noted when an animal has been calf-vaccinated with Strain 19. In this case 1:50 is considered negative, 1:100 suspicious, and 1:200 positive. The organism can usually be isolated from cattle showing reactions of 1:500 or higher.

In hogs it is easy to isolate Brucella from animals having reactions of 1:50 and sometimes in animals with reactions of 1:25; however, the disease in hogs is one of shorter duration than in cattle, and one may obtain cultures before the agglutination titer has reached a high level. A reaction of 1:50 in the hog should be considered significant, although Kernkamp and Roepke have shown that herds of swine apparently free of brucellosis may have some individuals whose sera will give a titer of 1:25 to 1:50. The application of the agglutination test to swine should be considered on a herd basis, and if any individuals in the herd show a titer of 1:100, the herd should be considered to be an infected one. Tests on individual sows or boars from a herd are of little value in determining the brucellosis status of the herd. In man a reaction of 1:80 or 1:100 indicates infection present or past. Some people with titers of 1:300 show no symptoms, even though, in a few such cases, the organism can be isolated from their blood streams. It should be remembered that all lesions and symptoms of disease cannot be attributed to Brucella merely because the organism is present; for example, it is known that cows affected with brucellosis may abort from other causes. It is often difficult to determine just which symptoms and lesions are due to Brucella infection and which are due to other causes.

The development of the ABR Test (Abortus Bang Ring) or the *Brucella abortus* Ring Test by Fleischhauer of Germany, in 1937, has provided another method of diagnosing brucellosis in cattle. This test consists of the use of a hemotoxylin-stained *Br. abortus* antigen which is added to 2 ml. of whole milk. Upon standing, the stained bacterial cells will rise with the cream, forming a purple layer if the animal is infected with brucellosis. In this positive reaction the bacteria have been agglutinated by the agglutinin in the milk serum forming clumps of bacteria large enough to be carried to the surface along with the fat globules. If the animal is not infected, the cream layer is white and the milk remains a light purple because the bacteria remain in suspension. This test can be applied to a composite sample of milk from the herd, thereby serving as an effective method of detecting herds of cattle in which one or more individual reactors exist. It is an effective screening test, allowing control officials to concentrate on certain herds during the interim between annual or semiannual routine serological tests. Furthermore, if the test is applied to milk samples monthly, the newly infected herds can be detected.

A combination of the ABR test and the plate test, whereby ring-test antigen and milk are placed on a glass plate, has been shown by Blake, Manthei, and Goode to be a satisfactory test.

The distinction between specific and nonspecific agglutination reactions in testing for brucellosis has been a problem since programs for the eradication of the disease were initiated. Unfortunately, this is true of all diagnostic tests for disease. Although those in charge of eradication programs do not wish to remove animals from herds without sufficient evidence, they do not wish to leave infected animals in the herd. Calfhood vaccination produces a positive agglutination in all calves. This reaction persists in some animals beyond breeding age. It has been shown that most of these animals do not harbor *Br. abortus,* so the positive titer of calfhood vaccinations has been changed from 1:100 to 1:200.

During his study of the various immunological reactions, the student learned that antibody in serum could be inactivated by heat and that complement was more sensitive to heat than antibody. In order to distinguish between specific and nonspecific reactions for brucellosis, a test known as the Heat-Inactivation Test (HIT) has been developed. In this test antigen-serum mixtures are heated to 65°C. for 15 minutes; cooled at 18°C. for 3 minutes; centrifuged at 2000 r.p.m. for 5 minutes; supernatant fluid above the bacterial mass is replaced with 2 ml. NaCl solution; the tube is gently shaken; and the reaction is read with a titration illuminator. Agglutination in the 1:25 antigen-serum dilution is considered positive and specific. No visible agglutination is considered negative and nonspecific. Amerault and coworkers found the above test valuable in distinguishing between specific and nonspecific reactions.

Nonspecific agglutinins are believed to be high-molecular weight proteins and may be found in serum and in milk whey.

### *Brucella ovis*

**Synonyms and History.** In most parts of the world where sheep have been found to have brucellosis, the etiologic agent has been *Br. melitensis.* In 1952 McFarlane and associates in New Zealand reported a gram-negative, pleomorphic coccobacillus which grew on blood agar, in 10 per cent $CO_2$, from cases of epididymitis, tunica vaginalis, orchitis, and inflammation of the vesiculae seminales of rams. This organism was found to be experimentally infective for rams and ewes. In the latter it caused abortion. Buddle and Boyes (1953) considered the organism to be a mutant strain of *Br. melitensis.* The first report of the isolation of the organism from ram epididymitis in the United States was by McGowan and Shultz in 1956 in California. Cultures of the organism were studied by Kennedy, Frazier, and McGowan (1956) who isolated them from the epididymis of rams in California. They found the organism to be characteristically pleomorphic upon initial isolation. They hesitated to place this organism in the genus Brucella, thinking it resembled the Hemophilae.

We did not include this organism in the 1961 edition of this textbook hoping that its correct classification would be forthcoming. It appears that no positive proof of its place in the genus Brucella has been published. Meyer and Cameron report that it does not utilize amino acids in a pattern similar to Brucella, fails to utilize glucose, lacks a urease system, and displays no serological relationship. They consider it closely related to the genus Neisseria. In the Fourth Report of the Joint FAO/WHO Expert Committee on Brucellosis (1964) and also in the review of brucellosis by Morgan (1964), the name *Br. ovis* is used. Many who have studied the disease in recent years use the name *Br. ovis.*

It is obvious that we have no authority to place the organism in any genus, but we think it is important enough so that students may learn about it, and for that reason it is being discussed in this chapter. Probably the next edition of Bergey's Manual may clarify the situation.

**Distribution and Transmission.** Abortion in ewes caused by *Br. ovis* has been reported only from Australia and New Zealand. Ram epididymitis associated with the organism has been reported from the United States, South Africa, and eastern Europe. The methods of transmission are not known, but the fact that the microorganism can be isolated from ram genitalia and that it may cause abortion in ewes suggests a venereal route. However, both rams and ewes may ingest it from contaminated pastures.

**Morphology and Staining.** *Br. ovis* is a small, pleomorphic coccobacillus 0.3μ in width and 0.7μ to 1.5μ in length. It is nonmotile, noncapsulated, and nonsporeforming. It usually occurs singly, but pairs and clumps have been described. It is gram-negative.

**Growth Requirements and Characteristics.** *Br. ovis* can only be isolated in primary culture in a 10 per cent $CO_2$ atmosphere, but cultures grow aerobically when adapted to laboratory media enriched with blood cells or serum. On blood agar small, circular, convex, entire, glistening, smooth, translucent, grayish colonies 0.2 to 0.4 mm. in diameter are formed in 3 to 5 days. Slight turbidity and a finely granular sediment occur in serum broth. Gelatin is not liquefied. No hemolysis is found in bovine, equine, or ovine erythrocytes.

**Biochemical Properties.** Every investigator has reported that *Br. ovis* is not able to ferment any of the carbohydrates. It does not utilize glucose, but does oxidize citrulline, arganine, and proline. It does utilize serine and D-aspartic acid. It is urease negative; $H_2S$ is not produced; nitrates are not reduced; litmus milk is unchanged; indol, methyl red, Voges-Proskauer, and ammonia tests are negative. It is catalase positive.

**Antigenic Structure and Toxins.** All strains of the organism which have been studied show them to be antigenically homogenous. None shows an antigenic relationship with other Brucella species nor with any other group of microorganisms.

Exotoxins have not been described, and it is presumed that the effect of endotoxin in producing tissue changes is similar to other gram-negative bacteria.

**Pathogenicity.** *Br. ovis* is characterized by epididymitis and inflammatory changes it produces in other genital tissues in the ram. Experimental infection of rams reproduces the natural disease. Following the intravenous inoculation of *Br. ovis* in pregnant ewes, it localizes in the hilar zone of the placentome, and in time exudate collects and the placenta becomes necrotic, which would eventually lead to fetal death. Molello *et al.* consider that "the pathogenicity of this organism does not appear to be great enough to cause serious trouble in pregnant ewes under usual field conditions. However, the possibility should not be overlooked when contending with stillbirths or abortion in sheep."

In guinea pigs, *Br. ovis* does not produce lesions of significance, but it may be recovered from the spleen, liver, and testicle 5 weeks after inoculation. Epididymitis, orchitis, and periorchitis are produced in the rat and are similar to the lesions which are produced in the ram. Mice are not susceptible.

No evidence has been presented to show that man is susceptible.

**Immunity.** Buddle, in New Zealand, has found that a salinin-oil adjuvant vaccine given in two doses of 1 ml. each, 8 weeks apart, appears the best of other vaccines he tested.

**Diagnosis.** A serious drawback in differentiating the disease or in diagnosing its presence in the live animal is that *Br. ovis* does not incite agglutinating antibody either naturally or experimentally.

The organism must be isolated and identified.

### *Brucella neotomae*

In 1957 Stoenner and Lachman reported an organism which they isolated from the

Desert Wood Rat *(Neotoma lepida)* sent to them from Utah. On the basis of morphological and biochemical characteristics, they concluded it belonged in the genus Brucella but differed from the other species. They named it *Brucella neotomae.*

Cameron and Meyer considered it different from *Br. abortus, Br. melitensis,* and *Br. suis* on the basis of dye bacteriostasis and oxidative rates on amino acid and carbohydrates. It is similar to *Br. suis* in that it produces $H_2S$.

Stoenner has shown that *Br. neotomae* is pathogenic for mice in much the same dosage as *Br. suis,* but it is not as pathogenic for guinea pigs. In the latter animal the organism persists in spleen and lymphoid tissue for at least 120 days.

## THE GENUS BORDETELLA

### *Bordetella bronchiseptica*

**Synonyms and History.** Although numerous types of organisms have been isolated from typical cases of canine distemper, the first organism which compares favorably with the one under discussion was isolated by Galli-Vallerio in 1896 and described again in 1908. He named his organism *Bacillus caniculae,* considered that it represented a position between the typhoid and hemorrhagic septicemia groups, and that it resembled *Bacillus pestis* in morphology. In 1901 Lignières considered an organism which he called *Pasteurella canina* as the cause of canine distemper. His organism did not ferment carbohydrates but exhibited many other characteristics similar to the organism of Galli-Vallerio.

The organism now recognized as *Bordetella bronchiseptica* was isolated and described in the United States by Ferry in 1911 and was called *Bacillus bronchicanis,* but was changed in 1912 to *Bacillus bronchisepticus.* Quite independently, in 1911, M'Gowan in England described the same type of organism as Ferry, but he did not propose a name. In 1912 Torrey and Rahe published an extensive study of canine distemper and of the organism *Bacillus bronchisepticus* which they considered to be the cause of the disease.

In 1918 Evans included *Bacillus bronchisepticus* among cultures of the Malta fever-contagious abortion group in a comparative study. She found morphological, physiological, and serological relationships among the different organisms; consequently, she assigned the canine organism to the genus Bacterium with *Bacterium melitensis* and *Bacterium abortus.*

The shakeup of the genus Bacterium and the formation of new generic names found the organism under the name *Alcaligenes bronchisepticus* in Bergey's Manual in 1923. This appeared to be a reasonable classification because many investigators, particularly Torrey and Rahe, noted a marked relationship to *Bacillus fecalis alkaligenes.* The organism was subsequently classified as *Brucella bronchiseptica.* In the 1957 edition of Bergey's Manual the new genus name Bordetella was established, and it is logical that this organism is now classified in this genus.

In 1905 Carré announced that the cause of canine distemper was a filterable virus. This discovery did not become established, however, because of the extensive research of Ferry, M'Gowan, and Torrey and Rahe. Largely because of the failure of the bacteriological agents to produce a durable immunity in young dogs against the disease, the question of etiology was reopened by Hardenberg in 1925. The question was promptly and securely closed in 1926 when Laidlaw and Dunkin published the results of their research in which they found that the primary cause of canine distemper was a filterable virus.

The results of Laidlaw and Dunkin have been universally accepted; consequently, the organism *Bordetella bronchiseptica* has been relegated to the role of an important secondary invader to the virus along with other microorganisms.

*Bord. bronchiseptica* infection is not confined to dogs. As early as 1922 Spray isolated it from swine lungs, as did Dorset *et al.* in the same year. Subsequently, it has been found associated with swine pneumonia, rhinitis, and turbinate atrophy.

The economic importance of the organism to the swine industry has become recognized by the research of Phillips (1944), Switzer (1956), Joubert *et al.* (1960), L'Ecuyer *et al.* (1961), Dunne *et al.* (1961), Cross and Claflin (1962), and Ross (1963). Duncan (1965) and Ross (1965) have contributed significantly to the pathology of *Bord. bronchiseptica* infection in swine.

**Distribution and Transmission.** *Bord. bronchiseptica* infection is frequently found in dogs, but it is not always present in cases of canine distemper. It is quite prevalent in swine herds of midwestern United States and has been isolated in England. It is transmitted from animal to animal by contact and by contaminated feed and water.

**Morphology and Staining.** The organism is a short, pleomorphic rod, showing coccoid shapes 0.5μ to 1.0μ and bacillary forms 0.5μ to 1.5μ in size. It usually occurs singly, but pairs are found, and in fluid media chains may be observed. It is motile by means of peritrichous flagella, is nonsporeforming, and noncapsuleproducing, although capsular material has been observed.

The organism is stained by the usual dyes, but many cells show decided bipolar staining. It is gram-negative.

**Growth Requirements and Characteristics.** *Bord. bronchiseptica* grows best under aerobic conditions, at a temperature of 37°C., and in a medium adjusted to a pH of 7.0 or 7.2. It requires a medium which is enriched with animal tissues or plasma.

The organism grows slowly upon primary isolation from the lung of an infected animal. No visible growth is present on the agar surface after 24 hours of incubation, but at the end of 48 hours, tiny, circular, dewdrop-like colonies appear scattered over the plate. As the cultures ages, the colonies increase in size up to 6 to 8 mm., becoming flat, glistening, and opalescent by reflected light and translucent with a smoky tinge by transmitted light.

In broth the organism produces a uniform turbidity with a finely granular sediment but no pellicle. Growth forms on the surface of the medium at the sides of the tube within 72 hours. The sediment in old cultures rises in a twisted cone when the tube is shaken. Old cultures of the organism liberate a stale odor similar to that of musty bread.

The growth of this organism is very characteristic on potato. In 24 hours the culture is abundant, moist, raised, glistening, and yellowish-brown in color accompanied by a greenish or grayish darkening of the potato. Upon aging, the growth becomes darker brown, and the potato also becomes darker.

**Resistance.** The organism is killed by 55°C. in 20 minutes, thereby showing less resistance to heat than other gram-negative, nonsporeforming rods. It is not resistant to light, desiccation, or the common disinfectants, and is not destroyed by freezing.

It is quite susceptible to mercuric chloride and other mercurial disinfectants.

Many of the sulfonamide compounds, especially sulfamethazine and sulfathiazole, can be used as effective therapeutic agents. It is sensitive to streptomycin, chloramphenicol, and oxytetracycline, but resistant to penicillin. It is sensitive to furazolidone, but not to furacin and furadantin.

**Biochemical Properties.** An outstanding property of this organism is its inability to ferment any of the carbohydrates. Another distinctive characteristic is its action on litmus milk. After 24 hours incubation a deep blue ring appears, extending about one-half inch from the surface of the medium. In 72 hours the ring is a deeper blue, and the rest of the medium is a deeper blue than the control. In 5 to 10 days the entire medium is blue-black in color. As the culture stands, the lower third of the medium bleaches to a faded blue color. The organism does not form indol or hydrogen sulfide. Torrey and Rahe divide the strains of the organism into two groups on the basis of nitrate reduction. Strains in Group A do not reduce nitrates and those in Group B reduce nitrates to nitrites. It is urease positive and is able to utilize citrate as a source of carbon. It is catalase and lysine decarboxylase positive.

**Antigenic Structure and Toxins.** The organism is homogenous antigenically according to the agglutination test. It shows some affinity to *Br. abortus,* but relatively little is known about its antigenic fractions.

Heat labile toxins which are lethal to guinea pigs are produced; also a dermonecrotic toxin lethal to rabbits is produced. The necrotizing ability of the organism is apparent by the necrosis of nasal turbinates of the pig. Beta hemolysis has been reported on blood agar of the sheep, cow, rabbit, dog, horse, and guinea pig, although washed erythrocytes are not so actively hemolyzed.

**Pathogenicity.** The original work on this organism indicated that it was the cause of canine distemper. Experimental inoculation of young dogs with the organism produced typical cases of distemper. Although the primary cause of the disease is a filterable virus, it is evident that *Bord. bronchiseptica* may be a secondary agent and that the fatality of the infection is largely attributed to the pneumonia which it causes.

M'Gowan reported finding the organism in the ferret, monkey, goat, guinea pig, rabbit, cat, and dog. He also reported the isolation of the organism from the nasal exudate of an attendant who had been handling rabbits and guinea pigs.

Previous mention has been made of the prevalence of *Bord. bronchiseptica* in the nasal turbinates and lungs of swine.

**Immunity.** Bacterins and immune serum were commonly used for the immunization of dogs until the work of Laidlaw and Dunkin. It was acknowledged before that time, however, that such immunizing agents were not satisfactory.

The organism is recognized as important in canine distemper, and for that reason animals in which canine distemper immune serum is produced are also immunized with *Bord. bronchiseptica* and other organisms which have been incriminated as secondary invaders.

Little is known concerning the immunity induced in pigs as a result of infection. Immunizing swine against infection is not a common practice, although the organism is incorporated in swine-mixed bacterins.

**Diagnosis.** The presence of a nasal secretion or pneumonia in an animal is not diagnostic for *Bord. bronchiseptica* infection because many bacteria and viruses can produce such symptoms.

For accurate diagnosis this microorganism must be isolated and identified. MacConkey's agar with the addition of 1 per cent dextrose was found by Ross to be a satisfactory medium for primary isolation. Bovine blood agar may also be used, but other infecting bacteria, particularly Pasteurella and Hemophilus species, will grow on it.

Farkas-Himsley recommends that the citrate lysine decarboxylase and oxidase tests be used to differentiate *Bord. bronchiseptica* from *Past. pseudotuberculosis.* The latter organism ferments rhamnose and hydrolyzes esculin while the former does not.

## Other Bordetella Species

*Bordetella pertussis* causes whooping cough which is characterized by tracheobronchitis and toxemia in children. Most adults have developed immunity due to previous exposure.

This organism is a small coccobacillus and is found in great numbers in the exudate during early stages of infection. The cell walls of the bacterium contain a heat-stable toxin, a protective antigen, and a histamine-sensitizing factor. A heat-labile toxin and other antigens are found in the protoplasm.

*Bord. pertussis* has not been isolated from animals.

*Bordetella parapertussis* is also associated with whooping cough, but produces a milder disease. It grows more readily on blood media, always produces catalase, and is not the same antigenically as *Bord. pertussis.*

## REFERENCES


AMERAULT, T. E., *et al.* A Heat-inactivation Test for Differentiating Specific and Non-specific Agglutination Reactions for Bovine Brucellosis. Amer. Jour. Vet. Res. 22:564–69, 1961.

ANDREWS, F. N., and HUTCHINGS, L. M. Amer. Jour. Vet. Res. 7:385, 1946.

BANG, B. Zeitschrift für Tiermedizin 1:241, 1897.

BASS, C. C., and WATKINS, J. A. Arch. of Intl. Med. 6:717, 1910.

BEAL, G. A., *et al.* Experimental Infection of Swine With *Brucella neotomae.* Amer. Jour. Vet. Res. 20:872, 1959.

BERGEY, D. H., *et al.* Bergey's Manual of Determinative Bacteriology. 7th Ed. Williams & Wilkins Co., 1957.

BERMAN, D. T., *et al.* Amer. Jour. Vet. Res. 15:406, 1954.

BLAKE, G. E., *et al.* Jour. Amer. Vet. Med. Assn. 120:1, 1952.

BORTS, I. H., *et al.* Jour. Amer. Med. Assn. 130 (Apr. 6, 1946) No. 14, p. 966.

BRUCE, D. Practitioner, London, 39:161, 1887.

BUDDLE, M. B. Production of Immunity in Rams Against *Brucella ovis* Infection. New Zealand Vet. Jour. 10: 111–15, 1962.

———, and BOYES, B. W. A Brucella Mutant Causing Genital Disease of Sheep in New Zealand. Austral. Vet. Jour. 29:145–53, 1953.

BUNNELL, D. E., *et al.* Amer. Jour. Vet. Res. 8:367, 1947.

CAMERON, H. S., and MEYER, M. E. Cornell Vet. 42:42, 1952.

———, and ———. Metabolic Studies on *Brucella neotomae* (Stoenner and Lackman). Jour. Bact. 76:546–48, 1958.

CAMPBELL, A. D., and RODWELL, A. W. Jour. Comp. Path. Therap. 55, 1945.

COTTON, CORNELIA M. An Intense Study of Post-Vaccination Responses in Groups of Calves Vaccinated Intracutaneously With Strain 19 Brucella. Amer. Jour. Vet. Res. 14:337, 1953.

COTTON, W. E. Jour. Amer. Vet. Med. Assn. 62:179, 1922.

———, and BUCK, J. M. Jour. Amer. Vet. Med. Assn. 80:342, 1932.

CROSS, R. F., and CLAFLIN, R. M. *Bordetella bronchiseptica*-induced Porcine Atrophic Rhinitis. Jour. Amer. Vet. Med. Assn. 141:1467–68, 1962.

CRUICKSHANK, J. C. Observations on Brucella Species Based on the Examination of 800 Strains. Jour. Hyg. 52:105–18, 1954.

DAMON, S. R., and FAGAN, R. Pub. Health Rept., Wash., 62:1097, 1947.

———, and SCRUGGS, J. H. Pub. Health Rept., Wash., 65:374, 1950.

DELEZ, A. L., *et al.* Amer. Jour. Vet. Res. 8:225, 1947.

DUNCAN, J. R. The Pathogenesis of *Bordetella bronchiseptica* Rhinitis and Pneumonia in Swine. Thesis. Iowa State Univ. Library, Ames, 1965.

EISELE, C. W., *et al.* Proc. Soc. Exp. Biol. Med. 61:89, 1946.

———, *et al.* Jour. Amer. Med. Assn. 135:983, 1947.

———, *et al.* Ann. Int. Med. 28:833, 1948.

ELBERG, S. S., and GLASSMAN, H. N. Amer. Jour. Vet. Res. 8:314, 1947.

EVANS, A. C. Jour. Inf. Dis. 22:580, 1918.

———. Pub. Health Rept., Wash., 38:1948, 1923.

———. Pub. Health Rept., Wash., 39:501, 1924.

FARKAS-HIMSLEY, H. Differentiation of *Pasteurella pseudotuberculosis* and *Bordetella bronchisepticum* by Simple Biochemical Tests. Amer. Jour. Vet. Res. 24:871–73, 1963.

FELSENFELD, O., *et al.* Amer. Jour. Vet. Res. 12:48, 1951.

FERRY, N. S. Amer. Vet. Rev. 37:499–504, 1910.

———. Etiology of Canine Distemper. Jour. Inf. Dis. 8:399–420, 1911.

FOSTER, J. W., and RIBI, E. Immunological Role of *Brucella abortus* Cell Walls. Jour. Bact. 84:258–68, 1962.

GALLI-VALERIO, B. Der Mikroörganismus der Hundestaupe. Zentralbl. f. Bakt. 19:694, 1896.

GERHARDT, P., and WILSON, J. B. Jour. Bact. 56:17, 1948.

———, and ———. The Nutrition of Brucellae. Bact. Rev. 22:81, 1958.

GILMAN, H. L., and LEGROW, W. R. Amer. Jour. Vet. Res. 8:192, 1947.

———, and WAGNER, W. C. The Evaluation of Brucellosis Vaccination at 4 to 8 Months of Age. Cornell Vet. 49:399, 1959.

GOOD, C. S., and SMITH, W. V. Jour. Bact. 1:415, 1916.

HALLMAN, E. T., *et al.* Mich. Agr. Exp. Sta. Tech. Bull. 93, 1928.

HARDY, A. V. Pub. Health Rept., Wash., 43:2459, 1928.

———, *et al.* Nat. Inst. of Pub. Health Bull. 158, 1930.

HARTLEY, W. J. The Pathology of *Brucella ovis* Infection in the Pregnant Ewe. New Zealand Vet. Jour. 9:115–20, 1961.

HENRICSSON, ERIK. Epizootic Abortion and Undulant Fever. Isaac Marcus Boktryckeri-Aktiebolag, Stockholm, 1932.

HOERLEIN, A. B. Amer. Jour. Vet. Res. 13:67, 1952.

HUDDLESON, I. F. Brucellosis in Man and Animals. New York, The Commonwealth Fund. Oxford Univ. Press, London, 1943.

———. Amer. Jour. Vet. Res. 7:5–10, 1946.

———. Amer. Jour. Vet. Res. 8:374, 1947.

———, *et al.* Studies in Brucellosis. III. Memoir 6, Mich. St. Agr. Exp. Sta., East Lansing, 1952.

HUTCHINGS, L. M., *et al.* Amer. Jour. Vet. Res. 7:11, 379, 388, 1946.

KEEFER, C. S. Bulletin of the Johns Hopkins Hospital, Baltimore 35:6, 1924.

KENNEDY, P. C., *et al.* Epididymitis in Rams: Pathology and Bacteriology. Cornell Vet. 46:303–19, 1956.

KERNKAMP, H. C. H., and ROEPKE, M. H. Amer. Jour. Vet. Res. 9:46, 1948

KRAFT, MARY E. Amer. Jour. Vet. Res. 16:295, 1955.

LAIDLAW, P. P., and DUNKIN, G. W. Jour. Comp. Path. Therap. 39:201–30, 1926.

LAMBERT, G., *et al.* Further Studies on the Persistence of *Brucella abortus* Infection in Cattle. Proc. 64th Ann. Meet. U.S. Livestock Sanit. Assn., 1960.

———, *et al.* Post-vaccinal Persistence of *Brucella abortus* Strain 19 in Two Bulls. Jour. Amer. Vet. Med. Assn. 145:909–11, 1964.

LAWRENCE, W. E. Ovine Brucellosis: A Review of the Disease in Sheep Manifested by Epididymitis and Abortion. Brit. Vet. Jour. 117:435–47, 1961.

MCCULLOUGH, N. B., *et al.* Jour. Bact. 53:5, 1947.

———, *et al.* Jour. Inf. Dis. 83:55, 1948.

———, *et al.* Pub. Health Rept., Wash., 64:537, 1949.

MCDIARMID, A. Vet. Rec. 60:227, 1948.

MCFARLANE, D., *et al.* Investigation Into Sheep Abortion in New Zealand During the 1950 Lambing Season. Austral. Vet. Jour. 28:221–26, 1952.

———, *et al.* Ram Epididymitis, Ewe Abortion and Lamb Neonatal Mortality. Austral. Vet. Jour. 28:226, 1952.

M'GOWAN, J. P. Jour. Path. Bact. 15:372–426, 1911.

MANTHEI, C. A. Amer. Jour. Vet. Res. 9:40, 1948.

———, *et al.* Proc. 87th Ann. Conv. Amer. Vet. Med. Assn., 1950.

MEYER, K. F., and SHAW, E. B. Jour. Inf. Dis. 27:173, 1920.

———, and ZOBELL, C. E. Jour. Inf. Dis. 51:72, 1932.

MEYER, M. E., and CAMERON, H. S. I. Statistical Evaluation of the Oxidative Rates by Which Type I of Each Brucella Species Can Be Identified. Jour. Bact. 82:387–95, 1961.

———, and ———. II. Oxidative Metabolic Patterns of the Described Biotypes of Brucella. Jour. Bact. 82: 396–400, 1961.

———, and ———. III. Oxidative Metabolism of Strains of Brucella That Show Anomalous Characteristics by Conventional Determinative Methods. Jour. Bact. 82:401–10, 1961.

———, and ———. IV. Correlation of Oxidative Metabolic Patterns and Susceptibility to Brucella Bacteriophage, Type Abortus, Strain 3. Jour. Bact. 82:950–53, 1961.

MOLELLO, J. A., *et al.* Placental Pathology of Sheep Experimentally Infected With *Brucella ovis*. Amer. Jour. Vet. Res. 24:897–904, 1963.

MORGAN, W. J. B. Reviews of the Progress of Dairy Science. Sec. E. Diseases of Dairy Cattle. Brucellosis. Jour. Dairy Res. 31:315–59, 1964.

MORSE, E. V., *et al.* Jour. Amer. Vet. Med. Assn. 122:18, 1953.

MUNOZ, J. J. Immunological and Other Biological Activities of *Bordetella pertussis* Antigens. Bact. Rev. 27:325–40, 1963.

MURRAY, C., *et al.* Jour. Amer. Vet. Med. Assn. 80:336, 1932.
OTTOSEN, H. E., and PLUM, H. Amer. Jour. Vet. Res. 10:5, 1949.
PAYNE, J. M. Changes in the Rat Placenta and Foetus Following Experimental Infection With *Brucella abortus*. Jour. Path. Bact. 73:141, 1957.
PHILLIPS, C. E. Canad. Jour. Comp. Med. 7:58–59, 1943.
PLASTRIDGE, W. N. Bovine Brucellosis: A Review of the Literature on Diagnosis and Control. Proc. 58th Ann. Meet. U.S. Livestock Sanit. Assn., 1954.
———, and MCALPINE, J. G. Jour. Inf. Dis. 49:127, 1931.
RABSTEIN, M. M., and COTTON, CORNELIA M. Proc. 46th Ann. Meet. U.S. Livestock Sanit. Assn., p. 129, 1942.
REPORT, JOINT FAO/WHO EXPERT COMMITTEE ON BRUCELLOSIS. World Health Org. Tech. Rept. Ser. 289, Geneva, 1964.
ROEPKE, M. H., *et al.* The Milk and Cream Ring Test for Brucellosis. Proc. 52nd Ann. Meet. U.S. Livestock Sanit. Assn., 1948.
ROSS, R. F. Incidence of *Bordetella bronchiseptica* in Swine and Experimental Production of Rhinitis With the Organism. Thesis. Iowa State Univ. Library, Ames, 1965.
SANDERS, E., and WARNER, J. Amer. Jour. Vet. Res. 14:388, 1953.
SCHROEDER, E. C., and COTTON, W. E. USDA Ann. Rept. of the Bur. of An. Ind., p. 139, 1911.
SMITH, T. Jour. Med. Res. 29:291, 1913.
STOENNER, H. G. Observations on the Behavior of *Brucella neotomae* in Laboratory Animals. Amer. Jour. Vet. Res. 26:347–52, 1965.
———, and LACHMAN, D. B. A New Species of Brucella Isolated From the Desert Wood Rat *Neotoma lepida* Thomas. Amer. Jour. Vet. Res. 18:947, 1957.
SYMPOSIUM ON BRUCELLOSIS. Amer. Assn. Adv. Sci., Washington, 1950.
TORREY, J. C., and RAHE, A. H. Jour. Med. Res. 27:291–364, 1912–13.
TOVAR, R. M. Amer. Jour. Vet. Res. 8:138, 1947.
TRAUM, J. USDA Ann. Rept. of the Bur. of An. Ind., p. 30, 1914.
VERWEY, W. F., and SCHEIDY, S. F. Jour. Amer. Vet. Med. Assn. 109:362, 1946
WASHKO, F. V., *et al.* Amer. Jour. Vet. Res. 9:342, 1948.

# 24

# The Genus Pasteurella

**GORDON R. CARTER,** ***D.V.M., M.S., D.V.Sc.***

*College of Veterinary Medicine*
*Michigan State University*
*East Lansing, Michigan*

MICROORGANISMS BELONGING TO THE GENUS Pasteurella are usually coccoid, short, plump rods; however, elongated cells are sometimes observed. They are generally capsulated, but noncapsulated forms have been reported. The majority of the species are nonmotile, and all are nonsporeforming. They are gram-negative and are stained more distinctly at either pole, giving rise to the term, bipolar, which is frequently used to characterize the group. The ability of these organisms to ferment carbohydrates is limited; although acid is produced in a number of sugar media, gas is never produced. The various species are parasitic and frequently pathogenic for animals and man.

The species of the Pasteurella group are conveniently divided into three subgroups on the basis of host relationship and type of disease.

A. The members of the hemorrhagic septicemia group are found in lower animals. There are two species in this group:

    *Pasteurella multocida*
    *Pasteurella hemolytica*

B. The members of the second group cause acute, subacute to chronic infections in rodents and are transmissible to man. There are two species in the group:

    *Pasteurella pestis*
    *Pasteurella tularensis*

C. The one species in the third category causes a chronic, focalized caseation necrosis in rodents. It is:

    *Pasteurella pseudotuberculosis*

In addition to the variable hosts and the types of disease, the above species can be distinguished on the basis of the characteristics given in Table 24.1.

### *Pasteurella multocida*

**Synonyms and History.** The organisms which produce a septicemia in the lower animals have been recognized as belonging to several genera such as Escherichia, Salmonella, Shigella, Streptococcus, and Bacillus. The term *hemorrhagic septicemia* designates a particular type of septicemia which is characterized by hemorrhage of the capillaries in the submucous and subserous membranes. The name was first used by Hueppe in 1886 to describe the disease produced by the bipolar organisms. The name *Pasteurellosis,* first proposed by Lignières in 1900, is a more appropriate term.

The isolation of different strains of *Pasteurella multocida* by different individuals from different hosts and at different times has introduced into the literature a number of names for the hemorrhagic septicemia group. They are scattered throughout the various systematic classifications of bacteria, but most of them are given in Bergey's Manual.

TABLE 24.1

DIFFERENTIAL CHARACTERISTICS OF THE PASTEURELLA

| | *Past. multocida* | *Past. hemolytica* | *Past. pestis* | *Past. tularensis* | *Past. pseudotuberculosis* |
|---|---|---|---|---|---|
| Motility | − | − | − | − | + |
| Hemolysis | − | + | − | − | − |
| Growth in bile | − | − | + | − | + |
| Indol formation | + | − | − | − | − |
| Litmus milk | neutral | acid | neutral | no growth | alkaline |
| Glucose | + | + | + | + | + |
| Saccharose | + | + | − | − | ± |
| Lactose | ± | ± | − | − | − |
| Raffinose | − | + | − | − | − |
| Rhamnose | − | − | + | − | + |

The first significant report of an organism of this group was made by Bollinger in 1878, following an investigation of a fatal disease among wild animals and cattle. The fowl cholera organism was described by Rivolta in 1877, by Perrincito in 1879, and also by Toussaint in the same year. The most complete description of fowl cholera and the organism was made by Pasteur in 1880. In the United States, Salmon and Smith observed the organism in 1880. Davaine, in 1880, and Gaffky, in 1881, described the rabbit septicemia organism. Loeffler and Schütz studied and described the organism of swine septicemia in 1882. In 1885 Kitt made a comparative study of the organisms producing fowl cholera, rabbit septicemia, swine septicemia, and the septicemia of wild animals and cattle. He concluded that they were similar in many respects and referred to them as *Bacterium bipolare multocidum*. In 1886 Hueppe noted the similarity of the diseases which were produced by these ovoid, bipolar organisms and suggested the name *septicemia hemorrhagica* for the disease. Poels described the organism of calf pleuropneumonia in 1886. Oreste and Armanni reported the buffalo strain in 1887, Galtier the sheep strain in 1887, and Lignières the equine strain in 1897. Much later, 1926, Meyer and Batchelder isolated a strain from rat septicemia.

In 1887 Trevisan used the name *Pasteurella* for the bipolar organisms and listed three species: *Pasteurella cholerae-gallinarum*, *Pasteurella davainei*, and *Pasteurella suilla*. In 1896 Flügge called the various hemorrhagic septicemia organisms *Bacillus boviseptica*, *Bacillus suisepticus*, etc. These classifications represent the early tendency to form a species name on the basis of the host affected. In following this procedure in detail, Lignières listed the organisms causing Pasteurellosis as follows:

- *Pasteurella aviaire*, producing natural infection in all the birds.
- *Pasteurella bovine*, producing hemorrhagic septicemia in wild animals and cattle, barbone of buffalo, and pleuropneumonia of calves.
- *Pasteurella ovine*, producing hemorrhagic septicemia, pneumoenteritis, and enzootic pneumonia in sheep.
- *Pasteurella porcine*, producing swine plague.

*Pasteurella equine,* producing contagious pleuropneumonia in the horse.

*Pasteurella canine,* producing all forms of disease in dogs.

This list of Lignières was too inclusive and obviously embraced organisms not belonging to the Pasteurella group. His system of nomenclature, however, was quite acceptable and had been adopted by most bacteriologists. The genus Pasteurella became established, and the species names were based upon the nomenclature of Flügge; hence, *Pasteurella aviseptica, -boviseptica, -oviseptica, -suiseptica, -equiseptica, -leptiseptica,* and *-muriseptica.*

During recent years comparative studies of strains of the organism isolated from the different animals have failed to support the zoological classification. All of the strains are morphologically, biochemically, serologically, and pathologically similar. As a consequence, there has been a tendency to use one name for the variety of strains. Lehmann and Neumann adhered to this method of classification throughout all of their early classifications and called the organism *Bacillus hemorrhagicae septicemiae.* In 1935 Gay and his associates suggested the use of *Pasteurella pluriseptica* or *septica,* and in 1936 Topley and Wilson suggested the name *Pasteurella septica* and that the animal origin be indicated where necessary. As a result of comparative studies, Rosenbusch in 1937, and Rosenbusch and Merchant in 1938 used the name *Pasteurella multocida* for the typical hemorrhagic septicemia organisms because the first inclusive name, *Bacterium bipolare multocidum,* was used by Kitt in 188[illegible].

**Distribution and Transmission.** The organism is encountered throughout the world and is frequently the cause of great economic loss. Since typical organisms have been isolated from respiratory and digestive tracts of normal animals, the primary relationship of the organism to the disease has been doubted frequently. These organisms may act as secondary invaders to other diseases or to debilitative predisposing factors such as severe weather, long truck or train rides, and faulty nutrition. The occurrence of epizootics and sporadic outbreaks, especially of fowl cholera, may indicate that these organisms can acquire virulence while being harbored in the animal, since the nature of these organisms requires continual parasitism for existence.

The organism is transmitted by contact and by the consumption of contaminated food and water. In some cases droplet infection is of significance.

**Morphology and Staining.** *Pasteurella multocida* is a small coccoid rod 0.25μ to 0.4μ by 0.6μ to 2.6μ in size (Fig. 24.1). After repeated culture on agar, the organism tends to form longer rods and to become more pleomorphic, forming chains, filaments, and rods of various sizes. When grown in bouillon or carbohydrate media for prolonged periods, marked pleomorphicity is noted. The organism usually possesses a capsule when recently isolated from disease processes. Capsules vary greatly in size and composition. The presence of hyaluronic acid in the large capsules of some strains was demonstrated independently by Carter and Bain (1960). Carter (1958) reported the decapsulation of Group A strains by means of staphylococcal hyaluronidase. Capsules are demonstrable by

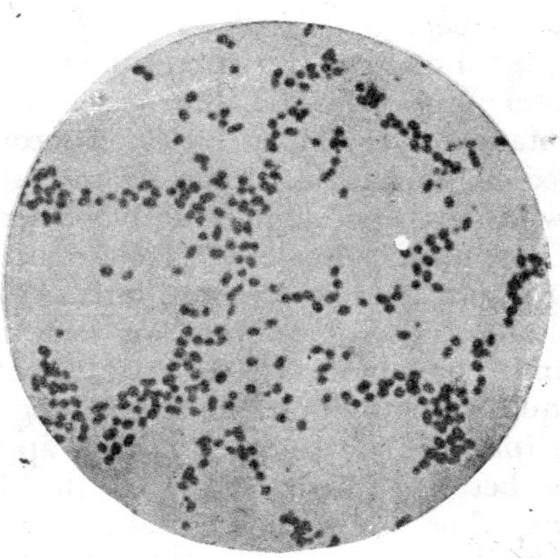

FIG. 24.1—**Pasteurella multocida** smear from agar culture, ×2,000. (From Nowak: Documenta Microbiologica, courtesy Gustav Fischer.)

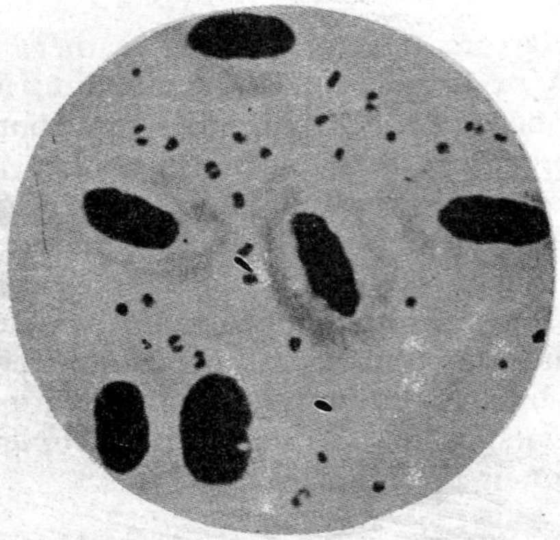

FIG. 24.2—**Pasteurella multocida** blood smear, fowl cholera, ×2,000. (From Nowak: Documenta Microbiologica, courtesy Gustav Fischer.)

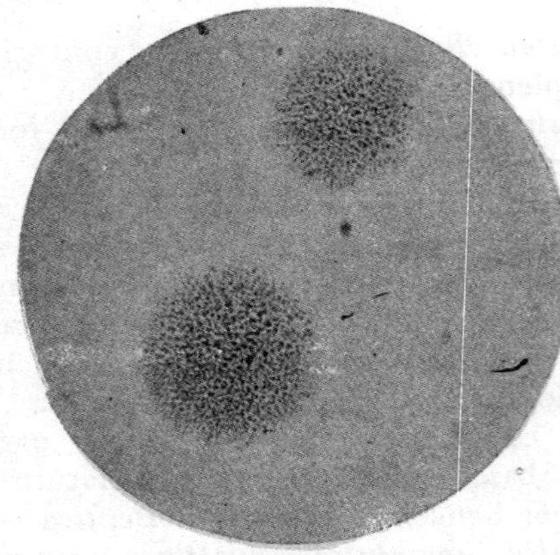

FIG. 24.3—**Pasteurella multocida** colony on agar plate, ×70. (From Nowak: Documenta Microbiologica, courtesy Gustav Fischer.)

Alcian Blue and negative stains employing India ink or nigrosin. Virulent strains may lose their capsular material after continued subculture on artificial media.

When smears of blood or other tissue are stained with methylene blue or carbol fuchsin, the organism is distinctly bipolar (Fig. 24.2). It is gram-negative.

**Growth Requirements and Characteristics.** The organism is an aerobe and faculative anaerobe. Its optimum temperature for growth is 37°C. The pH growth range is from 6 to 8.5 with an optimum of 7.2 to 7.4.

The use of digested protein media or proteose peptone stimulates the growth of the organism. The organism can be grown in beef infusion media, but better growth is obtained when blood or blood serum is added to the media. Some strains fail to grow in media not containing blood serum.

Three principal colony types are seen on clear serum agar: fluorescent, intermediate, and blue. The fluorescent, or iridescent, colonies are moderate in size, whitish, opaque, generally unstable and pathogenic. The intermediate colonies vary in appearance between fluorescent and the blue forms. The blue colonies, although not necessarily rough in appearance, correspond in many ways to the R forms of other species. They are smaller, dewdrop-like (Fig. 24.3), and of a relatively low virulence. Strains giving rise to blue colonies are most frequently recovered from chronic infections, while acute infections usually yield strains giving rise to fluorescent colonies. Many Group A strains produce mucoid variants on initial isolation on enriched media (Carter, 1958). The colonies are large, moist, and possess flowing margins. The capsules are composed for the most part of hyaluronic acid. Organisms yielding these variants vary greatly in virulence.

Carter (1957) correlated a number of older names used to denote the different variants with the widely used terms mucoid, smooth, and rough. Identification of the different variants was aided by oblique light and the use of acriflavine solution. All of the variants grow well on conventional media to which has been added 5 per cent serum. Growth in broth is usually diffuse but some strains form a flocculent precipitate which is characteristic of the rough phase of the organism. In old cultures a pellicle is often formed in broth, and a sticky sediment collects in the bottom of the tube.

The organism is not soluble in bile. There is usually no growth on potato.

**Resistance.** The organism is easily destroyed by 60°C. for 10 minutes or by 0.5

per cent phenol for 15 minutes. The organism remains infective in manure for a month and in decomposing carcasses for three months. A 1:5,000 solution of bichloride mercury and a 3.5 per cent solution of cresol are effective in a few minutes.

Stock cultures die shortly after being stored in the refrigerator; however, most air-tight cultures will survive for months and even years when stored at room temperature. Most cultures will lose their virulence on artificial media; however, it can usually be restored by animal passage.

This organism is sensitive to many of the commonly used antibiotics; however, considerable resistance to streptomycin, bacitracin, neomycin, and viomycin was reported by Muysson and Carter. The sulfa compounds, especially sulfathiazole, sulfamethazine, and sulfamerazine, are effective against it in vivo.

**Biochemical Properties.** Strains of this species show great variation in their fermentation of carbohydrates. Generally speaking, *Past. multocida* ferments glucose, saccharose, mannose, and mannitol. Variable results are obtained with lactose, xylose, arabinose, dulcitol, sorbitol, and fructose. Those substrates that are not usually split are: raffinose, trehalose, rhamnose, inositol, salacin, dextrin, and starch. It does not liquefy gelatin and only the lactose-fermenting strains alter litmus milk. $H_2S$ is not usually detectible in lead acetate agar or triple sugar iron agar but can be demonstrated if lead acetate paper is suspended over these media during incubation. Urease is not produced although Haagsma reported that some feline strains produce this enzyme.

Many attempts have been made to identify serological varieties of *Past. multocida.* Rosenbusch and Merchant, and Little and Lyon utilized the agglutination test with limited success. By means of a slide agglutination test Little and Lyon identified three serotypes which were referred to as Types 1, 2, and 3. Roberts divided his strains into four principal types or groups by means of serum-protection tests in mice.

Carter in 1955, employing an indirect hemagglutination test, was able to identify four different types on the basis of differences in capsular substances. These varieties and an additional one (Carter, 1961) were ultimately designated Groups A, B, D, and E (Carter, 1963) rather than Types when it was demonstrated by Namioka and associates that these categories contained more than one somatic variety. The latter employed agglutinin absorption tests using antigens made agglutinable by hydrochloric acid treatment. In their expanded classification the identification of a serotype requires the recognition of both the capsular and somatic components, the former being designated by a capital letter and the latter by an arabic number. Two important serotypes causing fowl cholera were designated 5:A and 8:A; the principal causes of epizootic hemorrhagic septicemia were referred to as 6:B (southeast Asia, principally) and 6:E (central Africa). The majority of the other serotypes were recovered from a number of animals and various infections.

Prior to the investigations of Namioka and associates, Heddleston showed that at least two immunogenic types of *Past. multocida* were encountered as important causes of fowl cholera. These two varieties were later found to correspond with Namioka's serotypes 5:A and 8:A.

It is now evident that the serology of *Past. multocida* is much more complex than was thought earlier. Additional studies will no doubt considerably increase the number of recognizable serotypes.

The organism does not produce exotoxin, but autolysed cultures contain endotoxin. Weil has demonstrated nontoxic aggressins or "infection-favoring" substances in the inflammatory exudates of Pasteurella-infected animals.

**Pathogenicity.** *Past. multocida* is pathogenic for a large number of different animals; however, the organism varies in virulence from the highly virulent to the comparatively avirulent types. The virulence of the organism can be increased by animal passage, chicken embryo passage, and growth upon blood or blood serum media. Spontaneous dissociative changes which occur in cultures also contribute to the loss of virulence in some strains. Probably the most important role that *Past. multocida* plays in disease is that of a secondary invader when the resistance of the animal has been reduced by various stresses.

The more susceptible of the experimental animals are the mouse, rabbit, and pigeon. Guinea pigs are more resistant. Chickens are more susceptible to fowl strains, although highly virulent ovine and bovine strains are able to produce death.

The acute infections caused by *Past. multocida* are characterized by a septicemia frequently accompanied by blood-vascular congestion, submucous and subserous hemorrhages, and an enteritis. The less acute form of the disease is accompanied by serofibrinous or hemorrhagic lesions in the mucosa and in tendon sheaths. The chronic type is characterized by necrotic areas, abscesses, and the accompanying debilitative conditions, such as anemia, diarrhea, and cachexia.

In chickens and turkeys cholera is seen in peracute, acute, and chronic forms. The less spectacular, but still destructive chronic type disease, is more frequently seen in some areas than the peracute form. Sporadic secondary infections of fowl are frequent in the air sacs and sinuses.

In addition to chickens, serious losses occur in domestic ducks and geese. Outbreaks of pasteurellosis may be encountered in wild fowl. Hudson has reported the disease in pheasants, and Quortrup, Queen, and Merovka observed an extensive epizootic in the wild duck in Texas.

In cattle, hemorrhagic septicemia occurs in either the pectoral or edematous forms. The pectoral form involves the lungs and the pleural cavity and is accompanied by petechial hemorrhages in those tissues. The edematous type appears as an extensive edema of the subcutaneous tissues and the organs and tissues of the peritoneal cavity. It appears that hemorrhagic septicemia seldom appears in the United States or Canada as an important epizootic. Recent observations have disclosed that shipping fever in Canada, once believed to have been a hemorrhagic septicemia, is nonsepticemic but is a bronchopneumonia. However, sporadic cases of hemorrhagic septicemia are still seen occasionally in the cow. The disease in calves is characterized by a typical pleuropneumonia. *Past. multocida* may localize in various tissues, including the brain. Isolation of the organism from a heifer showing symptoms of encephalitis has been recorded by Kingman. Numerous investigators have found the organism to be present in bovine mastitis.

Epizootic hemorrhagic septicemia of cattle, bison, and water buffaloes is an important and destructive disease most frequently seen in, but not limited to, central Africa and southeast Asia. This acute disease occurs infrequently in sheep and swine.

In sheep, *Past. multocida* is commonly encountered in pulmonary infections where it is usually thought to be a secondary invader. Biester, Schwarte, and Packer demonstrated that the organism may localize in the brain of a sheep, producing symptoms characteristic of encephalitis.

In swine, acute epizootic pasteurellosis is an infrequent disease on this continent. However, *Past. multocida* is an important secondary invader of the widespread virus pneumonia of pigs.

In horses, the organism is not common, although it has been found as a secondary invader in contagious pleuropneumonia.

In dogs and cats the organism is not considered as a common agent of disease. Its role as an occasional secondary invader in infections is no doubt related to the high carrier rate in the upper respiratory and digestive tracts of these species (Smith, 1955). Subcutaneous abscesses in cats, resulting from cat bites, frequently yield cultures of *Past. multocida.* Outbreaks of pasteurellosis in mink raised in captivity have been reported as initiated by feeding meat from another species of animal which had died of this disease.

In rabbits, *Past. multocida* is one of the causes of "snuffles," a disease of varying severity involving principally the upper and lower respiratory tracts, and often terminating as a septicemia. Subcutaneous abscesses in this species are frequently due to this organism.

Sporadic and epizootic infections occur in mice, rats, and other rodents. The animal species in which infections have been recorded are remarkably numerous.

In view of the broad range of animal species subject to *Past. multocida* infections, it is not surprising that occasional infections have been encountered in man. Olsen and Needham recovered the organism from cases of brochiectasis, empyema, chronic bronchitis, peritonsillar abscess, appendiceal abscess, and a joint infection. Other reports have dealt with pericarditis, pneumonia, pleurisy, peritonitis, and meningitis. The infections reported usually have been localized and chronic, indicating that man possesses considerable resistance to the organism. It is well known that dog and cat bites in man frequently result in infections with *Past. multocida*.

**Immunity.** Since Pasteur, in 1880, used an attenuated strain to immunize chickens against cholera, tissue aggressins, artificial aggressins, and bacterins have been employed for the prophylaxis of the pasteurelloses with usually disappointing results. Chemically killed broth bacterins prepared from a number of different strains of *Past. multocida* are still prepared, but no longer widely used unless combined with other species, e.g., *Cl. septicum* and *Cl. chauvoei*.

Bain, in 1954, developed an adjuvant type bacterin in which organisms were incorporated in lanolin and mineral oil. It has been used effectively in southeast Asia for the prevention of epizootic hemorrhagic septicemia in water buffaloes and cattle. A similar type adjuvant bacterin containing two different immunogenic or serologic types of *Past. multocida* was developed by Heddleston and associates (1958, 1959) for the prevention of fowl cholera. A bacterin consisting of lysed bacteria suspended in saponin has been used by Deply and Mir Chamsy for the prevention of epizootic hemorrhagic septicemia.

The latest information on serology and epizootiology suggests that the best success in active immunization should be expected in epizootic hemorrhagic septicemia. The variety of serotypes involved in the other pasteurelloses, including fowl cholera, suggests that immunization is of questionable value.

The use of hyperimmune serum to passively protect animals is no longer widely practiced.

**Diagnosis.** A tentative diagnosis of true hemorrhagic septicemia or fowl cholera can be made by demonstrating typical small bipolar coccobacillary organisms in blood smears stained by Wright's method. Organisms as a rule are readily recovered on blood agar, or by the subcutaneous inoculation of mice and rabbits and their subsequent culture. Morris, in 1958, described a selective medium containing tyrothricin, neomycin, and actidione for the isolation of *Past. multocida*. Definitive identification of *Past. multocida* is based on conformity to the differential characteristics given in Table 24.1.

### *Pasteurella hemolytica*

**Synonyms and History.** The first report of organisms typical of this species was made by Jones in 1921 when he reported a separate group of Pasteurella organisms which fermented lactose, did not produce indol, but did hemolyze blood. In 1932 Newsom and Cross isolated the organism from cattle and sheep and suggested the name *Pasteurella hemolytica*.

Several other reports of an organism which apparently belongs to this species have been made by a number of investigators. These include: Magnusson (1914) with an atypical hemorrhagic septicemia culture from a reindeer, Besemer (1917) with a calf strain, Spray (1923) with a group of *Pasteurella oviseptica* cultures, Jorgensen (1925) with organisms originating from the normal bacterial flora of cattle, Tanake (1926) with his buffalo cultures, Eddington (1930) with nine cattle cultures, Ochi (1931 and 1933) with six avirulent sheep strains, and Hellesnes (1935) with a virulent cattle strain. Rosenbusch and Merchant (1938) confirmed the results of Newsom and Cross with nine cultures.

**Distribution and Transmission.** Recent reports indicate that this organism has a wide host range and is probably worldwide in distribution. Like *Past. multocida* this organism apparently can be carried with impunity in the upper respiratory passages.

Transmission results from contact, inhalation, and by consumption of contaminated food and water.

**Morphology and Staining.** The organism is a short, nonmotile, encapsulated gram-negative rod which is indistinguishable from *Past. multocida* when recently isolated.

**Growth Requirements and Characteristics.** The growth requirements of this species are in general similar to those of *Past. multocida* although the need for enrichment of the media is greater with the former species.

On serum agar the colonies are round, smooth, and moist, resembling closely the smooth colonies of *Past. multocida*. Colonies composed of capsulated organisms are iridescent.

The so-called beta hemolysis is probably not a true hemolysis. A strain will lose its hemolytic capacity on repeated subculture. It returns, however, upon passage of the culture through mice or the chicken egg embryo. Hemolysis can sometimes be discerned only under the colony when the latter is scraped off the agar.

Growth in broth is usually diffuse.

**Resistance.** This organism does not survive on artificial media as long as *Past. multocida;* however, its resistance to antibiotics and other agents is essentially the same.

**Biochemical Properties.** Strains vary greatly in their fermentative capacity. Substrates that are usually fermented with the production of acid are lactose, maltose, saccharose, mannitol, glucose, dextrin, galactose, glycerol, inositol, fructose, raffinose, sorbitol, and xylose. Adonitol, salacin, rhamnose, and inulin are usually negative, while the fermentation of mannose, dulcitol, and arabinose is variable. Litmus milk is usually acidified and coagulated in 48 hours. This organism does not form indol; reduces nitrates to nitrites; does not produce methyl acetyl carbinol. All strains produce beta hemolysis on primary culture.

**Antigenic Structure and Toxins.** Carter, in 1956, found by means of an indirect hemagglutination technique that bovine strains of *Past. hemolytica* recovered from cases of shipping fever constituted one serological type on the basis of capsular substance. Later, employing a similar procedure, Biberstein and Gills identified 11 different capsular types from cattle, sheep, goats, pigs, and chickens. Upon employing a conventional agglutination test they found variation in the somatic antigens of the various types. Carter's and Biberstein's studies placed the pathogenic bovine strains in the Type 1 category. The remainder of Biberstein and Gills' strains from a variety of diseases were widely distributed among the 11 capsular serotypes.

Smith (1959, 1961) described two different varieties of *Past. hemolytica* on the basis of different cultural, biochemical, and pathological characteristics. He designated them Types A and T. In brief, the distinguishing features are:

Type A:
small gray colonies
arabinose + (7 days)
trehalose — (10 days)
more sensitive to penicillin
early loss of viability

Type T:
larger colonies, brownish centers
arabinose — (10 days)
trehalose + (2 days)
less sensitive to penicillin
viable for longer periods

Although these categories are not serological, Biberstein and Gills found that they contained different serotypes.

Exotoxins have not been reported.

**Pathogenicity.** *Past. hemolytica* is relatively nonpathogenic for mice and rabbits, and virulence is entirely lost after the cultures have grown on artificial media for some time.

This organism is frequently associated with pneumonias in cattle, sheep, goats, and occasionally swine. In these diseases it is usually considered an important secondary invader. The association of *Past. hemolytica* with pneumonia of cattle subjected to various stresses incidental to shipment is well known. As with *Past. multocida* infections, environmental factors are thought to be important in the initiation of infections. Investigations in Europe, Canada, and the United States by Florent and Godbille (1950), Carter (1954), Carter and McSherry (1955), and Collier *et al.* (1962) indicate that this organism has an important role in "shipping fever" or "stockyard's pneumonia."

A severe mastitis of ewes is caused by an organism originally referred to as *Past. mastididis,* but now considered identical to *Past. hemolytica.* A case of bovine mastitis due to this organism occurring during an outbreak of shipping fever was reported by Carter and Maplesden.

The primary role of *Past. hemolytica* in an important septicemic disease of lambs in Great Britain has been demonstrated (Stamp *et al.,* 1955). A similar disease of lambs was reported from California (Biberstein and Kennedy, 1959), and of pigs from England (Edwards, 1959).

Strains of *Past. hemolytica* are occasionally recovered from the respiratory tracts of chickens in the absence of any related abnormality. Cultures resembling *Past. hemolytica* but producing urease have been isolated from the upper respiratory tract and sputa of human beings (Henriksen and Jyssum, 1961). Their significance as pathogens is still in doubt.

**Immunity.** Strains of *Past. multocida* are included in some killed-culture bacterins for the prevention of pneumonias in cattle and sheep. The nature of the infections makes it difficult to determine by controlled experiments the efficacy of these products.

**Diagnosis.** This is based upon the isolation and identification of *Past. hemolytica* Of the various differential features listed in Table 24.1, beta hemolysis and failure to produce indol set this species apart from the more prevalent *Past. multocida.*

### *Pasteurella pestis*

**Synonyms and History.** *Bacterium pestis, Bacterium pestis bubonicae, Bacillus pestis.*

This organism has been the cause of numerous pandemics of bubonic plague or "black death" throughout periods in the history of man. It has been estimated that 10,000,000 persons died of this disease in India during the period 1896 to 1917. It was during this epidemic that the organism was first isolated and described by Kitasato and by Yersin, working independently, but reporting their work in 1894.

**Distribution and Transmission.** Although for many years *Past. pestis* was considered a homogeneous species, it is now known that three biologic varieties of epidemiological importance are recognizable. The following classification has been proposed (Girard): *Pasteurella pestis*:

var. *orientalis,* nitrite + glycerol —
var. *antiqua,* nitrite + glycerol +
var. *mediaevalis,* nitrite — glycerol +

Var. *orientalis* is found in southeast Asia, north Africa, and South America. Var. *antiqua* occurs in central Asia and central

Africa while var. *mediaevalis* is found in Turkey, Iraq, and southern Russia.

Widespread epidemics of bubonic plague have not occurred anyplace in the world since the turn of the present century. The organism has become established in the rodent population of various continents where a chronic type of the disease has become endemic in man. These areas include parts of China, India, Siberia, southern Russia, the Uganda district of east central Africa, western Africa, south Africa, and in Argentina.

In California Meyer and his coworkers have reported the organism from squirrels and other rodents in which it has caused sporadic cases of the disease known as sylvatic plague.

The transmission of plague to man governs the type of disease produced. The rat was recognized as being related to the disease in 1903, and in 1908 the rat fleas *Xenopsylla cheopsis* and *Ceratophyllus fasciatus* were found to be carriers of the organism. The bubonic form of the disease in man results from the bite of the flea. The pneumonic type of plague may result from the generalization of the disease due to flea bites, but is more common during cold seasons when there is direct transmission of the organism from person to person in close contact. The infection among rodents is transmitted by fleas, by contact, by food infection, and by cannibalistic practices.

**Morphology and Staining.** *Past. pestis* is a short, nonmotile rod measuring 0.5μ to 0.7μ in width and 1.25μ to 1.75μ in length. In body fluids it appears singly, in pairs, or in short chains. The organism is extremely pleomorphic in bubonic lesions and on salt agar, forming filaments, clublike forms, and yeastlike cells (Fig. 24.4). In the animal body the organism produces a thin layer of mucoid capsular material. It is nonmotile and nonsporeforming.

The organism is stained easily by ordinary dyes and is distinctly bipolar. It is gram-negative.

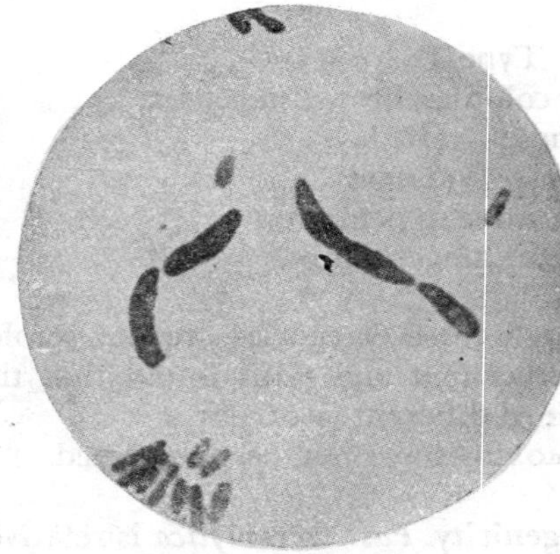

FIG. 24.4—**Pasteurella pestis** involution forms on salt agar, ×2,000. (From Nowak: Documenta Microbiologica, courtesy Gustav Fischer.)

**Growth Requirements and Characteristics.** This organism grows best at a temperature varying from 25° to 30°C. It is aerobic and facultatively anaerobic. A pH range of 6.2 to 7 is best suited for growth. It grows on all ordinary culture media, although growth is favored by the presence of serum.

On solid media, colonies of the organisms are flat, gray to grayish-white, translucent, iridescent, undulate with a notched margin and a raised center (Fig. 24.5). Variant colonies, considered rough and avirulent, are larger, more opaque, and have a crateriform center.

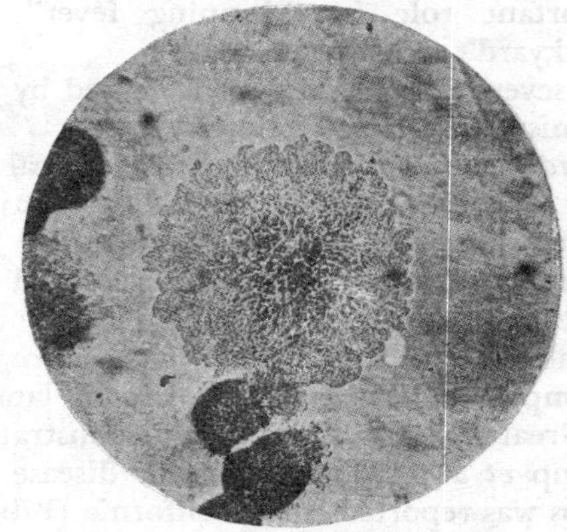

FIG. 24.5—**Pasteurella pestis** colony on gelatin plate, ×110. (From Nowak: Documenta Microbiologica, courtesy Gustav Fischer.)

In broth the organism grows moderately, producing a floccular deposit which does not disintegrate upon shaking.

The organism is not soluble in bile and grows on MacConkey's bile salt medium. A thin layer of growth is usually formed on potato.

**Resistance.** *Past. pestis* is killed by 55°C. in 5 minutes and immediately by 5 per cent phenol. It is not resistant to drying or to direct sunlight. Cultures of the organism kept in a refrigerator will survive for months if the culture tubes are sealed.

**Biochemical Properties.** The organism produces acid but no gas from glucose, maltose, mannitol, salicin, arabinose, and some strains from dextrin, glycerol, and xylose. It does not ferment lactose, saccharose, inulin, dulcitol, raffinose, adonitol, or sorbitol; does not produce indol; does not reduce nitrates; produces a small amount of $H_2S$. The organism is catalase positive, methyl red positive, and Voges-Proskauer negative. It produces $NH_3$; does not reduce methylene blue; does not change litmus milk; does not liquefy gelatin.

**Antigenic Structure and Toxins.** *Past. pestis* appears to be serologically homogeneous. The first antigenic components studied were thermolabile envelope and somatic factors which were identified by precipitin procedures (Schütze, 1932). Studies carried out in recent years and reviewed by Meyer have disclosed the presence of a toxin and also a Fraction 1 which is thought to be derived from the capsular envelope. The latter component can be used in various serological procedures. Injection of animals with toxin results in the production of antitoxin which does not confer protection without envelope antibodies. Treatment of the toxin with formalin results in a toxoid. Other antigens and substances referred to as pesticins have been identified.

The close serologic relationship of this organism with *Past. pseudotuberculosis* is indicated by the fact that of 16 antigens possessed by *Past. pestis,* 13 are shared with *Past. pseudotuberculosis* (Bhagavan *et al.,* 1956).

**Pathogenicity.** *Past. pestis* is pathogenic to man and various species of rodents including the rat, mouse, squirrel, wild guinea pig, rabbit, and hare. Experimentally, the organism produces infection readily in mice, rats, guinea pigs, rabbits, and monkeys, but cats, dogs, pigs, cattle, sheep, goats, and horses are difficult to infect. With the exception of the sparrow, birds are difficult to infect.

The disease in man is of primary importance. The septicemic and pneumonic forms of the disease are fatal in 60 to 95 per cent of the cases. The bubonic form of the disease is most common but is not as fatal.

Different forms of the disease are found in rats during natural infections. The acute type is characterized by blood-vascular congestion over the entire body. The subacute type causes enlargement of superficial lymph nodes accompanied by edema and hemorrhage. The spleen is enlarged, and the liver is covered with small hemorrhages and areas of focal necrosis. In the chronic form the organism localizes in the lymph nodes, liver, and spleen, where areas of caseation necrosis and abscess formation are produced.

Experimental animals, particularly guinea pigs, show typical buboes following subcutaneous inoculation, and the liver and spleen are studded with necrotic foci.

**Immunity.** One attack of the disease produces an immunity to further infections. In 1895 Yersin, Calmette, and Borrel produced an immunity in rabbits and horses by the injection of killed cultures. The serum taken from immune horses protected rabbits against inoculations of virulent organisms. Haffkine, in 1897, produced the first successful human vaccine consisting of heat-killed broth cultures prepared by repeated reinoculation of the medium over a period of six weeks. Avirulent and attenuated vaccines which are thought to produce a better immunity than heat-killed products have been used also.

Passive immunity by the use of hyperimmune horse serum has been reported by several investigators to be of value during the early stages of the disease.

**Diagnosis.** Direct smears which are made from material obtained by puncturing an enlarged lymph node often reveal the presence of this typical bipolar organism. Cultures and guinea pig inoculation are often essential for definite diagnosis.

Great care must be followed in the collection of suspected fluid and tissue from human cases and from dead rats for the purpose of laboratory examination. Such materials must be placed in tight containers which are distinctly labeled.

### *Pasteurella tularensis*

**Synonyms and History.** *Bacillus tularense, Bacterium tularense, Brucella tularense.*

*Pasteurella tularensis* was first observed by McCoy in 1911 in a plaguelike disease of the ground squirrel, *Citellus beechyi,* in Tulare County, California. In 1912 McCoy and Chapin succeeded in isolating the organism on egg-yolk medium. They named the organism *Bacterium tularense* and were able to reproduce the disease with cultures.

The greatest part of the literature concerning this organism and the disease which it produces has been contributed by Francis and his coworkers since 1919.

The position of this organism in the genus Pasteurella is open to serious question. Francis has shown that it has a definite antigenic relationship to the Brucella group and upon that basis Topley and Wilson refer to the organism as *Brucella tularensis.* Other investigators are reticent to follow this classification. Bergey's Manual listed the organism as *Pasteurella tularensis* in 1939; Zinsser and Bayne-Jones, 1939, prefer to take a course between the Brucella and Pasteurella and call it *Bacterium tularense.*

In 1932 Reimann published a comparative study of *Pasteurella pseudotuberculosis, Pasteurella tularensis,* and *Pasteurella pestis* in which he concludes that all three of the organisms are closely related and should be classified in the same group.

**Distribution and Transmission.** The organism is widely distributed throughout the world, having been reported from Japan, Russia, Norway, Sweden, and Austria. On this continent, it has been reported from Canada and from forty-six of the states and the District of Columbia.

*Past. tularensis* is transmitted in a variety of ways. It can be carried by bloodsucking flies, ticks, lice, and fleas. Cases result from contact with infected animals. The hair or fur from infected animals may carry the organism to the eyes or into the respiratory tract of man. The organism is not transmitted by contact from person to person.

Among wild animals the organism is usually transmitted by insect vectors and by cannibalism. It has been demonstrated that the organism passes from the parent tick with the eggs, thence to the larvae and the nymph stages, but not to the adult. The presence of the organism in insects results in the appearance of the greatest number of cases of the disease among wild animals during the late summer months. Cases of tularemia in man also occur during summer months, but the disease is most prevalent in the colder months during the hunting season for rabbits and squirrels. It is obvious that the infection remains endemic in rabbit and squirrel populations during the winter season or that resistant carriers of the organism exist.

An outbreak of tularemia in a human population in Russia was described by Tsareva as a water-borne infection. Presumably the water had been contaminated by water rats infected with the disease. The isolation of the organism from cold-water streams in western United States also indicates that the infection may be spread by water. Pahm found that the organism may be transmitted from an infected hog to man during the process of butchering.

**Morphology and Staining.** *Past. tularensis* is a small, pleomorphic, nonmotile rod, 0.2$\mu$ by 0.3$\mu$ to 0.7$\mu$ by 3$\mu$ in size. In young cultures ovoid and bacillary forms are found, but in old cultures the organism is coccoid. It is nonmotile and nonspore-forming. Clear zones around the organism considered capsules are observed in smears of animal tissue.

The organism is stained unevenly with most of the common dyes, revealing forms which appear swollen on one end and pointed on the other. Smears from animal tissues show the presence of many bipolar forms when methylene blue or carbol fuchsin is used. It is gram-negative.

**Growth Requirements and Characteristics.** The organism grows best at 37°C. and in a pH range of 6.8 to 7.3. Although considered aerobic, reduced oxygen tension and large inocula assist the growth of primary cultures.

*Past. tularensis* cannot be cultured on ordinary media. McCoy and Chapin found that egg yolk contained some essential growth substance. Francis subsequently demonstrated that when cystine or cysteine hydrochloride was added to the medium better growth resulted; consequently, either of those substances is incorporated in media which are used in the study of the organism. Traub and coworkers have listed 13 essential amino acids in a medium they recommend. Growth is also stimulated by the presence of a small piece of rabbit spleen in the medium. Larson has observed that the organism grows readily in the chicken embryo when introduced in the yolk sac. Ransmeier and Stekol demonstrated that thioglycollic acid and glutathione could be substituted for cystine or cysteine.

On a solid medium the organism forms minute, dewdrop-like, translucent colonies which vary from a viscid to a buttery consistency.

**Resistance.** The organism is killed in 10 minutes at 58°C. and is destroyed in 1 per cent tricresol in 2 minutes. The organism remains viable for years when present in spleen tissue preserved in glycerine and kept at —14°C. It has been found viable in the feces of bedbugs after drying for 26 days.

*Past. tularensis* is sensitive to streptomycin, some sulfonamides, and the tetracycline group of antibiotics.

**Biochemical Properties.** *Past. tularensis* is not as saccharolytic as the other members of the genus. It produces only a slight amount of acid from glucose, glycerol, maltose, mannose, fructose, and dextrin. Hydrogen sulfide is produced in a cystine medium. Catalase is produced.

**Antigenic Structure and Toxins.** The different strains of *Past. tularensis* are antigenically homogenous. An antigenic relationship exists with *Brucella abortus* and *Brucella melitensis*, but neither organism is able to absorb the homologous agglutinin from *Past. tularensis* antiserum.

Exotoxin is not produced.

**Pathogenicity.** The organism has been found to produce natural infection in the following animals: ground squirrels in California and Utah; wild rabbits and hares throughout the United States; wild rats and wild mice in California; sheep in Idaho; quail and grouse in Minnesota; wild rabbits in Japan, Norway, and Canada; water rats in Russia; beaver in Montana; beaver and muskrats in Canada; chipmunks in Idaho. McKeever and associates reported significant positive serum reactions in various wild mammals of southwestern Georgia and northwestern Florida. The organism is known to infect coyotes, foxes, and dogs which have eaten infected rabbits. Tularemia is a fatal septicemia in rodents, particularly in rabbits. The lesions of the disease are most predominant in the liver where numerous areas of focal necrosis are observed. Similar lesions are also found in the spleen, lungs, and bone marrow in some cases.

The etiological relationship of the Pasteurellae to horses has never been considered of any great importance, but occasional infections have been reported. Claus, Newhall, and Mee isolated *Past. tularensis* from a foal which had died following an acute illness. Other animals in the herd showed positive blood agglutination titers. These authors suggested that the infection may be found in areas where tularemia is endemic during tick seasons.

In a study of the comparative susceptibility of various laboratory animals, Downs and associates have found that white mice, rabbits, guinea pigs, hamsters, and cotton rats are all susceptible. Chicks and dogs are less susceptible than the above animals. In dogs the infection remains localized. Young monkeys succumb to an injection of as few as 20 bacteria but do localize the bacteria more effectively than any other experimental animal except the dog.

According to Lillie and Larson, the golden hamster is markedly susceptible to *Past. tularensis,* showing extensive lesions following experimental inoculation by a variety of routes.

In man, the disease has been divided into as many as five clinical types.

1. The *ulceroglandular type* is characterized by the formation of a papule in the skin which develops into an ulcer and is accompanied by enlargement of the regional lymph nodes.
2. The *oculoglandular type* is typified by a conjunctivitis accompanied by the enlargement of the regional lymph glands.
3. The *glandular type* is not accompanied by skin or eye lesions but presents enlargement of skeletal lymph glands.
4. The *typhoid type* is characterized by a high temperature and evidently represents the septicemic or bacteremic stage of the disease.
5. The *pneumonic type* is often an extension of any of the above types and represents the localization of the organism in the lungs. This type is the most fatal.

Lide has described a case of congenital tularemia which occurred in the mother during the eighth month of pregnancy causing the death of the fetus. Necrotic granulomatous lesions were found in various organs of the fetus, and organisms morphologically similar to *Past. tularensis* were found in chorionic villi.

**Immunity.** Recovery from tularemia results in a permanent immunity. This is true of wild animals, experimental animals, and man. Specific agglutinins remain in the circulation for years after recovery from the disease; this has resulted in the diagnosis of infections years after recovery has taken place.

An acetone-extracted vaccine prepared from peptone broth has been shown by Downs and his associates to be effective in producing immunity in the white rat against experimental infection. The essential antigenic substance was found to be protein in nature and the vaccine resisted heating to 100°C. and remained effective after storage in a refrigerator for eight months. Coriell, Downs, and Clapp noted that Swiss mice could be protected by vaccination, but a high percentage of the animals which survived the challenge inoculation continued to harbor virulent organisms for several weeks. Larson prepared an ether-extracted vaccine from yolk sacs of infected chicken embryos which was effective in immunizing white rats. A living vaccine consisting of avirulent organisms is used in the Soviet Union as part of the tularemia control program (Tigertt, 1962).

Hyperimmune serum prepared in horses, goats, rabbits, or sheep has been found effective experimentally, and according to Foshay is valuable in clinical cases of the disease in man. Larson has observed that if immune serum is withheld for 24 hours after the injection of *Past. tularensis* white rats are not protected against infection.

**Diagnosis.** The disease in rodents is more accurately diagnosed by the isolation of the organism. For this purpose it is necessary to inject the tissue emulsion from a suspected lesion into the guinea pig or white rat. This animal usually dies within a week, and cultures are made from the heart blood, spleen, and liver on blood-glucose, cystine agar, or coagulated egg-yolk media.

In human cases showing generalized symptoms, the blood may be injected into guinea pigs from which the organism can be isolated in case of death.

If the disease has passed the first week, the agglutination test can be used as a means of diagnosis in any animal or in man. Infected animals and man show allergic reactions to intradermal injections of oxidized bacillary suspensions of *Past. tularensis*; however, the value of such a test in the diagnosis of a suspected case is limited by the fact that skin allergy persists for some time following recovery from the disease.

### *Pasteurella pseudotuberculosis*

**Synonyms and History.** In 1883 Malassez and Vignal observed an organism which was isolated from guinea pigs after they had been injected with material taken from lesions of human tuberculosis. Whether this organism was the one under discussion is doubted. The first authentic report of the organism was made by Pfeiffer in 1889 when he referred to it as *Bacterium pseudotuberculosis rodentium*.

Since the organism is motile, some question its inclusion in the Pasteurella group. Reimann and Rose, however, have shown that it is quite similar to *Past. pestis* and *Past. tularensis* in many respects which offset the fact that flagella are present.

**Distribution and Transmission.** The organism is distributed throughout the world and produces spontaneous infections in rodents, turkeys, canaries, and pigeons. Infections occur less frequently in man and in some domestic animal species.

The organism is probably transmitted by the ingestion of infected food. It is not known to be transmitted by insects.

**Morphology and Staining.** *Past. pseudotuberculosis* is a small, pleomorphic coccobacillus which is similar to *Past. pestis.* The organism is motile in broth cultures incubated at 22°C. It is noncapsulated.

The organism is stained bipolar and is gram-negative.

**Growth Requirements and Characteristics.** The organism is aerobic and facultatively anaerobic. It grows well at 30°C. and at temperatures below and above this figure. It grows well on all ordinary culture media and is uninfluenced by serum or dextrose.

The colonies of the organism on an agar surface are round, umbonate, finely granular, translucent, grayish-yellow, even-bordered with an opaque center and a flat, clearer periphery showing striations. The colonies are buttery in consistency. A rough variant with an irregular surface and a crenated edge has been described. Cultural characteristics are considerably influenced by the incubation temperature. At 37°C., "R" forms predominate, while at 22°C. colonies are moist, slimy, and smooth.

At 22°C. growth in broth is diffuse, while at 37°C. there is considerable sedimentation and a pellicle may develop. Colonies on MacConkey's agar resemble those of the Salmonella. On potato the organism produces a thin, yellowish membranous growth which later turns brown.

**Resistance.** *Past. pseudotuberculosis* is not resistant to ordinary disinfectants. It is killed by a temperature of 60°C. in 10 minutes.

It is sensitive to streptomycin, neomycin, the tetracycline group, penicillin, and the sulfonamides.

**Biochemical Properties.** The organism

produces acid, but no gas, from glucose, maltose, mannitol, salicin, arabinose, fructose, galactose, rhamnose, and glycerol; some strains ferment saccharose. It does not ferment lactose, dulcitol, sorbitol, or raffinose; does not produce indol; reduces nitrates; produces $H_2S$ and $NH_3$. The organism is positive to the catalase test and the methyl red test but is negative to the Voges-Proskauer test. It reduces methylene blue; turns litmus milk slightly alkaline; does not liquefy gelatin.

**Antigenic Structure and Toxins.** The organism possesses two types of antigens, one a heat-labile H or flagellar antigen, and the other a heat-stable O or somatic antigen. The flagellar antigen is formed only at temperatures below 25°C. On the basis of the somatic antigens, five agglutination groups have been identified with a number of subtypes identified by agglutinin absorption procedures (Thal, 1954; Knapp, 1956). One of the somatic antigens is related to the O antigen of *Salmonella schottmeulleri*. This organism shares a number of antigens with *Past. pestis.*

An endotoxin was prepared by lysis of two different strains of *Past. pseudotuberculosis* with bacteriophage by Lazarus and Nozawa. The endotoxin produces marked circulatory changes and death in less than 12 hours in rabbits, guinea pigs, and white mice. In addition to death in experimental animals, the endotoxin in small doses produces skin necrosis of guinea pigs.

**Pathogenicity.** *Past. pseudotuberculosis* causes a condition called pseudotuberculosis in rodents, especially guinea pigs. The disease may be an acute septicemia or may follow a chronic course. In the chronic type of the disease the organism localizes in the mesenteric lymph nodes, the liver, the spleen, and the lungs, where it produces small necrotic nodules. A severe diarrhea usually accompanies the infection. Leader and Baker have reported a fatal disease in the chinchilla from which the organism was isolated.

Rosenwald and Dickinson isolated the organism from sick and dead turkeys in ten different flocks in Oregon. This organism has been isolated, likewise, from turkeys by Blaxland in England.

Other species of animals, in addition to those mentioned, are susceptible to this organism. Jamieson and Soltys have isolated it from cases of epididymo-orchitis in rams in Scotland. Watson and Hunter found it in an aborted lamb in Great Britain. Eieland, of Norway, has observed it in silver foxes and in swine. Experimentally, the organism has produced infection in the guinea pig, mouse, rabbit, wild rat, dog, cat, and horse. Guinea pigs which are inoculated with the organism usually die in two to three weeks.

Since the report of 17 cases by Hassig and associates in 1949, infections in man with *Past. pseudotuberculosis* have been recognized with increasing frequency. Infections assume one of two forms. The more serious is a typhoid-like disease with swelling of the spleen and liver, and terminal jaundice with death in two to three weeks. The less serious form simulates appendicitis and is characterized by an abscess-forming mesenteric lymphadenitis (Knapp, 1954; Knapp and Masshoff, 1954).

**Immunity.** Immunization against infections is mostly of academic interest. Laboratory animals can be protected by inoculation with avirulent organisms, and antitoxic immunity can be produced with toxoid.

**Diagnosis.** The differentiation of this organism from *Past. pestis* is most important. This can be done only after the organism is isolated in pure culture. The presence of flagella and the alkaline reaction produced in litmus milk serve to distinguish this organism from the one of bubonic plague. Identification of strains of *Past. pseudotuberculosis* by means of specific phages has been described by Girard (1943).

### Pasteurella-like Organisms

Bacteria closely resembling *Past. mul-*

*tocida* but not altogether typical are occasionally recovered from animals. They are probably commensals in the upper respiratory tract, and are encountered as opportunists or secondary invaders especially in respiratory disease. Their occurrence would appear to be more frequent in poultry than in the other domestic species.

Jawetz recovered an organism from the pneumonic lungs of mice which he called *Past. pneumotropica.* It was also isolated from guinea pigs, rats, and hamsters. In its cultural and biochemical characteristics it closely resembled *Past. multocida.* One departure from the majority of strains of *Past. multocida* was the consistent fermentation of lactose and a lower virulence for laboratory animals.

An organism tentatively referred to as *Past. gallinarum* was recovered by Hall and associates from chickens with lesions characteristic of cholera and from other respiratory infections. One feature which distinguishes it from *Past. multocida* is failure to produce indol.

### *Pasteurella anatipestifer*

This organism which has recently been placed in the Pasteurella genus was first recovered from ducklings by Hendrickson and Hilbert in 1932. They named it *Pfeifferella anatipestifer*. Bruner and Fabricant, in 1954, studied cultures of an organism isolated from ducklings which fitted the description of the above, and concluded it should be classified as *Moraxella anatipestifer.* There is still some question as to the significance of this organism in the highly acute disease with which it is associated.

*Past. anatipestifer* is a short, gram-negative rod occurring singly, in pairs, and in short chains. It is nonmotile and does not form spores. Growth is best obtained in a medium containing horse serum and in 5 to 10 per cent carbon dioxide. Colonies on solid media are small and dewdrop-like. In thioglycollate medium a ring of growth is noted 1 cm. below the surface. It does not ferment carbohydrates but does liquefy gelatin, coagulated blood serum, and coagulated egg medium.

## REFERENCES


AVI-DOR, Y., and YANIV, N. Jour. Bact. 63:751, 1952.

BAIN, R. V. S. Nature 173:584, 1954.

BELL, J. F., *et al.* Jour. Inf. Dis. 97:162, 1955.

BERGEY, D. H., *et al.* Bergey's Manual of Determinative Bacteriology. Williams & Wilkins Co., Baltimore, 1957.

BHAGAVAN, N. V., *et al.* Proc. Soc. Exp. Biol. Med. 91:353, 1956.

BIBERSTEIN, E. L., and GILLS, M. G. Jour. Comp. Path. 72:316, 1962.

———, and KENNEDY, P. C. Septicemic Pasteurellosis in Lambs. Amer. Jour. Vet. Res. 20:94, 1959.

BIESTER, H. E., *et al.* Amer. Jour. Vet. Res. 3:268–73, 1942.

BRUNER, D. W., and FABRICANT, I. Cornell Vet. 44:461, 1954.

CARTER, G. R. Canad. Jour. Med. Sci. 30:48, 1952.

———. Canad. Jour. Comp. Med. 18:359, 1954.

———. Amer. Jour. Vet. Res. 16:481, 1955.

———. Canad. Jour. Microbiol. 2:483, 1956.

———. Studies on *Pasteurella multocida.* II. Identification of Antigenic Characteristics and Colonial Variants. Amer. Jour. Vet. Res. 18:210, 1957. III. A Serological Survey of Bovine and Porcine Strains From Various Parts of the World. Amer. Jour. Vet. Res. 18:437, 1957.

———. Brit. Vet. Jour. 114:356, 1958.

———. Vet. Rec. 73:1052, 1961.

———. Vet. Rec. 75:1264, 1963.

———, and BAIN, R. V. S. Pasteurellosis (*Past. multocida*). A Review Stressing Recent Developments. Vet. Rev. Annot. 6:105, 1960.

———. and MCSHERRY, B. J. Canad. Jour. Comp. Med. 19:177, 1955.

CLAUS, K. D., *et al.* Isolation of *Pasteurella tularensis* From Foals. Jour. Bact. 78:294, 1959.

COGHLAN, J. D. Isolation of *Past. multocida* From Human Peritoneal Pus and a Study of Its Relationship to Other Strains of the Same Species. Jour. Path. Bact. 76:45, 1958.

COLLIER, J. R., *et al.* The Combined Effect of Infectious Bovine Rhinotracheitis Virus and *Pasteurella hemolytica* on Cattle. Amer. Jour. Vet. Res. 21:195, 1960.
———, *et al.* Jour. Amer. Vet. Med. Assn. 140:807, 1962.
CORIELL, L. L., *et al.* Jour. Immunol. 56:245, 1947.
DEPLY, L. P., and MIR CHAMSY, H Arch. Inst. Hessarek 6:32, 1949.
DOWNS, C. M., *et al.* Jour. Immunol. 56:217, 229, 1947.
EDWARDS, B. C. Vet. Rec. 71:208, 1959.
EVELETH, D F., *et al.* Vet. Med. 64:73, 1949.
FLORENT, A., and GODBILLE, M. Ann. Med. Vet. 94:337, 1950.
GALE, C., and SMITH, H. R. Studies on Shipping Fever of Cattle. Amer. Jour. Vet. Res. 19:815, 1958.
GAY, F. P., *et al.* Agents of Disease and Host Resistance. Chap. 34. Charles C Thomas, Baltimore, 1935.
GIRARD, G. Ann. Inst. Past. 69:52, 1943.
———. Ann. Rev. Microbiol. 9:253, 1955.
HAAGSMA, J. Tijdschr. Diergeneesk 89:1225, 1233, 1964.
HALL, W. J., *et al.* Amer. Jour. Vet. Res. 16:598, 1955.
HAMDY, A. H., and POUNDEN, W. D. Experimental Production of Pneumonia in Lambs. Amer. Jour. Vet. Res. 20:78, 1959.
———, *et al.* Microbial Agents Associated With Pneumonia in Slaughtered Lambs. Amer. Jour. Vet. Res. 20:87, 1959.
HASSIG, A., *et al.* Med. Wschr. 79:971, 1949.
HEDDLESTON, K. L., and HALL, W. J. Avian Dis. 2:322, 1958.
———, and REISINGER, R. C. Avian Dis. 3:397, 1959.
———, and ———. Avian Dis. 6:315, 1962.
HENDRICKSON, J. M., and HILBERT, K. F. Cornell Vet. 22:239, 1932.
HENRIKSEN, S. D., and JYSSUM, K. Acta Path. Microbiol Scand. 50:443, 1961.
HUDSON, C. B. Jour. Amer. Vet. Med. Assn. 104:211, 1944.
JAMIESON, S., and SOLTYS, M. A. Vet. Rec. 59:351, 1947.
JAWETZ, E. Jour Infect. Dis 86:172, 1950.
———, and BAKER, W. H. Jour. Infect. Dis. 86:184, 1950.
KITT, T. Ueber eine experimentelle, der Rinderseuche ähnliche Infectionskrankheit. Sitz. d. Gesell. f. Morph. u. Phy., I, 1885, Munchen.
KNAPP, W. Zentralbl. f. Bakt. I. Abt. (Orig.) 161:422, 1954.
———, and MASSHOFF, W. Dtsch. Med. Wschr. 79:1266, 1954.
———, and ———. Zeitschr. f. Hyg., Bd. 143:261, 1956.
LANGFORD, E. V. Canad. Jour. Comp. Med. 18:28, 1954.
LARSON, C. L. The Growth of *Past. tularensis* in the Yolk Sac of Developing Chick Embryo. Pub. Health Rept., Wash., 60:587, 1945.
———. Immunization of White Rats Against Infections With *Past. tularensis*. Pub. Health Rept., Wash., 60: 725, 1945.
———. A Serum Protection Test in Tularemia Infections in White Rats. Pub. Health Rept., Wash., 62:1793, 1947.
LAZARUS, A. S., and NOZAWA, M. M. Jour. Bact. 56:187, 1948.
LEADER, R. W., and BAKER, G. A. Paper No. 1275, Wash. Agr. Exp. Sta., Wash. St. Coll., Pullman, 1953.
LIDE, T. N. Arch. Path. 43:165, 1947.
LILLIE, R. D., and LARSON, C. L. Pub. Health Rept., Wash., 60:1243, 1945.
LITTLE, P. A., and LYON, B. M. Amer. Jour. Vet. Res. 4:110–12, 1943.
LUNDGREN, D. L., *et al.* Tularemia in the Coyote, *Canis lastrans lestes* Merriam. Jour. Inf. Dis. 101:154, 1957.
MCGEACHIE, J. Isolation of *Past. septica* (*Past. multocida*) From a Lion-Bite and Lion's Mouth. Jour. Path. Bact. 75:467, 1958.
MCKEEVER, S., *et al.* Jour. Inf. Dis. 103:120, 1958.
MAPLESDEN, D. C., and CARTER, G. R. Canad. Jour. Comp. Med. 19:295, 1955.
MEYER, K. F. *In* Dubos, Bacterial and Mycotic Infections of Man. 4th Ed., p. 663. J. B. Lippincott Co., Philadelphia, 1965.
MOLLERET, H. H., and DESTOMBES, P. L'Adenite Mesenterique aigue a *Pasteurella pseudotuberculosis*. Masson et Cie, Paris, 1960.
MORGAN, B. B. Tularemia in Wisconsin. Trans. Wis. Acad. Sci. Arts and Let., 39:1, 1949.
MORRIS, E. J. Jour. Gen. Microbiol. 19:305, 1958.

Muysson, J. R., and Carter, G. R. Canad. Jour. Microbiol. 5:122, 1959.
Namioka, S., and Murata, M. Cornell Vet. 51:498, 1961.
———, and ———. Cornell Vet. 51:507, 1961.
———, and ———. Cornell Vet. 51:522, 1961.
———, *et al.* Cornell Vet. 53:41, 1963.
Olsen, A. M., and Needham, G. M. Amer. Jour. Med. Sci. 224:77, 1952.
Owen, C. R., *et al.* Jour. Inf. Dis. 97:167, 1955.
Parker, R. R. Pub. Health Rept., Wash., 60:17, 1945.
Pestana, B. R., *et al.* Pasteurelose Humana. Revista do Inst. Adolfo Lutz, 1:357–60, 1941.
Priestley, F. W. Jour. Comp. Path. Therap. 49:348, 1936.
Pullen, R. L., and Stuart, B. M. Jour. Amer. Med. Assn. 129:495–500, 1945.
Quortrup, E. R., *et al.* Jour. Amer. Vet. Med. Assn. 108:94–100, 1946.
Ransmeier, J. C., and Stekol, J. A. Proc. Soc. Exp. Biol. 51:85, 1942.
Roberts, R. S. Jour. Comp. Path. 57:261, 1947.
Rosenbusch, C. T., and Merchant, I. A. Jour. Bact. 37:69, 1939.
Rosenwald, A. S., and Dickinson, E. M. Amer. Jour. Vet. Res. 5:246–49, 1944.
Smith, G. R. Nature 183:1132, 1959.
———. Jour. Comp. Path. 81:431, 1961.
Smith, H. C. Jour. Amer. Vet. Med. Assn. 124:147, 1954.
Smith, J. E. Jour. Comp. Path. 65:239, 1955.
Stagg, G., *et al.* Experimental Infections of Native Animals With *Pasteurella tularensis*. Jour. Inf. Dis. 99:34, 1956.
Stamp, J. T., *et al.* Jour. Comp. Path. 65:183, 1955.
Swartz, M. N., and Kunz, L. J. *Pasteurella multocida* Infections in Man: Report of 2 Cases—Meningitis and Infected Cat Bite. New England Jour. Med. 261:889, 1959.
Thall, E. Untersuchungen über *Pasteurella pseudotuberculosis* unter besonderer Beriicksicht igung ihres immunologischenverhaltens, Lund, Berlingska, Boktryckeriet, 1954.
Tigertt, W. D. Bact. Rev. 26:354, 1962.
Traub, A., *et al.* Jour. Bact. 70:68, 1955.
Tunnicliff, E. A. Pasteurella Mastitis in Ewes. Vet. Med. 44:498, 1949.
Watson, W. A., and Hunter, D. The Isolation of *Pasteurella pseudotuberculosis* From an Ovine Fetus. Vet. Rec. 72:770, 1960.

# 25

# The Genera Hemophilus and Moraxella

In classifying bacteria, it is often difficult to determine the appropriate place for all of them. Such is the case of the genera Hemophilus and Moraxella. The former genus has become well established because it has certain distinguishing characteristics. The latter, however, has not become as well established, especially in its relationship to the genus Hemophilus, yet both are classified in the family Brucellaceae. Representative species of both genera are coccobacilli, but the similarity appears to end with this characteristic. The fact that species of the genus Moraxella do not require X- and V-factors for growth would easily distinguish them from Hemophilus.

## THE GENUS HEMOPHILUS

It was because of the stimulating effect of hemoglobin on these organisms that the name Hemophilus was created. The substance in hemoglobin was not injured by heat and it became known as X-factor. It was then found that the iron complex in hemoglobin called *heme* (hemin) was the substance promoting growth. Vegetable juices and yeast extract were also found to contain a substance essential for the growth of many of the species of this genus. This was called V-factor. It is now known that this is a coenzyme 1 (see Chapter 3). Considerable research has centered around the Hemophilus group because of the dependence of many of the species on heme and coenzyme 1. Many species of bacteria are able to produce these enzymes and they function in the cellular metabolism of animals and plants. The organisms are small, coccoid, nonmotile, nonsporeforming bacilli that are found, for the most part, in the respiratory tracts of animals and man. They are frequently associated with the disease, influenza; consequently, they are often referred to as the influenza group.

Many of the species which are placed in this group are not significant as inciters of disease in animals and man. Some of them have been described by only a few investigators and are not considered of great importance; however, there are a few species which are important factors in human and animal infections.

The species which are of particular interest to students in veterinary bacteriology are:

*Hemophilus influenzae*—associated with human influenza.

*Hemophilus suis*—associated with swine influenza.

*Hemophilus canis*—found in prepucial secretions of dogs.

*Hemophilus gallinarum*—associated with infectious coryza of fowls.

*Hemophilus ovis*—isolated from a respiratory infection of sheep.

*Hemophilus cuniculi*—found in subcutaneous abscesses of rabbits.

### Relationship of *Hemophilus influenzae* to *Hemophilus suis*

A most unusual and interesting relationship exists between human influenza and swine influenza. The diseases in the two animals are symptomatically and pathologically alike, so definite interest is attached to the two organisms which have been isolated from typical cases of the disease in man and in swine.

*H. influenzae* was first described by Pfeiffer in 1892 and was conceded to be the cause of human influenza. This conclusion was accepted as true until the pandemic of influenza in 1918 when many investigators failed to find the typical organism in many cases of the disease. Filtrates of nasal exudate were found to reproduce the disease, and it was concluded that the primary cause was a filterable virus. The etiological role of *H. influenzae* in the infection has not been discarded by many; consequently, there is yet no unanimity of opinion in respect to the true cause of the disease. The most acceptable conclusion is that a virus is the primary inciting agent in the disease and that other organisms, such as *H. influenzae,* streptococci, and pneumococci, are important secondary invaders.

In 1918 Koen, working in the Federal Bureau of Animal Industry, now the Agricultural Research Service, as a field investigator of swine diseases in Iowa, observed a disease which was similar to human influenza, so prevalent at that time. He called the condition "flu" because of the similarity. In 1920 Murray isolated a small, gram-negative coccus which he considered the cause of the disease. McBryde, Niles, and Mosky, in 1928, isolated a pleomorphic, gram-positive bacillus and *Bacillus suisepticus* from the lungs of influenza swine. In 1930 Fulton also isolated a gram-positive organism from cases of swine influenza. A significant report was made in 1931 by Lewis and Shope concerning the etiologic factors responsible for swine influenza. They found that the disease was caused by the synergistic action of a filterable virus and an organism which they considered so similar to certain strains of *H. influenzae* that they called it *Hemophilus influenzae* (var. *suis).* In 1932 Köbe of Germany observed a similar organism in a chronic disease of pigs called "ferkelgrippe," and the following year Köbe and Kirchenbauer, independently, further emphasized the resemblance of this organism to *B. influenzae.* The first evidence to show that the two organisms were different antigenically was introduced by Schlüter in 1936 when he demonstrated antigenic differences by the use of complement-fixation and complement-fixation-absorption tests.

In 1938 Rosenbusch found that *H. influenzae suis* was distinguishable from *H. influenzae* on the basis of carbohydrate fermentation. The swine organism fermented maltose and sucrose but not xylose or dextrose, while the human strains fermented xylose and dextrose but not maltose or sucrose.

Hauduroy classified the swine influenza organism as *Hemophilus suis,* a name which Bergey's Manual also uses in the 1957 edition.

### *Hemophilus suis*

**Synonyms and History.** *Hemophilus influenzae* var. *suis, Hemophilus influenzae-suis, Bacterium influenzae suis.*

This organism was first isolated and described by Lewis and Shope in 1931.

**Distribution and Transmission.** Reports indicate that the organism is present in Germany and in the United States. Swine influenza was prevalent in the midwestern part of the United States following the epidemic of human influenza in 1918, but the disease has decreased among swine herds until only sporadic cases are reported at the present time.

The virus, which is the inciting factor in the disease, is transmitted by direct contact. The organism is considered a normal inhabitant of the upper respiratory tract of some animals, but it, too, is transmitted by contact during the active stage of an epizootic.

**Morphology and Staining.** *H. suis* is a small, slender rod, 0.2$\mu$ in thickness and varying from 0.5$\mu$ to 2$\mu$ in length. A few long, curved threadlike shapes are often observed. As the culture of the organism ages, coccoidal forms begin to appear, and when the culture is 48 hours old most of the organisms are coccoid in shape. Extremely large, coccoidal, and club-shaped

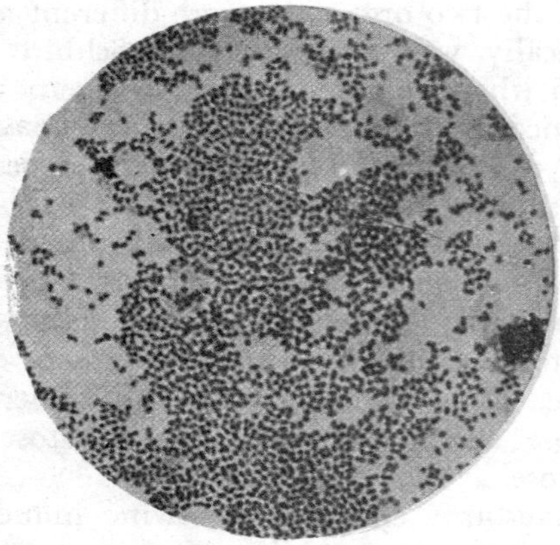

FIG. 25.1—**Hemophilus influenzae** from agar culture, ×2,000. (From Nowak: Documenta Microbiologica, courtesy Gustav Fischer.)

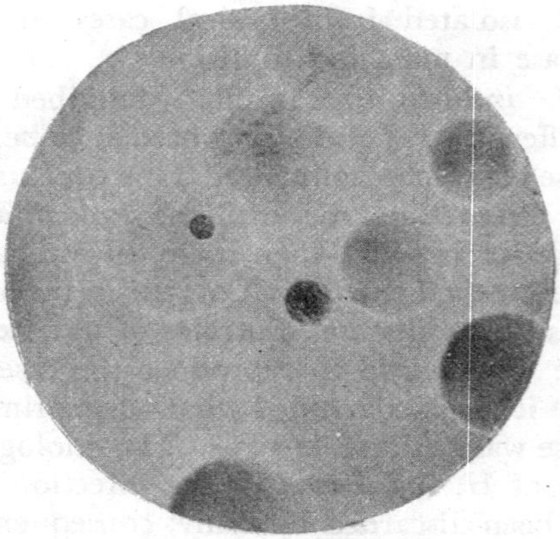

FIG. 25.2—**Hemophilus influenzae** colonies on agar plate, ×40. (From Nowak: Documenta Microbiologica, courtesy Gustav Fischer.)

forms are found in some cultures. The organism resembles the morphology of *H. influenzae* (Fig. 25.1).

The staining capacity of this organism is not as great as other similar types of bacteria. The ordinary alkaline methylene blue imparts only a faint blue color. A heavier stain is obtained by the use of phenolized methylene blue which is steamed during the staining process. The organism is gram-negative.

**Growth Requirements and Characteristics.** The swine influenza bacillus is a strict aerobe and grows best at 37°C. The reaction of the medium for maximum growth is pH 7.2.

On the surface of solid media *H. suis* produces small, circular, grayish, semitranslucent, flattened colonies that have a sharply contoured edge. They are similar to those produced by the human influenza organism (Fig. 25.2).

*H. suis* produces a faint turbidity in broth due to the feeble growth of the organism.

**Resistance.** This organism is similar to all of the gram-negative, nonsporeforming rods in resistance to heat, light, desiccation, and chemical disinfectants.

**Biochemical Properties.** In the study of any of the biochemical activities of this organism, it is emphasized that both X- and V-factors must be added to the media; failure to do so undoubtedly will yield variable results.

*H. suis* is not an actively saccharolytic microorganism. Shope and Lewis report no demonstrable action on glucose, lactose, saccharose, dulcitol, mannitol, glycerol, inulin, or arabinose. Rosenbusch reports the fermentation of maltose and traces of acidity in saccharose and a few strains in mannitol. The organism reduces nitrates to nitrites; does not produce hydrogen sulfide; does not liquefy gelatin. This organism does not produce indol; this is a characteristic similar to that of some of the strains of *H. influenzae*. Growth is scanty in litmus milk, and the medium remains unchanged.

**Antigenic Structure and Toxins.** The antigenic relationship of *H. suis* to *H. influenzae* has been subjected to careful study by a number of investigators. In their original work Lewis and Shope noted the antigenic heterogeneity of *H. suis;* this is also a characteristic of *H. influenzae* according to numerous reports. Rosenbusch observed that on the basis of agglutinin-absorption tests, the strains of *H. suis* were more homogenous than the strains of *H. influenzae;* however, he noted a definite cross agglutination between the two species.

The different antigenic fractions of *H. suis* have not been determined.

This organism does not produce a soluble toxin. It is not hemolytic.

**Pathogenicity.** The pathogenicity of *H. suis* depends upon the previous action of the filterable virus upon the mucous membranes of the respiratory tract. Shope demonstrated that the clinical and pathological pictures of swine influenza depend upon these two etiologic agents operating in synergistic action, and that neither the virus nor the organism can produce the disease when injected alone.

*H. suis* is variable in virulence to rabbits and guinea pigs. Some strains produce death in 24 hours while the majority do not produce any observable symptoms. The organism is pathogenic to white mice, producing a 50 per cent mortality, according to Shope. White rats are resistant.

Further discussion of the relationship of the virus to swine influenza will be found in the section of the book devoted to the filterable virus diseases.

**Immunity.** Swine which have recovered from attacks of influenza are immune. The presence of virus-neutralizing antibodies in the blood serum of these swine indicates that the immunity is a virus immunity and is not related to *H. suis*.

**Diagnosis.** The presence of *H. suis* can be detected only by demonstrating the organism by the inoculation of suitable culture media. For this purpose, chocolate agar or chocolate agar plus sterile potato infusion is recommended.

### *Hemophilus canis*

**Synonyms and History.** While working as an assistant to Pfeiffer in the period during which the human influenza bacillus was discovered, Friedberger, in 1903, isolated an organism, which he termed *Bacillus haemoglobinophilus canis,* from the prepucial exudate of the dog. In 1922 Rivers described the organism in more detail, called attention to its growth requirements, and suggested the name *Hemophilus canis.*

**Distribution and Transmission.** If the prevalence of prepucial exudate is the determining criterion of its presence, this organism is widely distributed throughout the dog world. Presumably it is transmitted by contact due to habits of male animals of the canine family.

**Morphology and Staining.** *H. canis* is a small, nonmotile rod which is very similar to *H. suis* and *H. influenzae.* The organism is gram-negative.

**Growth Requirements and Characteristics.** *H. canis* is aerobic and grows best at 37°C. and at a pH 7.0 to 7.2.

Rivers was the first to note that this organism differs from *H. influenzae* in its relationship to X and V growth factors. *H. canis* requires the presence of X-factor but, apparently, is able to synthesize V-factor or does not need it for growth.

On chocolate agar the organism produces small, round, grayish-white colonies which tend to become larger and more opaque as the culture ages.

A diffuse growth occurs in the proper fluid medium.

**Resistance.** The organism is typical of the other members in the group.

**Biochemical Properties.** *H. canis* forms acid without gas from glucose, fructose, galactose, mannitol, sucrose, and xylose; does not ferment maltose, lactose, dextrin, arabinose, or glycerol; forms indol and reduces nitrates.

**Antigenic Structure and Toxins.** Information concerning the antigenic relationship of this organism to others of the Hemophilus group is not available. It does not produce exotoxin.

**Pathogenicity.** *H. canis* is not considered pathogenic. Its presence in purulent prepucial exudate may indicate that it has a low-grade type of virulence. It has never been incriminated in the acute respiratory infections of the dog; however, this problem has not been completely explored. Even though Rivers speculated concerning the possibility of the organism becoming established in the respiratory tracts of people who handle dogs, it is not considered pathogenic to man.

The white mouse, the guinea pig, and the rabbit are not susceptible to *H. canis*.

**Immunity.** Nothing is known about the immunity produced by this organism.

**Diagnosis.** The isolation of the organism from the prepucial exudate is possible only by the use of a nutrient medium containing hematin. It is differentiated from the other species in the genus by means of carbohydrate fermentation.

### *Hemophilus gallinarum*

In 1932 DeBlieck reported finding an organism in the respiratory tract of chickens which showed a typical type of fowl pox. The organism was gram-negative and hemophilic so it was named *B. haemoglobinophilus coryza gallinarum*. Nelson, in 1932, observed the same type of an organism in an uncomplicated epizootic of coryza in the domestic fowl. In 1933 Delaplane and Stuart reported the organism from Rhode Island, and in the same year Pistor, Hoffman, Beach, and Schalm found it in California.

*H. gallinarum* shows the morphology which is typical of the group—small, coccoid, pleomorphic, gram-negative rods. Nelson reported the growth of the organism in blood at the base of agar slants which had been inoculated with a filtrate of nasal exudate. This may indicate that extremely small forms of the organism exist. Gregory has found that a medium containing filtered yeast extract and 1 per cent sodium chloride was more satisfactory for obtaining growth of the organism. This author observed that X-factor (hemin) was not essential for growth. On this medium the organism forms a fine confluent growth barely visible to the unaided eye. More abundant growth is obtained when the medium is incubated in a moist chamber to prevent desiccation.

Intranasal inoculation of cultures of the organism produces the typical disease in a susceptible chicken. Subcutaneous inoculation produces edema with subsequent suppuration at the point of injection. Turkeys, pigeons, sparrows, and crows are resistant. Rabbits and guinea pigs are also resistant.

The rhinitis produced by *H. gallinarum* is distinct from laryngotracheitis, produced by a filterable virus, as shown in cross-immunity tests by Delaplane, Erwin, and Stuart.

Page, Rosenwald, and Price have shown that a bacterin consisting of formalin-inactivated yolk-propagated cultures of *H. gallinarum* produces a marked resistance to air-sac infection and a significant resistance to coryza and lowered egg production.

It is essential to isolate and identify the organism to be able to differentiate infection by *H. gallinarum* from that produced by other agents. Yamamoto and Somersett have compounded a medium which produces bacterial yield sufficient for plate agglutination antigen. This shows promise as a diagnostic test for the disease.

### *Hemophilus ovis*

In 1925 Mitchell isolated from the respiratory tract of sheep an organism which he called *Hemophilus ovis*. Apparently this is the only report of the organism in the literature.

*H. ovis* is a short, coccoid, pleomorphic rod, quite typical of the influenza group. It is gram-negative and stains poorly with aniline dyes.

On chocolate agar, colonies are distinct, viscid, moist, and glistening, and about the size of a pinhead. After continued growth the colonies become flatter, with an elevated center, and lose their viscidity. In broth the organism produces a sight turbidity and forms in floating, ropy strands which settle to the bottom of the culture tube and form a slimy precipitate.

*H. ovis* produces acid but not gas from sorbitol, raffinose, fructose, galactose, glucose, maltose, mannitol, mannose, and sucrose; produces slight acidity in lactose and xylose; does not ferment inositol, salicin, inulin, arabinose, or rhamnose. It does not form indol; reduces nitrates to nitrites; does not liquefy gelatin; does not alter litmus milk to which blood is added.

The organism produces an acute bronchopneumonia in adult sheep. In addition to the lung lesions, degenerative changes are found in the liver, kidneys, and heart muscle. Intravenous inoculation of the organism into a sheep produces the typical form of the disease. The guinea pig and rabbit are susceptible. The chicken is resistant.

Intranasal instillation of the organism into the guinea pig produces death in four days, indicating that the organism gains entrance through the respiratory tract of sheep affected with the disease.

### *Hemophilus cuniculi*

In 1929 Gibbons isolated a hemophilic organism from subcutaneous abscesses in the domestic rabbit. Hauduroy lists the organism as *Hemophilus cuniculi*.

The organism is a short bacillus, 0.3$\mu$ to 0.4$\mu$ by 1.0$\mu$ to 1.2$\mu$ in size. It usually occurs singly, but chains are found. It is capsulated and nonmotile. The organism is gram-negative.

Blood agar is most suitable for artificial cultivation, and on this medium the organism forms round, smooth, watery, transparent colonies which are the size of a pin point. The growth is similar, although not as luxuriant, upon serum agar. After prolonged artificial cultivation upon blood agar the organism can be grown on ordinary beef-extract agar. A marked turbidity is produced in infusion broth.

*H. cuniculi* is aerobic and facultatively anaerobic. It produces acid but no gas from glucose, fructose, mannitol, maltose, lactose, sucrose, galactose, salicin, dextrin, and xylose; does not ferment dulcitol or inulin. It does not form indol; does not alter milk; does not liquefy gelatin.

Experimental subcutaneous inoculation of the organism into rabbits produces the typical, circumscribed, hard abscesses which persist for about a month. It causes death in mice within five days by producing a septicemia. Guinea pigs are relatively resistant.

### Miscellaneous Species

Brief mention is made of a few miscellaneous Hemophilus species. Dukes and Gardner have described an organism isolated from cases of human vaginitis. Serologically it is distinct from other members of the genus. The name *Hemophilus vaginalis* has been suggested for this new species. The classification of this organism in the genus Hemophilus has been questioned because it is not dependent on H- and V-factors. Furthermore, it shows a tendency to gram-positive, and therefore should be placed with the Corynebacteria. Edmunds, however, considers that if it is not a member of the Hemophilus group, a new genus should be created for it because it is not catalase positive, an essential characteristic of the genus Corynebacterium. Firehammer has reported the isolation of an organism from the aborted fetus of a dairy cow. This organism did not resemble any of the known species of the genus except *Hemophilus citreus*. A new species, *Hemophilus agni*, has been described by Kennedy *et al.* It was isolated from cases of septicemia in a flock of lambs. It was pathogenic for experimental lambs but not for mice, guinea pigs, or rabbits.

## THE GENUS MORAXELLA

Representative species of the genus Moraxella are coccobacilli commonly found in a diploid arrangement. They vary in size, especially in old cultures; many cells contain large vacuoles, peripheral chromatin granules, fat, and glycogen. Some strains are capsulated. They are gram-negative to gram-variable. Hemin or other growth factors considered essential to the various species of the genus Hemophilus are not required for the Moraxella.

### *Moraxella bovis*

In 1919 Allen isolated a small bacterium from bovine infectious keratitis. The organism was similar to the Morax-Axenfeld bacillus which is considered to be the cause of infectious conjuctivitis in man. Jones and Little found the same type of organism associated with the disease in 1923. Hauduroy classified the organism as *Hemophilus bovis* in 1927. As a result of his bacteriological study of bovine infectious keratitis in 1945, Baldwin demonstrated the etiological relationship of the organism to the disease, which was confirmed by Reid and Anigstein the same year.

The role of this organism as the primary infecting agent in infectious keratitis could not be confirmed by Farley *et al.* (1950). It is their belief that the organism is an important secondary invader in the disease, but there are other factors of primary importance. As an example, Hughes and associates have found that exposure of the eyes of experimental cattle to a mercury sunlamp made them more susceptible to infection. They contend that ultraviolet radiation has a primary etiologic role in the disease.

In the 1948 edition of Bergey's Manual this organism was placed in a new genus, Moraxella, because of its diplococcoid shape.

*M. bovis* is a short rod 0.5$\mu$ to 1.0$\mu$ in width and 1.5$\mu$ to 2.0$\mu$ in length. It is usually found in pairs, but short chains are observed. Pleomorphism is noted in old cultures. A definite capsule is present in young cultures. Neither flagella nor spores are produced. The organism is gram-negative.

Horse blood agar, pH 7.2 to 7.5, is the most satisfactory medium for isolation. On this medium small, round, translucent, grayish-white colonies develop in 24 hours. These colonies are surrounded by a narrow zone of beta hemolysis. As the culture ages, the colonies enlarge and develop a small raised area in the center. Growth is more scant on plain and serum agar media. On coagulated serum medium, the organism forms small colonies which sink into the medium, due to the liquefaction. As the culture ages, liquefaction is extended throughout the medium. The organism grows slowly in nutrient broth, forming a light turbidity and a coarse sediment.

*M. bovis* does not produce acid in any of the carbohydrates; in fact, the medium tends to become more alkaline. Litmus milk becomes alkaline with the development of three zones: the upper zone composed of deep blue fluid; the medium zone containing soft curd lighter in color; and the third zone white, coagulated casein. Nitrates are not reduced to nitrites; indol is not formed; gelatin is liquefied slowly.

The lesions typical of infectious keratitis have been reproduced in cattle by the use of cultures of the organism by Jones and Little, by Baldwin, by Reid and Anigstein, by Barner, by Jackson, and by Henson and Grumbles. Farley and coworkers were unable to reproduce the disease in cattle by using 24-hour cultures of the organism which were inoculated under the eyelids of normal cattle. Henson and Grumbles have reported a hemolytic toxin and a dermonecrotic toxin which are closely associated with the cell wall of *M. bovis*. The injection of both treated and untreated cultures of *M. bovis* intracorneally in rabbits and calves produced keratitis and conjunctivitis.

Rabbits and guinea pigs were refractory, likewise, to numerous intraocular exposures. These investigators found that *M. bovis* caused the death of 10- and 12-day-old chicken embryos when cultures were injected beneath the inner shell membrane. Sheep are not infected by artificial inoculation.

Baldwin noted that animals were resistant to the organism after recovery from the initial infection. However, some remain carriers of the organism, thus serving as reservoirs until the next season. Jones and Little observed that flies are agents of transmission.

In their study of calf pneumonia, Thorp, Shigley, and Farrell found an Hemophilus-like organism associated with the disease.

This organism is similar to *H. suis* in morphology and gives positive cross-agglutination results in titers of 1:300 and 1:640. As far as is known, no comparison has been made between this organism and cultures of *M. bovis* isolated from infectious keratitis.

## GENERA FLAVOBACTERIUM, MIMA, AND HERELLA

At times, most microbiologists isolate bacteria which do not fit into any of the commonly recognized genera. Such is the case with those given above. All of the reports concerning those organisms have come from isolations from man. Only one report by Ellis describing cultures he called *Bacterium anitratum* (B5w), which were isolated from the livers of chickens and from a calf head, has indicated that these bacteria may be found in animals. It is with this motive that these genera are included in this edition. About the only unanimous agreement concerning these organisms is that they are isolated from various tissues in man and that they should be correctly classified.

The use of the genus name Bacterium

TABLE 25.1

PROPERTIES OF MIMA, HERELLA, AND FLAVOBACTERIUM

| Property | Mima | Herella | Flavobacterium |
|---|---|---|---|
| Growth on SS agar | − | − | − |
| Blue colonies on EMB agar | ± | + | − |
| Yellow pigment on tryptose | − | + | + |
| Motility | ± | + | − |
| Growth at 23°C. | + | − | ± |
| Growth at 42°C. | − | + | + |
| Indol | − | − | − |
| Phenylalanine | − | − | − |
| Nitrate reduction | − | - | − |
| Catalase | + | + | ± |
| Oxidase | − | − | + |
| $H_2S$ | − | − | ± |
| Urease | − | ± | − |
| TSI | − | − | − |
| Dextrose | − | + | slow |
| Lactose 1% | ± | ± | slow |
| Lactose 10% | ± | + | ± |
| Maltose | − | − | slow |
| Sucrose | − | − | − |
| Galactose | − | + | − |
| Inocitol | − | − | − |
| Citrate | + | + | − |

was convenient but did not mean very much because this genus, which at one time included all gram-negative nonsporeforming rods, was eventually to become a sort of "pigeon hole" into which ill-defined, miscellaneous gram-negative, nonsporeforming rods were placed.

Space does not permit repeating the historical development of these genera. Ellis gives a good review, as do Nelson and Shelton. Wilson and Miles offer evidence which they believe places these bacteria in the genus Achromobacter. These genera are being appended to the chapter on the genera Hemophilus and Moraxella because they appear to be more closely related to them than to any other.

Small, gram-negative, coccobacillary rods which resemble the gram-negative diplococci and which are biochemically different from any other species are placed in one or the other of the above genera. Nelson and Shelton (1965) apparently have the last word about these organisms, so Table 25.1 has been adapted from their article to give those characteristics to keep in mind when a culture is isolated and which is not readily identified.

## REFERENCES

ALLEN, J. A. A Preliminary Note on Infectious Keratitis. Jour. Amer. Vet. Med. Assn. 54:307–13, 1919.

BAKOS, K. Studiern über *Haemophilus suis*. Appelbergs Boktryckeri A B, Stockholm, 1955.

BALDWIN, E. M. A Study of Bovine Infectious Keratitis. Amer. Jour. Vet. Res. 6:180–87, 1945.

BARNER, R. D. Amer. Jour. Vet. Res. 13:132, 1952.

BRUNER, D. W., and FABRICANT, I. Cornell Vet. 44:461, 1954.

DALY, A. K., *et al*. Infections Due to Organisms of the Genus Herella. Arch. Int. Med. 110:580–91, 1962.

DEBLIECK, L. A Haemoglobinophilic Bacterium as the Cause of Contagious Catarrh in the Fowl. Vet. Jour. 88:9–13, 1932.

DELAPLANE, J. P., *et al*. A Hemophilic Bacillus as the Cause of An Infectious Rhinitis (Coryza) of Fowls. R. I. Agr. Exp. Sta. Bull. 244, 1934.

DUKES, C. D., and GARDNER, H. L. Identification of *Haemophilus vaginalis*. Jour. Bact. 81:277, 1961.

EDMUNDS, P. N. The Biochemical, Serological, and Haemagglutinating Reactions of *Haemophilus vaginalis*. Jour. Path. Bact. 83:411–22, 1962.

ELLIS, E. M. The Recovery of *Bacterium anitratum* (B5w) From Animals. Amer. Jour. Vet. Res. 22:610–13, 1961.

FARLEY, H., *et al*. Amer. Jour. Vet. Res. 11:22, 1950.

FRIEDBERGER, E. Ueber ein Neues zur Gruppe des Influenzabacillus Gehöriges häemoglobinophiles Bakterium (*Bacillus haemoglobinophilus canis*). Zentralbl. f. Bakt. I. Abt. Orig. 33:401, 1903.

GIBBONS, N. E. *Hemophilus* sp. and *Neisseria* sp. in Skin Abscesses in Rabbits and Guinea Pigs. Jour. Inf. Dis. 45:288–92, 1929.

GREGORY, D. W. Nutrient Requirements of *H. gallinarum*. Amer. Jour. Vet. Res. 5:72–77, 1944.

HENDRICKSON, J. M., and HILBERT, K. F. Cornell Vet. 22:239, 1932.

HENSON, J. B., and GRUMBLES, L. C. Infectious Bovine Keratoconjunctivitis. I. Etiology. Amer. Jour. Vet. Res. 21:761, 1960.

———, and ———. Infectious Bovine Keratoconjunctivitis. III. Demonstration of Toxins in Moraxella (*Hemophilus bovis*) Cultures. Cornell Vet. 51:266–84, 1961.

HUGHES, D. E., *et al*. Ultraviolet Radiation and *Moraxella bovis* in the Etiology of Bovine Infectious Keratoconjunctivitis. Amer. Jour. Vet. Res. 26:1331–38, 1965.

JACKSON, F. C. Amer. Jour. Vet. Res. 14:19, 1953.

JONES, F. S., and LITTLE, R. B. An Infectious Ophthalmia of Cattle. Jour. Exp. Med. 38:139–48, 1923.

———, and ———. The Transmission and Treatment of Infectious Ophthalmia of Cattle. Jour. Exp. Med. 39:803–10, 1924.

KENNEDY, P. C., *et al*. A Septicemic Disease of Lambs Caused by *Hemophilus agni* (n. sp.). Amer. Jour. Vet. Res. 19:645, 1958.

LEWIS, P. A., and SHOPE, R. Swine Influenza. Jour. Exp. Med. 54:361–72, 1931.

MITCHELL, CHARLES, A. *Hemophilus ovis* (n. sp.) as the Cause of a Specific Disease in Sheep. Jour. Amer. Vet. Med. Assn. 68:8–18, 1925.

MURRAY, R. G. E., and TRUANT, J. P. Jour. Bact. 67:13, 1954.

NELSON, J. B. Etiology of Uncomplicated Coryza in the Domestic Fowl. Soc. Exp. Biol. Med. 30:306–7, 1932.

NELSON, J. D., and SHELTON, S. Cultural, Biochemical and Immunological Properties of Mima, Herella and Flavobacterium Species. Appl. Microbiol. 13:801–7, 1965.

PAGE, L. A., *et al.* Haemophilus Infections in Chickens. Avian Dis. 1963.

RIVERS, T. M. *Bacillus hemoglobinophilus canis* (Friedberger). Jour. Bact. 7:579, 1922.

ROSENBUSCH, C. T. Some Studies on Swine Influenza. I. Comparative Study of *Hemophilus influenza suis* and *Hemophilus influenzae*. Ph.D. Thesis, Iowa State Univ. Library, Ames, 1938.

SHOPE, R. Swine Influenza. Jour. Exp. Med. 54:349–60, 373–85, 1931.

THORP, W. T. S., *et al.* Studies on the Etiology and Pathology of Calf Pneumonia. Amer. Jour. Vet. Res. 3: 342–49, 1942.

WEED, L. A. Mimae—A Problem in Diagnosis and Taxonomy. Amer. Jour. Clin. Path. 35:447–48, 1961.

WILSON, G. S., and MILES, A. A. Topley's Principles of Bacteriology and Immunity. 5th Ed. Williams & Wilkins Co., Baltimore, 1964.

YAMAMOTO, R., and SOMERSETT, D. T. Antibody Response in Chickens to Infection With *Haemophilus gallinarum*. Avian Dis. 1964.

# 26

# The Genus Malleomyces

CLASSIFICATIONS OF BACTERIA ARE SUBJECTED to frequent changes. The glanders bacillus is an excellent example of how an organism may be shifted from one genus to another, from one family to another, and from one order to another. At the present time the organism is called *Malleomyces mallei*.

The genus Malleomyces includes the short rods, which sometimes form threads and show a tendency toward branching. They may be either motile or nonmotile; stain gram-negative; show a tendency toward bipolar staining; coagulate milk slowly; may liquefy gelatin; grow best on blood-serum media. These organisms are specialized for a parasitic existence on hosts in which they are capable of producing disease.

Two species are classified in this genus: *Malleomyces mallei* which causes glanders in the horse, and is infectious for man; *Malleomyces pseudomallei* which produces a glanders-like disease in rats, guinea pigs, rabbits, swine, and man, and has been reported only from India and Indo-China.

### *Malleomyces (Actinobacillus) mallei*

**History and Synonyms.** Loeffler and Shütz, in 1882, were the first to show that equine glanders was caused by an organism which they termed the glanders bacillus (rotzbacillus). Flügge called the organism *Bacillus mallei* in 1886. It was called *Corynebacterium mallei* by Lehmann and Neumann in 1899, *Bacterium mallei* by Migula in 1900, and *Mycobacterium mallei* by Chester in 1901. In 1918 the name *Pfeifferella mallei* was listed by Buchanan, although it was his intention to call the organism *Loefflerella mallei* in commemoration of the contributions of Loeffler to bacteriology. *Pfeifferella mallei* was becoming well established in the literature when Pacheco, in 1933, concluded that the organism should be called *Brucella mallei*. In the same year Thompson studied cultures of the glanders organism, of pseudoglanders, and of actinobacillosis and concluded that the three were similar enough to be placed in the same genus, Actinobacillus. This name was adopted by Bergey's Manual in 1934 and was becoming established in the literature.

In 1933 Pribram revived the name Malleomyces for the genus in which the glanders organism was placed. This was done because of the name *Malleomyces equestris* which was used by Hallier in 1870 as a result of his work on what he considered to be an organism causing glanders, but according to his descriptions he did not have a pure culture.

The inclusion of the glanders organism in the genus Actinobacillus, as proposed by Thompson, has been questioned by Topley and Wilson who still preferred the name *Pfeifferella mallei* in 1936. Holden, in association with Gay in 1935, sought to settle the controversy by proposing the name *Loefflerella mallei*. This appeared to be a happy solution, and many hoped that the name would be adopted. The 1939 edition of Bergey's Manual used the named *Malleomyces mallei*. In the 1957 edition the organism was again placed in the genus Actinobacillus. We prefer to leave it in the genus Malleomyces.

**Distribution and Transmission.** The disease glanders, which is caused by this organism, has been widely distributed throughout the world. In many countries where a concerted effort has been made to eradicate the disease, cases are extremely rare. In the United States the disease has ceased to be a major problem.

Glanders is a disease involving the respiratory tract and subcutaneous tissues. The organism is transmitted chiefly through the common watering trough, feed, and by direct contact. The isolation of the equine population on the farm has contributed a great deal to the disappearance of glanders. The perfection and use of adequate diagnostic methods with the subsequent destruction of the infected animals have also served as effective control measures. The practice of approved sanitary methods in places where large numbers of horses are kept together has proved an effective means of controlling the disease.

Human infection is usually obtained through skin cuts and abrasions during contact with glanders exudate.

The disease has been reported in dogs, cats, and other carnivora following the eating of meat from a glandered horse.

**Morphology and Staining.** *Malleomyces mallei* is a slender rod with rounded ends, and normally is 0.3μ to 0.5μ in breadth and 1.5μ to 5μ in length. Old cultures are pleomorphic; they are composed of forms which range from coccoid cells to extremely long filaments, some of which are slightly branched. Many of the cells, especially the filaments, present a beaded appearance, and numerous cells of normal size appear to have one or more minute vacuoles in the protoplasm (Fig. 26.1). Miller and coworkers have found, with the aid of the electron microscope, that the refractile bodies resemble lipoid globules. In smears which are made from a glanders lesion in a

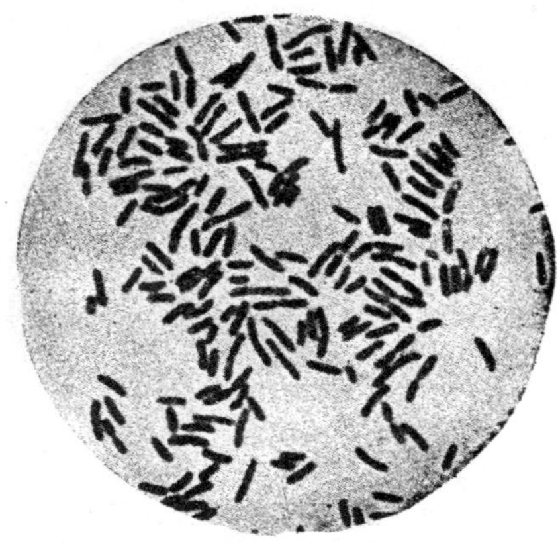

FIG. 26.1—**Malleomyces mallei** 24-hour agar culture, ×2,000. (From Nowak: Documenta Microbiologica, courtesy Gustav Fischer.)

mouse, the organism is definitely bipolar, but the polar granules are more distinct than in other bipolar staining cells. This organism is noncapsuleproducing, nonmotile, and nonsporeproducing. It is not stained easily by the common dyes and is gram-negative.

**Growth Requirements and Characteristics.** The glanders bacillus is aerobic and facultatively anaerobic. The most favorable temperature for artificial cultivation is 37°C., although some growth occurs between temperatures of 25° to 40°C. A slightly acid reaction, pH 6.6, is most conducive to satisfactory growth.

The organism grows well on most of the common laboratory media, but the addition of serum and glycerin yields a more rapid and abundant culture. After two days incubation upon glycerin agar the organism produces a small, round, amorphous, translucent colony (Fig. 26.2). Growth on solid media has a tendency to be slimy and tenacious in consistency. Surface colonies become yellowish-brown as the culture ages.

In glycerin bouillon the bacillus produces a light turbidity and forms a thin, delicate pellicle; the medium becomes darker brown as the culture stands.

The organism is distinctly characterized

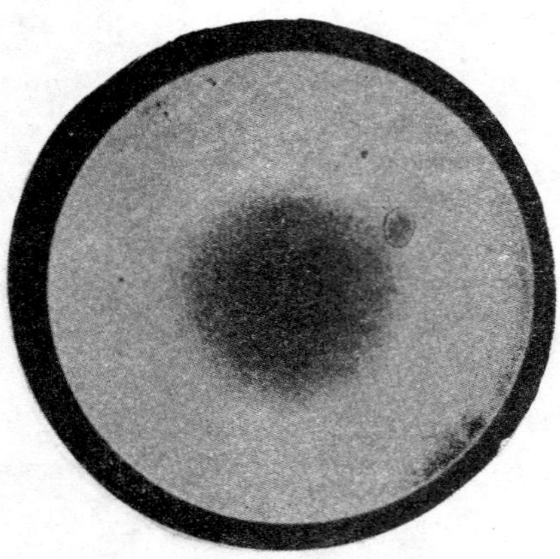

FIG. 26.2—**Malleomyces mallei** on agar plate, ×45. (From Nowak: Documenta Microbiologica, courtesy Gustav Fischer.)

by the growth which forms on potato. After 48 hours incubation, a yellowish, viscid, semitransparent growth appears and gradually turns a yellowish-brown and eventually to a rich mahogany. The potato medium is oxidized to a brownish-green color. *M. mallei* grows readily on the media used for the cultivation of tubercle bacilli; glycerol is definitely stimulating.

**Resistance.** This organism is not resistant to adverse conditions. It is killed by 55°C. in 10 minutes. Natural desiccation and sunlight do not permit the organism to live long outside the body. According to Miller *et al.* "roccal," hypochlorite, iodine, and mercuric chloride are highly effective as disinfectants, whereas phenol is less effective and lysol is ineffective. The organism remains viable in tap water for at least four weeks.

Streptomycin has been found of value in treating cases of glanders in man.

**Biochemical Properties.** An outstanding feature of *M. mallei* is its inability to ferment carbohydrate media, although some strains do produce a slight acid reaction in glucose and salicin after prolonged incubation. It does not produce indol; does not reduce nitrates; is negative to the methyl red and Voges-Proskauer tests. The organism produces a slight amount of $H_2S$, $NH_3$, and catalase. A slight acidity is formed in litmus milk, and in two to three weeks a soft curd is developed. The organism does not liquefy gelatin.

**Antigenic Structure and Toxins.** For practical diagnostic purposes the organism is antigenically homogenous when mallein or the complement-fixation test is used. The study of numerous strains of the organism by agglutination, precipitation, and complement fixation has revealed at least two antigenic types.

The glanders bacillus does not produce a true toxin, although an endotoxin is thought to be the cause of the emaciation and pyrexia which accompany the disease. This endotoxin, known as mallein, is better known as a diagnostic agent.

**Pathogenicity.** *M. mallei* is primarily pathogenic to horses and mules in which it produces a typical chronic infection. The disease is commonly classified into three types —pulmonary glanders, nasal glanders, and cutaneous glanders, or farcy.

Pulmonary glanders, which is observed in practically all cases of the disease, is characterized by the formation of round, grayish, firm, encapsulated nodules embedded throughout the lung tissue. These nodules are similar to the tubercles found in tuberculosis. Many of the nodules contain a yellowish, cheesy pus and are surrounded by a zone of inflammation, while others are firm and composed of fibrous connective tissue. In some cases, entire areas of the lungs may be replaced by this fibrous type of tissue.

Nasal glanders is typified by the formation of nodules in the mucous membrane of the nasal cavity, particularly of the septum. Many of these nodules rupture and liberate a mucopurulent exudate which becomes mixed with the serous or mucopurulent exudate already discharging from the nostrils. The ruptured nodules form ulcers with irregular, raised, and hyperemic borders. These ulcers heal slowly, but when they heal, a stellate scar is formed in the mucous membrane. The regional lymph nodes are commonly swollen in nasal glanders.

In farcy, or cutaneous glanders, the typical glanders nodules, or "farcy buds," form along the lymph vessels between affected lymph nodes. These often rupture through the skin and discharge a yellowish pus, and form into deep ulcers which heal slowly.

*M. mallei* is very pathogenic for the guinea pig and the field mouse, but is less so for the rabbit, cat, and dog.

In the male guinea pig the organism localizes in the testes, following intraperitoneal inoculation, and produces an orchitis characterized by swelling, which is followed by ulceration in approximately two weeks. This reaction was first described by Loeffler, but its diagnostic value was recognized by Strauss after whom it is named. In their study of the virulence of *M. mallei* and *M. pseudomallei,* Miller *et al.* observed that strains of these organisms varied in virulence and that the hamster was the most susceptible animal. Ferrets were also quite susceptible, but guinea pigs were only moderately so, by comparison. Rabbits, mice, rats, and monkeys were least susceptible. Lesions remain localized at the point of injection in dogs and cats.

Glanders in man is commonly confined to the formation of cutaneous ulcers at the point of invasion with subsequent enlargement of the regional lymph nodes. More acute and fatal cases have been described in which pulmonary lesions, similar to those in the horse, have been found.

**Immunity.** An immunity is not produced by the active disease. Many different types of immunizing agents have been used in glanders, but none of them has proved to be of value.

Antibodies are produced by the natural infection, but their presence in blood plasma does not halt the progress of the disease to any significant degree.

**Diagnosis.** From the viewpoint of prevention and eradication, the diagnosis of glanders is important due to the chronicity of the disease. The presence of the infection in the horse must be detected during the early stages so that the animal may be removed from the herd. A variety of diagnostic methods are available for glanders.

The method most commonly used is known as the *mallein test.* This test is an allergic reaction due to the sensitization of the cells of the animal by the end-products of bacteria during the natural infection. It is similar to the tuberculin test. Although the reactions are fundamentally the same, being due to an allergic condition, there are four different mallein tests. In the *subcutaneous test* mallein is injected beneath the skin, and a positive reaction is obtained by swelling at the point of injection and an increase in the temperature of the animal. The *ophthalmic test* involves the introduction of mallein, either in fluid or tablet form, under the eyelids. A positive reaction results in an intense reddening of the mucous membrane accompanied by a purulent, yellow exudate, usually within 6 to 8 hours after the introduction of the mallein. In the *cutaneous test,* mallein is injected into the skin or is rubbed into an abraded area on the skin along the side of the neck. An edematous swelling at the point of injection indicates a positive reaction. A modification of the cutaneous test is known as the *palprebral test.* In this test the mallein is injected into the skin close to the edge of the lower eyelid. A positive reaction, usually within 36 hours, is characterized by an extensive edema of the eyelid, accompanied by congestion of the conjunctiva and a mucopurulent secretion. The last test is the method used in routine testing of animals for glanders.

The *agglutination, precipitation, complement-fixation,* and *conglutination tests* have all been used for the diagnosis of glanders. These tests are technically the same as other similar tests; consequently, they need not be discussed here.

The *Strauss reaction* may be used for the diagnosis of glanders, but other organisms, such as *Brucella abortus,* can produce an orchitis in the guinea pig, and for that reason the test has lost much of its value.

The diagnosis of glanders by the use of

culturing methods has never gained prominence. This has been due to the presence of so many other types of bacteria in the nasal exudate of infected animals. However, Toyoshima and Shibuya have devised a medium containing thionine which they claim is of value for the isolation of *M. mallei* from the nasal discharge of infected horses.

### *Malleomyces (Pseudomonas) pseudomallei*

In 1913 Whitmore described a glanders-like disease in man at Rangoon and called it melioidosis. He proposed that the organism be called *Bacillus pseudomallei.* In 1925 Stanton and Fletcher observed the same organism in epizootics among laboratory animals in the Federated Malay States and considered that the most appropriate name was *Bacillus whitmori.* Since then the organism has been found in laboratory animals and in man in various localities in Indo-China and Ceylon.

The classification of this organism has been subjected to much of the same treatment as *M. mallei.* Its morphology and biochemical activity, however, have led some to doubt its close relationship with the glanders organism. In 1930 it was classified as *Flavobacterium pseudomallei* in Bergey's Manual. The comparative study of Thompson detected a relationship with the actinobacillus which led to the inclusion of the Whitmore bacillus in the genus Actinobacillus. Gay and Holden call it *Loefflerella whitmori;* Topley and Wilson use the name *Pfeifferella whitmori.* The 1957 edition of Bergey's Manual classifies it as *Pseudomonas pseudomallei.*

*M. pseudomallei* is a short, motile, gram-negative, aerobic rod. It forms thick, opaque, cream-colored colonies on solid media. On glycerin the growth tends to become wrinkled. In broth the organism produces a uniform turbidity and forms a pellicle. A heavy, cream-colored growth forms on potato.

This organism is able to produce acid from glucose, maltose, lactose, sucrose, and mannitol, but much of the saccharolytic power is lost by continued artificial growth. It does not produce indol, but does form $H_2S$; liquefies gelatin; acidifies litmus milk.

*M. pseudomallei* produces in rabbits and guinea pigs a natural infection which is similar to glanders in the horse but is more acute. In the septicemic form of the disease the animals live only a few days. In the more chronic form yellowish nodules are found in the nasal mucous membrane and in the lungs. The disease is nearly always fatal.

The occurrence of the organism in other animals has been reported. Stanton, Fletcher, and Symonds reported finding the organism in the nasal discharge of a horse, and Nicholls isolated it from an abscess in the spleen of a cow.

In man, *M. pseudomallei* produces a fatal infection characterized by a generalized distribution of nodules throughout the entire body, with the greatest number in the lungs.

The only certain method of diagnosis is the isolation of the organism. The rapidity of the disease does not allow the formation of antibody which may be used in the diagnosis of acute cases. The more chronic cases of the disease can be diagnosed by serological tests if the antigenic relationship of this organism and *M. mallei* is considered.

## REFERENCES


BERGEY, D. H., *et al.* A Manual of Determinative Bacteriology. 7th Ed. Williams & Wilkins Co., Baltimore, 1957.

FLETCHER, W. Melioidosis. A System of Bacteriology. 5:56–66. Med. Res. Council. His Majesty's Stationery Office, London, 1929.

HOLDEN, M. *In* Gay, F. P., *et al.*, Agents of Disease and Host Resistance, Chap. 36. Charles C Thomas, Baltimore, 1935.

KOLLE, W., and HETSCH, O. *In* Experimental Bacteriology, John Eyre (ed.), Chap. 39. George Allen and Unwin, Ltd., London, 1934.

MILLER, W. R., *et al.* Studies on Certain Biological Characteristics of *Malleomyces mallei* and *Malleomyces pseudomallei.* I. Morphology, Cultivation, Viability, and Isolation From Contaminated Specimen. Jour. Bact. 55:115, 1948.

———, *et al.* II. Virulence and Infectivity for Animals. Jour. Bact. 55:127, 1948.

MINNETT, F. C., and BULLOCK, W. Glanders. A System of Bacteriology. 5:13–55. Med. Res. Council. His Majesty's Stationery Office, London, 1929.

THOMPSON, L. Systematic Relationships of Actinobacillus. Jour. Bact. 26:221–27, 1933.

TOYOSHIMA, T., and SHIBUYA, U. A Simple Cultivation Method for the Isolation of *Bac. mallei.* Jour. Jap. Soc Vet. Sci. 16:136–53. English Summary, p. 19. Part 1, 1937.

# 27

# The Genus Actinobacillus

MICROORGANISMS PLACED IN THE GENUS Actinobacillus must show the following characteristics: they are medium-sized rods which vary in form from coccoid to long, filamentous cells; are aerobic; are stained gram-negative; ferment a number of carbohydrates forming acid but no gas; grow best in $CO_2$ on primary isolation; and are pathogenic for animals.

Only one species, *Actinobacillus lignicresi,* is of significance to animal health, although another, *Actinobacillus actinoides,* has been isolated from calves with pneumonia.

### *Actinobacillus lignieresi*

**Synonyms and History.** In 1902 Lignières and Spitz described an actinomycosis-like disease in cattle of Argentina. They referred to the organism as the Actinobacillus and called the disease actinobacillosis. Nocard confirmed their findings in 1902. Since then the organism has been isolated and described by numerous workers, and the disease is recognized as a rather prevalent one.

**Distribution and Transmission.** The particular type of infection due to *Actinob. lignieresi* is characterized by caseous abscesses in cervical lymph nodes, especially the submaxillary. This disease, widely spread throughout the cattle population of all countries, is more prevalent in some sections than others.

The invasive quality of the organism is low, and its method of transmission is not known.

**Morphology and Staining.** *Actinob. lignieresi* is extremely pleomorphic under natural circumstances. It varies in size from coccoid forms 0.4$\mu$ in diameter to elongated filaments up to 15$\mu$. It is nonmotile, noncapsulated, and nonsporeforming. An outstanding morphological characteristic of the organism is the tendency to form in aggregates, or clumps, in the infected tissue. When the caseous material from a typical abscess is carefully examined, these clumps are recognized as small, brownish-white granules. Examination of these granules under the microscope reveals that they are composed of a stellate arrangement of club-like processes. It is this morphology which is so confusing with similar granules formed by *Actinomyces bovis.* When these granules are broken and smears are made, *Actinob. lignieresi* is found to be a uniform, gram-negative rod as compared to the filamentous, branched, gram-positive cells of *Actinomyces bovis.*

**Growth Requirements and Characteristics.** *Actinob. lignieresi* is aerobic, but growth is increased by the presence of $CO_2$. The organism grows most abundantly at 37°C. and in a slightly alkaline serum medium.

On agar surfaces the growth is scant, bluish in color, transparent, and flat. Dwarf, granular, and fluorescent variants have been described by Ristic *et al.* In nutrient broth the organism grows abundantly and forms a distinct pellicle.

**Resistance.** The organism is killed by a temperature of 60°C. within 15 minutes. It is not resistant to disinfectants, sunlight, or desiccation. Laboratory cultures must be transferred to fresh medium each week, or they perish.

**Biochemical Properties.** *Actinob. lignieresi* produces acid from glucose, maltose, mannitol, fructose, galactose, and sucrose; does not ferment dulcitol, inulin, or salicin. After prolonged incubation, acid is produced in lactose, raffinose, and glycerol. Most strains produce no change in litmus milk, but some strains produce slight acid but no coagulation. Indol is not usually produced, but some strains may produce a faint reaction following prolonged incubation. Nitrates are reduced to nitrites. Phillips has described Actinobacillus-like organisms which he isolated from the bovine rumen. In addition to the carbohydrates listed above, these strains fermented dextrose, levulose, arabinose, xylose, and dextrin. In addition to those not fermented, he found trehalose. Negative results were obtained for indol, ammonia, and urease. Hydrogen sulfide was produced, and methylene blue was reduced. MacConkey's medium supported growth; nitrates were reduced to nitrites; and the methyl red test was negative.

**Antigenic Structure and Toxins.** Agglutinins are formed in the infected animal. Strains of the organism appear to be antigenically homogenous. It does not form toxin.

**Pathogenicity.** The Actinobacillus causes the formation of abscesses in the cervical region, particularly in the submaxillary lymph nodes. It also causes some of the cases of "wooden-tongue" in cattle. It may metastasize to other parts of the body and become localized. When experimentally inoculated into the udder, it has been reported as having produced chronic mastitis.

The recovery of this organism from the bovine rumen by Phillips suggests a commensal role and may explain infections of the cervical area. Hitherto it has been assumed that the organism was a normal inhabitant of the mouth.

Marsh and Wilkins report that the organism has been isolated in Montana from sheep which have an infection around the lips, with subsequent localization in the cervical lymph nodes. A similiar condition is reported from South Africa by Thomas, and in England by Taylor. Davis and Stiles isolated the organism from a typical outbreak of actinobacillosis in rams in New Mexico.

Pathak and Ristic have found that strains of *Actinob. lignieresi* of human and bovine origin were similar.

The organism has been found responsible for a considerable percentage of the cases of mammary abscesses in the sow. Wetmore and associates isolated an organism from the blood and/or synovial fluid of inflamed hocks of pigs which had been subjected to irradiation.

When inoculated into the male guinea pig, *Actinob. lignieresi* produces an orchitis very similar to that caused by the glanders bacillus. Rabbits, cats, and dogs are more resistant to the organism than guinea pigs, but they succumb to intravenous inoculation. The chicken embryo is susceptible.

**Immunity.** Immunity is not produced by the infection. Bacterins and immune serum are not used for this disease. The cases which occur are too sporadic to make general immunization worthwhile.

**Diagnosis.** It is emphasized again that the presence of the "sulfur granule" is not diagnostic of actinobacillosis. In order to distinguish the organism from *Actinomyces bovis,* it is necessary to break the granules and stain the smear with Gram stain. The presence of small, coccoid, gram-negative rods is indicative of *Actinob. lignieresi.*

The agglutination test has been used successfully for the diagnosis of the disease by some workers.

### *Actinobacillus actinoides* and *Actinobacillus seminis*

In 1918 Theobald Smith described an organism which he isolated from a peculiar type of pneumonia in the calf. The organism was similar in many respects to the Actinobacillus, so Smith called it *Bacillus actinoides.*

The bacillus forms typical ray-fungus colonies when grown in the condensation water of serum agar. The individual organism is 0.4$\mu$ to 0.5$\mu$ in diameter and is gram-negative. It can be grown only in a $CO_2$ atmosphere and in serum media which are kept sealed. Colonies on solid media are variable in size; some are minute and dew-drop-like; others are large and opaque. In the cultures the organism appears in three forms: as a bacillus; as a coccus-like endospore or arthrospore; and as a conglomerate Actinomyces-like flake, or colony, with peripheral clubs.

*Actinob. actinoides* has been reported by Smith as occurring in more than one herd of calves, but the extent of the infection is not known. The pneumonia is characterized by a suppurative bronchopneumonia with some encapsulation of older lesions. It is not pathogenic for laboratory animals.

Gunning found an organism typical of *Actinob. lignieresi* in an outbreak of bronchopneumonia in heifer calves. The lungs of the infected animals also contained lungworms *(Dictyocaulus* sp.) which this author considered as primary to the infection and suggested that the bacteria were secondary invaders.

In 1922 Jones described a similar organism which he isolated from an epidemic of rat pneumonia. In 1930 this organism was studied by Nelson who referred to it as *B. actinoides* var. *muris.*

Baynes and Simmons have reported an organism which is different from any other and which they have named *Actinobacillus seminis* n. sp. This organism was isolated in Australia from cases of ovine epididymitis. Livingston and Hardy, in Texas, isolated an organism from the semen of a ram with epididymitis, which was similar to that of Baynes and Simmons.

The growth and morphologic characteristics of the organism do not differ materially from *Actinob. lignieresi.* Acid was not formed in arabinose, xylose, rhamnose, glucose, fructose, mannose, galactose, sucrose, maltose, lactose, trehalose, raffinose, inulin, dextrin, glycogen, glycerol, adonitol, mannitol, dulcitol, sorbitol, salicin, aesculin, or inositol. After 28 days of incubation slight acid production was noted in arabinose, fructose, trehalose, and one strain in mannitol.

Litmus milk was not changed; urea was negative; indol was negative; Loeffler's serum was not liquefied. No growth appeared on potato, alkaline potato, or glycerol potato.

The organism was able to produce death in one of six mice, and guinea pigs were not affected.

Epididymitis was oberved in one of two rams by direct inoculation following an incubation period of about one week, but no systemic reaction was noted.

## REFERENCES


BAYNES, I. D., and SIMMONS, G. C. Ovine Epididymitis Caused by *Actinobacillus seminis* (n. sp.). Austral. Vet. Jour. 36:454, 1960.

DAVIS, C. L., and STILES, G. W. Actinobacillosis in Rams. Jour. Amer. Vet. Med. Assn. 95:754, 1939.

GUNNING, O. V. Vet. Rec. 58:447, 1946.

JONES, F. S. An Organism Resembling *Bacillus actinoides* Isolated From Pneumonic Lungs of White Rats. Jour. Exp. Med. 35:361, 1922.

LIGNIÈRES, J., and SPITZ, G. Actinobacillos. Revista de la Soc. Med. Argentina, No. 53, 1902.

———, and ———. Nouvelle Contribution a l'Étude des Champignons Produisant des Actinomycosis. Ann. de Parasit. 2:1, 1924.

LIVINGSTON, C. W., Isolation of *Actinobacillus seminis* From Ovine Epididymitis. Amer. Jour. Vet. Res. 25:660–63, 1964.

MARSH, H., and WILKINS, H. W. Actinobacillosis in Sheep. Jour. Amer. Vet. Med. Assn. 94:363–64, 1939.

NELSON, J. B. The Bacteria of the Infected Middle Ear in Adult and Young Albino Rats. Jour. Inf. Dis. 46:64–75, 1930.

———. The Biological Characters of *B. actinoides* var. *muris*. Jour. Bact. 21:183–95, 1931.

PATHAK, R. C. Detection of an Antibody to *Actinobacillus lignieresi* in Infected Human Beings and the Antigenic Characterization of Isolates of Human and Bovine Origin. Amer. Jour. Vet. Res. 23:310–13, 1962.

PHILLIPS, J. E. The Commensal Role of *Actinobacillus lignieresi*. Jour. Path. Bact. 82:205–8, 1961.

RISTIC, M., *et al.* Actinobacillosis. I. An Evaluation of Cultural Characteristics of Selected Strains of *Actinobacillus lignieresi*. Amer. Jour. Vet. Res. 17:555, 1956.

SHAHAN, M. S., and DAVIS, C. L. The Diagonal of Actinomycosis and Actinobacillosis. Amer. Jour. Vet. Res. 3:321–28, 1942.

SMITH, H. W. Penicillin Iodides and Sulfas for *Act. lignieresi*. Vet. Rec. 63:674, 1951.

SMITH, T. A Pleomorphic Bacillus From Pneumonic Lungs of Calves Simulating Actinomycosis. Jour. Exp. Med. 28:333, 1918.

———. The Capsules or Sheaths of *Bacillus actinoides*. Jour. Exp. Med. 34:593, 1921.

TAYLOR, A. W. Vet. Bull. 16:259, 1946.

THOMAS, A. D. Actinobacillosis and Other Complications in Sheep Which May Arise From the Feeding of Prickly Pear (*Opuntia* sp.). 17th Rept. Dir. Vet. Ser. and An. Ind., Union South Africa, Part 1, 215–29, 1931.

THOMPSON, L. Systematic Relationships of Actinobacillus. Jour. Bact. 26:221–27, 1933.

WETMORE, P. W., *et al.* Comparison of Selected Actinobacillus Species With a Hemolytic Variety of Actinobacillus From Irradiated Swine. Jour. Inf. Dis. 113:186–94, 1963.

# 28

# The Genus Spherophorus

IN THIS GENUS ARE PLACED THOSE VERY pleomorphic rods which are anaerobic, nonmotile, nonsporeforming, and gram-negative. In elongated cells metachromatic granules may be observed.

The genus name Spherophorus was used for the first time in the 1948 edition of Bergey's Manual. The classification of the type species, *Spherophorus necrophorus,* of the genus has presented a problem for systematic bacteriologists for some time. This organism appeared to have a rather firm place in the genus Actinomyces for many years. It has been classified in the genus Fusiformis but that name was not used to any extent.

There are a number of species listed under this genus but the only one of significance to animal disease is *Spherophorus necrophorus.*

## *Spherophorus necrophorus*

**Synonyms and History.** *Bacillus necrophorus, Bacillus diphtheriae vitulorum, Streptothrix cuniculi, Bacillus filiformis, Streptothrix necrophora, Fusiformis necrophorus.*

In 1884 Loeffler observed this organism in material taken from cases of calf diphtheria. He was able to obtain primary growth of the organism upon calf serum inoculated with necrotic tissue from mice in which he had succeeded in producing typical lesions. In 1891 Schmorl isolated an organism which he called *Streptothrix cuniculi* from necrotic lesions around the lips of the rabbit. Since that time the organism has been isolated from a large number of animals showing typical necrotic lesions which have given rise to the term necrobacillosis for the disease.

**Distribution and Transmission.** *Sph. necrophorus* is widely distributed throughout the world. It has been isolated from the intestinal tract of man and animals; thus it appears to be a normal inhabitant of animal tissues. Infections associated with this organism are also associated with filthy, insanitary conditions. These infections may reach epizootic proportions in certain animals, particularly in calves and horses. The organism is a frequent secondary invader in other diseases in which primary necrosis or destruction of tissue exists.

**Morphology and Staining.** *Sph. necrophorus* is a slender, pleomorphic organism varying from coccoid cells $0.5\mu$ to $1.5\mu$ in size to filaments $100\mu$ in length. In young cultures the filamentous forms are most prevalent, but as the culture ages these filaments appear to segment and to break up into numerous coccoid and bacillary forms (Fig. 28.1). This process of segmentation gives the organism a typical beaded appearance when stained with carbol fuchsin (Fig. 28.2). Numerous of the short rods contain granules in each end which give them a typical bipolar appearance. The organism is easily but not heavily stained by the aniline dyes and is gram-negative. It is nonmotile, nonsporeforming, and does not show branching.

**Growth Requirements and Characteristics.** This organism is a strict anaerobe and

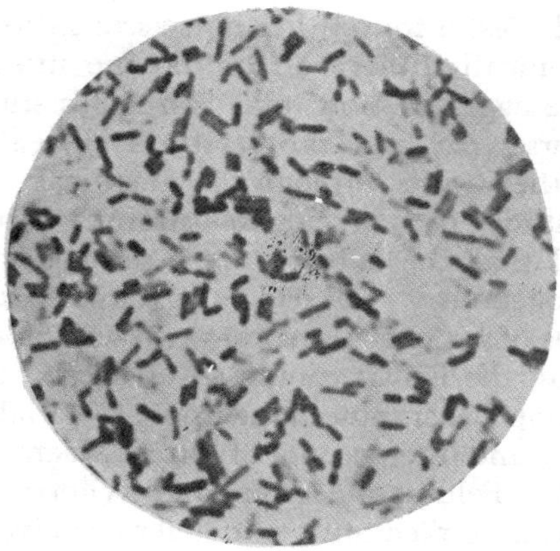

FIG. 28.1—**Spherophorus necrophorus** from an old bouillon culture, ×2,000. (From Nowak: Documenta Microbiologica, courtesy Gustav Fischer.)

grows at a temperature between 30° and 40°C. Hagan found that the organism produces enough hydrogen peroxide in the presence of air to cause inhibition of growth. Beveridge believes, however, that the oxygen intolerance of the organism is due partly to the oxidation-reduction potential and partly to the slight catalase formation by the organism. Catalase causes the decomposition of the peroxide. The organism grows most abundantly in a medium which is slightly alkaline, but growth occurs between pH 6.0 to 8.4.

It is difficult to obtain a pure culture of *Sph. necrophorus,* especially from skin and mucous membrane lesions, because of bacterial contamination. Pure cultures are more easily obtained from contaminated material by inoculating a rabbit subcutaneously with the necrotic material. Subcutaneous abscesses develop within a week, and in many cases isolated abscesses are formed in the liver. The organism can be isolated from these abscesses usually in pure culture. Feldman, Hester, and Wherry found that bovine liver abscesses were quite satisfactory sources of pure cultures. Necrotic material is transferred from the abscess to a number of tubes of Rosenow's dextrose-brain broth. These tubes are incubated at 37°C. for several days, and from them agar-shake cultures are made. Isolated colonies in the shake culture are then transferred to tubes of dextrose-brain broth for cultivation. On serum agar, incubated under anaerobic conditions, the organism forms small, round, opaque, circular colonies quite similar to those of the streptococci (Fig. 28.3). In broth the organism produces a uniform turbidity and the formation of a slight, fine, dirty-white sediment. As the culture ages, the medium clears, and the sediment increases in quantity and becomes darker in color.

**Resistance.** The necrophorus bacillus is killed in 15 minutes by a temperature of

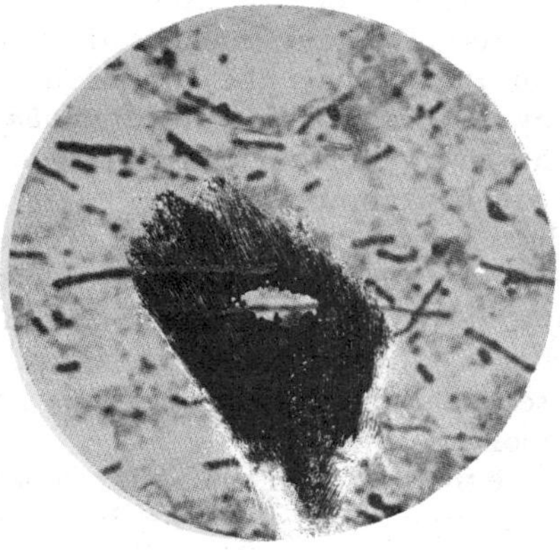

FIG. 28.2—**Spherophorus necrophorus** in smear of infected tissue, ×2,000. (From Nowak: Documenta Microbiologica, courtesy Gustav Fischer.)

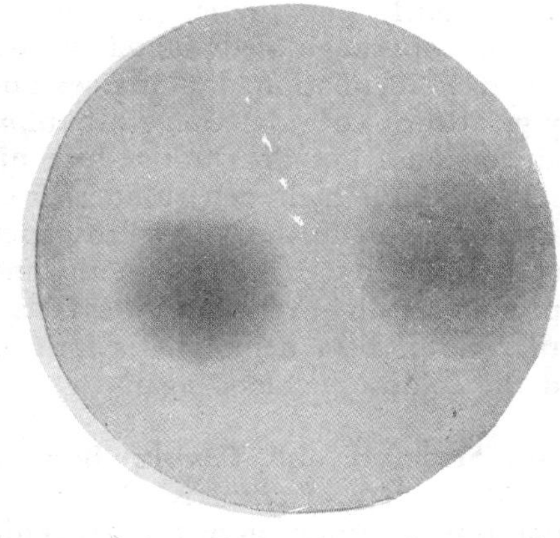

FIG. 28.3—**Spherophorus necrophorus** colonies on agar plate, ×50. (From Nowak: Documenta Microbiologica, courtesy Gustav Fischer.)

55°C. It is not resistant to chemical disinfectants. Kelser reports that 4 per cent acetic acid is a satisfactory germicide and is of value in treating necrotic dermatitis in the horse, which is caused by the organism.

It is difficult to maintain cultures of this organism on artificial media, and for that reason subcultures must be made at weekly intervals. The viability of this organism appears to be more pronounced in nature, for it persists in contaminated soil, and some believe that growth occurs under certain conditions. Beveridge sought to reveal the symbiotic action of aerobic organisms on the growth of *Sph. necrophorus* in air. He found that the necrophorus bacillus survived longer in the air when mixed with cultures of *Staphylococcus aureus* and *Escherichia coli* than when alone. This indicates that the organism is protected, at least from the action of oxygen, by the presence of aerobic bacteria and other substances which reduce oxygen tension.

**Biochemical Properties.** *Sph. necrophorus* produces acid and gas from glucose, maltose, and glycerol. Slight fermentation of lactose, galactose, fructose, arabinose, and mannitol has been reported by some investigators. It does not ferment xylose, rhamnose, mannose, raffinose, inulin, dulcitol, salicin, dextrin, erythritol, adonitol, sorbitol, inositol, or amygdalin. The organism is slightly proteolytic, causing the liquefaction of coagulated blood serum after ten days incubation, but it does not liquefy gelatin or coagulated egg albumin. It produces indol but does not reduce nitrates. It produces hydrogen sulfide; gives a negative reaction to the Voges-Proskauer and methyl red tests; reduces methylene blue; produces a slight reaction for catalase. A small zone of beta hemolysis is formed around the colony on blood agar.

**Antigenic Structure and Toxins.** Because of the wide variety of animals affected by this organism, the question of the antigenic relationships of various strains has been raised. Cesari found that horse strains were antigenically different from bovine strains, by the agglutination test. Harnach's study of horse, ox, and rabbit strains revealed that they were serologically identical. In the study of ten bovine strains Orcutt found that the cultures were serologically heterogenous. Beveridge grouped the strains of his organisms into two serological groups; the first is composed of five bovine and one Macropus (kangaroo or wallaby) strain, and the second of three Macropus strains. Feldman, Hester, and Wherry revealed a marked antigenic heterogeneity in fourteen bovine strains of the organism; however, they found a definite relationship between the agglutinins in the blood sera of sheep, swine, horses, and adult cattle for *Sph. necrophorus*.

The organism produces a soluble exotoxin which produces an edema when inoculated intradermally in rabbits. Endotoxins and killed suspensions of the organism produce subcutaneous necrosis in the rabbit and guinea pig.

**Pathogenicity.** *Sph. necrophorus* is responsible for necrotic and gangrenous lesions in a variety of species of animals. In all of the animals affected, the disease is characterized by a necrosis of tissue with the subsequent accumulation of cellular debris. The organisms do not progress far from the localized lesion, but in some cases metastasis occurs, and abscesses are formed within internal organs, such as the liver. In all of the animals the condition produced by this organism is called *necrobacillosis;* however, in some instances other names are in common use.

In horses *Sph. necrophorus* produces gangrenous dermatitis and necrotic processes about the lower extremities, known as "scratches." Ulceration of the intestines and a secondary necrotic pneumonia have been reported.

In cattle the organism has been recovered from numerous tissues of the body, but the most important condition is the necrosis in the mouth, larynx, and trachea of calves, commonly called "calf diphtheria." It produces liver abscesses in cattle of all ages and has been isolated from lesions in the intestinal tract, uterus, vulva, udder, teats, lungs, joints, and feet, either alone or as a secondary invader to other bacteria and traumatisms. Jensen, Flint, and Griner have clearly demonstrated that liver abscesses in cattle and sheep may be produced by the intraportal inoculation of a culture of the organism.

In sheep it is found in lip-and-leg ulceration, foot rot, necrotic hepatitis, necrotic vulvitis, and in a condition originating as necrosis of the ears due to fagopyrism.

In goats this bacillus has been isolated from ulcerative stomatitis, and in reindeer from foot lesions.

In pigs *Sph. necrophorus* is found in the intestinal lesions of enteritis probably as a secondary invader, in necrosis around the nose and the teeth, and in stomatitis and pharyngitis.

In fowls the organism has been reported as present in avian diphtheria as a secondary invader. Emmel has described an infection in young chickens in which necrotic lesions were present on the head. These lesions yielded an organism which had all the cultural characteristics of *Sph. necrophorus.*

In rabbits it produces a natural infection characterized by necrotic ulcers about the lips and mouth and extending to the skin and subcutaneous tissues.

*Sph. necrophorus* has been found in a variety of zoological animals including kangaroos, monkeys, antelopes, snakes, and tortoises. It has been reported as present in Australian kangaroos and wallabies by Beveridge.

In man the organism has been found in a number of necrotic processes. Dack, Dragstedt, Johnson, and McCullough compared strains isolated from cases of ulcerative colitis with animal strains and found them so similar that they were all grouped as *Bacterium necrophorum.* They found their strains were typical of an organism commonly called *Bacterium funduliforme.*

The rabbit is particularly susceptible to experimental inoculation with *Sph. necrophorus,* especially to the infected tissues of animals. On subcutaneous inoculation the tissue around the point of injection becomes necrotic, and the process progressively spreads until the skin and adjoining muscle tissue become involved. The animal becomes emaciated and usually dies within a week. On intravenous inoculation, necrotic abscesses are formed throughout the body; the animal becomes emaciated and dies within a week or is destroyed before that time. Mice are susceptible, and the same type of lesion is produced. Guinea pigs are somewhat resistant. Abscesses form subsequent to subcutaneous inoculation, and necrosis of skin occurs. The contents of the abscesses discharge and the lesions heal, but in some cases the infection spreads and the animal dies. McCullough has reported that guinea pigs placed on a vitamin C deficient ration until they were extremely scorbutic were more susceptible to *Sph. necrophorus* infection, and that vitamin C therapy produced prompt recovery in infected scorbutic guinea pigs.

**Immunity.** Agglutinating antibodies are produced in animals suffering with an infection produced by this organism. To what extent these antibodies protect the animal against more serious and fatal infection is not known. The presence of agglutinating antibodies in the serum of horses, cattle, sheep, and swine has been reported by Feldman, Hester, and Wherry; however, they found that the serum of cattle having hepatic abscesses did not show an appreciable increase in agglutinin.

Artificial immunizing agents have not been produced for this infection. Beveridge found that rabbits were not protected from experimental infection by two doses of formolized culture injected subcutaneously. This, according to him, is not surprising since the main lesion of the disease, necrosis, is produced by endotoxins of the organism. Scrivner and Lee found that the injection of bacterins into the rabbit delayed the formation of typical lesions following the inoculation with live cultures.

**Diagnosis.** The presence of this organism in necrotic tissue is substantial evidence of infection; however, since it occurs so frequently as a secondary invader, the primary cause should always be sought. Rabbit inoculation is sometimes essential for definite diagnosis. The presence of agglutinins in the blood serum of animals is not considered significant enough for the diagnosis of the presence of internal lesions produced by *Sph. necrophorus.*

## REFERENCES

BEVERIDGE, W. I. B. Jour. Path. Bact. 38:467, 1934.
EMMEL, M. W. Jour. Amer. Vet. Med. Assn. 113:169, 1948.
FELDMAN, W. H., *et al.* Jour. Inf. Dis. 59:159–70, 1936.
GAY, F. P., *et al.* Agents of Disease and Host Resistance, Chaps. 38, 39, 40, pp. 829–910. Charles C Thomas, Baltimore, 1935.
HAGAN, W. A. Jour. Inf. Dis. 35:390, 1924.
HARRIS, A. N. A. Austral. Vet. Jour. 23:152, 1947.
JENSEN, RUE, *et al.* Amer. Jour. Vet. Res. 15:5, 1954.
MCCULLOUGH, N. B. Jour. Inf. Dis. 63:34, 1938.
RYFF, J. F., and LEE, A. M. Amer. Jour. Vet. Res. 7:41, 1946.
SCRIVNER, L. H., and LEE, A. M. Jour. Amer. Vet. Med. Assn. 85:360–79, 1934.
TUNNICLIFF, E. A. Jour. Inf. Dis. 62:58, 1938.

# 29

# The Genus Listeria

IN THIS GENUS ONLY ONE SPECIES, *Listeria monocytogenes,* has been classified. This microorganism is a small, motile, gram-positive rod which grows readily on most culture media under aerobic and microaerophilic conditions. It produces acid but never gas from a number of carbohydrates, and is not proteolytic. It has been isolated from a large number of different species of animals and from man. In rodents it produces a mononucleosis from which it derived its name.

### *Listeria monocytogenes*

**Synonyms and History.** In March, 1910, Gustav Hülpers of Sweden isolated an organism which he called *Bacillus hepatis* from the liver of a rabbit. His description of the organism and the type of disease found in the rabbit clearly indicates that he may have been the first to isolate and describe *L. monocytogenes.* Unfortunately, his cultures were not retained and were not critically compared to any known strain of this microorganism. In 1926 Murray, Webb, and Swann, working in England, described an organism which produced a generalized infection characterized by a marked mononuclear leucocytosis in rabbits and occasionally in guinea pigs. They regarded the organism as one which had not been described previously and because of the effect on mononuclear cells, they coined the name *Bacterium monocytogenes.* This strain was given the number 53XXIII and has been recognized as the type culture of *L. monocytogenes.* It is pertinent to suggest that anyone who isolates a new microorganism should be certain he maintains several cultures for future reference.

In 1927 Pirie of South Africa observed that an organism was the cause of a generalized infection known as "Tiger River Disease" in which focal necrosis of the liver was the pronounced lesion in the gerbil, a small ratlike animal living in burrows in the ground. He could find no other species of organism similar to the one he isolated nor could he find a suitable genus in which to classify it; consequently, he suggested a new genus for the organism in honor of Lord Lister and formed the name *Listerella hepatolytica.* He called attention to the similarity of his organism to the one isolated by Murray, Webb, and Swann and suggested that if they were identical, the name *Listerella monocytogenes* be used. The name *Listerella monocytogenes* was used in Bergey's Manual in 1934. In 1937 Gill isolated the organism from sheep and suggested the name *Listerella ovis.*

The name Listerella has been used for other genera of plant life; consequently, Pirie suggested that the name Listeria would be more appropriate. In the 1948 edition of Bergey's Manual the genus name Listeria was adopted. This automatically changed the name of the disease from listerellosis to listeriosis.

The organism has been classified under the genus Erysipelothrix by some authors and also with the Corynebacteria by others. It is apparent that it is distinct from both of the above genera and the name as now used appears to be justified.

**Distribution and Transmission.** *Listeria monocytogenes* is found widely distributed in a number of different hosts in which it produces various types of diseases which are collectively called *Listeriosis.* In addition to the animals previously mentioned, the organism has been isolated from the following:

Sheep: Gill, 1931, 1933, 1937, in New Zealand; Ten Broeck, 1935, in New Jersey; Olafson, 1936, in New York; Jungherr, 1937, in Connecticut; Graham, Dunlap, and Brandly, 1938, in Illinois; Biester and Schwarte, 1939, in Iowa; Paterson, 1939, in England.

Cattle: Jones and Little, 1934, in New Jersey; Fincher, 1935, in New York; Olafson, 1936, in New York; Graham, Dunlap, and Brandly, 1938, in Illinois; Biester and Schwarte, 1938, 1941, in Iowa; Harbour, 1941, Wyan Jones, 1954, Britain.

Chickens: Ten Broeck, 1932, in New Jersey; Seastone, 1935, in New Jersey; Paterson, 1937, in England.

Swine: Biester and Schwarte, 1939, in Iowa; Jarrett *et al.*, 1959, Scotland.

Foxes: Cromwell, Sweebe, and Camp, 1939, in Illinois.

Chinchillas: Shalkop, 1950, in Washington, D.C.

Ferrets: Morris and Norman, 1950, in Washington, D.C.

Raccoons: Gifford and Jungherr, 1950, in Connecticut.

Horses: Grini, 1943, in Norway; Krage, 1944, in Germany; Belin, 1947, in France; Svenkerud, 1948, in Norway.

Man: Burn, 1934, 1935, 1936, in Connecticut; Schultz, Terry, Brice, and Gebhardt, 1934, in California; Gibson, 1935, in Scotland; Carey, 1936, in Massachusetts; Macgregor and Wright, 1938, in Scotland; Pons and Julianelle, 1939, in New Jersey.

According to Murray this organism has been isolated from 18 species of wild or domestic animals involving birds, rodents, ungulates, carnivores, and primates in 19 different countries and every continent. In Sweden Nilsson and Karlsson found it in 12 different species of animals during the period 1948–57.

In a Symposium on Listeric Infection held at Bozeman, Montana, in 1962, reports from many countries emphasize that *L. monocytogenes* is widespread throughout the world and infects many different species of animals and man. The student is referred to the published proceedings of this symposium and also the book, *Listeriosis,* by Seeliger for further reading.

The methods by which this organism is transmitted are unknown. Gill suggests that the larvae of *Oestrus ovis,* the "nasal bot" of sheep, may be a means by which the organism is transmitted among that species of animal. To what extent it is transmitted from one animal species to another is not known. Some human cases have revealed contact with sick animals; this indicates some degree of contagiousness and emphasizes the importance of the public health aspect of the disease. The name "opportunist" has been given to that type of organism which may be present in the body of the host, and under conditions of "stress" may produce cellular changes called disease. *L. monocytogenes* appears to be such an organism, and the carrier animal constitutes a hazard to itself and others, including man.

**Morphology and Staining.** *L. monocytogenes* is a small rod with rounded ends, 0.5$\mu$ in diameter by 1.0$\mu$ to 2.0$\mu$ in length. Filaments as long as 4$\mu$ are observed in some cultures. It occurs singly, in V-shaped or parallel pairs, and in short chains of three to six organisms (Fig. 29.1). It is nonsporeforming and noncapsuleproducing.

Griffin and Robbins have demonstrated that *L. monocytogenes* is peritrichous with a maximum of four flagella when grown at room temperature, but may produce no

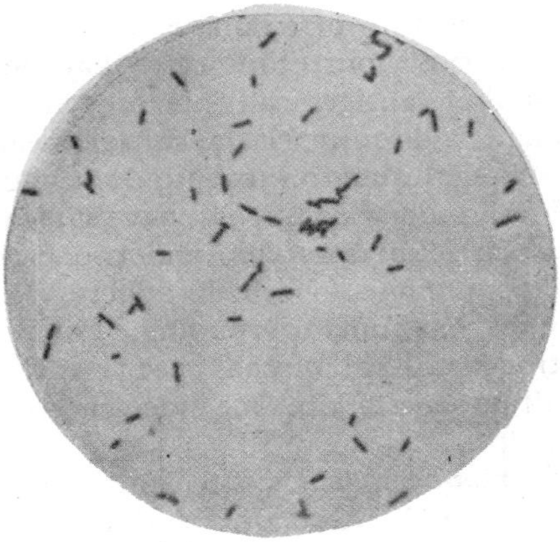

FIG. 29.1–**Listeria monocytogenes** from sheep, agar culture, ×1,200. (Photo by Schwarte.)

flagella at 37°C. with a small percentage of cells showing mono- and a few bi- and tri-flagellated forms.

This organism is easily stained by all of the aniline dyes and is gram-positive. Old cultures are more easily decolorized, and many of the cells show typical bipolar staining. It is not acid-fast.

**Growth Requirements and Characteristics.** The organism is aerobic and facultative; grows well at any temperature between 20°C. and 40°C.; grows best at pH 7.0 to 7.2. Any of the nutrient media which are used for the cultivation of pathogenic bacteria can be used for the growth of this organism. In order to obtain primary growth from infected tissue, it is essential to disperse the tissue in a Waring blender prior to inoculation of culture media; even then, only a few colonies are found on the inoculated surface. The presence of an inhibitory substance in fresh bovine brain tissue which prevents the growth of the bacteria is strongly indicated by the work of Gray and associates. These investigators found that more abundant growth was obtained from brain tissue after it had been refrigerated at 4°C. for a few weeks.

In another publication, Gray *et al.* found that the addition of 0.05 per cent potassium tellurite to tryptose agar was useful in isolating *L. monocytogenes*. This chemical inhibits the growth of most gram-negative bacteria. Listeria colonies appear black with a green color at the periphery; micrococci are pinkish-yellow at the periphery and intensely black at the center; streptococci are small, pinkish-gray in color, with a dull surface.

Various growth-promoting nutrients for *L. monocytogenes* have been studied. Friedman and Roessler recommend organic sulfur, valine, glutamine, and isoleucine; also leucine, histidine, arginine and methionine as stimulatory for some strains. Welshimer found that riboflavin, biotin, thiamine and thioctic acid were essential in growing cultures beyond the second passage.

On solid agar media, colonies of the organism are circular, smooth, and transparent; by reflected light they are gray in color; by oblique light they are blue-green.

On blood agar small colonies surrounded by a narrow zone of beta hemolysis are found.

In broth a slight turbidity is developed, and a fairly heavy granular sediment is formed.

On a semisolid medium the organism forms minute colonies surrounding the line of inoculation. In some cultures a clouding of the medium extends from the stab line (Fig. 29.2).

**Resistance.** The organism is destroyed by a temperature of 58° to 59°C. in 10 minutes. It is easily killed by the usual disinfectants.

The presence of the organism in soil is not known, but Welshimer has reported that it can survive for a period as long as 295 days, although many cells die during the first month of exposure. Although the evidence was somewhat circumstantial, Gray thought that poor-grade silage might have harbored the organism which was responsible for an outbreak of listeriosis in range cattle.

*L. monocytogenes* is sensitive to a number of antibiotics, but tetracycline is the most favorable therapeutic agent.

**Biochemical Properties.** *L. monocytogenes* produces acid from glucose, rhamnose, and

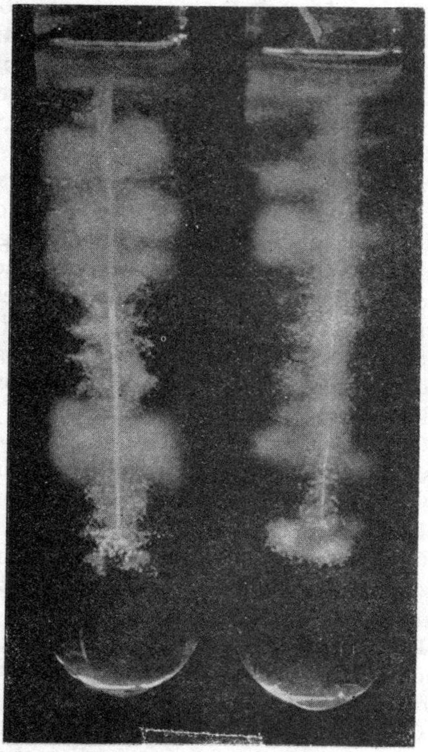

FIG. 29.2—**Listeria monocytogenes** culture in semisolid medium. (From Seastone, courtesy Journal Experimental Medicine.)

salicin within 24 hours after inoculation; produces acid in sucrose, maltose, lactose, glycerol, starch, and dextrin in 7 to 12 days; is slow and somewhat variable in the fermentation of galactose, trehalose, sorbitol, and xylose. Jungherr, Paterson, and Peterson all reported the fermentation of fructose, but Burn obtained negative results with human strains. All of the investigators reported the absence of fermentation of mannitol, dulcitol, inulin, inositol, and arabinose. The organism does not produce indol, does not reduce nitrates or form $H_2S$. It does not liquefy gelatin. Litmus milk is decolorized, and a slight amount of acid is formed, but the medium is not coagulated. The organism produces beta type hemolysis on blood agar.

**Antigenic Structure and Toxins.** The limited amount of investigation of the antigenic structure of strains of this organism from various sources indicates that they are somewhat antigenically heterogenous although a group relationship appears to exist. Agglutination techniques, using flagellar and somatic antigens, have shown that there are four serotypes and two or more subtypes, none of which adheres to any animal or human grouping. Fluorescent antibody technique has been used with medium success in the identification of serotypes.

*L. monocytogenes* does not produce a true exotoxin although filterable hemolysin is formed by all strains. McIlwain *et al.* have reported three proteinaceous fractions isolated from disrupted cells. One of these fractions, $P_1$, produced in rabbits cardiovascular symptoms, elevated temperature, and hyperglycemia followed by hypoglycemia and monocyte increase. The other fractions were without effect. A lipid substance in the organism, or produced by it, appears to have a bearing on the increase of monocytes in the blood vascular system as well as the accumulation of such cells in lesions found in various tissues.

The use of bacteriophage to classify strains of this organism into 8 phage types has been reported by Sword and Pickett.

**Pathogenicity.** *L. monocytogenes* is capable of producing natural infection in rabbits, guinea pigs, gerbils, chickens, turkeys, sheep, goats, cattle, foxes, swine, chinchillas, ferrets, raccoons, skunks, horses, and man.

The disease in all species of animals is somewhat varied as to type of tissue involved. In the rabbit, chinchilla, guinea pig, and gerbil, liver necrosis is a pronounced lesion. In the sheep, ox, and pig, lesions are confined to the central nervous system where a marked meningitis is produced, and monocytic infiltration with focalization is apparent. Graham and associates have reported finding the organism in an aborted bovine fetus. In the chicken, the organism causes an extensive necrosis of the myocardium. The report of the organism from the fox was not conclusive concerning the etiological relationship to an acute, distemper-like infection which was present in the young animals. It was isolated from the heart blood of five of the eight foxes which were observed. Morris and Norman have found that the organism is harbored in apparently healthy ferrets. In the course of distemper studies colonies of *L. monocytogenes* appeared in the cultures inoculated with lung and spleen tissues from distemper-infected ferrets. That the organism may be present in swine without causing symptoms of encephalitis is indicated by the report of Rhoades and Sutherland who isolated it from the liver, spleen, and kidney of a case of hog cholera. Bolin and Eveleth isolated the organism during the routine culturing of liver tissue from a pig. This organism has been isolated from meningitis in man. It is considered to be one of the causes of abortion and may produce consecutive abortions.

Guinea pigs, rabbits, mice, and rats are all susceptible to experimental inoculation. The animals usually die within 48 hours and postmortem examination reveals typical lesions of liver necrosis. Gray and coworkers have reported that abortion is produced in rabbits by ocular and oral inoculation with *L. monocytogenes*.

The respiratory virulence of the organism for mice, guinea pigs, and hamsters has been stressed by Kautter *et al.* Friedman and Kautter observed that the virulence for the guinea pig could be increased by decreasing the glucose concentration from 1.0 to 0.6 per cent and by including 0.1 per cent L-cysteine in the medium.

**Immunity.** Information concerning the immunity produced by this organism is variable. Olafson found that some sheep can be immunized to withstand subsequent injections of the organism, but just as many remain unprotected after the injection of 2.5 cc. of broth cultures two or three times a week for six weeks. The disease is so sporadic that wholesale immunization of flocks and herds is not indicated at the present time. In their experimental study of listeriosis, Olson, Cook, and Blore found that sheep were more resistant after having received one injection of *L. monocytogenes*. It is generally admitted that only living cultures, either virulent or avirulent, are capable of producing an effective immunity.

**Diagnosis.** The conditions which are produced by *L. monocytogenes* may be confused symptomatically with a number of diseases; consequently, the only certain method of diagnosis is the isolation and identification of the organism. Four significant characteristics of the organism must be emphasized: (1) It is a small, pleomorphic, G+ rod. (2) It is motile. (3) It is beta hemolytic. (4) Its isolation is augmented by storage of the suspected tissue in the refrigerator at 4°C. for a week if initial isolation is not successful.

Care must be shown in the examination of mice which die following the inoculation of suspected rabies brain tissue. If Negri bodies are not found in dead mice, they should be cultured for *L. monocytogenes* when the brain tissue is of ovine or bovine origin.

## REFERENCES


BAKULAV, A. A Study of the Sensitivity of the Agent of Listeriosis in Farm Animals to Various Antibiotics in Vitro. Antibiotics 4:575, 1959.

BARBER, M. Jour. Path. Bact. 48:11–23, 1939.

BELIN, M. Bull. Acad. Vet. Fr. 19:176, 1946.

BIESTER, H. E., and SCHWARTE, L. H. Jour. Inf. Dis. 64:135–44, 1939.

———, and ———. Jour. Amer. Vet. Med. Assn. 96:339–42, 1940.

———, and ———. No. Amer. Vet. 22:729–34, 1941.

BOLIN, F. M., and EVELETH, D. F. Jour. Amer. Vet. Med. Assn. 118:7, 1951.

BORMAN, G., *et al.* Amer. Jour. Vet. Res. 21:993, 1960.

BURN, C. G. Proc. Soc. Exp. Biol. Med. 31:1095, 1934.

BURN, C. G. Jour. Bact. 30:573–91, 1935.
———. Amer. Jour. Path. 12:341–48, 1936.
CAREY, B. W., JR. Jour. Pediatr. 8:626–29, 1936.
CROMWELL, H. W., *et al.* Science 89:293, 1939.
DICKIE, A. T., *et al.* Two Cases of *Erysipelothrix* (*Listeria*) *monocytogenes* Infection in Cattle. Vet. Rec. 70:1, 1958.
FINCHER, M. G. Cornell Vet. 25:61–63, 1935.
FRIEDMAN, M. E., and KAUTTER, D. A. Effect of Nutrition on the Respiratory Virulence of *Listeria monocytogenes*. Jour. Bact. 83:456–62, 1962.
———, and ROESSLER, W. G. Growth of *Listeria monocytogenes* in Defined Media. Jour. Bact. 82:528–33, 1961.
GIBSON, H. J. Jour. Path. Bact. 41:239, 1935.
GIFFORD, R., and EVELETH, D. F. Jour. Amer. Vet. Med. Assn. 101:413, 1942.
———, and JUNGHERR, E. Cornell Vet. 37:39, 1947.
GILL, D. A. "Circling Disease" of Sheep in New Zealand. Vet. Jour. 87:60–74, 1931.
———. Vet. Jour. 89:258–70, 1933.
———. Austral. Vet. Jour. 13:46, 1937.
GIRARD, K. F., and GAVIN, W. F. Jour. Path. Bact. 74:93, 1957.
GRAHAM, R. Jour. Amer. Vet. Med. Assn. 95:289–92, 1939.
———, *et al.* Listerellosis in Domestic Animals. Ill. Agr. Exp. Sta. Bull. 499. Urbana, 1943.
———, *et al.* Proc. Soc. Exp. Biol. Med. 89:163, 169, 1955.
GRIFFIN, A. M., and ROBBINS, M. L. Jour. Bact. 48:114, 1944.
GRINI, O. Norsk Vet. Tidsskr. Nr. 3, 1943.
HÜLPERS, GUSTAV. Lefvernekros hos kanin orsakad af en ej förut beskrifven bakterie. Svensk Veterinartidskrift 16:265, 1911.
JARRETT, W. F. H., *et al.* *Erysipelothrix* (*Listeria*) *monocytogenes* Infection in Piglets. Vet. Rec. 71:225, 1959.
JONES, F. S., and LITTLE, R. B. Arch. Path. 18:580–81, 1934.
JULIANELLE, L. A., and PONS, C. A. Proc. Soc. Exp. Biol. Med. 40:364–65, 1939.
JUNGHERR, E. Vet. Med. Assn. 91:73–87, 1937.
KAUTTER, D. A., *et al.* Virulence of *Listeria monocytogenes* for Experimental Animals. Jour. Inf. Dis. 112:167–80, 1963.
KEELER, R. F., and GRAY, M. L. Jour. Bact. 80:683, 1960.
KRAGE, P. Berl. Münch. tierärztl. Wsch./Wien. tierärztl. Wschr. Jan. 21, 30–31, 1944.
LAYMANN, V. Der Verlauf der experimentellen Infektion mit *Listeria monocytogenes* bei der weissen Maus. Inaug. Diss. Tierärztlichen Fakultät der Ludwig Maximilians-Universität, Munich, Germany.
MCILWAIN, P., *et al.* Pharmacologic Studies of a Toxic Cellular Component of *Listeria monocytogenes*. Amer. Jour. Vet. Res. 25:774–81, 1964.
MOLELLO, J. A., and JENSEN, R. Placental Lesions of Sheep Experimentally Infected With *Listeria monocytogenes*. Amer. Jour. Vet. Res. 25:441–49, 1964.
MORRIS, J. A., and NORMAN, M. C. Jour. Bact. 59:313, 1950.
MURRAY, E. G. D. A Characterization of Listeriosis in Man and Animals. Canad. Med. Assn. Jour. 72:99, 1955.
———. The Story of Listeria, Flavelle Medallists Address. Trans. Royal Soc. Canada. Vol. XLVII, Series III, June, 1953.
———, *et al.* Jour. Path. Bact. 29:407–39, 1926.
NILSSON, A., and KARLSSON, K. A. *Listeria monocytogenes* Isolations From Animals in Sweden During 1948–1957. Nord. Vet. Med. 11:305, 1959.
OLAFSON, PETER. Cornell Vet. 30:141–50, 1940.
OLSON, C., JR., *et al.* Amer. Jour. Vet. Res. 11:29, 1950.
———, *et al.* Amer. Jour. Vet. Res. 12:306, 1951.
———, *et al.* Amer. Jour. Vet. Res. 14:202, 1953.
———, *et al.* Amer. Jour. Vet. Res. 14:82, 1953.
———, *et al.* Amer. Jour. Vet. Res. 18:303, 1957.
OSEBOLD, J. W., and CORDY, D. R. Valvular Endocarditis Associated With *Listeria monocytogenes* Infections in Sheep. Jour. Amer. Vet. Med. Assn. 143:990–93, 1963.
———, *et al.* Jour. Amer. Vet. Med. Assn. 130:471, 1957.
———, *et al.* Amer. Jour. Vet. Res. 20:966, 1959.
PATERSON, J. S. Vet. Rec. 49:1533–34, 1937.
———. Jour. Path. Bact. 48:25–32, 1939.
———. Vet. Rec. 51:873–76, 1939.

PIRIE, J. H. H. Publ. S. African Inst. Med. Res. 3:163–86, 1927.

PONS, C. A., and JULIANELLE, L. A. Proc. Soc. Exp. Biol. Med. 40:360–61, 1939.

POUNDEN, W. D., *et al.* Jour. Amer. Vet. Med. Assn. 111:128, 1947.

PROCEEDINGS, SECOND SYMPOSIUM ON LISTERIC INFECTION. Bozeman, Montana. Publ. Mont. State College, Bozeman, 1963.

RHOADES, H. E., and SUTHERLAND, A. K. Jour. Amer. Vet. Med. Assn. 112:451, 1948.

RYFF, J. F., and LEE, A. M. Amer. Jour. Vet. Res. 9:147, 1948.

SCHOLTENS, R. G., and BRIM, A. Isolation of *Listeria monocytogenes* From Foxes Suspected of Having Rabies. Jour. Amer. Vet. Med. Assn. 145:466–69, 1964.

SCHULTZ, E. W., *et al.* Proc. Soc. Exp. Biol. Med. 31:1021–23, 1934.

SCHWARTE, L. H., and BIESTER, H. E. Amer. Jour. Vet. Res. 3:165–76, 1942.

SEASTONE, C. V. Jour. Exp. Med. 62:203–12, 1935.

SEELIGER, H. P. R. Listeriosis. Hafner Publ. Co., Inc., New York, 1961.

SEGRE, D., *et al.* Amer. Jour. Vet. Res. 17:299, 1956.

STOCKTON, J. J., *et al.* Jour. Amer. Vet. Med. Assn. 124:102, 1954.

SWORD, C. P., and PICKETT, M. J. The Isolation and Characterization of Bacteriophages From *Listeria monocytogenes*. Jour. Gen. Microbiol. 25:241–48, 1961.

WELSHIMER, H. J. Vitamin Requirements of *Listeria monocytogenes*. Jour. Bact. 85:1156–59, 1963.

OUNG, S., and FIREHAMMER, B. O. Jour. Amer. Vet. Med Assn. 132:434, 1958.

# 30

# The Genus Bacillus

The organisms which belong to the group of aerobic, sporebearing bacilli are cylindrical, usually flagellated, grow in chains, and produce large, irregular colonies on solid media. Practically all of the species liquefy gelatin. Only one species, *Bacillus anthracis,* is pathogenic.

The aerobic bacilli are probably the most common type of microorganism in existence. They are found in the soil and on decaying vegetation where they are most active in bringing about the decomposition of organic substances, particularly those changes grouped together under the term ammonification. They are, therefore, of great importance in the maintenance of soil fertility. Because of the resistance of the spores to high temperatures and desiccation, these organisms are among those which most frequently contaminate culture media in the laboratory.

The various species are differentiated from each other by the size, shape, and position of the spores, the tendency to chain formation, motility, by differences in cultural and physiologic characteristics, and in pathogenicity. *B. anthracis* can be separated, with certainty, from some of the common saprophytic soil species only by animal inoculation, by physiologic and serologic tests, or by careful observation of colony characteristics.

While it is true that the only definite pathogenic species is *B. anthracis,* there are a few other species which have been known to produce pathologic conditions. *Bacillus subtilis* may cause iridocyclitis and panophthalmitis, and has been known to produce a fatal septicemia. It has been isolated in pure culture from liver and mandibular abscesses in cattle and sheep. *Bacillus megatherium* is capable of producing death in guinea pigs by virtue of a potent hemolysin which it liberates. Pseudoanthrax bacilli, which are able to kill mice and guinea pigs when used in large doses, also have been described. The exact identity of such bacilli is unknown, but many of these bacteria are confused with the anthrax bacillus. Such bacilli are motile and noncapsuleproducing, while the reverse is true of anthrax bacilli. Salicin is more quickly fermented by pseudoanthrax bacilli. *B. anthracis* is considered to be nonhemolytic or weakly so, while the other type is strongly beta hemolytic. Many other characteristics may be used for differentiation but the above should suffice.

The student in veterinary bacteriology may study *B. subtilis* in lieu of *B. anthracis* in the laboratory since *B. subtilis* is not pathogenic to man. The virulence of *B. anthracis* to man makes the study of that organism in laboratory groups an unnecessary risk. *B. subtilis* is used often to portray the general characteristics of bacilli, so it will be given a rather complete description. The only other species described in detail will be *B. anthracis.*

### *Bacillus subtilis*

**Synonyms and History.** *B. subtilis* was first described by Ehrenberg as *Vibrio subtilis* in 1838, and is commonly known as the "hay bacillus."

**Distribution and Transmission.** The organism is found in the soil; hence it is on most vegetation. It is spread by water, wind, and normal traffic in feeds, and is present all over the world.

**Morphology and Staining.** The organisms occur as cylindrical rods, 1μ in diameter by 3μ to 4μ in length, straight or slightly curved, with rounded ends, singly or in chains. They are actively motile by peritrichic flagella. Spores are oval and centrally located. The sporangium quickly disappears after the spore is formed. Spores germinate laterally. The organism is gram-positive.

**Growth Requirements and Characteristics.** *B. subtilis* is easily cultured on any nutrient medium. Surface colonies on agar are small, grayish, amoeboid, with crenate margin and a wool-like edge. The surface is finely granular and dull. The growth is membranous, slightly sticky, and is emulsified with difficulty. A thick ring pellicle which usually sinks within 24 hours forms on broth. The pellicle swirls from the bottom of the tube in a twisted cone when the tube is rapidly rotated. On potato a luxuriant, warty, gray growth forms, which becomes pink with vesicles over the surface as the culture ages.

**Resistance.** The bacillus is extremely resistant to heat by virtue of the spores. Boiling kills it in 2 hours, or death may be brought about at 120°C. in 15 minutes. Spores remain viable for years in the dry state. Ordinary chemical disinfectants kill by prolonged contact.

It is sensitive to penicillin and is one of the organisms used in the assay of that antibiotic.

**Biochemical Properties.** Acid is formed from glucose, sucrose, and maltose; indol is not formed; nitrates are reduced; $H_2S$ is produced slightly. The organism is methyl red negative and Voges-Proskauer positive. It reduces methylene blue; coagulates litmus milk which is then slowly peptonized from the top downward; forms $NH_3$; liquefies blood serum slowly.

**Antigenic Structure.** Nothing definite is known concerning the antigenic structure, and no toxins are produced.

The production of the antibiotic, subtilin, by this organism is discussed in the chapter on antibiotics. The action of a substance in the filtrate of cultures of *B. subtilis* against the toxin of *Corynebacterium diphtheriae* was observed by Ramon and Richou. A similar but less marked effect was noted against *Clostridium tetani* and *Clostridium welchii* toxins.

### *Bacillus anthracis*

**History.** Rayer and his assistant Davaine in 1850 were the first to observe nonmotile, filiform bodies in the blood of animals having died of anthrax. Pollender, however, reported in 1855 that he had observed rod-like cells as early as 1849 in the blood of cows having died of anthrax. Brauell, in 1857–58, reported the transmission of anthrax from man to a sheep in which he found small, motionless organisms after death. In 1859 Fuchs claimed to have seen "Vibrions" in the blood of animals as early as 1842. Delafond, in 1860, found small bodies in the blood of numerous animals which had died of anthrax and in animals which had been artificially infected.

In a series of studies between the years 1863 and 1868, Davaine definitely established the presence of filiform bodies in the blood of animals which had died of anthrax. He gave the name "bacterides" to these bodies, and found he could produce the disease in rabbits. He observed the bodies in man having "malignant pustule," and he killed guinea pigs by injecting the "bacterides." Tiegel, in 1871, and Pasteur and Joubert, in 1877, showed that anthrax was caused by the small "bacterides" of Davaine because filtrates from which the organisms had been removed did not produce disease. Absolute proof of the etiology of anthrax was established by Koch in 1876–77 when he cultured *Bacillus anthracis* and reproduced the disease in animals by injecting suspensions of the organism. He proved his postulates by isolating the organism from the infected animal.

Contributions to the immunity of anthrax were made in 1880 by Chauveau and in the same year by Toussaint. Final and undoubted proof of the value of vaccination, however, resulted from the famous experiments of Pasteur at Pouilly-le-Fort in 1881.

**Distribution and Transmission.** Anthrax is found all over the world. It is particularly prevalent in countries where no organized control of animal diseases exists. India, China, Siberia, Russia, northern Africa, some parts of South America, and Mexico have anthrax as a major livestock problem. Germany, France, Italy, Great Britain, and the United States keep the disease well under control; however, in the United States anthrax is found in certain areas. Hansen believes that anthrax was introduced into the Ohio River Valley during the early days of westward migration, and he cites that Kercheval was the first person to describe an outbreak of the disease in cattle and infection in four farmers in the United States in 1824. The Mississippi and Missouri river valleys have endemic areas where anthrax is a problem. The disease has spread from the lower Mississippi region over the South where numerous sporadic cases occur. Other sections report cases from time to time. Such areas are strictly quarantined and have not developed into anthrax areas.

The prevalence of anthrax in the United States in 1945–54 was summarized by Stein (1955). Most of the well-known anthrax districts remained endemic areas with isolated outbreaks of the disease occurring in many of the states. Numerous cases of the disease appeared in swine in the midwestern states during 1951 and 1952. These isolated outbreaks were caused by raw bone meal which had been added to commercial feeds. An extensive epizootic of anthrax occurred in northeastern Oklahoma and southeastern Kansas in 1957, with a loss of 1627 animals on 741 premises as reported by Van Ness and associates. Attention is called to the drought conditions in this area for several years, followed by excessive rainfall just preceding the anthrax outbreak. The soil became abnormally alkaline, which Van Ness considers typical of anthrax areas.

The organism is spread by the soil-contaminated feeds, and by water. Pasture lands remain contaminated for years. Hay taken from such land has been known to transmit the disease. The spores of the organism are spread by water which has flooded over contaminated ground. Tanneries, wool-sorting establishments, rendering plants, and fertilizer plants have also been incriminated as sources of anthrax which has been spread by stream flow.

Carnivorous animals, dogs, cats, and hogs may contract anthrax by feeding on dead carcasses. Pinkerton has reported the disease in mink which had been fed horse meat. Birds spread the infection by carrying bits of flesh or by eating infected meat and eliminating the spores in their feces. Bloodsucking flies have been incriminated in the spread of the organism among animals, and in some cases from animals to man. Stiles has isolated the organism from colonies of spinose ear ticks *(Ornithodorus megnini)* which were attached to the ear of a cow dead with anthrax, thus indicating that ticks may be a vector of the organism.

Man contracts the disease by contact with infected animals, by handling infected hides, by sorting wool, from shaving brushes, from contamined furs and hair cushions, and from insect bites.

**Morphology and Staining.** The bacilli are cylindrical rods, $1\mu$ to $1.2\mu$ in diameter by $3\mu$ to $8\mu$ in length (Fig. 30.1). The capsule, which is formed in the infected animal, is demonstrated by suitable stains, such as Räbiger (Fig. 30.2). Spores are ellipsoidal, situated centrally in the cell, and are $0.7\mu$ to $0.8\mu$ by $1.5\mu$ in size (Fig. 30.3). They are not formed in the animal body. Spores germinate at the pole. Young cells are

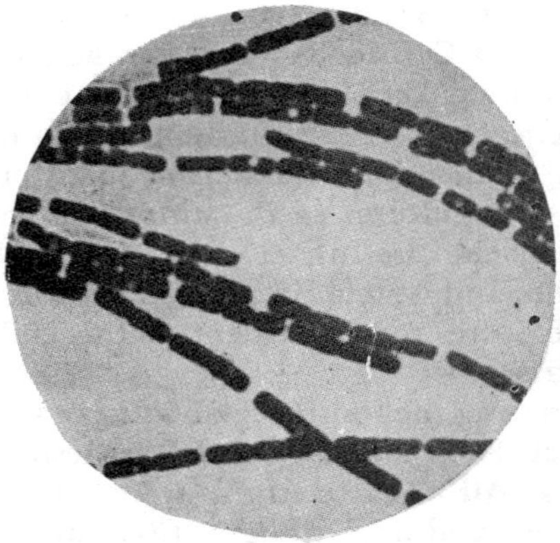

FIG. 30.1—**Bacillus anthracis** impression smear from a 48-hour-old agar plate colony, ×2,000. (From Nowak: Documenta Microbiologica, courtesy Gustav Fischer.)

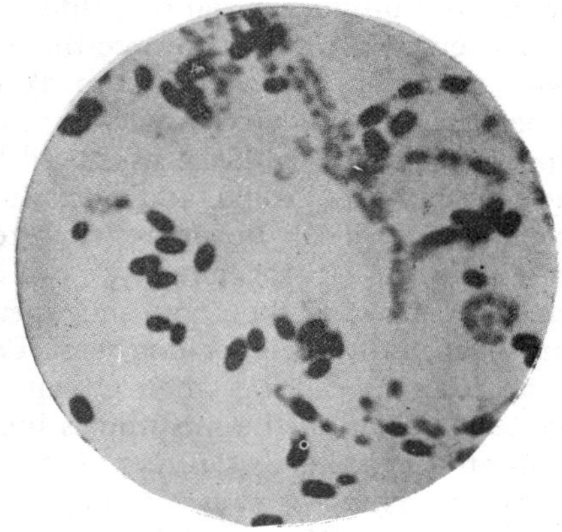

FIG. 30.3—**Bacillus anthracis,** an old potato culture showing many spores, ×2,000. (From Nowak: Documenta Microbiologica, courtesy Gustav Fischer.)

gram-positive, but old cells may decolorize easily.

**Growth Requirements and Characteristics.** *B. anthracis* grows readily on blood agar and is isolated easily from the blood or internal organs of an infected animal; it is aerobic, and the optimum temperature for growth is 37°C. A slightly alkaline medium, pH 7.5 to 7.8, is most conducive to good growth.

On the agar surface, colonies appear dull, opaque, grayish-white, with an irregular border from which long strands of cells are seen in parallel arrangement, giving the typical "medusa head" characteristic (Fig. 30.4). As the colony ages, "vesicles" may appear on the surface, giving it a contoured appearance. Broth is turbid with a floccular growth on the surface which sinks to the bottom of the tube within 24 hours. A thick, creamy growth occurs on potato; this growth later becomes granular, giving a mealy appearance. In a gelatin stab culture, filaments of growth radiate from the line of puncture and give the appearance of an inverted fir tree.

Aging and other treatment of stock labo-

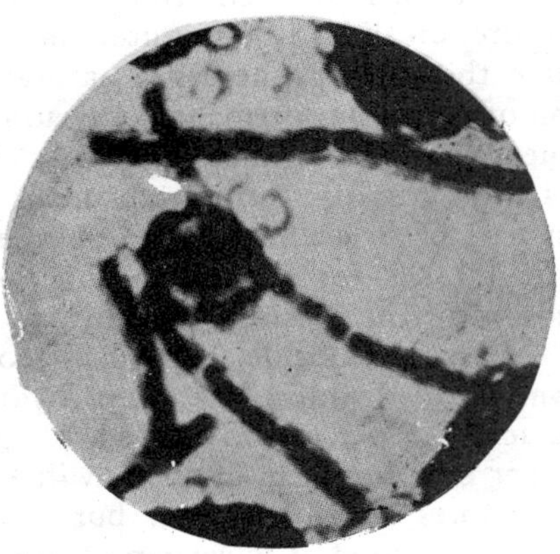

FIG. 30.2—**Bacillus anthracis** in smear from spleen, showing capsules, ×2,000. (From Nowak: Documenta Microbiologica, courtesy Gustav Fischer.)

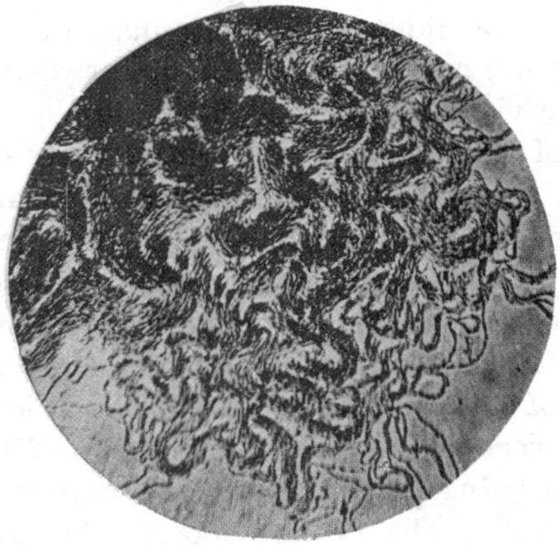

FIG. 30.4—**Bacillus anthracis,** edge of agar plate colony, ×210. (From Nowak: Documenta Microbiologica, courtesy Gustav Fischer.)

ratory cultures produce variants of different types. Pasteur was the first to note the loss of spore formation by exposure to 42°C. Chamberland and Roux observed that asporogenous strains could be produced by contact with phenol, 1:800, and potassium bichromate, 1:2,000. Bormans reported that a permanent asporogenous type can be produced by growing the organism repeatedly in sheep, calf, horse, or dog sera. The organism loses its capsule when grown on artificial media unless the medium is incubated in an atmosphere of 10 per cent carbon dioxide. This loss causes colony variation. Contrary to the usual type of variation, rough (R) is normal and virulent, whereas smooth (S) is avirulent.

**Resistance.** The vegetative cells of *B. anthracis* are not more resistant than similar cells of other bacteria; however, spores which are resistant are rapidly formed by this organism. All disinfection against anthrax must assume that the organism is in the spore state. Spores will remain viable for years and will be as virulent as the culture proved to be when originally isolated. Pasteur showed that spores remained viable in a buried carcass for 12 years. Gaiger reported that spores could be germinated after 15 to 24 years duration in the soil. Instances have been reported where animals became infected on premises 25 years after the original cases of the disease. Hair, wool, bones, and hides not treated sufficiently to kill spores may remain infective for years.

The viability of *B. anthracis* in the tissues of artificially infected guinea pigs exposed to decomposition, temperature, and desiccation has been recorded by Stein (1947). The organism is rapidly destroyed by decomposition in unopened carcasses after the third day, except under temperatures of 5° to 10°C. when it survives at least four weeks. Repeated freezing, —72°C., and thawing, 37.5°C., may kill vegetative cells but probably not spores. Anthrax spore suspensions were viable for 90 to 124 days when kept at —60° to —70°C. and for nine to ten years at either —5° to —6°C. or at 5° to 10°C. Blood swabs from field cases of anthrax kept in the light at room temperature were still virulent up to nine years. The author (Merchant) has found agar slant cultures of *B. anthracis* isolated from a field case in 1928, kept sealed with paraffin and stored in the dark at room temperature, to be virulent at the end of 38 years.

In testing the resistance of anthrax spores to heat, Stein and Rogers (1945) tested 43 strains. All of these strains were killed by vigorous boiling within 3 to 5 minutes. Spores from 31 strains were killed in 5 to 15 minutes at 100° to 101°C. in the steam sterilizer, but at 90° to 91°C. only 6 out of 12 strains were destroyed in 60 minutes. In the autoclave, at 120°C., all of the 31 strains tested were destroyed in 5 to 15 minutes. Insistence that cultures of *B. anthracis* must not be sterilized in an open vessel or glass tube is supported by the work of Stein and Rogers (1946) who found that viable spores escape with the steam from such cultures.

The report of Soltys is of considerable importance to those engaged in laboratory studies of *B. anthracis*. Soltys observed that spores of the organism in films on slides may withstand the temperature of the Bunsen flame for 5 to 6 seconds; that none of the common staining methods destroy all spores; that mercuric chloride, 1:1,000, killed spores on slides in 5 minutes and did not alter the smear, whereas a saturated solution of potassium permanganate ruined the smear for observation purposes. In view of these results it appears prudent to treat smears of *B. anthracis* with mercuric chloride, 1:1,000, for 5 minutes and then proceed with the desired staining technique. Mercuric chloride, 1:1,000, is more effective as a disinfectant when hydrochloric acid, 0.5 per cent, is added.

Ten per cent formalin at 40°C. will kill anthrax spores in 15 minutes, but when this chemical is used at lower temperatures more time must be allowed for disinfection. Freshly prepared sodium hydroxide in a 5 per cent solution is a satisfactory agent for disinfecting objects contaminated by the spores of this organism.

**Biochemical Properties.** *B. anthracis* forms acid but no gas from glucose, sucrose, maltose, fructose, trehalose, and dextrin. Some strains produce slight acid in glycerol and salicin. There is no fermentation of lactose, galactose, arabinose, rhamnose, mannose, raffinose, inulin, mannitol, dulcitol, sorbitol, inositol, and adonitol. Indol and $H_2S$ are not produced; nitrates are reduced to nitrites; $NH_3$ is produced. Methylene blue is reduced by some of the more virulent strains, and some strains hemolyze sheep blood. The organism is methyl red positive and Voges-Proskauer variable. Litmus milk is coagulated, decolorized, and slowly peptonized.

**Antigenic Structure and Toxins.** There appears to be two antigenic substances in *B. anthracis.* One protein-like material is found in the capsule, and the other is a somatic polysaccharide antigen. Both antigens act specifically with precipitating sera. No antigenic groups have been reported for the organism. Workers in Germany have reported the purification of anthrax capsular antigens. Antigens specific for the endospore phase of *B. anthracis* and *B. cereus* have been described by Lamanna and Eisler, and they were unable to distinguish between the two organisms by using agglutination tests. Thorne, Molnar, and Strange have demonstrated that *B. anthracis* produces two toxic substances when grown in a Casamino acid medium without serum or other protein. One component, called protective antigen, was present in the filtrate after passing through fritted glass filters; and the other, called filter factor, was adsorbed upon the filter. When tested alone each factor was nontoxic, but when used together skin reactions were noted on guinea pigs, and they were lethal to mice.

Stanley and Smith have found three factors in anthrax toxin. Factor I was not toxic when given alone, but when mixed with purified Factor II edema was produced in the skin of the rabbit, and mice were killed. Factor III was different antigenically from I and II. It was present in anthrax toxin produced in vivo, and was nonlethal to mice when injected alone. It was lethal to mice when mixed with II but not with I. All three factors were more virulent when mixed together than any other combinations.

In a series of studies on the nature of the infection produced by *B. anthracis,* Cromartie, Bloom, Watson, and associates have contributed significant information which is of aid in understanding the disease. Two substances are present in crude extracts of lesions produced by the organism: one an inflammatory factor capable of damaging tissue, and the other a protective antigen responsible for its immunizing property. The tissue-damaging factor is capable of interfering with the blood-clotting mechanism and inhibits an anthracidal substance produced by leucocytes and other cells. A disturbance in carbohydrate metabolism was observed in experimental cases of anthrax in rabbits, producing a state of hyperglycemia. Bacterial counts in the blood of rabbits fatally infected showed that the majority contained large numbers of bacilli in their blood at the time of death. Some animals died with relatively few bacilli in the blood, which tends to disprove the mechanical obstruction theory which has been advanced to explain the mechanism of death from anthrax.

The protective antigen migrates in an invisible component intermediate between the gamma and beta globulins; it is destroyed by heating at 57°C. for 30 minutes and by trypsin; it is not destroyed by formalin in a final concentration of 1.0 per cent, and is stable in the lyophilized state. This antigen has not been purified, but fractionation with ethanol in the cold suggests a method of concentration. The efficacy of the antigen in inducing active immunity in rabbits, sheep, guinea pigs, hamsters, and mice varies. The rabbit is protected against challenge doses of anthrax spores more than other animals. The protective antibodies present in hyperimmune rabbit serums fail to show any relationship to the antibody concerned in the precipitation and complement-fixation tests.

The role of leucocytes in eliminating anthrax bacilli from the body of both immune and normal animals is explained by the presence of an anthracidal substance in leucocytes. This substance appears to be a basic polypeptide, contains lysine, and can be prepared from the thymus gland of the calf. It has been shown to protect mice against lethal doses of anthrax bacilli.

The results of the investigators, briefly described, substantiate the known facts concerning anthrax. The presence of edema and hemorrhage makes it evident that a tissue-damaging factor operates in the disease, but the effect of this specific substance upon leucocytes and their extracts explains why the infection progresses so rapidly in the highly susceptible animal. That the tissue-damaging factor and anthracidal factor in leucocytes are two contending forces in the disease appears evident. In those species of animals which are more resistant to anthrax, the anthracidal factor in leucocytes appears to be in greater concentration because the bacilli do develop in these species; but the capsule is soon lost, and the bacilli disintegrate. The protective antigen appears to stimulate the production of a substance which does not allow the capsule to develop on the bacilli, but this substance does not seem to be allied with the antibody employed, or at least does not show the usual effects noted in the precipitation and complement-fixation tests. Obviously, these studies should be continued, and relationships noted to the various products of bacteria which are known to explain the different tissue reactions to infectious agents.

**Pathogenicity.** *B. anthracis* is pathogenic for cattle, sheep (except Algerian), horses, mules, swine, dogs, and cats. Anthrax appears as a septicemia in the first four species of animals in an apoplectic form, an acute form, and in a subacute form. Massive hemorrhagic swellings may be present in the subacute type but are not so common in the apoplectic and acute types. In swine the disease is manifested by an acute pharyngitis with extensive swelling and hemorrhage of the throat region. Anthrax in dogs and cats is similar to that in hogs with the exception of a severe gastroenteritis. The disease is rare in these animals, but cases have been reported. Irradiation of dogs makes them more susceptible to *B. anthracis*.

On postmortem examination, anthrax is characterized by edematous infiltrations in the subcutis; hemorrhages in various parts of the body, especially in serous membranes; marked swelling of the spleen, which is dark red and soft (raspberry-jam consistency). This characteristic spleen has given rise to the terms "splenic fever" and "milzbrand" (German) by which the disease is often known. The blood is dark red, tarry, and does not clot; these facts have led the French to call the disease "charbon."

In an electron microscope study of *B. anthracis* in the mouse spleen, Roth, Lewis, and Williams noticed a definite cytopathic effect on splenic cells characterized by disruption of the cell membrane and dissolution of cell substance. In Figure 30.5 this effect is seen as the clear area surrounding the two bacilli.

Hemorrhage is often observed from the natural body openings; this is of sanitary significance, for such pools of blood leave countless numbers of bacilli in the ground.

The type of anthrax in man usually depends on the avenue of infection. Pulmonary anthrax, or wool-sorters' disease, is contracted by the inhalation of anthrax spores. The disease runs its course as an atypical pneumonia and is usually fatal. Cutaneous anthrax, or malignant carbuncle, results from skin infection through scratches or other breaks in the skin. The pustule starts as a small red pimple and gradually spreads, forming a large swelling with a dark center surrounded by small vesicles. Regional lymph nodes are swollen and painful. If the organisms enter the blood stream, septicemia results. Most cases

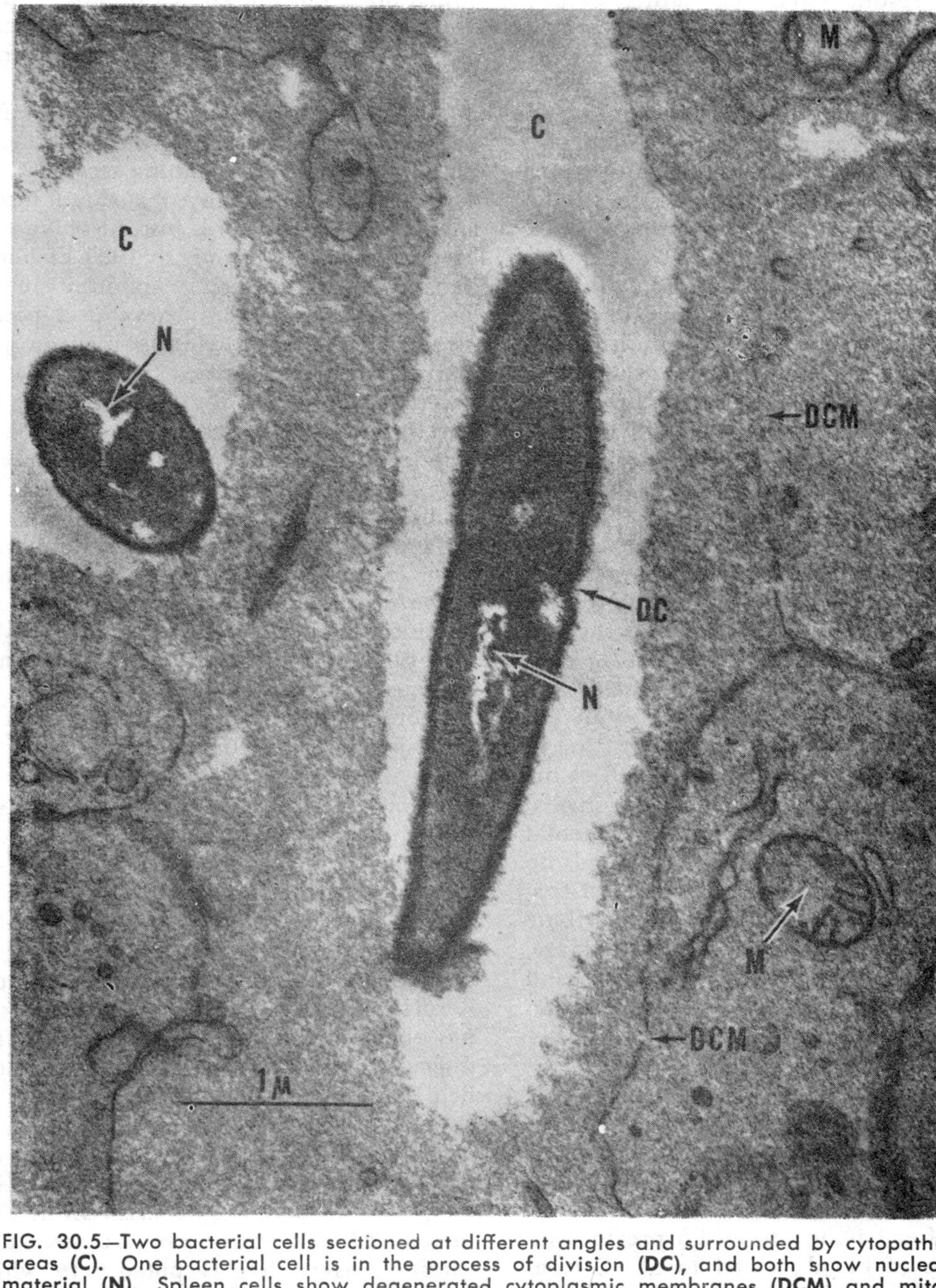


FIG. 30.5—Two bacterial cells sectioned at different angles and surrounded by cytopathic areas **(C)**. One bacterial cell is in the process of division **(DC)**, and both show nuclear material **(N)**. Spleen cells show degenerated cytoplasmic membranes **(DCM)** and mitochondria **(M)**. Approx. ×27,840. (Courtesy Roth, Lewis, and Williams, and Williams & Wilkins Co.)

of cutaneous anthrax recover. Intestinal anthrax results from the eating of uncooked meats from an anthrax carcass and is extremely rare in civilized countries.

Of the laboratory animals, the mouse is the most susceptible to *B. anthracis*. Guinea pigs are also highly susceptible, and are universally used for diagnostic purposes. Rabbits are less susceptible but do succumb. Rats are more resistant than rabbits, and the white rat is more so than gray or brown rats. Some white rats live for weeks before they die, and some survive in spite of comparatively large injections of living organisms. Marchette, Lundgren, and Smart, in Utah, have shown that many species of wild rodents are highly susceptible to this bacillus. Birds generally are resistant; however, sparrows and young pigeons have been infected.

It has been generally assumed that death of an animal or man following a rapid, septicemic course of anthrax is due to the changes produced in vital tissue such as spleen, liver, kidneys, and heart muscle. Furthermore it has been postulated that there are so many anthrax bacilli in the blood-vascular system that they, because of their aerobic nature, utilize so much of the oxygen that the subject dies of asphyxia. Nordberg *et al.* working with experimental anthrax in rabbits believe that animals do die of asphyxia, but not due to the utilization of oxygen by bacilli. They attribute asphyxia to hemolysis, renal damage, hepatic and myocardial degeneration, and perivascular and pericellular precipitation of mucopolysaccharides in the white matter of the brain.

**Immunity.** Anthrax was one of the first diseases for which a definite immunity was produced by the use of bacteria. Chauveau, in 1879, noticed that sheep were more resistant after having survived a previous inoculation of blood heated to 55°C. from animals dead of anthrax. Toussaint, in 1880, first attempted artificial immunization. Pasteur, with Chamberland and Roux, in 1881, proved that immunity did exist after using two vaccines: *Vaccine I,* attenuated by growing at 42°C. for 12 days, killed mice, but not guinea pigs or rabbits; *Vaccine II,* attenuated for a shorter time, so it killed mice and guinea pigs, but not rabbits or sheep.

Sobernheim, in 1904, improved on Pasteur's method by using Pasteur Vaccine II simultaneously with immune serum. Cienkowsy, in 1884, employed a simultaneous method but used spores instead of Vaccine II with immune serum. In 1925 Eichhorn reported that satisfactory immunity could be produced against anthrax if a potent strain of the bacillus were used in preparing the vaccine and if an edematous reaction resulted in the area in which the vaccine was injected. Spore vaccines standardized to compare with Pasteur Vaccine II, along with hyperimmune antianthrax serum, have been used in the United States for prophylactic immunization. In certain districts where the strain of *B. anthracis* appears to be more virulent, vaccines of greater virulence, called "Vaccine III" and "Vaccine IV," are used simultaneously with immune serum.

Spore vaccines, generally attentuated to correspond to Pasteur Vaccine II, may be given intradermally. This method of vaccination against anthrax has particular virtue when the function of the skin in this disease is considered. Furthermore, the skin is recognized as tissue in which antibody is produced, and it is so compact that the antigen is not quickly absorbed into the general circulation. Although the intradermal method of vaccination has merits, it has objectionable features, particularly the difficulty of making such an injection under field conditions into range animals. Subcutaneous and intramuscular methods of injection obviously are much easier to do.

The development of a special vaccine known as "carbozoo" by Mazzucchi in 1931 introduced a new anthrax vaccine. This vaccine was of No. II potency to which saponin was added. This glucoside has the property of causing tissue irritation, producing local edema, hence delaying the absorption of the vaccine. In addition to this reaction, Sterne of South Africa has observed that such an excipient as saponin or saturated sodium chloride decreases the virulence of virulent strains and increases the immunizing power of avirulent strains of anthrax bacilli. In many areas of the world saponized anthrax vaccine is used entirely.

Anthrax bacterins are prepared by using young, nonsporulated cultures attenuated with formalin. The duration of immunity produced by the bacterin is not as long as with spore vaccine, but its use is recommended in those areas which have not been contaminated by successive outbreaks of anthrax. In many instances the promiscuous use of spore vaccines of too great potency has been actually found to cause endemic anthrax areas when such vaccines have been used without immune serum. In other instances too great reliance has been placed on spore vaccines alone. In some instances the spore vaccine has been too impotent to produce immunity, thus allowing natural outbreaks of the disease to occur.

In 1935 Gochenour, Schoening, Stein, and Mohler conducted a comprehensive comparative study of the efficacy of various anthrax vaccines and antianthrax serum. Their results indicated that spore vaccine produced a more satisfactory immunity than the bacterin and that immune serum was highly efficacious for a few days, but its protective power was soon lost.

The use of capsule extracts and other purified antigenic fractions of *B. anthracis* appears to be promising according to Ivánovics. The gélosé-alum vaccine of Ramon and Staub also indicates a new departure in the preparation of anthrax vaccine.

Serum therapy in anthrax has been demonstrated to be dependable. The exact nature of the protection, however, has not been ascertained. There are numerous evidences that it is not a bacteriolytic effect. Precipitation of the two antigenic fractions of the bacillus is obtainable by the use of immune serum. The destruction of the microorganism is usually brought about by the phagocytes; so it is plausible that the "leucocyte-repelling" action of capsulated *B. anthracis* is neutralized by precipitation which, at the same time, sensitizes the cells for more rapid engulfment by phagocytes.

Investigators of animal diseases in South Africa are constantly confronted with anthrax, hence have been most active in developing satisfactory immunizing agents for the disease. The keeping qualities of the vaccines is one of their problems, for it usually must be transported long distances. In 1937 Sterne described the isolation of noncapsulated, avirulent immunogenic variants from virulent strains of *B. anthracis.* This investigator (1939) was able to produce an immunity with these strains in domestic animals that far surpasses the results obtained with the Pasteur type of spore vaccine. Sutton (1947) described a special medium, tryptic digest of casein (Brewer's yeast extract buffered by phosphates), which was of value in the maintenance of the immunogenic capacity of the variant strain of *B. anthracis.* The value of this type of vaccine has been confirmed by Boor and Tresselt. The Sterne strain is used widely in the United States, and according to Van Ness it was quite efficient in the control of the Oklahoma-Kansas outbreak in 1959.

**Diagnosis.** In submitting material for anthrax diagnosis, great caution must be exercised. It is an unnecessary risk to autopsy a carcass which has obviously died of anthrax. In England such autopsies are forbidden by law. Sending an ear packed in a tight suitable container is a universal practice; this method is satisfactory, but the practice of sending blood smears, cotton swabs, a small vial of blood, or tissue is preferable if sufficient caution is taken.

Laboratory diagnosis of anthrax may be obtained by any of the following:

1. Direct microscopic smears from the suspected material stained with a suitable capsule stain and observing definite capsules surrounding the bacilli.
2. Inoculation of blood agar where no hemolysis is produced and the typical curly edge of the colony is seen.
3. Subcutaneous inoculation of sus-

pected material into a guinea pig in which death is usually produced in 48 hours. Gelatinous edema and hemorrhage are found at the inoculation site, and numerous bacilli are seen in stained smears made from fluid in the area.

4. Some laboratories have specific bacteriophage W which can be used for diagnosis. A phage-fluorescent antiphage staining system or fluorescein-labeled antiglobulin may also be used.

## REFERENCES


Albrink, W. S. Pathogenesis of Inhalation Anthrax. Bact. Rev. 25:268–73, 1961.

Berdjis, C. C., *et al.* Modification of Anthrax by Ionizing Radiation. Jour. Inf. Dis. 113:219–27, 1963.

Biegeleisen, J. Z., *et al.* The Demonstration of *Bacillus anthracis* in Environmental Specimens by Conventional and Fluorescent Antibody Techniques. Amer. Jour. Hyg. 75:230–39, 1962.

Bonventre, P. F., *et al.* An Autographic Study of Anthrax Infection in the Mouse. Jour. Inf. Dis. 108:205, 1961.

Brachman, P. S., *et al.* An Epidemic of Inhalation Anthrax: the First in the Twentieth Century. Amer. Jour. Hyg. 72:6, 1960.

Burdon, K. L. Useful Criteria for the Identification of *Bacillus anthracis* and Related Species. Jour. Bact. 71:25, 1956.

Clark, Ada R. The Anthrax Bacillus. *In* Gay, F. P., *et al.* Agents of Disease and Host Resistance, Chap. 35. Charles C Thomas, Baltimore, 1935.

Cromartie, W. J., *et al.* Jour. Inf. Dis. 80:1–153, 1947.

Dowdle, W. R., and Hansen, A. A Phage-Fluorescent Antiphage Staining System for *Bacillus anthracis*. Jour. Inf. Dis. 108:125–35, 1961.

Eurich, F. W., and Hewlett, R. T. *Bacillus anthracis*. A System of Bacteriology. 5:439. Med. Res. Council, His Majesty's Stationery Office, London, 1929.

Gochenour, W. S., *et al.* Tech. Bull. 468, 1935, USDA, Washington, D.C.

Klein, D. M., and Klemm, W. R. A History of Anthrax. Jour. Amer. Vet. Med. Assn. 135:458, 1959.

Lamanna, C., and Eisler, D. Jour. Bact. 79:435, 1960.

Lantos, J., *et al.* Characterization of Anthrax Phages. Acta Microbiol. 7:31–42, 1960.

Marchette, N. J., *et al.* Jour. Inf. Dis. 101:148, 1957.

Nordberg, B. K. Studies of *Bacillus anthracis* in Regard to Its Properties of Diagnostic and Pathogenetic Importance. Gernandts Boktryckeri, Stockholm, 1951.

———, *et al.* Pathophysiological Investigations Into the Terminal Course of Experimental Anthrax in the Rabbit. Acta Path. Microbiol. Scand. 53:295–318, 1961.

Ramon, G., and Richou, R. Bull. Acad. Vet. Fr. 18:164, 1945.

———, and Staub, A. Sur une Nouvelle Méthode de Vaccination des Animaux Domestiques Contre le Charbon. Bull. Acad. de Méd., Ser. 3, 117, 299, 1937.

Roth, I. L., *et al.* Jour. Bact. 80:772, 1960.

Roth, N. G., *et al.* Jour. Bact. 72:666, 1956.

Schweiger, L. B., *et al.* Isolation of *Bacillus subtilis* From Actinobacillus-like Lesions in Cattle and Sheep. Amer. Jour. Vet. Res. 4:127–33, 1943.

Soltys, M. A. Jour. Path. Bact. 60:253, 1948.

Stanley, J. L., and Smith, H. Purification of Factor I and Recognition of a Third Factor of the Anthrax Toxin. Jour. Gen. Microbiol. 26:49–66, 1961.

Stein, C. D. Differentiation of *B. anthracis* From Non-pathogenic Aerobic Sporeforming Bacilli. Amer. Jour. Vet. Res. 5:38–54, 1944.

———. Vet. Med. 40:340, 1945.

———. Vet. Med. 42:13, 1947.

———. Vet. Med. 43:340, 1948.

———. Vet. Med. 45:205, 1950.

———, and Rogers, H. Vet. Med. 40:406, 1945.

———, and ———. Amer. Jour. Vet. Res. 7:481, 1946.

———, and Van Ness, G. B. Vet. Med. 50:579, 1955.

Sterne, M. Onderstepoort Jour. Vet. Sci. and An. Ind. 8:271, 1937.

———. Onderstepoort Jour. Vet. Sci. and An. Ind. 13:307, 313, 1939.

———. Jour. S. Afr. Vet. Med. Assn. 16:53, 1945.
———. Onderstepoort Jour. Vet. Sci. and An. Ind. 21:41, 1946.
STILES, G. W. Isolation of *B. anthracis* From Spinose Ear Ticks (*Ornithodorous megnini*). Amer. Jour. Vet. Res. 5:318–19, 1944.
SUTTON, G. D. Jour. S. Afr. Vet. Med. Assn. 18:79, 1947.
THORNE, C. B., *et al.* Jour. Bact. 79:450, 1960.
VAN NESS, G. B., and STEIN, C. D. Jour. Amer. Vet. Med. Assn. 128:7, 1956.
———, *et al.* Jour. Amer. Vet. Med. Assn. 134:125, 1959.

# 31

# The Genus Clostridium

IN THIS GENUS ARE PLACED THOSE SPOREFORMING rods which are anaerobes. By virtue of the resistant spore which they produce, the natural habitat of the majority of the species is the soil and intestinal tracts of animals. Some species are pathogenic to man, some to various animals in which they produce distinct types of disease, and some by the action of potent exotoxins produced either within or outside the animal body.

The spores of all the anaerobic bacilli are prevalent in the soil; consequently, the diseases which are caused by this group of bacteria are often called the soil-borne infections. This fact is best emphasized by the universal knowledge that the contamination of a wound by dirt may lead to tetanus or gas gangrene, both of which are caused by anaerobic bacilli.

The anaerobic bacilli are studied by specialized techniques, the most fundamental of which is the maintenance of anaerobic conditions. These methods have been listed and briefly discussed in the chapter on techniques and methods and should be reviewed by the student at this time.

A more thorough study of the "growth accessory substances" in the artificial cultivation of bacteria has revealed that the anaerobic bacteria may grow aerobically. For example, the addition of 0.025 per cent ascorbic acid powder or fluid to various fluid media will support the growth of anaerobes.

## GENERAL DESCRIPTION OF THE GROUP

These bacilli are variable in size, measuring $0.4\mu$ to $1.2\mu$ in diameter by $3\mu$ to $8\mu$ in length. They are usually plump in shape with round ends, but some are long, slender rods. Sporulation occurs in all species with a variable position of spores—central, subterminal, and terminal. Most of the species are motile by peritrichic flagella. They are gram-positive in young cultures but are easily decolorized when older. It is best to use only alcohol and not acetone-alcohol as a decolorizing agent in the Gram staining technique. Granulation is noted in the cells of some species, giving variations in the depth of staining when methylene blue is used.

On solid media, the clostridia grow in thin, irregular colonies, but when the medium is moist, spreading occurs. Variation in colony size and shape exists under different conditions. Fluid media are rendered uniformly turbid. In blood agar, hemolysis is first of the alpha type, which later develops into the beta type. Meat medium is reacted upon in two ways depending on the type of microorganism. It is digested and turned black by proteolytic varieties, whereas the saccharolytic types do not digest it, but they do turn the meat pink. Both of the above types of clostridia are capable of producing great quantities of gas in both protein and carbohydrate media. The gas ($CO_2$-$H_2$) ratio has been suggested by some workers as a means of differentiation.

Some of the common biochemical reactions of the Clostridia to be discussed in this chapter are given in Table 31.1.

Type specificity among the clostridia apparently depends on both O and H antigens. The use of soluble antigens and type-specific globulin in agar gel precipitin tests

TABLE 31.1

Biochemical Reactions of the Important Clostridia

| | Glucose | Maltose | Lactose | Salicin | $H_2S$ | Gel. Liq. | Nit. Red. | Indol | Lit. Milk |
|---|---|---|---|---|---|---|---|---|---|
| *Clost. chauvoei* | + | + | + | − | + | + | − | − | acid |
| *Clost. septicum* | + | + | + | + | + | + | + | − | acid |
| *Clost. novyi* | + | + | − | − | + | + | − | − | acid |
| *Clost. perfringens* | + | + | + | − | + | + | + | − | stormy |
| *Clost. hemolyticum* | + | − | − | − | + | + | − | + | acid |
| *Clost. tetani* | − | − | − | − | + | ± | − | + | no change |
| *Clost. botulinum* | + | + | − | − | + | + | − | − | acid |
| *Clost. sordellii* | + | + | − | ± | + | + | − | + | digested |

has been found effective in differentiating species.

The types of diseases caused by the Clostridia can be classified as toxigenic and histotoxic. *Clostridium tetani* and *Clostridium botulinum* cause toxigenic disease by the toxins they produce. In tetanus, toxin is liberated by the organism at the site of a wound and spreads throughout the body. In botulism, the toxin is formed in vegetables or meat which have been inadequately sterilized, and the disease results from the ingestion of the toxin-laden food. Those species which cause a histotoxic type of disease are frequently called the "gas edema" or "gas gangrene" group. They produce toxin which is injurious to muscle cells. They ferment muscle glucose, forming gas. Edema is produced by the damage to muscle capillaries, causing lymph to accumulate in the area. *Clostridium chauvoei* which causes blackleg and *Clostridium septicum* which causes malignant edema are excellent examples of those species which produce the histotoxic type of disease.

Antitoxin is prepared for use in immunizing against the toxin-producing species of anaerobes. Bacterial filtrates and antiserums are available for the less toxigenic types. Immunity against tetanus, botulism, and blackleg is widely and successfully practiced.

Only those members of the genus which are of significance to animal health will be discussed. There are many isolated and single reports of diseases produced by anaerobic, sporeforming bacilli, but the inclusion of all of them here is not feasible. The species given in the following list will be described:

*Clostridium chauvoei*
*Clostridium septicum*
*Clostridium novyi*
*Clostridium perfringens*
*Clostridium hemolyticum*
*Clostridium tetani*
*Clostridium botulinum*
*Clostridium sordellii*

### Clostridium chauvoei

**Synonyms and History.** *Bacillus chauvoei, Bacillus gangraenae emphysematosae, Clostridium feseri,* blackleg bacillus.

Blackleg was differentiated from anthrax and named "charbon symptomatique" by Chabert on the basis of clinical symptoms and postmortem lesions. Bollinger, in 1875, however, was the first to show that anthrax and blackleg had distinct etiologic agents. This conclusion was confirmed by Feser in 1876. Significant contributions were made to the literature concerning blackleg by Arloing, Cornevin, and Thomas in 1887, which accounts for the fact that they are often given the credit for the discovery of the organism. Even though they did contribute a great deal to the knowledge of blackleg, its cause and immunity, Roux is given the credit for being the first to cultivate the organism on artificial media in 1887. Improved methods for the cultivation of *Clostridium chauvoei* in pure cultures were contributed by Kitasato in 1889.

**Distribution and Transmission.** Blackleg in cattle is found in most parts of the world where animal husbandry is well established. In the United States the organism is scattered over the prairie states, being more prevalent in some areas than in others. The eastern Atlantic and southern Gulf states seem to be free of the infection. The disease is a typical soil-borne infection. The organism gains entrance by the digestive tract or through breaks in the skin. It may be artificially introduced by traumatisms of various sorts and has been found to follow shearing, docking, and castration in sheep.

**Morphology and Staining.** *Clost. chauvoei* is a rod 0.6$\mu$ in diameter by 3$\mu$ to 8$\mu$ in length, with rounded ends, and occurs singly or in short chains, but long filaments are common (Fig. 31.1). Swollen cells are often found, navicular and lemon shapes being most common. The spores of the organism are elongated, oval, subterminal or terminal, and wider than the cell, giving it a typical pear-shaped appearance. The bacillus is motile by means of peritrichous flagella. The organism is gram-positive but is easily decolorized in parts of the cell. Some cells show granular material in one or both poles. This is most apparent when stained with methylene blue. It does not form a capsule.

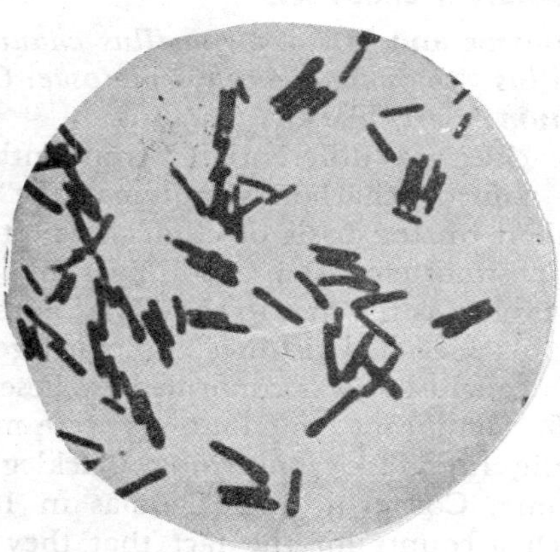

FIG. 31.1—**Clostridium chauvoei** from a young agar culture, ×2,000. (From Nowak: Documenta Microbiologica, courtesy Gustav Fischer.)

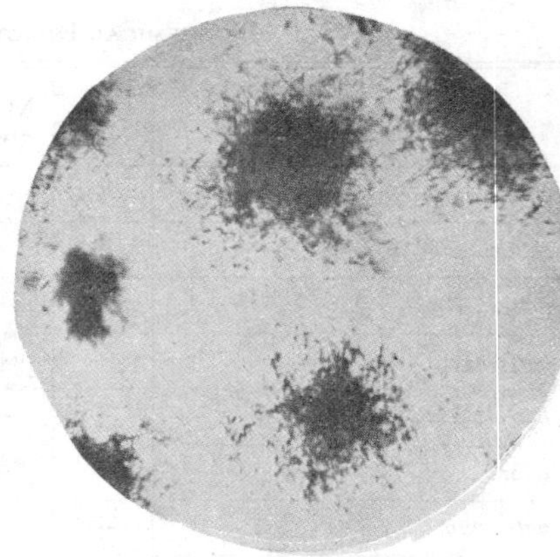

FIG. 31.2—**Clostridium chauvoei** colony on agar plate, ×50. (From Nowak: Documenta Microbiologica, courtesy Gustav Fischer.)

**Growth Requirements and Characteristics.** This organism is a strict anaerobe, and growth is improved by glucose and heart-meat infusion. Optimum temperature for growth is 37°C. The organism grows best in media which is slightly alkaline, although it has a rather wide pH range. It can be isolated in most instances in pure culture from deep muscle by seeding meat medium or brain medium.

On agar plates the organism forms a small, irregular colony, effuse, transparent, finely granular in the center, but becoming almost invisible toward the periphery (Fig. 31.2). The edges of the colony resemble wisps of hair. The colony is bluish-gray by transmitted light. In a glucose-gelatin shake culture, the colonies appear toward the bottom of the tube, each usually with its gas bubble, and surrounded by a liquefied area. These colonies show numerous radiating threads, or papillae, giving the appearance of a chestnut burr. The organism produces a uniform turbidity in bouillon, produces gas, and forms a flaky, white deposit.

**Resistance.** The vegetative form of the organism is not resistant to heat or chemicals. In the spore form it is quite heat resistant, not being killed for 10 minutes at 120°C. The spores are resistant to desiccation, living in the soil for years. In dried, infected muscle the spores have remained virulent for eight years. Bichloride of mercury, 1:500, kills spores within 10 minutes. The spores are killed by 3 per cent formalin in 15 minutes. The coal-tar disinfectants, in the strength in which they are used on infected premises, are effective and kill the spores readily.

**Biochemical Properties.** *Clost. chauvoei* produces acid and gas from glucose, fructose, maltose, lactose, and sucrose but not from mannitol, glycerol, dulcitol, salicin, or inulin. It coagulates milk into a flocculent curd but does not peptonize this medium. The organism turns meat medium pinker; acidifies but does not blacken Hibler's brain medium; produces a slight hemolysis on horse-blood-agar plates; does not produce indol; is methyl red negative and Voges-Proskauer negative; does not reduce nitrates; does not form $NH_3$; produces $H_2S$; does not reduce methylene blue; does not form catalase.

**Antigenic Structure and Toxins.** *Clost. chauvoei* is serologically homogenous. Differences in strains which some have found may have been due to the close relationship of this organism to *Clost. septicum*. By agglutination and complement-fixation tests, some antigenic relationships between *Clost. chauvoei* and *Clost. septicum* have been observed, especially in the lower dilutions. No antigenic fractions of the organism have been described.

That a true exotoxin is produced by *Clost. chauvoei* is open to question. Some strains undoubtedly do produce exotoxin, especially the more virulent ones. Grassberger and Schattenfroh claim to have succeeded in producing broth cultures containing a toxin that, in doses as small as those employed with diphtheria toxin, will kill laboratory animals. They have shown this toxin to be thermolabile. Kerrin, in 1934, also has shown that *Clost. chauvoei* produces toxin under suitable conditions. A dose of 0.025–0.5 cc. of toxin when injected intravenously into a mouse causes respiratory symptoms and death within a few minutes. Subcutaneous injection of the toxin into guinea pigs and mice is not fatal, but edema is produced. It is quite likely that this organism does produce exotoxin, but it is not as potent as that produced by other species of the gas-edema type, notably *Clost. septicum, Clost. perfringens,* and *Clost. novyi.*

**Pathogenicity.** Inoculation of pure cultures of this organism into laboratory animals results in death, with the production of many of the characteristic symptoms of blackleg. Guinea pigs, rabbits, white mice, and white rats can be infected. The guinea pig is the most susceptible and is commonly used as the experimental animal for the organism. Intramuscular injection of the guinea pig is followed by the first symptoms in about 14 hours consisting of a depressed attitude and ruffed hair coat; a soft inflamed swelling develops at the site of inoculation; in 24 to 30 hours the inflammation spreads to nearby muscles and these become emphysematous. Upon section, in typical cases, the tissues are found to be edematous and hemorrhagic, and the muscles contain many gas bubbles. Gas is also found in the subcutaneous fascia over the infected area.

Ryff and Lee have observed that the hamster is more susceptible to *Clost. chauvoei* than the guinea pig, succumbing to one-fifth the lethal dose required for the guinea pig.

Blackleg in cattle is characterized by a swelling, edema, and emphysema of the muscles and the subcutaneous tissues of the infected part. Infection occurs most commonly in the shoulder and hindquarters. The swelling increases rapidly in size, and the emphysema is soon detected by the crackling sound when the hand is drawn firmly across the affected part.

The organisms, along with other anaerobes, continue to grow after death, and the body becomes distended with gas. The subcutaneous tissues of the infected part are edematous, even gelatinous, and are permeated with blood and gas bubbles. The underlying muscles are dark brown or even blackish, whence the name, blackleg. A very characteristic, sweetish-sour, pungent odor can be detected from the infected tissue. The disease usually results fatally in cattle in one to three days after the first appearance of the symptoms.

In sheep and deer the infection due to this organism usually follows traumatic injuries and shows the same characteristic pathology as seen in cattle.

**Immunity.** Animals that have recovered from an attack of blackleg are immune during the remaining period of their lives. Very young cattle and aged cattle have a considerable degree of natural immunity. The reason for this immunity is not well understood; it probably is opsonic in nature in young animals, whereas in older cattle there is always the possibility that they have had an inapparent infection.

Active immunization by vaccination is extensively practiced for blackleg. Vaccines which have been used have included small pieces of blackleg muscle inserted under the skin of the animal; pulverized dry muscle attenuated with heat; muscle fluid collected and filtered; fluid from meat-bouillon cultures, filtered so it is germ-free.

During recent years a whole culture bacterin has given satisfactory results. It has been shown that blackleg is often complicated by the presence of *Clost. septicum.* For that reason a filtrate composed of the end-products of the growth of both organisms is used. Scheuber described the preparation of the filtrate as follows: "A liver-glucose medium is inoculated with *Clost. chauvoei* and incubated. The medium is fortified with glucose, and a pH of 8 is maintained throughout the process. At the end of one week of incubation, the culture is seeded with *Clost. septicum* and incubated for 8 to 10 days. A 0.4 per cent formalin is added, the culture is shaken, and then is allowed to settle for 24 hours. The supernatant fluid is drawn off, incubated for a week, and then tested for sterility by inoculation into brain medium." Breed has modified this technique by adding brain and a few more buffer salts to the liver medium. He also used a 1 per cent formalin for attenuation. His results with the mixed whole-culture bacterin are quite satisfactory. Rodrigues in Brazil has substantiated the value of formolized vaccine in producing immunity.

Immune serum is of aid in treating blackleg as well as producing a passive immunity for a period of about two weeks. It is prepared by hyperimmunization of cattle with any of the above products.

**Diagnosis.** The symptoms and the postmortem findings of blackleg are so characteristic that a laboratory diagnosis is often unnecessary. The organism is usually found in smears made directly from the infected muscle. Intramuscular inoculation of suspensions of infected tissue into guinea pigs produces characteristic lesions from which the organism can be isolated in pure culture. The differentiation of *Clost. chauvoei* and *Clost. septicum* is often necessary. *Clost. chauvoei* is shorter, plumper, and more ovoid than *Clost. septicum;* the former grows singly, whereas the latter frequently forms long chains. When injected subcutaneously into guinea pigs, *Clost. chauvoei* produces edema and gas in the injected area, whereas *Clost. septicum* produces more edema and not so much gas.

### *Clostridium septicum*

**Synonyms and History.** Pasteur and Joubert were the first to describe this organism in 1877, giving it the name *Vibrion septique.* Koch and Gaffky, in 1881, described it and originated the name *Bacillus oedematis maligni.* The organism has been called *Clostridium oedematis maligni* and *Clostridium oedematis* until recently, when there is a tendency to give the species name, *septique,* of Pasteur, the priority right after latinizing it to *septicum. Clostridium septicus* is found in some of the literature.

**Distribution and Transmission.** *Clost. septicum* causes malignant edema, is widely distributed over the earth, and, common to other anaerobic bacilli, is found in the soil. Certain areas are more heavily contaminated than others, and it has been observed that certain premises may be infective for indefinite periods. The organism gains entrance into deeper tissues through cuts and abrasions of the skin. It may be unknowingly injected into animals, and may gain entrance as a result of various surgical procedures. Infection may follow castration in all susceptible animals. Docking and shearing sheep are means by which that animal becomes infected. Horses may become infected during operations if aseptic technique is disregarded. Cows can become infected during parturition, especially when calf delivery is attempted by uninformed herdsmen whose knowledge of obstetrics embraces only forcible delivery. Since man is susceptible to the organism, care must be taken in the autopsy of infected animals as well as infected human beings. It is one of the organisms of the gas-edema group found particularly during wartimes.

In sheep the organism is one of the causes of bradsot or braxy. In such conditions the bacillus gains entrance through the mucous membrane of the abomasum due to penetration by sharp objects.

**Morphology and Staining.** *Clost. septicum* closely resembles *Clost. chauvoei* morphologically. It is a cylindrical rod $0.5\mu$ by $2\mu$ to $6\mu$ in size, with rounded ends, and arranged singly, although it may be found in long chains and filaments, especially from serous surfaces (Fig. 31.3). Spores are oval, subterminal, and slightly larger in diameter than the bacillus, giving "navicular" or "snowshoe" shapes. It is motile by means of 4 to 16 peritrichic flagella. It does not produce a capsule. The organism is gram-positive, although some parts of the cell may be decolorized. It does not stain uniformly, and with methylene blue, granules are observed in one end, or both ends, or in one-half of the cell.

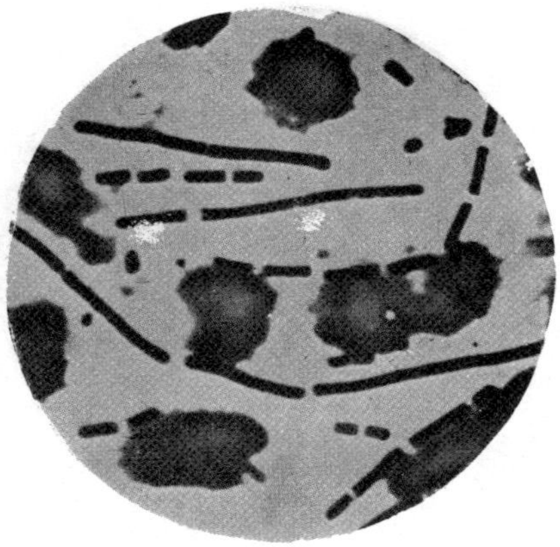

FIG. 31.3—**Clostridium septicum** impression smear from the surface of the liver of guinea pig, ×2,000. (From Nowak: Documenta Microbiologica, courtesy Gustav Fischer.)

**Growth Requirements and Characteristics.** *Clost. septicum* is an obligate anaerobe; grows well on meat infusion media at an optimum temperature of 37°C., although fair growth occurs at room temperature. The optimum pH is 7.6. Growth of the organism is improved by 1 per cent glucose in the medium.

Agar surface colonies are small, irregular, effuse, finely granular, translucent, and have a filamentous edge (Fig. 31.4). Both S and R colonies have been described. Smooth colonies have an amoeboid edge, and the colonies are gray, bluish-gray, and opaque at the center. Colonies in agar-shake cultures are delicate, arborescent, and floccose. Gelatin-shake colonies are large and floccose, with filaments later permeating the medium. A slight turbidity and a light, powdery sediment is formed in broth.

**Resistance.** This organism is the same as those sporeforming bacilli which have been previously described.

**Biochemical Properties.** *Clost. septicum*

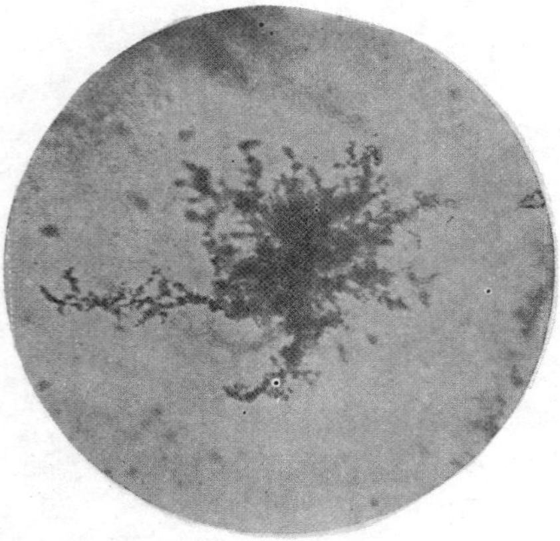

FIG. 31.4—**Clostridium septicum** agar colony, ×100. (From Nowak: Documenta Microbiologica, courtesy Gustav Fischer.)

produces acid and gas from glucose, fructose, galactose, maltose, lactose, and salicin, but not from sucrose (thus differing from *Clost. chauvoei*), mannitol, dulcitol, glycerol, or inulin. Milk is slowly acidified, coagulated, and slightly digested, and some gas is formed. Gelatin is slowly liquefied. Coagulated blood serum is not liquefied. Blood-agar plates show alpha hemolysis followed in a few days by the beta type. Cooked meat medium is turned pink; gas is produced but there is no digestion. Hibler's brain medium is turned black. The organism is indol negative, $NH_3$ slight, $H_2S$ positive, methyl red negative, and Voges-Proskauer negative. Nitrates are reduced; methylene blue is not reduced; the catalase test is negative.

**Antigenic Structure and Toxins.** Both O and H antigens for the organism have been described. On the basis of O antigen it can be divided into four distinct agglutinative groups. Each of these groups in turn is divided into subgroups on the basis of H antigen. Some antigenic component is common to both *Clost. septicum* and *Clost. chauvoei*, because positive cross agglutination and cross complement-fixation tests are observed.

Exotoxin is produced by the organism. A 48-hour-old filtrate will produce death in guinea pigs within 30 minutes in doses as small as 0.5 ml. The exotoxin produced seems to be common to all four antigenic types.

**Pathogenicity.** Experimentally, the organism produces disease in guinea pigs, rabbits, mice, and pigeons. Species which are naturally infected are man, the horse, sheep, cow, and pig. Dogs and cats are susceptible but rarely are infected.

Malignant edema is usually an acute, febrile disease that terminates fatally in two or three days. In man it may be so acute that death occurs in 24 hours.

Gas may not be present in great quantities, although some gas bubbles are always found. The edema is blood-stained and usually gelatinized. Muscle underlying subcutaneous infection is dark red in color and soft in consistency. Hemoglobin-stained fluid may be found in the body cavities and in the pericardial sac. The action of the toxin of this bacillus on the circulation of the cat and rabbit has been described by Kellaway, Reid, and Trethewie. They found that toxin has a specific cardiac action causing a fall in systemic blood pressure and a rise in cardiac pressure; it has a direct action on the heart, causing constriction of the coronary and pulmonary circulations (the latter more marked in the cat), leading to pulmonary edema. In the rabbit, but not in the cat, there is an initial peripheral vasoconstriction, causing a transient rise in systemic blood pressure. In the cat, but not in the rabbit, injection of toxin into the vessels supplying the adrenals causes the liberation of adrenalin, possibly as a result of the preliminary liberation of histamine.

*Clost. septicum* is one of the causes of braxy, a disease which is found in sheep on the western coast of Norway, in Iceland, the Faroe Islands, and Scotland. In this disease the lesions are confined to the tissues adjacent to the fourth stomach and the mucosa and submucosa of that organ. Intense inflammation characterized by edema and hemorrhage with some necrosis is noted. Degenerative changes are found in the visceral organs.

**Immunity.** Animals which recover from malignant edema are soundly immune. The use of immunizing agents is of little practical value except in sheep. The relationship to blackleg, as well as the preparation of the whole-culture bacterin, has been discussed previously.

Antiserum may be of some value in cases of *Clost. septicum* infection, especially if the case is diagnosed early. Otherwise, treatment is of little value.

**Diagnosis.** The isolation and identification of the organism is the only sure way to diagnose malignant edema. Guinea pig inoculation is commonly used to isolate the organism. Rabbits are more susceptible to *Clost. septicum* than to *Clost. chauvoei* and may be used to distinguish the two organisms. Serologic tests are of little value.

### *Clostridium novyi*

**Synonyms and History.** This organism was first described by Novy in 1894 and named *Bacillus oedematis maligni* II. Migula originated the name *Bacillus novyi* in his classification in 1900. The organism was isolated and described by Weinberg and Seguin in 1915 and named *Bacillus oedematiens.* Bergey's Manual recognizes *Clostridium novyi* as valid. *Bacillus gigas* of Zeissler and Raszfeld (1929) apparently is identical with this organism. Although *Clostridium oedematiens* is given as the name of the organism by English and European bacteriologists, it would seem that *Clostridium novyi* has priority rights and for that reason will be used here.

**Distribution and Transmission.** The organism appears to be rather widely spread throughout the world, but it is brought to attention in those areas where sheep are raised, especially those areas where the liver fluke is prevalent. The organism has been found in Montana by Marsh. In Colorado, Newsom, Cross, and Dobbins found it twice in the examination of 200 spleens of normal and diseased sheep. Shaw, Muth, and Seghetti have found the organism of considerable significance in Oregon. It is prevalent in Australia, where Turner has contributed much valuable data concerning it and the disease it produces. It is also found in areas in Germany.

The spores of the bacillus are found in the soil, and, no doubt, commonly are present in the intestinal tract of animals and man. The spores of the organism are probably carried into the bile duct and into the liver by flukes and, stimulated by the necrosis produced by that parasite, the spores germinate, multiply rapidly, and produce the toxin which causes the disease infectious necrotic hepatitis. A type of disease known as "stall braxy" has been described in Germany after castration of young lambs.

**Morphology and Staining.** *Clost. novyi* is one of the largest of the anaerobes, $0.8\mu$ to $1.5\mu$ in diameter and $5\mu$ to $10\mu$ in length. The edges of the organism are parallel, and the ends are rounded. It occurs singly, in pairs, and in long, jointed filaments. The spores of this bacillus are oval and subterminal. It is motile by peritrichous flagella (Fig. 31.5). A capsule is not produced. The organism is stained easily and uniformly and is gram-positive.

**Growth Requirements and Characteristics.** *Clost. novyi* grows well on ordinary media,

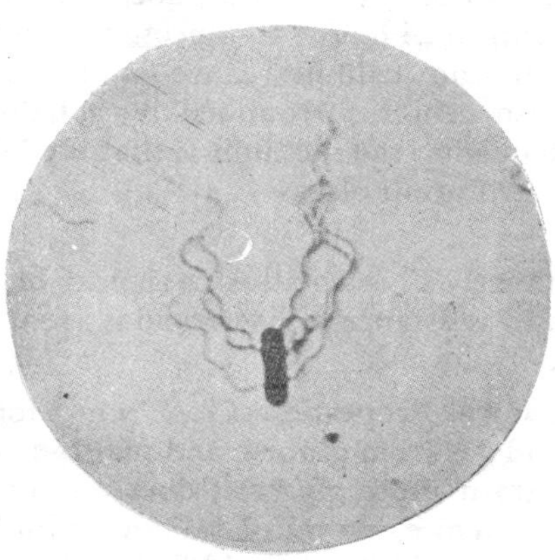

FIG. 31.5—**Clostridium novyi** showing flagella, ×2,000. (From Nowak: Documenta Microbiologica, courtesy Gustav Fischer.)

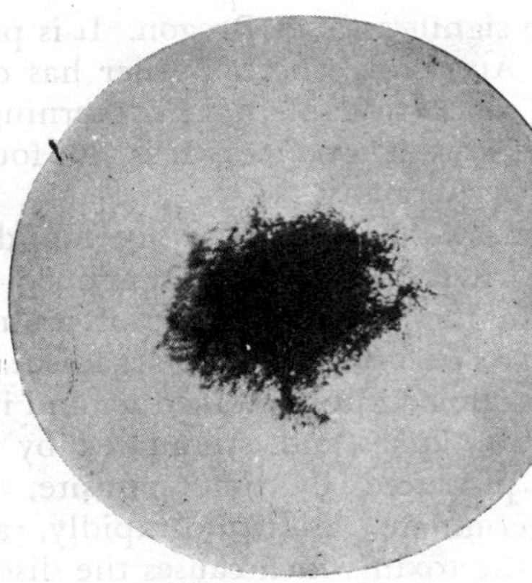

FIG. 31.6—**Clostridium novyi** colony on agar plate, ×80. (From Nowak: Documenta Microbiologica, courtesy Gustav Fischer.)

but glucose stimulates growth. Ferric salts, iron wire, and whole blood also aid growth. The optimum pH is 7.2 to 7.4 and the optimum temperature is 37.5°C. It is the most strictly anaerobic of the entire genus.

Agar plate colonies are small with irregular undulating borders and are finely granular in structure and grayish-blue in color (Fig. 31.6). On moist agar surfaces a thin scumlike colony is formed. Some strains have been described that form circumscribed mucoid colonies which are possibly due to dissociation.

In broth the organism forms slight turbidity during early hours of growth, but the cells form a light, loose, flocculent sediment within 24 hours. In glucose agar-shake cultures the colonies have a compact, yellowish center surrounded by a halo of fine filaments; the medium is shattered due to the evolution of gas.

**Resistance.** This bacillus is typical of the group in resistance to bactericidal agent

**Biochemical Properties.** *Clost. novyi* forms acid and gas from glucose and maltose, and some strains from glycerol; does not attack lactose, sucrose, mannitol, salicin, or inulin. Litmus milk is slowly acidified with some gas production but no digestion. Gelatin is rapidly and completely liquefied. Cooked meat medium is bleached or turned slightly pink with no digestion. Coagulated serum and egg are not liquefied. Brain medium is neither blackened nor digested. The organism is $NH_3$ negative; $H_2S$ slowly positive; indol negative; methyl red negative; and Voges-Proskauer negative. Beta hemolysis, turning to alpha when exposed to the air, is produced on blood-agar plates under anaerobic conditions. The organism does not reduce nitrates.

**Antigenic Structure and Toxins.** Different types of antigens have not been described for this bacillus. Agglutinating antiserum has been found to act only on the homologous strain. The auto-agglutinating characteristic of the organism, however, makes it difficult to use the agglutination test with any degree of success for study.

A lethal toxin (alpha toxin) is produced by *Clost. novyi* which is carried to all parts of the body in a naturally infected or experimentally inoculated animal.

**Pathogenicity.** *Clost. novyi* is pathogenic for guinea pigs, mice, and rabbits. When a 24-hour bouillon culture is injected intramuscularly into guinea pigs, death results within 24 to 48 hours. Experimentally, it has been found pathogenic for swine, cattle, and horses, producing rapid death and the formation of a pale, jelly-like edema of the subcutaneous and intramuscular connective tissue surrounding the point of inoculation. Degenerative changes are produced in visceral organs. The edema is not as hemorrhagic as in blackleg and malignant edema. The sheep is naturally susceptible and is the most commonly infected domestic animal. Parker has observed that the disease is most common in ewes more than 18 months old and rarely occurs in wethers.

Previous mention has been made of the relationship of the liver fluke, *Fasciola hepatica*, to infectious necrotic hepatitis of sheep. This disease is an extremely acute toxemia, the animal dying within 12 hours after symptoms have been noticed. Postmortem examination reveals marked venous congestion which gives the skin a dark color (black disease) and increased straw-colored fluid in the body cavities and pericardial sac. Greenish-colored areas of necrosis, about 1 cm. in size, in which immature liver flukes may be found, are found throughout the liver tissue. Larger, yellowish-white, necrotic foci, which are surrounded by a wide zone of venous congestion, may also be found in the liver.

**Immunity.** Antitoxin has a neutralizing effect on the toxin of *Clost. novyi.* The acute nature of the infection in which the organism is found, however, makes antitoxin therapy rather useless. However, Parker was able to control an outbreak of the disease in a flock of ewes with antiserum. Turner has prepared a formolized broth vaccine which has shown encouraging results. More satisfactory results are obtained when at least three injections of the vaccine are given.

In areas where the disease exists it has been found to be more effective to eliminate liver flukes than to depend on vaccination in order to prevent livestock losses.

**Diagnosis.** The presence of *Clost. novyi* infection can be diagnosed correctly only by the isolation and identification of the organism. Lesions produced in the guinea pig are not sufficiently different from those caused by *Clost. chauvoei* and *Clost. septicum* to be of value.

### *Clostridium perfringens*

**Synonyms and History.** *Bacillus aerogenes capsulatus, Bacillus welchii, Bacterium welchii, Bacillus phlegmonis emphysematosae, Bacillus enteritidis sporogenes, Bacillus perfringens, Granulo bacillus saccharo butyricus immobilis, Bacillus anaerobicus crytobutyricus, Bacillus cadaveris butyricus, Bacillus emphysematis vaginae, Clostridium welchii.*

The organism was first isolated and adequately described by Welch and Nuttall in 1892 following its isolation from a cadaver. The following year E. Fraenkel isolated an organism which he named *B. phlegmonis emphysematosae* from four cases of gas gangrene. In 1898 Veillon and Zuber named this organism *B. perfringens,* a name which is used in the 1948 edition of Bergey's Manual. In his classification of 1900, Migula referred to the organism as *B. welchii.* Since Welch's description, in 1900, of forty-six cases from which the organism was isolated, it has been found in a wide variety of conditions affecting man in all parts of the world.

*Clost. perfringens* and bacilli similar to it have been isolated from a variety of animal infections. Although it is usually considered a secondary invader, becoming especially active after the death of the animal, it has been found to be the direct cause of a variety of conditions. Dalling (1926) isolated an organism from sheep which he called *B. paludis.* Bennetts (1932) also isolated an anaerobe from sheep which he named *Clost. ovitoxicum.* Both of the above organisms are probably *Clost. perfringens,* differing only in the types of toxins produced.

**Distribution and Transmission.** This organism is the most ubiquitous of any of the anaerobic bacilli. It has been isolated from soil, feces, and the intestinal tracts of man and animals by numerous investigators. It also has been isolated from meats which have been incriminated in food poisoning outbreaks in human populations in various countries, including the United States.

**Morphology and Staining.** *Clost. perfringens* is a rod, 0.8$\mu$ to 1.5$\mu$ in diameter by 4$\mu$ to 8$\mu$ in length, with usually rather square ends (Fig. 31.7). Short, almost coccal forms, and long filaments may be found under certain growth conditions. Variant forms (club shapes, filaments, tadpole forms, granular types) are found frequently in old, coagulated serum cultures. It usually occurs singly, but may be found in pairs, short chains, and arranged in chains or filaments. It is absolutely nonmotile, differing from the other members of this genus. Spores are large and oval with slightly flattened ends, located subterminally or centrally. The spores are sometimes found in

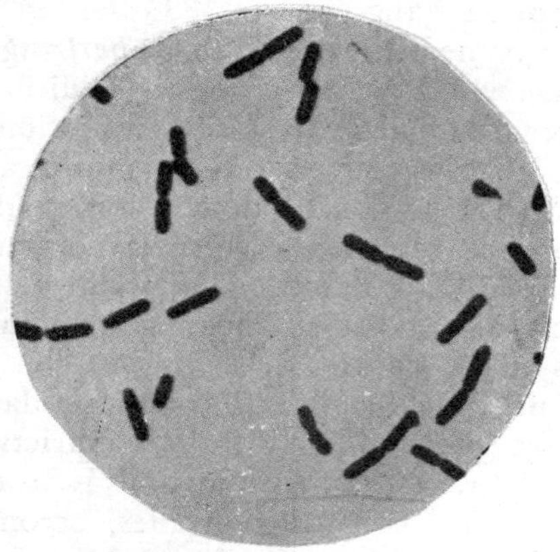

FIG. 31.7—**Clostridium perfringens,** ×2,000. (From Nowak: Documenta Microbiologica, courtesy Gustav Fischer.)

infected wounds, but are most readily formed in such media as casein broth, alkaline egg broth, and coagulated serum free from fermentable carbohydrate. Capsules may be demonstrated in body fluids and in media containing serum.

The organism stains readily with the common aniline dyes and is gram-positive in young cultures with the frequent occurrence of gram-negative cells in old cultures.

**Growth Requirements and Characteristics.** The organism grows well in ordinary media. According to McCampbell it is best isolated from soil and other material by successive inoculations into milk, followed by intravenous injection into a rabbit which is killed immediately after inoculation and placed in an incubator at 37°C. for 8 or 10 hours. The thorax of the animal is then opened, and cultures are made from the heart blood into glucose broth and placed under anaerobic conditions. The optimum growth temperature is 37°C. The organism grows best in alkaline media, and spore formation is inhibited at pH 6.6.

The colonies upon agar and gelatin plates are round, grayish, semitranslucent, and smooth, with an entire edge. Two types of colonies have been observed upon blood agar, one hemolytic and the other nonhemolytic. Colony variants have also been described. One type is a thin, filmy growth which spreads rapidly and is composed of long filaments. Another type is an extremely viscid, mucoid colony which adheres firmly to the medium. Bouillon is uniformly clouded, followed by a heavy precipitate.

**Resistance.** The organism is not significantly different from the group in resistance.

**Biochemical Properties.** *Clost. perfringens* forms acid and gas from glucose, fructose, galactose, maltose, lactose, and sucrose, but not from mannitol, dulcitol, or salicin. The aldehyde, acrolein, is produced from glycerol. Litmus milk is coagulated, and acid and gas are formed, giving a "stormy fermentation" within 24 hours. Cooked meat medium with iron is blackened. The organism produces slight $NH_3$; is strongly positive to $H_2S$ production; is indol negative; is methyl red negative; is Voges-Proskauer negative; reduces nitrates slightly; is methylene blue negative; is catalase negative.

**Antigenic Structure and Toxins.** There is no evidence that any definite antigenic groups exist on the basis of the agglutination test. By toxin-antitoxin neutralization tests, however, six different types of toxins have been described, but these types are not in agreement with any agglutination grouping.

The toxigenic types of *Clost. perfringens* have been summarized by MacLennan in Table 31.2 along with the name of the disease produced by each type. It will be observed that each toxigenic type may produce more than one toxin or axoenzyme which have detrimental effects on tissue cells. Of these, alpha toxin and epsilon toxin are of greatest significance in animal diseases.

**Pathogenicity.** *Clost. perfringens* is pathogenic for guinea pigs, mice, and pigeons, and to a lesser degree for rabbits. The orga-

TABLE 31.2

Toxigenic Types of Clostridium Perfringens

| Type | Toxin | | | | | | | | | | | | Disease |
|---|---|---|---|---|---|---|---|---|---|---|---|---|---|
| | $\alpha$ | $\beta$ | $\gamma$ | $\delta$ | $\epsilon$ | $\eta$ | $\theta$ | $\iota$ | $\kappa$ | $\lambda$ | $\mu$ | $\nu$ | |
| A | +++ | − | − | − | − | (+) | ++ | − | ++ | − | + or − | + | gas gangrene |
| B | + | +++ | + | + | ++ | ? | + | − | + or − | + | + | + | lamb dysentery |
| C | + | +++ | + | ++ | − | ? | ++ | − | + | − | − | + | struck |
| D | + | − | − | − | +++ | ? | + | − | + or − | + or − | + or − | + | enterotoxemia of sheep |
| E | + | − | − | − | − | ? | ? | ++ | ? | + | − | + | enterotoxemia of calves |
| F | + | +++ | +++ | − | − | ? | ? | − | + | ? | − | + | enteritis necroticans (gas gangrene) |

Source: MacLennan, J. D. Histoxic Clostridial Infections of Man. Bact. Rev. 26:177–276, 1962.

nism is one of those most commonly found in gas gangrene in man. It is pathogenic for sheep, producing a variety of conditions. It has also been involved in an acute toxemia in calves and in horses. The organism has been shown to be widely distributed in soil and in the intestinal tracts of animals and man. It may invade tissues quickly after death and give rise to a mistaken diagnosis. It has been isolated from cattle dead of anthrax, swine that have succumbed to cholera, and isolated together with *Clost. chauvoei* from blackleg lesions in cattle and in sheep. Gas gangrene in a dog, following the subcutaneous injection of calcium gluconate by an owner, has been reported.

Experimental infection in the guinea pig is characterized by a large, crepitant swelling at the point of inoculation. The skin is dark red and subcutaneous tissue surrounding and some distance from the site of inoculation is emphysematous, edematous, and blood-tinged. The suprarenal glands are congested. The underlying muscle is pale pink in color and shows evidence of liquefaction necrosis.

*Clost. perfringens* Type A has been associated with food poisoning in man in which meat has been contaminated with the organism. The report of Hall and associates following their study of 83 strains obtained from England, Europe, Asia, and the United States indicates that they comprise an antigenically heterogenic group and that antigenic typing is of limited epidemiological value.

The sheep appears to be the only domestic animal in which a definite disease is produced by more than one type of *Clost. perfringens*. A lamb dysentery which is characterized by an enteritis, ranging from a mild hyperemia to extensive necrosis and ulceration, has been described by Gaiger and Dalling of England. The organism associated with this disease produces a toxin which is classed as Type B. McEwen and Roberts have described a disease among sheep on the Romney Marsh in Kent, which occurs during the late winter and spring months. It is characterized by an acute toxemia with resulting enteritis and peritonitis, followed by typical lesions of gas gangrene after the animal has been dead for some time. The name *Clost. paludis* has been suggested for the organism found in this disease, but Topley and Wilson believe that it is best to refer to it as *Clost. perfringens* Type C. Griner and Bracken have observed that *Clost. perfringens* Type C can produce an acute toxemia in newborn calves. Bennetts (1932) described an infectious enterotoxemia found in sheep in Australia. The disease was due to the absorption of toxin which was liberated by the organism in the small intestine. The organism was identified as *Clost. perfringens* Type D of Wilsdon. This organism was found in lamb dysentery in Colorado by Newsom and Cross and in Montana by Marsh, Tunnicliff, and Jungherr. The condition known as pulpy kidney disease of lambs, which was observed in New Zealand by Gill (1932), in Wales by Montgomerie and Dalling (1933) and by Montgomerie and Rowlands (1933, 1934), and in Oregon by Shaw, Muth, and Seghetti (1939), was caused by the same organism. An acute toxemia of lambs, sheep, and horses was found to be due to a toxin obtained from filtrates of intestinal contents of those animals by Gordon (1934). This toxin was neutralized by an antitoxin of *Clost. perfringens* Type D. Griner has shown that Type D epsilon toxin produces small areas of liquefaction necrosis in the brain of experimental sheep. He has found white Swiss mice are the best experimental animals to use in studying the toxins produced by the organism. An enterotoxemia of pigs caused by *Clost. perfringens* Type C has been reported by Barnes and Moon. McGowan and associates in California isolated *Clost. perfringens* Type A from sheep which showed a condition similar to "enterotoxemic jaundice" described in Australia. Griner *et al.* have reported the isolation of *Clost. perfringens* Type D from Brown Swiss dairy calves.

**Immunity.** British workers have found effective the use of a formolized vaccine in immunizing pregnant ewes or the newborn lamb to prevent lamb dysentery. McEwen (1935) observed a formolized vaccine useful in immunizing sheep against "struck." The infectious enterotoxemia found in sheep of western Australia has been treated successfully by the use of specific antitoxin prepared by using *Clost. perfringens* Type D as the incitant. This has been confirmed by Shaw, Muth, and Seghetti in Oregon.

The use of an alum-precipitated toxoid by Muth and Morrill for enterotoxemia in sheep was reported in 1946. The same year Bythell and Parker found that an anaculture was an effective immunizing agent. In 1947 Whitlock and Fabricant also obtained favorable results with an anaculture. In 1948 Baldwin, Frederick, and Ray reported that a formolized bacterin was of significant value in immunizing feeder lambs against enterotoxemia. DeMello and associates, in 1952, reported that formalin-treated, alum-precipitated epsilon toxoid is a satisfactory immunizing agent for the disease in sheep.

**Diagnosis.** *Clost. perfringens* infection can be correctly diagnosed by the isolation and identification of the organism. This is best accomplished by the neutralization of the toxin by a known specific antitoxin. The diagnosis of enterotoxemia in sheep may be accomplished by mixing a quantity of the intestinal contents of the dead sheep with specific antitoxin and injecting into mice. Other mice are injected with intestinal contents not treated with antitoxin. If the former group of mice live and the latter group die, it is obvious that toxin is present in the intestine. If intestinal fluid cannot be used immediately after removal from the sheep, it should be frozen because toxins deteriorate rapidly.

Humphreys has described a diagnostic culture test using glycerol for the identification of *Clost. perfringens* which involves the detection of the formation of the aldehyde acrolein. He claims that in a large number of tests he has never known the test to mislead.

### *Clostridium hemolyticum*

**Synonyms and History.** This organism was first isolated and described by Vawter and Records in 1926, from which the following description is freely taken. They gave it the name *Clostridium hemolyticum-bovis*. Hall studied strains of the organism and named it *Bacillus haemolyticus*.

**Distribution and Transmission.** In the United States, *Clost. hemolyticum* is apparently confined to the mountain valleys of the western states—Nevada, Idaho, southwestern Montana, eastern Washington, eastern Oregon, and eastern California. Brown has reported the isolation of the organism from a liver infarct of a steer in Kentucky, but the animal had come from Texas two months previously. Sordelli, Ferrari, and Prado (1933) have observed the organism in South America from the Andes region in Chile. The disease, bacillary hemoglobinuria, occurs most frequently in swampy, poorly drained areas and irrigated pastures. The fact that animals become infected while grazing in swampy areas during the summer and early fall would indicate that the organism or its spores are taken in with the food or water in infected areas. However, Smith and Jasmin have isolated the organism from the livers of apparently healthy cattle from herds where bacillary hemoglobinuria had recently occurred and also from a normal animal from a ranch where the disease had not appeared for five years. The isolation of this organism, by Jasmin, from the bones of animals which had died of bacillary hemoglobinuria two years previously indicates a potential reservoir for the infection in range areas. Van Ness and Erickson believe that the organism persists in swampy valley areas where the soil is continually alkaline.

**Morphology and Staining.** The bacilli are rod-shaped, $1\mu$ to $1.3\mu$ in diameter by $3\mu$ to $5.6\mu$ in length, with rounded ends when organisms occur singly but truncate when in chains. Spores are heavily walled, globoid, oval, or slightly elongated and situated either terminally or subterminally. Spore formation decreases when the organism is grown on common artificial media, but this property is regained when the organism is grown on media containing serum or blood. This bacillus is sluggishly motile by means of six to sixteen long, peritrichous flagella. Capsules are not formed. The organism is gram-positive during the first 24 hours of growth and then it is gram-negative.

**Growth Requirements and Characteristics.** The organism is strictly anaerobic; it has an optimum temperature of 37°C. and an optimum pH of 7.5. Culture media which contain tryptophane or proteins, readily yielding this and other amino acids, are essential for growth and toxin production. Sulfur, likewise, appears to be utilized. Cooked liver medium containing sodium thioglycollate has proved to be satisfactory as a basic medium for routine culturing and toxin production.

On the surface of agar slants a light growth is present in 24 hours. In deep agar tubes growth is apparent after 24 hours incubation; colonies at first are homogeneous and lenticular, but rapidly develop an eccentric fluff, later appearing as dense, woolly masses with short peripheral filaments. These masses vary from 0.25 to 0.5 mm. in diameter, according to the number in the tube. In broth a complete clouding is present in 8 to 12 hours followed by autoagglutination. An abundance of gas with a cheesy odor is produced.

**Resistance.** *Clost. hemolyticum* loses its viability quickly on some types of media, especially in peptic-digest broth plus raw rabbit liver, sealed with petrolatum. Viability is maintained for long periods, however, in beef-heart, peptic-digest broth. Although no definite data are available, the spores of the organism probably do not differ from those of other anaerobes in respect to resistance to heat, desiccation, light, and chemicals.

**Biochemical Properties.** *Clost. hemolyticum* produces acid and gas from glucose and fructose. Records and Vawter previously had listed galactose as fermented, but their subsequent studies have proved this incorrect. Other carbohydrates not attacked are mannose, maltose, lactose, sucrose, mannite, raffinose, dulcitol, glycerin, arabinose, xylose, dextrin, inulin, and salicin. However, **Smith *et al.* have described a maltose-fermenting variant which resembled *Clost. hemolyticum* in every other respect. Blood agar shows diffuse hemolysis in 16 to 24 hours. Iron medium is blackened; gelatin is liquefied in two to six days; litmus milk is unchanged; coagulated serum is not**

liquefied; indol is produced in 16 to 18 hours; $H_2S$ is produced in large amounts; methyl red and Voges-Proskauer tests are negative; nitrates are not reduced.

**Antigenic Structure and Toxins.** Records and Vawter have shown that all strains of the organism studied by them are immunologically identical in respect to agglutination and toxin formation. They showed, also, by using specific antiserums in rabbits and then inoculating them with lethal doses of the organism, that no antigenic relationships exist between *Clost. hemolyticum* and *Clost. novyi, Clost. perfringens, Clost. chauvoei,* or *Clost. septicum.*

Two toxin fractions, which have not been separated in pure form, are produced in cultures and in the animal body. One fraction is markedly hemolytic but unstable. It is present in culture media at the eighth to tenth hour of incubation. Its maximum concentration is reached in 16 to 20 hours and disappears after 30 to 36 hours of incubation. The other fraction is recognized by its necrotizing action on tissues of rabbits and guinea pigs. It is present during the early stages of the growth of the culture but persists for a week longer.

Claus and Macheak found that *Clost. hemolyticum* toxin stimulated the formation of antitoxin in guinea pigs but toxoid did not.

The production of lecithinase by the *Clost. hemolyticum* has been reported by Jasmin who found that the production of opalescence in human serum and the flocculation of egg yolk solution by this enzyme paralleled the lethal and hemolytic action of the toxin produced by the organism.

**Pathogenicity.** *Clost. hemolyticum* is pathogenic to rabbits, guinea pigs, and white mice, but infection is dependent upon a high concentration of hemolytic toxin in the culture. The cow is the most susceptible of the domestic animals. The disease has been observed in sheep and swine.

Guinea pigs weighing 300 to 500 gms. are killed in 18 to 36 hours by 0.1 to 0.5 ml. of toxic culture. Rabbits weighing 1.5 to 2 kg. die in 16 to 24 hours after receiving 0.5 to 1.5 ml. of toxic culture. Mature white mice weighing 20 to 25 gm. die in 16 to 24 hours after inoculation with 0.1 ml. of culture. Upon autopsy an extensive, bloodstained edema without gas is found in the areolar tissue. The underlying muscle tissue is usually light colored but not so softened; bloodstained fluid is found in the body cavities; perivascular hemorrhages occur in the pleura and peritoneum; intestines are distended with gas, and the contents are bile stained, and sometimes are bloodstained; single or multiple infarcts occur in the liver; hemoglobinuria is a constant finding; the lungs are moderately congested.

The lesions produced by the natural infection in cattle, sheep, and swine are not unlike those described above. The most significant characteristics, however, may be repeated for emphasis. Light-colored infarcts are found in the liver from which the infection no doubt originates; extensive hemorrhages are found in the parietal peritoneum; subcutaneous connective tissue is icteric; pinhead-sized cortical hemorrhages are present in the kidneys; dark red-colored fluid accumulates in the urinary bladder.

**Immunity.** Records and Vawter (1945) have studied various types of vaccines and bacterins and have found that the aluminum hydroxide precipitated toxoid type of formolized bacterin gives the best results. Claus and Macheak believe that bacterins which are completely detoxified do not stimulate the formation of antitoxin.

A mineral oil adjuvant vaccine inactivated with formalin has been recommended by Claus because it gives a long-lasting immunity.

A potent antitoxic serum is produced in horses and when given intravenously in 500 to 1,000 ml. doses to infected animals proves to be an adequate treatment.

**Diagnosis.** The symptoms of the disease, the animal involved, and the section of the country are most valuable in diagnosis. The organism must be isolated and identified for absolute proof, however, because the disease may at times be confused with anthrax, hemorrhagic septicemia, and blackleg. *Clost. hemolyticum* resembles *Clost. novyi* and *Clost. sordellii* in some cultural characteristics as well as the effects produced in experimental animals. This organism is best identified by using a specific antiserum on young cultures obtaining a clear-cut agglutination reaction.

### *Clostridium sordellii (bifermentans)*

**Synonyms and History.** In 1922 Sordelli of Argentina isolated an organism which he called *Bacillus oedematiens sporogenes* from two fatal cases of gas gangrene in man. Meleney, Humphreys, and Carp, in 1927, unaware of Sordelli's work, described and named a similar organism, *Clostridium oedematoides.* In 1927 Hall and Scott suggested the name *Bacillus sordellii* after studying cultures isolated from cases of gas gangrene in man. Hall, in 1929, identified two cultures isolated from cases of icterohemoglobinuria of cattle as identical with those from human beings, and in the same year Hall, Rymer, and Jungherr found that cultures obtained from Meleney, from Sordelli, and from Nevada cattle were indistinguishable culturally and serologically. In 1931 Hall and Gray reported a fatal case of septic peritonitis in man due to this organism. This significance of *Clost. sordellii* as a pathogenic organism in animals was emphasized by Vawter in 1942 after his study of five cultures isolated from cattle and one from sheep in Nevada.

This organism is called *Clostridium bifermentans* by some authors who believe that it is only a pathogenic strain. Inasmuch as students in veterinary medicine are more concerned with pathogenic species, the name *Clost. sordellii* will be used.

**Distribution and Transmission.** The geographical distribution of this organism is not known, but its isolation from such widely separated areas as Argentina and Nevada suggests that more detailed studies of anaerobes isolated from cases of gas gangrene in man and animals may reveal its presence elsewhere.

In common with other bacilli of this group, it is presumed that the organism gains entrance through wounds and abrasions of the skin and mucous membranes, and originates from the soil.

**Morphology and Staining.** *Clost. sordellii* is a nonmotile, spore-forming bacillus $1\mu$ in diameter by $3.5\mu$ to $4.0\mu$ in length. Spores are located in a central or subterminal position. Capsules are not produced. Cultures 12 to 18 hours old are strongly gram-positive.

**Growth Requirements and Characteristics.** This organism grows readily and luxuriantly in media such as cooked meat medium and sodium thioglycollate agar. In cooked meat media, the meat particles first become bright red, then blacken and become partially digested or gelatinized. White crystals, resembling tyrosin, appear in meat cultures after ten days at room temperature. A black, veil-like stratum develops in fluid media containing sodium thioglycollate.

Colonies of the organism in deep agar cultures are pleomorphic, appearing as biconvex discs, multiplane discs, disc types with eccentric fluffs, or dense feathery masses. The agar column is usually broken by gas. The proteolytic action of the organism is notable and the characteristic valeric odor of cultures 20 to 48 hours old is typical.

**Resistance.** No data have been recorded to indicate that the spores of *Clost. sordellii* are different from those of other bacilli in respect to resistance. Vawter observed that cultures 10 to 12 years old grew readily when revived with liver digest broth and were fully virulent.

**Biochemical Properties.** Glucose, fructose, and maltose are fermented; galactose, lactose, sucrose, mannite, arabinose, xylose, inulin, salicin, dulcitol, and glycerol are not fermented. Gelatin is liquefied in 24 hours; litmus milk is coagulated in 24 hours and is peptonized in 5 to 7 days. Coagulated serum is liquefied in 5 to 7 days with the residual clot turning black. Indol is formed in 18 to 24 hours; $H_2S$ production is pronounced; methyl red test is positive; Voges-Proskauer reaction is negative; nitrates are not reduced. Red blood cells are hemolyzed in 4 to 6 hours.

**Antigenic Structure and Toxins.** All studies of the organism indicate that it is antigenically homogenous. However, Walker has been able to show that strains of *Clost. bifermentans* and *Clost. sordellii* could be differentiated on the basis of spore agglutinogens but not precipitinogens.

A very potent, moderately stable, filterable toxin is produced in 24 to 36 hours. This toxin is inactivated by 70°C. in 20 minutes and by 0.25 per cent formalin in 2 days at 37.5°C. The antigenic action of formolized cultures is not destroyed.

**Pathogenicity.** Guinea pigs and rabbits are susceptible to *Clost. sordellii* and the lesions produced are typical of a gas edema. Bacteremia is produced and death follows in 16 to 18 hours. Horses are killed by doses as small as 0.5 ml. of a toxic culture. Germ-free filtrates produce severe local reactions in horses when given subcutaneously. Cattle, likewise, are very susceptible.

Natural cases of the disease have been observed only in cattle and sheep by Vawter. Reference previously has been made to the strains isolated by him. Three of the cattle strains were isolated with either *Clost. hemolyticum* or *Clost. perfringens* from liver infarcts or other tissues of cattle which had died because of bacillary hemoglobinuria. One strain was isolated from a calf which showed atypical blackleg, and another strain from calves which had become infected by vaccination. An avirulent strain was isolated with *Clost. septicum* from a sheep.

**Immunity.** A highly potent antitoxic serum is produced in horses by the use of carefully attenuated cultures of the organism. Vawter has developed agglutinating antiserum in the rabbit by using formolized cultures.

**Diagnosis.** The presence of *Clost. sordellii* in an infection can be detected only by the isolation and identification of the organism.

### *Clostridium tetani*

**Synonyms and History.** Bacillus of Nicolaier; *Plectridium tetani; Bacillus tetani.*

Carle and Rattone, in 1884, produced tetanus in rabbits by injecting them with exudate taken from a wound of a man suffering with the disease. The description of the microorganism was contributed in 1884 by Nicolaier who produced tetanus in rabbits by injecting garden earth. He observed long, slender bacilli in the lesions of rabbits suffering from tetanus. Rosenbach, in 1886, provided the connecting link between the work of Carle and Rattone and of Nicolaier when he produced tetanus in guinea pigs by injecting them with the material from a woman who had died of tetanus following severe frostbite. He noted the bacillus and was probably the first to call attention to the "drumstick" nature of it. In 1889 Kitasato succeeded in growing the organism in pure culture and in transmitting the disease experimentally. Von Behring and Kitasato, in 1890, showed the toxic nature of the bacillus and also demonstrated that rabbits could be immunized against the toxin by the injection of small doses. More important was the fact that the blood serum from such rabbits could neutralize the toxin in vivo and in vitro; thus, these investigators laid the foundation for serum therapy.

During recent years, *Clost. tetani* has been investigated with the view of obtaining more information concerning its distribution, antigenic relationships, and toxic action as well as toxin and antitoxin standardization and the manufacture of tetanus toxoid.

**Distribution and Transmission.** *Clost. tetani* is widely distributed in nature. It has been isolated from the fecal material of man and herbivorous animals, particularly horses. Ten Broeck and Bauer have shown that the bacilli undergo multiplication in the intestinal tract of guinea pigs. Soils from various parts of the world have revealed the presence of the organism. It is possible that under certain conditions the bacillus may maintain, for a time, a saprophytic existence and multiply in the soil.

The organism gains entrance through skin wounds caused by objects which carry dirt into the deeper tissues. Some cases of tetanus occur in which the infection atrium is unknown.

**Morphology and Staining.** *Clost. tetani* is a long slender rod, 0.5μ in diameter by 2μ to 5μ in length, and long, filamentous forms occur which later break up into shorter rods. The ends of the organism are rounded. It occurs singly or in short chains which are sluggishly motile by means of peritrichic flagella (Fig. 31.8). The spores found in the organism are two or three times the diameter of the cell and are situated terminally, giving a "drumstick" appearance (Fig. 31.9). The organism stains readily by the ordinary aniline dyes and is gram-positive.

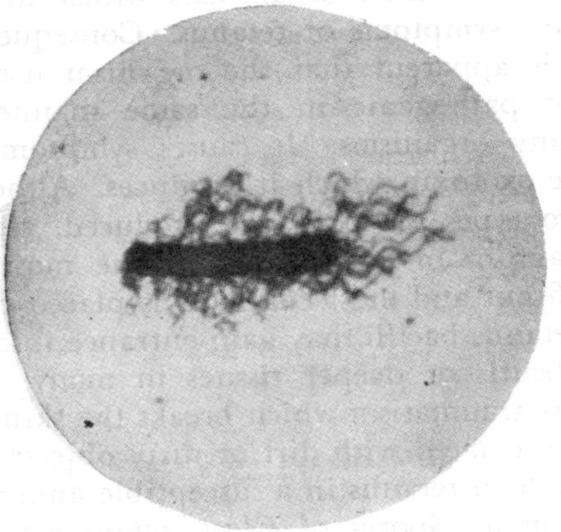

FIG. 31.8—**Clostridium tetani** showing mass of flagella, Van Ermengen stain, ×2,000. (From Nowak: Documenta Microbiologica, courtesy Gustav Fischer.)

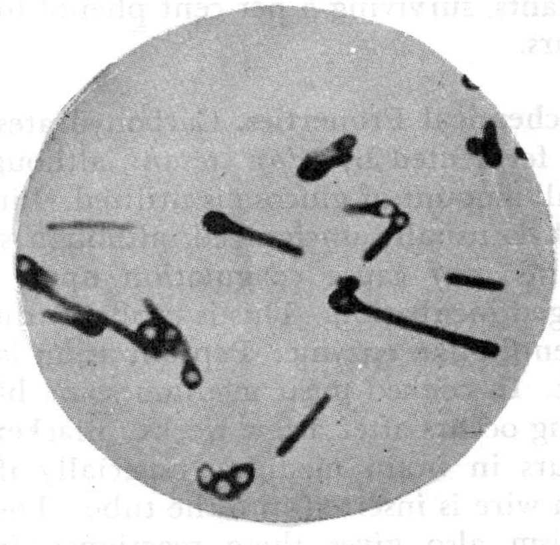

FIG. 31.9—**Clostridium tetani** showing polar spores, ×2,000. (From Nowak: Documenta Microbiologica, courtesy Gustav Fischer.)

**Growth Requirements and Characteristics.** *Clost. tetani* is an obligate anaerobe and is isolated with difficulty in pure culture from soil or infected animals. Heating the material taken from animals to 80°C. and subsequently placing it in broth is often required for isolation. The organism grows well in liquid media to which finely divided particles, such as meat, steel, or cotton, are added. A temperature of 37°C. is best suited for growth. The optimum pH is 7.0 to 7.6.

Colonies on agar surfaces are irregular, often spreading from a denser center (effuse), have a filamentous edge, are glistening and grayish-yellow, becoming brownish with age. Broth is uniformly clouded, and a slight, finely granular sediment forms. In gelatin stabs, a typical "fir-tree" growth occurs. The gelatin is slowly liquefied. Alpha type of hemolysis first appears but is followed in a few days by complete hemolysis.

**Resistance.** Spores of the tetanus bacillus resist desiccation indefinitely. They also resist boiling for some time (over 1 hour), but are killed at 105°C. in from 3 to 25 minutes. The age of the spore appears to be an important factor. The temperature of the autoclave kills the spores in 15 to 20 minutes. It is resistant to ordinary disinfectants, surviving 5 per cent phenol for 15 hours.

**Biochemical Properties.** Carbohydrates are not fermented by *Clost. tetani,* although a small amount of glucose is utilized. Litmus milk is usually unchanged, although some strains may cause coagulation upon prolonged incubation. This is probably due to a rennin-like enzyme. Peptonization is absent. In cooked meat medium some blackening occurs after a few weeks. Blackening occurs in brain medium, especially if an iron wire is inserted into the tube. The organism also gives these reactions: indol negative, methyl red negative, Voges-Proskauer negative, nitrates not reduced, $NH_3$ slight, $H_2S$ slight, methylene blue not reduced, and phenol positive.

**Antigenic Structure and Toxins.** *Clost. tetani* has been divided into nine types on the basis of the agglutination test. Felix and Robertson indicate that there are at least two antigenic substances in the bacterial body: one, a flagellar H antigen; the other, a somatic O antigen. The latter is common to the species. Toxin produced by all strains is only of one antigenic type; that is, antitoxin produced by the injection of one strain of toxin will neutralize the toxins of all strains.

Tetanus toxin, however, is known to attack two different types of tissue. *Tetanospasmin* has an affinity for nerve tissue, and *tetanolysin* produces hemolysis. Tetanus toxin is not absorbed from the intact digestive tract, and there is some evidence that it is inactivated or destroyed by gastric juices. The toxin is destroyed by heat at 65°C. for 5 minutes but resists 120°C. for 1 hour when dry. A temperature of 55°C. for 1 hour destroys its toxicity but does not alter its combining power with antitoxin. Freezing and thawing does not materially alter the potency of toxin, according to Hartley. Direct sunlight for 15 hours destroys tetanus toxin if the temperature is 40°C. Daylight weakens toxin. One of the most effective means of preserving tetanus toxin is by precipitation with ammonium sulfate, drying over sulfuric acid, and storing in the dark at 5°C. in vacuum tubes under pentophosphoric acid. The toxin is not resistant to acids or alkalies. Seventy per cent alcohol will destroy it in 1 hour. The potency of toxin may be decreased by certain chemicals, notably iodine trichloride, resulting in an anatoxin which may be used for immunization of horses in antitoxin production.

**Pathogenicity.** The injection of pure cultures of *Clost. tetani* or its toxin into muscle tissue of experimental animals causes the development of typical tetanus. The mouse is one of the most susceptible of animals, although the horse, guinea pig, and monkey are more susceptible to toxin when dosage and body weight are considered. Rabbits, sheep, cattle, and goats are susceptible. The pig is next to the horse in susceptibility, although this is sometimes contrary to popular opinion. Cats, dogs, and birds are resistant.

Cold-blooded vertebrates are not naturally affected by tetanus but are used in studies of the effects of tetanus toxin. Rowson, for example, has shown that frogs kept at a temperature above 15°C. are susceptible to the action of toxin, which appears to be the case with other cold-blooded animals.

*Clost. tetani* has been isolated from the intestinal tract of animals which do not show symptoms of tetanus. Consequently, it is apparent that the organism itself is not pathogenic in the same manner as many organisms. It causes symptoms by the exotoxin which it produces. Although two types of toxin are produced, tetanospasmin, or neurotoxin, is the most significant and most emphasis is placed on it. Tetanus bacilli may gain entrance into the subcutis or deeper tissues in many ways. Any traumatism which breaks the skin and is associated with dirt or dirty objects may result in tetanus in a susceptible animal or in man. Spores of *Clost. tetani* gain entrance; lacerated tissue provides excellent anaerobic conditions; the spores germinate; toxin is formed and is on its way. In rare cases tetanus is observed and there are no external injuries of any kind. Such cases may have resulted from an organism entering the blood stream and being carried to an area of the body low in oxygen, thereby permitting it to multiply and produce toxin. It also is possible for toxin to be produced in crypts and folds in the intestinal tract.

The absorption of the toxin and the mode by which it arrives at the central nervous system is controversial. Originally it was thought to be spread by the blood stream. The incubation period required for symptoms to appear after injection of toxin, however, made toxemia doubtful. Some have claimed that the toxin is absorbed by motor nerve endings and passes up the axis cylinders to the anterior horn cells, which explains why contractions are confined first to the affected limb or part. When the toxin becomes diffused through the cord and brain, the entire body may be affected. Abel and coworkers, however, contend that the toxin is absorbed by lymphatic vessels at the site of its liberation, then carried to the general circulation and distributed to the central nervous system by the arterial blood supply.

The period of incubation for the disease depends on the site of the injury. In man the average incubation period is seven days. In the horse the site of injury is more variable, and the incubation period varies from four to twenty days. The length of the incubation period is obviously hard to determine since so many factors seem to be responsible for the multiplication of the organism with subsequent toxin liberation. The phrase "period of incubation" is not the same in tetanus as it is in many diseases. In tetanus it is the period of time it takes for the toxin to migrate from the site of its production to local motor nerves or to the brain. The term "period of transfer" may be more appropriate.

The action of neurotoxin on nerve tissue is not known. A simple laboratory experiment shows that toxin is adsorbed by nerve tissue but not by liver tissue. Apparently some fraction in neurotoxin blocks the inhibitory hyperpolarization of motor neurones which alters their normal function (Brooks *et al.*). The identity of this fraction is unknown.

The characteristic symptom of tetanus in all animals is a stiffening of muscles due to contraction. The muscles at the site of inoculation may be the first, and in mild cases they may be the only ones, affected. In the horse the retraction of the eyes and protrusion of the nictitating membrane and spasmodic contraction of other parts of the body are diagnostic. As the toxin ascends, more motor nerves are affected, and when the toxin reaches the brain, generalized contractions are evident. When the diaphragm and intercostal muscles become affected the animal dies with asphyxia. Characteristic lesions are absent in tetanus upon postmortem examination.

**Immunity.** Some animals have the ability to resist the action of tetanus toxin. In some cases this appears to be a natural immunity as in the dog, whereas in others, the cow, there is some evidence that the blood serum contains antitoxin. Most cattle show more than 1/500 unit of antitoxin per milliliter of blood serum. Sheep and goat serum likewise may contain small quantities. The presence of antitoxin in the blood of these animals has been explained by the assumption that tetanus bacilli may grow and multiply in the forestomachs, especially the rumen, and liberate enough toxin to stimulate antitoxin formation. The resistance of cows, sheep, and goats to tetanus, therefore, may be due to a slight immunity and not natural resistance. In this connection it is interesting to note that the blood of man, horses, pigs, guinea pigs, rabbits, and monkeys does not contain antitoxin.

When tetanus toxin becomes adsorbed to nerve tissue, it cannot be removed except by maceration of the tissue, and it cannot be neutralized by antitoxin unless the antitoxin is injected directly into the nerve sheath. The use of antitoxin, therefore, is mainly prophylactic. It is for this reason that antitoxin is given immediately after any lacerating injury in animals or in man. The presence of antitoxin in the body will neutralize any toxin formed at the site of injury if tetanus bacilli are there.

Tetanus toxoid is widely used in man, and it should be used more than it is in animals. After an initial dose of toxoid is given, the level of antitetanus immunity can be kept up with "booster shots" given every three years.

The preparation of tetanus toxin, antitoxin, and toxoid is described in the chapter on toxin-antitoxin, to which the student can refer.

**Diagnosis.** The symptoms of tetanus are so characteristic that laboratory methods are rarely, if ever, used for diagnosis. The organism can be recognized in stained smears of exudate from the infected wound of an animal showing typical tetanus.

### *Clostridium botulinum*

**Synonyms and History.** This organism was first isolated from brine-preserved ham in 1896 by Van Armengen who named it *Bacillus botulinus.* The following year Kempner was able to show that a potent antitoxin was produced in goats against the toxin liberated by the bacillus. The next most significant contribution was the recognition by Leuchs in 1910 that toxins of different strains were antigenically different. In 1915 Burke distinguished two distinct toxigenic strains which he designated A and B. A third strain, Type C, was discovered by Bengston in 1922 in fly larvae and was named *Clostridium luciliae.* In 1923 Graham and Boughton isolated the same bacillus from chickens and ducks. In 1926 Theiler and his associates in South Africa cultivated an organism, which they designated *Clostridium parabotulinum* Type D, from cattle affected with lamziekte. Theiler and Robinson, in 1928, isolated an anaerobic bacillus, which they called *Clostridium parabotulinum equi,* from horses and mules having died as a result of eating hay contaminated by decomposed rats. The name *Clostridium botulinum* Type E has been suggested for the last organism.

**Distribution and Transmission.** The detailed surveys of Meyer and coworkers have shown that the spores of *Clost. botulinum* are widely distributed in many parts of the world. The presence of most of the spores of anaerobic bacilli is attributed to the habitation of the area by people and animals. The spores of Type A of this organism, however, are more prevalent in virgin soil in the forests and mountains, especially in the western part of the United States. The spores of Type B are more prevalent in heavily manured soils and seem to be confined to the eastern United States and to Europe. Type C has been found in American and Australian soils. The other two types apparently are found only in South Africa. The spores of *Clost. botulinum* are rare throughout the midwestern part of the United States. Reported cases of botulism are often prone to be something else upon close analysis.

The persistence of botulism toxin in the bodies of animals which have died of botulism has been observed by many investigators. Reference is made above to decomposed rats in hay. Fourie has found toxin in the carcass of a hare after 54 days and in an iguana for 90 days. The toxin persisted in the body of a dead tortoise for over a year and Fourie believes that this is a most significant source of lamziekte which occurs in Bechuanaland, South Africa.

The organism is a saprophyte and under anaerobic conditions produces a potent toxin which is responsible for the disease botulism, which follows the consumption of contaminated food materials. Animal, fish, and vegetable foods are most commonly incriminated. In the United States, Meyer found vegetable foods incriminated in 72 per cent of the cases, animal products in 18 per cent, and the remaining of unknown origin. In Europe the greater percentage of cases of botulism is caused by contaminated animal products.

**Morphology and Staining.** *Clost. botulinum* is a large bacillus, 0.9$\mu$ to 1.2$\mu$ by 4$\mu$ to 6$\mu$, with rounded ends. It commonly occurs singly or in pairs, sometimes in short chains. Oval spores, usually greater than the cell in diameter, are situated terminally (Fig. 31.10). The organism is sluggishly motile by means of four to eight peritrichic flagella. Capsules have not been demonstrated. Young cultures are gram-positive, and some cells vary in depth of staining.

**Growth Requirements and Characteristics.** This bacillus is a strict anaerobe. It grows best at 25° to 30°C. and poorly at 37°C. Slightly alkaline medium is most suitable. The organism grows well on most common media, but growth is enhanced by 0.5 per cent glucose and 0.5 per cent $K_2HPO_4$ in beef heart and peptic-digest liver broth.

Colonies on agar surfaces are irregular, small, translucent, grayish-white to yellowish-brown, glistening, and have a fimbriate edge. Glucose agar-shake culture colonies vary in size, are opaque, and have a brown center with a less dense periphery. Types C, D, and E have woolly edges. Broth cultures are uniformly turbid with a moderate, powdery sediment. Types C, D, and E are lightly turbid and form a more flaky deposit in the tube.

Bonventre and Kempe found that the normal growth cycle of *Clost. botulinum* was characterized by a period of cell multiplication followed by active autolysis of the cells. The latter was responsible for the liberation of toxin. Mechanical disruption of cells following the active logarithmic growth phase also liberated toxin.

**Resistance.** The spores of this bacillus are killed in 5 hours at 100°C., 2 hours at 105°C., 1½ hours at 110°C., 40 minutes at 115°C., and in 10 minutes at 120°C. It is apparent that boiling for a few hours will not kill the spores.

**Biochemical Characteristics.** The different strains of *Clost. botulinum* produce different types of changes in carbohydrate and protein media. Type A produces acid and gas from glucose, maltose, fructose, dextrin, and glycerol. Types B and C do not ferment salicin; C does not ferment glycerol. None of the strains ferments raffinose, inulin, mannitol, dulcitol, galactose, xylose, rhamnose, or arabinose. Litmus milk is

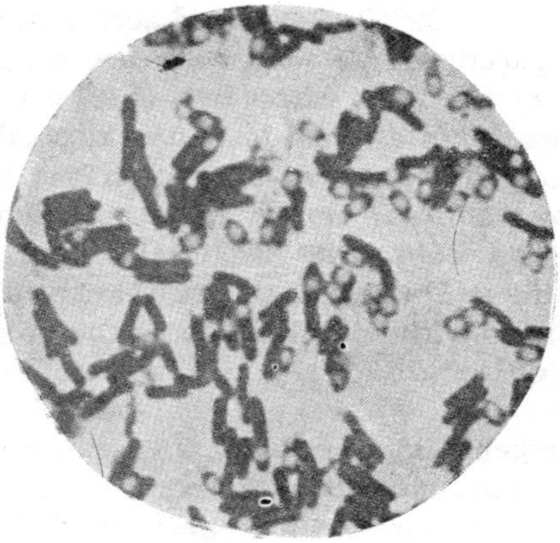

FIG. 31.10—**Clostridium botulinum** from agar culture, ×2,000. (From Nowak: Documenta Microbiologica, courtesy Gustav Fischer.)

coagulated with resulting digestion and alkalinity. Blood medium is hemolyzed. Cooked meat medium is digested and blackened by Types A and B, but not changed by C, D, and E. The liquefaction of coagulated egg-white medium is variable and has been suggested as a means of classifying the various types. Bengston suggests the designation of liquefying types as *Clost. parabotulinum* in which are placed all American Types A and B strains and all European Type A strains. European B strains and all C and D Types fail to liquefy coagulated egg white and are designated as *Clost. botulinum*. All types liquefy gelatin. Coagulated serum is liquefied by Types A and B, but not by C, D, and E. The organism is $NH_3$ positive, $H_2S$ strongly positive, indol negative, nitrate reduction negative, methyl red negative, Voges-Proskauer negative, methylene blue reduction negative, and catalase negative.

**Antigenic Structure and Toxins.** *Clost. botulinum* is divided into two main types on the basis of toxin produced. Antitoxin for A does not neutralize the toxin of B, nor does antitoxin for B neutralize the toxin of A. The other three types mentioned also produce specific toxins which are antigenically distinct. The two main types also can be distinguished on the basis of agglutination and complement-fixation tests. The toxin is destroyed by heating 6 minutes at 80°C. Prolonged action of sunlight decreases potency in a few months. One of the most important characteristics of the toxin is that it is not affected by acidity equivalent to that of gastric juice or by peptic or tryptic digestion, thereby differing from other bacterial toxins. According to Duff *et al.* the incubation of the organism with trypsin increases the production of toxin.

**Pathogenicity.** Toxins of Types A and B *Clost. botulinum* produce botulism in man. Type A produces limberneck in chickens. Type $C_a$ has been associated with botulism in wild ducks and limberneck in chickens. Type $C_b$ produces forage poisoning in horses. Type D causes lamziekte in cattle. Type E is responsible for a forage poisoning in horses and mules. All toxins are capable of producing death in guinea pigs, rabbits, mice, mink, ferrets, and muskrats. Foxes, coyotes, and wildcats were found to be resistant by Quortrup and Gorham.

*Clost. botulinum* Type E and Type B were found to be the cause of outbreaks of botulism in Indian families in northern British Columbia by Dolman and his associates. The organisms were isolated from raw salmon eggs. Dolman and Iida have summarized the epidemiology of Type E botulism which has been found in various parts of the world due to the consumption of inadequately sterilized fish and fish products.

Botulism is produced only after the organism has grown in favorable food materials where the toxin has been eliminated. Although vegetable, fruit, and animal foods may be involved, the former has been found to be most important in the United States. Meyer has found that home-canned string beans are more commonly involved, followed by corn, olives, spinach, asparagus, beets, apricots, and pears. Of the animal products, pork has been most commonly incriminated. The above foods are of more significance to man than to animals; however, cases of botulism (limberneck) in chickens have usually followed the feeding of spoiled foods primarily intended for human use. The condition in chickens is characterized by weakness, muscular incoordination, a drooping head, prostration, coma, and death.

Forage has been incriminated in the death of horses. Buckley and Shippen (1917) isolated a bacillus resembling *Clost. botulinum* from oat hay and ensilage which had caused symptoms suggestive of botulism in horses. Graham and Brueckner (1919) found corn ensilage caused botulism in horses. Experimental botulism could be produced by giving horses 2 ml. of a broth culture of the organism they isolated. The animals showed general muscular weakness, difficulty in mastication, pharyngeal paresis, inability to control the tongue, viscid discharge from the nostrils and mouth, inability to stand, emaciation, enuresis, and finally coma and death. Mention has been made previously of the observation by Theiler and Robinson (1928) of the cases of forage poisoning in horses following the eating of hay in which rats had decomposed, which certainly suggests a rather unusual source of the toxin.

Botulism in cattle, following the eating of corn ensilage, has been observed by Graham and Schwarze (1921). Although they did not suggest the organism was responsible for icterohemoglobinuria, Dubovsky and Meyer (1922) isolated *Clost. botulinum* from the livers and mesenteric lymph nodes of two cows with that disease. Seddon (1922) isolated a botulism organism from cattle in Australia afflicted with an impaction of the omasum (dry bible). The organism he isolated was very similar to the one found in South Africa by Theiler and coworkers in cattle suffering with lamziekte. The latter disease results from the eating of "green" skeletons by cattle afflicted with phosphorus starvation. The disease in cattle is characterized by paralysis of the locomotor system with difficult mastication and general weakness.

Botulism of wild ducks has been found in the western part of the United States. The birds obtain the toxin from feeding along the muddy shores of lakes. Whether the toxin is liberated by the growth of the organism in the mud or whether the ducks consume infected fly larvae in sufficient numbers to cause death is not known.

There are no significant lesions produced by botulism. General hyperemia is constant and microscopic thrombosis is found in some blood vessels; hemorrhages may be observed in the lungs.

**Immunity.** Antitoxin can be prepared which neutralizes *Clost. botulinum* toxin. The antitoxin is active for the homologous strain only, a fact which must be considered in treatment. Experimentally it has been found that antitoxin will prevent death when given immediately after the injection of toxin. No outstanding results have been obtained, however, by using antitoxin in treating field cases of botulism. In man, large doses, 50 ml., given intravenously each day have proved to be of curative value. When the disease is diagnosed early in a food-poisoning epidemic, a prophylactic dose of 10 ml. of antitoxin should be given all those who have taken food and do not show symptoms.

**Diagnosis.** In man, botulism must be differentiated from other types of food poisoning. The only certain diagnosis of the disease is the demonstration of toxin by injecting a filtrate of the suspected food or forage into mice or guinea pigs simultaneously with protective doses of the various types of antitoxin. The organism may be isolated from the suspected food material and from the intestinal tract of those having died of the disease. The mere presence of *Clost. botulinum* in the intestinal tract of animals is not a safe diagnostic criterion, however, due to the prevalence of the organism in food materials consumed by animals in some regions. The symptoms observed in the animals before death and the food consumed must always enter into the diagnostic procedure.

### *Clostridium histolyticum*

*Clost. histolyticum* was first described by Weinberg and Seguin in 1916. It is not considered to be of great significance in animal infections but has been encountered as a secondary invader. The ability of the organism to produce extensive liquefaction necrosis in tissue is its outstanding characteristic. This is due to a number of different proteinase enzymes produced by the organism. These proteinases have been used experimentally for the debridement of burns produced in guinea pigs and show promise of being effective in other animals and in man. The organism is not significantly different from the other members of this group in regard to morphology and colony appearance. It does not ferment carbohydrates. Frank and Scott have reported two cases of *Clost. histolyticum* infection in the horse.

### *Clostridium sporogenes*

This organism is another of the extremely active proteolytic species which is often encountered in wounds. It may be involved in *Clost. perfringens* and *Clost. septicum* infections in animals. It grows so easily and abundantly that other species are overgrown; consequently, it is difficult to isolate the true etiologic agent when contamination with this one is present. It is similar to other anaerobic bacilli in morphology and colony characteristics but is able to liquefy all protein materials with the production of a very offensive odor. Toxin production by the organism has never been proved. Although Weinberg has shown that some freshly isolated strains are capable of killing guinea pigs, most investigators claim that *Clost. sporogenes* is entirely nonpathogenic.

## ISOLATION PROCEDURES FOR THE CLOSTRIDIA

Due to the anaerobic nature of the Clostridia and also to the tissue changes produced by them and contaminating anaerobes, the isolation of the causative Clostridium species is a difficult procedure. Baldwin has presented a valuable discussion on this subject and his suggestions are summarized below.

1. Procedures for isolating the Clostridia which produce tissue changes in the

host, *Clost. chauvoei, Clost. hemolyticum, Clost. novyi, Clost. septicum,* and *Clost. sordellii.*

(a) Precautions to be observed.

(1) Do not use a water-washed gas to achieve anaerobic conditions. It may contain oxygen. Use a pure dry gas if available, otherwise pass the gas through a wash bottle of alkaline pyrogallol to remove the oxygen. Nitrogen is the gas of choice.

(2) Gram stains should be prepared using 95 per cent alcohol as a destaining agent. The Clostridia are easily destained by the reagents that act rapidly.

(3) Do not rely upon results obtained from specimens that are partially decomposed. Several of the pathogenic Clostridia are found in the intestine and soil. They can become postmortem contaminants. This is particularly true of liver specimens.

(4) Check the accuracy of the biochemical test media regularly by using known species of Clostridia.

(5) Always exercise aseptic measures in handling specimens and cultures. Laboratory facilities once contaminated are very difficult to clean.

(6) Do not use mature guinea pigs for inoculation tests. Latent infections may be activated in them and give erroneous findings. Use clean stock weighing approximately 300 to 400 grams.

(7) Animal test cages should be sterilized. Contaminated cages can give rise to spontaneous Clostridial infections and/or immunity to them.

(8) Do not endeavor to make a diagnosis from the gross lesions observed in test guinea pigs. They are not reliable. The offending organism must be isolated and identified before a diagnosis can be rendered.

(b) Culture media must be suitable for Clostridia and be placed in screw-cap tubes. Modified Brewer's media are recommended for growth and toxin production. Three separate examinations are made of tissue extract:

(1) Cultures are made directly into modified Brewer's liquid media.

(2) Streak plates are made on freshly prepared blood agar. These are incubated in an anaerobe jar. Suspicious colonies are subcultured into modified Brewer's media.

(3) Guinea pigs are inoculated intramuscularly with approximately 0.5 ml. of tissue extract.

Following the death of guinea pigs smears are made of lesions, and blood agar plates and modified Brewer's media are inoculated from the livers of dead animals. When pure cultures are obtained, differential media are inoculated.

2. The noninvasive clostridia, ***Clost. botulinum, Clost. perfringens,*** and ***Clost. tetani.***

(a) The identification of botulism can be made only if the causative food material or a specimen of gastrointestinal fluid is available. A filtrate is injected into the guinea pig (not mice) which will develop a flaccid paralysis if botulinum toxin is present. The type of antitoxin can be determined by neutralization tests.

(b) The diagnosis of enterotoxemias due to the toxins of *Clost. perfringens* is made by collecting material from the intestine (ileum), centrifuging, and injecting the supernatant into mice. Neutralization tests of the filtrate may be made to determine the toxigenic type.

## REFERENCES


Aikat, B. K., and Dible, J. H. The Pathology of *Clost. welchii* (perfringens) Infection. Jour. Path. Bact. 71:461, 1956.

Baldwin, E. M. Procedures for Clostridium Infections. Proc. 96th Ann. Meet. U.S. Livestock Sanit. Assn., 1965.

———, *et al.* Amer. Jour. Vet. Res. 9:296, 1948.

Barnes, D. M., and Moon, H. W. Enterotoxemia in Pigs Due to *Clostridium perfringens* Type C. Jour. Amer. Vet. Med. Assn. 144:1391–94, 1964.

Bell, J. F., *et al.* A Polyvalent Toxoid for Botulism in Mink. Amer. Jour. Vet. Res. 18:167, 1960.

Blenden, D. C., and Merilan, C. P. Isolation of Clostridia by Crystal Violet Inhibition of Aerobic Spore-forming Bacteria. Amer. Jour. Vet. Res. 22:944–47, 1961.

Bonventre, P. F., and Kempe, L. L. Jour. Bact. 79:18, 1960.

Brooks, M. E., *et al.* A Re-assessment of the Criteria Used for Type Differentiation of *Clostridium perfringens.* Jour. Path. Bact. 74:185, 1957.

Brooks, V. B., *et al.* The Action of Tetanus Toxin on the Inhibition of Motorneurones. Jour. Physiol. 135:655, 1957.

Bullen, J. J., and Batty, I. The Effect of *Clost. welchii* (perfringens) Type D Culture Filtrates on the Permeability of the Mouse Intestine. Jour. Path. Bact. 71:311, 1956.

———, *et al.* The Effect of Normal and Immune Sera on the Growth of *Clostridium welchii* (perfringens) Type A in the Allantoic Cavity of Embryonated Hen Eggs. Jour. Path. Bact. 82:383–401, 1961.

Bythell, D. W. P., and Parker, W. H. Vet. Rec. 58:367, 1946.

Claus, K. D. A Mineral Oil Adjuvant for Bacillary Hemoglobinuria. Amer. Jour. Vet. Res. 25:699–703, 1964.

———, and Macheak, M. E. Nonantigenic Nature of *Clostridium hemolyticum* Toxoid. Amer. Jour. Vet. Res. 26:353–56, 1965.

Collee, J. G. The Nature and Properties of the Haemagglutinin of *Clostridium welchii* (perfringens). Jour. Path. Bact. 81:297–312, 1961.

Crawford, R. A Field Trial of Enterotoxaemia Vaccines. New Zealand Vet. Jour. 10:53–58, 1962.

DeMello, G. C., *et al.* Proc. 56th Ann. Meet. U.S. Livestock Sanit. Assn., p. 295, 1952.

Dolman, C. E., and Iidea, H. Type E Botulism: Its Epidemiology, Prevention and Specific Treatment. Canad. Jour. Pub. Health. 54:293–308, 1963.

———, *et al.* Jour. Inf. Dis. 106:5, 1960.

Duff, J. T., *et al.* Jour. Bact. 72:455, 1956.

Ellner, P. D. A Medium Promoting Rapid Quantitative Sporulation in *Clostridium perfringens.* Jour. Bact. 71:495, 1956.

Fourie, J. M. Jour. S. Afr. Vet. Med. Assn. 17:85, 1946.

Gill, D. A. New Zealand Jour. Sci. Tech. 18:106–19, 1936.

Gochenour, R. B., *et al.* Debridement of Burns on Various Species by *Clostridium histolyticum* Proteinases. Amer. Jour. Vet. Res. 23:1089–96, 1962.

Griner, L. A. Effects of *Clostridium perfringens* Type D Toxin on the Brains of Sheep and Mice. Amer. Jour. Vet. Res. 22:429–42, 1961.

———. *Clostridium perfringens* Type D Antitoxin Titers of Normal, Nonvaccinated Lambs. Amer. Jour. Vet. Res. 22:447–48, 1961.

———, and Bracken, F. K. Jour. Amer. Vet. Med. Assn. 122:99, 1953.

Hall, H. E., *et al.* Characteristics of *Clostridium perfringens* Strains Associated With Food and Food-borne Disease. Jour. Bact. 85:1094–1103, 1963.

Hartley, P. Quart. Jour. Pharm. 18:359, 1945.

Jayko, L. G., and Lichstein, H. C. Nutritional Factors Concerned With Growth and Licithinase Production by *Clostridium perfringens.* Jour. Inf. Dis. 104:142, 1959.

Kellaway, C. H., *et al.* Austral. Jour. Exp. Biol. Med. Sci. 19:297, 1941.

Kerrin, J. C. Jour. Path. Bact. 38:219, 1934.

LARSEN, A. E., *et al.* Successful Immunization of Mink With a Toxoid Against *Clostridium botulinum* Type C. Amer. Jour. Vet. Res. 16:573, 1955.

MACLENNAN, J. D. The Histotoxic Clostridial Infections of Man. Bact. Rev. 26:177–276, 1962.

MARSH, H., *et al.* Jour. Inf. Dis. 51:330–35, 1932.

MEYER, K. F., and DUBOVSKY, BERTHA. Jour. Inf. Dis. 31:641, 1922.

MILLER, P. A., *et al.* Formation of Tetanus Toxin Within the Bacterial Cell. Jour. Bact. 77:733, 1959.

MOUSSA, R. S. Complexity of Toxins From *Clostridium septicum* and *Clostridium chauvoei.* Jour. Bact. 76:538, 1958.

NEWSOM, I. E., and THORP, FRANK, JR. Jour. Amer. Vet. Med. Assn. 93:165–67, 1938.

———, *et al.* Jour. Inf. Dis. 45:386, 1929.

OAKLEY, C. L. The Toxins of *Clost. welchii.* A Critical Review. Bull. Hyg. 18:781–806, London, 1943.

PARKER, W. H. Vet. Rec. 60:497, 1948.

PERCIVAL, R. C., *et al.* Amer. Jour. Vet. Res. 15:574, 1954.

QUORTRUP, E. R., and GORHAM, J. R. Amer. Jour. Vet. Res. 10:268, 1949.

———, and GUDHEIMER, R. L. Jour. Amer. Vet. Med. Assn. 102:264, 1943.

RECORDS, E., and VAWTER, L. R. Nev. Agr. Exp. Sta. Bull. 113, 1928.

———, and ———. Bacillary Hemoglobinuria of Cattle and Sheep. Agr. Exp. Sta. Bull. 173. Univ. of Nevada, Reno, 1945.

RODRIGUES, C. Arq. Inst. Biol., S. Paulo, 16:217, 243, 255, 265, 297, 1945.

ROSE, A. L. Enzootic Botulism Among Wild Birds. Austral. Vet. Rec. 10:76, 1935.

ROWSON, K. E. K. The Action of Tetanus Toxin in Frogs. Jour. Gen. Microbiol. 25:315–29, 1961.

RYFF, J. F., and LEE, A. M. Science 101:361–62, 1945.

———, and ———. Jour. Amer. Vet. Med. Assn. 111:283, 1947.

SCHUCHARDT, L. F., *et al.* Amer. Jour. Vet. Res. 15:316, 1954.

SHAW, J. N. Pulpy Kidney Disease in Oregon Lambs. Oreg. Agr. Exp. Sta. Bull. 367, 1939.

———, *et al.* Oreg. Agr. Exp. Sta. Bull. 360, 1939.

SMITH, D. D., and MATSUOKA, T. Amer. Jour. Vet. Res. 20:91, 1959.

SMITH, L. D., and JASMIN, A. M. Jour. Amer. Vet. Med. Assn. 129:68, 1956.

———, *et al.* Jour. Bact. 72:809, 1956.

SMITH, L. DS. Introduction to the Pathogenic Anaerobes. The Univ. Chicago Press, Chicago, 1955.

———. Clostridial Diseases of Animals. Advances in Veterinary Science. Vol. III, 1957.

———, *et al.* *Clostridium sordellii* Infection in Sheep. Cornell Vet. 52:62–68, 1962.

SMITH, L. O. S., and MATSUOKA, T. Amer. Jour. Vet. Res. 15:361, 1954.

STERNE, M., *et al.* Immunization of Sheep With Multicomponent Clostridial Vaccines. Vet. Rec. 74:909–13, 1962.

TUNNICLIFF, E. A. Jour. Inf. Dis. 52:407–12, 1933.

TURNER, A. W. Black Disease (Infectious Necrotic Hepatitis) of Sheep in Australia. Austral. Council Sci. Ind. Res. Bull. 46, 1930.

TURNER, G. C., and WONG, M. M. Intestinal Excretion of Heat-Resistant *Clostridium welchii* (perfringens) in Hong Kong. Jour. Path. Bact. 82:529–31, 1961.

VAN NESS, G. B., and ERICKSON, K. Ecology of Bacillary Hemoglobinuria. Jour. Amer. Vet. Med. Assn. 144: 492–96, 1964.

VAWTER, L. R. Jour. Amer. Vet. Med. Assn. 75:201–15, 1929.

———. Amer. Jour. Vet. Res. 3:382–85, 1942.

———, and RECORDS, E. Jour. Amer. Vet. Med. Assn. 68:494–514, 1926.

WALKER, P. D. The Spore Antigens of *Clostridium sporogenes*, *Cl. bifermentans* and *Cl. sordellii.* Jour. Path. Bact. 85:41–49, 1963.

WEBSTER, M. E., *et al.* Enzymatic Debridement of Third-degree Burns on Guinea Pigs by *Clostridium histolyticum* Proteinases. Jour. Bact. 83:602–8, 1962.

WEINBERG, M., *et al.* Les Microbes Anaerobies. Masson & Co., Paris, 1937.

WHITLOCK, J. H., and FABRICANT, J. Cornell Vet. 37:211, 1947.

WILLIS, A. T., and HOBBS, G. A Medium for the Identification of Clostridia Producing Opalescence in Egg-Yolk Emulsions. Jour. Path. Bact. 75:299, 1958.

———, and ———. Some New Media for the Isolation and Identification of Clostridia. Jour. Path. Bact. 77:511, 1959.

WILSDON, A. J. Observations on the Classification of *Bacillus welchii.* Univ. Cambridge Inst. An. Path., 2nd Rept. Director. W. Heffer & Sons, Cambridge, 1931.

———. The Relationship of *Bacillus ovitoxicus* (Bennetts) to the *Clostridium welchii* Group. Univ. Cambridge Inst. An. Path., 3rd Rept. Director. W. Heffer & Sons, Cambridge, 1932–33.

# 32

# The Genus Corynebacterium

DIPHTHERIA IN MAN IS PRODUCED BY AN ORganism which is rodlike and frequently filamentous with a tendency toward the development of branches. Many of the individual cells in a culture of this organism are swollen, clubbed, and irregular, and show a decided tendency to form in clumps and parallel groups. When grown upon certain types of media and stained with special stains, the organism contains metachromatic granules in one or both poles. Numerous cells in a culture stain unevenly, giving a segmented or barred appearance. It is gram-positive. This organism, known as *Corynebacterium diphtheriae,* represents the type species of the genus; consequently, all other bacteria which are similar to it are placed in this group. Because of the resemblance of many species to the diphtheria bacillus, the members of the group are commonly called the "diphtheroid" group.

The genus Corynebacterium is composed of species of bacteria which are found in man and animals. Many of them are nonpathogenic, being found on mucous membranes. A few are pathogenic and are associated with both acute and chronic diseases of man and animals. Only the most significant ones will be discussed in this text.

The most important member of the group, from the viewpoint of human health, is *Corynebacterium diphtheriae,* the cause of diphtheria. This organism is not of significance in animal health, but animals are frequently used in the production and standardization of diphtheria antitoxin and in the diagnosis of the disease; furthermore, methods which have been developed in the study of this organism are of value in the study of related forms from animals.

Among the strictly animal species, four have been found to be of greatest importance, *Corynebacterium pyogenes, Corynebacterium renale, Corynebacterium pseudotuberculosis,* and *Corynebacterium equi.* A few other species have been described and named, but since they are not of great importance to animal health, they will be referred to under the title Miscellaneous Corynebacteria.

There is usually no occasion to differentiate *Corynebacterium diphtheriae* from the four animal species; however, there are numerous instances when the animal strains may be found in the same species and in the same tissue. Differential laboratory methods can be used for their identification. Some of the most valuable reactions are given in Table 32.1.

## Corynebacterium diphtheriae

**Synonyms and History.** *Bacillus Diphtheriae, Bacterium diphtheriae,* diphtheria bacillus, Klebs-Loeffler bacillus.

The diphtheria bacillus was first observed by Klebs in 1883 but was isolated and completely described by Loeffler in 1884. The discovery of the production of a potent toxin by the organism was made by Roux and Yersin in 1888. In 1890 von Behring demonstrated that recovery from the disease resulted in the formation of a specific antitoxic substance in the blood

TABLE 32.1

DIFFERENTIATION OF THE CORYNEBACTERIA

| | *C. diphtheriae* | *C. pyogenes* | *C. pseudo-tuberculosis* | *C. renale* | *C. equi* |
|---|---|---|---|---|---|
| Hemolysis | − | + | ± | − | − |
| Gelatin liq. | − | + | − | − | − |
| Litmus milk | no change | coag. acid. digestion | no change | alkaline digestion | no change |
| Nitrate rdc. | − | − | − | − | + |
| Dextrose | + | + | + | + | − |
| Maltose | + | + | + | − | − |
| Galactose | + | + | ± | − | − |
| Lactose | − | + | − | − | − |

stream, thus paving the way for antitoxin therapy.

**Distribution and Transmission.** Diphtheria is worldwide in prevalence. Many countries, notably the United States, have controlled the disease by toxoid or toxin-antitoxin immunization, and as a consequence, widespread epidemics of the disease are rare where this procedure is followed.

The organism is transmitted by personal contact with infected individuals and by contact with fomites handled by infected individuals. Immune carriers of the organism are sometimes sources of epidemics of the disease.

**Morphology and Staining.** *C. diphtheriae* is a pleomorphic rod, 0.3$\mu$ to 0.8$\mu$ by 1.0$\mu$ to 8.0$\mu$ in size. The rods are usually straight or slightly curved, and are frequently swollen on both ends (Fig. 32.1). Numerous cells show segmentation and the presence of metachromatic granules. The organism is nonmotile, noncapsulated, and nonspore-producing.

When stained with methylene blue, the barred characteristic is particularly apparent. It stains well with the ordinary dyes and is gram-positive.

**Growth Requirements and Characteristics.** This organism is aerobic and facultatively

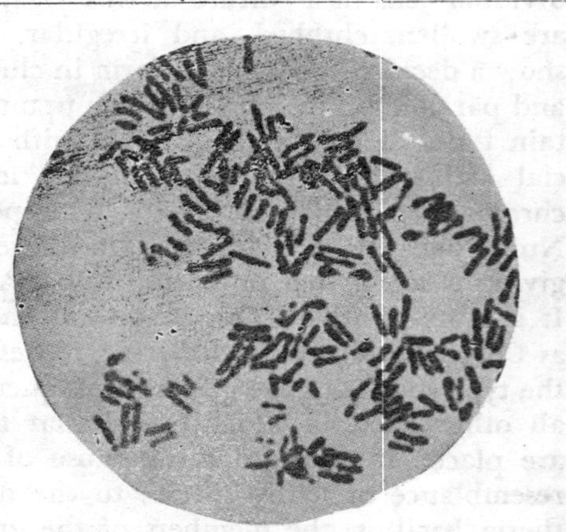

FIG. 32.1—**Corynebacterium diphtheriae** serum agar culture, ×2,000. (From Nowak: Documenta Microbiologica, courtesy Gustav Fischer.)

anaerobic. It grows most abundantly at 37°C. in media which are adjusted to pH 7.0 to 7.2. It can be isolated from throat lesions of active cases of diphtheria by the use of media to which blood serum has been added. The most universally used medium for the primary growth of *C. diphtheriae* is Loeffler's coagulated blood serum. One of the difficulties encountered in the isolation of the organism is the growth of contaminating organisms. In order to overcome this objection, potassium tellurite may be added to the isolation medium. This salt prevents the growth of other organisms to some extent, but is valuable in that the colonies of *C. diphtheriae* are grayish-black which facilitates subculturing.

On serum agar this organism grows in small, finely granular, translucent colonies which have an irregular border. Old colonies frequently reveal a peripheral secondary growth; this gives the surfaces of such colonies a concentrically ringed appearance.

In broth a uniform turbidity is produced during the first 24 hours of growth, and then a thin pellicle is formed.

**Resistance.** The diphtheria bacillus is similar to the vegetative forms of other bacteria in resistance to heat and chemicals.

**Biochemical Properties.** *C. diphtheriae* forms acid, but not gas, from glucose, maltose, arabinose, and galactose, and many strains ferment dextrin and glycerol; does not ferment sucrose, lactose, or mannitol; does not form indol, although some investigators report a color reaction with sulfuric acid and potassium nitrite as the test substances. Nitrates are not generally reduced to nitrites, although positive results have been obtained with some strains. Gelatin is not liquefied. The organism grows in litmus milk but does not alter that medium.

**Antigenic Structure and Toxins.** The antigenic structure of this organism is heterogenous; that is, the numerous strains are antigenically distinct. These strains, in turn, can be divided into antigenic subtypes by agglutination technique. This heterogony of antigenic structure appears to be characteristic among many other species of Corynebacteria. The author noted a slight cross agglutination between one strain of *C. diphtheriae* (Park 8) and two strains of *C. renale* and one strain of *C. pseudotuberculosis.* It is quite probable that antigenic fractions are common to various species of the genus during certain phases of growth.

*C. diphtheriae* is characterized, more than in any other way, by the toxin which it produces. The lesions which are produced in the disease are due to this potent toxin. It diffuses through the body and produces lesions in numerous tissues far removed from the localized throat lesion of the primary disease. Different strains of the organism produce toxins of varying potency but not of different antigenic structure. The variation in the antigenic structure of the bacterial cells has no relationship to the toxins which are liberated by the different antigenic strains.

Diphtheria toxin is heat labile and is easily destroyed by chemicals. It can be attenuated, however, by formalin and precipitated by alum with the formation of toxoid, which is of value in immunization.

**Pathogenicity.** The diphtheria bacillus is pathogenic primarily to man, and the disease is most frequent in the susceptible child population. In an infected individual the organism remains localized in the region of the tonsils, larynx, and upper part of the trachea. From this focus of infection the toxin is absorbed and spread throughout the body, producing degenerative changes such as albuminous and fatty degeneration in parenchymatous tissues. The disease is, in all respects, the most perfect example of a toxemia.

The toxin of the organism produces death in guinea pigs and rabbits, but mice and rats are resistant. Dogs and cats are moderately susceptible. The guinea pig is killed by doses as small as 0.002 ml. of a broth filtrate. In this animal the degenerative changes found in the disease in man are observed. The guinea pig is used universally as the test animal in the determination of the potency of diphtheria toxin and in the standardization of antitoxin. The unit of measurement of toxin is called the M.L.D. (minimum lethal dose) and is defined as: *The least amount of toxin which, when injected subcutaneously, will cause the death of a 250-gram guinea pig in 96 hours.*

The pathogenicity of *C. diphtheriae* for animals has been a subject of considerable study. Many diphtheria-like organisms have been isolated from numerous animals. *C. diphtheriae* of the *mitis* variety has been reported from horses; this is considered significant in view of negative Schick reactions in that animal. Epidemics of diphtheria in man have been associated with milk supplies. Most often these epidemics have resulted from the contamination of the utensils or the milk by the dairyman or milk plant operators who are immune carriers of the organism. In some instances cows have been incriminated. Inasmuch as diphtheroid bacilli are commonly present in the bovine udder, any report incriminating *C. diphtheriae* must be substantiated by correct identification which must include toxicity tests. Pfeiffer and Viljoen, in South Africa, found that an epidemic of diphtheria in a localized community was associated with a diphtheritic mastitis in two cows, thus emphasizing that the bovine udder may become infected with this bacillus.

**Immunity.** Recovery from an attack of diphtheria results in durable immunity. Prophylactic treatment, however, is the modern method of combating the disease. For this purpose a variety of immunizing products are used.

Fundamental to immunization is the determination of the susceptibility of the individual. Some persons may have had the disease and have not been aware of it. The *Schick Test* is used to detect diphtheria susceptibility. In this test a small amount of toxin, 1/50 M.L.D., is injected into the skin of the forearm. A positive test, that is, susceptibility, is characterized by a local area of erythema at the point of injection within 24 to 48 hours and is well marked at the end of the fourth day.

The products which are used in active diphtheria immunization are:

1. Toxin-antitoxin mixtures (T.A.T.) which are rarely used now but were in the original method of von Behring.
2. Formol-toxoid (F.T.), which was originated by Ramon, and is used extensively in France.
3. Alum-precipitated-toxoid (A.P.T.) is a precipitated toxin prepared by the addition of alum. The toxin in this preparation is liberated slowly into the tissues surrounding the point of injection, thereby producing a durable active immunity. It has an added value in that only one dose is necessary.

In the treatment of an active case of diphtheria, antitoxin must be used. Antitoxin is usually prepared by the immunization of horses, but goats may be used by the injection of toxoid followed by toxin. The production of diphtheria antitoxin is basically the same as that of tetanus antitoxin, which has been described in the chapter on toxin-antitoxin. The student is referred to this chapter. More detailed information can be obtained in one of the various texts of medical bacteriology given in the reference list at the end of this chapter.

**Diagnosis.** Diphtheria is diagnosed by isolating and identifying the causal organism. The organism must be isolated in pure culture. Then 0.5 ml. of an emulsified growth is injected subcutaneously into each of two guinea pigs for a virulence test. One of these animals is given a protective dose of antitoxin. If the organism is *C. diphtheriae* the unprotected guinea pig will die in 96 hours and show typical lesions of the disease. The protected guinea pig remains alive.

### *Corynebacterium pyogenes*

**Synonyms and History.** *Bacillus pyogenes, Bacterium pyogenes, Hemophilus pyogenes.*

Kitt, in 1890, was apparently the first to observe this organism in caseous pneumonia in the pig. It was isolated from the cow and described by Lucet in 1893. Poels, in 1897, called the organism *Bacillus polyarthritidis* because he found it in arthritis in calves. In 1902 Grips found the organism in swine pneumonia, and in 1903 Kunneman observed it in cases of suppuration in the cow. Glage studied bovine and swine strains of the organism in 1903, concluded that they were identical, and used the name *Bacillus pyogenes*. Since that time numerous studies of the organism, isolated chiefly from chronic suppurative lesions in the cow and swine but occasionally from goats and sheep, have been made.

This organism had been considered to be pleomorphic and gram-positive by most investigators; however, Priewe, in 1911, considered it to be related to the influenza bacillus; in fact, he reported that antiserum of *Bacillus pyogenes* agglutinated suspensions of *Bacillus influenzae*. The organism was first included in the diphtheroid group and called *Corynebacterium pyogenes* (Glage) by Eberson in 1918.

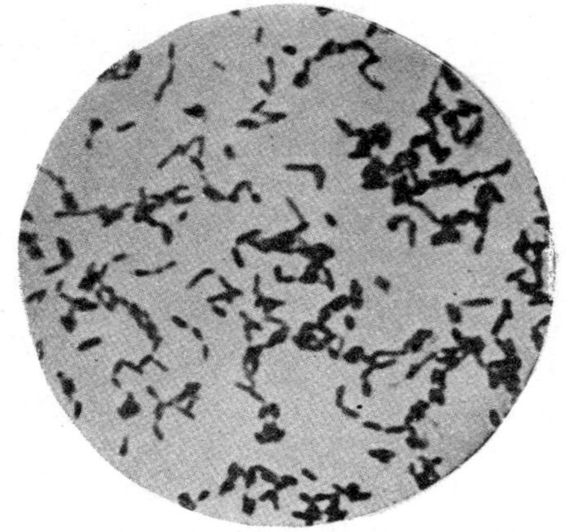

FIG. 32.2—**Corynebacterium pyogenes** serum agar culture, ×2,000. (From Nowak Documenta Microbiologica, courtesy Gustav Fischer.)

**Distribution and Transmission.** Reports of this organism have been contributed from all quarters of the world where animals have been domesticated. In most cases the disease which it causes is chronic and occurs sporadically in the herd. Acute types of pneumonia in swine have been reported, however, which indicates that the organism may be of herd significance at times. In such cases transmission may be directly from one animal to another. In most cases it appears probable that the infection is due to the presence of the organism normally upon mucous membranes and skin. Hancock and Kelly have isolated *C. pyogenes* from the semen of apparently healthy bulls. Ruebke, and likewise Morgan, Johansson, and Emerson, have found it to be present in the sheath of normal bulls.

**Morphology and Staining Characteristics.** *C. pyogenes* is a small, coccoid, pleomorphic bacillus varying from 0.2μ to 0.3μ in breadth by 0.5μ to 2.0μ in length. Cells with swollen ends and those with pointed ends are common (Fig. 32.2). The organisms are usually single but show a decided tendency to form clumps; palisade arrangements are frequently observed. It is nonmotile and noncapsuleproducing.

Young cultures of this organism are decidedly gram-positive, but old cultures are easily decolorized. It stains unevenly with methylene blue. Metachromatic granules are not found as frequently as in most of the other species of the genus.

**Growth Requirements and Characteristics.** This bacillus is aerobic and microaerophilic. Growth is more abundant in an atmosphere of reduced oxygen tension. A neutral pH is more conducive to growth. The optimum temperature is 37°C.

The organism can be isolated from most tissue without much difficulty if serum media are used. Continued growth on artificial media is more difficult to obtain. Blood agar, blood bouillon, and milk are best suited for the maintenance of laboratory cultures. The incorporation of tellurium salts in the isolation medium is helpful in isolating pure cultures of the organism. When coagulated serum plus potassium tellurite is used, the organism forms small, black colonies which sink in a few days into a liquefied trough in the medium.

On serum agar, *C. pyogenes* forms minute dewdrop-like colonies which resemble colonies of streptococci (Fig. 32.3). With age, however, the colonies become opaque and tend to become dry. Small zones of beta hemolysis are observed around colonies on blood agar in four days. In serum bouillon the organism forms a light, pow-

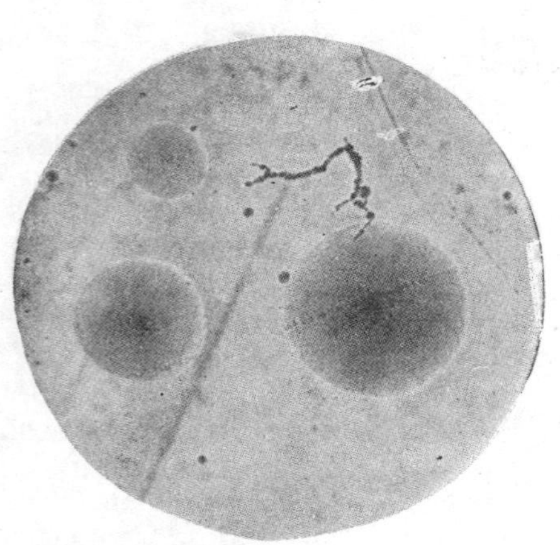

FIG. 32.3—**Corynebacterium pyogenes** colonies on serum agar, ×45. (From Nowak: Documenta Microbiologica, courtesy Gustav Fischer.)

dery sediment along the walls and in the bottom of the test tube. It does not form a pellicle.

**Resistance.** The organism is similar to other vegetative cells in resistance. The survival of the organism in heavy tenacious exudates from infected tissues has been noted by Roach. This author observed that iodine and lysol were the best disinfectants, but it was difficult to rid contaminated instruments of the organism except by thorough cleaning and disinfection.

*C. pyogenes* is extremely sensitive to penicillin but the nature of the infectious process and the purulent exudate apparently prevent this antibiotic from coming in contact with the organism.

**Biochemical Properties.** *C. pyogenes* produces acid but no gas from glucose, maltose, galactose, lactose, fructose, mannose, sucrose, and dextrin, but none from arabinose, xylose, inulin, salicin, dulcitol, mannitol, or glycerol. Ryff and Browne have found that after cultures of *C. pyogenes* have become adjusted to unenriched media, they have greater saccharolytic properties. Many of their cultures fermented arabinose, xylose, salicin, mannitol, and glycerol. Dulcitol was the only carbohydrate not being fermented. The organism does not form indol; does not reduce nitrates; does not form $H_2S$; is negative to the methyl red and Voges-Proskauer tests. The reaction on milk is distinctive. Milk is first acidified and coagulated; subsequently, the clot is digested, and within a week the medium is clear. Gelatin is slowly liquefied; coagulated blood serum is liquefied.

**Antigenic Structure and Toxins.** This organism is antigenically homogenous by agglutination technique. Cross-agglutination with other diphtheroids has not been reported. A major and a minor antigen have been found in some strains.

An exotoxin lethal to rabbits and capable of hemolyzing red blood cells has been reported by Lovell. This exotoxin likewise produces necrosis of the skin in guinea pigs and is lethal to mice. The potency of the exotoxin may be determined by a hemolysin test. Antitoxin may be found in the serum of animals infected with this organism.

**Pathogenicity.** *C. pyogenes* has been isolated from numerous tissues in swine, cattle, sheep, and goats. In swine it may cause pneumonia characterized by the formation of small focal, encapsulated abscesses, followed by extensive caseous pneumonia. Polyarthritis is also due to the organism in many cases. In the cow it has been found to be responsible for chronic, abscessing mastitis, suppurative pneumonia, actinomycosis-like lesions, abscesses in the peritoneal and thoracic cavities caused by traumatism, and arthritis. *C. pyogenes* has been found associated with abortion in cows by Maxwell and by Boyd and Kelly. In the calf it causes chronic suppurative pneumonia, umbilical infection, and arthritis. It has been isolated from mastitis and pneumonia in sheep and goats. The horse is rarely infected with the organism, but Karlsson has reported the isolation of it from a case of sinusitis. Fowls are likewise considered resistant, but the above author isolated it from abscesses in the head of the chicken.

This organism produces subcutaneous abscesses in the rabbit and localizes in the joints, producing a deforming arthritis. Guinea pigs and rats are resistant. Abscesses are formed on the omentum and in the livers of mice following intraperitoneal inoculation. Morse and coworkers have found strains of the organism from calf pneumonia more pathogenic to mice than those from bovine mastitis.

**Immunity.** The sporadic nature of the conditions produced by the organism makes it difficult to observe immune animals. Bacterins and vaccines have been used in infected animals without influencing the course of the disease. Lovell has reported the presence of *C. pyogenes* antitoxin in the serum of infected animals, and Weitz has demonstrated the presence of antitoxin in dairy cows following the injection of alum-precipitated toxoid. Weitz and Langridge have reported that the injection of toxoid decreased the number of experimental udder infections in lactating ewes.

**Diagnosis.** *C. pyogenes* infection can be diagnosed correctly only by the isolation and identification of the organism. The characteristic morphology, colony size, and reaction on milk are significant in diagnosis.

### *Corynebacterium pseudotuberculosis*

**Synonyms and History.** *Bacillus pseudotuberculosis ovis, Bacillus pseudotuberculosis, Corynebacterium ovis.* Preisz-Nocard bacillus.

In 1888 Nocard isolated an organism from bovine farcy which no doubt was *Corynebacterium pseudotuberculosis.* In 1891 Preisz and Guinard isolated a similar organism from the kidney of a sheep. Nocard, in 1893, observed his organism in equine pseudofarcy. Preisz, in 1894, was the first to describe the organism completely and to observe its resemblance to the diphtheria bacillus. At that time he called the organism *Bacillus pseudotuberculosis ovis.* Since then the organism has been found to be the cause of caseous lymphadenitis in sheep and deer and ulcerative lymphangitis in horses, and in various suppurative conditions in the cow, including skin lesions resembling tuberculosis.

In 1911 Buchanan called the organism *Bacillus pseudotuberculosis.* Eberson classified it with the diphtheroids in 1918 under the name *Corynebacterium pseudotuberculosis* (Preisz) Eberson.

**Distribution and Transmission.** *C. pseudotuberculosis* is widely distributed but most prevalent in regions such as Australia, Argentina, New Zealand, South Africa, and the western United States where sheep are raised in large flocks. The organism appears to be a skin contaminant, for skin wounds caused by docking, castration, and shearing are predisposing to infection.

Among horses the organism is most prevalent in Europe; relatively few cases of ulcerative lymphangitis have been reported from the North American continent. The method of transmission among horses is not known, although the use of a currycomb and brush for a number of horses may well be suspected.

This organism has been found to be the cause of pseudotuberculosis of deer in the western mountain states of North America. It is believed to be transmitted to these animals from ground on which sheep are kept. Lacerations on the legs of deer due to brush offer an excellent avenue of infection for the organism.

Humphreys and Gibbons have shown that engorged female ticks *(Dermacentor albipictus)* harbored the organism, and that by guinea pig inoculation larval ticks reared from such females were also shown to contain the organism.

**Morphology and Staining.** This bacillus is a coccoid to filamentous rod, 0.5$\mu$ to 0.6$\mu$ by 1.0$\mu$ to 3.0$\mu$ in size (Fig. 32.4). It shows a tendency to form in clumps and in a palisade formation. In natural lesions the organism is notably pleomorphic, but is uniformly coccoid on artificial media. Metachromatic granules are distinctly observed in the bacillary forms but are absent from coccoid cells. The organism is non-

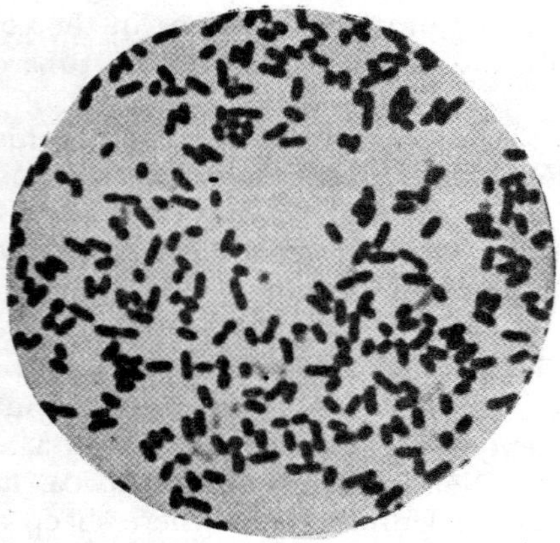

FIG. 32.4—Corynebacterium pseudotuberculosis agar culture, ×2,000. (From Nowak: Documenta Microbiologica, courtesy Gustav Fischer.)

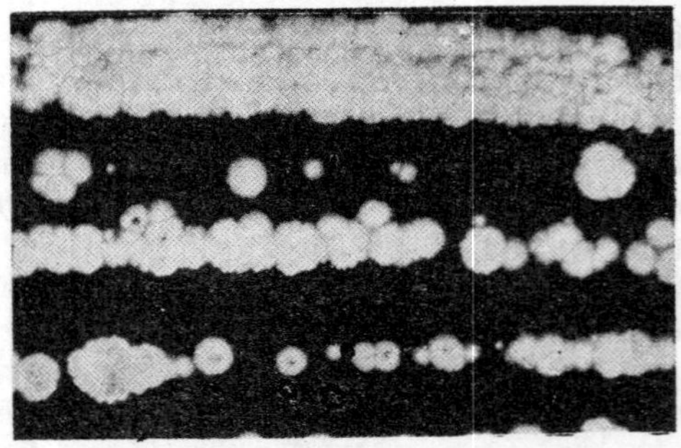

FIG. 32.5—Corynebacterium pseudotuberculosis four-day growth on serum agar, ×2½.

motile and noncapsuleforming.

It is stained easily but unevenly by the ordinary dyes, and is gram-positive.

**Growth Requirements and Characteristics.** *C. pseudotuberculosis* is aerobic and facultatively anaerobic. It grows best at 37°C. and in a medium adjusted to pH 7.0 to 7.2. More abundant growth is obtained by the addition of serum to culture media. It can be isolated from primary lesions of the disease, but only a few colonies develop on the agar surface. When these are smeared over the surface of the medium a uniform and abundant growth results.

On the surface of serum agar this organism forms colonies which, when young, are typical of *C. diphtheriae.* As the colonies age they become opaque, concentrically ringed, dry, and crumbly (Fig. 32.5). Many of the colonies are rosette-like. Such colonies are cream- to orange-colored, depending on the strain. Variant smooth strains have been observed from cultures of the organism. These cultures are smooth and glistening and are bright pink to red in color.

The organism produces a thick, crumbly pellicle in serum bouillon. The growth extends up on the sides of the tube a short distance from the surface of the medium. Some of the surface growth settles to the bottom of the tube, forming a coarsely granular sediment. The intervening medium remains clear.

**Resistance.** This organism is typical of the group in resistance.

**Biochemical Properties.** *C. pseudotuberculosis* is variable in fermenting ability. All strains produce acid but not gas from glucose, fructose, maltose, mannose, and sucrose; some strains ferment galactose, dextrin, and glycerol; none ferments arabinose, xylose, raffinose, lactose, rhamnose, inulin, salicin, dulcitol, adonitol, mannitol, or soluble starch. It does not produce indol; does not reduce nitrates, although a few positive strains are reported; forms $H_2S$ slowly; is negative to the methyl red and Voges-Proskauer tests. This organism is not proteolytic; consequently, it does not liquefy gelatin, coagulated blood serum, or milk casein. It grows in milk but does not alter the medium. The organism is slightly hemolytic, producing a narrow zone of beta hemolysis. Carne reports that the red blood cells of animals decrease in sensitivity to the hemolytic activity of the organism in the following order: guinea pig, rabbit, horse, and sheep. The hemolysin does not have a relationship with the exotoxin formed by the organism.

**Antigenic Structure and Toxins.** The antigenic structure of the organism is not known but it appears to be somewhat heterogenous. This bacillus produces an exotoxin which is lethal for guinea pigs, rabbits, and sheep. The lesions produced in experimental animals are similar to those produced by diphtheria toxin. In 1907 Dassonville, who was one of the first to describe the toxin, reported that diphtheria antitoxin neutralized the toxin of the Preisz-Nocard bacillus. Toxin-neutralizing antibodies have been reported from the horse, showing lesions of ulcerative lymphangitis. It has also been shown that the blood serum from normal horses has this property. Some horses are negative to the Schick test, and it is interesting to speculate concerning the relationship between this fact, the presence of neutralizing antitoxin for *C. pseudotuberculosis* toxin in horses, and the means by which it is produced in horses free from apparent infection.

Doty *et. al.* have observed that toxin is uniformly produced by strains of this organism and that the toxin of one strain is the same as other strains. They have proposed a skin test, the reverse of the Schick test, which could be used to diagnose the presence of the disease in animals. Experimentally the test on rabbits showed considerable promise.

The presence of acid-fast variants of this bacillus in tuberculosis-like lesions of sheep and cattle has suggested that this type of infection may be responsible for no-lesion reactors to tuberculin. However, Larsen and Johnson could not detect any reaction to johnin and tuberculin in goats infected with *C. pseudotuberculosis*.

**Pathogenicity.** *C. pseudotuberculosis* causes caseous lymphadenitis in sheep, a disease characterized by the presence of caseation necrosis in the lymph glands. The lesions are frequently confined to superficial glands, but generalized cases of the disease are not uncommon in which abscesses are distributed throughout the body. Marsh found that arthritis and bursitis present in lambs in Montana during July and August were due to this organism.

In the horse the organism causes ulcerative lymphangitis, a disease which is confined to the lymph vessels of the extremities, particularly the hind legs. The lymph vessels and regional lymph nodes enlarge and ulceration occurs, producing a condition similar to the skin lesions of glanders.

Rapidly occurring equine abscesses have been reported by Wisecup, Blanchard, and Neil, and two cases of generalized infection in mares were observed by Hughes, Biberstein, and Richards.

The infection in goats is similar to that in sheep.

In deer the organism causes a disease similar in pathology to that in sheep with the exception of the presence of subcutaneous abscesses of the extremities.

Intravenous injection of the organism into the guinea pig causes death in four to ten days, with the formation of abscesses in the lungs and liver. Intraperitoneal injection of this bacillus into the male guinea pig produces the orchitis typical of the glanders bacillus.

The magpie *(Pica pica)*, so common in the western mountain states of North America, is killed within 24 hours following intraperitoneal injection of the organism.

**Immunity.** Bacterins and vaccines have been used to produce an immunity against this disease. Formolized toxin (toxoid) has been reported valuable in immunizing sheep.

**Diagnosis.** The conditions produced by the organism are so similar to many others that it is essential to isolate and identify the causal agent.

Awad has described a slide agglutination test which he found reliable in diagnosing the disease in sheep.

### *Corynebacterium renale*

**Synonyms and History.** *Bacillus pyelonephritis boum, Bacillus renalis, Corynebacterium renalis, Bacillus renalis bovis.*

In 1877 Dammann observed small bacteria in lesions of typical pyelonephritis of the cow, and in 1890 Hess observed a curved bacillus in the urine and kidneys of cows suffering with the disease. Bollinger reported an organism in 1890 under the name of *Bacillus renalis bovis.* Enderlen is given the credit for being the first to cultivate the organism upon artificial media and to describe it in detail in 1891. In the same year Höflich, independent of Enderlen, isolated and described the same organism. The most complete early description of pyelonephritis and of the organism was made by Ernst in 1905 and 1906. This investigator pointed out the relationship of the organism to the diphtheria bacillus and proposed the name *Corynebacterium renalis.*

**Distribution and Transmission.** The organism is widely distributed throughout the bovine population. It was first observed in the United States by Boyd, in Minnesota, in 1918. Jones and Little, in New Jersey, studied a number of cases of the disease and the organism in 1925 and 1926. Numerous cases of pyelonephritis have been observed in Iowa.

Jones and Little were able to isolate the organism from the vaginal mucous membrane of normal cattle. Ruebke, as well as Morgan, Johansson, and Emerson, have isolated it from the genital tracts of bulls. Ernst observed in his study that the infection was an ascending one. It is believed that certain predisposing factors, such as feeding and pregnancy, are responsible for the establishment of the organism in the pelvis of the kidney, the ureters, and urinary bladder where it produces pyelonephritis and cystitis. Most cases of the disease occur during the late winter and early spring months, which further substantiates the importance of predisposing factors.

**Morphology and Staining.** *C. renale* is a pleomorphic rod, 0.5$\mu$ to 0.7$\mu$ by 1.5$\mu$ to 3$\mu$ in size. This organism is more like the diphtheria bacillus than any of the animal diphtheroids, although it is slightly larger. It occurs singly, but clumps and palisade formations are common, especially in direct smears from kidney exudate (Fig. 32.6). Barred cells are usually observed, and large, distinct metachromatic granules are formed

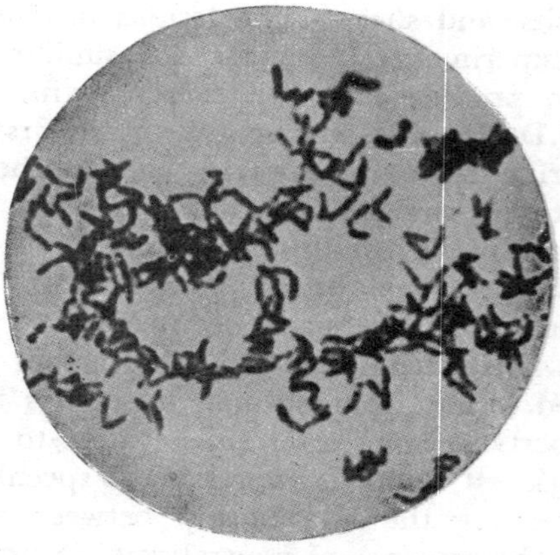

FIG. 32.6—**Corynebacterium renale** smear of kidney exudate, ×2,000. (From Nowak: Documenta Microbiologica, courtesy Gustav Fischer.)

when the organism is grown on Loeffler's medium. The organism is nonmotile and noncapsuleproducing.

When smears of kidney exudate are stained with methylene blue the organisms are stained unevenly, and many cells with swollen ends are observed. The organism is gram-positive, but the granules are more difficult to decolorize than the other part of the cell.

**Growth Requirements and Characteristics.** This bacillus is aerobic and facultatively anaerobic, and grows best in serum media adjusted to pH 7.0 to 7.2. The optimum temperature for growth is 37°C.

On primary isolation upon serum agar the organism forms small, dewdrop-like colonies. These enlarge within two days and become opaque and ivory colored. They are moist at first and later become dry, but never as dry as the colonies of *C. pseudotuberculosis.* The colonies are granular and have an uneven border (Fig. 32.7). Although the colonies of this bacillus cannot be considered smooth in the sense of the gram-negative bacteria, some may be designated smooth as contrasted with those which are more rough. In a study of the colonial phase variant of the organism, Feenstra, Thorp, and Gray observed that the culture designated as "smooth" showed the weakest fermentation of glucose, the

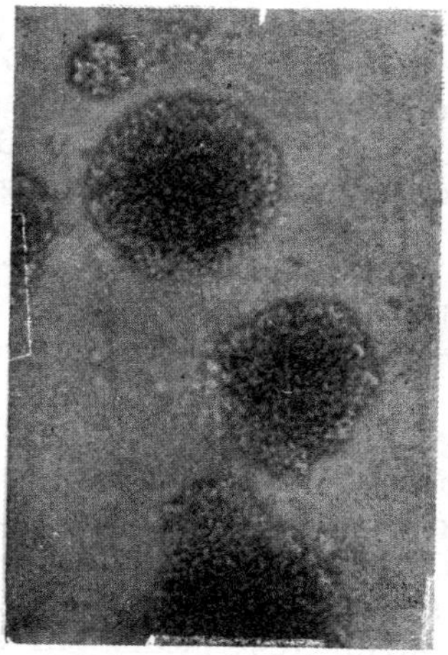

FIG. 32.7—**Corynebacterium renale,** colony on serum agar, ×220.

digestion of casein, the least resistance to the bactericidal action of bovine plasma, and was the least pathogenic to rabbits. Two cultures which they designated as "rough" showed the most resistance to the bactericidal action of bovine plasma and were the most pathogenic to rabbits.

In broth a fine powdery sediment collects on the walls and in the bottom of the test tube. Some strains form a thin pellicle.

**Resistance.** This organism is similar to the group in respect to resistance. *C. renale* is sensitive to penicillin, and this antibiotic would seem to be a most effective agent for treating cattle affected with pyelonephritis, inasmuch as it is eliminated through the renal circulation so rapidly. Morse has found that the drug is effective in those cases of the disease which are detected in the early stages.

**Biochemical Properties.** *C. renale* produces a slight amount of acid in glucose, and some strains are able to attack fructose and mannose. Many strains, however, appear to be devoid of saccharolytic ability. The organism does not form indol; does not reduce nitrates; does not form $H_2S$; is negative to the methyl red and Voges-Proskauer tests. It does not hemolyze red blood cells. Some strains do not alter litmus milk, while others are able to digest casein with the formation of a subsequent alkalinity. It is able to split urea.

**Antigenic Structure and Toxins.** The organism is antigenically heterogenous, and numerous strains cross agglutinate with bovine strains of *C. pseudotuberculosis.*

Toxins are not produced.

**Pathogenicity.** *C. renale* causes pyelonephritis in cattle; it has been isolated from kidney abscesses in swine. The disease is not prevalent, and is first manifested by hemoglobinuria and the voiding of blood clots. The infection is confined to the urinary bladder, the ureters, and the pelvis of the kidney. It may be unilateral or bilateral.

The pathogenicity of *C. renale* for rabbits was first reported by Enderlen, but the marked and typical renal pathology produced in that animal has since been described by Feenstra, Thorp, and Gray (1949). By intravenous inoculation of the organism these investigators produced papillitis and pyelitis characterized by necrosis. Bacteria were found in the necrotic debris of the lesions and in the pelvis of the kidney.

Lovell and Cotchin were able to infect mice when extremely large doses (20 million per ml.) of the organism were inoculated intravenously. The bacillus showed an affinity for renal tissue where the greatest concentration was reached in three days, with a gradual reduction in numbers up to the 16th day. Morse and Morgan have found that cystitis and pyelonephritis are produced in mice.

C. *renale* has not been found to be pathogenic for the guinea pig. Little or no growth is obtained in the chicken embryo.

**Immunity.** The disease caused by this organism is not a type which produces immunity or responds to immunizing treatment.

**Diagnosis.** Smears made from the exudate present in hemoglobin-stained urine from the cow reveal large numbers of this organism. Pure cultures of the organism can usually be obtained from such material. The fermentation of dextrose, the alkalinization of milk, and marked urease activity are considered differential characteristics.

### *Corynebacterium equi*

**Synonyms and History.** In 1923 Magnusson, in Sweden, isolated this organism from suppurative pneumonia of a foal. He gave it the name *Corynebacterium equi.* The same year Lutje recovered an organism from suppurative pneumonia in three foals. He called his organism *Corynebacterium pyogenes (equi) roseum.*

Dimock and Edwards, in 1931, were the first to isolate the organism from cases of suppurative pneumonia of foals in the United States. Since that time they have found the organism frequently in Kentucky.

In 1936 Holth and Amundsen, of Denmark, observed a small coccobacillus in tuberculosis-like lesions of the cervical lymph nodes of swine. In 1938 Bendixen and Jepsen, of Denmark, found that the Holth bacilli were really *C. equi.* This has been confirmed by Karlson, Moses, and Feldman in Minnesota.

**Distribution and Transmission.** The distribution of *C. equi* is not known because the presence of the organism has undoubtedly been overlooked often in the past. In foals it is apparently confined to the Kentucky region and to eastern United States. The presence of the organism in swine was a new discovery. If the cervical lesions first described by Holth and Amundsen are any criterion, the organism is widely spread among American swine herds, for such lesions are extremely common. Karlson, Moses, and Feldman found it present in 23.2 per cent of 114 submaxillary lymph nodes of swine.

The transmission of *C. equi* is not known; presumably it gains entrance through the respiratory tract in foals, although hematogenous origin of the pulmonary infection is possible. Bruner, Dimock, and Edwards isolated the organism from the os uteri of barren mares and from aborted equine fetuses. This strongly suggests that prenatal infection of foals occurs. Bendixen and Jepsen isolated the organism from garden soil, which introduced a sanitation problem as far as swine were concerned.

**Morphology and Staining.** *C. equi* is a coccoid rod measuring $0.8\mu$ to $1.5\mu$. It is extremely pleomorphic, however, and different shapes are observed to be more common on different media. In exudate from a typical lesion of purulent pneumonia, *C. equi* is short and plump. On solid culture media it is coccoid, although bacillary forms are present (Fig. 32.8). In fluid media, large, swollen bacillary shapes are most common. The organism is capsuleproducing, nonsporeforming, and nonmotile.

*C. equi* is stained easily with the common dyes and is gram-positive. Metachromatic granules are demonstrated by a suitable stain, but they are not numerous. It is not acid-fast.

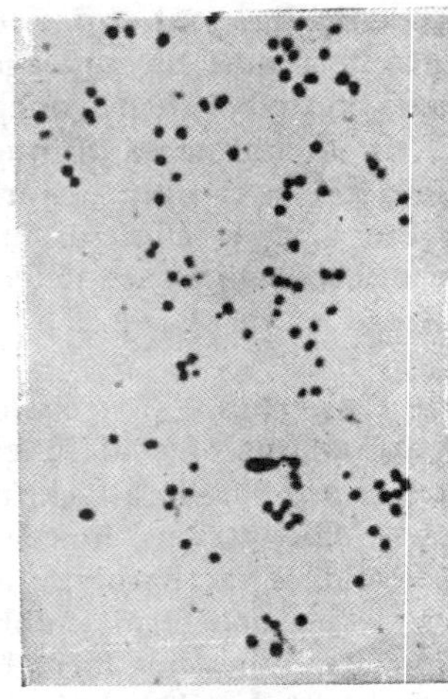

FIG. 32.8—**Corynebacterium equi** from serum agar culture, ×1,400.

**Growth Requirements and Characteristics.** This organism is cultivated upon any of the nutrient medium which is used for pathogenic organisms; in fact, it grows quite readily upon any laboratory medium. It is aerobic and facultatively anaerobic; grows best at 37°C., although quite abundantly at 30°C. Ottosen has found that suppurative exudate from cervical abscesses of swine treated with 5 per cent sulfuric acid for 10–14 minutes and then inoculated onto agar plates was a satisfactory method of isolating *C. equi.*

Colonies on solid media are large, moist, and viscid with an entire edge. In 24 hours, growth is creamy-white, but as the culture ages it turns to pink, and in a few days time the color is a salmon-pink. Pigmentation is accentuated when the organism is grown on coagulated egg-yolk medium and is incubated at room temperature. When the organism is grown on an agar slant, the growth is so viscid it flows from the surface of the medium and collects in the bottom of the tube. Growth on the inverted Petri dish is so abundant and viscid that some of the culture drops onto the dish below.

In bouillon the organism produces a heavy turbidity, and a scant viscid sediment collects in the tube.

**Resistance.** The organism is killed within 15 minutes at 60°C. and is readily destroyed by chemical disinfectants. It is resistant to 5 per cent oxalic acid for 60 minutes. This permits the use of oxalic acid in the isolation of the organism from less resistant bacteria.

**Biochemical Properties.** *C. equi* is devoid of any ability to ferment carbohydrates although it is able to utilize glucose without producing an acid reaction. It differs from the other members of the group in being able to reduce nitrates to nitrites. The organism does not liquefy gelatin or coagulated blood serum; does not alter milk; does not form indol; $H_2S$ forms in three to four days; does not react to the methyl red and Voges-Proskauer tests; is catalase positive.

**Antigenic Structure and Toxins.** This organism does not reveal any antigenic relationship with other members of the diphtheroid group.

Bruner, Dimock, and Edwards demonstrated by complement-fixation tests that the organism possesses species-specific and type-specific antigens. By using agglutination and precipitation tests, these investigators were able to divide the strains of *C. equi* into four main serologic types. Cultures from the genital tract of mares, from aborted equine fetuses, and from pneumonia of foals were found to belong to the same serologic type. In their studies of swine strains, Karlson, Moses, and Feldman observed antigenic heterogeneity with the agglutination test; however, in the complement-fixation test, with an antigen treated with acid and heat, the typical swine strains appeared antigenically homogenous. The type-specific component of the antigen is destroyed by acid and heat.

The antigenic heterogenity of the organism has also been emphasized by Ottosen who has reported six major groups in the study of 217 strains.

The organism is not toxin-producing.

**Pathogenicity.** *C. equi* is capable of producing bronchopneumonia in foals. The pneumonia is accompanied by the formation of small abscesses scattered throughout the lung tissue. Abscess formation is also observed in the mediastinal lymph glands, and in some cases lymph nodes in the peritoneal cavity are involved. Subcutaneous injection of the organism produces an abscess filled with typical, thick, yellow pus. Instillation of the organism into the upper air passages of the foal may not reproduce the disease, although Magnusson reports that it is possible to produce infection by intratracheal inoculation. Flatla has found that *C. equi* infection can be produced experimentally by feeding cultures of the organism to foals. In the infected animal extensive ulcerative enteritis was observed, and abscesses were present in the mesenteric lymph nodes. This author considers the infection as primary in the intestinal tract with metastasis to the lungs. *C. equi* has been isolated from the os uteri of barren mares and from the fetuses of mares which have aborted.

In the pig, *C. equi* is associated with small, soft, encapsulated abscesses which are commonly found in the submaxillary lymph glands. It has also been found in pneumonia of the pig by Thal and Rutqvist. Bendixen and Jepsen have been able to reproduce abscess formation by the subcutaneous inoculation of the organism into pigs. Plum has emphasized that the differentiation of *C. equi* infection in pigs from tuberculosis is only possible by microscopic examination.

Experimental animals, especially the rabbit and rat, are not susceptible. Some strains of the organism are able to kill mice and guinea pigs, according to the report by Thal and Rutqvist. Chicken embryos are killed within 4 to 6 days following inoculation.

**Immunity.** No data are available concerning the immunity produced by the organism either naturally or artificially. The sporadic nature of the infection eliminates any great need of immunizing agents.

**Diagnosis.** Infection produced by *C. equi* can be accurately diagnosed only by the isolation and identification of the organism. Such characteristics as morphology, viscid pigmented growth, lack of carbohydrate fermentation, and marked nitrate reduction are considered outstanding and most valuable.

## Miscellaneous Corynebacteria

The diphtheroid organisms form a large group of bacteria which are rather common on the mucous membranes and skin of man and animals. In man the identification of the various species is essential in order to arrive at a correct diagnosis of diphtheria. In animals the presence of other diphtheroids may confuse the diagnosis of the diseases which are known to be caused by certain species. The isolation of a diphtheroid organism may lead to a false diagnosis in some cases. The ubiquity of such bacteria emphasizes the need of the careful study of numerous strains of an organism before conclusions of etiologic relationships are made.

Cystitis and pyelonephritis of swine are frequently observed, and it has been generally assumed that the etiologic agents have been a mixture of bacteria, such as streptococci, staphylococci, *E. coli,* and *C. pyogenes.* In 1957 Soltys and Spratling described an anaerobic diphtheroid bacillus isolated from cases of cystitis and pyelonephritis. In 1961 Soltys gave a quite complete description of the organism and suggested the name *Corynebacterium suis.* Although it may be erroneous to assume that the organism is confined to the British Isles, this is the only area of the world from where it has been reported.

*C. suis* is a pleomorphic, gram-positive bacillus. It can be grown on blood agar or serum-enriched media only under anaerobic conditions. Therefore, it has the distinction of being the only anaerobic corynebacterium. It produces acid from maltose, but does not ferment lactose, salicin, mannitol, levulose, or galactose. Slight alkalinity is produced in litmus milk after 7 days incubation. The methyl red and Voges-Proskauer tests are negative; indol is not produced; gelatin, coagulated blood serum, or egg media are not liquefied; nitrates are not reduced; catalase test is negative.

Upon studying numerous strains by means of the precipitation test, Soltys found that *C. suis* was not antigenically related to *C. renale.* It is difficult to study this organism, as well as other corynebacteria, with the agglutination test because of their tendency to autoagglutinate.

Corynebacteria have been isolated from pulmonary abscesses in mice, from throat lesions in chickens and other birds, from the conjunctiva of dogs and horses, and from abscesses in numerous animals. Many of these organisms have been considered the causes of the conditions from which they were isolated. It is apparent, therefore, that other species of Corynebacteria may be recognized in the future.

One organism which is not specifically identified as yet, although it appears to be identical with the *C. pseudodiphtheriticum* of man, has been found in the lungs of swine, cattle, and sheep by numerous investigators. It was first described by Ray who considered it to be the cause of pulmonary edema of cattle.

Lesbouyries of France has reported the isolation of an organism he called *Corynebacterium metritis* from female rabbits. Chief symptoms were fever, loss of condition, unsteady gait, partial paralysis of the hind limbs, congestion of the vulva, and a mucopurulent discharge. Abortion occurred frequently. The significant lesions consisted of petechial hemorrhages of the vaginal mucous membrane and vulva, enlargement of the uterus and abdominal lymph nodes, and small multiple areas of abscessation and necrosis in the liver. Seventy-five per cent of the affected animals died or were destroyed.

## REFERENCES


Andrews, F. W., *et al.* Diphtheria, Its Bacteriology, Pathology and Immunology. His Majesty's Stationery Office, London, 1923.

Awad, F. I. Serologic Investigation of Pseudotuberculosis in Sheep. I. Agglutination Test. Amer. Jour. Vet. Res. 21:251, 1960.

Backsdale, W. L., *et al.* The Mutation of *Corynebacterium pyogenes* to *Corynebacterium haemolyticum*. Jour. Gen. Microbiol. 16:749, 1957.

Benham, C. L., *et al.* *Corynebacterium pseudotuberculosis* and Its Role in Diseases of Animals. Vet. Bull. 32:645, 1962.

Boyd, W. L., and Kelly, M. D. Isolation of *Corynebacterium pyogenes* From a Fetus and Later From the Mammary Gland of the Dam. Jour. Amer. Vet. Med. Assn. 103:24, 1943.

Brown, J. Howard, and Orcutt, Marion L. A Study of *Bacillus pyogenes*. Jour. Exp. Med. 32:219–48, 1920.

Bruner, D. W., and Edwards, P. R. Classification of *Corynebacterium equi*. Ky. Agr. Exp. Sta. Bull. 414, Lexington, 1941.

———, *et al.* The Serological Classification of *Corynebacterium equi*. Jour. Inf. Dis. 65:92–96, 1939.

Carne, H. R. A Bacteriological Study of 134 Strains of *Corynebacterium ovis*. Jour. Path. Bact. 49:313–26, 1939.

Cobb, R. W. Cultural Characteristics of Some Corynebacteria of Animal Origin, With Special Reference to *C. bovis* and *C. pyogenes*. Jour. Med. Lab. Tech. 20:199, 1963.

Cowie, R. S. A Generalized *Corynebacterium pyogenes* Disease of Cattle. Vet. Rec. 74:258, 1962.

Dimock, W. W., and Edwards, P. R *Corynebacterium equi* in Foals. Jour. Amer. Vet. Med. Assn. 79:809–12, 1931.

Doty, R. B., *et al.* A Comparison of Toxins Produced by Various Isolates of *Corynebacterium pseudotuberculosis* and the Development of a Diagnostic Skin Test for Caseous Lymphadenitis of Sheep and Goats. Amer. Jour. Vet. Res. 25:1679, 1964.

Eberson, F. A Bacteriologic Study of the Diphtheroid Organisms With Special Reference to Hodgkin's Disease. Jour. Inf. Dis. 23:1–42, 1918.

Ernst, W. Ueber Pyelonephritis Diphtherica Bovis und die Pyelonephritisbacillen. Zentralbl. f. Bakt. I. Abt. Orig. 39:549, 1905; 40:79, 1906.

Feenstra, E. S., and Thorp, F., Jr. Amer. Jour. Vet. Res. 7:432, 1946.

———, *et al.* Mich. State Coll. Vet. 5:147, 1945.

———, *et al.* Jour. Bact. 56:697, 1948.

———, *et al.* Amer. Jour. Vet. Res. 10:12, 1949.

Flatla, John L. Infeksjon med *Corynebacterium equi* hos foll. Norsk. Veterinair-Tidsk. 6:249–91, 1942.

Hancock, J. L., and Kelly, W. R. Vet. Rec. 60:669, 1948.

Hughes, J. P., and Biberstein, E. L. Chronic Equine Abscesses Associated With *C. pseudotuberculosis*. Jour. Amer. Vet. Med. Assn. 135:559, 1959.

———, *et al.* Two Cases of Generalized *Corynebacterium pseudotuberculosis* Infection in Mares. Cornell Vet. 52, 1961.

Humphreys, F. A., and Gibbons, R. J. Some Observations on Corynebacterial Infections. Canad. Jour. Comp. Med. 6:35–45, 1942.

Jewett, Walter. *Bacillus pyogenes* and Its Relation to Bovine Mastitis. Jour. Comp. Path. Therap. 38:180, 1925.

JONES, F. S., and LITTLE, R. B. Specific Infectious Cystitis and Pyelonephritis of Cows. Jour. Exp. Med. 42: 593–607, 1925.

———, and ———. The Organism Associated With Specific Infectious Cystitis and Pyelonephritis of Cows. Jour. Exp. Med. 43:11–20, 1926.

KARLSON, A. G., *et al.* Jour. Inf. Dis. 66:243, 1940.

KARLSSON, K. F. Skand. Vet. Tidsskr. 35:129, 1945.

LARSEN, A. B., and JOHNSON, H. W. Amer. Jour. Vet. Res. 8:184, 1947.

LOVELL, R. The *Corynebacterium pyogenes* Antitoxin Content of Animal Sera. Jour. Path. Bact. 49:329–38, 1939.

———. Studies on *Corynebacterium pyogenes* With Special Reference to Toxin Production. Jour. Path. Bact. 45: 339–55, 1937.

———. Jour. Comp. Path. 56:196, 1946.

———, and COTCHIN, E. Jour. Comp. Path. 56:205, 1946; 57:20, 1947.

MAGNUSSON, H. Spezifische Infektiose Pneumonie beim Fohlen, In Neurer Eitererreger beim Pferde. Arch. f. Wiss. Prakt. Tier. 50:22–38, 1923.

MARSH, H. Amer. Jour. Vet. Res. 8:294, 1947.

MAXWELL, H. The Occurrence, in Cattle, of Abortion, Macerated Fetuses and Acute Suppurative Mastitis Associated With *Corynebacterium pyogenes.* Cornell Vet. 33:315–18, 1943.

MERCHANT, I. A. The Corynebacteria Associated With Diseases of Domestic Animals. Jour. Bact. 30:95–117, 1935.

MINNETT, F. C. Immunological Studies With the Preisz-Nocard Bacillus and Their Application to Ulcerative Lymphangitis in the Horse. Jour. Comp. Path. Therap. 35:71–197, 1922.

MORGAN, B. B., *et al.* Mich. State Coll. Vet. 6:68, 72, 1946.

MORSE, E. V. Cornell Vet. 38:135, 1948.

———, and MORGAN, B. B. Cornell Vet. 41:59, 1951.

———, *et al.* Cornell Vet. 42:368, 1952.

NORGAARD, V. A., and MOHLER, JOHN R. The Nature, Cause and Economic Importance of Ovine Caseous Lymphadenitis. USDA 16th Ann. Rept. Bur. An. Ind., 1899.

OTTOSEN, H. E. Abstr. Vet. Bull. 17:523, 1947.

PARVANTA, M. F. Zur Frage der Aktiven Immunisierung mit Vaccinen von *Corynebacterium pyogenes.* Inaug. Diss., Munich, 1962.

PFEIFFER, D. H., and VILJOEN, N. F. Jour. S. Afr. Vet. Med. Assn. 16:148, 1945.

PREISZ, HUGO, and GUINARD, M. L. Pseudo-tuberculose chez le Mouton. Jour. de Med. Vet. 42:563–72, 1891.

RAY, J. D. Specific Pulmonary Edema of Cattle. A Bacterial Infection Due to Unnamed Diphtheroids or Corynebacteria. Vet. Med. 23:490, 1928.

ROACH, R. W. Vet. Rec. 58:169, 1946.

ROLLE, M. Biology der *Bacterium pyogenes.* Inaug. Diss., Hannover. M. & H. Shaper, Hannover, 1929.

RUEBKE, H. J. Bacterial Flora of the Bovine Male Genitalia. M.S. Thesis, Iowa State Univ. Library, 1950.

RYFF, J. F., and BROWN, J. Amer. Jour. Vet. Res. 15:617, 1954.

SOLTYS, M. A. *Corynebacterium suis* Associated With a Specific Cystitis and Pyelonephritis in Pigs. Vet. Rec. 81: 441, 1961.

———, and SPRATLING, F. R. Infectious Cystitis and Pyelonephritis of Pigs: A Preliminary Communication. Vet. Rec. 69:500, 1957.

THAL, E., and RUTQVIST, L. Nord. Vet. Med. 11:298, 1959.

THOMSON, DAVID, and THOMSON, ROBERT. The Corynebacteria (Diphtheria Bacillus and "Diphtheroids"). The Importance of Microphotography as an Aid to Their Classification and Identification. Annals, Pickett-Thomson Res. Lab., Vol. II. Bailliere, Tindall and Cox, London. Williams & Wilkins Co., Baltimore, 1929.

WEITZ, B. Jour. Comp. Path. 57:279, 1947.

———. Vet. Rec. 61:123, 1949.

———, and LANGRIDGE, R. Jour. Comp. Path. 57:286, 1947.

WISECUP, W. G., *et al.* *Corynebacterium pseudotuberculosis* Associated With Rapidly Occurring Equine Abscesses. Jour. Amer. Vet. Med. Assn. 144:152, 1964.

# 33

# The Genus Mycobacterium

**ALFRED G. KARLSON, D.V.M., Ph.D.**
*Section of Microbiology*
*Mayo Clinic and Mayo Foundation*
*Rochester, Minnesota*

One outstanding characteristic differentiates the organism in the genus Mycobacterium from other bacteria. When any of the members of this group are stained with a suitable dye, such as carbol fuchsin, they are not decolorized by the action of acids. This property has led to the designation *acid-fast* for this group of microorganisms. In addition to this characteristic, the mycobacteria are recognized as slender rods which may be beaded, clavate, and branched. They are strictly aerobic, and most strains grow slowly on artificial media.

Acid-fast bacteria are widely distributed in nature; a few are pathogenic for man and animals; some are pathogenic for cold-blooded animals; and others are saprophytes found in animal excretions and tissue and in the soil. The following species of interest to veterinarians are conveniently listed in the three categories:

A. Species pathogenic for man and animals.

*Mycobacterium tuberculosis* causes tuberculosis in man and in other animals.

*Mycobacterium bovis* is pathogenic primarily for cattle, although man and other animals may become infected.

*Mycobacterium avium* is the cause of tuberculosis in the avian family and in various mammals.

*Mycobacterium paratuberculosis* causes paratuberculosis, otherwise known as Johne's disease or chronic bacillary dysentery, in cattle and sheep.

*Mycobacterium leprae* is the cause of leprosy in man.

*Mycobacterium lepraemurium* is the cause of leprosy which occurs in wild rats.

*Mycobacterium microti* is an acid-fast microorganism found in the vole, in which it produces lesions typical of tuberculosis.

*Mycobacterium fortuitum* has been isolated from lesions in man, cattle, and cold-blooded animals. It is found in the soil and water.

B. Species parasitic and pathogenic for cold-blooded animals.

*Mycobacterium piscium* is pathogenic for frogs, toads, turtles, lizards, snakes, salamanders, and carp.

*Mycobacterium marinum* (formerly *balnei*) has been isolated from fish. It has also been isolated from swimming pools and from skin lesions in man.

*Mycobacterium cheloni* is found in lesions of turtles.

*Mycobacterium thamnopheos* has been isolated from garter snakes and probably from other snakes.

The naming of mycobacteria from cold-blooded animals is based on the species of host, such as *Mycobacterium piscium* from fish. It is not known that such strains are actually different species; they may be *Mycobacterium marinum.*

C. Sarophytic species.

*Mycobacterium smegmatis* includes a number of strains of saprophytic bacteria which have been known under other species' names (see Bergey's Manual, p. 697, 1957). The organism is found in soil, dust, water, and smegma. *Mycobacterium phlei* is widely distributed in hay, grass, and in the soil and dust. It was originally isolated from timothy hay and is commonly called the timothy hay bacillus.

The student in veterinary bacteriology is primarily interested in the pathogenic species of mycobacteria; however, it must be remembered that saprophytic species do exist, and that they may resemble pathogenic species. The species which produce disease in cold-blooded animals are of especial interest to naturalists and others concerned with the diseases of zoological specimens. Information on this special field may be obtained by referring to the work of Vogel, Ippen, and Parisot and Wood.

### *Mycobacterium tuberculosis*
### *Mycobacterium bovis*
### *Mycobacterium avium*

**Synonyms and History.** *Bacillus tuberculosis, Mycobacterium tuberculosis* var. *hominis,* var. *bovis,* and var. *avium.*

The tubercle bacillus and tuberculosis of man and animals have been studied more than all the other microorganisms and diseases combined. Entire books are written on the subject, and entire journals are devoted to past and current literature.

Tuberculosis is one of the oldest diseases of which there is any record. References are made to the disease in the earliest literature, and Egyptian mummies show lesions of the infection. The contagious nature of the disease was recognized by early peoples, and it was but natural that some confusion existed during the Middle Ages between tuberculosis and such diseases as syphilis.

Conclusive proof of the infectiousness of tuberculosis was contributed by Villemin of France[1] in 1865 and more completely in 1868, when he produced the disease in the rabbit by inoculation with human and bovine tuberculous exudates. He was the first to demonstrate that rabbits have a greater resistance to the human tubercle bacillus than to bovine microorganisms. Villemin concluded that (1) tuberculosis is a specific disease; (2) it is caused by an inoculable agent; and (3) it can be transmitted from man and from cattle to rabbits and guinea pigs.

The announcement of the discovery of the cause of tuberculosis by Robert Koch in 1882 stands out as the most important contribution to the study of this disease. It was this discovery which opened the doors to others who have contributed to the subject since that time.

Robert Koch succeeded in staining the tubercle bacillus with alkaline methylene blue and with vesuvin as a counterstain. He was able to cultivate the microorganism on coagulated blood serum, and he proved the etiologic relationship of the microorganism to the disease by inoculating the cultures into guinea pigs. During the early years of his work, Koch erroneously considered that the human and bovine tubercle bacilli were identical. In 1898 Theobald Smith revealed that the human and bovine strains of tubercle bacilli could be differentiated by growth on acidified glycerin broth. He showed that the bovine strains grew more slowly and decreased the acidity of the broth. This difference was not accepted by Koch and his school; consequently, considerable controversy over the subject existed until 1901 when Koch admitted that the human and bovine bacilli represented different types. Ehrlich is given credit for having shown the acid-fast characteristics of this microorganism in 1882. His staining technique was later adopted by Koch. In 1890 Koch prepared a concentrated glycerin-broth extract of the tubercle bacillus. This he called tuberculin, and he hoped that it would serve as a pro-

[1] Early work on tuberculosis and acid-fast bacteria is historically important and may be found in the publications of Calmette, Feldman (1938), and Rich.

tective and curative agent in the disease. Injection of tuberculin into infected animals and man, however, produced characteristic local and systemic reactions, and it was soon realized that tuberculin was a valuable diagnostic agent instead of a curative one.

In 1872 Paulicki observed the similarity between avian tuberculosis and the human and bovine disease. Koch, however, considered that birds were infected with the human or bovine organism. Little significance was attached to the avian disease until Rivolta in 1889, Strauss and Gamaleia in 1891, and Maffucci in 1892 demonstrated that the avian organism was different from the human and bovine types.

Present-day classification uses the name *Mycobacterium tuberculosis* for the human type, *Mycobacterium bovis* for the bovine type, and *Mycobacterium avium* for the microorganism found in chickens and other avian species. For convenience of discussion the avian tubercle bacillus will be considered with the bovine and human types.

**Distribution and Transmission.** Tubercle bacilli are distributed throughout human and bovine populations in most parts of the world. The disease is one which has been introduced by civilization. It is rarely found in native peoples of a country unless it has been introduced by those from the Old World. Bovine herds are comparatively free of the disease in countries with few cattle. Crowding appears to be a definite factor in the prevalence of tuberculosis. In man the disease is most common in heavily populated cities and in people living in an unsanitary environment and in close contact. In cattle the disease is most frequent in animals stabled together or kept in close contact in pens. This fact has been emphasized after it was revealed that tuberculosis among cattle in the southern part of the United States is comparatively rare except in herds of work oxen which were stabled together. Avian tuberculosis is prevalent in chicken flocks of most countries of the world. In the United States the disease is most common in the midwestern states surrounding the Great Lakes. It is a disease prevalent in temperate zones, probably because of the necessity for housing the animals during unfavorable weather.

In man, the microorganism is transmitted by sputum or other exudate containing bacilli. This is illustrated by the prevalence of tuberculosis in families; in fact, the ease by which the infection becomes established in families has given rise to the belief that it is inherited. Tuberculosis is not inherited, but family predisposition and close contacts make it appear to be. It is obvious that coughing, sneezing, spitting, the contamination of the hands by mouth and nasal exudates, and the handling of food and cooking utensils by a person with open lung lesions of tuberculosis are means of transmitting the organism. The human tubercle bacillus may be transmitted to dogs, swine, and cattle by tuberculous persons; generally, such infections are not extensive, but the animals will react to the tuberculin test.

Among cattle the bacillus is transmitted through feed and, in some cases, water. Pulmonary exudates in the cow are usually swallowed; hence, the organism passes with the feces and contaminates the ground and feed. The organisms may be washed from the mouth while the animal is drinking and in this manner contaminate the water tank.

The bovine type of the organism is pathogenic to man. Cases of bovine tuberculosis in man may be caused by drinking milk from a cow with tuberculous mastitis or milk which has been contaminated with bovine fecal matter containing the microorganism. Swine may be infected with the bovine type of bacillus when they feed in the same lot with tuberculous cattle, and with the human type when they feed on garbage from tuberculosis sanatoria or from residences housing human cases. Persons infected with bovine tubercle bacilli may be a source of infection for swine and cattle.

Tuberculosis is spread through the avian family by the medium of feed and water contaminated with fecal material. Swine obtain the avian organisms by contact with infective droppings and by eating diseased chickens.

**Morphology and Staining.** *Myco. tuberculosis* is a slender rod, 0.2μ to 0.6μ in diameter, and 1.5μ to 4μ in length. *Myco. bovis* is considered to be shorter and thicker than the human forms, but this cannot be taken as a definite diagnostic criterion because strains of both types show variation in size (Figs. 33.1 and 33.2). The organism is uneven in size, and forms ranging from coccoid to filamentous are frequently observed in the same culture. *Myco. avium* is similar to the human and bovine types, although it is considered more pleomorphic. It is usually uniform in size in smears made from infected tissue (Fig. 33.3), but on artificial media short, coccoid cells and long, beaded filaments are common. The nature of these filaments was observed by Brieger and Fell by growing the avian tubercle bacilli in a hanging drop of dilute chicken embryo extract on a warm stage. The colonies develop as follows: (1) The original rods elongate into filaments. (2) The filaments multiply by ordinary fission and also by forming fine, pinlike terminal sprouts which grow into independent bacilli. (3) After division the daughter filaments usually remain in contact at the site of fission; their terminal growth continues at an angle to the former cleavage plane, and the colony thus acquires its characteristic structure. (4) The colony enlarges, and ramification becomes increasingly complex until about the fifth day of incubation, when growth declines. The bacilli remain filamentous. (5) When transferred to embryo extract of normal concentration, the pseudomycelial colonies pass through a phase of filamentous proliferation followed by disintegration of the filaments into short, discrete rods.

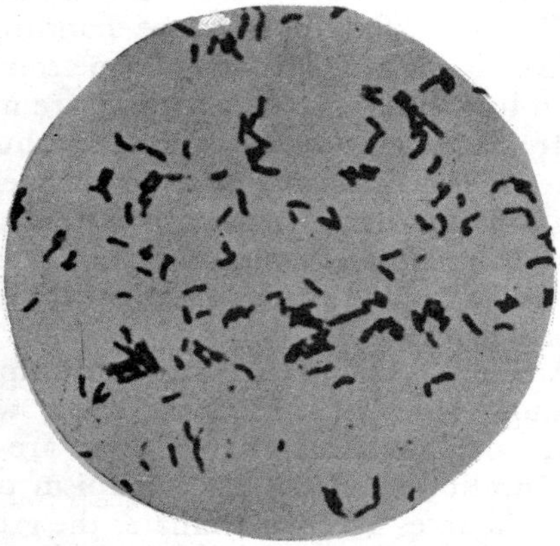

FIG. 33.1—**Mycobacterium bovis** glycerin bouillon culture, ×2,000. (From Nowak: Documenta Microbiologica, courtesy Gustav Fischer.)

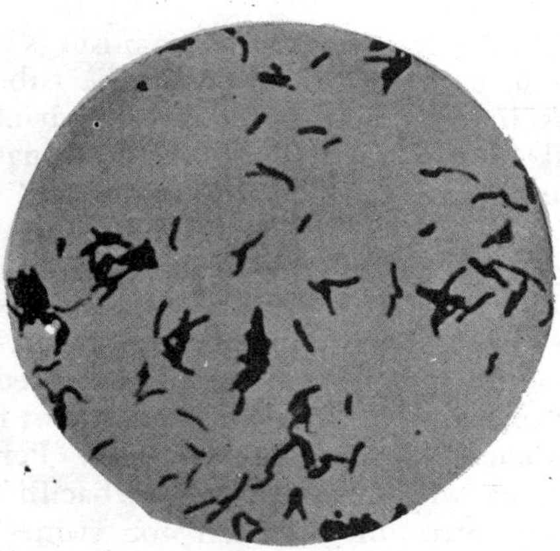

FIG. 33.2—**Mycobacterium tuberculosis** glycerin potato culture, ×2,000. (From Nowak: Documenta Microbiologica, courtesy Gustav Fischer.)

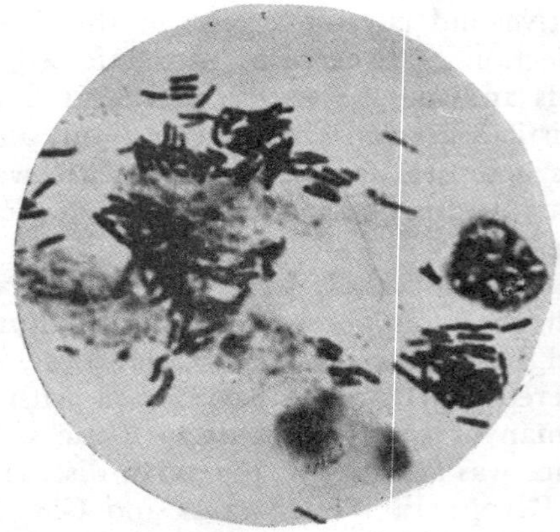

FIG. 33.3—**Mycobacterium avium** tissue smear, ×2,000. (From Nowak: Documenta Microbiologica, courtesy Gustav Fischer.)

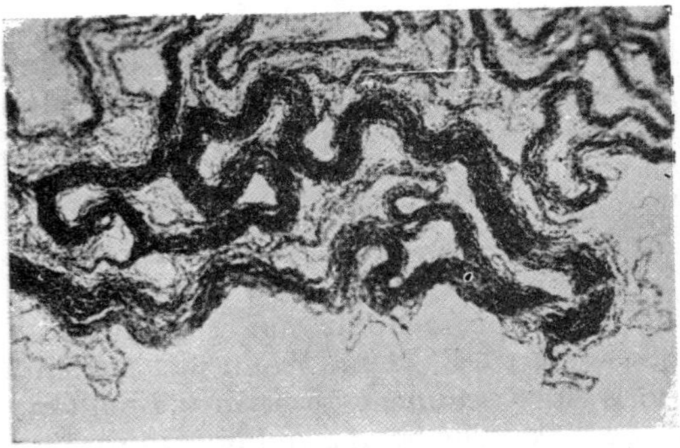

FIG. 33.4—**Mycobacterium tuberculosis** in Proskauer and Beck liquid medium. Cord formation in 14-day-old culture. This arrangement in tightly packed bundles or cords is characteristic of mammalian tubercle bacilli; other acid-fast bacteria usually do not grow in this arrangement, ×400.

It has been observed that mammalian tubercle bacilli grow in liquid media, in which they form tight bundles or cords of bacilli in close parallel arrangement (Fig. 33.4). Although Koch first described this characteristic, Middlebrook associated it with the virulent strains of tubercle bacilli. When such cultures are treated with petroleum ether, the strands of bacilli disrupt and reveal the lipid nature of the substance that causes individual cells to adhere.

Tubercle bacilli are nonsporeforming and nonmotile. Extremely pleomorphic types of tubercle bacilli have been described. These forms range through small filterable granules, diplococcoid shapes, diphtheroid shapes, and normal-sized bacilli.

The most important staining characteristic of this microorganism is its resistance to acidified decolorizing agents. This resistance or acid-fast nature is due to the presence in the organism of a waxy substance which prevents the ready adsorption of dyes. In order to stain the bacillus, smears must be placed in hot staining solutions or remain in contact with the stain for several hours. The heated stain is quicker and therefore preferable. Numerous staining techniques are available for staining this microorganism, but the Ziehl-Neelsen stain is the one commonly used in most laboratories.

**Growth Requirements and Characteristics.** *Myco. tuberculosis, Myco. bovis,* and *Myco. avium* all require aerobic conditions for artificial growth. An atmosphere containing approximately 5 per cent carbon dioxide aids growth.

The optimal temperature for growth is 37°C., although the microorganism does grow slowly at a temperature as low as 30°C. Avian tubercle bacilli grow well at temperatures between 25° and 45°C. The human and bovine strains of tubercle bacilli differ in the optimal pH for growth. Human strains grow best in a medium adjusted to pH 7.4 to 8.0, while bovine strains grow best at a pH of 5.8 to 6.9. Avian strains prefer a slightly alkaline medium.

Tubercle bacilli can be cultivated on artificial media directly from infected tissues, but the organism frequently is not present in a pure culture. Various methods have been devised to overcome the presence of contaminants which grow more rapidly than tubercle bacilli. One of the methods commonly used is to add an equal volume of 3 per cent solution of sodium hydroxide to the tissue or exudate, shake the tube vigorously, and allow it to stand for about 30 minutes. It is neutralized with 3N hydrochloric acid and centrifuged. The supernatant fluid is poured off, and the sediment is then "seeded" over the surface of slants of suitable culture medium. Other methods for decontaminating tissue and body fluids are described by Darzins and by Willis and Cummings in the Veterans Administration *Handbook for Tuberculosis Laboratory Methods.* Gentian violet and malachite green are commonly incorporated in media used for the isolation of tubercle bacilli in order to prevent growth of contaminants not killed by treatment with alkali.

The growths of the various types of tubercle bacilli on solid media have many characteristics in common. On many specialized media, however, there are sufficient

FIG. 33.5—The three types of tubercle bacilli on egg-yolk agar slant cultures; left to right, bovine, human, and avian. (From Feldman, Avian Tuberculosis Infections, courtesy Williams & Wilkins Co.)

differences among the three types for presumptive identification. On solid medium, the human type produces a dry, rough, crumbly growth; the bovine type produces a scant, dry growth even after prolonged incubation; the avian type produces a smooth, moist, grayish-white growth (Fig. 33.5). Glycerin is commonly incorporated into many of the media used to cultivate tubercle bacilli. It was first used to prevent desiccation during long periods of incubation. Glycerin is definitely stimulating to the human and the avian tubercle bacilli. However, the amount of glycerin ordinarily incorporated in media for the growth of human strains retards the growth of bovine strains; glycerin is usually omitted from media intended for the cultivation of bovine strains.

For methods of preparing various media for tubercle bacilli, the reader is referred to the Veterans Administraton *Handbook of Tuberculosis Laboratory Methods* and to Willis and Cummings.

The relative ease with which the growth of each of the three types of bacilli is miscible in water is considered of differential significance. The avian type forms a uniform homogeneous suspension, but the human and bovine varieties are notoriously difficult to put into suspension.

In liquid media, such as Proskauer and Beck medium, the three types present some differences. The avian culture and most of the saprophytic strains form a soft, viscid pellicle on this medium, and as the culture ages, stalactites extend from the pellicle and a viscid sediment forms in the bottom of the flask. The bovine and human strains produce a crumbly pellicle, parts of which fall to the bottom of the flask and form a granular sediment. Slightly acidified, glycerin bouillon is rendered more acid in reaction by the growth of human strains, while an alkaline reaction is produced by the growth of bovine strains. The growth of strains of the tubercle bacillus used for the manufacture of tuberculin is quite abundant in Dorset's synthetic medium (see chapter on Bacteriological Techniques and Methods).

**Resistance.** The presence of a lipid substance in *Myco. tuberculosis* increases its resistance to conditions that are detrimental to other nonsporeforming types of bacteria. When present in exudate which becomes thoroughly dried, the microorganism may be viable for months. Although direct sunlight kills the bacillus after a few minutes exposure, much of the animal exudates and fecal matter in which the microorganism is present usually protects it from the direct rays of the sun. The tubercle bacillus remains alive in putrefying material for months; consequently, it is hazardous to spread manure on pasture land if such material has come from tuberculous animals. Well-rotted manure is considered free of the microorganism. Watering tanks may remain contaminated for months if the bacillus has been introduced into them by infected animals.

The necessity of thorough disinfection of barns and chicken houses following the removal of tuberculous individuals is a fundamental and difficult procedure in the eradication of tuberculosis. Before the application of a disinfectant, all litter must be removed and burned. The tubercle bacillus is quite sensitive to high temperatures, and therefore live steam is an effective sterilizing agent for solid surfaces. The cresol compounds in a 2 to 3 per cent solution are effective against this organism. Sodium hydroxide or lye in the 2 per cent solution which is so effective against some bacteria and viruses cannot be relied on to kill tubercle bacilli. In fact, exudates to be examined for the presence of *Myco. tuberculosis* may be treated with 3 per cent sodium hydroxide in order to destroy contaminating bacteria.

Alcohol has been found to be an effective disinfectant against tubercle bacilli. Smith has demonstrated that these bacilli in water or sputum suspension are killed in 15 to 30 seconds in absolute, 95 per cent, and 70 per cent alcohol. Bacilli in smears dried from sputum or water suspensions were usually killed by 50 and 70 per cent ethyl or 30 to 80 per cent isopropyl alcohol in 1 to 2 minutes, sometimes in 15 to 30 seconds. He concluded that 95 per cent alcohol is best for wet surfaces, 50 per cent for dry, and 70 per cent for wet or dry surfaces.

Laboratory cultures of tubercle bacilli under optimal conditions usually remain viable for at least 6 months, but it is advisable to transplant cultures at more frequent intervals to assure viability. Since these organisms must be incubated longer than more rapidly growing bacteria, the media which are used must be protected against desiccation. It has been noted that glycerin, which is a nutrient for human and avian types of tubercle bacilli, reduces the rate of drying. Cultures may be incubated in a chamber in which a high humidity is maintained. Screw cap tubes or small bottles that prevent evaporation are commonly used. Culture tubes may be opened and a few drops of sterile water may be added in order to maintain a moist atmosphere. Sealing tubes with paraffin or with rubber caps to prevent evaporation, although commonly done, is not conducive to maximal growth of this organism because of the reduction in oxygen tension. Cultures of tubercle bacilli grow more abundantly in an atmosphere of 5 per cent $CO_2$.

**Chemotherapy of Tuberculosis.** For authoritative discussions on the chemotherapy of tuberculosis in man and the development of antituberculosis drugs, the reader is referred to the texts by Hinshaw and Garland and by Baum. The following is a brief historical sketch. The value of chemical agents in the treatment of mammalian tuberculosis was shown in 1940 by William H. Feldman and associates, who demonstrated that the experimental disease in guinea pigs was benefited by 4-4′-diaminodiphenylsulfone and derivatives of this compound. Parenthetically, it may be noted that this agent is now the treatment of choice in another mycobacterial disease, leprosy. The discovery of streptomycin in 1944 by Albert Schatz and associates and the demonstration in 1944 of the tuberculostatic effect of this agent in guinea pigs are significant developments.

The usefulness of streptomycin in treating clinical tuberculosis in man is somewhat circumvented by the emergence of streptomycin-resistant tubercle bacilli during the course of treatment. It was subsequently found that the occurrence of such drug-resistant strains could be curtailed by the administration of para-aminosalicylic acid (PAS), an antituberculosis agent described in 1946 by Jörgen Lehmann.

A third important antituberculosis drug is isonicotinic acid hydrazide, also called isoniazid, whose spectacular effects were announced in 1952 (Editorial, New Antituberculosis Drug, *J.A.M.A.* 148:1034, 1952). Isoniazid is usually administered with PAS and streptomycin. The combination of drugs potentiates the antituberculosis effect and also curtails the emergence of drug-resistant tubercle bacilli. A peculiarity of isoniazid-resistant tubercle bacilli is a loss of virulence for guinea pigs. Isoniazid has been recommended as a drug for prophylactic use when tuberculosis is a constant threat. It is given orally and is relatively nontoxic and inexpensive.

In Italy, South America, and South Africa attempts have been made to control bovine tuberculosis by prophylactic use of isoniazid, but the results have not been promising. In zoological gardens and in laboratory colonies of primates, isoniazid has been used to treat tuberculous animals and also as a prophylactic measure. Information on the control and treatment of tuberculosis in primates has been summarized by Ruch.

**Biochemical Properties.** Surprisingly little data are available concerning the biochemical activities of the tubercle bacilli. Human and avian strains have been known to produce a slight acid reaction in glucose, maltose, trehalose, and glycerol. Tubercle bacilli are catalase-positive, and some strains form a slight amount of hydrogen sulfide. Results of the methyl red and Voges-Proskauer tests are negative. Growth of the organisms occurs in milk, but the medium is not changed in appearance. For discussions on the growth and metabolism of tubercle bacilli, see Darzins, and also Drea and Andrejew.

**Antigenic Structure and Toxins.** It has been found that the common agglutination reaction is not sufficient to separate the three types of tubercle bacilli. This indicates that they must share common antigens. Agglutinin absorption, however, distinguishes the mammalian from the avian strains. The human and bovine varieties have been shown to be antigenically similar by cross-tuberculin reactions. The avian tubercle bacillus, *Myco. avium,* however, is distinctly different. The avian organism can be subdivided into groups on the basis of serologic reactions, but the human and bovine varieties are antigenically homogenous. According to Karlson (1963) avian tubercle bacilli appear to be antigenically similar to so-called Battey bacilli of Runyon's Group III isolated from human patients.

The nature of the toxic substances produced by tubercle bacilli in the natural disease remains unknown. The most important reaction produced by the end-products of bacterial growth is the allergic reaction observed in sensitized individuals following the injection of tuberculin. This reaction and its significance will be discussed later in the chapter.

**Pathogenicity.** The three types of tubercle bacilli are characterized by their pathogenicity for the three hosts—human, bovine, and avian. In addition to the primary host, each type is able to produce disease in other species of animals.

***Mycobacterium tuberculosis.*** The human type of tubercle bacilli is primarily pathogenic for man, anthropoid apes, monkeys, and certain species of parrots. It has been found to be pathogenic in naturally infected cattle. Lesslie attributed the occurrence of tuberculin reactors in five different herds of cattle to infection with human type of tubercle bacilli. In each instance a tuberculous person was found to have had contact with the animals. No additional reactors were found after the source of the infection had been removed. Although this is not considered to be a frequent occurrence in the United States, it is obvious that tuberculous people must be kept out of contact with cattle, for if this is not done, this may be one source of persistent tuberculin reactors in a herd. The reports on human-type infection in cattle and the relationship to tuberculin reactors have been reviewed by Karlson (1962).

The human type of the organism is also pathogenic for swine. The lesions produced in that animal are generally confined to the lymph nodes of the mesentery and the cervical region and are found, for the most part, in hogs which are fed uncooked garbage (Karlson, 1963).

Tuberculosis of any type is rare in the horse, and most cases are due to the bovine type of the microorganism. The human type has been recovered from horses. The same is true of sheep and goats. Birds, other than the parrot, are resistant to the human strain. Parrots are known to become infected after long years of close association with a tuberculous person. House dogs kept in close contact with human cases may become infected with tubercle bacilli. The human type is found more frequently in dogs than the bovine because of the greater possibility for infection with the human type of the organism. Cats are generally considered highly resistant to the human strain by both experimental and natural infection.

Rabbits are but slightly susceptible to the human type, and when infected they rarely succumb to the infection. The hamster, which has come into use in experimental procedures, has been found to be as susceptible as the guinea pig to the human type of the microorganism. Guinea pigs are highly susceptible to human tubercle bacilli, which produce, even with extremely small doses, an irreversible, eventually fatal disease. Mice can be infected with the human type of the microorganism, and by intravenous inoculation marked lesions are produced in the lungs. Susceptibility varies with the strain of mice used. The albino rat is generally considered to be markedly resistant to this organism. Significant lesions have been produced, however, by injecting 5-mg. doses of bacilli intraperitoneally into that animal.

***Mycobacterium bovis.*** This organism is primarily pathogenic for cattle, but swine are readily infected when in contact with tuberculous cows. Cases of tuberculosis in horses and sheep have been reported as being caused by the bovine microorganism, but these animals are generally considered resistant to the microorganism. Cases of bovine tuberculosis also have been observed in dogs and cats. Chickens are resistant to the bovine bacillus, but parrots and related birds are highly susceptible.

The pathogenicity of the bovine tubercle bacillus for man has been recognized as a public health problem in all countries where milk and milk products are important articles of food. In the United States this danger to health has been reduced to a minimum as a result of the eradication of tuberculosis from cattle herds and of widespread pasteurization of milk. Children less than 16 years of age are most susceptible to bovine tubercle bacilli, and in them the microorganism usually produces lesions of a nonpulmonary nature. However, in sections of the world where infections due to the bovine type are common, a significant percentage of pulmonary tuberculosis is reported. The tissues most commonly involved are the cervical and abdominal lymph nodes and the bones, although generalized tuberculosis due to bovine tubercle bacilli is by no means rare.

Bovine tubercle bacilli can produce generalized tuberculosis in the rabbit even when given in extremely small doses. The guinea pig is also very susceptible to the bovine organism. Mice are usually infected by intraperitoneal inoculations, but rats are resistant. The hamster is susceptible to virulent strains of the bovine type of organism.

***Mycobacterium avium.*** The avian tubercle bacillus is primarily pathogenic for the domestic fowl, although the organism is capable of infecting all species of birds and some species of mammals (Table 33.1). It is quite likely that the factors which determine the prevalence of tuberculosis in

TABLE 33.1

RELATIVE PATHOGENICITY OF THE AVIAN TUBERCLE BACILLUS FOR DIFFERENT ANIMALS

| Animal | Degree of Suscepti-bility | Animal | Degree of Suscepti-bility |
|---|---|---|---|
| Chicken | marked | Rat | slight |
| Pheasant | marked | Mink | moderate |
| Turkey | marked | Sheep | moderate |
| Parrot | moderate | Horse | moderate |
| Duck | moderate | Cow | slight |
| Goose | moderate | Guinea pig | slight |
| Pigeon | moderate | Dog | not susceptible |
| Swine | moderate | Cat | not susceptible* |
| Rabbit | marked | Goat | slight |
| Mouse | slight | | |

Source: Feldman, W. H. Avian Tuberculosis Infections, courtesy Williams & Wilkins Co.

* One case of avian tuberculosis has been reported in the cat.

many species of the avian family are the environmental conditions, particularly crowding, under which they live. The pheasant in its wild state is not often found to be infected, but the disease is apt to be quite severe in pheasants that have access to and mingle freely with infected chicken flocks. The disease may be found in turkeys that are raised in contact with infected chickens. The pigeon, which is rather common on some farms, may become infected, and the same is true of sparrows and crows. Water fowl, such as ducks, geese, and swans, even though living in close contact with infected chickens, rarely become infected. House birds such as canaries, parrots, and love birds are susceptible to the avian tubercle bacillus, although they have rare opportunities to become infected. Tuberculosis is the most common cause of death in aviaries of some zoological gardens.

Among the mammals, swine and rabbits are the most susceptible. Tuberculosis in swine in the United States is predominantly due to the avian bacillus. The prevalence of tuberculosis in swine is emphasized by the report of the United States Meat Inspection Division for the fiscal year 1964, which reported 5,527 total swine carcasses and 339,221 parts of swine carcasses condemned out of 72,156,009 inspected postmortem. Tuberculosis in swine due to avian tubercle bacilli is predominantly a disease of the lymph nodes. However, generalization may occur with lesions involving the liver, spleen, lungs, and kidneys. The rabbit may become infected with the avian type of the microorganism as a result of close contact with infected chickens. Intravenous inoculation with a suspension of avian tubercle bacilli usually produces an acute disease, the rabbit dying within 2 to 4 weeks. In this acute type of the disease, macroscopic tubercles are usually absent, but the spleen is enlarged and the animal has lost considerable weight. Stained smears of the splenic pulp reveal numerous acid-fast bacilli.

The susceptibility of cattle to *Myco. avium* has been the subject of considerable research because of cross reactions to the routine tuberculin test. In general, it can be concluded that cattle are not readily infected with the avian microorganism under natural conditions to the extent that generalized macroscopic lesions are developed. It is believed that natural infection with the avian type of the bacillus will sensitize cattle sufficiently to cause them to react to mammalian tuberculin. Therefore, it is prudent to keep chickens separated from cattle herds and to eliminate the disease from poultry flocks by carefully culling older birds, or by tuberculin testing. The maintenance of completely negative tuberculin-tested cattle herds appears unlikely unless avian tuberculosis is also eradicated (Feldman, 1960).

It is evident that few species of bacteria can infect so many hosts as this organism does. This may be partially due to the feeding of chickens or chicken offal to animals. Illustrating this point is a report by Hall and Winkel stating that infection was caused in mink by feeding them chicken livers.

Cases of tuberculosis in the horse caused by *Myco. avium* have been reported, but this animal is considered refractory to the organism following natural exposure. Sheep may be infected, but goats, dogs, and cats are considered quite resistant. Mice and rats possess slight susceptibility to the avian bacillus. Guinea pigs can be infected with inoculations of avian tubercle bacilli, but the disease is mild and nonprogressive. This fact is of great importance in the typing of an unknown tubercle bacillus.

Case histories are given in the literature which show that man may be infected with *Myco. avium*. However, when compared with the virulence for man of the human and bovine types of the microorganism, it is generally conceded that the avian type is of little consequence in human tuberculosis (Feldman, 1963).

**Differentiation of Types.** The relative virulence for laboratory animals of the four types of tubercle bacilli responsible for tuberculosis in warm-blooded animals is

TABLE 33.2

RELATIVE VIRULENCE, IN LABORATORY ANIMALS, OF THE FOUR TYPES OF MYCOBACTERIA RESPONSIBLE FOR TUBERCULOSIS OF WARM-BLOODED ANIMALS*

| Bacillary Type | Animal | | | |
|---|---|---|---|---|
| | Guinea pig | Rabbit | Chicken | Vole |
| Human | + | ∓ | 0 | 0 |
| Bovine | + | + | 0 | + |
| Avian | ∓ | + | + | 0 |
| Vole | 0 | 0 | 0 | + |

Source: Feldman, W. H. Animal Tuberculosis and Its Relationship to the Disease in Man, courtesy New York Academy of Science.

* 0 = very resistant; ∓ = slightly susceptible; + = definitely susceptible.

shown in Table 33.2. In distinguishing the various types of tubercle bacilli by animal pathogenicity tests, the relative susceptibility of the following animals must be determined for each bacterial strain studied—two guinea pigs, two rabbits, and two chickens. These animals should have been tested previously with avian tuberculin and found negative. Guinea pigs should receive the infecting inoculum subcutaneously; rabbits and chickens are inoculated intravenously. If the vole bacillus is suspected, mice may be included in the typing series and given the inoculum intravenously. Guinea pigs living 8 weeks after inoculation are killed for autopsy, while the rabbits and chickens are examined for lesions 90 days after inoculation.

The human type of tubercle bacillus is distinguished from all other mycobacteria, including the bovine strain, by its ability to produce niacin in vitro as determined by the Konno test (Karlson, 1964). The bovine strain differs from the human strain by its sensitivity in vitro to thiophene-2-carboxylic acid, by its failure to produce niacin, and by the lack of nitrate reductase and of nicotinamidase (Bönicke, 1962). These in vitro tests for differentiation of *Myco. tuberculosis* and *Myco. bovis* are less time-consuming and less expensive than are animal pathogenicity tests.

It is obviously important to differentiate between *Myco. tuberculosis* and *Myco. bovis.* For example, if it can be shown that *Myco. tuberculosis* is responsible for an infection in animals, one must look for a tuberculous person as the source of infection. If *Myco. bovis* is demonstrable as the cause of an outbreak, it is likely that infected cattle or other animals may be the source. It must be borne in mind, however, that the bovine type of tubercle bacillus may be transmitted by an infected person.

## Immunity

***Natural Resistance.*** It is obvious that many species of animals possess natural resistance to tuberculosis. According to Lurie this natural resistance may be of three types. First, there are those species in which the bacilli do not grow or do so to a limited degree. The inability of the bovine type to grow in the chicken, partly due to the high normal temperature, is an example. Second, in some animals the organisms grow but do not produce serious injury to the tissues. This has been found true of the growth of the human type of tubercle bacilli in the rat. Ordinarily, this animal is considered to be resistant to tuberculosis, yet the symbiotic relationship of bacillus and animals is now recognized. Third, in most susceptible species there is evidence of natural resistance to the disease, manifested by the ability of the natural body defense mechanism to phagocytize the bacilli and to encapsulate and calcify the lesion they may have produced. However, it is not possible to eliminate the probability that resistance can be acquired during the active phases of the infection. This may be partly responsible for the fact that progressive tuberculosis does not develop in every animal infected with the disease.

***Koch's Phenomenon.*** In a normal guinea pig the injection of living bacilli produces typical lesions of tuberculosis throughout the lymph system as well as in the lungs, liver, and spleen. In contrast, injection of tubercle bacilli into a tuberculous guinea pig causes marked necrosis and sloughing of the tissue at the point of injection without any generalization or localization of the baçilli in the regional lymph nodes. Koch found that this reaction was also produced by the injection of dead tubercle bacilli; he subsequently demonstrated a similar but less severe type of reaction to protein extracts of the microorganism. Koch's phenomenon revealed two things: first, that some degree of resistance to a second inoculation may be produced in the guinea pig by an active infection; second, that a hypersensitivity to the bacteria, or to the products of the bacteria, is produced in an infected animal. This last reaction, commonly known as a *tuberculin reaction,* is known to be an allergic phenomenon and is of value in the diagnosis of the disease.

***Acquired Resistance.*** The progressive nature of tuberculosis in animals and man indicates that immunity is not produced by the infection in quite the same degree as is observed in other diseases. But, as emphasized by Rich, a total acquired resistance is rarely developed in any disease, and there is evidence that significant resistance is developed in tuberculosis. The recovery of people who have had small pulmonary lesions, found in later life by the X-ray examination, is considered to be due, at least partially, to acquired resistance.

Since the initial publications of Robert Koch, many attempts have been made to develop an immunizing agent which would be of value as a prophylactic in tuberculosis. In fact, Koch was searching for an immunizing agent when he discovered the effects produced by tuberculin. Numerous types of immunizing products have been used against tuberculosis, but it is not feasible to discuss them all here. The reader is referred to the book by Calmette for a list of such agents.

One product which has been prepared for artificial immunization is known as BCG (Bacille Calmette-Guerin); Calmette and Guerin were two French scientists who prepared the vaccine. This vaccine is composed of living microorganisms of a bovine strain which was attenuated by growth in potato-glycerin bile medium for several hundred transfers. It is claimed that it is without harmful effect in calves and children and that it produces an increased resistance to tuberculosis. While BCG may be an aid in preventing tuberculosis in parts of the world where the disease is quite prevalent in human and bovine populations, it has never found favor in the United States.

The experimental results of Watson and of Cotton and Crawford in cattle indicated that BCG should not be used as a means of controlling bovine tuberculosis in America. The detection of infected animals by the tuberculin test and the slaughter of reactors is the most satisfactory method. In a review of methods for controlling bovine tuberculosis, Ritchie concluded that vaccination can play no useful part in plans for eradicating the disease.

Mention should be made of the most recent immunizing agent advocated for tuberculosis. The vole bacillus, *Myco. muris,* described by Wells in 1937, has been shown to produce resistance in guinea pigs against virulent human and bovine strains of tubercle bacilli.

**Diagnosis.** The diagnostic method employed for tuberculosis varies. In the packing plant the veterinarian engaged in postmortem inspection of cattle, swine, and poultry detects the disease by the gross appearance of the lesions; in the laboratory direct smears, cultures, and animal inoculations are used; in the field the presence of the disease in the living animal is diagnosed by the tuberculin test, or in chickens by an agglutination test. Each of these methods will be discussed.

The unit lesion in tuberculosis is known as a *tubercle,* which in its beginning is microscopic in size. The newly developing lesion is composed of tubercle bacilli intermingled with epithelioid cells. Many bacilli may be phagocytized by the epithelioid cells. As the lesion develops, necrosis of the initial concentration of epithelioid cells occurs and giant cells appear around the area of necrosis. In the next stage the area of necrosis and the giant cell zone are surrounded by a loosely arranged zone of lymphocytes, monocytes, and fibrocytes which are supported in a newly formed reticulum of connective tissue. As the central necrotic process continues, this primary tubercle becomes larger, newly developed tubercles form in the adjacent tissue, and ultimately the tubercle attains macroscopic size. The macroscopic lesion of tuberculosis may be caseous or calcified. In some instances liquefaction necrosis results in the production of large cavities, particularly in the lungs. In numerous cases healed lesions of long duration are evident by the presence of nodules composed of compact fibrous tissue and calcification.

With certain anatomic modifications, the development of the tubercle in the avian species is the same as in mammals. The primary lesions are usually confined to the wall of the intestine, whence the organism is spread to other parts of the body and may form massive lesions in the liver, spleen, bone marrow, and lungs, but not in the muscles. Lesions do not become calcified. However, lesions of tuberculosis in mammals, caused by the avian type of tubercle bacilli, may become calcified.

In mammals, primary tuberculosis is confined usually to the lymph system and the lungs. The escape of tubercle bacilli from a lesion via the blood or lymph stream enables them to reach the general circulation and results in widely disseminated tuberculosis, with the formation of lesions in various parts of the body. In mammals, lesions of tuberculosis are rarely found in muscle and brain or in the thymus, thyroid, pancreas, or salivary glands. The presence of tubercles on serous membranes of the thoracic and peritoneal cavities gave rise to the name *pearly disease,* because of the resemblance of the nodular lesions to pearls. In some cases of generalized tuberculosis the lesions are small and evenly distributed; they resemble millet seeds, hence the term *miliary* tuberculosis.

While the presence of the previously described lesions are most suggestive of tuberculosis, other infectious agents produce caseation and calcification. Unrefuted diagnosis of tuberculosis is accomplished only by the detection of tubercle bacilli. In the laboratory this is accomplished by three procedures. *First,* smears of suspected tissue are stained with the Ziehl-Neelsen stain and examined for acid-fast bacilli. In some preparations organisms are few, so that prolonged examination is often necessary. It may be necessary to treat the material with sodium hydroxide and centrifuge it in order to concentrate the bacilli before smears are made. The finding of acid-fast bacteria, although highly suggestive, is not absolutely diagnostic, because other mycobacteria may resemble tubercle bacilli microscopically. *Second,* suitable media are inoculated in order to obtain a culture of the microorganism. The material to be cultured is usually treated with 3 per cent sodium hydroxide, 5 per cent oxalic acid, or 10 per cent trisodium phosphate solutions in order to kill other types of bacteria present. Cultures should be incubated at least 8 weeks. *Third,* guinea pigs are injected subcutaneously, and suspected material is treated as described above. Those guinea pigs that are living at the end of 8 weeks are killed, but this period may be shortened if the animal is given Old Tuberculin (0.5 ml.) intramuscularly at the end of the fourth week; tuberculous guinea pigs given this amount of tuberculin will die in 12 to 18 hours and may then be examined for tuberculous lesions.

If avian tuberculosis is suspected, chickens or rabbits are used as the test animal.

***The Tuberculin Test.*** In the field, the diagnosis of tuberculosis is confined to the use of tuberculin. The value of tuberculin as a diagnostic agent has been proved by the successful eradication of tuberculosis from most of the cattle herds of the United States. The percentage of tuberculin reactors in cattle was 4.9 in 1918; in 1965 the percentage of reactors was 0.08.

Tuberculin as originally prepared by

Koch is an extract of the soluble bacterial products of the bacilli which have been grown in glycerinated veal broth. After being allowed to grow for 8 weeks, the bacilli are killed by streaming steam, they are removed from the broth by filtration, and the filtrate is evaporated to one tenth its original volume. This represents Koch's Old Tuberculin, commonly called K.O.T. In order to produce tuberculin that is free from the proteins of the medium, a synthetic medium (see chapter on Bacteriological Techniques and Methods) was adopted in 1934 as the official medium for tuberculin manufacture. This is recognized as the official United States Department of Agriculture method of preparing intradermal tuberculin. Three strains of human type tubercle bacilli are used. In brief the procedure is described below:

1. The inoculated medium is incubated for 8 weeks.
2. The cultures are heated in steam for 3 hours, cooled, and filtered through fine-mesh copper gauze.
3. Glycerin is added to the filtrate, 1.2 ml. for each 100 ml. of original culture medium, and the mixture is evaporated to one fifth the original volume.
4. Phenol, 0.5 per cent, is added as a preservative.
5. The tuberculin is centrifuged until perfectly clear and then filtered through a Mandler filter.
6. The finished product is tested for sterility, samples are centrifuged, and the sediment is examined for the presence of dead tubercle bacilli. If any are found, the tuberculin is refiltered.
7. The tuberculin is dispensed in 10-ml. vials and is ready to be used for intradermal testing.

Three different tuberculin tests can be used in the diagnosis of bovine tuberculosis: the *subcutaneous*, the *intradermal*, and the *ophthalmic*.

In the *subcutaneous* test (also known as the thermal or temperature test), which is of historical importance only, a dose of 2 ml. of Koch's Old Tuberculin is injected subcutaneously. Previous to the injection, however, the temperature of the animal is taken three times at 2-hour intervals. If the temperature of the animal is normal, the tuberculin is injected. Eight hours after the injection, temperatures are again taken at 2-hour intervals through the eighteenth hour after injection. A positive reaction is noted by an increase in temperature of at least 2°F. during the interval between the eighth and eighteenth hours after injection.

In the *intradermal* test, at least 0.1 ml. and not more than 0.2 ml. of tuberculin is injected into the dermal layer of the skin of the animal. In cattle the thin skin of the caudal fold or of the vulva is used. The skin of the cervical area has been found to give a more pronounced reaction but is not used in routine testing, except in a recheck of suspected reactors. A positive reaction is apparent by a small to large firm swelling at the point of injection within 72 hours. In the tuberculin test of chickens, avian tuberculin is injected into the wattle. A positive reaction is noted by the swelling of the wattle within 48 hours. In swine, tuberculin is injected intradermally in the skin of the ear or of the vulva.

In the *ophthalmic* test, tuberculin is inserted into the conjuctival sac with a soft camel's-hair brush or with a medicine dropper. The concentrated tuberculin may be mixed with a suitable substance, such as lactose, and molded into a small disk which dissolves readily in the eye. These ophthalmic-tuberculin disks are commonly used for the eye test. In the ophthalmic test, two applications of tuberculin are required. The first application is for the purpose of sensitization, for it has been shown that a more marked reaction is obtained by this procedure. The second application is given 2 or 3 days later for the purpose of diagnosis. The animal is kept under close observation for 8 hours after the instillation of the diagnostic dose. A positive reaction is characterized by marked inflammation of the conjunctiva, profuse lacrimation, and a mucopurulent exudate.

It is apparent that the intradermal

tuberculin test is the most economical and practical for routine diagnosis. The other two tests are seldom used except in cases of doubtful reactions to the intradermal test.

Old Tuberculin (OT) is merely the concentrated medium in which tubercle bacilli have been grown. A so-called Purified Protein Derivative (PPD) is used for testing in man, and in some countries in domestic animals. PPD is prepared by precipitating the protein from the culture medium by trichloroacetic acid or by ammonium sulfate. The precipitate can be weighed, and measured amounts can be given. In Great Britain, cattle are tested by the intradermal injection of 0.2 mg. of PPD in 0.1 ml. of solution. In the United States, almost all tests in man are done with PPD, and 0.00002 mg., or one Tuberculin Unit (TU), is used as the first test. In some patients a second test is done in doubtful cases, for which 0.005 mg., or 250 TU, is used. For diagnostic purposes there seems to be no significant difference between OT and PPD.

***Serologic Tests.*** The preparation of a suitable suspension of mammalian tubercle bacilli is difficult, and this prevents the use of the agglutination test as a method of diagnosing tuberculosis in animals. Experimentally it has been shown that collodion particles and erythrocytes may be coated with tuberculin; this procedure prepares an antigen suitable for agglutination purposes. Such a diagnostic test has not come into practical use because of low sensitivity and also because of cross reactions with other mycobacteria, particularly *Myco. paratuberculosis.*

*Myco. avium* is readily miscible in salt solution, so that a stable suspension can be made for a rapid agglutination test. In 1950 Karlson, Zinober, and Feldman explored this test and demonstrated that a whole-blood, rapid agglutination test has real merits as a diagnostic test for avian tuberculosis.

Complement-fixation tests for tuberculosis have been studied for many years, but none has been sensitive enough for diagnosis. Vardaman and Larsen (1964) found that of 28 tuberculosis-free herds only 2 contained animals with a significant titer of complement-fixing antibodies; in contrast, of 15 infected herds, all but 1 had animals with significant titers. They concluded that the test would be of no value in detecting individual tuberculous cattle but that it could be used to detect infected herds.

The most recent serologic test is the gel-diffusion test proposed by Parlett and Youmans. The antigen is a concentration of liquid culture of *Myco. tuberculosis* which is incorporated in agar gel. Serum to be tested is overlaid on a column of the agar; a positive test is indicated by the development of precipitate rings. Application of the gel-diffusion precipitin test to diagnosis of tuberculosis in domestic animals must await further research on preparation of antigens and on field tests to demonstrate reliability.

### *Mycobacterium paratuberculosis*

**Synonyms and History.**[2] Johne's bacillus. *Bacillus paratuberculosis.*

During the study of chronic dysentery of cattle in Germany, Johne and Frothingham, in 1895, demonstrated the presence of masses of acid-fast bacteria in the infected intestine. They considered that these organisms were either avian tubercle bacilli or bovine tubercle bacilli which had become changed in some way so that infection in the intestinal tract was produced. However, in 1906 Bang, of Denmark, recognized the disease as an infection distinct from tuberculosis, and he suggested the name paratuberculosis. The disease then came to the attention of investigators in England, and in 1907 McFadyean described it in some detail. The organism was first isolated in pure culture by Twort in 1910 by the use of medium containing dead tubercle bacilli.

Although primarily a bovine disease, paratuberculosis is also found in sheep,

[2] A brief history and many references to the literature may be found in the report by Doyle.

goats, deer, and camels. Eveleth and Gifford have reported in their study of Johne's disease in Arkansas that clinical cases of the infection were found only in cattle and sheep but that swine, goats, horses, and mules may be sensitive to the intradermal johnin test.

It will be noted in this discussion that three names are used interchangeably: chronic bacillary dysentery, paratuberculosis, and Johne's disease. The latter is more commonly used.

**Distribution and Transmission.** *Myco. paratuberculosis* has been reported from most of the countries on the European continent and from the British Isles and neighboring islands. It is found in the United States, but the extent is not known. The disease does not spread rapidly through a herd; only a few animals show symptoms at a time. Calves may become infected but do not show symptoms until they become adults. This chronic nature of the disease is a most outstanding characteristic, and for this reason the infection is known to persist in a herd for years. Because of this, many cases probably pass unrecognized.

Johne's disease is characterized by a persistent diarrhea which may extend over a period of a year. The animal becomes progressively thin and emaciated. Lesions of the infection are confined to the ileum and the colon, and in some cases extend posteriorly as far as the rectum. The intestinal mucous membrane is hyperemic and is so greatly thickened that it presents a corrugated appearance. The mesenteric lymph nodes are usually swollen and edematous. The organisms are present in the mucous membrane, and large numbers of them pass out with fecal material and thereby contaminate feed and water.

**Morphology and Staining.** *Myco. paratuberculosis* is a short, thick rod, 0.5$\mu$ in diameter and 1$\mu$ to 2$\mu$ in length. In smears made from an infected intestinal mucous membrane, the organism is found in clumps, although numerous single cells are scattered over the preparation (Fig. 33.6). The bacillus is comparable in size to the avian tubercle bacillus. It is stained with the usual acid-fast stains. Most of the cells are stained evenly, but an occasional beaded form may be seen. The microorganism is considered gram-positive.

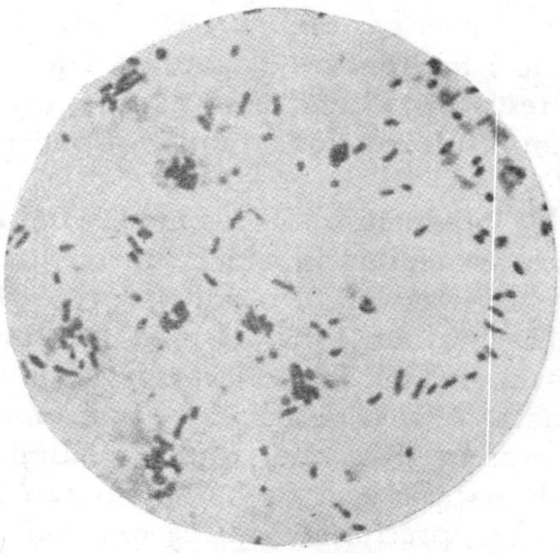

FIG. 33.6 – **Mycobacterium paratuberculosis** smear of mucous membrane, ×2,000. (From Nowak: Documenta Microbiologica, courtesy Gustav Fischer.)

**Growth Requirements and Characteristics.** This bacillus is aerobic and grows at a temperature of 37°C. It has a rather wide growth-temperature range, however, since it will grow in temperatures as low as 28°C. and as high as 43°C.

An outstanding characteristic of *Myco. paratuberculosis* is the difficulty with which it is cultivated on artificial media. Twort obtained growth only after he incorporated dead tubercle bacilli in his culture medium. Subsequently, it was found that tuberculin supplied the essential growth factors and later that the extracts of saprophytic acid-fast bacteria were satisfactory. Snow has given the name "mycobactin P" to the growth factor formed by *Myco. phlei*. Merkal and associates (1964) recommended egg-yolk agar containing glycerin extracts of *Myco. phlei* for isolation of *Myco. paratuberculosis*.

On a suitable egg medium containing extracts of mycobacteria, the organism produces tiny dull-white colonies which are rarely visible in 4 weeks. As the culture ages, the colonies increase in size, form a central elevation, and become yellowish white.

In glycerin broth containing extracts of *Myco. phlei* or other mycobacteria, the bacillus forms a thin pellicle which becomes thick and folded as the culture ages.

**Resistance.** *Myco. paratuberculosis* resembles the tubercle bacillus in resistance to heat and chemical disinfectants. Vardaman reports that cresylic compounds in 1:64 dilution, phenol 1:40, sodium ortho-phenylphenate 1:100, alcohol 95 per cent, mercury bichloride 1:1,000, calcium hypochlorite 1:50, and methylene blue 1:500 prevent growth after 15 minutes exposure. Lovell, Levi, and Francis have found this bacillus viable after 9 months exposure in tap water-mud suspension, after 163 days in ditch water in open air, and after 152 to 246 days in feces.

In a study of the survival time of the organism under various exposures, Larsen and associates (1956) found the following: In a mixture of bovine urine and feces, survival time was less than 30 days; in bovine urine, less than 30 days; in tap water or saline, 17 to 19 months; in tap water at pH 5 or 8.5 or containing 1 per cent gelatin, 14 to 17 months; in a desiccator over sulfuric acid, 47 months. The microorganism survived for 12 months when stored at —14°C., for 5 months at 4°C., and for 8 months at 38°C. When placed on filter paper and exposed to sunlight through cellophane, the microorganism was viable after 65 hours but not after 100 hours of exposure.

**Biochemical Properties.** The difficulty with which this organism is cultured artificially has retarded investigation concerning its biochemical properties. Presumably it is similar to the other acid-fast bacteria in not being able to produce changes in the various substances that are used in the study of bacteria.

**Antigenic Structure and Toxins.** Little is known concerning the antigenic structure of this organism. Positive reactions are obtained by the use of avian tuberculin in a large percentage of the cases of Johne's disease. This indicates an antigenic relationship with the avian tubercle bacillus. Some cases will also react to mammalian tuberculin. The effect of Johne's disease on the routine test for bovine tuberculosis is discussed by Karlson (1962).

Toxins are not produced by this organism.

**Pathogenicity.** *Myco. paratuberculosis* produces chronic bacillary dysentery in cattle and to some extent in sheep, goats, and other ruminants. The disease can be produced artificially in the cow by injecting the organism intravenously, subcutaneously, or intraperitoneally.

Mohler has observed that guinea pigs, rabbits, mice, rats, chickens, and pigeons could be infected with the organism when it was thoroughly suspended in paraffin oil. For further information, including a review of the literature on experimental infections with *Myco. paratuberculosis,* the paper by Harding should be consulted. He found that in mice the most common site of infection was the liver but that in rabbits the pulmonary lesions were most marked. Lesions resembling the natural infection in ruminants were seen in only one mouse.

**Immunity.** The chronic nature of paratuberculosis indicates that any immunity that is formed by the disease is not significant. Very few animals ever recover from the infection; however, some reports of apparent recovery have been made.

Artificial immunizing agents for this disease are not in common use. French investigators have reported that some resistance was produced in cattle following the injection of organisms suspended in pumice and oil. Sigurdsson (1960) found that a vaccine composed of killed bacteria suspended in light mineral oil gave excellent protection against the disease in sheep. Vaccination against Johne's disease may interfere with the tuberculin test in cattle because of cross-sensitivity reactions, but for sheep this is not important. Larsen (1965) has reported that vaccination against Johne's disease in sheep has definite value, and he recommends its use in sheep when this disease is a problem.

**Diagnosis.** Paratuberculosis can be diagnosed by making smears from the intestinal mucosa. In the live animal a positive diagnosis may be obtained by pinching out a small piece of the rectum, washing the piece thoroughly with sterile saline solution, and then mashing it thoroughly between two slides. The smears thus made are stained with an acid-fast stain. This method is dependable only in cases in which lesions are present in the rectum. A possible source of error is the presence of saprophytic acid-fast bacilli in the feces.

Previous mention has been made of the positive reaction which may be obtained in response to the injection of avian tuberculin. In the use of tuberculin for this disease, intravenous injection is made, and a positive reaction is indicated by restlessness, shivering, diarrhea, and pyrexia. The temperature usually reaches its peak 4 to 8 hours after the injection of the tuberculin.

An extract of the bacillus called "johnin" was produced in England and has been used to a limited extent in the United States as an intravenous temperature test; the same technique is employed as was used with avian tuberculin. A more specific intradermal johnin, purified protein derivative (PPD), has been prepared by Larsen, Baisden, and Merkal by the precipitation of *Myco. paratuberculosis* culture filtrate with trichloroacetic acid.

Johnson observed that the skin of the neck region was more sensitive to johnin than the caudal fold. This fact has been confirmed by numerous investigators; consequently, the intradermal test is applied in that region. Larsen (1965) has found that some infected cattle fail to react to johnin and that responses to the test may vary.

In applying the test, 0.2 ml. of intradermal johnin is injected into the skin of a clipped area on the neck. After 48 hours the test is read. A positive reaction consists of an increase in skin thickness of 3 mm. or more greater than the original thickness; an increase of 3 to 2 mm. is considered suspicious; and less than 2 mm. is negative. An injection of johnin desensitizes the skin at that site so that subsequent tests must be applied at other sites.

Sigurdsson (1956) has described an antigen prepared from the intestinal wall of sheep infected with Johne's disease. By using this antigen in the complement-fixation test, they found it of value in diagnosing the disease in sheep. According to Larsen (1965), for cattle, the complement-fixation test is not of great value in the control of Johne's disease.

Important discussions on the diagnosis, prevention, and control of Johne's disease are given in the report of the Seminar by the European Productive Agency.

### *Mycobacterium leprae*

*Myco. leprae* is considered to be the cause of leprosy, one of the diseases mentioned in the earliest history of mankind. Leprosy is a generalized disease of man which affects principally the skin and peripheral nerve trunks. It is an exceedingly chronic disease, having an incubation period as long as 20 years. As far as is known, it is transmitted only by close contact. However, with due caution physicians and nurses work among leprous patients for years without contracting the infection. The disease is still quite prevalent throughout the world. This infection is found in the United States, where it is most prevalent in the Gulf states and California.

*Myco. leprae* was first observed by G. A. Hansen in 1874 in Norway. The infection is sometimes called Hansen's disease. The acid-fast staining characteristic of the organism was not discovered, however, until after Koch had published his work on the tubercle bacillus. *Myco. leprae* is a small, slender microorganism $0.3\mu$ to $0.5\mu$ thick and $1\mu$ to $7\mu$ long. It is often curved, and many cells present a beaded appearance. The bacteria occur in clumps and packets in the infected tissue in lepromatous leprosy but are hard to find in the tuberculoid type. There is considerable doubt whether or not the leprosy bacillus has even been successfully cultivated on artificial media. Although acid-fast bacilli have been cultured from leprosy lesions, such cultures are probably saprophytes from the skin. Many attempts have been made to transmit *Myco. leprae* to animals, but without success. Recently, however, Shepard reported that the microorganism will multiply when lepromatous material is injected in the foot-pads of mice.

Leprosy is commonly diagnosed by the symptoms and lesions found in the patient. Of much importance in establishing the diagnosis is the demonstration of acid-fast bacilli in tissue scrapings from the lobes of the ears or the alae nasi. Less dependable is the finding of acid-fast bacilli in smears from the nasal mucosa. Allergy tests have been extensively investigated, but at present none is specific for the disease. The complement-fixation test is also used, but this, too, is not considered specific enough for accurate diagnosis.

During recent years 4,4′-diaminodiphenylsulfone and certain derivatives of this compound have been found to be quite effective against leprosy, and their use is gradually being extended throughout the areas of the world where leprosy exists. The disease is best controlled by the separation of children from leprous parents and by the isolation of patients in leprosy colonies where modern treatment is often followed by marked resolution of the visible lesions. The comprehensive text on leprosy by Cochrane and Davey may be consulted for additional information.

### *Mycobacterium lepraemurium*

In 1901 W. K. Stefansky, while examining wild rats for plague in Odessa, observed a disease which showed many lesions similar to human leprosy and which was caused by an acid-fast bacillus. The disease has been found in rats in London, Berlin, Japan, and in New South Wales. In the United States the disease has been reported from San Francisco. Rat leprosy is characterized by swelling of lymph nodes, subcutaneous swelling, and induration with ulceration, by falling of the hair, and by emaciation during the later stages of the disease. The condition is exceedingly chronic, extending as long as one year in some cases. Upon postmortem examination the swollen lymph nodes are not suppurative. Increased numbers of epithelioid cells are present, among which the bacilli are found in large numbers. Subcutaneous swellings are similar to adipose tissue in appearance, but are also composed of epithelioid cells, among which the bacilli are found. Nodules may be found in the liver and lungs.

The rat leprosy bacillus, to which the name *Myco. lepraemurium* has been given, is 3$\mu$ to 5$\mu$ long and is slender and curved. It is gram-positive and decidedly acid-fast. Numerous beaded or granular cells are observed in a tissue smear. The microorganism has not been cultivated artificially on nonliving media, but it will multiply in tissue cultures of rat and mouse cells (Garbutt and associates).

This disease has no etiologic relationship with human leprosy.

### *Mycobacterium microti*

In 1937 Wells reported the presence of lesions resembling those of tuberculosis in the vole, in England. An acid-fast bacillus was isolated from such lesions, and the common name "the vole bacillus" was given to it. In an extensive report on the murine type of tubercle bacillus in 1946 Wells pointed out the specific nature of the organism, and he left no doubt that a new organism had been discovered. The disease was identified in more than 900 small animals in four different species—the wild vole *(Microtus agrestis),* the bank vole *(Clethrionomys glareolus),* the wood mouse *(Apodemus sylvaticus),* and the shrew *(Sorex araneus).*

*Myco. microti* in infected lesions is an extremely pleomorphic rod ranging from 1$\mu$ to 5$\mu$ in length and 0.5$\mu$ to 0.6$\mu$ in width. No branching forms have been described.

On culture media the organism is less pleomorphic and is shorter and thicker. It is nonmotile, noncapsulated, and nonsporeforming. This bacillus is markedly acid-fast; it resists decolorization in 25 per cent sulfuric acid for 24 hours. The typical beading of tubercle bacilli is observed in the vole bacillus in smears made from natural lesions and from artificial cultures.

Growth of *Myco. microti* is obtained on the types of media used for the cultivation of bovine tubercle bacilli. Glycerin, 5 per cent or more, inhibits growth of the organism, so that it resembles the bovine type of the tubercle bacillus in that respect. The microorganism is difficult to grow on fluid media, where it forms a thin, unpigmented pellicle. Two types of colonies are formed on solid media. One is a round, smooth, white colony with an entire edge which becomes wartlike and a crateriform center. The other is irregular in shape and has a fluted edge. This bacillus is killed by 60°C. in 20 minutes, by 0.5 per cent phenol in 24 hours, and by 5 per cent acetic acid. It is resistant to 6 per cent sulfuric acid, 5 per cent oxalic acid, and 3 per cent sodium hydroxide.

The appearance of the natural disease is typical of tuberculosis—it shows the presence of epithelioid cells, giant cells, caseation necrosis, and calcification. Most of the lesions observed in captured animals are confined to the lymph nodes, but the skin and subcutaneous tissue, lungs, spleen, liver, suprarenals, and kidneys are also affected. Artificial infection may be produced in the white mouse, white rat, golden hamster, and in certain wild rodents.

It is not possible to separate the vole bacillus from the human and bovine types of tubercle bacilli by serologic tests. Animals infected with the vole bacillus show a sensitivity to human and bovine tuberculin. Conversely, animals infected with the human or bovine tubercle bacillus are sensitive to tuberculin prepared from the vole bacillus. No significant antigenic relationships exist between this organism and the avian tubercle bacillus.

Previous mention has been made of the use of the vole bacillus as an immunizing agent against tuberculosis in guinea pigs, cattle, and man. There is evidence that the vole bacillus produces resistance to tuberculosis in man. It has also been shown that in the early stages of virulent infection in guinea pigs, vaccination with the vole bacillus leads to a greater retardation of the disease than does BCG; in the later stages the degree of resistance is approximately equal. In cattle, the vole bacillus may confer more resistance than BCG (Wells and Wylie).

### *Mycobacterium fortuitum*

This is a rapidly growing acid-fast microorganism that is commonly present in soil and water. It grows well on ordinary media at 37°C. and forms large, rough, colorless colonies in several days. On liquid medium a rough, crumbly pellicle is formed in 1 to 3 days. The cells are rod-shaped, and they vary in length from 2$\mu$ to 5$\mu$. *Myco. fortuitum* may be distinguished from other rapidly growing mycobacteria by its ability to split phenolphthalein sulfate in 72 hours or less (Wayne).

Various rapidly growing mycobacteria have been isolated from disease processes in man and animals and given separate names, but Gordon and Smith found that many such strains were actually *Myco. fortuitum*. Experimental infections in mice may be produced by intravenous inoculation, which causes death in 10 to 21 days with involvement of the kidneys.

*Myco. fortuitum* has been recovered from cases of mastitis in cattle. Peterson described an epizootic of such infection in a herd of 260 animals in which the disease was spread by unsanitary teat tubes. There were several deaths and 38 cows were slaughtered; the mastitis continued to spread and the entire herd was eventually disposed of.

### Other Acid-Fast Bacilli

In addition to the few mycobacterial diseases mentioned in this chapter, there are others found in animals and in man.

Their importance is not known, and few complete bacteriologic studies have been done on the acid-fast bacteria involved. Some have not been cultured on artificial media. Leprosy-like diseases have been seen in such a variety of animals as water buffalo, frogs, wood pigeons, and a parrot.

So-called "skin tuberculosis" in cattle is a granulomatous lesion of the subcutaneous tissue which occurs usually on the lower part of the legs. Acid-fast bacilli may be seen in smears of a high percentage of such lesions, but not in all. Attempts to culture and characterize the acid-fast bacilli have failed. These lesions have been implicated as the cause of nonspecific tuberculin reactions in cattle, but the relationship is not understood (Karlson, 1962).

In man the so-called "swimming pool granuloma" has been seen which involves the arms and legs. The acid-fast organism isolated from such lesions was originally called *Myco. balnei,* but it has been shown to be *Myco. marinum,* the water mycobacterium previously known to cause disease in fish (Clark and Shepard).

A saprophytic acid-fast bacillus of this group is an organism described by Karlson and Feldman in 1940. This bacillus was consistently isolated from swine tonsillar tissue. It resembles the avian bacillus in morphology and in many culture characteristics. Moreover, it sensitizes guinea pigs to avian tuberculin and gives a positive cross-agglutination reaction with avian tubercle bacilli. The bacillus is not pathogenic to chickens, mice, or calves, and it produces only a localized focal necrosis when guinea pigs and rabbits are inoculated subcutaneously. Its relationship to swine infection is not known.

In 1948 a mycobacterium previously unrecorded was found by MacCallum and associates in ulcerated lesions of the skin in human beings in a rural area of Australia. The organism was strongly acid-fast, and the optimal temperature for artificial growth was 33°C. It has been named *Myco. ulcerans.* In addition to man this bacillus was found to be pathogenic for rats and mice but not for guinea pigs. The nutritive requirements were comparable to those necessary for growing tubercle bacilli.

A mycobacterial disease in salmonoid fish has been reported by Parisot and Wood. This condition has been found to be more prevalent than expected. The infection may result in death of the fish, or debilitate them and thereby make them easier to catch by fishermen and also by predators. Sexual underdevelopment is also observed in the infected fish. In comparing the staining characteristics of the microorganisms and the microscopic lesions with those in human tuberculosis and leprosy, they suggested that the condition be referred to as fish mycobacteriosis rather than fish tuberculosis.

The list of other acid-fast organisms to be found in the literature is too great to be given here. Even snails have a mycobacterial disease! Further information on these various mycobacteria from animals may be found in the paper by Feldman (1964).

Many unnamed and unclassified mycobacteria have been isolated from diseased animals and man as well as from apparently healthy individuals. These mycobacteria are sometimes designated as "unclassified," or as "anonymous" mycobacteria. The term "atypical" mycobacteria is sometimes used, but this term is not appropriate. A convenient method of grouping these anonymous mycobacteria was devised by Runyon, based on chromogenicity and rate of growth, as follows:

Group I. Photochromogen. Slowly growing, requiring 2 to 4 weeks of incubation; colonies become yellow when exposed to light; also called "yellow bacillus" or *Myco. kansasii.*

Group II. Skotochromogen. Slowly growing, requiring 2 to 4 weeks of incubation; colonies are yellow or orange when grown in darkness as well as when exposed to light.

Group III. Nonphotochromogenic. Slowly growing, requiring 2 to 4 weeks of incubation. Colonies are colorless to light buff or, in older cultures, slightly yellow. The pigment, if any, is not affected by exposure to light; also called "Battey bacilli" after Battey General Hospital, Rome, Georgia, where many cases of infection with this organism have been studied.

Group IV. Rapid growers. Growth is evident in 1 to 4 days; colonies are colorless or pigmented.

The mycobacteria in Groups I and III are implicated as the cause of a granulomatous disease in man which may be undistinguishable from tuberculosis by roentgenogram or by histologic examination. Persons infected with these organisms may react to the Mantoux test, especially with 250 TU doses of tuberculin. The Group II organisms are generally considered to be nonpathogenic, although there are some reports of their being found in tuberculosis-like lesions, especially in cervical adenitis of children. For additional information and references to the literature on these groups of mycobacteria, the reader is referred to the reviews by Chapman and by Brown.

It is of utmost importance that the anonymous mycobacteria be differentiated from tubercle bacilli. Disease due to the anonymous organisms is not known to be transmissible, whereas tuberculosis is a contagious disease. The public health laws relating to tuberculosis do not apply to infections with anonymous mycobacteria. In addition, it is important to make a bacteriologic differentiation, because the usual antituberculosis agents are often not effective against the anonymous mycobacteria.

It is necessary that research be encouraged in order to determine what role these anonymous or any other mycobacteria may play in sensitizing cattle and other animals to tuberculin. It is appealing to assert that the so-called "nonspecific" reaction in cattle is due to mycobacteria other than tubercle bacilli, but the data available do not permit more than conjecture on this point.

It becomes more and more evident that the mycobacteria represent a most extensive group of bacteria affecting mammals, birds, fish, and reptiles and that many years of research must be spent on this very interesting group.

## REFERENCES

Baisden, L. A., *et al.* Comparison of the Potencies and Specificities of Human and Bovine Tuberculins. Jour Amer. Vet. Med. Assn. 13:338, 1952.

Baum, G. L. Textbook of Pulmonary Diseases. Little, Brown and Co., Boston, 1965.

Bönicke, R. Differentiation of Mycobacteria by Biochemical Methods. Bull. Intl. Union Against Tuberc. 32: 13, 1962.

Brieger, E. M., and Fell, H. B. Warm-Stage Observations on the Initial Development of the Avian Tubercle Bacillus Cultivated in Embryo Extract. Jour. Hyg. 44:158, 1945.

Brown, R. C. Atypical Mycobacteria and Human Disease—A Review. Intl. Path. 6:86, 1965.

Calmette, Albert. Tubercle Bacillus Infection and Tuberculosis in Man and Animals. Williams & Wilkins Co., Baltimore, 1923.

Chapman, J. S. The Present Status of the Unclassified Mycobacteria. (Editorial.) Amer. Jour. Med. 33:471, 1962.

Clark, H. F., and Shepard, C. C. Effect of Environmental Temperatures on Infection With *Mycobacterium marinum* (Balnei) of Mice and a Number of Poikilothermic Species. Jour. Bact. 86:1057, 1963.

Cochrane, R. G., and Davey, T. F. Leprosy in Theory and Practice. 2nd Ed. Williams & Wilkins Co., Baltimore, 1964.

Cotton, W. E., and Crawford, A. B. Second Report on the Calmette-Guerin Method of Vaccinating Animals Against Tuberculosis. Jour. Amer. Vet. Med. Assn. 80:18, 1932.

Darzins, Egons. The Bacteriology of Tuberculosis. Univ. of Minn. Press, Minneapolis, 1958.

Doyle, T. M Johne's Disease. *In* Stableforth, A. W., and Galloway, I. A., Infectious Diseases of Animals: Diseases Due to Bacteria. Vol. I, pp. 319–45. Academic Press, Inc., New York, 1959.

Drea, W. F., and Andrejew, Anatole. The Metabolism of the Tubercle Bacillus. Charles C Thomas, Springfield, Ill., 1953.

EDITORIAL. Isonicotinic Acid Hydrazide. Lancet 1:702, 1952.

ELLIS, E. M., and YODER, W. D. Distribution and Significance of the Mycobacteria Isolated From Cattle and Swine in the United States. (Abst.) Amer. Rev. Resp. Dis. 90:294, 1964.

EUROPEAN PRODUCTIVITY AGENCY, PROJECT NO. 207. Control of Johne's Disease in Cattle, Sheep and Goats. The Organization for European Economic Co-operation, Paris, 1956.

EVELETH, D. F., and GIFFORD, REBECCA. Johne's Disease in Farm Animals. Jour. Amer. Vet. Med. Assn. 102: 27, 1943.

FELDMAN, W. H. Avian Tuberculosis Infections. Williams & Wilkins Co., Baltimore, 1938.

———. Avian Tubercle Bacilli and Other Mycobacteria: Their Significance in the Eradication of Bovine Tuberculosis. Amer. Rev. Resp. Dis. 81:666, 1960.

———. Tuberculosis. *In* Hull, T. G., Diseases Transmitted From Animals to Man. 5th Ed. Pp. 5–81. Charles C Thomas, Springfield, Ill., 1963.

———, and KARLSON, A. G. The Importance of the Isolation and Identification of Tubercle Bacilli. Journal-Lancet 67:239, 1947.

FRANCIS, JOHN. Tuberculosis in Animals and Man: A Study in Comparative Pathology. Cassell and Co., Ltd., London, 1958.

GARBUTT, ELIZABETH W., *et al.* Growth of *Mycobacterium lepraemurium* Maintained in Cultures of Rat Fibroblasts. Jour. Gen. Microbiol. 27:259, 1962.

GORDON, RUTH E., and SMITH, MILDRED M. Rapidly Growing, Acid-Fast Bacteria. II. Species' Description of *Mycobacterium fortuitum* Cruz. Jour. Bact. 69:502, 1955.

HALL, R. E., and WINKEL, F. Avian Tuberculosis in Mink—A Case Report. Jour. Amer. Vet. Med. Assn. 131:49, 1957.

HARDING, H. P. The Histopathology of *Mycobacterium johnei* Infection in Small Laboratory Animals. Jour. Path. Bact. 78:157, 1959.

HINSHAW, H. C., and GARLAND, L. H. Diseases of the Chest. 2nd Ed. W. B. Saunders Co., Philadelphia, 1963.

IPPEN, RUDOLF. Vergleichende Pathologische Untersuchungen über die spontane und experimentelle Tuberkulose der Kaltblüter. Abhand. Deutsch. Akad. d. Wissenchaft. Berlin Akademie Verlag, Berlin, 1964.

JOHNSON, H. W. Studies on Johnin. V. Producing and Standardizing a Potent Product. Amer. Jour. Vet. Res. 5:320, 1944.

KARLSON, A. G. Tuberculosis Caused by Human, Bovine and Avian Tubercle Bacilli in Various Animals. Proc. 64th Ann. Meet. U.S. Livestock Sanit. Assn., pp. 194–201, 1960.

———. Nonspecific or Cross-Sensitivity Reactions to Tuberculin in Cattle. Adv. Vet. Sci. 7:147, 1962.

———. Cross Sensitivity Reactions Between *Mycobacterium avium* and Nonchromogenic Mycobacteria (Battey Bacilli) in Guinea-Pigs. (Abst.) Excerpta Medica Intl. Cong. Ser. No. 63, pp. 321–22. 17th Conf. Intl. Tuberc., 1963.

———. Tuberculosis. *In* Dunne, H. W., Diseases of Swine. 2nd Ed. Pp. 472–87. Iowa State Univ. Press, Ames, 1964.

———, and FELDMAN, W. H. Studies on an Acid-Fast Bacterium Frequently Present in Tonsillar Tissue of Swine. Jour. Bact. 39:461, 1940.

———, *et al.* A Whole Blood, Rapid Agglutination Test for Avian Tuberculosis—A Preliminary Report. Amer. Jour. Vet. Res. 11:137, 1950.

———, *et al.* Identification of Mycobacterium Tuberculosis With One Tube of Liquid Medium. Proc. Staff Meet., Mayo Clin. 39:410,1964.

KOCH, ROBERT. Die aetiologie der Tuberculose. Berl. klin. Wchnschr. 19:221, 1882.

KUBICA, G. P., and JONES, W. D., JR. Differential Colonial Characteristics of Mycobacteria on Oleic Acid—Albumin and Modified Corn Meal Agars. I. Investigation of Slowly Growing Mycobacteria. Zentralbl. f. Bakt. 196:53, 1965.

LARSEN, A. B. Recent Developments in Paratuberculosis (Johne's Disease) Research. Proc. 68th Ann. Meet. U.S. Livestock Sanit. Assn., pp. 342–47, 1965.

———, *et al.* Allergic Response to Johnin and Tuberculin of Various Skin Regions of Cattle. Amer. Jour. Vet. Res. 11:301, 1950.

———, *et al.* A Comparison of Regular Intradermic Johnin and a Purified Protein Derivative of Intradermic Johnin on Artificially and Naturally Sensitized Ruminants. Amer. Jour. Vet. Res. 16:35, 1955.

———, *et al.* Survival Time of *Mycobacterium paratuberculosis*. Amer. Jour. Vet. Res. 17:549, 1956.

LESSLIE, I. W. Tuberculosis in Attested Herds Caused by the Human Type Tubercle Bacillus. Vet. Rec. 72: 218, 1960.

LOVELL, R., *et. al* Studies on the Survival on Johne's Bacilli. Jour. Comp. Path. 54:120, 1944.

LURIE, M. B. Immunology of Tuberculosis. *In* The Cyclopedia of Medicine, Surgery Specialties. Vol. VII, pp. 1–30. F. A. Davis Co., Philadelphia, 1964.

MACCALLUM, P., *et al.* A New Mycobacterial Infection in Man: Parts I–IV. Jour. Path. Bact. 60:93, 1948.

MALLMANN, VIRGINIA H., *et al.* Relationship of Atypical Bovine and Porcine Mycobacteria to Those of Human Origin. Health Lab. Sci. 1:11, 1964.

MERKAL, R. S., *et al.* Improvements in the Techniques for Primary Cultivation of *Mycobacterium paratuberculosis*. Amer. Jour. Vet. Res. 25:1290, 1964.

MIDDLEBROOK, GARDNER. The Mycobacteria. *In* Dubos, R. J., and Hirsch, J. G., Bacterial and Mycotic Infections of Man. 4th Ed. Pp. 490–529. J. B. Lippincott Co., Philadelphia, 1965.

MOHLER, W. M. Johne's Disease Infection of Laboratory Animals With Aid of Paraffin Oil. Jour. Amer. Vet. Med. Assn. 94:590, 1939.

MOULTON, F. R. Tuberculosis and Leprosy: The Mycobacterial Diseases. Symp. Ser., Vol. I, Amer. Assn. Adv. Sci., Washington, D.C., 1938.

MYERS, J. A. Man's Greatest Victory Over Tuberculosis. Charles C Thomas, Springfield, Ill., 1940.

PARISOT, T. J., and WOOD, E. M. A Comparative Study of the Causative Agent of a Mycobacterial Disease of Salmonoid Fishes. II. A Description of the Histopathology of the Disease in Chinook Salmon (*Oncorhynchus tshawytscha*) and a Comparison of the Staining Characteristics of the Fish Disease With Leprosy and Human Tuberculosis. Amer. Rev. Resp. Dis. 82:212, 1960.

PARLETT, R. C., and YOUMANS, G. P. An Evaluation of the Specificity and Sensitivity of a Gel Double-Diffusion Test for Tuberculosis: A Double-Blind Study. Amer. Rev. Resp. Dis. 80:153, 1959.

PETERSON, K. J. *Mycobacterium fortuitum* as a Cause of Bovine Mastitis: Tuberculin Sensitivity Following Experimental Infections. Jour. Amer. Vet. Med. Assn. 147:1600, 1965.

RICH, A. R. The Pathogenesis of Tuberculosis. 2nd Ed. Charles C Thomas, Springfield, Ill., 1951.

RITCHIE, J. N. Eradication of Bovine Tuberculosis. *In* Stableforth, A. W., and Galloway, I. A., Infectious Diseases of Animals: Diseases Due to Bacteria. Vol. II, pp. 713–44. Academic Press, Inc., New York, 1959.

RUCH, T. C. Diseases of Laboratory Primates. W. B. Saunders Co., Philadelphia, 1959.

RUNYON, E. H. Anonymous Mycobacteria in Pulmonary Disease. M. Clin. North America 43:273, 1959.

SCHAEFER, W. B. Serologic Identification and Classification of the Atypical Mycobacteria by Their Agglutination. Amer. Rev. Resp. Dis. 92:85, 1965.

SCHWALBE, J. Gesammelte Werke von Robert Koch. George Thieme, Leipzig, 1912.

SHEPARD, C. C. The Experimental Disease That Follows the Injection of Human Leprosy Bacilli in Foot-Pads of Mice. Jour. Exper. Med. 112:445, 1960.

SIGURDSSON, BJÖRN. Immunological Problems in Paratuberculosis. Bact. Rev. 20:1, 1956.

———. A Killed Vaccine Against Paratuberculosis (Johne's Disease) in Sheep. Amer. Jour. Vet. Res. 21:54, 1960.

SMITH, C. R. Alcohol as a Disinfectant Against the Tubercle Bacillus. U.S. Pub. Health Rept. 62:1285, 1947.

SNOW, G. A. The Structure of Mycobactin P, a Growth Factor for *Mycobacterium johnei*, and the Significance of Its Iron Complex. Biochem. Jour. 94:160, 1965.

UNITED STATES DEPARTMENT OF AGRICULTURE, PROGRESS REPORT. Cooperative State-Federal Tuberculosis Eradication Fiscal Year 1965, ARS 91–44–2, Oct., 1965.

VARDAMAN, T. H. The Effect of Various Chemical Agents on the Viability of *Mycobacterium paratuberculosis* In Vitro. Amer. Jour. Vet. Res. 15:159, 1954.

———, and LARSEN, A. B. The Complement-Fixation Test for Detecting Tuberculosis in Cattle. Amer. Jour. Vet. Res. 25:690, 1964.

VETERANS ADMINISTRATION. Handbook of Tuberculosis Laboratory Methods. Dept. of Med. and Surg., Washington, D.C., Nov., 1962.

VOGEL, HENRY. Mycobacteria From Cold-Blooded Animals. Amer. Rev. Tuberc. & Pulm. Dis. 77:823, 1958.

WATSON, E. A. Bovine Tuberculosis and B.C.G. Vaccination. 12th Internat. Vet. Cong., New York, 1934. Vol. II, pp. 2–14. U.S. Govt. Printing Off., Washington, D.C., 1935.

WAYNE, L. G. Recognition of *Mycobacterium fortuitum* by Means of a Three-Day Phenolphthalein Sulfatase Test. Amer. Jour. Clin. Path. 36:185, 1961.

WELLS, A. Q. The Murine Type of Tubercle Bacillus (the Vole Acid-Fast Bacillus). Med. Res. Council 259:1 1946.

———, and WYLIE, J. A. H. Vaccination Against Tuberculosis With the Vole Bacillus. Brit. Med. Bull. 10: 96, 1954.

WILLIS, H. S., and CUMMINGS, M. M. Diagnostic and Experimental Methods in Tuberculosis. Charles C Thomas, Springfield, Ill., 1952.

WILSON, G. S., and MILES, A. A. Topley's Principles of Bacteriology and Immunity. 5th Ed. Williams & Wilkins Co., Baltimore, 1964.

YEGIAN, DIRAN, and VANDERLINDE, R. J. The Nature of Acid-Fastness. Jour. Bact. 54:777, 1947.

# 34

# The Genus Erysipelothrix

**ALFRED G. KARLSON, *D.V.M., Ph.D.***

*Section of Microbiology*
*Mayo Clinic and Mayo Foundation*
*Rochester, Minnesota*

BACILLI CLASSIFIED IN THE GENUS ERYSIPELOTHRIX are slender rods, which may be curved or straight, and which show a marked tendency to form elongated filaments with only slight tendency toward branching. They are nonmotile, nonsporeforming, and do not form capsules. The organisms are gram-positive and, when stained by Gram's method, many of the elongated filaments show granulation. They are microaerophilic and are not active biochemically under artificial conditions. These organisms are variable in size and shape, so for that reason they are classified in the family Corynebacteriaceae.

It is a rule of bacteriological nomenclature that the name of an organism which was first used must have priority over all other names. For many years the genus Erysipelothrix included three species, *E. rhusiopathiae, E. muriseptica,* and *E. erysipeloides.* Numerous investigators have revealed that there was not sufficient evidence to show that these were separate species. The 1957 edition of Bergey's Manual has included all three in a single species which has been given the name *Erysipelothrix insidiosa.* This was the first species name used for the organism by Trevisan in 1885. This change is too recent for its adoption by all scientists, so it is expected that even in current literature the name for the swine erysipelas organism *Erysipelothrix rhusiopathiae* may be used.

Within the last three decades *Erysipelothrix insidiosa* has become recognized as important to animal health in America. It is now known that the disease is widespread and constitutes a serious menace to the swine-raising industry. In addition to swine, *Erysipelothrix insidiosa* has been isolated in cases of arthritis of lambs in the western sheep-raising areas. Infection in turkeys results in serious losses. Many cases of infection in man are reported in the literature of this country.

## *Erysipelothrix insidiosa*

**Synonyms and History.** *Bacillus rhusiopathiae suis, Bacterium erysipelatos suum, Bacterium rhusiopathiae, Erysipelothrix porci.* The names *Bacterium murisepticus* and *Erysipelothrix murisepticus* were formerly used to designate the species when isolated from mice. The name *Erysipelothrix erysipeloides* was given to the microorganism when isolated from man.

In 1876 Robert Koch described a "mouse septicemia bacillus" obtained from mice which had been injected with putrid meat. No relationship to swine disease was then known for this bacillus. In 1882 Pasteur described a slender, curved rod which he isolated from swine showing symptoms of swine erysipelas. Vaccines made from this microorganism protected swine against natural infection, but from the descriptions of the bacillus it is assumed that Pasteur worked with impure cultures. Credit for the first accurate description of the swine erysipelas microorganism is given to Loeffler. In 1885 and 1886 he published the results of his work which demonstrated that the disease in swine is caused by a bacillus identical to, or closely resembling, the mouse septicemia bacillus of Koch. Loeffler repeatedly emphasized the similarity between the two.

In 1909 Rosenbach described a bacillus obtained in a case of erysipeloid of man as being almost identical to the one isolated by Koch from mice. On the basis of his studies on the causes of swine erysipelas, mouse septicemia, and erysipeloid in man, Rosenbach concluded that there were three closely related species. *E. porci, E. murisepticus,* and *E. erysipeloides.* Studies that have since been made on the relationships of the microorganisms isolated from the above sources show that the strains are identical.

The history of swine erysipelas and of infections due to this microorganism in other animals in the United States is of some interest because, prior to 1930, it had been stated by many writers that the disease did not exist in America. In retrospect, however, it is likely that infections due to *E. insidiosa* were not uncommon, but were not recognized. As a matter of fact, in 1885 Smith reported the isolation from a sick pig of microorganisms which he said closely resembled the bacillus of swine erysipelas. In Minnesota, in 1894, there occurred a serious outbreak of a swine disease with mortality of 60 to 100 per cent, from which the swine erysipelas microorganism was isolated by Smith. There are at least five other reports of the occurrence of infections, due to microorganisms we now call *E. insidiosa,* in the United States prior to 1930. Additional historical data on *E. insidiosa* and on its occurrence in America may be found in the bulletin by Van Es and McGrath and in the paper by Shuman (1964).

**Distribution and Transmission.** Swine erysipelas and infections due to *E. insidiosa* in other animals are known to occur in many parts of the world. In Europe the infection in swine appears in epizootic proportions in certain countries from spring until early fall, and sporadic outbreaks are observed during the colder months of the year. The disease has been reported from North Africa, China, and Japan. In Australia and New Zealand, as well as in America, polyarthritis in sheep due to *E. insidiosa* is of some economic importance. The microorganism has been isolated from various species of fowl in Europe and, especially in America, it is known to cause serious losses among turkeys.

In North America the disease in swine is most commonly seen in the late summer months, but the chronic forms of swine erysipelas have been recognized throughout the entire year. The infection in turkeys is most frequently seen in the late fall or early winter.

Natural infection in swine and perhaps in other animals occurs commonly via the alimentary tract. Soil, food, and water are readily contaminated by sick animals because the feces and urine contain the microorganism. Soil, which may retain viable and virulent microorganisms, serves as an excellent medium for conveying the infection to the animal body by way of the digestive tract. Surface waters may also be incriminated in transmitting the disease from one farm to another. *E. insidiosa* has been isolated from fish meal used in the preparation of animal foods which are, therefore, potential sources of infection. Swine with subclinical infection and those that have the chronic form of swine erysipelas may live for a long time and be a constant source of infection. The role in the transmission of the disease, played by healthy animals which harbor *E. insidiosa* in their tissues, has not been clarified, but it has been repeatedly demonstrated that the microorganism can be isolated from swine that have no demonstrable disease.

Infections in man are largely limited to packing plant workers and others who handle animal products. The ubiquity of *E. insidiosa* is demonstrated by the number of cases of erysipeloid among those who

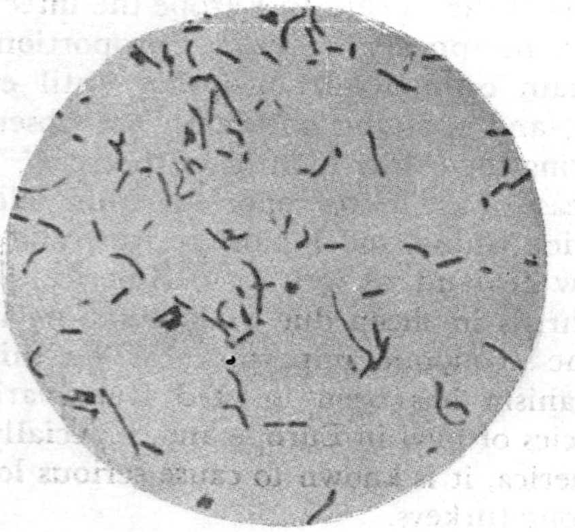

FIG. 34.1—**Erysipelothrix insidiosa** agar culture, ×2,000. (From Nowak: Documenta Microbiologica, courtesy Gustav Fischer.)

handle fish. In man, the disease is largely limited to the hands and arms where the microorganism has gained entrance via wounds. There are, however, several instances where the infection could be traced to the ingestion of pork. Of particular interest is the report that a group of veterinary students became infected with *E.-insidiosa* as the result of dissecting an improperly embalmed horse in an anatomy laboratory.

**Morphology and Staining.** *E. insidiosa* is variable in form. In smears from blood and tissue it appears as a short, slender, straight or bent rod, 1μ to 2μ in length; it often appears in pairs or groups (Fig. 34.1). On culture media a mixture of short rods and elongated, thickened filaments, measuring 5μ to 20μ, may be found. In liquid media the filamentous forms of some cultures are bent and twisted into a mass resembling a mycelium. In young, actively growing cultures, pairs of rods often form an angle as though they had snapped off during fission. Branching is not common but has been observed. As has been noted, the microorganism is nonmotile and does not produce spores or capsules. Some investigators have demonstrated a waxlike covering. The microorganism stains well with ordinary dyes and is gram-positive. Old cultures are easily decolorized by acetone alcohol. The thickened, elongated filaments are characteristically beaded when stained with Gram's stain. The organism has no metachromatic granules and is not acid-fast.

**Growth Requirements and Characteristics.** *E. insidiosa* grows sparingly on ordinary culture media. The addition of serum to nutrient broth or agar enhances the growth. The presence of the amino acid, tryptophane, favors rapid and abundant development on solid or liquid media. It is microaerophilic, as shown by the tendency of recently isolated cultures to grow beneath the surface of solid media, although older cultures grow well under atmospheric conditions. Growth occurs well at room temperature, as well as at 37°C. The optimal reaction of media is pH 7.4.

Two types of colonies are formed. The short rods, the so-called "S" or smooth types, form small, round, discrete, translucent colonies with entire edges, seldom more than 1 mm. in diameter. The elongated filamentous forms are found in colonies that are opaque, have uneven surfaces and edges, and tend to become confluent. They may measure 2 to 4 mm. in diameter. These large, irregular colonies are referred to as the "R" or rough forms. In broth the short rods, or the "smooth" type of the microorganism, form a uniform turbidity with no pellicle and very little sediment. The elongated, or "rough" type, produce a heavy, turbid growth with sediment in broth. In gelatin stabs the growth radiates from the line of inoculation to form a characteristic test-tube brush appearance.

**Resistance.** *E. insidiosa* is remarkably resistant for a nonsporeforming microorganism. It resists drying at room temperature for several months. When kept moist, cultures will remain alive for six months or more. A broth culture has been reported to be viable and able to kill mice after standing for seventeen years. Exposure to sunlight destroys the organism in twelve to fourteen days. It is readily destroyed by boiling. A temperature of 70°C. kills the microorganisms in five to ten minutes, but the fact that they remain alive in smoked or pickled meat for several months is important. Pieces of pork 6 inches thick require cooking for two and a half hours to destroy the bacillus in the tissues. It has been found alive in cadavers seven months after death. In alkaline soil, which may be a source of infection, the organism lives and multiplies during the warmer months.

Certain strains have been found to survive, and even multiply, in concentrations of phenol that are destructive to many other microorganisms. Bichloride of mercury 1:100, formalin 2 per cent, cresol compound 3.5 per cent, and phenol 5 per cent will destroy the organism in five to fifteen minutes. The various sulfonamide preparations appear not to be effective in vivo against *E. insidiosa*. The microorganisms are sensitive to penicillin, streptomycin, and broad spectrum antibiotics.

**Biochemical Properties.** *E. insidiosa* is not active in producing changes on the differential media in common use. It does not form indol; does not reduce nitrates; is negative to the Voges-Proskauer, the methyl red, the methylene blue reduction, and the catalase tests; and does not hydrolyze esculin. The production of $H_2S$ by this organism depends upon the type of medium under which it is cultured. No detectable $H_2S$ is produced in some media, but when the culture is grown upon a medium containing lead acetate and serum, $H_2S$ is apparent after four days incubation. It forms acid but no gas from glucose, galactose, fructose, and lactose and produces a delayed reaction in mannose and cellobiose.

An important study was made by White and Shuman who found that the fermentation pattern of *E. insidiosa* varied, depending upon the medium and the indicator. There was no correlation between virulence and any variation in fermentation reactions. There is no surface growth or liquefaction of gelatin. Litmus milk may show a slight acid reaction, but there is usually no change. A narrow green zone of hemolysis occurs around deep colonies in blood agar.

**Antigenic Structure.** The results of cross-agglutination tests using unabsorbed serum indicate that all strains of *E. insidiosa* have at least one common antigen. It can be demonstrated that there are separate serologic types of *E. insidiosa* which may be due either to type-specific antigens or to quantitative differences in the antigens common to all. The serologic groups are designated as Types A, B, and N; there are also subgroups of A and of B. Hubrig has found, as have others, that Type A is most commonly isolated from acute cases of swine erysipelas whereas Types B and N are found in the chronic cases or in symptomless carriers. It is suggested that Type A loses its A antigenic component and then becomes less virulent. In a discussion on the serologic grouping of *E. insidiosa,* Shuman (1964) concluded that a system of classifying the antigens of the microorganism is needed, and that with improved serologic techniques there would be a more effective method of studying the disease.

Serologic specificity has been reported by Nelson and Shelton using fluorescein-conjugated antiserum. There was no cross reaction with *Listeria monocytogenes* nor with a variety of other bacteria.

**Pathogenicity.** Pigs from the age of three to eighteen months are more readily infected with the swine erysipelas bacillus, but the resistance shown by the very young is only a relative one, and many outbreaks of the disease among suckling pigs have been reported.

Swine erysipelas presents itself in three recognizable forms: the acute or septicemia type, the chronic form with endocarditis and arthritis, and the skin form or "diamond skin disease" which may be followed by gangrenous dermatitis.

The *acute* form is characterized by its sudden onset, high temperature, rapid course, and high mortality which varies from 25 to 75 per cent. Areas of hemorrhage may appear on the ventral portions of the animal which become dark red as the disease progresses. Accompanying symptoms are loss of appetite, general depression, and often discharge from the eyes. Postmortem examination reveals hemorrhagic gastroenteritis and marked enlargement of the spleen which has become dark red. The lymph nodes are swollen and hemorrhagic. Petechial hemorrhages may be found on the serous surfaces of the organs. The lungs are usually congested and edematous. If the course of the disease is prolonged, the organs and fat become icteric, and this manifestation is accompanied by perirenal edema.

The *chronic* form of swine erysipelas is characterized by vegetative endocarditis of the heart valves, particularly the mitral. This may also be accompanied by chronic arthritis, in which the joints of the limbs become enlarged, giving the swine a characteristic stilted walk. The arthritis occurs without the heart lesions in many instances. Chronic swine erysipelas is not often fatal, but the affected animals do not gain weight rapidly.

The arthritis of swine caused by *E. insidiosa* has been studied extensively by Sikes and by others because the lesions resemble those of rheumatoid arthritis in man. In addition to lesions of joints in the limbs, it has been found by Grabel and associates that arthritis of the spine is common.

The *urticarial* form of swine erysipelas, called "diamond skin disease," is a mild infection characterized by the development on the skin of well-defined, diamond-shaped spots 1 to 5 cm. in diameter; these appear on the back and sides of the animal as dark red or purple areas which become raised. Extensive gangrene, with subsequent sloughing of the skin, often follows the "diamond skin disease."

The reproduction of the disease in swine by intravenous, intramuscular, or subcutaneous inoculation with virulent cultures is not routinely successful. In 1944 Fortner and Dinter demonstrated that cultures applied to skin scarifications resulted in a severe erythematous lesion along the scratch and in case of the virulent cultures in generalized infection. This technique has been confirmed by Shuman (1951), who has found it valuable in the study of immunity. In 1955 Hughes reported that generalized swine erysipelas could be produced by the inoculation of a virulent culture into the ear vein.

In sheep the infection with *E. insidiosa* is characterized by chronic polyarthritis. The infection is probably soil-borne and enters the body through the umbilicus at birth. Lambs up to 3 months of age appear to be most commonly stricken. In spite of the extensive polyarthritis that may occur, the parenchymal organs are not involved.

In addition to causing outbreaks of disease in swine and sheep, *E. insidiosa* has been isolated in sporadic cases of infection of horses, cattle, dogs, reindeer, kangaroo, porpoise, and wild boar.

Natural infections in turkeys, geese, ducks, chickens, and pigeons are of an acute nature. The postmortem appearance in birds is that of peracute septicemia. Attempts to infect poultry artificially are not always successful, however, and many authors conclude that fowls are relatively resistant to infection with the swine erysipelas bacillus.

Of the laboratory animals, mice and pigeons are highly susceptible to experimental infection. Both die in eighteen to ninety-six hours of acute septicemia. Rabbits are quite resistant, although Goldie and Collins were able to produce granulomatous joint lesions by repeated small intravenous injections. Subcutaneous injections into rabbits may give rise to local inflammation and edema, and highly virulent cultures may cause death in a period of from several days to a week. Intravenous injections are more often fatal to rabbits, and death often occurs in two or three days. Guinea pigs are markedly resistant to infection with the swine erysipelas bacillus. Horses, cattle, dogs, and cats are reactive to artificial inoculation of virulent strains.

Erysipeloid, as the disease is known in man, is characterized by a painful swelling at the point of inoculation in the skin. The area becomes reddened, turns purple, and some necrosis of the skin and subcutis occurs. The regional lymph nodes may become enlarged and painful. Arthritis may develop in the nearby joints. The disease is not often fatal and rarely becomes generalized. Additional information and illustrations of the lesions in man are presented by Morse.

**Immunity.** Animals that recover from swine erysipelas remain permanently immune, although many may continue to harbor and disseminate the causative agent. Swine of more than eighteen months of age show a relative resistance which possibly may be attributed to early exposure.

Pasteur and Thuiller devised the first method of immunization in 1882, which is of historical interest only. They found that the swine erysipelas microorganism could be attenuated by passage through rabbits and that its virulence could be exalted by passage through pigeons. Their method of immunization consisted of injecting a live culture of an attenuated strain, followed in twelve days by injection of a virulent strain. The method has been abandoned because the injection of the virulent culture was found to be capable of actually causing the disease in some instances. Serious losses were known to result, and the disease actually was propagated in new localities by use of virulent cultures for vaccines.

The simultaneous method of vaccination against swine erysipelas is now commonly used. The method of Lorenz, who introduced the simultaneous, or serovaccination method, consists of, first, injecting a virulent culture, followed immediately by injection of immune serum. A modification of this method is to mix the vaccine with the immune serum immediately before use and to employ the mixture for inoculation in a single dose. In the swine-raising section of the midwestern part of the United States, herds may be given two injections of vaccine along with immune serum after the disease has been found to be present on the premises. It has been observed by Shuman (1964) that the vaccination of gilts with culture and serum, just before breeding, will afford protection to the newborn pigs until weaning time. The immune serum made by hyperimmunizing horses is very effective in treating sick animals. Symptoms of acute swine erysipelas may be caused to abate in twenty-four hours or less by the use of immune serum.

Gray and Norden have reported an immunizing agent called erysipelas vaccine avirulent (EVA) which is composed of a living avirulent but highly antigenic strain of *E. insidiosa*. Experimental and field trials with this vaccine indicate that it is an effective immunizing agent. It may be used simultaneously with immune serum or used alone.

The production of immunity against any disease by the use of a living culture has a number of disadvantages. This fact is true of swine erysipelas. The report of the value of a formalin-killed aluminum hydroxide adsorbed bacterin, by Traub in 1947 and by Dinter in 1948, was viewed with great interest. The application of this method experimentally by Cooper and associates and by Shuman has revealed that satisfactory immunity may be produced.

It has been apparent for some time that vaccination of swine does prevent the acute type of the disease, but arthritis may be observed later. Neher and Swenson believe that the high incidence of arthritis in vaccinated animals lends support to the theory that sensitization plays a role in the development of joint lesions. These workers also state that under farm conditions some pigs may develop arthritis without an acute stage of swine erysipelas as a result of sensitization by multiple natural exposures. Neher and Swenson conclude from their studies that although vaccination is beneficial in preventing mortality from the acute infection, it may actually contribute to, rather than solve, the arthritis problem.

Shuman (1964) has made extensive studies on the problems involved in immunization against swine erysipelas. In a survey of his own work and that of others he concludes that there is now no adequate immunizing agent for effective long-term protection, although each procedure has some merit. Shuman believes that improved or new prophylactic biologics will be developed from newer knowledge of the antigens of *E. insidiosa.*

Prophylactic use of the immune serum is valuable in swine-raising, but the passive immunity is of short duration and cannot be relied on for longer than two weeks. Specific immune serum has been used prophylactically and for treatment of turkeys and ducks, with some reported beneficial results, but there seems to be no agreement as to the practicability of such procedures.

**Diagnosis.** The diagnosis of infections due to *E. insidiosa* may be made with certainty only by bacteriologic or serologic procedures. Swine erysipelas may readily be confused with other acute septicemic infections. The chronic forms of the disease, accompanied by valvular lesions, arthritis, or skin manifestations may also be caused by other microorganisms.

The slender, gram-positive rods may sometimes be found in smears of tissue. Large clumps of the bacteria often are observed in smears of blood from pigeons (Fig. 34.2) and in smears from the spleen or kidneys of mice which have been inoculated with material obtained in cases of swine erysipelas. The microorganism can be demonstrated by inoculation of blood or serum agar. The tiny, smooth colonies, which may not be seen for several days, may then be transferred to suitable differential mediums for identification. Packer has shown that *E. insidiosa* may be more easily isolated from contaminated tissues if sodium azide and crystal violet are incorporated in the medium.

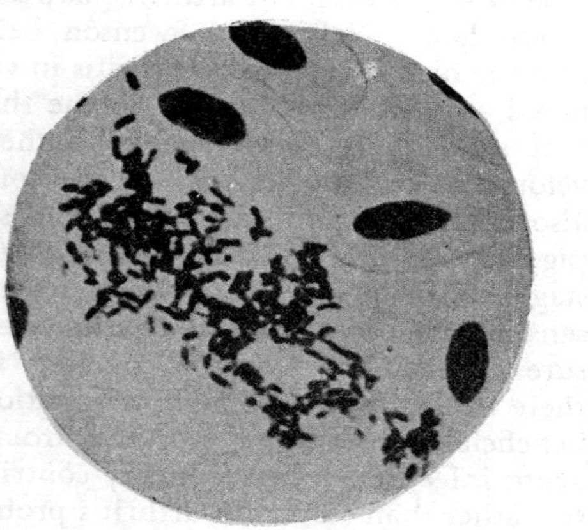

FIG. 34.2—**Erysipelothrix insidiosa** smear of pigeon blood, ×2,000. (From Nowak: Documenta Microbiologica, courtesy Gustav Fischer.)

Fuze recommends incorporation of 100 micrograms per ml. of neomycin or 400 micrograms per ml. of kanamycin in blood agar for the isolation of the microorganism; these antibiotics prevent growth of most other bacteria but do not inhibit *E. insidiosa.*

Serologic tests are of value only in the chronic infections. The agglutination test has been found to be a useful procedure for detecting chronically infected animals in herds where, if allowed to remain, they may be constant sources of the infection.

The antigen for the laboratory tube test is made by centrifuging the microorganisms out of broth cultures and resuspending them in formolized physiologic saline solution. Serum dilutions are made in the ordinary manner with the antigen and incubated for four hours at 37°C. The tubes are then centrifuged for a short time before being read. In positive tests the supernatant fluid will be cleared, while in negative tests it will remain turbid. A rapid serum or whole blood test is made by mixing a drop of serum or blood with a drop of antigen 50 times heavier than that used for the tube test. A positive reaction is indicated in a few minutes by the formation of clumps. This rapid agglutination test which may be used in the field for chronic swine erysipelas is more commonly used than the laboratory tube test.

A rapid laboratory test may be made by using as the antigen a twelve-hour to twenty-four-hour broth culture of the smooth type of the organism. Hanging drops are made of serial dilutions of suspected serum and the broth cultures. After incubation for five to fifteen minutes the hanging drops are examined microscopically. A positive test is indicated by marked clumping of the microorganisms. In a negative test the bacilli remain evenly distributed throughout the field with no tendency to form clumps.

Care should be taken in making the hanging drops to prevent contamination of the hands.

## REFERENCES


Barber, Mary. A Comparative Study of Listerella and Erysipelothrix. Jour. Path. Bact. 48:11, 1939.

Blackmore, D. K., and Gallagher, G. L. An Outbreak of Erysipelas in Captive Wild Ducks and Mammals. Vet. Rec. 76:1161, 1964.

Brill, J., and Politynska, E. Die Differenzierung von *Erysipelothrix rhusiapathiae*-Stämmen mit. Bakteriophagen. Zentralbl. f. Bakt. I. Orig. 181:473, 1961.

Callaway, H. P., *et al.* Field Use of An Adsorbed Swine Erysipelas Bacterin. Vet. Med. 50:39, 1955.

Cooper, M. S., *et al.* Laboratory Studies on Erysipelas. I. Immunization Against Swine Erysipelas and Susceptibility of Swine to Challenge. Amer. Jour. Vet. Res. 15:594, 1954.

———, *et al.* Laboratory Studies on the Vaccination of Mice and Turkeys With an *Erysipelothrix rhusiopathiae* Vaccine. Canad. Jour. Comp. Med. 18:83, 1954.

Dinter, Z. Zur Schutzimpfung gegen Schweinrotlauf mit einer Adsorbatvaksine. Tierärztl. Umschau 17-18: 279, 1948.

Fortner, J., and Dinter, Z. Ist. das Rotlaufbakterium der alleinige Erreger des Schweinerotlaufs. Ztschr. f. Infektionskr. 60:157, 1944.

Füzi, M. Über die selektiv Züchtung der Schweinrotlaufbakterien. Zentralbl. f. Bakt. I. Orig. 188:387, 1963.

Goldie, W., and Collins, D. H. Erysipelothrix Arthritis in Rabbits: Experimental Induction and the Response to Cortisone. Jour. Path. Bact. 71:425, 1956.

Grabel, I., *et al.* Discospondylitis and Arthritis in Swine Erysipelas. Acta Vet. Scand. 3:33, 1962.

Gray, C. W., and Norden, C. S. Erysipelas Vaccine Avirulent—A New Agent for Erysipelas Control. Jour. Amer. Vet. Med. Assn. 127:506, 1955.

Grey, C. G., *et al.* Swine Erysipelas, the Agglutination Test for Its Diagnosis, and a Report on a Study of Arthritis in Swine. Amer. Jour. Vet. Res. 2:74, 1941.

Hubrig, T. Über die Veränderlichkeit der serologischen Rotlaufbakterientypen. Zentralbl. f. Bakt. I. Orig. 186:344, 1962.

Hughes, D. L. Arthritis in Pigs. The Experimental Disease Induced by *Erysipelothrix rhusiopathiae*. Brit. Vet. Jour. 111:183, 1955.

Kalf, G. F., and Gréce, Mary Ann. The Antigenic Components of *Erysipelothrix rhusiopathiae*. III. Purificationof B- and C-Antigens. Arch. Biochem. and Biophys. 107:141, 1964.

Karlson, A. G., and Merchant, I. A. The Cultural and Biochemic Properties of *Erysipelothrix rhusiopathiae*. Amer. Jour. Vet. Res. 2:5, 1941.

Langford, G. C., and Hansen, P. A. The Species of Erysipelothrix. Antonie van Leeuwenhoek 20:89, 1954.

Levine, N. D. Erysipelas. *In* Biester, H. E., and Schwarte, L. H. (eds.), Diseases of Poultry, pp. 461–69. Iowa State Univ. Press, Ames, 1965.

Lorenz. Ein Schutzimpfungsverfahren gegen Schweinrotlauf. Zentralbl. f. Bakt. 13:357, 1893.

Morrill, C. C. Erysipeloid: Occurrence Among Veterinary Students. Jour. Inf. Dis. 65:322, 1939.

Morse, Erskine Y. Swine Erysipelas. *In* Hull, T. G., Diseases Transmitted From Animals to Man. 4th Ed., pp. 188–209. Charles C Thomas, Springfield, Ill., 1963.

Moulton, J. E., *et al.* Erysipelatous Arthritis in Calves. Jour. Amer. Vet. Med. Assn. 123:335, 1953.

Neher, G. M., and Swensen, C. B. Does Vaccination Against Swine Erysipelas Afford Protection Against Arthritis? Lab. Investigation 8:1419, 1959.

Nelson, John D., and Shelton, Sharon. Immunofluorescent Studies of *Listeria monocytogenes* and *Erysipelothrix insidiosa*. Jour. Lab. Clin. Med. 62:935, 1963.

Packer, R. A. The Use of Sodium Azide ($NaN_3$) and Crystal Violet in a Selective Medium for Streptococci and *Erysipelothrix rhusiopathiae*. Jour. Bact. 46:343–49, 1943.

Rowsell, H. C. The Effect of Stomach Contents and the Soil on the Viability of *Erysipelothrix rhusiopathiae*. Jour. Amer. Vet. Med. Assn. 132:357, 1958.

Sadler, W. W., and Corstvet, R. E. The Effect of *Erysipelothrix insidiosa* Infections on Wholesomeness of Market Turkeys. Amer. Jour. Vet. Res. 26:1429, 1965.

SHUMAN, R. D. Swine Erysipelas Induced by Skin Scarification. Proc. 88th Ann. Meet. Amer. Vet. Med. Assn., p. 153, 1951.

———. Swine Erysipelas. *In* Dunn, H. W., Diseases of Swine. 2nd Ed., Chap. 24. Iowa State Univ. Press Ames, 1964.

SIKES, DENNIS. A Rheumatoidlike Disease in Swine. Lab. Investigation 8:1406, 1959.

SMITH, THEOBALD. Investigations of Diseases of Domestic Animals. Swine Erysipelas or Mouse Septicemia Bacilli From an Outbreak of Swine Disease. USDA, U.S. Bur. of An. Ind., 12th and 13th Ann. Repts., pp. 166–74, 1895–1896.

SPEARS, H. N. Carriers of Swine Erysipelas. Jour. Comp. Path. Therap. 64:152, 1955.

TEN BROECK, CARL. Studies on *Bacillus murisepticus*, or the Rotlauf Bacillus, Isolated From Swine in the United States. Jour. Exp. Med. 32:331, 1920.

TRAUB, E. Immunizierung gegen Schweinrotlauf mit Konzentrierten Adsorbatimpfstoffen. Monatsh. f. Veterinärmed. 10:165, 1945.

TRUSZCZYNSKI, M. The Antigenic Structure of Virulent and Avirulent Strains of *Erysipelothrix rhusiopathiae*. III. The Agar Gel Diffusion-Precipitation Test. Amer. Jour. Vet. Res. 22:846, 1961.

VAN ES, L., and MCGRATH, C. G. Swine Erysipelas. Nebr. Agr. Exp. Sta. Res. Bull. 128, Lincoln, 1942.

WATTS, P. S. Studies on *Erysipelothrix rhusiopathiae*. Jour. Path. Bact. 50:355, 1940.

WHITE, T. A., and SHUMAN, R. D. Fermentation Reactions of *Erysipelothrix rhusiopathiae*. Jour. Bact. 82:595, 1961.

WILSON, G. S., and MILES, A. A. Topley's Principles of Bacteriology and Immunity. 5th Ed. Williams & Wilkins Co., Baltimore, 1964.

# 35

# The Genera Actinomyces, Nocardia, and Dermatophilus

**ALLAN C. PIER, *D.V.M., Ph.D.***
*National Animal Disease Laboratory*
*Ames, Iowa*

THESE GENERA INCLUDE MICROORGANISMS which morphologically bridge the gap between bacteria and fungi. Their size and chemical composition distinguish them as bacteria; however, they resemble the molds morphologically by forming a branched mycelium during early growth. The young mycelium of all three genera is slender, approximating 0.5μ to 1.0μ in diameter. The mycelium fragments into rod or coccoid elements resembling spores or, as in the case of Dermatophilus, motile spores are formed following multidimensional cleavage of mature mycelial elements. Species of both Actinomyces and Nocardia may be encountered as either saprophytes or pathogens; species of Dermatophilus appear to be obligate parasites since they have been isolated only from animal lesions.

Organisms of the genus Actinomyces are anaerobic to microaerophilic; they form soft friable colonies on solid media and a slender mycelium which is not acid-fast. The Nocardia are aerobic organisms which form friable to adherent colonies; the slender mycelium of young cultures of most pathogenic species is partially acid-fast. Dermatophilus grows aerobically, forming adherent colonies which soften with age; the slender mycelium of the young colony widens with maturity, and forms multidimensional septations and motile spores. The mycelium of Dermatophilus is not acid-fast.

## THE GENUS ACTINOMYCES

There are two prominent pathogens in this genus, *Actinomyces bovis* and *Actinomyces israelii*. These are closely related organisms; but distinct differences in their host affinity, colonial morphology, and biochemical reactions mark them as separate species. Actinomycosis of cattle is nearly always the result of *A. bovis* infection, while human actinomycosis is usually the result of *A. israelii* infection. The early literature did not distinguish between these two species, thus confusing present knowledge of host relationships. Additional species capable of pathogenicity, *Actinomyces baudetii, Actinomyces ericksonii,* and *Actinomyces propionicus,* as well as a nonpathogenic species, *Actinomyces naeslundii,* have been described.

### *Actinomyces bovis*

**Synonyms and History.** *Discomyces bovis, Nocardia actinomyces, Streptothrix actinomyces, Streptothrix bovis,* the "ray fungus."

Actinomycosis, as a disease, was reported long before the organism was known to exist; in fact, Moodie reported finding bone necrosis, simulating actinomycosis, in the fossil remains of a rhinoceros. In 1845 Langenbeck reported finding a ray fungus in a young man suffering with Pott's disease. The presence of sulfur granules in actinomycosis of the cow was reported by Rivolta in 1868. He considered that such granules were organisms and coined the name *Discomyces bovis*. It must be noted that this organism might have been *Actinobacillus lignieresi*. The real significance of the organism as a specific agent of disease was determined in 1877 by Bollinger who called the disease actinomycosis. Bollinger took specimens containing the organism to Harz, a botanist who noted the ray fungus characteristic and suggested the name, *Actinomyces bovis*. In 1878 Israel observed a similar organism in a suppurative lesion in man, and in 1891 Wolf and Israel were able to culture it on artificial media under anaerobic conditions. These workers are credited, by some, as being the first to discover the organism. In 1891 considerable confusion was introduced by Bostroem, by the isolation of an aerobic organism from typical actinomycotic lesions in man and in cattle. He believed his organism was *Actinomyces bovis*. It was present upon various grasses as a saprophyte and was considered to be introduced into deeper tissues of the buccal cavity by the penetrating action of sharp awns. Bostroem's organism was not pathogenic for guinea pigs or rabbits, and its relationship to actinomycosis was doubted first by Wright in 1905. Since then, the etiological relationship of the organism to actinomycosis has been completely disproved by many investigators. Bostroem's organism is considered under the name *Actinomyces hominis (Actinomyces graminis* of Topley and Wilson), a contaminating saprophyte which can be isolated frequently from actinomycotic lesions. *Actinomyces bovis* is considered to be the organism first observed by Bollinger, described and named by Harz, and isolated in pure culture by Wolf and Israel.

**Distribution and Transmission.** *A. bovis* is widely distributed throughout the world in regions devoted to the grazing of cattle herds. It is common in south Russia, the Scandinavian countries, England, Holland, and Italy, but uncommon in France and Germany. In the United States the organism is found in the north central states and in the western grazing states.

The organism is a normal inhabitant of the mucous membranes of the upper respiratory and digestive tracts. It has been found in the tartar of teeth and in decaying food material on the gums. The relationship of the awns of the bearded grasses to the infection is considered mechanical. Such sharp objects penetrate the tissues of the buccal cavity, afford a channel of entry, and produce primary necrosis of tissue which is essential to the development of the organism. In this respect the anaerobic conditions necessary for the multiplication of this organism are similar to those for the Clostridium group

**Morphology and Staining** *A. bovis* is a branching, filamentous organism when grown under artificial conditions. Many of the filaments are beaded, and fragment readily into smaller rod and coccoid forms which are considered to function as conidia (Fig. 35.1). In the infected tissues the organism forms typical "ray fungus" granules

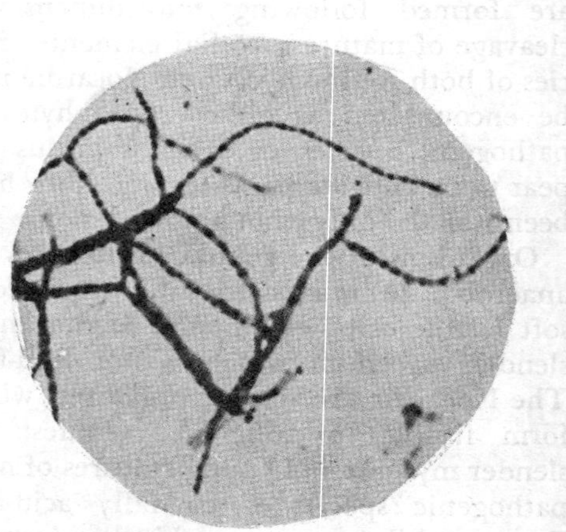

**FIG. 35.1—Actinomyces bovis** agar culture showing beaded filaments, ×2,000. (From Nowak: Documenta Microbiologica, courtesy Gustav Fischer.)

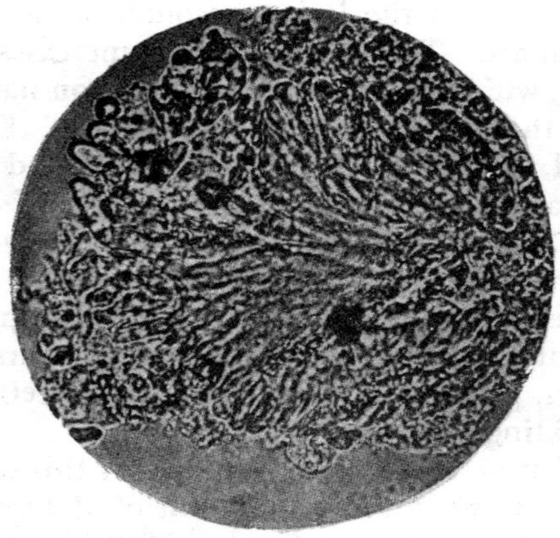

FIG. 35.2—**Actinomyces bovis** unstained granule in actinomycotic pus, ×110. (From Nowak: Documenta Microbiologica, courtesy Gustav Fischer.)

from 1 to 2 mm. in size. When an unstained preparation is examined under the microscope, these granules are found to be composed of a mass of clublike processes originating at the center of the granule. Many of the processes are well formed while others are small and ill defined (Fig. 35.2). When granules were examined in ultrathin sections with the electron microscope, in stained sections with the light microscope, or in wet mounts before and after chemical extraction with the light and phase microscope, Pine and Overman found that the granule is a mycelial mass of *A. bovis* cemented together by a polysaccharide plus protein complex, and contains about 50 per cent calcium phosphate. The granules are compact, and many are calcified, but when placed between two slides they are easily crushed. If a smear which has been made in this manner is stained with the Gram stain, the long, slender, filamentous type of organism is found. The organism is gram-positive and nonacid-fast.

**Growth Requirements and Characteristics.** The organism grows best upon primary isolation under anaerobic or microaerophilic conditions, but when adjusted to artificial media it may grow aerobically. The presence of 10 per cent $CO_2$ is stimulating to the organism. Original growth is slow, taking several days for a colony of any significant size to form. A favorable medium for the cultivation of the organism contains 1 per cent glycerin, 1 per cent blood serum, and 1 per cent dextrose added to a nutrient agar base and adjusted to pH 7.3 to 7.6. When a shake culture is made of the organism in this medium, numerous small colonies are formed about 1 cm. under the surface of the medium. Larger and scattered colonies which are irregular in shape and with a knobby surface are observed throughout the medium. The organism is frequently associated with numerous other species of bacteria which make the isolation of a pure culture difficult. A considerable number of contaminating bacteria are eliminated by placing the actinomycotic exudate in sterile water and washing the granules free from tissue cells. This may be repeated until only a thin layer of granules is left in the bottom of the tube. These granules are then crushed with a sterile rod, and cultures are made of this material.

*A. bovis* forms small, smooth, round, convex, opaque, amorphous colonies on the surface of the agar plate. As the colony of some strains ages, the center may become elevated, the surface nodular, and the periphery lobular, giving the colony a rosette appearance.

Growth in thioglycollate broth is typically soft and diffuse; some strains produce soft mulberry-like granules in broth medium, which are easily disintegrated upon shaking.

Coagulated serum medium and Dorset's egg medium support a moderate growth of the organism. The appearance of the cultures on these media is similar to that on agar but is usually more glistening; some strains may have a pink tinge of color. The media are not liquefied.

**Resistance.** The organism is killed at 60°C. in 10 minutes. It is not resistant to the mercurial disinfectants but is resistant to phenolic compounds. It is killed by a 1:1,000 solution of $HgCl_2$ in 5 minutes. Artificial cultures of the organism must be transferred often in order to maintain them. The granules are resistant to desiccation and more resistant to chemicals than the filamentous forms. *A. bovis* shows sensitivity to the same antibiotics as the gram-positive cocci, penicillin, and the broad spectrum antibiotics.

**Biochemical Properties.** *A. bovis* hydrolyzes starch and produces acid, but not gas, from glucose, maltose, lactose, salicin, and occasionally from glycerol, but not from xylose, mannitol or raffinose under anaerobic conditions. It does not reduce nitrates to nitrites or ammonia, and gives a negative reaction for indol, to the methyl red and Voges-Proskauer tests, and for $H_2S$ and catalase production. The organism grows slowly in litmus milk with slight acid production and no coagulation or peptonization.

**Antigenic Structure and Toxins.** Little data are available concerning the antigenic structure of the organism. Colebrook found three strains of the organism antigenically different. Magnusson reported three serological types; Type A was found in cattle, and Types B and C in swine. Slack and associates were able to determine serological groups A, B, C, and D by using fluorescent antibody techniques in their study of strains of actinomyces from animals and man. *A. bovis* strains were placed in Group A.

**Pathogenicity.** *A. bovis* is most frequently pathogenic for cattle and swine; infections of the horse, dog, and cat are seen occasionally but this organism rarely infects man.

The lesions produced by the organism in cattle are most prevalent in the mandible and in the tongue, although they may be found in any of the tissues of the cervical region, and on rare occasions are quite generalized throughout the internal organs. The organism is spread from localized lesions by continuity of tissue or by the blood stream. Lesions of actinomycosis in animals and in man are characterized by abscess formation with encapsulation. As the process advances, connective tissue increases, and the lesion becomes dense and compact. The affected part increases in size, which has given rise to common names for the disease, such as "lumpy jaw." Kimball, Twiehaus, and Frank have found the organism in orchitis of the bull.

Cases of actinomycosis due to *A. bovis* have been reported from swine, horses, and sheep. In swine it is considered most prevalent as a mammary infection of nursing sows, presumably due to the sharp teeth of suckling pigs.

Kimball and Frank report that this organism was recovered in 40 out of 55 typical, previously unopened cases of fistulous withers and poll evil in the horse. The relationship of the organism with *Br. abortus* and *Br. suis* in producing a bursitis in the supraspinous bursa of the horse has been shown by Roderick, Kimball, McLeod, and Frank. In a case of pulmonary actinomycosis in the dog, Menges, Larsh, and Habermann observed the organism and considered it to be the cause of the condition.

Teng has reported two cases of cerebral actinomycosis in man, although most lesions are found in the cheek and neck. His cases survived after the removal of the lesion and antibiotic therapy. Human actinomycosis is usually caused by *A. israelii*.

*A. bovis* is pathogenic for the rabbit and guinea pig, and when it is inoculated intraperitoneally into those animals, it produces encapsulated nodules similar to tubercles over the omentum.

**Immunity.** Actinomycosis is so chronic that it is apparent that some degree of resistance is possessed by the normal animal. The resistance is not increased by the infection, apparently, because the disease progresses continuously. Artificial immunization is not practical.

**Diagnosis.** The presence of *A. bovis* in the cervical region of cattle is detected by the demonstration of gram-positive filamentous cells. Other organisms, notably *Actinobacillus lignieresi, Staphylococcus aureus,* and *Corynebacterium pyogenes* may be found in cervical lesions.

It must be reemphasized that thc presence of sulfur granules is not diagnostic of actinomycosis, inasmuch as such bodies are also found in other infections.

### *Actinomyces israelii*

Previous mention has been made of the history of this organism. While the majority of strains of Actinomyces which produce infection in man probably are *A. israelii,* it is believed that *A. bovis* occasionally may be found in typical cases of actinomycosis of the human family.

The morphology of *A. bovis* and *A. israelii* is not significantly different. The colonies of *A. bovis* are usually smooth and soft in consistency as contrasted to those of *A. israelii* which are rough and have a pebbled surface as the culture ages.

In brain broth *A. bovis* grows slowly without producing any appreciable change in the medium. *A. israelii* grows more abundantly in this medium, producing a slight acid reaction. *A. bovis* produces a diffuse growth in thioglycollate medium but *A. israelii* forms discrete, compact colonies, irregularly round, and variable in size. Most strains of *A. israelii* produce acid from glucose, xylose, and mannitol, reduce nitrates but do not hydrolyze starch. Porteous, Keir, and Christie report that *A. israelii* (Wills strain) grows best if the growth factors biotin, inositol, nicotinic acid, pyridoxal, and riboflavin in a modified Howell and Pine medium.

### Other Actinomyces Species

Four other species of Actinomyces have been described. Georg and associates recently isolated and described *A. ericksonii;* this organism was isolated from several human cases of pleuritis and pulmonary abscessation. In addition to biochemical and antigenic differences, *A. ericksonii* does not form granules in infected tissues. Two other pathogens, *A. baudetii* and *A. propionicus,* have been described. The propriety of *A. baudetii* as a species is questionable; it has been isolated from canine and feline infections. *A. propionicus* was isolated from a human lesion.

## THE GENUS NOCARDIA

In 1888 Nocard isolated a filamentous, aerobic organism from a cattle disease known as *farcin de boeuf* or bovine farcy. The disease was characterized by enlargement and ulceration of the lymphatics and regional lymph nodes of the extremities. The organism was named *Nocardia farcinica.* In 1891 Eppinger isolated a similar organism from a human brain abscess; this organism, known as *Cladothrix asteroides,* was renamed *Nocardia asteroides* in 1891. Recent work of Gordon and Mihm (1962) indicate that *N. asteroides* and *N. farcinica* are not separable. The name *N. asteroides* has become established by use for the species. The genus Nocardia contains two other notable pathogens, *Nocardia brasiliensis* and *Nocardia caviae.* Of the remaining 41 or more species of this genus that have been described, some appear to be more closely related to the genus Mycobacterium, others to the genus Streptomyces, and the remainder unimportant pathogens of animals. This genus promises to benefit by further taxonomic evaluation.

Nocardiosis is an important disease of animals and man. Cattle appear to be the most frequently affected domestic animals. Bovine nocardiosis is seen as a severe, chronic mastitis, as bovine farcy, and as a pulmonary disease. Canine nocardiosis occurs commonly in young dogs and is seen in the form of a pulmonary disease accompanied by proliferative pleuritis; visceral organs, subcutaneous tissues, bone, and the central nervous system may become infected. Nocardiosis of the goat, horse, and cat is recognized occasionally, and infection of the pig apparently is rare. In human nocardiosis, pulmonary involvement is common but other organ systems are less frequently involved. A subcutaneous form of actinomycotic mycetoma is caused by *N. brasiliensis* infection. The lesions of nocardiosis typically present a granulomatous tissue reaction with suppuration.

The three pathogens discussed in this section, *N. asteroides, N. brasiliensis,* and *N. caviae,* have all been isolated from the soil.

Infection may be opportunistic in nature, following inhalation or mechanical introduction of the organism. Infection is not considered to be contagious; however, these organisms are capable pathogens once they become established in the tissues.

### *Nocardia asteroides*

*N. asteroides* is the most common animal pathogen of the genus. It is widely distributed throughout the soils of the United States and has been isolated from diseased tissues in many countries. Infections by *N. asteroides* commonly involve cattle, dogs, and man. In cattle, mammary and cutaneous infections are prominent. Nocardial mastitis often results from unsanitary infusion practices. In bovine farcy the organism is frequently called *N. farcinica* which is currently considered to be synonymous with *N. asteroides*.

**Morphology and Staining.** *N. asteroides* is a branching filamentous organism which fragments into rod and coccoid elements (Fig. 35.3). The mycelial filaments are slender, approximating 0.5$\mu$ to 1.0$\mu$ in width. All forms are gram-positive, but the filamentous forms may stain unevenly, imparting a beaded appearance. Most strains are partially acid-fast, but the degree of acid-fastness is less pronounced than is that of mycobacteria. Acid-fastness of nocardia is best determined using Kinyoun's stain and 1 per cent aqueous $H_2SO_4$ for decolorizing; alcohol should be specifically excluded from the decolorizing solution. Under these conditions some mycelial elements and many coccoid elements retain the fuchsin stain.

**Growth Requirements and Characteristics.** The Nocardia are aerobic organisms which grow well on a variety of bacteriologic and mycologic media. On blood agar *N. asteroides* grows slowly, forming raised, wrinkled, waxy colonies which reach 2 cm. in diameter after 2 weeks incubation at 37°C.; the colonies are nonhemolytic, tend to adhere to the medium, are tan to orange in color, and may have a white, powdery surface if aerial hyphae are abundant. Similar colonies are formed on Sabouraud's dextrose agar which does not contain antibiotics. In serum broth *N. asteroides* typically forms a waxy, flaky pellicle and a granular sediment. Discrete microcolonies approximating 1 mm. in diameter are formed in broth by many strains, and some strains produce a soluble brown pigment. Nearly all strains of *N. asteroides* form aerial hyphae, but in many strains this for-

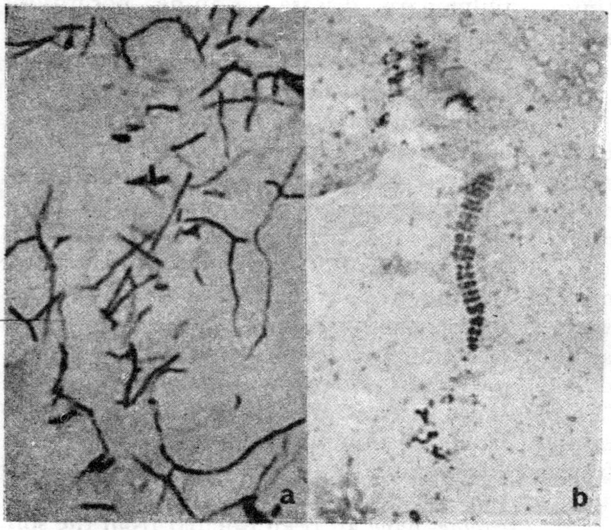


FIG. 35.3—a. **Nocardia asteroids** from broth culture, Gram stain, ×950. b. **Dermatophilus congolensis** from exudate, Giemsa stain, ×950.

mation is not grossly obvious; Bennett's agar is used to detect the formation of aerial hyphae.

**Resistance.** *N. asteroides* is relatively heat tolerant. Nearly all strains will grow at 40°C., many grow at 45°C., and a few grow at 50°C. Suspensions of most cultures exposed to 50°C. for 8 hours, or 60°C. for 4 hours, remain viable. The organism in culture suspension is more heat resistant than are organisms in infectious exudates. Exposure to 100 parts per million available chlorine for 5 minutes or 100 p.p.m. benzalkonium chloride for 10 minutes is germicidal. Sulfonamides are the preferred drug for treating nocardiosis; antibiotics are not consistently effective, although many strains of *N. asteroides* are sensitive to novobiocin.

**Biochemical Properties.** Nearly all strains of *N. asteroides* produce acid from glucose and glycerol but not from lactose and rarely from inositol, maltose, and mannitol. Most strains reduce nitrates to nitrites, but do not decompose casein, tyrosine, or xanthine. Paraffin can be utilized as a carbon source when placed in Sohngen's medium, a feature that facilitates isolation from soil samples. While most strains do not liquefy gelatin, studies have shown too much variability in this reaction to be a recommendable test.

**Antigenic Structure.** Cummings has shown antigenic similarities between cell wall preparations of Nocardia, Mycobacteria, and Corynebacteria that contain arabinose and galactose in their cell walls. Pier and Keeler have shown that a culture filtrate antigen which is free of cell wall antigens is active in precipitin, complement fixation, and skin tests in cattle experimentally infected with *N. asteroides*. This latter antigen has been used successfully in serologic and skin tests of naturally infected cattle, and does not cross react when used to test cattle infected with Mycobacteria. Common antigens exist between *N. asteroides* and *N. brasiliensis*, and antigenic differences appear to exist between some strains of *N. asteroides*.

**Pathogenicity.** *N. asteroides* is pathogenic for cattle, goats, horses, dogs, cats, and man. Rare instances of infection occur in swine, fish, and other marine life. Pathogenicity studies in the laboratory are usually conducted by intraperitoneal inoculation of guinea pigs. When strains of low pathogenicity are used, the inoculum may be mixed with sterile gastric mucin to enhance the pathogenicity.

### *Nocardia brasiliensis*

*N. brasiliensis* is not known to be an important pathogen of animals. Ajello and associates have reported isolation of the organism from subcutaneous lesions in a cat. The most common lesion caused by *N. brasiliensis* is actinomycotic mycetoma of man. These infections primarily involve the cutaneous and subcutaneous tissues with occasional osteitis; draining sinus tracts are formed, and mineralized granules containing *N. brasiliensis* are found in the lesion and exudates.

**Morphology and Staining.** On the basis of colony morphology and staining reactions, *N. brasiliensis* is indistinguishable from *N. asteroides*. In tissues and exudates, *N. brasiliensis* tends to form granules which are microcolonies surrounded by an organic and mineralized matrix. Such granules are not often seen in *N. asteroides* infections, but nonorganized microcolonies are.

**Cultural Characteristics and Resistance.** The cultural characteristics of *N. brasiliensis* are essentially the same as those listed for *N. asteroides;* however, *N. brasiliensis* is less heat resistant. Most strains will not grow at 45°C., and do not survive exposure at 50°C. for 8 hours.

**Biochemical Properties.** Nearly all strains of *N. brasiliensis* produce acid from glucose, glycerol, inositol, and mannitol but not from lactose and rarely from maltose

Most strains reduce nitrates to nitrites; decompose casein and tyrosine but not xanthine; and liquefy gelatin.

**Antigenic Structure.** Zamora and associates have shown the existence of polysaccharide antigens in cell extracts of *N. brasiliensis* and *N. asteroides,* some of which are common to both species and some of which are species specific.

### *Nocardia caviae*

Gordon and Mihm have published methods for the identification of *N. caviae* which was originally described as an isolate from infected guinea pigs. The organism has been isolated from cases of bovine mastitis and human mycetoma and has been shown to be pathogenic for mice following intraperitoneal inoculation.

The morphological, staining, and cultural characteristics of *N. caviae* are similar to those of *N. asteroides* and *N. brasiliensis.* The heat tolerance resembles that of *N. asteroides* in that most strains of *N. caviae* survive exposure to 50°C. for 8 hours; they do not grow when incubated at 50°C., but most strains will grow at 45°C. *N. caviae* produces acid from glucose, glycerol, inositol, mannitol, and usually from maltose but not from lactose. Nitrates are reduced to nitrites; and xanthine is decomposed but casein and tyrosine are not.

## THE GENUS DERMATOPHILUS

In 1915 Van Saceghem isolated and described an aerobic, filamentous organism from *impetigo contagieux* of African cattle. The infection is common in cattle, sheep, hor and goats and is typified by an exudative dermatitis. Accumulations of dried exudate build up along tufts of hair or wool in the affected areas. Mild cases exhibit only small accumulations of exudate in the hair or wool; in more severe cases the skin is eroded, microabscesses are present, and the animal may die possibly as the result of secondary invaders. The disease in cattle, horses, and goats called cutaneous streptothricosis; the condition in sheep known as "lumpy wool" or mycotic dermatitis; and the second condition in sheep, "strawberry foot-rot," affecting the feet and lower extremities, collectively are named dermatophilosis.

Austwick examined isolates from cutaneous streptothricosis, mycotic dermatitis, and strawberry foot rot and proposed that all three belonged to the same genus. Accordingly three species were proposed: *Dermatophilus congolensis* (Van Saceghem, 1915), the agent of cutaneous streptothricosis; *Dermatophilus dermatonomus* (Austwick, 1958), the agent of mycotic dermatitis; and *Dermatophilus pedis* (Austwick, 1958), the agent of strawberry foot rot. Application of this proposal substantially clarified a nomenclature which had previously included references to such generic terms as Actinomyces, Nocardia, Streptothrix, and Polysepta for these organisms. In 1964 Gordon published the results of comparative studies of members of the genus Dermatophilus and concluded that all members can be accommodated by the single species *Dermatophilus congolensis.*

### *Dermatophilus congolensis*

*D. congolensis* is known to exist in many areas of the world, including Africa, Australia, Europe, India, and North and South America. The organism may be an obligate parasite in that it has been isolated only from animal lesions and not from soil or other saprophytic locations. In lesions on infected animals, *D. congolensis* may be demonstrated in exudative crusts and in superficial layers of the affected skin. The interesting and rather complex life cycle of *D. congolensis* has been described by Roberts and is depicted in Fig. 35.4.

**Morphology and Staining.** Motile zoospores approximating 1$\mu$ in diameter are formed in and released from mature hyphal elements. These spores are propelled by a group of polar flagellae. The spores enlarge and eventually germinate, producing slender, 0.5$\mu$ to 1.0$\mu$ wide, branching filaments. These filaments elongate, and trans-

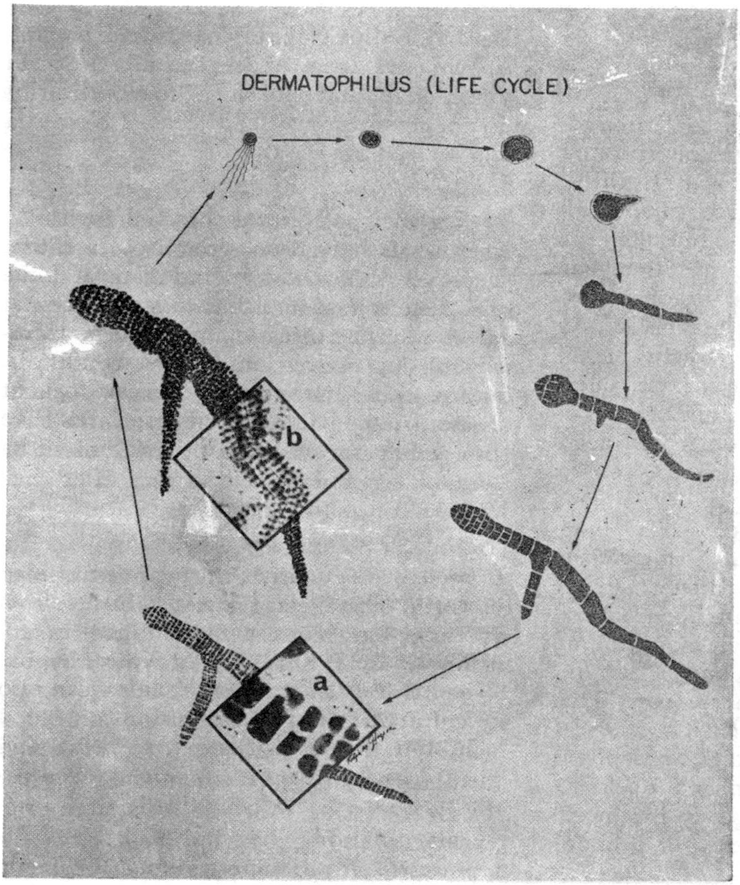


FIG. 35.4—Life Cycle of **Dermatophilus congolensis.** a. Inset electron micrograph of thin section, ×12,000. b. Inset photomicrograph, ×950. (Courtesy J. L. Richard.)

verse septa are formed in decreasing frequency from the spore end to the tip of the tapering hyphae. The hyphae widen and additional septations occur in several planes until the hyphae are divided into a series of packets. At this time the hyphae may have 4 to 8 or more packets across its diameter and measure up to $3\mu$ in width. Motile zoospores are released and the morphological cycle continues under favorable conditions of growth (Fig. 35.4). The mature hyphae and young zoospores are encapsulated. All forms are gram-positive, but Giemsa's stain is recommended to demonstrate the organism in clinical materials. The organism is not acid-fast.

**Growth Requirements and Characteristics.** *D. congolensis* grows aerobically at 37°C. on whole blood agar, serum broth, or other serum containing media. It will not grow on Sabouraud's medium or media containing antibiotics. On blood agar *D. congolensis* grows relatively slowly, forming small, gray to orange, raised, granular colonies which approximate 1 mm. in diameter by 48 to 72 hours. The colonies tend to sink into the agar surface, are adherent to the medium, and produce a limited zone of $\beta$ hemolysis. Mature colonies approximating 1 cm. in diameter after 1 to 2 weeks incubation are orange, wrinkled to crateriform, and waxy in consistency, with central or apical liquefaction. In serum broth a soft flocculent sediment or microcolonies are formed; many strains form a delicate waxy surface film. The organism is negatively aerotactic and is capable of anaerobic as well as aerobic growth.

**Resistance.** In exudative crusts, *D. congolensis* resists desiccation over concentrated sulfuric acid for 9 days. Exposure to chlorhexidine diacetate at 100 p.p.m., benzalkonium chloride at 230 p.p.m., and 2 per cent solutions of phenol derivatives in detergent carriers for 10 minutes kills the organism. Many antibiotics, including penicillin and streptomycin, prevent the growth of *D. congolensis* in culture media but are generally ineffective in treatment; intramuscular streptomycin has shown some beneficial effects when used in diseased sheep prior to shearing.

**Biochemical Properties.** *D. congolensis* produces acid from glucose, fructose, galactose, inulin, and serum-enriched maltose but not from dulcitol, lactose, mannitol, or salicin; occasional strains have been reported to produce acid in sucrose. This organism is quite proteolytic; it hydrolyzes urea, peptonizes litmus milk, hydrolyzes casein, and liquefies gelatin and Loeffler's inspissated serum. Catalase is produced, but nitrates are not reduced, nor is indol formed.

**Antigenic Structure.** Gordon has shown common precipitinogens in all types of Dermatophilus isolates tested, and precipitins in sera from experimentally infected sheep, goats, and rabbits. These precipitins do not cross react with antigens of Nocardia and Actinomyces.

**Pathogenicity.** Natural infections with *D. congolensis* have been recognized in cattle, sheep, goats, horses, deer, and man. Rabbits and mice are susceptible to experimental infection. The disease appears to be transmissible by contact, and moist conditions of the skin and existing lesions benefit transmission. Richard and associates have shown that infection can be transmitted by both biting and nonbiting flies after they have fed on moist lesions.

**Diagnosis.** Exudative crusts are emulsified in sterile saline, and Giemsa-stained smears of these emulsions are examined microscopically for the presence of typical hyphal elements (Fig. 35.3). The organism can also be cultured from these emulsions on blood agar, but the lack of selective media and the propensity of contaminants to overgrow the slow-growing *D. congolensis* often complicate isolation. Pier and associates have reported a filtration technique that facilitates cultural isolation and the application of fluorescent antibody techniques for microscopic identification of *D. congolensis*.

## REFERENCES


Ajello, L., *et al*. Isolation of *Nocardia brasiliensis* From a Cat With a Review of Its Prevalence and Geographic Distribution. Jour. Amer. Vet. Med. Assn. 138:370, 1961.

Austwick, P. K. C. Cutaneous Streptothricosis, Mycotic Dermatitis and Strawberry Foot Rot and the Genus Dermatophilus Van Saceghem. Vet. Rev. Annot. 4:33, 1958.

Christie, A. O., and Porteous, J. W. The Cultivation of a Single Strain of *Actinomyces israelii* in a Simplified and Chemically Defined Medium. Jour. Gen. Microbiol. 28:443–60, 1962.

Cope, Zachary. Actinomycosis. Oxford Univ. Press, New York, 1938.

Cummings, C. S. Chemical Composition and Antigenic Structure of Cell Walls of Corynebacterium, Mycobacterium, Nocardia, Actinomyces, and Arthrobacter. Jour. Gen. Microbiol. 28:35, 1962.

Erikson, D. Pathogenic Anaerobic Organisms of the Actinomyces Group. Med. Rec. Council Spec. Rep. Ser. 24D, 1940.

Georg, L. K., *et al*. A New Pathogenic Anaerobic Actinomyces Species. Jour. Inf. Dis. 115:88, 1965.

Gordon, M. A. The Genus Dermatophilus. Jour. Bact. 88:509, 1964.

Gordon, R. E., and Mihm, J. M. The Type Species of the Genus Nocardia. Jour. Gen. Microbiol. 27:1, 1962.

———, and ———. Identification of *Nocardia caviae* (Erickson) *Nov. Comb*. Ann. N.Y. Acad. Sci. 98:628, 1962.

Kier, H. A., and Porteous, J. W. The Amino Acid Requirements of a Single Strain of *Actinomyces israelii* Growing in a Chemically Defined Medium. Jour. Gen. Microbiol. 28:193–201, 1962.

KIMBALL, ALICE, and FRANK, E. R. Amer. Jour. Vet. Res. 6:39, 1945.

———, *et al.* Amer. Jour. Vet. Res. 15:551, 1954.

MENGES, R. W., *et al.* Jour. Amer. Vet. Med. Assn. 122:73, 1953.

PIER, A. C. Nocardiosis in Animals. Proc. 66th Ann. Meet. U.S. Livestock Sanit. Assn., 409, 1962.

———, and KEELER, R. F. Extracellular Antigens of *Nocardia asteroides.* I. Production and Immunologic Characterization. Amer. Rev. Resp. Dis. 91:391, 1965.

———, *et al.* Fluorescent Antibody and Cultural Techniques in Cutaneous Streptothricosis. Amer. Jour. Vet. Res. 25:1014, 1964.

PINE, L., and OVERMAN, J. R. Determination of the Structure and Composition of the "Sulphur Granules of *Actinomyces bovis.*" Jour. Gen. Microbiol. 32:209–23, 1963.

———, *et al.* Studies on the Morphological, Physiological and Biochemical Characteristics of *Actinomyces bovis.* Jour. Gen. Microbiol. 23:403, 1960.

RICHARD, J. L., and PIER, A. C. Transmission of *Dermatophilus congolensis* by *Stomoxys calcitrans* and *Musca domestica.* Amer. Jour. Vet. Res. 27:419, 1966.

ROBERTS, D. S. The Life Cycle of *Dermatophilus dermatonomus,* the Causal Agent of Ovine Mycotic Dermatitis. Austral. Jour. Exp. Biol. Med. Sci. 39:463, 1961.

RODERICK, L. M., *et al.* Amer. Jour. Vet. Res. 9:5, 1948.

SLACK, J. M., *et al.* Serological Grouping of Actinomyces by Means of Fluorescent Antibodies. Jour. Bact. 82:54–65, 1961.

TENG, P. Actinomycotic Cerebral Abscesses. Jour. Amer. Med. Assn. 175:807–10, 1961.

THOMPSON, L. Proc. Staff Meet., Mayo Clin. 25:81, 1950.

WAKSMAN, S. A. *In* Bergey's Manual of Determinative Bacteriology. 7th Ed. Williams & Wilkins Co., Baltimore, 1957.

WILSON, G. S., and MILES, A. A. Topley's Principles of Bacteriology and Immunity. 5th Ed. Williams & Wilkins Co., Baltimore, 1964.

ZAMORA, A., *et al.* Immunologically Active Polysaccharides From *Nocardia brasiliensis.* Jour. Bact. 85:549, 1963.

# 36
# The Spirochetes

**SAM G. KENZY, *D.V.M., Ph.D.* and LEIF M. RINGEN, *Ph.D.***

*Department of Veterinary Microbiology*
*College of Veterinary Medicine*
*Washington State University*
*Pullman, Washington*

SPIROCHETES ARE MICROORGANISMS WHICH are slender and spiral in shape, motile by means of a flexuous motion, and they multiply by transverse fission. Most of the forms which have been described are saprophytic upon plant and animal life; some are parasitic, and a few are pathogenic for man and animals.

The spirochetes were among the first types of microscopic life observed and described by Leeuwenhoek in 1681. The large forms which are representative of the group were seen in various types of plant infusions by the early microscopists, and as early as 1837, Donne observed spiral-shaped microorganisms in smears from genital lesions. In 1833 Ehrenberg used the name *Spirochaeta* for a large, free-living, spiral-shaped organism. The first spirochete of any pathogenic significance was described by Obermeir in 1873. This organism was found in the blood of patients suffering with relapsing fever. In 1891 Sakharoff found that a spirochete was the cause of a goose septicemia in Russia, and in 1902 Theiler observed a spiral-shaped organism in a febrile condition of cattle in South Africa.

The spirochetes were considered bacteria until 1905 when Schaudinn and Hoffmann concluded studies on the spiral organism of syphilis. They compared the organism with a flexuous protozoan parasite, a trypanosome of birds, and concluded that it, too, was a protozoan. As a result of their classical studies, the spirochetes were claimed by the protozoologists. During the past twenty years it has become obvious that these microorganisms are closely related to the bacteria and at the present time they are classified as bacteria in the order *Spirochaetales*. It is freely admitted, however, that the spirochetes show some of the characteristics of the flexuous protozoa.

The differentiation of the spirochetes is difficult because they are not cultivated with ease on artificial media and are devoid of marked biochemical activity. Present-day classifications are based upon the morphology of the different types, and on these characteristics two families are recognized.

These families are listed and described in Bergey's Manual, 1957, as follows:

FAMILY I. *Spirochaetaceae:* spirals $30\mu$ to $500\mu$ in length, having definite protoplasmic structures.

FAMILY II. *Treponemataceae:* spirals $4\mu$ to $16\mu$ in length, having no obvious protoplasmic structure.

None of the genera in the family *Spirochaetaceae* has species which are pathogenic for animals, although some have been isolated from oysters, shell-fish, and mollusks.

The family *Treponemataceae* contains three genera which do have species pathogenic for animals and man. These genera are differentiated as follows:

I. Stains easily with aniline dyes.
   Genus I. *Borrelia.*

II. Stain with difficulty except with Giemsa's stain or by silver impregnation.
   Genus II. *Treponema,* strict anaerobes.
   Genus III. *Leptospira,* aerobes.

The species in each of these genera which are related to specific diseases in animals and man will be discussed.

## THE GENUS BORRELIA

### *Borrelia anserina*

**Synonyms and History.** *Spirochaeta gallinarum, Spironema gallinarum, Spirochaeta anserina, Treponema anserina, Borrelia gallinarum.*

In 1891 Sakharoff described a spirochete which he considered to be the cause of an acute septicemia in geese. He called the organism *Spirochaeta anserina.* In 1903 Marchoux and Salimbeni, in Brazil, reported a septicemia in domestic fowls. The disease was caused by a spirochete which they named *Spirochaeta gallinarum.* It is quite probable that the organism described by Sakharoff from geese and the one from fowls are identical.

**Distribution and Transmission.** *Bor. anserina* is responsible for the disease commonly known as fowl spirochetosis. It has been observed in South America, Africa, Australia, Java, in parts of Asia, and to some extent in European Russia, the Balkan countries, and in Germany.

In the United States the organism has been found in Texas, California, and New Mexico.

This organism is transmitted from one bird to another by the bite of ticks belonging to the genus Argas. The mechanical transmission of the spirochete by the chicken mite, *Dermanyssus gallinae,* and by the ingestion of fecal material from infected ticks has been considered probable.

If ectoparasite vectors are controlled, recovered chickens could be moved within 30 days to new premises without danger of disease transmission (Dickie and Barrera). The organism can be transmitted by the contact of susceptible birds with the feces of those infected. Loomis observed in his study of the disease in turkeys in California that the infection was not transmitted by the tick *Argas persicus,* and concluded that the feces of infected turkeys constituted the chief source of infection.

**Morphology and Staining.** *Bor. anserina* is a long, spiral organism, $10\mu$ to $20\mu$ in length, with an average of one spiral per $1.5\mu$ (Fig. 36.1). The organism is not flagellated but does possess terminal filaments. It is actively motile. In old cultures, small granules or coccoid bodies which are considered to be representative of pleomorphism have been found. These same bodies have been observed in ticks. The organism is stained readily with dilute carbol fuchsin and Giemsa's stain. It is also easily demonstrated by the silver impregnation method of Levaditi and by the use of India ink. It is gram-negative and nonacid-fast.

**Growth Requirements and Characteristics.** This spirochete is grown only under anaero-

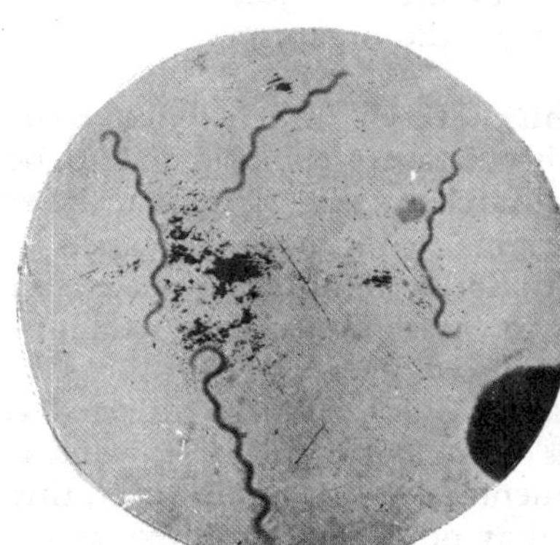

FIG. 36.1—**Borrelia anserina** in blood of goose, Giemsa stain, ×2,000. (From Nowak: Documenta Microbiologica, courtesy Gustav Fischer.)

bic conditions at a temperature of 37°C. It is cultivated with some difficulty, but the use of ascitic fluid containing pieces of rabbit kidney or heart muscle has been found satisfactory. It does not produce any characteristic type of growth, and nothing is known concerning its biochemical properties.

The organism is not resistant, and subcultures must be made weekly in order to maintain viability.

**Pathogenicity.** *Bor. anserina* is found most often in chickens but has been reported in ducks, turkeys, and geese. The disease is characterized by an acute septicemia which is fatal within three or four days. The disease is most fatal to young birds. It is accompanied by a rise in temperature, drowsiness, diarrhea, and emaciation. Anemia and enlargement of the spleen are commonly observed, due to the destruction of red blood cells by the toxic products liberated from the disintegrating organisms. The spleen is usually mottled in appearance.

Experimentally, the organism has been found to be pathogenic for ducks, geese, chickens, guinea fowls, turtledoves, sparrows, pheasants, pigeons, and canaries. It is not pathogenic for mammals. Although it multiplies to some extent in rabbits after parenteral injection, it does not produce any significant disease. McNeil *et al.* were not able to infect rabbits, rats, lambs, or lizards with the organism.

**Immunity.** Fowls which have recovered from the disease are considered to be immune. Marchoux and Salimbeni showed in their original work that fresh blood heated to 55°C. for 5 minutes produced an immunity in susceptible birds. Immune serum produced in horses and goats by the inoculation of blood from infected chickens has been found to be of value under experimental conditions; however, this procedure has not been employed as a practical means of controlling the disease in chicken flocks.

**Diagnosis.** The type of septicemia produced by *Bor. anserina* in the avian family can be diagnosed accurately only by the demonstration of the organism in blood smears. Agglutinin is produced by the infection, but the agglutination test is not used as a method of diagnosis.

### *Borrelia theileri*

**Synonyms and History.** *Spirochaeta theileri, Spironema theileri, Treponema theileri.*

In 1902 Theiler, in South Africa, found a long, spiral organism associated with a minor febrile disease of cattle. In some respects the disease was similar to piroplasmosis, or tick fever. This organism is transmitted from the infected host to susceptible animals by the bite of ticks, such as *Rhipicephalus decoloratus* and *Rhipicephalus evertsi.* A similar organism was found in the horse and in sheep by Theiler, and in 1906 Stordy observed the organism in a horse. These organisms have been called *Spirochaeta ovis* and *Spirochaeta equi,* respectively, by Novy and Knapp. The cross-agglutination results obtained by Todd and others have indicated that the organism *Bor. theileri* occurs in cattle, sheep, and horses.

This spirochete is a slender organism with pointed ends, measuring 0.25μ to 0.3μ by 20.0μ to 30.0μ. It is actively motile by means of polar filaments and a flexuous motion. It is stained by the Giemsa stain or other suitable blood stains.

### *Borrelia hyos*

In 1913 King and Baeslack, by means of dark-field illumination, observed a spirochete in the blood of hogs with hog cholera. They considered the organism to be of some etiological significance to the disease and suggested the name *Spirochaeta suis.*

According to the above investigators *Bor. hyos,* as named by Bergey, is a large spirochete 5μ to 7μ in length by 1μ in width. It is flexible and round on its ends; however, a polar flagellum was observed on one cell by the India-ink method. In addition to the spirochete, these authors observed distinct, highly refractive bodies in hog cholera blood and suggested that these granular bodies may represent certain stages in the life cycle of the spirochete.

Hoskins cultivated this organism in an anaerobic medium composed of human ascitic fluid and fresh rabbit tissue. This investigator could find no etiological relationship of the spirochete with hog cholera.

## THE GENUS TREPONEMA

None of the species in the genus Treponema is of any significance to animal health. One organism, *Treponema cuniculi,* has been isolated from rabbits but is not prevalent or of great importance. *Treponema pallidum,* the cause of syphilis in man, is of great health significance to the human race and warrants a brief consideration here.

### *Treponema pallidum*

**Synonyms and History.** *Spirochaeta pallidum, Spirillum pallidum.*

In 1905 Schaudinn and Hoffmann observed a spirochete in the primary chancres of syphilis and in enlarged regional lymph nodes. They considered this organism as the cause of syphilis; this fact was subsequently proved by numerous investigators. Up to this time different agents were described as the cause of syphilis. These were, for the most part, the various bacteria which existed as saprophytes upon external genitalia.

**Distribution and Transmission.** *Trep. pallidum* is widely distributed throughout the civilized world. It is generally agreed that, quite contrary to other diseases, syphilis had its origin on the American continent, for it made its appearance in the Old World after the return of Columbus from the discovery of this continent. The infection is transmitted readily by sexual intercourse and other sexual contacts. Intrauterine infection of the fetus occurs in syphilitic mothers.

The disease may be transmitted non-

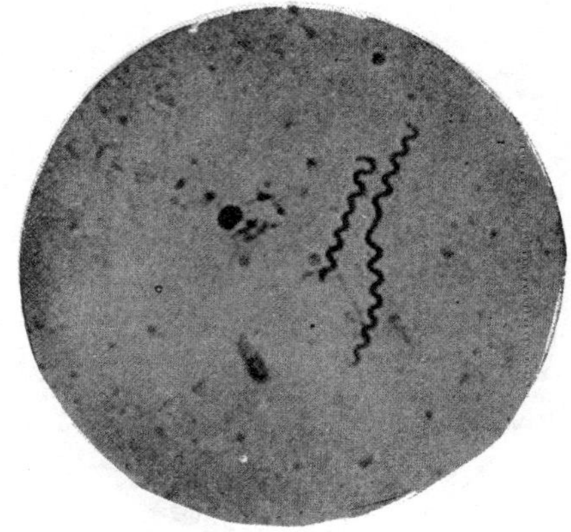

FIG. 36.2—**Treponema pallidum** in primary chancre, Giemsa stain, ×2,000. (From Nowak: Documenta Microbiologica, courtesy Gustav Fischer.)

venereally. This form is not uncommon and may predominate where social and economic conditions result in poverty and overcrowding. Nonvenereal syphilis may reach epidemic proportions, especially among children.

**Morphology and Staining.** This spirochete is $0.25\mu$ to $0.3\mu$ in diameter and $8\mu$ to $15\mu$ long. It is tightly coiled into eight to fifteen spirals which are rigid, and with an amplitude of approximately $1\mu$. The organism is actively motile by means of an undulating and rotating motion. It is not flagellated, although long, polar filaments are often observed (Fig. 36.2). Granular forms of the organism have been described, but whether these forms are a part of a life cycle has not been determined. Multiplication occurs by transverse fission. No spores are formed.

*Trep. pallidum* is rendered visible in an unstained preparation by dark-field illumination. The brilliant, silvery appearance of the organism against the dark background is quite characteristic. A number of the more penetrating stains, such as Giemsa and Wright, are suitable to demonstrate the organism in smears. In tissue sections, silver impregnation methods are commonly employed. In such preparations the orga-

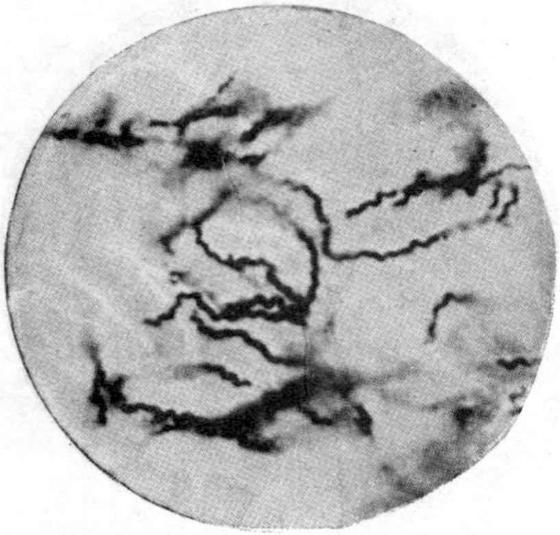

FIG. 36.3—**Treponema pallidum** in lung of syphilitic fetus, silver impregnation stain, ×2,000. (From Nowak: Documenta Microbiologica, courtesy Gustav Fischer.)

nism is stained a dense black color (Fig. 36.3).

**Growth Requirements and Characteristics.** *Trep. pallidum* is cultivated with difficulty under artificial conditions. Reports of the growth of the organism on Noguchi's medium have been made, but it is doubtful if the organisms grown were actually the syphilis spirochete. It is commonly agreed, at the present time, that the organism has not been grown artificially.

**Resistance.** This spirochete is not resistant to heat, drying, or the action of chemicals.

The organism is susceptible to arsenical and bismuth compounds, which are extensively used in the treatment and cure of the disease. *Trep. pallidum* is sensitive to penicillin in vivo, and this drug is used extensively in treating syphilis. Some cases of the disease treated with penicillin relapse, however, and it is believed that resistance to this antibiotic is developed by some strains of the organism.

**Pathogenicity.** Under natural conditions man, only, is susceptible to *Trep. pallidum.* All races of mankind have been afflicted with the disease produced by the organism, but some individual and racial examples of resistance have been noted. The disease was particularly severe on the European continent after its first appearance, but resistance, apparently, has been developed since that time.

The organism is pathogenic to monkeys. Rabbits are susceptible and are used experimentally in the study of the organism and the disease. All types of the disease can be produced in rabbits by appropriate avenues of inoculation. Guinea pigs are susceptible to the organism, but they are not used to any great extent in experimental studies of the disease.

**Immunity.** Recovery from one attack of syphilis produces immunity, and persons suffering with an active case of the disease are refractive to a second inoculation. Artificial immunizing agents have never proved practical as a prophylaxis in the disease.

**Diagnosis.** Syphilis is diagnosed by two laboratory methods. Primary lesions of the disease are diagnosed by the use of darkfield illumination in the demonstration of the characteristic spirochete. Approximately two weeks after the first chancre, the presence of antibodies in the blood serum can be detected by appropriate serological tests. For this purpose the Wassermann test has been universally employed. During recent years the Kahn precipitation test has been used for routine diagnosis. Opinion is somewhat divided concerning the relative reliability of the complement-fixation (Wassermann) and the precipitation tests for the diagnosis of syphilis. Both tests are suitable, but neither can be relied upon as an absolutely accurate diagnostic aid. They are used to supplement clinical observations. It must be emphasized that there are two periods when both reactions are negative: first, during the first two weeks of the developing chancre and, second, during the latent period of the disease following treatment. The student is referred to textbooks devoted to the human pathogens for additional information concerning these and other diagnostic tests.

### *Treponema cuniculi*

This organism was first observed by Ross in 1912 and by Bayon in 1913. Noguchi named it *Treponema cuniculi* in 1921.

It is practically the same size as *Trep. pallidum,* and for this reason may lead to some confusion in experimental study. The organism produces about the genitalia of rabbits superficial lesions which are characterized by slight elevation and desquamation. Generalization of the infection has not been observed. There is no antigenic relationship between this organism and the syphilis spirochete, and rabbits infected with *Trep. cuniculi* do not give a positive Wassermann reaction.

## THE GENUS LEPTOSPIRA

In 1962 the Leptospira subcommittee of the International Committee on Bacteriological Nomenclature recommended that the genus Leptospira be divided into two species: *L. interrogans,* representing the parasitic types; and *L. biflexa,* the saprophytic. These two species can be differentiated on the basis of resistance *(L. biflexa)* or susceptibility *(L. interrogans)* to the bacteriostatic action of divalent copper ions in a solution of copper sulfate diluted 1:100,000. These species are further subdivided into groups, serotypes, and subserotypes, based upon cross-agglutination and agglutinin-adsorption techniques. The division into groups is arbitrarily used for practical purposes of preliminary diagnostic procedures. At the present time, *L. interrogans* is divided into 13 groups containing 85 serotypes and 37 subserotypes. Undoubtedly this number will continue to grow with improved techniques for isolations and extended epidemiologic studies.

Table 36.1 lists the various groups of leptospira. Except for groups *icterohaemorrhagiae, canicola,* and *pomona,* only the representative serotypes, subserotypes, and type strains are given. A complete listing is available through the World Health Organization reports.

It is quite evident that diagnostic laboratories must continually be alert to detect the presence of new serotypes which may become responsible for further livestock losses. We must also be cognizant of the continual disease-producing potential that leptospirae have for man, since, for example, it has been estimated that almost 30 per cent of his canine pets experience leptospirosis.

Under the joint sponsorship of the World Health Organization (WHO) and the Food and Agriculture Organization (FAO), six reference laboratories throughout the world have been established for the identification of leptospiral isolates and for the dissemination of information to workers in leptospirosis. These laboratories are located in The Netherlands, England, Italy, Japan, Australia, and the United States. The Division of Veterinary Medicine, in the Walter Reed Army Institute of Research, serves as a reference laboratory in this country.

Three serotypes are known to be of particular significance to animal health in the United States: *icterohaemorrhagiae, canicola,* and *pomona.* Other serotypes which have been isolated from either wild or domestic animals in this country include: *hardjo, ballum, autumnalis, grippotyphosa, australis, naam, hebdomadis, mini, atchafalaya, hyos,* and *bataviae.*

### Serotypes: *icterohaemorrhagiae, canicola,* and *pomona*

#### Synonyms and History

Serotype *icterohaemorrhagiae.* A disease in man characterized by fever, jaundice, and petechial hemorrhages was observed as early as 1800 by Larrey. That this disease was different from other similar conditions was first seen by Stimson in 1907 in sections of kidney from a patient who was believed to have died of yellow fever in New Orleans. Stimson thought he had discovered the causal organism of that disease and named it *Spirochaeta interrogans.* The cause of Weil's disease was determined in 1916 by Inada and coworkers to be an organism they called *Spirochaeta icterohaemorrhagiae.* This disease was confused with yellow fever as late as 1928 by Noguchi and his associates, who referred to their spirochete as *Spirochaeta icteroides.* These organisms are considered identical with *Leptospira interrogans* serotype *icterohaemorrhagiae.*

A canine disease similar to the human infection was described as early as 1850 by

TABLE 36.1

PATHOGENIC LEPTOSPIRA *

| Group | Serotype | Subserotype | Type Strain † |
|---|---|---|---|
| Icterohaemorrhagiae | icterohaemorrhagiae | incompleta ‡ | RGA |
| | icterohaemorrhagiae | icterohaemorrhagiae | M 20 |
| | icterohaemorrhagiae | mankarso | Mankarso |
| | icterohaemorrhagiae § | ndahambukuje | Ndahambukuje |
| | naam | naam | Naam |
| | naam § | mwogole | Mwogole |
| | naam | dakota | Grand River |
| | sarmin | | Sarmin |
| | birkini | birkini | Birkin |
| | birkini | smithii | Smith |
| | ndambari | | Ndambari |
| Javanica | javanica | | Veldrat Batavia 46 |
| Canicola | canicola | | Hond Utrecht IV |
| | schueffneri | | Vleermuis 90C |
| | benjamin | | Benjamin |
| | jonsis | | Jones |
| | sumneri | | Sumner |
| | malaya | | H–6 |
| | kamituga § | | Kamituga |
| | bafani § | | Bafani |
| | kahendo § | | Kahendo |
| | broomi | | Patane |
| | bindjei | | Bindjei |
| Ballum | ballum | ballumensis | Mus 127 |
| Pyrogenes | pyrogenes | | Salinem |
| Cynopteri | cynopteri | | 3522C |
| Autumnalis | autumnalis | autumnalis | Akiyami A |
| Pomona | pomona | pomona | Pomona |
| | pomona | cornelli | C B |
| Australis | australis | | Ballico |
| Grippotyphosa | grippotyphosa | | Moskva V |
| Hebdomadis | hebdomadis | hebdomadis | Hebdomadis |
| Bataviae | bataviae | | Swart |
| Hyos | hyos | hyos | Mitis Johnson |

* Abstract of Leptospira Subcommitte Annex II.
† The first type strain listed in each serotype is regarded as the type strain of that serotype.
‡ The serotype *incompleta* is listed before *icterohaemorrhagiae* because of the prior discovery of its type strain (RGA).
§ Provisional classification.

Hofer. It became epidemic in Germany in 1898 when it was first called Stuttgart disease. This infection did not attract much attention until it was shown that the etiologic agent was the same as in Weil's disease. In 1917 Courmont and Durand found that puppies could be infected with the spirochetes which produced typical jaundice in man. Lukes, in 1924, and Drivacek, in the same year, observed, in the tissues of dogs which had died of Stuttgart disease, organisms which were morphologically identical to Leptospira. In 1925 Okell, Dalling, and Pugh found the organism in epizootic jaundice in hunting dogs in England. The canine strain of the organism was studied in 1928 by Klarenbeek of Holland, who referred to it as *Spirochaeta ictero-uraemia canis.* This organism was subsequently admitted to be the classical organism *Leptospira interrogans* serotype *icterohaemorrhagiae.*

Serotype *canicola.* In 1931 Klarenbeek and Schuffner recognized serologically that another serotype, later called canicola, was the cause of a considerable percentage of the leptospirosis of dogs. In 1937 this serotype was isolated by Meyer and associates in San Francisco and has been described bv them in subsequent publications.

Serotype *pomona* (named after the township of Pomona, North Queensland, Australia). Clayton and coworkers, in 1937, isolated this serotype from dairymen with the seven-day fever. The Mezzano strain from rice-field workers in northern Italy, isolated by Babudieri and Bianchi (1940), was found to be identical. Savino and Rennella (1944) proposed the name *L. suis* for leptospirae isolated from swine in Argentina, which they later recognized as being the same as the *pomona* serotype. Swineherd's disease in man, recognized in Switzerland since 1914, was found through Gsell's investigations (1944) to be caused by this organism.

In the United States, Gochenour *et al.* (1950) identified the *pomona* serotype as the cause of a bovine leptospirosis outbreak reported in 1948 by Baker and Little. Soon after this, infections in swine and other domestic animals were reported. By 1960 every state, except Alaska, had reported evidence of leptospirosis.

**Distribution and Transmission.** Human leptospirosis has been found in Africa, America, Asia, Australia, and many European countries. Most domesticated and wildlife mammals, as well as cold-blooded animals, are susceptible to infection with leptospirae. Although some serotypes appear to be limited geographically and show a host specificity, this can be complicated by the presence of mixed infections. An apparent simultaneous infection by serotypes *hardjo* and *icterohaemorrhagiae* was noted by Clark *et al.* in cattle. Dogs were experimentally exposed to both *pomona* and *canicola* serotypes, resulting in simultaneous infection (Menges *et al.*).

Roth *et al.*, during a leptospirosis survey, isolated leptospirae from 57.4 per cent of 650 skunks. The following serotypes (listed in decreasing frequency of isolation) were reported: *pomona, hyos, ballum, canicola, icterohaemorrhagiae, mini georgia, grippotyphosa,* and the *australis* group.

The primary serotype infecting cattle and swine in the United States appears to be *pomona,* although agglutinins against serotypes *autumnalis, canicola, sejroe, grippotyphosa,* and *icterohaemorrhagiae* have also been reported (Roberts *et al.*).

Human and canine leptospirosis due to serotype *icterohaemorrhagiae* is usually associated with infection of rats, while the serotype *canicola* is usually transmitted by infective dog urine. Human leptospiral infection, apparently contracted through examination of a canefield soil specimen shipped over 1,100 miles, has been reported (Galton).

Contact with urine from animals with leptospiruria is considered the most important method of transmission, particularly when such urine gains access to surface waters. It is believed that the leptospirae gain entrance through mucous membranes of the nose and mouth, conjunctivae, and broken skin surfaces while drinking, swimming, or wading. Leptospirosis has been reported in abbatoir and sewer workers. The inhalation of aerosols produced by urination of dairy cows on concrete floors has also been suggested as a means of spread. The infective potential of a bovine shedder is readily appreciated when we realize that a single cow may excrete more than 6 trillion leptospirae in a 24-hour period and continue to shed at usually a decreasing rate for 30 to over 100 days. In the southern United States Roth has observed shedding in many of the skunks and other wild animals, which may serve as a reservoir of infection to man and domestic animals.

In a Washington study about 30 per cent new leptospirosis infections were observed each month during the summer months in a beef herd on irrigated pastures. Obviously, the rate of spread in a herd must depend on many variables, including surface water pH and drainage, crowding of animals in barns or pastures, nutritional status, and weather changes.

Since fish and snakes have been experimentally infected, cold-blooded animals may provide a means for overwintering of leptospirae. Snakes developed a leptospiremia and possibly a leptospiruria when transmission occurred to contact controls. Infection persisted for at least 17 days in fish (Maestrone and Benjaminson) and in snakes for more than 6 months, including 70 days of induced hibernation (Abdulla and Karstad).

Gsell has outlined 10 epidemiological principles concerning leptospirosis in man and animals with which the student should be familiar:

1. Leptospiral infections are zoonoses.
2. The number of animal species naturally infected by leptospirae is less than the number which can be infected experimentally.
3. In a given area one animal species generally harbors predominantly one serotype of leptospira, or at most only a few serotypes which are weakly differentiated.
4. The intensity of the infection varies considerably in different animals.
5. The danger of infection from animals is due to the emission of leptospirae in the urine.
6. The epidemiological importance of animal carriers of leptospirosis depends upon their collective mode of life.
7. Epidemics in man are possible under (a) natural conditions, and (b) artificial conditions created in animal husbandry.
8. Infection of man can occur either directly from an infected animal, or indirectly through water or soil contaminated by animals.
9. Infection attacks man chiefly through abrasions of the skin and mucous membranes.
10. Epidemiologically, human leptospirosis has characteristic features related to age, season, sex, and occupation.

**Morphology and Staining.** The various serotypes of leptospirae are indistinguishable on the basis of morphology. They are from $8\mu$ to $12\mu$ long and vary from $0.1\mu$ to $0.2\mu$ in thickness. They are closely spiraled, with the ends commonly bent into the shape of a hook (Fig. 36.4). Electron micrographs (Fig. 36.5) indicate that leptospirae consist of an axial filament coiling spirally around a protoplasmic spiral and an enveloping sheath (Swain, 1957; Simpson and White, 1964; Ritchie and Ellinghausen, 1965).

These unflagellated organisms, which are best studied by dark-field illumination, are actively motile by means of a spinning action on the long axis, giving the "buttonhook" ends a flasklike appearance. There may also be a serpentine undulating motion. Some forms are capable of passing through the pores of Berkefeld N filters.

Leptospirae do not stain with the aniline

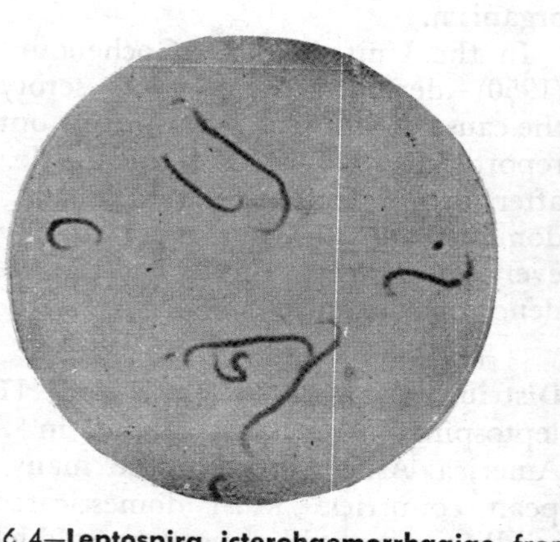

FIG. 36.4—**Leptospira icterohaemorrhagiae** from blood agar culture, Giemsa stain, ×2,000. (From Nowak: Documenta Microbiologica, courtesy Gustav Fischer.)

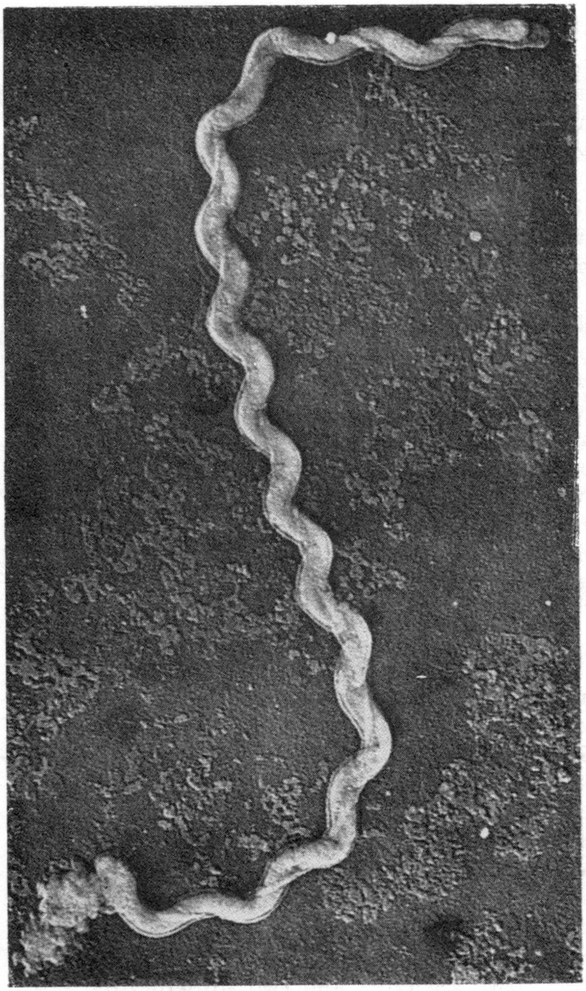

FIG. 36.5—Electron micrograph of intact **Leptospira canicola.** Freshly fixed, gold-paladium shadowing. (Courtesy R. H. A. Swain and the Jour. Path. and Bact.)

dyes. However, Hoyer's Congo Red (negative stain), Giemsa, or impregnation with silver are effective means of demonstrating their morphology (Babudieri, Blendon, and Goldberg).

One of the simplest procedures employs Giemsa stain which is diluted 20 times, applied to a methanol-fixed smear, and allowed to act for 25 minutes. Leptospirae take on a reddish-violet stain.

Basic fuchsin stain is effective if the smears are first formalin fixed and treated with sodium bicarbonate (Ryu).

**Growth Requirements.** Many types of media are described, most of which require 5 to 10 per cent serum (usually rabbit). Both Stuart's and Fletcher's are available as commercial products to which hemoglobin and serum are added. The simplicity of Fletcher or Ringen and Gillespie media formulas makes these media applicable for the routine diagnostic laboratory. A pH of 7.2 to 7.4 and an incubation temperature of 28.5° to 29.5°C. is optimal.

These media may be stored in the frozen state to prevent deterioration. After inoculation with blood, tissues, or urine, cultures may be held six weeks before growth occurs. Organisms adapted to laboratory media may produce satisfactory growth in several days.

In choosing a medium, such factors as growth support for initial isolation, maintenance of stock cultures, and antigen production should be considered.

For the primary isolation of pathogenic leptospirae, the use of both direct culture and laboratory animal inoculation is recommended. Alexander *et al.* reported on a pathogenic serotype which would grow only in the presence of 20 per cent serum. Cox described a saprophytic serotype which was completely inhibited by serum, and postulated that many of the laboratory strains are a selected population due to adaptation to growth in the presence of serum.

Serum-free media have been devised, but are of a complex nature and not applicable for routine use in a diagnostic laboratory (Ellinghausen and McCullough).

**Resistance.** Like the spirochetes, leptospirae do not withstand dryness or heat. Alkaline surface waters with a pH 7.0 to 8.0 favor survival of these organisms in nature.

Serotype *icterohaemorrhagiae* survived 12 hours in domestic sewage, and when present in surface waters proved infective 22 days for guinea pigs. Residual iodine of 0.7 p.p.m. for 10 minutes or 3 to 5 p.p.m. of residual chlorine was found to kill this serotype, while 10 p.p.m. of cationic detergents proved effective in 30 minutes and 2.2 per cent salt destroyed viability in 18 to 20 hours (Chang *et al.*)

Urine with an acid pH has been observed to kill serotype *icterohaemorrhagiae* within a few hours unless diluted with a buffered solution (Fuhner). This serotype was able to survive at —27°C. for 9 months, while 45°C. for 30 minutes proved lethal (Chang *et al.*). Streptomycin in doses of 40 mg. per kg. of body weight for 3 to 5 days eliminated serotype *canicola* from kidneys of infected dogs (Brunner and Meyer). Chemotherapy is considered effective if initiated before the third or fourth day of illness and continued every 6 hours until patient is free of clinical signs. Comparable effectiveness is reported for penicillin at a level of 600,000 units, or 0.5 gm. of either chlortetracycline or oxytetracycline (Alston and Broom).

Serotype *pomona* was found to persist in streams serving as a source of water for cattle infected with *pomona* for 19 days after an outbreak (Gillespie). The same serotype survived 183 days in supersaturated soil, 5 days in damp soil, 2½ hours in dry soil, and 7 to 10 days in fecal-contaminated water (Okazaki and Ringen).

Dilution of urine from shedder cattle with distilled or buffered (pH 6.8) water preserves the infectivity of *pomona.* Urine from clinically normal cattle may inhibit the viability of this serotype within hours, while in other cases the leptospirae may still be viable after 2 months of storage at 5°C. (Gillespie). Okazaki and Ringen found the survival time of serotype *pomona* greater at pH 6.2 from 7° to 10°C. than at 20° to 26°C., while at pH 8.4 the reverse effect was noted. Gillespie reports *pomona* serotype to remain viable for at least 10 years when stored in a dry-ice chamber.

**Antigenic Structure.** The *icterohaemorrhagiae* group consists of 9 subserotypes, with RGA as the type strain, while the *canicola* group consists of 11 serotypes but no subserotypes. The *pomona* group has two serotypes and two subserotypes.

Leptospirae are classified on the basis of cross-agglutination and agglutinin-adsorption techniques, employing antisera prepared in rabbits. From Table 36.1 we note that this would be an exacting and laborious procedure in view of the numerous serotypes and subserotypes. Two strains are considered to belong to different serotypes if, after cross absorption with heterologous antigen, 10 per cent or more of the homologous titer regularly remains in each of the two antisera in repeated tests. A subserotype is a strain within a serotype where, in repeated tests, less than 10 per cent of the homologous titer regularly remains in one antiserum but 10 per cent or more remains in the other antiserum after cross absorption with heterologous antigen (within the serotype).

An antigen specific for the genus Leptospira is recognized through the hemolytic test based on erythrocyte sensitization by extracts of Leptospira (Chang).

**Pathogenicity.** Natural leptospiral infections are recognized in almost all animals. Although signs of acute infection are quite evident, undetected or subclinical infections are more common.

In man, Weil's disease or epidemic jaundice is more common than infection due to serotype *canicola*. However, Meyer and coworkers point out that canicola fever cases may be mild and difficult to diagnose clinically, since the majority of cases have no jaundice, but resemble influenza or undulant fever and are accompanied by a meningitis.

Swineherd's disease of man in Switzerland due to the serotype *pomona* produces a disease very similar to *canicola*. In fact some affected humans have been hospitalized as polio suspect cases. Yager reported that an outbreak of *canicola* leptospirosis occurred in children who bathed in a stream in Georgia. Serum samples from swine and cattle on the stream's watershed were positive to the *canicola* serotype. Tjalma described 77 human cases of *pomona* leptospirosis associated with swimming in surface waters subjected to contamination by upstream cattle with *pomona* titers. Over 80 *pomona* cases were recognized in high school students in Washington associated with swimming in irrigation waters that were contaminated by upstream cattle demonstrated to be shedders of the *pomona* serotype.

Although subclinical infections due to *icterohaemorrhagiae* and *canicola* serotypes occur in swine, cattle, sheep, and horses in the United States, much more serious clinical disease may be associated with the *pomona* serotype.

Serotype *pomona* infections are also recognized in dogs, foxes, skunks, deer, and rodents. The skunk particularly appears to be an endemic host of significance.

In cattle a wide variety of disease expressions may be observed, including fever, inappetence, flaccid udder with loss of milk production and even bloody milk, abortion, hemoglobinuria, hemolytic anemia, death, and rarely icterus. Infection in range cattle may only be recognized through serologic tests unless abortion losses occur. Expelled fetuses are usually 2 to 3 months early, although 4- to 5-month-old fetuses may be noted in *pomona* outbreaks. Although "abortion storms" of 10 to 40 per cent have been observed, such losses are often less than 5 per cent. Hemoglobinuria, apparently observed only in ruminants, appears to be associated with the presence of hemolysin which is produced by some strains of *pomona*. Although *pomona* has been isolated from aborted bovine fetuses, it is usually quite difficult to isolate.

Serotype *pomona* infection in swine is characterized by abortion and death of newborn pigs. Fever, joint stiffness, and inappetence may also be noted. Apparently sows that are exposed during the second month of pregnancy experience the most severe abortion and stillborn losses (Ferguson and Powers). Isolation of *pomona* from swine fetuses and dead pigs, however, is quite successful. Swine are considered as an important source of infection since shedding of leptospirae is heavy and may persist for a year (Bryan *et al.*).

Fever, inactivity, jaundice, abortion, and periodic ophthalmia (moon-blindness) appear to be associated with *pomona* infection in the horse. The moon-blindness is considered as a sequela of leptospiral infection in the horse (Roberts *et al.*).

Experimental animals such as guinea pigs, hamsters, and rats have been widely used for the study of leptospiral infections. Serotype *icterohaemorrhagiae* produces a typical and fatal icterus in the guinea pig, whereas *canicola* produces lesions only after the organism has been increased in virulence by passage through that animal. Larson has observed that the golden hamster

*(Cricetus aceratus)* is susceptible to serotype *canicola,* dying in 4–10 days after intraperitoneal inoculation with the organism. This information is of aid in the use of experimental animals for differential diagnosis. Serotype *icterohaemorrhagiae* kills guinea pigs, mice, and hamsters, while *canicola* kills hamsters but only produces a febrile reaction with a loss of weight in guinea pigs, and fails to infect mice.

Guinea pigs and hamsters infected by *pomona* may exhibit a febrile response of variable duration, and occasionally death. Through serial passages, virulence may increase sufficiently to cause death consistently. These laboratory animals are valuable and necessary for experimental studies in leptospirosis, particularly when inocula are contaminated so that cultural methods cannot be readily employed.

The brown rat, *Rattus norvegicus,* is recognized as being the reservoir for serotype *icterohaemorrhagiae* and is easily infected with the organism which becomes localized in the kidneys and is eliminated in great numbers from the urine. This rat, however, is not susceptible to serotype *canicola* which persists for a short time in inoculated tissues but does not localize in kidney tissue and has never been recovered from rat urine. The reaction of the mouse to the two organisms is similar to that of the rat.

The dog is susceptible to both organisms which produce the natural disease. According to all reports *canicola* infection is much more prevalent in dogs than *icterohaemorrhagiae.* The type of disease produced by each of the organisms is also somewhat different. Serotype *canicola* produces uremia but very little or no jaundice, whereas serotype *icterohaemorrhagiae* produces the typical jaundice of Weil's disease. Meyer and coworkers described a number of typical cases of *canicola* infection in which hemorrhage and faint icterus were found. Chronic types of canine leptospirosis have been described in which large numbers of the organisms are excreted with the urine.

**Immunity.** In their original work on the disease in man, Inada and Ito demonstrated that the disease responded favorably to the injection of blood from convalescent cases. Later they were able to produce in horses an antiserum which reduced the severity of the infection but did not prevent kidney lesions. Heat and phenol-killed cultures have been used successfully in Japan for the purpose of immunizing mine workers against the disease.

Larson found that specific anti-*canicola* rabbit serum would protect hamsters against infection and proved of value as a therapeutic agent if used within three days after infection. The use of 10-day-old cultures to which 0.2 per cent formalin is added for attenuation gives satisfactory immunity in dogs, according to Alicata. In regions where both types of the organism are present, polyvalent biologics should be used.

Animals recovering from leptospirosis are considered immune to the homologous serotype for life, but may still be susceptible to infection with other nonantigenically related serotypes. The presence of agglutination-lysis (AL) antibodies indicates that the animal will be resistant to infection by the homologous serotype; however, some animals may be immune although AL antibodies are not demonstrable in the sera. York and coworkers (1955) reported on the development of a bacterin that was effective in preventing leptospirosis in cattle. Bacterins for immunization of cattle and swine have now been commercially available since the early 1950's. Generally such bacterins stimulate an effective immunity which protects cattle about 12 months against fever and leptospiruria, although experimental studies indicate that some cattle may be immune for 20 months and some susceptible at 8 months after vaccination (Gillespie and Kenzy). These workers also found that calves less than 3 months of age failed to develop an effective immunity when given *pomona* bacterin.

During "abortion storms" bacterins may not prove effective for 3 to 5 weeks since cattle may be infected before or shortly after vaccination. Field reports, however, indicate that abortion outbreaks are usually stopped within 7 to 10 days. Reinhard (1954) pointed out that cows receiving an egg-passaged vaccine were immune for at least 17 months and no adverse effects were observed. Since then Kenzy *et al.*, employing a 543rd egg-passaged culture vaccine, observed persistence of immunity for about 4 years. As might be expected, the living vaccine stimulates an earlier AL antibody response which is demonstrated by the fourth day, while about 10 to 14 days elapse before a bacterin stimulates demonstrable AL antibodies. When yearlings are vaccinated, a few of these shed limited numbers of leptospirae for 1 to 3 weeks, detectable only by inoculation of urine into laboratory animals. No evidence of contact transmission has been observed. The living culture was found to be about three times as effective as the bacterin in controlling *pomona* abortions following vaccination during an outbreak.

**Diagnosis.** Leptospirosis may be diagnosed serologically by agglutination-lysis, capillary tube, slide or plate agglutination, serum hemolytic, urine hemolytic, or complement-fixation tests. Jones and coworkers used the plate test to detect the presence of leptospiral antibodies in war dogs. Of 4,368 dogs tested, 58 reactors (1.33 per cent) were found.

The demonstration of antibodies does not necessarily indicate the presence of active leptospiral infection since recovered animals may carry agglutination-lysis antibodies for years, if not for life. With the modification of the Cox hemolytic test (HL) for bovine and porcine sera by Ringen, it appears that a positive HL test is very closely associated with the shedder state in cattle and swine. It is interesting that the HL test is genus specific; thus, acute infections with all serotypes should be recognized. The final diagnosis of leptospirosis must depend on the isolation or demonstration of the leptospira. Fluorescent-labeled antibody technique has been used to demonstrate the presence of leptospira in urine and tissues (White and Ristic).

Blood, tissue, or urine from an infected animal may be cultured directly or inoculated into laboratory animals such as hamsters or guinea pigs. After 3 to 4 weeks the sera from such inoculated laboratory animals are tested for leptospiral antibodies, and the kidney tissues may be subcultured in leptospiral media for isolation of the infecting serotype.

When urine is collected from leptospirosis-infected animals, immediate dilution with sterile buffered water to give a pH of 7.0 to 7.4 is recommended. Intraperitoneal or subcutaneous inoculation of laboratory animals with this diluted urine should be completed with as little delay as possible.

By culturing the urine through serial dilutions in media, contaminants may be diluted out and the effect of inhibitive substances minimized. Urine dilution also reduces the inhibitive effect of any specific antibody which apparently interferes with the infection of laboratory animals (Ringen *et al.*).

Leptospiral inhibitive substances which are lytic in nature have been noted in extracts of renal tissue and in milk, thus interfering with the culturing of such materials unless properly diluted (Salheim).

The addition of 5-fluorouracil, a selective inhibitive agent, to contaminated materials aids in the isolation of leptospirae (Johnson and Rogers).

Solid media in petri dishes have been used for pure colony isolation of leptospira (Cox and Larson). This has been a helpful tool for the detection of leptospiral infections associated with two different leptospiral serotypes (Roth *et al.*). Excellent references such as Wolf, Babudieri, and Alston and Broom are recommended for further study.

## REFERENCES


Abdulla, P. K., and Karstad, L. Experimental Infections With *Leptospira pomona* in Snakes and Turtles. Zoonoses Res. 1:295–306, 1962.

Alexander, A. D., *et al.* A New Pathogenic Leptospira, Not Readily Cultivated. Jour. Bact. 83:754–60, 1962.

Alicata, J. E. Active Immunization of Dogs Against Leptospirosis by the Use of Formolized Leptospira Antigen. Jour. Amer. Vet. Med. Assn. 102:472–73, 1943.

ALSTON, J. M., and BROOM, J. C. Leptospirosis in Man and Animals. E. & S. Livingstone, Ltd., Edinburgh and London, 1958.

BABUDIERI, B. Laboratory Diagnosis of Leptospirosis. Bull. World Health Org. 24:45–58, 1961.

———, and BOANCHI, L. Untersuchungen tiber ein epidemisches Vorkommen der Reisfelderleptospirose in der Provinz Pavia. Z. Immun. Forsch. 98:37, 1940. *In* Alston and Broom, Leptospirosis in Man and Animals, 1958.

BAKER, J. A., and LITTLE, R. B. Leptospirosis in Cattle. Jour. Exp. Med. 88:295–307, 1948.

BERGEY, D. H. Bergey's Manual of Determinative Bacteriology. 7th Ed. Williams & Wilkins Co., Baltimore, 1957.

BERNKOPF, H., *et al.* Studies on Bovine and Human Leptospirosis. Jour. Inf. Dis. 80:53–63, 1947.

BLENDEN, D. C., and GOLDBERG, H. S. Silver Impregnation Stain for Leptospira and Flagella. Jour. Bact. 89:899–900, 1965.

BOHL, E. H. The Incidence and Clinical Aspects of Leptospirosis in Cattle and Swine in Ohio. Proc. 92nd Ann. Meet. Amer. Vet. Med. Assn., pp. 167–72, 1955.

BORG-PETERSEN, C. Leptospirenuntersuchungen in Danemark. Congr. int. Med. trop., 3, Amsterdam, Acta 1:396, 1938. *In* Alston and Broom, Leptospirosis in Man and Animals, 1958.

———, and FENNESTAD, K. L. A Field Rodent (*Apodemus agrarius*) as a Carrier of *Leptospira pomona* in Denmark. Jour. Amer. Vet. Med. Assn. 128:204–5, 1956.

BROOM, J. C. The Protective Value of Leptospiral Vaccines in Hamsters. Vet. Rec. 61:127–28, 1949.

———, and MACINTYRE, A. B. A Survey of Canine Leptospirosis in England. Vet. Rec. 60:487–88, 1948.

BRUNNER, K. T., and MEYER, K. F. Streptomycin in the Treatment of Leptospira Carriers. Experiments With Hamsters and Dogs. Proc. Soc. Exp. Biol Med., N.Y. 70:450–52, 1949.

BRYAN, H. S., *et al.* Studies on Leptospirosis in Domestic Animals. II. Isolation of *Leptospira pomona* From Aborted Swine Fetuses. Vet. Med. 48:438, 1953.

CHAMBERLAND, H. La Leptospirose du chien et du renard ictere infectieux et typhus canin. Canad. Jour. Comp. Med. 7:39–46, 1943.

CHANG, R. S., *et al.* Amer. Jour. Trop. Med. Hyg. 6:101, 1957.

CHANG, S. L., *et al.* Studies on *Leptospira icterohaemorrhagiae.* IV. Survival in Water and Sewage: Destruction in Water by Halogen Compounds, Synthetic Detergents, and Heat. Jour. Inf. Dis. 82:256–66, 1948.

CLARK, L. G., *et al.* Leptospirosis in Cattle and Wildlife on a Pennsylvania Farm. Jour. Amer. Vet. Med. Assn. 139:889–91, 1961.

CLAYTON, G. E. B., *et al.* The Presence of Leptospirosis of a Mild Type (Seven-Day Fever) in Queensland. Austral. Med. Jour. 1:647, 1937. *In* Alston and Broom, Leptospirosis in Man and Animals, 1958.

COURMONT, J., and DURAND, P. La Spirochetose icterohemorragique chez le chien. C. R. Soc. Biol., Paris, 80:275, 1917. *In* Alston and Broom, Leptospirosis in Man and Animals, 1958.

COX, C. D. Standardization and Stabilization of an Extract From *Leptospira biflexa*, and Its Use in the Hemolytic Test for Leptospirosis. Jour. Inf. Dis. 101:203–9, 1957.

———. Some Aspects of the Growth of Leptospira on Solid Media. Bact. Proc. 54, 1965.

DICKIE, C. W., and BARRERA, J. A Study of the Carrier State of Avian Spirochetosis in the Chicken. Avian Dis. 8:191–95, 1964.

ELLINGHAUSEN, H. C. Nephelometry and a Nephelo-Culture Flask Used in Measuring Growth of Leptospires. Amer. Jour. Vet. Res. 20:1072–76, 1959.

———, and MCCULLOUGH, W. G. Growth of Leptospira in a Medium Devoid of Whole Serum. Bact. Proc. 54, 1965.

ESSEVELD, H., and COLLIER, W. A. Z. Immun. Forsch. 93:512–28, 1938.

FERGUSON, L. C., and POWERS, T. E. Experimental Leptospirosis in Pregnant Swine. Amer. Jour. Vet. Res. 17:471–77, 1956.

FIELD, H. J., and SELLERS, K. C. Leptospira Icterohaemorrhagiae in the Calf. Vet. Rec. 62:311–13, 1950.

FLETCHER, W. Recent Work on Leptospirosis, Tsutsugamushi Disease, and Tropical Typhus in the Federated Malay States. Trans. R. Soc. Trop. Med. Hyg. 21:265, 1928. *In* Alston and Broom, Leptospirosis in Man and Animals, 1958.

FREUND, S. Leptospirosis in Cattle in Palestine. Jour. Comp. Path. Therap. 57:62–66, 1947.

FUHNER, F. Epidemiologische Untersuchungen zur Netterlnburger Weil-Badeepidemie. Stadtehygiene 1:218, 1950. *In* Alston and Broom, Leptospirosis in Man and Animals, 1958.

GALTON, M. Recent Advances and Needs for Future Emphasis in Research on Leptospirosis. Proc. 67th Ann Meet. U.S. Livestock Sanit. Assn., pp. 201–19, 1963.

GAY, F. P. Agents of Disease and Host Resistance. Chap. 44, Charles C Thomas, Baltimore, 1935.

GILLESPIE, R. W. H., and KENZY, S. G. Immunization of Cattle Against Leptospirosis. Vet. Med. I, 53:401–9, 1958; II, 53:611–16, 1958; III, 54:12–16, 1959.

———, and RYNO, J. W. Further Observations on the Occurrence of *L. pomona* in Surface Waters. Proc. 14th Ann. Meet. Internatl. Northwest Conf. on Diseases in Nature Communicable to Man. Pp. 95–98, Aug., 1960.

———, and RYNO, JOANNE. Unpublished data.

GOCHENOUR, W. S., JR., *et al.* Antigenic Similarity of Bovine Strains of Leptospirae (United States) and *Leptospira pomona.* Proc. Soc. Exp. Biol. Med. 74:199–202, 1950.

GSELL, O. R. Epidemiology of the Leptospirosis. P. 34. Symp. on the Leptospiroses. Med. Sci. Publ. 1, U.S. Govt. Print. Off., Washington, D.C., 1953.

GUTHE, T., and WILCOX, P. R. A World Problem Chronicle. World Health Org. 8:37–114, 1954.

HINDLE, E. The Spirochaetes. A System of Bacteriology 8:101–295. Med. Res. Council, His Majesty's Stationery Office, London, 1929.

HOWARTH, J. A. Effect of Aureomycin and Polytic in an Outbreak of Leptospirosis of Swine. Jour. Amer. Vet. Med. Assn. 129:268–71, 1956.

INADA, R., *et al.* The Etiology, Mode of Infection, and Specific Therapy of Weil's Disease (Spirochaetosis Icterohaemorrhagica). Jour. Exp. Med. 23:377–402, 1916.

JOHNSON, R. C., and ROGERS, P. 5-Fluorouracil as a Selective Agent for Growth of Leptospires. Jour. Bact. 87:422–26, 1964.

JOINT WHO/FAO EXPERT COMMITTEE ON ZOONOSES, 2ND REPT. World Health Org. Tech. Rept. Ser. 169, Geneva, 1959.

JONES, T. C., *et al.* Control of Leptospirosis in War Dogs. Amer. Jour. Vet. Res. 6:120–28, 1945.

JUNGHERR, E. Observations on Canine Spirochetosis in Connecticut. Jour. Amer. Vet. Med. Assn. 91:661–73, 1937.

———. Bovine Leptospirosis. Jour. Amer. Vet. Med. Assn. 105:276–81, 1944.

KAUFMANN, O. Z. Immun. Forsch. 93:354–67, 1938.

KENZY, S. G., *et al.* Problems in Treatment and Control of Leptospirosis. Jour. Amer. Vet. Med. Assn. 136: 253–55, 1960.

KING, W. E., and BAESLACK, F. W. Studies on the Virus of Hog Cholera. Jour. Inf. Dis. 12:39–41, 1913.

KLARENBEEK, A. Leptospirae (*Spircchaeta icterouraemiae canis*) als oorzaak van icterus, nephritis en uraemie van den hond. Tijdschr. Diergeneesk. 55:227, 1928. *In* Alston and Broom, Leptospirosis in Man and Animals, 1958.

———, and SCHUFFNER, W. A. P. Het voorkomen van een afwijkend Leptospiraras in Nederland. Ned. Tijdschr. Geneesk. 7:4271, 1933. *In* Alston and Broom, Leptospirosis in Man and Animals, 1958.

LARSON, C. L. Experimental Leptospirosis in Hamsters (*Cricetus aurdus*). Pub. Health Rept. 59:522–27, 1944.

LITTLE, R. B., and BAKER, J. A. Leptospirosis in Cattle. Jour. Amer. Vet. Med. Assn. 116:105–11, 1950.

LOOMIS, E. C. Avian Spirochetosis in California Turkeys. Amer. Jour. Vet. Res. 14:612–15, 1958.

LUKES, J. Sur la presence des spirochetes chez les chiens atteints de gastroenterite et sur le role pathogene possible de ces microorganismes. Ann. Inst. Pasteur 38:523, 1924. *In* Alston and Broom, Leptospirosis in Man and Animals, 1958.

MAESTRONE, G., and BENJAMINSON, M. Leptospira Infection in the Gold Fish (*Carassius auratus*). Nature 190: 719–20, 1962.

MARSH, H. Leptospira in Bovine Icterohemoglobinuria. Jour. Amer. Vet. Med. Assn. 107:119–21, 1945.

MATHEWS, F. P. A Contagious Disease of Cattle Associated With Leptospira. Amer. Jour. Vet. Res. 7:78–93, 1946.

MCNEIL, E., *et al.* A Study of Borrelia Anserina Infection (Spirochetosis) in Turkeys. Jour. Bact. 57:191–206, 1949.

MENGES, R. W., *et al.* Cultural and Serologic Studies on Four Dogs Inoculated With Two Leptospiral Serotypes, *Leptospira pomona* and *Leptospira canicola.* Amer. Jour. Vet. Res. 21:371–76, 1960.

MEYER, K. F., *et al.* Canine Leptospirosis in the United States. Jour. Amer. Vet. Med. Assn. 95:710–29, 1939.

MILLS, SUSAN. Clinical Aspects of Canine Leptospirosis. Vet. Rec. 60:267–72, 1948.

MOLNER, J. G., *et al.* Leptospiral Infections (A Survey). Jour. Amer. Med. Assn. 136:814–19, 1948.

MONLUX, W. S. I. The Incidence of Leptospirosis in the Rat Population of Ithaca, New York, and Vicinity. Cornell Vet. 38:57–68, 1948.

MORCOS, Z., *et al.* A Concise Investigation of Fowl Spirochetosis in Egypt. Jour. Amer. Vet. Med. Assn. 109: 112–16, 1946.

MORSE, E. V. The Economic Significance of Leptospirosis in Domestic Animals. Proc. 92nd Ann. Meet. Amer. Vet. Med. Assn., pp. 162–67, 1955.

NOGUCHI, H. The Newer Knowledge of Bacteriology and Immunology. E. O. Jordan and I. S. Falk (eds.). Univ. of Chicago Press, p. 452, 1928. *In* Alston and Broom, Leptospirosis in Man and Animals, 1958.

———. The Survival of Leptospira (Spirochaeta) Icterohaemorrhagiae in Nature; Observations Concerning Microchemical Reactions and Intermediate Hosts. Jour. Exp. Med. 27:609–25, 1918.

NOVY, F. G., and KNAPP, R. E. Studies on Spirillum Obermeieri and Related Organisms. Jour. Inf. Dis. 3:291–393, 1906.

OKAZAKI, W., and RINGEN, L. M. Some Effects of Various Environmental Conditions on the Survival of *Leptospira pomona*. Amer. Jour. Vet. Res. 18:219–23, 1957.

OKELL, C. C., *et al.* Leptospiral Jaundice in Dogs (Yellows). Vet. Jour. 81:3, 1925.

RINEHARD, K. R. Epidemiology of the Leptospiroses. P. 126. Symp. on the Leptospiroses, Med. Sci. Publ. 1, U.S. Govt. Print. Off., Washington, D.C., 1953.

———, and HADLOW, W. J. Experimental Bovine Leptospirosis—Pathological, Hematological, Bacteriological, and Serological Studies. Proc. Jour. Amer. Vet. Med. Assn., pp. 203–16, 1954.

RINGEN, L. M. A Preliminary Report on a Comparison of Agglutination-Lysis, Capillary Tube, and Hemolytic Tests for the Diagnosis of Bovine Leptospirosis. Proc. 63rd Ann. Meet. U.S. Livestock Sanit. Assn., pp. 120–25, 1959.

———, and GILLESPIE, RUSSELL W. H. A Simple Medium for the Cultivation of Leptospira. Jour. Bact. 67: 252–53, 1954.

———, *et al.* Studies on Bovine Leptospirosis. I. Some Effects of Dihydrostreptomycin and Terramycin on the Carrier Condition in Bovine Leptospirosis. Jour. Amer. Vet. Med. Assn. 126:272–76, 1955.

RITCHIE, A. E., and ELLINGHAUSEN, H. C. Electron Microscopy of Leptospires. I. Anatomical Features of *Leptospira pomona*. Jour. Bact. 89:223–33, 1965.

ROBERTS, C. S., *et al.* Bovine Leptospirosis in Alabama—A Five-Year Study. Jour. Amer. Vet. Med Assn. 139:877–83, 1961.

ROBERTS, S. J., *et al.* An Outbreak of Leptospirosis in Horses on a Small Farm. Jour. Amer. Vet. Med. Assn. 121:237–42, 1952.

ROTH, E. E., *et al.* The Use of Agar Plates as an Aid for the Isolation of Leptospires. Amer. Jour. Vet. Res. 22:308–12, 1961.

———, *et al.* The Bacteriologic and Serologic Incidence of Leptospirosis Among Striped Skunks in Louisiana. Zoonoses Res. 2:13–19, 1963.

RYU, E. A Simple Method for Staining Leptospira and Treponema. Jap. Jour. Microbiol. 7:81–85, 1963.

SAVINO, E., and RENNELLA, E. Studies on Leptospira (Abst.) Vet. Bull. 16:297–98, 1946.

———, and ———. Leptospira y Leptospirosis in la Republica Argentina. Buenos Aires: Thomas Palumbo. 1944. *In* Alston and Broom, Leptospirosis in Man and Animals, 1958.

SCHMID, G., and GIOVANELLA, R. Schweiz. Arch. Tierheilk. 89:1, 1947.

STALHEIM, H. A. V. Leptospiral Lysis by Lipids of Renal Tissue and Milk. Jour. Bact. 89:545, 1965.

STOENNER, H. G. Application of Serology to the Diagnosis of Leptospirosis. Proc. 92nd Ann. Meet. Amer. Vet. Med. Assn., pp. 172–77, 1955.

SUTHERLAND, A. D., and MORRILL, C. C. An Outbreak of Leptospirosis in Cattle Jour. Amer. Vet. Med. Assn. 113:468–71, 1948.

THEILER, A. Spirillosis of Cattle. Jour. Comp. Path. Therap. 17:47–55, 1904.

TJALMA, R. A. Personal communication.

VERGE, J. Avian Spirochaetosis. Rec. Med. Vet. 112:257–70, 1936.

WALCH-SORGDRAGER, B. Leptospirosis, League of Nations Bull., World Health Org. VIII. Pp. 1–2, 143–386, 1939.

WEIL, A. Uber eine eigentumliche, mit Milztumor, Icterus und Nephritis einhergehende akute Infektionskrankheit. Dtsch, Arch. klin. Med. 39:209, 1886. *In* Alston and Broom, Leptospirosis in Man and Animals, 1958.

WHITE, F. H., and RISTIC, M Detection of *Leptospira pomona* in Guinea Pig and Bovine Urine With Fluorescein-Labeled Antibody. Jour. Inf. Dis. 105:118–23, 1959.

WOLFF, J. W. The Laboratory Diagnosis of Leptospirosis. Charles C Thomas, Springfield, Ill., 1954.

YAGER, R. H. Epidemiology of the Leptospiroses, p. 221. Symp. on Leptospiroses. Med. Sci. Publ. 1, U.S. Govt. Print. Off., Washington, D.C., 1953.

YORK, C. J., *et al.* The Use of Vaccine in the Control of Leptospirosis in Cattle and Swine. Proc. 92nd Ann. Meet. Amer. Vet. Med Assn., pp. 169–72, 1955.

# 37

# The Order Rickettsiales

**LESLIE A. PAGE, *Ph.D.***
*National Animal Disease Laboratory*
*Ames, Iowa*

THE NAME RICKETTSIALES HONORS HOWARD Taylor Ricketts, an American pathologist who elucidated the transmission of the agent of Rocky Mountain spotted fever between arthropods and man.

Some microorganisms of this order were once considered as viruses because of their apparent inability to grow outside of living host cells, and others were considered to be primitive protozoans because of certain "life-cycle" characteristics, but all of these organisms are now thought to have features of such fundamental similarity to those of bacteria that they should be placed in the bacterial class Schizomycetes.

In regard to morphology, organisms of the order Rickettsiales are spherical, ranging from 0.2μ to 2.0μ in diameter, or rod shaped, ranging from 0.3μ to 4.0μ in length. In terms of fine structure, all are procaryotic; that is, they contain morphologically undefined or primitive nuclei without evidence of other internal structures such as mitochondria or endoplasmic reticula. This distinguishes them from more advanced eucaryotic organisms such as protozoa. For propagation, most of the organisms can be cultivated only within living host cells, although several species grow and multiply on lifeless media. Many species multiply by fission entirely, but others have a developmental cycle where multiplication by fission is only part of a multistage maturation process. All of the species exhibit metabolic reactions independent of those of the host cell, but the capabilities of the expressed metabolic systems vary greatly between different families of organisms. All of the species contain both DNA and RNA and most of them are susceptible to tetracycline antibiotics. Tinctorially, all are gram-negative. For light microscopy, they stain best using Giemsa's, Macchiavello's, or Castenada's method.

The order has four families, Rickettsiaceae, Chlamydiaceae, Bartonellaceae, and Anaplasmataceae, which are differentiated by their morphology, their mode of transmission between hosts, and by their cytotropism. In many cases, arthropods are the natural primary hosts and mammals are incidental hosts.

Organisms of the family Rickettsiaceae usually are parasites of the gut cells of arthropods which transmit the agents to other hosts. The agents that affect mammals, especially man, attack the capillary endothelium resulting in characteristic red skin rashes. On the other hand, organisms of the family Chlamydiaceae commonly are transmitted between animals by inhalation of dried infectious excrement or by other nonvector means. In birds and mammals these agents affect the epithelial cells of the lung or mucosal membranes as well as vascular endothelium and mobile phagocytes.

Organisms of the other two families, the

Bartonellaceae and the Anaplasmataceae, parasitize mammalian erythrocytes primarily, although transmission between mammalian hosts in nature is dependent upon an intermediate arthropod host. Organisms of the family Bartonellaceae are rod-shaped and multiply by division either inside or outside of the host cell, whereas organisms of the family Anaplasmataceae are spherical and only multiply intracellularly. Some strains have saclike appendages which may reach 8$\mu$ in length. The essential difference between these obligate red cell parasites and the most elementary protozoan red cell parasites is revealed by studies of their fine structure. The anaplasma organisms contain no morphologically defined organelles such as are found in protozoans. They are placed in the order Rickettsiales, therefore, because of their primitive morphological characteristics and their similarity to other organisms of the order with respect to mode of multiplication, arthropod transmission, and sensitivity to tetracyclines.

The student should be aware that some investigators currently maintain that anaplasma organisms are protozoa and not bacteria. This reasoning appears to be related to the traditional inclusion of red blood cell parasites which have complex life cycles into the class Protozoa. These investigators also dispute the presently available evidence on the fine structure, reproductive cycle, and physiology of these organisms, which suggests their proper placement in the order Rickettsiales. Future research on the fine structure may resolve the morphological questions and serve to guide taxonomists. Should such evidence point strongly to the exclusion of organisms of the family Anaplasmataceae from the order Rickettsiales, then the discussion of these organisms will be deleted from future editions of this book. In the meantime, it is desirable that students become acquainted with these complex organisms.

Each of these families contains numerous genera, many of which have species which are pathogenic to animals and to man. Each family group will be described and those species of particular significance will be discussed.

## THE FAMILY RICKETTSIACEAE

Organisms in this family usually are small, ovoid rods, 0.2$\mu$ to 0.6$\mu$ in length which are gram-negative, but are readily stained by Giemsa's, Castenada's, or Macchiavello's methods. Their principal natural hosts are insects and arachnids which transmit the organisms to incidental mammalian hosts. According to Luria (1953) any classification of these agents based on the diseases they cause in man (typhus, spotted fever, Q fever, etc.) is probably artificial, for the organisms that are infectious for man probably represent only a small sample of a large group of microorganisms symbiotic with a variety of arthropods. For this reason, new generic names for the nonpathogenic symbiotic rickettsiae were created by Philip (1956) for the 7th edition of *Bergey's Manual of Determinative Bacteriology*.

Metabolically, these organisms are one evolutionary step away from true bacteria because of their dependence upon host cells for growth. At present, however, one species, *Rickettsia quintana,* can be cultivated on lifeless media (Vinson and Fuller, 1961); all of the others require living cells for multiplication. Nevertheless, the rickettsiae are sharply different from viruses in that they, like bacteria, contain numerous enzymes involved with energy-producing oxidations. The host cell, when necessary, probably supplies essential substrates rather than enzymes. The small, fastidious gram-negative bacterium, *Pasteurella tularensis,* whose natural habitat also is an arthropod, is probably the closest bacterial relative of the rickettsiae. Chemically, the cell envelopes of rickettsiae are qualitatively similar to walls of gram-negative bacteria. The envelopes contain, for example, muramic acid, which has been found only in bacteria and some algae.

At present, the family Rickettsiaceae is divided into seven genera: Rickettsia, Coxiella, Ehrlichia, Cowdria, Neorickettsia, Wolbachia, Symbiotes, and Rickettsiella.

### The Genus Rickettsia

There are ten species in this genus. They are separated on the basis of whether they can be propagated in chicken embryos, whether they reproduce in the cytoplasm or nucleus of host cells, by which species of arthropod vector they are transmitted, and what disease syndrome they produce in man.

Of those species that can be propagated in the chicken embryo, three species are intracytoplasmic only: *R. prowazekii* which is louse-borne; *R. typhi* which is chiefly transmitted by the flea; and *T. tsutsugamushi* which is transmitted by trombiculid mites. The first two are insects in which the agent does not pass transovarially. However, this type of passage does occur in arachnids such as mites. The next four rickettsial species multiply either in the cytoplasm or nucleus of the host cell and pass transovarially in mites: *R. rickettsii* which is borne by ticks of the genus *Dermacentor; R. conori* which is chiefly borne by the Mediterranean dog tick *Rhipicephalus sanguineus; R. australis* which is similar to *R. rickettsii* except antigenically; and *R. akari* which is borne only by the Dermanyssid mite in urban areas of the eastern United States. Lackman *et al.* (1965) have arranged four subgroups of rickettsiae of the spotted fever agents and created two new species, *R. parkeri* and *R. montana,* based upon serologic and neutralization differences among isolates.

The tenth species, *R. quintana,* does not multiply in the chicken embryo, but can be cultivated on lifeless media (Vinson and Fuller, 1961).

### *Rickettsia prowazekii*

*R. prowazekii* is the cause of typhus fever, an acute infectious disease of man characterized by high fever, severe headaches, and a generalized macular or maculopapular rash. The disease occurs endemically in Korea, Japan, China, Indo-China, Serbia, Russia, Central Europe, North Africa, Egypt, Ethiopia, South Africa, Mexico, Guatemala, Colombia, Peru, Boliva,

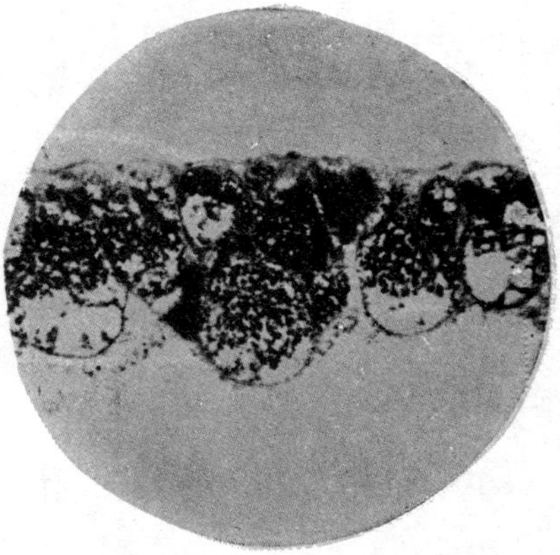

FIG. 37.1—**Rickettsia prowazekii** in epithelial cells of louse intestine, Giemsa stain, ×500. (From Nowak: Documenta Microbiologica, courtesy Gustav Fischer.)

and Chile. The organism has not become established upon the North American continent.

This organism is transmitted by the common body louse and the head louse from an infected person to a susceptible one. Although such lice neither fly nor jump, they do crawl considerable distances, hence may become lodged in clothing and crawl directly from person to person in close contact. Lice spend their life on the human body, deriving nutrition from the blood of their hosts. The organism multiplies in the tissue cells lining the intestine of the louse (Fig. 37.1), causing a rupture of the infected cells and the liberation of masses of rickettsia. The feces of the louse contain large numbers of the organism by which other lice may become infected. The organism is transmitted to man by the infected lice at the time of feeding and, obviously, the lice become infected from man in the same process.

*R. prowazekii* is a minute, coccoid, ovoid rod although long rods and filamentous forms may be seen (Fig. 37.2). Single cells are $0.25\mu$ by $0.4\mu$ in size. They are nonmotile. When stained with Giemsa stain the organism is light purple. It does not stain well by the Gram stain but is considered gram-negative.

The organism can be cultivated artificially in tissue cultures of mammalian cells,

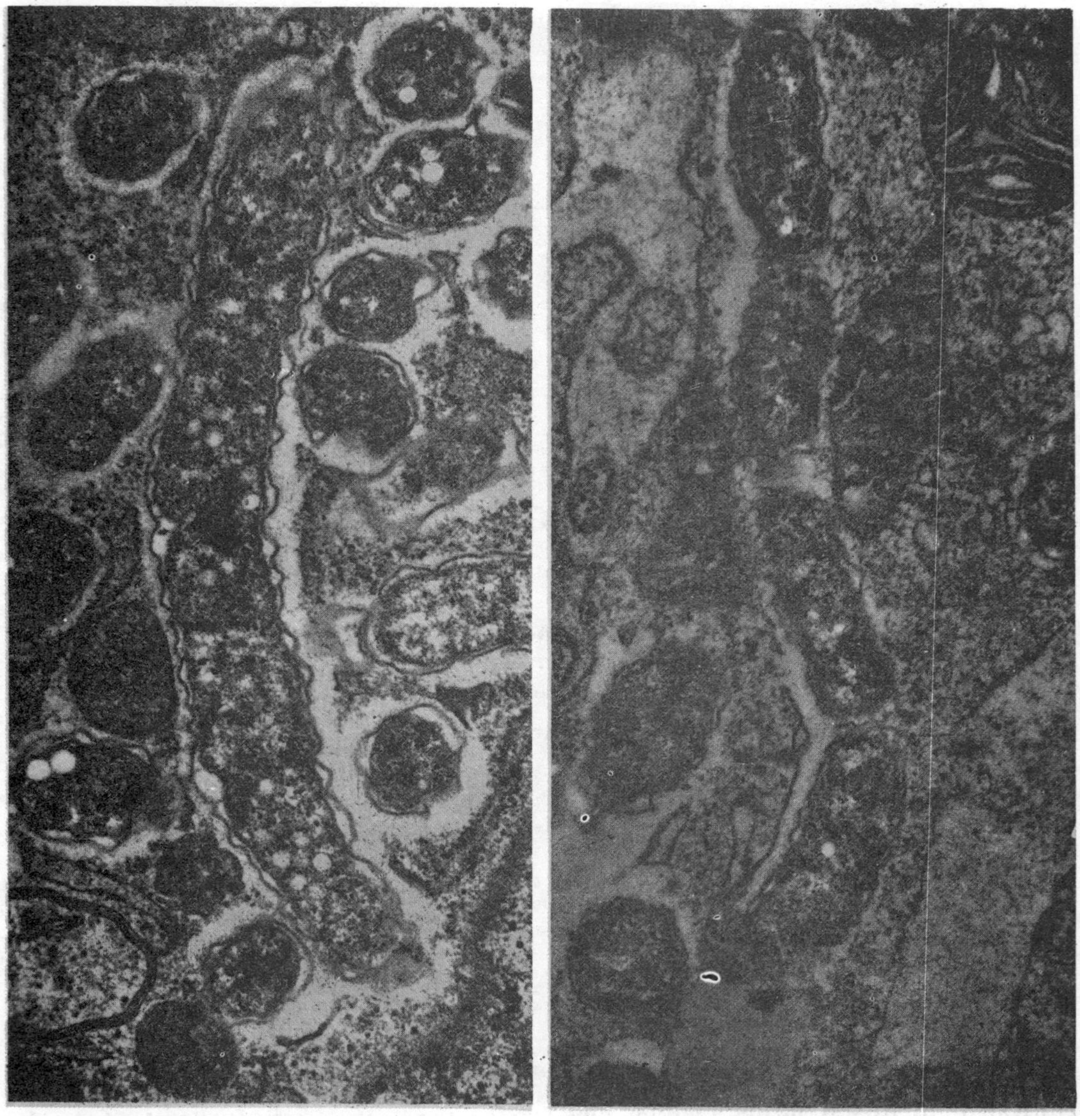

FIG. 37.2—Electron micrographs of ultrathin sections of **Rickettsia prowazekii. Left,** longitudinal section through a cell which is 4μ long. Several cross sections are also included in the field. A rippled cell wall is obvious, and the underlying plasma membrane which bounds the rickettsial cytoplasm is easily seen in several places. The internal material consists of ribosomes and DNA strands, and some electron-lucent spherical structures, ×45,000. **Right,** section through chain of short rods of **R. prowazekii,** ×45,000. (From Anderson **et al.,** 1965. Used by permission.)

in the intestine of the louse, in modified Maitland media with and without agar, on the chorioallantoic membrane, and in the yolk sac of the chicken embryo.

In addition to man and lice, the organism is pathogenic for apes, monkeys, guinea pigs, cotton rats, and the gerbil.

Immunity is produced in man by an attack of the disease. Killed vaccines, formerly produced from artificially infected lice, but now from infected yolk-sac material of the chicken embryo, are valuable immunizing agents. The disease is prevented in many areas of the world by prophylactic vaccination.

Antibodies are produced by the fifth or

eighth day of illness, so agglutination and complement-fixation tests may be used for diagnosis, using antigens composed of the organism. Serum from a patient with typhus fever agglutinates (Weil-Felix reaction) suspensions of *Proteus vulgaris,* strain OX19, revealing an antigenic component which is common to both organisms. Diagnosis is confirmed by the isolation of *R. prowazekii* from blood clots inoculated into guinea pigs or into embryonated chicken eggs.

#### *Rickettsia typhi*

*R. typhi* is the cause of murine typhus, a relatively mild, acute febrile disease of man, of 9 to 15 days duration, characterized by headache and a macular rash. The disease is worldwide in distribution and occurs endemically throughout certain sections of the southern part of the United States and in Mexico. It has been frequently confused with epidemic typhus.

The organism produces a natural infection in rats and mice, among which it is transmitted by the rat flea and also the rat louse. It is transmitted to man from the rat by the rat flea, although the body louse of man is also known to be a transmitting agent.

*R. typhi* does not differ from *R. prowazekii* in morphology and staining characteristics, and it can be cultivated on the same types of media. Growth has been obtained in the peritoneal cavity of X-rayed rats, in the lungs of white rats and white mice following intranasal inoculation, and in the lungs of rabbits following intratracheal inoculation.

In addition to rats, mice, fleas, lice, rabbits, and man, the following animals have been shown susceptible: ape, monkey, guinea pig, gerbil, woodchuck, flying squirrel, gray squirrel, fox squirrel, gopher, cottontail rabbit, swamp rabbit, chipmunk, skunk, opossum, and cat. In the guinea pig the organism produces, by intraperitoneal inoculation, a febrile reaction and testicular swelling without necrosis.

Immunity is produced by an infection caused by this organism. Antibodies developed are indistinguishable from those produced by *R. prowazekii* infection. The comparatively mild nature of the disease serves to differentiate murine typhus from epidemic typhus, otherwise accurate diagnosis is difficult.

#### *Rickettsia rickettsii*

*R. rickettsii* is the cause of Rocky Mountain spotted fever of man, an acute febrile disease characterized by marked prostration, chills, myalgia and arthralgia, and a distinctive rash which develops into rose-red maculopapular lesions from which the name was derived. The disease is found in most of the states of North America. In Brazil the disease is known as Sao Paulo typhus and Minas Gerais typhus, and in Colombia it is called Tobai fever. The greatest number of cases in the United States occur in the western mountain states where the disease is endemic in the tick population.

The organism is present in numerous species of ticks. In the western mountain region the common wood tick *Dermacentor andersoni* is involved; the dog tick *D. variabilis* is found throughout the midwestern and eastern states; the rabbit tick *Haemaphysalis leporis palustris* is found throughout the United States, north into Canada and Alaska, and south into South America. Numerous other species of ticks are known to harbor the organism and are agents for its transmission among animal hosts from which it may be transmitted to those various ticks which attack man. *R. rickettsii* is transmitted through the life cycle of the tick from the ova to the adult. It is present in all the tissues of the tick and in the feces; hence, man may become infected not only by the bite of the tick but also by crushing ticks or by handling tick-infested animals.

Morphologically, *R. rickettsii* is a small, lanceolate rod, often occurring in pairs. It is $0.2\mu$ to $0.3\mu$ in width by $1\mu$ in length. When stained by the Giemsa method the organism is blue with purple polar granules. It occurs in the cytoplasm of infected cells in dense masses of coccoid forms. The organism can be cultivated in ticks, in tissue cells of mammalian origin, in Maitland media, on the chorioallantoic membrane, and in the yolk sac of the chicken embryo.

In addition to man and the ticks themselves, the organism is known to infect various species of rabbits, squirrels, and mice. These animals are not considered to have a natural infection but serve as temporary passive carriers during the active life cycle of the tick. Mammalian blood does apparently contain an "activator" substance which serves to stimulate the growth of the organism in the tick. It is during this period of tick activity that man becomes accidentally infected. He does not enter into the cycle by which the organism is perpetuated. The large domestic animals are not susceptible to *R. rickettsii.* However, dogs and cats have been found susceptible to experimental infection. In Brazil dogs are found to be naturally infected and are considered to play a role in the transmission of the disease. The best experimental animal is the guinea pig in which the organism produces fever, scrotal rash, necrosis of the tips of the ears and foot pads, and a markedly enlarged spleen. Monkeys and rabbits are susceptible and may be used as experimental animals in studying the disease.

A permanent immunity is developed in man by an attack of the disease. Vaccines prepared from infected ticks and from the yolk sacs of fertile chicken eggs are used for immunization. The disease is diagnosed by symptoms with the aid of the inoculation of guinea pigs and egg embryos, the Weil-Felix reaction, the serum-neutralization test, and the complement-fixation test.

### *Rickettsia conorii*

*R. conorii* is the cause of Boutonneuse fever of man, a benign disease characterized by a maculopapular eruption on the palms and soles and a black hemorrhagic area at the site of the tick bite. This disease is also known as Marseilles or Mediterranean typhus. It is found in various countries bordering on the Mediterranean Sea.

The organism is transmitted almost exclusively by the dog tick, *R. sanguinius,* in which it may live during the entire life cycle of the tick. Dogs do not show an apparent infection and are of significance in the disease only by serving as hosts for ticks. Rabbits, sheep, pigs, and pigeons have been found resistant to the disease. The guinea pig is susceptible, and the same type of disease, except milder, is produced as by *R. rickettsii.*

*R. conorii* is similar to *R. rickettsii* in morphology and staining properties and may be cultivated upon the same types of media.

The disease is diagnosed by its peculiar symptomatology, by complement fixation, and by the Weil-Felix reaction. Vaccines are not used for the control of the infection.

### *Rickettsia tsutsugamushi*

This organism causes tsutsugamushi fever and scrub typhus in man, an acute febrile disease characterized by exanthema and enlargement of the lymph nodes near the site of bite wounds. The disease is also known as Japanese flood fever, flood fever, and Kedani fever. In addition to Japan the disease is found in Formosa, Sumatra, the Malay States, and probably other regions of the Orient and the islands of the Southwest Pacific.

*R. tsutsugamushi* is transmitted by a mite, and there is evidence that the organism passes through the life cycle of the mite. It is a small bacterium-like organism $0.3\mu$ to $5\mu$ in width by $0.8\mu$ to $2\mu$ in length; it is nonmotile and gram-negative. Artificial growth is obtained upon tissue cultures, chicken egg embryo, in the rabbit testis, and the endothelial cells overlying Descemet's membrane of the rabbit eye.

In addition to man and the animals mentioned, the organism is pathogenic for monkeys, gibbons, guinea pigs, hamsters, rats, voles, mice, gerbils.

The immunity produced in man is not as permanent as with the other rickettsia, and it is believed that different antigenic strains of the organism exist.

### *Rickettsia akari*

*R. akari* is the cause of rickettsialpox of man, an acute but not fatal disease characterized by fever and a maculopapular rash which develops into vesicles with black scabs. The organism is transmitted by the mite, *Allodermanyssus sanguineus*. The disease has been found only in New York City.

The organism is a minute diplobacillus, found intracellularly and also intranuclearly in yolk sac cells. It is nonmotile. Growth has been obtained only in the yolk sac of the chicken egg. Mice and guinea pigs have been infected experimentally but attempts to produce the disease in monkeys have been unsuccessful.

### The Genus Ehrlichia

*Ehrlichia bovis* was first described by Donatien and Lestoquard at Algiers, North Africa, in 1936. It is found as tightly massed irregular forms in monocytic cells of the cow in which it produces a slight febrile disease. It is transmitted by ticks of the genus Hyalomma.

*Ehrlichia canis* was also described by Donatien and Lestoquard in 1935, being found in experimental dogs. They considered it to be transmitted by the dog tick. The organism occurred as spherical masses in the monocytic cells of the dog in which it produced an acute fatal disease.

*Ehrlichia ovina* was first described by Donatien and Lestoquard in 1936. It likewise was found in monocyte cells of sheep in Algeria. The tick *Rhipicephalus bursa* was considered to be the vector.

### The Genus Coxiella

This genus was established for the etiologic agent of Q fever which is an obligate intracellular parasite like Rickettsia, but does not produce a skin rash in man nor is it dependent upon arthropod transmission in the infectious cycle. There is only one species, *Coxiella burnetii*.

### *Coxiella burnetii*

*Coxiella burnetii* is the cause of Q fever in man—an acute, febrile, influenza-like disease characterized by sudden onset, malaise, headache, anorexia, weakness, and an interstitial pneumonitis.

This disease was first noted by Australian investigators in the province of Queensland in 1935, and the etiologic agent was observed and named *Rickettsia burnetii* by Derrick of Australia in 1939. During the same period an organism was isolated from the tick, *Dermacentor andersoni*, by Davis in 1935, and described by Davis and Cox in Montana in 1938. This organism was named *Rickettsia diaporica* by Cox in 1939. Subsequently the two organisms were shown to be identical by Dyer and by Bengston, and the name *Coxiella burnetii* was given to it in honor of Cox and Burnet.

In addition to Australia and Montana, previously mentioned, the organism has been found to produce infection in western Europe, the Mediterranean area, the Balkans, the Near East, Spain, and Panama. In the United States Q fever has been reported from numerous parts of the country. It was found to produce an infection in packinghouse workers in Texas and Illinois. It is endemic in dairy cattle in southern California. The testing of serums from cattle and human beings in Washington has given positive results. Cases of the disease have occurred among laboratory workers in Washington, D.C., and Fort Bragg, South Carolina, and two cases were reported among people who had contact with one of the workers in Washington, D.C. (Beeman). In a study of Q fever in Iowa, Tjalma and Smith found positive reactors to the Luoto capillary agglutination test in various parts of the state. Undoubtedly, future surveys will reveal the presence of the organism in many other areas.

Morphologically, *C. burnetii* is a small, pleomorphic organism varying in shape from coccoid to short rod forms (Fig. 37.3). It occurs in large numbers in the cytoplasm of infected cells and particularly in the monocytes, pushing the nucleus of the cell over to one side. When observed extracellularly, diplobacillary, lanceolate, segmented bacillary forms and short chains are apparent. Sizes varying from $0.25\mu$ to $1.5\mu$ have been described. When stained with Giemsa stain it is reddish-purple and with Macchiavello's stain it is bright red

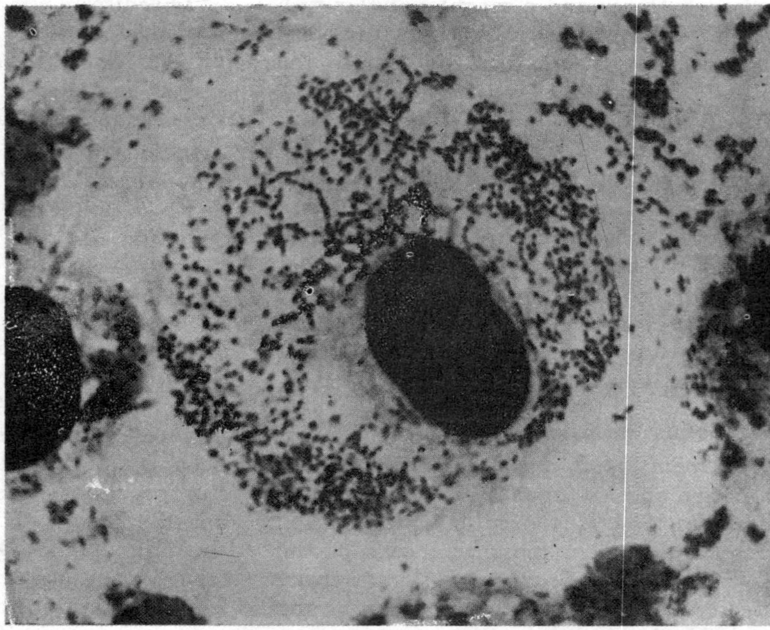

FIG. 37.3—**Coxiella burnetii**, ×960. Subcutaneous exudate from guinea pig. (Courtesy H. R. Cox.)

against a blue background. The organism is gram-negative. Artificial culture is obtained in plasma tissue cultures, in modified Maitland media, in the yolk sac, and in all tissues of the chicken embryo. All strains are similar antigenically, although some are more antigenic than others.

*C. burnetii* is transmitted by numerous species of ticks to the various animals which serve as natural reservoirs. In Australia the tick, *Haemaphysalis humerosa*, is considered the most important vector. This tick is commonly found on the bandicoot (Smith, Derrick *et al.)*, an animal which is found to be naturally infected, and also on cattle and rats. In the United States the ticks *Dermacentor andersoni, Ambeyomma americanum, Haemaphysalis leporis palustris, Dermacentor occidentalis, Ixodes dentatus,* and *Otobius megnini* are recognized as transmitting agents. Many other species of ticks have been found to transmit *C. burnetii* experimentally, so it is quite likely that most ticks are vectors if the infection is present in an area. In common with other Rickettsia, ticks remain infected with *C. burnetii* for long periods of time and their feces contain the organism.

Mantovani and Benazzi have shown that ticks *(Rhipicephalus sanguineus)* which had fed on dogs suffering a natural infection of Q fever harbored the organisms and were capable of transmitting them to susceptible hosts.

The cycle of transmission of Q fever in the natural state involves many species of animals. The bandicoot in Australia has been mentioned, and cattle have been persistently present in the picture in all areas where the disease exists. Experimentally, numerous species of rodents have been infected with the organism, but the role they play in the natural disease is not known. Reports also indicate that goats, sheep, horses, mules, dogs, and cats may be hosts for the organism. Of the avian species, the chicken and parakeet have been found susceptible experimentally. The transmission of *C. burnetii* to man may be made directly by the bite of ticks, by the handling of cattle whose hides have been contaminated by tick bites, and by contact with the flesh of cattle which are infected with the organism. The observation of Q fever in southern California among dairy workers and the investigations of Huebner and his associates have revealed that the disease may be transmitted by milk. However, it has been demonstrated by Stoenner and Lackman that the dairy cow cannot be infected by bathing the ends of the teats in infective material. This method of transmission is all the more important since it has been shown that *C. burnetii* is resistant to pasteurization at 143°F. for 30 minutes. The discovery (Luoto and Huebner, 1950) of this organism in placental tissues of cows serologically positive to Q fever antigen has revealed another potential source of infection.

In addition to the obvious methods of transmission just described, Parker, Bell, and Stoenner indicate that results with experimental animals suggest: "(1) that the eyes, nostrils, digestive tract, and the abraded or even the unabraded skin may be avenues of infection; (2) that the Rickettsia remains highly infectious for long periods in dry tick feces, in dry blood, and probably in other dried materials, and that dried infectious materials can contaminate the ground, inanimate objects, burrows, nests, etc., and can be in the air as dust particles; (3) that tissues of animals dead from Q fever, or of live animals in which the Rickettsia has persisted following recovery, may be a source of infection for scavenger and predaceous animals; (4) that it is possible, as in the case of sheep, goats and cattle, that milk from infected animals may be infectious for their young; and (5) that there is at least a possibility that infected male animals may sometimes be able to transmit infection to females during copulation and perhaps vice versa."

The nature of Q fever in man has been briefly described at the beginning of the discussion of the organism. Other details of the infection may be found in medical texts of which the description by Smadel is typical. The pathology of natural Q fever in domestic animals, particularly cattle, is not thoroughly known. Allusions are made in the literature to a "slight illness." It has been apparent to all observers that the disease in the natural state is a very benign one and that the infected animal is best described as one having an "inapparent infection." Experimentally, Parker, Bell, and Stoenner obtained the following results in four cows following the inoculation via the milk ducts of 5 billion guinea pig doses of a yolk-sac culture of the organism: "(1) the blood of all 4 cows was infectious on two or more of the first five days (later on, all tests were negative); (2) the milk of each of the inoculated quarters of each cow was infectious from the first day to the date of sacrifice, or to such date as the tests were completed; (3) the systemic reaction was of brief duration preceding and accompanying an acute phase of mastitis and was characterized by marked pyrexia, slight serous nasal and lacrimal discharges, moderate to severe depression, partial inappetence, infrequent rumination and shallow rumen movements, moderate tachycardia, and a moderate polypnea accompanied only by a definite increase in vesicular murmur; (4) the disease produced temporary metabolic changes in the activity of the mammary gland as far as the constituents of milk were concerned; (5) the cows, except for the one sacrificed on the 5th day, all became positive serologically; (6) on autopsy, gross lesions were confined chiefly to the mammary gland and regional lymph nodes; (7) by titration of milk in guinea pigs, the milk was shown to be infective in dilutions of at least $10^{-5}$ and $10^{-4}$ on the 2nd and 7th day postinoculation, respectively, and thereafter at five-day intervals was infective at $10^{-1}$; and (8) in the cow sacrificed on the 63rd day, the milk of the uninoculated right rear quarter became infectious on the 7th day and remained infectious until the cow was sacrificed." In addition to the experiment described above these authors were able to infect calves with infective milk. One calf became febrile on the 13th day while the other one did not develop symptoms.

The guinea pig is the experimental animal of choice in Q fever studies. This animal is readily infected by subcutaneous or intradermal inoculation, and a marked inflammatory reaction occurs at the point of inoculation. Mortality is low in inoculated guinea pigs; those dying reveal a marked splenic enlargement. As previously mentioned, *C. burnetii* grows well in embryonated chicken eggs, and death of the embryo results four to five days after inoculation. Chicken embryo cultures are routinely used for infection experiments, cross-immunity tests, and for experimental vaccine production. Berman and coworkers also found the chicken embryos were useful in testing vaccines for viable organisms because of their marked susceptibility.

Monolayer cultures of 4-day-old chicken embryo entodermal cells have been found by Weiss and Pietryk to be valuable for the study of *C. burnetii.*

The diagnosis of Q fever in man is accomplished by the isolation of the organism and by serologic tests. The antigen used in serologic tests is prepared in chicken embryos. Either the agglutination test or the complement-fixation test may be used. Surveys of animal populations to obtain data relative to the presence of Q fever in an area are made with the agglutination or complement-fixation tests.

### The Genus Cowdria

The genus Cowdria is composed of one species which produces disease in animals, *Cowdria ruminantium.*

#### *Cowdria ruminantium*

In 1925 Cowdry described a small microorganism which he found in the endothelial cells of animals that had succumbed to "heartwater." He found the organism resembled those of typhus and Rocky Mountain spotted fever; consequently, he named it *Rickettsia ruminantium.* The genus Cowdria was originated by Bengston in honor of Cowdry in 1948.

This organism is the cause of an acute septicemia which has been observed in cattle, sheep, and goats in various parts of Africa. The name "heartwater" is given to this disease because of the most characteristic lesion, hydropericardium, found on autopsy. The disease is further characterized by a high temperature and by nervous symptoms. The microorganisms are found in the endothelial cells of the capillaries of the renal glomeruli, in the endothelial cells of the large blood vessels, and in the superficial gray matter of the cerebral cortex. It is not found in blood smears from the infected animal.

*Cowdria ruminantium* is transmitted by ticks of the genus Amblyomma. If the ticks are infected during the larvae stage they remain infective after moulting to the nymph stage; if infected in the nymph stage they are infective in the adult stage. The organism multiplies within the cells of the intestine of the tick and probably to some extent in the lumen. It is not transmitted from one generation of ticks to another through the egg, thereby differing from the microorganism of Rocky Mountain spotted fever.

This organism is $0.2\mu$ to $0.3\mu$ by $0.4\mu$ to $0.5\mu$ in size. Diplococcoid forms are commonly observed. The organisms are usually contained within the cell, but a few scattered ones are occasionally seen in the surrounding tissue. It is stained a dark blue by Giemsa stain and is gram-negative. It cannot be cultivated upon artificial media.

*Cowdria ruminantium* rarely survives more than 36 hours at laboratory temperatures; however, it will live as long as 12 days in brain tissue stored in a refrigerator.

The disease produced by this Rickettsia is most prevalent during the warm months of the year during the tick season. Goats are the most susceptible, then sheep and cattle. In goats and sheep mortality is often 100 per cent, while 60 per cent of the cattle may die. Experimentally, the organism is infective for the guinea pig, the rabbit, the white rat, the ferret, and some of the species of antelope.

An animal which recovers from an attack of "heartwater" is resistant to further attacks, but the organism has been known to persist in recovered animals for as long as 105 days. The immunity is apparently cellular in nature, for passive immunity cannot be transferred from an immune to a susceptible animal. Experimentally it has

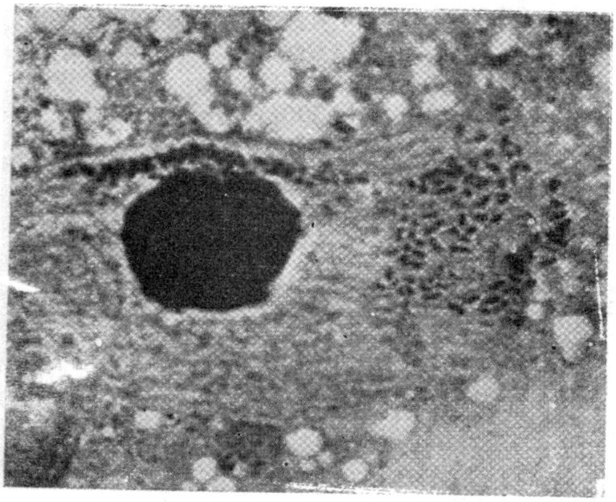

FIG. 37.4—**Cowdria ruminantium** in endothelial cell of vena cava of sheep, ×1,800. (From Donatien and Lestoquard, Arch. Inst. Past. d'Algérie.)

been found necessary to cause a reaction in order to produce an immunity against the disease.

The diagnosis of this disease is facilitated by the epizootic and the pathologic features of the infection. The organisms can be seen usually in the endothelial cells of the jugular vein and the vena cava (Fig. 37.4).

#### The Genus Neorickettsia

This genus, which contains a single species *N. helminthoeca,* was created by Philip, Hadlow, and Hughes (1953) for the etiologic agent of a helminth-borne disease of dogs, called salmon-poisoning, or salmon disease, which occurs along the coast of northwestern United States. Canines pick up the disease by eating salmon which contain the rickettsia-infected helminth fluke, *Troglotrema salmincola.* The disease in dogs has the appearance of an intoxication and is nearly always fatal. Foxes and coyotes are highly susceptible, but only a mild response is obtained in guinea pigs, hamsters, and white mice when they are injected with infectious material from dogs or fish.

The rickettsial etiology of the disease was elucidated by Cordy and Gorham (1950), although an association between the disease and the intestinal fluke was first observed by Donham (1925). Chapin (1926) observed that the fluke became encysted in the musculature of the fish (family Salmonidae) and when the fish was eaten by carnivores, the adult form of the fluke developed in the intestines. Escaping ova were ingested in turn by a snail *Goniobasis plicifera* var. *silicula,* which was eaten by the fish. The availability of the snail was the controlling factor in the spread of the fish infestation. Donham, Simms, and Miller (1926) found that in addition to chinook, silver, chum, or dog salmon being parasitized by the fluke, brook, mountain rainbow, and steelhead trout were also infested. Only one species of the genus Goniobasis snail was observed in the region where infested fish were found. It is not known whether the Neorickettsia survive throughout all the developmental stages of the fluke, but they are present in mature flukes and in large numbers in the reticular cells of lymph nodes of infected dogs.

**The Disease in Dogs.** Within 6 to 8 days after eating infective fish, dogs develop the first signs of the disease. A slight febrile response is noted, followed within 24 hours by a marked rise in temperature (104°–107°F.) with anorexia and depression. The temperature may decline temporarily followed by an exudative conjunctivitis characterized by a "sunken eye" appearance. During this time vomiting alternated by avid drinking of water occurs. Diarrhea also appears by the 5th clinical day. The discharge may be blood-tinged at first, but later contains large amounts of blood. Death occurs in more than 90 per cent of the infected animals.

Necropsy reveals extensive intestinal inflammation with profuse hemorrhage, although ulceration is rare. Large numbers of flukes and ova may be found in the intestinal content. Enlargement of ileocecal, mesenteric, portal, and internal iliac lymph nodes, due to reticular proliferation, is invariable. Numerous coccoid bodies, 0.3μ to 0.4μ in diameter, are observed in the cytoplasm of infected cells in node-impression smears stained by Giemsa's or Macchiavello's method.

Finding fluke ova in the feces of a dog with characteristic clinical signs is the surest method for diagnosis. The ova are oval-shaped averaging 50μ wide and 77μ long. Sick dogs are quickly relieved by oral administration of aureomycin or terramycin; as little as 250 mg. in a 15-pound beagle is effective (Philip, Hughes, Locker, and Hadlow, 1954).

The finding of intracytoplasmic coccoid bodies in stained node-impressions is also significant.

### The Genera Wolbachia, Symbiotes, and Rickettsiella

These genera were named for rickettsia-like intracellular parasites of various arthropods. As far as is known, they have no relationship to any disease of animals, therefore the reader is referred to texts and research papers devoted to these arthropod infections.

## THE FAMILY CHLAMYDIACEAE

The organisms of this family are now considered to be members of a single genus, Chlamydia, and are commonly known as the psittacosis-lymphogranuloma-venereum-trachoma agents (Page, 1966a). They are related in that they have a common morphology, developmental cycle, and group antigen. They are spherical, intracytoplasmic parasites ranging in size from 200mμ to approximately 1000mμ. After entry of the small elementary body (200mμ to 300mμ in diameter) into the host cell (Fig. 37.5), an intracytoplasmic inclusion, which may range up to 12μ across, is formed. The inclusion becomes filled with amorphous forms (1000mμ in diameter) of very low infectivity. These bodies appear to undergo various sequential changes: division, reduction in size, and development of a dense central mass, until the highly infectious elementary bodies are formed (Tajima, *et al.*, 1957). According to Moulder (1964), this cycle takes 30 hours. Other research workers suggest a 17-hour multiplication cycle (Tanami, Pollard, and Starr, 1961) for tissue culture-grown agents and insist that the lower infectivity of the initial forms of these agents represent the eclipse phase typical of virus multiplication. Unfortunately, they continue to refer to them as viruses.

The chlamydiae, however, are fundamentally distinct from the viruses because of their structure, chemical composition, mode of reproduction, and independent metabolic activities. They have cell walls similar in composition to those of gram-negative bacteria. They contain both forms of nucleic acids, RNA and DNA, are susceptible to many antibiotics, and can catabolize glucose when separated from host cells. They are known as "energy parasites" (Moulder, 1964), dependent upon the host cell for high energy compounds such as ATP.

All species of the group can be propagated in the yolk sac of embryonated chicken eggs. During growth, they form an antigenic lipoprotein-carbohydrate complex which is serologically similar in all species and known as the common group antigen. The antigen is stable at 100°C. for 30 minutes or more, and after such treatment can be used as an antigen to test for group antibodies produced as a result of stimulation by any other species of the group. Other antigens with less heat stability which are specific for certain strains reside in the membranes surrounding the infectious particles. These envelopes or semirigid walls (Fig. 37.6) have a high lipid content with some protein and carbohydrate, hence they are highly sensitive to

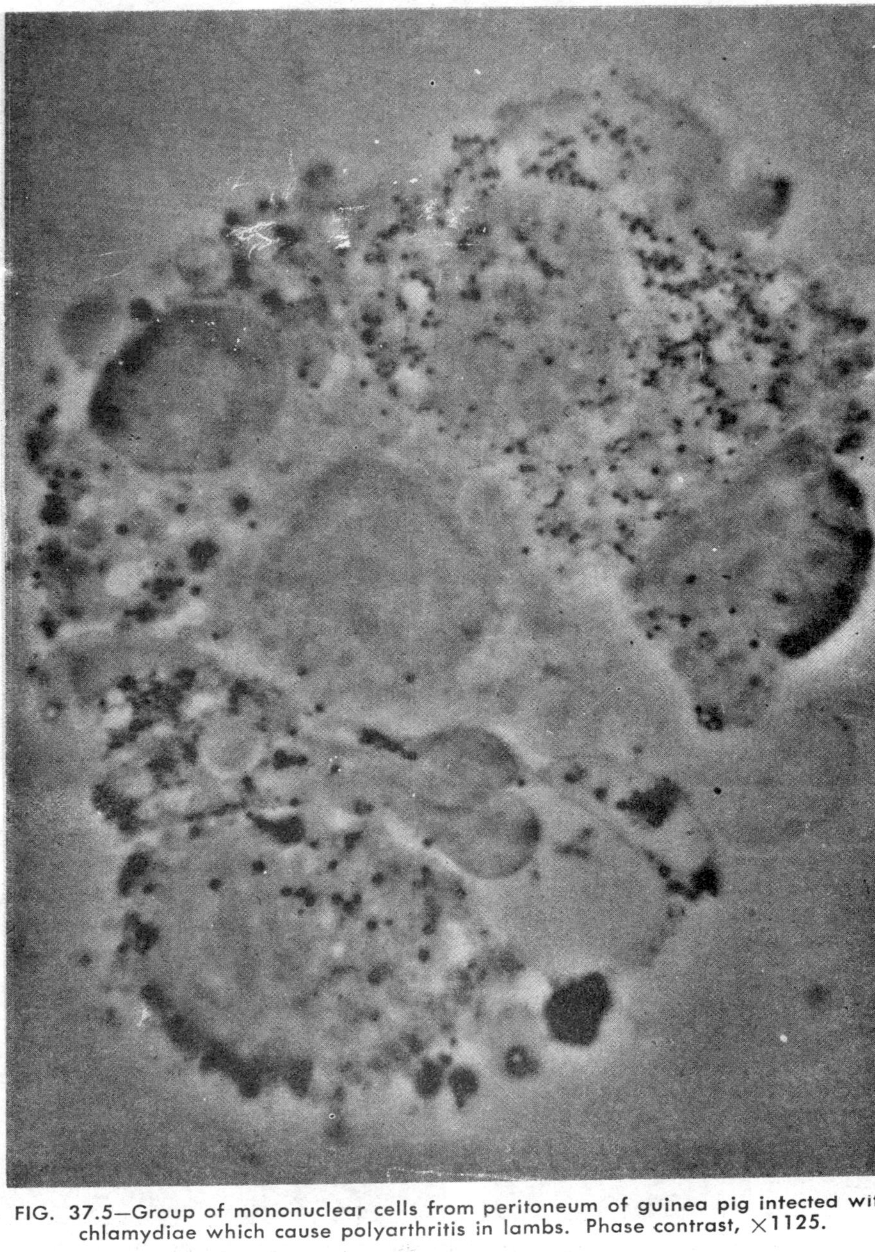

FIG. 37.5—Group of mononuclear cells from peritoneum of guinea pig infected with chlamydiae which cause polyarthritis in lambs. Phase contrast, ×1125.

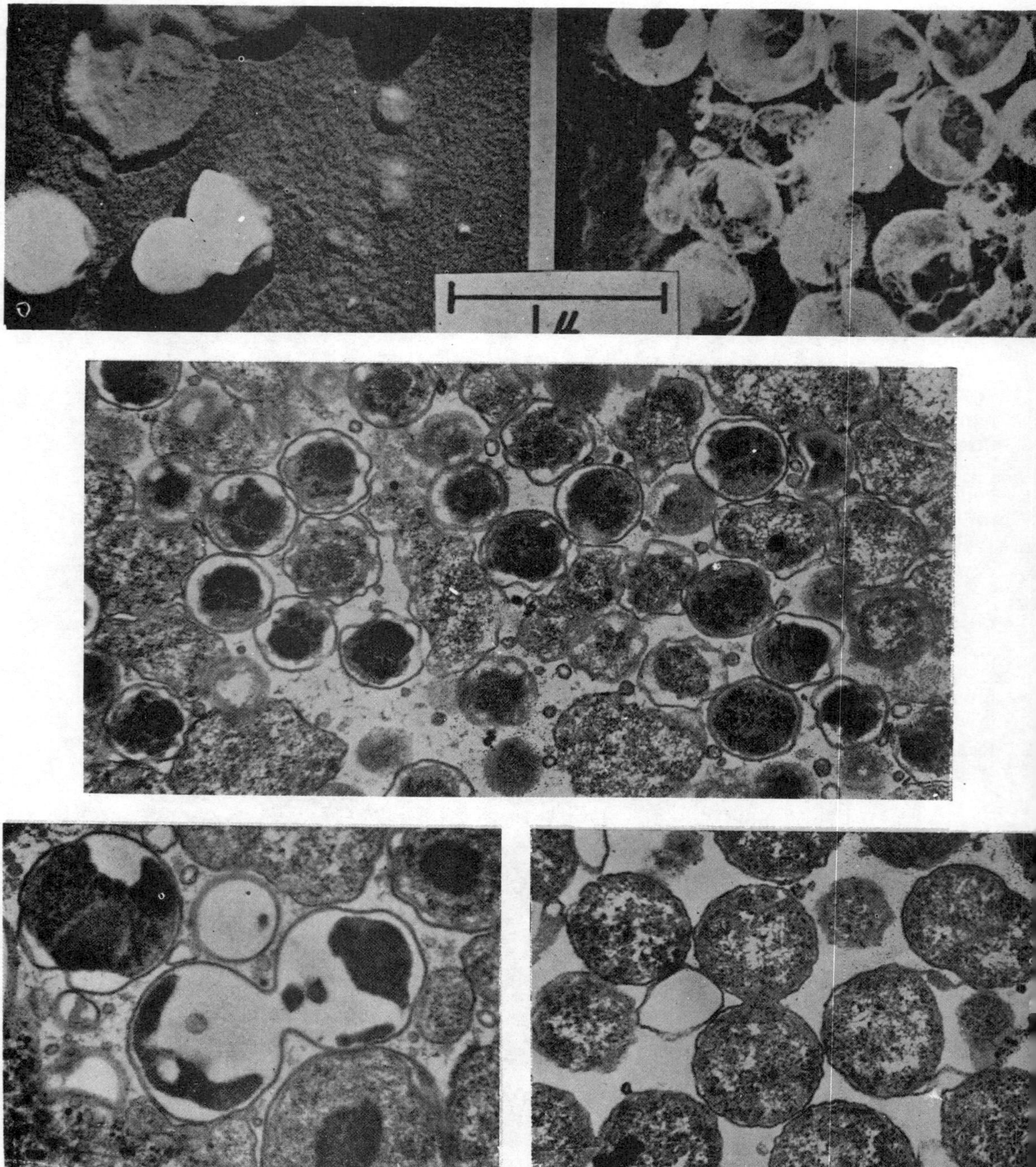


FIG. 37.6—Electron micrographs of various chlamydial isolates from birds. **Upper left,** a cell wall shaken of an organism by ultrasonic vibration is shown. **Upper right,** empty shells of cell walls from which the dens central mass was enzymatically removed are shown, ×15,000. (From Page, 1961). **Center,** ultrathin sectio showing internal structures (prominent ribosomes are the small dots). **Bottom left** and **right** show fission form of elementary bodies and initial bodies, ×45,000. (Latter three pictures from Anderson **et al.,** 1965.)

lipid solvents and detergents (Jenkin, 1963; Benedict and O'Brien, 1956). The organisms are highly resistant to proteolytic enzymes, such as trypsin.

The organisms are weakly gram-negative, but, like rickettsiae, readily stain purple by Giemsa's method, blue by Castenada's method, or red by Macchiavello's method. They are clearly visible in the cytoplasm of host cells in wet mounts under phase-contrast microscopy (Fig. 37.5); therefore, it is not necessary to stain them for microscopic examination.

Many chlamydial isolates from different animal species possess a lipoprotein component which, when injected intravenously into susceptible animals such as laboratory mice, cause severe damage to the vascular endothelium of the host, resulting in a rapid "toxic" death (Manire and Meyer, 1949). The antigenic specificity of this component has been useful in grouping strains, but does not regularly permit the separation of species.

Studies of the nomenclature of the PLT group indicate that there is no sound basis for their separation into two genera (Chlamydia and Miyagawanella) as suggested by Rake in the 7th edition of Bergey's Manual (1957), or into four genera as proposed by Levaditi, Roger, and Destombes (1964). Therefore, for purposes of this book they will be considered as members of a single genus, Chlamydia, which was proposed by Jones, Rake, and Stearns (1945) for the etiologic agents of trachoma, psittacosis, and lymphogranuloma venereum. At present, only two species are justified and they are separated on the basis of their intracellular colonial morphology, their ability to produce glycogen, and their susceptibility to sodium sulfadiazine.

### *Chlamydia trachomatis*

This is the type species of the genus. It is the cause of trachoma in man, a disease characterized by prolonged conjunctival inflammation and development of destructive lesions of the conjunctiva and cornea. Masses of spherical organisms are clearly visible in the cytoplasm of inflammatory cells in scrapings from infected areas. The organism can be cultivated in the yolk sac of chicken embryos after multiple blind passage of the original material in eggs incubated at 35°C. The organism may be adapted to tissue cultures. It is pathogenic only for primates. All strains form compact intracellular microcolonies, produce glycogen, and are susceptible to sulfadiazine.

Other strains cause acute conjunctivitis and urethritis in man. It is transmitted venereally and by other means associated with close contact.

Strains of either *C. trachomatis* or *C. psittaci* have been isolated from cases of lymphorganuloma venereum, a veneral disease of humans, although it can be experimentally transmitted to primates. The organism affects chiefly the lymphatic tissues of the iliac and inguinal regions, producing a lesion characterized by masses of granulation tissue, which bleeds easily. Elephantiasis of the genitalia and strictures of the rectum may occur. The agent is similar to other chalamydiae except for its highly limited host range. In the laboratory, the agent can be propagated only in the lungs of young mice, in the yolk sac of embryonating chicken eggs, and in tissue culture.

The organisms are very susceptible to penicillin and tetracyclines, the former being the drug of choice for treatment.

This species, as well as the following species, was originally placed in the genus Miyagawanella Brumpt.

### *Chlamydia psittaci*

This organism causes psittacosis, a disease of man and numerous birds of the psittadae family (parakeets, parrots, etc.). The organism is commonly carried by normal-appearing psittacine birds in their spleens and kidneys. When these birds are subjected to physiologic and environmental stresses, the organisms multiply and are excreted by their avian hosts in large numbers into the environment.

The excreta dries, becomes infectious dust, and is inhaled by other susceptible avian or mammalian hosts. In man and other mammals, the organisms rapidly multiply in the epithelial cells lining the alveoli of the lung, causing a pneumonitis. From the lungs they spread via the blood stream to other parts of the body causing a severe systemic disease (20 per cent mortality in untreated humans). The infection in birds is usually inapparent or chronic, affecting only the spleen or kidney, until stress factors cause it to become acute and systemic (Fig. 37.7). Then the birds usually die, especially if secondary infection develops. This classic sequence of events often follows the purchase of the "dime-store" parakeet which has been subjected to crowded, insanitary conditions, and radical change in diet, or to intensive breeding. The bird is brought to a new environment in which it spreads infectious dust, and dies. Such birds have caused sickness in entire households with mortality in numerous cases. Fortunately, all isolates thus far have been found susceptible to tetra-

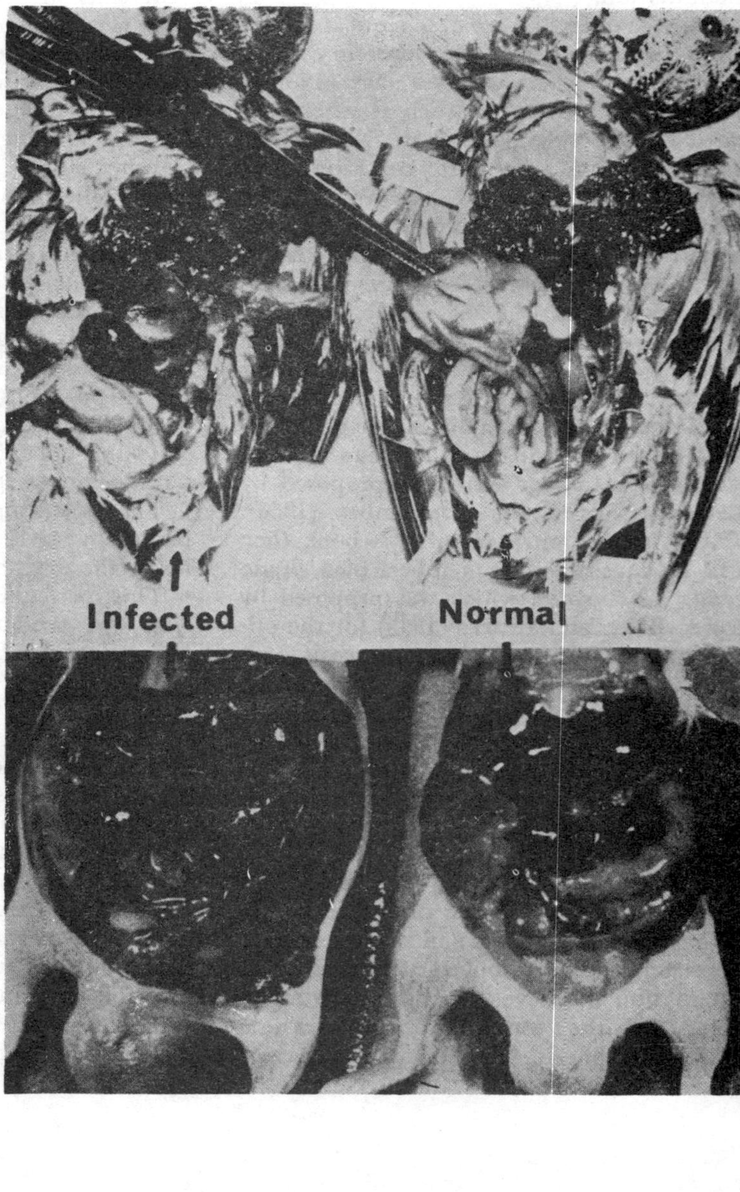


FIG. 37.7—Lesions caused by chlamydiae in parakeets and mice. Infected hosts are on left. The infected parakeet shows the classic enlarged spleen characteristic of psittacosis. Chlamydiae from the parakeet produced the typical gross lesions of experimental chlamydosis in mice inoculated by the intraperitoneal route: enlarged spleen, peritoneum filled with serofibrinous fluid containing infected, inflammatory cells. (From Page, 1966.)

cyclines, and this class of drug is the treatment of choice in birds, mammals, or man.

The organisms may be isolated by inoculating infected tissue homogenates into any of a number of tissue line cell cultures, into embryonating chicken eggs (yolk-sac route), into mice (intracerebral, intranasal, or intraperitoneal route), or into normal parakeets (intraperitoneal route). The organisms multiply to high titer in tissue line cell cultures, but usually do not cause visible cytopathogenicity. Intracytoplasmic inclusion and elementary bodies can be seen microscopically, however, and identified by means of treatment with specific antibodies conjugated with fluorescein dyes. The organisms multiply in the yolk membrane of eggs and eventually kill the embryo within 6 to 10 days, depending upon the number of organisms inoculated. They multiply on the meninges, in the lungs, or in the peritoneal serosa of mice and cause inflammatory exudates to accumulate as well as enlargement of liver and spleen (Fig. 37.7). They produce severe airsacculitis, splenomegaly, and peritonitis in parakeets. Microscopic examination of the exudates with phase-contrast optics characteristically reveals numerous intracytoplasmic elementary bodies within mononuclear cells.

Other organisms similar to *C. psittaci* in every respect, except serologic specificity of the lipoprotein in their cell walls, have been isolated from numerous species of nonpsittacine birds such as turkeys, chickens, ducks, sparrows, pigeons, pheasants, gulls, herons, and other wild birds. The most common carrier of such organisms is the pigeon. Serologic surveys indicate that over 90 per cent of flocks of pigeons have been exposed to chlamydial agents. These isolates from nonpsittacine birds were given the species epithet *ornithosis* by Rake after a suggestion by Meyer (1940) that they be distinguished from the psittacine isolates. Since these organisms cause a disease in man and birds that is identical to that caused by *C. psittaci*, they are not differentiated taxonomically.

Epizootics in turkeys caused by similar agents produced severe economic loss as well as a public health hazard in the poultry industry during the 1950's. Highly infectious, virulent chlamydiae were found in turkeys, usually breeding hens, which caused drastic lowering of egg production, depression, weight loss, drop in market value and severe lesions in affected birds with up to 30 per cent mortality. Moreover, when infected, untreated birds were sent to processing plants, the personnel handling the birds between the shipping trucks to the eviscerating tables were subjected to heavy exposure of infectious dust and aerosols. Many persons became infected and some died. In 1954 over 217 overt cases of psittacosis in humans were reported to the Public Health Service as being associated with the processing of poultry (Andrewes, 1957). There probably were many more inapparent or undetected infections. Since 1960, the disease in turkeys has abated somewhat, but up to 50 per cent of flocks in some states become infected every year.

The source of the infection to annually replaced poultry flocks has never been satisfactorily determined. Feral pigeons and migratory water birds such as gulls, herons, egrets, and ducks harbor similar organisms and could serve as an infection source when they intermingle with domestic birds (Moore *et al.*, 1959). Agents carried by wild birds readily transfer to domestic birds and have been implicated in epizootics among turkeys (Page, 1960).

No evidence exists for transovarial transmission of the organism in turkeys (Page, 1960). On the other hand, arachnids, such as nest mites or turkey mites surviving in nest boxes of marketed, infected birds, may retain the infectious particles in or on their bodies until a new group of birds arrives. How the disease agents are transmitted to the new group of birds has not been proved, but these mites may play a role (Eddie *et al.*, 1961).

The disease in turkeys or other nonpsittacine birds may be diagnosed on the basis of clinical history (depression, anorexia, hyperthermia, drop in egg production, yellow-green gelatinous droppings), 3 to 30 per cent mortality, gross pathology (airsacculitis, perihepatitis, pericarditis, hepatomegaly, splenomegaly), microscopic examination of inflammatory exudates for intracytoplasmic elementary bodies, and complement-fixing antibodies in the serums of affected individuals. Fluorescent-antibody techniques may also be applied to identify the etiologic agent (Ross and Borman, 1963). The organisms may readily be isolated by inoculation of tissue homogenates into chicken embryos or into mice by any route. Lesions and mortality of the inoculated animals are the same as for *C. psittaci*. The virulent turkey isolates usually have a high pathogenicity and lethality for mice, guinea pigs, turkeys, and chicken embryos. The pigeon isolates of low virulence usually fail to kill turkeys or mice and have no effect on guinea pigs (Page, 1966b). The public health hazard is much greater when the virulent strains are affecting the birds.

Several methods may be used for testing serums of infected birds: the indirect complement-fixation test of Karrer *et al.* (1950), the direct complement-fixation tests of Benedict (1958) or Brumfield and Pomeroy (1957), and a capillary tube agglutination test of Mason (1956). Individual titers of infected birds vary, depending upon the intensity of the antigenic stimulus, the length of time after stimulation, and the method used for testing (Page and Bankowski, 1960). Serology is more useful for diagnosis on a flock basis. During a current epizootic, 95 per cent or more of the birds may show some degree of serologic reaction to any of the tests. Titers may range between 1:4 to 1:1,000, the highest in chronically diseased birds.

Treatment of infected flocks consists of incorporating tetracyclines in the turkey feed at the rate of 400 grams per ton or more, for a period of one to three weeks, depending on the virulence of the strain currently affecting the birds. If the birds are marketed at the end of the treatment period, the birds may show numerous healing or residual organism-free lesions which may be a cause for condemnation but do not make them a public health hazard.

Numerous immunologically distinct strains of *C. psittaci* have been isolated from humans with pneumonia for which no mammalian or avian reservoir could be established. These isolates are similar to *C. psittaci* in every respect except the specificity of the lipoprotein in their cell walls.

### Diseases of Mammals Caused by Chlamydiae

In recent years chlamydial infections of domestic mammals have become of considerable economic importance. All of the agents associated with these diseases fit the description of chlamydiae in relation to their morphology, developmental cycle, and group antigen. They appear to have a more limited host range than avian strains which undergo many interspecies transfers. Most of the isolates associated with different disease entities can be shown to be serologically distinct by neutralization tests, although several isolates associated with a single disease entity may show similar variation.

All the mammalian strains may be isolated in the yolk sac of chicken embryos or in tissue cultures, although several blind passages may be necessary before death patterns or high titers are established. Many strains can also be propagated in mice, if inoculated by the intranasal route.

Serology of the affected animal species may be readily performed, utilizing antigens prepared with homologous strains, if an unusual degree of specificity is required; otherwise, commercial or experimental antigens prepared with standard psittacosis strains may be used to test for antibodies to the group antigen. Methods for preparing such group antigens have been described by Meyer and Eddie (1956) and for specific antigens by Jenkin (1960) and Fraser and Berman (1965).

**Murine Pneumonitis *(C. psittaci)*.** A number of similar agents causing this disease have been isolated from the lungs of mice in certain infected colonies (Gönnert, 1941; Nigg, 1942). Ordinarily, the agents cause a mild disease and do not produce lethal pneumonia unless serially passaged in young mice by the intranasal route of inoculation. It is important to examine mouse colonies for the presence of these organisms, for infected mice should not be used for experimental chlamydial infections.

**Feline Pneumonitis *(C. psittaci)*.** This agent causes an infectious disease of domestic cats characterized clinically by conjunctival and nasal discharges and anorexia. At necropsy, consolidated portions of the lung have a grayish appearance (Baker, 1944). Kittens are susceptible to intranasal inoculation of infectious exudate. The disease is probably transmitted naturally between cats and may be prevented by use of commercially produced vaccines, or treated by the use of tetracycline antibiotics.

**Ovine Pneumonitis and Abortion.** Agents causing pneumonitis or abortion in sheep have been repeatedly isolated from diseased lungs of sheep (McKercher, 1952; Boidin, 1957) and from aborted ovine fetuses (Stamp *et al.,* 1950; McKercher *et al.,* 1964. It has been shown experimentally that chlamydiae recovered from diseased ovine lungs can cause abortion in pregnant ewes (Dungworth, 1963), and that chlamydiae isolated from aborted ovine fetuses are capable of producing pneumonia in lambs (Page, 1966b). Therefore, it would appear that the two syndromes (pneumonia and abortion) are caused by similar, if not identical agents, although some serotypic differences exist between so-called "ovine pneumonitis" and "ovine abortion" strains.

**Ovine Arthritis.** An arthritic disease of sheep characterized clinically by lameness and stiffness and pathologically as polyarthritis was observed in 1957 in Wisconsin by Mendlowski and Segre (1960). The disease was also found by Storz *et al.* (1963) to be widespread in the intermountain region of western United States. Both investigators and their colleagues recovered the etiologic agent—a microorganism belonging in the genus Chlamydia—and reproduced the disease. The disease affected lambs up to 6 months of age with mortality ranging between 3–7 per cent. Lameness was the most prominent sign, with other signs ranging from tetanus-like spasms and death in the most severely affected to mild lameness of one leg and spontaneous recovery. Affected animals were also depressed and anorexic with elevated body temperatures. A constant necropsy finding was a serous to serofibrinous or fibrinous synovitis. Excessive serous exudate in the joints was associated with periarticular edema and pinpoint hemorrhages. Microscopic examination of wet mounts of joint exudates with phase-contrast optics revealed numerous mononuclear inflammatory cells whose cytoplasm contained elementary bodies typical of the chlamydiae. Significant cellular changes occurred in the spleens and livers of infected lambs. The spleen showed a marked hyperplasia of reticular cells, some of which contained large numbers of chlamydiae. The liver showed widespread parenchymatous degenerative changes, edema, and scattered hemorrhages (Mendlowski and Segre, 1960).

Methods for the control of this disease in sheep are still under investigation.

**Epizootic Bovine Abortion.** In the 1950's a persistently high rate of abortions among cattle in central California was investigated by Howarth *et al.* (1956). These workers could not associate the abortion etiology with known abortion agents such as bacteria of the genera Brucella, Leptospira, or Vibrio. One cause of the abortions, however was later shown by Storz *et al.* (1960) to be an organism of the psittacosis-lymphogranuloma venereum group now assigned to the genus Chlamydia. The disease in gravid cows resulting in abortion was reproduced by inoculation of pure cultures of chlamydiae isolated from naturally aborted fetuses by Storz and McKercher (1961). These investigators observed that the incidence of abortion among California cows was seasonal, following the practice by husbandrymen of transferring mated cows to foothill and mountain areas for summer grazing and returning them in the late fall to valley areas for winter grazing and calving, where the majority of abortions occurred. Within infected herds, the average abortion rates were 2 per cent observed in adult cows, with a probable additional 2 per cent unobserved; in either first or second calf heifers, the abortion rate was 20 per cent observed, with a probable additional 20 per cent unobserved. Occasionally adult cows had as high an abortion rate as heifers. In the experimental disease, Storz and McKercher observed that gravid cows showed a marked febrile response one to four days after inoculation and aborted from 11 to 126 days later regardless of the route of inoculation (except by oral administration which produced no detectable effect).

By inoculating infected tissue homogenates into chicken embryos, the agent was recovered from uterine contents of infected cows and from many organs of the aborted fetus, especially the spleen, liver, and kidney. Fetal pathology was characterized by subcutaneous edema, ascites, generalized hemorrhage, and hepatopathy.

The disease was not transferred from infected cows to normal cows by close pen contact. This fact combined with field observations has led investigators to suspect certain species of cattle ticks as vectors in the transmission of the disease agent, and considerable effort by researchers is being made to resolve this basic question. The use of vaccines against this disease has been considered, but previous trials of various vaccines against ovine abortion (Stamp *et al.*, 1950), turkey ornithosis, and human psittacosis have indicated that good vaccine immunity against agents of the genus Chlamydia is very difficult to obtain, although some natural immunity against reinfection is occasionally observed. Current research has also shown that abortion in cattle and sheep can be produced experimentally with chlamydial strains derived from birds, and that the characteristics of strains isolated from various abortion epizootics in cattle differ in their pathogenicity and serologic specificity. In view of the variety of strains of chlamydial agents that may be involved in cattle abortions, it is not possible as yet to assign species names to specific isolates and relate them to a specific syndrome or disease.

**Sporadic Bovine Encephalomyelitis *(C. psittaci)*.** In the early 1950's, a disease of calves characterized by hyperthermia, anorexia, depression, labored respiration, excessive salivation, and diarrhea followed by paralysis was described by Menges *et al.* (1953) and others. Necropsy revealed peritoneal ascites and a fibrin film on the omentum and covering the liver and spleen. Encephalomyelitis represented a residual complication. All of the manifestations of the disease (including the encephalomyelitis) were difficult to reproduce in calves with pure cultures of the etiologic agent. Isolates of this agent were typical members of the genus Chlamydia and were isolated by inoculating homogenized suspensions of infected tissues into embryonating chicken embryos by the yolk-sac route or into guinea pigs by the intraperitoneal route.

**Other Chlamydial Isolates Associated With Diseased Mammals.** In 1949 Roca Garcia isolated an agent of the genus Chlamydia from the brains of several species of opossums which died of convulsions and paralysis. York and Baker, in 1951, recovered from the feces of apparently normal calves a chlamydial microorganism *(C. bovis)* which was lethal to calves when administered orally. Omori and his coworkers (1953) isolated another chlamydial agent from the lungs of diseased goats, and with it was able to reproduce a pneumonitis in the natural host as well as in a number of laboratory animals.

More recently Murray (1965) isolated another chlamydial agent from the diseased conjunctiva of hamsters. Also various colonies of guinea pigs have been reported to be chronically infected with similar agents causing conjunctivitis. Guinea pig agents were also found to be transmitted transovarially (Storz, 1961).

It is readily apparent to the student that agents of the genus Chlamydia are widely distributed in nature and cause a variety of pathologic effects. It is uncertain whether the affected host species represent incidental hosts which were randomly exposed to chlamydial agents carried by vectors or intermediate host species; or are by themselves carrier species, individuals of which developed signs of disease.

### Other Genera

Bergey's Manual (7th edition) lists three other genera in the family Chlamydiaceae for rickettsia-like organisms that have been found by Coles, and others, in conjunctival scrapings of fowls, cattle, swine, sheep, and goats. Little is known of them except their morphology and apparent natural host range. They have never been cultivated. They are classified as follows: *Ricolesia conjunctivae,* associated with acute conjunctivitis and keratitis in fowls; *Ricolesia bovis,* associated with keroto-conjunctivitis in cattle; *Ricolesia lestoquardii,* associated with kerato-conjunctivitis in swine; *Colettsia pecoris,* found as a nonpathogenic inhabitant of the conjunctiva of cattle, sheep, and goats; and *Colesiota conjunctivae,* associated with acute kerato-conjunctivitis in sheep. The relationships, if any, between these organisms have not been established, nor have their differences, except for some variation in their natural host and degree of parasitism.

## THE FAMILY BARTONELLACEAE

This family consists of markedly pleomorphic microorganisms which parasitize erythrocytes of man and lower animals. Under Giemsa's stain they may appear as rods, cocci, filamentous forms, or ring-shaped forms, their shape probably depending upon their nutritional and chemical environment and the stage of growth. Within erythrocytes they stain solidly, thereby appearing to have no cytoplasm. This serves to differentiate them from protozoa. Some species are transmitted by insect vectors.

Four genera are listed in Bergey's Manual (7th edition). These are: (1) Bartonella, consisting of organisms that parasitize erythrocytes and vascular endothelium of man, but have also been found in sand flies. These organisms are bacteria-like in that they can be propagated on lifeless media, can multiply by binary fission, are polar-flagellate rods, and are sensitive to antibiotics. (2) Grahamella, consisting of nonpathogenic organisms that parasitize erthrocytes of rodents. Splenectomy or treatment with arsenicals does not affect the course of infection. One species can be cultivated on lifeless medium. (3) Haemobartonella, consisting of organisms which parasitize erythrocytes of animals in which splenectomy and arsenicals alter the course of the disease. There are nine species separated on the basis of their host relationships. (4) Eperythrozoon, consisting of blood parasites found in and around erythrocytes of rodents and domestic cattle, sheep, and swine. Splenectomy activates latent infections. There are seven species separated on the basis of host relationships.

### *Bartonella bacilliformis*

This organism is the cause of bartonellosis in man which is characterized by any of three conditions: anemia (Oroyo fever), cutaneous eruptions (Verruga Peruana), or a mixture of the two. The strict limitation of its occurrence to Peru, Colombia, and Ecuador is possibly related to the habitat restrictions of its probable insect vector, the sandfly (*Phlebotumus*).

In stained films of blood, the organisms appear as slender rods, either curved, bent or straight, or as ellipsoidal forms (Fig. 37.8). The rods may be beaded, or swollen at both ends, and often occur in chains. They may be as long as $3\mu$. They are independently motile, deriving their motion from undulations of tufted polar flagella. They may be cultivated in semisolid agar containing fresh rabbit serum and hemoglobin or in chicken embryos. They are nonfermentative and obligately aerobic. (See Peters and Wigand, 1955).

### The Genus Grahamella

Organisms of this genus have been found in erythrocytes of moles and other rodents. They resemble the bartonellae but are less pleomorphic. Several strains have been cultivated aerobically on lifeless media. Growth is favored by the presence of hemoglobin. The ends of the organisms are enlarged, giving dumbbell, wedge, and club-shaped forms which are arranged irregularly, 6 to 20 in number, in the erythrocyte. They are $0.1\mu$ to $1.0\mu$ in size, and are gram-negative, nonacid-fast, and nonmotile. Two species are listed, *Grahamella talpae* which is found in moles, and *Grahamella peromysci* which is found in deer mice, although the latter species is considered provisional.

### The Genus Haemobartonella

This genus is composed of numerous species which are named and classified according to the animal they infect. These organisms cause haemobartonellosis and anemia in the various animals infected, but do not cause eruption. As a group they are characterized as slender rods with rounded ends in which darker granules may be found, producing club, dumbbell, or diplococcoid shapes. They vary in size from $0.1\mu$ to $0.25\mu$ by $0.7\mu$ to $4\mu$ in length. Short chains and filamentous segmented forms are observed in some species. In an infection they are found distributed over the erythrocyte and have been observed within the cell. Some of them have been cultivated upon artificial media, especially semisolid, rabbit-blood agar. Artificial infection is difficult to produce in experimental animals without splenectomy. They are usually transmitted by insect vectors. They are sensitive to arsenicals.

The reader is referred to Bergey's Manual (1957) for greater details concerning the various species. The species names of Haemobartonella and their hosts are as follows: *H. muris,* the white rat; *H. canis,* the dog; *H. microtii,* the vole; *H. tyzzeri,* the guinea pig; *H. bovis,* cattle; *H. sturmanii,* buffalo; *H. peromyscii,* the deer

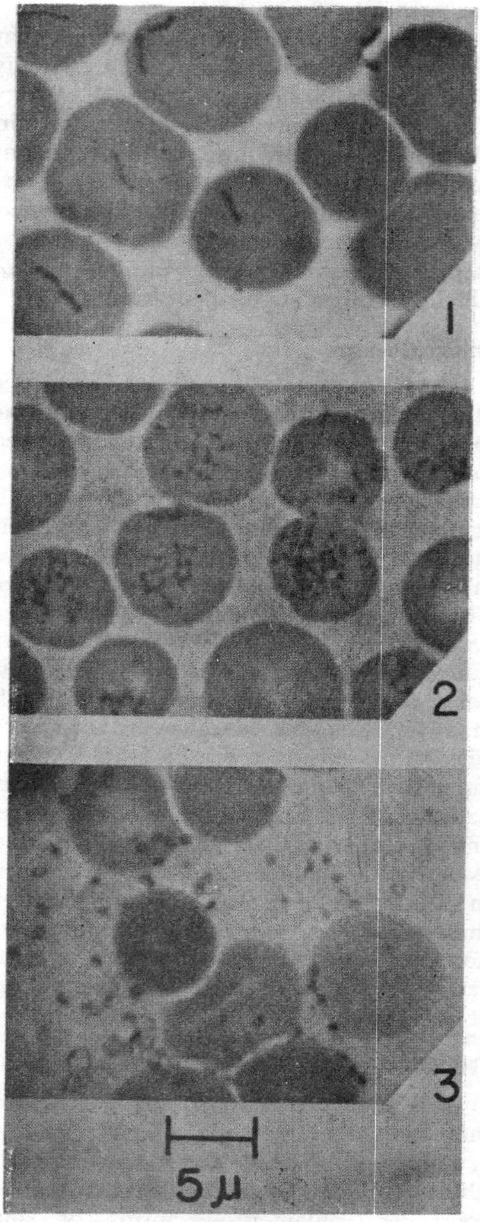


FIG. 37.8—Giemsa-stained blood smears containing **Bartonella bacilliformis, 1; Haemobartonella muris, 2;** and **Eperythrozoon coccoides, 3.** The smears are of human, hamster, and mouse blood, respectively. (From Peters and Wigand, Bact. Rev. 19:156, 1955.)

mouse; *H. peromyscii* var. *maniculati*, the gray-backed deer mouse; *H. blarinae*, the short-tailed shrew; *H. sciurii*, the gray squirrel.

### The Genus Eperythrozoon

The microorganisms classified in this genus are found in the plasma and on the erythrocytes of animals in which they produce anemia, eperythrozoonosis. These organisms are coccoid short rods, 1$\mu$ to 2$\mu$ long, often appearing in ring shapes. They stain bluish or pinkish violet by the Giemsa stain and are gram-negative. Splenectomy of susceptible animals activates latent infections. They have not been grown on cell-free media. Six different species have been described: *E. coccoides*, in white mice; *E. ovis*, in sheep; *E. wenyoni*, in cattle; *E. suis*, in swine; *E. varians*, in gray-backed deer mice; *E. dispar*, in voles and dwarf mice.

*Eperythrozoon suis* has been found by Splitter in naturally occurring outbreaks of eperythrozoonosis among swine in Kansas. The disease is characterized by a severe icteroanemia and marked debility. Swine which recover from the infection are considered to be permanent carriers.

The disease is usually diagnosed in a herd by the appearance of a large number of cases of anemia. Upon necropsy the spleen is enlarged and smears will reveal the organism. Splitter has found that the complement-fixation test, similar to the technique used for the diagnosis of anaplasmosis, may be used for the diagnosis of eperythrozoonosis.

## THE FAMILY ANAPLASMATACEAE

Philip, in Bergey's Manual (7th edition), placed these parasites of the erythrocytes of ruminants in the order Rickettsiales because of the similarity in certain aspects of their morphology, reproductive cycle, physiology, and parasitism to members of other families of the order. The organisms of this monogeneric family are distributed worldwide and affect numerous species of ruminants, especially cattle and sheep. They may be transmitted by a variety of species of arachnids and insects.

As observed inside the infected erythrocyte, the organism consists of a membrane-limited oval or spherical body measuring 0.25$\mu$ to 1.5$\mu$ in diameter. The size depends upon the development of progeny within the parent body. As the number of progeny, or "initial bodies," increases, the size of the parent body enlarges. The "initial bodies" (Fig. 37.9) range between 0.25$\mu$ to 0.58$\mu$ in diameter and upon maturing become an infectious unit. In some strains, most of the organisms have saclike, thin appendages 1.0$\mu$ wide by 1.3$\mu$ to 8.0$\mu$ long which resemble tails (Fig. 37.10). Thus an infectious unit appears to have a small "head" and a long "tail."

The mode of multiplication has not been conclusively established, but is postulated for one species at least that after the infectious unit enters the red cell, it localizes or attaches itself to the inner wall of the host cell. The organism develops two to seven progeny within its cytoplasm. The mode of multiplication of the progeny is presumed to be by fission. The saclike appendages develop from one or more of the maturing initial bodies which then become other infectious units. The function of the appendage is not known. For further details, the reader is referred to articles by Ristic *et al.* (1963, 1965), Ritchie (1962), and Simpson *et al.* (1965).

Much controversy has accompanied the exclusion of Anaplasma organisms from the protozoa, and it was not until the early 1960's when techniques for examination of the fine structure of microorganisms became sufficiently developed to make definitive distinctions based on morphological considerations. The principal reason for separating the Anaplasma organisms from protozoa is that the primary infectious unit does not contain endoplasmic reticula or a membrane-limited nucleus. The absence of these fundamental morphologic features places them among the procaryotic bacteria which have primitive, undifferentiated nuclei. All eucaryotic protozoa have such features. In an elementary protozoan such as *Babesia canis*, which is also a parasite of mammalian erythrocytes, a nucleus sur-

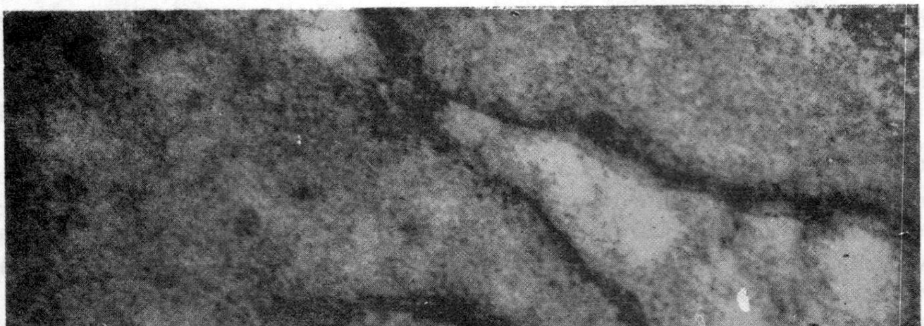

FIG. 37.9—Electron micrograph of ultrathin section of part of an erythrocyte containing an anaplasm with three initial bodies, ×15,000. (Courtesy M. Ristic.)

rounded by a double membrane, and endoplasmic reticulum has been clearly demonstrated (Bayer and Dennig, 1962). In other protozoan parasites of erythrocytes, organisms of the genus Plasmodia which cause malaria, mitochrondria, and other complex structures are demonstrable (Rudzinska and Trager, 1957). Moreover, the Anaplasma organisms appear to have respiration rates much lower than those of the genus Plasmodia, and they are sensitive to tetracyclines (Pilcher, 1961).

There is a single genus, Anaplasma, in which three species are recognized, *A. marginale, A. centrale,* and *A. ovia.* The generic name, which means "without plasma," was given to the organisms by Theiler (1910). The first two species were separated on the basis of their location in the host cell—at the periphery of erythrocytes or in the central portion of the host cell. The third species was so named for its specific host, although it was morphologically similar to *A. marginale.*

### *Anaplasma marginale*

This organism causes an acute, sometimes chronic, disease of cattle characterized by hyperthermia, anemia, and icterus with variable mortality. Cases in animals under one year of age are rare, although splenectomy removes the natural resistance of calves. In acute cases, in older animals, mortality may exceed 50 per cent, especially

FIG. 37.10—Individual anaplasma organisms in host red cell stroma showing lysis of the saclike structure and possible subdivision of a terminal round body in the cell on the right, ×10,000. (From Ritchie, 1962.)

in hot climates. Death may occur within 3 days after the first signs appear. In chronic cases, the disease lingers, and the animals become emaciated, anemic, and icteric. Erythrocyte count may fall to 14 per cent of normal with a corresponding decrease in hemoglobin. Seriously affected animals show pale and yellowish mucous membranes and may excrete dark, blood-tinged, mucous-covered feces. Diagnosis is confirmed by the microscopic observation of marginally located dark bodies in erythrocytes of suspect animals. Artifacts may be eliminated from consideration by use of fluorescein-labeled antibody and ultraviolet microscopy (Ristic, 1960).

The morphology of the organism fits that mentioned in the family description.

The organisms are transmitted by at least 19 species of ticks, in three of which the organisms pass through the egg *(Margaro annulatus, Dermacentor occidentalis,* and *Dermacentor andersoni).* Seven species of horseflies *(Tabanidae)* and five species of mosquitoes *(Psorophora)* have been implicated in the mechanical transmission of the disease (Piercy, 1956) Any means by which blood from infected animals is transferred to normal animals, including surgical procedures, dehorning, inoculations, etc., is to be carefully avoided.

The organisms are influenced by chlortetracycline and oxytetracycline, but treatment of acutely diseased or chronically infected animals ameliorates the severe aspects of the disease but does not necessarily effect a cure. Treatment prevents continued intravenous multiplication, thereby relieving clinical signs, but relapse may occur later (Miller, 1956). To be most effective it should be given at the first sign of disease. Successful use of whole blood transfusions (5 cc. per pound body weight) in alleviating the disease has been reported by Lotze (1947).

### *Anaplasma centrale*

This organism resembles *A. marginale* very closely but differs from it by its slightly greater size and its preference for the central portion of the host red cell. Some degree of cross immunity exists between *A. centrale* and *A. marginale.* This organism is also arthropod-borne, is infectious for cattle, and is found in Africa, Palestine, and Roumania.

### *Anaplasma ovis*

This species also resembles *A. marginale* but differs in its host preference and its position in erythrocytes. About 65 per cent of the organisms are found in the periphery of erythrocytes, while the remaining percentage are found in the central position. It is found in arthropods and in the erythrocytes of sheep of the Rocky Mountain area, and in sheep and goats in Africa, Southern Europe, and Asia.

## REFERENCES

ANDERSON, D. R., *et al.* Comparison of the Ultrastructure of Several Rickettsiae, Ornithosis Virus, and *Mycoplasma* in Tissue Culture. Jour. Bact. 90:1387, 1965.

ANDREWES, J. M. The Importance of Psittacosis in the United States. Jour. Amer. Vet. Med. Assn. 130:109, 1957.

BAKER, J. A. A Virus Causing Pneumonia in Cats and Producing Elementary Bodies. Jour. Exp. Med. 79:159, 1944.

BENEDICT, A. A., and MCFARLAND, C. Newer Methods for Detection of Avian Ornithosis. Annals N.Y. Acad. Sci. 70:501, 1958.

———, and O'BRIEN, E. Antigenic Studies on the Psittacosis-Lymphogranuloma Venereum Group of Viruses. II. Characterization of Complement-Fixing Antigens Extracted With Sodium Lauryl Sulfate. Jour. Immunol. 76:293, 1956.

BERGEY'S MANUAL OF DETERMINATIVE BACTERIOLOGY. 7th Ed. Williams & Wilkins Co., Baltimore, 1957.

BOIDIN, A. G. Ph.D. Thesis. Univ. of Calif., Davis, 1957.

BRUMFIELD, H. P., and POMEROY, B. S. Direct Complement Fixation by Turkey and Chicken Serums in Viral Systems. Proc. Soc. Exp. Biol. Med. 94:146, 1957.

CHAPIN, E. A. A New Genus and Species of Trematode, the Probable Cause of Salmon-Poisoning in Dogs. North Amer. Vet. 7:36, 1926.

CORDY, D. R., and GORHAM, J. R. The Pathology and Etiology of Salmon Disease in the Dog and Fox. Amer. Jour. Path. 26:617, 1950.

COWDRY, E. V. Jour. Exp. Med. 42:231, 253, 1925.

COX, H. R. Pub. Health Rept., Wash. 54:1822, 1939.

DAVIS, G. E., and COX, H. R. Pub. Health Rept., Wash. 53:2259, 1938.

DERRICK, E. H. Austral. Med. Jour. Jan. 7, p. 14, 1939.

DONATIEN, A., and LESTOQUARD, F. Bull. Soc. Path. Exot. 28:418, 1935.

———, and ———. Bull. Soc. Path. Exot. 29:1057, 1936.

DONHAM, C. R., *et al.* So-called Salmon Poisoning in Dogs. Jour. Amer. Vet. Med. Assn. 68:701, 1926.

DUNGWORTH, D. L. The Pathogenesis of Ovine Pneumonia. III. Placental Infection by Pneumonitis Virus. Jour. Comp. Path. Therap. 73:68, 1963.

EDDIE, B., *et al.* Isolation of Ornithosis Bedsoniae From Mites Collected in Turkey Quarters and From Chicken Lice. Jour. Inf. Dis. 110:231, 1962.

FRASER, C. E. O., and BERMAN, D. T. Type Specific Antigens in the Psittacosis Lymphogranuloma Venereum Group of Organisms. Jour. Bact. 89:943, 1965.

HOWARTH, J. A., *et al.* Epizootic Bovine Abortion Characterized by Fetal Hepatopathy. Jour. Amer. Vet. Med. Assn. 128:441, 1956.

JENKIN, H. M. Preparation and Properties of Cell Walls of the Agent of Meningopneumonitis. Jour. Bact. 80: 639, 1960.

JONES, H., *et al.* Studies on Lymphogranuloma Venereum. III. The Action of the Sulfonamides on the Agent of Lymphogranuloma Venereum. Jour. Inf. Dis. 76:55, 1945.

KARRER, H., *et al.* The Complement Fixation Inhibition Test and Its Application to the Diagnosis of Ornithosis in Chickens and in Ducks. I. Principles of the Test. Jour. Inf. Dis. 87:13, 1950.

LACKMAN, D. B., *et al.* The Rocky Mountain Spotted Fever Group of Rickettsias. Health Lab. Sci. 2:135, 1965.

LESTOQUARD, F., and DONATIEN, A. Bull. Soc. Path. Exot. 29:108, 1936.

LEVADITI, J. C., *et al.* Tentative de Classification des *Chlamydiaceae* (Rake, 1955) Tenant Compte de Leurs Affinites Tissulaires et de leur Epidemiologie. Ann. Inst. Past. 107:656, 1964.

LOTZE, J. C. Blood Transfusions in Bovine Anaplasmosis. Amer. Jour. Vet. Res. 8:284, 1947.

LUOTO, L., and HUEBNER, R. J. Q-fever Studies in Southern California. IX. Isolation of Q-fever Organisms From Parturient Placentas of Naturally Infected Dairy Cows. Pub. Health Rept., Wash. 65:541, 1950.

McKercher, D. G. A Virus Possibly Related to the Psittacosis-Lymphogranuloma-Pneumonitis Group Causing a Pneumonia in Sheep. Science 115:543, 1952.

———, *et al.* Isolation of the Virus of Enzootic Abortion of Ewes From California and Oregon Sheep. Jour. Amer. Vet. Med. Assn. 145:564, 1964.

Manire, G. P., and Meyer, K. F. The Toxins of the Psittacosis-Lymphogranuloma Group of Agents. III. Differentiation of Strains by the Toxin Neutralization Test. Jour. Inf. Dis. 86:241, 1950.

Mason, D. M. A Capillary Tube Agglutination Test for Detecting Antibodies Against Ornithosis in Turkey Serum. Jour. Immunol. 83:661, 1959.

Mendlowski, B., and Segre, D. Polyarthritis in Sheep. I. Description of the Disease and Experimental Transmission. Amer. Jour. Vet. Res. 21:68, 1960.

Menges, R. W., *et al.* Sporadic Bovine Encephalomyelitis. Studies on Pathogenesis and Etiology of the Disease. Amer. Jour. Vet. Med. Assn. 122:294, 1953.

Meyer, K. F. Psittacosis. Auk. 57:330, 1940.

Miller, J. G. The Prevention and Treatment of Anaplasmosis. Annals N.Y. Acad. Sci. 64:49, 1956.

Moore, R. W., *et al.* Experimental Ornithosis in Herons and Egrets. Amer. Jour. Vet. Res. 20:884, 1959.

Moulder, J. W. The Psittacosis Group as Bacteria. 95 pp. John Wiley & Sons, Inc., New York, 1964.

Murray, E. S. Guinea Pig Inclusion Conjunctivitis Virus. I. Isolation and Identification as Member of the Psittacosis-Lymphogranuloma-Trachoma Group. Jour. Inf. Dis. 114:1, 1964.

Omori, T., *et al.* Study on an Infectious Pneumonia of Goats Caused by a Virus. I. Isolation of the Causative Agent and Its Characteristics. Exp. Rept. 27, Govt. Exp. Sta. An. Hyg., 1953.

Page, L. A. Ecologic Considerations in Turkey Ornithosis. Amer. Jour. Vet. Res. 21:618, 1960.

———. Revision of the Family *Chlamydiaceae* Rake (*Rickettsiales*): Unification of the Psittacosis-Lymphogranuloma Venereum-Trachoma Group of Organisms in the Genus *Chlamydia.* Jones, Rake, and Stearns, 1945. Intl. Jour. Systematic Bact. 16:223, 1966a.

———. Interspecies Transfers of Psittacosis Group Agents. Pathogenicity of 2 Avian and 2 Mammalian Strains for 8 Species of Birds and Mammals. Amer. Jour. Vet. Res. 27:397–406, 1966b.

———, and Bankowski, R. A. Factors Affecting the Production and Detection of Ornithosis Antibodies in Infected Turkeys. Amer. Jour. Vet. Res. 21:971, 1960.

———, *et al.* Electron Microscopic Survey of Thirteen Strains of *Miyagawanella.* Avian Dis. 5:121, 1961.

Parker, R. R., *et al.* Jour. Amer. Vet. Med. Assn. 114:55, 124, 1949.

Peters, D., and Wigand, R. Bartonellaceae. Bact. Rev. 19:150, 1955.

Philip, C. B. Comments on the Classification of the Order Rickettsiales. Canad. Jour. Microbiol. 2:261, 1956.

———, *et al.* Riassunti delle Communicezioni. VI. Congresso Internaz. di. Microbiol. Roma 2:256, 1953.

———, *et al.* Salmon-poisoning Disease of Canines. II. Further Observations on Etiologic Agent. Proc. Soc. Exp. Biol. Med. 87:397, 1954.

Piercy, P. L. Transmission of Anaplasmosis. Annals N. Y. Acad. Sci. 64:40, 1956.

Pilcher, K. S., *et al.* Studies on the Morphology and Respiration of *Anaplasma marginale.* Amer. Jour. Vet. Res. 22:298, 1961.

Ristic, M. *Anaplasma marginale*—A Non-Protozoan Blood Parasite in Progress in Protozoology. Pp. 32–33. Intl. Cong. Ser. 91 Excerpta Medica Foundation. Mouton, The Hague, Netherlands, 1965.

———, and Watrach, A. M. Anaplasmosis. VI. Studies and a Hypothesis Concerning the Cycle of Development of the Causative Agent. Amer. Jour. Vet. Res. 24:267, 1963.

Ritchie, A. E. Simplified Specimen Preparation for Electron Microscopic Studies of an Intra-erythrocytic Parasite *Anaplasma marginale.* Proc. Soc. Exp. Biol. Med. 110:532, 1962.

Ross, M. R., and Borman, E. K. Direct and Indirect Fluorescent-Antibody Techniques for the Psittacosis-Lymphogranuloma Venerum-Trachoma Group of Agents. Jour. Bact. 85:851, 1963.

Simpson, C. F., *et al.* The Nature of Bands in Parasitized Bovine Erythrocytes. Jour. Cell Biol. 27:225, 1965.

Smith, D. J. W., and Derrick, E. H. Austral. Jour. Exp. Biol. Med. Sci. 18:1, 99, 103, 119, 193, 1940.

Splitter, E. J. *Eperythrozoon suis*, the Etiologic Agent of Icteroanemia or an Anaplasmosis-like Disease of Swine. Amer. Jour. Vet. Res. 11:324, 1950.

———. The Complement-Fixation Test in Diagnosis of Eperythrozoonosis in Swine. Jour. Amer. Vet. Med. Assn. 132:47, 1958.

Stamp, J. T., *et al.* Enzootic Abortion in Ewes. I. Transmission of the Disease. Vet. Rec. 62:251, 1950.

Storz, J. The Diplacental Transmission of Psittacosis-Lymphogranuloma Group of Viruses in Guinea Pigs. Jour. Inf. Dis. 109:129, 1961.

———, and McKercher, D. G. Etiological Studies on Epizootic Bovine Abortion. Zent. für Veterinärmed. 9:411, 1962.

STORZ, J., *et al.* Polyarthritis of Sheep in the Intermountain Region Caused by a Psittacosis-Lymphogranuloma Agent. Amer. Jour. Vet. Res. 24:1201, 1963.

TAJIMA, M., *et al.* Structure and Development of Viruses of the Psittacosis-Lymphogranuloma Group Observed in the Electron Microscope. Jour. Bact. 74:605, 1957.

TANAMI, Y., *et al.* Replication Pattern of Psittacosis Virus in a Tissue Culture System. Virology 15:22, 1961.

THEILER, A. *Anaplasma marginale* (Genus Nov. et Species Nov.) Un Nouveau protozoaire du betail. Bull. Soc. Path. Exot. 3:135, 1910.

VINSON, J. W., and FULLER, H. S. Studies on Trench Fever. I. Propagation of Rickettsia-like Microorganisms From a Patient's Blood. Path. Microbiol. (Suppl.) 24:152, 1961.

WEISS, E., *et al.* Glucose Metabolism by Members of the Psittacosis-Trachoma Group. Virology 22:551, 1964.

WILSON, M. R., and DUNGWORTH, D. L. Psittacosis Lymphogranuloma-Venereum Group Viruses in Sheep. Comparison Between a Faecal and an Enzootic Abortion Strain. Jour. Comp. Path. Therap. 73:277, 1963.

YORK, C. J., and BAKER, J. A. A New Member of the Psittacosis-Lymphogranuloma Group of Viruses That Causes Infection in Calves. Jour. Exp. Med. 93:587, 1951.

# 38

# The Genus Mycoplasma

**WILLIAM P. SWITZER, *D.V.M., Ph.D.***

*Veterinary Medical Research Institute*
*Iowa State University*
*Ames, Iowa*

THE MEMBERS OF THIS GENUS MAY BE EITHER parasitic or saprophytic organisms. They have a minimal cell wall that is morphologically very similar to the cytoplasmic membrane of mammalian cells. This results in the development of polymorphic forms including ring, globules, filaments, and small elementary bodies. Many of these forms pass bacteria-retaining filters. Most members of this group grow both aerobically and anaerobically, but an occasional strain may be stimulated by 10 per cent $CO_2$ atmosphere and one obligate anaerobic species has been reported from man.

The parasitic species of this group of organisms require a medium with a high protein content. This is customarily supplied by serum protein. This requirement probably reflects an inability of this group to synthesize certain protein complexes. Recent studies have suggested that some of these organisms may require certain essential lipids for growth. Initial studies of the optimum osmotic requirements for the growth of mycoplasma indicate that a tonicity of about 10 atmospheres pressure results in the best growth.

At the present time there are three metabolic pathways described for various members of this genus. They are: glycolysis with lactic acid accumulation the major end product under anaerobic conditions; the conversion of arginine to ornithine; and the utilization of urea. The hemolysin produced by *Mycoplasma pneumoniae* and *Mycoplasma gallisepticum* has been found to be hydrogen peroxide. Members of this genus can be neutralized by specific antisera but the necessary conditions vary. Some members require the presence of a labile accessory factor (not complement) present in some fresh sera, especially guinea pig sera. Most members of the group that have been studied were found to be resistant to penicillin, thallium acetate, sulfathiazol, and sometimes crystal violet and methylene blue. Most mycoplasma are moderately susceptible to the action of tetracycline antibiotics.

It is customary to exclude from this group those organisms that will revert to typical bacterial forms.

Members of the group may be cultivated either in suitable liquid media or on solid media. On the latter, small, glistening colonies that often have a faint surface marking and some degree of either a central elevation or depression occur, usually after several days incubation. These colonies are usually difficult to remove from the surface of the medium since they tend to grow into the medium. A few organisms of this group have been observed to form a film on the surface of suitable solid media.

Fluid medium is usually more satisfactory for the cultivation of members of this group. In some cases the organisms will produce enough turbidity in the medium so that growth may be readily detected. However, in most instances only a faint turbidity is produced and control tubes should always be available for comparison purposes. A more certain method of detecting growth is to stain the sediment centrifuged from the culture and to observe typical organisms. In most cases Giemsa's stain has been used to stain these organisms since they stain very poorly with analine dyes. The colony morphology can be visualized with greater clarity following staining with Dienes' stain or with 1:1,500 neutral red.

Workers dealing with this group of organisms refer to them as pleuropneumonia or pleuropneumonia-like organisms (PPLO), since the first and only known member of this group for many years was the agent producing bovine pleuropneumonia.

Nocard and coworkers, in 1898, were the first to cultivate the causal agent of bovine pleuropneumonia in a cell-free medium. This agent had been considered to be a filterable virus up to that time. The studies of Bordet and of Borrel in 1910 disclosed the polymorphic characteristics of the organism. Elford demonstrated in 1929 that this organism possessed filterable forms 125 m$\mu$ to 150 m$\mu$ in size which were capable of developing into larger structures. It was for this reason, no doubt, that the agent of contagious pleuropneumonia was classified as a filterable virus.

In 1923 Bridré and Donatien demonstrated that the causal agent of contagious agalactia of sheep and goats was quite similar to the cause of pleuropneumonia.

Shoetensack, in 1934, isolated an organism fulfilling the characteristics of this group from dogs suffering with distemper; however, he did not infer that the organism alone was the cause of distemper.

In 1935 Klieneberger reported that a pleuropneumonia-like organism ($L_1$) was present in all the cultures of *Streptobacillus moniliformis* which she had studied. The latter is a pleomorphic, gram-negative organism found in the nasopharynx of rats and associated with at least one type of rat-bite fever in man. She was able to isolate the $L_1$ organism in pure culture and was able to maintain it in pure culture, although she considered it a symbiont of *S. moniliformis.* Other investigators—Dawson and Hobby, Dienes and Edsall—have suggested that the microorganism is a variant of *S. moniliformis.*

The discovery that organisms of this group are not confined to parasitic species was made by Laidlaw and Elford in 1936, who isolated typical cultures from raw sewage. These observations were confirmed by Seiffert when he isolated similar microorganisms from soil, compost, manure, and decomposing leaves.

In 1938 Sabin and Findlay *et al.,* working independently, isolated pleuropneumonia-like organisms from mice which had developed nervous symptoms during the passage of lymphocytic choriomeningitis virus. It was subsequently discovered that the microorganisms had a special affinity for the mesenchymal cells of the pleura, peritoneum, and joints, but produced a neurotropic exotoxin which caused the choreiform symptoms. Other strains which localize in the mesenchymal cells of the joints of the mouse, producing a proliferative and chronic ankylosing arthritis, have been described by Sabin.

Interest in the mycoplasma received a major advance when Chanock *et al.* (1962) demonstrated that the Eaton agent was a member of this group. It has subsequently been found that *M. pneumoniae* is the major cause of primary atypical pneumonia associated with cold agglutinating antibodies in man. Research on this disease has been vigorous and successful, so that today it is our best understood model of mycoplasmal disease.

Nelson (1936a,b) described coccobacillary bodies associated with slowly developing coryza in poultry. These organisms were probably pleuropneumonia-like organisms. Van Herick and Eaton (1945) isolated a pleuropneumonia-like organism from chicken embryo material, which they believed to be a contaminant carried by the chicken embryo. It was not until 1952 that Markham and Wong showed that pleuropneumonia-like organisms would experimentally produce mild upper-respiratory-tract lesions in chickens and turkey sinusitis. Since that time, this group has been recognized as being of major importance to the poultry industry, and consequently, considerable research has been in progress on this group.

Edward *et al.* (1947) isolated pleuropneumonia-like organisms from the bovine genital tract and suggested that they caused an inflammation that predisposed to infertility. In 1953 Switzer isolated a pleuropneumonia-like organism from the nasal cavities of swine and later showed it to be the cause of certain fibrinous lesions on the serous membranes of swine, especially the pericardium, and to occur in pneumonic swine lungs (Switzer, 1953a,b, and 1954a).

Carter (1954) demonstrated that members of this group of organisms occurred in certain cases of bovine bronchopneumonia.

Cordy *et al.* (1955) described a highly fatal disease due to a pleuropneumonia-like organism in a herd of dairy goats. This disease was characterized by septicemia and arthritis.

Greig (1955) reported the isolation of a pleuropneumonia-like organism from the respiratory tract of sheep.

At the present time this group of organisms is receiving an ever-increasing amount of attention with new species recently described as causes of swine arthritis, poultry arthritis, bovine mastitis, and swine metritis—mastitis agalactiae. Much current interest is directed toward the possible role of mycoplasma as a cause of human arthritis. Many new species of mycoplasma will undoubtedly be discovered and characterized in the future.

There are three general criteria that are used to identify various species of mycoplasma. The first of these is host-infected since very few mycoplasma are known to infect more than one species. In those few cases the species of hosts are usually closely related. The second general criterion used for recognition of individual species is the biological characteristics of the isolates. These would include such factors as morphology of colony; morphology of individual organisms; presence of hemolysins; resistance to methylene blue; hemagglutinating ability; action on certain cell cultures; action on embryonating hens eggs; lesions produced in the host; utilization of certain carbohydrates, amino acids, urea, or special growth factors; and aerobic growth. The third criterion for recognition of the species of mycoplasma is serological comparison of an unknown isolate with a prototvpe isolate. This procedure has been utilized most extensively in the study of the mycoplasma from poultry and man. It is likely that serologic identification will be used more extensively in the future study of mycoplasma isolates from other species. The growth inhibition, metabolic inhibition, tube agglutination, and hemagglutination-inhibition tests have so far proved to be the most useful tests, while the indirect hemagglutination and complement-fixation tests have resulted in less clear-cut differentiation between species.

## CLASSIFICATION AND NOMENCLATURE

The classification and nomenclature of this group of organisms are not firmly established. The classification given here is expanded from that suggested by Freundt (1955) and Edward (1955).

Order *Mycoplasmatales*
Genus *Mycoplasma*
Individual species

1. *Mycoplasma mycoides*—organism causing contagious bovine pleuropneumonia
   *M. mycoides* var. *capri*—organism causing pleuropneumonia in goats
2. *M. agalactiae*—organism causing contagious agalactia of sheep and goats
3. *M. agalactiae* var. *bovis*—organism causing mastitis and infertility in cattle
4. *M. iners* and *M. gallinarum*—organisms found in respiratory tract of chickens
5. *M. gallisepticum* and *M. mele-*

*agridis*—organisms associated with chronic respiratory disease, air sac infection, and sinusitis in poultry
6. *M. hyorhinis*—organism producing fibrinous pericarditis, pleuritis, peritonitis, and arthritis in swine
7. *M. bovigenitalium*—frequent inhabitant of the bovine lower genital tract, both in males and females and one cause of bovine mastitis
8. *M. spumans, M. canis,* and *M. maculosum*—pleuropneumonia-like organisms isolated from dogs
9. *M. pulmonis*—organism from the respiratory tract of rats
10. *M. neurolyticum*—organism producing nervous symptoms in mice
11. *M. arthritidis*—organism producing arthritis in rats
12. *M. laidlawii*—sewage and other saprophytic strains
13. *M. hominis* I, *M. hominis* II, *M. oralis, M. fermentans, M. salivarium,* and *M. pneumoniae*—pleuropneumonia-like organisms isolated from man: the latter organism is a significant cause of pneumonia
14. *M. synoviae*—organism causing an infectious synovitis in poultry
15. *M. hyopneumoniae*—organism causing a chronic pneumonia in swine
16. *M. granularum* and *M. hyoarthrinosa*—organisms causing arthritis in swine

Other Mycoplasma not yet named or with only preliminary information available from

(a) bovine pneumonia
(b) sheep respiratory tract
(c) acute septicemia and arthritis of goats
(d) T forms from human genital tract
(e) *M. hyogenitalium* from swine metritis-mastitis
(f) cell cultures, especially the G.D.L. mycoplasma isolate

In this discussion of Mycoplasma, only those species that are currently known to have significance to domestic or laboratory animals will be considered.

### *Mycoplasma mycoides*

The presence of this organism in bovine pleuropneumonia was first demonstrated by Nocard in 1898. The pleomorphic nature of the organism was recognized in 1910 by Bordet, who considered it allied to the spirochetes. The varied forms of the organism were recognized in 1910 by Borrell, who considered the coccal forms of *the* organism in coining the name *Asterococcus mycoides.* Other names which have been used for the organism are: *Coccobacillus mycoides peripneumoniae* (Martzinovski, 1911), *Micromyces peripneumoniae bovis contagiosae* (Frosch, 1923), *Mycoplasma peripneumoniae* (Nowak, 1929), *Asteromyces peripneumoniae bovis* (Wroblewski, 1931), and *Borrelomyces peripneumoniae* (Turner, Campbell, and Dick, 1935). In his classification of this group of organisms, Sabin first used the name *Bovimyces pleuropneumoniae* but subsequently suggested that *Asterococcus mycoides* had priority. Since the generic name *Asterococcus* had been used previously for a genus of algae, it now appears that the first valid generic name given to this organism was *Mycoplasma* (Nowak, 1929).

Bovine pleuropneumonia, the disease caused by *M. mycoides,* has been a well-recognized disease on the European continent for the past two centuries. In all countries where the disease has appeared, great losses of cattle have resulted. It has been eradicated in many of the sections of Europe, and before World War II was localized in Russia, Spain, and Poland. The condition is widespread in Mongolia and Manchuria, and epizootics occur in India and China. It is still present in Egypt and Central Africa. The disease is found in South American countries.

Intensive current efforts to eradicate this disease from Australia have resulted in enough reduction in incidence that hope is held that the disease may be completely eradicated from this continent in the future.

It was introduced into the United States

as early as 1843, and by 1886 had spread as far west as Missouri. Stringent action was taken by the newly formed Bureau of Animal Industry, and in March, 1892, a proclamation was issued stating that the country was free of the disease. The presence of this disease in various parts of the world, the marked infectiousness of it, and increased animal traffic are all factors which may result in the introduction of the infection again. All animal disease agencies must be constantly alert in order to prevent the establishment of the disease in the cattle herds of this country.

The microorganism is transmitted by direct contact and by water and feed recently contaminated by an infected animal. Chronic cases of the disease remain carriers because the organism is present in the exudate from healing lung lesions. Apparently healthy animals may remain infectious for 2 to 3 years.

At certain stages in the development of *M. mycoides,* filterable forms 125 m$\mu$ to 150 m$\mu$ in size are present. Large oval or rounded bodies 0.2$\mu$ to 0.8$\mu$ are seen in artificial cultures. These develop into a mycelium composed of hyphae up to 240$\mu$ in length which become curled and twisted, forming various shapes (Fig. 38.1). The organism can be stained with the commonly used bacterial stains and is gram-negative. Deeper stained preparations are obtained with Giemsa's method. Masses of growth can be noted in tissue sections but it is essential to fix such sections with Zenker's

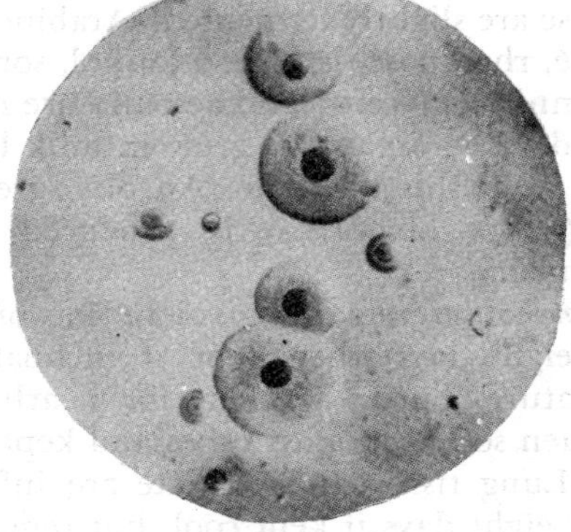

FIG. 38.2—Colonies of **Mycoplasma mycoides** on serum agar, ×40. (From Nowak: Documenta Microbiologica, courtesy Gustav Fischer.)

fluid, for the organisms are not observed when formalin fixation is used. On solid medium, containing at least 10 per cent bovine serum, the organism produces minute colonies which are smooth and transparent with an entire edge. In well-isolated colonies a nipple-like darker center is present (Fig. 38.2). The colonies are firmly adherent to the medium, due to the penetration of the organism below the surface. In serum bouillon, light turbidity is observed after the second day of incubation. Upon successive transplants the turbidity becomes more dense and forms filmy swirls when the tube is agitated. Optimum growth occurs at 37° to 38°C., with no growth below 27°C.

Acid but no gas is produced from glucose, maltose, mannose, fructose, dextrin,

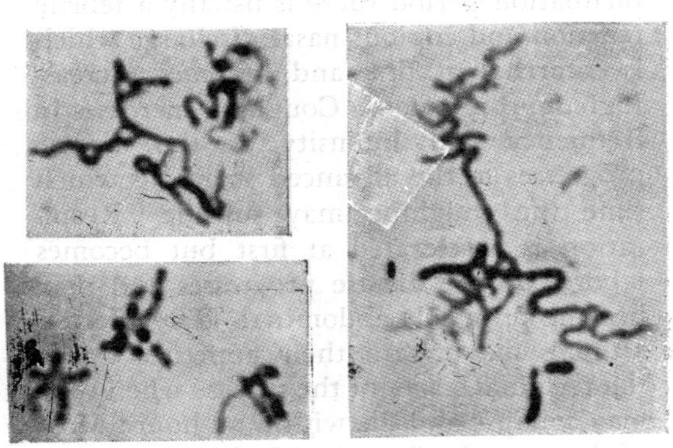

FIG. 38.1—**Mycoplasma mycoides** showing pleomorphism, ×3,000. (From Nowak: Documenta Microbiologica, courtesy Gustav Fischer.)

and starch. Galactose, xylose, sucrose, and trehalose are slightly fermented. Arabinose, raffinose, rhamnose, lactose, adonitol, sorbitol, mannitol, glycerol, and aesculin are not attacked. The organisms grow in milk but do not alter this medium. An olive-green color (alpha hemolysis) is produced in blood media.

*M. mycoides* remains virulent for only six to eight days when kept at incubator temperature, but is virulent for nearly a year when sealed in glass tubes and kept at 12°C. Lung tissue and exudate are infective for eight days if kept cool, but remain virulent for at least three months if kept at —5°C. The organism remains virulent in tissue kept in concentrated glycerin and 0.5 per cent phenol. A temperature of 58°C. kills the organism and it is easily destroyed by the various disinfecting chemicals. It is destroyed by exposure to air and sunlight.

The production of a toxin has been suggested by some investigators. The cachexia produced in cattle is given as evidence, and a similar condition is produced in rabbits following the installation of the organism contained in collodion sacs in the peritoneal cavity. It has been shown, also, that exudate contains a toxic principle which is precipitated by alcohol. It retains its activity at 80°C. and causes marked intoxication when injected intravenously into sheep and goats.

Under natural conditions this organism produces pleuropneumonia in cattle and related animals—the buffalo, yak, reindeer, and bison. Experimentally sheep and goats have been infected. Other animals and man are resistant.

Although in naturally occurring epizootics of the disease, cattle become easily infected, it has not been easy to produce the disease artificially. Subcutaneous inoculations produce a rise in temperature and edema at the site of inoculation. In calves such inoculations produce acute reactions characterized by localization in the joints. Injection of lung exudates into the udder cistern produces severe inflammation and the organism persists in the purulent viscid milk for two months. The intravenous injections of cultures contained in finely divided agar produce pulmonary emboli with resulting lesions typical of the disease. Sabin has suggested that pulmonary parasites may be factors in the establishment of infection in the lungs.

Animals which have recovered from pleuropneumonia are resistant to subsequent attacks. Artificial immunization was practiced long before the causal agent was discovered. This consisted of the inoculation of lung exudate subcutaneously, preferably in the tail, from which absorption was slow. Cultures kept in peptone-serum bouillon become attenuated after the twenty-fifth passage and may be used for vaccination. Calves vaccinated at too young an age may develop arthritis, myocarditis, and valvulitis. Hyperimmunization of cattle is accomplished by the injection of massive doses of culture and the resulting antiserum is effective for passive immunization.

The type of lesion found in bovine pleuropneumonia is rather distinctive but cannot be depended upon for accurate diagnosis. Isolation of *M. mycoides* is possible in the majority of cases of the disease if all of the precautions are taken to obtain the growth of the organism. The precipitation, agglutination, complement-fixation, and indirect hemagglutination tests have been used with success for diagnosis.

### *Mycoplasma mycoides* var. *capri*

This organism produces a highly fatal disease in goats. Following a 3- to 10-day incubation period there is usually a febrile reaction and copious nasal discharge which is catarrhal at first and becomes increasingly mucopurulent. Coughing increases in frequency and intensity as the disease progresses to the advanced stages, at which time the coughing may subside. Respiration is accelerated at first but becomes labored as the disease progresses and may become primarily abdominal. The affected animals may retain their appetites up to the terminal stages of the disease when they may collapse and die within an hour. Most of the animals affected with this disease die.

The lesions observed in cases of this disease are primarily pneumonia and pleuritis, with pericarditis present in some cases. There are usually no other lesions except small hemorrhages on the mucous and serous surfaces.

Death of the animal usually occurs within 1 to 4 weeks after the onset of the symptoms.

This disease was thought to be caused by a virus until Longley (1951) isolated a pleuropneumonia-like organism and reproduced the disease with cultures of the organism. The disease is of considerable economic importance in parts of Europe, Asia, and Africa.

Workers dealing with this disease report that *M. mycoides* and *M. mycoides* var. *capri* have similar properties except for host-infected and antigenic structure. The possibility has been suggested that the disease in goats may be caused by a bovine organism which has become adapted to goats.

A pathogenic pleuropneumonia-like organism from goats was reported in the United States by Cordy *et al.* (1955). This organism was recovered from a herd of goats affected with a highly fatal septicemia and arthritis. They reproduced a similar disease syndrome in experimental goats by inoculation of the organism. This organism appeared to resemble that of goat pleuropneumonia in many biochemical reactions but had a different antigenic structure.

### *Mycoplasma agalactiae*

This organism, which is the cause of contagious agalactia of sheep and goats, was first reported by Bridré and Donatien in 1923. The disease is known to occur in the mountainous areas of Italy, France, Switzerland, and in Algeria.

*M. agalactiae* is a minute pleomorphic microorganism possessing granules, globules, ring-structures, and filaments characteristic of the group. It stains faintly by the Gram method and is negative to that stain. The Giemsa stain gives a better preparation than the ordinarily used bacterial stains. The organism can be observed best by dark-field illumination. Minute colonies, which are best observed under low-power magnification of the microscope, develop along the needle path on solid medium.

This microorganism can be isolated from infected tissues by using fluid medium containing at least 10 per cent serum. Bridré and Donatien have shown that it grows in media containing up to 10 per cent serum, but undiluted serum will not promote growth.

Cows and goats milk may be used as culture media but no change is produced by the growth of the organism. Some of the carbohydrates—lactose, mannitol, and erythritol—promote growth, but others—glucose, fructose, galactose, raffinose, arabinose, xylose, sucrose, and maltose—retard growth. Good growth occurs in the presence of staphylococci and other organisms and can be separated from them by filtration.

*M. agalactiae* produces natural infection in sheep and goats. These animals also can be infected artificially by intravenous inoculation and by feeding infected tissues. The disease in these animals is best known because of the effect on the mammary gland in which fibrosis and atrophy are produced. Arthritis, keratitis, and in some cases vesiculopustular skin lesions are also produced. The arthritis in many cases becomes chronic, resulting in deformity. The organism may localize in the testes and abortion has been observed.

Bridré and Donatien have demonstrated that this organism is antigenically distinct from the agent of bovine pleuropneumonia. Attempts to develop immunity have been unsuccessful with the exception of a transient resistance which is produced by immune serum.

### *Mycoplasma agalactiae var. bovis*

This organism was isolated by Hale *et al.* (1962) from an acute bovine mastitis outbreak. It culturally resembles *M. agalactiae* and produces an acute mastitis followed by marked fibrosis of the affected mammary gland. Transmission of the acute mastitis can readily be accomplished by introduction of the organism into the teat canal. Infusion of the organism into the uterus of the cow results in little clinical effect but may produce varying degrees of endometritis, salpingitis, and salpingoperitonitis. These lesions may result in sterility. The organism will survive in bull semen during storage and will infect cows when inseminated. Natural infection in bulls has not been adequately investigated.

Greig (1955) reported the occurrence of a pleuropneumonia-like organism in the respiratory tract of sheep. This organism produced a diffuse turbidity in enriched fluid medium. It grew on nutrient agar supplemented with 5 per cent rabbit or sheep blood. It fermented dextrose, sucrose, and maltose but not lactose, galactose, fructose, xylose, mannose, rhamnose, sorbitol, or mannitol. This organism was propagated in chicken embryos. It usually killed the embryos 3 or 4 days postinoculation when administered by way of the chorioallantoic sac. This organism does not appear to have a pathogenic effect on sheep.

### Mycoplasma gallinarum
### Mycoplasma gallisepticum
### Mycoplasma iners
### Mycoplasma meleagridis
### Mycoplasma synoviae

Nelson (1936a, b) reported the cultivation in tissue culture of a small coccobacillary organism from coryza of chickens. This organism was probably a pleuropneumonia-like organism. Delaplane and Stuart (1943) isolated a pleuropneumonia-like organism in chicken embryos from a clinical condition they termed chronic respiratory disease of poultry.

Groupé *et al.* (1948) isolated a similar agent from cases of turkey sinusitis and reproduced the condition with it. Since that time numerous investigators have confirmed the role pleuropneumonia-like organisms play in the production of respiratory infections in poultry. However, in many cases there appear to be additional stress factors necessary to produce some of the severe clinical conditions observed in field flocks.

In the period of 1948–55 the studies of various workers suggested that these diseases were due to a single organism. However, since 1955 an ever-increasing number of workers have established that over twenty distinct serotypes of Mycoplasma are present in poultry. Of these serotypes, five have been given species designation. *M. gallinarum* was originally believed to be the pleuropneumonia-like organism infecting poultry. Several of the prototype strains studied were found to be nonpathogenic. Further studies evolved that the typical poultry pathogens differed considerably from these prototype strains, so other species and serotype designations have been established.

***Mycoplasma gallinarum*** is present in the respiratory tract of chickens. The presence of this organism is not correlated with clinical evidence of disease. This organism is not pathogenic for embryonated hens eggs, experimental chickens, or turkeys. Abundant growth of this organism occurs in suitable fluid media and on enriched agar media. The colonies formed on solid media are relatively large, attaining a maximum diameter of 1 mm. They develop a prominent central elevation. The surface of the colony is smooth with an entire periphery. The cellular morphology of all of the Mycoplasma of avian origin is reasonably similar, consisting of spherical to coccobacillary forms approximately 0.25$\mu$ to 0.5$\mu$ in diameter, which affords little basis for species or serotype differentiation. *M. gallinarum* does not produce acid from lactose, sucrose, dextrose, maltose, mannite, galactose, trehalose, levulose, mannose, dextrin, starch, dulcitol, salicin, or xylose. It produces complete hemolysis of horse red blood cells incorporated into solid medium. Cell suspensions of this organism do not hemagglutinate avian erythrocytes. A prototype of this organism is represented by isolate 54-537 of Kleckner (1960).

***Mycoplasma gallisepticum*** is a pathogenic avian pleuropneumonia-like organism. A prototype strain of this organism is the $S_6$ isolate of Adler (1955). This organism produces air-sac lesions in chickens, turkeys, and other avian species, as well as sinusitis in turkeys, and occasionally produces a tendovaginitis in the area of the hock joint of turkeys and chickens. Embryonated hens eggs inoculated with this organism regularly succumb within 4 to 8 days postinoculation. The embryos exhibit congestion, hepatitis, and splenomegaly. Some embryos develop various degrees of pericarditis. Colonies of this organism are approximately 0.25 to 0.3 mm. in diameter with an elevated central portion, a smooth surface, and an entire periphery. *M. gallisepticum* produces acid from dextrose, maltose, galactose, trehalose, levulose, mannose, dextrin, starch, and xylose. Delayed acid formation occurs in sucrose and mannite. Lactose, dulcitol, and salicin are not fermented. This organism produces complete hemolysis of horse red blood cells incorporated in solid medium. Cell suspensions of avian erythrocytes are hemagglutinated. This organism is transmitted by direct contact with infected poultry or contaminated equipment. In addition, a limited but significant transmission from hen to offspring occurs by way of the egg. Serological tests have been devised to eliminate infected flocks in order to break the egg transmission cycle.

***Mycoplasma iners*** is the third species recognized as occurring in chickens. It is similar to *M. gallinarum* in that no recognized clinical manifestations are associated with the presence of this organism in chickens. *M. iners* causes sporadic deaths in inoculated embryonated hens eggs. Many of the dead or surviving embryos exhibit periarticular cellular infiltration. It has been isolated from respiratory tract and pericardial lesions in chickens, but its etiological significance is not established. This organism resembles *M. gallinarum* in colony morphology. It likewise fails to ferment any of the usual carbohydrates and does not hemagglutinate avian erythrocytes. In contrast to *M. gallinarum* this organism does not produce hemolysis of horse red blood cells incorporated in solid medium. In addition, *M. iners* is serologically distinct from *M. gallinarum* and *M. gallisepticum*. These characteristics have been utilized to establish *M. iners* as a distinct species. A prototype of this species is represented by the O isolate of Yamamoto and Adler (1958).

***Mycoplasma meleagridis.*** As intensive efforts were made to eradicate *M. gallisepticum* it was apparent that mild air-sac lesions were very common in commercial turkey poults at the time of hatching. Repeated attempts to cultivate mycoplasma resulted in development of agar slant broth overlay techniques that would grow a mycoplasma from these lesions. These isolates have been termed "N" strain and "H" strain by various workers. The organism is now called *M. meleagridis*. This organism is capable of producing air-sac lesions in turkey embryos and in young turkeys. Some information suggests that this organism may be present in the upper respiratory tract of older turkeys and may on occasion produce sinusitis. *M. meleagridis* is not known to infect chickens, although inoculated chickens develop antibody titers against the organism. This infection is transmitted through the egg to the poult. Experimental antigens for detection of infected turkey hens are being evaluated. The principal control measure now available is the elimination of reactor hens from breeding flocks. The fact that this infection is extremely widespread and the disease produced is comparatively mild may retard eradication efforts.

In addition to these five recognized species of avian Mycoplasma there exist at least fifteen other distinct serotypes. These serotypes vary in colony morphology, utilization of carbohydrates, action on horse red blood cells, hemagglutination of avian erythrocytes, and pathogenicity for embryonated hens eggs. There is evidence that some of these serotypes may possess pathogenic potential for the production of respiratory tract lesions. In addition, lesions may occur in the periarticular structures. Representative isolates of the reasonably well-established serotypes are the SA, C, and N isolates of Yamamoto and Adler (1958), the DPR#2 and NY isolates of Kleckner (1960), and the Iowa 695 isolate of Yoder and Hofstad (1961).

Recognition of the existence of the numerous serotypes of avian Mycoplasma is essential for the eventual development of adequate diagnostic and control procedures. Much additional work will be required before a reasonably complete understanding of the avian Mycoplasmae is possible. It will not be surprising if intensive efforts establish fully as complex Mycoplasma flora in other hosts as have been established in poultry.

Nelson (1942) reported that the coccobacilliform bodies of rat infectious catarrh could be transferred to chickens with the production of a mild coryza. After the second transfer in chickens, the infection failed to transmit to other chickens. This is of special interest since it represents the apparent successful transmission of mycoplasma between two quite unrelated species.

***Mycoplasma synoviae*** was thought to be a viral agent until Chalquest and Fabricant (1960) cultivated the organism on artificial medium. It has been found that this organism requires an available source of soluble diphosphonucleotide for growth. The disease produced by this organism is important in high broiler production areas. Some states report 150 or more outbreaks per year with many more unreported. The pathogenesis of the natural infection is not clearly defined, but the organism appears to first localize in the upper respiratory tract. It invades from these sites and produces anemia and diarrhea. At about this time the tendon sheaths and joints, especially in the hock region, become inflamed and distended with a grayish mucoid exudate. The birds are acutely lame. Chickens necropsied at this stage have swollen spleens and focal accumulations of hepatic reticulocytes. The affected birds become emaciated. The morbidity and mortality can be very high in some outbreaks. The use of broad spectrum antibiotics, especially the tetracyclines administered by feed or water, will suppress the clinical manifestations of an outbreak. The disease may reoccur when medication is discontinued. *M. synoviae* can be grown in embryonating hens eggs and in artificial medium enriched with 0.1 to 0.01 per cent soluble diphosphonucleotide. There is a slight antigenic relationship between this organism and *M. gallisepticum*. The inoculation of *M. gallisepticum* into the foot-pad of young chickens produces an infection of the joints and tendon sheaths that resembles that caused by *M. synoviae*. Most natural outbreaks of infectious synovitis appear to be due to *M. synoviae* infection.

### *Mycoplasma hyorhinis*

This is a small coccoid organism that was first described by Switzer (1953a, b; 1954a). It frequently exhibits ring forms. No filamentous forms have been observed. It is common in the nasal cavities of swine, where it does not appear to cause any appreciable damage. It is a very common secondary invader in swine pneumonia but it does not markedly enhance the severity of the pneumonia. However, when it gains entrance into the body it may produce an inflammation of various serous surfaces. The most severe lesion is usually pericarditis, but pleuritis, peritonitis, and arthritis may occur. In many respects these lesions resemble the disease syndrome that occurs in Europe and is referred to as Glässer's disease. The polyserositis produced by this organism and by *Hemophilus* sp. are somewhat similar. The use of the term Glässer's disease for the *Hemophilus* sp. polyserositis has priority. Therefore, the serous surface lesions elicited by *M. hyorhinis* are properly referred to as mycoplasmal polyserositis and not Glässer's disease. Clinical observations suggest that turbinate atrophy and pneumonia predispose to invasion of this organism. The possibility of louse transmission of this agent has been suggested by Willigan (1955).

This organism produces very small, smooth, glistening colonies on suitable solid medium. These colonies have an indefinite central elevation. This organism is slightly inhibited by the addition of lactose, sucrose, dextrose, maltose, or mannite to the medium. It is readily stained by Giemsa's stain. Satisfactory growth occurs in an ox heart-chicken serum medium described by Switzer (1955) or in a medium described by Edward (1947a). In addition, inoculation of this organism into the yolk sac of 6- or 7-day-old chicken embryos results in death of about half of the inoculated embryos during 4 to 13 days postinoculation. Embryos succumbing from the seventh to thirteenth day postinoculation usually have pericarditis. Giemsa-stained smears of this pericardial exudate are suitable for demonstration of the organism. A contradiction exists about the ability of *M. hyorhinis* to utilize glucose. In some laboratories this organism appears to utilize glucose while in other laboratories it does not. It is possible that conditions of cultivation or supplemental factors supplied by some media influence the ability of this organism to utilize glucose. This group of organisms is not a serologically homogenous group.

The primary mode of transmission of this organism is by inhalation of infective aerosols. It has been found that baby pigs may harbor the organism in their nasal cavities after remaining in contact with infected dams for only a few hours. The occurrence of visceral lesions due to this organism in the United States has not been adequately evaluated, although in one survey it was found that as many as 8 per cent of the swine hearts were being condemned in one large Iowa packing plant because of pericarditis typical of that produced by this organism.

*M. hyorhinis* has been found to be the most common secondary invader in swine pneumonia in Iowa. It is not capable of initiating a primary pneumonia. In one survey conducted by L'Ecuyer *et al.,* over 50 per cent of the pneumonic lungs harbored this organism. Roberts *et al.* have demonstrated that there is a statistically significant increase in bronchiolar epithelial damage when *M. hyorhinis* occurs as a secondary invader in field cases of pneumonia believed to be initiated by *M. hyopneumoniae.*

### *Mycoplasma granularum*

This organism is the most common cause of arthritis in Iowa swine between 75 and 225 pounds in weight. Case histories of such herds indicate that the condition may reoccur in subsequent groups of pigs. The arthritis may affect only an occasional pig or may involve up to 20 per cent of the herd. Numerous cases recover after a rather protracted period of lameness, but a considerable weight loss occurs. This type of arthritis usually occurs without any other serous surface lesions.

The colonies produced by *M. granularum* are of the same general size as those formed by *M. hyorhinis;* however, in *M. granularum* the central elevation appears to be more prominent. This organism does not produce the distinctive cytopathogenic effect in primary swine kidney cell cultures that *M. hyorhinis* does. In addition it does not multiply or produce lesions in embryonating hens eggs.

Different laboratories report variable results on the ability of *M. granularum* to utilize glucose. Some isolates of this organism decolorize phenol red. Growth of this organism is greatly stimulated by the addition of one-half per cent swine gastric mucin to the medium. Fluid cultures of this organism produce small granules and may develop an extremely delicate waxy pellicle. A distinct film is formed on solid medium. Inoculation of *M. granularum* into young pigs does not produce any lesions of polyserositis or pneumonia. A portion of older pigs inoculated intravenously with cultures of this organism develop typical arthritis, but the factors necessary for more consistent incidence of lesion production are not well worked out. There is no significant temperature elevation associated with the arthritis in either naturally occurring or experimentally produced cases.

The larger articulations of the limbs are the most commonly involved, especially the stifle joints. It is a common clinical observation that extremely lean, extremely heavily muscled pigs are most frequently affected. Treatment of affected animals within 18 hours of onset of the arthritis with parental Tylosin will often result in rapid recovery. After the arthritis has existed for over 48 hours, the clinical response is very minimal. *M. granularum* arthritis tends to reoccur in subsequent groups of swine and poses a grave problem in many of the very best meat-type swine herds.

### *Mycoplasma hyopneumoniae*

This organism has been recently recognized by Maré and Switzer (1965). It was isolated from swine pneumonia believed to be typical of the condition previously termed "virus pneumonia of pigs." Pure cultures of this organism inoculated into respiratory disease-free pigs reproduce all aspects of uncomplicated "virus pneumonia of pigs." This is a chronic bronchopneumonia characterized by peribronchiolar lymphoid hyperplasia, septal cell proliferation, and mild neutrophilic infiltration. Whittlestone (1965) has subsequently reported cultivation of an apparently similar organism from swine pneumonia. He has proposed the name *M. suipneumoniae*. Comparisons of the organisms will be necessary to adequately evaluate the relationship of these two isolates.

The optimum growth requirements of this organism are not well defined. At the present time, media for growth usually have a cell-culture, balanced-salt-solution base, and are enriched with swine serum, yeast hydrolysate, and lactalbumin hydrolysate. Growth in fluid media is very scant for several passages. Adapted cultures produce a faint, smooth sediment. There is no apparent utilization of glucose and no hemolysis of red blood cells. Colonies of the organism grown on solid media are extremely minute and are enhanced by the presence of *Micrococcus* sp. colonies.

This organism is somewhat sensitive to the tetracycline antibiotics. Swine receiving adequate levels of these antibiotics are resistant to infection by this organism, but the administration of these drugs to swine with established pneumonia does not eliminate the organism.

### *Mycoplasma hyoarthrinosa*
### *Mycoplasma hyogenitalium*

These two organisms have been recovered by Moore *et al.* (1965) from swine.

*Mycoplasma hyoarthrinosa* resembles *M. granularum* in several respects but appears to produce an alkaline reaction in fluid medium, suggesting that it has somewhat different metabolic pathways than *M. granularum*. In addition it appears to be more pathogenic to experimental pigs and is believed to be the cause of considerable swine arthritis in Texas. The disease produced by this organism is believed to be less responsive to antibiotic treatment than is *M. granularum* arthritis.

*Mycoplasma hypogenitalium* was recovered by Moore *et al.* (1965) from uterine biopsy material. The organism is believed to have reproduced mastitis-metritis-agalactiae in experimental sows.

### *Mycoplasma bovigenitalium*

Edward *et al.* (1947) reported the isolation of two different pleuropneumonia-like organisms from both male and female bovine genitalia. One of these organisms produced rather large colonies and did not require enrichment fluid for growth. This organism was considered to be a saprophyte and was designated as organism S. The second pleuropneumonia-like organism produced a film effect on horse serum agar with precipitation of portions of the serum. It developed very small colonies. This organism appeared to be parasitic and to be concerned in the production of infertility in the herd studied. Therefore, the organism was given the name P. This latter organism is now named *M. bovigenitalium*.

*M. bovigenitalium* forms unstable, sparsely branching mycelium with very short filaments that may measure 2μ to 5μ in length. It produces an alpha hemolysis of horse red blood cells and does not attack any of the more commonly employed carbohydrates. Ten strains investigated serologically shared common antigens, but at least three different serological types appear to exist.

Circumstantial evidence indicates it may be involved in the production of infertility in both male and female cattle, but experimental inoculation of cultures have not been completely convincing in this respect. It has been observed that isolates from cases where a diseased condition exists are often very difficult to subculture, and therefore, the laboratory cultures employed may simply represent avirulent strains that are capable of growing in artificial medium. More study of this organism is necessary before its true significance as a pathogen can be determined.

In 1963 an isolation of *M. bovigenitalium* was made from a naturally occurring mastitis epizootic. This organism produced mastitis when inoculated into the teat canal of normal cows. This is one of the first reports to clearly establish that this organism is a bovine pathogen.

Several laboratories in the United States have isolated pleuropneumonia-like organisms from bull semen. These isolates appear to be of at least two serological types. It is likely that some of these organisms are *M. bovigenitalium*. Research workers have cautioned that the presence of these organisms in bull semen is not desirable and that they should remain under suspicion as possible causes of lowered fertility until additional information is available.

Carter (1954) isolated a pleuropneumonia-like organism from cases of bovine bronchopneumonia. The published photographs of the colonies of this organism show a close resemblance to those of the S organism isolated by Edward from bovine genitalia. Carter used enrichment media to grow his organism. The possible significance of pleuropneumonia-like organisms in bovine bronchopneumonia has not been determined.

### *Mycoplasma pulmonis*
### *Mycoplasma arthritidis*
### *Mycoplasma neurolyticum*

Several different pleuropneumonia-like organisms have been isolated from rats and mice. Many of these appear to be distinct species but at least one organism has been recovered from both rats and mice. Adequate comparisons of the various strains isolated in different laboratories have not been made in most cases. Therefore the number of species that should be recognized is largely a matter of opinion and will undoubtedly undergo considerable alteration as comparative studies are made.

The pleuropneumonia-like organisms of rats and mice are of very real importance to laboratory workers attempting to establish infectious agents in these animals by intranasal inoculation. Some members of this group will produce pneumonic lesions. In addition, members of this group have been isolated from material being serially passaged from brain to brain of mice. This group also produces naturally occurring pneumonia, infectious catarrh, and otitis media.

***Mycoplasma pulmonis.*** *M. pulmonis* is defined as the organism isolated by Klieneberger and Steabben (1937) from the lungs of tame rats with bronchopneumonia and bronchiectasis. This organism was also isolated from normal appearing rat lungs. The organism was named $L_3$. It failed to produce lesions when inoculated into rats. In 1940 Klieneberger and Steabben reported additional studies on the lungs of 251 laboratory rats and 17 wild rats. Lung lesions were present in 108 of the laboratory rats but they recovered the organism from 138 lungs. Only 1 wild rat had lung lesions and it yielded the organism.

This organism fails to grow on serum-free medium. On suitable solid medium the colonies tend to coalesce and form a filmlike growth. It grows better near the surface of semisolid agar medium with a granular growth. It produces hemolysis of horse blood agar and ferments glucose, maltose, mannose, dextrin, starch, and glycogen. It does not ferment fructose or galactose. The surface of the colony is somewhat rough with surface markings tending to obscure the central spot.

This organism also occurs in mice where it has been isolated from the brain and from the nasal cavity.

Other studies on bronchopneumonia of rats describe additional agents. Thus, Nelson (1940) described infectious catarrh and otitis media of rats due to small gram-negative coccobacilliform bodies present in the cytoplasm of the leucocytes. He cultivated this organism in minced chicken embryo tissue suspensions and reproduced the disease with these cultures. His reason for thinking that this organism was different from the $L_3$ organism described by Klieneberger was that very little growth occurred in cell-free fluid medium, no growth occurred on solid medium, and the organism was stained by Gram's stain using dilute carbolfuchsin as the counterstain. He observed that elimination of this agent from a colony of rats markedly reduced the incidence of otitis media and also the severity of the naturally occurring bronchopneumonia. This coccobacilliform organism could be transferred to mice where it produced a rhinitis, otitis, and a fatal progressive pneumonia. It did not become established in chickens.

Nelson (1937a, b) also described natural occurrence of infectious catarrh of mice which was due to coccobacilliform bodies which closely resembled those from the rat and were transferrable to rats (Nelson, 1942). He found these bodies associated with a pleuropneumonia-like organism in the nasal cavities of some mice. This latter organism was localized primarily in the conjunctival sac where, in one inbred strain, it seemed to intensify a conjunctivitis (Nelson, 1950a, b).

Edward (1940) studied infectious catarrh of mice and also found it to be a transmissible disease. Edward (1947b) reproduced the disease with early subcultures of pleuropneumonia-like organisms isolated from the respiratory tract. He reported the occurrence of coccobacilliform bodies in the lesions produced by the cultures.

In addition to coccobacilliform bodies, Nelson (1946) described a virus-like agent present in laboratory rats with endemic pneumonia. This agent produced a reaction in susceptible mice very much like the coccobacilliform bodies of mouse and rat infectious catarrh. However, no coccobacilliform bodies were present in the cytoplasm of the leucocytes. This virus-like agent is regarded by Nelson as the cause of endemic pneumonia in laboratory rats and the rat coccobacilliform bodies are considered to be a separate disease entity commonly superimposed on the pneumonia. Rats under 8 months of age frequently carry the virus-like agent in their lungs but show no lesions. As the rat matures the virus-like agent produces pneumonia. Some commercial suppliers of laboratory animals are attempting to eliminate the virus-like agent and coccobacilliform bodies from their stock by breaking the cycle of transmission. Young rats are delivered by cesarian section, placed on clean foster dams, and reared in isolation. This program has been referred to as "Nelson testing."

It appears that the organisms from chickens, mice, and rats, that Nelson termed coccobacilliform bodies, are members of the pleuropneumonia group but their requirements for growth in cell-free medium are not certain. Most workers contend they are the same as pleuropneumonia-like organisms already studied, although some think they have not been grown in cell-free medium. Nelson (1954) reported that the intra-abdominal inoculation of 4 strains of murine pleuropneumonia-like organisms of the catarrhal type (or coccobacilliform bodies) regularly resulted in the production of oophoritis and salpingitis in weanl ng mice. No lesions occurred in the genital organs of male mice inoculated intraperitoneally.

***Mycoplasma arthritidis.*** This organism was originally designated as $L_4$ when isolated by Klieneberger (1938) from a submaxillary gland of a rat. It was found to be serologically identical with a pleuropneumonia-like organism isolated by Findlay *et al.* (1939) and a filter-passing pyogenic agent isolated by Woglom and Warren (1938) from a transmissible sarcoma. This organism produces abscesses when inoculated into rats and mice. In the inoculated rats there is a tendency to localize in the joints. The intracerebral injection of mice causes encephalitis. The "Preston" strain of this organism examined by Edward did not grow on serum-free medium, did not produce a film on solid medium, and grew throughout semisolid medium. It did not ferment glucose, fructose, galactose, maltose, or dextrin. It produced smooth growth in semisolid medium.

The natural habitat of this organism has not been determined, but it has been recovered from abscesses, swollen submaxillary glands, and septicemias in rats. The mouse is even more susceptible to this organism than the rat, but guinea pigs, pigs, rabbits, moles, hedgehogs, rhesus and cercapithecus monkeys were refractive.

This organism has been cultivated on the chorioallantoic membrane of the chicken embryo. It is said to produce inclusions in the epithelial cells of the skin overlying the abscesses produced in the rat and mouse.

***Mycoplasma neurolyticum.*** This organism was first encountered by Sabin (1938) and Findlay *et al.* (1938) in the brains of mice used for passaging other agents. It has since been found in the nasal cavity, lungs, and especially the conjunctiva of mice. On one occasion it has been recovered from a normal mouse brain. The relationship of this organism to the one recovered from conjunctivitis of mice by Nelson is not clear, although Nelson believed the organisms were not the same. It is believed that newborn mice do not harbor this organism but become infected by contact. The eyes do not become infected until the lids open. Mice probably remain carriers of this organism throughout life but do not show any spontaneous disease.

Intracerebral inoculation of this organism into mice produces a very characteristic turning or rolling on the long axis of the body with or without other nervous signs. This usually occurs 2 or 3 days postinoculation. The majority of the mice recover but some nervous symptoms may persist for months.

Intra-abdominal or intrathoracic injection of this organism results in similar symptoms in 20 to 40 per cent of the inoculated mice. Glucose-serum broth cultures of this organism produce a true exotoxin that causes the same nervous symptoms following intravenous inoculation.

According to Sabin, fluid cultures of this organism consist chiefly of elementary bodies, minute rings, or ovals with condensed bodies at one or both poles and occasionally triangular or quadrangular structures in which the elementary bodies are linked by thinner bonds. The fully developed colonies range from $20\mu$ to $300\mu$ and present central areas that are circumscribed, elevated, and darker than the rest of the colony. There appears to be a variation in the exotoxin-producing ability of different isolates of this organism.

Edward (1954) studied a strain of this organism that had been maintained for several years in artificial medium and found that it did not form a film on solid medium, hemolyzed horse blood agar, fermented glucose, maltose, and mannose, but not fructose or galactose. It gave a granular growth that was best near the surface of semisolid medium.

### *Mycoplasma spumans*
### *Mycoplasma canis*
### *Mycoplasma maculosum*

Pleuropneumonia-like organisms were first isolated from dogs by Shoetensack (1934, 1936a, b). They were found in secretions of the upper respiratory tract and in lesions of the respiratory tract of dogs suffering from canine distemper. It was believed by this worker that they were the cause of canine distemper, but it is now known that a virus is the primary cause of this disease. His isolates seemed to be of two distinct types and they were named *Asterococcus canis* I and II.

Edward and Fitzgerald (1951) undertook the investigation of sterility and epididymitis in a male dog and isolated a pleuropneumonia-like organism from his semen. A survey was made of the occurrence of this organism in the throats and genital tracts of the dogs in this breeding kennel. They isolated 3 distinct types of organisms from these sites. They called these organisms, α, β, and γ.

All three organisms were recovered from the vagina. Only *M. canis* and *M. maculosum* were recovered from the throat swabs. About one-half of the vaginal swabs and about three-fourths of the throat swabs were positive for pleuropneumonia-like organisms.

None of the three organisms grows at room temperature or on media devoid of serum. They seem to grow as well anaerobically as aerobically. The organisms have a slight granularity in semisolid medium that tends to disappear on repeated subculture. None of the organisms ferments glucose, and all three produce some degree of hemolysis of horse blood agar.

Identification of the three organisms is based on colony morphology, especially on primary isolation, and serological reactions. a close correlation is observed between these two criteria.

***Mycoplasma spumans*** is distinguished by having a coarse surface reticulum. In young colonies only the centers have the heavy markings, leaving the periphery conspicuously translucent with the surface resembling a drop of water. This organism was isolated from the genitalia and is considered to warrant additional study as a possible pathogen.

***Mycoplasma canis*** was isolated from both the throat and genital tract. The colonies are large, flattened, and translucent. They have no center spot but have fine surface markings. On repeated subculture some strains of *M. spumans* and *M. canis* become somewhat similar in appearance.

***Mycoplasma maculosum*** was isolated from both the throat and vagina. It forms a film on the surface of horse serum enriched solid medium with precipitation of a portion of the medium to form small dark spots. This organism has a well-developed central tip.

These three organisms are distinct serologically. Their pathogenicity has not been investigated.

Greig (1954) reported his observations on the pathogenicity of cultures of pleuropneumonia-like organisms isolated from the respiratory tracts of dogs. The cultural characteristics of the organisms were not described but were said to elicit at most only transient bouts of sneezing and occasional coughing in inoculated dogs.

Switzer (1954b) isolated pleuropneumonia-like organisms from pneumonic lungs of dogs clinically affected with canine distemper. This organism grew well in ox heart-chicken serum medium and produced distinct colonies on the surface of solid medium enriched with Difco serum fraction. Fluid cultures of this organism were composed primarily of small coccoid forms that stained well with Giemsa's stain and were faintly gram-negative. Colonies of this organism had a well-marked central elevation. This organism passed a Selas No. 02 filter, grew with a uniform turbidity in fluid medium, produced no lesions or deaths in chicken embryos, and produced no lesions when inoculated into the air sacs, sinus, nostril, or conjunctiva of turkeys.

This organism did not survive for an appreciable length of time at —40°C. or in the lyophilized state.

What appeared to be a completely distinct pleuropneumonia-like organism was isolated by Switzer (1954c) from the pneumonic lung of a 6-week-old kitten that had evidenced a chronic cough. This organism passed a Selas No. 02 filter but did not produce visible lesions in chicken embryos. It produced a very faint turbidity in ox heart-chicken serum medium and did not survive at —40°C. or in the lyophilized state. The individual organisms in fluid medium were stained rather lightly with Giemsa's stain and had numerous ring forms. On solid medium enriched with Difco serum fraction the colonies were very small and translucent without well-developed center spots. Fluid cultures of this organism produced no lesion in 7-week-old kittens when administered intranasally. The kittens were observed 3 weeks. The organism was not recovered from the respiratory tract of the inoculated kittens.

## REFERENCES


Adler, H. E. Ph.D. Thesis. Univ. of Calif., Davis, 1955.

Argaman, M., and Razin, S. Cholesterol and Cholesterol Esters in Mycoplasma. Jour. Gen. Microbiol. 38: 153–68, 1965.

Bordet, J. La Morphologie du microbe de la peripneumonie des bovides. Ann. Inst. Past. 24:161–67, 1910.

Borrell, Dujardin-Beaumetz, Jeantet et Jouan. Le Microbe de la peripneumonie. Ann. Inst. Past. 24: 168–79, 1910.

Bridré, J., and Donatien, A. Le Microbe de l'agalaxie contagieuse du mouton et de la chevre. Ann. Inst. Past. 39:925–51, 1925.

Carter, G. R. Science 120:113, 1954.

Chalquest, R. R., and Fabricant, J. Avian Dis. 4:515–39, 1960.

Chanock, R. M., *et al.* Mycoplasma Pneumoniae: Proposed Nomenclature for Atypical Pneumonia Organism (Eaton Agent). Science 144:662, 1962.

Clyde, W. A. Mycoplasma Species Identification Based Upon Growth Inhibition by Specific Antisera. Jour. Immunol. 92:958–65, 1964.

Cordy, D. R., *et al.* Cornell Vet. 45:50–68, 1955.

Daubney, R. Contagious Bovine Pleuropneumonia. Note on Experimental Reproduction and Infection by Contact. Jour. Comp. Path. Therap. 48:83–96, 1935.

Delaplane, J. P., and Stuart, H. O. Amer. Jour. Vet. Res. 4:325–32, 1943

Dienes, L. Organisms of Klieneberger and *Streptobacillus moniliformis*. Jour. Inf. Dis. 65:24–42, 1939.

———. Cultivation of Pleuropneumonia-like Organisms From Female Genital Organs. Proc. Soc. Exp. Biol. Med. 44:468–69, 1940.

Dinter, Z., *et al.* Differentiation of Porcine Mycoplasma Strains. Jour. Gen. Microbiol. 41:77–84, 1965.

Edward, D. G. Jour. Path. Bact. 50:409–18, 1940.

———. Jour. Gen. Microbiol. 1:238–43, 1947a.

———. Jour. Path. Bact. 59:209–21, 1947b.

———. Jour. Gen. Microbiol. 10:27–64, 1954.

———. Int. Bull. Bact. Nomenclature and Taxonomy 5:85–93, 1955.

———, and Fitzgerald, W. A. Jour. Gen. Microbiol. 5:566–75, 1951.

———, and Kanarek, A. D. N.Y. Acad. Sci. 79:696–702, 1960.

———, *et al.* Vet. Rec. 59:329–30, 1947.

Fabricant, J. Avian Dis. 4:505–14, 1960.

Findlay, G. M., *et al.* Lancet 235:1511–13, 1938; 237:7–10, 1939.

Forsyth, B. R., *et al.* Etiology of Primary Atypical Pneumonia in a Military Population. Jour. Amer. Med. Assn. 191:364–68, 1965.

Freundt, E. A. Intl. Bull. Bact. Nomenclature and Taxonomy 5:67–78, 1955.

Grayston, J. T., *et al.* Mycoplasma Pneumonia Infections: Clinical and Epidemiologic Studies. Jour. Amer. Med. Assn. 191:369–74, 1965.

Greig, A. S. Canad. Jour. Comp. Med. 18:275–78, 1954; 19:265–71, 1955.

Groupé, V., *et al.* Proc. Soc. Exp. Biol. Med. 67:397–98, 1948.

Hale, H. H., *et al.* Bovine Mastitis Caused by a Mycoplasma Species. Cornell Vet. 52:582–91, 1962.

Hirth, R. S., *et al.* Genital Mycoplasmosis in Cattle and Man. Jour. Amer. Vet. Med. Assn. 148:277–82, 1966.

Hofstad, M. S. Unpublished observations, cited in discussion of "Infectious Bronchitis" by Hofstad, M. S., in Diseases of Poultry, 5th Ed., p. 605, Biester, H. E., and Schwarte, L. H. (eds.). The Iowa State Univ. Press, Ames, 1965.

Hutyra, F., *et al.* Special Pathology and Therapeutics of the Diseases of Domestic Animals. Vol. I, pp. 455–71 Alexander Eger, Chicago, 1938.

JENSEN, K. E., *et al.* An Inactive Mycoplasma Pneumoniae Vaccine. Jour. Amer. Med. Assn. 194:134–38, 1965.

KLECKNER, A. L. Amer. Jour. Vet. Res. 21:274–80, 1960.

KLIENEBERGER, E. The Colonial Development of the Organisms of Pleuropneumonia and Agalactia on Serum Agar, etc. Jour. Path. Bact. 39:409–20, 1934.

———. Jour. Hyg. 38:458–76, 1938.

———. The Pleuropneumonia-like Organisms: Further Comparative Studies and a Descriptive Account of Recently Discovered Types. Jour. Hyg. 40:204–22, 1940.

———, and STEABBEN, D. B. Jour. Hyg. 37:143–52, 1937; 40:223–27, 1940.

LEACH, R. H. The Osmotic Requirements for Growth of Mycoplasma. Jour. Gen. Microbiol. 27:345–54, 1962.

L'ECUYER, C., *et al.* Microbiological Survey of Pneumonic and Normal Swine Lungs. Amer. Jour. Vet. Res. 22:1020–25, 1961.

LONGLEY, E. O. Colonial Research Publ. 7, His Majesty's Stationery Office, London, 1951.

MARÉ, C. J., and SWITZER, W. P. New Species: *Mycoplasma hyopneumoniae.* A Causative Agent of Virus Pig Pneumonia. Vet. Med./Small Animal Clinician 60:841–46, 1965.

MARKHAM, F. S., and WONG, S. C. Poultry Sci. 31:902–4, 1952.

NELSON, J. B. Jour. Exp. Med. 63:515–22, 1936a; 64:749–58, 1936b; 65:843–49, 1937a; 65:851–60, 1937b; 72:655–62, 1940; 76:253–62, 1942; 84:15–23, 1946; 91:309–20, 1950a; 92:431–39, 1950b; 100:311–20, 1954.

NOCARD, ROUX, *et al.* Le Microbe de la peripneumonie. Ann. Inst. Past. 12:240–62, 1898.

NOWAK, J. Ann. Inst. Past. 43:1330–52, 1927.

OLSON, N. O., *et al.* Antigenic Relationship Between *Mycoplasma synoviae* and *Mycoplasma gallisepticum.* Amer. Jour. Vet. Res. 26:195–98, 1965.

ROBERTS, E. D., *et al.* Influence of *Pasteurella multocida* and *Mycoplasma hyorhinis* (PPLO) on the Histopathology of Field Cases of Swine Pneumonia. Cornell Vet. 52:306–21, 1962.

ROSS, R. F. M.S. Thesis. Iowa State Univ., Ames, 1961.

SABIN, A. B. Science 88:575–76, 1938.

———. The Pleuropneumonia Group. Bact. Rev. 5:1–68, 331–35, 1941.

SCHIMKE, R. T., and BARILE, M. F. Arginine Metabolism in Pleuropneumonia-like Organisms Isolated From Mammalian Cell Culture. Jour. Bact. 86:195–206, 1963.

SHOETENSACK, H. M. Kitasato Arch. Exp. Med. 11:277–90, 1934 :13:269–80, 1936a; 13:175–84, 1936b.

SMITH, S. L., *et al.* Respiratory Pathways in the Mycoplasma. I. Lactate Oxidation by *Mycoplasma gallisepticum.* Jour. Bact. 86:893–97, 1963.

SOMERSON, N. L., *et al.* Hemolysin Production as an Aid in the Identification and Quantitation of Eaton Agent (*Mycoplasma pneumoniae*). Amer. Jour. Hyg. 77:122–28, 1963.

SWITZER, W. P. Jour. Amer. Vet. Med. Assn. 123:45–47, 1953a.

———. Vet. Med. 48:392–94, 1953b.

———. Iowa Vet. 25:9–11, 1954a.

———. Unpublished data, 1954b.

———. Unpublished data, 1954c.

———. Amer. Jour. Vet. Res. 16:540–41, 1955.

———. Mycoplasmosis. *In* Diseases of Swine. 2nd Ed. H. W. Dunne (ed.). Iowa State Univ. Press, Ames, 1964.

TIETHEWIE, E. R. Preventive Tail-tip Inoculation of Calves Against Bovine Contagious Pleuropneumonia. Austral. Vet. Jour. 37:27–36, 1961.

VAN HERICK, W., and MONROE, D. E. Jour. Bact. 50:47–55, 1945.

WILLIGAN, D. A. Studies on a Transmissible Agent Isolated From Pericarditis of Swine. M.S. Thesis. Univ. of Ill., Urbana, 1955.

WOGLOM, W. H., and WARREN, J. Jour. Exp. Med. 68:513–28, 1938.

YAMAMOTO, R., and ADLER, H. E. Jour. Inf. Dis. 102:143–52, 1958.

———, and BIGLAND, C. H. Infectivity of *Mycoplasma meleagridis* for Turkey Embryos. Amer. Jour. Vet. Res. 27:326–30, 1961.

YODER, H. W., JR., and HOFSTAD, M. S. A Previously Unreported Serotype of Avian Mycoplasma. Avian Dis. 6:147–60, 1962.

# 39

# The Pathogenic Fungi

**ALLAN C. PIER, *D.V.M., Ph.D.*, and JOHN L. RICHARD, *M.S., Ph.D.***

*National Animal Disease Laboratory*
*Ames, Iowa*

THE FUNGI ARE A LARGE GROUP OF NUCLEATED plant organisms which lack chlorophyll and are not differentiated into roots, stems, or leaves. With the exception of certain forms, the fungus body is composed of filaments, known as hyphae, which may or may not branch. The filaments possess a cell wall primarily composed of either cellulose or chitin. Nearly all formed elements of the fungal body may initiate growth. Individual hyphae elongate by apical growth. The entire mass of hyphae is called a mycelium. In the majority of the fungi the hyphae are divided into numerous individual cells by transverse septa. Some of the fungi do not form regular septa; in these coenocytic molds the nuclei are scattered throughout the cytoplasm of the plant body.

Reproduction in the fungi is accomplished by spores of two types: sexual and asexual. Typically, a fungus reproduces by both methods, although asexual spores are most important in the propagation of the organism due to the greater number of reproductive elements formed. Sexual reproduction involves the fusion of two nuclei with the eventual formation of reproductive elements. Asexual spores are formed by constriction or extrusion from specialized hyphal structures, by fragmentation of the hyphae, or by budding.

## CLASSIFICATION

The fungi pathogenic for animals and man are generally grouped according to one of two methods; one is based upon the area of the body they infect and the other is based upon the morphology of the infecting fungus. The former method groups together the agents of the cutaneous mycoses, the subcutaneous mycoses, and the deep or systemic mycoses. There are obvious disadvantages to this system. Many taxonomically divergent fungi may be involved in a single group such as the systemic mycoses; furthermore, this method may require consideration of a single genus in all three groups.

The latter method, classification on the basis of morphology, sporulation, and similar taxonomic criteria, is a more sound approach even in medical mycology. Morphological variations among these organisms are complex, and clinicians and pathologists are not as a rule primarily interested in taxonomy. However, the mycoses are generally named after the genus of the causative agent as in Candidiasis (genus Candida), Histoplasmosis (genus Histoplasma), and Coccidioidomycosis (genus Coccidioides). Prominent exceptions to this nomenclature remain deeply entrenched in the literature, such as Phycomycosis (named for the taxonomic class) and Dermatophytosis (named for a tissue affinity). The generic nomenclature of the mycoses has much to recommend it and promises to prevail; however, reorganizations of taxonomy pose a continuing threat to the permanency of the name of a given agent or disease.

Although the classification of the fungi is in a state of flux, five classes will be discussed: the Myxomycetes, Phycomycetes, Ascomycetes, Basidiomycetes, and the Deuteromycetes (Fungi Imperfecti). These groups encompass such fungi as yeast, molds, mushrooms, mildews, rusts, smuts, etc.

### Myxomycetes

The Myxomycetes are commonly known as slime molds because in the vegetative stage of their life cycle they are nonmycelial multinucleate masses of protoplasm which lack cell walls and possess ameboid-like motility. This vegetative stage eventually produces sporebearing bodies which have a more typical fungal architecture. The Myxomycetes are not known to produce animal diseases and will not be considered further in this chapter.

### Phycomycetes

The Phycomycetes typically produce branched hyphae which are nonseptate or sparsely septate; young hyphae are usually nonseptate. Motile, flagellate reproductive elements are produced by many species of this class. Asexual reproduction is accomplished primarily by sporangiospores and occasionally by conidia. Sexual reproduction occurs in one of three ways, all of which result in the formation of a zygote: (1) The formation of a zygospore resulting from the fusion of two similar, specialized, hyphal branches (gametangia) along with their contained nuclei. (2) The formation of oospores resulting from fertilization of female nuclei by male nuclei which pass from a male structure, the antheridium, into a female structure, the oogonium. (3) The formation of a zygote resulting from fusion of two motile gametes. In addition to many plant pathogens, this class also includes a number of fungi which occasionally infect members of the animal kingdom including amoebae, insects, fish, man, and other mammals.

### Ascomycetes

The Ascomycetes are a large class of fungi including both molds and the true yeasts characterized by the possession of sexual spores produced within an enlarged, saclike structure known as an ascus. Usually, eight ascospores are produced within a single ascus. The asci are typically formed within or upon a specialized fruiting body, the ascocarp. Asexual reproduction is accomplished by budding, fission, fragmentation, or by the formation of arthrospores, chlamydospores, or conidia. The majority form conidia produced on specialized hyphae called conidiophores. The Ascomycetes contain a large number of saprophytic forms and plant pathogens; however, some are parasites of insects, man, and other animals. Some Ascomycetes are important producers of mycotoxins.

### Basidiomycetes

Within this class of the fungi are placed the familiar mushrooms and the puffballs, the rusts and the smuts. The cells of the mature mycelium are typically binucleate, and sexual basidiospores are borne externally on a club-shaped hyphal end called a basidium. Typically, four basidiospores are formed on a single basidium. Many of the Basidiomycetes produce their basidia in or on a specialized fruiting body called a basidiocarp; the common mushroom is a basidiocarp. Asexual reproduction occurs by means of budding, fragmentation, and by the formation of conidia or arthrospores. Although this group contains important plant disease agents, only two animal pathogens have been reported, both of which cause infections in man. There are many important toxin-producing species which cause deleterious effects and even death of animals and man.

### The Deuteromycetes (Fungi Imperfecti)

This is a form-class composed of fungi which are known to reproduce only by asexual means. Many members of this form-class are probably Ascomycetes for which sexual reproductive elements have not been discovered or which have lost their ability to reproduce sexually. Occasionally sexual stages are found in members of this class; this results in confusion of nomenclature since the imperfect name remains in popular use while another name must be used for the perfect state of the same fungus (e.g., *Monosporium apiospermum* and *Allescheria boydii*, *Microsporum nanum* and *Nannizzia obtusa*). Closely related fungi are often improperly listed under two taxonomic classes by the same generic name (e.g., *Aspergillus chevalieri* and *Aspergillus fumigatus*). *A. chevalieri* is actually an Ascomycete and should be known generically as Eurotium.

The asexual spores of the Deuteromycetes are usually called conidia, although special names are often given to some of these spores based on shape, color, septation, or method of formation. Most of the animal pathogens are in this class and are contained within the order Moniliales. Several toxin-producing species are also included.

## THE PHYCOMYCETES

Several fungi of the class Phycomycetes have been isolated from animal lesions. Notable among these are members of three genera of the order Mucorales, namely, Absidia, Mucor, and Rhizopus. These fungi are widely distributed in nature and cause sporadic infections which are not considered to be communicable but are contracted from environmental sources. Infection may occur by ingestion or inhalation of spores or by implantation of viable elements into wounds of the skin or mucous membranes. These are opportunistic pathogens which most frequently invade subjects debilitated by other diseases or those with substantial flaws of the epithelial surfaces.

Reference to these infections is implied by the terms "phycomycosis," "mucormycosis," or the description of "mucoraceous" hyphae in pathologic specimens. In many cases of "mucormycosis" the causative agent has been unidentified, inadequately identified, or, when identified, found to be nonpathogenic. Because of their prominence in nature, evidence for pathogenicity of the Phycomycetes must be firmly established to avoid crediting a saprophytic contaminant with pathogenic significance.

Several Phycomycetes have been found to be pathogenic for domestic animals and man. Among the better established phycomycoses of animals are mycotic abortion in cattle and granulomata of the lymph nodes and abdominal viscera of cattle, swine, and guinea pigs. Phycomycetes have been associated, probably secondarily, with gastric ulcers of swine and cattle and have been found in lesions of the nasal or paranasal sinuses of the dog and horse, subcutaneous lesions in mink, and cutaneous and mucocutaneous lesions of horses.

### Cultural Features

The more important genera of animal pathogens, Absidia, Mucor, and Rhizopus, grow rapidly on Sabouraud's medium at 25°C. and produce a coarse, woolly mycelium which fills the culture tube within a few days. The growth of these fungi is inhibited by media containing cycloheximide. They form broad ($5\mu$ to $20\mu$) hyphae which are usually devoid of septa; these two features are of diagnostic importance when seen in clinical exudates or histopathologic sections. The genera Absidia and Rhizopus form rootlike structures (rhizoids) at nodes along stolons which are vinelike vegetative hyphae. All three genera produce numerous sporangiospores within terminal enclosures (sporangia) borne on specialized hyphal branches (sporangiophores) (Fig. 39.1a). The sporangiophore protrudes into the sporangium forming a structure known as the columella. Sexual reproduction is accomplished by the formation of zygospores. These genera are differentiated on the basis of the origin of the sporangiophore, the shape of the sporangia and columellae, and by morphological features of the zygospores and their associated structures.

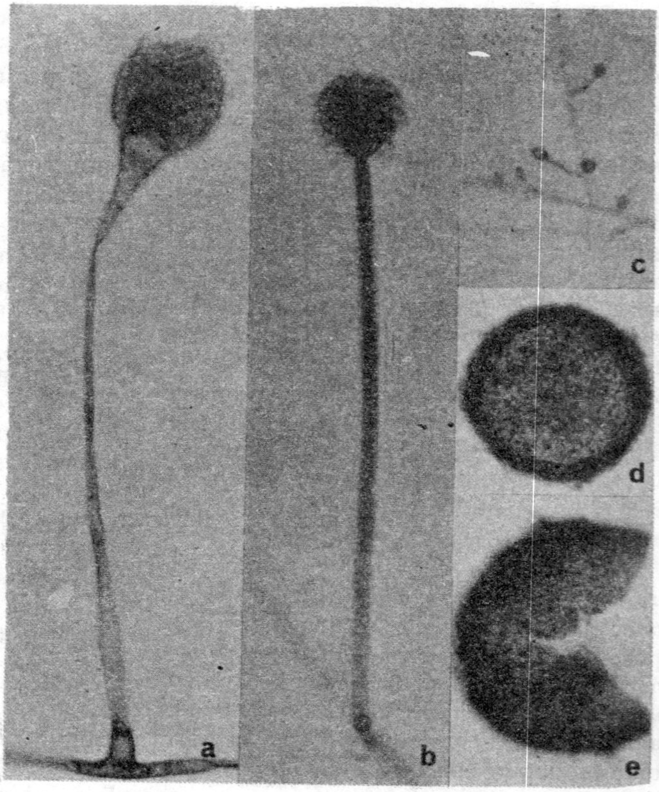


FIG. 39.1—Phycomycetes and Ascomycetes: a, **Mucor** sp. sporangium and sporangiophore, ×250; b, **Absidia** sp. sporangium and sporangiophore, ×250; c, **Allescheria boydii** mycelium and conidia, ×250; d, **Allescheria boydii** cleistothecium, ×125; e, **Allescheria boydii** ruptured cleistothecium, ×125.

### The Genus Absidia

Two species of Absidia are established pathogens of animals. *Absidia ramosa* and *Absidia corymbifera* are the phycomycetes most frequently described in animal infections. They are prominent agents in bovine mycotic abortion and have been described in infections of swine, guinea pigs, and mink.

The genus Absidia produces pear-shaped sporangia borne terminally on unbranched sporangiophores; the columella is typically conical in shape (Fig. 39.1b). Stolons are present with rhizoids occurring at the nodes; the sporangiophores arise from the stolon between these nodes.

### The Genus Mucor

Of several Mucor species isolated from animal lesions, *Mucor pusillus* is the species best established as a pathogen. This species has been demonstrated in mycotic abortion in cattle, a lung nodule in a horse, and from lesions in the calf and pig; the species has been shown to be pathogenic by experimental inoculation into rabbits. Other species of Mucor, notably *Mucor racemosus* and *Mucor spinosus*, have been associated with animal lesions, but evidence of their pathogenicity is less well established.

The genus Mucor produces globose sporangia borne terminally on sporangiophores which arise singly from the mycelium; the terminal sporangiophore may be branched or unbranched (Fig. 39.1a). Columellae with basal collarettes, comprised of remnants of the ruptured sporangia, are typical in mature cultures. The nonseptate mycelium of Mucor does not form rhizoids.

### The Genus Rhizopus

Three species, *Rhizopus arrhizus, Rhizopus cohnii*, and *Rhizopus microsporus*, have been described as the causative agents of occasional cases of mycotic abortion in cattle. *Rhizopus arrhizus* and *Rhizopus oryzae* are known to be pathogenic for man, and both *R. oryzae* and *R. microsporus* have been found to be pathogenic in experimentally inoculated laboratory animals.

The genus Rhizopus produces globose sporangia borne terminally on unbranched sporangiophores. The sporangiophores arise in groups at the nodes of the stolon opposite the rhizoids.

#### Other Phycomycetes

*Entomophthora coronata* has been isolated from nasal lesions in horses; these lesions take the form of granulomatous nodules of the nasal mucosa and the mucocutaneous junction. In lesions, the hyphae of *E. coronata* are relatively nonseptate while in culture the hyphae develop considerably more septa than do those of Absidia, Mucor, and Rhizopus. Sporangia are not formed but asexual conidia are developed which are forcibly discharged from the conidiophore.

*Hyphomyces destruens* has been isolated from granulomatous lesions of the skin and subcutaneous tissues of the extremities of horses. The hyphae of this pathogen are relatively nonseptate, and although the method of sporulation has not been described, it is believed to be a phycomycete.

Organisms of the genus Mortierella have been isolated from cutaneous ulcers in man, and the phycomycete *Basidiobolus ranarum* has been found in subcutaneous processes in man. Neither of these has been verified as a pathogen of lower animals.

### THE ASCOMYCETES

The Ascomycetes do not contain many animal pathogens. Only two are important as pathogens of man or animals. *Allescheria boydii (Monosporium apiospermum)* produces mycetomas (localized swollen lesions of the skin and underlying tissue which usually form draining sinuses) in man. The organism is a common soil inhabitant in many areas of the United States and Canada. Entrance of the organism into the host tissue usually results from penetrating wounds caused by thorns or other sharp objects. *A. boydii* has caused mycotic abortion in the mare. In culture, *A. boydii* grows rapidly, producing a dark, smoky-gray colony; ascocarps, known as cleistothecia, containing asci and ascospores, are imbedded in the soft, woolly, mycelial colony. Light brown oval conidia, approximating 8$\mu$, are borne in small groups or singly on the tips or sides of simple or branched conidiophores (Fig. 39.1c,d,e).

*Piedra hortae* is the agent of black piedra, a disease characterized by the formation of a hard mass of fungus cells on a hair shaft. The fungal mass contains locules in which asci and characteristic ascospores are contained. The growth of the fungus into the hair shaft weakens the shaft and it breaks easily. The disease occurs primarily in tropical countries in chimpanzees, monkeys, and man. *Piedra hortae* grows slowly, producing a small, heaped, black or brownish colony on Sabouraud's medium which may contain asci in the more dense areas of the colony. The dark-colored hyphae are closely septate and contain chlamydospore-like enlargements.

Some Ascomycetes may be toxigenic. Ergotism, a classic disease known during the eleventh century as "St. Anthony's Fire," is caused by ingestion of sclerotia of *Claviceps purpurea*. This fungus is parasitic on cereal grains and other grasses. The fungus invades and replaces the ovary of the plant with a hardened, horn-shaped, purple to black mass of fungal tissue, a sclerotium. Affected animals exhibit lameness and dry gangrene of the extremities which may be followed by shedding of the distal portion. Other effects include central nervous symptoms, paralysis, lesions in the mouth, intestinal irritation, and diarrhea. The ergot alkaloids have been commercially prepared and used as drugs in veterinary and human medicine.

### THE BASIDIOMYCETES

Although widely distributed in nature and causing many important plant diseases, the Basidiomycetes are not important agents n the mycoses of animals. Only two genera have been reported as being agents of mycoses in man. A smut organism of the genus Ustilago has been reported to cause an infection of the central nervous system in man, and *Schizophyllium commune,* another Basidiomycete, was reported to be the agent of a fingernail infection in man.

In this group are several fungi toxic for man, but little is known as to their effects on animals. Two species, *Russula emetica* and *Amanita verna,* were thought to be involved in poisoning of reindeer and cattle, respectively. *Amanita phalloides* is known to be highly toxic for man. Members of the order Ustilaginales (smut fungi) are toxic for cattle, birds, dogs, man, and other animals.

## THE DEUTEROMYCETES (FUNGI IMPERFECTI)

The majority of established animal pathogens are found in the form-class Deuteromycetes. As previously indicated this is an extremely diverse group which essentially embodies those fungi not known to produce sexual spores. The majority of the fungi known to be pathogenic for animals and man are found in this class. Important groups are the dermatophytes, the pathogenic yeasts, the Aspergilli, and the dimorphic fungi.

### The Dermatophytes

Dermatophytoses (ringworm) are among the oldest and best recognized mycoses. These differ from most of the mycoses in that they are definitely contagious. The causative fungi, the dermatophytes, are keratinophilic and preferentially parasitize keratinized epithelium, hair, and nails of animals and man. Certain species, the zoophilic dermatophytes, usually parasitize animals while the anthropophilic dermatophytes usually parasitize man; however, host predilection is not absolute and man or animals may share infections by various agents. A third group of dermatophytes normally resides in the soil and is capable of infecting either animals or man; this group is termed geophilic.

There are more than 20 species of pathogenic dermatophytes; these are assigned to four genera, namely, Epidermophyton, Keratinomyces, Microsporum, and Trichophyton. Sexual reproduction has been recognized in several dermatophytes and has resulted in the development of further taxonomic diversity; however, the parasitic species continue to be known in medical mycology by the generic names listed above.

The geographic distribution of the dermatophytes is variable. Some, such as *Microsporum canis,* are distributed worldwide, while others, such as *Trichophyton concentricum,* are known to exist only in restricted geographic areas.

#### Cultural Features

The dermatophytes may be grown on either Sabouraud's medium or on a similar medium containing cyclohexamide and chloramphenicol; the latter medium inhibits many contaminants and facilitates isolation of dermatophytes and certain other fungal pathogens. Most dermatophytes develop typical colonies following 2 to 4 weeks incubation at 25°C. Colonial color and morphology are useful criteria in identification. Nutritional tests such as the requirement of *Trichophyton equinum* for nicotinic acid and of *Trichophyton verrucosum* for thiamin and inositol are used for specific identification.

Asexual spore development is of three types: macroconidia, microconidia, and arthrospores. Macroconidia are large multicellular spores borne terminally either singly or in clusters; their configurations are useful for identification, although some species and individual strains rarely produce typical macroconidia (Fig. 39.2 a, b, c). Microconidia are produced in abundance by several Trichophyton species; these are small, single-celled spores borne on short conidiophores along the hyphae and in terminal clusters. The microconidia are less useful in species differentiation than are the macroconidia.

Microscopic examination of potassium hydroxide wet mounts prepared from plucked hairs or scrapings from skin and nails constitutes one of the most helpful methods of diagnosis. A branching, septate

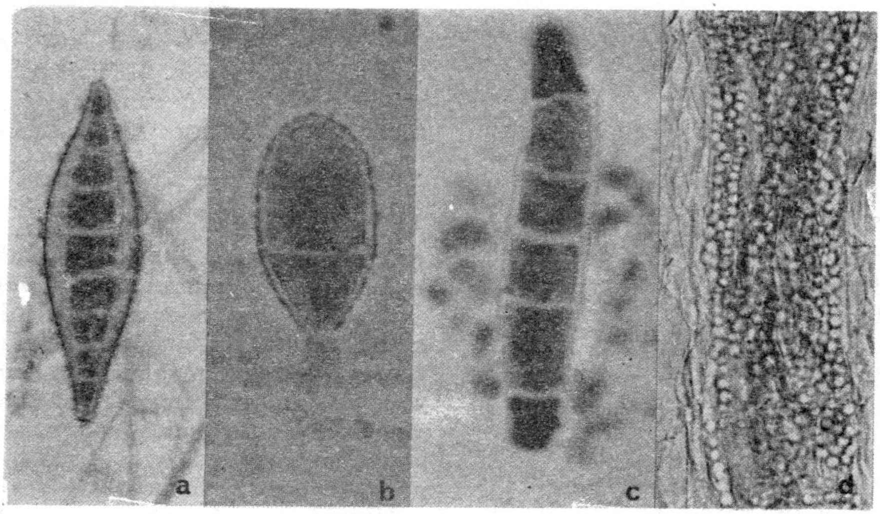

FIG. 39.2—Dermatophytes: **a, Microsporum canis** macroconidium, ×400; **b, Microsporum nanum** macroconidium, ×900; **c, Trichophyton equinum** macroconidium and microconidia, ×900; **d,** Ectothrix of bovine hair caused by **Trichophyton verrucosum** infection, ×400.

mycelium approximately 3μ wide invades the keratinized tissue and forms arthrospores. External sheaths of arthrospores commonly form about the hair shafts in certain animal and human infections; this formation is known as ectothrix (Fig. 39.2d). The diameter of the arthrospores vary according to the infecting agent.

## The Genus Epidermophyton

*Epidermophyton floccosum* is the only member of this genus. This anthropophilic dermatophyte infects the toenails and hairless areas of human skin, notably the feet and groin. Hairs are not invaded and infection of lower domestic animals is unknown. Mature colonies of *E. floccosum* are yellow-green, folded, and velvety to granular in texture. Macroconidia are abundant and are borne in clusters. They appear as two- to four-celled club-shaped spores approximately 6μ in width by 30μ in length. Their walls are relatively thin with a smooth exterior surface. Microconidia are not formed.

## The Genus Keratinomyces

*Keratinomyces ajelloi* is the only known member of the genus. This geophilic dermatophyte may rarely infect the skin and hair of animals. Infected hairs and skin scales are reported to contain mycelia and chains of arthrospores; ecothrix is not seen, and infected hairs do not fluoresce under filtered ultraviolet light (Wood's light). Mature colonies of *K. ajelloi* are tan to golden with a colorless to dark blue-black reverse side; they are flat and granular to downy in texture. Macroconidia are abundant; they have eight or more cells, are boat-shaped, and are approximately 6μ wide and 40μ long. The walls of the macroconidia are thick with smooth exteriors. Microconidia are formed in relatively small numbers.

## The Genus Microsporum

Of eight recognized species of Microsporum only three are important pathogens of animals; these are *Microsporum canis, Microsporum gypseum,* and *Microsporum nanum.* Members of this genus typically produce macroconidia which have rough projections on the exterior wall; the walls are usually thick. Microconidia are either absent or inconspicuous. A few species produce a fluorescent pigment, pteridine, in infected hairs which causes the infected hair to fluoresce yellow-green under Wood's light and constitutes a useful diagnostic criterion.

#### Microsporum canis

*Microsporum canis,* a zoophilic dermatophyte, frequently infects cats, dogs, and man; horses and lower primates are involved less frequently. *M. canis* infection is readily transmissible from animal to animal and to man. Infected hairs exhibit ectothrix, with spores 2μ to 3μ in diameter surrounding the shaft. Such hairs fluoresce typically under Wood's light. The fungus may be found also in skin scales and toenails.

*M. canis* grows rapidly, forming a downy white colony with a yellow pigment on the reverse side by the second week of growth. Macroconidia are abundant in most strains; they are canoe-shaped with thick walls, rough exteriors, and usually contain eight or more cells (Fig. 39.2a).

#### Microsporum gypseum

*Microsporum gypseum,* a geophilic dermatophyte, infrequently infects dogs, horses, cats, and man. The infection may be transmitted, but infection from a common soil source is an equally possible cause for group involvement. Infected hairs exhibit ectothrix with spores approximating 5μ to 8μ, forming chains along the hair shaft; such hairs do not fluoresce typically under Wood's light. The fungus may also be found in skin scales.

*M. gypseum* grows rapidly, forming a flat, powdery, orange-tan colony in a week. Macroconidia are abundant; they are boat-shaped with relatively thin walls, rough exteriors, and usually contain four or more cells.

#### Microsporum nanum

*Microsporum nanum* appears to be a geophilic dermatophyte which frequently causes mild infections in swine and infrequently involves man. The fungus invades the keratinized skin of swine but apparently does not invade the hair; lesion specimens do not fluoresce under Wood's light.

*M. nanum* grows rapidly, forming a powdery, tan colony in a week; the reverse side of the mature colony has a reddish-brown pigmentation. Macroconidia are abundant; they are elliptical with thin, rough walls, and nearly invariably contain two cells (Fig. 39.2b).

#### Other Microsporum Species

Notable among the other pathogenic species of Microsporum is *Microsporum audouinii.* This organism frequently parasitizes children and is a prominent agent of tinea capitis; lower animals are rarely involved. Hairs parasitized by *M. audouinii* fluoresce typically under Wood's light. The organism grows slowly, and macroconidia are infrequently produced.

*Microsporum distortum,* named for the bizarre distorted forms of its macroconidia, is an occasional pathogen of man and lesser primates and a rare pathogen of the dog. Hairs parasitized by *M. distortum* fluoresce typically under Wood's light.

*Microsporum vanbreuseghemii* is a rare pathogen, and the remaining species of this genus are considered to be saprophytes.

### The Genus Trichophyton

There are 14 recognized species of Trichophyton; only four are important as animal pathogens, namely, *Trichophyton equinum, Trichophyton gallinae, Trichophyton mentagrophytes* (granular variety) and *Trichophyton verrucosum.* Members of this genus typically produce club-shaped macroconidia with thin walls and smooth exteriors. Microconidia are abundant in some species. Hairs and other keratinized tissues infected by Trichophyton species do not produce a typical fluorescence under Wood's light. The vitamin requirements for the growth of certain species are important in species identification.

#### Trichophyton equinum

*Trichophyton equinum,* a zoophilic dermatophyte, frequently infects horses; human infections occur occasionally and canine infections occur rarely. Infected hairs exhibit ectothrix, with spores approximating $6\mu$ forming sheaths or chains along the hairshaft.

*T. equinum* grows rapidly, forming a downy white colony with a yellow pigment at the periphery and on the reverse side. This organism has a requirement for nicotinic acid. Macroconidia are produced but are rare on many strains; they are club-shaped with thin walls, smooth exteriors, and usually contain three or more cells (Fig. 39.2c).

### Trichophyton gallinae

*Trichophyton gallinae,* a zoophilic dermatophyte, infects poultry and infrequently involves other birds and man. Infection in birds is limited to the skin, usually of the comb and wattles, and does not invade the feathers.

*T. gallinae* grows fairly rapidly, producing a downy white colony and a striking red pigment which diffuses through the medium by the third week. Macroconidia are produced and are more abundant when the organism is grown on a thiamin-enriched medium; they are club-shaped, thin walled with smooth exteriors, and often contain six or more cells.

### Trichophyton mentagrophytes

*Trichophyton mentagrophytes* is unusual in that it has two major varieties each with a different host predilection. The downy variety, distinguished by a downy white colony, is primarily a pathogen of man which infects the feet and other essentially hairless regions of the body. The granular variety, distinguished by a flat powdery colony, has a wide host range and is primarily zoophilic. The latter variety is of primary interest in veterinary medicine. *T. mentagrophytes* (granular variety) is a frequent pathogen of rodents and dogs; occasional infections of cats, horses, cattle, and man, particularly farmers, are observed. Wild rodents are a natural reservoir and infected hairs or scales from these animals contaminate granaries, feed grains, stalls, and cages. Such contamination introduces infection into laboratory colonies of guinea pigs, mice, and other animals and may involve their human attendants. Infected hairs exhibit ectothrix; chains of spores approximating $5\mu$ in diameter are formed on the infected hair shaft.

The granular variety grows rapidly, forming a flat, powdery, whitish colony with a yellow to red pigment appearing on the reverse side within 2 weeks. Macroconidia are produced by most strains; they are club-shaped with thin walls and smooth exteriors and contain three or more cells.

### Trichophyton verrucosum

*Trichophyton verrucosum,* a zoophilic dermatophyte, causes the vast majority of dermatophytosis in cattle and occasionally involves horses, dogs, and other domestic animals; human handlers of infected cattle often become infected. The spores in infected hairs and scales may lodge on wooden posts and remain viable for several years and thus act as a perpetual source of infection. Infected hairs exhibit ectothrix, with spores approximating $8\mu$ in diameter.

*T. verrucosum* grows slowly, producing a white to yellow heaped and folded colony after 3 to 4 weeks. Growth is enhanced by incubation at 37°C., and the organism requires thiamin or a combination of thiamin and inositol in some strains. Macroconidia are formed rarely.

### Other Trichophyton Species

*Trichophyton rubrum,* a common pathogen of man, frequently infects the feet and nails; infections in lower animals are rare. *Trichophyton schoenleinii* is an infrequent pathogen of man and rarely a pathogen of animals in the United States; this organism is the cause of true "favus," an infection which involves deep layers of the epidermis and produces cup-shaped scabs and scar formation. *Trichophyton tonsurans,* once an infrequent human pathogen in this country, is now seen more frequently, particularly in immigrants and inhabitants of portal cities. *Trichophyton violaceum* is an infrequent human pathogen in the United States; rare infections of cattle in Europe by this organism have been reported.

The remaining Trichophyton species are those of extremely limited geographic distribution and which appear to be inconsequential pathogens of animals or, in some cases, are frankly saprophytic.

## The Pathogenic Yeasts

There are four genera of imperfect yeastlike fungi which infect animals. These yeastlike pathogens resemble the true yeasts in colony morphology and in the production of blastospores or budding forms by most genera. Unlike the true yeasts, three of the four genera produce a mycelium or pseudomycelium and none of the four produces sexual spores. The genera Cryptococcus and Candida are important pathogens of animals and man; the two remaining genera, Trichosporon and Geotrichum, are infrequently pathogenic.

## The Genus Cryptococcus

Of several species in this genus, only *Cryptococcus neoformans* is a recognized pathogen. Cryptococcosis, the disease resulting from *C. neoformans* infection, is seen commonly in both animals and man. Cryptococcosis usually results from inhalation of the yeast in contaminated dust; primary foci in the respiratory organs are often the source of systemic disseminations which may involve the central nervous system, boney structures, the skin, or other organs. Cryptococcosis is a notable disease of mature cats; dogs and horses also have been infected, and cryptococcal mastitis has been reported in cattle.

*C. neoformans* has been isolated from the environment, particularly from areas contaminated with pigeon droppings. The organism grows well on Sabouraud's medium, producing a soft, creamy to mucoid colony in 1 to 2 weeks. Chloramphenicol may be added to the medium to facilitate isolation from contaminated specimens. Growth is obtained with incubation at either 25° or 37°C., a fact which is helpful in differentiating *C. neoformans* from saprophytic species. Among the more important differential criteria for identification are the ability of this genus to hydrolyze urea and the specific ability of *C. neoformans* to kill or cause lesions in mice following intracerebral or intraperitoneal inoculation.

*C. neoformans* does not produce mycelial elements. Microscopically, the organism appears as single spherical or budding yeast cells approximating 5μ to 8μ in diameter. India ink wet mounts of clinical materials or materials from inoculated mice demonstrate clear halos of capsular material; these capsules are not evident in cultural material (Fig. 39.3b).

## The Genus Candida

Several species of the genus Candida are capable of causing infection in animals and man. The most frequent pathogen of the genus is *Candida albicans*. Candidiasis, the disease resulting from Candida infection, commonly affects the skin and mucous membranes of many species of domestic animals and of man. Candidiasis of the alimentary canal, often referred to as "thrush," is a prominent disease of poultry and has been reported in swine. Candidiasis is known to involve the skin of dogs, the uterus of the mare, and the reproductive tract and mammary gland of the cow. Systemic infection may result by dissemination from superficial foci. Predilection to infection has been attributed to diabetes or other debilitating diseases and to systemic therapy with certain antibiotics.

*C. albicans* may be isolated from the environment and is a frequent resident of normal skin and mucous membranes. The organism grows well on many bacteriological mediums and on Sabouraud's medium. Soft, glistening white colonies appear after 2 to 7 days incubation at either 25° or 37°C. All members of the genus produce mycelial elements, called pseudomycelia, and blastospores (budding yeast cells). Microscopic examination of exudates or culture material reveals strongly gram-positive oval yeast cells, approximating 3μ by 5μ, budding forms, and pseudomycelia. Mature cultures of *C. albicans* on cornmeal agar contain

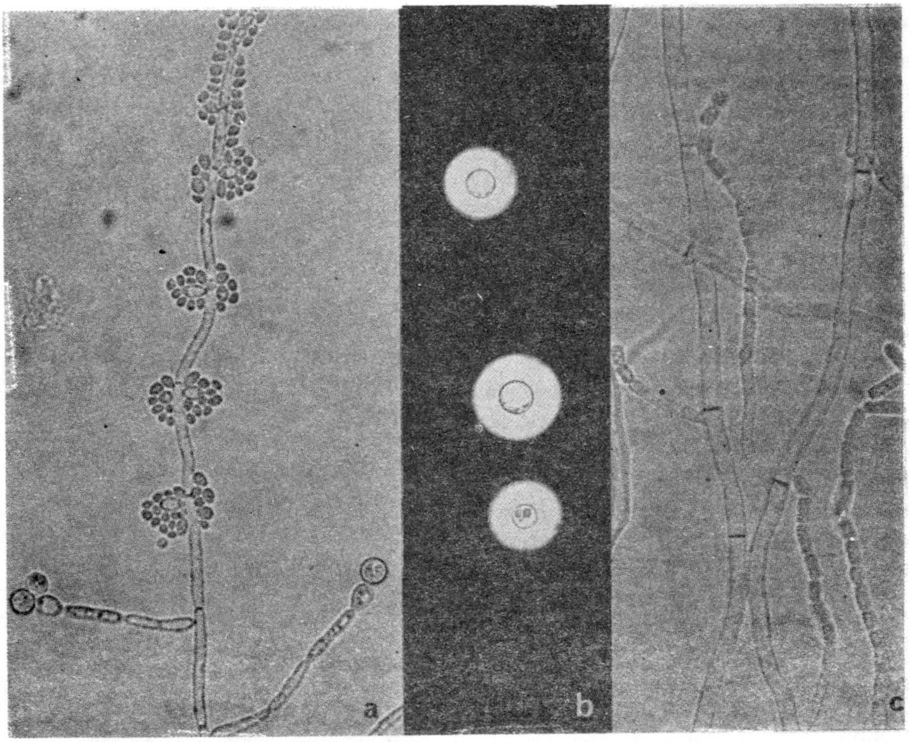


FIG. 39.3—Pathogenic yeasts: **a, Candida albicans** with chlamydospores and clusters of blastospores, ×250; **b, Cryptococcus neoformans** yeast cells with capsules. India ink mount from mouse brain, ×250; **c, Geotrichum candidum** mycelium and chains of arthrospores, ×250.

clusters of blastospores at the juncture of mycelial elements and large, thick-walled chlamydospores (Fig. 39.3a). Sugar fermentation tests are helpful for the identification of Candida species; *C. albicans* typically produces acid and gas in dextrose and maltose, variably produces acid in sucrose, and does not ferment lactose. References for more definitive identification of *C. albicans* and other potentially pathogenic species of Candida have been included.

## The Genus Trichosporon

*Trichosporon cutaneum* causes infections of the hair of man and lesser primates; members of this genus also cause infrequent cases of bovine mastitis. Trichosporon species grow rapidly on Sabouraud's medium, forming soft white to tan colonies that become wrinkled or crateriform. Mycelial elements, blastospores and arthrospores, are produced.

## The Genus Geotrichum

*Geotrichum candidum* is the only member of the genus. This organism has been isolated from the soil, from cases of respiratory and intestinal geotrichosis, and infrequently from cases of bovine mastitis. The organism grows rapidly on Sabouraud's medium, forming moist yeastlike colonies which may develop a cottony aerial mycelium with age. Chains of rectangular arthrospores approximating $4\mu$ by $10\mu$ are formed and may be seen in culture materials or in Gram-stained films of exudates (Fig. 39.3c). Older arthrospores tend to have rounded ends, or germ tubes may be seen extending from the corner of the rectangular forms.

## The Aspergilli

Members of the genus Aspergillus are responsible for both infections and intoxications of a variety of domestic and wild animals and man. Aspergillosis is the infectious disease. Primary infection usually involves the respiratory system with subsequent dissemination to other organ systems. Infection of the alimentary canal, skin, or other organs may occur opportunistically following occurrence of flaws in the epithelial surfaces or debilitating diseases. Aspergillosis is known to affect nearly all domestic animals, many wild species, and man. Numerous species of birds have been affected by respiratory infection and in many instances severe economic losses have resulted. Members of the genus Aspergillus are a major cause of mycotic abortion in mammalian species, particularly in cattle. The Aspergilli are common saprophytes and, when conditions of temperature and humidity are favorable, they grow profusely in hay, feed, and decaying plant and animal debris. They produce prodigious quantities of spores which readily form aerosols in the environment. The agents as well as the disease are worldwide in distribution. *Aspergillus fumigatus* is the chief agent of avian and mammalian aspergillosis. Inhaled spores of *A. fumigatus* may produce infections of the lungs or air sacs. Signs of infection are neither definitive nor constant. Lesions of internal organs typically present necrosis and granulomatous reaction.

In the case of mycotic abortion where *A. fumigatus* is the chief agent, the spores presumably gain entry into the body by the respiratory route, with subsequent hematogenous dissemination to the placenta, establishing a mycotic placentitis. The disease is symptomless in the dam until abortion occurs. Diagnosis of mycotic abortion is made by cultural and microscopic examination of placental tissue more often than by examination of fetal stomach contents. Species of Aspergillus which are toxigenic are discussed later in this chapter with the toxigenic Deuteromycetes.

*A. fumigatus* grows rapidly on Sabouraud's medium at 27°C., forming a fuzzy white colony which becomes blue-green and powdery as the conidial heads develop. Older colonies become gray colored. The mycelium is septate and approximates 3$\mu$ in width. The conidial heads are columnar and compact with parallel chains of conidia (Fig. 39.4). The rough, globose conidia approximate 3$\mu$ in diameter and are borne on a single row of sterigma situated on the terminal portion of a flask-shaped vesicle. The growth of *A. fumigatus* is inhibited by media containing cylohexamide.

## The Dimorphic Fungi

Certain pathogenic fungi develop substantially different forms when they infect animal or human tissues as compared to the form they maintain in the free-living state. These fungi are called dimorphic, and the morphological phases are known as the tissue or yeast form and the mold form, re-

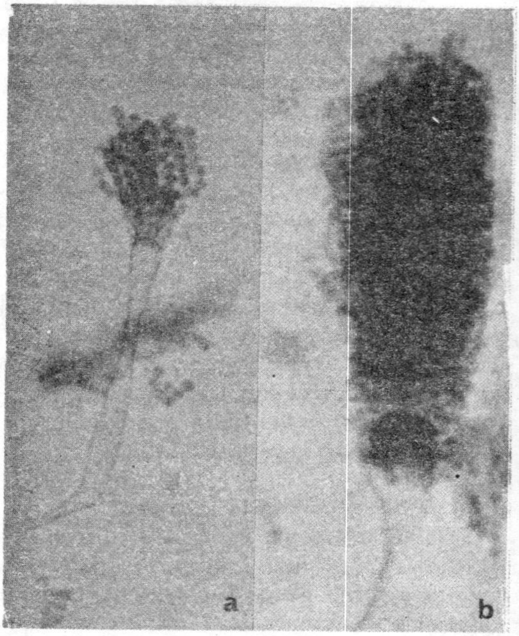


FIG. 39.4—Aspergillus: a, **Aspergillus fumigatus** conidiophore with vesicle, single row of sterigmata and a few conidia, ×400; b, A mature conidial head of **A. fumigatus** with long column of conidia in parallel chains, ×400.

spectively. The tissue form of most of the dimorphic pathogens can be reproduced by incubating the fungus at 37°C. on an enriched medium such as brain heart infusion agar or blood agar; the mold form may be produced by incubating the fungus at 25°C. on Sabouraud's medium. The dimorphic fungi include virulent pathogens capable of causing systemic disease; they must be handled with considerable respect in the laboratory. Infections by the dimorphic fungi are not ordinarily considered to be contagious, but arise from environmental sources. The genera considered here are all in the form-class Deuteromycetes; they include Blastomyces, Paracoccidioides, Sporotrichum, Histoplasma, and Coccidioides.

### The Genus Blastomyces

*Blastomyces dermatitidis* is the causative agent of North American blastomycosis. This disease appears to be endemic in certain regions of the central United States extending from the Mississippi River to the mid-Atlantic coast. The organism is thought to live saprophytically in the soil or other environmental loci, although this fact awaits definitive proof. Blastomycosis is a chronic granulomatous disease which frequently involves the lungs with subsequent dissemination to the skin, lymph nodes, and visceral organs. Infection apparently originates in most instances by inhalation of infectious fungal elements. Dogs and man are most frequently affected and the disease has been reported in the horse.

*B. dermatitidis* grows rather slowly from clinical materials, forming a fluffy tan colony which may be marked by concentric waves after 3 to 4 weeks of incubation at 25°C. on Sabouraud's medium or selective mediums containing cyclohexamide and chloramphenicol. The mold form is comprised of a slender, segmented mycelium which bears single oval conidia approximating $3\mu$ to $5\mu$ in diameter (Fig. 39.5b). The mold form can be converted to the tissue form by cultivation on brain heart infusion agar containing 5 per cent whole blood and incubating at 37°C. The tissue form develops a heaped, warty, yeastlike colony. Microscopically, the tissue or yeast form appears as a spherical budding yeast cell approximating $5\mu$ to $15\mu$ in diameter (Fig. 39.5f). The buds are typically attached to the parent cell by a broad base and only a single bud is formed per parent cell.

For the laboratory identification of *B. dermatitidis,* both the mold form and the tissue or yeast form should be demonstrated. Sensitins for skin testing and serologic antigens are available as clinical diagnostic aids.

### The Genus Paracoccidioides

The fungus *Paracoccidioides brasiliensis* is the South American counterpart of *B. dermatitidis*. South American blastomycosis in animals is not well documented and apparently does not exist, or occurs only rarely in this country. The fungus is extremely slow growing, producing a heaped white mold colony and a typical glabrous, yeast form colony. The yeast or tissue form produces multiple buds around the parent cell.

### The Genus Sporotrichum

Of several species in this genus, only *Sporotrichum schenckii* is a notable pathogen of animals and man. Infection has been observed in horses, mules, and man; dogs and cattle are less frequently involved. The disease occurs as ulcerating or nonulcerating subcutaneous lesions, often following lymphatic channels, and may also be seen as a systemic disease with respiratory involvement. *S. schenckii* is a widely distributed organism which lives saprophytically on timbers, plants, and in other environmental loci. Infection results from skin penetration by contaminated slivers or thorns and by inhalation of infectious elements.

The mold form of *S. schenckii* grows fairly rapidly on Sabouraud's medium or selective mediums containing cyclohexamide and chloramphenicol, forming glistening, white, membranous colonies after incubation for 1 week at 25°C.; these colonies

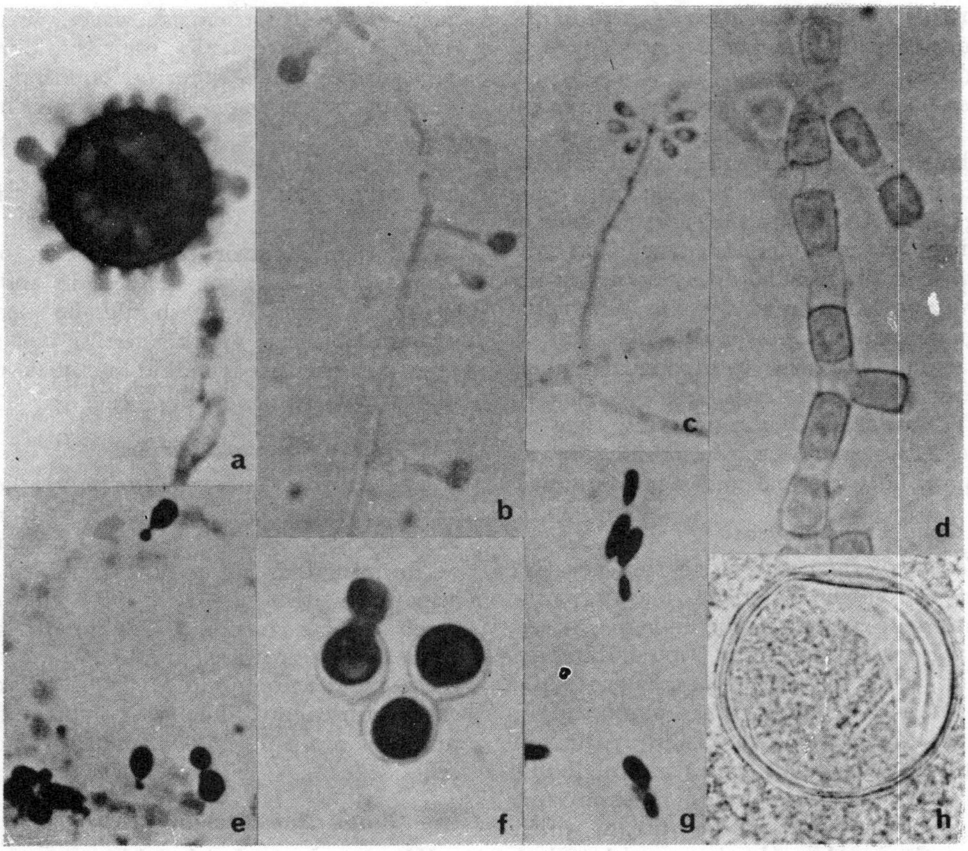


FIG. 39.5—Dimorphic Fungi: a, **Histoplasma capsulatum** mold form tuberculate macroconidium, ×900; b, **Blastomyces dermatitidis** mold form mycelium and conidia, ×900; c, **Sporotrichum schenckii** mold form mycelium and conidia, ×900; d, **Coccidioides immitis** mold form arthrospores in intermittent chains, ×900; e, **Histoplasma capsulatum** yeast form, ×900; f, **Blastomyces dermatitidis** yeast form, ×900; g, **Sporotrichum schenckii** yeast form, ×900; h, **Coccidioides immitis** tissue form, ×250.

usually become wrinkled, and the central portions develop brown to black pigmentation as they mature. The mold form is distinguished microscopically by the development of a slender, segmented mycelium with pyriform conidia borne on delicate sterigmata occurring in rows along the mycelium and in terminal clusters (Fig. 39.5c).

The yeast or tissue form may be produced by persistent culturing on fresh blood agar at 37°C. or by animal inoculation. The yeast cells are oval to elongate cigar-shaped elements approximating 2$\mu$ by 4$\mu$ (Fig. 39.5g). These forms are not often seen in clinical materials but are readily demonstrable in materials from experimentally infected laboratory animals. Both forms of the organism should be demonstrated for diagnostic surety.

## The Genus Histoplasma

*Histoplasma capsulatum* is the most prominent pathogen of the genus and is the causative agent of histoplasmosis in dogs, man, and less frequently in cats and other domesticated animals. This fungus lives saprophytically in confined geographical areas of the United States, Central and South America, Africa, and the Near East.

Notable among the endemic areas in the United States are the Mississippi and Ohio valleys of the Midwest and the Appalachian region of the East. *H. capsulatum* resides in soil and compost particularly that which is admixed with the excreta of birds or bats. Histoplasmosis of animals or man usually results from inhalation of spore-laden dust. Despite a high incidence of infection in man and susceptible animals in endemic areas, relatively few cases develop clinical manifestations and fewer still progress to severe or fatal termination. Following inhalation of spores, primary respiratory foci are formed with concomitant dissemination to the reticuloendothelial system. The infection causes the formation of nonsuppurative granulomata and the tissue form of the organism is usually seen intracellularly in phagocytes.

The mold form of *H. capsulatum* is produced on Sabouraud's medium or selective media containing cyclohexamide and chloramphenicol after incubation at 25°C. The colony develops slowly; the young colony is white and fluffy, but a buff to tan color develops with maturity. The mold form is comprised of a slender, segmented mycelium which bears microconidia approximating $3\mu$ in diameter and distinctive tuberculate macroconidia approximating $10\mu$ to $20\mu$ in diameter (Fig. 39.5a). The mold form should be handled with caution by wetting with sterile saline solution and working under a properly ventilated safety hood to avoid contamination of both the laboratory and personnel.

The yeast or tissue form can be produced by culture on blood agar at 37°C. or by animal inoculation. The mouse is a particularly susceptible laboratory animal for inoculation experiments. The yeast form appears as oval, budding yeast cells approximating $2\mu$ by $3\mu$ (Fig. 39.5e). These cells are not encapsulated as their name implies, but staining artifacts give the appearance of capsule formation.

Both the mold form and the tissue or yeast form should be demonstrated for definitive diagnosis. Diagnostic antigens are available to detect cutaneous hypersensitivity, precipitins, and complement-fixing antibodies. Antigenic differences are apparent between the mold form and the yeast form and antigenic cross reactions with *B. dermatitidis* have been observed.

*Histoplasma farciminosum* causes epizootic lymphangitis of horses in Africa and Asia; this condition resembles sporotrichosis. *Histoplasma duboisii* is found in Africa where it has produced lesions of the skin, bones, and lymph nodes of man; this organism produces larger tissue forms than does *H. capsulatum*, some of which may approximate $15\mu$ in diameter.

### The Genus Coccidioides

*Coccidioides immitis* is the causative agent of coccidioidomycosis. This disease is endemic in restricted areas of the western hemisphere, including the Pacific southwestern United States, northern Mexico, Central and South America. Within these regions, *C. immitis* resides in the soil of semiarid locales closely corresponding with the lower sonoran life zone. The fungus is seasonally prevalent in surface soil of endemic areas; in the dry season it becomes air-borne in dust, and may be prevalent near rodent burrows or other sites where the soil has been freshly turned. Infection is nearly invariably the result of inhaling spore-laden dust. As with histoplasmosis, there is a high incidence of infection among human and animal residents of endemic areas. Fortunately, relatively few of these cases develop clinical manifestations and fewer still progress to severe disseminated disease or fatal termination.

Coccidioidomycosis most frequently affects dogs and man. Cattle often become infected but rarely develop clinical disease. Wild burrowing rodents in endemic areas may contract infection. In both dogs and man there is evidence of racial susceptibility to disseminated disease. Coccidioidomycosis causes febrile and allergic manifestations and produces suppurative granulomatous lesions of the lungs and bronchial lymph nodes; dissemination to the skin, bone, and other organ systems, with the notable exception of the enteric canal, may occur. Disseminated infection in the dog frequently produces a distinctive chronic osteomyelitis.

*C. immitis* grows rapidly on Sabouraud's medium or selective media containing cyclohexamide and chloramphenicol, forming a flat, fuzzy, white colony after incubation at 25°C. for one week. The aerial mycelium collapses back on the medium of older cultures, imparting a moth-eaten appearance; some fully mature cultures may become tan or brown colored. The mold form mycelium is comprised of a septate mycelium which bears barrel-shaped arthrospores, approximating 3$\mu$ by 5$\mu$, in intermittent chains at the ends of mature hyphae (Fig. 39.5d). The occurrence of the intermittent chains of arthrospores and blank spaces in the terminal hyphae are features which readily distinguish *C. immitis* from other arthrospore-forming fungi such as Geotrichum. Fragmentation of the chain leaves small tags of the blank hypha attached to the ends of the arthrospore. These arthrospores are readily aerosolized, constituting a serious laboratory hazard. This mold colony should be moistened with sterile saline and handled under a properly ventilated safety hood.

The tissue form of *C. immitis* is best demonstrated by animal inoculation; intratesticular inoculation of mold phase culture material or clinical specimens into male guinea pigs is the usual method. Following inoculation, the arthrospore becomes round, enlarges, and develops into a thick-walled spherule varying in size between 10$\mu$ and 200$\mu$ (Fig. 39.5h). The mature spherule develops internal spores known as endospores; when the spherule ruptures in the tissue these endospores are released and renew the cycle by forming additional spherules. In naturally or experimentally infected tissues the spherule constitutes a distinctive diagnostic element and may be seen extracellularly in the exudates or, particularly with smaller spherules, may be contained within macrophages or giant cells.

Coccidioidin is a culture filtrate antigen produced on a synthetic medium. The antigen is used effectively in skin tests and for detecting precipitins and complement-fixing antibodies in individuals suspected of having coccidioidomycosis. The demonstration of humoral antibodies appears to be dependent on sufficient tissue involvement to engender a detectable serologic titer. Serologic and allergic tests for coccidioidomycosis, histoplasmosis, and blastomycosis should be conducted as comparative tests using a battery of fungal antigens; such a procedure often clarifies the results of possible antigenic cross reactions.

### The Genus Rhinosporidium

The organism, *Rhinosporidium seeberi,* causes the development of tumorous enlargements of mucous membranes of cattle, horses, and man. These lesions, seen mostly in tropical climates, may reach from one to several inches in diameter. The lesions contain small white specks which are thick-walled sporangia which contain small globose spores. The sporangia vary in size between 10$\mu$ and 400$\mu$. *Rhinosporidium seeberi* is presumed to be a fungus, but to date, cultural methods have not permitted its growth in the laboratory.

### Toxigenic Deuteromycetes

The occurrence of mycotoxins has been recognized since ancient times and the mycotoxicoses have regained prominence in recent years. The known toxigenic Deuteromycetes and the important effects of their toxins on animal recipients are summarized below.

**Rhizoctonia.** Toxic factors of *Rhizoctonia leguminicola,* an organism which produces "blackpatch" disease on legumes, are known to cause excessive salivation, diarrhea, and frequent urination in cattle when ingested. The symptoms are reproducible in guinea pigs fed toxin; the effects resemble those of parasympathomimetic drugs and may be counteracted by atropine.

**Stachybotrys.** A toxin produced by *Stachy-*

*botrys atra,* a worldwide-occurring, cellulolytic organism, has produced a condition in horses manifested by such symptoms as swelling and cracking of the lips, necrosis of the mucosa of the oral and gastrointestinal tracts, elevated temperature, followed by death. The toxin depresses hematopoesis; it is ether soluble and relatively heat stable.

**Sporodesmium.** Toxins of *Sporodesmium bakerii* syn. *Pithomyces chartarum* are known to cause a photosensitivity disease of sheep known as "facial eczema." The toxin produces a cholangiohepatitis and necrosis of the liver which results in accumulation of sensitizing phyloerythrins in the blood. The water-soluble toxin is contained in the hyphae and spores of the fungus growing on pasture grasses.

**Fusarium.** *Fusarium sporotrichoides* produces a toxin, when grown on overwintered cereal grains, which causes irritation and necrosis of the oral mucosa, hematopoetic depression, and frequently death. This condition is known as "alimentary toxic aleukia" of man. Another species, *Fusarium graminearum (Gibberella zeae),* produces a uterotrophic compound causing an enlargement of the uterus in animals fed grain infested with this organism. The effect on both male and female recipients, particularly swine, is that of an estrogen.

**Aspergillus.** Several species of Aspergillus produce toxins which have varied effects on animals. Some strains of *Aspergillus flavus* produce a series of closely related toxins known as "aflatoxins" which cause hepatic necrosis and bile duct proliferation in many animals fed grain concentrates and other substances infested with the organism. Among the animals most susceptible to aflatoxicosis are ducklings, turkey poults, pigs, calves, and trout. Hepatic tumors have been produced in trout and rats experimentally fed aflatoxins. Aflatoxin is chloroform soluble and relatively heat stable. *Aspergillus fumigatus, Aspergillus chevalieri,* and *Aspergillus clavatus* produce toxins which cause a hyperkeratosis-like condition in calves. *Aspergillus niger* and some strains of *A. flavus* produce toxins which cause tremors in mice followed by death. These and other species produce large quantities of oxalic acid.

**Penicillium.** *Penicillium puberulum, Penicillium rubrum,* and *Penicillium islandicum* strains are known to produce toxins, some of which are similar to the aflatoxins produced by *A. flavus.* In addition, *Penicillium notatum* and other species are renowned for their ability to produce antibiotic substances.

## REFERENCES FOR FURTHER STUDY

The references included in this chapter are not intended to represent a complete or exhaustive list. The references selected are authoritative texts, classical treatises, or exclusive monographs on a specific agent or disease. Individual reports have been included only where more complete works do not exist. Use of these references should provide the interested student with an adequate *entre* to the current literature. The important historical literature pertaining to fungal diseases in animals has been well summarized in the text by Ainsworth and Austwick.

## REFERENCES

AINSWORTH, G. C. A Dictionary of the Fungi. Commonwealth Mycological Institute, Kew, Surry, 1961.

———, and AUSTWICK, P. K. C. Fungal Diseases of Animals. Commonwealth Agr. Bur., Farnham Royal, Bucks, England, 1959.

AJELLO, L. Present-Day Concepts of the Dermatophytes. Mycopath. et Mycol. Appl. 17:315, 1962.

———, *et al.* Laboratory Manual for Medical Mycology. 2nd Ed. U.S. Dept. Health, Educ. and Welfare, Communicable Disease Center, Atlanta, Ga., 1962.

———, *et al.* The Natural History of Microsporum Nanum. Mycologia 56:873, 1964.

ALEXOPOULAS, C. J. Introductory Mycology. 2nd Ed. John Wiley & Sons, Inc., New York, 1962.

AUSTWICK, P. K. C., and VENN, J. A. J. Mycotic Abortion in England and Wales, 1954–1960. Proc. 4th Intl. Cong. of An. Reproduction, The Hague, 1961.

BAKER, R. D., and CHICK, E. W. (eds.). Intl. Symp. on Opportunistic Fungus Infections. Lab. Invest. 11:1017, 1962.

BRIDGES, C. H., and EMMONS, C. W. A Phycomycosis of Horses Caused by *Hyphomyces destruens*. Jour. Amer. Vet. Med. Assn. 138:579, 1961.

———, *et al.* Phycomycosis of Horses Caused by *Entomophthora coronata*. Jour. Amer. Vet. Med. Assn. 140:673, 1962.

CHRISTIANSEN, M. Mucormykose beim Schwein. I. Mitteilung. Virchorus Arch. 273:829, 1929.

CHUTE, H. L., *et al.* A Bibliography of Avian Mycosis. (Partially annotated.) Misc. Publ. 655, Maine Agr. Exp. Sta., Orono, 1962.

DAVIS, C. L., *et al.* Mucormycosis in Food-Producing Animals. A Report of Twelve Cases. Jour. Amer Vet. Med. Assn. 126:261, 1955.

EMMONS, C. W., *et al.* Medical Mycology. Lea & Febiger, Philadelphia, 1963.

FIESE, M. J. Coccidioidomycosis. Charles C Thomas, Springfield, Ill., 1958.

FURCOLOW, M. L., and RHUE, J. S. Histoplasmin Sensitivity Among Cattle. Amer. Jour. Pub. Health 39:719, 1949.

GEORG, L. K. Animal Ringworm in Public Health. Diagnosis and Nature. U.S. Dept. Health, Educ. and Welfare, Communicable Disease Center, Atlanta, Ga., 1959.

HUGENHOLTZ, P. G., *et al.* Experimental Coccidioidomycosis in Dogs. Amer. Jour. Vet. Res. 19:433, 1958.

LODDER, J., and KREGER-VAN RIJ, N. W. J. The Yeasts—A Taxonomic Study. Interscience Publ., Inc , New York, 1953.

MADDY, K. T. Coccidioidomycosis. Adv. Vet. Sci. (Acad. Press, New York.) 6:251, 1960.

MAHAFFEY, L. W., and ROSSDALE, P. D. An Abortion Due to *Allescheria boydii* and General Observations Concerning Mycotic Abortion of Mares. Vet. Rec. 77:541, 1965.

MENGES, R. W. Histoplasmin Sensitivity in Animals. Cornell Vet. 44:21, 1954.

———. Blastomycosis in Animals. Vet. Med. 55:45, 1960.

OLANDER, H. J., *et al.* Feline Cryptococcosis. Jour. Amer. Vet. Med. Assn. 142:138, 1963.

POUNDEN, W. D., *et al.* A Severe Mastitis Problem Associated With *Cryptococcus neoformans* in a Large Dairy Herd. Amer. Jour. Vet. Res. 13:121, 1952.

ROBERTS, E. D., *et al.* Feline Cryptococcosis. Iowa State Univ. Vet. 26:30, 1963.

SALVIN, S. B. Immunologic Aspects of the Mycoses. Prog. in Allergy (Karger & Basel, New York.) 7:213, 1963.

SASLAW, S., *et al.* Experimental Histoplasmosis in Large Domestic Animals. Proc. Soc. Exp. Biol. Med. 105: 76, 1960.

STRAUB, M., *et al.* Incidence and Pathology of Canine Histoplasmosis. Arch. Path. 71:685, 1961.

SWEANY, H. C. Histoplasmosis. Charles C Thomas, Springfield, Ill., 1960.

WOGAN, G. N. (ed.). Mycotoxins in Foodstuffs. Mass. Inst. Tech. Press, Cambridge, 1965.

PART 4

# The Viruses

# 40

# General Characteristics of Viruses

**JOHN B. GRATZEK, *D.V.M., Ph.D.***
*Department of Veterinary Microbiology and Preventive Medicine*
*University of Georgia*
*Athens, Georgia*

THE WORD VIRUS IS DERIVED FROM THE LATIN, meaning a slimy, liquid poison such as venom. The term was used in ancient times to denote various types of noxious agents. It was also applied to pathogenic bacteria in the early days of medical bacteriology as well as to the invisible infectious agents which were described about 1900. Gradually the term has taken on a restricted meaning until now it is applied only to those obligate parasitic agents which are below 300 m$\mu$ in size and contain only one type of nucleic acid.

The viruses are widely distributed in nature, causing infection of animals, insects, and bacteria. Many hundreds of viruses have been described.

Credit for the first discovery of a virus is given to Iwanowski who in 1892 reported that the agent which produced the mosaic disease of tobacco plants could be freely passed through bacteria-retaining filters. In 1898 the Dutch bacteriologist, Beijerinck, recognized that the agent producing mosaic disease of tobacco represented a new type of microorganism, referring to it as *contagium vivum fluidum*—a living contagious fluid. Also in 1898, the first animal virus, the foot-and-mouth disease virus, was described by Loeffler and Frosch.

Since this time the study of viruses has steadily progressed, due in large part to technical achievements by various researchers. Certainly the development of the electron microscope by Ruska and Knoll in 1931 was a most significant contribution to present-day concepts of virus morphology. Goodpasture's discovery that viruses could be propagated in embryonating hens eggs and Enders' discovery that poliovirus would kill cells which were propagating in vitro began an era of research where virus-cell interactions could easily be studied at the biochemical level.

## GENERAL PROPERTIES OF VIRUSES

A strict definition of a virus has been difficult because only recently have their structural, biochemical, and reproductive characteristics been discovered. Mature viruses, also called *virions,* vary considerably in size. Foot-and-mouth virions are approximately 27 m$\mu$ in diameter, while the animal poxviruses are nearly 300 m$\mu$. Size differences between an average-sized mammalian cell (10$\mu$–15$\mu$) and various viruses are appreciable.

Viruses contain protein and one type of nucleic acid, which is either desoxyribonucleic acid (DNA) or ribonucleic acid (RNA). Smaller viruses are composed only of these two constituents, while more complex viruses may contain lipid, polysaccharides, and trace elements. It is well established that animal viruses contain no enzymatic systems. Thus, viruses demonstrate no independent metabolism.

The simple composition of a virus requires that it utilize the metabolic machinery of a living cell for its reproduction. This requires that the virion first penetrate into a living cell. The external protein coat of the virion is then broken down, releasing the viral nucleic acid into the cell. The viral nucleic acid uses the cellular metabolic machinery to reproduce itself and viral protein molecules. The final step includes the assembly of these constituents to form hundreds of new virus particles in each infected cell.

## STRUCTURE OF VIRUSES

The fine structure of the virion of many viruses has been studied during the past several years by high resolution microscopy of negatively stained virus particles, using phosphotungstic acid as an electron dense material. From these studies as well as from biological and X-ray diffraction data, information has been obtained relative to the organization and function of the virion and its components. Several features of virus morphology and structure are well established. The infectious component of the virus is its nucleic acid, either RNA or DNA. The viral nucleic acid is enclosed in a symmetrically arranged protein shell called the *capsid*. The capsids of animal viruses are constructed of small protein subunits called *structure units*. Structure units may be organized in the form of icosahedral shells representing *cubic symmetry*, or in elongated tubules representing *helical symmetry*. *Capsomeres* are the surface components of cubic viruses which are easily visualized by electron microscopy and are composed of symmetric clusters of structural units. The capsid along with the nucleic acid is often called the *nucleocapsid*. The nucleocapsid of helical viruses would include the nucleic acid and the surrounding structure units. Virions of the picornavirus, reovirus, papovavirus, and adenovirus groups consist of nucleic acid with the surrounding capsid. Virions of the myxovirus, arbovirus, herpesvirus, and poxvirus groups have long helical nucleocapsids which are enclosed in an envelope. The main structural features of viruses are diagrammatically presented in Figure 40.1. Table 40.1 presents the major characteristics of the eight groups of animal viruses. The relationship between ether sensitivity and the presence of a lipoprotein envelope will be noted. Virions possessing envelopes mature at a cellular membrane site. Although cellular in origin, the envelope con-

TABLE 40.1

CHARACTERISTICS OF THE MAJOR GROUPS OF ANIMAL VIRUSES

| Virus Group | Size mμ | Ether Sensitivity | Site of Maturation * | Presence of Envelope | Capsid Symmetry | Number Capsomeres |
|---|---|---|---|---|---|---|
| RNA Viruses | | | | | | |
| Picornavirus | 17–30 | — | C | — | cubic | . . . |
| Reovirus | 74 | — | C | — | cubic | 92 |
| Arbovirus | 20–100 | + | C | + | helical | . . . |
| Myxovirus | 80–200 | + | C | + | helical | . . . |
| DNA Viruses | | | | | | |
| Papovavirus | 40–55 | — | N | — | cubic | 42 |
| Adenovirus | 70–85 | — | N | — | cubic | 252 |
| Herpesvirus | 120–180 | + | N | + | cubic | 162 |
| Poxvirus | 150–300 | + or — | C | + | helical † | . . . |

Modified from Green, M. Major Groups of Animal Viruses. *In* Viral and Rickettsial Diseases of Man. Horsfall, F. L., and Tamm, I. (eds.). J. B. Lippincott Co., Philadelphia, 1965.

* C = Cytoplasm
N = Nucleus

† Poxviruses are structurally complex and the nature of the capsid is speculative.

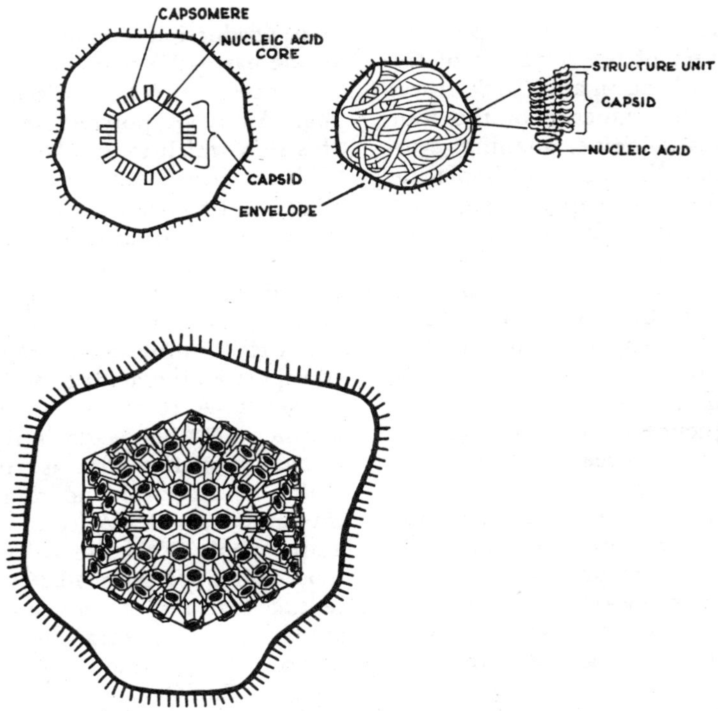


FIG. 40.1—Structural characteristics of animal viruses. **Top left:** Schematic cross-sectional diagram of an icosahedral virus with an envelope. **Top right:** Diagram of a helical virus showing the helical arrangement of the capsid and enclosed nucleic acid. **Bottom:** Three-dimensional appearance of an enveloped icosahedral virus (herpesvirus) showing the surface arrangement of the hollow, hexagonal-shaped capsomeres. (Adapted from diagrams by R. W. Horne. Sci. Amer. 208:48, 1963.)

tains virus-specific antigens against which virus-neutralizing antibodies are directed.

## FUNCTIONAL CHEMISTRY OF VIRUSES

The protein coat of a virus (capsid) serves as a protective container for the viral nucleic acid which is the functionally infectious component of the virion. It has been demonstrated with many viruses that cells may be infected with the viral nucleic acid alone. Nucleic acids from poliovirus will infect a broad spectrum of cell types from many different animal species, while the intact virion will infect only cells derived from primates. In this case, infectivity is dependent on the breakdown of the protein capsid by lipoprotein receptors which are present in primate cells but absent in nonprimate cells. This relationship is one explanation of natural resistance to various viruses.

Since viral nucleic acid alone can infect cells, it must contain the genetic information for at least three types of macromolecular components: viral nucleic acid, viral structural subcomponents, and enzymes which must be induced in the infected cell and play an essential role in virus replication.

## BIOCHEMICAL AND CELLULAR BACKGROUND

The basic concepts upon which all modern biology is based concern the genetic information for normal cellular components. After the discovery of the structure of the DNA molecule by Watson and Crick, it was postulated that the sequence of the four nitrogenous bases (adenine, guanine, cytosine, and thymine) in the DNA molecule must be aligned in some specific sequence and that the language or code must contain enough sequence patterns or "words" to provide at least one word for each of 20 amino acids. The four nitrogenous bases in RNA (adenine, guanine, cytosine, and uracil) provide the letters of the words. It was later determined that the code words do consist of sequences of three nitrogenous bases or multiples of three. The existence of a code was proved by demonstrating a definite association between a nitrogenous base sequence and the incorporation of a specific amino acid into protein. The first major breakthrough was made in 1961 when workers showed that when polyuridylic messenger RNA was added to the protein-synthesizing system of *E. coli,* a protein containing only the amino acid phenylalanine was obtained. This proved that only uracil was necessary in the code word for phenylalanine and that the triplet sequence must therefore be UUU. This was the first code word, and other discoveries followed rapidly.

The sequence of events leading to protein production include the transcription of the particular sequence of the DNA base to a messenger RNA molecule by base pairing. An RNA polymerase is required for this step which takes place in the nucleus. This messenger RNA passes into the cytoplasm and attaches to the ribosomes. Many ribosomes are attached to a messenger RNA strand. This ribosome cluster is called a polyribosome. In the cytoplasm the amino acids are activated with ATP and then react with transfer-RNA molecules which transport amino acids to the ribosome-messenger RNA complex. Somewhere in the transfer-RNA molecule is the coding site, a base sequence that is specific for the amino acid carried and complementary to the messenger RNA code word for that amino acid. This site is probably in the loop region. Figure 40.2 presents the essential features of this process. For example, an alanine-transfer RNA complex is shown to have the bases GGC at the coding site. The GGC is complementary to the CCG of the ribosomal messenger RNA, which is now located at the "active site" of the ribosomes, and binding occurs. The messenger RNA moves along the ribosome and brings the next code word to the active site, UGA. This is complementary to the coding site for methionine-transfer RNA and it attaches next, followed in a similar

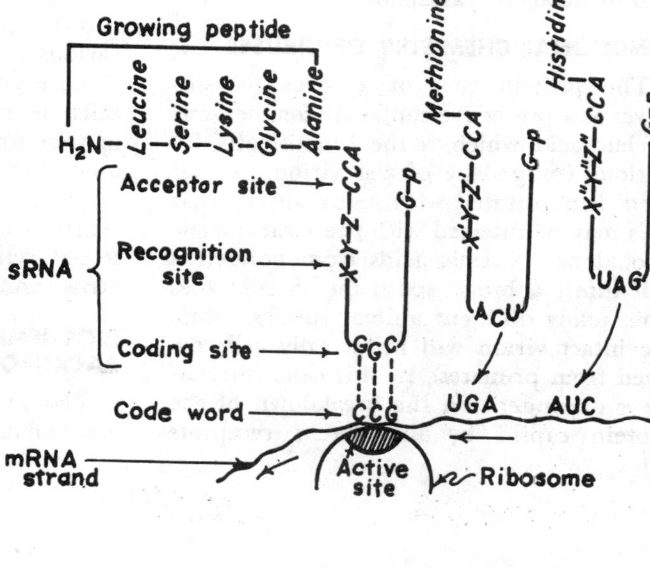


FIG. 40.2—Scheme of protein synthesis. The messenger RNA (m-RNA) strand contains information in the form of particular base sequences (code words). The coding site of the transfer RNA (s-RNA) attaches to the complementary site (code word) on the m-RNA strand. Amino acids which are transported to the ribosome site by specific s-RNA's are then enzymatically released and polymerized into peptide chains. (Courtesy Brotman and McGill. Proc. Mayo Clin. 39:777, 1964.)

manner by histidine. Using their stored energy, the amino acids combine by peptide linkage. The polypeptide chain thus formed is freed from the ribosome, and the transfer RNA dissociates, completing the cycle: DNA has dictated the specific sequence of combination of amino acids into protein.

## VIRUS REPLICATION

The sequential events in viral multiplication are intimately associated with cellular functions. In order for a successful virus infection to occur, a series of events must take place which include: (1) virus attachment, (2) penetration and release of the nucleic acid, (3) viral nucleic acid replication and coding of virus-specific products, (4) assembly and maturation of virus particles, and (5) virus release. Table 40.2 summarizes the events in viral replication according to site of viral synthesis, role of cellular membranes and type of virus release.

Attachment of virus particles to cells is initially an electrostatic phenomenon as evidenced by the requirements for divalent cations. Virus particles and cell surfaces have net negative charges. The function of cations is most probably to reduce the mutual electrostatic repulsion between virus and cell. After the initial electrostatic union of virus with the cell surface, the virus associates with a specific receptor which may be a protein or a lipoprotein. A receptor has a specific electrostatic charge arrangement complementary to that of the virus, which results in the weakening of the virus capsid and the eventual release of the nucleic acid. The ability of the cell receptor to disrupt the virus capsid is most important in the initiation of virus infections. For example, it has been demonstrated with poliovirus that nonprimate cells which lack a lipoprotein receptor are unable to break down the capsid of the virus, whereas RNA extracted from poliovirus will infect these cells. It has also been shown that vaccine strains of poliovirus will not attack cells of the nervous system. This evidence suggests that the capsid

TABLE 40.2

CHARACTERISTICS OF VIRAL MULTIPLICATION

| Nucleic acid | Site of Virus Synthesis | | | Roll of Cell Membrane in Maturation | | Virus Release | |
|---|---|---|---|---|---|---|---|
| | Cytoplasm | Nucleus and cytoplasm | Nucleus | Independent | Dependent | Extensive | Slight |
| RNA | Picornavirus<br>Reovirus<br>Arbovirus<br>Myxovirus* Subgroup II | Myxovirus Subgroup I | | Picornavirus<br>Reovirus | Arbovirus<br>Myxovirus I and II | Picornavirus<br>Myxovirus I and II | Reovirus |
| DNA | Poxvirus | | Herpesvirus<br>Papovavirus<br>Adenovirus | Papovavirus<br>Adenovirus<br>Poxvirus | Herpesvirus | Herpesvirus | Papovavirus<br>Adenovirus<br>Poxvirus |

* The myxovirus group is subdivided into two groups. Group I includes influenza A, B, C; fowl plague, and swine influenza. Group II includes mumps, Newcastle disease virus, parainfluenza 1, 2, 3, 4; simian myxovirus, distemper, rinderpest and measles. Composed from tables by Tamm, I. and Eggers, H. J. Biochemistry of Virus Reproduction. Amer. Jour. Med. 38:678, 1965.

structure of the poliovirus vaccine strains is unable to be disoriented by receptors on nerve cells, and most probably is related to configurational differences in the capsid of the vaccine strains.

## PENETRATION

Available evidence indicates that upon attachment to host cells animal viruses are transferred intact, with their nucleic acid component protected, into phagocytic vacuoles. This transfer into the cell is an active, unspecific, temperature-dependent process which suggests that the virus plays a passive role in penetration. It is during this time of engulfment, called *pinocytosis,* that the virus is being uncoated by capsid breakdown. There is good evidence that each type of virus, once it has been engulfed by pinocytosis, reacts with the cell in a particular way. A good example is provided by vaccinia virus—a representative of the poxvirus group. The DNA of this virus is released in a three-stage process which involves uptake of intact virus, breakdown of an outer coat which enables the DNA-containing core to enter the cytoplasm, and separation of the DNA from the core. Disruption of viral capsids within pinocytotic vesicles is also indicated for myxoviruses and reoviruses in addition to picornaviruses and poxviruses. Since herpesviruses, adenoviruses, and papovaviruses replicate in the nucleus, transfer of the nucleic acid to the nucleus is required for infection. It has been shown that virus particles of adenovirus Type 7 penetrate into the nucleus of the cells without rupture of their capsid, indicating that release of the viral DNA must occur in the vicinity of the nucleus or possibly within the nucleus.

## NUCLEIC ACID REPLICATION

After the release of the viral nucleic acid from the viral capsid the biosynthetic events involved in the reproduction of the virus commence. These events in general follow a predictable pattern:

(1) Viral DNA or RNA serves as a template for the production of many nucleic acid molecules in reactions catalyzed by DNA polymerase or RNA synthetase—a viral-induced enzyme.

(2) "Viral messenger RNA" is synthesized in a reaction catalyzed by RNA polymerase, using viral DNA (from DNA viruses) as a template; the viral RNA from certain RNA viruses can serve directly as messenger RNA.

(3) Viral messenger RNA from both DNA- and RNA-containing viruses acts as a template for the synthesis of (a) viral protein structure units which eventually form capsomeres, and (b) enzymes involved in virus replication.

The entire replication scheme is dependent upon a viable cell, and generally follows the normal pattern of cellular nucleic acid metabolism, i.e., the viral messenger RNA acts like normal cellular RNA in that it must associate with ribosomes in order to produce viral specific components and enzymes needed for their synthesis, assembly, and maturation.

The final step in the multiplication cycle involves the packing together of the viral protein subunits and the nucleic acid molecule (in the case of simple nucleocapsids) by means of noncovalent bonds to form the mature virus particle. The exact mechanism of this process has not been established, but it is likely that the viral protein subunits coalesce by a process of self-assembly. The self-assembly process is a natural result of the uniformity of viral subunits and their identical bonding sites. These features lead automatically to highly symmetric, minimum-energy structures for which no external or guiding principle is necessary to account for the economy, efficiency, and simplicity of these designs. Self-assembly has been demonstrated in vitro with tobacco mosaic virus which had been degraded into its protein and nucleic acid components and then reassembled into fully infectious virus.

This scheme implies that virus capsids may not necessarily enclose their nucleic acid component. Electron microscopy and density gradient centrifugation studies show clearly that many particles in an infectious preparation have empty capsids or incomplete components of nucleic acids. Such particles are often called *incomplete* virus forms.

The mechanism of assembly of helical viruses such as myxoviruses, arboviruses, and possibly poxviruses is not well defined, but most probably a self-assembly process is involved. Viruses which have outer envelopes (myxoviruses, arboviruses, herpesviruses) mature at a cell membrane site. The available evidence indicates that the viral envelope is a portion of the cell membrane intermixed with viral specific protein.

## VIRUS RELEASE

There are marked differences among viruses as to their pattern of release. Herpesvirus particles are enveloped and mature at the nuclear membrane. Their pattern of egress from the nuclear surface may involve the attachment of particles to a membrane with subsequent transport to the exterior of the cell in vesicles or by attachment to the endoplasmic reticulum and transport to the exterior by a dynamic flow mechanism. Adenoviruses, which develop and mature within nuclei, have no such mechanism for release and tend to be retained by the cell. In general, the progeny particles of DNA viruses tend to be retained in the cells even after viral cytopathic effects have occurred, whereas RNA virus progeny are released in considerable numbers. Exceptions to this rule are the reoviruses which contain double-stranded RNA and behave like a DNA virus, and herpesvirus which is released from the cell in large quantities.

## BIOCHEMICAL CHANGES INDUCED IN VIRUS-INFECTED CELLS

The basic question of concern to virologists is in the mechanism of virus-induced alterations leading to cell death or accelerated growth. The ultimate explanation is found in the activities of the various proteins coded by the virus genome. For some of the smallest viruses, such as the picornaviruses where the nucleic acid contains 4,000 to 6,000 nucleotides, there is enough genetic information (assuming a triplet code) to code for 1,500 to 2,000 amino acids, or 10 to 15 proteins. On the other hand, the DNA of vaccinia virus contains approximately 250,000 nucleotide pairs which theoretically could provide the information for 400 to 600 proteins. These proteins may be placed in two general classes, early and late. It appears that most of the synthesis of early proteins is due primarily to the genetic functioning of the parental viral genomes and that the synthesis of the late proteins is due primarily to the functioning of the viral progeny genomes. The early proteins include those which inhibit host-cell DNA replication, host-cell RNA formation, and host-cell protein biosynthesis. Also included are enzymes on the nucleic acid biosynthetic pathway and proteins of viral *inclusion bodies*—areas where virus replication, assembly, and maturation proceed. Late proteins include viral structural proteins, and proteins which function in the repression or "switching off" of the formation of virus-induced enzymes. It is well that the student recall that the synthesis of all these proteins is under the control of viral nucleic acids. By the use of inhibitors such as actinomycin, which prevents the transcription of RNA from a DNA template, and puromycin or para-fluorophenylalanine (PFA), which inhibits translation of the genetic message from messenger RNA into protein, the formation of these various virus-induced proteins may be blocked. Selective blocking of early or late proteins is possible by addition of inhibitors early or late in the replication cycle. These inhibitors have been used to study biochemical alterations of cells by viruses.

## INHIBITION OF HOST CELL RNA SYNTHESIS

In cells infected with certain picornaviruses (mengovirus, or mouse encephalitis virus), host cell RNA synthesis is inhibited almost immediately, whereas in cells infected with poliovirus it is inhibited after approximately two hours. It has been shown that when mengovirus infects mouse-origin L cells, there is a marked decrease in the activity of the cellular enzyme which polymerizes RNA from a DNA template (DNA-dependent RNA polymerase). The inhibition of this enzyme does not occur if viral protein synthesis is inhibited, which suggests that the viral genome codes for the protein causing this inhibition. The mechanism of this inhibition could be by a destruction of the template activity of the host cell DNA or by the interference with the functioning of the DNA-dependent RNA polymerase. The latter alternative is most likely because it has been shown that DNA of infected cells retains its template activity. Furthermore, there is evidence for the synthesis, shortly after infection of L cells with mengovirus, of a basic protein with histone-like properties. This protein was able to inhibit in vitro the activity of the DNA-dependent RNA polymerase. Histones in uninfected cells are thought to exert control over DNA metabolism by a repression mechanism.

## INHIBITION OF HOST CELL PROTEIN SYNTHESIS

According to current concepts most cellular protein is assembled and synthesized on aggregates of ribosomes called polyribosomes. Cellular protein synthesis therefore can be blocked by the interference with the synthesis of messenger RNA and by the interference with the action of messenger RNA. If cellular messenger RNA synthesis is blocked, the rate of decrease of protein synthesis will reflect the rate of decay of messenger RNA formed prior to inhibition. If the action of cellular messenger RNA is blocked, the rate of decrease of protein synthesis could be appreciably faster than the rate of decay of messenger RNA. The half-life of messenger RNA in actinomycin-treated HeLa (human origin) and L cells is approximately three hours. If HeLa cells are infected with poliovirus, the rate of decrease of protein synthesis is faster than in cells treated with actinomycin which stops messenger RNA synthesis. The implication of this finding is that in poliovirus-infected HeLa cells there is a factor (protein) which interferes with the function of messenger RNA. The mechanism by which a virus-associated protein can alter this function is speculative at present. Two possibilities which may explain the mechanism are (1) that structural protein of the virus in high concentrations has a blocking effect, by steric hindrance, on the function of messenger RNA, or (2) that a specific inhibitor protein encoded by the viral genome elicits this effect. Evidence has been presented that the cellular protein inhibitory effect of Newcastle disease virus and poliovirus on HeLa cells is blocked by PFA or puromycin which presumably inhibit the translation of a virus-inhibitor protein from the viral RNA template.

## ENZYME METABOLISM OF VIRUS-INFECTED CELLS

Cellular infection by a virus is often followed by the induction of new enzymes which may catalyze a reaction not found in the uninfected cell, or have an additive effect to a naturally occurring enzyme. There is good evidence that some of the enzymes are induced *de novo* from information encoded by the viral genome; however, rigorous proof utilizing cell-free systems is, at present, lacking. The observed enzyme changes may be a secondary effect from the overall disorganization of the cell brought about by viral development. Particular enzyme activities thought to be regulated by information encoded in the viral genome are discussed below.

## ENZYME CHANGES IN VIRUS-INFECTED CELLS (RNA-SYNTHETASE)

### RNA-dependent RNA Polymerase

In the normal cell all RNA is transcribed directly from cellular DNA. In cells infected with RNA viruses which replicate in the cytoplasm (picornaviruses, arboviruses, and myxoviruses—subgroup II) it is theoretically mandatory that an enzyme be present that catalyzes the polymerization of viral RNA from a cellular RNA template. This enzyme is not found in normal cells but has been found in cells infected with the above-mentioned viruses.

### DNA Polymerase

The function of DNA polymerase in the normal cell is to catalyze the polymerization of nucleotides on a cellular DNA template. Increased levels of this enzyme are seen in cells infected with poxviruses and herpesviruses. If puromycin is added shortly after infection of HeLa cells with vaccinia virus, the expected increase in enzyme is inhibited, suggesting that the information for this enzyme is encoded in the virus genome. Since poxviruses replicate in the cytoplasm where DNA polymerase may not normally exist, the survival advantage of the enzyme being encoded in the viral genome is obvious.

### Thymidine Kinase

Infection of various cells with poxviruses and herpesviruses causes an increase in the levels of thymidine kinase. The exact function of thymidine kinase in the normal cell at this writing is not known. It may phosphorylate the free deoxyribonucleoside (thymine dexoyribose) to a usable DNA precursor. The end result may be the reduction of free thymidine which in some way controls the enzymes involved in DNA synthesis. Whatever its exact function may be, the survival advantage associated with increased levels of thymidine kinase is not large in that cellular mutants lacking the enzyme multiply satisfactorily and viral mutants not inducing the enzyme multiply to good titer in cells lacking the enzyme.

An interesting facet with thymidine kinase induced by vaccinia virus is that it is subject to a control mechanism. Normally, in infected cells, enzyme production is switched off at ten hours. The switch-off function can be inhibited if actinomycin or puromycin are added after enzyme induction and before the normal control mechanism is effective. In this case there is a 40-fold increase of the enzyme. This suggests that the control mechanism is caused by a protein coded for by a messenger RNA transcribed from viral DNA molecules. The nature of the protein causing the switch-off mechanism is not presently known.

### Arginase

Rabbit papilloma virus is able to induce high levels of arginine in squamous epithelium—a tissue which normally contains very little arginine. The induced enzyme differs immunologically and physicochemically from the normal enzyme and apparently is released from normal cellular control mechanisms. It is speculated that the net effect is the depletion of cellular arginine which results in reducing the amount of arginine-rich histones synthesized. Since histones are thought to be largely instrumental in regulating normal cellular DNA synthetic activity, their absence could be related to the increased cellular growth rate which follows infection with this virus.

## CHANGES IN STRUCTURAL PROTEIN

In many cases examination of virus-infected cells by either light or electron microscopy reveals areas of virus multiplication and maturation referred to as inclusions or "factories." These inclusions may be large (poxviruses) or small (picornaviruses) and may be limited by a membrane. The virus may code for the membrane as well as for the matrix which is structurally different from the surrounding cytoplasm. New proteins are frequently associated with tumors induced by viruses. Such proteins can also be detected in cells which have been transformed to cancerous cells in vitro by oncogenic viruses. They are detected by complement fixation, fluorescent antibody labeling, and graft rejection. These proteins are most probably under the control of the viral genome, but the possibility remains that they are cellular-response products activated as a result of virus infection. However, it is impossible to associate the tumor antigen with any phase of the process of malignant transformation. One hypothesis which has been presented is that these new proteins alter the surface of cells, resulting in the loss of *contact inhibition*—a phenomenon whereby normal cells in vitro stop dividing when in contact with one another. When oncogenic viruses are added to normal susceptible cells, the infected cell undergoes a morphological transformation which is associated with an accelerated growth, loss of mitotic inhibition, multilayered growth, and chromosomal aberrations.

## FACTORS INFLUENCING VIRUS MULTIPLICATION

Whether or not a virus is capable of infecting a cell depends on many factors. In many virus-cell systems, one infectious unit is usually associated with the presence of from $10^3$ to $10^5$ noninfectious virus particles. This low ratio may be associated with the inefficient uncoating of virus particles and the subsequent degradation of viral nucleic acid by cellular nucleases. An exception is provided by vaccinia virus where nearly every virus particle is capable of infecting a cell.

In some virus-cell systems, blocks in viral development occur after the viral genome has already started to function. For example, herpes simplex virus infects dog kidney cells with the development of cytopathic effects, inhibition of cell division, synthesis of viral antigen, but with negligible synthesis of viral DNA and progeny virus. A reason for this may be related to the failure of the viral DNA to replicate in dog kidney cells, for the virus replicates normally in many other cells. It is possible that the viral DNA is acted upon by a cellular nuclease or that sufficient DNA polymerase is not present for replication.

Another interesting example of abortive infections is provided by the influenza-HeLa cell system. Influenza virus can infect these cells with the production of the nucleoprotein antigen and a hemagglutin but with no yield of infectious particles. It is likely that the viral genome fails to code for a product necessary for viral maturation.

Elevated temperatures often affect expression of the host genome. At 40°C., poliovirus will inhibit cellular RNA synthesis, but viral RNA fails to replicate and no viral progeny are produced. It has been suggested that the monomer forms of the virus-induced RNA-dependent RNA polymerase fail to polymerize at this temperature. This phenomenon may well be associated with recovery from virus infections where body temperature elevations are produced.

Many particles in a virus population have incomplete virus genomes. Influenza viruses provide outstanding examples of this. Cells infected with such particles produce nucleoprotein, hemagglutinin, but no mature virus. By density gradient centrifugation studies, such particles are found to be less buoyant than complete particles, suggesting a deletion of a portion of the RNA helix.

## VIRAL INTERFERENCE

The phenomena of virus interference has been demonstrated in vitro and in vivo between related and unrelated viruses. The effect is generally demonstrated by infecting cells with a virus, followed by the addition of a second virus. Viral interference is demonstrated when the second virus either fails to replicate or is greatly inhibited. It is becoming increasingly apparent that various mechanisms of virus interference exist. In general, these can be categorized into two groups: (1) interference mediated by a virus-induced cellular protein called *interferon,* and (2) interference which apparently is noninterferon mediated, but is related to the presence in the cell of the virus or virus-related components.

Interferons are approximately 20,000 molecular weight proteins produced by cells in response to infection by various viruses which act as inducing agents. The genetic information for interferon production apparently resides in the host cell genome. Viral nucleic acids, bacterial nucleic acids, whole bacteria, and endotoxins stimulate cell cultures to produce interferon-like substances, possibly by the derepression of a normally repressed segment of cellular DNA. Interferons are not virus specific, but they exhibit strict cell specificity; that is, they are effective in inhibiting viruses in cells of the same animal species in which they were produced. For example, chicken fibroblast cell interferon is inactive in mouse cells but is inhibitory for viruses grown in chicken fibroblast cell cultures. Many theories relative to the mechanism of action of interferon have been proposed and rejected. There seems to be no doubt that its function as an inhibitor is related to a very early step in the replication of the virus genome. Evidence available suggests that interferon blocks the translation of the viral genome since early functions of virus-induced specific proteins are blocked. The basic mechanism, however, remains speculative. The finding that interferon does not bind to naked viral RNA nor reduce its infectivity suggests that the inhibitory action takes place at a cellular site. There is evidence that it prevents the viral RNA from associating with ribosomes to form polyribosomes, possibly through a steric hindrance mechanism. The role of interferon in recovery from viral diseases is being investigated. A promising avenue of investigation in virus disease research is the induction of circulating interferon by non-virulent viruses or defined chemical substances to bolster natural host defenses.

Noninterferon-mediated interference is differentiated from interferon-mediated interference in that the presence of a replicating genome and fully mature virus is required. An example of this type of interference is that between noncytopathic strains of bovine virus diarrhea virus and cytopathic strains of bovine virus diarrhea or vesicular stomatis virus. Another example of this type of interference is between the noncytopathic rubella virus and Newcastle disease virus. The basic mechanism for this *intrinsic interference* is speculative, but it may be related to competition for replicative sites within the cellular matrix, or to a failure of the second virus to absorb due to changes in cellular receptor sites induced by the interfering virus.

## GENETICS OF VIRUSES

A constant feature of animal virology is the observed variation among strains of viruses. With appropriate selective conditions, viral mutants can easily be obtained. Properties of virus strains which may vary are many and include variations in virulence, hemagglutinability, antigenicity, resistance to heat, and resistance to chemical inhibitors. There is no doubt that these variations are a result of alterations of the viral genome which result in various viral end-product differences. Modern biologists accept the principle of mutation and selection without reservation. There are several possibilities explaining virus variation at the genetic level. A segment of a viral genome could be *translocated;* i.e., exchange positions with another segment, disturbing the nucleotide sequence and resulting in a difference of one or more virus-related proteins. Similarly, a nucleotide segment could be completely *deleted*, or *inverted* where an end of a broken segment would be joined to the normal terminus of the segment. Purine and pyrimidine bases may exchange positions with other purines and pyrimidines respectively. This is called *transition*. When a purine base substitutes for a pyrimidine base or vice versa, the process is called *transversion*. It is likely that in an unselected population of viruses numerous mutant forms exist which can be detected only by careful selection procedures. Most natural mutants probably occur from "mistakes" in virus nucleic acid replication. Mutant forms can be induced by exposure to UV light and various oxidants such as nitrogen mustard.

*Genetic recombination* has proved to be a powerful tool in the study of animal virus genetics, with special reference to myxoviruses. By multiple infection of cells with two virus strains, each having at least two characteristics distinct from one another, viral progeny will be produced which inherit characteristics of both parental viruses. Frequencies of recombination can be calculated and genetic maps can be constructed.

The importance of virus variation in medical virology is great. Vaccine strains of many viruses differ in essential properties from wild virulent strains. The failure of poliovirus vaccine strains to adsorb to neuronal cells must be a function of a difference of the capsid protein and ultimately of the nucleotide sequence. Conversely, virulent strains have the capability of adsorbing to and penetrating neuronal tissues.

The epidemiological significance of antigenic variation in influenza viruses is well established. A population which is immune to a predominant serotype of virus will select out and be susceptible to antigenic mutants which are no longer neutralized by antiserum to the parental type. This phenomenon has been termed *antigenic drift.* Its existence in viruses other than influenza has been suggested to explain recurrent infections with a particular virus. The origin of new serotypes which are refractory to neutralization by antiserum produced against parental types could come about by virus recombination in vivo.

## ALTERATION IN CELL STRUCTURE AND DEATH OF CELLS

Many different kinds of fine structural changes in cells are known to be induced by viral infections, but the most common among them involved formation of membrane complexes, or extensive networks of cisternae. Infections by polioviruses and other small RNA viruses elicit this type of response. Membranous lamellar formations are induced by herpesviruses, but a large variety of inorganic toxic agents (silica, dyes) are capable of inducing similar changes. The ultimate reason for such changes is the biochemical modification of cellular structures leading to altered function. It seems that the end result of the structural changes is an attempt to segregate and dispose of toxic materials. In most cases this response is inadequate because the cells die.

Cell death is related to the alterations of intermediary metabolism induced in infected cells. These changes include shutoff of RNA, DNA, and protein metabolism. The basic question referrable to how these functions are altered is, at this time, speculative. Both "early" proteins and "late" proteins (structural proteins) have been incriminated. Good evidence has been presented indicating that the structural proteins of adenoviruses inhibit cellular DNA, RNA, and subsequent protein production by binding to host cell DNA, and thus inhibiting the function of DNA-dependent RNA polymerase in the transcription of messenger RNA. It is probable that many classes of essential intermediates react with virus-induced proteins, and by steric interference inhibit their normal function.

Many viruses will infect cells without inducing cell death. Certainly it is not advantageous for the virus to kill its host, and a certain amount of variation in virulence capabilities of strains of viruses is expected. Ultimately, the basic reason why viruses do not kill cells is that viral metabolism and cellular metabolism are noncompetitive. Avirulent strains most probably lack the genetic information for various inhibitors, and their viral structural proteins are not toxic to the host cell, or never accumulate to toxic levels within the cell.

Many viruses induce cellular proliferation and tumor formation. Both DNA viruses (adenovirus, papovavirus) and RNA viruses (myxovirus) have been incriminated. The biology of viral oncogenesis is interesting, especially in regard to the "masking" of the virus. In many instances virus cannot be recovered from tumors originally induced by viral inoculation. Tumors induced by Rous sarcoma virus (RSV), an RNA virus, provide a good example of this phenomenon. There are two reasons why infective virus cannot be reisolated from such tumors. In one case, new antigens associated with virus infections induce a delayed hypersensitivity reaction, resulting in the sensitization of lymphocytes which then destroy virus-containing transformed cells, which leads eventually to the regression of the tumor. This finding suggests an immunological approach to the treatment of cancer. The second reason why virus may not be isolated from induced tumors is that RSV virus is defective; that is, by itself it lacks the information which is responsible for its maturation and release. It was determined that RSV is almost always associated with an antigenically related helper virus—Rous associated virus (RAV)—which provides the information required for maturation and release of RSV. RSV will by itself induce cellular transformation and tumor induction, but no complete mature virus is produced without the help of RAV.

Similarly, recovery frequencies of DNA viruses from viral-induced tumors are low. Although virus antigens are associated with transformed cells, it has been shown that the virus particle cannot be detected by routine isolation procedures or even by electron microscopy. Recent work with DNA hybridization has indicated that the DNA tumorigenic adenoviruses have a high degree of complementarity with the DNA of cells. This finding suggests that a segment of viral DNA, probably no more than .0001 to .00001 per cent of total cellular DNA, is incorporated *into* the nucleotide chain of the host cell DNA, and subsequently replicates along with cell DNA. It has been suggested that the segment of viral DNA may act as a repressor to cellular DNA, and also code for proteins related to cell transformation.

Immunological tolerance to various tumor-inducing viruses plays a critical role in tumor induction. Nontolerant individuals, upon virus inoculation, will not develop tumors, while tolerant individuals will.

## REFERENCES


Beijerinck, M. W. Ueber ein Contagium vivum fluidum als Urasache der Fleckenkrankheit der Tabaksblatter. Verh. Akad. Wetensch. Amsterdam, II, 6:1–21, 1898.

Berger, E., and Melnick, D. L. (eds.). Progress in Medical Virology. Vols. I–VII. S. Karger, New York, 1959–1965.

Brotman, M., and McGill, D. B. Protein Biosynthesis and the Genetic Code. Mayo Clin. Proc. 39:777, 1964.

Cold Spring Harbor Symposia on Quantitative Biology. Vol. XXVII. The Biological Laboratory, Cold Spring Harbor, L.I., New York, 1962.

Enders, J. F., *et al.* Cultivation of the Lansing Strain of Poliomyelitis Virus in Cultures of Various Human Embryonic Tissues. Science 109:85, 1949.

Fraenkel-Conrat, H. Design and Function at the Threshold of Life: The Viruses. Academic Press, New York, 1962.

Horsfall, F. L., and Tamm, I. Viral and Rickettsial Infections of Man. 4th Ed. J. B. Lippincott, Co., Philadelphia, 1965.

Iwanowski, D. Uber die Mosaikkrankheit der Tabakspflanze. Bull. Acad. Imp. Sci., St. Petersburg, 3:67–70 1892.

Levintow, L. Biochemistry of Virus Replication. Ann. Rev. Biochem. 34:487, 1965.

Loeffler, F., and Frosch, P. Berichte der Kommission zur Erforschung der Maul-und-Klauenseuche bei dem Institut fur Infektionskrankheiten in Berlin. Zentralbl. f. Bakt. Abt. I. Orig. 23:371–91, 1898.

Loewy, A. G., and Siekevitz, P. Cell Structure and Function. Holt, Rinehart, and Winston, New York, 1963.

M. D. Anderson Tumor Institute. Viruses, Nucleic Acids and Cancer. Williams & Wilkins Co., Baltimore, 1963.

Pollard, M. Perspectives in Virology. Vols. I–IV. Harper and Row, New York 1959–1965.

Prier, J. E. Basic Medical Virology. Williams & Wilkins Co., Baltimore, 1966.

Rhodes, A. J., and Van Rooyen, C. E. Textbook of Virology. 4th Ed. Williams & Wilkins Co., 1962.

Ruska, E., and Knoll, M. The Magnetic Concentrating Electromagnet for Fast Electrons. Z. Tech. Physik 12:389, 1931.

Smith, K. M., and Lauffer, M. A. (eds.). Advances in Virus Research. Vols. I–XI. Academic Press, New York, 1953-1965.

Steiner, R. F. The Chemical Foundations of Molecular Biology. D. Van Nostrand Co., Inc., Princeton, 1965.

Tamm, I. Symposium on Viruses. Amer. Jour. Med. 38:649–766, 1965.

Woodruff, A. M., and Goodpasture, E. W. Susceptibility of Chorioallantoic Membrane of Chick Embryos to Infection With Fowl-pox Virus. Amer. Jour. Path. 7:209, 1931.

# 41

# General Aspects of Viral Diseases

**JOHN B. GRATZEK, D.V.M., Ph.D.**
*Department of Veterinary Microbiology and Preventive Medicine*
*University of Georgia*
*Athens, Georgia*

GENERALLY, ALL ASPECTS OF CLINICAL DISease induced by viruses are related to the particular way in which a given virus strain reacts with a population of cells, or various tissues. In the preceding chapter, basic properties of the virus-cell relationship were discussed. Various diseases which are induced by viral infections are nothing more than the result of differences in the ways that viruses react with cells. The basic reactions which may be observed in cell cultures are quite simple compared to the effects of a virus in an animal. There are many factors which play a role in the eventual outcome of a virus infection. Consider, for example, the diverse tissues in the body and the particular way in which the virus would affect their metabolism. Other factors which must be considered are the presence of viral inhibitors in serum and on epithelial surfaces, the presence or absence of specific cell receptors in cells of a particular tissue, the effects of hormonal imbalances induced by stress, the effects of multiple virus infections, or the synergistic effect of virus and bacterial infections, and finally the differences in immunological capabilities of individual host animals. These are but a few of the factors which are involved in the inducton of viral disease, and in part explain the varied and diverse clinical responses observed in groups of animals infected with a pure strain of virulent virus.

## VIRUS RESERVOIRS

Interepidemic survival of viruses is a problem of concern to epidemiologists. Since viruses in general do not survive for long periods outside an animal host, it follows that the interepidemic survival of viruses depends largely on *inapparent infections* of *carrier* animals. In acute generalized virus infections it is usual for virus to be excreted during the acute phase of the disease and sometimes during convalescence, but in many cases excretion ceases soon thereafter. In certain infections, however, virus may continue to be excreted continuously or intermittently from localized sites for months or years. In general, antibody in the serum prevents dissemination of virus within the body, although occasionally virus and antibody may coexist in the blood. Bovine virus diarrhea is an example of a virus disease in which virus within leucocytes is protected by the neutralizing effects of serum antibodies. Virus can be recovered from the leucocytes of apparently normal animals. Similarly, if viral replication is taking place in cells located at an epithelial surface where antibody is not present, virus excretion can be prolonged over extended periods even though specific neutralizing antibodies are present in the blood.

The mode of spread of virus to new hosts

is related to the route by which the virus leaves the body of infected hosts. For example, infectious bovine rhinotracheitis virus generally is excreted in nasal mucus and is most probably spread to the nasal or oral pharyngeal epithelium of uninfected cattle by direct contact. Similarly, strains of this virus which have a wider tissue spectrum could be spread from the nose of infected cattle to the vaginal tract of other cattle by direct contact.

Excretion of virus from generalized infections will depend largely on the target organs where virus replication finally takes place. In a few diseases, virus may be excreted from the saliva because of its localization in the salivary glands. Examples of this type of excretion are provided by rabies, mumps, and salivary gland diseases of animals. Many classes of viruses are excreted in feces and include picornaviruses (enteroviruses), reoviruses (respiratory-enteric viruses), herpesviruses, adenoviruses, and myxoviruses. The exact site of multiplication of these viruses in most cases is unknown, but they could be derived from infected cells of the gastrointestinal epithelium, respiratory tracts, liver, or pancreas. In many generalized viral infections virus is excreted in the urine. In canine distemper and canine hepatitis, virus can be isolated from the urine. In cases of generalized bovine viral diarrhea, virus is present in the leucocytes found in milk and in urine. Whether or not this represents spillover of virus from the circulation is not known. It is interesting to note that virus-like particles have been observed in milk from cows with lymphosarcoma.

Insects may be reservoirs for viral infections. In arbovirus infections, where a viremia is a disease characteristic, the insect vector provides a suitable host for further virus replication as well as a means of introducing virus to a new host.

## PORTALS OF ENTRY

In general the routes of entry are considered to be: (1) all mucous membranes, (2) skin, (3) subcutaneous tissues following wounds, insect bites, or inoculation, and (4) the placenta in intrauterine infections.

The respiratory tract may serve as a portal of entry not only of viruses which produce lesions in that system (influenza, adenoviruses, herpesviruses), but also may serve as a portal of entry for agents producing lesions elsewhere in the body and, in some cases, generalized infections. Examples of this include, among others, canine distemper, smallpox, and infectious bovine rhinotracheitis. In these instances a primary locus of infection may be involved, but the possibility exists that the virus is carried to local lymph nodes by a phagocyte prior to extensive multiplication.

In many cases it is not known whether the virus enters the body via the respiratory tract or mouth. It is becoming increasingly evident that the primary site of virus multiplication in many virus diseases is the tonsil. Examples of virus infections which are thought to gain entry through the tonsils are poliomyelitis, hog cholera, infectious bovine rhinotracheitis, and canine distemper.

Some viruses gain entry by direct implantation to the tissues underlying the skin. Examples of such viruses are rabies pseudorabies, and herpes B virus. Pseudo rabies infections in cattle are transmitted by swine kept on the same premises with cattle. The virus is present on the snouts of the swine and is transmitted to cattle through skin abrasions. Herpes B virus is transmitted to man by monkey bites. The virus is present in the saliva of monkeys undergoing an inapparent infection. The disease is fatal to man.

Arthropod transmission of animal viruses, when it occurs, is usually effected by bloodsucking mosquitoes, sandflies, or ticks. Transmission may be mechanical or may not occur until after the virus has multiplied in the vector. This is called *biological transmission*. Mechanical transmission of viruses by biting insects has been shown to occur in fowl pox, rabbit fibroma, rabbit papilloma, and myxomatosis of rabbits. Bloodsucking lice apparently are able to transmit swine pox. In these instances the virus is present in and around the area of the insect's stylet, but the virus does not multiply and will fail to be transmitted after a period of time.

In biological transmission, the virus multiplies in the arthropod vector and eventually reaches the salivary glands of its host where it can be transmitted at the time of stylet penetration. After initial infection of the vector, there is a time during which it is unable to transmit the virus, which roughly corresponds to the time it takes for the virus to reach the salivary glands. Virus may be transmitted during the entire life of the insect. Arbovirus (arthropod-borne) viruses are transmitted in this way.

Viruses may enter fetuses *in utero* via the placenta and may cause death and subsequent abortion, or in some cases induce anatomical or immunological anomalies. It has been suggested that mice infected *in utero* with lymphocytic choriomeningitis virus fail to develop antibodies to this virus through a tolerance mechanism and remain virus carriers throughout their lives. This mechanism may be responsible for persistent carriers of equine infectious anemia, and possibly for bovine virus diarrhea.

## VIRUS EXTENSION WITHIN THE HOST

After the virus has entered the host, the spread of the virus is determined by the nature of the virus and the way in which it reacts with various cells of the host. These considerations have been discussed in the preceding chapter and have been shown to be extremely variable. A virus may not invade the host tissues much beyond the point of entry in an animal that is naturally insusceptible or in one which has acquired immunity. In a susceptible host the extension and spread of the virus to various tissues in the body are quite variable among the main groups of viruses as well as among members of the same group. A virus infection may produce clinical signs by local multiplication and limited extension as in the case of warts. It may only spread along mucous membranes as in influenza, or to deeper tissues and distant organs by lymph and blood vessel pathways.

Local extension of viruses after entry into the host may be facilitated by the presence of intracellular bridges, or direct cell-to-cell spread by syncytium formation. A classical example of local extension is afforded by herpesvirus (coldsore) infections in man. The virus apparently exists intracellularly and is able to extend itself without being exposed to specific neutralizing antibodies. One theory relating to the mechanism of this survival is that infected cells are able to fuse their plasma membranes with those of uninfected cells, which results in virus extension and provides continuous protection from neutralizing antibody. The result of cell fusion is a multinucleate cell called a syncytium.

Many respiratory virus infections, such as those caused by the influenza group, are spread by extension over mucosal surfaces and never penetrate deeply into underlying tissues. It has been shown that many viruses which do not penetrate have optimal growth at temperatures lower than normal body temperatures. This would explain why such viruses propagate at epithelial surfaces where temperatures are lower. The failure of these viruses to grow at higher temperatures is probably related to a failure of viral-induced enzyme monomers to polymerize. It is most likely that virus is spread by mucus flow and ciliary action. Many viruses which infect respiratory epithelium have a surface enzyme, *neuraminidase,* which is capable of digesting the protective layer of mucus overlaying the cells.

In many generalized virus infections, the symptomatic phase of illness is associated with involvement of organs and tissue at a distance from the portal of entry, for example, the liver in canine hepatitis, the intestine in bovine virus diarrhea, and various organs in hog cholera. The localization and multiplication of virus in these sites must follow dissemination of virus by the blood stream. It would appear that virus may gain entry to the circulation in several ways: (a) by lymph pathways via the thoracic duct, (b) within leucocytes passing from local sites of virus multiplication into blood capillaries, or (c) from direct involvement of the vascular epithelium near the site of initial entry.

It appears that many viruses which produce generalized infections gain access to the blood via the thoracic duct. In general the following sequence of events would apply to many of these infections: Viruses infecting the animal by the oral or respiratory route initially replicate in the region of the nasopharynx, specifically the tonsils in poliomyelitis, hog cholera, infectious bovine rhinotracheitis, and many others. The viruses then pass to lymph nodes draining this site as free particles in the lymph, but most probably they are carried via leucocytes to these nodes in which they replicate. After multiplication of viruses in these lymphatic tissues, the viruses pass into the circulation as free particles and within leucocytes. The extent of viremia at this time may be so minimal as to preclude detection of the virus by isolation attempts. This virus is rapidly removed from the circulation by cells of the reticuloendothelial system, including those in the spleen and in the sinuses of the lymph nodes. Multiplication proceeds in these secondary sites and most probably accounts for the leucopenia and primary temperature response observed in many virus infections. After the virus multiplies in these tissues there is a secondary viremia which corresponds to the onset of illness and may be sufficiently extensive to be detected by virus isolation. Virus at this time can be found free or in leucocytes. Undoubtedly, leucocytes serve to carry viable virus to many and diverse sites within the body; whether or not the virus is capable of replicating at these sites will be dependent on basic mechanisms considered previously. This second wave of virus replication is usually accompanied by a second temperature elevation. The viruses of bovine virus diarrhea and infectious bovine rhinotracheitis may be found in leucocytes. Virus diarrhea virus has been isolated from leucocytes in the milk, but apparently not from the fluid portion. Infectious bovine rhinotracheitis virus can be isolated from leucocytes and it is most likely that virus is carried to various target organs by these cells and is responsible for the generalization and various syndromes frequently observed with this virus.

## LOCALIZATION OF VIRUS IN TARGET ORGANS

In generalized virus infections, dissemination usually occurs via the blood stream. From the blood the virus localizes with subsequent multiplication in target tissues or organs, damage to which will determine the clinical picture of the disease. The factors which determine this localization are complex and inevitably related to basic virus-cell interactions. These will be determined by host variation and strain variation and include among others: temperature limitations, inhibitor susceptibility, interactions with cell receptors, production and sensitivity to interferon, stability of viral DNA within cells of various tissues, and the ability to form complete virus in various cells.

Specific examples of thermal limitations are provided by the poxviruses and some myxoviruses. Many poxviruses will not grow in the chick chorioallantosis at a temperature of 39°C. or higher. Localization in the skin after the rise in temperature in human smallpox and animal pox diseases might be a consequence of the increased internal body temperature at this time. Indeed the distribution of poxvirus lesions of swine would suggest that a thermal factor is operative, i.e., lesions are usually restricted to the belly region and the natural folds of the body. Smallpox lesions in man, on the other hand, tend to be more profuse on the extremities and on the extensor aspects of the limbs rather than the flexor aspects where warmer conditions might be expected. It has been previously suggested that the basic reason for the failure of the virus to propagate at higher temperatures may be related to the failure of induced enzymes to be polymerized from monomer forms. The same mechanism may explain why various myxoviruses fail to penetrate into deeper tissues.

Spread of viruses to the central nervous system may be either via the blood stream or by spread along nerve trunks. Many systemic virus infections occasionally involve the central nervous system. Picornavirus infections (poliovirus, Teschen disease of swine), canine distemper, and infectious bovine rhinotracheitis virus may be cited as examples. In most virus encephalitides there is no evidence of passage of virus by nervous pathways to the central nervous system. There is usually no specific localization of lesions within the central nervous system, and since viremia is a common feature of these infections, it seems likely that spread to the brain or meninges is secondary to infection of the vascular endothelium of the vessels of the brain.

Certain viruses such as rabies virus and some neurotropic herpesviruses of man (herpesvirus B, herpes zoster) may travel along nerve trunks to the central nervous system. There is overwhelming evidence that these viruses do not migrate within the axon proper, but most likely spread along the nerve by progressively infecting the cells in the connective tissue or Schwann cells. This type of spread would provide an explanation for the long incubation period observed in some cases of rabies.

## HOST RESPONSES TO VIRUS INFECTIONS

During the initial phases of a virus infection, the infected individual may react normally. This period is called the *incubation period* and includes the time of initial infection until symptoms of disease are observed. The clinical symptomatology for any given virus is usually not pathognomonic in that many different viruses induce disease syndromes which are similar. The clinical characteristics of some virus infections are so typical to the eye of a trained clinician as to allow an accurate diagnosis to be made from observation of the patient. In a significant number of instances virus infection is inapparent or "silent" and no outward signs of disease are observed.

The nature and extent of the lesions induced in target organs by a virus is determined by the virus involved and its reaction with individual host cells. Viruses are generally considered to elicit a lymphocytic response, which appears to be proliferative in nature, rather than an exudative response involving neutrophils. The reason for this is most probably related to the fact that viruses can kill cells without producing great amounts of soluble protein products which attract neutrophils (leucotoxin). The mechanism of recovery from virus infections and limitation of virus spread is most complex.

The role of antibodies in recovery from virus infections is not well understood in that many animals may harbor and undergo virus infections in the presence of neutralizing levels of antibody. Mechanisms for this have been previously discussed. Evidence which suggests that antibody may not be the prime factor in virus clearance is provided by the observation that human beings suffering from agammaglobulinemia recover quite normally from virus infections, whereas bacterial infections are generally lethal unless treated. There are various factors at a local site of virus replication which would tend to limit virus replication and spread. These include changes in cell types, many of which are insusceptible to virus attack; pH; inhibitor-containing exudates; increase in local temperature; lowered oxygen tension; and interferon production. It has been shown that various leucocytes are efficient producers of interferon, especially under adverse conditions such as lowered pH, higher temperatures, and lowered oxygen tension. The role of antibodies may be merely to neutralize virus which is free in the blood stream. The plasma cells which often surround areas of virus proliferation probably are producing specific virus-neutralizing antibody and would serve further to localize the spread of virus.

## APPROACHES TO THE CONTROL OF VIRAL DISEASE

### Immunization

Immunization of animals can be effected by the injection of either killed or live viruses which have been modified in some way. The modification process is most generally accomplished by the process of passing a virus in various cell cultures or, in some cases, in animals not normally susceptible to the disease. There are many ways in which a virus becomes modified. Many vaccine strains have a different receptor affinity than wild types. Poliovirus vaccines lack affinity for neuronal tissues while wild strains retain this affinity. Wild strains of yellow fever virus have a marked hepatic cell tropism, whereas the vaccine strain lacks this affinity. Many avirulent vaccine viruses produce more interferon and are more sensitive to it than virulent strains. There are many other factors which control the virulence of a virus that have been mentioned in Chapter 40. With this fundamental knowledge, the selection of avirulent strains can be accomplished with a minimum of manipulation, and the extensive passaging of viruses will eventually be replaced with the careful selection of virus populations following specific treatments designed to allow the replication of avirulent strains. These could include selection for thermal-sensitive mutants, interferon production, ability to induce incomplete forms, and many others.

Modified live-virus vaccines are generally best adapted to the prevention of diseases caused by viruses where few antigenic types exist, where there is a systemic virus infection in the natural disease, and where lifelong immunity following infection is the rule. Examples are smallpox, poliomyelitis, canine distemper, bovine virus diarrhea, and hog cholera. In these cases administration of vaccines induces circulating antibodies which are effective in preventing systemic dissemination of a wild strain. It is probably true that the unattenuated wild strains are capable of replication at epithelial sites of vaccinated animals, but are neutralized if extension into deeper tissues takes place. This superficial replicating virus would serve as a continual antigenic stimulation and most probably explains why serum-neutralizing antibody titers in man and animals remain elevated over periods of time which far surpass their normal half-life. There are some disadvantages to modified live-virus vaccines. They may induce severe responses in a few animals which, for unknown reasons, react as they would to unmodified strains. There may be synergistic effects with virus infections present at the time of vaccination, or preexisting virus infections may interfere with the vaccine virus. Reversion to virulence, while possible, has not been a problem with human and veterinary vaccines. Possibly the greatest disadvantage to the use of live vaccines is for the prevention of virus infections where numerous antigenic wild types (those occurring in nature) exist and where the disease is normally a superficial infection. These diseases generally lend themselves better to the use of killed vaccines. An example is provided by the many different respiratory viruses of man. Transmissible gastroenteritis virus in piglets is an example where circulating antibody will not protect against disease, whereas maternal antibodies in ingested milk will prevent infection. This suggests that antibody must be present at or near the site of virus replication (gastrointestinal epithelium) to neutralize it and prevent disease. It is likely that many enteric virus diseases present the same problem.

### Chemotherapy

The chemotherapeutic approach to the treatment of virus disease is beset with many difficulties. The basic problem concerns the intimate relationship between host-cell and virus metabolism and finding a chemical agent which selectively blocks the virus infection mechanism without altering the host cell. The complexity of this problem is multiplied by the biochemical differences of individual cells in the host and by the vast variety of strains, types, and families of viruses which affect mammals. The use of antiviral drugs would be limited from a clinical viewpoint in that many viruses have already replicated in tissues by the time clinical symptoms are apparent.

Many chemicals have been tested in various cell culture systems for antiviral activities, and many have been shown to be active. However, the vast majority of these chemical agents have a toxic effect in vivo. A group of chemicals which has shown some promise in the treatment of some DNA-virus infections are the halogenated pyrimidines. One such compound, 5-iodo-2′-deoxyuridine (IDU), has been studied extensively in the suppression of superficial corneal lesions in rabbits caused by herpesvirus infections. IDU as a thymidine analog interferes with the utilization of thymidine. IDU is incorporated into viral DNA, producing a fraudulent and presumably nonfunctional DNA. The drug apparently has the same effect on host cells in this respect.

Recovery from virus infection is the result of ill-defined, nonspecific host defense mechanisms and antibody production. It is probable that the nonspecific mechanisms play a greater role in recovery than antibody production. This concept has led immunologists to the idea of bolstering normal host defense mechanisms. Stimulation of interferon production by the administration of interferon-inducing substances such as foreign nucleic acids, certain bacteria, polysaccharides, and lipopolysaccharides has been considered both as a preventative and therapeutic measure.

## REFERENCES

Andrewes, C. H. Viruses of Vertebrates. Williams & Wilkins Co., Baltimore, 1964.

Berger, E., and Melnick, D. L. (eds.). Progress in Medical Virology. Vols. I–VII. S. Karger, New York, 1959–1965.

Burnet, F. M., and Stanley, W. M. The Viruses. Vols. I, II, III. Academic Press, New York, 1959.

Horsfall, F. L., and Tamm, I. Viral and Rickettsial Infections of Man. 4th Ed. J. B. Lippincott Co., Philadelphia, 1965.

M. D. Anderson Tumor Institute. Viruses, Nucleic Acids and Cancer. Williams & Wilkins Co., Baltimore, 1963.

Rhodes, A. J., and Van Rooyen, C. E. Textbook of Virology. 4th Ed. Williams & Wilkins Co., Baltimore, 1962.

Smith, K. M., and Lauffer, M. A. (eds.). Advances in Virus Research. Vols. I–XI. Academic Press, New York, 1953–1965.

Smith, W. (ed.). Mechanisms of Virus Infection. Academic Press, New York, 1963.

# 42

# Methods Used in the Study of Viruses

## DETERMINATION OF SIZE AND MORPHOLOGY

KNOWLEDGE OF THE SIZE AND MORPHOLOGY of viruses has increased as the tools and techniques have been discovered and developed. Scientists in the early part of this century were aware that living agents capable of inciting disease existed that were smaller than objects seen with the light microscope. However, in spite of this limitation, many of the physical properties of the various viruses were determined with remarkable accuracy.

## STAINING OF VIRUSES

A number of techniques for staining elementary bodies and inclusion bodies have been used. (See Van Rooyen and Rhoades, Chapter III.) These techniques are most useful in visualizing elementary bodies of the larger viruses or aggregates of them in infected cells by the light microscope. Such procedures are of no value for smaller viruses which cannot be resolved by the light microscope.

For preparations to be viewed by the electron microscope, phosphotungstate and uranyl sulfate have been used to give contrast to the viruses.

The negative staining technique as described by Brenner and Horne has been particularly useful in bringing out some of the detailed structures of virus elementary bodies. Virus preparations are mixed with 2% phosphotungstic acid and sprayed onto the films to be observed in the electron microscope.

Fluorescent antibody to specific viruses can be added to cell suspensions or tissue sections, and the location of the virus within cells or its presence or absence can be determined with a microscope using ultraviolet light sources. Acridine orange can be used to aid in visualizing aggregates of viruses and to determine whether a virus possesses single- or double-stranded nucleic acid.

## FILTERS AND FILTRATION

Filtration experiments were used by Iwanowski (1892) in his original work which proved the existence of a virus. He used filters having a pore size which retained bacteria, yet an infectious agent passed through into the filtrate. This technique has been used since that time to separate viruses from bacteria and for many years as a criterion for the presence of a virus. If a filtrate proved infectious and no bacteria could be demonstrated, then a virus was presumed to be present. Filters of various porosities were manufactured and by passing a virus through a series of filters having pores of known size, the approximate size of the virus was determined by noting which filter allowed the passage of the virus and which one retained it.

There are several types of filters in use. The molded candle type includes the Berkefeld, Mandler, Selas, and Pasteur-Chamberland filters. These are made of porcelain or diatomaceous earth. Several types of asbestos pads are used, such as the Seitz, Boerner, and Swinney. Collodion and cellulose membranes are also used to advantage in many instances.

### The Berkefeld Filter

This filter is manufactured of diatomaceous earth and is graded into three porosities. The V (viel) grade is coarse and is used for preliminary filtration to remove some bacteria or large particles from a solution. The N (normal) grade is most useful since it retains most bacteria while nearly all viruses will pass through. The W (wenig) grade has very small pores and will retain all bacteria as well as some large viruses.

### The Mandler Filter

This type is also made of diatomaceous earth and is very similar to the Berkefeld. Three grades—preliminary, regular, and fine—are manufactured.

### The Pasteur-Chamberland Filter

This filter is made of porcelain, molded into a candle form, and graded in porosities of $L_1$, coarse grade, to $L_{13}$, the finest grade.

### Selas Filters

These filters are a porcelain product made in seven grades of porosity. They are graded from XF, XFF, No. 10, and No. 01 which are coarse grades to No. 015, No. 02, and No. 03 which retain bacteria.

### Seitz Filters

These filters are asbestos pads manufactured in two grades, K which is coarse and EK which retains bacteria. These pads are held in a metal holder and are discarded after being used once to eliminate cleaning.

### Boerner Filters

These filters are the same as the Seitz except that they are small and are fitted in a small metal receptacle which adapts onto a test tube and are centrifuged in order to force the liquid through them.

### Swinney Filters

These filters consist of a small Seitz pad placed in a metal receptacle which adapts onto a syringe, and the material to be filtered is forced through the pad by positive pressure.

### Collodion Filters

The collodion filter is composed of nitrocellulose. The pore diameter may be varied by the addition of various amounts of alcohols, ether, acetone, and acetic acid. Filters of pore diameter ranging from $3\mu$ to $10m\mu$ can be made. This type of filter has been most useful in determining the size of virus particles.

### Cellulose Filters

Filter membranes of pure cellulose or cellulose derivatives are manufactured in a variety of porosities. Those used in virology are: coarse with the pore diameter $3\mu$ to $0.75\mu$, medium $0.75\mu$ to $0.5\mu$, dense $0.5\mu$ to $0.2\mu$, and very dense below $0.2\mu$.

**Preparation of Filters for Use.** Before a filter is used, it must be clean, sterile, and free from leaks. New filters of the Berkefeld or Mandler type should be washed free of dust by passing distilled water through them from the outside to the inside of the filter and then reversing the flow. One method of testing for leaks is to apply air pressure to the inside of the filter candle while it is submerged in water. The air pressure should be started low and gradually increased. If there are cracks in the candle, air will pass through them on low pressure and the air bubbles will emerge from one spot. An actual test for the retention of small bacteria is sometimes used. A diluted broth culture of *Serratia marcescens* is filtered and the filtrate cultured. This organism is a small gram-negative rod which produces a red pigment. It is also nonpathogenic, so it can be handled easily and detected on cultures of filtrates. Sterilization of filters of the molded candle type is usually accomplished by autoclaving for one-half hour at 121°C. after which they are gradually cooled and allowed to dry.

Sterilization of asbestos pad filters is done by autoclaving the pad assembled in its receptacle for 30 minutes at 121°C.

Collodion filters are sterilized by boiling or by treatment with ultraviolet light.

### Technique of Filtration

The ideal condition of virus filtration is to remove bacteria but to allow the passage of all of the virus present in the solution. This condition is seldom reached.

The efficiency of filtration is dependent upon the following factors:

1. Size of virus to be passed.
2. Amount of virus present.
3. Diameter of the pores of the filter.
4. Electrical charge of the filter.
5. Electrical charge of the virus.
6. Amount of negative or positive pressure applied.
7. Viscosity and pH of the solution.
8. Duration of the filtering operation.

Successful filtration is to a great extent dependent upon knowledge of the properties of the various filters and of the virus to be filtered. Obviously, a filter must be chosen which has pores larger than the virus to be passed into the filtrate. On the other hand, the filter pores must be small enough to withhold bacteria which may be present.

Trouble is often encountered with certain virus-filter combinations because they are of the opposite electrical charge and the virus is adsorbed onto the filter. In this case little or no virus passes into the filtrate unless the concentration of virus is quite high. Filters made of diatomaceous earth are negatively charged while the asbestos pads have a positive charge. Most viruses are negatively charged. The application of negative pressure to the inside of the filter increases the rate of filtration. However, it should be measured by a mercury manometer or other suitable device and not allowed to become excessive, or bacteria may be drawn through a filter which would otherwise withhold them. Ordinarily pressures of more than 5 cm. of mercury should not be used and, if possible, lower pressures are more desirable.

Cleaning of filters after their use varies. If the material being filtered is infectious, the sterilization or disinfection of the filter must precede the cleaning process. Boiling the filter in 2 per cent sodium carbonate is satisfactory. Immersion in 2 per cent phenol is used also. After bactericidal or virucidal treatment, the filter should be washed with a brush and then distilled water used to wash out the pores by reversing the flow on the filter. The asbestos pads are not cleaned but are disinfected and then discarded.

Selas filters can be freed of organic material by firing in a furnace at around 1,200°F. Collodion membranes are more difficult to prepare but in many ways are more satisfactory than the other types because they absorb less virus and do not become clogged as easily.

## CENTRIFUGATION

Centrifugation of virus-containing material may be done for two reasons: to concentrate the virus particles in the process of purification for detailed study and to determine the rate of sedimentation which will aid in estimating the size of the elementary body. If other constants are known, it is possible to calculate the size of a virus particle by its rate of sedimentation.

There are four types of centrifuges which are used in sedimentation of viruses. The *Sharples type* consists of a cylinder which is mounted in a vertical position and is driven by a high-speed electric motor. Fairly large amounts of solution may be passed through this type at speeds up to 50,000 r.p.m.

The *angle centrifuge* is the most efficient and will sediment many of the viruses. The head rotates at an angle of about 28° from the vertical so that any particle will have only a short distance to travel to be deposited on the wall of the tube. A small *air-driven type* is in the form of a turbine which has small vanes which compressed air strikes, propelling the turbine at speeds up to 60,000 r.p.m. Only small amounts of material can be centrifuged in this apparatus.

The *bucket type* is driven directly by an electric motor or a geared motor. The material to be centrifuged is contained in plastic or hard glass test tubes of about 5 ml. capacity. Speeds of 40,000 r.p.m. are possible and will sediment many viruses in 1 hour.

Centrifuges have been modified to advantage in several ways such as the vacuum centrifuge in order to reduce air resistance, refrigeration of the chamber to protect the virus material from excessive heat, and the optical centrifuge in which the progress of sedimentation can be photographed at intervals during the operation.

## MICROSCOPY

### Light Microscope

It is possible to observe the elementary bodies of some viruses under the ordinary light microscope. Techniques have been devised for staining the larger viruses such as the pox group. As with the bacteria, differential staining aids a great deal in distinguishing the virus particles from other small particles seen in tissue preparations. Although it is possible to resolve particles as small as 250 m$\mu$, which is within the range of size of viruses, it is very difficult to identify them with certainty. The practical limit of magnification for the light microscope is in the region of 1,200 to 1,500 diameters.

Dark-field illumination of virus specimens has some advantage over the ordinary application of light microscopy. By employing this technique, the limits of visibility and resolution are increased; however, its use has been limited.

A magnification of $\times$3,200 with good resolution has been obtained by using ultraviolet light. Instruments of this kind have not come into use because direct view of the object is not possible and photographic plates must be used.

### Electron Microscope

The use of electron rays instead of visible light rays has made possible overall magnifications up to $\times$5,000,000 with good definition. Microscopes of this type have been developed since the work of Marton in 1934.

The electron microscope is a very highly specialized instrument requiring considerable technical training and skill to operate. The basic principle of magnification of the electron microscope is similar to the light microscope except that electrons are used in place of light rays and the electron rays are focused by magnetic fields instead of the lens of glass in the light microscope. The source of electrons is a hot filament and they are accelerated by very high voltages of 50 kilovolts or more. This voltage must be controlled to within 1 to 2 volts.

The objects to be observed are placed on a carbon, formvar or collodion membrane which is supported by a small disc of 200-mesh screen. This screen is then placed in a holder which is inserted into the microscope, and high vacuum is pumped in the tube. The electrons pass from the filament through the specimen and are focused on the fluorescent screen below. A shadow appears where the electrons strike an object in the specimen and are scattered so they do not reach the screen.

A process known as "shadow casting" has been used. Before the specimen is placed in the electron microscope, it is placed in a vacuum chamber and a metal, usually gold or chromium, is evaporated by heating it to incandescence so that a very thin layer of the metal coats the surface of particles, such as a virus. The coating on the surface of the object is not uniform since more of the metal is deposited on the side of the particle nearest the source of the metal vapor while very little is deposited on the opposite side. When such objects are observed in the electron microscope a third dimension can be determined.

In addition to viewing viruses on the fluorescent screen of the electron microscope, photographs are usually taken and even more detail may be observed. Also pictures of viruses may be photographically enlarged several times. From such photographs the size may be calculated and the morphology can be observed.

Although the electron microscope is important as a virus research tool, it is not used in routine diagnosis of virus diseases.

## DETERMINATION OF ESSENTIAL LIPIDS

An important characteristic used in the identification and classification of animal viruses is the presence or absence of essential lipids. This is determined by mixing virus preparations with either ether or chloroform. Sufficient ethyl ether is added to the virus preparation to make a 20 per cent solution. The mixture is allowed to stand 18 to 24 hours at 4°C. after which it is poured into a Petri dish and the ether is allowed to evaporate.

To expose a virus to chloroform 0.05 ml. of reagent grade chloroform is added to 1.0 ml. of virus preparation, mixed for 10 minutes at 4°C. The chloroform is removed by centrifugation.

## DETERMINATION OF NUCLEIC ACID TYPE

A common method used to determine which type of nucleic acid a virus possesses is the use of DNA inhibitors such as 5-fluoro-2′-deoxyuridine (FUDR), 5-bromo-2′-deoxyuridine (BUDR), or 5-iodo-2′-deoxyuridine (IUDR). These substances act as specific inhibitors of viral DNA synthesis when added to cell culture medium. If growth of the virus is inhibited it is presumed to contain DNA; if not, it possesses RNA.

## CONCENTRATION AND PURIFICATION OF VIRUSES

In order to study many of the properties of viruses, a purified preparation must be used. One of the problems is to separate the virus elementary bodies from the components of the cells in which the virus has grown. Centrifugation of crude virus-containing material at various speeds will serve to remove much of the extraneous material. By experiment, the speed at which the majority of elementary bodies are sedimented can be determined. Resuspension of the virus in fresh diluent and resedimentation through several cycles will remove much of the unwanted tissue material.

The use of density gradients composed of sucrose or glycerol has enabled the separation of viruses from tissues as well as the separation of different components of certain viruses. The gradient is made by carefully layering fluids of different density one over the other in a centrifuge tube, with the one of greatest density on the bottom. The virus-containing material is placed on top and then the tube is centrifuged at high speed. Depending on their relative density, the virus and the tissue materials placed in the top of the tube will become stratified, each settling in the zone of fluid of equal density. Since plastic tubes are used for this technique, it is possible to use a syringe and needle to draw off the desired layer through the wall of the tube.

Another method of concentration of viruses, hemagglutination-elution, can be applied to those viruses which are attracted to erythrocytes. A large volume of virus-containing fluid and washed erythrocytes from an appropriate source are mixed together. The elementary bodies become attached to the surfaces of the erythrocytes and are carried to the bottom of the tube as it is centrifuged. The virus is allowed to dissociate or elute from the erythrocytes and is then taken up in a small volume of diluent. The erythrocytes are removed by centrifugation while the virus remains in the supernatant fluid.

There are several chemical methods for the purification. Precipitation with cold ethyl alcohol of various concentrations has been used to purify certain viruses. Extraction of tissues or fluids with fluorocarbons such as Genetron and freons has been quite successful in selectively removing viruses in relatively pure form from tissues in which they have been grown.

## CULTIVATION OF VIRUSES

Viruses may be cultivated in three ways: animal inoculation, tissue cultures, and the inoculation of chicken embryos. Some viruses can be successfully propagated by any of the three methods while others can be grown only in the natural host animal.

### Animal Inoculation

Animal inoculation was the first method of virus cultivation and for many years was the only means of virus propagation. This method is not as convenient and is also more expensive than embryo methods. Besides serving to propagate the virus, the inoculation of various animal hosts is important in the identification of an unknown virus. This procedure is used in distinguishing between viruses which produce similar lesions such as foot-and-mouth disease and vesicular stomatitis of cattle. In such cases calves and horses are inoculated. Calves are susceptible to both viruses while horses are insusceptible to foot-and-mouth virus but readily contract vesicular stomatitis.

Rabies diagnosis in some cases must be made by the inoculation of laboratory animals because Negri bodies cannot always be demonstrated in the brain tissue of the infected animal. There are many techniques and routes of animal inoculation used for virus studies. The type of tissue attacked and the animal to be inoculated will determine the method employed.

Viruses which produce encephalitis are usually inoculated intracerebrally, the poxviruses intradermally, and those of the respiratory group intranasally. Examples of other types of inoculation include inoculation into the scarified cornea of a rabbit, scarified epithelium of the mouth and tongue of calves, or the foot pad of the guinea pig.

In poultry, inoculation of live virus vaccines is made into defeathered follicles on the legs, the web of the wing, or in the case of laryngotracheitis vaccine, into the cloacal bursa.

In addition to the above-mentioned special methods of inoculation, the more common routes such as intravenous, subcutaneous, or intramuscular injections are used occasionally.

The materials used for animal inoculation may consist of filtered or unfiltered suspensions of organs or exudates. If the materials are unfiltered, it is important to add antibacterial substances, such as penicillin and streptomycin, to prevent contaminating or associated bacterial agents from becoming established. This is especially important in intracerebral inoculations. Some bacteria which are ordinarily considered nonpathogenic may cause infection when directly introduced into the brain tissue of the living animal.

A general procedure for preparation of inoculum is as follows: the infected tissue or exudate is removed from the animal with sterile instruments and placed in a sterile container. The tissue is cut into small pieces and placed in a sterile mortar. An abrasive such as sterile alundum (90 mesh) is sprinkled over the tissue which is ground to a paste and then suspended in tryptose phosphate broth or other buffered liquid to make a 10 to 20 per cent suspension. Centrifugation at 3,000 r.p.m. for 3 to 5 minutes will clarify the material so that the supernatant can be used in a syringe for injection. After centrifugation the supernatant fluid is transferred to another tube and the antibiotics are added. A period of 15 to 30 minutes incubation at room temperature is allowed before the mixture is injected. However, if the material is collected relatively free of contamination, it can be inoculated immediately into animals and chicken embryos.

### Cultivation of Viruses in Tissue Culture

There are many techniques for the artificial cultivation of viruses. The virus to be grown and the materials available may modify the technique used. Most of the methods employ the following ingredients:

1. Tissue cells—avian or mammalian, embryonic, adult, or neoplastic.
2. Lactalbumin hyrolysate (enzymic).
3. Serum—often necessary to use serum homologous to cells but not in all systems.
4. Balanced salt solution.

Other ingredients such as ascitic fluid,

amniotic fluid, and serum ultrafiltrate are sometimes used. It is possible to cultivate certain tissue cells in a chemically defined medium composed of amino acids, vitamins, glucose, and inorganic salts. The addition of penicillin and streptomycin to control growth of any bacteria present is standard procedure.

The tissue culture techniques which are most often used will be briefly described. For additional details of the procedures, the student is referred to one or more of the reference books listed at the end of this chapter.

It is of utmost importance that the glassware used in cultivating tissue cells be absolutely clean and free from film and toxic substances. The chemicals and the distilled water used must be free from toxic ions. The various manipulations of handling tissues and media should be carried out in a room which is free from dust and air currents. All instruments and other equipment must be sterile and handled in such a manner as to avoid contamination.

**Slide Cultures.** One of the simplest types of tissue culture is the slide culture. This type is recommended for the beginner because the culture can be observed frequently under the microscope and its progress noted. Tissue fragments cut with a sharp knife and no larger than 1 to 2 mm. in diameter are placed on a sterile coverglass and a drop each of heparinized plasma, serum, embryo extract, and balanced salt solution is added. The plasma will clot the entire mixture and thereby stabilize the tissue on the coverglass. A slide which has a deep depression in it is placed over the coverglass so that the plasma clot is in the center of the depression. The coverglass is sealed and held fast to the slide by a thin film of petrolatum applied around the edge of the hollow depression.

After a few hours in the 37°C. incubator, the culture will show evidence of growth (Fig. 42.1). Proliferation and migration of cells will be observed around the edge of the tissue fragment. Growth of the tissue cells will continue for 2 to 3 days, and then a portion of the tissue must be transferred to a fresh medium; if not, the accumulation of waste products of cell metabolism will kill the tissue.

**Flask Cultures.** Various types of flasks have been used to contain cell cultures. Erlenmeyer, Carrel, and Porter flasks are most commonly used. A suspended cell culture is quite easily prepared by dropping small tissue fragments into a flask containing a suitable nutrient medium. Under such conditions the cells do not proliferate to any extent but survive long enough to support

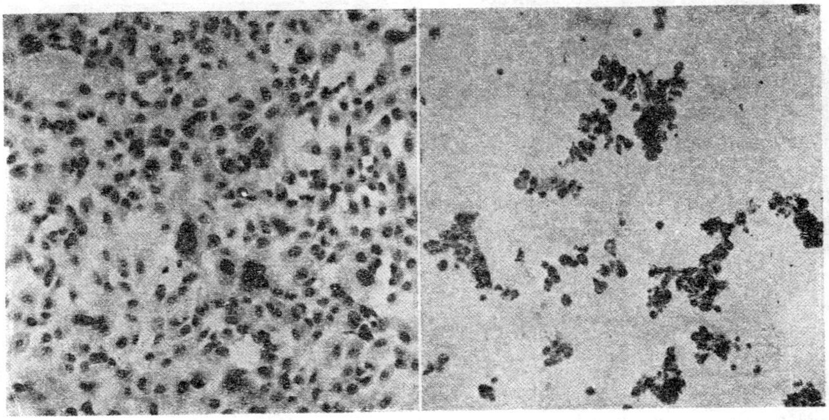

FIG. 42.1—**Left.** Normal growth in tissue culture of human liver cells. **Right.** Same culture showing cytopathic effect after infection with poliomyelitis virus. (Courtesy J. T. Syverton, Univ. Minn.)

virus multiplication. Tissue fragments may be placed in flasks and then embedded in plasma clots if desired.

Another common method of tissue culture is the type in which the cells are grown on the glass surface of the inside of the flask. For this type of culture, trypsinized kidney cells may be used. Preparation of the cells consists of finely mincing the tissue with scissors, followed by treatment with trypsin. The action of the trypsin is to liberate the cells from the minced tissue particles so that uniform suspensions of cells can be prepared. In this way such suspensions can be standardized so that a uniform inoculum is available. The suspended cells are transferred into nutrient fluid contained in flasks. The cells will settle to the bottom and grow in a single layer, forming a sheet of cells which adheres to the glass surface.

**Roller-Tube Cultures.** Tissue cultures may be grown in test tubes which are rotated during incubation. Tissue explants are first placed in the tube and a small amount of plasma or agar is distributed over the inside surface of the tube so that the fragments remain in place. A quantity of nutrient fluid is then added to the tube to fill it approximately 1/10 to 1/8 full. The culture is then placed in a horizontal position in a rotating drum at 37°C. As the tube is rotated 8 to 12 r.p.m., the tissue explants are submerged in the nutrient medium only a portion of the time. Some cells do not grow satisfactorily if they are entirely submerged. Other cells, especially those cultivated through many transfers, will stick to the glass surface and will grow when continuously submerged. In such instances rotation is unnecessary.

**Monolayer Tissue Cultures.** In 1952, Dulbecco devised a method of growth and titration of certain animal viruses which produce a cytopathic effect (Fig. 42.2). Fibroblasts (other cells may be used) obtained from chicken embryos are first grown in a single layer on the glass surface of a flask. The nutrient fluid used for growth of the cells is then replaced with nutrient fluid containing virus. After a short period of incubation to allow attachment of the virus to the cells, the fluid is poured off and replaced with a layer of melted agar. Following an additional period of incubation, areas of necrotic cells

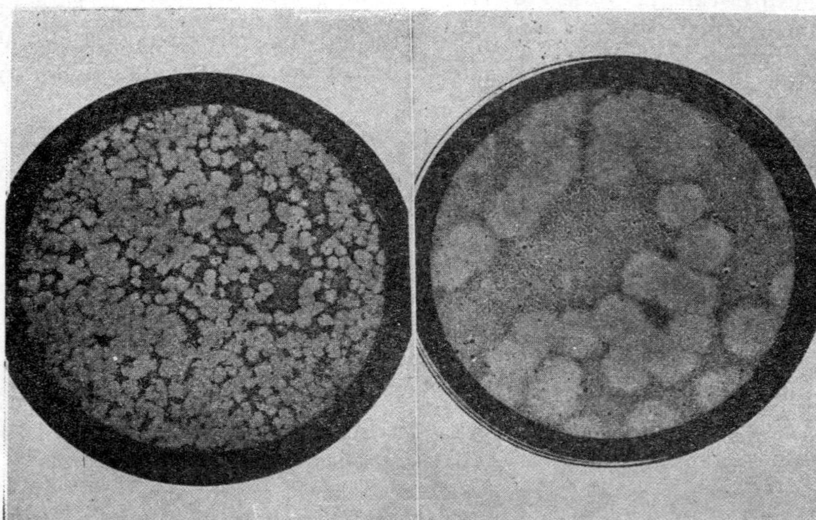

FIG. 42.2—Plaque formation in monolayer cultures of embryonic chick fibroblasts. **Left.** Plaques of Newcastle disease virus. **Right.** Plaques of western equine encephalomyelitis virus. (Courtesy W. W. Kirkham and L. N. Brown.)

will be found which are the result of virus growth in the tissue cells. The addition of a solution of neutral red differentiates the dead from the living cells. If the virus has been sufficiently diluted, these areas of necrosis can be counted to determine the number of elementary bodies present in the original virus inoculum, since it is assumed that each area of necrosis or *plaque* results from one elementary body.

## Virus Propagation in Chicken Embryos

The chicken embryo has been found susceptible to a great many viruses and has become most useful in virus diagnosis, research, and in vaccine production.

Eggs for the purpose of embryo inoculation should be procured from disease-free flocks since some infectious agents may pass from the infected hen into the egg. Antibodies may be present in eggs layed by recovered birds, which will interfere with growth of certain avian viruses. Eggs from flocks in which the fertility rate is high are more satisfactory and economical.

Incubation of the eggs before inoculation is usually at 38° to 39°C. in a regular egg incubator. Humidity should be kept at 60 per cent. The eggs should be turned at least once or preferably twice a day. After inoculation the conditions of incubation may be varied. The temperature of incubation is usually 35° to 37°C. and the eggs are not turned. Incubation after inoculation may be done in an ordinary bacteriological incubator.

Eggs can be held for several days before starting incubation but should be kept at cool temperatures of about 10–12°C.

The length of incubation before inoculation depends upon the type of inoculation to be made and the virus to be cultivated. For example, inoculation into the yolk sac is usually made in 7- to 9-day-old embryos while chorioallantoic inoculation is made on 10- to 13-day embryos. The extreme range for inoculations is from 6- to 15-day embryos.

Before eggs are inoculated, they must be examined to determine that a viable embryo is present. This is done by candling in a darkened room. After 5 or 6 days of incubation, the blood vessels of the chorioallantois are readily distinguishable in a fertile egg, but none is found in an infertile egg which will be quite translucent.

**Techniques of Embryo Inoculation.** The methods of inoculation are as follows:

1. Chorioallantoic membrane.
2. Allantoic cavity.
3. Amniotic sac.
4. Yolk sac.
5. Intraembryonic.
6. Intracerebral.
7. Intravenous.

The first four methods are in common use and will be described briefly. The other three methods require considerable experience and skill to perform and are limited to special work.

***Chorioallantoic Inoculation.*** A number of viruses grow best on the chorioallantois; the pox group is a good example. The chorioallantoic membrane is useful not only for the isolation and propagation of many viruses but also lesions are formed and can be studied.

It is possible to assay the quantity of virus present in unknown material by making dilutions of such material and inoculating onto the chorioallantoic membrane. After a period of incubation the lesions or *pocks* are counted and the amount of virus in the original material is calculated. It is assumed that on membranes where the pocks are well separated each lesion originated from a single elementary body.

Embryos 10 to 14 days of age may be selected for chorioallantoic membrane inoculation. In order to inoculate onto the membrane, a portion of it must be exposed. The technique of "dropping the membrane" is ordinarily used. This is accomplished by first candling the egg and marking a triangular area of 1 to 1.5 cm. on the side, taking care to avoid the large blood vessels. A small electric drill with a suitable cutting disc is used to cut through the shell along the lines of the triangle. It is important to avoid cutting too deeply so that the delicate chorioallantoic membrane is not injured. An inoculating needle can be used to remove the triangular piece of shell and then with a gentle downward pressure with the end of the needle a slit is made in the shell membrane. A small hole is then drilled in the end of the egg through the shell and shell membrane into the air cell. By using a rubber bulb, suction is applied to the opening in the end of the egg. As the air is exhausted from the natural air cell an artificial air cell is formed over the embryo by the air entering the slit in the shell membrane on the top of the egg, thereby separating the chorioallantoic and shell membranes. The chorioallantoic membrane is "dropped" and the contents of the egg displaced into the natural air cell (Fig. 42.3).

The inoculum is placed directly onto the exposed membrane from a pipette or syringe and the openings sealed with melted paraffin, collodion, household cement, or cellulose tape. Eggs inoculated in this manner should be handled carefully and incubated in a horizontal position so

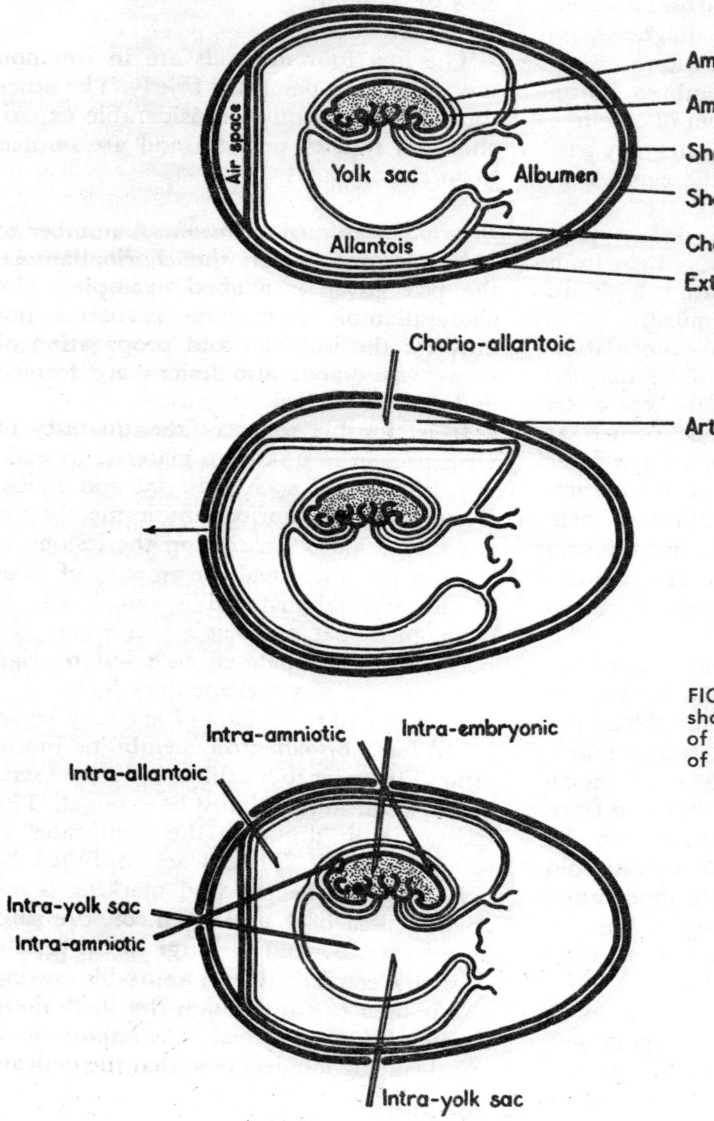


FIG. 42.3—Sketch of chicken embryo showing position and relationship of structures to the various routes of inoculation.

that the position of the membrane will not be disturbed.

*Allantoic Cavity Inoculation.* This is easily made by drilling a small hole through the shell into the air cell about 3 mm. from its border. The position and extent of the air cell is marked in the candler. A tuberculin syringe with a 25-gauge ⅝-inch needle is suitable for this type of inoculation. The needle is directed into the allantoic cavity by inserting it through the drilled hole and parallel to the long axis of the egg. Amounts of inoculum may vary from 0.05 to 0.5 ml., but 0.2 to 0.3 ml. are average for the allantoic cavity. If the larger amounts are injected, it is advisable to drill a second hole in the air cell near the first to allow for expansion or some of the inoculum may leak back past the needle.

Allantoic cavity inoculation may be made through a hole drilled on the side of the egg, but this may produce injury and hemorrhage. After inoculation the holes are closed and the eggs incubated in the same manner as described previously.

*Amniotic Sac Inoculation.* This is more difficult and detailed than either of those already described. One method is to candle eggs with 10- to 12-day-old embryos and mark the extent of the air cell. By using a drill, the entire top of the egg is cut off, exposing the air cell. A small area of the shell membrane is made transparent by the application of sterile mineral oil so that the embryo can be viewed below. Sterile forceps are used to pierce the shell membrane and the chorioallantoic membrane in order to pick up the amniotic membrane and pull it through the opening. The inoculation is made into the amniotic sac by injecting through the amniotic membrane as it is held in the forceps. Following inoculation, the membrane is released and allowed to go back to its normal position. The top of the egg is covered with a suitable cap of rubber or paper, or a small glass funnel which is cemented or paraffined onto the shell.

Another method is to approach the amniotic sac through a "window" cut as for chorioallantoic inoculation. By using transillumination from below, so that the embryo can be viewed during the inoculation, the embryo is approached with the needle of the syringe. As the point of the needle reaches the embryo, a short quick thrust will strike the embryo and it will move away from the end of the needle. The point of the needle is in the amniotic sac and the inoculation is then made. The normal swallowing movements of the embryo places part of the inoculum in contact with respiratory epithelium. Some viruses grow best when inoculated by this route.

*Intraembryonic, Intracranial, and Intravenous Inoculation.* These inoculations of embryos are not widely used and will not be described here. For more detailed description of these and other methods of inoculation the student should refer to the work of Burnet.

Following inoculation, embryos are incubated for a period of one to six days during which they are observed twice daily for evidence of death of the embryo. Some viruses, such as equine encephalomyelitis, kill the embryo within 24 hours while others kill in 2 or 3 days. Still other viruses grow readily in the tissues of the embryo but seldom are they lethal.

Embryo death is accompanied by collapse of the large blood vessels of the chorioallantois so that they are difficult to see upon candling the egg, whereas they are quite distinct while the embryo is alive. Normal movements of the embryo are no longer observed if the embryo is moribund or dead.

If the embryo is not dead after 5 or 6 days incubation, it is killed and examined for lesions.

Examination of the embryo should be done soon after death or certain lesions may be obscured by postmortem changes.

Some of the lesions and changes which may be induced by virus growth are listed below.

1. Embryo death.
2. Hemorrhages of subcutaneous tissues, feather follicles, occipital region.
3. Congestion of vessels of the wings and feet or of entire embryo.

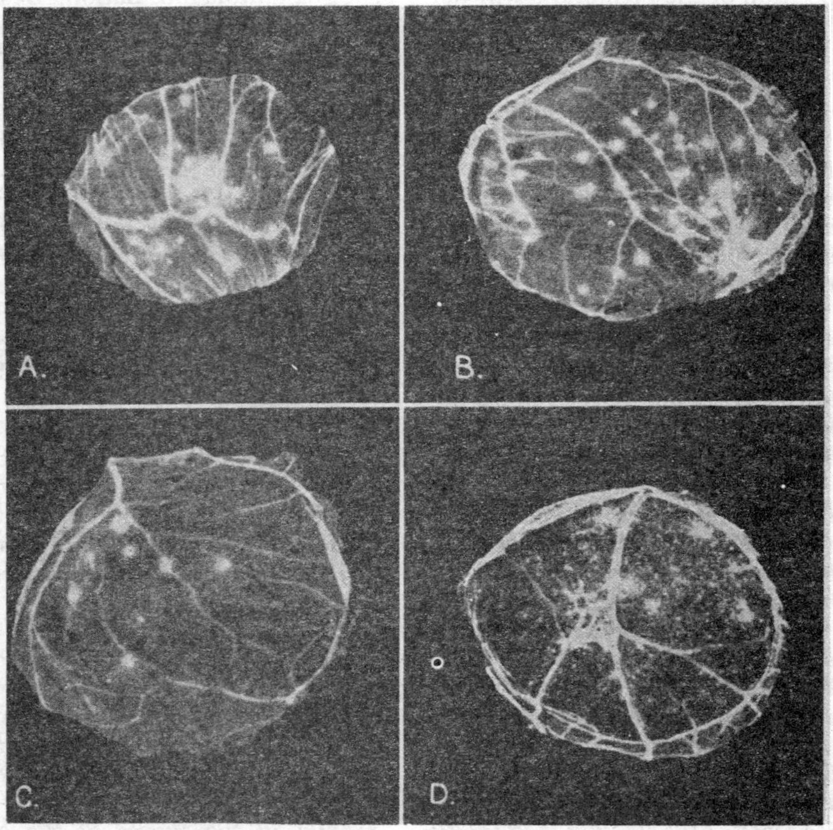


FIG. 42.4—Chorioallantoic membrane lesions, natural size. A. Herpesvirus. B. Virus B. C. Pseudorabies virus, early passage. D. Late passage pseudorabies virus, showing primary and secondary foci. (Burnet, Lush, and Jackson. Austral. Jour. Exp. Biol. Med. Sci. 17:35, 1939.)

4. Growth of the embryo is stunted.
5. Tucking of the embryo.
6. Decreased amount of amniotic fluid.
7. Increased amount of allantoic fluid.
8. Thickening and edema of chorioallantoic membrane.
9. Pocks or areas of leucocytic infiltration, often with central necrosis (Fig. 42.4).
10. Microscopic lesions.
11. Formation of inclusion bodies.

It is desirable to refrigerate the embryos for four or five hours before examination. This will reduce hemorrhage into the fluids if the embryo is still alive. If materials are to be saved for further passage or for vaccine production, it is important to disinfect the shell with alcohol or tincture of iodine before opening the egg so as to avoid bacterial contamination. Allantoic fluid may be removed by a syringe or pipette directly from the egg by removing the shell over the air cell, then by breaking the shell membrane and the chorioallantoic membrane beneath. Forceps or other suitable instruments are used to hold back the embryo and its membranes from obstructing the end of the pipette or syringe. Following the removal of fluids the embryo is removed from the shell in order to detect gross lesions. Various portions of the embryo or the extra-embryonic membranes may be collected for microscopic sections.

Observation of inoculated chorioallantoic membranes is accomplished by cutting away the shell over the artificial air cell. The exposed membrane may be removed by cutting it at the border with a pair of scissors. Lesions in the membrane may be more clearly demonstrated by floating it on saline in a Petri dish which is placed over a black background.

If materials are to be held for a time before reinoculation, they should be stored in an ice chest. Although some viruses will remain viable for months when stored in the ordinary refrigerator, storage at temperatures of —35°C. or below is better. Lyophilization and storage *in vacuo* is also recommended for preservation of viruses.

Cultures, aerobic and anaerobic, should be made of all embryo materials harvested, since many species of bacteria may produce lesions or death of embryos which may simulate those produced by viruses.

It should be pointed out that up to 10 per cent of the deaths in embryos may occur from nonspecific causes. Deaths due to such causes must not be confused with those produced by viruses. Passage of material from such embryos will fail to kill on second transfer.

Some viruses fail to produce lesions in the first passages so several "blind" passages must be made in order to establish them in embryos.

## SEROLOGICAL METHODS

The viruses are good antigens and readily stimulate the production of antibodies. The detection of specific antibody to a virus by various serological techniques is useful not only for the diagnosis of virus infection but also for the identification of an unknown virus by reacting it with known immune serum. The discovery that a number of viruses will agglutinate erythrocytes in the absence of antibody has added a valuable tool in the study and identification of viruses.

The serological methods commonly employed in virus studies are as follows:

1. Agglutination and precipitation.
2. Complement fixation.
3. Serum neutralization.
4. Virus neutralization.
5. Protection tests.
6. Hemagglutination and hemagglutination-inhibition.
7. Cytopathogenicity in tissue culture.

### Agglutination and Precipitation

It has been shown that viruses may be sensitized by specific antibody and in the presence of an electrolyte the virus particles cling to each other forming aggregates which can be seen by either microscopic or macroscopic examination. The mechanism in this case is not different from that already described as occurring with bacteria (agglutination) or with protein molecules (precipitation). Since the size of viruses is intermediate between the bacteria and protein molecules, neither term will precisely fit the condition of virus aggregation in the presence of immune serum. The term flocculation which is more inclusive might be appropriate. The term agglutination is most often used, however, and is a valuable aid to the identification of certain viruses and for the detection of their antibodies. The preparation of the antigen for agglutination tests is often difficult because the viruses must be grown in the tissues of animals rather than on agar culture as for most bacterial antigens. The virus must be separated as completely as possible from the host cells in which it is grown. This is usually accomplished by centrifugation and washing in buffered solution followed by recentrifugation. The antigen is standardized and the agglutination technique carried out in a manner similar to agglutination testing with bacterial antigens. Suitable controls on the materials must be used in order to avoid error in conclusions.

The agglutination of virus elementary bodies is useful in two ways. If the virus is known, antibodies for it can be detected in an unknown serum. On the other hand, if known immune serum is available, an unknown virus can be identified by this technique.

So far only a few viruses such as vaccinia

and varicella have been studied by using ag glutination technique.

Soluble antigens of a number of viruses have been identified by precipitation procedures.

### Complement Fixation

There is little basic difference in the technique of complement fixation using viruses as antigens than that employed with bacterial antigens. Virus antigen for this test is obtained from infected animal tissues, such as lung or brain, or from the tissues or fluids of infected chicken embryos. The exact technique of preparation of viral antigens is too diverse to be described here. The complement-fixation procedure is otherwise the same as described in Chapter 11.

Complement-fixation tests are useful in detecting the presence of antibodies in serum by employing a known antigen, or for the identification of an unknown virus by using known antibody.

### Neutralization Tests

Neutralization tests are quite useful in virus studies and are more often applied than flocculation or complement-fixation procedures. There are two neutralization techniques employed: serum neutralization (SN) and virus neutralization (VN).

Serum neutralization tests employ known virus to which unknown serum is added. If antibodies for the virus are present in the serum, the virus will be neutralized or rendered noninfective. The technique for neutralization tests will vary according to the virus to be used. The amounts of virus, the amount of serum, the test animal, and the route of inoculation employed must be modified to suit the conditions necessary for virus growth and to obtain satisfactory end-points. The basic principles of testing are in general the same and may be illustrated as follows:

1. Preliminary titration of the infectivity of the virus is necessary to determine dilutions to be used. A wide enough range of dilutions is used so that 100 per cent survival as well as 100 per cent mortality will be determined.
2. Equal volumes, usually 0.2 to 0.3 ml., of each virus dilution and known negative serum are mixed.
3. Equal volumes of each virus dilution and immune serum are mixed.
4. Incubate the mixtures 30 minutes at 37°C.
5. Inoculate 5 or 6 test animals, cell cultures, or chicken embryos with a dose which should be infective as determined in the preliminary titration. Twice the volume of inoculum will be necessary to account for the dilution by the serum.
6. Inoculate an equal number of controls with each virus dilution which contains no serum.
7. Observe the animals, cell cultures, or embryos for lesions or lethal effect and calculate the amount of virus neutralized by the serum after determining end-points of reaction.

For comparison purposes, end-points of 50 per cent death ($LD_{50}$) or 50 per cent infectivity ($ID_{50}$) are usually calculated. Reference to Table 42.1 shows the virus killed 50 per cent of the embryos or animals when diluted $10^{-7}$ or 1 to 10 million. In other words, the original virus suspension contained 10 million $LD_{50}$ doses per ml. of inoculum. The virus and the normal serum mixture also killed 50 per cent in a dilution of $10^{-7}$, showing that there were no antibodies in the normal serum for the virus. The virus mixed with serum from the immune animal showed a titer of only $10^{-3}$, indicating a neutralization of the virus by the serum. In this case there was a difference of $10^{-4}$ $LD_{50}$'s between the immune serum and the control; thus, 10,000 $LD_{50}$'s had been neutralized.

Virus neutralization tests may be conducted in a manner similar to the one described above for serum neutralization, except that the serum is known and the virus unknown.

### Protection Tests

Protection tests, although not strictly serological, are used in the study and identification of those viruses which can be used to produce a successful vaccine.

TABLE 42.1

HYPOTHETICAL SERUM NEUTRALIZATION TEST

| | Virus Dilutions | | | | | | | |
|---|---|---|---|---|---|---|---|---|
| | $10^{-2}$ | $10^{-3}$ | $10^{-4}$ | $10^{-5}$ | $10^{-6}$ | $10^{-7}$ | $10^{-8}$ | $LD_{50}$ |
| Virus + saline | 6* | 6 | 6 | 6 | 6 | 3 | 0 | $10^{-7}$ |
| Virus + normal serum | 6 | 6 | 6 | 6 | 6 | 3 | 0 | $10^{-7}$ |
| Virus + immune serum | 6 | 3 | 0 | 0 | 0 | 0 | 0 | $10^{-3}$ |

* The number in each space indicates the number of deaths with each dilution. Six were inoculated.

This procedure is also employed for the testing of many commercial serum and vaccine products.

The protection test involves first the production of either active or passive immunity in an animal which is followed by a challenge dose of the virulent virus. It is, in a way, an in vivo neutralization test.

An example of the use of a protection test for the identification of a virus is to distinguish the three equine encephalomyelitis viruses.

In this instance vaccines are prepared from all three types and a series of guinea pigs immunized with each one. When satisfactory immunity is developed they are all challenged with the unknown virus which has been isolated from horse brain and is suspected of being one of the three.

In the example given in Table 42.2, the unknown virus would be identified as western equine encephalomyelitis since the animals immunized with vaccine prepared from known western virus were resistant to the challenge dose while the others, including the controls, were not.

Commercial products, such as rabies and hog cholera vaccines, are routinely tested for potency by using them to produce active immunity in test animals which are then given challenge doses of the living virus.

The passive immunizing property of anti-hog cholera serum is tested by injecting it in graded doses into a series of susceptible pigs simultaneously with a challenge dose of live hog cholera virus.

### Virus Hemagglutination (HA Test)

Hirst, in 1941, observed that agglutination of the chicken embryo erythrocytes occurred when they mixed with amniotic and allantoic fluids, provided these fluids were high in influenza virus content. Subsequent research has shown that many viruses will agglutinate the erythrocytes of the adult fowl and certain mammals (Table 42.3). Hemagglutination has become a valuable test for the presence of some viruses and also can be used to show the quantity present in a given fluid.

The mechanism by which a virus may agglutinate erythrocytes is not completely understood. It is known that virus hemagglutination differs from hemagglutination by antibody. It has been theorized that erythrocytes possess receptors which attract virus particles. The union of the virus with these receptors alters the properties of the

TABLE 42.2

A HYPOTHETICAL PROTECTION TEST FOR THE IDENTIFICATION OF EQUINE ENCEPHALOMYELITIS VIRUS

| Immunized Guinea Pigs Given | Virus Dilution Used | | | | |
|---|---|---|---|---|---|
| | $10^{-3}$ | $10^{-4}$ | $0^{-5}$ | $10^{-6}$ | $10^{-7}$ |
| Eastern type vaccine | 5* | 5 | 2 | 1 | 0 |
| Western type vaccine | 1 | 0 | 0 | 0 | 0 |
| Venezuelan type vaccine | 5 | 5 | 3 | 0 | 0 |
| Controls | 5 | 5 | 3 | 1 | 0 |

* The number in each space represents the number of animals killed; five were inoculated.

erythrocytes so that they agglutinate. Hemagglutination by influenza virus has been studied in some detail, others to a lesser extent. A number of properties and characteristics of virus hemagglutination may be listed.

1. Ability to produce hemagglutination rests with the virus particle itself in some cases but can be separated from infectivity in others.
2. Hemagglutination by variola and vaccinia is produced by a product of the virus rather than the elementary body.
3. Union of virus and erythrocyte is not stable. After a period of time, the virus leaves the red blood cell and is again present in the suspending fluid. This is known as *elution* of a virus.
4. Following elution of the virus, the agglutinated cells fail to adhere to each other.
5. Red blood cells from which a virus has been eluted cannot be reagglutinated by the same virus, but may be agglutinated by an unrelated virus.
6. A virus killed by formalin retains its hemagglutinative property.
7. Heat inactivation reduces or completely destroys hemagglutination, depending upon the temperature and duration of treatment.

The quantity of a virus which will produce hemagglutination can be quite accurately titrated by HA test.

In the performance of the HA titration, doubling dilutions of the virus-containing material are made in saline using a separate pipette for each dilution. After the suspension of washed erythrocytes is added, the tubes are shaken and then allowed to stand at room temperature until sedimentation of the cells occurs and the results can be read. The period of incubation is usually 40 to 75 minutes. If agglutination is present, a granular mat, often with curling at the edges, will be observed in the bottom of the tube. Absence of agglutination is shown by the cells settling to the very bottom of the tube in a rather compact round "button."

Rapid HA tests are useful as a quick presumptive test for the presence of certain viruses in embryo fluids. The rapid test may be done on a slide or spot plate by adding equal volumes, 1 to 2 drops, of embryo fluids and a 4 per cent suspension of washed erythrocytes. If a fairly high concentration of virus is present, hemagglutination will be evident, usually within one minute.

### Hemagglutination-Inhibition (HI)

The discovery that certain viruses would agglutinate erythrocytes was promptly followed by the observation that antibodies to the virus would inhibit the reaction. HI tests have been a convenient method of detecting the presence of specific antibody in the serum of infected, or convalescent, individuals. Furthermore, by diluting the serum, the comparative amount of antibody can be determined.

Although the serum from infected or recovered individuals will inhibit hemagglutination and also neutralize the virus, there is evidence that these reactions are the result of separate antibodies.

The virus antigen used in the above test must be titrated accurately by using the HA

TABLE 42.3

VIRUS HEMAGGLUTINATION OF ERYTHROCYTES OF VARIOUS ANIMALS

| Source of R.B.C. | Newcastle of Fowl | Fowl Pest | Swine Influenza | Vaccinia |
|---|---|---|---|---|
| Chicken | + | + | + | ± |
| Man | + | + | + | + |
| Cow | + | + | — | + |
| Sheep | + | + | — | ± |
| Rabbit | — | ... | + | ± |
| Guinea pig | + | + | + | + |

TABLE 42.4

A SAMPLE HEMAGGLUTINATION TEST

| Dilution 1 to | 10 | 20 | 40 | 80 | 160 | 320 | 640 | 1,280 | 2,560 | 5,120 |
|---|---|---|---|---|---|---|---|---|---|---|
| ml. of each virus dilution... | .5 | .5 | .5 | .5 | .5 | .5 | .5 | .5 | .5 | .5 |
| ml. of 0.25% washed chicken R.B.C. ........ | .5 | .5 | .5 | .5 | .5 | .5 | .5 | .5 | .5 | .5 |
| hemagglutination | + | + | + | + | + | + | + | + | — | — |

+ = hemagglutination; — = no hemagglutination. Hemagglutination titer is 1:1,280.

test previously described. A satisfactory amount of virus for the test is 20 hemagglutinating units to be contained in the 0.5 ml. which is added to tubes 3 to 10 inclusive. A *hemagglutinating unit* is the smallest amount of virus contained in 0.5 ml. of saline which will completely agglutinate the erythrocytes in 0.5 ml. of 0.25 per cent of suspension. Reference to Table 42.4 shows 0.5 ml. of the 1:1,280 dilution to contain 1 hemagglutinating unit of virus. Therefore 0.5 ml. of 1:64 dilution of the original virus will be used in the test.

Forty units of virus should be added to tube 2 to keep the amount of virus constant in each tube. Tube 1 is a serum control to check the red blood cell suspension. If agglutination should occur in tube 1, the serum should be absorbed first by the erythrocytes to remove the natural hemagglutinins and then retested. Tubes 10 and 11 are controls on the virus and red blood cell suspension respectively.

It should be noted that interference with hemagglutination may occur which may be due to one of several factors:

1. Chemical contamination of tubes or ingredients such as acids.
2. Inhibitory substances in tissue extracts.
3. Peculiarities of R.B.C.'s from certain individuals.
4. Heat-labile components of serum.
5. Bacterial enzymes and toxins.
6. Species incompatability between R.B.C. used and serum tested.

### Hemadsorption

This is a technique, similar to hemagglutination, devised by Shelokov *et al.* It is used for detection of certain viruses grown

TABLE 42.5

A SAMPLE HEMAGGLUTINATION-INHIBITION TEST

| | 1 | 2 | 3 | 4 | 5 | 6 | 7 | 8 | 9 | 10 | 11 |
|---|---|---|---|---|---|---|---|---|---|---|---|
| Serum ml. ..... | .2 | doubling dilutions are made 0.5 ml. taken from tube 1 and mixed with tube 2, etc. | | | | | | | | 0 | |
| Saline ml. ..... | .8 | | | | | | | | | 0 | .5 |
| Virus ml. ...... | | .5 | .5 | .5 | .5 | .5 | .5 | .5 | .5 | .5 | |
| 0.25% washed R.B.C. ml. | .5 | .5 | .5 | .5 | .5 | .5 | .5 | .5 | .5 | .5 | .5 |
| Final dilution of serum. 1 to... | 10 | 20 | 40 | 80 | 160 | 320 | 640 | 1,280 | 2,560 | | |
| Positive serum... | — | — | — | — | — | — | + | + | + | + | — |
| Negative serum.. | — | + | + | + | + | + | + | + | + | + | — |

+ = hemagglutination; — = no hemagglutination.

in tissue culture. Those viruses producing hemagglutinin will adsorb erythrocytes to the surface of cells in which the virus has grown. To conduct the test, a suspension of washed erythrocytes is added to tissue culture tubes in which a virus has grown. If a hemadsorbing virus is present, the erythrocytes will form clusters and rosettes around the infected cells of the culture and can be observed microscopically. This technique is most useful for detection of viruses which produce only small amounts or weak hemagglutinins. The term hemadsorption virus has been applied to such viruses.

The hemadsorbing reaction can be inhibited by specific antibody, hence hemadsorption-inhibition tests have been devised for the detection of antibody.

## REFERENCES

ANDREWES, C. H., and HORSTMANN, D. M. The Susceptibility of Viruses to Ethyl Ether. Jour. Gen. Microbiol. 3:290, 1949.

BEVERIDGE, W. I. B., and BURNET, F. M. The Cultivation of Viruses and Rickettsiae in the Chick Embryo. Med. Res. Council Spec. Rept. 256. His Majesty's Stationery Office, London, 1946.

BRAKKE, M. K. Density Gradient Centrifugation Technique. Jour. Amer. Chem. Soc. 73:1847, 1951.

BRENNER, S., and HORNE, R. W. A Negative Staining Method for High Resolution Microscopy of Viruses. Biochem. and Biophys. Acta. 34:103, 1959.

CUNNINGHAM, C. H. A Laboratory Guide in Virology. 6th Ed. Burgess Publ. Co., Minneapolis, 1966.

DE ST. GROTH, S. F. The Neutralization of Viruses. Adv. Virus Res. 9:1, 1962.

DULBECCO, R. Production of Plaques in Monolayer Tissue Cultures by Single Particles of an Animal Virus. Proc. Natl. Acad. Sci. 38:747, 1952.

———, and VOGT, M. Plaque Formation and Isolation of Pure Lines With Poliomyelitis Viruses. Jour. Exp. Med. 99:167, 1954.

———, *et al.* A Study of the Basic Aspects of Neutralization of Two Animal Viruses, Western Equine Encephalitis Virus and Poliomyelitis. Virol. 2:162, 1956.

FELDMAN, H. A., and WANG, S. S. Sensitivity of Various Viruses to Chloroform. Proc. Soc. Exp. Biol. Med. 106:736, 1961.

GESSLER, A. E., *et al.* A New and Rapid Method for Isolating Viruses by Selective Fluorocarbon Deproteinization. Trans. N.Y. Acad. Sci. 18:701, 1958.

HAMPARIAN, V. V., *et al.* Contributions to the Characterization and Classification of Animal Viruses. Proc. Soc. Exp. Biol. Med. 112:1040, 1963.

HARRIS, R. J. C. (ed.). Techniques in Experimental Virology. Academic Press, New York, 1964.

HIRST, G. K. The Agglutination of Red Cells by Allantoic Fluid of Chick Embryos Infected With Influenza Virus. Science 94:22, 1941.

HORNE, R. W., and WILDY, P. Virus Structure Revealed by Negative Staining. Adv. Virus Res. 10:101, 1963.

HSIUNG. G. D Diagnostic Virology. Yale Univ. Press, 1964.

MERCHANT, D. J., *et al.* Handbook of Cell and Organ Culture. Burgess Publ. Co., Minneapolis, 1964.

PARKER, R. C. Methods of Tissue Culture. 2nd Ed. Paul B. Hoeber, Inc., New York, 1950.

REED, L. J., and MUENCH, H. A Simple Method of Estimating Fifty Percent Endpoints. Amer. Jour. Hyg. 27:493, 1938.

SALZMAN, N. P. The Rate of Formation of Vaccinia Deoxyribonucleic Acid and Vaccinia Virus. Virol. 10: 150, 1960.

SHELOKOV, A., *et al.* Hemadsorption (Adsorption-Hemagglutination) Test for Viral Agents in Tissue Culture With Special Reference to Influenza. Proc. Soc. Exp. Biol. Med. 97:802, 1958.

VAN ROOYEN, C. E., and RHODES, A. J. Virus Diseases of Man. Thomas Nelson & Sons, New York, 1948.

WHITE, P. R. The Cultivation of Animal and Plant Cells. Ronald Press, New York, 1954.

# 43

# The Classification of Animal Viruses

FOLLOWING THE DISCOVERY OF VIRUSES AT the beginning of this century, many years elapsed before any characteristics of the viruses other than their filterability, disease-producing capabilities, and tissue affinities were determined. Such meager information could not be used for classification of the animal viruses except for broad groupings as to type of disease produced and tissues affected.

As technical methods improved, beginning in the 1930's and 1940's, more of the properties of the viruses became known. These methods included the use of the embryonating chicken egg, filters of known porosity, invention of the electron microscope, development of cell culture techniques, and improvements in biochemical methodology.

The first extensive effort at classification of the animal viruses was made by F. O. Holmes of the Rockefeller Institute who published a scheme in Bergey's Manual in 1948. Genus and species names were proposed in accordance with the International Rules of Bacterial Nomenclature. These names were used in previous editions of this textbook since they were the first and only scientific names that had been published. Objection was raised by many virologists because the basis of the Holmes classification was largely on pathogenicity, host relationships, tissue affinities, and lesions produced.

In the 1950's improvements in technology enabled the virologists to determine morphological and biochemical properties of the animal viruses which have been used to form groupings of viruses with similar characteristics. Committees composed of investigators having special knowledge of specific groups of viruses have formulated descriptions of the major groupings. These have been modified and extended by many others. There is general acceptance of the basis for major groupings by virologists the world over. Much work is yet to be done. Many viruses will be added and revisions will be necessary as additional data become available. Listed below are the major groupings of animal viruses and the members of each. The placement of some viruses is uncertain and controversial, which only added knowledge can resolve.

## GROUPINGS

**Poxviruses.** DNA, 200 mμ × 300 mμ, envelope variable, usually ether resistant.

**Mammalian Poxes.** Smallpox and vaccinia, specific poxviruses infecting cattle, sheep, swine, horses, goats, mice, monkeys, rabbits, and camels.

**Avian Poxes.** Fowl, turkeys, canaries, and pigeons.

**Viruses Similar to the Poxviruses.** Ecthyma, bovine papular stomatitis, lumpy skin, paravaccinia, rabbit myxoma and fibroma, and squirrel fibroma.

**Herpesviruses.** DNA, enveloped, 110 mμ, cubic symmetry, ether sensitive.

Herpes simplex
Pseudorabies

Virus B
Infectious rhinotracheitis
Malignant catarrhal fever
Equine rhinopneumonitis
LK
Laryngotracheitis
Canine herpes
Feline herpes
Cytomegaloviruses
Herpes zoster

**Papovaviruses.** DNA, 40 mμ to 50 mμ, cubic symmetry, ether resistant, nonenveloped.

Common wart
Bovine papilloma
Canine oral papilloma
Rabbit oral papilloma
Rabbit papilloma
Polyoma
SV 40
Genital papilloma of swine

**Adenoviruses.** DNA, 70 mμ to 80 mμ, cubic symmetry, ether resistant, nonenveloped.

Adenoviruses of man
Canine hepatitis
Bovine adenovirus
Simian adenovirus
Avian adenovirus

**Arboviruses.** RNA, 40 mμ to 50 mμ, symmetry probably cubic, ether sensitive, enveloped, usually vector transmitted.

*Group A*
Western equine encephalitis
Eastern equine encephalitis
Venezuelan equine encephalitis
Other Group A viruses

*Group B*
Japanese B
St. Louis
West Nile
Murray Valley
Louping-ill
Russian spring-summer
Yellow fever
Rift Valley fever
Wesselsbron
Dengue
Powassan
Other Group B

*Ungrouped Arboviruses*
California encephalitis
African horse sickness
Blue tongue
Colorado tick fever

**Myxoviruses.** RNA, 80 mμ to 200 mμ, helical symmetry, enveloped, ether sensitive, affinity for mucoproteins.

*Influenza Viruses*
Human
Swine
Equine
Duck
Fowl plague
Virus N
Tern virus

*Parainfluenza Viruses*
Parainfluenza—5 types
Mumps
Newcastle
Yucaipa

*Other Myxoviruses*
Measles
Canine distemper
Rinderpest
Respiratory syncytial

**Picornaviruses.** RNA, 13 mμ to 35 mμ, cubic symmetry, ether resistant, nonenveloped.

*Enteroviruses*
Poliomyelitis
Coxsackie
Echoviruses
Bovine enteroviruses
Swine enteroviruses
Avian enteroviruses
Simian enteroviruses

*Rhinoviruses*
Human "cold" viruses
Equine rhinoviruses

Bovine rhinovirus
Foot-and-mouth disease
Vesicular exanthema

*Other Picornaviruses*
Avian encephalomyelitis
Mouse encephalitis
Feline picornavirus

**Reoviruses.** Double-stranded RNA, 70 mμ to 85 mμ, cubic symmetry, ether resistant.

**Unclassified Viruses.** Viruses not conforming in characteristics to established grouping and those which are incompletely studied.

Hog cholera
African swine fever
Equine arteritis
Infectious bronchitis
Borna disease
Scrapie
Aleutian disease
Hemorrhagic disease of deer
Visna and madei
Transmissible gastroenteritis of swine
Panleucopenia
Ulcerative dermatosis
Equine anemia
Avian leucosis
Rous sarcoma
Lymphocytic choriomeningitis
Duck hepatitis
Mucosal disease—bovine virus diarrhea complex
Hemagglutinating encephalitis of swine
Rabies, Vesicular stomatitis } Suggested as members of the Rhabdovirus group.

**Picodnavirus.** A possible new group of small viruses 20 mμ to 24 mμ, DNA, ether resistant, icosahedral symmetry.

Hamster osteolytic virus H
Kilham (RV) rat virus
Adeno-associated viruses

## REFERENCES


ANDREWES, C. H. Viruses of Vertebrates. Williams & Wilkins Co., Baltimore, 1964.

———, *et al.* A Short Description of the Myxovirus Group. Virol. 1:176, 1955.

BECKER, Y. An Approach to the Organization and Classification of Vertebrate Viruses. Nature 210:1019, 1966.

CABASSO, U. J. The Emerging Classification of Animal Viruses—A Review. Avian Dis. 9:471, 1965.

COOPER, P. D. A Chemical Basis for the Classification of Animal Viruses. Nature 190:302, 1961.

FENNER, F., and BURNET, F. M. A Short Description of the Poxvirus Group. Virol. 4:305, 1957.

HAMPARIAN, V. V., *et al.* Contributions to Characterization and Classification of Animal Viruses. Proc. Soc. Exp. Biol. Med. 112:1040, 1963.

HOLMES, F. O. Order Virales. *In* Bergey's Manual of Determinative Bacteriology. 6th Ed. Williams & Wilkins Co., Baltimore, 1948.

HUCK, R. A. The Classification of Viruses. Vet. Bull. 34:239, 1964.

JAWETZ, E., *et al.* Review of Medical Microbiology. 7th Ed., p. 288. Lange Medical Publications, Los Altos, Calif., 1966.

MINER, R. W. (ed.). Virus and Rickettsial Classification and Nomenclature. Ann. N.Y. Acad. Sci. 56:383–622, 1953.

WILNER, B. I. A Classification of the Major Groups of Human and Other Animal Viruses. 3rd Ed. Burgess Publ. Co., Minneapolis, 1965.

ZHDANOV, B. M. Opredelitel Virusov Cheloveka i Zhivotnykh Izd-Uo Akademiimedisinskikh nauk, Moscow, USSR, 1953.

# 44

# The Poxviruses

MEMBERS OF THE POX GROUP OF VIRUSES ARE the largest of the "true viruses," being just within the limits of visibility under the light microscope. Their nucleic acid is of the DNA type. The structure of the poxviruses is complex, some features of which are not understood. Electron micrographs show a central dense area surrounded by several layers of lesser electron density. On the surface are strands of nucleoprotein which appear to be tubular. On some of the poxviruses they may be wound in spiral fashion around the elementary body, while on others they are distributed in a random fashion over the surface. Apparently all poxviruses possess an envelope or outer covering; however, some members of the group are ether sensitive, while others are not.

Most of the poxviruses are easily cultivated under artificial conditions. Laboratory animals, cell cultures, and chicken embryos are in general use for that purpose. Replication takes place in the cytoplasm of the host cell. A hemagglutinin is produced by the smallpox virus and by other members of the group which are immunologically closely related to it.

The poxviruses have definite predilection for surface epithelium; however, they may infect various other tissues. Typical lesions begin as a papule and then progress through vesicular and pustular stages, followed by scab formation and healing. Several members of the pox group induce cell proliferation which is followed by necrosis.

## MAMMALIAN POXVIRUSES

Smallpox
Vaccinia
Cow pox
Mouse pox
Monkey pox
Rabbit pox
Sheep pox
Goat pox
Camel pox
Horse pox
Swine pox

The mammalian poxviruses are related morphologically, contain a common antigen, and produce similar lesions in their natural hosts. The first six viruses listed above are quite closely related antigenically, exhibiting cross immunity and the ability to "hybridize" when grown together in the same cell culture.

It has been reported by many investigators that smallpox virus (variola) can be converted to vaccinia by passage in animals, while others using carefully controlled experiments have failed.

Cow pox, once considered to be identical with vaccinia, is a distinct virus as shown by antigenic studies.

Sheep pox and goat pox are similar and may be host-adapted variants of the same virus.

Swinc-pox virus is distinct from all other mammalian poxviruses.

### Smallpox Virus, Variola, Vaccinia

**Proposed Names.** *Borreliota variolae, Poxvirus variolae, Poxvirus officinale.*

**Diseases Produced.** Smallpox, alastrim, vaccinia.

**Hosts Affected.** Man and monkey are susceptible to smallpox. Experimentally all mammals and chickens are susceptible to vaccinia. Natural disease occurs in cattle and swine.

**Properties of Virus.** The elementary bodies measure approximately 225 m$\mu$ $\times$ 300 m$\mu$ and are oval in shape (Fig. 44.1). Smallpox elementary bodies are often termed *Paschen bodies.* Inclusions consisting of collections of elementary bodies are found in abundance in infected tissue. These have been termed *Guarnieri bodies.* Various stains such as Giemsa, methylene blue, or carbol fuchsin, and many special stains can be used to demonstrate these bodies. The variola virus is filterable through Berkefeld V, N, and W, and Chamberland $L_3$ but not through the Mandler type. There is considerable absorption of the virus by most filters. Filtration of vaccinia material through Seitz pads allows the passage of soluble antigen into the filtrate. The soluble antigen is not infective but is flocculated by antivaccinial serum. Two portions of the soluble antigen are distinguishable: "L" which is labile at 56°C. and "S" which is stable at 95°C.

Thermal inactivation of the virus occurs by exposure to 55°C. for 20 minutes. The virus is preserved at freezing temperatures for prolonged periods. It has been known to survive in dried crusts for over one year. Ultraviolet rays rapidly destroy the virus. Both vaccinia and variola may agglutinate chicken erythrocytes; however, the erythrocytes from different chickens vary in their agglutinability. Hemagglutination occurs at 37°C.

**Cultivation.** Animal inoculation is one of the methods of cultivation. Monkeys are quite susceptible to variola. Inoculation of the scarified cornea of the rabbit (Paul's test) is used. Vaccinia can be propagated in nearly all animals, but calves are commonly used for vaccine production.

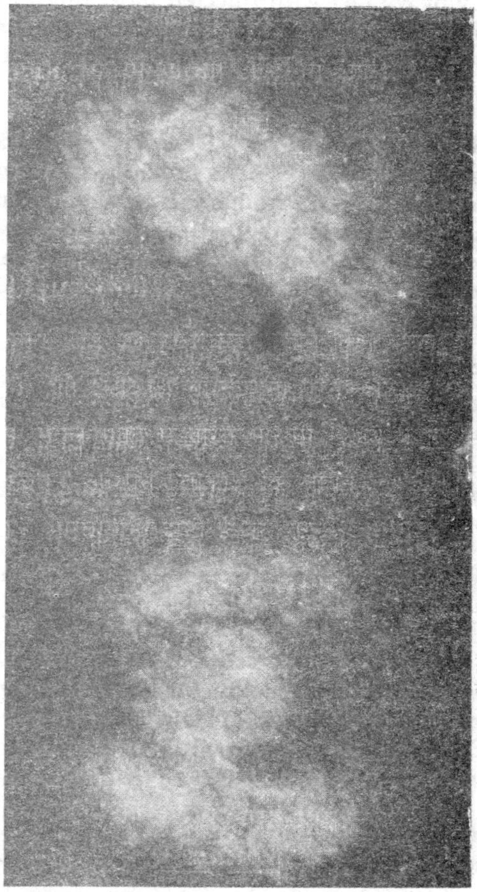

FIG. 44.1—Vaccinia virus, $\times$200,000. (Courtesy Nagington and Horne. Virol. 16:248, 1962.)

Vaccinia can be cultivated by intratesticular inoculation. Certain strains of vaccinia have been converted to neurovaccinia by brain-to-brain passage in rabbits.

The chorioallantoic membrane of the chicken embryo will support a good growth of either variola or vaccinia. Growth of the virus on the membrane produces thickening, edema, leucocytic infiltration, and necrosis, and may or may not be lethal to the embryo.

The virus can be grown successfully in tissue cultures and produces cytopathic changes.

**Transmission.** Smallpox is transmitted usually by contact with infected individuals or contaminated fomites, but also may be transmitted by droplets from the respiratory tract.

**Characteristics of the Disease.** Smallpox has occurred in all parts of the world and has been known throughout the ages, often in serious epidemics causing many deaths. General use of vaccine has reduced the incidence to a very low figure in the United States and European countries.

### Ectromelia Virus

**Proposed Name.** *Borreliota marmorans, Poxvirus muris.*

**Diseases Produced.** Mouse ectromelia, mouse pox.

**Hosts Affected.** White mouse. Experimentally the rat and chicken embryo.

**History and Distribution.** Ectromelia is a disease of laboratory mice which has been described in England. The first descriptions of the disease and the virus were by Marchal in 1930.

**Properties of the Virus.** Direct measurements from electron photographs of the virus show it is 232 $m\mu \times 172\ m\mu$ in size. It is filterable through Berkefeld N, Chamberland $L_2$, and Mandler filters. The virus is inactivated if heated to 55°C. for 30 minutes. It remains viable for 6 months in a dried state, for 2 months if frozen at —10°C., and for at least 5 months if stored in 50 per cent glycerin. Mouse-pox virus is resistant to 1 per cent phenol for 20 days but is killed by 40 days exposure.

Ectromelia virus will produce hemagglutination of fowl erythrocytes. The hemagglutinin in this case is a soluble substance which can be removed from the elementary bodies. The hemagglutination occurs best at 37°C. and there is no evidence of elution of the virus from the erythrocytes. In these respects ectromelia closely resembles the hemagglutinating properties of vaccinia. Sera from mice which have recovered from ectromelia will inhibit hemagglutination by vaccinia virus.

**Cultivation.** Mouse-pox virus has been successfully propagated in tissue cultures which employ mouse embryonic tissue. The virus can also be grown on the chorioallantoic membrane of chicken embryos on which it produces small opaque foci. If the embryos are incubated at 36° to 37°C. death occurs in 3 to 4 days, whereas the embryos survive if incubated at higher temperatures. Inclusion bodies can be demonstrated from the lesions of the membrane.

**Transmission.** The virus of ectromelia is transferred by contact with infected mice.

**Characteristics of the Disease.** The infection is characterized by lesions in the skin, usually on the feet. They begin as localized swellings which become moist, then dry with scab formation and separation of the skin by a line of demarcation between the infected and noninfected areas. There is also mottling of the liver and spleen. Inclusion bodies can be demonstrated in skin lesions. Young mice are most susceptible.

**Immunity.** Specific immunity follows recovery. Mice which have been vaccinated with vaccinia virus are refractory to ectromelia virus.

**Diagnosis.** A diagnosis of ectromelia is made by the appearance of the typical lesions and by transmission of the virus to other mice and to chicken embryos. Demonstration of hemagglutinins for avian erythrocytes and agglutinins for elementary bodies is also used.

### Cow Pox Virus

This disease is worldwide in distribution and is enzootic, especially in dairy cattle. Cow pox is always a local infection on the udder and teats. It may be caused by either cow-pox or vaccinia strains which have been shown by Downie to differ antigenically. Lesions are indistinguishable, but the cow pox is believed to be the naturally occurring strain. Pox in cows has been observed shortly after the vaccination of persons milking them. Cow-pox virus is transmissible to man and produces immunity against smallpox as has been shown by the classical work of Jenner. Cow-pox lesions usually heal, leaving no scar. Ordinarily the disease is considered quite benign but occasionally predisposes the teat to the entrance of mastitis organisms. Immunization of cattle against cow pox is practiced in some countries.

### Vaccinia-like Swine Pox Virus

Two viruses which produce pox lesions in swine are described. One is closely related to the vaccinia-variola group; the other is apparently unrelated antigenically and has a limited host range.

The vaccinia-like swine-pox virus has been described in outbreaks of the disease in Europe and Japan. The relationship of the virus in these reports is indicated by its transmissibility to rabbits and immunity to it which is conferred by vaccinia. It is seen more frequently in young pigs. The lesions produced are typical of the pox diseases, starting with a small red papule followed by vesicle and pustule formation. The eruptions may involve the mouth and pharynx and occasionally the lungs, which may account for some deaths. Skin lesions become black and encrusted, followed by healing if uncomplicated by bacterial infection.

Transmission is by contact and by the hog louse.

### Horse Pox Virus

Horse pox is also known under the names contagious pustular dermatitis and "grease heel." The virus attacks the buccal mucous membrane, skin of the lips and nares, producing vesicles, papules, and pustules. The virus also attacks the skin in the pastern-fetlock region and occasionally over the back where the saddle or harness may abrade it. Ulcers and pustules are produced in these regions. The virus may be transmitted by contaminated brushes, combs, saddles, and harness as well as other contaminated materials. Horses are susceptible to inoculation with vaccinia, but the natural cases are believed due to a specially adapted equine virus.

### Rabbit Pox Virus

Rabbit pox occurs in laboratory and domestic rabbits, producing some death losses. The virus is closely related to vaccinia. It is suggested that it may be a host-adapted strain of vaccinia virus.

### Monkey Pox Virus

Outbreaks of pox in laboratory monkeys has been found due to a virus related to vaccinia.

A poxlike virus has been isolated from "subcutaneous tumors" observed in rhesus monkeys and dog-faced baboons (Niven *et al.*, 1961). This virus, also known as the Yaba monkey virus, is distinct from vaccinia.

### Swine-Pox Virus

**Proposed Name.** *Borreliota suis.*

**Disease Produced.** Swine pox.

**Hosts Affected.** Only swine are naturally susceptible to this virus. The rabbit, horse, calf, sheep, dog, cat, mouse, fowl, guinea pig, rat, and man are insusceptible by direct inoculation.

**Properties of the Virus.** The morphology of swine-pox virus is similar to other poxviruses (Fig. 44.2).

**Cultivation.** Swine-pox virus can be isolated and grown in cell cultures from swine kidney, lung, brain, and testes. Intracytoplasmic inclusion bodies and intranuclear vacuoles are produced in cultures of swine kidney. Distinct plaques are produced in monolayer cultures of swine kidney. Mayr reported the successful transfer of the virus to the chorioallantoic membrane of chicken embryos but could not maintain the virus in serial passage in that host.

FIG. 44.2—Swine poxvirus, ×110,000. (Courtesy A. E. Ritchie and J. O. Norman, National Animal Disease Lab., Ames, Iowa.)

**Transmission.** Swine-pox virus is most often transmitted by the hog louse *Haematopinus suis*. Flies and mosquitoes have been suggested as vectors. Contact transmission is also possible.

**Characteristics of the Disease.** Outbreaks of swine pox due to this virus have been reported in Europe and in the United States. It occurs in young pigs and is usually limited to occasional outbreaks. Lesions are found in the skin of the abdomen and over the sides and back. There is usually hemorrhage into the lesion, producing a dark center. The infection may spread to many pigs in a group which are in close contact. The infection is usually not severe enough to produce death losses unless complicated by other infections, but may account for reduced weight gains for a short period.

**Pathological Changes.** Lesions on the underline are typical of the pox diseases passing successively through papule, vesicle, and pustule formation. The lesions on the back are not as characteristic. These develop into small, hard, smooth elevations which become encrusted and soon drop off.

**Immunity.** Immunity results from having recovered from the disease. Artificial immunization is not practiced. No cross immunity is produced against the vaccinia-like swine-pox virus.

**Diagnosis.** The disease is usually diagnosed by the characteristic lesions. It is differentiated from pox produced by vaccinia-like virus by cross-immunity tests and by determining the host range.

### Sheep-Pox Virus

Sheep-pox virus is distinct from members of the vaccinia-smallpox group. Goat pox and the "Neethling" virus of cattle are related antigenically. Sheep pox has been grown in cell cultures composed of sheep embryo or mouse embryo. Cytoplasmic inclusions are formed in cell cultures and a cytopathic effect is observed. The virus has also been adapted to growth in chicken embryos.

Sheep pox occurs in many areas of the Mediterranean, Middle East, and in Africa. It is a disease which is generalized and shows many skin lesions typical of the poxes, the nonwooled areas showing the greatest number of eruptions.

In some countries chicken embryo-propagated virus or live modified virus is incorporated into immunizing agents.

### Goat Pox Virus

A pox disease occurs in goats which closely resembles sheep pox. It is found in Norway, Africa, and the Middle East.

## AVIAN POXVIRUSES

Fowl pox
Turkey pox

Canary Pox
Pigeon pox

The avian poxviruses form a distinct group. Although they are quite similar in size, morphology, and type of tissue response, they do not infect mammals and are antigenically unrelated to the mammalian poxes.

In addition to the four avian pox strains listed above, isolations of related viruses have been made from many species of wild and domestic birds.

### Fowl-Pox Virus, Turkey Pox, Pigeon Pox, Canary Pox

**Proposed Names.** *Borreliota avium, Poxvirus avium.*

**Diseases Produced.** Fowl pox, avian diphtheria.

**Hosts Affected.** Chicken, turkey, pigeon, canary, duck, goose, guinea fowl, pheasant, and many wild birds.

**Properties of the Virus.** The elementary bodies, which are coccoid-shaped, are approximately 250 m$\mu$ in diameter. They often are referred to as *Borrel bodies.* Aggregates of Borrel bodies occur in the lesions and are called *Bollinger bodies.* Digestion of the Bollinger body with 1 per cent trypsin releases the elementary bodies.

The fowl-pox virus will pass through the coarser grade filters, such as Berkefeld V, but fails to pass finer grades. It is killed by 60°C. in 8 minutes or 56°C. in 30 minutes. Storage of the virus at 0° to 4°C. in dried material retains its viability for 2 years.

The following chemicals are reported to inactivate the virus in 10 minutes exposure: 1:500 sodium hydroxide, 1:1,000 crystal violet, 70 per cent ethyl alcohol, and 1:400 cresol.

Phenol in 3 per cent concentration kills in 30 minutes but not in 10 minutes. Formaldehyde, 3 per cent, does not kill by exposure for 20 minutes; 50 p.p.m. of chlorine and 1:400 tincture of iodine are reported effective against fowl pox.

Three strains of fowl-pox virus are responsible for natural outbreaks of the disease among various species of fowl. Fowl-pox virus is found in chickens and is probably the same in turkeys. Pigeon pox and canary pox are strains which produce disease in pigeons and canaries respectively. All three strains are immunologically related and are intertransmissible by artificial inoculation.

**Cultivation.** Fowl pox can be readily passed from one bird to another by inoculation onto the scarified epithelium of the comb or wattles or defeathered feather follicles. It can also be grown on the chorioallantoic membrane of chicken embryos where it produces thickening, edema, and necrosis of the membrane, but the virus usually is not lethal to the embryo. Tissue cultures can also be used to propagate the virus of fowl pox.

**Transmission.** Contact with infected birds or objects contaminated by them may transmit the disease. Injury to the epithelium predisposes to infection; in fact, it has been reported essential for the initiation of fowl pox. Mosquitoes and biting flies have been shown to transmit the virus. Artificial inoculation, intramuscular or intravenous, will result in infection. Droplet transmission is possible from cases of pox infection of the mouth and pharynx.

**Characteristics of the Disease.** Fowl pox occurs widely throughout the world, attacking adult or young adult birds. The disease is more prevalent in fall and winter months. Mortality rates are usually low, but may be as high as 50 per cent. However, losses from decreased egg production and loss in weight may be considerable. Deaths most often occur in birds having lesions in the mouth, pharynx, orbit, and sinuses. Infection of this type is called avian diphtheria. Occasionally lesions will be seen on the feet. The course of the disease usually runs 3 to 4 weeks.

**Pathological Changes.** The lesions are characterized by the proliferation of the surface epithelial structures followed by degeneration. The basal layer of epithelium is usually undamaged unless secondary bacterial invasion occurs. Cells of the infected area become swollen and exhibit vacuoles in which Bollinger bodies can be demonstrated. Healing takes place usually without scar formation.

**Immunity.** Recovery from an attack of fowl pox results in immunity. Artificial immunization is practiced in certain areas, especially those in which the disease appears quite regularly each year. There are two products in general use: pigeon-pox vaccine and fowl-pox vaccine.

Pigeon-pox vaccine is prepared by inoculating the virus into defeathered follicles in young pigeons or by propagating it on the chorioallantoic membrane of chicken embryos. The material harvested for vaccine is either preserved in 20 per cent glycerin or is dried. The dried vaccine can be kept viable several months and is diluted just before use.

Fowl-pox vaccine may be prepared by growing the virus on the comb of young cockerels or on the chorioallantoic membrane of chicken embryos. These materials are harvested, then dried and stored. They are prepared for use by diluting in water.

Pigeon-pox vaccine produces less reaction in vaccinated birds, so is usually recommended for use in laying flocks. Fowl-pox vaccine is used in young birds before they come into production and it is considered to produce better immunity than pigeon-pox vaccine. The vaccines are applied by subcutaneous inoculation into the shank (stick method), by brushing the vaccine into defeathered follicles, or by piercing the web of the wing with a needle dipped in the vaccine.

**Diagnosis.** The lesions on the comb and wattles are usually so characteristic as to be sufficient for diagnosis. However, when lesions are present in the mouth, pharynx, or orbit, diagnosis may be more difficult. In these cases transmission of material from the lesions to susceptible birds or chicken embryos will produce typical lesions if the disease is fowl pox. Bollinger and Borrel bodies in the infected tissue may be demonstrated microscopically. Agglutination of Borrel bodies is occasionally used as an aid to the identification of the virus.

## OTHER VIRUSES OF THE POX GROUP

Ecthyma
Bovine papular stomatitis
Bovine lumpy skin (Neethling virus)
Bovine paravaccinia
Rabbit myxoma
Rabbit fibroma
Squirrel fibroma

### Ecthyma Virus

**Proposed Name.** *Borreliota ecthymatis.*

**Diseases Produced.** Contagious ecthyma, contagious pustular dermatitis, sore-mouth, and orf.

**Hosts Affected.** Sheep, goats, man, and possibly the rabbit.

**History and Distribution.** Although contagious ecthyma of sheep had been known many years, Aynaud was the first to describe the virus in 1923. The disease is widely distributed in the sheep-raising areas of the United States,. Australia, Europe, Great Britain, and Africa.

**Properties of the Virus.** The ecthyma virus is comparatively large, probably being nearly the size of vaccinia (Fig. 44.3). Elementary bodies have been observed with the light microscope by staining as for Paschen bodies of variola.

The virus will pass the Berkefeld V filter with difficulty, but is retained by Berkefeld N and W, Chamberland $L_2$, and Seitz types. It will pass through the Mandler (6–9 lb.) if the diluent used is adjusted to pH 7.6 but it is retained by this filter if the pH is 8.2. As with vaccinia, the digestion of ecthyma-infected tissue with trypsin is often necessary to liberate the elementary bodies from the

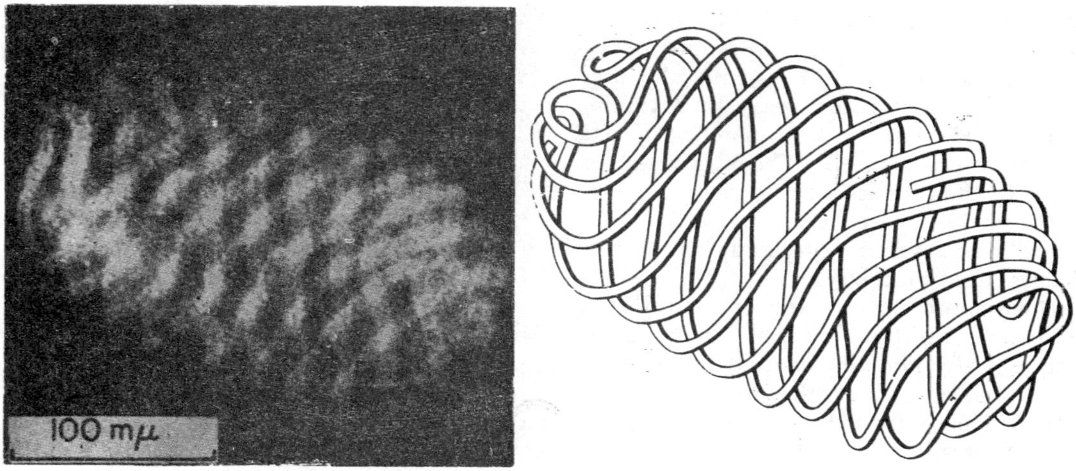


FIG. 44.3—Ecthyma (Orf) virus. (Courtesy Nagington and Horne. Virol. 16:248, 1962.)

tissue cells before filtration of the virus is accomplished. Ecthyma virus is quite resistant to desiccation. Observations are recorded in which the virus remained viable for 4 years and 8 months in one instance, and for 15½ years in another. A temperature of 56°C. for 30 minutes kills the virus, but material held at 55° for 20 minutes remains infective.

Ecthyma virus is antigenically related to vaccinia and ectromelia viruses as shown by complement-fixation and agar-diffusion precipitation tests.

**Cultivation.** Ecthyma virus has been cultivated in cell cultures derived from sheep kidney, human amnion, human embryonic kidney and liver, and monkey kidney. Cytopathic changes are observed. Attempts to adapt the virus to laboratory animals and chicken embryos have been unsuccessful.

**Transmission.** Ecthyma is spread by contact with infected sheep. Transmission from the ewe's udder to the mouth of suckling lambs and vice versa may occur.

**Characteristics of the Disease.** Lesions of ecthyma of sheep usually appear on the lips but are also frequent on the coronary band of the feet. Occasionally lesions are observed on other parts of the body such as the udder, teats, eyes, ears, nostrils, and vulva. Young animals are most susceptible and suffer from the disease because they cannot eat or nurse without great difficulty and this results in severe loss of weight and thriftiness. Foot lesions cause lameness in infected animals. Older animals show a milder form of the disease. Death losses are low unless secondary bacterial infection is serious or screw worms attack the infected area. *Spher. necrophorus* or *Staph. aureus* are usually found in cases of bacterial complications. There are no generalized symptoms noted in uncomplicated cases of ecthyma, differing from sheep pox in this respect. The duration of the disease is usually about 25 days.

Man is susceptible to ecthyma virus, and a number of proven cases of the disease have been reported. The lesions are usually on the hands, arms, or fingers, occurring in cuts or abrasions. The disease is not serious and complete recovery occurs in about 6 weeks.

**Pathological Changes.** The successive pathological stages observed in ecthyma are papule, vesicle, pustule, and scab formation. These changes are analogous to the changes seen in the pox diseases. In some cases there are proliferative changes in the infected areas of the lips, giving rise to pseudopapillomas or wartlike lesions.

**Immunity.** Recovery from ecthyma is accompanied by permanent immunity. Artificial immunization is successful and is used in many sheep-raising areas. Live vaccine is prepared from the scab material of artificially infected sheep. The vaccine is applied to the scarified skin of the medial aspect of the thigh. Lesions indicating a "take" of the vaccine should appear in 6 to 7 days after vaccination.

Cross-immunity tests show that strains of ecthyma virus from various countries are antigenically homologous and no relationship to sheep pox or ulcerative dermatosis can be demonstrated. Complement-fixing and neutralizing antibodies have been demonstrated in the serum of immune animals.

**Diagnosis.** A diagnosis of ecthyma is based on the appearance of typical lesions on the lips and feet or lips alone and differentiation of the virus from ulcerative dermatosis by cross-immunity tests. Elementary bodies have been demonstrated in some cases of ecthyma in stained preparations of exudate.

### Papular Stomatitis Virus

**Disease Produced.** Papular stomatitis of cattle.

**Hosts Affected.** Cattle. The horse, pig, sheep, goat, mouse, rabbit, and guinea pig are not susceptible.

**History and Distribution.** Papular stomatitis of cattle has been reported by various European investigators since 1884. Griesmer and Cole, in 1960, reported a high incidence of the disease in Ohio cattle and were able to isolate a virus from typical lesion material. Many other reports of similar conditions, ulcerative and proliferative stomatitis, appear in the literature prior to 1960 but do not describe a specific viral agent.

**Properties of the Virus.** It is a large virus (300 mμ × 170 mμ) and is morphologically similar to ecthyma virus.

**Cultivation.** The virus has been cultivated in cell cultures of bovine kidney and bovine testicle. Cytopathic changes are observed. Attempts to propagate the virus in chicken embryos have been unsuccessful.

**Transmission.** The method of natural transmission is not precisely known. Experimental transmission is accomplished by introduction of the virus into the oral mucosae by injection or scarification. Inoculation of external epithelium does not produce infection. Parenteral inoculation of the virus results in the production of typical lesions.

**Characteristics of the Disease.** Papular stomatitis of cattle is a mild disease of varying duration. Usually the epithelium of the oral region is affected. Lesions sometimes disappear in a few days; in other instances they persist for several months. Grossly the lesions are proliferative in character. Microscopically, hydropic degeneration, hyperplasia of the mucosa, and intracytoplasmic inclusions are observed.

**Immunity.** Some animals are refractory to a second attack of papular stomatitis, while reoccurrence of lesions has been observed in others.

**Diagnosis.** Diagnosis is usually made on the basis of gross and microscopic lesions. Virus isolation in cell cultures should be attempted.

### Neethling Virus

A virus responsible for lesions designated as lumpy skin disease of cattle has been reported in Africa. The virus possesses properties similar to the pox group. Immunization of cattle with sheep-pox vaccine is reported to protect cattle against experimental infection. Other viruses are also reported from lumpy skin lesions of cattle and will be discussed in other chapters.

### Bovine Paravaccinia Virus

A poxvirus which occurs in cattle but differs from cow pox or vaccinia is called paravaccinia. This virus is transmissible to man, producing the condition known as "milkers nodules." The virus has been isolated in cultures of bovine cells. Morphology of the virus is similar to bovine papular stomatitis virus. Nagington *et al.* present evidence that paravaccinia and orf (ecthyma) viruses are the same.

### Rabbit-Myxoma Virus

**Proposed Names.** *Borreliota myxomae, Poxvirus myxomatis.*

**Disease Produced.** Rabbit myxomatosis.

**Hosts Affected.** Wild European rabbit, hare, domestic rabbit. Experimentally the cottontail and jackrabbit.

**History and Distribution.** Sanarelli, in 1898, reported on myxomatosis of rabbits and showed that the disease was transmissible and suggested that the causative agent was too small to be seen by ordinary microscopic methods. Myxomatosis has been reported in South America, United States, Great Britain, Europe, and Australia. The disease has been deliberately introduced into wild rabbits of Australia in order to aid in the control of the "rabbit plague" of that country.

**Properties of the Virus.** The morphology and structure of myxomavirus closely resemble the poxviruses. Elementary bodies measure 296 m$\mu$ $\times$ 254 m$\mu$. The surface appears convoluted and is composed of tubular structures which are usually arranged in random fashion but sometimes are arranged in a regular spiral. A covering membrane is often observed.

Myxomavirus passes Berkefeld V and N filters, but not Chamberland $L_5$ or $L_7$ types. The size of fibroma strains is 125 m$\mu$ to 175 m$\mu$. Thermal inactivation takes place at 55°C. in 10 minutes or at 50°C. for 1 hour. The virus is inactivated by ether.

**Cultivation.** The rabbit-myxoma virus can be cultivated in tissue cultures which contain rabbit tissues such as mononuclear cells, testicular, kidney, or lymphoid tissue. Plaques are produced in kidney cell cultures. It is also readily cultivated by chorioallantoic inoculation of chicken embryos. Discrete foci of ectodermal proliferation appear in the chorioallantoic membrane 3 days after inoculation. No changes are noted in the embryo itself.

**Transmission.** The myxomavirus can be transmitted by contact with infected rabbits or their discharges. The virus has been recovered from flies. In some cases the disease has been transmitted by fleas. In Australia the successful use of myxomatosis as a rabbit control measure is due to the spread of the virus by mosquitoes.

**Characteristics of the Disease.** Myxomatosis is characterized by tumors which appear in the skin around the eyes, mouth, nose, and genitalia. There is conjunctivitis, edema of the eyelids, nasal discharge, and dyspnea. The central nervous system is invaded by extension of the virus from the blood stream. The disease is fatal in 1 to 2 weeks. However, if the animals are kept in a room which is held at a temperature of 36° to 42°C., there are few deaths, and there is retrogression of the lesions.

**Pathological Changes.** The tumor masses produced by the myxomavirus are gelatinous in appearance and consist largely of loosely arranged connective tissue cells. Infected epithelial cells in or adjacent to the tumor contain cytoplasmic inclusions.

**Immunity.** Rabbits which recover from myxomatosis are immune to the disease. Neutralizing antibodies are produced which are effective against both the myxoma and fibroma viruses. If fibroma virus is injected 48 to 96 hours before myxoma, protection against fatal myxomatosis results. This may be explained by the phenomenon of virus interference.

**Diagnosis.** The appearance of soft tumors in the skin of rabbits suggests myxomatosis.

Transmission experiments to rabbits and to chicken embryos are confirmatory. Demonstration of cytoplasmic inclusions in the infected tissue cells may also be used.

### Squirrel-Fibroma Virus

A naturally occurring fibroma of gray squirrels has been described by Kilham *et al.* The virus is immunologically related to Shope's rabbit-fibroma virus. It is transmissible to woodchucks and to domestic rabbits. However, in the latter-named host the virus is not transmissible beyond one passage.

## REFERENCES

### Mammalian Poxviruses

Barnard, J. E., and Elford, W. J. The Causative Organism in Infectious Ectromelia. Proc. Roy. Soc., London, Ser. B., 109:360, 1931.

Bedson, H. S., and Duckworth, M. J. Rabbit Pox: An Experimental Study of the Pathways of Infection in Rabbits. Jour. Path. Bact. 85:1, 1963.

Borrel, A. Epithelioses Infectieuses et Epitheliomas. Ann. Inst. Past. 17:81, 1903.

Herrlich, A., *et al.* Experimental Studies on the Transformation of the Variola Virus Into the Vaccinia Virus Arch. ges. Virusforsch. 12:579, 1963.

Horgan, E. S. The Experimental Transformation of Variola to Vaccinia. Jour. Hyg., Cambridge, 38:702, 1938.

Kasza, L., *et al.* Isolation and Cultivation of Swine Pox Virus in Primary Cell Cultures of Swine Origin. Amer. Jour. Vet. Res. 21:269, 1960.

Marchal, J. Infectious Ectromelia. Jour. Path. Bact. 33:713, 1930.

McNutt, S. H., *et al.* Swine Pox. Jour. Amer. Vet. Med. Assn. 74:752, 1929.

Nagington, J., and Horne, R. W. Morphological Studies of Orf and Vaccinia Viruses. Virol. 16:248, 1962

Paschen, E. Was wissen wir uber den Vakzineerreger? Münch. med. Wschr. 53:2391, 1906.

Paul, G. Eine neve Untersuchungs-methode der variolierten Hornhaut des kanin-chenauges zur objektiven Sicherung der Varioladiagnose. Berl. Klin. Wschr. 53:874, 1916.

Reczko, E. Morphology of Pox Viruses. Arch. ges. Virusforsch. 12:269, 1962.

Rondle, C. J. M., and Dumbell, K. R. Antigens of Cowpox Virus. Jour. Hyg. 60:41, 1962.

Sabban, M. S. Sheep Pox and Its Control in Egypt. Bull. Off. Int. Epiz. 53:1527, 1960.

Schwarte, L. H., and Biester, H. E. Pox in Swine. Amer. Jour. Vet. Res. 2:136, 1941.

Woodroofe, G. M., and Fenner, F. Genetic Studies With Mammalian Poxviruses. IV. Hybridization Between Several Different Poxviruses. Virol. 12:272, 1960.

———, and ———. Serological Relationships Within the Poxvirus Group: An Antigen Common to All Members of the Group. Virol. 16:334, 1962.

### Avian Poxviruses

Beaver, D. L., and Cheatham, W. J. Electron Microscopy of Junco Pox. Amer. Jour. Path. 42:23, 1963.

Cavill, J. P. Canary Pox: Report of an Outbreak in Roller Canaries (*Serinus canarius*). Vet. Rec. 76:463–65, 1964.

Cunningham, Charles H. Fowl Pox. *In* Diseases of Poultry. 5th Ed. Biester, H. E., and Schwarte, L. H. (eds.). Iowa State Univ. Press, Ames, 1965.

Goodpasture, E. W., and Anderson, K. Isolation of a Wild Avian Pox Virus Inducing Both Cytoplasmic and Nuclear Inclusions. Amer. Jour. Path. 40:437, 1962.

Govinda, Rao, C. Studies on Pox in Ducks in Andhra Pradesh. Indian Vet. Jour. 42:151, 1965.

Hyde, J. M., *et al.* Fine Structure of the Coat and Nucleoid Material of Fowlpox Virus. Jour. Bact. 89:1557, 1965.

Mayr, A., and Kalcher, K. Plague-Bildung bei den Geflugelpocken viren. Arch. ges. Virusforsch. 11:307, 1961.

———, *et al.* A Canary Pox Vaccine Developed From Attenuated Culture Virus. Zentbl. Vet. Med. 12B:41, 1965.

### Other Viruses Similar to Poxviruses

Aynaud, M. La Stomatite Pustuleuse Contagieuse Des Ovins. Ann. Inst. Past. 37:498, 1923.

Bearcroft, W. G. C., and Jamieson, M. F. An Outbreak of Subcutaneous Tumours in Rhesus Monkeys. Nature 182:195, 1958.

BOUGHTON, I. B., and HARDY, W. T. Contagious Ecthyma (Sore Mouth) of Sheep and Goats. Jour. Amer. Vet. Med. Assn. 85:150, 1934.

BUTTNER, D., *et al.* The Fine Structure of the Virions of Contagious Pustular Dermatitis and Bovine Papular Stomatitis. Arch. ges. Virusforsch. 14:657–73, 1964.

GRIESMER, R. A., and COLE, C. R. Bovine Papular Stomatitis. Jour. Amer. Vet. Med. Assn. 137:404, 1960.

MOSCOVICI, C., *et al.* Isolation of a Viral Agent From Pseudocowpox Disease. Science 141:915, 1963.

NAGINGTON, J., *et al.* The Morphology of Bovine Papular Stomatitis Virus. Virol. 17:361, 1962.

———, *et al.* The Structure of Orf Virus. Virol. 23:461, 1964.

———, *et al.* Milker's Nodule Virus Infections in Dorset and Their Similarity to Orf. Vet. Rec. 78:305, 1966.

NEWSOM, I. E., and CROSS, F. Sore Mouth in Feeder Lambs Due to a Filtrable Virus. Jour. Amer. Med. Assn. 84:233, 1934.

NIVEN, J. S. F., *et al.* Subcutaneous "Growths" in Monkeys Produced by a Pox Virus. Jour. Path. Bact. 81:1, 1961.

PETERS, DIETRICH, *et al.* The Fine Structure of Paravaccinia Viruses. Virol. 23:609, 1964.

## Myxoma and Fibroma Viruses

KILHAM, L. Metastasizing Viral Fibromas of Gray Squirrels: Pathogenesis and Mosquito Transmission. Amer. Jour. Hyg. 61:55, 1955

MARSHALL, I. D., and FENNER, F. Studies in the Epidemiology of Infectious Myxomatosis of Rabbits. VII. The Virulence of Strains of Myxoma Virus Recovered From Australian Wild Rabbits Between 1951 and 1959. Jour. Hyg. 58:485, 1960.

PADGETT, B. L., *et al.* Electron Microscopic Structure of Myxoma Virus and Some Reactivable Derivatives. Jour. Bact. 87:454, 1964.

SHOPE, R. E. A Filtrable Virus Causing A Tumor-like Condition in Rabbits and Its Relationship to Virus Myxomatosum. Jour. Exp. Med. 56:803, 1932.

# 45

# The Herpesviruses

VIRUSES OF THE HERPES GROUP ARE COMPOSED of double-stranded DNA, surrounded by a capsid showing icosahedral shape and possessing 162 capsomeres. The complete virions, including the envelope, measure 180 mμ to 250 mμ in diameter (Figs. 45.1 and 45.2). They are sensitive to ether and are pH and heat labile.

Replication of the viruses of this group begins with the formation of the nucleocapsid in the nucleus of the host cell. The envelope of the virus is acquired during its passage from the nucleus through the cytoplasm of the cell.

Herpesviruses have a predilection for surface epithelium, mucous membranes, and respiratory tissues. Some members of the group may infect nervous tissue and others the salivary glands of various animals.

### Herpes Simplex Virus

**Proposed Name.** *Herpesvirus hominis.*

Herpes-simplex virus causes "fever blisters" or "cold sores" of man. It does not cause natural disease in animals, but rabbits, guinea pigs, mice, and cats have been experimentally infected. The virus can be grown on the chorioallantoic membrane of chicken embryos and in tissue cultures.

### Pseudorabies Virus

**Diseases Produced.** Pseudorabies, Aujeszky's disease, mad-itch, infectious bulbar paralysis.

**Hosts Affected.** Cattle, swine, brown rats, dogs, cats, horses, sheep, and, rarely, man.

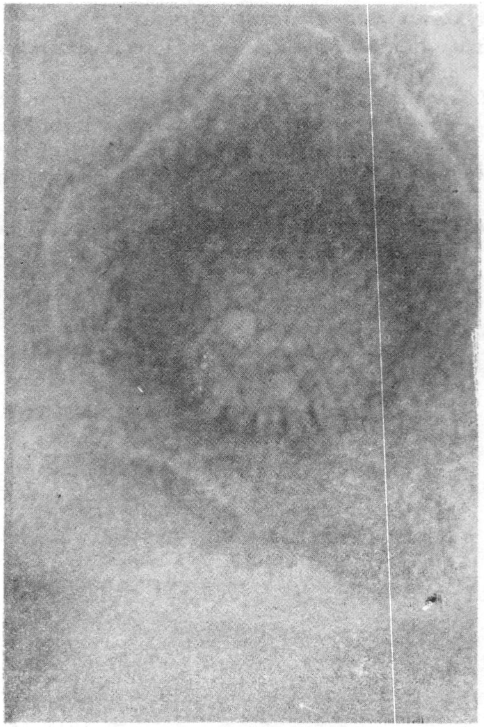

FIG. 45.1—Herpesvirus showing envelope, ×350,000. (Courtesy Wildy, Russell, and Horne. Virol. 12:204, 1960.)

Experimentally the rabbit, guinea pig, mouse, monkey, chicken, and chicken embryo may be infected.

**History and Distribution.** Pseudorabies was first described by Aujeszky in Hungary in 1902. The work of Schmeidhoffer in 1910 showed the etiological agent to be a virus. The disease occurs sporadically in many

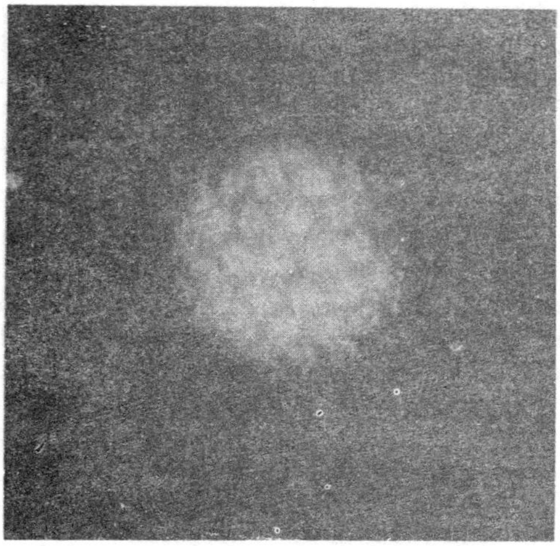

FIG. 45.2—Herpesvirus nonenveloped, ×370,000. (Courtesy Wildy, Russell, and Horne. Virol. 12:204, 1960.)

parts of the world. It has been reported in Europe, the British Isles, South America, and the United States.

**Properties of the Virus.** The morphology of pseudorabies virus is typical of the herpes group. Elementary bodies measure approximately 100 mμ without the envelope and 150 mμ to 180 mμ including it. It is preserved in 50 per cent glycerin stored at 0°C. for several years. In fluid from pulmonary edema it is viable after 797 days storage in a refrigerator. Heating to 55°–60°C. for 30 to 50 minutes, 70° for 10 minutes, or 80° for 3 minutes destroys the virus, and at 100° the virus is killed instantly. Phenol in a 5 per cent concentration will destroy the virus in 2 hours, 1 per cent in 15 hours, and 0.3 per cent in 61 days. One per cent sodium hydroxide destroys the virus immediately. Putrefaction destroys the virus in 11 days.

**Cultivation.** Animal passage in rabbits by skin or cerebral inoculation can be used to propagate the virus. Tissue cultures which employ rabbit or guinea pig testicular tissue will support growth of pseudorabies virus. Chicken embryos can be infected by various routes of inoculation and pock lesions are produced when the virus is inoculated onto the chorioallantoic membrane (Fig. 42.3). The egg-adapted virus may be lethal to the embryo, killing it in 3 to 5 days after inoculation, but recently isolated strains may fail to kill or do so irregularly.

**Transmission.** Transmission of pseudorabies in cattle usually takes place when the virus is introduced into the injured skin or mucous membrane. Shope and others have called attention to rats and swine as disseminators of the virus, these hosts being readily infected by feeding. Shope has also drawn particular attention to the presence of pseudorabies virus in the nasal secretions of swine and to the fact that the secretions are the usual source of the virus for other swine and cattle. Dogs and cats have been known to contract the disease following the consumption of infected tissues of cattle. Commercial hog cholera virus vaccines have been contaminated with pseudorabies virus, and transmission to swine has occurred through the use of such products.

**Characteristics of the Disease.** Pseudorabies is a highly fatal, relatively noncontagious disease of cattle and laboratory animals and a highly contagious, mild disease of swine. Its occurrence in swine, according to Shope, is quite widespread and is usually not detected. The disease is seldom fatal in swine, but in artificially infected hogs a definite temperature increase and inappetence is observed. Local paralysis may result if the virus is injected intramuscularly. In other animals, there is intense itching at the point of skin infection which is accompanied by self-mutilation by gnawing or rubbing. These symptoms are so characteristic in cattle and laboratory animals that they are considered diagnostic of the disease. Mania is often observed in cattle and sometimes other animals so it is confused with rabies, hence the name pseudorabies has been used. In the final stages of the disease the virus involves the brain and the animal becomes paralyzed. This is followed by coma and death. The virus has been isolated from human infection in laboratory workers. However, the disease is mild and of short duration.

**Pathological Changes.** There are no characteristic lesions in pseudorabies. The kind and extent of lesions depend upon the animal species infected and the duration of the disease. In animals with skin infection, the lesions may include hyperemia, edema, and necrosis which are usually accompanied by severe traumatic lesions. Depending upon the duration of the disease, there may be meningitis and perivascular, leucocytic infiltration of the brain tissue. In sheep and swine pulmonary edema may be observed.

**Immunity.** Resistance apparently follows recovery in swine. Neutralizing antibodies have been demonstrated in the serum of large numbers of swine. A majority of the samples of commercial anti-hog cholera serum tested by Shope showed the presence of neutralizing antibodies for pseudorabies.

Artificial immunizing agents are used in some countries for the prevention of this disease. Live modified-virus vaccines have been used to a limited extent.

**Diagnosis.** The diagnosis can be made in cattle and sheep and laboratory animals from the symptoms of intense itching of the skin. Rabbits which are inoculated subcutaneously with pseudorabies material should exhibit characteristic symptoms of intense pruritus in 3 to 7 days if the virus is present.

### Virus B

**Proposed Name.** *Herpesvirus simiae.*

**Disease Produced.** Encephalitis.

**Hosts Affected.** Man, captive monkeys, and, experimentally, guinea pigs, mice, rabbits, and chicken embryos.

**History and Distribution.** Virus B was first isolated from a fatal case of encephalitis, patient B, a laboratory worker who had been bitten by a monkey.

Several fatal cases of virus B infection have occurred in laboratory workers and caretakers of monkeys. Surveys reveal a significant number of monkeys are naturally infected with the virus. Isolations of the virus from the central nervous system and from kidney tissue of monkeys have been reported.

**Properties of the Virus.** B virus is approximately 125 m$\mu$ in size and is filterable through Berkefeld V and N candles, Seitz and Chamberland $L_3$ filters. The virus can be preserved in 50 per cent glycerin, by storing in dry ice at $-70$°C., or by lyophilization. Virus B is antigenically related to herpes-simplex and pseudorabies viruses.

**Cultivation.** Virus B can be cultivated on the chorioallantoic membrane of the chicken embryo where it produces pocks similar to those of herpes simplex and pseudorabies.

The virus can also be propagated in tissue cultures, and will produce a cytopathic effect in the cells of the culture.

**Transmission.** The virus occurs in the saliva of some monkeys and is transferred to man by biting. Other hosts are infected only by artificial inoculation.

**Pathological Changes and Characteristics of the Disease.** Vesiculopustular lesions appear at the site of the monkey bites, followed by lymphangitis and lymphadenitis. A week later meningoencephalitis develops, followed by death. There are also focal necrotic lesions in the spleen, adrenals, and lymph nodes. Intranuclear inclusions are described in experimental infections.

**Immunity.** Neutralizing antibodies can be demonstrated from the sera of some normal monkeys. Artificially infected monkeys are immune following recovery from the infection.

**Diagnosis.** A diagnosis of virus B infection would necessitate isolation of the virus and its differentiation from other viruses.

### Infectious Bovine Rhinotracheitis Virus

**Diseases Produced.** Infectious bovine rhinotracheitis (IBR), infectious pustular vaginitis (IPV), conjunctivitis, encephalitis, abortion.

**Hosts Affected.** Cattle. Possibly deer. Horses, swine, goats, mice, and guinea pigs are not susceptible.

**History and Distribution.** Infectious bovine rhinotracheitis virus was first described by Madin, York, and McKercher in 1956. The disease had been observed earlier by others in both Colorado and California. The virus has since been isolated from many countries throughout the world. The disease which was originally thought to infect only the upper respiratory tract of cattle has been isolated from a variety of tissues, especially those of the genital tract. The condition originally described in Africa as "Epi-vag" is caused by the IBR virus.

**Properties of the Virus.** The morphology and structure of IBR virus is typical of the herpes group. The elementary bodies are reported to be 120 mμ to 180 mμ in size. The virus loses its infectivity after 50 days at 22°C. and after 10 days at 37°C. It is inactivated by a 21-minute exposure to 56° C. At —60° C. it survives for 9 months. It is sensitive to the action of ether, acetone, and ethyl alcohol. It is stable at pH 6 to 9 but loses activity below pH 6.

Antigenic comparison of various isolates of IBR and IPV viruses does not reveal marked differences among them. However, several investigators suggest there is variation among certain strains. An antigenic relationship between IBR and other herpesviruses has been shown by complement-fixation procedures.

**Cultivation.** The IBR virus can be grown in a variety of cell cultures. Kidney cells of bovine origin are in common use. Cells from pig, sheep, and goat kidney will support growth. HeLa cells have also been used. A cytopathic effect is produced. Cell cultures of chicken embryo fibroblasts or intact chicken embryos do not support growth of the virus.

**Characteristics of the Disease.** The respiratory form of the disease is usually of sudden onset with high temperature, congested nasal mucous membranes, salivation, and nasal discharge. Recovery usually occurs in about 10 days. Death losses are usually low. Conjunctivitis is not infrequently observed in outbreaks of IBR. Abortion may occur in pregnant cows at 6 to 7 months of gestation.

Occasionally the virus produces encephalitis.

**Pathological Changes.** Infection of the female genital tract (IPV) is evidenced by lesions in the vagina and vulva characterized by circumscribed ulcerative areas accompanied by mucopurulent discharge. In the bull there may be lesions of the genitalia similar to those observed in the cows. Inclusion bodies may be observed in infected cells.

**Immunity.** Recovery from IBR usually results in immunity. A live modified-virus vaccine is widely used for the prevention of the disease.

Reduction of virulence of the virus for the production of vaccine is accomplished by passage in cell cultures.

**Diagnosis.** The diagnosis of infectious bovine rhinotracheitis may be made by the isolation of the virus in bovine kidney cell cultures and its subsequent identification by determination of its specific characteristics. Diagnosis is also made by comparison of the neutralizing capacity of paired serum samples. One sample is collected during the acute phase of the disease and the other during convalesence.

### Malignant Catarrhal Fever Virus

**Disease Produced.** Malignant catarrhal fever. Snotsickte (Africa).

**Hosts Affected.** Cattle and the wildebeest.

**History and Distribution.** Malignant catarrhal fever of cattle probably occurred as early as the 1850's according to Piercy. Difficulties in artificial transmission and cultivation of the virus have impeded the study of the disease. The disease occurs worldwide, but its overall incidence in any locality is not high.

**Properties of the Virus.** The malignant catarrhal fever virus has been described by Plowright as being typical of the herpes group, resembling most closely the varicella-zoster and the cytomegalic subgroups. The virion, complete with its envelope, measures 140 mμ to 240 mμ and 100 mμ exclusive of envelope. The virus is more susceptible to physical destruction than most. It survives for only a few days in blood stored at 4°C. Freezing destroys infectivity unless the virus is protected by mixing with serum or glycerine. Sonication of cells carrying the virus destroys infectivity. The virus is inhibited by IDUR and is sensitive to ether.

Malignant catarrhal fever virus is quite strongly cell-associated, especially with leucocytes. Serum or erythrocytes separated from infective whole blood are usually non-infectious when administered to susceptible animals. By neutralization tests the virus shows no relationship to infectious bovine rhinotracheitis virus.

**Cultivation.** The malignant catarrh virus has been grown in calf thyroid and calf kidney cell cultures. Serial transfer is more successful in the thyroid cells and more of the virus appears in the cell culture fluids than with kidney cells in which the virus is mainly cell-associated. Intranuclear inclusions and syncytium formation are observed in cell cultures. The virus cannot be grown in chicken embryos.

**Transmission.** Transmission apparently occurs by contact with discharges from diseased or carrier animals. Vector transmission has been suggested but not proved. In Africa the wildebeest is an important inapparent carrier of the virus.

**Characteristics of the Disease.** Malignant catarrhal fever is a sporadic, acute disease of cattle. It does not usually spread to very many animals in a herd. Febrile reaction, depression, anorexia, upper respiratory congestion, and nasal discharges are most frequently observed in affected cattle. Nervous symptoms are also quite common. Mortality rate is high in those animals infected.

**Pathological Changes.** Marked inflammatory and destructive changes occur in the upper respiratory areas. Lesions of meningoencephalitis are also observed.

**Immunity.** Recovered animals are resistant to reinfection. Neutralizing antibodies can be demonstrated. Although killed vaccines have been used, they are not widely employed.

**Diagnosis.** Clinical and pathological features have most often been used as a basis of diagnosis. However, resemblances of malignant catarrhal fever and other bovine diseases, such as infectious bovine rhinotracheitis and mucosal disease, may require isolation and identification of the virus for accurate diagnosis.

### Equine Rhinopneumonitis Virus

**Diseases Produced.** Rhinopneumonitis. Abortion.

**Hosts Affected.** Horse. Experimentally, the hamster, mouse, and guinea pig.

**History and Distribution.** Although respiratory disease of horses has been recognized and recorded in the early writings of the diseases of animals, the complex etiology of this condition was not appreciated until about 1954 when improved virological methods were developed and applied. While it had been shown by Basset, in 1911, that a filterable agent was a cause of equine respiratory disease and Dimock and Edwards, in 1922, suggested that equine abortions were the result of virus infection, the techniques for the isolation and characterization of the viruses concerned were not available. Investigations since 1954 have revealed that there are several viruses which are associated with respiratory disease of the equine, one of which is designated as rhinopneumonitis virus. This virus is also an important cause of abortion. Rhinopneumonitis virus has been isolated and identified in many countries, so it is worldwide in occurrence. On horse farms yearly outbreaks of the disease in young horses may occur.

**Properties of the Virus.** The morphology and structure of the rhinopneumonitis virus is typical of the herpes group. Electron microscopic studies show the elementary bodies to be variable in size, ranging from approximately 100 m$\mu$ to 200 m$\mu$ in diameter, with the average being 167 m$\mu$. The nucleic acid is of the DNA type.

Plummer (1964) was unable to show by cross-neutralization tests any antigenic relationship between the rhinopneumonitis virus (equine herpesvirus type I) and other members of the herpes group. Those compared included herpes simplex, virus B, IBR, pseudorabies, and equine herpesvirus type II (LK virus). However, complement-fixation tests showed an antigenic relationship between rhinopneumonitis, IBR, and pseudorabies. Antigenic variants of rhinopneumonitis virus have not been reported.

**Cultivation.** Rhinopneumonitis virus can be cultivated in cell cultures derived from equine, rabbit, or hamster kidneys. Cytopathic changes are observed, consisting of ballooning of cells and syncytium formation. Pock lesions are produced by inoculation of the chorioallantoic membrane of chicken embryos. Inoculation of suckling hamsters with the virus results in a fatal hepatitis in 18 to 24 hours. Suckling mice are killed by intracerebral inoculation. Local erythema is produced by the intradermal inoculation of rabbits.

**Transmission.** The virus of rhinopneumonitis is usually transferred through respiratory droplets and discharges. Older literature suggests transmission via the semen from carrier stallions.

**Characteristics of the Disease.** Rhinopneumonitis is primarily a respiratory disease of young horses. It is quite contagious and has an incubation period of 2 to 10 days. Fever, depression, and nasal discharge are common signs of the infection. Reinfection of adult horses is usually asymptomatic. It is during these reinfections that the virus may pass from the mare to the fetus. Abortions usually occur after the eighth month of gestation.

**Pathological Changes.** Most of the lesions of rhinopneumonitis are found in the respiratory tract. The mucosa of the upper respiratory tract is congested, covered by excessive mucus, and may show petechial hemorrhages. Adjacent lymph nodes are edematous and hyperemic.

Aborted fetuses show liver necrosis and hemorrhages on the heart and in the lungs. Microscopically, acidophilic intranuclear inclusion bodies can be demonstrated in the hepatic cells and epithelium of the bronchi.

**Immunity.** Resistance to rhinopneumonitis virus results from infection and recovery. However, such immunity wanes rather rapidly, and recovered animals are again susceptible in 3 to 4 months.

Vaccines consisting of live hamster-adapted virus have been used with success if administered twice yearly.

**Diagnosis.** The isolation and identification of rhinopneumonitis virus are necessary for accurate diagnosis. Differentiation of virus from equine influenza, parainfluenza, equine rhinoviruses, and "LK" virus must be made.

### Equine Herpesvirus "LK"

A herpesvirus isolated from a horse with respiratory catarrh was reported by Plummer and Waterson (1963). The properties of this isolate (LK) are very similar to rhinopneumonitis except that it is antigenically distinct and is not pathogenic for suckling mice or chicken embryos. The importance of this virus as a pathogen of the horse must await further investigation.

## Laryngotracheitis Virus

**Disease Produced.** Laryngotracheitis.

**Hosts Affected.** Chickens and pheasants. Other birds and laboratory animals are refractory to inoculation.

**History and Distribution.** Laryngotracheitis was first recognized as a disease entity in 1925 by May and Tittsler. Beach reported in 1930 that the disease was produced by a filterable virus.

The disease is widespread in poultry throughout the United States and Canada. It also has been identified in Japan and Australia and European countries.

**Properties of the Virus.** The morphology and structure of the laryngotracheitis virus is reported to be identical with other herpesviruses (Cruickshank *et al.,* 1963). Elementary bodies are 100 mμ to 110 mμ in diameter, exclusive of the envelope.

Heat inactivation of the virus occurs by exposure to 55°C. for 15 minutes and to 75°C. for 30 seconds.

Five per cent phenol kills in 1 minute and 3 per cent cresol and 1 per cent sodium hydroxide are lethal in 30 seconds.

The virus remains viable at 4° to 10°C. for 217 days and in the dried state for 661 days. It does not survive in the carcass of dead birds long after decomposition is evident.

**Cultivation.** The virus of laryngotracheitis can be cultivated in chicken embryos. Chorioallantoic inoculation is best since the virus produces pock lesions, and this fact is an aid in its differentiation from other viruses which attack the respiratory system of chickens.

**Transmission.** The transmission of laryngotracheitis is by droplets from the respiratory tract which contain the virus and are inhaled by susceptible chickens. Contaminated food and water also play a part in transmission. Recovered birds have been shown to harbor the virus for as long as 16 months, and are capable of transmitting the disease to susceptible birds.

**Characteristics of the Disease.** Laryngotracheitis is a disease of adult and young adult birds. More outbreaks occur in the fall and winter months. Symptoms of gasping and coughing are outstanding. Infected birds are depressed, and in laying flocks egg production is sharply reduced and ceases entirely in some cases. The disease usually spreads rapidly and the morbidity rate is high, but death rates average about 15 per cent. Death results from occlusion of the lumen of the larynx or trachea with blood and exudate.

**Pathological Changes.** Lesions of laryngotracheitis are limited to the larynx and trachea. There is marked hyperemia and congestion of the mucous membrane of these organs. These changes are accompanied by hemorrhage, excessive mucous secretion, and caseous exudation. Intranuclear inclusion bodies are described as occurring in tracheal epithelium.

**Immunity.** Recovery from laryngotracheitis confers immunity.

Artificial immunization is practiced. Live virus, usually embryo propagated, is inoculated onto the cloacal mucous membrane or wing web. The virus produces an infection at this site but does not involve the respiratory system. Birds so vaccinated are immune to tracheal infection.

**Diagnosis.** Laryngotracheitis must be distinguished from infectious bronchitis and Newcastle disease, with which it may be confused at times. Isolation and identification of the virus in chicken embryos is most accurate (Table 45.1).

A serum neutralization test described by Hitchner *et al.* may be helpful in diagnosis.

## Virus III

**Disease Produced.** Virus III infection.

**Host Affected.** Domestic rabbit.

**History and Distribution.** Virus III was

TABLE 45.1

DIFFERENTIATION OF AVIAN RESPIRATORY VIRUSES IN CHICKEN EMBRYOS

| Virus | Chorioallantoic Membrane | Effect on Embryo | Agglutination of Avian R.B.C. by Allantoic Fluid |
|---|---|---|---|
| Newcastle | no lesions | lethal 48–72 hrs. | + |
| Bronchitis | no lesions | dwarfed | — |
| Laryngotracheitis | thickened with pock lesions | no gross changes | — |

first described by Rivers and Tillet in connection with attempts to infect rabbits with chicken-pox virus of man. At first these investigators thought they had transferred the chicken-pox virus to rabbits, but later found they were propagating a virus which was latent in the rabbits and did not produce lesions until it had been concentrated by successive passages.

**Properties of the Virus.** Virus III is filterable through Berkefeld V and N and Chamberland $L_2$ candles. It is inactivated at 55°C. in 10 minutes. The virus is preserved for 6 weeks in 50 per cent glycerin and for 16 months when frozen and dried.

**Cultivation.** Cultivation of virus III is by inoculation of rabbits or in tissue cultures employing rabbit testicular tissue.

**Transmission.** The injection of filtrates of diseased tissues or in some cases blood and tissues from apparently normal rabbits is the source of the virus.

**Characteristics of the Disease.** After 4 to 6 days incubation, anorexia, emaciation, diarrhea, and fever result. Reddened spots and papules appear in the skin. Recovery occurs in a few days, the disease being nonfatal.

**Immunity.** Specific neutralizing antibodies are present in the blood serum after recovery.

**Diagnosis.** Diagnosis of virus III infection is possible only by transmission to susceptible rabbits and differentiation from other viruses by cross-immunity experiments.

### Canine Herpesvirus

Isolates of a virus from pups and from dog kidney cell cultures reported by several investigators have been classified as a herpesvirus.

The virus has a particle size of 144 mμ and is morphologically typical of the herpes group. It does not agglutinate the erythrocytes of the horse, cow, guinea pig, dog, mouse, fowl, sheep, or man. It is serologically distinct from canine hepatitis virus and from other herpesviruses.

The virus can be grown in dog kidney cell cultures and produces cytopathic changes. The chorioallantoic membrane of chicken embryos does not support growth. Suckling mice and ferrets are resistant.

Fatal hemorrhagic disease in newborn pups has been reported to result from infection with the virus. However, the virus has also been isolated from clinically healthy pups. The transplacental passage of the virus has been reported.

### Feline Herpesvirus

A viral agent isolated by Crandell and Maurer (1958) from respiratory disease of cats was later found by Ditchfield and Grinyer to belong to the herpesvirus group. Isolates from cats in Canada and Europe are closely related or identical immunologically.

The name feline rhinotracheitis for the disease has been suggested by Crandell *et al.*

Feline rhinotracheitis virus particles measure approximately 100 mμ in diameter.

Some particles exhibit a "tailed" appearance. The virus is chloroform and acid sensitive and its growth is inhibited by IUDR. It can be isolated and grown in kitten kidney cells in which cytopathic changes occur, including the formation of intranuclear inclusions. Rabbit kidney cell cultures will also support the growth of the virus.

The disease in cats is characterized by a febrile reaction, depression, and anorexia, accompanied by acute respiratory signs which include sneezing, coughing, profuse lacrimation, nasal discharge, and difficult breathing. The mucous membranes of the upper respiratory tract are congested and covered with mucopurulent exudate. Intranuclear inclusions can be demonstrated in epithelial cells of the upper tract.

A number of viral isolates have been obtained from the respiratory tract of cats which have been found antigenically distinct from the feline rhinotracheitis virus. Until they have been adequately studied, their role in disease or their classification cannot be determined.

The relationship of the feline rhinotracheitis virus to the feline distemper virus described by Hindle and Findley in 1932 cannot be determined. While the clinical features are very similar, the viruses have not been compared.

## CYTOMEGALOVIRUSES

A group of viruses which induce the production of abnormally large cells in the host tissue or in cell cultures have been designated as cytomegaloviruses. These viruses have been determined by electron microscopy to be similar in structure to the herpesviruses. A prominent characteristic of the cytomegalic virus infection is the presence of enlarged cells 25μ to 40μ and the appearance of intranuclear inclusions within these cytomegalic cells.

Most members of this group have a predilection for the epithelium of the salivary glands and so have previously been referred to as *salivary gland viruses*. Other members of the group occur in the upper respiratory tissues.

The cytomegaloviruses can be cultivated in cell cultures and usually grow best in cultures derived from the natural host of the particular virus. The viruses are strongly cell-associated, and therefore, fluids obtained from infected cell cultures may contain little or no virus.

The detailed characteristics of the viruses of this group have not been determined.

### Cytomegalovirus (Salivary Gland Virus) of Man

Apparently widespread in man. Usually inapparent infections occur, but fatal neonatal infection is recorded.

### Cytomegalovirus of Swine

Inclusion body rhinitis of swine has been recognized in many parts of the world and has been associated with upper respiratory disease in that species. The young pig is susceptible, and substantial death losses due to the infection have been reported.

### Cytomegaloviruses of Small Laboratory Animals

Salivary gland viruses have been described from guinea pigs, mice, hamsters, and rats.

Usually these viruses produce only an inapparent infection. However, generalized infection may occur as a result of the stress of various experimental procedures to which these animals may be subjected. Intracerebral inoculation of the salivary gland virus of guinea pigs into young guinea pigs will produce a fatal meningitis.

### Cytomegaloviruses of Monkeys

Isolation of a virus from the African Green Monkey has been reported by Black *et al.* The virus which was recovered from kidney cell cultures and from salivary glands possesses the general characteristics of a cytomegalic virus. A shared antigen with a cytomegalic virus of human origin and the ability to grow in cell cultures derived from human tissues differs from the rather strict host specificity of other members of the group.

Cellular inclusions in the salivary glands of other primate species have been observed, and the existence of cytomegalic viruses is suggested.

## MISCELLANEOUS HERPESVIRUSES

### Herpes Zoster-Varicella Virus (*Herpes varicellae*)

This virus is the cause of chicken pox and herpes zoster in man. Chicken pox occurs primarily in children and herpes zoster chiefly in adults. Animals are not susceptible.

### *Herpesvirus platyrrhinae*

Holmes *et al.* (1966) have described a new member of the herpes group which infects monkeys. The virus apparently is widespread among several varieties of New World monkeys producing nonfatal infections. Marmosets in captivity are highly susceptible and suffer high mortality. The name *Herpesvirus platyrrhinae* is suggested for this virus.

## REFERENCES


### Herpes Simplex Virus

Scott, T. F. M., and Tokumaru, T. The Herpesvirus Group. *In* Viral and Rickettsial Infections of Man. 4th Ed. Horsfall, F. L., and Tamm, I. (eds.). J. B. Lippincott Co., Philadelphia, 1965.

### Pseudorabies Virus

Aujeszky, A. Ueber eine neve Infektionskrankheit bei Haustieren. Zentralbl. f. Bakt. Abt. I. Orig. 32:353, 1902.

Bartha, A., and Koinok, J. Active Immunization Against Aujeszky's Disease. Proc. 17th World Vet. Cong., Hanover, 1:531, 1963.

Ben-Porat, T., and Kaplan, A. S. The Chemical Composition of Herpes Simplex and Pseudorabies Viruses. Virol. 16:261, 1962.

Remlinger, P., and Bailly, J. La Maladie d'Aujeszky. Massom and Co., Paris, 1938.

Saunders, J. R., *et al.* An Unusual Outbreak of Aujeszky's Disease in Swine. Proc. 67th Ann. Meet. U.S. Livestock Sanit. Assn., p. 331, 1963.

Shope, R. E. An Experimental Study of "Mad Itch" With Especial Reference to Its Relationship to Pseudorabies. Jour. Exp. Med. 54:233, 1931.

———. Experiments on the Epidemiology of Pseudorabies. Jour. Exp. Med. 62:85, 1935.

Singh, K. U. A Plaque Assay Method of Pseudorabies Virus in Monolayers of Porcine Kidney Cells. Cornell Vet. 52:237, 1962.

### Virus B

Buthala, D. A. I. Studies on *Herpesvirus simiae* (B virus): Inactivation Attempts and Vaccine Production. II. Hyperimmunized Horse Anti-B Virus Globulin: Preparation and Effectiveness. Jour. Inf. Dis. 111:95. 101, 1962.

Hartley, E. G. Naturally-occurring "B" Virus Infection in Cynomolgus Monkeys. Vet. Rec. 76:555, 1964.

Keeble, S. A. Virus B Infections of Monkeys: A Disease Communicable to Man. Vet. Rec. 73:618, 1961.

Sabin, A., and Wright, A. M. Acute Ascending Myelitis Following a Monkey Bite, With the Virus Capable of Reproducing the Disease. Jour. Exp. Med. 59:115, 1934.

### Infectious Bovine Rhinotracheitis Virus

Abinanti, F. R., and Plumer, G. R. The Isolation of Infectious Bovine Rhinitis Virus From Cattle Affected With Conjunctivitis—Observations on Experimental Infection. Amer. Jour. Vet. Res. 22:13, 1961.

Armstrong, J. A., *et al.* Observations on the Virus of Infectious Bovine Rhinotracheitis and Its Affinity With the Herpesvirus Group. Virol. 14:276, 1961.

Kendrick, J. W., *et al.* Infectious Pustular Vulvovaginitis of Cattle. Cornell Vet. 48:458, 1958.

Madin, S. H., *et al.* Isolation of the Infectious Bovine Rhinotracheitis Virus. Science 124:721, 1956.

McKercher, D. G. Studies of the Etiologic Agents of Infectious Bovine Rhinotracheitis and Bläschenausschlag (Coital Vesicular Exanthema). Amer. Jour. Vet. Res. 24:501–9, 1963.

———, and Wada, E. M. The Virus of Infectious Bovine Rhinotracheitis as a Cause of Abortion in Cattle. Jour. Amer. Vet. Med. Assn. 144:136, 1964.

Maré, C. J., and van Rensburg, S. J. The Isolation of Viruses Associated With Infertility of Cattle. Jour. S. Afr. Vet. Med. Assn. 32:201, 1961.

### Malignant Catarrhal Fever Virus

PIERCY, S. E. Studies in Bovine Malignant Catarrh. Brit. Vet. Jour. 108:35, 1952.

PLOWRIGHT, W. Studies on the Virus of Malignant Catarrhal Fever in Africa. Proc. 17th World Vet. Cong., Hanover, 1:276, 1963.

———, *et al.* Blue Wildebeest and the Etiological Agent of Bovine Malignant Catarrhal Fever. Nature 188: 1167, 1960.

———, *et al.* Growth and Characterization of the Virus of Bovine Malignant Catarrhal Fever in East Africa. Jour. Gen. Microbiol. 39:253, 1965.

### Equine Rhinopneumonitis Virus

BASSET, J. Cause determinante de la fievre typhoide du cheval (influenza, grippe, pasteurellose; pferdestaupe; pinkeye). Compt. rend. Acad. sci. 153:485, 1911.

DIMOCK, W. W. The Diagnosis of Virus Abortion in Mares. Jour. Amer. Vet. Med. Assn. 96:665, 1940.

———, and EDWARDS, P. R. Infections of Fetuses and Foals. Ky. Agr. Exp. Sta. Bull. Supp. 333:297, 1933.

DOLL, E. R., and BRYANS, J. R. Epizootiology of Equine Viral Rhinopneumonitis. Jour. Amer. Vet. Med. Assn. 142:31, 1963.

———, and ———. Immunization of Young Horses Against Viral Rhinopneumonitis. Cornell Vet. 53:24, 1963.

———, and WALLACE, M. E. Cultivation of Equine Abortion and Equine Influenza Viruses on the Chorioallantoic Membrane of Chicken Embryos. Cornell Vet. 44:453, 1954.

———, *et al.* Cultivation of the Equine Influenza Virus in Suckling Syrian Hamsters. Its Similarity to the Equine Abortion Virus. Cornell Vet. 44:133, 1954.

———, *et al.* Thermal, Hematological, and Serological Responses of Weanling Horses Following Inoculation With Equine Abortion Virus: Its Similarity to Equine Influenza. Cornell Vet. 44:181, 1954.

MANNINGER, R. Studies on Infectious Abortion in Mares Due To a Filterable Virus. Acta Vet. Hungarica 1:62, 1949.

PLUMMER, G. Serological Comparison of the Herpes Viruses. Brit. Jour. Exp. Path. 45:135, 1964.

———, and WATERSON, A. P. Equine Herpes Viruses. Virol. 19:412, 1963.

### Laryngotracheitis Virus

BEACH, J. R. Infectious Bronchitis of Fowls. Jour. Amer. Vet. Med. Assn. 68:570, 1926.

———. The Virus of Laryngotracheitis of Fowls. Science 72:633, 1930.

BEAUDETTE, F. R., and HUDSON, C. B. Experiments on Immunization Against Laryngotracheitis in Fowls. Jour. Amer. Vet. Med. Assn. 82:460, 1933.

CHOMIAK, T. W., *et al.* Tissue Culture and Chicken Embryo Techniques for Infectious Laryngotracheitis Studies. Avian Dis. 4:235, 1960.

CRUICKSHANK, J. G., *et al.* The Fine Structure of Laryngotracheitis Virus. Virol. 20:376, 1963.

GELENCZEI, E. F., and MARTY, E. W. Studies on a Tissue-Culture Modified Infectious Laryngotracheitis Virus. Avian Dis. 8:105, 1964.

HOFSTAD, M. S. Infectious Laryngotracheitis. *In* Diseases of Poultry. 5th Ed. Biester, H. E., and Schwarte, L. H. (eds.). Iowa State Univ. Press, 1965.

MAY, H. G., and TITTSLER, R. P. Tracheo-laryngitis in Poultry. Jour. Amer. Vet. Med. Assn. 67:229, 1925.

SHIBLEY, G. P., *et al.* A Study of Infectious Laryngotracheitis Virus. I. Comparison of Serologic and Immunogenic Properties. Avian Dis. 6:59, 1962.

WATRACH, A. M., *et al.* The Structure of Infectious Laryngotracheitis Virus. Virol. 21:601, 1963.

### Virus III

RIVERS, T. M., and TILLET, W. S. Studies on Varicella. Jour. Exp. Med. 38:673, 1923.

### Canine Herpesvirus

CARMICHAEL, L. E., *et al.* Identification of a Cytopathic Agent Infectious for Puppies as a Canine Herpesvirus. Proc. Soc. Exp. Biol. Med. 120:644, 1965.

SPERTZEL, R. O., *et al.* Recovery and Characterization of a Herpes-like Virus From Dog Kidney Cell Cultures. Proc. Soc. Exp. Biol. Med. 120:651, 1965.

STEWART, S. E., *et al.* Herpes-like Virus Isolated From Neonatal and Fetal Dogs. Science 148:1341, 1965.

STRANDBERG, J. D., and CARMICHAEL, L. E. Electron Microscopy of a Canine Herpesvirus. Jour. Bact. 90: 1790, 1965.

### Feline Herpesvirus

BITTLE, J. L., *et al.* Serological Relationship of New Feline Cytopathogenic Viruses. Amer. Jour. Vet. Res. 21:547, 1960.

CRANDELL, R. A., and DESPEAUX, E. W. Cytopathology of Feline Viral Rhinotracheitis Virus in Tissue Cultures of Feline Renal Cells. Proc. Soc. Exp. Biol. Med. 101:494, 1959.

———, and MADIN, S. H. Experimental Studies on a New Feline Virus. Amer. Jour. Vet. Res. 21:551, 1960.

———, *et al.* Experimental Feline Rhinotracheitis. Jour. Amer. Vet. Med. Assn. 138:191, 1961.

DITCHFIELD, J., and GRINYER, I. Feline Rhinotracheitis Virus: A Feline Herpes Virus. Virol. 26:504, 1965.

### Cytomegaloviruses

ANDREWES, C. H. Viruses of Vertebrates. Williams & Wilkins Co., Baltimore, 1964.

BLACK, P. H., *et al.* Isolation of a Cytomegalovirus From African Green Monkey. Proc. Soc. Exp. Biol. Med. 112:601, 1963.

CORNER, A. H., *et al.* A Generalized Disease in Piglets Associated With the Presence of Cytomegalic Inclusions. Jour. Comp. Path. 74:192, 1964.

SMITH, M. G. The Salivary Gland Viruses of Man and Animals. Prog. Med. Virol. 2:171, 1959.

WRIGHT, H. T., *et al.* Human Cytomegalovirus. Morphology by Negative Staining. Virol. 23:419, 1964.

### Miscellaneous Herpesviruses

HOLMES, A. W., *et al.* Isolation of a New Herpes-like Virus From South American Marmosets. Fed. Proc. 22: 234, 1963.

———, *et al.* The Epidemiology of a Herpes Virus Infection of New World Monkeys. Jour. Immunol. 90: 668–71, 1966.

HUNT, R. D., and MELENDEZ, L. V. Spontaneous Herpes-T Infection in the Owl Monkey. Pathologia Vet. 3:1, 1966.

WELLER, THOMAS. Varicella-Herpes Zoster Virus. *In* Viral and Rickettsial Infections of Man. Horsfall, F. L., and Tamm, I. (eds.). J. B. Lippincott Co., Philadelphia, 1965.

# 46
# The Papovaviruses

THE DESIGNATION OF THIS GROUP IS derived from papilloma-polyoma-vacuolating agents. Viruses classified in this group are composed of a DNA core surrounded by a capsid of icosahedral symmetry. Forty-two capsomeres make up the capsid. Particle size ranges from 40 mμ to 58 mμ. The viruses are stable in the presence of ether and at low pH. Agglutination of erythrocytes occurs when they are mixed with certain members of the group.

Replication occurs in the nucleus of the cell. The papovaviruses produce infections of surface epithelium, resulting in proliferative changes. Some members of the group produce neoplastic growths, especially in species of animals other than the natural host.

## Common-Wart Virus

**Disease Produced.** Warts.

**Host Affected.** Man.

The common warts of man are transmissible but have a long incubation period of one to twenty months. They are usually quite benign and usually disappear spontaneously. Acquired immunity to the virus is thought to play a part in recovery. Vaccines have been tried, but unsuccessfully. Attempts to transmit warts of man to animals are usually unsuccessful. Laryngeal warts of man have been reported transferable to the vagina of dogs, but this has not been confirmed.

## Bovine Papilloma Virus

**Disease Produced.** Cattle warts.

**Hosts Affected.** Cattle. The horse is susceptible but rabbits, mice, guinea pigs, and man are insusceptible to experimental inoculation.

**History and Distribution.** Cattle warts apparently occur in all countries. Royère, in 1902, was able to transmit experimentally the warts of cattle, horses, and dogs. Magalhães, in 1920, was able to transmit cattle warts by using Berkefeld filtrates of wart material.

**Properties of the Virus.** Bovine papilloma virus is typical of the papovavirus group since it possesses a DNA core and a capsid of 42 capsomeres. The virion is 48 mμ in diameter. The virus is resistant to chloroform and remains viable for 180 days at —70°C. and 90 days at 4°C.

**Cultivation.** The virus can be grown in cell cultures derived from a variety of sources. No cytopathic changes are produced. The virus has been adapted to grow in chicken embryo tissues.

**Transmission.** It is believed that warts are spread by contact with infected animals or objects contaminated by them. Injuries to the skin favor the establishment of the infection.

**Characteristics of the Disease.** Warts are more common in young cattle, especially in calves under one year. Affected areas are usually on the head, neck, and shoulder regions, often near or surrounding the eyes.

They may also occur on the udder and teats or on other parts of the body. The infected skin first becomes thickened, then rough and nodular, with the loss of hair. Sometimes the warts become large, pendular, and cauliflower-like in appearance. In such cases the growth and development of the host may be retarded. Frequently, spontaneous recovery occurs.

**Immunity.** Acquired immunity probably plays a part in spontaneous recovery. Vaccines are commercially available which are made by grinding fresh wart tissue in saline and then treating it with formalin to kill the virus. A wart vaccine of chicken embryo origin is also available. Although spontaneous recoveries often occur, the use of these vaccines is claimed to result in rapid disappearance of the warts.

**Diagnosis.** A clinical diagnosis of warts is ordinarily sufficient.

### Canine Oral-Papillomatosis Virus

**Disease Produced.** Canine oral papillomatosis.

**Host Affected.** Dog.

**History and Distribution.** Canine warts probably occur in all countries. Their contagiousness was recognized by McFadyean and Hobday and also Penberthy in 1898. Findlay, in 1930, reported the transmission of canine warts by Berkefeld filtrates of wart material.

**Properties of the Virus.** Canine oral-papillomatosis virus will pass through Berkefeld N filters. It is inactivated by a temperature of 45° to 58°C. in one hour. The virus remains viable upon storage in the refrigerator either in dried material or in 50 per cent glycerin for 63 days (Fig. 46.1).

**Cultivation.** The virus is transmissible to young dogs by inoculation into the scarified mucous membrane.

**Transmission.** Transmission of canine oral papilloma is presumed to occur through contact with infected dogs.

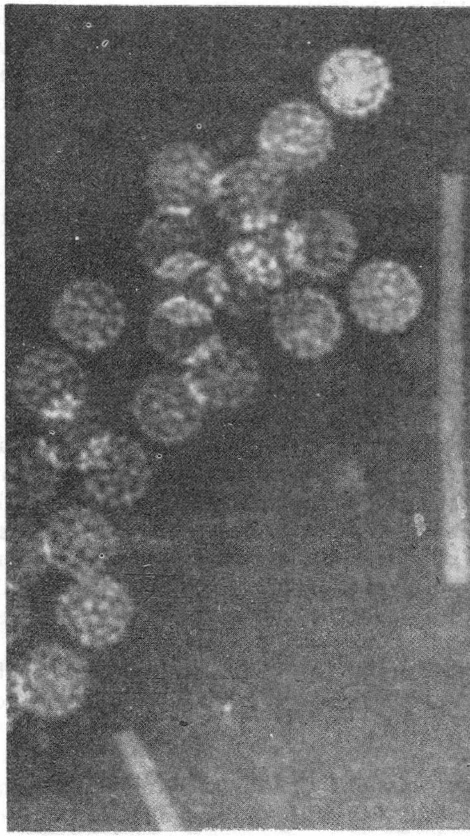

FIG. 46.1—Canine oral-papilloma virus and rods of tobacco mosaic (TMV ca. 180A wide) for size comparison, ×200,000. (Courtesy A. E. Ritchie and N. F. Cheville, A.R.S., National Animal Disease Lab., Ames, Iowa.)

**Characteristics of the Disease.** In experimentally inoculated dogs, the lesions appear in the mouth after incubation of one month. Areas which were inoculated become blanched and raised, then become roughened, finally resulting in a mass of closely packed papillae. In naturally occurring cases the warts may appear on the lips, tongue, palate, or buccal mucosa. The warts are quite benign and recovery with immunity results. Secondary warts often appear in other parts of the mouth after the primary ones have appeared.

**Immunity.** Dogs which have recovered from infection with canine oral-papilloma virus are resistant to reinfection; therefore, immunity probably is concerned with the disappearance of the papillomas. Artificial immunizing agents are not used to any extent. Wart vaccines prepared as for bovine use have been suggested for use in dogs.

**Diagnosis.** A clinical diagnosis is ordinarily made in canine oral papillomatosis.

### Rabbit Oral-Papillomatosis Virus

**Disease Produced.** Rabbit mouth warts.

**Hosts Affected.** Rabbits.

**History and Distribution.** The virus of oral papillomatosis of rabbits was discovered by Kidd and Parsons in 1936 in a rabbit with induced vitamin A deficiency. Later these investigators found similar papillomas in the oral mucous membranes of "normal" domestic rabbits.

**Properties of the Virus.** Rabbit oral-papilloma virus measures 50 mμ in diameter and passes Berkefeld V and N filters.

**Transmission.** Usually transmission accompanies injury of the mucous membrane and simultaneous exposure to the virus. Older animals are more resistant to exposure.

**Characteristics of the Disease.** Benign papillomas occur on the lower surface of the tongue and occasionally on the gums or floor of the mouth.

**Immunity.** Resistance to the rabbit oral-papilloma virus results after recovery from the infection.

**Diagnosis.** A diagnosis of oral papillomatosis of rabbits would consist of the appearance of the typical lesions of the mouth and the demonstration of their transmissibility to other rabbits.

### Rabbit-Wart Virus or Rabbit-Papilloma

**Disease Produced.** Rabbit warts.

**Hosts Affected.** Cottontail rabbit and experimentally the domestic rabbit.

**History and Distribution.** Rabbit-papilloma virus was isolated from cottontail rabbits by Shope in 1932. The specimens which yielded the virus were collected from rabbits in northwestern Iowa and later from some in southern Kansas. The disease is apparently confined to midwestern United States.

**Properties of the Virus.** The elementary bodies of rabbit-papilloma virus are nearly spherical in shape and are approximately 44 mμ in diameter. They will pass all grades of the Berkefeld type filter. The virus withstands a temperature of 65° to 67°C. for 30 minutes, but it is killed at 70°C. exposure.

**Cultivation.** Rabbit-papilloma virus can be passed serially in wild cottontail rabbits. It will produce lesions in domestic rabbits, but cannot be passed serially in that species.

**Transmission.** Transmission of rabbit-papilloma virus can be accomplished by intradermal inoculation in rabbits. Scarification or application of benzene to the skin increases its susceptibility to the virus.

**Characteristics of the Disease.** Rabbit-papilloma virus is specific for the skin epithelium of the rabbit. At first there are minute elevations in the skin which become keratinized and wrinkled, followed by cornification, forming large "horns" in some cases. Some papillomas become malignant and metastasize to internal organs.

**Immunity.** Specific immunity can be produced by intraperitoneal injection of the virus. No antigenic relationships have been noted with other viruses such as vaccinia, fibroma, or myxoma.

**Diagnosis.** The appearance of the cornified warts are characteristic and need little confirmation. Transmission experiments to rabbits may confirm a diagnosis of rabbit papilloma.

### Polyoma Virus

**Disease Produced.** Polyoma (multiple tumors).

**Hosts Affected.** Laboratory mice and wild mice by natural exposure. Experimentally, hamsters, rats, guinea pigs, and rabbits can be infected.

**History and Distribution.** While working with mouse leukemia, Gross (1953) and Stewart (1953) independently noted the occurrence of neoplasms in mice inoculated with cell-free extracts and filtrates prepared from mice with leukemia. Upon further investigation, experimental inoculation of the virus was found to produce many neoplasms in mice and in other laboratory animals. The virus is apparently widely distributed, occurring frequently in wild house mice.

**Properties of the Virus.** The general shape of the virus is round. It measures 45 m$\mu$ in diameter and is reported to possess 42 capsomeres which cover the DNA core (Fig. 46.2).

The polyoma virus agglutinates the erythrocytes of several species when placed at 4°C. Elution takes place when the erythrocyte-virus mixture is raised to 37°C. The virus is sensitive to interferon.

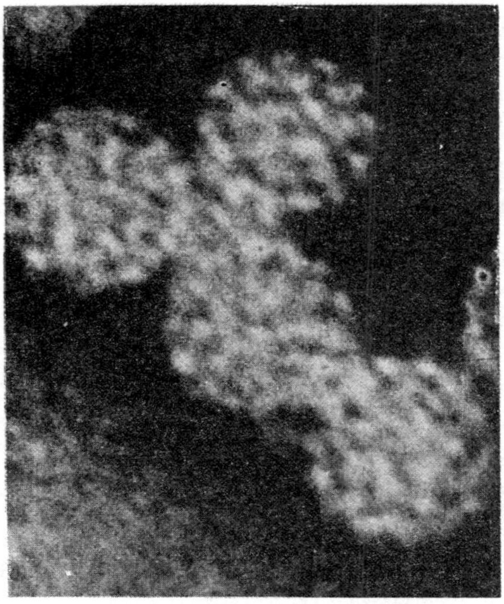

FIG. 46.2—Polyoma virus, ×550,000. (Courtesy Wildy, Stoker, Macpherson, and Horne. Virol. 11:444, 1960.)

The polyoma virus is resistant to ether and is somewhat more tolerant of heat and chemicals than many viruses.

**Cultivation.** Cell cultures of mouse embryo are most often employed for growth of the virus; however, other mouse tissues and tumor tissue from hamsters and rats will support growth. Cytopathic changes are observed in mouse embryo cell cultures, and plaques will form in monolayer preparations.

No disease of monkeys is caused by the virus.

**Transmission.** Polyoma virus is eliminated from the body of infected mice in urine, saliva, and feces. Contact with these discharges or consumption of contaminated feed and water are the usual sources of the virus to susceptible mice. The virus has been isolated from floor sweepings from premises where infected mice are found.

Wild mice have been found to be infected with polyoma.

**Characteristics of the Disease.** Other than tumor formation, there are usually no signs of infection in laboratory or wild mice. Many infected animals do not show tumor growths.

**Pathological Changes.** A great variety of neoplasms are induced by experimental polyoma virus infection. Most frequent are mixed tumors of the parotid salivary gland. Subcutaneous sarcomas, mammary tumors, thymic epitheliomas, and osteogenic sarcomas are also produced.

**Immunity.** Polyoma virus stimulates the formation of complement-fixing and neutralizing antibodies.

**Diagnosis.** Isolation of the virus and its identification by its characteristic features would be necessary for diagnosis. The virus cannot always be recovered from tumors induced by the infection.

## SV40 Virus

A virus isolated from monkey kidney cultures which produces marked vacuolation of the cells has been found to possess characteristics of the papilloma group.

The simian vacuolating virus has been isolated from both live and killed polio vaccines, but when such vaccines are administered to human beings no disease has been observed.

### Genital Papilloma Virus of Swine

A viral agent has been isolated by Parrish from genital papillomas of pigs. The virus passes filters having an average pore diameter of 175 m$\mu$.

The virus consistently reproduced lesions by experimental inoculation of pigs but failed to infect man, calf, guinea pig, rabbit, mouse, or chicken embryos. Lesions produced in pigs regressed and disappeared. Recovered animals proved to be immune to reinfection.

## REFERENCES


### Common Wart Virus

FINDLAY, G. M. Warts. A System of Bacteriology. 7:252 His Majesty's Stationery Office, London, 1930.

MAGALHAES, A. Brazil Med. 34:431, 1920.

### Bovine Papilloma Virus

CREECH, G. T. Experimental Studies of the Etiology of Common Warts in Cattle. Jour. Agr. Res. 39:723, 1929.

HUCK, R. A. Bovine Papillomatosis. Vet. Bull. 35:475, 1965.

SEGRE, D., *et al.* Neutralization of Bovine Papilloma Virus With Serums From Cattle and Horses With Experimental Papillomas. Jour. Amer. Vet. Res. 16:517, 1955.

### Canine Oral-Papilloma Virus

CHAMBERS, V. C., *et al.* Canine Oral Papillomatosis. II. Immunological Aspects of the Disease. Cancer Res 20:1083, 1960.

DEMONBREUN, W. A., and GOODPASTURE, E. W. Infectious Oral Papillomatosis of Dogs. Amer. Jour. Path 8:43, 1932.

McFADYEAN, J., and HOBDAY, F. Note on the Experimental Transmission of Warts in the Dog. Jour. Comp Path. Therap. 11:341, 1898.

PENBERTHY, J. Contagious Warty Tumours in Dogs. Jour. Comp. Path. Therap. 11:363, 1898.

### Rabbit Oral-Papilloma Virus

PARSON, R. J., and KIDD, J. G. Oral Papillomatosis of Rabbits: A Virus Disease. Jour. Exp. Med. 77:233, 1943.

### Rabbit-Wart Virus

CHAMBERS, V. C., and ITO, Y. Morphology of Shope Papilloma Virus Associated With Nucleic Acid Induced Tumors of Cotton-tailed Rabbits. Virol. 23:434, 1964.

SHOPE, R. E. Infectious Papillomatosis of Rabbits. Jour. Exp. Med. 58:607, 1933.

———. Immunization of Rabbits to Infectious Papillomatosis. Jour. Exp. Med. 65:219, 1937.

### Polyoma Virus

DMOCHOWSKI, L., *et al.* Studies on a Virus (Polyoma) Inducing Multiple Tumors in Animals. Proc. Soc. Exp. Biol. Med. 102:575, 1959.

DULBECO, R., and FREEMAN, G. Plaque Production by the Polyoma Virus. Virol. 8:396, 1959.

EDDY, B. E., *et al.* Hemagglutination With the S.E. Polyoma Virus. Virol. 6:290, 1958.

GROSS, L. A Filterable Agent Recovered From AK Leucemic Extracts, Causing Salivary Gland Carcinomas in C3H Mice. Proc. Soc. Exp. Biol. Med. 83:414, 1953.

ROWE, W. P. The Epidemiology of Mouse Polyoma Virus Infection. Bact. Rev. 25:18, 1961.

STEWART, S. E. Leukemia in Mice Produced by a Filterable Agent Present in AKR Leukemic Tissues With Notes on a Sarcoma Produced by the Same Agent. Anat. Rec. 117:532, 1953.

———. Neoplasma in Mice Inoculated With Cell-free Extracts or Filtrates of Leucemic Mouse Tissues. Jour. Natl. Cancer Inst. 15:1391, 1955.

———, and EDDY, B. E. Properties of a Tumor-producing Virus Recovered From Mouse Neoplasms. Persp. Virol. 2:245, 1959.

WILDY, P., *et al*. The Fine Structure of Polyoma Virus. Virol. 11:444, 1960.

### Simian Vacuolating Virus

HSIUNG, G. D., and GAYLORD, W. H., JR. The Vacuolating Virus of Monkeys. I. Isolation, Growth Characteristics and Inclusion Body Formation. Jour. Exp. Med. 114:975, 1961.

### Genital Papilloma Virus of Swine

PARRISH, W. E. A Transmissible Genital Papilloma of the Pig Resembling Condyloma Acuminatum of Man. Jour. Path. Bact. 81:331, 1961.

———. An Immunological Study of the Transmissible Genital Papilloma of the Pig. Jour. Path. Bact. 83:429, 1962.

# 47

# The Adenoviruses

THE ADENOVIRUSES WERE FIRST ISOLATED from the adenoid tissues of children. They have been associated with a number of conditions in human beings but primarily with respiratory infections. Except for the canine hepatitis virus, adenoviruses found in various animals are not particularly pathogenic.

Members of the adenovirus group are composed of a double-stranded DNA core surrounded by a capsid of 252 capsomeres. The virus particles are 60 mμ to 85 mμ in size, and their symmetry is icosahedral. The viruses of the group are resistant to ether, sensitive to heat, pH stable, and agglutinate the erythrocytes of one or more species of animals. All members of the adenovirus group, except avian types, possess a common soluble antigen.

## ADENOVIRUSES OF MAN

Adenoviruses are widely distributed among the human population. They have most frequently been associated with acute respiratory disease involving the pharyngeal and upper respiratory areas. Often they have been found to be latent in tonsillar and adenoid tissues. Keratoconjunctivitis is produced especially by certain serotypes.

There are at least 45 different serotypes which have been isolated from human sources. A limited number of these serotypes have been found pathogenic for laboratory and domestic animals. Types 1, 2, 5, and 6 were found by Betts to produce lesions in pigs, and types 12 and 18 have been reported by Trentin to produce tumors in hamsters.

## ADENOVIRUSES OF ANIMALS

### Canine Hepatitis Virus

**Diseases Produced.** Fox encephalitis, canine hepatitis.

**Hosts Affected.** Fox (silver and red), dog, and coyote. The raccoon, gray fox, and black bear are slightly susceptible by intraocular inoculation. Cats, ferrets, white rats, gray squirrels, mink, sheep, monkeys, and rabbits are insusceptible.

**History and Distribution.** An epizootic disease of the silver fox was reported by Green in 1925 in which there were symptoms of encephalitis. An organism of the genus Salmonella and later a streptococcus were suggested as causes of the disease. In 1930, Green described a filterable virus as the etiological agent. Three years later Green reported the transmissibility of fox encephalitis to dogs and described focal liver necrosis and intranuclear inclusions in various endothelial cells. Cowdry and Scott had reported in 1930 inclusions in the hepatic cells of two dogs, but no transmission experiments were tried. Rubarth of Sweden published an extensive study of canine hepatitis as found in that country and suggested that the viruses of fox encephalitis and canine hepatitis were the same. Siedentopf and Carlson compared the viruses of these two diseases and concluded that they are identical.

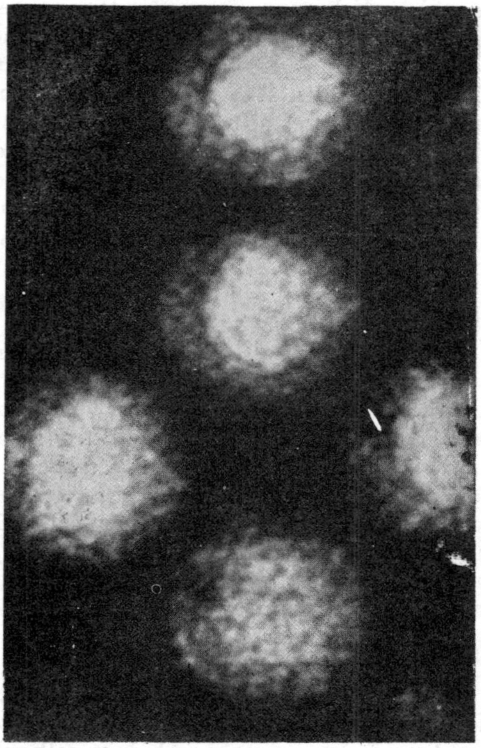

FIG. 47.1—Canine hepatitis virus, ×480,000. (Courtesy Horne. Ann. N.Y. Acad. Sci. 101:475, 1962.)

**Properties of the Virus.** The morphology and structure is typical of the adenovirus group (Fig. 47.1). The size of the elementary bodies is reported to be 82 mμ. They are filterable through common filter types.

The virus is quite stable on storage, retaining its viability in 50 per cent glycerine for several years. Under controlled conditions of pH and temperature the virus will agglutinate the erythrocytes of chickens, rats, and man.

**Cultivation.** Canine hepatitis virus can be cultivated in cell cultures derived from the kidney tissue of a number of animals including the dog, pig, ferret, raccoon, and guinea pig.

Cytopathic changes or intranuclear inclusions are observed in infected cell cultures.

Growth in chicken embryos has also been reported.

**Transmission.** The virus is probably transmitted by discharges from the respiratory tract. Blood, urine, and nasal secretions are consistently infectious during the disease.

**Characteristics of the Disease.** Canine hepatitis virus infection in the fox is of sudden onset. Some foxes are found dead without having shown symptoms, since wild animals in general do not readily exhibit signs of sickness until disease is well advanced. Those animals which are noted sick may show loss of appetite, lethargy, weakness, and finally coma. Nervous symptoms include hyperexcitability, paralysis, convulsions, and muscular twitchings. Nasal discharge and diarrhea are frequently observed. Mortality rates are usually within 10 to 25 per cent.

The disease in dogs runs an acute, rapid, fatal course within a week. There is apathy, vomition, and diarrhea, and there are nasal and eye discharges which are often copious and become purulent. Nervous symptoms include spasms, excitability, and "running fits." Respiratory symptoms with acute tonsillitis have been described by Coffin.

**Pathological Changes.** A postmortem examination of animals dying of fox encephalitis may not show a definite pathological picture. There is general congestion of many tissues, and hemorrhages, especially of the brain.

In the dog, outstanding changes will be found in the liver, which is grossly enlarged, with a lighter color and a distinct lobular design. Tissues of the nervous system show cellular infiltration. Acute tonsillitis is usually observed.

Green has described intranuclear inclusions which regularly appear in both dogs and foxes as well as other infected species. These inclusion bodies are found in the vascular endothelium and meningeal and hepatic cells. Their demonstration is of value in diagnosis of the disease.

**Immunity.** Animals which recover from fox encephalitis or canine hepatitis are immune.

Siedentopf and Carlson report reciprocal

neutralization of virus from cases of fox encephalitis and canine hepatitis by their respective antisera. There is no immunological relationship between canine hepatitis and canine distemper viruses. Hyperimmune serum is available and it is recommended for use both as a prophylactic and a therapeutic agent for fox encephalitis or canine hepatitis.

Simultaneous serum-virus vaccination has been attempted, but many delayed cases of the disease followed this method.

A modified live virus vaccine produced in either dog or swine kidney cell cultures is widely used for the immunization of animals against canine hepatitis. Inactivated virus vaccines are also used.

**Diagnosis.** Since both foxes and dogs are susceptible to canine hepatitis and to canine distemper, differential diagnosis is important. Ferrets are highly susceptible to canine distemper virus but are insusceptible to fox encephalitis-canine hepatitis virus. If ferrets are available, the inoculation of this animal is helpful in the differential diagnosis.

Green has pointed out that the inclusion bodies of canine distemper may be either intracytoplasmic or intranuclear, while those of fox encephalitis-canine hepatitis are only intranuclear. He further notes that distemper inclusions are not found in hepatic cells, but those of canine hepatitis and fox encephalitis are usually abundant in those cells.

### Bovine Adenoviruses

A number of investigators have isolated viruses from cattle feces which have the properties of the adenovirus group. Serological investigations indicate that the adenoviruses may be widespread among cattle.

The adenoviruses of bovine origin can be cultivated in calf kidney cell cultures and produce intranuclear inclusions in these cells. The viruses agglutinate rat and mouse erythrocytes but not those of the chicken, sheep, cattle, guinea pig, or man.

A complement-fixing antigen which is shared with human types of adenoviruses has been demonstrated. Inoculation of the bovine adenoviruses back into cattle usually produces little or no visible reaction but results in an antibody response. However, the inoculation of colostrum-deprived calves produces mild disease symptoms and lesions of the respiratory tract. The virus has been found to persist in calves for as long as 3 weeks postinoculation.

### Porcine Adenovirus

Haig *et al.* and also Kasza have isolated viruses from pigs which have the characteristics of the adenovirus group. The isolates are distinct immunologically from known human adenoviruses but share the adenovirus group antigen. The viruses can be cultivated in swine kidney cell cultures. Their size is approximately 100 m$\mu$ in diameter and they have icosahedral symmetry. A hemagglutinin is produced.

### Simian Adenoviruses

At least 12 serotypes of adenoviruses have been identified from the stools of monkeys and from monkey kidney cell cultures. They are distinct from other adenoviruses though they possess a common soluble antigen. These isolates produce cytopathic changes with intranuclear inclusions. Hemagglutinins are produced. The role of the Simian viruses in disease is not great; however, illness such as pharyngoconjunctival fever has been observed.

### Avian Adenovirus

A virus isolated and described by various workers from avian lymphomatosis materials was determined not to be the lymphomatosis virus. Burmeister *et al.* suggested the term GAL virus (Gallus Adeno-Like) be used to designate these isolates because of their close similarity to the adeno group. It is approximately 85 m$\mu$ in size, polyhedral in shape, ether stable, and develops within the nucleus of host cells.

According to Petek *et al.* two additional avian viruses, chicken embryo lethal orphan (CELO) and quail bronchitis, belong to the adenovirus group.

## REFERENCES


### Adenoviruses of Man

ENDERS, J. F., *et al.* "Adenoviruses": Group Name Proposed for New Respiratory-Tract Viruses. Science 124: 119, 1956.

PEREIRA, H. G., *et al.* A Short Description of the Adenovirus Group. Virol. 20:613, 1963.

SOHIER, R., *et al.* Adenoviruses. Status of Current Knowledge. Prog. Med. Virol. 7:253, 1965.

TRENTIN, J. J., *et al.* The Quest for Human Cancer Viruses. Science 137:835, 1962.

### Canine Hepatitis Virus

COFFIN, D. L. The Pathology of So-Called Acute Tonsillitis of Dogs in Relation to Contagious Canine Hepatitis (Rubarth). Jour. Amer. Vet. Med. Assn. 112:355, 1948.

DAVIES, M. C., *et al.* Electron Microscopic Structure of Infectious Canine Hepatitis (ICH) Virus, A Canine Adenovirus. Virol. 15:87, 1961.

ESPMARK, J. A., and SALENSTEDT, C. R. Hemagglutination-Inhibition Test for Titration of Antibodies Against Hepatitis Contagiosis Canis. Arch. ges. Virusforsch. 11:64, 1961.

FIELDSTEEL, A. H., and EMERY, J. B. Cultivation and Modification of Infectious Canine Hepatitis Virus in Roller Tube Cultures of Dog Kidney. Proc. Soc. Exp. Biol. Med. 86:819, 1954.

GREEN, R. G. Distemper in the Silver Fox (*Culpes vulpes*). Proc. Soc. Exp. Biol. Med. 22:546, 1925.

KAPSENBERG, J. G. Relationship of Infectious Canine Hepatitis Virus to Human Adenovirus. Proc. Soc. Exp. Biol. Med. 101:611, 1959.

LEVINE, S., *et al.* Plaque Formation by Infectious Canine Hepatitis Virus. Proc. Soc. Exp. Biol. Med. 100:600, 1959.

RHUBARTH, S. An Acute Virus Disease With Liver Lesion in Dogs. Acta Path. Microbiol. Scand. Suppl. No. 69, 1947. (In English.)

SALENSTEDT, C. R. Studies on the Virus of Hepatitis Contagiosa Canis (HCC). II. Susceptibility of Guinea Pigs to Experimental Infection With HCC Virus. Arch. ges. Virusforsch. 8:600, 1959.

SIEDENTOPF, H. A., and CARLSON, W. E. A Comparative Study of the Fox Encephalitis Virus and the Virus of Infectious Canine Hepatitis. Jour. Amer. Vet. Med. Assn. 115:109, 1949.

### Bovine Adenoviruses

DARBYSHIRE, J. H., *et al.* Association of Adenoviruses With Bovine Respiratory Disease. Nature 208:307, 1965.

KLEIN, M., *et al.* Isolation From Cattle of a Virus Related to Human Adenovirus. Proc. Soc. Exp. Biol. Med. 102:1, 1959.

MOHANTY, S. B., and LILLIE, M. G. Experimental Infection of Calves With a Bovine Adenovirus. Proc. Soc. Exp. Biol. Med. 120:679, 1965.

### Porcine Adenoviruses

BETTS, A. O., *et al.* Inoculation of Pigs With Adenoviruses of Man. Nature 193:45, 1962.

HAIG, D. A., *et al.* Isolation of an Adenovirus From a Pig. Jour. Comp. Path. 74:81, 1964.

KASZA, L. Isolation of an Adenovirus From the Brain of a Pig. Amer. Jour. Vet. Res. 27:751, 1966.

### Simian Adenoviruses

GINSBERG, H. S., and DINGLE, J. H. The Adenovirus Group. *In* Viral and Rickettsial Infections of Man. Horsfall, F., and Tamm, I. (eds.). J. B. Lippincott Co., Philadelphia, 1965.

### Avian Adenovirus

BURMEISTER, B. R., *et al.* Virus Isolated From Avian Lymphomas Unrelated to Lymphomatosis Virus. Jour. Natl. Cancer Inst. 24:1443, 1960.

DUBOSE, R. T., and GRUMBLES, L. C. The Relationship Between Quail Bronchitis Virus and Chicken Embryo Lethal Virus. Avian Dis. 3:321, 1959.

KOHN, A. Gallus Adeno-like Virus in Chickens. Studies on Infection, Excretion and Immunity. Amer. Jour. Vet. Res. 23:562, 1962.

PETEK, M., *et al.* Further Studies on CELO Virus: Its Relationship to the Adenovirus Group. Arch. ges. Virusforsch. 14:637, 1964

SHARPLESS, G. R., *et al.* GAL Virus: Its Growth Cycle in Tissue Culture and Some of Its Properties. Virol. 13:315, 1961.

YATES, V. J., and FRY, D. E. Observations on Chicken Embryo Lethal Orphan (CELO) Virus. Amer. Jour. Vet. Res. 18:657, 1957.

# 48

# The Arboviruses

THE ARTHROPOD-BORNE VIRUSES COMPRISE A group which in addition to being vector-borne possess other similar characteristics. They are composed of a single-stranded core of RNA, a protein coat, and a lipid-containing envelope. The particle size of most of the arboviruses falls between 30 $m\mu$ and 50 $m\mu$; however, some may be as large as 100 $m\mu$. Though some members of the groups are reported to be cubic in symmetry, others are helical. A majority of the arboviruses have not yet been examined in morphological detail. A hemagglutinin is produced by many members of the group.

Mosquito transmission is the only means of natural spread for certain viruses in the group, while others are transmitted by ticks and a few by gnats. Multiplication of these viruses within the vectors is of importance. Some viruses of the group exhibit a definite predilection for central nervous tissue, while others produce generalized febrile conditions. Inapparent infection is common.

By immunological tests, the arboviruses have been grouped into A, B, C, and Ungrouped categories.

Approximately 200 different viruses have been described and classified as arboviruses.

## GROUP A ARBOVIRUSES

### Equine Encephalomyelitis Viruses

#### Western Equine Encephalomyelitis Virus
#### Eastern Equine Encephalomyelitis Virus
#### Venezuelan Equine Encephalomyelitis Virus

**Disease Produced.** Encephalomyelitis, "sleeping sickness."

**Hosts Affected.** Horse, man, rarely pheasant and pigeon. Experimental hosts include the guinea pig, white mouse, hamster, rat, domestic and wild rabbit, monkey, squirrel, gopher, wild mouse, deer, sheep, calf, pig, goat, dog, and prairie chicken. Domestic fowl and some wild birds show only a viremia following inoculation with no symptoms. Cats are resistant.

**History and Distribution.** Epizootics of encephalitis in horses had been known in the United States for many years previous to 1931, but it was in that year Meyer, Haring, and Howitt were able to recover a filter-passing virus from the brain of infected horses involved in a California outbreak. The incidence of encephalitis increased sharply in the western states in the next few years and spread eastward to the Middle West until, in 1937 and 1938, 173,889 and 184,662 cases, respectively, were reported. In 1939 a sharp drop to 8,008 cases was attributable to resistance developed by earlier attacks and especially to widespread vaccination with chicken embryo vaccine.

In 1933 Ten Broeck and Merrill, also Giltner and Shahan, reported on a virus responsible for equine encephalitis which occurred in New Jersey, Virginia, Delaware, and Maryland. Ten Broeck and Merrill demonstrated distinct antigenic differences between the eastern and western strains of the virus. The eastern type spread over the eastern and southern states, and in 1939 it spread westward to some extent.

The western type virus has occurred in at least 20 states which includes nearly all of those west of the Mississippi River and a few east of it. The eastern type has been found chiefly in eastern and southern states. Both viruses have been identified from several states.

Coincident with the disease in the horse, both viruses have been isolated from cases of encephalitis in man. In 1941 an epidemic of human encephalitis due to the western type virus occurred in the Dakotas, Minnesota, and adjacent areas of Canada. Over 3,000 cases were diagnosed, with a mortality rate of 8 to 15 per cent. These viruses have spread widely among wild and domestic animals and fowl, and so a reservoir of the virus remains and the disease is enzootic in many areas.

An outbreak of eastern encephalitis occurred in 1959 on the southern coastal region of New Jersey. Thirty-six cases with 21 fatalities were reported. During this same period 66 cases of encephalitis were reported in horses, and numerous isolations of eastern virus were made from captive flocks of pheasants.

A third type of equine encephalomyelitis has been reported from Venezuela, S. A., which is caused by a virus with similar properties to those of the eastern strain, but it is antigenically distinct.

Equine encephalomyelitis occurs in the United States, Canada, Panama, and South America.

**Properties of the Virus.** By collodion membrane filter studies, the elementary bodies of western type virus have been reported as being 20 mμ to 35 mμ in diameter. Measurements made from photographs taken in the electron microscope show the eastern type is 40 mμ to 47 mμ in diameter and the western type 40 mμ to 53 mμ. Both viruses are spherical in shape.

Klimenko *et al.* have shown the Venezuelan encephalitis virus to be enveloped with a spherical nucleoid. The complete virion is 60 mμ to 75 mμ in diameter and the nucleoid measures 30 mμ to 40 mμ. Disrupted particles yield helical structures; however, the internal arrangement is not like that of the myxoviruses.

The equine encephalitis viruses are comparatively resistant. They withstand a temperature of 70°C. for 10 minutes when in suspension and resist 2 per cent phenol, 0.05 per cent mercuric chloride, and 1:500 merthiolate. Formalin in a concentration of 0.4 or 0.2 per cent will inactivate the viruses in three to four days. The viruses are preserved by refrigeration for at least one year in chicken embryo fluids. They are also preserved in 50 per cent buffered glycerin or by lyophilization.

Chanock and Sabin have reported that eastern and western viruses will agglutinate the erythrocytes of the chickens if the pH of the suspending liquid is 6.1. The age of the chicken used for the donor of the erythrocytes is also important since erythrocytes from newly hatched chicks are essential. Goose erythrocytes are also agglutinable.

Eastern and western viruses are susceptible to the action of interferon.

The three equine encephalomyelitis viruses are considered to be antigenically distinct from each other, but serological cross reactions and cross protection among them have been reported. Antigenic variation within the western and eastern types has been established. Also antigenic relationships between the equine viruses and other members of Group A have been found.

Equine encephalomyelitis occurs in Argentina and Brazil. The Argentine strains of the virus closely resemble the western type, while the Brazilian strains are of the eastern variety.

**Cultivation of the Virus.** The equine encephalitis viruses can be cultivated in tissue cultures of various types and produce a marked cytopathic effect. The viruses are readily cultivated in chicken embryos by any method of inoculation and are lethal in 18 to 24 hours. Hemorrhage, thrombosis, and necrosis are observed in the dead embryos. Half-day-old chicks are very sensitive hosts and are used for isolation of the viruses.

**Transmission.** The encephalitis viruses are eliminated in nasal secretions of infected horses, and contact with such secretions may result in transmission of the virus. However, the disease is usually thought to be transmitted by bloodsucking arthropods in a majority of cases. Encephalitis viruses have been isolated repeatedly from mosquitoes trapped in endemic areas. Species of mosquitoes of the genera Aedes, Anopheles, Culex, and Culiseta have yielded the virus. In addition to mosquitoes, ticks such as *Dermacentor andersoni* and mites *Dermanyssus americanus and Dermanyssus gallinae* have also yielded the virus. Experimental transmission has been proved with these insects. Mosquitoes become infective 7 to 20 days after feeding on an animal which shows viremia. There is evidence of multiplication of the equine encephalitis virus in the mosquito, and it remains infected for life. Transovarial transmission of the virus occurs in ticks, but probably does not in mosquitoes. The virus may be transmitted from chicken to chicken by infected mites.

The "reservoir" of the viruses which exists in mosquitoes and inapparent hosts constitutes a problem in control.

Western virus has been reported by Thomas and Ecklund to persist in garter snakes through the winter hibernation period and for at least 66 days following the beginning of spring activity.

**Characteristics of the Disease.** Equine encephalomyelitis is seasonal, occurring in the summer and early fall months. In the horse, there is at first high temperature accompanied by viremia which is followed by typical symptoms of encephalomyelitis. These include depression, sleepiness, pharyngeal paralysis, incoordination, and paralysis of the lips and legs. Death may occur in 3 to 8 days after onset. Complete recovery or survival with nervous sequelae may occur. Some cases are mild and of short duration with rapid recovery. Infection by the eastern type is more severe and rapid than that produced by western strains. Mortality rates are about 90 per cent with eastern type and approximately 27 per cent with western type infection.

Experimental infections in mice and guinea pigs have been studied extensively. The induced disease in these hosts is evidenced by depression, paralysis, rapid dehydration, and death.

Human infection has been contracted under natural conditions as well as by laboratory accidents.

Typical symptoms of encephalitis occur in man. Headache, sweating, drowsiness, mental confusion, and paralysis are usually observed. The mortality rate is about 10 per cent. The eastern type infection in man is usually more severe and intense than the western type.

The Venezuelan type virus often produces a generalized infection not necessarily accompanied by encephalitis. Laboratory-acquired infection in man is more apt to occur with this virus than with eastern or western types.

Naturally occurring infections in pheasants and turkeys by eastern encephalitis virus have been reported by Jungherr. The infection of fowl is usually of the inapparent type.

**Pathological Changes.** The pathological changes which occur in equine encephalomyelitis are chiefly microscopic and confined to the brain and meninges. In the brain there is mononuclear infiltration and leucocytic perivascular cuffing. There is congestion and edema of the meninges.

**Immunity.** Antibodies which fix complement or neutralize the virus appear with recovery from the disease or by vaccination. In many hosts such as fowl, serological demonstration of these antibodies is the only evidence of virus invasion. Active immunization by chicken embryo-propagated virus has been widely used and with success. Monovalent eastern, monovalent western, or polyvalent vaccines are available. The type of vaccine chosen depends upon the type or types of the virus which occur in the area where it is to be used. Formolized chicken embryo vaccine was at first prepared from the whole embryo and its fluids which included allantoic, amniotic, and yolk sac contents. This practice was abandoned because of the development of hypersensitivity to egg proteins in some vaccinated horses. The vaccine was otherwise successful, however.

The whole embryo vaccine was succeeded by a purified intradermal vaccine. This vaccine is formolized, 0.4 per cent, and the virus is recovered from the infected embryo contents by high speed differential centrifugation.

The immunity produced by the killed vaccine is considered durable for only one season, so animals in enzootic or epizootic areas must be vaccinated each year.

The same vaccine which is used in horses is useful in immunizing laboratory workers who work in research or in vaccine production.

Killed vaccines for the prevention of eastern or western encephalitis are also produced by propagation in chicken embryo cell cultures.

Animals which recover from natural infection are resistant to reinfection.

**Diagnosis.** A diagnosis of equine encephalomyelitis depends upon isolation and identification of the virus or by satisfactory serological evidence. Actual isolation of the virus can be made from the central nervous tissue obtained at postmortem. Isolation of the virus from the blood of naturally infected animals is rare because the stage of viremia is transient and usually precedes the onset of symptoms. Half-day-old chicks or weanling mice are the most suitable test animals for isolation of the virus and are inoculated intracerebrally with brain tissue from the suspected case. These animals should show symptoms in about 4 days following inoculation. Chicken embryos may be inoculated directly with the brain of the infected animal and should die in about 48 hours if the virus is present.

A virus isolated from the nervous tissue of an animal with encephalitis should be identified and specifically differentiated from other viruses by cross-immunity, complement-fixation, and serum neutralization tests.

Serological tests are used in the diagnosis of nonfatal or inapparent infections. However, the mere demonstration of antibodies does not constitute a diagnosis of present infection, but may in some cases reflect a past contact with the virus and a persistence of antibody. If possible, sera collected early in the disease should be compared with the antibody content of that collected in convalescence. A distinct increase in the titer of antibodies in the latter would carry significance. However, a positive serological test indicates contact with the virus at some time and is useful in epidemiological surveys.

### Other Group A Arboviruses

A number of viruses apparently belonging to Group A have been isolated from man or mosquitoes in various parts of the world, especially Africa. Studies concerning their occurrence and properties are quite incomplete. None has been related to disease of animals; however, serological evidence of infection for some has been reported. The names which have been attached to these isolates are listed below.

Sindbis—Africa
Chikungunya—Africa
Mayaro—Trinidad
Semliki Forest—Africa
O'Nyong-Nyong—Africa
Mucambo—Brazil
Middleburg—S. Africa
Ndumu—Africa
Sagiyama—Japan
Una—Brazil
Aura—Brazil
Pixuna—Brazil

## GROUP B ARBOVIRUSES

### Japanese B Virus

**Disease Produced.** Japanese B encephalitis.

**Hosts Affected.** Man and horse. Experimentally cattle, sheep, swine, rabbits, hamsters, monkeys, mice, chickens, and chicken embryos.

**History and Distribution.** A "summer encephalitis" which had been described as occurring among the Japanese population for the last 100 years was not accurately identified as of virus etiology until 1936. The virus is widely spread over Japan and has also occurred in Korea, Okinawa, China, Taiwan, India, and far eastern Russia. The disease is known to occur in horses and there is considerable evidence of the existence of the virus in cattle, sheep, hogs, and goats. The virus has not been found in North or South America, Europe, or Africa.

**Properties of the Virus.** The elementary bodies of Japanese B virus are reported as 20 mμ to 30 mμ in size by filtration studies. The virus is filterable through Berkefeld N, W, Seitz, and Mandler filters. Exposure to 56°C. for 30 minutes inactivates the virus. It is preserved for long periods by freezing at —70°C. and by lyophilization, but it is less stable at ordinary refrigerator temperatures. At 0°C. it lives for about 3 weeks. It is more stable in 10 per cent serum or skim milk than in saline suspension. Antigenic relationship between Japanese B, West Nile, and St. Louis viruses has been demonstrated.

Sabin has reported that Japanese B virus will agglutinate the erythrocytes of chickens, pigeons, and sheep, if the conditions of the test are carefully controlled.

**Cultivation.** Japanese B virus can be cultivated in either tissue cultures or chicken embryos. Chorioallantoic inoculation of the embryo is preferable but the yolk sac route is satisfactory. Embryos die within 2 to 3 days following inoculation. The greatest concentration of the virus occurs in the embryo itself.

**Transmission.** Japanese encephalitis virus is transmitted by mosquitoes. It has been possible to experimentally transmit the disease to mice, horses, and swine by bites of infected mosquitoes.

Swine and fowl are considered important reservoirs of the virus. However, neither is visibly affected by the virus during periods of viremia.

**Characteristics of the Disease.** Japanese B encephalitis in man may show a few days of prodromal symptoms or the onset may be sudden. The symptoms include high fever, general impairment of mental faculties, and often paralysis. Death occurs in many cases. Mortality rates range from 40 to 90 per cent with the highest rate among the aged. Japanese B and St. Louis encephalitis are closely related both epidemiologically and clinically. In the horse, there is evidence that inapparent infection is widespread in Japan. However, there are reports of outbreaks of encephalomyelitis in Japanese horses in which the mortality rate reaches 50 per cent in those horses clinically affected with the disease. The symptoms in the horse include high temperature, excitement followed by apathy, depression, and spastic or flaccid paralysis of the legs.

**Pathological Changes.** The pathological changes are those of meningitis and encephalitis. The meninges are edematous and congested. The brain proper is congested, and microscopically there is cellular infiltration and perivascular cuffing of the blood vessels.

**Immunity.** Animals which recover from experimental inoculation or vaccination are resistant to reinoculation.

Neutralizing and complement-fixing antibodies are formed following infection or vaccination.

Vaccines may be produced from virus propagated in chicken embryos or from formolized mouse brain. These vaccines have been used to some extent in man and experimentally in mice. Neutralizing antibodies are produced by the use of vaccines, but the value of such vaccines has not been determined.

**Diagnosis.** A diagnosis of Japanese B infection is made by isolation and identification of the virus. Isolation can be made by intracerebral inoculation of rabbits and young mice or by yolk sac or chorioallantoic inoculation of chicken embryos. Serological and immunological differentiation from related viruses must be done.

## St. Louis Encephalitis Virus

**Disease Produced.** St. Louis encephalitis.

**Hosts Affected.** Man and horse. Experimentally mice, hamsters, monkeys, and chicken embryos. Rabbits and guinea pigs, and wild and domestic fowl show no symptoms, but a viremia may be present for a time after inoculation.

**History and Distribution.** An outbreak of encephalitis of man occurred in 1932 in the vicinity of Paris, Illinois. The following year over 1,100 cases of the disease were diagnosed in the St. Louis area, and the virus was isolated from brain material by Webster and Fite. Since 1933 the disease has remained endemic and has spread widely throughout the United States. A reservoir of the virus has been shown to exist in many wild and domestic fowl.

**Properties of the Virus.** The virus measures 20 m$\mu$ to 30 m$\mu$ in size. It is filterable through Berkefeld V, N, and Seitz filters. The virus is killed by 56°C. for 30 minutes or 0.1 per cent formalin in 10–18 hours, but resists 1 per cent phenol for 25 days and 0.5 per cent for 50 days. The infectivity is rapidly lost in the refrigerator. However, it is preserved by lyophilization or if stored at — 70°C. The virus will live longer in serum or skimmed milk than in saline suspension. Penicillin does not affect the virus.

St. Louis encephalitis virus will produce the agglutination of chicken, pigeon, or sheep erythrocytes if tested under proper conditions.

**Cultivation.** St. Louis virus multiplies in tissue cultures which employ either chicken or mouse embryonic tissues. Chicken embryos can be readily infected by any of the usual routes of inoculation. Inoculation of the virus onto the chorioallantoic membrane results in edema, opacity, diffuse proliferation, and necrosis of the membrane after 3 to 4 days incubation. The embryo itself is usually little affected by the virus.

**Transmission.** St. Louis encephalitis is seasonal in occurrence, most of the cases occurring in summer and early fall. This period coincides with greatest insect activity. It has been shown that mosquitoes, especially *Culex tarsalis* and *Culex pipiens*, can transmit the virus and are considered the chief vectors. Nine species of mosquitoes have transmitted the infection under experimental conditions. Repeated isolations of the virus have been made from *Culex tarsalis* mosquitoes trapped in nature. The virus has been isolated from chicken mites, *Dermanyssus gallinae*, which have been collected in nature and so may play a part in spread of the disease. Transovarian infection has been demonstrated in the mites.

**Characteristics of the Disease.** The incubation period in man ranges from 9 to 21 days. Onset of the illness is sudden with headache, high fever, neck rigidity, mental confusion, and tremors. This is usually followed by encephalitis, with the symptoms of apathy and sleepiness in some patients or sleeplessness and excitement in others.

Some cases are abortive and the encephalitic symptoms do not appear. Mortality rates in the early epidemics of 1932, 1933, and 1937 were 37, 20, and 23.7 per cent, respectively. In the horse, St. Louis virus produces a disease characterized by high temperature, depression, sleepiness, incoordination, and paralysis, and in some cases death. Many horses, however, develop neutralizing antibodies to the virus without showing any signs of illness.

**Pathological Changes.** The pathological changes are almost entirely confined to the brain and cord. The outstanding changes are those of congestion with occasional petechial hemorrhage, of leucocytic infiltration, and perivascular cuffing of the blood vessels.

**Immunity.** Complement-fixing and neutralizing antibodies are produced following infection and recovery, and remain in high titer for several years. Horses which have developed neutralizing antibodies are refractory to the virus. Mice can be successfully immunized by the inoculation of formolized or ultraviolet-treated virus. Neutralizing antibodies are readily produced by vaccination of mice or hamsters, but resistance to intracerebral challenge does not always parallel the appearance and disappearance of these antibodies.

Convalescent serum has been used for treatment of St. Louis encephalitis in man.

Vaccines are not commercially available for the immunization of animals or man.

**Diagnosis.** Accurate diagnosis of St. Louis encephalitis depends upon isolation and identification of the virus. Isolation of the virus may be accomplished by intracerebral inoculation of mice or chorioallantoic inoculation of chicken embryos with brain material from the infected host.

Complement-fixation or serum neutralization tests are often used in diagnosis of the nonfatal case as well as inapparent infections in many hosts.

It is important to differentiate St. Louis encephalitis from the other encephalitis viruses which may be encountered in clinically identical cases in man or animals.

### West Nile Virus

**Disease Produced.** Encephalitis.

**Hosts Affected.** Man, and possibly the horse. Experimentally monkeys, mice, and hamsters are susceptible. Rabbits and guinea pigs are insusceptible.

West Nile virus was isolated in 1937 by Smithburn from the blood of a human patient in Africa. Several isolations of the virus have been reported, and epidemiological surveys show serological evidence of the existence of West Nile virus in many parts of Africa, the Middle East, and India. The virus has neurotropic tendencies when injected into mice, monkeys, or hamsters.

West Nile virus is 21 $m\mu$ to 31 $m\mu$ in size and is antigenically related to Japanese B and St. Louis viruses. There is also some similarity to louping-ill and Russian Far Eastern viruses. The virus will produce hemagglutination if placed under proper conditions.

The West Nile virus can be grown in tissue culture or in chicken embryos.

High antibody titers to West Nile virus have been found by Schmidt and El Mansoury in many Egyptian horses. They also report the isolation of the virus from one case.

### Murray Valley Encephalitis Virus

A virus isolated from outbreaks of human encephalitis occurring in Northern Australia and New Guinea is related to Japanese B, St. Louis, and West Nile viruses. The virus is pathogenic for monkeys, mice, hamsters, and sheep. Horses, rabbits, and birds develop viremia without visible signs of disease. Characteristics of the virus closely resemble those of other Group B arboviruses.

### Louping-Ill Virus

**Disease Produced.** Louping-ill.

**Hosts Affected.** Sheep, cattle, deer, wild rodents, and man. Experimentally horses, swine, mice, dogs, monkeys, rats (inapparent), and chicken embryos.

**History and Distribution.** Louping-ill was described in Scotland in 1807 by Duncan, but the etiology was discovered to be a virus only after many years of controversy and experimental work. Pool, Brownlee, and Wilson in 1931 were the first to reproduce the disease in sheep by injecting Berkefeld filtrates. Louping-ill occurs in Scotland, northern England, and some areas of Russia.

**Properties of the Virus.** Louping-ill virus is comparatively small, measuring approximately 20 $m\mu$ to 27 $m\mu$ in size. The virus passes all grades of Berkefeld filters and the Chamberland $L_2$ and $L_3$ candles. The virus is heat sensitive, being destroyed at 58°C. in 10 minutes, at 60°C. in 2 to 5 minutes, and at 80°C. in 30 seconds.

The virus may not survive more than 2 weeks in the refrigerator, but will live for 4 to 6 months in glycerin.

An antigenic relationship has been shown between louping-ill virus and Russian spring-summer virus.

**Cultivation.** Louping-ill virus can be cultivated in tissue cultures which employ minced chicken embryo in Tyrode's solution. Inoculation of the virus onto the chorioallantoic membrane results in the growth of the virus and the death of the embryo within 6 days. Lesions of the embryo include liver necrosis, generalized edema, and jaundice.

**Transmission.** Under natural conditions the virus of louping-ill is transmitted only by the bite of ticks *(Ixodes ricinus)*. Experimentally the virus can be transferred in sheep by intracerebral, ocular, intravenous, and subcutaneous inoculation.

**Characteristics of the Disease.** Louping-ill occurs in the spring and fall among lambs and yearlings and occasionally in older sheep. The disease exhibits a diphasic febrile reaction in most cases. At first, the infected sheep shows depression and increased temperature, followed by a second temperature increase which is accompanied by symptoms of encephalitis. The mortality of this type of the disease is high. However, the disease may be abortive in some cases and only the first phase is noted; no nervous symptoms occur.

The disease has been described in man. It has been most frequently diagnosed in laboratory workers and seldom among people who have contact with sheep. The disease in man is not serious. There is fever, malaise, headache, and mild nervous symptoms.

**Pathological Changes.** Most of the pathological changes occur in the central nervous system. These changes include congestion and leucocytic infiltration of the meninges, perivascular cuffing, and degeneration of the cells in the cerebrum, cerebellum, and medulla. Inclusion bodies have been demonstrated in the central nervous tissue of infected mice.

**Immunity.** Animals which have recovered from louping-ill are resistant to reinoculation. Complement-fixing and neutralizing antibodies are demonstrable in the serum of recovered and immunized animals. Formolized chicken embryo vaccine is used to produce artificial immunity to the disease. Tick eradication is very important in control.

**Diagnosis.** In addition to symptoms of the disease, the diagnosis of louping-ill is based on isolation of the virus by intracerebral inoculation in mice or by chicken embryo inoculation. Serologic reactions are helpful in the differentiation of louping-ill from Russian Far Eastern encephalitis virus.

### Russian Spring-Summer Virus or Far Eastern Encephalitis Virus

**Disease Produced.** Russian Far Eastern encephalitis.

**Hosts Affected.** Man, cattle, horses, sheep, goats, dogs, wild carnivora, wild rodents, also grouse and other birds. Rabbits and pigeons are insusceptible.

**History and Distribution.** Russian spring-summer virus is apparently confined to various parts of the U.S.S.R. The disease it produces was known about 1914, but did not become a problem until about 1935. It has been found in many animals—man is only an accidental host. Men who work in the forests as lumbermen are among the most frequently infected.

**Properties of the Virus.** The Russian spring-summer virus will pass all three grades of Berkefeld filter, Seitz and Chamberland $L_2$, $L_3$, and $L_5$ candles. The elementary bodies of the virus are 15 m$\mu$ to 25 m$\mu$ in size. A temperature of 60°C. for 10 minutes will kill the virus. There are definite antigenic relationships between louping-ill and Russian virus. St. Louis, Japanese, and West Nile viruses show some relationships but are less pronounced.

**Cultivation.** The Russian spring-summer virus can be grown in tissue cultures employing minced chicken embryo and Tyrode's solution as well as in chicken embryos.

**Transmission.** Ticks *(Ixodes ricinus)* are the vectors of Russian virus. Transovarial transmission of the virus in ticks from one generation to another has been shown.

**Characteristics of the Disease.** The disease in animals is usually of the inapparent type and is not diagnosed clinically. Evidence of the disease is most often based on serological tests, but the virus has been isolated from the brain of cattle. Intracerebral inoculations of the virus in white mice result in convulsions and paralysis in 5 to 13 days, and death.

The infection in man is manifest after a 10- to 14-day incubation period. Symptoms include fever, nausea, and headache which are followed by flaccid paralysis and other signs of encephalitis.

Some infections are abortive, ending in complete recovery within a few days. Others terminate in death or permanent neurologic injury.

**Immunity.** Formolized virus is used for the production of artificial immunity. The control of ticks is an important control measure.

**Diagnosis.** Isolation and identification of the virus constitutes a diagnosis of infection. Serological differentiation of the virus from louping-ill is necessary.

### Yellow Fever Virus

**Disease Produced.** Yellow fever.

**Hosts Affected.** Man. Mice and members of the monkey family can be experimentally infected.

Yellow fever occurs only in man under natural conditions. Its occurrence is usually limited to the warmer climates of the tropical and subtropical regions, but at times it has been spread into southern United States and, during summer months, northward into the middle Atlantic regions. The virus is transmitted by mosquitoes. This fact was dramatically demonstrated by the U.S. Army Medical Commission to Cuba in 1901 under the direction of Walter Reed. Certain members of this Commission allowed themselves to be used in experiments to prove that the mosquitoes which fed on yellow fever patients could transmit the disease.

The virus is relatively small, measuring 38 mμ in size. It can be isolated from the blood of patients by intracerebral inoculations of mice. Strains of the virus which have been adapted to mice can be successfully transferred to the chicken embryo for propagation. Chicken embryo vaccine was used extensively for immunization purposes during World War II.

### Rift Valley Fever Virus

**Disease Produced.** Rift Valley fever.

**Hosts Affected.** Man, sheep, cattle, and goats. Experimentally, the monkey, mouse, ferret, white rat, and hamster are susceptible. The horse, pig, guinea pig, and chicken have been found insusceptible.

**History and Distribution.** The disease Rift Valley fever and the virus were described in 1931 by Daubney, Hudson, and Garnham. A disease of sheep which occurred in the Rift Valley, East Africa, became epizootic in that area. A similar disease to that in the sheep was contracted by those who investigated the outbreak as well as among the sheepherders who tended the infected flocks.

A particularly severe epizootic occurred in 1959; the loss of 100,000 sheep and cattle was reported.

So far the disease has not been identified outside eastern or central Africa.

**Properties of the Virus.** Rift Valley fever virus is approximately 23 mμ to 35 mμ in diameter. It is able to pass all grades of Berkefeld and Chamberland candles.

Thermal inactivation of the virus occurs at 56°C. for 40 minutes.

The virus remains viable for 8 months in glycerin when stored at 4°C., 1 month in dried tissue, or 6 months in 0.5 per cent phenol.

**Cultivation.** Rift Valley fever virus can be cultivated in tissue cultures derived from a variety of animal species. Plaques are produced in cultures of lamb and hamster kidney and chicken embryo fibroblasts. It can be readily cultivated on the chorioallantoic membrane of the chicken embryo. In the embryo the virus produces hyperplasia and necrosis of the membrane. Liver necrosis is noted in the embryo.

**Transmission.** Rift Valley fever is transmitted under natural conditions by mosquitoes, and the virus has been isolated from these arthropods which have been caught in nature. Infection has been reported in laboratory workers, but the mode of transmission was unknown. It is not transmitted among animals by contact.

**Characteristics of the Disease.** The disease in sheep is characterized by listlessness, anorexia, and prostration. In the newborn lamb, the death rate may be high due to extensive liver necrosis. Abortion occurs in pregnant ewes. In man, the onset may be sudden after an incubation period of 5 to 6 days. Symptoms are malaise, chilling, headache, and fever. There may be extreme pain in the arms, legs, and joints. The temperature curve is of the saddle-back type. Leucopenia is characteristic. The disease runs a benign course with complete recovery in a few days.

**Pathological Changes.** In animals, the chief pathological changes are in the liver. Necrosis of the liver is most outstanding with scattered petechial hemorrhages. The kidneys, spleen, and lymph nodes may show minor degenerative changes.

**Immunity.** Antibodies are produced as a result of infection and are capable of neutralizing the virus. There is no antigenic relationship between Rift Valley fever virus and yellow fever or dengue. A vaccine produced in chicken embryos and a formalin-killed cell culture product are used to prevent the disease. Immune serum is used to some extent in this disease.

**Diagnosis.** A diagnosis of Rift Valley fever depends upon isolation and identification of the virus by mouse inoculation, complement-fixation and serum neutralization tests.

### Wesselsbron Virus

A virus responsible for death losses in newborn lambs and abortions and deaths of ewes was isolated in the Wesselsbron area of Orange Free State, South Africa. It resembled Rift Valley fever virus in some respects but was found to be distinct from it.

Infant mice are killed by the virus. Adult mice, rabbits, and guinea pigs show no symptoms. However, pregnant rabbits and guinea pigs either aborted or lost their young following injection of the virus. Cattle, horses, and swine show only a transient reaction to virus inoculation.

Human infection may be acquired during laboratory procedures dealing with the virus. A moderately severe influenza-like illness is produced.

Mosquito transmission of the virus to sheep is most likely since it has been isolated from naturally infected mosquitoes trapped in several areas of South Africa.

### Dengue Virus

**Disease Produced.** Dengue (Hemorrhagic Fever).

**Hosts Affected.** Man. Experimentally monkeys and mice.

Extensive outbreaks of dengue have occurred in man in various countries of the world which lie in the tropical or subtropical areas. The virus is mosquito-borne and has the general characteristics of the Group B arboviruses. In man, a febrile, generalized illness is produced. The disease may be severe in some persons, but in others only a mild or inapparent infection results. Control of the disease is based largely on mosquito eradication.

### Powassan Virus

A virus isolated by McLean *et al.* from a case of human encephalitis occurring in the Powassan region of Ontario, Canada, has been designated as Powassan virus. Similar, if not identical, isolates have been reported from Colorado, South Dakota, and New York.

This virus is the first of the Russian spring-summer type to be isolated in North America. The virus is presumed to be tick-borne since it has been isolated from them. It has also been isolated from snowshoe rabbits, woodchucks, and foxes. Serological evidence of infection has been obtained by neutralization tests conducted on blood serum collected from a wide variety of wild animals and from man in the northeastern United States and Ontario regions.

The virus can be cultivated in hamster kidney cells and is quite pathogenic for young mice. It produces a hemagglutinin which is active on goose erythrocytes.

#### Other Group B Arboviruses

Ilhéus virus—South America
Turkey meningoencephalitis—Israel
Central European tick fever virus—Central Europe
Kyasanur Forest virus—India
Omsk hemorrhagic fever virus—U.S.S.R.
Langat virus—Malaya

### UNGROUPED ARBOVIRUSES

#### California Virus

A virus isolated by Hammon and Reeves in 1952 from mosquitoes was originally of doubtful pathogenicity, although serological evidence of infection was present in man and animals of the region in California where it was isolated. Since 1961 isolations of the virus and serological surveys indicate that it may be rather widespread in the United States and parts of Canada. The first isolation of California virus from a human case of encephalitis has been reported by Thompson and Evans. They also reported the presence of antibodies to the virus in 25.9 per cent of 637 human sera obtained in the Wisconsin area.

Other viruses found to be related to California virus are:

Trivittatus virus—Mosquitoes—U.S.
Lumbo virus—Mosquitoes—Africa
Tahnya virus—Mosquitoes and man—Czechoslovakia
Melao virus—Mosquitoes—Trinidad

#### African Horse-Sickness Virus

**Disease Produced.** African horse sickness.

**Hosts Affected.** Horse. Mules are somewhat resistant. Mice, rats, and guinea pigs can be infected by intracerebral inoculation. Dogs and goats can be infected.

**History and Distribution.** African horse sickness causes serious losses in horses and mules in Africa. It has been known for several centuries in that region. The virus which is the etiological agent in the disease was first described by M'Fadyean in 1900. The disease does not ordinarily occur except in southern Africa. However, it has been known in Egypt, and in 1944 it was identified in horses in Palestine. In 1960 an epizootic reaching from Turkey to India resulted in the loss of two to three hundred thousand horses and mules.

**Properties of the Virus.** Polson has studied the virus of horse sickness and described it as spherical in shape and measuring 46 $m\mu$ in diameter. It is filterable through Berkefeld, Seitz EK, and Chamberland filters.

The virus is destroyed by a temperature of 70°C. for 5 minutes or 50°C. for 10 minutes. Slow drying at room temperature also is destructive, but rapid drying at low temperatures has no effect on viability.

Plurality of the virus has been established and must be considered in immunity production. Nine antigenic types have been identified.

**Cultivation.** African horse-sickness virus has been adapted to guinea pigs and mice by intracerebral passage. Such neurotropic strains have been cultivated in chicken embryos. Neurotropic tendencies of the virus are retained in the embryo since nearly all of the multiplication takes place in the brain of the embryo. No deaths or specific lesions are noted in the infected embryo.

Cell cultures derived from kidney tissues of young hamsters, lambs, calves, horses, and monkeys will support growth of the virus and show cytopathic effects. Chicken embryo fibroblast cultures will also support growth but show no visible effects of infection.

**Transmission.** African horse sickness is not spread by contact. It is readily transmissible by injection of blood or nasal discharges from an infected animal. Arthropod vectors have long been suspected since the occurrence of the disease coincides with the coming of the summer season, and it promptly disappears after the first frost. Mosquitoes trapped in the wild state have been shown to harbor the virus, and successful transmissions by artificially fed mosquitoes have been reported. Several species of the genus *Culicoides* are also vectors of the virus.

**Characteristics of the Disease.** African horse sickness is an acute or subacute febrile disease which is classified as one of four forms. The pulmonary form begins with temperature increase to 105° to 106°F., depression, dyspnea, profuse sweating, and a large amount of serous discharge from the nose. The cardiac form is the subacute type with edema of the subcutaneous tissues about the head and neck. Sometimes a combined attack of the pulmonary and cardiac forms occurs. In others the disease is mild, with only a short period of fever and recovery. Death rates and complications are higher in the pulmonary type of the disease. In some outbreaks mortality may be 90 to 95 per cent, while in others it may be only 25 per cent.

**Pathological Changes.** The most common changes in horse sickness are severe pulmonary edema, subcutaneous edema, and cardiac hemorrhage.

**Immunity.** Animals which have recovered from the disease are immune to the homologous strain but may contract the disease as a result of exposure to a strain of different antigenic type. Foals receive passive immunity to the homologous virus through colostrum from immune mares.

Live vaccine attenuated by intracerebral inoculation of mice and guinea pigs has been used. Mice are ordinarily used for this purpose, and a polyvalent vaccine is produced. This neurovaccine is reported safe and effective. Live-modified vaccines produced in monkey or hamster kidney cell cultures have been used with promising results.

**Diagnosis.** A diagnosis of African horse sickness is made upon clinical symptoms, lesions, and the absence of other agents such as *B. anthracis* or protozoan parasites. In cases suspected in areas where the disease has been identified previously, isolation of the virus by transmission to other horses and identification by protection tests are necessary.

### Blue Tongue Virus

**Diseases Produced.** Blue tongue, pseudo foot-and-mouth disease.

**Hosts Affected.** Sheep and cattle. Experimentally suckling mice and hamsters, also chicken embryos.

**History and Distribution.** Blue tongue of sheep has been known in South Africa since 1876 and it probably existed for some years before. The virus was discovered in 1905 by Theiler. The disease is most prevalent during wet years and during the summer months. Until 1932 it was thought that under natural conditions blue tongue occurred only in sheep, but Bekker, De Kock, and Quinlan reported its occurrence in cattle over a wide area of South Africa. Blue tongue has also been reported in East Africa, the island of Cyprus, Syria, Turkey, Israel, and in six states of southwestern and western United States.

**Properties of the Virus.** The elementary bodies of blue tongue virus are reported as being approximately 100 m$\mu$ in size.

The details of the structure of the blue tongue virus have not been resolved; however, the electron micrograph (Fig. 48.1) illustrates the general morphology.

At least 16 antigenic types of the virus have been identified.

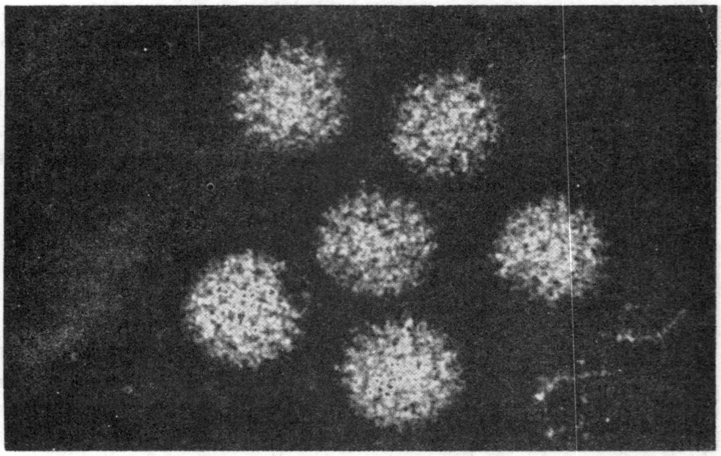

FIG. 48.1—Bluetongue virus, ×364,000. Cluster of unenveloped capsids showing compact icosahedral form with ultrafine projections extending from the capsid surface. (Courtesy A. E. Ritchie, A.R.S., National Animal Disease Lab., Ames, Iowa; and J. G. Bowne, USDA, ADRL, Denver, Colorado.)

The fact that blue tongue virus is not sensitive to the action of either ether or sodium desoxycholate sets it apart from other members of the arbovirus group or indicates that it is not properly classified with them.

The virus is quite resistant to aging. Blood which contains the virus will remain infective for at least two years when kept at room temperature, and Neitz has reported it viable after 25 years.

**Cultivation.** Blue tongue virus has been adapted to grow in chicken embryos. McKercher reports that the blue tongue virus adapts more readily to the chicken embryo if chorioallantoic inoculation is used. However, satisfactory growth has been obtained by the yolk sac route. Tissue cultures of sheep kidney will support the growth of chick embryo-adapted virus, according to Haig, McKercher, and Alexander. Cytopathic changes are observed in the cells of the culture.

**Transmission.** Blue tongue is not spread by contact. Susceptible sheep which drink from the same trough as infected ones do not contract the disease. Drenching a susceptible sheep with virulent blood does not transmit it. Field observations as long ago as 1905 suggested insect transmission. Several species of mosquitoes are thought to be capable of transmitting the infection, and mosquitoes trapped in nature have been shown to contain the virus. However, in Africa and the United States species of the genus *Culicoides* are considered the most common vectors. The fact that some sheep and cattle and also the wild blesbok may carry the virus without showing symptoms presents a problem. Cattle have been shown to retain the virus in their blood for at least 22 days after inoculation, and sheep for 60 days. Goats also may harbor the virus for some time following inoculation.

**Characteristics of the Disease.** Blue tongue of sheep begins with a temperature rise 2 to 4 days after exposure. Some animals show only the temperature increase and then quickly recover. Others will develop the typical disease. Symptoms include sore mouth and reluctance to eat; swelling and cyanosis of the tongue, lips, and gums; eye and nasal discharge; diarrhea; and loss of weight. Lameness is observed, caused by swelling and tenderness about the coronary area. Mortality rates may reach 30 per cent among infected sheep.

As pointed out by DuToit, blue tongue virus usually does not produce clinical disease in cattle. However, cattle are readily infected under natural conditions and are thought to be an important reservoir of the virus.

**Pathological Changes.** The principal lesions of blue tongue are found in the mouth and tongue. They are characterized by hyperemia of the mucous membranes followed by loss of epithelium. Ulcers appear on the inside of the lips, dental pad, and tongue. The tongue may lose most of its epithelium and becomes blue and occasionally gangrenous. The mucous membranes of the gastrointestinal tract may be hyperemic, edematous, with occasional small hemorrhages.

**Immunity.** Early investigations of blue tongue showed that immunity resulted from a recovery from a natural case of the disease.

Serum-virus injections were the first means of immunization. Serum alone was found to be of some value as a therapeutic agent. Live virus which was attenuated by several passages through sheep was used successfully for many years. Occasional animals will suffer mild reactions to the injection of the vaccine and these reactions are more severe in animals exposed to intense sunlight. Immunity induced by the vaccine is not effective for more than a season, and annual or semiannual vaccination is recommended.

Modification of the blue tongue virus by serial passage in chicken embryos has made possible a live-virus vaccine. In Africa a quadrivalent vaccine is used extensively, while in the United States only one antigenic type apparently exists and so a monovalent vaccine is used. Schultz and DeLay have reported losses in newborn lambs in instances where the chicken embryo vaccine was used to vaccinate pregnant ewes. The fetal lamb is most susceptible at 5 to 6 weeks gestation.

**Diagnosis.** A diagnosis of blue tongue depends upon isolation and identification of the virus by transmission to susceptible sheep and protection tests in immunized sheep. Blue tongue is sometimes confused with foot-and-mouth disease or rinderpest. However, both of these diseases spread rapidly by contact while blue tongue does not.

## OTHER VIRUSES OF THE ARBO GROUP

Colorado tick fever—U.S.
Tacaribe—Trinidad
Junin—Argentina, S.A.
Phlebotomus fever—Middle East
Nairobi sheep disease—Africa

## REFERENCES

### General

CASALS, J. Procedures for Identification of Arthropod-borne Viruses. Bull. World Health Org. 24:723, 1961.

———, *et al.* The Arboviruses. *In* Viral and Rickettsial Infections of Man. Horsfall, F. L., and Tamm, I. (eds.). J. B. Lippincott Co., Philadelphia, 1965.

CLARKE, D. H., and CASALS, J. Techniques for Hemagglutination and Hemagglutinin-Inhibition With Arthropod-borne Viruses. Amer. Jour. Trop. Med. Hyg. 7:561, 1958.

SABIN, A. B. Hemagglutination by Viruses Affecting the Human Nervous System. Fed. Proc. 10:573, 1951.

SYMPOSIUM ON THE EVOLUTION OF ARBOVIRUS DISEASES I. Origin and Evolution of Viruses, C. D. Darlington. II. Ecological Aspects of the Evolution of Mosquito-borne Virus Diseases, P. F. Mattingley. III. Factors in the Past and Future Evolution of the Arboviruses, C. E. Gordon Smith. Trans. Roy. Soc. Trop. Med. Hyg. 54:89, 1960.

### Equine Encephalitis Viruses

CASALS, J. Antigenic Variants of Eastern Equine Encephalitis Virus. Jour. Exp. Med. 119:547, 1964.

GILTNER, L. T., and SHAHAN, M. S. Transmission of Infectious Equine Encephalomyelitis in Mammals and Birds. Science 78:63, 1933.

———, and ———. The Immunological Relationship of Eastern and Western Strains of Equine Encephalomyelitis Virus. Science 78:587, 1933.

———, and ———. The Outbreak of Infectious Equine Encephalitis in the Eastern States. N. Amer. Vet. 14:25, 1933.

HENDERSON, J. R. Immunologic Characterization of Western Equine Encephalomyelitis Virus Strains. Jour. Immunol. 93:452, 1964.

Karabatoss, N., *et al.* Antigenic Variation Among Strains of Western Equine Encephalomyelitis. Amer. Jour. Trop. Med. Hyg. 12:408, 1963.

Klimenko, S. M., *et al.* Architecture of Venezuelan Equine Encephalomyelitis Virus. Virology 27:125, 1965.

Meyer, K. F., *et al.* The Etiology of Epizootic Encephalomyelitis of Horses in the San Joaquin Valley, 1930. Science 74:227, 1931.

Porterfield, J. S. Cross-neutralization Studies With Group A Arthropod-borne Viruses. Bull. World Health Org. 24:735, 1961.

Ten Broeck, C., and Merrill, M. H. A Serological Difference Between Eastern and Western Equine Encephalomyelitis Virus. Proc. Soc. Exp. Biol. Med. 31:217, 1933.

Thomas, L. A., and Eklund, C. M. Overwintering of Western Equine Encephalomyelitis Virus in Garter Snakes Experimentally Infected by *Culex tarsalis*. Proc. Soc. Exp. Biol. Med. 109:421, 1962.

## Other Group A Arboviruses

Causey, O. R., *et al.* Aura and Una, Two New Group A Arthropod-borne Viruses. Amer. Jour. Trop. Med. Hyg. 12:777, 1963.

Shope, R. E., *et al.* The Venezuelan Equine Encephalomyelitis Complex of Group A Arthropod-borne Viruses Including Mucumbo and Pixuna From the Amazon Region of Brazil. Amer. Jour. Trop. Med. Hyg. 13:723, 1964.

## Japanese Encephalitis Virus

Burns, K. F., and Matumoto, M. Survey of Animals for Inapparent Infection With the Virus of Japanese B Encephalitis. Amer. Jour. Vet. Res. 10:146, 1949.

Lee, H. U., *et al.* Porcine Kidney Cell Cultures for Propagation and Assay of Japanese Encephalitis Virus. Proc. Soc. Exp. Biol. Med. 99:579, 1958.

Sherer, W. F., *et al.* Ecologic Studies of Japanese Encephalitis Virus in Japan. VI. Swine Infection. Amer. Jour. Trop. Med. Hyg. 8:698, 1959.

Taniguchi, T., *et al.* A Virus Isolated in 1935 Epidemic of Summer Encephalitis of Japan. Jap. Jour. Exp. Med. 14:185, 1936.

Tigertt, W. D., and Berge, T. O. Japanese B Encephalitis. Amer. Jour. Pub. Health 47:713, 1957.

## St. Louis Encephalitis Virus

Chamberlain, R. W., *et al.* St. Louis Encephalitis Virus in Mosquitoes. Amer. Jour. Hyg. 70:221, 1959.

Cox, H. R., *et al.* Susceptibility of Horses to St. Louis Encephalitis Virus. Pub. Health Rept., Wash., 56:1391 1941.

Rhim, J. S. Plaque Assay of Japanese B Encephalitis Virus on Hamster Kidney Monolayers. Proc. Soc. Exp. Biol. Med. 109:887, 1962.

Shinner, J. J. St. Louis Encephalomyelitis. Arch. Path. 75:309, 1963.

Sudia, W. D. The Virus of St. Louis Encephalitis in Chickens. Amer. Jour. Hyg. 70:197, 1959.

Webster, L. T., and Fite, G. L. A Virus Encountered in the Study of Material From Cases of Encephalitis in the St. Louis and Kansas City Epidemics of 1933. Science 78:463, 1933.

## West Nile Virus

Marburg, K., *et al.* The Natural History of West Nile Fever. Amer. Jour. Hyg. 64:259, 1956.

Schmidt, J. R., and el Mansoury, H. K. Natural and Experimental Infection of Egyptian Equines With West Nile Virus. Ann. Trop. Med. Parasit. 57:415, 1963.

## Murray Valley Encephalitis Virus

French, E. L. Murray Valley Encephalitis: Isolation and Characterization of the Etiological Agent. Austral. Med. Jour. 1:100, 1952.

## Louping-Ill Virus

Gordon, W. S., *et al.* Studies in Louping-Ill. Jour. Comp. Path. Therap. 45:106, 1932.

Pool, W. A. The Etiology of Louping-Ill. Vet. Jour. 87:177, 1931.

———. The Etiology of Louping-Ill. Vet. Jour. 87:222, 1931.

———, *et al.* The Etiology of Louping-Ill. Jour. Comp. Path. Therap. 43:253, 1930.

### Russian Spring-Summer Virus

KERR, J. A. Yellow Fever and *Aedes aegypti* in the Western Hemisphere. Proc. 6th Intl. Cong. Trop. Med. & Malar. 5:219, 1959.

KOVAC, W., *et al.* Die Electronenmikroskopische Darstellung des Virus der Fruhsommermeningoencephalitis in HeLa Zellen. Arch. ges. Virusforsch. 11:544, 1961–62.

VAN ROOYEN, C. E., and RHODES, A. J. Virus Diseases of Man. Thomas Nelson and Sons, New York, 1948.

### Yellow Fever Virus

REED, W., *et al.* Papers Relating to Yellow Fever. U.S. 61st Cong., 3rd Sess., Senate Doc. No. 822, Washington, D.C., 1911.

STRODE, G. K. (ed.). Yellow Fever. McGraw-Hill, New York, 1951.

TRUBY, A. E. Memoir of Walter Reed, the Yellow Fever Episode. P. B. Hoeber Inc., New York, 1943.

### Rift Valley Fever Virus

DAUBNEY, R., *et al.* Enzootic Hepatitis or Rift Valley Fever. Jour. Path. Bact. 34:545, 1931.

EASTERDAY, B. C. Rift Valley Fever. Adv. Vet. Sci. 10:65, 1965.

RANDALL, R., *et al.* Rift Valley Fever Virus Vaccine. Amer. Jour. Trop. Med. Hyg. 12:611, 1963.

WEISS, K. E. Rift Valley Fever: A Review. Bull. Epizootic Dis. Afr. 5:431, 1957.

### Wesselsbron Virus

WEISS, K. E., *et al.* Wesselsbron Virus—A Virus Not Previously Described, Associated With Abortion in Animals. Onderstepoort Jour. Vet. Res. 27:183, 1956.

### Dengue Virus

SABIN, A. B. Recent Advances in our Knowledge of Dengue and Sandfly Fever. Amer. Jour. Trop. Med. Hyg. 4:198, 1955.

### Powassan Virus

CASALS, J. Antigenic Relationship Between Powassan and Russian Spring-Summer Encephalitis Viruses. Canad. Med. Assn. Jour. 82:355, 1960.

MCLEAN, D. M., and DONOHUE, W. L. Powassan Virus: Isolation of Virus From a Fatal Case of Encephalitis. Canad. Med. Assn. Jour. 80:708, 1959.

———, *et al.* Powassan Virus: Surveys of Human and Animal Sera. Amer. Jour. Pub. Health 50:1539, 1960.

———, *et al.* Powassan Virus: Field Investigations During Summer 1963. Amer. Jour. Trop. Med. Hyg. 13: 747, 1964.

WHITNEY, E., and JAMBACK, H. The First Isolations of Powassan Virus in New York State. Proc. Soc. Exp. Biol. Med. 119:432, 1965.

### California Encephalitis Virus

BARDOS, V., and DANIELOVA, V. L. The Tahnya Virus, A Virus Isolated From Mosquitoes in Czechoslovakia. Jour. Hyg. Epidem. Microbiol. Immunol. 3:264, 1959.

CASALS, J. Immunological Relationship Between Tahnya and California Encephalitis Viruses. Acta Virol. 6:140, 1962.

MCHAMMON, W. McD., and REEVES, W. C. California Encephalitis Virus. A Newly Described Agent. I. Evidence of Natural Infection in Man and Other Animals. Calif. Med. 77:303, 1952.

NEWHOUSE, V. F., *et al.* California Encephalitis Virus. Serological Survey of Small Wild Mammals in Northern United States and Southern Canada and the Isolation of Additional Strains. Amer. Jour. Hyg. 78:123, 1963.

THOMPSON, W. H., and EVANS, A. S. California Encephalitis Virus Studies in Wisconsin. Amer. Jour. Epidem. 81:230, 1965.

### African Horse-Sickness Virus

ALEXANDER, R. A. Studies on Neurotropic Virus of Horsesickness. VI. Propagation in the Developing Chick Embryo. Onderstepoort Jour. Vet. Sci. An. Ind. 11:9, 1938.

HOWELL, P. G. The 1960 Epizootic of African Horse-sickness in the Middle East and S.W. Asia. Jour. S. Afr. Vet. Med. Assn. 31:329, 1960.

Howell, P. G. The Isolation and Identification of Further Antigenic Types of African Horse-sickness Virus. Onderstepoort Jour. Vet. Res. 29:139, 1962.

M'Fadyean, J. African Horse Sickness. Jour. Comp. Path. Therap. 13:1, 1900.

———. The Susceptibility of the Dog to African Horse Sickness. Jour. Comp. Path. Therap. 23:27, 1910.

Ozawa, Y., and Hazrati, A. Growth of African Horse-sickness Virus in Monkey Kidney Cell Cultures. Amer. Jour. Vet. Res. 25:505, 1964.

———, *et al.* African Horse-sickness Live-virus Tissue Culture Vaccine. Amer. Jour. Vet. Res. 26:154, 1965.

## Blue Tongue Virus

Bekker, J. G., *et al.* The Occurrence and Identification of Bluetongue in Cattle—the So-called Pseudo-Foot and Mouth Disease in South Africa. Onderstepoort Jour. Vet. Sci. 2:393, 1934.

Brown, J. G., *et al.* Current Status of Bluetongue in Sheep. Jour. Amer. Vet. Med. Assn. 144:759, 1964.

———, *et al.* Current Aspects of Bluetongue in Cattle. Jour. Amer. Vet. Med. Assn. 148:1177, 1966.

Cox, H. R. Bluetongue. Bact. Rev. 18:239, 1954.

DuToit, R. M. The Role Played by Bovines in the Transmission of Blue Tongue in Sheep. Jour. S. Afr. Vet. Med. Assn. 33:483, 1962.

Foster, N. M., *et al.* Preliminary Investigations on Insect Transmission of Bluetongue Virus in Sheep. Amer. Jour. Vet. Res. 24:1195, 1963.

Haig, D. A., *et al.* The Cytopathic Action of Bluetongue Virus on Tissue Cultures and Its Application to the Detection of Antibodies in Serum in Sheep. Onderstepoort Jour. Vet. Res. 27:171, 1956.

McKercher, D. G., *et al.* Studies on Bluetongue. I. Isolation, Identification, and Typing of the Bluetongue Virus and a Preliminary Report on the Serodiagnosis of the Disease. Proc. 91st Ann. Meet. Amer. Vet. Med. Assn., p. 167, 1954.

Owen, N. C., *et al.* Blue Tongue in Cattle: Typing of Viruses Isolated in Cattle Exposed to Natural Infections. Onderstepoort Jour. Vet. Res. 32:3, 1965.

Spreull, J. Malarial Catarrhal Fever (Bluetongue) of Sheep in South Africa. Jour. Comp. Path. Therap. 18: 321, 1905.

Studdert, M. J. Sensitivity of Bluetongue Virus to Ether and Sodium Desoxycholate. Proc. Soc. Exp. Biol. Med. 118:1006, 1965.

## Other Viruses of the Arbovirus Group

Casals, J., and Clarke, D. H. Arboviruses Other Than Group A and B. *In* Viral and Rickettsial Diseases of Man. Horsfall, F. L., and Tamm, I. (eds.). J. B. Lippincott Co., Philadelphia, 1965.

Causey, O. R., *et al.* The Isolation of Arthropod Viruses Including Members of Two Hitherto Undescribed Serological Groups in the Amazon Region of Brazil. Amer. Jour. Trop. Med. Hyg. 10:227, 1961.

Dick, G. W. A., and Haddow, A. J. Uganda S. Virus. A Hitherto Unrecorded Virus Isolated From Mosquitoes in Uganda. Trans. Roy. Soc. Trop. Med. Hyg. 46:600, 1952.

Holden, P., and Hess, A. D. Cache Valley Virus. A Previously Undescribed Mosquito-borne Agent. Science 130:1187, 1959.

Whitney, E. Flanders Strain, An Arbovirus Newly Isolated From Mosquitoes and Birds of New York State. Amer. Jour. Trop. Med. Hyg. 13:123, 1964.

———. Arthropod-borne Viruses in New York State: Serological Evidence of Groups A, B and Bunyamwera Viruses in Dairy Herds. Amer. Jour. Vet. Res. 26:914, 1965.

# 49

# The Myxoviruses

THE NAME MYXOVIRUS REFERS TO THOSE VIRUSES which have an affinity for the mucoproteins of the stroma of erythrocytes. The attachment of the virus to erythrocytes in suspension causes them to temporarily stick together (hemagglutinate) and is an important property of the group.

While the original myxovirus members produced hemagglutinins, several viruses having similar morphology and structure but lacking hemagglutinin have since been classified with them.

The myxoviruses are composed of a single-stranded RNA core with the capsid wound in a helical fashion inside a lipoprotein envelope. Projecting radially from the envelope are spikes of protein (hemagglutinin and neuraminidase) which are responsible for attachment and enzymic elution from susceptible erythrocytes.

The size of the various members of the myxovirus group ranges from 80 m$\mu$ to 250 m$\mu$. The site of replication of the nucleoprotein portion of the myxoviruses varies; with some the process of replication begins in the nucleus of the cell while with others replication occurs in the cytoplasm. The envelope is added as the nucleocapsid is extruded through the cell membrane.

Most members of the myxovirus group produce respiratory infections in man or lower animals, while a few characteristically produce generalized disease.

## INFLUENZA A VIRUSES

Influenza A—Man. *Myxovirus influenzae A-hominis* subtypes A, $A_1$, $A_2$ (Asian)

Swine influenza—Swine. *Myxovirus influenzae A-suis*

Equine influenza—Horses. *Myxovirus influenzae A-equi* subtypes—A-equi 1/Prague/56; A-equi 2/Miami/63

Duck influenza—Ducks. *Myxovirus influenzae A-anatis*

Fowl pest (Fowl plague)—Fowl.

Tern Virus—European Tern.

Virus N—Chickens.

### Influenza A Viruses

**Proposed Name.** *Myxovirus influenzae A-hominis.*

**Disease Produced.** Influenza, "flu."

**Hosts Affected.** Man, swine, horse. The monkey, ferret, mouse, and hamster can be experimentally infected. Rabbits, guinea pigs, and rats show inapparent infection.

**History and Distribution.** Human influenza has been recognized as a disease entity for many centuries. The etiology was thought by Pfeiffer to be *Hemophilus influenzae;* he first described this organism in 1893. However, this organism could not be isolated from many typical cases of influenza, and much doubt arose as to its role in the disease. In 1931 Shope reported on the isolation of the virus of swine influenza and showed that a virus and a hemophilic organism were responsible for the disease in swine, which was clinically similar to human influenza. Smith, Andrewes, and

Laidlaw, in 1933, were the first to isolate influenza virus from a human source. These workers produced a respiratory infection in ferrets by injecting throat washings from human cases of influenza. Since the first isolation and description of the influenza virus, an immense amount of work has been published on the virus and the disease.

Influenza is worldwide in occurrence. While it is usually endemic, it has been known to produce several pandemics, that of 1918 being the most severe. It has been estimated that up to half the world's population was attacked in that outbreak, with the death of some 20 million persons. In the United States 550,000 deaths occurred during the 1918 pandemic.

A pandemic which originated in Asia in 1957 and spread worldwide within a year rivaled the attack rate of the 1918 virus. It has been estimated that in the United States 45 million persons were infected with the Asian (A-2) virus during October and November, 1957. The mortality rate of the "Asian type" influenza was very low compared to the 1918 pandemic.

Influenza A viruses are generally spherical in shape, though elongated and filamentous forms are seen (Fig. 49.1). The particles are 80 mμ to 120 mμ in size. They are composed of a nucleoprotein which is helical in shape and is wound rather tightly inside the lipoprotein envelope. The nucleoprotein is also referred to as *soluble antigen*. On the surface of the virus particle are spikes projecting radially which can be removed by ether treatment of the virus and which can be shown to possess marked hemagglutinin activity. Human and chicken erythrocytes are most often used to demonstrate hemagglutination.

Dissociation of virus-erythrocyte complexes results from the action of the enzyme neuraminidase which is among the surface components of the virus particle.

The dominant antigens are to be found in the surface components of the virus which include the envelope and the surface proteins.

The virus is inactivated by exposure for 30 minutes at 56°C. It may be preserved by freezing and drying or freezing alone at low temperatures. Simple drying of the virus does not preserve it for more than several days unless it is kept cool and in a dark place, in which case it may survive for weeks.

Various chemical disinfectants are able to destroy influenza virus in the commonly used concentrations.

Penicillin, streptomycin, or tyrothricin have no effect upon the virus. The first two mentioned are used to aid in its isolation in pure culture from bacteria-contaminated materials.

**Cultivation.** Chicken embryos are often used for cultivation of the virus. The most sensitive method is amniotic sac inoculation and it is recommended for pri-

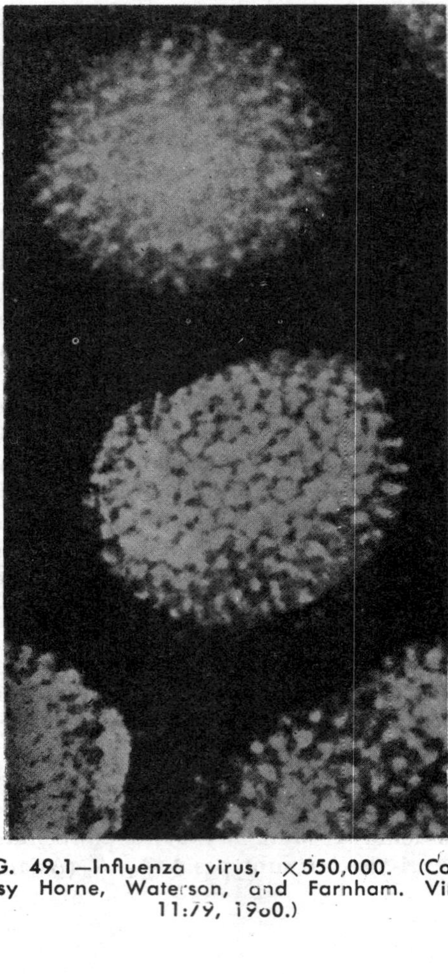

FIG. 49.1—Influenza virus, ×550,000. (Courtesy Horne, Waterson, and Farnham. Virol. 11:79, 1960.)

mary isolation. Allantoic cavity and chorioallantoic membrane inoculation are also used. Incubation at 35°–36°C. after inoculation is preferable to 37°C. Influenza virus may be lethal to the embryo in 3 to 5 days, but may fail to kill. Some embryos will show retarded development, and microscopic lesions are pronounced in the epithelial cells of the respiratory tract. Certain strains of influenza virus produce typical pocks when inoculated in the chorioallantoic membrane. Hemagglutination tests of the amniotic or allantoic fluid are the usual methods of detecting virus multiplication in the embryo.

Influenza A can also be cultivated in tissue cultures composed of chicken embryo tissue, human embryonic lung or kidney, or monkey kidney cells. Tissue cultures can be used for the primary isolation of influenza virus. Visible plaques are produced in monolayer cell cultures.

**Transmission.** Influenza is essentially a droplet-spread infection. The virus is expelled into the air by persons in late incubation period or early stages of the disease. Direct contact with contaminated clothing or eating utensils may also spread the infection. The disease is most prevalent in the winter and it is thought that weather conditions are a predisposing factor. The incubation period is 24 to 48 hours.

**Characteristics of the Disease.** Human influenza usually begins with headache, chills, "ache all over" feeling, and temperature increases, and there may be dizziness and vomition. Cough develops which may last for many days. There is a distinct leucopenia. The fever lasts 3 to 5 days, and recovery usually takes place in a week or ten days. Bacterial complications sometimes occur. Secondary bacteria include *H. influenzae, Dip. pneumoniae,* hemolytic streptococci, and *Staphylococcus aureus.*

**Immunity.** Resistance to influenza follows recovery from the disease but it is often of short duration.

A number of vaccines have been prepared and used for active immunization, but embryo-propagated virus has been used most extensively for vaccine manufacture.

Various methods of vaccine preparation include formolized allantoic fluid, alum-precipitated products, and vaccines prepared by concentration methods such as freezing and thawing, high speed centrifugation, and red cell absorption and elution. Some vaccines employ only strains of influenza A, but bivalent A and B vaccines have been used in others. The results of the use of vaccines have been varied. Some workers report negative results, but more recent work with more concentrated vaccines has generally shown a significant reduction in the attack rate.

**Diagnosis.** A diagnosis of influenza is ordinarily based on clinical symptoms. More accurately it must include isolation of the virus in chicken embryos and its identification by hemagglutination and hemagglutination-inhibition procedures.

Serum neutralization, hemagglutination-inhibition, and complement-fixation tests are of some value in determining recent contacts or in following the immune response to vaccination or infection.

### Swine Influenza Virus

**Proposed Name.** *Myxovirus influenzae A-suis.*

**History and Distribution.** Coincident with the 1918 pandemic of influenza in man, a similar disease was recognized in swine in Iowa by Koen and the name "hog flu" was ascribed to it. Several investigators attempted unsuccessfully to determine the etiology of the disease. In 1931 Shope studied the disease and recovered a virus. This virus was unable to produce typical swine influenza when inoculated alone in the form of a filtrate. A mild indefinite illness, "filtrate disease," was produced. In the same year Lewis and Shope reported the isolation of a hemophilic organism, *Hemophilus suis,* which occurred consistently along with the virus and that these two agents together were responsible for the clinical swine flu. *Hemophilus suis* alone was found incapable of producing the disease.

Swine influenza is widely distributed among swine in the United States. It also occurs in swine in Europe, Great Britain, and in Ireland.

**Properties of the Virus.** The general properties of swine influenza virus are identical to influenza A.

The only difference between swine influenza and influenza A is on the basis of antigenicity and pathogenicity; however, even these differences are not always clear-cut.

COMPARISON OF SWINE INFLUENZA AND INFLUENZA A VIRUSES

1. They are closely related antigenically. They share antigenic components, and more difference may be in quantity of these components than in kind.
2. Antibodies which react serologically with swine virus are widely prevalent in man.
3. Antibodies which react serologically with influenza A have been demonstrated in swine sera, and a natural infection due to influenza A virus is presumed.
4. Influenza A virus isolated from human cases is pathogenic for swine by inoculation, but does not spread by contact to other swine.
5. Immunization of animals with swine virus gives protection against the swine virus, but does not regularly protect against influenza A.

Swine influenza virus possibly represents specially adapted strains of human influenza A virus which are epizootic in swine. Koen in his original description of swine influenza called particular attention to the occurrence of influenza in the farm families and swine on the same farm during the 1918 pandemic. Shope and others have suggested that swine influenza virus is a persistence of the 1918 pandemic virus in swine. It has been suggested that swine may be a source of influenza virus to man, but this has not been proved

Surveys made during the 1957 outbreak of Asian influenza revealed naturally acquired hemagglutinating-inhibiting antibodies in both swine and horses. However, it was concluded that although inapparent infection occurred in these hosts, they did not play any role in the spread of the disease in man. By complement-fixation tests and hemagglutinins for horse erythrocytes, the A-2 virus of the 1957 pandemic appears more closely related to swine strains than to other human A isolates.

**Cultivation.** Swine influenza virus can be cultivated in the same manner as influenza A. Chicken embryo propagation is the most often employed. A higher proportion of deaths of embryos occurs if *H. suis* and the virus are inoculated together.

The virus alone can be transmitted to mice or ferrets without difficulty. In these species of animals typical respiratory infection is produced.

**Transmission.** Droplet infection is the most common method of transmission of swine influenza. An unusual method of transmission in this disease has been carefully studied by Shope. He found that the virus was latent in some swine and that the disease could be "precipitated" by intramuscular injections of *H. suis.* This was possible only in the fall and winter months. More extended investigation found that the lungworm of swine may act as a carrier of the virus and perpetuate the disease from one year to another. The virus has been isolated from lungworm ova and also lungworm larvae found in earthworms in the vicinity of hog lots. Hogs which may feed on earthworms then become infested with lungworms, and at the same time they are exposed to the swine influenza virus carried directly to the lungs by the lungworms.

**Characteristics of the Disease.** Swine influenza is prevalent in the fall and winter months. It is quite contagious; usually close to 100 per cent of the susceptible swine become infected. Morbidity is high, but the mortality is low, usually 2 per cent or less. The symptoms appear suddenly and there is fever, anorexia, extreme prostration, cough, rapid respiration, and a peculiar abdominal breathing. The course of the disease is usually 2 to 6 days with rapid recovery except in complicated cases. There is some loss in fattening hogs and also reduced fertility in sows which are bred near the time of the outbreak.

Although Shope has emphasized the synergistic action of *H. suis* in producing swine influenza, Scott showed that a Pasteurella could act in a similar manner but the disease produced did not spread among swine. British workers have also suggested that organisms other than *H. suis* could act in the same role.

**Pathological Changes.** The pathological changes in uncomplicated swine influenza are confined to the respiratory tract. Exudative bronchitis and bronchiectasis with extensive pulmonary consolidation and atelectasis are characteristic. Leucopenia is a constant finding early in the disease.

**Immunity.** Animals which recover from swine influenza are resistant to reinfection. Antibodies can be demonstrated in their serum.

Artificial immunization with chicken-embryo propagated virus has been tried experimentally, but has not come into general use.

**Diagnosis.** Clinical diagnosis of swine influenza is ordinarily made. For accuracy, isolation by chicken embryo inoculation, and identification of the virus by hemagglutination and hemagglutination-inhibition tests is necessary.

### Equine Influenza Virus

**Proposed Name.** *Myxovirus influenzae A-equi.*

**Disease Produced.** Equine influenza.

**Hosts Affected.** Horses, possibly man.

**History and Distribution.** Respiratory disease in horses was described in the veterinary literature of the 12th century. The disease, designated as equine influenza in the past, has been found to be etiologically complex; several viruses being capable of producing similar clinical conditions. Not until the middle 1950's was evidence presented that more than one virus is concerned with respiratory disease of the horse. In 1956 Sovinová *et al.* reported the isolation of a myxovirus which was associated with an epizootic of influenza in horses in Czechoslovakia. The new agent was found to be related to the influenza A virus of man. Since 1956 many outbreaks of equine influenza throughout Europe and North America have been found to be caused by viruses belonging to the influenza A group. (See discussion under Rhinopneumonitis, Chapter 45.)

**Properties of the Virus.** The general characteristics of equine influenza virus are assumed to be like those of the A group but are not precisely known. The ability of the virus to agglutinate the erythrocytes of the horse, pig, and calf indicates a closer relationship to $A_2$ type than to other members of the A group.

Two antigenically different strains of the virus are represented by equi 1/Prague/56 and equi 2/Miami/63.

**Cultivation.** Equine influenza virus can be cultivated in chicken embryos and in cell cultures composed of chicken embryo fibroblasts or monkey kidney cells.

**Transmission.** Transmission of equine influenza occurs most often by inhalation of droplet nuclei expelled into the air by the sneezing and coughing of infected animals.

**Characteristics of the Disease.** The symptoms exhibited by horses infected with influenza virus are those of an acute upper respiratory disease. A febrile reaction is observed for 3 to 5 days accompanied by depression, coughing, sneezing, and nasal discharge. Recovery is uneventful unless complicated by secondary infections or the stresses of shipping and fatigue.

Experimental exposure of human volunteers to A-equi virus has been reported by Kasel *et al.* as producing clinical illness and an immunological response.

**Immunity.** Recovered horses are immune to the virus for a period of a few months.

A bivalent vaccine which incorporates both the Prague 56 and the Miami 63 strains is used for prophylaxis of equine influenza. The viruses are propagated in chicken embryos and then killed by chemical treatment.

**Diagnosis.** Equine influenza must be diagnosed by virus isolation and identification or by serological evidence gained from hemagglutination-inhibition tests which are conducted on serum samples collected during acute and convalescent periods of the disease.

### Duck Influenza Virus

**Proposed Name.** *Myxovirus influenzae A-anatis.*

A virus disease of ducklings first reported by Koppel *et al.* is related to the influenza A group. Morphologically it resembles influenza A, occurring generally as spheres of 80 mμ to 100 mμ in diameter, though filamentous forms are occasionally observed.

In hemagglutinin activity the virus resembles the A-equi and $A_2$ subgroups since it is active on horse, pig, and calf erythrocytes.

The disease has occurred in epizootics in Czechoslovakia. Sinusitis is the outstanding manifestation of the infection. Outbreaks of duck sinusitis have also been reported from Great Britain by Roberts.

### Fowl Pest Virus

**Proposed Name.** *Myxovirus pestis-galli.*

**Disease Produced.** Fowl pest, fowl plague.

**Hosts Affected.** Chickens and turkeys are most commonly infected. Water fowl such as ducks and geese are susceptible, as are guinea fowl, sparrows, owls, blackbirds, canaries, and pigeons. Some mammals can be experimentally infected. These include mice, rats, rabbits, ferrets, monkeys, and hedgehogs.

**History and Distribution.** Fowl pest was first recognized in Italy in 1878. The virus was described by Centanni in 1901 and 1902 in reports on the disease and on experiments which proved that the etiological agent would pass Chamberland filters.

Fowl pest has spread worldwide, occurring in many countries at some time during the last 50 years. The disease made its first appearance in the United States in 1924–25 and again in 1929. It was first recognized in New York, New Jersey, and Pennsylvania, and spread westward to Michigan, Illinois, and Indiana. The disease was brought under control in all instances by eradication methods, and no occurrences have been recorded since 1929.

Fowl pest remains enzootic in countries of Europe, in the Mediterranean and Danube areas, and also in many areas of Asia.

**Properties of the Virus.** The elementary bodies of fowl pest may be round or filamentous in shape and are reported to vary between 80 mμ and 100 mμ in size. They will pass through Berkefeld, Chamberland, and Seitz filters.

Thermal inactivation of the virus occurs at 60°C. in 5 minutes, but at 55°C. it remains viable after 15 minutes exposure.

The virus is preserved at —70°C. for at least 242 days. Infectivity is lost at storage temperatures of 6°C. and 37°C. within 85 and 92 days respectively. One per cent phenol or 0.02 per cent merthiolate does not kill the virus in 1 hour. Five per cent phenol is lethal in 10 minutes exposure. Formalin, 0.1 per cent, inactivates the virus in 18 to 24 hours and 0.2 and 0.4 per cent concentrations within 6 hours.

Exposure to 10,000 Oxford units of penicillin for 1 hour is without effect.

Fowl pest virus will produce hemagglutination of erythrocytes of the following animals: chicken, chicken embryo, turkey, duck, man, dog, cat, rabbit, swine, horse, ox, sheep, guinea pig, and monkey. The cells of the rabbit and swine are least satisfactory. Hemagglutination is specifically inhibited by immune sera.

Variant strains have been described on the basis of antigenicity and virulence. No antigenic relationship to Newcastle virus has been shown, but cross reactions with the influenza A group have been reported.

**Cultivation.** Fowl pest virus can be readily grown in chicken embryos by the usual methods of inoculation. The virus multiplies very rapidly and high concentrations are present in the fluids and tissue of the embryo. The virus is uniformly lethal to the embryo within 24 to 48 hours. Hemorrhage is the most common lesion observed in the dead embryo.

**Transmission.** Fowl pest is usually transmitted by contact with infected birds. The virus is present in eye and nasal secretions as well as in blood, urine, and feces. Contaminated food and water are common sources of the virus. Insect vectors have been suspected of transmission in some cases. Immune carriers also play a part in the dissemination of fowl pest. Wild birds such as owls, sparrows, and blackbirds may spread the virus.

**Characteristics of the Disease.** Fowl pest is an acute infection with sudden onset. Some birds may die before definite symptoms are noted. A majority of the infected birds will show depression, anorexia, loss of egg production, diarrhea, ruffled feathers, and an unsteady gait. The comb and wattles become cyanotic. Edema of the head region and gasping and coughing are common. Nervous symptoms are sometimes observed, especially in the less susceptible species of birds. Mortality rates in chickens are very high and deaths occur in 24 to 48 hours after onset of the disease.

**Pathological Changes.** A postmortem examination of birds dying of fowl pest will show lesions of a septicemia. Petechial hemorrhages may be found in organs such as the lungs, heart, proventriculus intestines, and in the fat around the gizzard and in the mesentery. Subcutaneous edema of the head region is usually observed.

**Immunity.** The few birds that recover from fowl pest are immune.

Serum-neutralizing and hemagglutination-inhibiting antibodies are readily demonstrated in immune birds. Several methods of active immunization have been studied. Live virus and immune serum injected simultaneously confer immunity, but the method is not considered practical because of the expense and the losses of birds following the inoculation.

Killed vaccines of various kinds have been of limited value. Formolized virus confers some protection against the disease but it is not highly effective. Other vaccines which have been heat killed, ultraviolet killed, or chemically killed have been even less successful.

Living virus vaccine produced from a variant of a Dutch East Indies strain of fowl pest virus has been studied by Moses, Brandly, Jones, and Jungherr. Under experimental conditions, this virus appeared to produce satisfactory resistance to challenge with highly virulent virus.

**Diagnosis.** A diagnosis of fowl pest requires isolation and identification of the virus. Chicken embryo inoculation with blood and tissue material will isolate the virus. The addition of suitable antibiotics such as penicillin and streptomycin to the inoculum is desirable if not always required. If fowl pest virus is present in the inoculum it should produce death of the embryos in 24 to 48 hours. Hemagglutination tests of allantoic fluid should be positive if fowl pest is present. However, Newcastle disease virus may be isolated from birds showing similar symptoms and under the same conditions of isolation. Since both fowl pest and Newcastle viruses will produce hemagglutination, it is necessary to differentiate them by serum neutralization and hemagglutination-inhibition tests, using known immune sera.

It is also necessary to eliminate bacteria as a cause of rapid deaths among fowl, since fowl pest and fowl cholera are sometimes confused clinically.

## OTHER VIRUSES RELATED TO INFLUENZA A

### Virus N

A virus which was isolated from chickens by Dinter in 1949 has characteristics which are similar to the influenza A group. The virus particles are spherical and measure 100 m$\mu$ to 200 m$\mu$ in diameter. The size and arrangement of the ribonucleoprotein of virus N is similar to influenza A and is also immunologically related. The hemagglutinins, however, appear to be unrelated.

### Tern Virus

Rowan has described a disease occurring in the European common tern which was responsible for substantial death losses among these migratory birds. The virus resembles the influenza A group morphologically, and the ribonucleoprotein antigen is serologically related to it.

## INFLUENZA B VIRUS

**Proposed Name.** *Myxovirus influenzae B.*

**Disease Produced.** Influenza.

**Hosts Affected.** Man. Mice and ferrets can be experimentally infected.

**History and Distribution.** In 1940 Francis isolated an influenza virus which proved to be immunologically distinct from influenza A. In addition to its occurrence in the United States, it has been identified in various countries.

**Characteristics of Influenza B.** Influenza B is similar in every respect to influenza A in its properties. It is not as widely distributed nor is the disease produced as severe. Otherwise, the two viruses cannot be differentiated except on immunological bases.

Influenza B has been incorporated in many of the recent influenza vaccines.

## INFLUENZA C VIRUS

An influenza virus isolated by Taylor, also by Francis, Quilligan, and Minuse, differs from either A or B types. This virus has been designated as influenza C.

## PARAINFLUENZA VIRUSES

The parainfluenza group of viruses comprises those which closely resemble the "true" influenza virus in morphology, structure, and general characteristics. Points of similarity are: RNA type nucleic acid, helical ribonucleoprotein, ether sensitive envelope, surface hemagglutinin, affinity for mucoproteins of erythrocytes, and the erythrocyte receptors for both groups are destroyed by "receptor-destroying enzyme." Points of difference are the larger size of parainfluenza viruses (150 mμ to 250 mμ), loose coiling of ribonucleoprotein inside the envelope, and that the diameter of the ribonucleoprotein is twice that of influenza A (18 mμ).

The hemagglutinin activity of the parainfluenza viruses compared to influenza is "weaker" and can be demonstrated in some instances only by hemadsorption methods. Laboratory-adapted strains give stronger reactions.

Syncytium formation is often observed in cell cultures as a result of cell coalescence due to a cell-wall-destroying enzyme. Based on antigenic structure there are at least 5 parainfluenza viruses.

### Parainfluenza 1 Virus (Sendai Virus

Parainfluenza 1 virus occurs in upper respiratory infections of children, is common as a latent virus in mice, and has been isolated from swine (Fig. 49.2).

### Parainfluenza 2 Virus (CA. Croup-Associated Virus)

Parainfluenza 2 is most often associated with acute laryngotracheobronchitis in children.

### Parainfluenza 3 Virus

Parainfluenza 3 occurs in man, cattle, and horses. Though strains from cattle sources are closely related to those found in children, they can be distinguished serologically.

Parainfluenza 3 virus has been repeatedly isolated from "shipping fever" of cattle. The virus alone is not able to reproduce the typical disease, but when accompanied by *Past. multocida* the "shipping fever" syndrome is produced.

Experimental immunizing products which incorporate both parainfluenza 3 virus and *Past. multocida* bacterin have been reported to give promising results in the laboratory but not in field trials. According to Hamdy variation in strains isolated from field cases may have a bearing on the failure of vaccines to protect.

FIG. 49.2—Sendai virus (Parainfluenza 1) showing helical elements from disrupted particle, ×200,000. (Courtesy Horne and Waterson. Jour. Mol. Biol. 2:75, 1960.)

### Parainfluenza 4 Virus

A hemadsorption virus isolated by Johnson *et al.* from the upper respiratory tract of man has been found to be distinct from other parainfluenza viruses and designated as parainfluenza 4.

### Parainfluenza 5 Virus (DA, SA, and SV5 Viruses)

A fifth type of parainfluenza has been proposed which includes viruses isolated from both human and simian sources.

### Mumps Virus

**Proposed Name.** *Myxovirus parotitidis.* Mumps or epidemic parotitis is a common virus disease of man and other primates. The virus is typical of the myxoviruses in its general properties. It is variable in size but averages around 140 mμ in diameter. It is composed of RNA type nucleic acid. The nucleoprotein is arranged in the form of a helix and is covered by a lipid-containing outer coat. A hemagglutinin active on human and fowl erythrocytes can be readily demonstrated.

Growth occurs in chicken embryos and in a variety of cell cultures derived from monkey or human tissues.

Infection of the salivary glands is most common, but encephalitis, orchitis, oöphoritis, and pancreatitis may occur.

Natural infection in animals apparently does not occur but has been suspected in dogs.

Inactivated vaccines of chicken embryo origin have been used for prophylaxis.

### Newcastle Disease Virus

**Proposed Name.** *Myxovirus multiforme.*

**Disease Produced.** Newcastle disease, avian pneumoencephalitis.

**Hosts Affected.** Chickens chiefly, also turkeys, pheasants, quail, pigeons, parakeets, doves, ducks, geese, sparrows, starlings, and chukar partridge are susceptible. The virus has been reported to attack some mammals such as man and experimentally has been transferred to hamsters, sheep, swine monkeys, and mice.

**History and Distribution.** The close clinical similarity between Newcastle disease and fowl pest probably prevented the recognition of Newcastle disease as a separate entity for several years. It was recognized in the Dutch East Indies and in England almost simultaneously, but Doyle, in 1927, was the first to identify the disease and to describe the virus as it occurred on a farm near Newcastle, England. Since the first description, Newcastle disease has been recognized in many countries including the United States, Canada, South Africa, China, Japan, most European countries, the Philippine Islands, Australia, and throughout the East Indies.

Newcastle disease was first reported in the United States by Beach in 1940 in California. Beach further proved the relationship of the virus isolated from the California outbreak to Newcastle virus isolated in England. Since 1940, Newcastle disease has spread widely over the United States and each year accounts for considerable losses in poultry.

**Properties of the Virus.** The morphology of Newcastle virus may vary. Spherical forms are observed in electron micrographs (Fig. 49.3). The spherical particles measure about 180 mμ. Elongated and filamentous forms are often observed. The virus will pass Berkefeld V and N candles as well as Chamberland $L_3$ and Seitz filters. Newcastle virus is more resistant to heat than many other viruses. A majority of strains resist 56°C. for 30 minutes, and occasional strains have been found viable after 180 minutes.

The Newcastle virus has been found by Moses, Brandly, and Jones to be quite stable to comparatively wide pH ranges. After a 1-hour exposure at pH values of 2 to 12, the virus was unaffected. This is contrasted with the fowl pest virus which was found to remain viable only within the range of pH 6 to 11.

The following chemicals are reported to

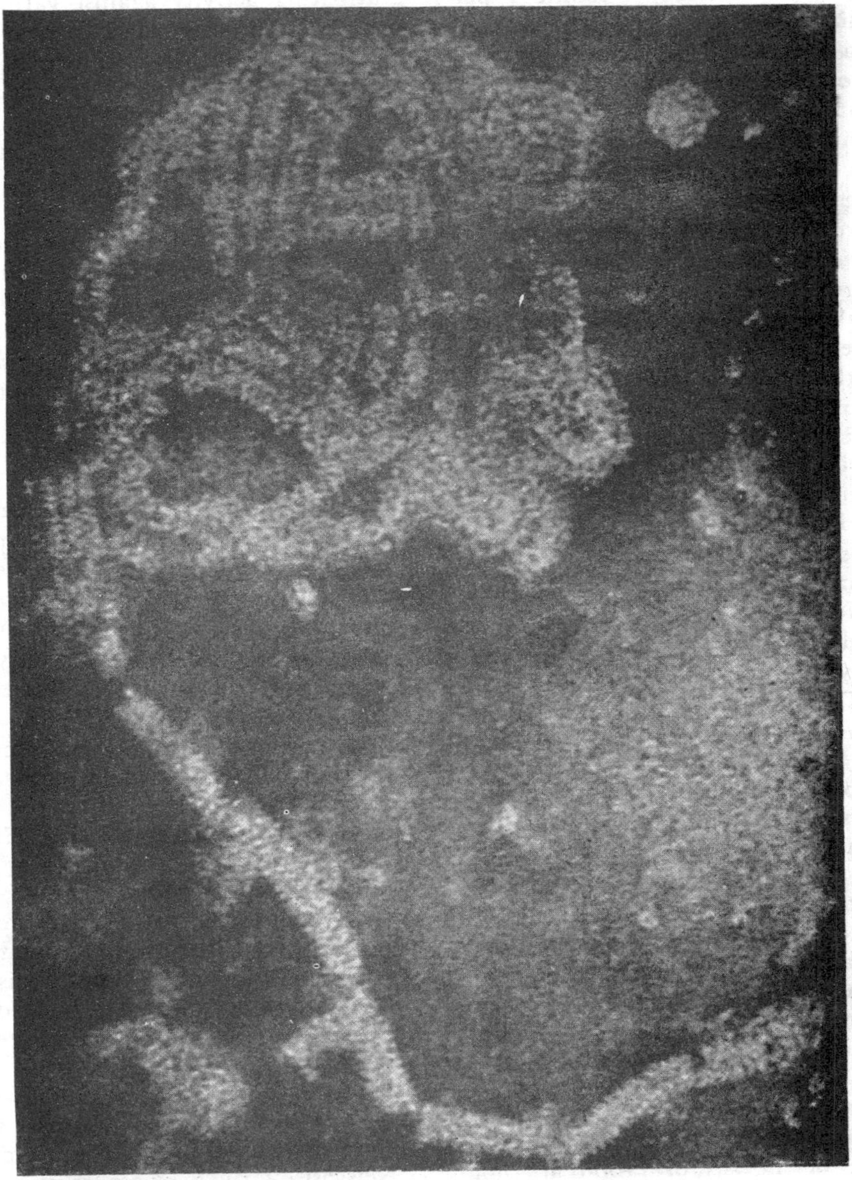

FIG. 49.3—Newcastle disease virus showing helical nucleoprotein components, ×300,000. (Courtesy Horne and Waterson. Jour. Mol. Biol. 2:75, 1960.)

kill the virus in 3 minutes: ethyl alcohol 70 and 95 per cent, phenol 3 per cent, cresol 3 per cent, and tincture of iodine 1 per cent. Sodium hydroxide in 2 per cent concentration is reported as effective by some investigators but not by others.

Fumigation with formaldehyde at 100 per cent humidity destroys the virus under incubator conditions and triethylene glycol is effective in destroying it in the air.

The virus will remain viable in embryo fluids stored at 5°C. for at least a year and for longer periods at —70°C. It has remained alive in fecal material for 5½ months kept at 40°F.

Newcastle virus will remain alive in the carcasses of slaughtered birds for 300 days when held at —4°F. When dried on various materials and held at room temperature, the virus lives 30 days, and if temperatures are lowered to freezing, it remains alive for as long as a year.

Penicillin and streptomycin are without effect on Newcastle virus.

A hemolysin which is capable of lysing chicken erythrocytes has been described by Kilham. The amount of hemolysin activity of the virus is found to parallel its concentration.

An important property of the Newcastle disease virus is that of hemagglutination. Avian, usually chicken, erythrocytes are commonly used for hemagglutinating work, although turkey and other avian species can be used. Certain mammalian erythrocytes are also agglutinated by the virus. In this case, hemagglutination is variable, depending on the strain of virus tested and the individual animal used. Human, guinea pig, and mouse erythrocytes are most satisfactory. Cow, bison, elk, horse, dog, goat, and sheep erythrocytes are quite irregular, while those of the fox or rabbit are not agglutinated by the virus.

Hemagglutination by Newcastle virus is quantitative, and under standardized conditions the amount of virus present in a fluid can be determined. Furthermore, the hemagglutination reaction is inhibited by specific immune serum which is also quantitative.

Various strains of Newcastle virus have been shown to vary in virulence, in hemagglutinating activity against various mammalian erythrocytes, and in heat stability of the hemagglutinating property. Asiatic and European strains of the virus are more virulent than the American ones. No significant antigenic difference among strains has been reported.

**Cultivation.** Newcastle virus is readily cultivated in chicken embryos. The conditions of growth of this virus are not critical. It can be grown by any route of inoculation, at a fairly wide range of temperatures of incubation, and requires no adaptation to the embryo. The usual method of inoculation is into the allantoic cavity. The virus is usually lethal to the embryo in 48 to 72 hours, and hemorrhages of the feather follicles, subcutaneous tissues, occipital region, yolk sac membrane, and general congestion of the embryo are common lesions.

The virus has been grown in tissue cultures composed of chicken embryo fibroblasts and produces a cytopathic effect.

**Transmission.** Under natural conditions Newcastle spreads rapidly by airborne droplets coughed or sneezed from the respiratory system. Beach has succeeded in isolating the virus from the air of a chicken house.

The virus may be introduced into a flock and also spread by means of contaminated food. Outbreaks of Newcastle disease in England have been initiated by feeding the offal from dressed chickens imported from the Continent to other poultry.

Poultry culling and testing personnel who travel from farm to farm may transfer the virus on clothing and equipment.

Newcastle virus has been recovered from eggs laid by hens during the early stages of the disease. However, the virus usually kills the embryo and so these eggs seldom hatch. Even though the eggs do not hatch they may spread the infection if they are accidentally broken in the incubator or if the shell of the egg is contaminated by the virus.

Attempts to isolate the virus from the eggs produced by recovered birds have been unsuccessful.

Carriers of Newcastle disease seldom are found but are believed to exist. Although the carrier rate is very low it still must be considered as a method of spread of the disease.

**Characteristics of the Disease.** Newcastle disease is an acute, highly contagious disease of chickens and occasionally of other fowl. It begins with sudden onset after an incubation period of about 5 days. The first symptoms noted are dullness, coughing, sneezing, and gasping. In laying flocks, egg production drops sharply in two or three days time. The infection spreads rapidly to all susceptible contact birds. Nervous symptoms occur in some birds, especially young ones, within a few days after onset of the disease. Paralysis of the legs or wings or often torticollis resulting in a complete twisting of the neck is observed. Morbidity rates are usually near 100 per cent and mortality rates are variable, ranging from 5 to 50 per cent. Death losses are ordinarily higher in baby chicks than in adult or young adult birds.

In European and Asiatic countries the mortality rates are 70 to 100 per cent—much higher than those in the United States—and there is more tendency for the virus to produce lesions of a generalized nature in outbreaks which occur in those countries.

Several reports of Newcastle infection in man have been substantiated by the isolation of the virus. The conjunctiva is apparently the tissue most often involved. Although the disease is mild and usually localized, Quin *et al.* have reported evidence of generalized infection since Newcastle virus has been isolated from blood, saliva, and urine in some instances. Spontaneous recovery results in a few days.

Infection of other animals by Newcastle virus does not occur under natural conditions but has been produced by experimental inoculation. Intracerebral inoculation of hamsters, mice, monkeys, swine, and sheep has produced fatal infection. The virus has been adapted to hamsters and mice and has been passed in series in these animals until it produces a rapidly fatal disease.

The virus produces death in sheep and swine after intracerebral inoculation, but the virus cannot always be recovered from the brain tissue, and serial passage has not been accomplished in these animals.

**Pathological Changes.** The most marked pathological changes occur in the respiratory system. There is hyperemia and congestion throughout, with much mucus in the trachea. In European and Asiatic outbreaks the lesions are much more pronounced and in addition to the respiratory lesions, hemorrhages, especially of the lymph follicles of the intestinal tract, will be observed. Cloudiness of the air sac membranes is a usual finding, and petechial hemorrhages may be seen in the respiratory tract on the epicardium and in the digestive tract. Catarrhal enteritis is also observed.

The brain shows microscopic cellular infiltration of lymphocytes and hemorrhage.

**Immunity.** Birds which recover from a natural case of Newcastle disease are solidly immune. HI and SN antibodies are demonstrable in the serums of recovered birds for several months after recovery. The eggs from recovered hens contain antibodies and can be demonstrated by the HI test as described by Schmittle and Millen. Chicks which are hatched from these eggs may show antibodies in their serum for a period of 3 or 4 weeks.

Active immunization to Newcastle disease is widely used. Both live and killed types are available and have their particular advantages and disadvantages.

Killed vaccines are made from infected tissues or embryo-propagated virus. A variety of chemicals such as formalin or phenol, as well as physical methods, have been employed to kill the virus.

Killed vaccines have the advantage of being completely safe to use, but immunity is apparently not as effective or as lasting as is desirable unless 2 doses are given, spaced 2 to 3 months apart. Formalin-inactivated vaccine is in common use.

Live vaccines include avirulent strains and modified virus.

Two types of live virus vaccine are used, one more virulent than the other. The more virulent type is administered by application to the web of the wing. The other type is quite avirulent and may be administered intranasally or by mass inoculation methods such as aerosol, dusting with the dried virus, or in the drinking water. Immunity conferred by the wing-web vaccine is more durable than the intranasal type. Losses from the infection by the vaccine strain occur, especially in unthrifty flocks. Egg production is substantially lowered in laying flocks, and the disease is perpetuated and in some cases introduced into new flocks through vaccination.

Combination of live Newcastle vaccine and other live vaccines such as fowl pox, laryngotracheitis, or bronchitis has been tried.

**Diagnosis.** The most dependable diagnosis of Newcastle disease is the isolation and identification of the virus. The virus is abundant in the respiratory tissues during the initial stages of the disease. It is also present in the blood, spleen, brain, and liver during the early stages but is in less concentration than in the respiratory tract. Inoculation of chicken embryos with emulsions of pooled organs will isolate the virus. The addition of penicillin and streptomycin is necessary in most cases to prevent bacterial contamination of the embryos. Presumptive evidence of the presence of the virus can usually be obtained in about 48 hours by conducting a hemagglutination test on the allantoic fluid. In areas where fowl pest does not occur, a positive diagnosis of Newcastle disease is made on the basis of the isolation of a virus from poultry which produces hemagglutination.

Confirmatory tests for identification of Newcastle virus should include HI and SN tests, using known immune serum or protection tests with immune birds.

It is difficult to isolate the virus from the tissues of infected birds after antibodies are detectable in the serum. The virus is not often isolated from birds showing advanced nervous symptoms.

Serological evidence of the disease can be obtained by HI or SN tests upon serum of sick, convalescent, or recovered birds. However, such evidence must be carefully interpreted only after other findings and history are considered. The presence of antibodies in the serum may result from previous infection in older birds, vaccination, or passive egg transfer in chicks.

Newcastle disease may be confused with fowl pest, infectious bronchitis, or laryngotracheitis.

### Myxovirus Yucaipa

A virus which possesses properties similar to those of Newcastle and the parainfluenza group was isolated by Bankowski *et al.* The virus was recovered from an outbreak of respiratory disease in three-week-old chickens but was considered to be of secondary importance to laryngotracheitis virus which was also isolated.

The virus is structurally similar to Newcastle and is approximately the same size (175 m$\mu$). It agglutinates the erythrocytes of chickens, guinea pigs, and man. Growth of the virus occurs in chicken embryos by allantoic inoculation and in cell cultures derived from pig, chicken, and monkey kidney. A cytopathic change is observed in the infected cell cultures, and acidophilic inclusion bodies can be demonstrated in the cytoplasm of infected cells.

The Yucaipa virus is serologically distinct from Newcastle, the influenza, and the parainfluenza viruses. Its occurrence has not been reported outside the area of Yucaipa, California.

## VIRUSES SIMILAR TO THOSE OF THE MYXOVIRUS GROUP

A number of important animal viruses have been found to resemble the myxoviruses in morphology and certain other features, but do not completely satisfy the definition of the myxovirus group. Viruses placed in this group resemble the myxoviruses in being approximately the same size, possessing RNA, being ether sensitive, and disrupted particles showing helical internal components similar to the parainfluenza-Newcastle viruses. Some of the viruses placed here produce hemagglutination as do the myxoviruses, but do not elute from erythrocytes by enzyme digestion. Syncytium formation is observed in infected cell cultures.

While they have been tentatively classified by some authors with the myxoviruses, they have not been so included by others. Until such time as these viruses have been more completely studied and their taxonomic position agreed upon, they will be discussed as a group separate from the myxoviruses.

### MEASLES—CANINE DISTEMPER—RINDERPEST GROUP

These three viruses are quite similar in their morphology and are related antigenically.

Persons recovering from measles usually show neutralizing antibodies for canine distemper. Dogs vaccinated with measles vaccine show resistance to canine distemper. Likewise dogs vaccinated with rinderpest vaccine or which have close contact with cattle infected with rinderpest are resistant to canine distemper. Distemper virus used in cattle may show an immunity to rinderpest. Measles and rinderpest viruses are also reported to cross immunize to some extent.

### Measles Virus

Only man and other primates are susceptible to measles. The virus morphology is like that of the parainfluenzas. Hemagglutination of erythrocytes of various primates occurs. Receptor-destroying enzymes applied to susceptible erythrocytes does not destroy their agglutinability. Formaldehyde treatment of measles virus destroys its hemagglutinin while such treatment of myxoviruses does not have this effect.

Measles virus can be cultivated in cell cultures of human and monkey tissue origin. It has been adapted to grow in chicken embryos and in cell cultures of chicken embryo. Virus for vaccine production is obtained by these methods. The disease is worldwide in occurrence and commonly attacks children at ages 3 to 5 years. Generalized infection with fever, rash, and conjunctivitis are usual manifestations. Encephalitis may occasionally follow generalized measles infection.

### Canine Distemper Virus

**Disease Produced.** Canine distemper. "Hard pad" disease.

**Hosts Affected.** Dog, fox, mink, ferret, wolf, coyote, raccoon, weasel, skunk, binturong, and the dingo.

**History and Distribution.** Canine distemper has been recognized as a disease of dogs in Europe since the 18th century, having been introduced from Asia or Peru. Its distribution is worldwide. For many years, the cause of the disease was ascribed to several different bacteria. Carré, in 1905, found that filtrates of nasal discharges would reproduce the disease and proposed that the etiological agent was a virus. The role of the virus as the primary agent has been well established for many years. However, secondary bacteria may be a factor in the natural disease.

**Properties of the Virus.** The virus of canine distemper resembles the parainfluenza and measles viruses in structural and morphological features. It is generally round in shape, though filamentous, crescent, and ring forms are observed. The round forms measure 115 m$\mu$ to 230 m$\mu$ in diameter. A double-contoured membrane 75 to 85 Å thick with surface projections radiating from it covers the helical inner components. A hemagglutinin has not been demonstrated.

Field strains of the virus are preserved for at least a year when stored at 7°C. in oxygen-free nitrogen, for a year and a half by lyophilization, and for 2 years when stored at —24°C. At 10°C. it will remain viable for a month or two.

Celiker and Gillespie, using embryo-adapted distemper virus, report the following effects of pH, chemicals, and heat. Exposure to 50°C. for 60 minutes or 55°C. for 10 minutes destroys the infectivity. Virus held at 25°C. is inactivated in 7 to 8 days, and at 4°C. 7 to 8 weeks are required to inactivate it. The virus remains viable for 24 hours when the pH of the suspending liquid is 4.4 to 10.4, whereas a pH of 4.2 or 10.9 inactivates it in 2 hours. The virus is destroyed by 0.1 per cent formalin in 1 to 2 hours, 0.5 per cent phenol in 48 to 72 hours, 0.3 per cent chloroform in 10 minutes, and Roccal 0.2 per cent in 30 minutes.

**Cultivation.** Canine distemper virus is ordinarily kept viable by passage in susceptible dogs or ferrets. Haig, also Cabasso and Cox, have reported that ferret-passaged strains can be adapted to grow in the chorioallantoic membrane of chicken embryos. No significant lesions are noted until 9 or 10 "blind" passages are made. Subsequent passages show increased thickening and whitish areas in the chorioallantoic membranes. Material beyond the 28th passage fails to produce illness in ferrets but does produce immunity to the virulent virus.

Canine distemper virus has been adapted to grow in cell cultures of dog kidney, ferret tissue, and chick fibroblasts. Cytopathic changes are produced. An avianized strain of the virus has been adapted to suckling mice by Morse.

Cultivation of the virus in dog kidney cell cultures results in the attenuation of the virus at the 20th passage level. Intranuclear and cytoplasmic inclusions and syncytium formation are observed in cell cultures.

**Transmission.** The disease is quite contagious, with transmission occurring by droplet transfer and by contact. The average incubation period is four days.

**Characteristics of the Disease.** Canine distemper is an acute, highly infectious disease of dogs, foxes, mink, and occasionally other carnivora. It more often infects young animals.

The symptoms include fever, depression diarrhea, loss of appetite, purulent conjunctivitis, and rhinitis. A diphasic temperature curve is characteristic. At the onset of the disease there is a sharp rise in temperature and a watery discharge from the eyes and nose. This phase is of 1 to 2 days duration and is often not observed. A second and sustained fever occurs about 2 or 3 days following the first, and it is during this period that symptoms are most pronounced. Secondary bacterial invasion may contribute to the symptoms and the lesions observed. *Brucella bronchiseptica* and *Past. multocida* are organisms which may assume this role in some cases.

Some infected animals will show skin eruptions which occur usually on the posterior abdominal wall and inner aspect of the thighs.

In other cases, the skin of the foot pads and the nose become very thick and hard. This condition is called "hard pad disease." A feature of hard pad disease is a demyelinating encephalitis with a high mortality. This type of the disease was first thought to be due to a virus other than canine distemper. However, Cabasso has compared the hard pad strains with those from a typical case of canine distemper and found them to be closely related, immunologically.

Some cases are abortive and mild, lasting only a few days, with complete recovery.

**Pathological Changes.** The pathological changes may vary, depending on whether or not secondary bacterial invasion occurs. In uncomplicated cases the lesions are less pronounced. Most animals show involvement of the respiratory system. The mucous membranes are red, swollen, and covered with mucopurulent exudate. There is often bronchitis and occasionally pneumonia. Purulent conjunctivitis is a rather constant finding. Catarrhal enteritis is usually present. Occasionally there are encephalitis and meningitis.

Inclusion bodies were described in canine distemper by Lenz in 1908 and were considered at that time to be diagnostic of the disease. Demonstration of inclusions is still an important aid to the diagnosis of distemper These inclusion bodies are most often found in epithelial cells and may be either intranuclear or cytoplasmic. Epithelial cells of the urinary bladder, kidney, renal pelvis, and the lining membrane of the gallbladder or bile ducts are the usual sites, although they may occur in other tissues. Goss *et al.* describe their occurrence in the epithelium of the tongue and conjunctiva and suggests the use of stained smears as an aid to diagnosis of canine distemper in the sick animal. The inclusion bodies of distemper may be confused with those of fox encephalitis or occasionally rabies if only the brain is examined.

**Immunity.** Animals which recover from canine distemper are immune for life.

Artificial immunization is widely practiced, and a variety of products and procedures are available.

***Passive immunity.*** Serum from dogs which have been hyperimmunized by repeated injections of distemper virus is useful in preventing the disease in exposed animals and to some extent for the treatment of the sick. It is injected with live virus for active immunization by the serum-virus method. Many serum producers also hyperimmunize their dogs used for serum production against the common secondary bacteria.

***Active immunization.*** The method of Laidlaw and Dunkin has been used with success. This method consists of the subcutaneous injection of formolized virus of canine origin followed by intradermal injection of living virus of ferret origin two weeks later.

Another method which has been widely used is the injection of live virus followed by immune serum 24 to 48 hours later.

Others recommend two or three doses of killed vaccine spaced at 2-week intervals for active immunization.

A live virus modified by continued ferret passage is also used. This vaccine, called distemperoid vaccine, prepared by the method of Green, is ferret virus of 60 or more continuous passages. It is highly pathogenic for ferrets and will also produce severe disease in mink and skunks, but is avirulent when injected into dogs and foxes. The injection of distemperoid virus in dogs or foxes produces active immunity to canine distemper. It has been further observed that the administration of distemperoid vaccine is of value in preventing distemper in exposed animals as well as apparent curative properties in sick animals. These effects of distemperoid virus are explained by the phenomenon of virus interference.

Distemper virus of blood origin is also used in the live state and will confer active immunity. In this case the dose is graded according to the size of the animal, with no antiserum being used.

*Avianized vaccine.* The adaptation of the canine distemper virus to growth in the chicken embryo has made possible the development of a live vaccine for use in the prevention of the disease. Since its introduction in 1951, it has been accepted as a useful immunizing agent.

*Tissue culture vaccine.* A modified-live-virus vaccine produced in dog kidney tissue cultures is reported to give good immunity.

**Diagnosis.** Canine distemper is diagnosed by the correlation of clinical symptoms and microscopic demonstration of inclusion bodies in the epithelial cells of the urinary bladder or gallbladder. It must be differentiated from canine hepatitis infection in foxes or dogs.

## Rinderpest Virus

**Disease Produced.** Rinderpest.

**Hosts Affected.** Cattle, sheep, goats, deer, camel, buffalo, and swine.

**History and Distribution.** Rinderpest of cattle has been one of the most devastating of all diseases in certain areas of the world. It apparently had its origin in Asia, and with the migration of peoples and cattle during the Middle Ages, the disease was carried into Europe. In the 18th and 19th centuries it ravaged the cattle population of Europe, and great losses from the disease were reported. In the years 1711 to 1714, Holland lost nearly all its cattle. In 1865 rinderpest was reintroduced into Great Britain after 20 years freedom from the disease, and within 2 years time 500,000 cattle died. The disease spread to Africa in the 1890's and millions of cattle were destroyed. The institution of successful immunity procedures, in about 1900, and of strict quarantine measures brought the disease under control in most areas. The disease still is enzootic in many areas of Asia and Africa. European areas have been free of the disease since shortly after the end of World War I.

Rinderpest has been introduced into Brazil and Australia but it has been promptly eliminated. It has not occurred in the United States.

The virus of rinderpest was discovered in 1902 by Nicolle and Adil-Bey.

**Properties of the Virus.** Rinderpest virus is similar to measles, canine distemper, and to the larger myxoviruses. It measures 120 mμ to 300 mμ in diameter. An internal helical component is about 175 Å in diameter and is covered by an outer membrane. Filamentous forms are observed, although round forms are most common.

Heating of the virus to 60°C. quickly destroys it. The virus is fairly resistant to phenol. In 2 per cent concentration, phenol fails to kill in 5 days, but if glycerin is added to the mixture, the virus is destroyed in 48 hours. One per cent phenol does not destroy the virus in 21 days and in 0.5 per cent concentration the virus may live at least 271 days. It is killed by formalin and by chloroform. The virus apparently does not survive long in nature after it leaves the host. It is quickly destroyed by putrefaction.

**Cultivation.** Rinderpest virus has been adapted to grow on the chorioallantoic membrane of chicken embryos. No specific lesions are produced, though some deaths occur. The virus can also be grown in the yolk sac of 6- to 7-day-old embryos if the virus is first adapted to eggs by chorioallantoic passage. The rinderpest virus has been adapted by Plowright and Ferris to grow in tissue cultures of calf kidney. A cytopathic effect is produced and attenuation of the virus for cattle is noted after approximately 20 passages.

**Transmission.** Rinderpest virus is usually transmitted by contact between infected and noninfected animals through a medium of food or water which has been contaminated with virus-bearing discharges from the infected animal.

**Characteristics of the Disease.** Rinderpest is an acute, highly fatal disease of cattle. It is also a disease of sheep, goats, buffalo, other ruminants, and swine, but infection of these animals is less severe and occurs less frequently than in cattle.

A sharp rise in temperature precedes the appearance of other symptoms by a day or two. The symptoms are usually marked depression, stupor, loss of appetite, emaciation, conjunctivitis, mucopurulent nasal discharge, and diarrhea. Mucous membranes are hyperemic and show necrotic areas.

The course of the disease runs from 4 to 8 days, with occasional cases running a prolonged course. Mortality rates are usually high, up to 90 per cent, but some animals recover.

**Pathological Changes.** Erosive and necrotic lesions in the mucous membranes, beginning in the oral cavity and extending throughout the alimentary tract are characteristic. Peyer's patches may be severely affected because of the destructive action of the virus on lymphoid tissue. Petechial and ecchymotic hemorrhages may occur in various mucous membranes.

**Immunity.** Immunity to rinderpest has been studied for many years and many immunizing agents have been tried.

Recovered animals are usually immune to second attacks.

Active immunity was first produced by the injection of immune serum and the virus simultaneously. Although this method was successful, it was later abandoned because of the high cost of serum, because the use of live virus spread the infection to new areas, and because of the losses which occurred from protozoan diseases spread by injecting virus blood which was frequently contaminated with protozoa.

Chemically killed vaccines have been used in the past. Boynton's tissue vaccine is prepared by the addition of phenol and glycerin to lymphoid tissues of cattle which have been inoculated with the virus. The mixture is heated to 42°C. and held for 3 hours to accomplish attenuation. The final concentration of phenol is 0.5 per cent.

Chloroform-inactivated vaccine prepared according to Kelser's method has been useful in producing active immunity. Cattle which have been inoculated with virulent rinderpest virus are sacrificed during the acute stages of the disease and the lymphoid tissues removed and finely ground. Chloroform is added to the tissue emulsion to make 0.75 per cent concentration. After 48 hours the vaccine is ready to use.

Formalin-treated vaccine has been useful in some areas.

Live-modified virus vaccines are most commonly used for immunization against rinderpest. Desiccated goat spleen given in graded doses is effective as long as the virus in it remains alive.

Lapinized and avianized rinderpest vaccines were a result of adaptation of the virus to rabbits and to chicken embryos by Shope, Griffiths, and Jenkins of the American-Canadian Commission working at Grosse Isle during World War II. A vaccine composed of modified Nakamura III strain of the virus is used in Asiatic countries and tissue culture modified vaccine has come into use in Africa.

**Diagnosis.** In localities where the disease is known to exist, rinderpest is diagnosed largely upon the clinical and postmortem manifestations.

Accurate diagnosis depends upon isolation of the virus in cell cultures of either calf kidney or peripheral leucocytes. Complement-fixation, immuno-diffusion and fluorescent antibody procedures are also employed.

### RESPIRATORY SYNCYTIAL VIRUS

An agent first isolated from laboratory chimpanzees with coryza has been called the respiratory syncytial virus (Morris *et al.*, 1956). Since 1956 the virus has been frequently isolated from children with respiratory infections. It is considered to be the most important cause of respiratory infection in children up to 6 months of age. Antibodies are present in serum of a large percentage of persons over 4 years of age.

The virus particles range in size from 120 mμ to 300 mμ. Its structure is like that of the parainfluenza and the measles-rinderpest-distemper group. It contains an internal helical component and an envelope with radiating spikes. The virus is ether sensitive and resistant to inhibition by IUDR and FUDR— the latter character indicating the presence of RNA. Hemagglutination has not been demonstrated.

The virus can be cultivated in cell cultures of human tissue origin. Syncytium formation is common in infected cultures.

Monkeys, baboons, chimpanzees, ferrets, mink, chinchillas, guinea pigs, hamsters, and mice can be experimentally infected. Chicken embryos are not susceptible.

## REFERENCES

### Influenza A Viruses

Davenport, F. M., *et al.* Epidemiologic and Immunologic Significance of Age Distribution of Antibody to Antigenic Variants of Influenza Virus. Jour. Exp. Med. 98:641, 1953.

Hirst, G. K. The Agglutination of Red Cells by Allantoic Fluid of Chick Embryos Infected With Influenza Virus. Science 94:22, 1941.

Horne, R. W., *et al.* The Structure and Composition of the Myxoviruses. I. Electron Microscope Studies of the Structure of Myxovirus Particles by Negative Staining Techniques. Virol. 11:79, 1960.

HOYLE, L., *et al* The Structure and Composition of the Myxoviruses. II. Components Released From the Influenza Virus Particle by Ether. Virol. 13:448, 1961.

SMITH, W., *et al.* A Virus Obtained From Influenza Patients. Lancet 2:66, 1933.

WATERSON, A. P., *et al.* The Fine Structure of Influenza A, B and C Viruses. Arch. ges. Virusforsch. 12:487, 1963.

## Swine Influenza Virus

DORSET, M., *et al.* Remarks on "Hog Flu." Jour. Amer. Vet. Med. Assn. 62:162, 1922–23.

GLOVER, R. E., and ANDREWES, C. H. The Antigenic Structure of British Strains of Swine Influenza Virus. Jour. Comp. Path. Therap. 53:329, 1943.

KOEN, J. S. A Practical Method for Field Diagnosis of Swine Diseases. Amer. Jour. Vet. Med. 14:468, 1919.

LEWIS, P. A., and SHOPE, R. E. Swine Influenza. Jour. Exp. Med. 54:361, 1931.

SHOPE, R. E. Swine Influenza. Jour. Exp. Med. 54:349, 1931.

———. Swine Influenza. Jour. Exp. Med. 54:373, 1931.

———. The Swine Lungworm as a Reservoir and Intermediate Host for Swine Influenza Virus. Jour. Exp. Med. 77:111, 127, 1943.

———. Birth of New Disease. *In* Newcastle Disease Virus. R. P. Hanson (ed.). Univ. of Wis. Press, Madison, 1964.

## Equine Influenza Virus

DITCHFIELD, J., *et al.* Upper Respiratory Disease in Thoroughbred Horses: Studies of Its Viral Etiology in the Toronto Area, 1960–1963. Canad. Jour. Comp. Med. Vet. Sci. 29:18, 1965.

DOLL, E. R. Influenza of Horses. (Intl. Conf. on Asian Influenza.) Amer. Rev. Resp. Dis. 83:48, 1961.

KASEL, J. A., *et al.* Experimental Infection of Human Volunteers With Equine Influenza Virus. Nature, London, 206:41, 1965.

LIEF, F. S., and COHEN, D. Equine Influenza. Amer. Jour. Epid. 82:225, 1966.

SOVINOVA, O., *et al.* Isolation of a Virus Causing Respiratory Disease in Horses. Acta Virol. 2:52, 1958.

TUMOVA, B., and SOVINOVA, O. Properties of Influenza Viruses A/Asia/57 and A-Equi/Praha/56. I. Agglutination of Red Blood Cells. Bull. World Health Org. 20:445, 1959.

WADDELL, G. H., *et al.* A New Influenza Virus Associated With Equine Respiratory Disease. Jour. Amer. Vet. Med. Assn. 143:587, 1963.

WILSON, J. C., *et al.* Recovery of Influenza Virus From Horses in the Equine Influenza Epizootic of 1963. Amer. Jour. Vet. Res. 26:1466, 1965.

## Duck Influenza Virus

BLASKOVIC, D., *et al.* Antigenic Relationships to Myxoviruses of a Virus Isolated From Respiratory Infection in Ducks. Acta Virol. 3:17, 1959.

FRANO, J., *et al.* Virus 550, Isolated From a Respiratory Disease in Ducklings. Vet. Cas. 7:411, 1958.

KOPPEL, Z., *et al.* A Mass Infection in Ducklings in E. Slovakia Characterized by Signs of Infectious Sinusitus Veterinárství 6:267, 1956.

PEREIRA, H. G., *et al.* Avian Influenza A Viruses. Bull. World Health Org. 32:855, 1965.

ROBERTS, D. H. The Isolation of an Influenza A Virus and a Mycoplasma Associated With Duck Sinusitis. Vet. Rec. 76:470, 1964.

## Fowl Pest Virus

CENTANNI, E. Die Vogel Pest. Zentralbl. f. Bakt. Abt. I. Orig. 31:182, 1902.

STUBBS, E. L. Fowl Plague in Pennsylvania. Jour. Amer. Vet. Med. Assn. 67:180, 1925

———. Fowl Plague. *In* Diseases of Poultry. 5th Ed. Biester, H. E., and Schwarte, L. H. (eds.). Iowa State Univ. Press, Ames, 1965.

WATERSON, A. P., *et al.* The Structure of Fowl Plague Virus and Virus N. Zeit. Naturforsch. 16b:154, 1961.

## Tern Virus

BECKER, W. B. The Morphology of Tern Virus. Virol. 20:318, 1963.

ROWAN, M. K. Mass Mortality Among European Common Terns in South Africa. Brit. Birds 55:103, 1962.

### Virus N

DINTER, Z. Eine variante des virus der Geflugelpest in Bayern. Tierarztl. Umschau. 4:185, 1949.

———, and BAKOS, K. Uber die Beziehungen des Virus N Zu dem Virus der Klassischen Geflugelpest Berlin u. Münch. tierarztl. Wschr. 6:101, 1950.

ROTT, R., and SCHAFER, W. Physikalisch-Chemische und biologische eigenschaften des Virus N und seine Bezichungen zur Influenza A—Untergruppe der Myxoviren. Zlb. Veterinarmed. 7:237, 1960.

WATERSON, A. P. Two Kinds of Myxoviruses. Nature 193:1163, 1962.

———, *et al.* The Structure of Fowl Plague Virus and Virus N. Zeit. Naturforsch. 166:154, 1961.

### Parainfluenza Viruses

ABINANTI, F. R., and HUEBNER, R. J. The Serological Relationship of Strains of Parainfluenza 3 Virus Isolated From Humans and Cattle With Respiratory Disease. Virol. 8:391, 1959.

HAMDY, A. H. Variants of Myxovirus Parainfluenza 3 Isolated From Calves Clinically Affected With Shipping Fever. Cornell Vet. 55:623, 1965.

———, *et al.* Attempted Immunization of Cattle Against Shipping Fever: A Field Trial. Amer. Jour. Vet. Res. 26:897, 1965.

HSIUNG, G. D., *et al.* Studies of Parainfluenza Viruses. III. Antibody Responses of Different Animal Species After Immunization. Jour. Immunol. 94:67, 1965.

JOHNSON, K. M., *et al.* Studies of a New Human Hemadsorption Virus. I. Isolation, Properties and Characterization. Amer. Jour. Hyg. 71:81, 1960.

REISINGER, R. C., *et al.* A Myxovirus (SF) Associated With Shipping Fever of Cattle. Jour. Amer. Vet. Med. Assn. 135:147, 1959.

### Mumps Virus

CANTEL, K. Mumps Virus. Adv. Virus Res. 8:123, 1961.

### Newcastle Disease Virus

BEACH, J. R. Avian Pneumoencephalitis. Proc. U.S. Livestock Sanit. Assn. 46:203, 1942.

BRANDLY, C. A., and HANSON, R. P. Newcastle Disease. *In* Diseases of Poultry. 5th Ed. Biester, H. E., and Schwarte, L. H. (eds.). Iowa State Univ. Press, Ames, 1965.

———, *et al.* Immunization of Chickens Against Newcastle Disease. Amer. Jour. Vet. Res. 7:307, 1946.

DOYLE, T. M. A Hitherto Unrecorded Disease of Fowls Due to a Filter-Passing Virus. Jour. Comp. Path. Therap. 40:144, 1927.

HANSON, R. P. (ed.). Newcastle Disease Virus, An Evolving Pathogen. Univ. of Wis. Press, Madison, 1964.

JUNGHERR, E. L., *et al.* The Comparative Pathology of Fowl Plague and Newcastle Disease. Amer. Jour. Vet. Res. 7:250, 1946.

### Yucaipa Virus

BANKOWSKI, R. A., and CORSTVET, R. Isolation of a Hemagglutinating Agent Distinct From Newcastle Disease From the Respiratory Tract of Chickens. Avian Dis. 5:253, 1961.

———, *et al.* Isolation of an Unidentified Agent From the Respiratory Tract of Chickens. Science 132:292, 1960.

DINTER, Z., *et al.* Studies on Myxovirus Yucaipa: Its Classification as a Member of the Paramyxovirus Group. Virol. 22:297, 1964.

### Measles Virus

KATZ, S. L., and ENDERS, J. F. Measles Virus. *In* Viral and Rickettsial Infections of Man. Horsfall, F. L., and Tamm, I. (eds.). J. B. Lippincott Co., Philadelphia, 1965.

### Canine Distemper Virus

BITTLE, J. L., *et al.* Adaptation and Modification of a Strain of Canine Distemper Virus in Tissue Culture. Cornell Vet. 51:359, 1961.

CARRÉ, H. Sur La maladie des jeunes chiens. Compt. rend. Acad. sci. 140:689, 1905.

CELIKER, A., and GILLESPIE, J. H. The Effect of Temperature, pH, and Certain Chemicals on Egg-Cultivated Distemper Virus. Cornell Vet. 44:276, 1954.

CRUICKSHANK, J. G., *et al.* The Structure of Canine Distemper Virus. Res. Vet. Sci. 3:485, 1962.

HOPPER, P. K. The Propagation of Canine Distemper Virus in Tissue Culture. Jour. Comp. Path. Therap. 69:78, 1956.

INAGAWA, D. T., *et al.* Immunological Relationship of Measles Distemper and Rinderpest Viruses. Proc. Natl Acad. Sci., U.S., 46:1119, 1960.

LAIDLAW, P. P., and DUNKIN, G. W. Studies in Dog Distemper. Jour. Comp. Path. Therap. 44:1, 1931.

NORRBY, E., *et al.* The Ultrastructure of Canine Distemper Virus. Arch. ges. Virusforsch. 13:335, 1963.

ROCKBORN, G. Canine Distemper Virus in Tissue Culture. Arch. ges. Virusforsch. 8:407, 1958.

## Rinderpest Virus

BOYNTON, W. H. Rinderpest, With Special Reference to Its Control by a New Method of Prophylactic Treatment. Philippine Jour. Sci. 36:1, 1928.

DAUBNEY, R. Observations of Rinderpest. Jour. Comp. Path. Therap. 41:228, 1928.

JOINT UNITED STATES-CANADIAN COMM. AND CHEM. WARFARE SERVICE, U.S. ARMY. Rinderpest, the Preparation of Tissue and Egg Vaccines. Amer. Jour. Vet. Res. 7:133, 1946.

NICOLLE, M., and ADIL-BEY. Etudes Sur La Peste Bovine. Ann. Inst. Past. 16:56, 1902.

PLOWRIGHT, W., *et al.* The Morphology of Rinderpest Virus. Virol. 17:118, 1962.

POLDING, J. B., *et al.* Links Between Canine Distemper and Rinderpest. Vet. Rec. 71:643, 1959.

## Respiratory Syncytial Virus

CHANOCK, R. M., *et al.* Recovery From Infants With Respiratory Illness of a Virus Related to Chimpanzee Coryza Agent (CCA). I. Isolation, Properties and Characterization. Amer. Jour. Hyg. 66:281, 1957.

MORRIS, J. A., *et al.* Recovery of Cytopathogenic Agent From Chimpanzees With Coryza. Proc. Soc. Exp. Biol. Med. 92:544, 1956.

# 50

# The Picornaviruses

THE PICO (SMALL) RNA (RNA) VIRUS GROUP includes the enteroviruses and the rhinoviruses of man and animals and certain other viruses having similar properties. Common characteristics of these viruses are small size (15 mμ to 35 mμ), cubic symmetry (30 to 42 capsomeres), single-stranded RNA, and ether resistance. Subdivision of picornaviruses is possible on the basis of antigenic structure, hemagglutination, pH sensitivity, stability to heat in the presence of $MgCl_2$, pathogenicity and tissue affinities. Viruses placed under the enterovirus heading are heat stable at pH 3.0 to 5.0. In addition they have definite affinity for the intestinal tract. Those in the rhinovirus group are not stabilized to heat in the presence of $MgCl_2$, are sensitive to acid, and show little ability to replicate in intestinal tissue. They are found primarily in the upper portion of the respiratory and alimentary tracts. The main groupings are:

A. Enteroviruses
   1. Human origin
      - Polioviruses, 3 types
      - Coxsackie viruses A and B
      - ECHOviruses (enteric cytopathogenic human orphan)
   2. Animal origin
      - ECBO (enteric cytopathogenic bovine orphan)
      - Swine enteroviruses
        - Teschen and talfan viruses
        - Pig polioencephalitis strains
        - ECPO (enteric cytopathogenic porcine orphan)
      - Avian enteroviruses
      - Simian enteroviruses

B. Rhinoviruses
   - Human "cold" viruses
   - Equine rhinoviruses
   - Bovine rhinovirus
   - Foot-and-mouth disease virus
   - Vesicular exanthema

C. Other picornaviruses
   - Avian encephalomyelitis (epidemic tremor)
   - Mouse encephalitis
   - Feline picornaviruses

### Poliovirus

Since poliovirus does not produce disease in any nonprimate animal host under natural conditions of exposure, it will be only briefly reviewed.

Poliovirus is apparently distributed among all populations of the world. Until about 1940 it was generally thought that the virus was strictly neurotropic causing paralytic symptoms only. As research on the disease progressed, it became evident that poliovirus infection was common and that paralytic cases were uncommon. It is now recognized that most persons infected suffer only from pharyngeal and intestinal involvement which is often so mild in character it is never brought to the attention of physicians.

The poliovirus is an RNA type virus, 28 mμ in diameter and possesses icosahedral symmetry (Fig. 50.1). It is resistant to ether and fails to agglutinate erythrocytes. It can be cultivated in a variety of types of cell culture in which cytopathic effects are produced. Certain strains have been adapted to grow in chicken embryos, ham-

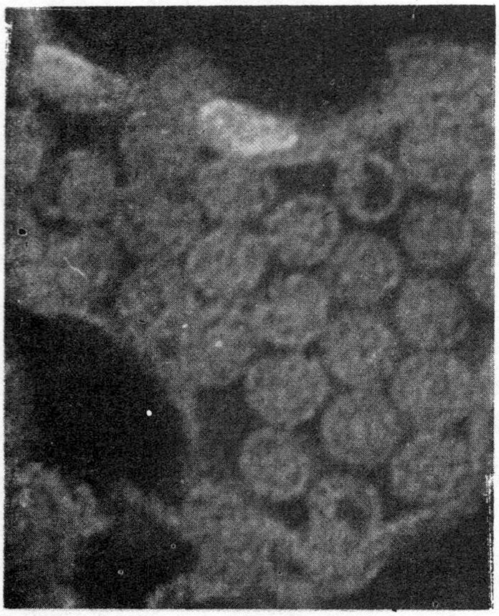

FIG. 50.1—Poliovirus, ×320,000. (Courtesy Horne and Nagington. Jour. Mol. Biol. 1:333, 1959.)

sters, and cotton rats. Primates other than man can be infected. Three antigenic types are established.

Improvement of cell culture methods for artificial growth of the virus and recognition of three antigenic types were important developments which led to the introduction of a killed vaccine (Salk) in 1953 and its widespread use.

A live attenuated polio vaccine which was first tested in 1952 by Koprowski and further developed by Sabin has largely supplanted the killed vaccine. All three antigenic types have been successfully "tamed" for use in orally administered vaccine preparations. Their general use has reduced the incidence of paralytic poliomyelitis in many countries to very low figures.

### Coxsackie Virus

An enterovirus isolated in 1948 by Dalldorf and Sickles from patients with paralytic polio was found to differ from the classical polio viruses. The patients were from Coxsackie, New York, and so the virus was named for the town where it was first recognized.

The coxsackie virus is an RNA type and measures about 28 mμ in diameter. It differs from polio in that it is pathogenic for infant mice and other laboratory rodents, and some strains produce hemagglutination. It can be grown in cell cultures such as HeLa and monkey kidney and a cytopathic effect is produced.

Two distinct groups, A and B, of the virus are distinguished on the basis of their pathological effects in mice. Group A produces paralysis with marked necrosis of skeletal muscle, while Group B virus produces spastic paralysis, fat necrosis, and pancreatitis. Twenty-three serotypes of Group A and six of Group B are recognized.

In children an aseptic meningitis which often suggests poliomyelitis infection is observed. Herpangina, myocarditis, and laryngitis are often described.

The disease conditions associated with the coxsackie virus are self-limiting. No vaccines are used for prophylaxis.

### The ECHO Viruses

Man is host to a group of viruses which possess the properties of the picornavirus group; they generally inhabit the alimentary tract, but often cannot be associated with a definite clinical syndrome. They have been isolated from persons with enteric disturbances, fever, aseptic meningitis, etc.; however, their role in the illness observed may not be clear-cut. There is mounting evidence that some types can cause disease of some severity and the number of true "orphans" among the group is declining. Over 30 antigenic types have been identified.

The isolation of a virus which apparently is ECHO type 6 has been reported from healthy dogs.

### Bovine Enteroviruses

Viral agents from cattle which have the properties of the picornavirus group have been isolated and studied in various countries. These viruses are of the RNA type; small in size, in the order of 20 mμ to 40 mμ; ether and chloroform resistant; and have the capacity to replicate in the alimentary tract of cattle. They can be cultivated in cell cultures of bovine kidney and testicular origin and produce cytopathic effects. Some isolates can be grown in cultures of monkey, swine, or guinea pig kidney. Certain viruses of this group will agglutinate the erythrocytes of various animals, but others do not possess this property. Many different antigenic types of bovine enteroviruses have been described.

Bovine enteroviruses are quite common among cattle and are considered to be "orphan" agents (ECBO) of little significance in disease. However, mild symptoms have been observed in some instances when calves have been artificially exposed. Vander Maaten has suggested a role in calf enteritis. Bouters has reported an association with bovine infertility, and Straub reported that the introduction of a bovine enterovirus into the udder produced acute mastitis. Evaluation of the bovine enteroviruses in disease and their classification must await additional research.

### Swine Enteroviruses

A rather large number of viral agents isolated from swine have been found to possess all of the characteristics of the picornavirus group. Some are associated with disease conditions such as polioencephalitis, enteritis, and reproductive disorder, while others have been placed in the "orphan" class since they have not been proved to cause disease. Teschen disease virus and other viruses related to it will be discussed separately. Other viruses of the group have not been sufficiently studied and characterized so as to form distinct groups.

Many investigators have isolated viruses from swine exhibiting signs and lesions of polioencephalitis. They have also found that certain strains isolated from "normal" swine will produce neurologic symptoms when inoculated into germ-free or specific-pathogen-free pigs. Dunne *et al.* have isolated enteroviruses from various reproductive disorders in swine. A number of serologically distinguishable enteroviruses have been reported from the conditions mentioned above. Additional investigation and comparison of isolates will be required before they can be evaluated as causes of disease, or completely classified.

### Teschen Disease Virus

**Diseases Produced.** Teschen disease of swine. Encephalomyelitis of swine. Talfan disease.

**Hosts Affected.** Domestic and wild swine. Mice, rats, guinea pigs, rabbits, monkeys, and hamsters are insusceptible.

**History and Distribution.** The first report of Teschen disease was published by Trefney in 1930 and it occurred near the town of Teschen in Czechoslovakia. Klobouk, in 1931, was the first to artificially transmit the disease and demonstrate the etiological agent as a virus. The disease is reported to have spread rapidly throughout Czechoslovakia, and in 1938 it spread to Germany, Austria, Hungary, Yugoslavia, Switzerland, and France. A disease called talfan, occurring in England, and similar encephalitic diseases were reported in Sweden, Denmark, and Poland. Virus isolates from pigs in the United States and Canada have been found related to talfan virus.

**Properties of the Virus.** The Teschen disease virus is spherical in shape and measures 30 mμ in diameter. It is resistant to the effects of penicillin and streptomycin, to ether, and to drying. It is destroyed by exposure to a temperature of 70°C. for 30 minutes.

Infectious RNA has been extracted from the Teschen disease virus. Three serological types of the virus have been described.

**Cultivation.** Teschen disease virus has been propagated in susceptible swine and tissue cultures of porcine kidney. A cytopathic effect is produced by the virus. Loss of virulence for pigs is reported at the 130th tissue culture passage level.

**Transmission.** The virus is transmitted by contact. Experimentally the virus will reproduce the disease if inoculated intracerebrally, intranasally, or orally. The virus is shed in the feces.

**Characteristics of the Disease.** Teschen disease most often attacks young pigs. An incubation period of 4 to 28 days is noted in artificially infected pigs. If the virus content is high in the inoculum, the incubation period is short—6 days—and becomes longer as the virus is diluted. First evidence of the disease is a temperature increase, 104°–106°F., followed by stiffness, ataxia, tremors, convulsions, and prostration. Death follows in 3 to 4 days in many cases. The mortality rate ranges from 50 to 70 per cent but may reach 90 to 100 per cent in some outbreaks.

**Pathological Changes.** There are no macroscopic lesions characteristic of Teschen disease. Microscopic changes are found only in the central nervous system. A striking resemblance between the histopathological changes of Teschen disease and those seen in human poliomyelitis has been reported. Degeneration of nerve cells, perivascular infiltration, and glial proliferation are most common. Cells of the anterior horn, particularly of the lumbar region, are markedly affected.

**Immunity.** Many of the animals infected with Teschen disease and which do not die may fully recover, although convalescence is prolonged. Immunity results from such an attack. A live vaccine has been used for the prevention of the disease with good results. It is made from brain tissue of an artificially infected pig and is administered intramuscularly. A vaccine produced from virus modified by tissue culture passage is reported to give good immunity.

**Diagnosis.** Teschen disease may be confused with hog cholera, pseudorabies, and certain nutritional deficiencies. The isolation of an encephalitic virus should be suspected as being Teschen disease virus. Further comparison with known strains of Teschen disease would be necessary in order to positively identify it.

### Avian Enteroviruses

Viruses which apparently belong to the enterovirus group have been isolated from the alimentary tract of chickens. Their relationship to disease and their complete characterization must wait further research.

### Simian Enteroviruses

Enteroviruses are widespread among monkey populations. There are at least 13 serotypes described, but none is related to those isolated from human sources. The role of these viruses in clinical disease of monkeys is not established.

### Rhinoviruses of Man

The common cold is said to be the most frequent virus infection of man. These viruses are approximately 30 mμ in diameter and are of the RNA type. They can be grown in cell cultures derived from human tissues. Cytopathic effects are produced at 33°C. incubation. At least 57 different serotypes have been distinguished.

The pathogenesis of colds is not well understood. Oral and subcutaneous introduction of the virus does not result in infection. Person-to-person spread of the virus undoubtedly occurs, but experimental exposure of volunteers results in surprisingly few infections.

Secondary bacterial infection and allergy are believed to play important roles in the symptomatology.

The multiplicity of serologic types may account for the apparent lack of immunity observed with some individuals.

The chimpanzee is the only other host for the human rhinoviruses.

### Equine Rhinovirus

Certain viruses isolated from the respiratory tract of horses in England and Canada have been determined to have properties of the rhinovirus subgroup of the picornaviruses. The isolates are approximately 30 mμ in diameter, and are ether resistant. They do not agglutinate erythrocytes, are unstable at pH 5.0, and are not stabilized to heat in the presence of 1M. $MgCl_2$. The viruses can be readily cultivated in monkey kidney cells.

Experimental inoculation of horses results in a viremia lasting 4 to 5 days with accompanying fever and nasal discharge. Monkeys, rabbits, and man are susceptible, showing viremia with fever, acute pharyngitis and lymphadenitis when inoculated intranasally.

The equine rhinoviruses are apparently common, although surveys for the virus in most countries have not been made.

### Bovine Rhinovirus

A virus having the characteristics of the rhinovirus group has been isolated from cattle by Bögel and Böhm in Europe.

### Foot-and-Mouth Disease Virus

**Diseases Produced.** Foot-and-mouth disease, aphthous fever.

**Hosts Affected.** Cattle, swine, sheep, goats, deer, buffalo, and rarely man. Experimentally the guinea pig, rabbit, hedgehog, rat, suckling mice, and domestic poultry may be infected. The guinea pig and white mouse are used in experimental studies.

**History and Distribution.** The first disease of animals proved to be of virus etiology was foot-and-mouth disease and was determined by Loeffler and Frosch. In 1897 these investigators showed that bacteria-free lymph collected from infected animals could be used to transmit the infection and, in the following year, that the causative agent of foot-and-mouth disease could be passed through filters which retained bacteria. The disease has occurred in all parts of the world and is still endemic in many countries. It is completely controlled in the United States and Canada by vigorous eradication methods. Nine outbreaks of the disease were recorded in the United States between the years 1870 and 1932. A serious outbreak occurred in Mexico in 1946 and a limited one in Canada in 1951. Australia and New Zealand have remained free of the the disease.

**Properties of the Virus.** Foot-and-mouth disease virus appears to be rounded or hexagonal in shape and measures 22 mμ to 25 mμ in diameter. A noninfectious protein component 7 mμ in size is present in infected tissues or in cultures. Degradation of the infectious virus yields similar 7 mμ structures. The virus is of the RNA type and is ether and chloroform resistant. According to Dimopopoullos *et al.,* the virus may survive 85°C. exposure for 4 hours in the presence of protective colloids. Virulent as well as modified strains produce interferon, but the modified strains used as vaccines are more active in this respect.

Foot-and-mouth disease virus remains viable for long periods of time in frozen meat products. It is quite resistant to aging and drying. It will remain infective one month on infected hair, 4 to 5 months on hay and grains, and for one month or more in the soil. In one instance the survival of the virus was demonstrated on a farm 345 days after an outbreak.

Foot-and-mouth virus is comparatively resistant to chemical disinfection. Exposure of the virus to mercuric chloride 1 to 1,000 or 3 per cent cresol solution fails to kill the virus in 6 hours. It also resists 1 per cent phenol for 5 months and 70 per cent alcohol for 2 to 3 days. Although the virus is resistant to these chemicals, it is easily destroyed by alkalies, 1 per cent sodium hydroxide killing it within one minute. Therefore, sodium hydroxide is commonly used for disinfection following outbreaks of the disease.

There are three classical types of the virus: A, O, and C which are immunologically distinct. Several strains within these types have been described. In South Africa, types S.A.T. 1, 2, and 3 have been identified. A type, Asia-1, has been reported.

**Cultivation.** The cultivation of foot-and-mouth virus is usually accomplished by the inoculation of scarified areas of the buccal mucosa and tongue of calves or by foot-pad inoculation of guinea pigs. Suckling white mice are quite susceptible and are very useful in conducting titrations of foot-and-mouth disease virus and for serum neutralization tests.

The virus has been adapted to newborn rabbits and then to young rabbits. After 90 passages in rabbits the virulence of the virus for cattle is lost but it still stimulates antibody formation.

It is also possible to cultivate the virus in tissue cultures which employ bovine kidney cells or epithelial tissues taken from either bovine or guinea pig embryos. A cytopathic effect is produced in the cells of the tissue culture as a result of the growth of the virus. Gillespie has shown that all three strains of foot-and-mouth disease virus can be adapted to grow in chicken embryos if they are first adapted to grow in tissue cultures and day-old chicks. Type O virus has been adapted to chicken embryos directly from bovine tissue cultures without first adapting it to day-old chicks. Virus in the 25th embryo passage was found to be nonpathogenic for cattle but did stimulate immunity.

**Transmission.** Foot-and mouth disease is quite highly contagious, especially among cattle. Dilutions of 1 to 10 million of virus-containing material have been found infective. Vesicular fluid and saliva contain the most virus, but during febrile stages, the blood, milk, urine, and feces also contain it. Contact with infected animals and especially the ingestion of contaminated food and water transmits the disease. Indirect infection may take place by contact with inanimate objects of various kinds. The virus can penetrate the intact mucous membrane, but its entrance is facilitated by abrasions. Artificial inoculation by almost any route will result in infection.

Transmission of the disease is complicated by the fact that some clinically recovered animals may harbor the virus for some time and act as reservoirs of the infection.

The sources of the virus in the outbreaks of foot-and-mouth disease in the United States include imported cattle; ships' garbage, containing meat scraps, which was brought ashore and fed to nogs; contaminated straw and hay brought from foreign countries, and imported smallpox vaccine in the form of calf lymph.

**Characteristics of the Disease.** Foot-and-mouth disease infects all cloven-hoofed animals and occasionally other animals, but it rarely infects man. The disease is characterized by the formation of vesicular lesions in the mouth, on the muzzle, in the interdigital space and coronary band of the feet, on the udder and teats of cows, and the snout of swine. The virus may also infect the parenchyma of the mammary gland, resulting in complete loss of function.

Upon entry of the virus into the body, one or more primary vesicles are formed and often they are not observed. The virus gains entrance to the blood stream from these primary vesicles and is distributed to all parts of the body, localizing chiefly in the skin and mucous membranes, producing a large number of secondary vesicles.

Losses due to foot-and-mouth disease may be quite high in young animals, but in older animals deaths are usually 5 per cent or less. However, losses due to emaciation, debility, abortion, reduced milk flow, and complicating conditions may be considerable.

**Pathological Changes.** The formation of vesicles on the buccal mucous membrane and tongue is followed by ulceration, erosion, and healing. Lesions of the feet are similar to those in the mouth, being first vesicular and then ulcerative. The lesions of both the mouth and feet are accompanied by swelling, redness, and pain which account for lameness and reluctance of the animal to eat and move about. In the malignant form of the disease there is marked myocardial degeneration which results in many deaths in young animals.

**Immunity.** Immunity begins to develop in about 6 days following the onset of infection, and plays a definite role in recovery. Such immunity is variable in duration, but usually lasts for at least a year. However, the fact that there are several antigenic types of the virus means that recovery from an attack by one type confers no protection against another. Monovalent, bivalent, or trivalent vaccines are used to produce active immunity in cattle, depending upon the type or types of the virus which prevail in the locality.

For many years formolized vaccines made from infected tongue epithelium have been used with relative success. Chemicals other than formaldehyde have been used to kill the virus for vaccine preparation and are reported to produce less change in the immunogenicity of the virus. Acetylethyleneimine, beta propiolactone, and glycidaldehyde are examples.

Considerable research leading to the development of live-modified vaccines has been reported since 1960. Adaptation of foot-and-mouth virus to rabbits, mice, chicken embryos, and various types of cell cultures are promising.

Convalescent and hyperimmune serums have proved valuable in treating the malignant form of foot-and-mouth disease and are also useful in exposed animals to prevent a generalized infection, although local vesicle formation occurs in animals so treated.

**Diagnosis.** The characteristic appearance of vesicles in the mouth and feet usually narrows the possibilities to two or three viruses. In the United States three viruses must be differentiated in a vesicular disease of swine, and in cattle two viruses must be considered. Determination of the host range in three or four species of animals is the first step in diagnosis. Those species used in such a test and their susceptibility to the three viruses are presented in Table 50.1.

Complement-fixation tests have been shown by Brooksby and by Bankowski and Kummer to be useful in the rapid differentiation of the vesicular viruses.

Differential filtration may aid in distinguishing foot-and-mouth and vesicular stomatitis viruses since elementary bodies of the latter are about 10 times the size of the foot-and-mouth disease virus. The fact that vesicular stomatitis virus can be cultivated in chicken embryos and the foot-and-mouth disease virus cannot is useful in diagnosis.

It has been shown that the virus of foot-and-mouth disease will regularly produce typical lesions following intramuscular inoculation into a susceptible calf, while the virus of vesicular stomatitis fails to do so. This fact, also, must be considered of importance in diagnosis.

Cross-immunity, complement-fixation, or neutralization tests must be made in order to determine the identity of the strain causing a particular outbreak.

### Vesicular-Exanthema Virus

**Disease Produced.** Vesicular exanthema.

**Hosts Affected.** Swine. Horses are susceptible to A and C types. Some strains have been shown to be pathogenic for hamsters. Cattle, sheep, and guinea pigs are not susceptible.

TABLE 50.1

HOST RANGE OF THE VIRUSES PRODUCING VESICULAR LESIONS*

| | Cattle | Swine | Horses | Guinea pigs |
|---|---|---|---|---|
| Foot-and-mouth | +++ | ++ | — | +± |
| Vesicular stomatitis | ++ | ++ | +++ | ++ |
| Vesicular exanthema | — | +++ | ± | — |

* Confirmatory tests may include protection tests in guinea pigs immunized with a known virus.

**History and Distribution.** Vesicular exanthema was first observed in California in garbage-fed swine in the years 1932–33. At first, 1932, it was diagnosed as foot-and-mouth disease and handled as such. The following year it was recognized as a different virus disease by Traum and the name vesicular exanthema was suggested. Six years after the first outbreak of the disease it reappeared and spread in California, infecting approximately one-fourth of the swine of that state. Other outbreaks have been recorded since 1939–40, but none occurred outside the state of California until 1952 when the disease spread to many states. The disease was declared to be eradicated in October, 1959. Except for brief threats of introduction into Hawaii and Iceland, vesicular exanthema has not occurred outside the United States.

**Properties of the Virus.** The virus will pass Berkefeld N filters. Several types of the virus are differentiated immunologically: A, B, C, and D were originally described. During the 1952–53 outbreaks other strains were isolated and found immunologically different from each other but could not be compared with some of the original strains because they were lost. Types which have been studied are designated A-48, B-51, C-52, D-53, E-54, F-55, and G-55. Thirteen different types have been reported.

According to Madin and Traum, the vesicular exanthema virus is approximately 14 mμ to 22 mμ in size. The virus is also reported by them to remain viable at ordinary refrigerator temperatures for two years but not for three years. The virus remains viable for six weeks stored at room temperature, and for twenty-four hours at 37°C. The virus is noninfective after fifty-four hours at 37°C.

**Cultivation.** Cultivation of vesicular exanthema virus has usually been carried out by the inoculation of swine. Some strains have been grown in hamsters by intradermal inoculation. Tissue cultures composed of swine embryo tissue cells have supported the growth of the virus and a cytopathic effect is produced by the virus.

**Transmission.** Vesicular exanthema is transmitted by contact with or by consumption of food and water contaminated with the virus. Uncooked garbage which contains pork trimmings has often been the source of the virus. It is also thought to be carried by inanimate objects and by persons going directly from farm to farm.

**Characteristics of the Disease.** Lesions of vesicular exanthema are almost identical to those of foot-and-mouth disease. The vesicles appear on the snout, in the nostrils, around the coronary band, interdigital space and digital pads of the feet, also on the udder of nursing sows. Animals become lame and the hoofs are sometimes shed. Death losses are low except in suckling pigs. Recovery follows after the vesicles rupture and heal, but gains in weight are retarded for some time afterward. Sows in advanced pregnancy may abort.

**Immunity.** Hogs are resistant after recovery from an attack, but for only a few months duration. An experimental vaccine has been used by Madin and Traum with encouraging results.

**Diagnosis.** Animal inoculation is necessary for accurate diagnosis. Swine and horses are usually inoculated with vesicular fluid from suspected cases, and if the virus is present the swine should show lesions within 48 hours. Since calves and guinea pigs are insusceptible to vesicular exanthema, but are easily infected with foot-and-mouth or vesicular stomatitis viruses, they should be used also as test animals.

## Avian Encephalomyelitis Virus or Epidemic Tremor Virus

**Diseases Produced.** Avian encephalomyelitis, epidemic tremor.

**Hosts Affected.** Chickens. Experimentally turkey poults, ducklings, and young pigeons are susceptible.

**History and Distribution.** Avian encephalomyelitis was first observed in the New England states in 1930 by Jones who later described the disease and the virus causing it, in 1932. Since this first occurrence, the disease has spread and has been diagnosed in many states. The disease has also been reported in Australia, England, Canada, Japan, Sweden, and Union of South Africa.

**Properties of the Virus.** The elementary bodies of avian encephalomyelitis virus are 20 m$\mu$ to 30 m$\mu$ in size and will pass Berkefeld V and N as well as Seitz filters.

The virus survives for at least 88 days in 50 per cent glycerin and for 68 days in lyophilized material.

No relationship between the avian and equine encephalomyelitis viruses has been shown.

**Cultivation.** Avian encephalomyelitis virus can be cultivated in tissue cultures composed of minced whole embryo tissue and chicken serum. Newly hatched chicks are uniformly susceptible to the virus by intracerebral inoculation, whereas chicken embryos are infected irregularly by the usual techniques of inoculation. This fact has been pointed out by Olitsky as a striking reversal of the general rule, since many viruses will grow readily in the developing embryo, but will not affect the newly hatched chick or adult bird.

**Transmission.** The mechanism of transmission of avian encephalomyelitis is not definitely known. Transmission by contact with infected birds has been thought to be of importance by some investigators, but is discounted by others. Van Roekel, also Jungherr and Minard, suggest that the virus is egg-borne. The virus was found in the unabsorbed yolk of naturally infected chicks. Jungherr and Minard also report the production of typical lesions in the brain of chicks inoculated with saline suspensions of feces collected from infected flocks. However, clinical symptoms were not observed, nor was the virus isolated in these cases.

**Characteristics of the Disease.** Avian encephalomyelitis is a disease of young chicks which occurs within the first six weeks of life. Most of the clinical cases are noted in chicks between one and three weeks of age. Older birds are refractory even to artificial inoculation.

Tremor of the head is one of the most often-noted symptoms. Incoordination and leg weakness are frequently observed. General debility, prostration, and death may follow. Mortality rates range from 0 to 50 per cent with an average of about 17 per cent.

Many cases of the disease are asymptomatic but will show histopathological evidence of infection if the brain is carefully examined.

**Pathological Changes.** The only lesions observed in avian encephalomyelitis are microscopic lesions of the brain. There is marked degeneration of the neuron cells of the brain proper and of the cord. There is also perivascular cuffing of the blood vessels of the meninges and the brain.

**Immunity.** Neutralizing antibodies have been demonstrated in the serum of birds which are vaccinated with killed virus. However, no protection to intracerebral challenge is demonstrable in such birds.

Schaaf has described an experimental vaccine produced from virus grown in chick brains. Beta propiolactone is used as the inactivating agent. A live chicken embryo-modified vaccine which is given orally has been described by Calnek *et al.* and used successfully for immunization of breeder flocks.

**Diagnosis.** A diagnosis of avian encephalomyelitis is based on the appearance of characteristic symptoms, typical histopathological lesions of the brain, and demonstration of the presence of the virus by intracerebral inoculation of susceptible chicks.

### Mouse Poliomyelitis Virus

**Proposed Name.** *Poliovirus muris.*

**Diseases Produced.** Mouse poliomyelitis. Theiler's encephalomyelitis.

**Hosts Affected.** White mouse. Wild gray mouse may be an intestinal carrier.

**History and Distribution.** Mouse encephalomyelitis was first noted in the United States by Theiler in 1934 who reported that the etiology of the disease was a virus. The virus is widespread, probably occurring wherever white mice are raised. It has been identified in the United States, South America, Europe, and Japan.

**Properties of the Virus.** Mouse encephalitis virus is of the RNA type and measures about 28 mμ in diameter. It is resistant to ether and chloroform and to detergents. Some strains agglutinate human "O" erythrocytes. The virus passes all grades of the Berkefeld type filter and the Chamberland $L_3$ type. The virus retains its viability for 14 months at —78°C., and at least 150 days in 50 per cent glycerin stored at 2° to 4°C. It is readily inactivated by 1 per cent hydrogen peroxide and by heating to 55°C. for 30 minutes.

**Cultivation.** Mouse encephalitis virus can be cultivated in tissue cultures of mouse embryo brain or in the chicken embryo by allantoic, yolk sac, or chorioallantoic membrane inoculation.

**Transmission.** The virus is eliminated in the feces, and this constitutes the usual source of the virus which is spread to other susceptible mice. It has been reported that the virus is present mainly in the small intestine and that the virus content of the ingesta is about 10 times greater than that of the adjacent intestinal wall. The virus is found in the central nervous system of paralytic cases but not in the "carrier" animal.

**Characteristics of the Disease.** Encephalomyelitis or poliomyelitis of mice closely parallels human poliomyelitis in many respects, and so has been fairly well studied for that reason. As in human poliomyelitis, this disease of mice is characterized by intestinal infection, with a few individuals exhibiting nervous symptoms. In infected stocks of mice, a high percentage of the animals become intestinal carriers with about one in a thousand becoming paralytic. The paralysis observed in this disease is a flaccid type involving the hind legs. However, young mice may die without showing paralysis. The virus has been found in wild gray mice and kangaroo rats housed near white mice which were carriers.

**Pathological Changes.** The pathological changes are similar to human poliomyelitis. There is necrosis of ganglionic cells of the anterior horn. There may be inflammatory changes with perivascular and focal leucocytic infiltration in the central nervous system.

**Immunity.** Recovery from mouse poliomyelitis usually confers immunity to the disease, but the virus may persist in the animal for at least one year.

**Diagnosis.** Mouse encephalitis infection is diagnosed by isolation and identification of the virus. It must be differentiated from other viruses which infect the central nervous system of mice.

## Picornaviruses of Cats

Burke has reported on the occurrence of viruses isolated from the respiratory tract of cats. Five serotypes were distinguished and all had properties which would place them in an intermediate position between the enterovirus and rhinovirus groups. Their behavior in experimentally inoculated cats was more like the rhinovirus group than the enterovirus group.

## REFERENCES

### Poliovirus

BODIAN, D., and HORSTMAN, D. M. Polioviruses. Chap. 18. *In* Viral and Rickettsial Infections of Man. Horsfall, F. L., and Tamm, I. (eds.). J. B. Lippincott Co., Philadelphia, 1965.

———, *et al.* Differentiation of Types of Poliomyelitis Viruses. III. The Grouping of Fourteen Strains Into Three Basic Immunological Types. Amer. Jour. Hyg. 49:234, 1949.

KOPROWSKI, H., *et al.* Immune Responses in Human Volunteers Upon Oral Administration of a Rodent-Adapted Strain of Poliomyelitis. Amer. Jour. Hyg. 55:108, 1952.

MAYOR, H. D. Picornavirus Symmetry. Virol. 22:156, 1962.

PLOTKIN, S. A., *et al.* The Polioviruses of Man. Ann. N. Y. Acad. Sci. 101:357, 1962.

SABIN, A. B. Oral Polio Vaccines, Recent Results and Recommendations for Optimum Use. Jour. Roy. Soc. Promot. Health 82:51, 1962.

### Coxsackie Virus

DALLDORF, G., and MELNICK, J. L. Coxsakie Viruses. Chap. 19. *In* Viral and Rickettsial Infections of Man. Horsfall, F. L., and Tamm, I. (eds.). J. B. Lippincott Co., Philadelphia, 1965.

PLAGER, H. The Coxsackie Viruses. Ann. N.Y. Acad. Sci. 101:390, 1962.

### ECHO Viruses

MELNICK, J. L. Echoviruses. Chap. 20. *In* Viral and Rickettsial Infections of Man. Horsfall, F. L., and Tamm, I. (eds.). J. B. Lippincott Co., Philadelphia, 1965.

PINDAK, F. F., and CLAPPER, W. E. Isolation of Enteric Cytopathogenic Human Orphan Virus Type 6 From Dogs. Amer. Jour. Vet. Res. 25:52, 1964.

WERNER, H. A. The ECHO Viruses. Ann. N.Y. Acad. Sci. 101:398, 1962.

### Bovine Enteroviruses

BOUTERS, R. A Virus With Enterogenic Properties Causing Degeneration of the Germinal Epithelium in Bulls. Nature 201:217, 1964.

BURKI, F. Studien uber bovine enteroviren. Zentbl. Vet. Med. 9:748, 1962.

FALK, V. Isolierung und Charakterisierung zytopathogener enteroviren von Rinderen einer Klinisch gesunden herde. Arch. Exp. Veterinärmed. 18:582, 1964.

KALTER, S. S. Animal "Orphan" Viruses. Bull. World Health Org. 22:319, 1960.

KLEIN, M., and FARLEY, E. The Isolation of Enteric Cytopathogenic Bovine Orphan (ECBO) Viruses From Calves. Bacteriol. Proc. 31:73, 1957.

KUNIN, C. M., and MINUSE, E. The Isolation in Tissue Culture, Chick Embryo and Suckling Mice of Filterable Agents From Healthy Dairy Cattle. Jour. Immunol. 80:1, 1958.

LAPLACA, M., *et al.* Isolation and Characterization of Enteroviruses From Cattle. Giorn. di Microb. 12:93, 1964.

MCFERRAN, J. B. Bovine Enteroviruses. Ann. N.Y. Acad. Sci. 101:436, 1962.

MOLL, T., and ULRICH, M. I. Biologic Characteristics of Certain Bovine Enteric Viruses. Amer. Jour. Vet. Res. 24:545, 1963.

MOSCOVICI, C., and LAPLACA, M. Further Studies of Bovine Enteroviruses—Tentative Scheme of Classification. Amer. Jour. Vet. Res. 23:645, 1962.

STRAUB, O. C., and KIELWEIN, G. Bovine enterviren als Mastitis-erreger. Berl. Munch. tierartzl. Wschr. 78: 386, 1965.

VANDER MAATEN, M. Characterization of Some Bovine Enteric Viruses. Ph.D. Thesis. Iowa State Univ. Library, 1964.

### Swine Enteroviruses

BERAN, G. W., *et al.* Enteroviruses of Swine. I. Their Recognition, Identification and Distribution in a Herd of Swine. Amer. Jour. Vet. Res. 19:545, 1958.

BETTS, A. O., *et al.* The Isolation and Characterization of Some Enteroviruses From Pigs. Vet. Rec. 73:752, 1961.

———, *et al.* Porcine Enteroviruses Other Than the Virus of Teschen Disease. Ann. N.Y. Acad. Sci. 101:428 1962.

DUNNE, H. W., *et al.* Porcine Reproductive Failure Associated With a Newly Identified "SMEDI" Group of Picorna Viruses. Amer. Jour. Vet. Res. 26:1284, 1965.

HUCK, R. A., *et al.* Porcine Polioencephalomyelitis. Jour. Amer. Vet. Med. Assn. 144:612, 1964.

KASZA, L. Swine Polioencephalitis Viruses Isolated From the Brains and Intestines of Pigs. Amer. Jour. Vet. Res. 26:131, 1965.

———, and ADLER, A. Biological and Immunological Characterization of Six Swine Polioencephalomyelitis Viruses. Amer. Jour. Vet. Res. 26:625, 1965.

KELLY, D. F. Studies on Enteroviruses of the Pig. VII. Some Properties of a Porcine Enterovirus (F7). Res. Vet. Sci. 5:56, 1964.

L'ECUYER, C. L., and GREIG, A. S. Serological and Biological Studies on Porcine Enteroviruses Isolated in Canada. Canad. Vet. Jour. 7:148, 1966.

MAYR, A. Degrees of Variation of the Virus of Teschen Disease and Relationship to Other Enteroviruses of Swine. Bull. Off. Intl. Epiz. 56:106, 1961.

MEYER, R. C., *et al.* Electron Microscopy of a Pathogenic Porcine Enterovirus. Virol. 22:163, 1964.

SWITZER, W. P. Incidence and Economic Effects of Enterovirus in Iowa Swine. Proc. U.S. Livestock Sanit. Assn., p. 393, 1960.

ZZAWA, H., *et al.* Porcine Enteroviruses. I. Properties of Three Isolates From Swine With Diarrhea and One From Apparently Normal Swine. Amer. Jour. Vet. Res. 23:1131, 1962.

———, *et al.* Porcine Enteroviruses. II. Pathogenesis of Viral Agents Isolated From the Intestinal Tract of Swine. Amer. Jour. Vet. Res. 23:1142, 1962.

## Teschen Disease Virus

CARTWRIGHT, S. F., and HUCK, R. A. Studies of Enterovirus of Swine. Isolation in Tissue Culture of a Strain ($Fs_{65}$) of the Teschen Group of Viruses. Jour. Comp. Path. 73:27, 1963.

GREIG, A. S. Tissue Culture Studies and Electron Microscopy of the Virus of Teschen Disease. Canad. Jour. Comp. Med. 25:3, 1961.

KAPLAN, M. M., and MERANZE, D. R. Porcine Virus Encephalomyelitis and Its Possible Biological Relationship to Human Poliomyelitis. Vet. Med. 43:330, 1948.

MAYR, A. The Virus of Teschen Disease. Ann. N.Y. Acad. Sci. 101:423, 1962.

## Avian Enteroviruses

BURKE, C. N., *et al.* Avian Enteric Cytopathogenic Viruses. I. Isolation. Avian Dis. 3:412, 1959.

KHANNA, P. N. Studies on Cytopathogenic Avian Enteroviruses. I. Their Isolation and Serological Classification. Avian Dis. 8:632, 1964.

SARMA, P. S., and POMEROY, B. S. Enteroviruses of Chickens; Isolation and Characterization of Two Isolates. Poult. Sci. 41:1679, 1962.

TAYLOR, P. J., and CALNEK, B. U. Isolation and Classification of Avian Enteric Cytopathogenic Agents. Avian Dis. 6:51, 1962.

## Simian Enteroviruses

HEBERLING, R. L., and CHEEVER, F. S. Some Characteristics of the Simian Enteroviruses. Amer. Jour. Epidem. 81:106, 1965.

## Human Rhinoviruses

ANDREWES, C. H., and TYRELL, D. A. J. Rhinoviruses. Chap. 21. *In* Viral and Rickettsial Infections of Man. Horsfall, F. L., and Tamm, I. (eds.). J. B. Lippincott Co., Philadelphia, 1965.

TYRELL, D. A. J., and CHANOCK, R. M. Rhinoviruses: A Description. Science 141:152, 1963.

## Equine Rhinovirus

DITCHFIELD, J., and MACPHERSON, L. W. The Properties and Classification of Two New Rhinoviruses Recovered From Horses in Toronto, Canada. Cornell Vet. 55:181, 1965.

PLUMMER, G. An Equine Respiratory Virus With Enterovirus Properties. Nature 195:519, 1962.

———. An Equine Respiratory Enterovirus: Some Biological Pro[illegible]es. Arch. ges. Virusforsch. 12:694, 1963.

## Bovine Rhinovirus

BÖGEL, K., and BÖHM, H. Ein Rhinovirus des Rir[illegible] bl. f. Bakt. I. Orig. 187:2, 1962.

## Foot-and-Mouth Disease Virus


BRADISH, C. J., *et al.* Concentration and Electron Microscopy of the Characteristic Particle of Foot-and-Mouth Disease. Jour. Gen. Microbiol. 22:379, 1960.

BROOKSBY, J. B Vesicular Stomatitis and Foot-and-Mouth Disease Differentiation by Complement Fixation. Proc. Soc Exp. Biol. Med. 67:254, 1948.

———. The Virus of Foot-and-Mouth Disease. Adv. Virus Res. 5:1, 1958.

BROWN, F., and CRICK, J. Application of Agar Gel Precipitation Tests to the Study of the Virus of Foot-and-Mouth Disease. Virol. 5:133, 1958.

BURROWS, R. The Behavior of Some Modified Strains of Foot-and-Mouth Disease Virus in the Pig. Bull. Off. Intl. Epiz 61:1251, 1964.

CUNHA, R. G., *et al.* Studies on Rabbit-Adapted Foot-and-Mouth Virus of Type C Waldmann. Canad. Jour. Comp. Med. 28:288, 1964.

DIMOPOPOULLOS, G. T., *et al.* Thermal Inactivation and Antigenicity Studies of Heated Tissue Suspensions Containing Foot-and-Mouth Disease Virus. Amer. Jour. Vet. Res. 20:510, 1959

GILLESPIE, J. H. Propagation of Type C Foot-and-Mouth Disease Virus in Egg-Cultivated Virus on Cattle. Cornell Vet. 45:170, 1955.

LOEFFLER, F., and FROSCH, P. Summarischer Bericht uber die Ergebnisse der Unter suchunger der kommission zur Erforschung der Maul-und-Klavenseuche bei der Institut fur Infektionskrankheiten in Berlin. Zentralbl .f. Bakt. 22:257, 1897.

———, and ———. Berichte der kommission zur Erforschung der Maul-und-Klavenseuche bei dem Institut fur Infektionskrankheiten in Berlin. Zentralbl. f. Bakt. 23:371, 1898.

MOHLER, J. R. Foot-and-Mouth Disease. USDA Dept. Circ. 400, 1926.

OLITSKY, P. K., *et al.* Report of the Foot-and-Mouth Disease Commission of the United States Department of Agriculture. USDA Tech. Bull. 76, 1928.

ROSENBUSCH, C., *et al.* Intradermal Foot-and-Mouth Disease Vaccine. Jour. Amer. Vet. Med. Assn. 112:45, 1948.

SCHULZE, P., and GRALHEER, H. Untersuchungen Zur Feinstruktur des Maul-und-Klavenseuche-Virus. Arch. Exp. Veterinärmed. 18:1449, 1964.

SKINNER, H. H. Infection of Domestic Poultry With the Viruses of Foot-and-Mouth Disease and Vesicular Stomatitis. Arch. ges. Virusforsch. 9:92, 1959.

TRAUM, J. Foot-and-Mouth Disease: Specific Treatment, Eradication and Diagnosis. Rept. 12th Internatl. Vet. Cong. 2:87, 1934

ZAHRAN, G. E. D. Foot-and-Mouth Disease Virus. I. Propagation of 3 Immunologic Types of Virus in Chicks. II. Propagation and Modification of 3 Immunologic Types of Virus in Embryonating Chicken Eggs. Amer. Jour. Vet. Res. 22:518, 1961.


## Vesicular-1 Exanthema Virus


BANKOWSKI, R. A. Vesicular Exanthema. Adv. Vet. Sci. 10:23, 1965.

MADIN, S. H. Vesicular Exanthema. Chap. 11. *In* Diseases of Swine. 2nd Ed. H. W. Dunne (ed.). Iowa State Univ. Press, 1964

———, and TRAUM, J. Experimental Studies With Vesicular Exanthema of Swine. Vet. Med. 48:395, 1953.

——— and ———. Experimental Studies With Vesicular Exanthema of Swine. II. Stability. Vet. Med. 48:443, 1953

———. and ———. Vesicular Exanthema of Swine. Bact. Rev. 19:6, 1955.

MCCLAIN, M. E., *et al. In vitro* Cultivation and Cytopathogenicity of Vesicular Exanthema Virus. Proc. Soc. Exp. Biol. Med. 86:771, 1954.

MOHLER, J. R., and SNYDER, R. The 1932 Outbreak of Foot-and-Mouth Disease in Southern California. USDA Misc. Publ. 163, 1, 1933.

TRAUM, J. Foot-and-Mouth Disease: Specific Treatment, Eradication and Differential Diagnosis. Proc. 12th Intl. Vet. Cong., New York, 2:87, 1934.


## Avian Encephalomyelitis Virus


BURKE, C. N., *et al.* The Multiplication of Avian Encephalomyelitis Virus in Chicken Embryo Tissues. Avian Dis. 9:104, 1965.

CALNEK, B. U., *et al.* Studies on Avian Encephalomyelitis. V. Development and Application of an Oral Vaccine. Avian Dis. 5:297, 1961.

JONES, E. E. An Encephalomyelitis in the Chicken. Science 76:331, 1932.

JUNGHERR, E., and MINARD, E. L. The Present Status of Avian Encephalomyelitis. Jour. Amer. Vet. Med. Assn. 100:38, 1942.

SCHAAF, K. Avian Encephalomyelitis Immunization With Inactivated Virus. Avian Dis. 3:245, 1959.

TAYLOR, J. R. E., and SCHELLING, E. P. Distribution of Avian Encephalomyelitis in North America as Indicated by an Immunity Test. Avian Dis. 4:122, 1960.

VAN ROEKEL, H. Avian Encephalomyelitis. (Epidemic Tremor.) Chap. 24. *In* Diseases of Poultry. Biester, H. E., and Schwarte, L. H. (eds.). Iowa State Univ. Press. 1965.

## Mouse Encephalitis Virus

LEYON, H. Some Physico-Chemical Properties of Spontaneous Mouse Encephalomyelitis Virus Strain FA. Exp. Cell Res. 2:207, 1951.

THEILER, M., and GARD, S. Encephalomyelitis of Mice. I. Characteristics and Pathogenesis of the Virus. II. Epidemiology. Jour. Exp. Med. 72:49, 79, 1940.

## Picornaviruses of Cats

BURKE, F. Picornaviruses of Cats. Arch. ges Virusforsch. 15:690, 1965.

# 51

# The Reoviruses

THE REOVIRUSES (RESPIRATORY-ENTERIC-orphan) constitute a distinct group because they are composed of double-stranded RNA rather than single-stranded nucleic acid as are other RNA viruses. They are also distinct from other animal viruses in that they appear to have a double capsid which is similar to the clover wound-tumor virus. They are cubic in symmetry and measure about 70 mμ to 82 mμ across. Ninety-two capsomeres can be distinguished in the outer capsid. Hemagglutination is produced by all members of the group. Most isolates agglutinate human erythrocytes but are inactive on fowl, sheep, ox, and guinea pig cells. However, type 3 reovirus is reported to agglutinate bovine erythrocytes and not those of man. The hemagglutinin is distinctly different from that of the myxoviruses.

The reoviruses are ether resistant, resembling the picornaviruses in this respect. It was this characteristic which led to their inclusion with the enteroviruses when they were first described. The reoviruses are also resistant to the action of sodium desoxycholate and to pH 3.

The reoviruses are most easily cultivated in cell cultures derived from the tissues of monkeys, pigs, dogs, cats, and guinea pigs. A cytopathic effect is observed, and cytoplasmic inclusion bodies are characteristic in infected cells. Many strains can be grown on the chorioallantoic membrane of chicken embryos or in the amniotic sac. Pock lesions are produced in the chorioallantoic membrane.

All strains of reoviruses possess a common complement-fixing antigen. By hemagglutinin-inhibition tests three groups have been distinguished.

The reoviruses are widely distributed in the human and animal populations but their significance in disease is not fully established. The isolation of the same serotype of virus from man and animals suggests that they may be intertransmissible. Isolations have been made from both the respiratory and alimentary tracts of "normal" as well as clinically ill hosts. Hosts from which reoviruses have been recovered include man, monkeys, chimpanzees, cattle, dogs, mice, and chickens. Experimental inoculation of these isolates into various hosts have in a few cases reproduced the original clinical syndrome. In other trials only a mild febrile reaction is noted, while no illness is observed after some exposures.

## REFERENCES


GOMATOS, P. J., and TAMM, I. Reactive Sites of Reovirus Type 3 and Their Interaction With Receptor Substances. Virol. 17:455, 1962.

HARTLEY, J. W., *et al.* Recovery of Reoviruses From Wild and Laboratory Mice. Proc. Soc. Exp. Biol. Med. 108:390, 1961.

KAWAMURA, H., *et al.* Avian Reovirus: Its Properties and Serological Classification. Natl. Inst. An. Health Quar., Tokyo, 5:115–24, 1965.

LERNER, A. M., *et al.* Hemagglutination With Reoviruses. Virol. 19:58, 1963.

MASSIE, E. L., and SHAW, E. D. Reovirus Type I in Laboratory Dogs. Amer. Jour. Vet. Res. 27:783, 1966.

MAYOR, H. D., *et al.* Reoviruses. II. Structure and Composition of the Virion. Jour. Bact. 89:1548, 1965.
RHIM, J. S., and MELNICK, J. L. Plaque Formation by Reoviruses. Virol. 15:80, 1961.
ROSEN, L., Serologic Grouping of Reoviruses by Hemagglutination-Inhibition. Amer. Jour. Hyg. 71:242, 1961.
———. *et al.* Further Observations on the Natural Infection of Cattle With Reoviruses. Amer. Jour. Hyg. 77:38, 1963.
SABIN, A. B. Reoviruses. Science 130:1387, 1959.

# 52

# Unclassified Viruses

THERE ARE A NUMBER OF IMPORTANT ANImal viruses which are presently unclassified either because they are incompletely characterized or are sufficiently different in their known characters as to exclude them from established groups.

The virus of hog cholera, rabies vesicular stomatitis, and members of the mucosal disease-virus diarrhea complex are reported to possess helical symmetry resembling the myxoviruses. However, none of these viruses has been shown to have affinity or enzymic activity for mucoproteins of erythrocytes, a basic characteristic in the definition of the myxovirus group.

The viruses of vesicular stomatitis and infectious bronchitis are each morphologically and structurally quite different from any other animal virus so far described.

Until new groups are formed and additional characteristics are determined, it seems best not to attempt classification of these viruses.

## Hog Cholera Virus

**Disease Produced.** Hog cholera, swine fever (Europe).

**Hosts Affected.** Swine. Wild hogs are susceptible to some extent and sometimes are inapparent carriers.

**History and Distribution.** Hog cholera was first recognized as a disease in the United States in 1833 in Ohio, but the exact origin of the disease in that state is not known. The first accounts of the disease in England were in 1862, and from England the disease spread over Europe and then to Africa. The etiological agent was first thought to be *Salmonella choleraesuis* or possibly *Pasteurella multocida,* since cultures of these organisms were recovered from many typical cases and injection of them into other hogs would frequently produce a disease with similar lesions. However, immunity experiments which employed bacterins made from these organisms showed that their use afforded no protection against hog cholera. In 1903 de Schweinitz and Dorset in their investigations of the disease in southwestern Iowa found that filtrates made of swine body fluids would consistently reproduce the disease. They also proved by cultural examination and by laboratory animal inoculation that such filtrates were free of any bacteria. This discovery was of great significance and quickly led to an entirely new concept of the disease. The following months witnessed the production of the first successful antiserum, and by 1908 the process of anti-hog cholera serum manufacture and simultaneous serum-virus immunization procedure were established.

Hog cholera is still most prevalent in the chief swine-raising area, the midwestern United States. It has spread worldwide in all areas where swine are kept. Certain countries, notably Canada, have been quite successful in controlling it by vigorous quarantine measures.

**Properties of the Virus.** The virus of hog cholera is usually reported as 30 m$\mu$ to 35 m$\mu$ or less in size. The virus is destroyed in one hour by 2 per cent cresol, but solutions of sodium hydroxide are considered to be effective disinfectants. Hog cholera virus is resistant to phenol, surviving long periods of contact with 0.5 per cent phenol. Torrey and Prather (1963) recorded thermal inactivation of the virus in defibrinated blood at 69°C. in 30 minutes, 68°C. in 45 minutes, or 66°C. in 60 minutes. A temperature of 68°C. applied for 30 minutes killed the virus when diluted to 80 per cent with saline.

The virus is resistant to aging if the temperature is low. In saline-glycerin solution at —15°C., it will live for 5 years. It will survive in meat products for months, and it is also resistant to pickling, salting, and smoking for at least 6 months. Putrefactive processes destroy the virus in a few days, except in the bone marrow where it has been known to survive for 15 days.

Variation in virulence of the virus is well known. The American strains are considerably more virulent than the European. Variation among American strains has been reported by Dale *et al.* However, definite antigenic types of the virus have not been distinguished. An antigenic relationship between the soluble antigens of hog cholera virus and bovine virus diarrhea virus has been shown by Darbyshire (1960).

**Cultivation.** Hog cholera virus has been cultivated in tissue cultures which employ various swine tissues such as lymph node, bone marrow, spleen, kidney, testicle, and chorioid plexus.

**Transmission.** Hog cholera is a highly contagious disease of swine and it spreads rapidly and easily among them. Eye and nasal secretions, blood, urine, and feces all contain the virus during the disease and for a period before symptoms are shown. Under natural conditions contact with these secretions or excretions may result in transmission. Very minute quantities of the virus will reproduce the disease in susceptible pigs. Blood from hog cholera pigs can be diluted to 1:1,000,000 and regularly produce the disease when injected, and dilutions of 1:50,000,000 occasionally are infective.

Birds, such as pigeons, also insects, have been suspected of playing some role in the transmission of hog cholera, but experimental evidence has so far failed to incriminate any of these.

Pigs which have recovered from clinical hog cholera or serum-virus vaccination are possible disseminators of the virus. The urine of such animals may remain infective for other swine for 20 to 30 days after inoculation with the virus, and the blood has been found to contain the hog cholera virus for some time after injection—in one instance, up to 10 months. Pigs inoculated at an early age with live virus may become tolerant to the virus and thereby remain as carriers. Hog cholera virus has also been shown by Carbrey *et al.* to persist in the tissues of exposed pregnant sows with transmission to their offspring.

Wild pigs are often inapparent carriers of the virus and so are a distinct menace to domestic swine.

Other farm animals have been suspected of transmitting the virus of hog cholera. Jacotot has reported that hog cholera virus can be transmitted to sheep, goats, horses, dogs, rabbits, pigeons, and calves by injection and by contact, that the virus could be recovered from these animals and would produce the disease in swine. Zichis also reported the passage of hog cholera virus through sheep and calves and back to swine with evidence of its multiplication in these hosts. However, neither of these investigators noted any symptoms of disease in animals used except swine.

Transmission of hog cholera is not infrequently by way of infected scraps of pork in uncooked garbage which is fed to susceptible pigs. Introduction of the virus into hog-cholera-free areas has occurred in this manner.

**Characteristics of the Disease.** Hog cholera begins with a rise in temperature which reaches 106° to 107°F. and remains high until just before death. Depression, loss of appetite, stilted gait, incoordination, purulent conjunctivitis, and diarrhea are usually characteristic of the disease. Mortality rates are generally around 90 per cent in the United States. In European countries the death loss is often lower.

Hog cholera is frequently complicated by secondary bacterial infection. *Salmonella choleraesuis* is most common, but other organisms such as *Past. multocida, Ery. rhusiopathiae,* or *S. necrophorus* may be found. Chronic hog cholera which runs a prolonged clinical course is sometimes observed.

**Pathological Changes.** The outstanding pathological change in hog cholera is the appearance of hemorrhages, usually petechial, but ecchymotic in some cases. These may appear on any or nearly all serous surfaces. Hemorrhages of the bladder, kidney, epiglottis, and epicardium are commonly noted. Hemorrhagic lymphadenitis and a leucopenia are usual findings. Neurologic damage is a fairly common finding in swine with acute cholera. "Tremors" in newborn pigs has been related to the presence of hog cholera virus.

Cases with secondary bacterial invasions may show severe enteritis, and even more extensive hemorrhages.

Inclusion bodies have been described by Boynton *et al.* in the epithelial cells of the duct of the gallbladder of cholera hogs.

**Immunity.** The development and use of successful immunizing agents for hog cholera has been of inestimable value to the swine-raising industry. The first successful method of producing immunity to hog cholera was through the simultaneous injection of live virulent virus and serum from swine hyperimmunized against the virus. This method which originated in 1905 was used very successfully until the late 1950's. As serious efforts to eradicate the disease began in the United States it was necessary to discontinue the methods which employed live virulent virus.

***Crystal-violet vaccine.*** Cole and McBryde found that crystal violet would attenuate the hog cholera virus without destroying its antigenic properties. Their method consists of preparing a 0.5 per cent solution of crystal violet and a 3 per cent solution of disodium phosphate; 100 ml. of each solution is added to 800 ml. of defibrinated virus blood. The mixture is incubated at 37°C. for 14 days, with agitation once daily. At the end of 14 days the virus no longer produces the disease and is given alone for the production of immunity. Two doses are recommended, to be given about 2 weeks apart.

***Tissue vaccine. B.T.V.*** Boynton devised a vaccine for hog cholera patterned after his anti-rinderpest vaccine for cattle. This vaccine is prepared from lymphoid tissues of cholera-infected pigs, and the virus is attenuated by 1 per cent oil of eucalyptol. The period required for inactivation varies but generally takes about 8 weeks at refrigerator temperatures.

Crystal-violet and tissue vaccines are used in about the same manner. They are used in unexposed hogs and two doses are recommended, to be given without serum.

***Lapinized hog cholera virus.*** Baker, in 1947, succeeded in adapting the hog cholera virus to the rabbit by the alternate passage technique. It was observed that after many such passages the virulence of the virus for swine was lost, while the immunogenic properties were retained. Swine inoculated with the lapinized virus showed no symptoms following the injection and were later resistant to challenge by the fully virulent hog cholera virus. This rabbit-adapted strain of the virus has been successfully used as an immunizing agent for the disease. While it has been used without an accompanying dose of antiserum, it is not recommended procedure.

Although the lapinized hog cholera virus is nonpathogenic for young and adult swine, it has been reported by Sautter *et al.* that it can infect the fetal pig, causing edema, ascites, and congenital malformations.

***Modified live virus vaccine.*** The lapinized virus has also been used in a similar immunizing product that employs virus which has gone through fewer rabbit passages, thus retaining some pathogenicity. This product is produced in swine and is harvested in the form of blood and spleen emulsion. This emulsion is lyophilized and then reconstituted with distilled water just before use. An administration of immune serum is necessary when modified live virus is used.

***Tissue culture vaccine.*** A live vaccine prepared in tissue cultures of swine origin is used to some extent for immunization. Although the virus is reduced in virulence by passage in cultures, it is necessary to give immune serum at the same time as the vaccine is administered.

***Passive immunity.*** Hyperimmune serum is used chiefly for active immunization procedures, but is also administered as a therapeutic agent to sick animals or occasionally alone to confer passive immunity for a short period.

Passive immunity is usually conferred on suckling pigs by transfer of antibodies through the milk of immune sows. This has been shown by experimental trials as well as field observations. Dunne has called attention to interference of vaccines by the presence of maternal antibody.

**Diagnosis.** The diagnosis of hog cholera depends upon the demonstration of the presence of the virus. This can be accomplished by injection of blood or tissues from suspected cases into known susceptible pigs. It is necessary to protect other pigs with known anti-hog cholera serum and inject a similar amount of the suspected material into them. The suspected blood and tissue suspensions must be rendered bacteria-free by filtration or by the addition of antibiotics such as penicillin and streptomycin. If the pigs which received no antiserum die with lesions typical of hog cholera, and those given immune serum live, a diagnosis of the disease is made. Cultures of the inoculum and of the dead pigs should be made to exclude any role bacteria might play in the results.

An agar-diffusion precipitation test described by Molnar is useful as an aid to the diagnosis of hog cholera. Pancreatic tissue from infected swine contains a soluble antigen which will precipitate with serum from hyperimmunized swine. Other tissues, such as lymph nodes, can be used but do not contain as much of the antigen.

Diagnostic procedures which employ fluorescent antibodies in the detection of hog cholera virus have been described by a number of workers. A procedure which uses a stable pig kidney cell line and fluorescent hog cholera antibody has been described by Mengling *et al.* (1963). Hog cholera virus may be grown from infected tissues by the inoculation of pig kidney cells propagated on coverslips in Leighton tubes. The infected cells can be detected by their specific fluorescence following the application of fluorescent hog cholera antibody to the coverslip preparation 16 to 48 hours after inoculation. This test has been found highly reliable in the diagnosis of hog cholera when compared with swine inoculation tests. A similar technique in which fluorescent hog cholera antibody is applied directly to tissue sections or smears of tissues from swine with the disease has been reported by Aiken *et al.* (1964).

Kumagai *et al.* (1961) have devised a method referred to as Enhancement Newcastle Disease (END) for the detection and and assay of hog cholera virus in infected tissues. This procedure employs the phenomenon of enhancement of cytopathic effects observed when two different viruses infect the same cell culture. Newcastle disease virus produces a cytopathic effect when inoculated onto monolayers of pig testicular cells at 6 to 8 days incubation but has no visible effect when inoculated on monolayers 4 to 5 days old. Monolayers infected with hog cholera virus which is noncytopathic will show cytopathic effects when Newcastle disease virus is inoculated as early as 2 days incubation. Thus the effects of Newcastle virus are enhanced by the presence of hog cholera virus in the cells.

### African Swine Fever Virus

**Disease Produced.** African swine fever

**Hosts Affected.** Swine. Bush pig, wart hog inapparent. Cattle, horses, sheep, goats, cats, and fowl are insusceptible.

**History and Distribution.** An acute infectious disease closely resembling American hog cholera occurs in East and South Africa. The disease was recognized by Montgomery in 1910 as differing from ordinary swine fever (hog cholera), and he determined the etiological agent to be a filterable virus in 1911. In 1957 the disease appeared outside Africa. It was identified in Portugal and then spread to Spain and France.

**Properties of the Virus.** Breeze and DeBoer describe the African swine fever virus as having a hexagonal outer membrane measuring 175 mμ to 215 mμ surrounding an electron lucent region with a dense nucleoid which is 72 mμ to 89 mμ in diameter. They compare the morphological appearance of the virus with the herpes group.

The virus has been shown by Malmquist and Hay to hemadsorb pig erythrocytes. The virus will pass through Berkefeld, Chamberland, and Seitz filters. The dried virus is not destroyed by exposure to 40°C. in 15 days or 50°C. in 3½ hours. It is preserved in 0.5 per cent phenol—50 per cent glycerin mixture at room temperature for 536 days. It is quite stable to aging since it remains viable for 11 days at room temperature, 15 weeks in carcasses, 5 months in processed hams, and 6 months in bone marrow. The virus has been found viable after 6 years storage in the refrigerator.

It has been suggested that multiple antigenic types of the virus exist in Africa but only one in Europe.

**Cultivation.** McIntosh has reported the successful cultivation of the virus in chicken embryos. He used virus which was partially rabbit-adapted for the work. The embryos used were 8 days old and were incubated at 33°C. following inoculation.

Malmquist and Hay have cultivated the virus in tissue cultures of swine bone marrow and leucocytes obtained from the buffy coat layer of centrifuged circulating blood. Definite cytopathic effects are produced in the cell cultures and hemadsorption is observed.

**Transmission.** The transmission of the virus is considered to be through ingestion. Montgomery muzzled healthy pigs and placed them in contact with pigs sick with African swine fever, and they did not contract the disease. Most of the outbreaks of African swine fever can be related to contact with either the African wart hog or bush pig, which have been proved inapparent carriers of the virus.

The virus has been isolated from ticks collected in the vicinity of swine infected with African swine fever, but their role in transmission is not established.

**Characteristics of the Disease.** African swine fever is characterized as an acute generalized infection accompanied by high temperature, dullness, loss of appetite, cyanosis, and incoordination of the hind legs. The incubation period is three to four days and the duration of the disease three to four days. Mortality is usually 100 per cent, with only an occasional animal surviving. The lesions are most pronounced in the blood vascular system which shows extensive hemorrhage.

**Immunity.** Artificial immunization has been attempted but has not been successful.

In Spain and Portugal vaccines of live-modified virus have been produced by cell culture passage. Such vaccines have not proved satisfactory because of the delayed cases of the disease which develop 4 to 5 months later.

### Rabies Virus

**Disease Produced.** Rabies.

**Hosts Affected.** All mammals. Fowl can be experimentally infected. Reptiles and fish are insusceptible.

**History and Distribution.** Rabies is a disease which has been recognized since ancient times. The disease was described as early as 500 B.C. in dogs. The relationship of rabies in animals to human rabies was recognized in A.D. 100 and cauterization of dog-bite wounds was recommended.

Zinke, in 1804, reported the transmission of rabies to a normal dog by the inoculation of saliva from a rabid one. Thus the infectiousness of the disease was proved and quarantine measures on dogs were instituted in the Scandinavian countries as early as 1826. Consequently, these countries have been free of the disease for over 100 years.

The classical work of Pasteur, in the 1880's, which showed that the virus could be modified to produce immunity without the hazard of producing the disease is one of the milestones in medicine.

Although Pasteur had theorized that the etiological agent of rabies was smaller than bacteria, Remlinger, in 1903, showed that Berkefeld filtrates of brain tissue were infective. Also in 1903 Negri described intracytoplasmic inclusion bodies in the nerve cells of rabid animals, which are of diagnostic significance. These inclusion bodies known as *Negri bodies* are found only in rabies. There have been periods in history when rabies became epizootic in European areas, but the disease usually is enzootic or sporadic in occurrence. Rabies is distributed generally throughout the world, but the British Isles, Australia, and the Scandinavian countries have been free of the disease for many years.

**Properties of the Virus.** Rabies elementary bodies are rounded, elongated, rod-shaped particles of varying lengths. They are 100 m$\mu$ to 150 m$\mu$ in diameter and may be 250 m$\mu$ to 1,000 m$\mu$ in length. Electron micrographs show a structure which is similar to the myxoviruses; i.e., they appear to consist of a saclike membrane with radial projections on its surface and internal filamentous components arranged in the form of double helices. Thin sections of infected cells show the virus only in the cytoplasm.

The rabies virus is of the RNA type and contains essential lipid material. No hemagglutinins have been demonstrated and therefore does not qualify for inclusion in the myxovirus group as suggested by some investigators. A soluble noninfectious antigen measuring 12 m$\mu$ can be obtained from rabies-infected tissues. Rabies virus will pass all grades of Berkefeld filters, also Mandler and Chamberland types, but the virus is retained by Seitz pads. The virus is killed by exposure to 70°C. for 15 minutes, but if dried it may withstand 100°C. for 2 to 3 minutes. The virus is preserved in 50 per cent glycerin for about one year and by freezing for more than one year. Quick freezing followed by desiccation preserves the virus, but it is attenuated by slow drying.

Ultraviolet radiation rapidly destroys rabies virus. Mercuric chloride, formalin, acids, and bases readily inactivate the virus. Phenol, chloroform, and ether are effective but require considerable time to kill.

Sulfonamides, penicillin, and streptomycin do not affect the virus and are frequently used in its isolation from contaminated materials.

Various strains of the rabies virus have been shown to vary in their pathogenic properties and in the amounts of antigenic constituents, but distinct antigenic types have not been described.

There are two types of the virus which are well known. *Street virus* is the rabies virus as it occurs in nature. *Fixed virus* is a laboratory-adapted virus which is developed by continued passage of a street strain by brain-to-brain inoculation in an animal such as the rabbit. Street virus in the rabbit usually has an incubation period of 15 to 21 days. As fixation occurs through passage, the incubation period becomes progressively shorter until it becomes "fixed" at 6 to 8 days. Strains of street virus vary considerably in their ability to become fixed. Some become fixed in 20 passages, while others require 50 or more, and still others do not become fixed at all. Ordinarily, the more virulent street strains are apt to become fixed in a few passages.

Fixed virus is also modified in other ways than by a shortened incubation period. It multiplies faster and a greater quantity of virus is found in the brain tissue. It also loses most of its ability to form Negri bodies and becomes less virulent for hosts other than the one in which it has become fixed.

Fixed virus is quite stable and it is very difficult to effect a change back to a street form. Fixed virus is used almost exclusively for vaccine production.

**Cultivation.** Rabies virus can be cultivated in tissue cultures composed of brain from the embryo rabbit, mouse, rat, or chicken suspended in Tyrode's solution, serum, and plasma. Kidney cell cultures derived from the dog, cat, hamster, pig, and guinea pig will support growth of the virus. A cytopathic effect may be observed in hamster kidney cells and in neuron cells of cultured cat brain. Such effects which are irregular occur after several passages. Giant cell formation in swine kidney cultures is reported.

Chicken embryos are infected irregularly, but the virus can be adapted to grow successfully, though no specific lesions are produced. Infectivity for animals is reduced by cultivation in chicken embryos.

**Transmission.** The transmission of rabies is almost invariably through the bite of an infected animal. The fact that the virus is eliminated in the saliva is of great significance, and unless saliva is introduced beneath the skin, the disease is seldom transmitted. The virus has been demonstrated in the saliva of dogs 3 to 8 days before the onset of symptoms. However, it has also been reported that only about 50 to 60 per cent of the infected dogs shed the virus in the saliva. Rare cases of rabies have been reported where only clawing and scratching occurred, or where the skin was contaminated with saliva.

The virus is most concentrated in the central nervous system and saliva, but it has also been demonstrated in various organs of the body as well as in the blood and milk from infected animals.

The dog is a most important animal as a disseminator of rabies virus, not only to man but also to other animals. Wild carnivora may be infected and transmit the disease. In the United States foxes and skunks are the most commonly involved. These animals are sometimes responsible for infecting domestic farm animals.

On the island of Trinidad, a paralytic form of rabies in domestic animals and man is transmitted by blood-lapping vampire bats which carry the virus in their saliva and prey on animals and man, especially children. This same situation has also been described in Brazil and Mexico.

In the United States, rabies virus has been isolated from the brain of insectivorus bats. These animals have been reported to attack human beings on a number of occasions.

The incubation period in natural cases of rabies is variable. In general, the greater the quantity of virus introduced into the wound the shorter is the incubation period. The location of the wound is also correlated with the length of incubation before symptoms occur. Virus introduced into wounds on the legs is less dangerous and requires a longer incubation period. In dogs, the minimum period is 10 days, the average 21 to 60 days, but may be as long as 6 months. In man, the period of incubation varies between 1 and 3 months, with the minimum of 10 days. Virus ordinarily reaches the central nervous tissue by way of the nerves leading from the area of the bite wound, although other routes such as the blood vascular may occur.

**Characteristics of the Disease.** In animals rabies may be manifest in one of two forms: furious, and dumb or paralytic types.

Furious rabies in animals, especially in the dog, is characterized by altered behavior such as restlessness, hiding, depraved appetite, excitement, unprovoked biting, aimless wandering (sometimes for many miles), excessive salivation, altered voice, pharyngeal paralysis, staggering, general paralysis, and finally death. Death usually occurs within 3 to 4 days after the onset of symptoms. There are probably no recoveries in natural cases of rabies, although some experimentally inoculated animals

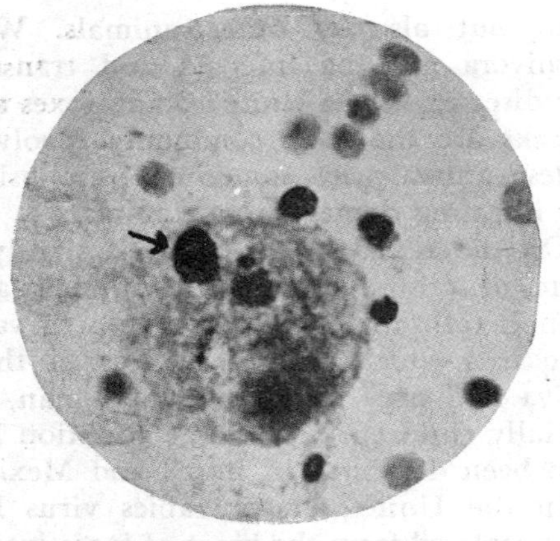

FIG. 52.1—Negri bodies in Purkinje cell of bovine cerebellum, ×540. (Photo by Benbrook.)

may show an abortive type of illness and recover. The dumb or paralytic form of rabies is frequently observed in animals inoculated with fixed virus, and is occasionally observed in other animals with street virus contracted under natural conditions. Animals showing this type usually show a short period of excitement which is followed by incoordination, ataxia, paralysis, dehydration, and loss of weight, followed by death.

**Pathological Changes.** The pathological changes are not marked in rabies. There are degenerative changes in the cells of the brain, accompanied by hyperemia and edema of the meninges. There are also leucocytic infiltration and "cuffing" of the blood vessels of the brain tissue.

The *Negri body* (Fig. 52.1) is an eosinophilic cytoplasmic inclusion body found only in rabies and is of great significance in diagnosis. Although the Negri body is pathognomonic of the disease, its precise nature is not yet established. It varies in size from 0.25$\mu$ to 20$\mu$, is round in form, and typically has an internal granular structure. Most evidence indicates that the Negri body is the product of altered cellular metabolism which results from infection. Electron photographs have not revealed rabies virus in these cell inclusions.

**Immunity.** The fact that there are virtually no recoveries from rabies has no doubt been an important driving force in the large amount of research on this disease and particularly with respect to immunization procedures. Pasteur, with the assistance of Chamberland and Roux, in 1884, showed that dogs could be protected against rabies by injecting suspensions of dried spinal cord of the rabbit infected with the disease. In the next year Pasteur made the historic injections of his vaccine into a 9-year-old boy who had been exposed by the bite of a rabid dog, and the vaccine was given credit for saving the boy's life.

In the years following, thousands of exposed persons have received antirabies vaccine, and the results have been quite satisfactory. Although several modifications of Pasteur's rabies vaccine have been made, the name "Pasteur treatment" is still usually applied to any human antirabic vaccine treatment. Many rabies vaccines have been prepared for use in the prevention of this disease, some of which are as follows:

*Desiccated cord or Pasteur type vaccine.* Rabbits are injected subdurally with fixed virus and in 6 to 7 days they are killed and the cords are harvested intact. They are cut into 2 or 3 pieces and placed in jars with potassium hydroxide for the required desiccation and incubated at 23°C. The loss of virulence parallels loss of moisture from the cord.

Originally, Pasteur started with injections of cord dried 14 days and gave daily injections with progressively less attenuation until 1-day cord was given on the 11th day. In recent years 7- to 8-day cord is used at the beginning and 2-day cord at the end. The number of injections varies with the exposure. Cases with least risk may be treated for 14 days, while those more severely exposed are treated 21 to 25 days.

*Phenolized type.* Examples of this type are the Fermi, Semple, and Umeno-Doi vaccines. The phenolized type of vaccine has been widely used in both human and veterinary medicine. In the preparation of this vaccine, fixed virus is inoculated intracerebrally into animals such as horses, rabbits, or goats and their brain and cord is removed when they have reached the last stages of the disease. Techniques of processing vary, but ordinarily this type of product contains 20 per cent brain suspension with 0.5 per cent phenol added. A period of 30 days at 37°C. is allowed for the phenol to kill the virus. Depending on the risk involved, the frequency, duration, and dose may be varied in the human treatment. In animals a prophylactic dose of 5 ml. is administered yearly in dogs. If animals are exposed the dose is increased.

*Ultraviolet-treated vaccine.* Webster and his coworkers found that rabies virus was readily killed by exposure to ultraviolet light, yet retained its immunizing properties. The technique of preparation of this type vaccine has been modified by Habel and others to produce a highly antigenic vaccine which is superior to other types of killed vaccines.

Ultraviolet rabies vaccine is prepared from the brains of animals which have been inoculated intracerebrally with fixed virus. Vaccines of this type have been found suitable for "single dose" immunization procedures.

*Live vaccines.* In some of the early work with rabies vaccines, it was found that live fixed virus could be peripherally injected into an animal without producing the disease. It was also observed that the live vaccines were superior in stimulating immunity. Several methods for the use of live fixed virus vaccines have been devised. One of these is the Hoegyes vaccine which uses dilutions of the virus to keep it below the infective level as the series of injections begin. Usually a 1:10,000 dilution of the virus is used first, and as the treatment is continued, progressively lower dilutions are injected until 1:100 dilution is administered at the end of 14 to 20 days.

The Harris method employs fixed virus in the form of rabbit brain which is frozen, quickly dried, and powdered. The minimum infective dose for rabbits is determined, and in large animals 500 doses are injected on the first day of treatment and then gradually increased to 5,000 doses at the end of 15 days. In dogs, the dose is 100 minimum infective doses in the beginning and increased to 1,500. Live vaccines are quite antigenic and for that reason are preferred by some over killed virus products. However, there have been some cases of fixed virus rabies which occur following treatment, and this danger, though somewhat remote, has been a point against the use of this type of vaccine.

*Avianized vaccines.* The adaptation of rabies virus to growth in the chicken embryo by Koprowski and Cox led to the development of a live virus vaccine. It was found that a strain of the virus, designated as the Flury strain, was altered in its pathogenicity after its adaptation to the chicken embryo. After 40 to 50 embryo passages the virus was no longer pathogenic for rabbits and dogs if introduced extraneurally. However, it would still produce rabies if injected intracerebrally. After 180 or more embryo passages the virus was further reduced in pathogenicity, being nonpathogenic when injected intracranially, except in suckling mice.

Avianized rabies vaccine is reported to be completely safe when injected intramuscularly into dogs. It has the following advantages: It possesses high antigenic properties in common with other live vaccines. There is no danger from neuroparalytic accident, which occasionally occurs with vaccines prepared from nervous tissues. Also, an immunity of longer duration is claimed.

Living avianized vaccine of high embryo passage (HEP) has been used to some extent in human beings. Low embryo passage (LEP) virus is not considered safe in any animal except the dog.

An inactivated avianized vaccine for use in man has been described by Peck *et al.* This vaccine is produced by the propagation of fixed rabies virus in duck embryos. The virus is inactivated by beta propiolactone. Fourteen daily doses are usually prescribed. This type of vaccine has come into common use in man because of the reduced hazard of allergic encephalitis which may accompany vaccines made from infected nervous tissues. The use of vaccines in exposed persons and animals has generally been successful—however, there have been failures. In cases of severe exposure, especially about the face, occasional deaths occur despite prompt and intensive treatment. In those fatal cases, death usually occurs after a relatively short incubation period. Vaccine treatment almost never fails in cases in which the incubation period would be over 30 days.

Occasionally, death results during vaccine treatment of dogs and human beings, due to an ascending paralysis. The explanation usually given is that of hypersensitivity, which develops from the repeated injection of brain tissue. The nervous tissue, which is tissue specific rather than host specific, stimulates in certain individuals antibodies to its own nerve tissue. These antibodies, then, are thought to be responsible for the demyelinization of the nerves, and paralysis and death result.

These accidents occur more often in persons receiving more than one series of antirabic treatment and in those who have allergic tendencies. The allergic theory has been strengthened by research which has shown that the substances responsible for the paralysis can be removed from vaccines by various calcium salts, by extraction with benzene, or by differential centrifugation.

*Immune serum.* Serum from hyperimmunized horses has been found useful in the prevention of rabies if administered within 24 hours after exposure. Infiltration of the tissues in the surrounding area of bite wounds is sometimes done. Gamma globulin from persons who have taken antirabic vaccines is also used for prophylaxis and has the advantage that it does not contain protein foreign to human beings.

*Local wound treatment.* For many centuries the wounds inflicted by rabid animals have been cauterized in an attempt to destroy the virus before it is absorbed by the tissues. Nitric acid, phenol, or heat cautery have been used. Such treatment, though drastic, has been considered beneficial.

Trials by Dean *et al.* using a variety of chemicals for wound prophylaxis showed that prompt, thorough washing with soap and water or 1 per cent aqueous benzalkonium chloride were quite effective in this role.

**Diagnosis.** Accurate diagnosis of rabies is important especially in instances where human beings are definitely exposed by animal bites.

Demonstration of Negri bodies in the cells of the hippocampus major constitutes a diagnosis of the disease. The demonstration of Negri bodies is more successful if the animal is confined and allowed to die. Smears are made of the hippocampus and cerebellum of the brain and stained with a differential stain such as Lenz, Sellers, or Giemsa (see chapter on Techniques and Methods). The Negri bodies can also be demonstrated in paraffin sections stained with hemotoxylin and eosin.

It is not always possible to demonstrate Negri bodies in the brain tissue of rabid animals. It is reported that 10 to 12 per cent of infected animals fail to show microscopic evidence of the disease. In these cases mouse inoculation is used. A small amount of the brain tissue is emulsified in a mortar and a mixture of streptomycin and penicillin is added to inhibit any bacteria present. The amounts of antibiotic used varies between 1,000 and 5,000 units of each per ml. of material. Following centrifugation of the material, .02 to .03 ml. of the supernatant is inoculated intracerebrally into 5 or 6 Swiss albino mice. If rabies virus is present in the inoculum, the mice will usually show symptoms of paralysis, depression, and dehydration in 6 to 16 days, with death occurring in 1 or 2 days following the appearance of symptoms. Occasionally symptoms may not appear until 17 to 25 days, and inoculated mice should be observed for 21 days before reporting them as negative.

Negri bodies can be demonstrated usually at 5 to 15 days in mice, if the virus is present. In cases where early diagnosis is important, 1 or 2 mice are sacrificed at 5 days and their brains examined for Negri bodies.

Serological procedures hold promise as an aid to rapid diagnosis of rabies. Agar diffusion precipitation and complement-fixation tests which employ known hyperimmune antirabic serum have been described. A soluble complement-fixing antigen is present in infected brain tissue.

Fluorescent antibody techniques are applicable to brain tissue for rabies diagnosis and are in common use. Antibody to rabies is conjugated with a fluorescene dye and is applied to smears of the brain from animals suspected of rabies. Cells exhibiting fluorescence are interpreted as rabies-infected cells.

### Vesicular-Stomatitis Virus

**Diseases Produced.** Vesicular stomatitis, pseudo foot-and-mouth disease.

**Hosts Affected.** Horses, mules, cattle, man, deer, raccoon, and swine. Experimentally sheep, goats, guinea pigs, occasionally cats, rats, and rabbits.

**History and Distribution.** Vesicular stomatitis was first observed in South Africa in 1884 by Hutcheon. It was first recognized as occurring in the United States by French veterinarians who examined horses imported to France from the United States and Canada during World War I (1915). It was diagnosed in horses in Colorado in 1916. The disease is enzootic in southeastern United States and extends westward to Louisiana and Texas. Occasional outbreaks are reported in eastern and midwestern areas. It occurs in Canada, Mexico, and several Central and South American countries. A virus (cocal virus) resembling vesicular stomatitis virus has been isolated from mites obtained from rodents on Trinidad. Cotton and Olitsky, Traum and Schoening reported simultaneously, in 1926, on the filterability of the agent of vesicular stomatitis, proving the existence of the virus.

**Properties of the Virus.** The vesicular stomatitis virus is rod-shaped, measuring 68 m$\mu$ × 175 m$\mu$. One end of the virus particle is rounded and the other shows central hollow area 17 m$\mu$ in diameter. Surface projections 10 m$\mu$ long cover the outside of the virus (Fig. 52.2). The internal structure is apparently in the form of a helix.

The virus resists 0.5 per cent phenol for 23 days, but is rendered noninfective by 0.05 per cent crystal violet as used in hog cholera vaccine production. Vesicular stomatitis is inactivated at 58°C. for 30 minutes.

There are two antigenic types of vesicular-stomatitis virus recognized: the New Jersey and Indiana types. Complement-fixation tests using hyperimmune serum for each of the two antigenic types have been

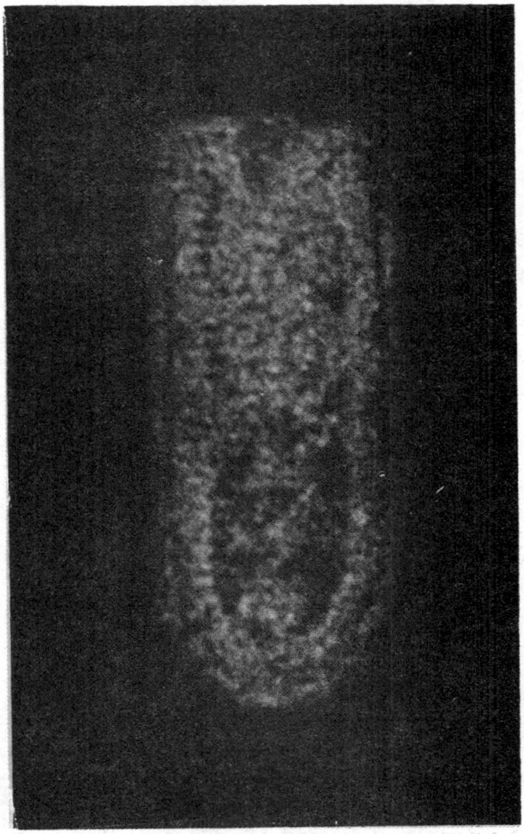

FIG. 52.2—Vesicular stomatitis virus showing degraded particle with striated and double concentric layered construction, ×620,000. (Courtesy A. E. Ritchie and A. L. Fernelius. A.R.S., National Animal Disease Lab., Ames, Iowa.)

found useful in their differentiation from each other and from foot-and-mouth disease virus.

**Cultivation.** The virus can be cultivated in guinea pigs by foot-pad inoculation. Inoculation of vesicular-stomatitis virus onto the chorioallantoic membrane of the chicken embryo results in growth of the virus and death of embryos. The infected membrane becomes thickened, and hemorrhages may be observed in the embryo itself.

Cell cultures derived from chicken embryos, cattle, swine, monkey, and guinea pig tissues readily support growth. The virus is destructive to the cells of the culture, producing distinct plaques in monolayers.

**Transmission.** Vesicular-stomatitis virus is transmitted by contact with contaminated objects. Abrasions of the mucous membranes of the mouth greatly favor the entry of the virus. Ferris, Hanson, Dicke, and Roberts have presented evidence that the virus can be transmitted by bites of flies and mosquitoes.

**Characteristics of the Disease.** Vesicular stomatitis virus is pathogenic for horses and mules, but it is frequently found in cattle and swine. It occurs chiefly in the United States although it was first described in South Africa. In cattle and swine the disease closely resembles foot-and-mouth disease from which it must be differentiated. Vesicular stomatitis is usually quite benign. Complete recovery results in one to two weeks after the onset of symptoms, except in an occasional case in which there is secondary bacterial infection of the vesicles. The vesicles are usually confined to the mouth, but they may appear on the feet and udder.

Olitsky and Sabin have demonstrated the neurotropic properties of vesicular stomatitis in guinea pigs and mice, but these tendencies are not known in other animals.

**Pathological Changes.** Vesicle formation is the first change noted. The vesicles rupture and erosion of the surface epithelium follows. These eroded areas are covered with new epithelium in three to four days.

**Immunity.** Recovered animals are immune to reinfection by the same type of virus.

Experimental vaccines have been used to prevent vesicular stomatitis but have not come into general use.

**Diagnosis.** Since the horse is not susceptible to foot-and-mouth disease, the diagnosis of vesicular stomatitis is usually not difficult in the horse, although it has been confused with horse pox.

If the disease is confined to cattle or swine it is essential that it be accurately identified. In such instances host range, differential filtration, cell culture, and chicken embryo inoculation procedures may be used. The realkalinization technique of Pyl, which consists of acidification of the virus material to pH 3 and return to pH 7.5, kills foot-and-mouth virus but not vesicular stomatitis.

## Equine Arteritis Virus

**Diseases Produced.** Equine viral arteritis, abortion.

**Host Affected.** Horse. Other animals not susceptible.

**History and Distribution.** A disease of horses occurring at Bucyrus, Ohio, in 1953 was investigated by Doll *et al.* and found to be due to a virus which had not been previously described. In retrospect, the condition described by Doll as equine viral arteritis has in the past been included under the diagnosis of "equine influenza." The disease has so far been reported only in the United States.

**Properties of the Virus.** The arteritis virus has not been characterized. It is reported to have remained viable in fetal spleen held at –20°C. for 6 years, and for 75 days in cell culture medium at 4°C. It survives only 2 days at 37°C., and for 20 minutes at 56°C.

**Cultivation.** The virus can be isolated and grown in horse or rabbit kidney cell cultures. After adaptation of the virus to horse kidney cells it can be propagated in hamster kidney cultures. A marked cytopathic effect is produced by the virus in the cell cultures.

**Transmission.** The arteritis virus is believed to be transmitted through discharges from the respiratory tract. It is not shed in the urine or intestinal contents. The incubation period ranges from 5 to 10 days.

**Characteristics of the Disease.** While the symptoms of equine viral arteritis are variable, fever, conjunctivitis, palpebral edema, congested and hemorrhagic nasal mucosa, edema of the legs, weakness, depression, and prostration are usual. Invasion of the fetus by the virus is quite common. Up to 50 to 75 per cent of pregnant mares may abort. Death losses may reach 30 per cent of those infected.

**Pathological Changes.** The most characteristic lesions of equine arteritis occur in the small arteries of the body. Necrosis of the medial layer of the vessel wall and degeneration of the intima and endothelium result in edema, hemorrhage, thrombosis, and infarction.

**Immunity.** Animals which recover from viral arteritis are immune to challenge. Passage of the virus in cell cultures results in its attenuation. At the 116th passage McCollum *et al.* report that only a mild febrile reaction occurs following inoculation of the virus into susceptible horses. While immunity to challenge was shown, the attenuated virus still retained its ability to infect the fetus of pregnant mares.

**Diagnosis.** Equine viral arteritis, rhinopneumonitis, and equine influenza may exhibit some of the same clinical symptoms and so virus isolation and identification are necessary to accurately differentiate these conditions. Growth of a cytopathogenic virus in horse or rabbit kidney cell cultures and which does not agglutinate erythrocytes would indicate the presence of the arteritis virus. The absence of inclusion bodies in hepatic cells would constitute additional evidence for the presence of arteritis virus, since inclusions are regularly found in rhinopneumonitis infection.

### Infectious Bronchitis Virus

**Disease Produced.** Infectious bronchitis.

**Host Affected.** Chicken.

**History and Distribution.** Infectious bronchitis was first recognized by Schalk and Hawn in North Dakota in 1931.

There was some confusion in nomenclature of the early 1930's because laryngotracheitis was also being referred to as infectious bronchitis by some investigators. A few years later laryngotracheitis was found not to involve the bronchi but lesions were confined to the larynx and trachea, and was distinct from infectious bronchitis. So the name infectious bronchitis as originally suggested by Schalk and Hawn is applied to the disease which they described.

Infectious bronchitis is widely distributed in the poultry-raising areas of the United States and Canada and has also been reported from Great Britain and Europe.

The disease was originally thought to be confined to baby chicks, but it is also of considerable importance in adult chickens.

**Properties of the Virus.** Infectious bronchitis virus is circular in shape, measuring 80 mμ to 120 mμ in diameter (Fig. 52.3). According to Berry *et al.* it is unique in its morphological characteristics and cannot be placed in any established group. It is about the size of the myxoviruses but does not possess neuraminidase activity nor helical internal components. It has bulbous projections, but no rosette structures are formed as a result of disruption of particles as is observed with the viruses of the influenza group.

Corbo and Cunningham report that he-

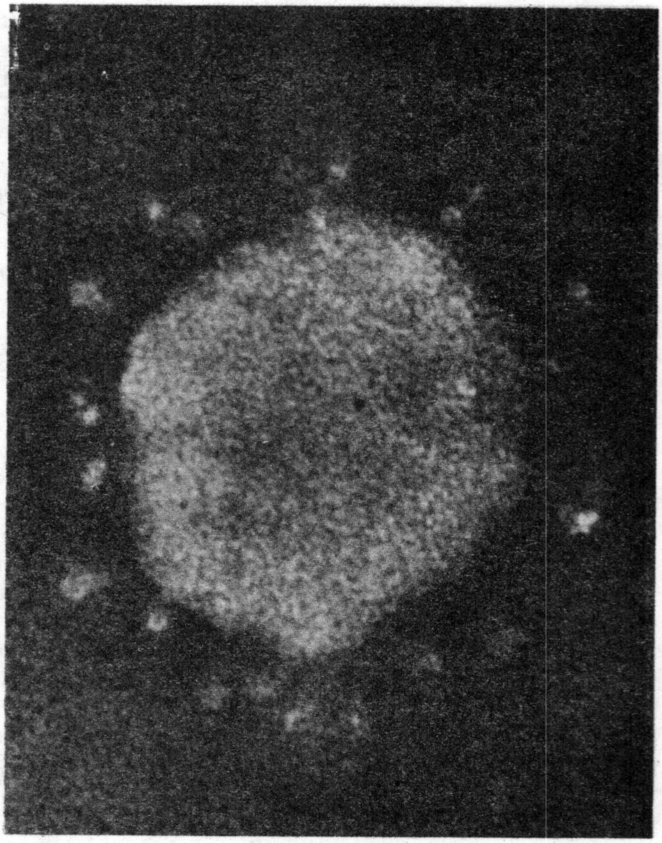

FIG. 52.3—Infectious bronchitis virus. Intact particle showing sparse superficial projections. (Courtesy A. E. Ritchie and P. D. Luckert. A.R.S., National Animal Disease Lab., Ames, Iowa.)

magglutination by bronchitis virus will occur if it is treated with trypsin. Inhibition of the reaction was observed with both normal and immune serum. The virus is filterable through all grades of Berkefeld candles as well as Seitz pads. The virus is not resistant to heat and dies in a short time at 37°C. The following chemicals are lethal in 3 minutes or less: one per cent phenol, cresol, formalin, Lugol's solution, or metaphen, also mercuric chloride 1 to 1,000, or potassium permanganate 1 to 10,000 concentration, and 5 per cent NaOH.

Antigenic variation among strains of bronchitis virus have been described by Jungherr and also by Hofstad.

**Cultivation.** Infectious bronchitis virus can be readily cultivated in chicken embryos. Allantoic cavity inoculation is preferable. Outstanding changes in the infected embryo are stunting or dwarfing and tucking of the embryo. These changes may not be evident in the first passage but are almost always present by second or third passage. Embryo-adapted strains become increasingly virulent for embryos on passage, and the virus may consistently kill in 3 to 4 days after inoculation.

The virus can be cultivated in cell cultures of epithelial cells of chicken, but not in fibroblast cells. Plaques are produced in liver, lung, and kidney cell cultures.

**Transmission.** Infectious bronchitis is usually transmitted by infective droplets from the respiratory system which are expelled by the coughing of sick birds. Food and water which may be contaminated with nasal secretions may also play a part in transmission. The incubation period in artificially exposed birds is about 24 hours.

**Characteristics of the Disease.** Infectious bronchitis is of sudden onset and spreads rapidly, affecting the entire flock in a short time. Gasping, wheezing, nasal discharge, and distinct bronchial rales are characteristic. In older birds, the symptoms may be less distinct, but rales are definite, and in laying flocks egg production is reduced to one-half or more. Mortality may be high in baby chicks, but is negligible in older birds. The greatest loss in older birds is in lowered egg yield and quality.

**Pathological Changes.** Lesions are confined to the respiratory system. Usually there is a clear mucoid exudate in the trachea, congestion of the lungs, with bronchi entirely filled with exudate, and the air sacs show a definite "cloudiness."

**Immunity.** Birds which have recovered from infectious bronchitis are immune. Chicks hatched from eggs laid by immune stock are passively immune for at least 2 weeks but are usually susceptible at 5 weeks.

Neutralizing antibodies can be readily demonstrated in the serum of immune chickens.

Artificial immunization is used to some extent in the prevention of infectious bronchitis.

Live virus which has been modified by many chicken embryo passages is also employed as an immunizing agent. It may be administered by spraying the birds with dried virus in the form of dust, or it may be sprayed as an aerosol or added to drinking water.

**Diagnosis.** Accurate diagnosis of infectious bronchitis depends upon the isolation of the virus and its differentiation from Newcastle and laryngotracheitis viruses (see Table 45.1). Trachea and lungs from suspected cases should be removed and an emulsion prepared and, after adding antibiotics, inoculated into embryos. Allantoic cavity inoculation is preferable for bronchitis or Newcastle viruses, but chorioallantoic inoculation should be done in case laryngotracheitis virus is present. If susceptible chicks are available, a portion of the inoculum introduced into the trachea will produce bronchial rales and other symptoms in about 24 hours if bronchitis virus is present. If Newcastle or laryngotracheitis virus is present, the incubation period is longer.

### Borna-Disease Virus

**Disease Produced.** Borna disease.

**Hosts Affected.** Horses, sheep, and possibly cattle and deer. Rabbits, guinea pigs, mice, monkeys, rats, and possibly fowl are susceptible to experimental inoculation.

**History and Distribution.** Borna disease is so named because of a particularly severe outbreak of the disease near the town of Borna, Germany, in 1894. The disease was known in Germany for many years before but under different names. It is a disease primarily of the equine species, but also may occur in sheep. Cases of the infection have been reported in cattle and deer but are not well substantiated. The etiology of the disease was suggested to be a virus by Joest in 1911 and was confirmed by Zwick, Seinfried, and Witte in 1926. The disease occurs in central European countries.

Borna disease and equine encephalomyelitis are so similar that cases of the latter disease which occurred in the United States were thought at first to be Borna disease, but the two were soon differentiated.

**Properties of the Virus.** The elementary bodies of Borna-disease virus are 85 m$\mu$ to 125 m$\mu$ in size. They will pass collodion filters and also Berkefeld, Mandler, and Chamberland filters, but only with irregularity. A small complement-fixing component measuring 15 m$\mu$ to 30 m$\mu$ has been described by von Sprockhoff. The virus is inactivated by exposure to 57°C. for 30 minutes or 70°C. for 10 minutes.

It is killed by 1 per cent phenol in 4 weeks, but not in 2 weeks. It is resistant to drying and survives in the dried state or in glycerin for 6 months to 1 year.

Borna-disease virus is antigenically distinct from other encephalitis viruses.

**Cultivation.** The Borna-disease virus can be cultivated on the chorioallantoic membrane of chicken embryos. Incubation of inoculated embryos at 35°C. favors growth of the virus. No data regarding tissue culture cultivation of the virus are available. The virus for most experimental work is propagated by intracerebral inoculation of rabbits.

**Transmission.** The Borna-disease virus is eliminated from the infected animal in the saliva, nasal secretions, milk, and urine. The saliva and nasal secretions are considered most important in transmission. Contamination of food and water with these secretions has transmitted the disease. The incubation period is about 30 days.

**Characteristics of the Disease.** The onset of definite symptoms of the disease may be preceded by a slight fever and other mild signs of illness. These are followed by typical symptoms of meningitis and encephalomyelitis such as dullness, incoordination, paralysis, and altered behavior. The course of the disease is usually 1 to 3 weeks and death occurs in 90 per cent of the cases.

**Pathological Changes.** The lesions of Borna disease are confined to the central nervous system. Gross lesions are not marked nor characteristic. Microscopic lesions of the brain and meninges consist of areas of leucocytic infiltration and degeneration of nerve cells.

Intracytoplasmic inclusion bodies can be demonstrated in some of the ganglion cells of the hippocampus major.

**Immunity.** Recovery from an attack of Borna disease confers temporary immunity. A brain tissue vaccine prepared from rabbits has been of some value in immunizing horses. Such immunity may last for 6 months to 1 year.

**Diagnosis.** Accurate diagnosis of Borna disease depends upon the isolation of the virus by rabbit or guinea pig inoculation and differentiation from other viruses. The demonstration of intracytoplasmic inclusion bodies from the brain tissue is of value.

### Panleucopenia Virus

**Diseases Produced.** Panleucopenia, agranulocytosis, infectious enteritis of mink, feline enteritis.

**Hosts Affected.** Domestic cat, leopard, mink, and raccoon. The guinea pig, ferret, rabbit, and mouse are insusceptible.

**History and Distribution.** Lawrence and Syverton, in 1938, described a disease of cats characterized by leucopenia and also a virus as its etiological agent. Others in this country have described epizootics of panleucopenia in cats. Kikuth *et al.* report an identical disease in Germany. Johnson has described a disease in a leopard from which the virus of panleucopenia was isolated.

Wills has shown that the etiological agent of infectious enteritis of mink appears to be identical to the panleucopenia virus of cats.

**Properties of the Virus.** Panleucopenia virus passes all grades of the Berkefeld type filter as well as Seitz EK pads. Its size has been estimated to be 35 mμ or less.

The virus can be preserved for 138 days in 50 per cent glycerin and also by desiccation at —80°C.

**Cultivation.** The virus of panleucopenia has been cultivated in susceptible cats. It has been reported that the virus can be grown in cat kidney tissue cultures.

**Transmission.** The disease is highly contagious and is probably spread by respiratory droplets and contaminated food. The virus is present in blood, nasal secretions, feces, and irregularly in the urine of infected cats. Some difficulty has been experienced in the experimental reproduction of the typical clinical syndrome with panleucopenia virus alone. When panleucopenia virus is accompanied by certain other viruses (herpesviruses) a severe disease is produced.

**Characteristics of the Disease.** After a period of 5 to 6 days of incubation, infected animals become listless, refuse food, and may show vomition, diarrhea, nasal and eye discharge. Temperature increase is usually noted but not marked. Death occurs in 50 to 90 per cent of those cats infected. Some animals recover after a mild illness of 2 to 4 days.

**Pathological Changes.** Most pronounced changes occur in the blood picture. Leucopenia, especially neutropenia, is characteristic. Leucocyte counts of the circulating blood drop sharply from 10,000 to 13,000 down to as low as 1,000 or less in 3 to 4 days.

Bone marrow changes are marked by a change from a fairly firm red marrow to a nearly fluid, hemorrhagic type. Intranuclear inclusion bodies in the epithelial cells of the mucosa of the intestinal tract can be found in a majority of cases.

**Immunity.** Cats which recover from panleucopenia are immune.

Immune serum is commercially available for prophylactic and therapeutic uses. This serum is effective in many cases if given 3 days before symptoms begin, but if given later it is less effective.

Formolized tissue vaccine is available for the active immunization of cats against the disease. Two doses given 7 to 10 days apart are recommended.

**Diagnosis.** The diagnosis of panleucopenia of cats is usually based on leucocyte counts associated with clinical features of the disease.

### Ulcerative-Dermatosis Virus

**Diseases Produced.** Ulcerative dermatosis, lip-and-leg ulceration, posthitis, vulvitis.

**Host Affected.** Sheep.

**History and Distribution.** Ulcerative dermatosis has been known to occur in sheep in England since 1894 and was described in Montana by Knowles in 1907. In these early publications the term "lip-and-leg ulceration" was used to denote the condition, and *Spher. necrophorus* was believed to be the causative agent. Tunicliff and Matisheck, in 1941, proved the etiological agent to be a virus.

**Properties of the Virus.** The size and shape of the virus are not known, but it is filterable through Berkefeld V and N filters. The virus is ether resistant. Guinea pigs, hamsters, and mice are insusceptible.

**Cultivation.** The ulcerative-dermatosis virus can be cultivated in cell cultures of ovine kidney cells and bovine kidney, skin, and muscle cells. A cytopathic effect is observed as an indication of virus growth.

**Transmission.** It is transmitted by contact with infected tissues and from the ram to ewes by breeding.

**Characteristics of the Disease.** The ulcerative-dermatosis virus infects only the surface epithelial structures, producing ulcerations of the lips, interdigital space and pastern area, vulva, and prepuce. Erosion and destruction of the epithelium occur. The ulcers which are produced often require several weeks to heal. The disease is not fatal, but lameness, unthriftiness, and breeding difficulties may result.

**Pathological Changes.** The basic pathological changes are those of tissue destruction and ulceration, followed by surface scab formation and slow healing.

**Immunity.** If immunity follows recovery it is temporary, since the disease has been observed more than once in the same animals. Artificial immunizing agents are not used for the prevention of this disease.

**Diagnosis.** Usually a clinical diagnosis of ulcerative dermatosis is made. This condition must be differentiated from contagious ecthyma of sheep, which it closely resembles, by conducting protection tests using ecthyma vaccine in one group and leaving another group unvaccinated. If ulcerative-dermatosis virus is inoculated into both groups, both will show infection. On the other hand, if those given ecthyma vaccine show no lesions following inoculation and the control group becomes infected, the virus in question is that of contagious ecthyma.

### Equine Infectious Anemia Virus

**Disease Produced.** Equine infectious anemia, "swamp fever."

**Hosts Affected.** Horse, mule, donkey, and, rarely, man. Experimentally, the guinea pig and rabbit can be infected but show only mild reactions.

**History and Distribution.** Equine infectious anemia has been recognized in Europe for a little over 100 years and for at least 50 years in the United States. It has occurred in at least 34 states and in Canada. The disease has spread widely throughout Europe and also occurs in Africa and Japan.

The infectious nature of the disease was recognized for many years before Carré and Vallée reported that the etiological agent was a filterable virus in 1904.

**Properties of the Virus.** The elementary bodies are reported by Reagan *et al.* to be rounded particles which measure from 11 mμ to 59 mμ, with the average being 30 mμ in diameter.

Using differential filtration methods, Mohlmann and Gralheer have determined the size of the virus as 60 mμ to 95 mμ in diameter. The virus will pass the Chamberland and Berkefeld V filters.

Equine anemia virus is comparatively resistant. A temperature of 58°C. for one hour is necessary to inactivate it. An exposure of 30 days in 0.5 per cent phenol will inactivate the virus, while 0.1 or 0.2 per cent formalin is lethal after 33 days.

The virus survives at 5°C. for 3 months or if 20 per cent glycerin is added it is viable after 15 months storage. Freezing at low temperatures, followed by desiccation, is not detrimental to the virus and it is preserved for at least 16 months in this condition.

**Cultivation.** Equine anemia virus has not been cultivated in chicken embryos or tissue cultures. The virus has been carried through 20 rabbit passages by Reagan and his coworkers.

**Transmission.** It is believed that under natural conditions equine anemia is spread by vectors and by ingestion, but vectors or other means of introducing infectious material beneath the skin are most important. It is known that the virus escapes from the infected host by the blood, urine, feces, milk, spermatic fluid, saliva, and nasal secretions. Transfer of the virus by blood may occur by biting flies, mosquitoes, lice, or by bleeding needles or surgical instruments which have been used on infected animals. Transfer of the virus from mare to foal may occur through the milk or *in utero*. Secretions and excretions may contaminate food or water with resulting transmission. The chronic carrier of the virus is of great importance in the dissemination of the disease because it may show no definite symptoms of the disease and there is no reliable test for its detection except horse inoculation.

**Characteristics of the Disease.** Equine anemia may be an acute, subacute, or chronic disease of horses, mules, or donkeys. The incubation period is usually from 12 to 15 days but in some cases may be as long as 2 months. The acute form begins with a temperature increase, which is followed by weakness, incoordination, rapid respiration, with loss in weight, anemia, and subcutaneous edema. Pregnant mares may abort during a period of febrile reaction. Death may result in 15 to 30 days or the animal may develop a subacute form of the disease and in such cases the anemia may be marked. Some animals show the chronic forms with or without acute flare-ups of the disease. However, chronic cases have been shown to carry the virus in their blood for periods of 11 to 14 years. Such animals are a menace to other horses and if found should be destroyed.

In rabbits infected by artificial exposure, a temperature rise is the only manifestation of the disease. Guinea pigs which have been inoculated with the virus may show a febrile reaction, loss in weight, and death in some cases. A Japanese commission reported that swine are susceptible to the virus, but this was not confirmed by Stein.

A few cases of equine anemia in man are reported. The symptoms include headache, fever, anemia, edema, general debility, and loss of weight. A case of infection in a veterinarian, proved by horse inoculation, is reported by Peters.

**Pathological Changes.** The pathological changes which are seen at postmortem of acute or subacute cases include general emaciation and edema, hemorrhages of mucous membranes, enlarged spleen and liver. The liver may be quite friable and will be a yellowish-brown color.

Gross changes in chronic cases are not marked or are entirely absent.

**Immunity.** A degree of resistance to equine anemia apparently exists in the chronic cases of the disease, but such resistance does not enable the animal to rid itself of the virus.

Numerous attempts to produce immunity by a variety of common methods have all been unsuccessful.

**Diagnosis.** The only reliable diagnosis of equine infectious anemia is by horse inoculation. This is not an economical procedure, so temperature curves, clinical symptoms, blood counts, and sedimentation rates of erythrocytes are used in areas where the disease has been proved to exist or as presumptive evidence of the disease.

### Avian-Leucosis Virus

**Diseases Produced.** Avian leucosis complex, fowl leucosis.

**Hosts Affected.** Chicken, also pheasant, and possibly turkey.

**History and Distribution.** Avian leucosis was described by Marek in 1907, and Ellerman and Bang, in 1908, reported that the disease was transmissible and that the etiological agent was a virus. The filterability of the agent of avian leucosis has been repeatedly confirmed by other workers.

The fact that the word *complex* is retained in the designation of this disease is appropriate, and there is still much to be clarified with respect to the virus as the etiological agent as well as the relationship of the pathological manifestations to each other. It is not within the scope of this text to present the mass of data regarding the disease or the pathology. However, some of the characteristics of the virus are known and there is fairly general agreement on some phases of the disease which can be presented.

Avian leucosis is widespread among flocks of chickens in the United States and European countries. Death losses, unthriftiness, and lowered egg production as the result of this disease take a heavy annual toll from the income of poultry flocks.

**Properties of the Virus.** The particle size of leucosis virus is reported as about 72 m$\mu$ by Stern and Kirschbaum. It will pass all grades of Berkefeld and Seitz filters.

The virus is inactivated by a temperature of 56°C. applied for 30 minutes. It is preserved for at least 54 days in the dried state and for 104 days in glycerin at 4°C. or at —60°C. for 6 months or more. Viability is lost after 14 days at 37°C.

**Cultivation.** Avian leucosis virus has been cultivated in chicken embryos and monolayer tissue cultures of chick liver cells.

**Transmission.** Higher incidence of leucosis has been shown among chickens reared on premises in contact with infected birds. Progeny of infected stock show a high incidence of leucosis. Transmission through the egg occurs and the virus has been identified from eggs.

**Characteristics of the Disease.** The general types of the leucosis complex are:

1. Neural lymphomatosis—with cellular infiltration of the nerves, and paralysis.
2. Ocular lymphomatosis—infiltration of the iris.
3. Visceral lymphomatosis—cellular infiltration involving visceral organs, especially the liver, spleen, kidney, and ovary.
4. Osteopetrotic lymphomatosis—involving the bones, especially the shanks.
5. Erythroblastic form—characterized by anemia.
6. Granuloblastic form—characterized by increase in leucocytes of the granuloblastic type in the circulating blood.
7. Myelocytomatosis—characterized by the formation of tumor masses in various organs.

According to the "unitarian theory," the same virus is the etiological agent of all the various types of the disease listed above, and there is much evidence to support this theory. On the other hand, some investigators have been able to isolate "pure virus" which will consistently reproduce one type of lesion. Whether there may be more than one virus or a single virus which rapidly undergoes variation or whether the host itself influences the type of pathological change produced is not clear. Much of the work on leucosis is hampered by the extreme difficulty in securing and maintaining leucosis-free experimental birds. Rubin *et al.* (1962) observed that congenitally infected chickens became tolerant to the leucosis virus. Such birds exhibited a constant viremia over a period of months and did not develop antibodies. In contrast, birds which were infected by contact developed a transient viremia followed by antibody formation and clearance of the virus from the blood.

**Pathological Changes.** Briefly stated, the outstanding character of leucosis is the growth of cells of leucocytic types which infiltrate the various tissues of the infected bird, giving rise to various symptoms and lesions depending upon the site of infection.

**Immunity.** Immunizing agents are not used.

**Diagnosis.** A diagnosis of leucosis depends upon the finding of characteristic lesions and by blood studies.

### Rous-Sarcoma Virus

**Disease Produced.** Rous sarcoma.

**Hosts Affected.** Chicken. Experimentally the pheasant, turkey, quail, and duck can be infected. Possibly mammals.

**History and Distribution.** The original virus was described by Rous in 1911 from an adult hen. Since its discovery this virus has been studied in considerable detail. Although the disease is of no economical importance as far as poultry are concerned, the extensive research which has been done on the virus has been a valuable contribution to the study of viruses and to the fundamental knowledge of certain neoplasms. The virus occurs in the United States, and similar strains have been isolated in England and Japan.

**Properties of the Virus.** Rous-sarcoma virus contains RNA and is reported as being 60 mμ to 100 mμ in size. It will pass Berkefeld V filters. Heating the virus to 54°C. for 30 minutes will inactivate it. At 37°C. the virus becomes inactive in about 48 hours. Spontaneous degradation occurs at refrigerator temperatures, due to oxidation; therefore, the addition of reducing substances has a preserving effect upon the virus.

The Rous virus is morphologically indistinguishable from the leucosis viruses. It is closely related antigenically to the leucosis group and therefore should be considered as a member of that group of agents.

**Cultivation.** Rous-sarcoma virus can be cultivated on the chorioallantoic membrane of the chicken embryo, with the production of focal lesions. Cell cultures derived from chicken embryos support growth of the virus. Infected cells of the culture are transformed to malignant types which no longer grow in monolayers. Foci of transformed cells can be counted for purposes of assay. Hanafusa *et al.* have described a "helper" or Rous-associated virus which is required for the production and release of mature Rous virus. The Rous-associated virus is apparently an avian leucosis virus.

**Transmission.** The injection of tissue cells or a filtrate of the infected tissue will transmit the disease.

**Characteristics of the Disease.** Rous-sarcoma virus induces tumor formation of connective tissue which metastasizes readily to various organs of the body. Death may result in 2 to 5 weeks following inoculation of the virus. All birds which are artificially exposed do not develop tumors, and it has been shown that resistance to infection is sometimes attributable to genetic factors.

**Pathological Changes.** The parent cell of the sarcoma is the normal histiocyte. At the point of infection a nodule is formed which enlarges and becomes necrotic or cystic and often contains a brownish sanguinous fluid mixed with mucoid exudate. Metastatic lesions occur in the heart, liver, and lungs, and the infected bird becomes emaciated, weak, and depressed, and finally dies.

**Immunity.** Rous-sarcoma virus is antigenic, and antibodies have been demonstrated which will neutralize the virus. Antigenic relationships have been shown between Rous-sarcoma virus and other sarcoma viruses such as the Fujinami, Mill Hill 1 and 2 strains which have been isolated from fowl tumors.

**Diagnosis.** A diagnosis of transmissible tumor of fowl depends upon reproduction of the condition by the injection of cell-free filtrates of infected tissue.

## Lymphocytic Choriomeningitis Virus

**Disease Produced.** Lymphocytic choriomeningitis.

**Hosts Affected.** Mouse and man. Experimentally guinea pig, rat, monkey, and hamster. Inapparent infection results from inoculation of the dog and ferret. Insusceptible hosts include the pig, chicken, rabbit, canary, parakeet, and the vole.

**History and Distribution.** Armstrong and Lillie, in 1934, while working with material from a fatal human case of St. Louis encephalitis discovered a new virus. This virus, which was found in the 5th monkey passage, had previously been thought to be the St. Louis virus, since the original case was clinically typical and occurred during the 1933 epidemic of St. Louis encephalitis. A virus was isolated in 1935 from mice by Traub and from a case of meningitis in man by Rivers and Scott and shown to be identical with that isolated by Armstrong and Lillie. Numerous isolations of the virus have been made from laboratory and wild mice. One isolation from a cow's brain is reported by Alice and McNutt. The virus is widely distributed. It has been isolated from many parts of the United States, also from England, France, Japan, and North Africa.

**Properties of the Virus.** The elementary bodies of lymphocytic choriomeningitis (LCM) virus are calculated to be between 40 m$\mu$ and 60 m$\mu$ in size. They will pass Berkefeld V, N, W, Chamberland $L_1$, $L_2$, $L_3$, and Seitz filters. It is probably an RNA type virus.

The virus is inactivated by exposure to 55°C. for 20 minutes, also by ultraviolet light, and by ether.

LCM virus is preserved in 50 per cent glycerin for 7 months and in the frozen state for 1 year.

**Cultivation.** Lymphocytic choriomeningitis virus can be grown in tissue cultures which employ either mouse or chicken embryo tissues in Tyrode's solution. It can also be grown on the chorioallantoic membrane. The virus may kill the embryo in 8 to 9 days but without the formation of pocks or specific lesions.

**Transmission.** It has been suggested that the mouse is the primary host for the virus of lymphocytic choriomeningitis and is thought to be the usual source of the virus. LCM virus has been isolated from house mice trapped in homes where human infection has been diagnosed. The virus escapes from the infected mouse in the nasal secretions, semen, urine, and feces. It is believed that these infected materials, especially urine, become dried and that they are carried into the air and inhaled by man or enter the eye. *In utero* infection of mice has been shown to occur. The virus can also be transmitted by vectors such as lice, bedbugs, ticks, and possibly mosquitoes, since the virus circulates in the blood for a time after an animal becomes infected. Transovarial transmission of the virus from one tick to another has been reported.

The virus has also been found as a contaminant in canine distemper virus, which was passed in dogs and ferrets, and from tissue cultures of rabies virus which employed mouse brain or monkey serum.

**Characteristics of the Disease.** Natural disease in mice is usually inapparent with death losses not exceeding 2 per cent. Experimental infection is variable depending on the route of inoculation. Intracerebral inoculation of mice at birth usually results in a "tolerant persistent infection." A viremia persists for many weeks or often for the lifetime of the mouse. No symptoms are exhibited. Older mice injected intracerebrally often show high mortality rates. Intraperitoneal injection of the virus produces a lower mortality rate and often infection is inapparent. Growth retardation or stunting is a frequent result of nonfatal infection. No antibody response occurs in the tolerant infections of infant mice but complement-fixing and neutralizing antibodies are produced in older mice which survive.

Symptoms of infection in mice are emaciation, dullness, tremors, convulsions, and death.

Autoimmune mechanisms of disease are operative in lymphocytic choriomeningitis infection, according to Hochin.

In man, there are usually prodromal symptoms such as sore throat, tonsilitis, bronchitis, and cough, which simulate influenza. These symptoms are followed by meningeal symptoms of headache, vomiting, and neck rigidity. Recovery usually occurs in a few weeks. In some cases there are recurrent attacks. Neutralizing antibodies for the virus of lymphocytic choriomeningitis have been demonstrated in the blood of about 12 per cent of normal people in the United States, indicating widespread subclinical infection.

**Pathological Changes.** The outstanding pathological changes are observed in the meninges and choroid plexuses which show lymphocytic infiltration. The brain may show perivascular cuffing and degeneration of nerve cells.

Naturally infected mice often show mild leucocytic infiltrations of the meninges and focal liver necrosis.

**Immunity.** Mice which have recovered from an attack of lymphocytic choriomeningitis are usually refractory to a second inoculation. Complement-fixing and neutralizing antibodies are formed in response to the virus. Artificial immunity can be produced in mice with live virus, but immunity is less durable in guinea pigs which receive formolized virus.

**Diagnosis.** The diagnosis of lymphocytic choriomeningitis infection depends upon isolation and identification of the virus in susceptible mice or guinea pigs. It is very important to determine the absence of latent infection in any mouse stock used for diagnostic purposes. Intracerebral inoculation of ordinary nutrient broth into mice with latent choriomeningitis will give rise to meningeal symptoms and lesions. The possibilities of the presence of this virus in laboratory mice stocks must be considered when any intracerebral inoculations are to be made.

### Duck Hepatitis Virus

**Disease Produced.** Hepatitis.

**Host Affected.** Ducks.

**History and Distribution.** Viral hepatitis of ducks was first reported in New York by Levine and Fabricant in 1950. Reports of the occurrence of the disease from many other countries indicate its worldwide distribution.

**Properties of the Virus.** Some properties of the virus are known. It is reported to be 20 mμ to 40 mμ in size, but its structure is not determined. It is apparently an RNA type virus. Hansen *et al.* report the virus is comparatively stable. It survives storage at —20°C. for 7 years, 4 weeks at 25°C., and 7 days at 37°C.

**Cultivation.** The virus can readily be grown in chicken or duck embryos in which it produces stunting and edema as well as lethal effects. Cell cultures of chicken embryos are suitable for propagation of the virus but no cytopathic effects are observed. Duck embryo kidney cell cultures infected with the virus show degenerative changes and finally necrosis of the cells occurs. Interferon can be demonstrated from cell culture fluids. No hemagglutinins have been demonstrated in virus preparations.

**Transmission.** The oral route is presumed to be the portal of entry of duck hepatitis virus. Injection of the virus reproduces the disease. Isolation of the virus from yolk and from dead embryos taken from the incubator suggests egg transmission (Vindel and Aycardi, 1962).

**Characteristics of the Disease.** Duck hepatitis is an acute disease of ducklings 3 days to 3 weeks old. It is highly fatal in those birds which become affected.

**Pathological Changes.** The gross lesions observed are found chiefly in the liver. Hemorrhage edema and necrosis are most often seen.

**Immunity.** Live modified vaccines have been used to prevent the disease. The modification of the virus is accomplished by repeated passage in chicken embryos. Ducklings hatched from eggs laid by immune birds are passively resistant to infection. Immune serum has been used successfully in controlling outbreaks.

**Diagnosis.** Isolation and identification of the hepatitis virus by either chicken or duck embryo inoculation would constitute an accurate diagnosis.

### Mucosal Disease—Bovine Virus Diarrhea Complex

Similar clinical and pathological syndromes described by various investigators as either mucosal disease or bovine virus diarrhea are undoubtedly related etiologically but may not be identical as some suggest. Olafson *et al.* (1946) were the first to call attention to a filterable agent as a cause of enteric infection in cattle. However, the agent which was assumed to be a virus, was never isolated or characterized. Ramsey and Chivers, in 1953, described a disease syndrome which was designated as mucosal disease because of the marked lesions noted in various mucous membranes. Pritchard *et al.* (1956) investigated outbreaks of diarrhea among cattle of Indiana. Gillespie *et al.* were the first to isolate a cytopathogenic virus from cases of enteritis in cattle. Since these early accounts, mucosal disease and bovine virus diarrhea have been reported throughout the world.

Numerous viral agents have been isolated from cattle which exhibit the clinical signs and lesions of mucosal disease or virus diarrhea. However, no single agent isolated has been found which is capable of reproducing both syndromes. Comparison of detailed characteristics of the various isolates show considerable variation (Table 52.1). While the various isolates from the mucosal disease-virus diarrhea syndrome vary in many respects, they are reported to be related antigenically to each other

TABLE 52.1

COMPARISON OF SOME VIRUSES ISOLATED FROM MUCOSAL DISEASE AND VIRUS DIARRHEA

| Author | Strain Studied | Size (mμ) | Symmetry | Nucleic Acid | Sensitivity to Lipid Solvent |
|---|---|---|---|---|---|
| Ditchfield and Doane | C24V and MAC | 150–250 | helical | RNA | + |
| Dutta *et al.* | BVDMJ | 75–85 | helical | RNA | |
| Hermonsson and Dinter | C24V | 40 | helical | | + |
| Huck | M6 | 30 | | | − |

and to hog cholera virus. Darbyshire and others have noted that soluble antigens of hog cholera and those obtained from mucosal disease-virus diarrhea are closely related. The use of bovine virus diarrhea virus for vaccination of swine against hog cholera has been proposed by Sheffy *et al.* The viruses can be isolated in bovine testicular or kidney cell cultures. Some strains are cytopathogenic, others are not. Noncytopathogenic strains can be assayed by virus interference methods.

The clinical and pathological characteristics of acute mucosal disease are very similar to rinderpest; however, no relationship between the etiological agents has been shown.

Mucous membranes of the alimentary tract show erosion of epithelium as an important lesion. Infected animals show fever, anorexia, salivation, lameness, corneal opacity and diarrhea. There is leucopenia and all lymphoid tissues show destructive changes. Mortality is high in animals showing typical mucosal disease, while it is relatively low in animals with virus diarrhea syndrome. A live modified vaccine is used for immunization of cattle against virus diarrhea.

## Hemagglutinating Encephalomyelitis Virus of Swine

A viral agent responsible for outbreaks of encephalomyelitis in neonatal pigs has been described by Canadian investigators. The virus has not been characterized except that it produces hemagglutinin for chicken erythrocytes. It can be grown in pig kidney cell cultures in which it produces cytopathic effects. No growth occurs in cell cultures of bovine or lamb kidney. While pigs of any age can be infected, only those less than 2 weeks of age show signs of encephalomyelitis.

The fact that 30 per cent of the sera obtained from swine at slaughter in the Ontario swine-raising regions contain antibodies for the virus indicates the virus is apparently widespread.

## Scrapie Virus

A virus disease of sheep known in Europe since the early 1700's has been called scrapie because the outstanding symptom is that of scratching or scraping the skin. The virus is neurotropic and produces characteristic degenerative changes in the central nervous system, causing incoordination, paralysis, and death of the infected animal.

The disease was reported in North America for the first time by Schofield of Ontario, Canada, in 1939. It was reported in Michigan in 1947 and in California in 1952. Several other states have reported the occurrence of scrapie, but the number of sheep that have been infected has been small.

The etiological agent of scrapie is believed to be a virus with somewhat unusual properties. That the disease is transmissible. there now seems to be no doubt; however, this point has long been debated.

The agent is very small, probably smaller than any other infectious agent: 7 mμ to 11 mμ has been suggested. It is remarkably resistant. It resists exposure to 75°C. for one hour with very little loss of infectivity and is not completely inactivated at 100°C. for one hour. Brain material containing the agent placed in 10 to 12 per cent formalin still contains viable particles after 4 to 28 months. The agent is also ether resistant. Transmission of scrapie is possible by feeding and by inoculation intracerebrally or intraperitoneally. The agent could not be demonstrated in saliva, milk, urine, or feces (Pattison, 1964). Congenital transmission is considered most likely under natural conditions. The incubation period ranges from 18 months to 2 years.

Adult sheep are the chief hosts, but goats are susceptible. Experimentally mice, rats, and hamsters can be infected.

All of the symptoms exhibited by the infected animal are referable to damage to the nervous system. The affected sheep will rub the skin on various objects such as fences and will show the attitude of the "scratch reflex" when rubbed. They may become excitable, with the head carried higher than normal. Convulsions may occur in some animals. The disease usually lasts for several weeks or as long as 6 months, becoming progressively more severe until death ensues.

Histopathological examination of the central nervous system will show marked vacuolation of the neuron cells which is diagnostic of the disease. More of the cells of the medulla show this change than those from other parts of the brain. Apparently no immunity results from having the disease, since there are no recoveries.

### Aleutian Disease Virus

This is a disease of mink, designated Aleutian disease because of its greater occurrence in certain fur color mutants known as Aleutians. The disease is characterized as a plasmacytosis with resulting hypergammaglobulinemia. The viral agent is not well characterized, but it can be grown in cell cultures of either mink testis or kidney. Growth in cell cultures results in a visible destructive effect in infected cells. The virus is small since it passes a 50 mμ filter but is retained by a filter having an A.P.O. of 10 mμ.

Transmission can be accomplished by injection of emulsions of infected tissues or cell culture fluids containing the virus. Aerosols and virus-contaminated food will also infect susceptible mink. However, there are factors other than mere exposure to the virus which influence the attack rate in field outbreaks (Gorham *et al.*, 1964).

Attempts to immunize mink with a formolized tissue vaccine have failed. An iodine agglutination test which reveals hypergammaglobulinemia has been found useful in diagnosis of Aleutian disease.

### Epizootic Hemorrhagic Disease Virus

A virus disease of deer has been reported from various areas of the United States. In southern parts a disease known as "black tongue" has been known for many years and is probably the same as that described by Shope in 1960. Fay *et al.* reported the occurrence of a similar if not identical disease in Michigan in 1956. Pirtle and Layton in 1961 were able to cultivate the virus in cell cultures of deer spleen and determined that the virus was a small, spherical one, measuring about 20 mμ to 40 mμ in size.

Mettler *et al.* report that the New Jersey type of the virus can be grown in HeLa cells and is transmissible to mice by intracerebral inoculation. They suggest that because of its sensitivity to sodium desoxycholate the virus may belong to the arbovirus group.

### Visna and Maedi Viruses

Two chronic diseases of sheep of virus etiology have been described from Iceland: visna virus, which produces a chronic degenerative disease of the central nervous system; and maedi virus, isolated from chronic progressive pneumonia. These two conditions were so different in their clinical and pathological manifestations that the viruses were at first not suspected of being related. Comparison of the viruses finds them very similar in all physical and chemical characters and related antigenically.

Electron micrographs of the visna virus show it to be spherical and to measure 90 mμ to 100 mμ in size. Surface projections resembling those of the myxoviruses are observed. Internal structure shows concentrically arranged components but they may not be helical.

Both viruses are ether sensitive and are inhibited by BUDR and actinomycin D indicating that DNA is required in the synthesis of their nucleic acids. The nucleic acid type of the viruses has not been determined.

Erythrocytes from a variety of species of animals have been employed for the detection of hemagglutinin activity of the viruses, but none has been demonstrated.

Visna and maedi viruses have been cultivated in cell cultures of sheep choroid plexus. The viruses are slow to develop in cultures, but visible changes include giant cell formation and later cell destruction. The viruses mature at the cell membrane and apparently acquire a lipid-containing envelope as they leave the cell.

### Transmissible Gastroenteritis Virus

A disease of neonatal pigs characterized by diarrhea, vomition, dehydration, and high mortality was described in 1946 by Doyle and Hutchings. The virus has been difficult to cultivate and study; consequently, it has not been as well characterized as many animal viruses. According to Ristic *et al.* it is hexagonal in outline and measures 98 mμ in diameter; 165 mμ including its envelope. It is ether sensitive and acid resistant. These characteristics suggest that the virus belongs to the herpesvirus group. The virus can be cultivated in cell cultures of swine or hamster kidney. A cytopathic effect is produced.

Animals other than swine do not show clinical signs following exposure to the virus, but dogs and foxes harbor the virus for several days.

Greatest losses are among newborn pigs, but older swine are susceptible and often show symptoms when exposed. The disease is not often fatal in older swine.

Recovery from transmissible gastroenteritis confers immunity. Colostrum or serum from immune sows is protective when ingested, but serum fails to protect if given parenterally.

An experimental vaccine prepared from inactivated virus propagated in cell cultures has been shown to produce some resistance to infection.

## REFERENCES

### Hog Cholera Virus

Aiken, J. M., *et al.* Rapid Diagnosis of Hog Cholera: A Tissue-Impression Fluorescent-Antibody Technique. Jour. Amer. Vet. Med. Assn. 144:1395, 1964.

Baker, J. A., and Sheffy, B. E. A Persistent Hog Cholera Viremia in Young Pigs. Proc. Soc. Exp. Biol. Med. 105:675, 1960.

Birch, R. R. Hog Cholera. Macmillan Co., New York, 1922.

Carbrey, E. A., *et al.* Transmission of Hog Cholera by Pregnant Sows. Jour. Amer. Vet. Med. Assn. 149:23, 1966.

Darbyshire, J. H. A Serological Relationship Between Swine Fever and Mucosal Disease of Cattle. Vet. Rec. 72:331, 1960.

De Schweinitz, E. A., and Dorset, M. A Form of Hog Cholera Not Caused by the Hog-Cholera Bacillus. USDA Circ. 41 (BAI), 1903.

———, and ———. New Facts Concerning the Biology of Hog Cholera. USDA Circ. 72 (BAI), 1905.

Dorset, M., *et al.* The Etiology of Hog Cholera. USDA Bull. 72 (BAI), 1905.

———, *et al.* Further Experiments Concerning the Production of Immunity From Hog Cholera. USDA Bull. 102 (BAI), 1908.

Dunne, H. W. Hog Cholera. *In* Diseases of Swine. Iowa State Univ. Press, Ames, 1964.

Gillespie, J. H., *et al.* Propagation of Hog Cholera Virus in Tissue Culture. Proc. Exp. Biol. Med. 105:679, 1960.

Jacotot, H. Sur la Transmissibilité de la Peste Porcine à Diverses Espéces Animales. Ann. Inst. Past. 62:516, 1939.

Kumagai, T., *et al.* A New *in Vitro* Method (END) for Detection and Measurement of Hog Cholera Virus and Its Antibody by Means of Effect of HC Virus on Newcastle Disease Virus in Swine Tissue Cultures. I. Establishment of Standard Procedure. Jour. Immunol. 87:245, 1961.

MENGLING, W. L. Evaluation of the Fluorescent Antibody Technique for the Diagnosis of Hog Cholera. Ph.D. Thesis. Iowa State Univ. Library, 1966.

———, *et al*. Identification of Hog Cholera Viral Antigen by Immunofluorescence. Application as a Diagnostic and Assay Method. Canad. Jour. Comp. Med. Vet. Sci. 27:249, 1963.

OSE, E. E., *et al*. Characterization of a New Tissue Culture Hog Cholera Vaccine. Vet. Med. Small An. Clin. 59:606, 1964.

SAUTTER, J. H., *et al*. The Experimental Production of Malformations and Other Abnormalities in Fetal Pigs by Means of Attenuated Hog Cholera Virus. Proc. 90th Ann. Meet. Amer. Vet. Med. Assn., p. 146, 1953.

TORREY, J. P., and PRATHER, J. K. Heat Inactivation of Hog Cholera Virus. I. Studies With Defibrinated Blood and Serum. Proc. 67th Ann. Meet. U.S. Livestock Sanit. Assn., p. 414, 1963.

## African Swine Fever Virus

ANONYMOUS. Summary of the Proceedings of the Conference on African Swine Fever. Bull. Off. Int. Epiz. 55:223, 1961.

BOTIJA, C. S. Reservorios del virus de la Peste Porcina Africana. Bull. Off. Int. Epiz. 60:895, 1963.

———, Modification del virus de la Peste Porcina Africana en cultivos celulares. Bull. Off. Int. Epiz. 60:901, 1963.

BREEZE, S. S., JR., and DEBOER, C. J. Electron Microscope Observations of African Swine Fever Virus in Tissue Culture Cells. Virol. 28:420, 1966.

LARENAUDIE, B., *et al*. Identification en France Métropolitaine de la Peste Porcine Africaine ou Maladié de Montgomery. Bull. Acad. Vet. Fr. 37:257, 1964.

MALMQUIST, W. A. Serologic and Immunologic Studies With African Swine Fever Virus. Amer. Jour. Vet. Res. 24:450–59, 1963.

———, and HAY, D. Hemadsorption and Cytopathic Effect Produced by African Swine Fever Virus in Swine Bone Marrow and Buffy Coat Cultures. Amer. Jour. Vet. Res. 21:104, 1960.

MONTGOMERY, R. E. On a Form of Swine Fever Occurring in British East Africa (Kenya Colony). Jour. Comp. Path. Therap. 34:159, 1921.

RIBEIRO, J. M., *et al*. Vaccination Contre la Peste Porcine Africaine. Bull. Off. Int. Epiz. 60:921, 1963.

SCOTT, G. R. Symposium: The Smallest Stowaways. I. African Swine Fever. Vet. Rec. 77:1421, 1965.

## Rabies Virus

ABELSETH, M. K. An Attenuated Rabies Vaccine for Domestic Animals Produced in Tissue Culture. Canad. Vet. Jour. 5:279, 1964.

———. Propagation of Rabies Virus in Pig Kidney Cell Culture. Canad. Vet. Jour. 5:84, 1964.

ALMEIDA, J. D., *et al*. Electron Microscope Observations on Rabies Virus by Negative Staining. Virol. 18:147, 1962.

BEAUREGARD, M., *et al*. The Use of Fluorescent Antibody Staining in the Diagnosis of Rabies. Canad. Jour. Comp. Med. 29:141, 1965.

CABASSO, V. J., *et al*. Tissue-Culture Rabies Vaccine (Flury LEP) in Dogs. Amer. Jour. Vet. Res. 26:24, 1965.

CONSTANTINE, D. G. Rabies Transmission by the Non-Bite Route. Pub. Health Rept., Wash., 77:287, 1962.

DAVIES, M. C., *et al*. The Electron Microscopy of Rabies Virus in Cultures of Chicken Embryo Tissues. Virol. 21:642, 1963.

DEAN, D. J., *et al*. The Use of Mice for the Potency Testing of Modified Live-Virus Rabies Vaccine. Amer. Jour. Vet. Res. 24:614, 1963.

———, *et al*. Studies on the Local Treatment of Rabies-Infected Wounds. World Health Org. Bull. 28:477, 1963.

———, *et al*. Pathogenesis of Rabies. World Health Org. Bull. 29:803, 1963.

———, *et al*. Studies on the Low Egg Passage Flury Strain of Modified Live Rabies Virus Produced in Embryonating Chicken Eggs and Tissue Culture. Amer. Jour. Vet. Res. 25:756, 1964.

FERNANDES, M. V., *et al*. Mechanism of the Cytopathic Effect of Rabies Virus in Tissue Culture. Virol. 21:128, 1963.

HABEL, K. Evaluation of a Mouse Test for the Standardization of the Immunizing Power of Anti-Rabies Vaccine. Pub. Health Rept., Wash., 55:1473, 1940.

JOHNSON, H. N. Rabies Virus. *In* Viral and Rickettsial Infections of Man. Horsfall, F. L., and Tamm, I. (eds.) J. B. Lippincott Co., Philadelphia, 1965.

KISSLING, R. E. Growth of Rabies Virus in Non-Nervous Tissue Culture. Proc. Soc. Exp. Biol. Med. 98:2231, 1958.

———, and REESE, D. R. Antirabies Vaccine of Tissue Culture Origin. Jour. Immunol. 91:362, 1963.

KOPROWSKI, H., and COX, H. R. Studies on Chick Embryo Adapted Rabies Virus. I. Culture Characteristics and Pathogenicity. Jour. Immunol. 60:533, 1948.

Laboratory Techniques in Rabies. World Health Org., Monograph Ser. 23, Geneva, 1954.

MCQUEEN, J. L., *et al.* Rabies Diagnosed by Fluorescent Antibody. I. Its Evaluation in a Public Health Labora tory. Amer. Jour. Pub. Health. 50:1743, 1960.

NEGRI, A. Beitrag zum Studium der Aetiologie der Tollwut. Zeit. für Hyg. Infections Krankh., 43:507, 1903.

PARKER, R. L., and WILSNACK, R. E. Pathogenesis of Skunk Rabies: Quantitation in Skunks and Foxes. Amer. Jour. Vet. Res. 27:33, 1966.

PASTEUR, L. Lettre de M. Pasteur sur la Rage. Ann. Inst. Past. 1:1, 1887.

PECK, F. B., JR., *et al.* New Antirabies Vaccine for Human Use. Clinical and Laboratory Results Using Rabies Vaccine Made From Embryonated Duck Eggs. Jour. Lab. Clin. Med. 45:679, 1955.

PINTERIC, L., and FENJI, D. The Visualization of Rabies Virus in Mouse Brain. Virol. 20:208, 1963.

REMLINGER, P. Le Passage du Virus Rabique à Travers les Filtres. Ann. Inst. Past. 17:834, 1903.

SOAVE, O. A. Transmission of Rabies to Mice by Ingestion of Infected Tissue. Amer. Jour. Vet. Res. 27:44, 1966.

SULKIN, S. E., *et al.* Studies on the Pathogenesis of Rabies in Insectivorous Bats. I. Role of Brown Adipose Tissue Jour. Exp. Med. 110:369, 1959.

VAN ROOYEN, C. F., and RHODES, A. J. Virus Diseases of Man. Thomas Nelson and Sons, New York, 1948.

VAUGHN, J. B., JR., *et al.* Excretion of Street Rabies Virus in the Saliva. Jour. Amer. Med. Assn. 193:363–68, 1965.

VEERARAGHAVAN, N., and SUBRAMANYAN, T. P. The Value of Duck-Embryo Vaccine and High-Egg-Passage Flury Vaccine in Experimental Rabies Infection in Guinea Pigs. World Health Org. Bull. 29:323, 1963.

## Vesicular-Stomatitis Virus

COTTON, W. E. The Causal Agent of Vesicular Stomatitis Proved To Be a Filter-Passing Virus. Jour. Amer. Vet. Med. Assn. 70:168, 1926.

EICHHORN, E. A., and MANTHEI, C. A. Propagation of the Virus of Vesicular Stomatitis in the Chick Embryo. Jour. Amer. Vet. Med. Assn. 94:608, 1939.

FERRIS, D. H., *et al.* Experimental Transmission of Vesicular Stomatitis Virus by Diptera. Jour. Inf. Dis. 96:184, 1955.

FRANK, A. H., *et al.* Vesicular Stomatitis. Amer. Jour. Vet. Res. 6:28, 1945.

HANSON, R. P. The Natural History of Vesicular Stomatitis. Bact. Rev. 16:179, 1952.

HOWATSON, A. F., and WHITMORE, G. F. The Development and Structure of Vesicular Stomatitis Virus. Virol. 16:466, 1962.

HUTCHEON, D. Aphtha or Vesicular Stomatitis of Horse. Vet. Jour. 47:54, 1898.

JONKERS, A. H., *et al.* Cocal Virus Epizootiology in Bush Forest and the Nariva Swamp, Trinidad. Amer. Jour. Vet. Res. 26:758, 1965.

LAUERMAN, L. H., JR., and HANSON, R. P. Field Trial of Live Virus Vaccination Procedure for Prevention of Vesicular Stomatitis in Dairy Cattle. II. Second Year Evaluation in Panama. III. Evaluation of Emergency Vaccination in Georgia. Proc. 67th Ann. Meet. U.S. Livestock Sanit. Assn., New Mexico, 1963, pp. 473–82 483–90.

MCCOMBS, R. M., *et al.* Biophysical Studies of Vesicular Stomatitis Virus. Jour. Bact. 91:803, 1966.

MOHLER, J. R. Vesicular Stomatitis of Horses and Cattle. Jour. Amer. Vet. Med. Assn. 52:410, 1918.

PYL, G. Vergleichende Untersuchungen uber den Realkalisierungseffekt bei Virusarten. Hoppe-Seyler's. Zeit. f. Physiol. Chemie. 226:18, 1934.

RECZKO, E. Electron Microscopy of the Virus of Vesicular Stomatitis. Arch. ges. Virusforsch. 10:588, 1961.

SHAHAN, M. S. Effect of Temperature, Phenol, and Crystal Violet on Vesicular Stomatitis Virus. Amer. Jour. Vet. Res. 7:27, 1946.

———, *et al.* Studies of Vesicular Stomatitis With Special Reference to a Virus of Swine Origin. Jour. Amer. Vet. Med. Assn. 108:5, 1946.

## Equine Viral Arteritis

DOLL, E. R., *et al.* Isolation of a Filterable Agent Causing Arteritis of Horses and Abortion by Mares. Its Differentiation From the Equine Abortion (Influenza) Virus. Cornell Vet. 47:3, 1957.

———, *et al.* An Outbreak of Abortion Caused by the Equine Arteritis Virus. Cornell Vet. 47:69, 1957.

JONES, T. C., *et al.* The Lesions of Equine Viral Arteritis. Cornell Vet. 47:52, 1957.

MCCOLLUM, W. H., *et al.* The Recovery of Virus From Horses With Experimental Cases of Equine Arteritis Using Monolayer Cell Cultures of Equine Kidney. Amer. Jour. Vet. Res. 23:465, 1962.

———, *et al.* Isolation and Propagation of Equine Arteritis Virus in Monolayer Cells of Rabbit Kidney. Cornell Vet. 52:452, 1962.

WILSON, J. C., *et al.* Propagation of Equine Arteritis Virus Previously Adapted to Cell Cultures of Equine Kidney in Monolayer Cultures of Hamster Kidney. Cornell Vet. 52:200, 1962.

## Infectious Bronchitis Virus

BEACH, J. R. Infectious Bronchitis of Fowls. Jour. Amer. Vet. Med. Assn. 68:570, 1926.

BERRY, D. M., *et al.* The Structure of Infectious Bronchitis Virus. Virol. 23:403–7, 1964.

CUNNINGHAM, C. H. Recent Studies on the Virus of Infectious Bronchitis. Amer. Jour. Vet. Res. 21:498, 1960

HOFSTAD, M. S. Antigenic and Immunological Studies on Several Isolates of Avian Infectious Bronchitis Virus. Avian Dis. 5:102, 1961.

———. Infectious Bronchitis. *In* Diseases of Poultry. Biester, H. E., and Schwarte, L. H. (eds.) Iowa State Univ. Press, Ames, 1965.

SCHALK, A. F., and HAWN, M. C. An Apparently New Respiratory Disease of Baby Chicks. Jour. Amer. Vet. Med. Assn. 78:413, 1931.

## Borna-Disease Virus

ELFORD, W. J., and GALLOWAY, I. A. Filtration of the Virus of Borna Disease Through Graded Collodion Membranes. Brit. Jour. Exp. Path. 14:196,1933.

NITZSCHKE, E. Experimental Borna Infection in Rats. Zentbl. Vet. Med. 10B:470, 1963.

ROTT, R., and NITZSCHKE, E. Untersuchungen uber die Züchtung des virus der Bornaschen Krankheit im bebrütenen. Huhnerer' unter verschiedenen Bedingungen. Zentbl. Vet. Med. 5:629, 1958.

VON SPROCKHOFF, H. Experimentelle Befunde bei der Bornaschen Krankheit. Z. Immun. forsch. 115:161, 1958

ZWICK, W., and SEIFRIED, O. Untersuchungen uber die in Hessen gehauft auftretende Seuchen hafte Gehirn-und Ruckenmarksentzundung Bornasche Krankheit bei Pferden. Berl. tierarztl. Wschr. 40:465, 1924.

## Panleucopenia Virus

BITTLE, J. L., *et al.* Comparative Study of Feline Cytopathogenic Viruses and Feline Panleucopenia Virus. Amer. Jour. Vet. Res. 22:374, 1961.

BOUILLANT, A., and HANSON, R. P. Epizootiology of Mink Enteritis. III. Carrier State in Mink. Canad. Jour. Comp. Med. Vet. Sci. 29:183, 1965.

HAMMON, W. D., and ENDERS, J. F. A Virus Disease of Cats, Principally Characterized by Aleucocytosis Enteric Lesions and the Presence of Intranuclear Inclusion Bodies. Jour. Exp. Med. 69:327, 1939.

JOHNSON, R. H. Feline Panleucopenia. Res. Vet. Sci. 6:466, 1965.

KIRKUTH, W., *et al.*Infektiose Aleukozytose der Katzen. Zentralbl. f. Bakt. Abt. I. Orig. 146:1, 1940.

LAWRENCE, J. S., and SYVERTON, J. T. Spontaneous Agranulocytosis in the Cat. Proc. Soc. Exp. Biol. Med. 38:914, 1938.

LEASURE, E. E., *et al.* Feline Infectious Enteritis. No. Amer. Vet. 15, No. 7, p. 30.

SYVERTON, J. T., *et al.* The Virus of Infectious Feline Agranulocytosis. Jour. Exp. Med. 77:41, 57, 1943.

WILLS, C. G. Notes on Infectious Enteritis of Mink and Its Relationship to Feline Enteritis. Canad. Jour. Comp. Med. 16:419, 1952.

## Ulcerative Dermatosis Virus

FILMER, J. F. Ovine Posthitis and Balano-Posthitis. Some notes on field investigations. Austral. Vet. Jour. 14:47, 1938.

MELVIN, A. D., and MOHLER, J. R. Lip and Leg Ulceration of Sheep. USDA Bur. An. Ind. Circ. 160, 1910.

TRUEBLOOD, M. S., and CHOW, T. L. Characterization of the Agents of Ulcerative Dermatosis and Contagious Ecthyma. Amer. Jour. Vet. Res. 24:47, 1963.

———, *et al.* An Immunologic Study of Ulcerative Dermatosis and Contagious Ecthyma. Amer. Jour. Vet. Res. 24:42, 1963.

TUNICLIFF, E. A. Ulcerative Dermatosis of Sheep. Amer. Jour. Vet. Res. 10:240, 1949.

———, and MATISHECK, P. H. A Filterable Virus Demonstrated To Be the Infective Agent in Ovine Balano-Posthitis. Science 94:283, 1941.

## Equine Infectious Anemia Virus

CARRÉ, H. J., and VALLEE, H. P. Sur la Nature Infectieuse de l'anemic du Cheval. Comp. rend. Acad. Sci. 139:331, 1904.

ISHII, S. Equine Infectious Anemia or Swamp Fever. Adv. Vet. Sci. 8:263, 1963.

JOHNSON, A. W. Equine Infectious Anemia: An Annotation. Vet. Bull. 36:465, 1966.
PETERS, J. T. Equine Infectious Anemia Transmitted to Man. Ann. Int. Med. 23:271, 1945.
STEIN, C. D. Infectious Anemia or Swamp Fever in Horses. Jour. Amer. Vet. Med. Assn. 87:312, 1935.
———. The History and Distribution of Equine Infectious Anemia in the United States. Vet. Med. 36:410, 1941.
———, and MOTT, L. O. Studies on Congenital Transmission of Equine Infectious Anemia. Vet. Med. 37:370, 1942.
———, and ———. Susceptibility of Animals Other Than Solipeds to Infectious Anemia. Vet. Med. 39:408 1944.
———, and ———. Equine Infectious Anemia in the United States With Special Reference to the Recent Outbreak in New England. Proc. U.S. Livestock Sanit. Assn. 51:37, 1947.
———, and OSTEEN, O. L. Studies on Immunization in Equine Infectious Anemia. Amer. Jour. Vet. Res. 2:344, 1941.
———, *et al.* Studies on the Possible Role of Ectoparasites in the Transmission of Infectious Anemia. Jour. Amer. Vet. Med. Assn. 95:536, 1939.
———, *et al.* Transmission of Equine Infectious Anemia by the Stablefly, *Stomoxys Calcitrans*, the Horsefly, *Tabanus Sulcifrons* (Macquart), and by Injection of Minute Amounts of Virus. Amer. Jour. Vet. Res. 3:183 1942.
———, *et al.* Experimental Transmission of Equine Infectious Anemia by Contact and Body Secretions and Excretions. Vet. Med. 39:46, 1944.
———, *et al.* Action of Chemical and Physical Agents on the Virus of Equine Infectious Anemia. Amer. Jour. Vet. Res. 5:291, 1944.

## Avian-Leucosis Virus

ANDREWES, C. H. Viruses of Vertebrates. Williams & Wilkins Co., Baltimore, 1964.
BEARD, J. W. Avian Virus Growths and Their Etiologic Agents. Adv. Cancer Res. 7:1–127, 1963.
BURMESTER, B. R. Review of the Avian Leucosis Complex. Paper No. 22. *In* Report of Scrapie Seminar. Agr. Res. Serv. USDA, 1964. ARS 91–53, 1966.
DMOCHOWSKI, L. Electron Microscope Studies of Avian Leucosis Tumors. *In* Diseases of Poultry. Biester, H. E., and Schwarte, L. H. (eds.). Iowa State Univ. Press, Ames, 1965.
ELLERMAN, V., and BANG, O. Experimentelle Leukamie bei Huhner. Zentralbl. f. Bakt. Abt. I. Orig. 46:4 595, 1908.
FURTH, J. Lymphomatosis, Myelomatosis and Endothelioma of Chickens Caused by a Filterable Agent. Jour. Exp. Med. 58:253, 1933.
JUNGHERR, E. L., and HUGHES, W. F. The Avian Leucosis Complex. Chapter 19. *In* Diseases of Poultry. Biester, H. E., and Schwarte, L. H. (eds.). Iowa State Univ. Press, Ames, 1965.
LEE, C. D., *et al.* Fowl Leukosis. Jour. Inf. Dis. 61:1, 1937.
RUBIN, H., *et al.* Tolerance and Immunity in Chickens After Congenital and Contact Infection With an Avian Leucosis Virus. Virol. 17:143, 1962.
STERN, G., and KIRSCHBAUM, A. On the Nature of the Agent Causing Leucosis in Fowls. Science 89:610, 1939.
STOKER, M. G. P. Studies on Avian Lymphoma Virus in Tissue Culture. Virol. 8:250, 1959.

## Rous-Sarcoma Virus

AMIES, C. R. The Particulate Nature of Avian Sarcoma Agents. Jour. Path. Bact. 44:141, 1937.
ANDREWES, C. H. The Immunological Relationships of Fowl Tumors With Different Histological Structure. Jour. Path. Bact. 34:91, 1931.
CLAUDE, A. Properties of the Causative Agent of a Chicken Tumor. Jour. Exp. Med. 66:59, 1937.
———, and MURPHY, J. B. Transmissable Tumors of Fowl. Physiol. Rev. 13:246, 1933.
HANAFUSA, H., *et al.* The Defectiveness of Rous Sarcoma Virus. Proc. Natl. Acad. Sci. 49:572, 1963.
KEOGH, E. V. Ectodermal Lesions Produced by the Virus of Rous Sarcoma. Brit. Jour. Exp. Path. 19:1, 1938.
ROUS, P. A Sarcoma of the Fowl Transmissible by an Agent Separable From the Tumor Cells. Jour. Exp. Med. 13:397, 1911.
RUBIN, H. A Virus in Chick Embryos Which Induces Resistance *in Vitro* to Infection With Rous Sarcoma Virus. Proc. Natl. Acad. Sci. 46:1105, 1960.
———, and VOGT, P. K. An Avian Leucosis Virus Associated With Stocks of Rous Sarcoma Virus. Virol. 17:184, 1962.

### Lymphocytic Choriomeningitis Virus

ALICE, F., and MCNUTT, S. H. A Study of Lymphocytic Choriomeningitis Virus. Amer. Jour. Vet. Res. 6:54, 1945.

ARMSTRONG, C., and LILLIE, R. D. Experimental Lymphocytic Choriomeningitis of Monkeys and Mice Produced by a Virus Encountered in Studies of the 1933 St. Louis Encephalitis Epidemic. Pub. Health. Repts. 49:1019, 1934.

———, and SWEET, L. K. Lymphocytic Choriomeningitis. A Report of Two Cases With Recovery of the Virus From Grey Mice Trapped in the Two Infected Households. Pub. Health Rept., Wash., 54:673, 1939.

HAAS, V. H. Some Relationships Between Lymphocytic Choriomeningitis Virus and Mice. Jour. Inf. Dis. 94:187, 1954.

HOCHIN, J. The Biology of Lymphocytic Choriomeningtitis Infection: Virus-Induced Immune Disease. Cold Spring Harbor Symp. on Quanat. Biol. 27:479, 1962.

———, and WEIGAND, H. Studies of Lymphocytic Choriomeningitis of Mice. I. Relationship Between Age at Inoculation and Outcome of Infection. Jour. Immunol. 86:392, 1961.

RIVERS, T. M., and SCOTT, T. F. M. Meningitis in Man Caused by a Filterable Virus. Science 81:439, 1935.

TRAUB, E. A Filterable Virus Recovered From White Mice. Science 81:298, 1935.

VAN ROOYEN, C. E., and RHOADES, A. J. Virus Diseases of Man. Thomas Nelson and Sons, New York, 1948.

VOLKERT, M., and LARSEN, J. H. Immunological Tolerance to Viruses. Prog. Med. Virol. 7:160, 1965.

### Duck Hepatitis Virus

FITZGERALD, J. E., *et al.* Cytopathic Effects of Duck Hepatitis Virus in Duck Embryo Kidney Cell Cultures. Proc. Soc. Exp. Biol. Med. 114:814, 1963.

HANSEN, L. E., and ALBERTS, J. O. Virus Hepatitis in Ducklings. Jour. Amer. Vet. Med. Assn. 128:37, 1956

———, *et al.* Properties of Duck Hepatitis Virus. Avian Dis. 8:196, 1964.

HWANG, J., and DOUGHERTY, E., JR. Serial Passage of Duck Hepatitis Virus in Chicken Embryos. Avian Dis. 6:435, 1962.

KAEBERLE, M. L., *et al.* Cultivation of Duck Hepatitis Virus in Tissue Culture. Proc. Soc. Exp. Biol. Med. 106:754, 1961.

LEVINE, P. P. Duck Virus Hepatitis. Chap. 30. *In* Diseases of Poultry. Biester, H. E., and Schwarte, L. H (eds.). Iowa State Univ. Press, Ames, 1965.

———, and FABRICANT, J. A Hitherto Undescribed Virus Disease of Ducks in North America. Cornell Vet. 40:71, 1950.

REUSS, U. Virusbiologische Untersuchungen bei der entenhepatitis. Zentbl. Vet. Med. 6:209, 1959.

VINDEL, J. A., and AYCARDI, J. Transmission Naturelle ab ovo du virus de l'hepatite infecteuse du Caneton. Comp. rend. Acad. Sci. 255:800, 1962.

### Mucosal Disease—Virus Diarrhea Complex

BAKER, J. A., *et al.* Virus Diarrhea in Cattle. Amer. Jour. Vet. Res. 15:525, 1954.

DARBYSHIRE, J. H. Serological Relationship Between Swine Fever and Mucosal Disease of Cattle. Vet. Rec. 72:331, 1960.

DELAY, P. D., and KNIAZEFF, A. J. Response of Virus Diarrhea-Mucosal Disease-Convalescent Calves and Rinderpest-Vaccinated Calves to Inoculation With Heterologous Virus. Amer. Jour. Vet. Res. 27:512, 1966.

DINTER, Z. Relationship Between Bovine Virus Diarrhea Virus and Hog Cholera Virus. Zentralbl. f. Bakt. Orig. 188:475, 1963.

DITCHFIELD, J., and DOANE, F. W. The Properties and Classification of Bovine Virus Diarrhea Virus. Canad. Jour. Comp. Med. 28:148, 1964.

DUTTA, S. K., *et al.* Electron Microscopic Structure of Bovine Diarrhea Virus. Bact. Proc., p. 111, 1965.

GILLESPIE, J. H., *et al.* A Cytopathogenic Strain of Virus Diarrhea Virus. Cornell Vet. 50:73, 1960.

HERMONDSSON, S., and DINTER, Z. Properties of Bovine Virus Diarrhea Virus. Nature 194:893, 1962.

HUCK, R. A. Mucosal Disease Complex. Jour. Comp. Path. Therap. 67:267, 1957.

———. Mucosal Disease. Bull. Off. Int. Epiz. 56:5, 1961.

KNIAZEFF, A. J., and PRITCHARD, W. R. Antigenic Relationships in the Bovine Viral Diarrhea-Mucosal Disease Complex. Proc. U.S. Livestock Sanit. Assn. 64:344, 1960.

MENGLING, W. L., *et al.* Demonstration of an Antigenic Relationship Between Hog Cholera and Bovine Viral Diarrhea Viruses by Immunofluorescence. Canad. Jour. Comp. Med. 27:162, 1963.

MILLS, J. H. L., *et al.* Current Status of Bovine Mucosal Disease. Jour. Amer. Vet. Med. Assn. 146:691, 1965.

OLAFSON, P., *et al.* An Apparently New Transmissible Disease of Cattle. Cornell Vet. 36:205, 1946.

PRITCHARD, W. R. The Mucosal Disease of Cattle. Epizootiology, Symptomatology and Experimental Studies. Proc. Amer. Vet. Med. Assn. 92:37, 1955.

———. Bovine Viral Diarrhea-Mucosal Disease Complex. Adv. Vet. Sci. 8:1, 1963.

RAMSEY, F. K., and CHIVERS, W. H. Mucosal Disease of Cattle. No. Amer. Vet. 34:629, 1953.

SHEFFY, B. M., *et al.* Protection of Pigs Against Hog Cholera With Virus Diarrhea Virus of Cattle. Proc. 65th Ann. Meet. U.S. Livestock Sanit. Assn., p. 347, 1961.

TAYLOR, D. O. N., *et al.* Properties of Some Viruses of the Mucosal Disease-Virus Diarrhea Complex. Amer. Jour. Vet. Res. 24:143, 1963.

TYLER, D. E., and RAMSEY, F. K. Comparative Pathologic Immunologic and Clinical Responses Produced by Selected Agents of the Bovine Mucosal Disease-Virus Diarrhea Complex. Amer. Jour. Vet. Res. 26:903, 1965.

## Hemagglutinating Encephalomyelitis Virus

ALEXANDER, T. J. L., *et al.* Encephalomyelitis of Suckling Pigs in Ontario. Canad. Jour. Comp. Med. Vet. Sci. 23:316, 1959.

APPEL, M., *et al.* Encephalomyelitis in Swine Caused by a Hemagglutinating Virus. IV. Transmission Studies. Res. Vet. Sci. 6:482, 1965.

GIRARD, A., *et al.* Encephalomyelitis of Swine Caused by a Hemagglutinating Virus. III. Serological Studies. Res. Vet. Sci. 5:294–302, 1964.

GREIG, A. S., *et al.* A Hemagglutinating Virus Producing Encephalomyelitis in Baby Pigs. Canad. Jour, Comp. Med. 26:49, 1962.

## Scrapie Virus

CUILLE, J., and CHELLE, P. L. La tremblante du mouton. Son etiologie. Rev. Path. Comp. 38:1358, 1938.

DARCEL, C. le Q., *et al.* Scrapie. 1. Transmission and Pathogenesis. Canad. Jour. Comp. Med. Vet. Sci. 27:81, 1963.

GUSTAFSON, D. P., and KANITZ, C. L. In Vitro Studies of Scrapie Virus. Fed. Proc. 24:248, 1965.

HUNTER, G. D., and MILLSON, G. C. Studies on the Heat Stability and Chromatographic Behaviour of the Scrapie Agent. Jour. Gen. Microbiol. 37:251, 1964.

MORRIS, J. A., *et al.* Spread of Scrapie From Inoculated to Uninoculated Mice. Proc. Soc. Exp. Biol. Med. 120:108, 1965.

PATTISON, I. H. The Spread of Scrapie by Contact Between Affected and Healthy Sheep, Goats or Mice. Vet. Rec. 76:333–36, 1964.

———. Resistance of the Scrapie Agent to Formalin. Jour. Comp. Path. 75:159, 1965.

PLUMMER, P. J. G. Scrapie—A Disease of Sheep. Canad. Jour. Comp. Med. 10:49, 1946.

Report of Scrapie Seminar. Agr. Res. Serv. USDA, ARS 91–53, 1966.

Report of Special Meetings on Scrapie. Agr. Res. Serv. USDA, ARS 91–22, June, 1960.

SCHOFIELD, F. W. A Case of Scrapie in an Imported Ewe. Rept. Ontario Vet. Coll. for 1938, p. 34, 1939.

STAMP, J. T. Scrapie: A Transmissible Disease of Sheep. Vet. Rec. 74:357, 1962.

———, *et al.* Further Studies on Scrapie. Jour. Comp. Path. 69:268, 1959.

THORP, F., *et al.* Scrapie in Sheep. Mich. State Univ. Vet. 13:36, 1952.

ZLOTNIK, I., and RENNIE, J. C. Experimental Transmission of Mouse-Passaged Scrapie to Goats, Sheep, Rats and Hamsters. Jour. Comp. Path. 75:147, 1965.

## Aleutian Disease Virus

BASUR, P. K., *et al.* Aleutian Disease (plasmacytosis) of Mink. III. Propagation of the Virus in Mink Tissue Cultures. Canad. Jour. Comp. Med. 27:301, 1963.

GORHAM, J. R., *et al.* The Experimental Transmission of a Virus Causing Hypergammaglobulinemia in Mink: Sources and Modes of Infection. Jour. Inf. Dis. 114:341, 1964.

HARTSOUGH, G. R., and GORHAM, J. R. Aleutian Disease in Mink. Natl. Fur News 28:10, 1956.

HELMBOLDT, C. F., and JUNGHERR, E. L. The Pathology of Aleutian Disease in Mink. Amer. Jour. Vet. Res. 19:212, 1958.

KARSTAD, L., *et al.* Aleutian Disease (plasmacytosis) of Mink. II. Responses of Mink to Formalin-Treated Diseased Tissues and to Subsequent Challenge With Virulent Inoculum. Canad. Jour. Comp. Med. 27:124, 1963.

OBEL, A. Studies on a Disease in Mink With Systemic Proliferation of the Plasma Cells. Amer. Jour. Vet. Res. 20:384, 1959.

RUSSELL, J. D., *et al.* The Etiology and Diagnosis of Aleutian Disease in Mink. Proc. 66th Ann. Meet. U.S. Livestock Sanit. Assn., p. 462, 1962.

## Epizootic Hemorrhagic Disease Virus

FAY, Z. D., *et al.* An Epizootic of Deer in Michigan. Trans. 21st N. Amer. Wildlife Conf., p. 173, 1956.

METTLER, N. E., *et al.* The Propagation of the Virus of Epizootic Hemorrhagic Disease of Deer in Newborn Mice and HeLa Cells. Jour. Exp. Med. 116:665, 1962.

PIRTLE, E. C., and LAYTON, J. M. Epizootic Hemorrhagic Diseases in White-Tailed Deer—Characteristics of the South Dakota Strain of Virus. Amer. Jour. Vet. Res. 22:104, 1961.

SHOPE, R. E., *et al.* A Virus-Induced Epizootic Hemorrhagic Disease of the Virginia White-Tailed Deer. Jour. Exp. Med. 111:155, 1960.

## Visna and Maedi Viruses

SIGURDARDOTTIR, B., and THORMAR, H. Isolation of a Viral Agent From the Lungs of Sheep Affected With Maedi. Jour. Inf. Dis. 114:55, 1964.

SIGURDSSON, B. Maedi, a Slow Progressive Pneumonia of Sheep: An Epizoological and Pathological Study. Brit. Vet. Jour. 110:255, 1954.

———, *et al.* Maedi, A Chronic Progressive Infection of Sheep's Lungs. Jour. Inf. Dis. 90:233, 1952.

THORMAR, H. Stability of Visna Virus in Infectious Tissue Culture Fluid. Arch. ges. Virusforsch. 10:501, 1961.

———. The Growth Cycle of Visna Virus in Monolayer Cultures of Sheep Cells. Virol. 19:273, 1963.

———. A Comparison of Visna and Maedi Viruses. I. Physical, Chemical and Biological Properties. Res. Vet. Sci. 6:117, 1965.

———. Effect of 5–Bromodeoxyuridine and Actinomycin D on the Growth of Visna Virus in Cell Cultures. Virol. 26:36, 1965.

———, and CRUICKSHANK, J. G. The Structure of Visna Virus Studied by the Negative Staining Technique. Virol. 25:145, 1965.

———, and HELGADOTTIR, H. A Comparison of Visna and Maedi Viruses. II. Serological Relationship. Res. Vet. Sci. 6:456–65, 1965.

## Transmissible Gastroenteritis Virus

DOYLE, L. P., and HUTCHINGS, L. M. A Transmissible Gastroenteritis in Pigs. Jour. Amer. Vet. Med. Assn. 108:257, 1946.

FULLER, D. A., and WELTER, C. J. T.G.E. of Swine. II. Clinical Field Trials With an Inactivated Tissue Culture Vaccine. Vet. Med. 61:257, 1966.

HAELTERMAN, E. O. Epidemiological Studies of Transmissible Gastroenteritis of Swine. Proc. 66th Meet. U.S. Livestock Sanit. Assn., p. 305, 1962

———. Transmissible Gastroenteritis of Swine. Proc. 17th World Vet. Cong. 1:615, 1963.

LEE, K. M. Propagation of Transmissible Gastroenteritis Virus in Tissue Culture. Ann. N.Y. Acad. Sci. 66:191, 1956.

McCLURKIN, A. W. Studies on Transmissible Gastroenteritis of Swine. I. The Isolation and Identification of a Cytopathogenic Virus of Transmissible Gastroenteritis in Primary Swine Kidney Cell Cultures. Canad. Jour. Comp. Med. 29:46, 1965.

RISTIC, M., *et al.* Electron Microscopy and Ether Sensitivity of Transmissible Gastroenteritis of Swine. Amer. Jour. Vet. Res. 26:609, 1965.

# 53

# The Bacteriophages or Bacterial Viruses

AN INTERESTING PHENOMENON WAS reported in 1915 by Twort who was working with a staphylococcus isolated from calf-lymph vaccine. He observed a visible change in some of the colonies which was found to be transmissible and it suggested a "disease of bacteria." Furthermore, it was found that filtrates of the changed cultures would also initiate the "disease" of the staphylococcus.

D'Herelle, working independently, made similar observations on colonies of a coccobacillus isolated from an intestinal disease of locusts. In areas of confluent growth of this organism on agar, there would occasionally be small areas where no growth would occur.

In another experiment D'Herelle was searching for a virus in dysentery and typhoid fever of man. He thought a virus might be associated with these diseases in the same way as the hog cholera virus had a few years earlier been found to be associated with *Sal. choleraesuis* as the cause of hog cholera. To test his hypothesis, D'Herelle injected *Shig. dysenteriae* and *Sal. typhosa* together with filtrates of fecal materials collected from cases of the disease into laboratory animals to try to reproduce the disease. He also tried mixtures of these organisms and the filtrates on agar plates. It was found that filtrates from patients recovering from the disease would produce the same phenomena as seen with the organisms from the locusts. The addition of filtrates at the time of inoculation of broth cultures resulted in failure of growth and, furthermore, if the filtrates were added in the early stages of growth, the bacterial cells were observed to undergo lysis with consequent clearing of the tubes. This was the beginning of many years work in which D'Herelle found bacteriophages from many sources. The name *bacteriophage* was proposed by D'Herelle because of the disappearance of the bacterial cells in the presence of these viruses.

Since the work of Twort and D'Herelle, much work has been done on the bacterial viruses which has contributed significantly to the knowledge of viruses in general as well as having many practical applications.

## Properties of the Bacterial Viruses (Bacteriophages)

**Size and Morphology.** The size of the bacterial viruses varies from those which are 10 m$\mu$ to 20 m$\mu$ to some nearly 100 m$\mu$. Most of those which have been photographed under the electron microscope have a "tadpole" or sperm-shaped particle (Fig. 53.1). The body of the particles in Figure 53.1 is spherical, 70 m$\mu$ in diameter, and a distinct tail is observed which is 30 m$\mu$ wide and 150 m$\mu$ in length. The nucleic acid of the phages is of DNA type.

**Cultivation.** The bacterial viruses cannot be cultivated except in the presence of living susceptible bacteria. Growth rates are quite rapid upon the addition of a virus to a culture of its host organism. Viral DNA enters the bacterial cell and causes replication of the complete virus until it bursts the cell and liberates the newly formed particles. The *burst times* vary with

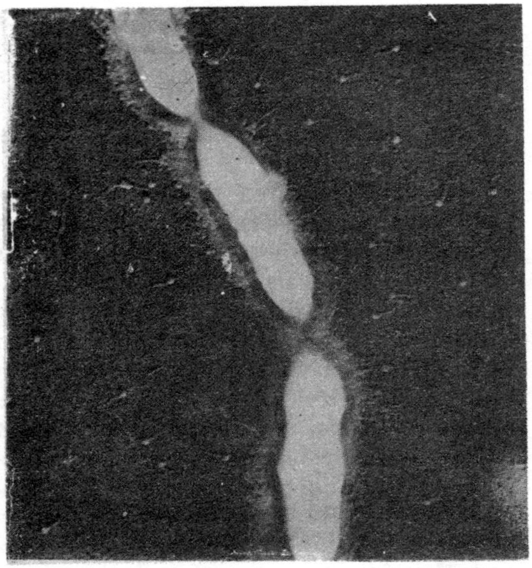

FIG. 53.1—**Strep. lactis** and bacteriophage, ×15,000. (Courtesy Parmellee, Carr, and Nelson. Jour. Bact. 57:391, 1949.)

various viruses, but may be from 13 to 40 minutes, and the yield of virus per cell varies from 120 to 400 particles.

**Resistance.** The bacterial viruses are in general more resistant to heat than the animal viruses. Whereas a majority of the animal viruses are killed by exposure to a temperature of 56°C. for 30 minutes, many of the bacterial viruses require 60°C. for 30 minutes or even higher temperatures. *Strep. lactis* phages, for example, resist milk pasteurization temperatures, 62°C., for 30 minutes.

A majority of bacteriophages are resistant to aging and to drying.

**Antigenic Structure.** Like most viruses, the bacteriophages are antigenic when injected into the animal body. Antiphage serum is specific and neutralizes the action of the phage against its host bacteria. Different strains of phage which attack the same bacterial species have been distinguished by means of serological tests.

**Specificity of the Bacterial Viruses.** Among the bacterial viruses are examples of the extreme in host specificity. Certain phages are able to distinguish strains of bacteria within a species which cannot be distinguished by any other means. On the other hand, some phages attack different species of bacteria within the same genus, especially if the bacteria are antigenically similar.

**Interference Phenomena of Bacterial Viruses.** It has been shown that the phenomena of virus interference occurs among the bacterial viruses. If two serologically distinguishable viruses which are capable of attacking the same species of bacteria are inoculated together, one may predominate in the progeny.

**Genetic Variation of Bacterial Viruses.** The observation by Hershey and others that genetic recombination occurs between different strains of bacterial viruses has led to a great deal of research on the genetics of viruses including those which infect animals.

It has also been observed that bacteriophages can act as "carriers" of genetic material between two strains of the same species of bacteria. This phenomenon has been called *transduction.* Bacterial antigens and the ability to produce toxins have been transferred by phages from one organism to another.

**Pathological Changes.** The effect of a bacterial virus on a susceptible bacterial cell is lysis. The virus grows and multiplies until the cell bursts, expelling the cell contents and the newly developed virus particles. Electron micrographs have clearly shown bacterial cell disintegration as the result of phage attacks.

Broth cultures which show turbidity may be seen to clear in a matter of minutes as a result of lytic action. Lysis may occur in agar colonies, and variation in colony characteristics is sometimes observed.

The appearance of resistant mutants among susceptible strains of bacteria is frequently noted.

### Enumeration of Bacterial Viruses

The usual method of determining the amount of virus present in a solution is the plaque-counting technique. A *plaque* is the clear area showing no growth on an agar plate which is seeded with the host organism and the virus which will attack it. By making appropriate dilutions of materials, the plaques can be counted in a manner similar to a bacterial plate count.

It is presumed that each plaque counted is from a single particle of virus in the original inoculum.

The size and other characteristics of the plaques are useful in classification and recognition of the phages. Some of the species of bacteria associated with animals and man for which bacteriophages have been demonstrated are *E. Coli, Sal. typhosa, Sal. pullorum, Sal. paratyphi, Sal. enteritidis, Sal. choleraesuis, Shig. dysenteriae, Aerob. aerogenes, Klebs. pneumoniae, Past. multocida, Past. pestis, Past. pseudotuberculosis, V. comma, B. subtilis, B. anthracis, Coryn. diphtheriae, Strep. pyogenes, Strep. equisimilis, Strep. lactis, Staph. aureus, Br. abortus,* and *Myco. tuberculosis.* There are many soil and plant bacteria from which phages have been isolated.

## Habitat of Bacterial Viruses

As with animal or plant viruses, the bacterial viruses are found with their hosts. It appears that nearly all bacterial cells may carry viruses to which they are resistant. Such bacteria are referred to as being *lysogenic.* Although a particular strain of bacteria may be resistant to the virus it is carrying, this same virus may be pathogenic for other strains of the bacterial species. Many phage strains have been recovered by the cross-culture technique described by Fisk. A number of isolates of a given species of bacteria are streaked on the same agar plate in such a way that the colonies of the various strains cross each other. If one strain carries a phage which is virulent for another isolate, evidence of lysis of the colony can be observed and the bacteriophage recovered by filtration. For many bacteria of the intestinal group, sewage is a good source of phages. Milk is a source of *Strep. lactis* phages.

## Practical Considerations

D'Herelle conceived the idea from his early work that a bacteriophage would be a great weapon in the fight against diseases of man and animals. He investigated outbreaks of animal disease and held the view that recovery from infection and cessation of the outbreak were related to the occurrence of a bacteriophage which was active against the organism producing the disease. D'Herelle further reported resistance to infection by the injection of phage into susceptible animals. In spite of the encouraging work of D'Herelle, the use of bacteriophage for the treatment of disease has been quite limited. One of the difficulties has been the high host specificity of the phages, and the fact that a phage may act only on a single strain of the disease-producing organism. This would necessitate typing of the organism causing each outbreak and the maintenance of many phage strains.

Bacteriophage has been used successfully in typhoid fever in man, but the difficulties mentioned above, as well as other factors, have prevented its general use in the treatment of the disease. The problem of bacteriophage activity against *Strep. lactis* is very important to the dairy industry which uses this organism to ripen cream, for butter-making, and in cheese-making.

In some milk plants, phage prevents proper development of the cultures and as a result considerable economic loss is suffered from inferior products.

Phage studies have aided in the classification of several species of bacteria. Differences in phage susceptibility have been shown between strains of bacteria which are otherwise indistinguishable.

## REFERENCES

ADAMS, M. H. Bacteriophages. Interscience Publ., Inc., New York, 1959.

BLAIR, J. E., and CARR, M. The Bacteriophage Typing of Staphylococci. Jour. Inf. Dis. 93:1, 1953.

COHEN, S. S. The Biochemistry of Bacteria Infected by Viruses. Chap. 7. *In* Viral and Rickettsial Infections of Man. J. B. Lippincott Co., Philadelphia, 1965.

D'HERELLE, F. The Bacteriophage and Its Behavior. English translation by Smith, G. H. Williams & Wilkins Co., Baltimore, 1926.

FISK, R. T. Studies on Staphylococci. I. Occurrence of Bacteriophage Carriers Among Strains of *Staphylo coccus aureus*. Jour. Inf. Dis. 71:153, 1942.

GROMAN, N. B. Evidence for the Induced Nature of the Change From Nontoxigenicity to Toxigenicity in *Corynebacterium diphtheriae* as a result of Exposure to Bacteriophage. Jour. Bact. 66:184, 1953.

HERSHEY, A. D. Mutation of Bacteriophage With Respect to Type of Plaque. Genetics 31:620, 1946.

LURIA, S. E. General Virology. John Wiley & Sons, Inc., New York, 1953.

RIFKIND, D., and PICKETT, M. J. Bacteriophage Studies on the Hemorrhagic Septicemia Pasteurellae. Jour. Bact. 67:243, 1954.

SMITH, P. B., and CHERRY, W. B. Identification of Malleomyces by Specific Bacteriophages. Jour. Bact. 74:668, 1957.

STINEBRING, W. R., and BRAUN, W. Brucellaphage. Jour. Bact. 78:736, 1959.

TAKEYA, K., and YOSHIMURA, T. Isolation of Bacteriophage Against All Types of *Mycobacterium tuberculosis*. Jour. Bact. 74.540, 1957.

TWORT, F. W. An Investigation of the Nature of Ultramicroscopic Viruses. Lancet 2:1241, 1915.

WILSON, G. S., and MILES, A. A. The Bacteriophage. *In* Topley's Principles of Bacteriology and Immunity. 5th Ed. Williams & Wilkins Co., Baltimore, 1964.

# Index

# B

# C

# D



# E

# H

# M

# W



# X



# Y



# Z